JIMMY HATLO CARTOONS

JIMMY HATLO

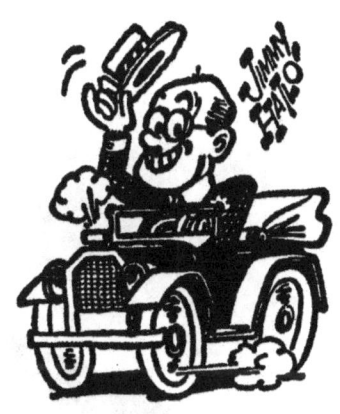

JIMMY HATLO CARTOONS

They'll Do It Every Time ®

COACHWHIP PUBLICATIONS
Greenville, Ohio

Jimmy Hatlo Cartoons
© 2018 Coachwhip Publications

Jimmy Hatlo (1897-1963)
No claims made on public domain material.

CoachwhipBooks.com

ISBN 1-61646-458-5
ISBN-13 978-1-61646-458-5

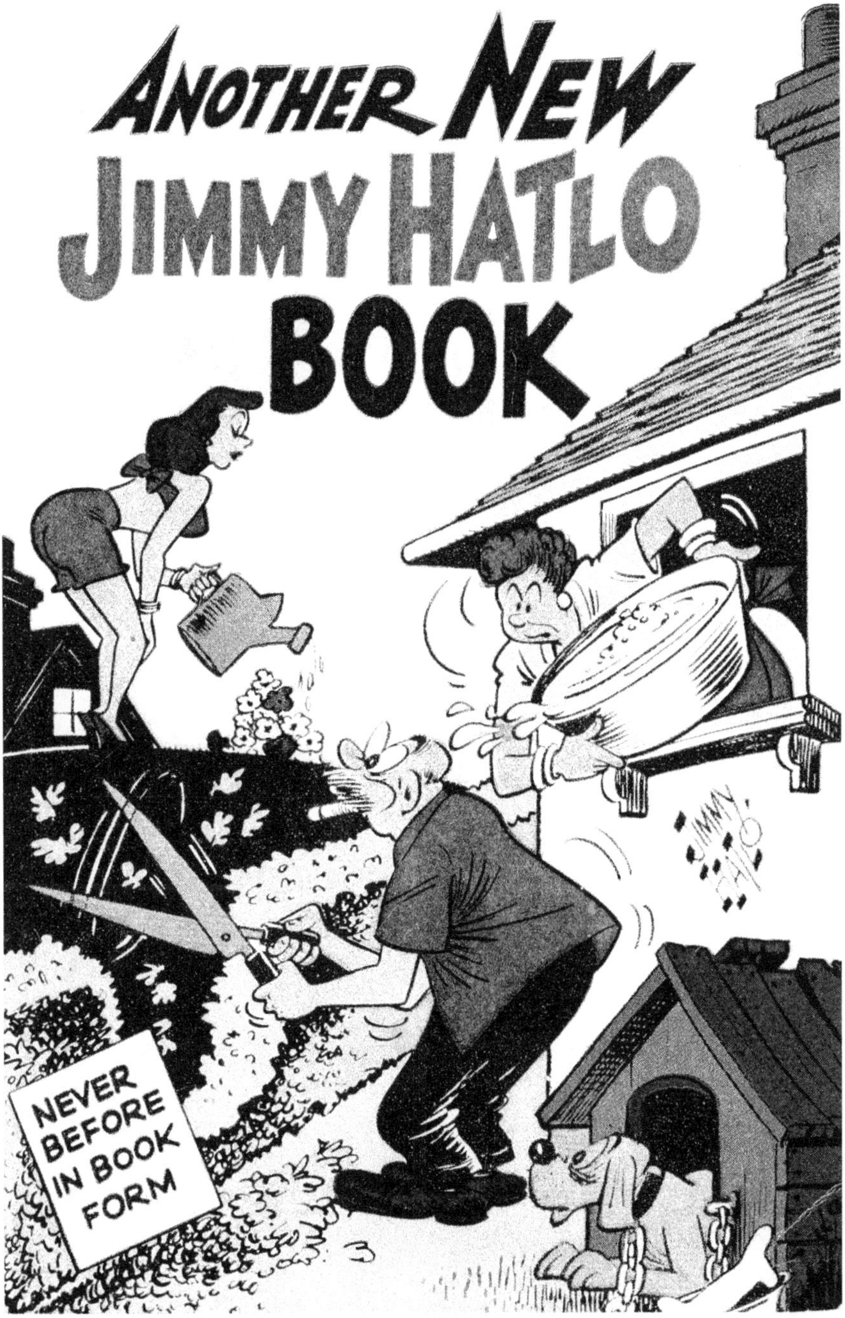
ANOTHER NEW
JIMMY HATLO
BOOK
NEVER BEFORE IN BOOK FORM
JIMMY HATLO

Another New

Jimmy Hatlo Book

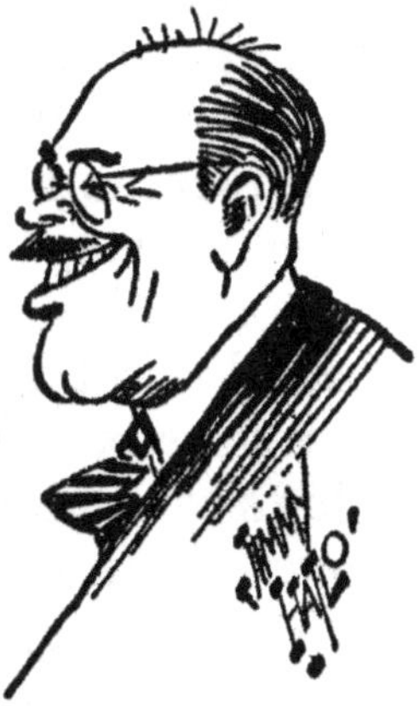
JIMMY HATLO

Foreword

BY DAN PARKER
Sports Editor, New York Daily Mirror

If Jimmy Hatlo, who draws "They'll Do It Every Time," had to pay space rates for all the green baize acreage his cartoons cover on office bulletin boards throughout America, he'd have to switch from India to red ink. There may be some doubt as to whom the Nation's No. 1 pin-up girl is, but by unanimous agreement, Jimmy is the most pinned-up boy. To a cartoonist dealing in a pleasantly satirical vein with the foibles of the human race, this is the supreme tribute. Every bulletin-board pin-up of a Hatlo cartoon means that Jimmy has hit another bull's-eye in caricaturing a stuffed shirt or office nuisance.

Perhaps the next highest compliment paid Jimmy is that oft heard remark: "He reminds me of Tad." A generation to whom Tad Dorgan, the great satirist of the sports pages, is but a name, may not grasp the full significance of this comparison. To be mentioned in the same breath with Tad is the highest accolade most comic artists would want.

Like Tad, Hatlo sees through all that is phony in everyday life and impales each piece of fraud on his sharp pen for the world to laugh at. One of the reasons for the widespread success of "They'll Do It Every Time" is that Jimmy is shrewd enough to depend on the public for much of his inspiration. After all, there's nothing like going to the source. In every office or business organization, there's a shrewd observer who sees through the petty artifices of the pompous fraud with whom he is associated. Human failings follow the same general patterns the world over. So when a keen judge of character sends Jimmy Hatlo the material for a lampoon on his pet office aversion, he is unwittingly describing a thousand other pests out of the same mold, and when Jimmy sets it down in black and white, a million recognize the character Jimmy's ink-spouting scalpel dissects.

In any collection of Hatlo's best, there's no question but that some of the characters satirized will cause the reader to say to himself: "That guy reminds me of So and So at the office."

The reason I'm sure Hatlo's cartoons will produce this effect is that (to borrow a line from Hatlo himself) "They'll Do It Every Time."

(This tribute of Mr. Parker's was written for a hardbound book collection of Hatlo cartoons.)

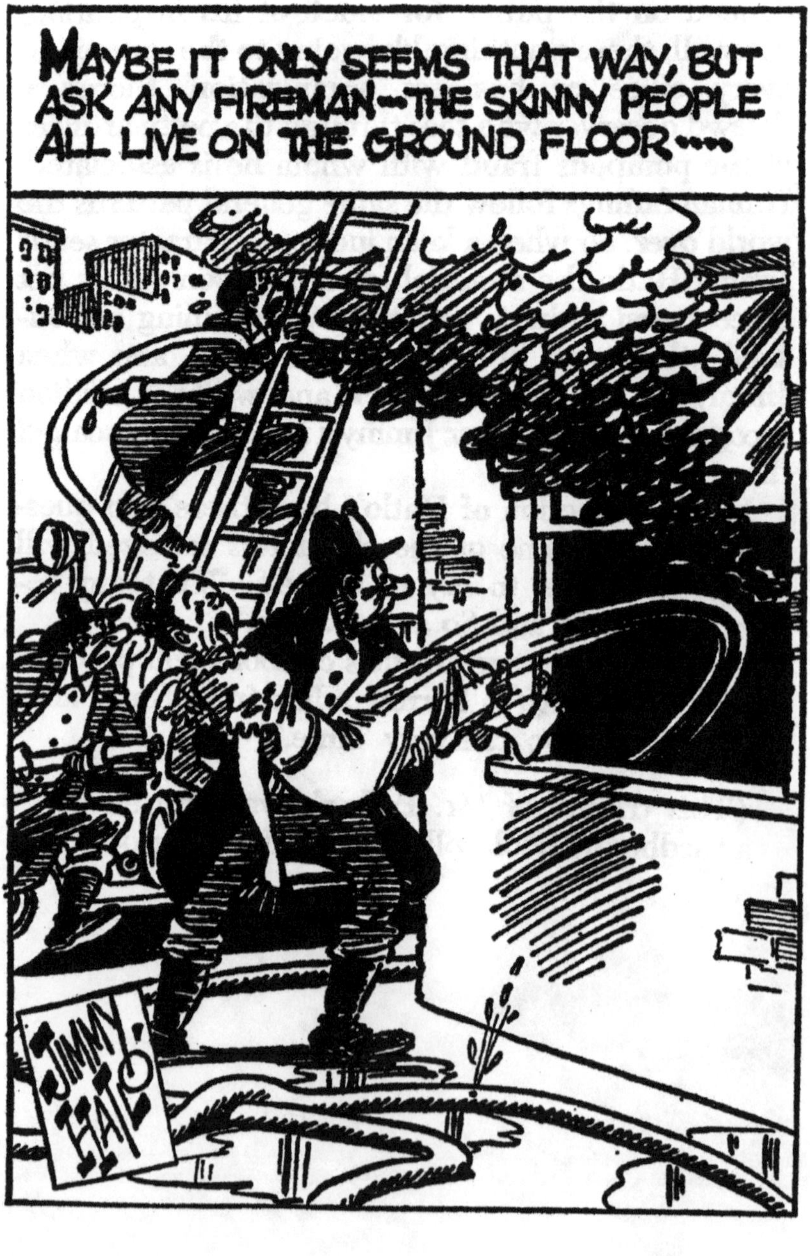
MAYBE IT ONLY SEEMS THAT WAY, BUT ASK ANY FIREMAN--THE SKINNY PEOPLE ALL LIVE ON THE GROUND FLOOR....
JIMMY HATLO

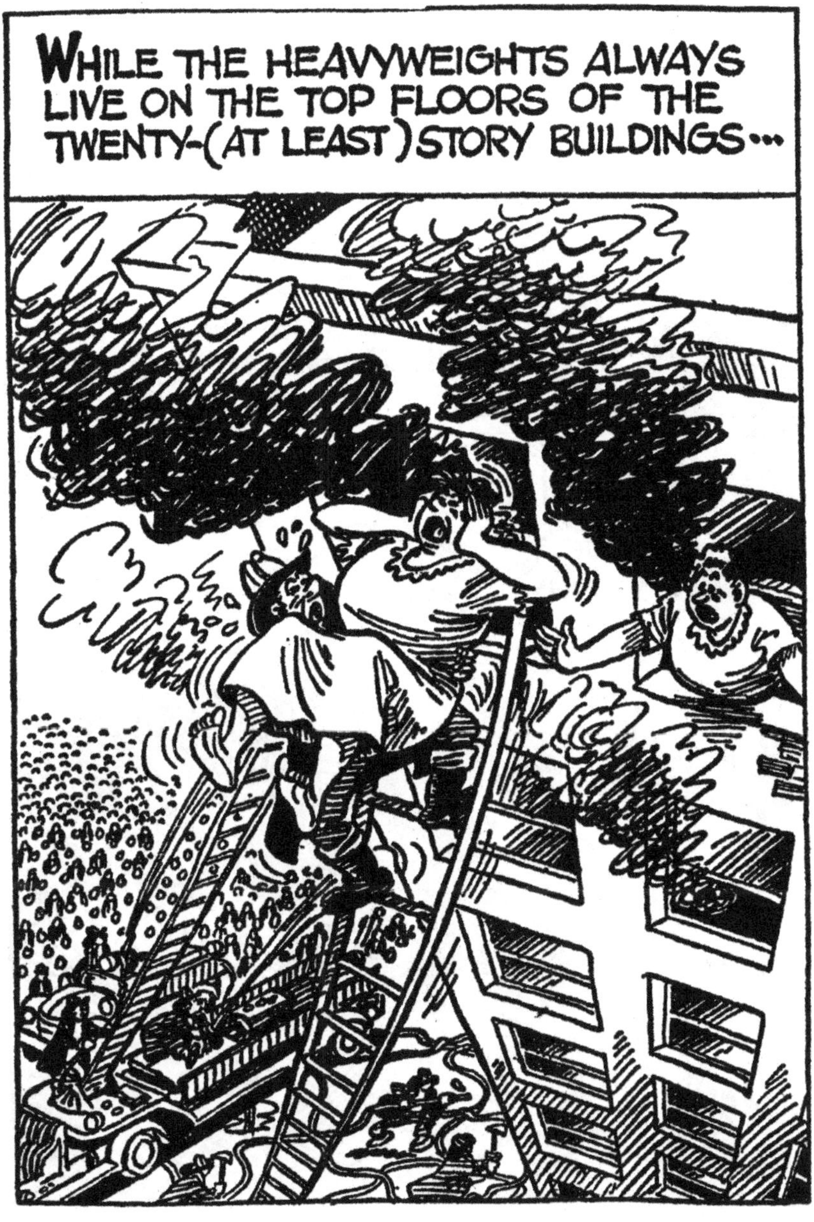
WHILE THE HEAVYWEIGHTS ALWAYS LIVE ON THE TOP FLOORS OF THE TWENTY-(AT LEAST) STORY BUILDINGS...

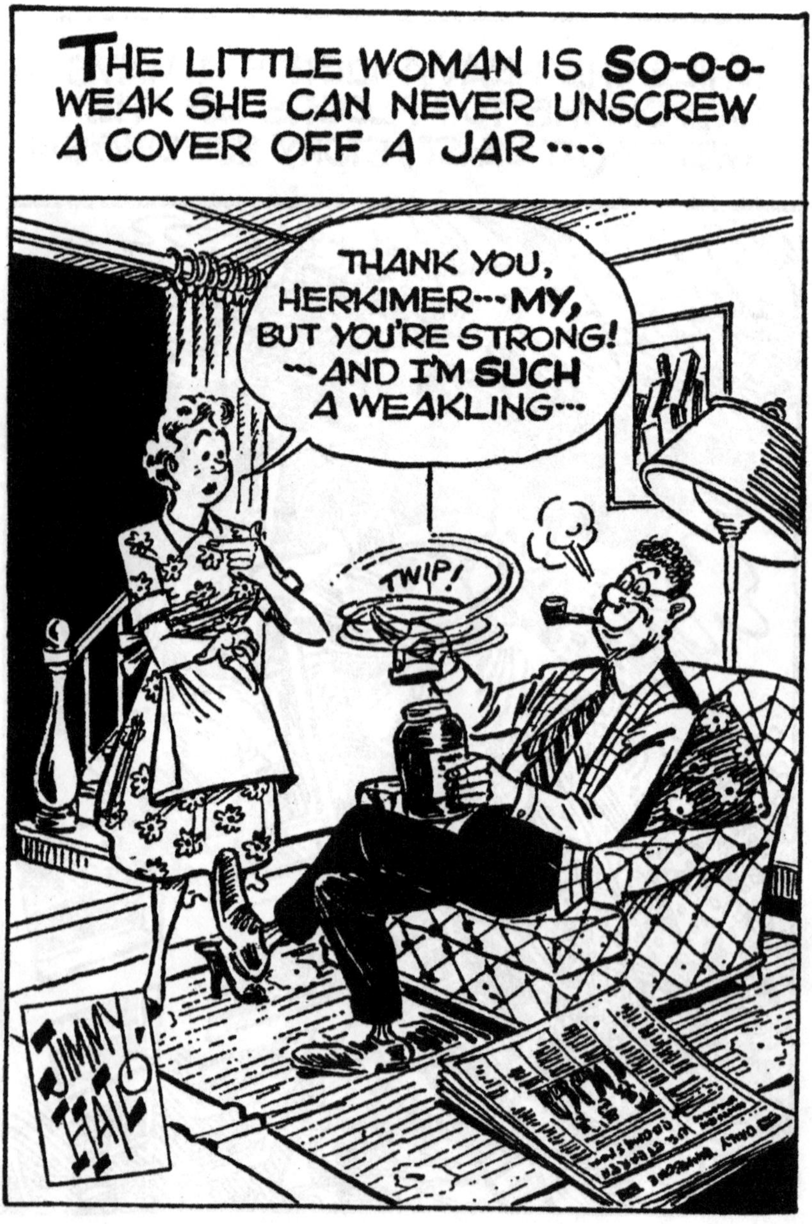
THE LITTLE WOMAN IS SO-O-O-WEAK SHE CAN NEVER UNSCREW A COVER OFF A JAR....
THANK YOU, HERKIMER---MY, BUT YOU'RE STRONG! ---AND I'M SUCH A WEAKLING---
TWIP!
JIMMY HATLO

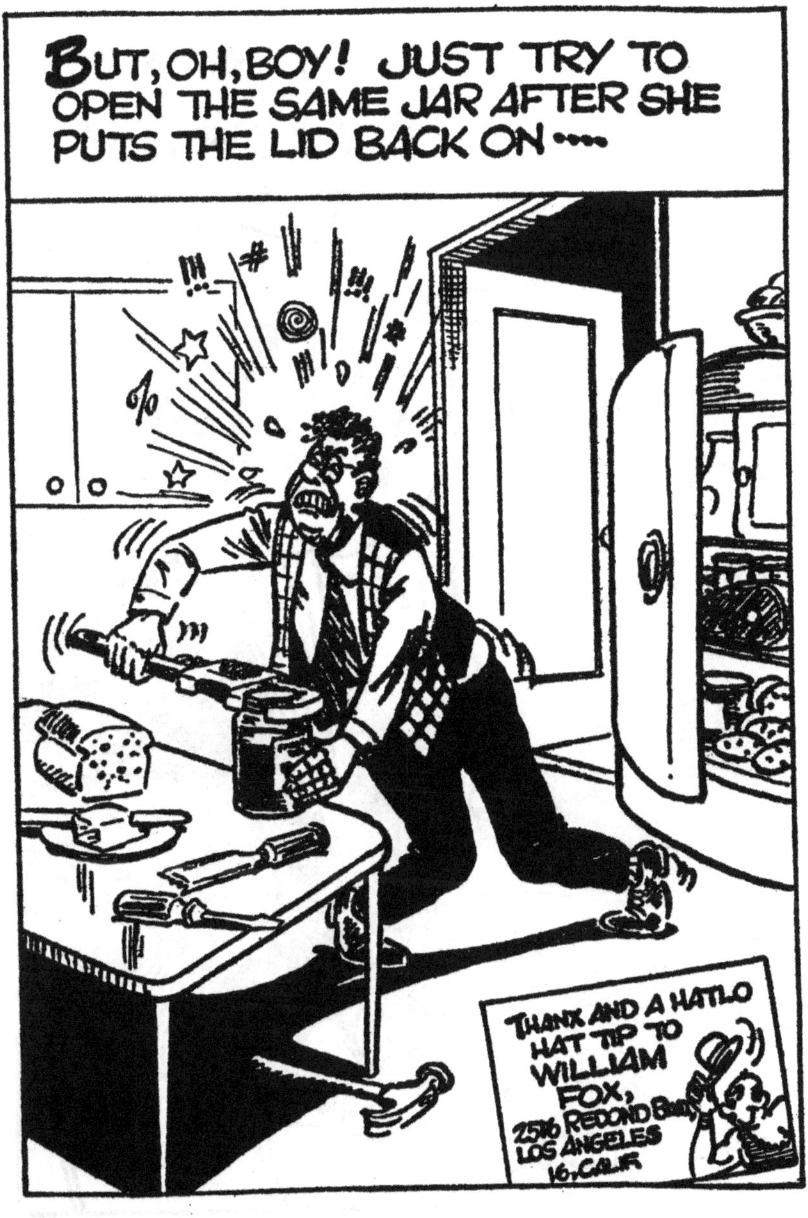
BUT, OH, BOY! JUST TRY TO OPEN THE SAME JAR AFTER SHE PUTS THE LID BACK ON....
!!!
#
!!!
%
THANX AND A HATLO HAT TIP TO WILLIAM FOX, 2516 REDOND
LOS ANGELES 16, CALIF.

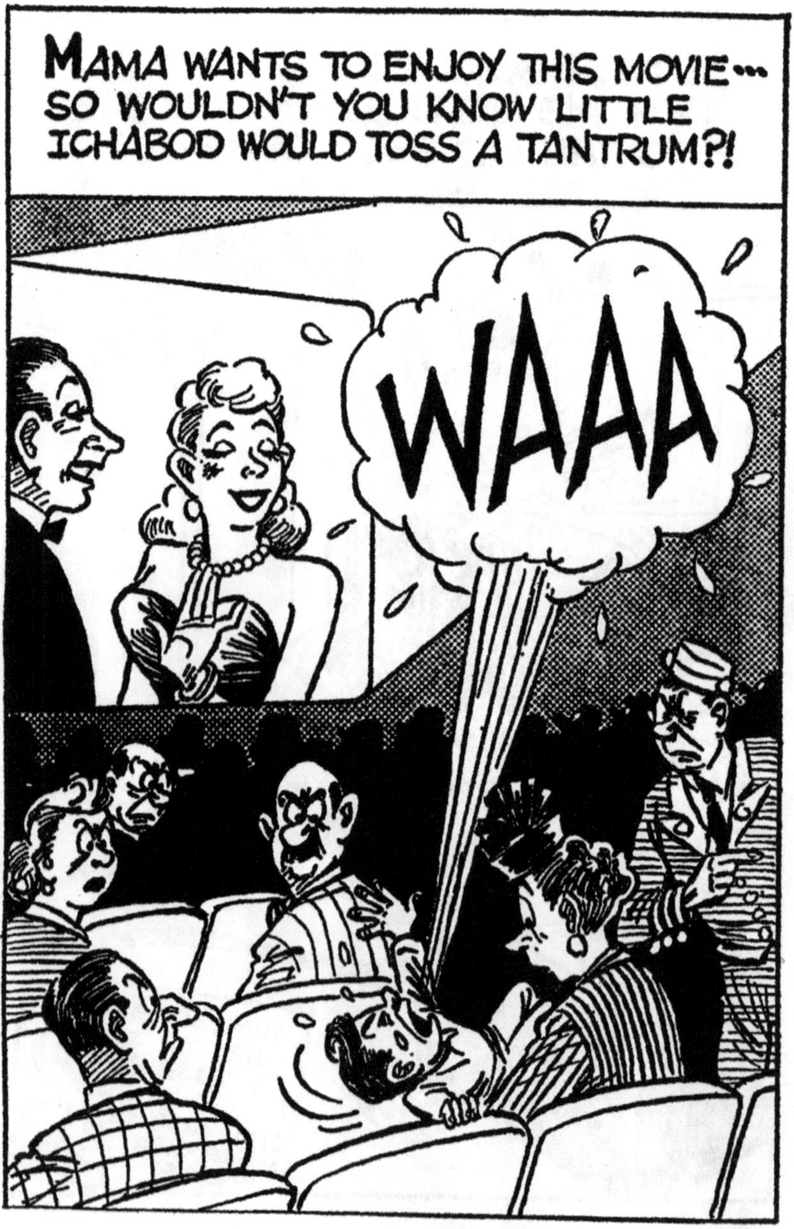
MAMA WANTS TO ENJOY THIS MOVIE...
SO WOULDN'T YOU KNOW LITTLE
ICHABOD WOULD TOSS A TANTRUM?!
WAAA

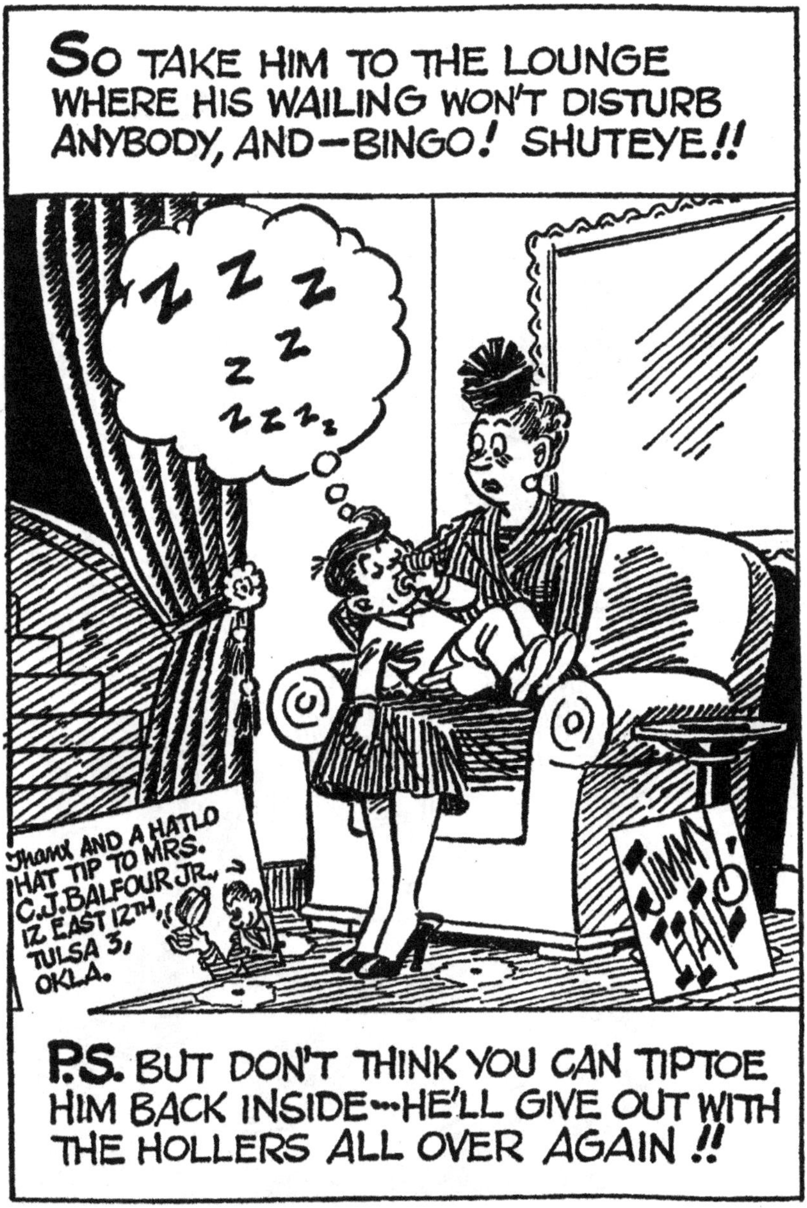
SO TAKE HIM TO THE LOUNGE WHERE HIS WAILING WON'T DISTURB ANYBODY, AND—BINGO! SHUTEYE!!
Z Z Z Z Z Z Z Z Z
Thanx AND A HATLO HAT TIP TO MRS. C.J. BALFOUR JR., 12 EAST 12TH, TULSA 3, OKLA.
JIMMY HATLO
P.S. BUT DON'T THINK YOU CAN TIPTOE HIM BACK INSIDE--HE'LL GIVE OUT WITH THE HOLLERS ALL OVER AGAIN!!

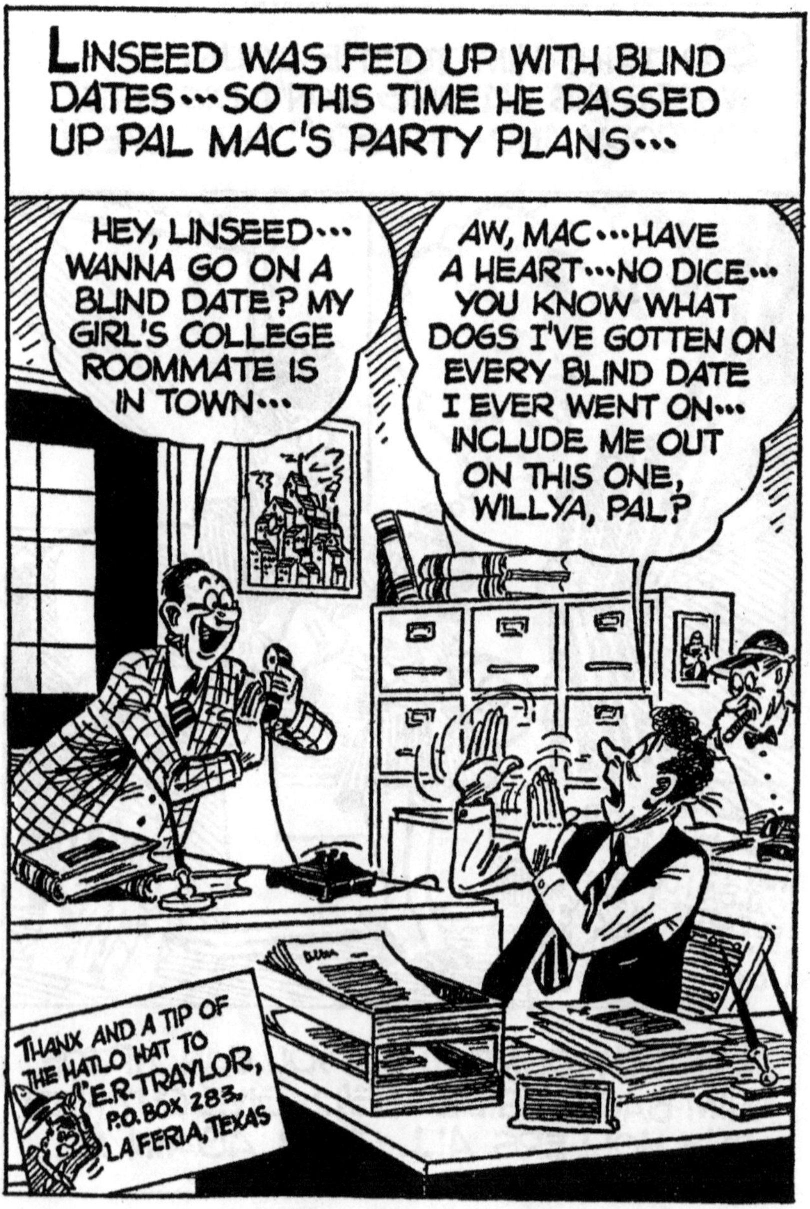
LINSEED WAS FED UP WITH BLIND DATES··· SO THIS TIME HE PASSED UP PAL MAC'S PARTY PLANS···
HEY, LINSEED··· WANNA GO ON A BLIND DATE? MY GIRL'S COLLEGE ROOMMATE IS IN TOWN···
AW, MAC···HAVE A HEART···NO DICE··· YOU KNOW WHAT DOGS I'VE GOTTEN ON EVERY BLIND DATE I EVER WENT ON··· INCLUDE ME OUT ON THIS ONE, WILLYA, PAL?
THANX AND A TIP OF THE HATLO HAT TO E.R. TRAYLOR, P.O. BOX 283, LA FERIA, TEXAS

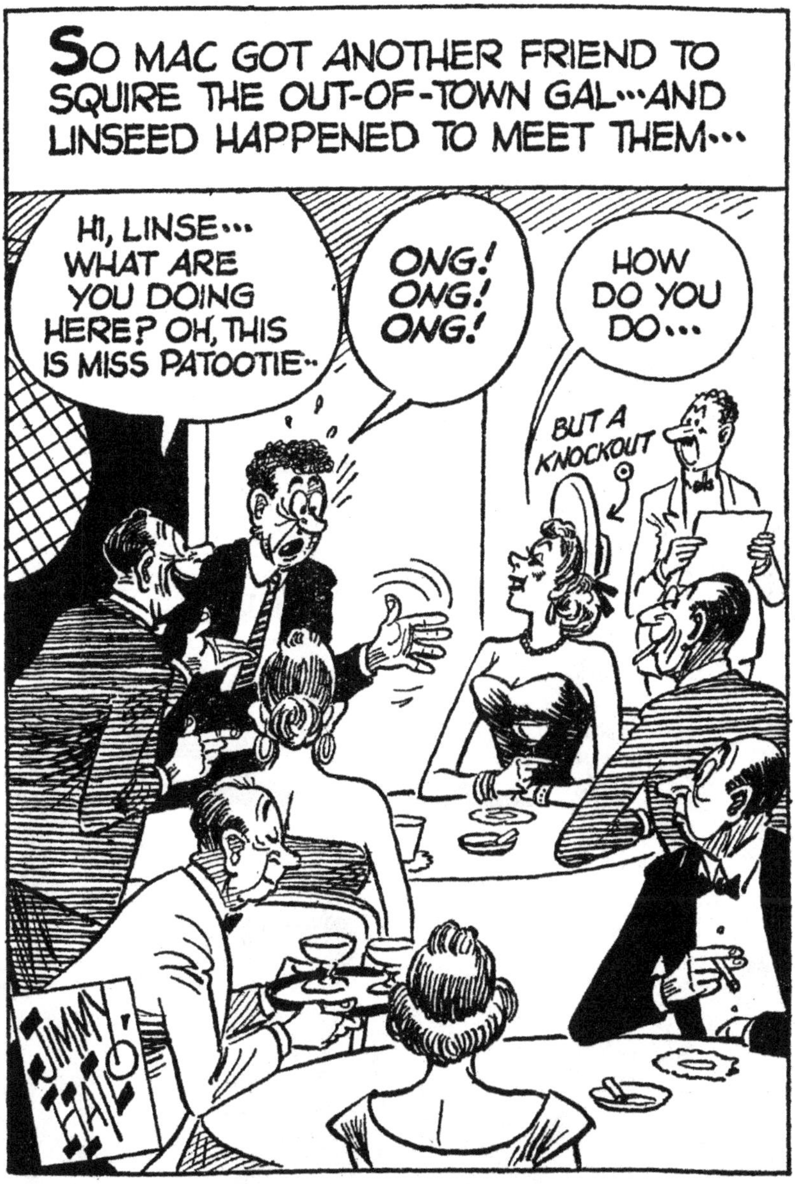
SO MAC GOT ANOTHER FRIEND TO SQUIRE THE OUT-OF-TOWN GAL···AND LINSEED HAPPENED TO MEET THEM···
HI, LINSE··· WHAT ARE YOU DOING HERE? OH, THIS IS MISS PATOOTIE··
ONG! ONG! ONG!
HOW DO YOU DO···
BUT A KNOCKOUT
JIMMY HATLO

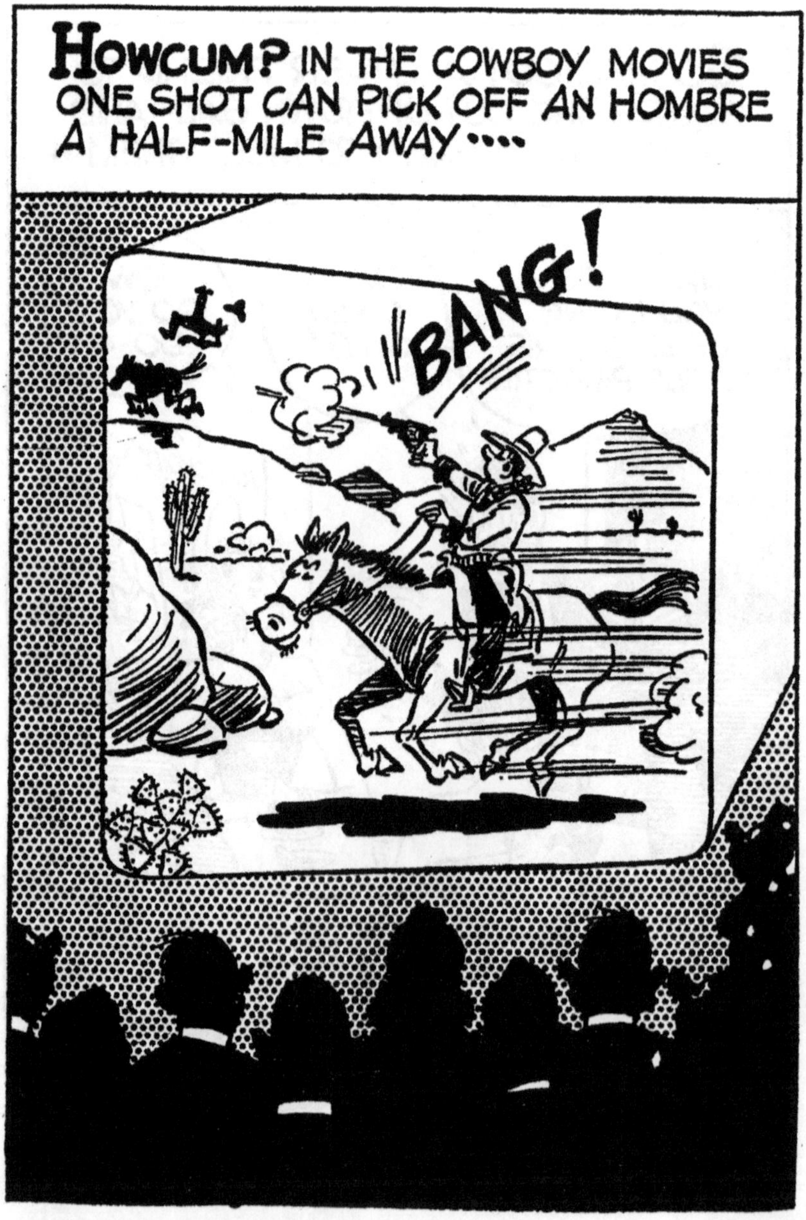
HOWCUM? IN THE COWBOY MOVIES ONE SHOT CAN PICK OFF AN HOMBRE A HALF-MILE AWAY....
BANG!

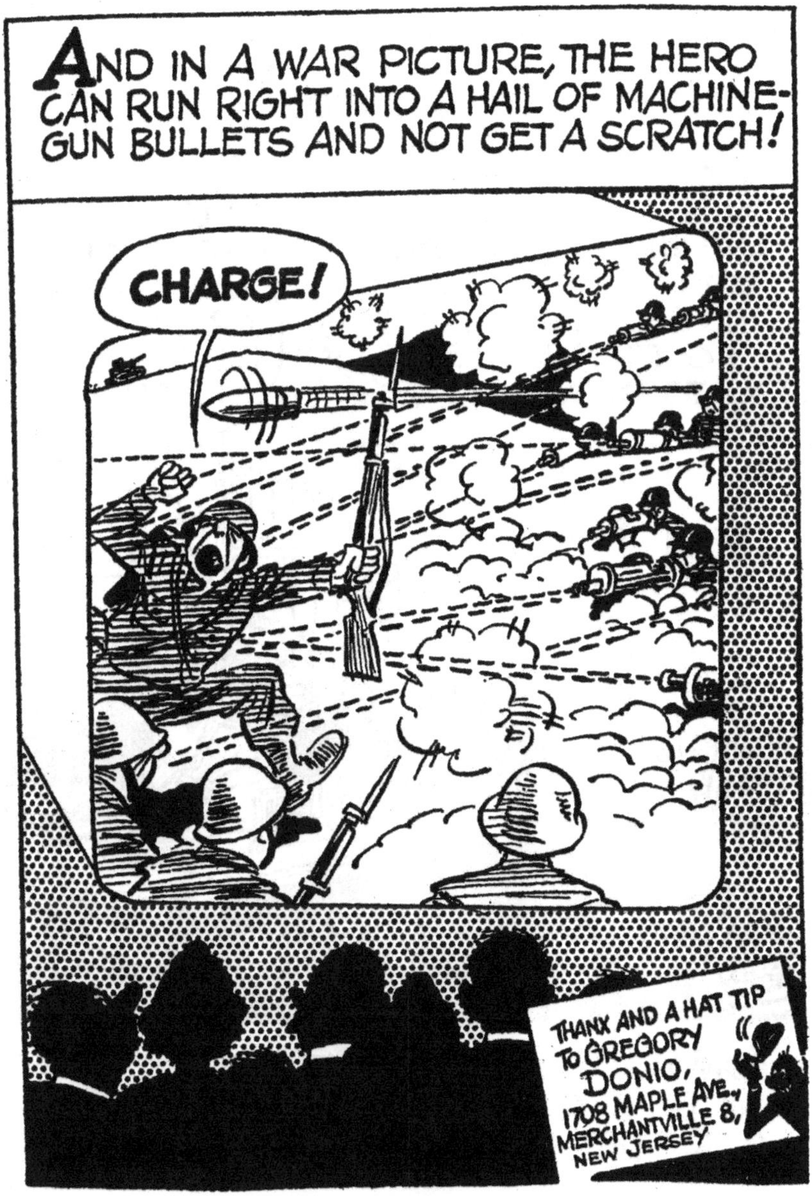
AND IN A WAR PICTURE, THE HERO CAN RUN RIGHT INTO A HAIL OF MACHINE-GUN BULLETS AND NOT GET A SCRATCH!
CHARGE!
THANX AND A HAT TIP TO GREGORY DONIO, 1708 MAPLE AVE., MERCHANTVILLE 8, NEW JERSEY

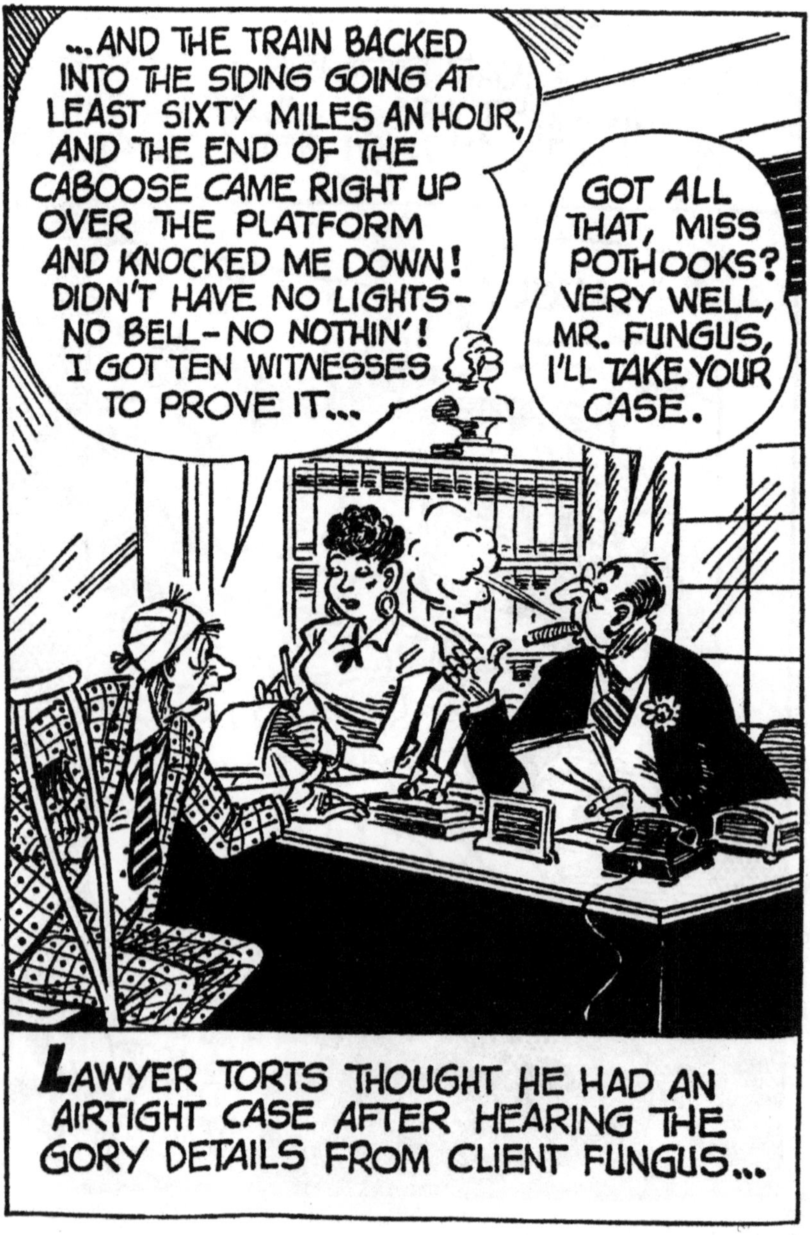
...AND THE TRAIN BACKED INTO THE SIDING GOING AT LEAST SIXTY MILES AN HOUR, AND THE END OF THE CABOOSE CAME RIGHT UP OVER THE PLATFORM AND KNOCKED ME DOWN! DIDN'T HAVE NO LIGHTS- NO BELL-NO NOTHIN'! I GOT TEN WITNESSES TO PROVE IT...
GOT ALL THAT, MISS POTHOOKS? VERY WELL, MR. FUNGUS, I'LL TAKE YOUR CASE.
LAWYER TORTS THOUGHT HE HAD AN AIRTIGHT CASE AFTER HEARING THE GORY DETAILS FROM CLIENT FUNGUS...

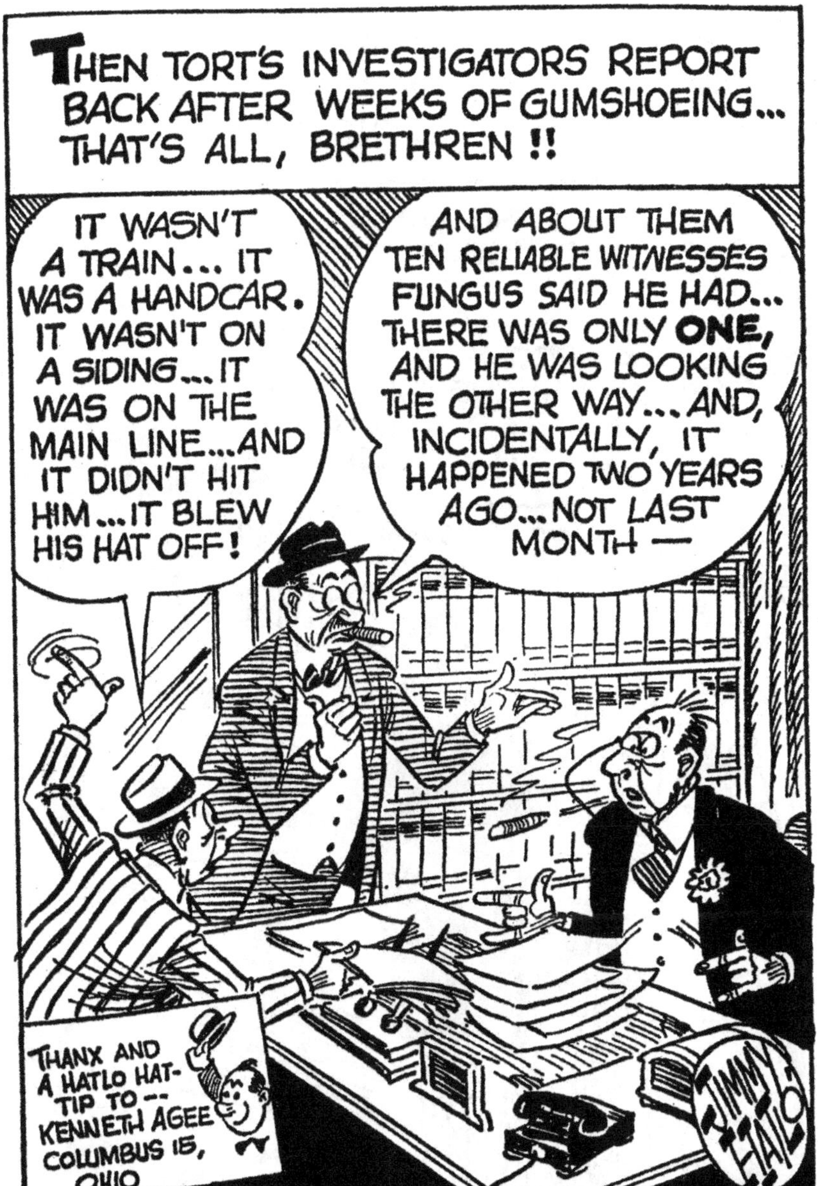
THEN TORT'S INVESTIGATORS REPORT BACK AFTER WEEKS OF GUMSHOEING... THAT'S ALL, BRETHREN !!
IT WASN'T A TRAIN... IT WAS A HANDCAR. IT WASN'T ON A SIDING... IT WAS ON THE MAIN LINE...AND IT DIDN'T HIT HIM...IT BLEW HIS HAT OFF!
AND ABOUT THEM TEN RELIABLE WITNESSES FUNGUS SAID HE HAD... THERE WAS ONLY ONE, AND HE WAS LOOKING THE OTHER WAY... AND, INCIDENTALLY, IT HAPPENED TWO YEARS AGO... NOT LAST MONTH —
THANX AND A HATLO HAT-TIP TO-- KENNETH AGEE COLUMBUS 15, OHIO
JIMMY HATLO

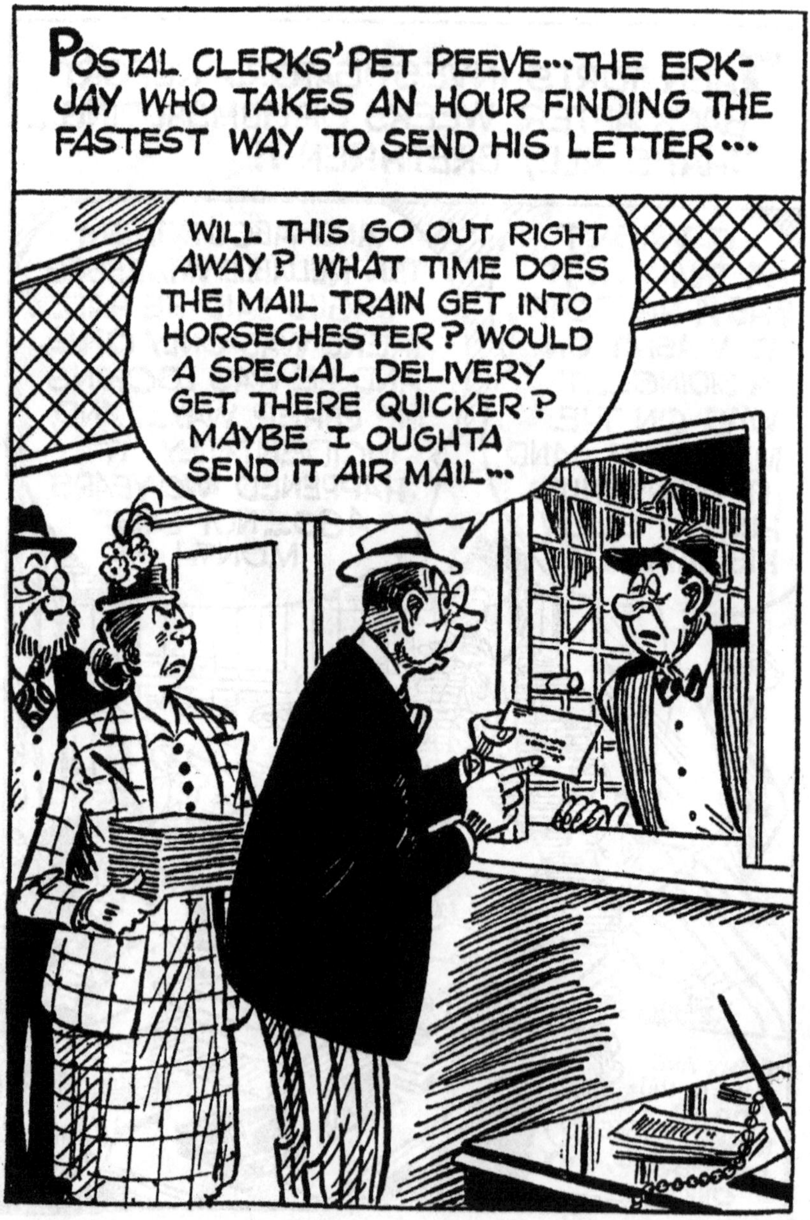
POSTAL CLERKS' PET PEEVE...THE ERK-JAY WHO TAKES AN HOUR FINDING THE FASTEST WAY TO SEND HIS LETTER...
WILL THIS GO OUT RIGHT AWAY? WHAT TIME DOES THE MAIL TRAIN GET INTO HORSECHESTER? WOULD A SPECIAL DELIVERY GET THERE QUICKER? MAYBE I OUGHTA SEND IT AIR MAIL...

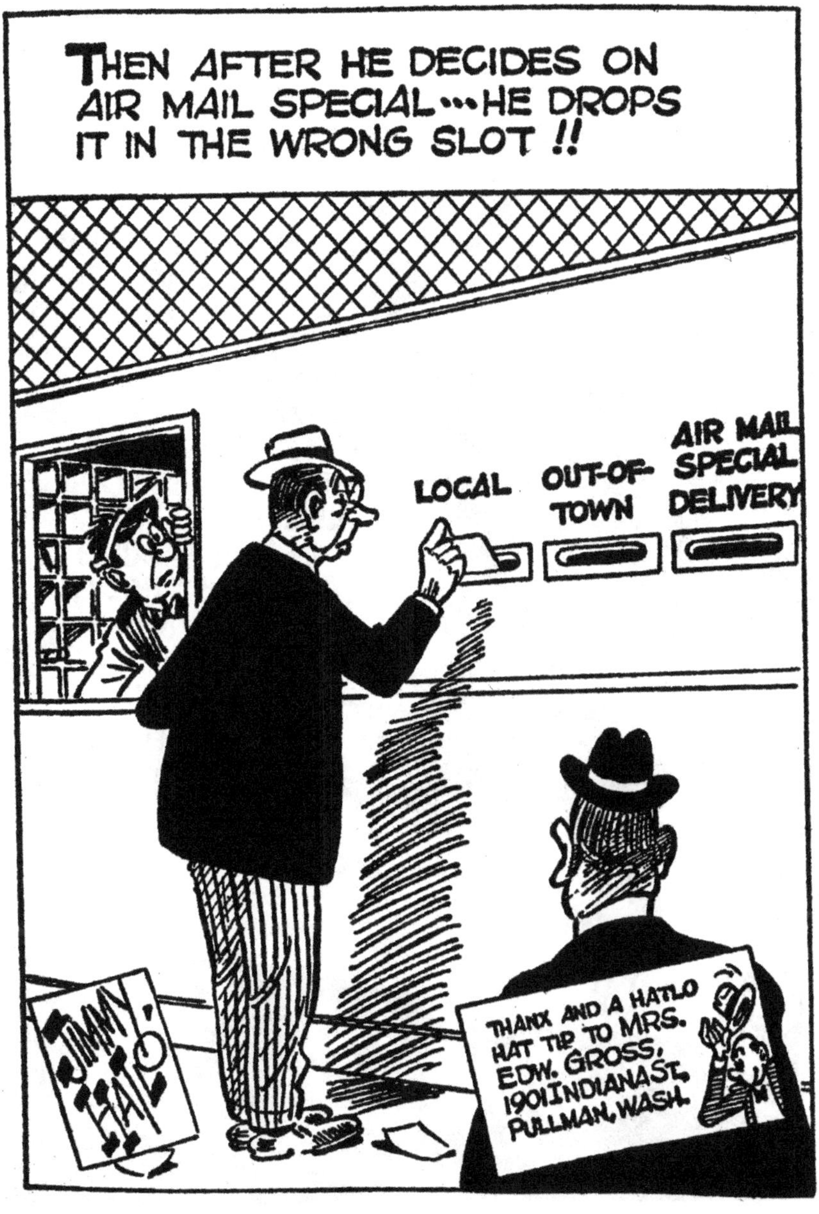
THEN AFTER HE DECIDES ON AIR MAIL SPECIAL... HE DROPS IT IN THE WRONG SLOT !!
LOCAL
OUT-OF-TOWN
AIR MAIL SPECIAL DELIVERY
THANX AND A HATLO HAT TIP TO MRS. EDW. GROSS, 1901 INDIANA ST., PULLMAN, WASH.
JIMMY HATLO

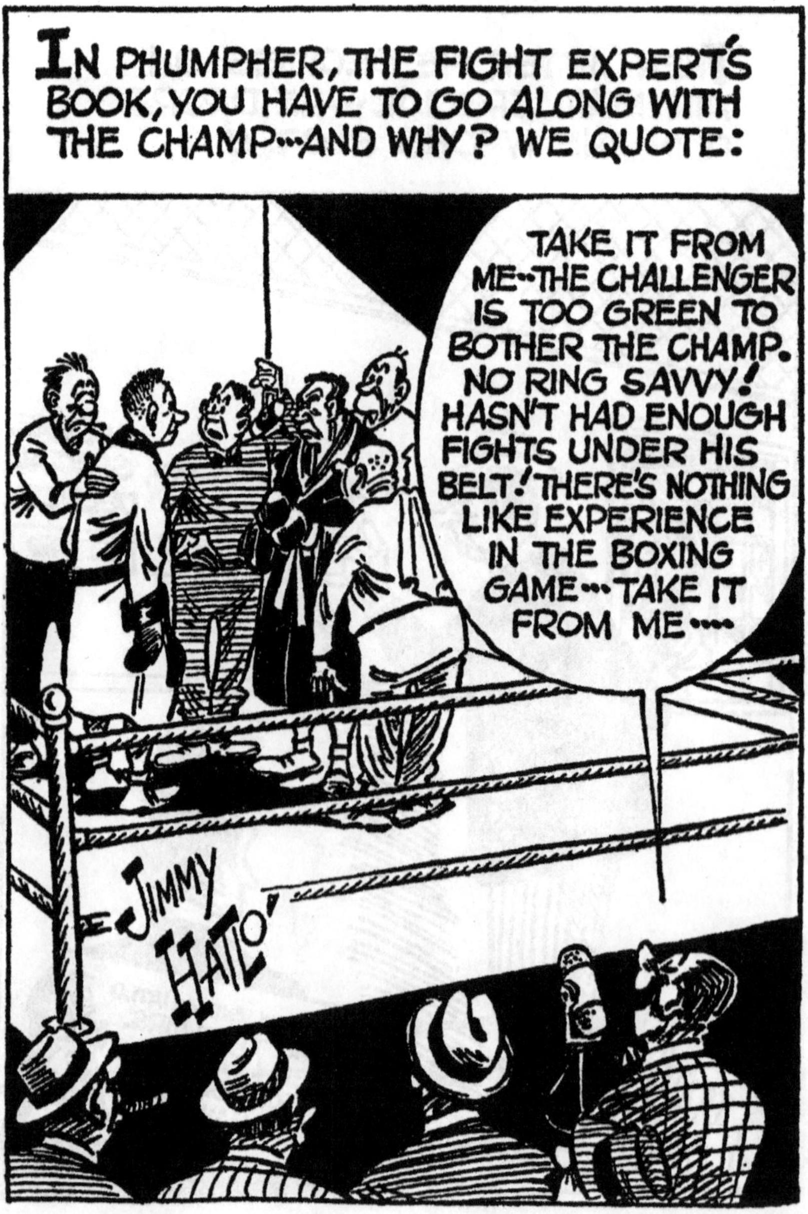
IN PHUMPHER, THE FIGHT EXPERT'S BOOK, YOU HAVE TO GO ALONG WITH THE CHAMP--AND WHY? WE QUOTE:
TAKE IT FROM ME--THE CHALLENGER IS TOO GREEN TO BOTHER THE CHAMP. NO RING SAVVY! HASN'T HAD ENOUGH FIGHTS UNDER HIS BELT! THERE'S NOTHING LIKE EXPERIENCE IN THE BOXING GAME--TAKE IT FROM ME....
JIMMY HATLO'

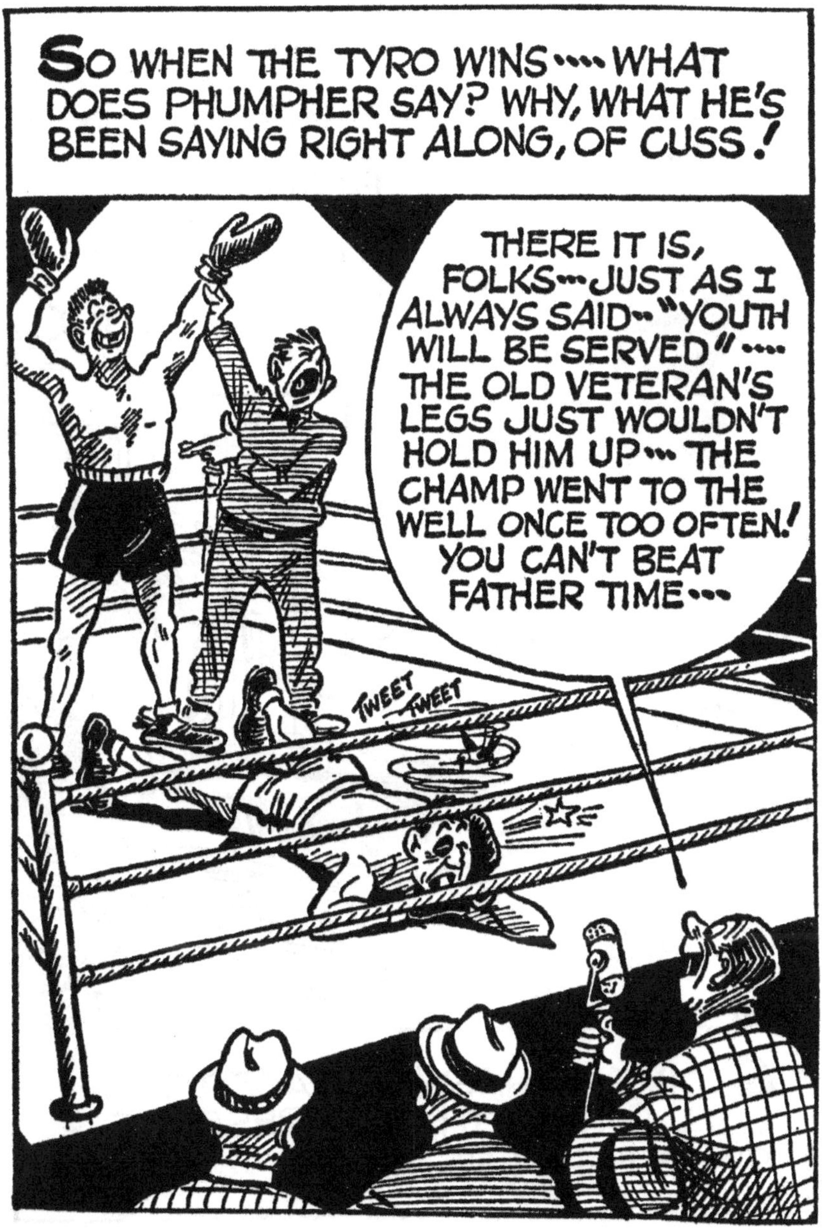
SO WHEN THE TYRO WINS···· WHAT DOES PHUMPHER SAY? WHY, WHAT HE'S BEEN SAYING RIGHT ALONG, OF CUSS!
THERE IT IS, FOLKS··· JUST AS I ALWAYS SAID·· "YOUTH WILL BE SERVED"···· THE OLD VETERAN'S LEGS JUST WOULDN'T HOLD HIM UP··· THE CHAMP WENT TO THE WELL ONCE TOO OFTEN! YOU CAN'T BEAT FATHER TIME···
TWEET TWEET

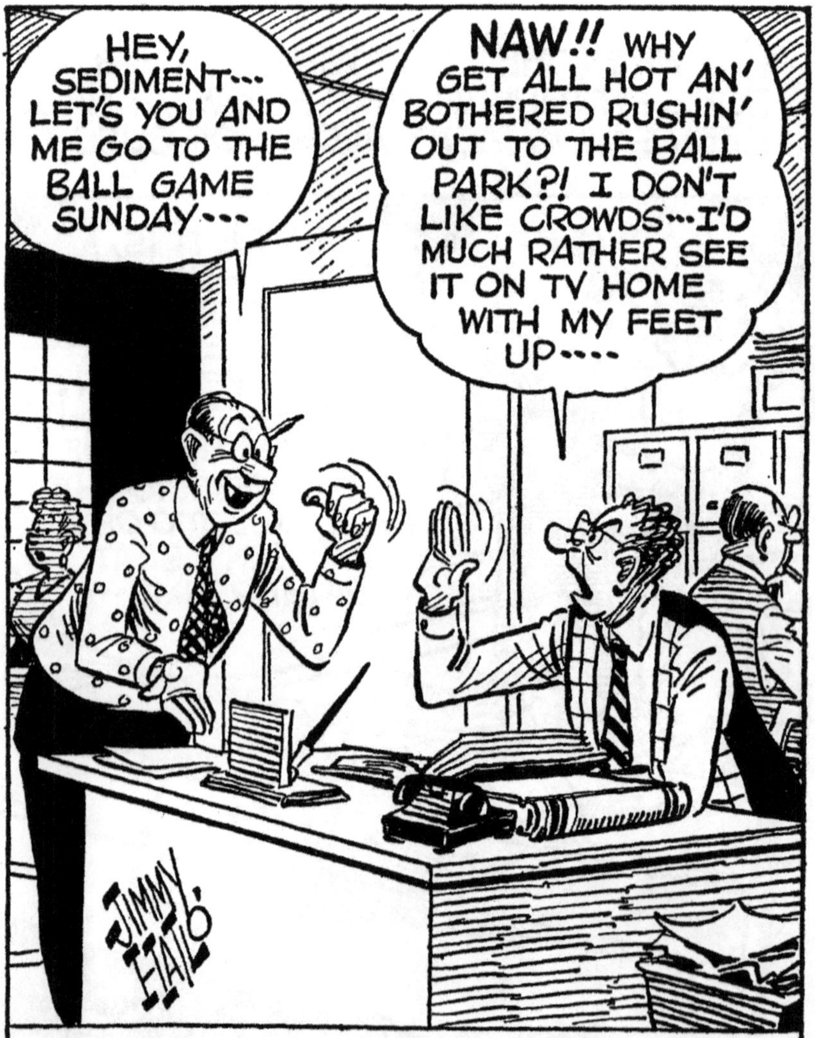
HEY, SEDIMENT--- LET'S YOU AND ME GO TO THE BALL GAME SUNDAY---
NAW!! WHY GET ALL HOT AN' BOTHERED RUSHIN' OUT TO THE BALL PARK?! I DON'T LIKE CROWDS---I'D MUCH RATHER SEE IT ON TV HOME WITH MY FEET UP----
JIMMY HATLO

SEDIMENT HASN'T GRACED THE BALL PARK WITH HIS PRESENCE SINCE 1949 (P.S. HE HAD A PASS)

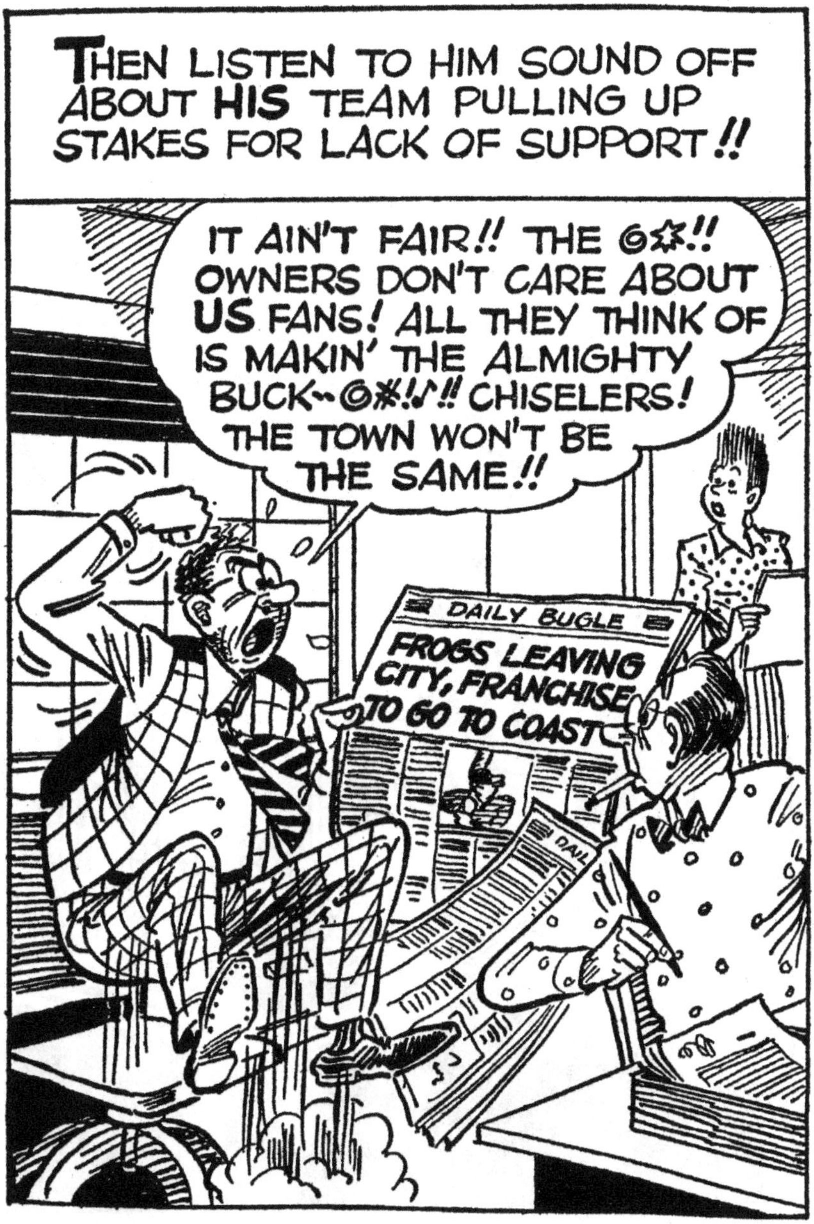
THEN LISTEN TO HIM SOUND OFF ABOUT HIS TEAM PULLING UP STAKES FOR LACK OF SUPPORT!!
IT AIN'T FAIR!! THE @☆!! OWNERS DON'T CARE ABOUT US FANS! ALL THEY THINK OF IS MAKIN' THE ALMIGHTY BUCK--@#!♪!! CHISELERS! THE TOWN WON'T BE THE SAME!!
DAILY BUGLE
FROGS LEAVING CITY, FRANCHISE TO GO TO COAST

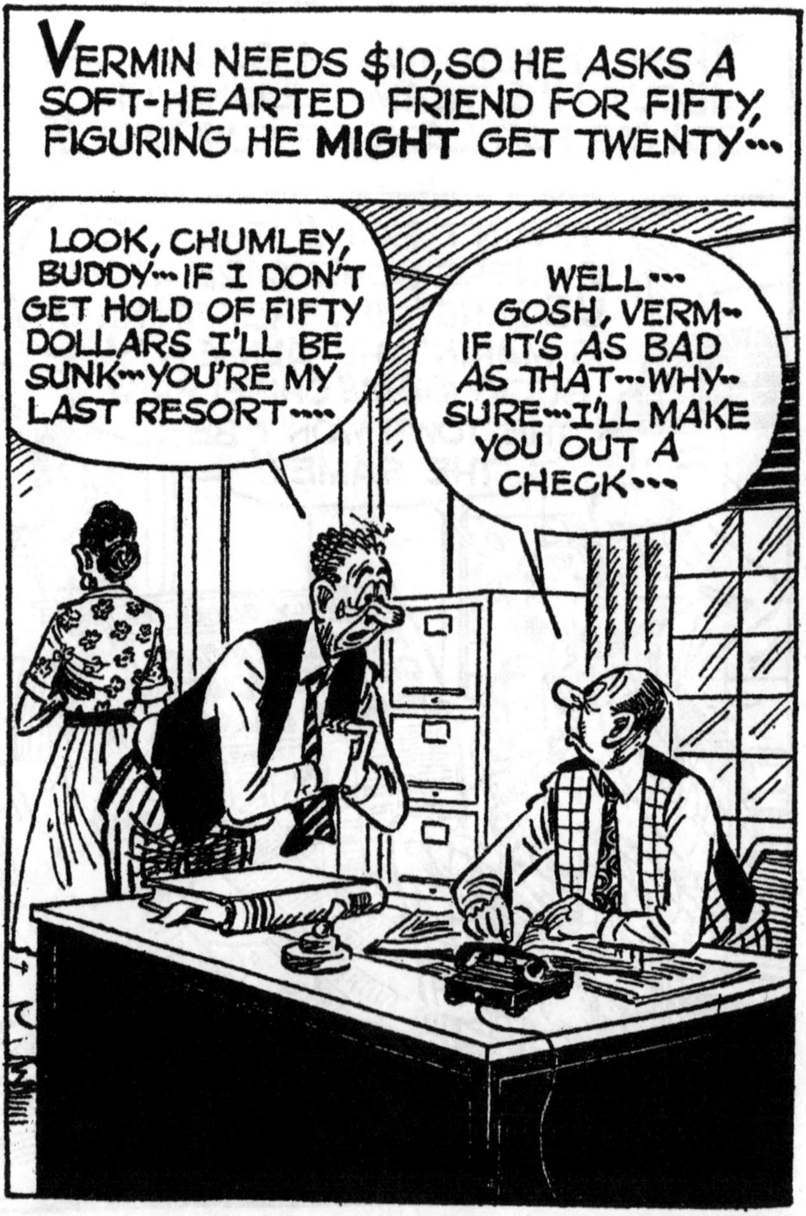
VERMIN NEEDS $10, SO HE ASKS A SOFT-HEARTED FRIEND FOR FIFTY, FIGURING HE MIGHT GET TWENTY…
LOOK, CHUMLEY, BUDDY… IF I DON'T GET HOLD OF FIFTY DOLLARS I'LL BE SUNK… YOU'RE MY LAST RESORT…
WELL… GOSH, VERM… IF IT'S AS BAD AS THAT… WHY… SURE… I'LL MAKE YOU OUT A CHECK…

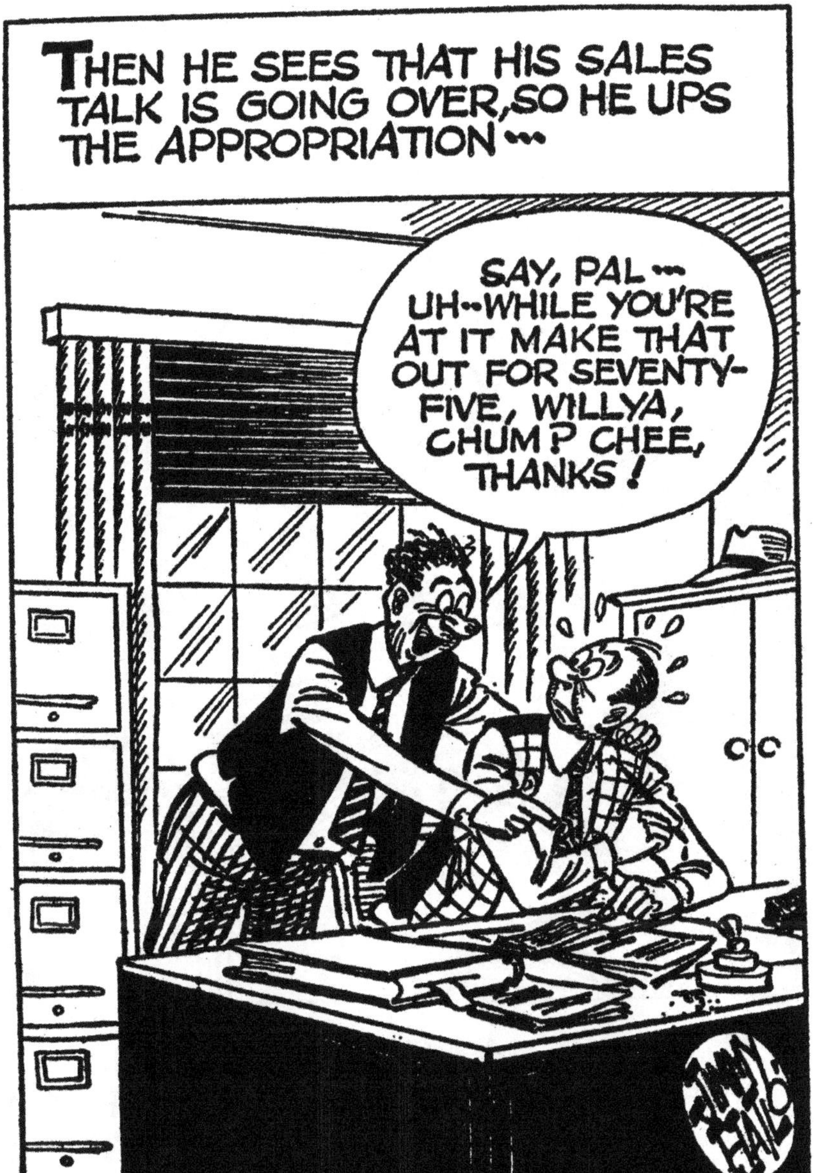
THEN HE SEES THAT HIS SALES TALK IS GOING OVER, SO HE UPS THE APPROPRIATION...
SAY, PAL... UH--WHILE YOU'RE AT IT MAKE THAT OUT FOR SEVENTY-FIVE, WILLYA, CHUM? CHEE, THANKS!

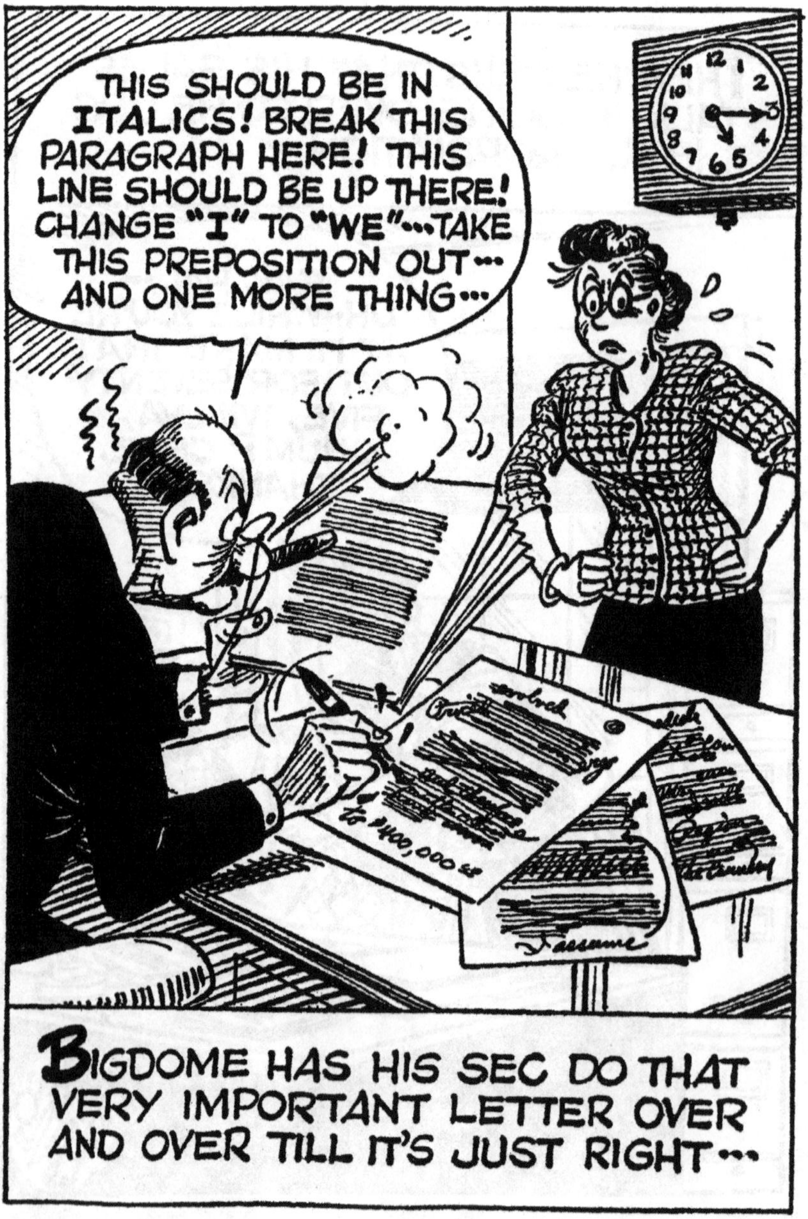
THIS SHOULD BE IN ITALICS! BREAK THIS PARAGRAPH HERE! THIS LINE SHOULD BE UP THERE! CHANGE "I" TO "WE"...TAKE THIS PREPOSITION OUT... AND ONE MORE THING...
BIGDOME HAS HIS SEC DO THAT VERY IMPORTANT LETTER OVER AND OVER TILL IT'S JUST RIGHT...

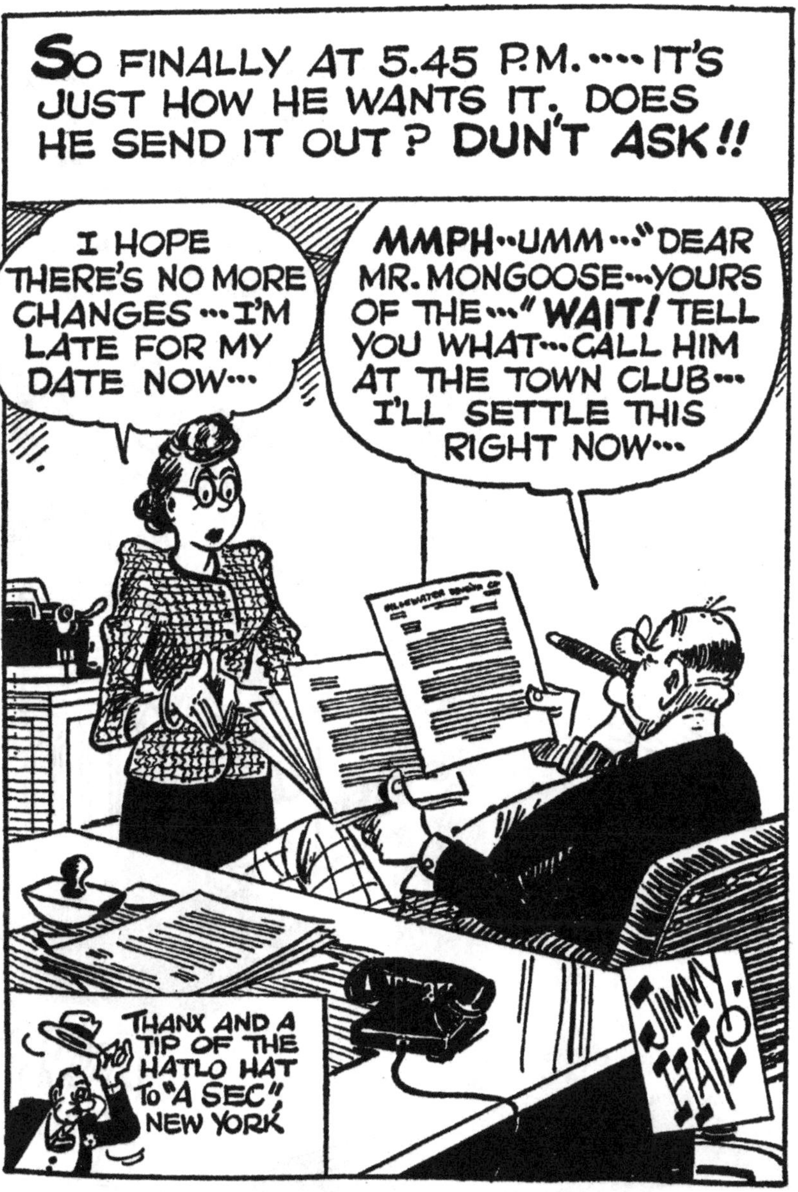

SO FINALLY AT 5.45 P.M. .... IT'S JUST HOW HE WANTS IT. DOES HE SEND IT OUT? DUN'T ASK!!
I HOPE THERE'S NO MORE CHANGES ... I'M LATE FOR MY DATE NOW ...
MMPH .. UMM ... "DEAR MR. MONGOOSE ... YOURS OF THE ..." WAIT! TELL YOU WHAT ... CALL HIM AT THE TOWN CLUB ... I'LL SETTLE THIS RIGHT NOW ...
THANX AND A TIP OF THE HATLO HAT TO "A SEC," NEW YORK
JIMMY HATLO

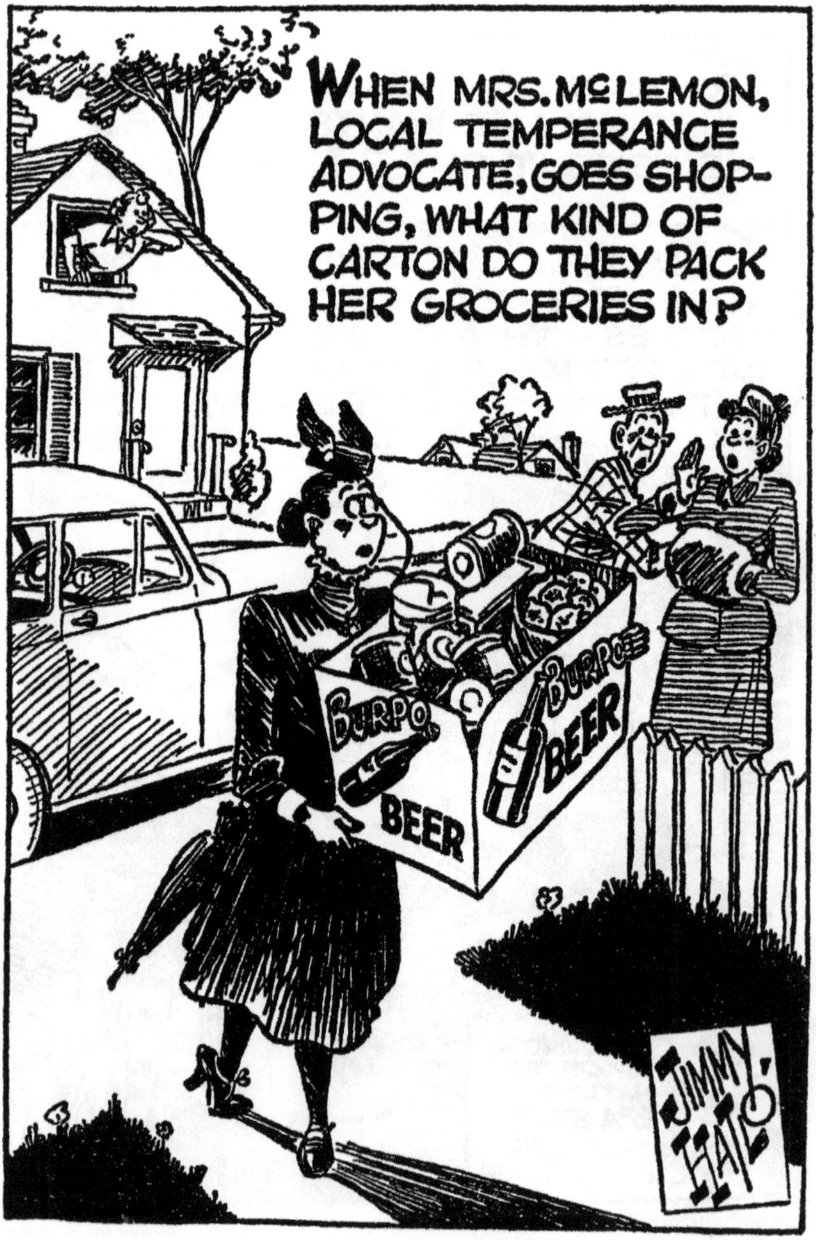
WHEN MRS. McLEMON, LOCAL TEMPERANCE ADVOCATE, GOES SHOP-PING, WHAT KIND OF CARTON DO THEY PACK HER GROCERIES IN?
BURPO BEER
BURPO BEER
JIMMY HATLO

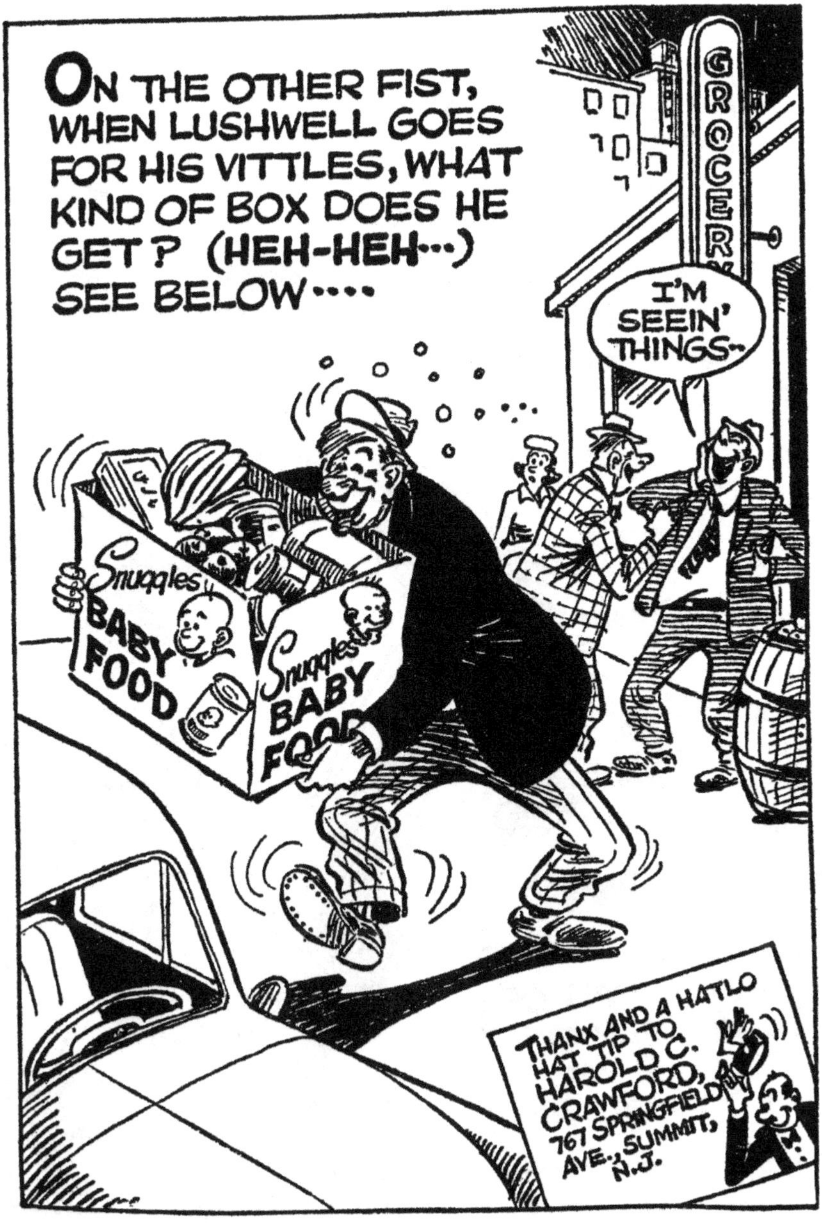
ON THE OTHER FIST, WHEN LUSHWELL GOES FOR HIS VITTLES, WHAT KIND OF BOX DOES HE GET? (HEH-HEH...) SEE BELOW....
GROCER
I'M SEEIN' THINGS--
Snuggles BABY FOOD
Snuggles BABY FOOD
THANX AND A HATLO HAT TIP TO HAROLD C. CRAWFORD, 767 SPRINGFIELD AVE., SUMMIT, N.J.

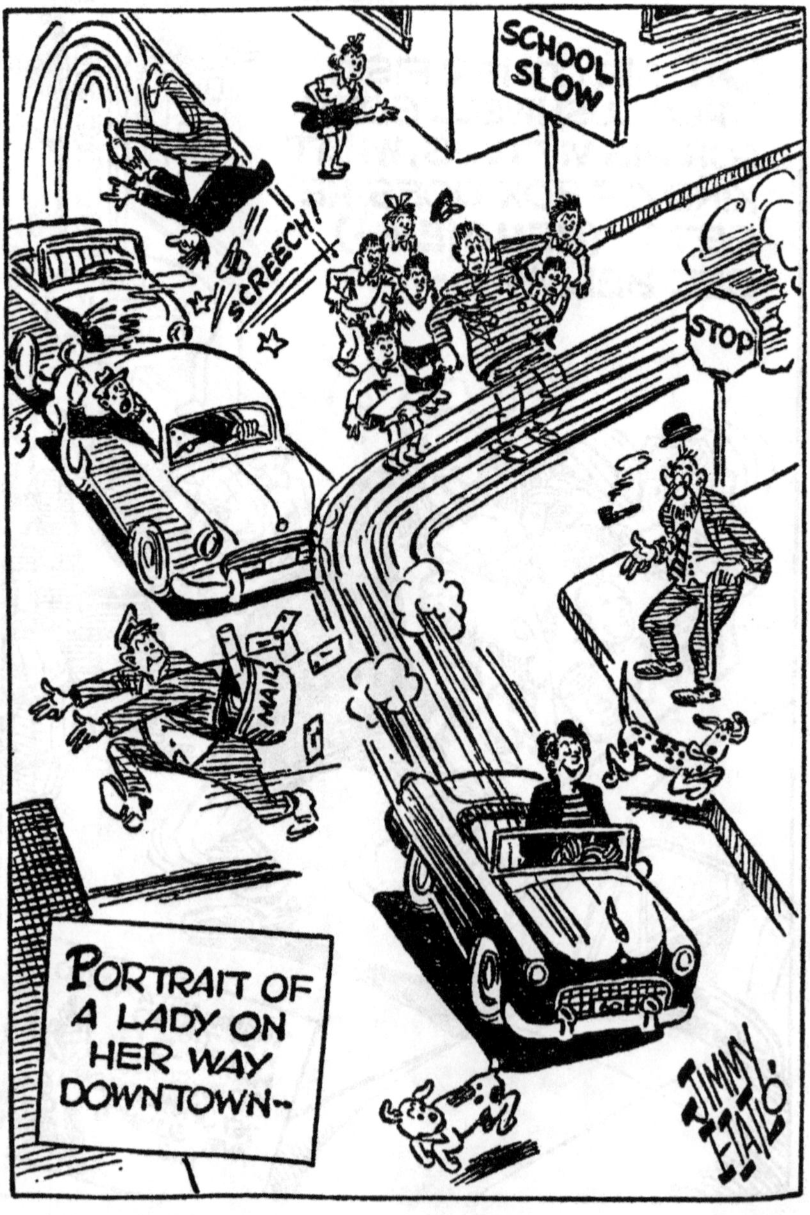
SCHOOL
SLOW
SCREECH!
STOP
MAIL
PORTRAIT OF
A LADY ON
HER WAY
DOWNTOWN--
JIMMY HATLO

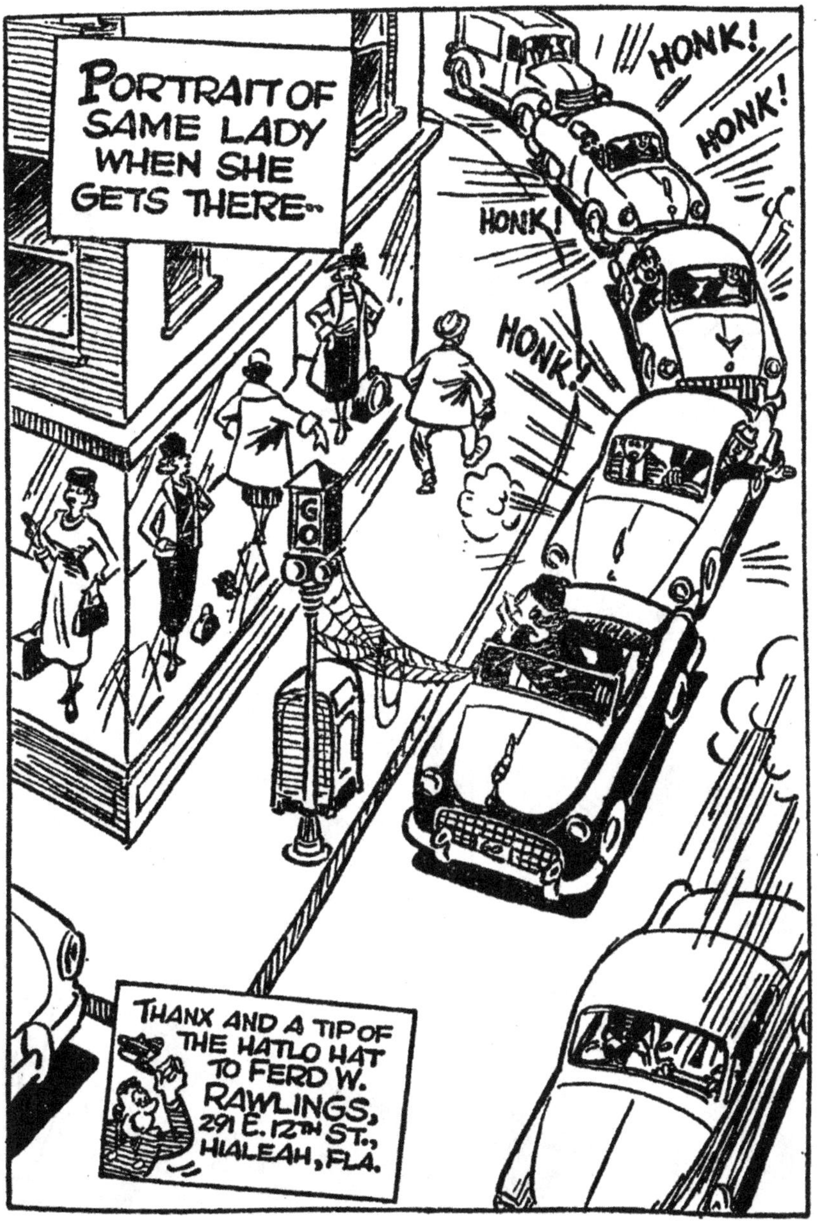
PORTRAIT OF SAME LADY WHEN SHE GETS THERE--
HONK!
HONK!
HONK!
HONK!
GO
THANX AND A TIP OF THE HATLO HAT TO FERD W. RAWLINGS, 291 E. 12TH ST., HIALEAH, FLA.

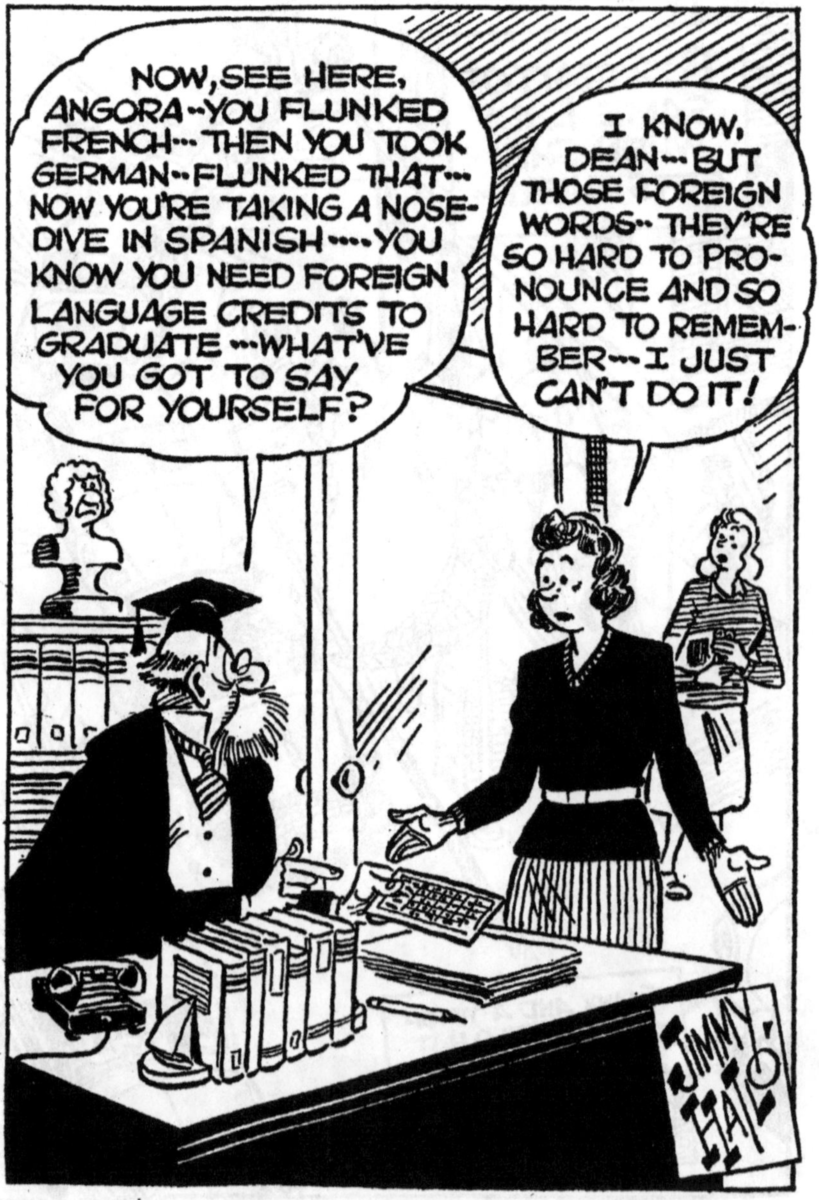
NOW, SEE HERE, ANGORA--YOU FLUNKED FRENCH--- THEN YOU TOOK GERMAN--FLUNKED THAT--- NOW YOU'RE TAKING A NOSE-DIVE IN SPANISH----YOU KNOW YOU NEED FOREIGN LANGUAGE CREDITS TO GRADUATE ---WHAT'VE YOU GOT TO SAY FOR YOURSELF?
I KNOW, DEAN--- BUT THOSE FOREIGN WORDS-- THEY'RE SO HARD TO PRONOUNCE AND SO HARD TO REMEMBER--- I JUST CAN'T DO IT!
JIMMY HATLO

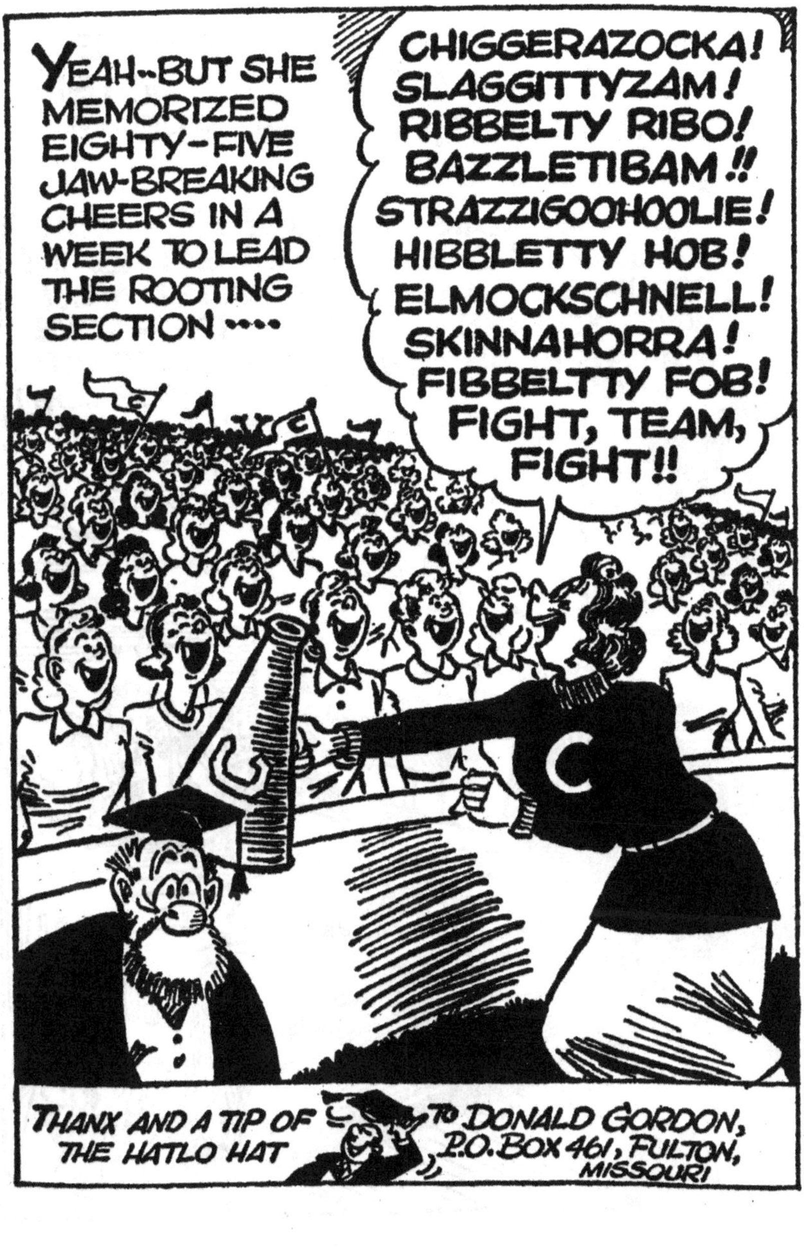

YEAH--BUT SHE MEMORIZED EIGHTY-FIVE JAW-BREAKING CHEERS IN A WEEK TO LEAD THE ROOTING SECTION ....
CHIGGERAZOCKA! SLAGGITTYZAM! RIBBELTY RIBO! BAZZLETIBAM!! STRAZZIGOOHOOLIE! HIBBLETTY HOB! ELMOCKSCHNELL! SKINNAHORRA! FIBBELTTY FOB! FIGHT, TEAM, FIGHT!!
THANX AND A TIP OF THE HATLO HAT TO DONALD GORDON, P.O. BOX 461, FULTON, MISSOURI

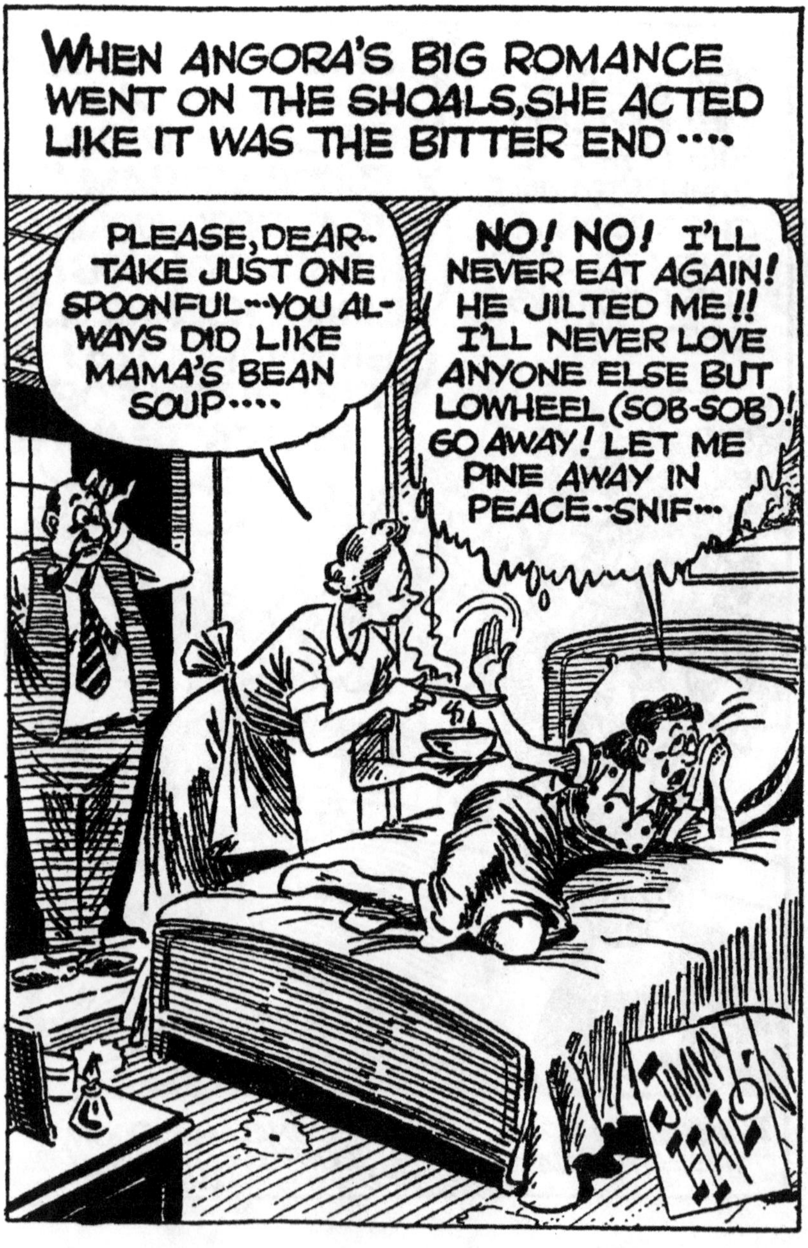
WHEN ANGORA'S BIG ROMANCE WENT ON THE SHOALS, SHE ACTED LIKE IT WAS THE BITTER END....
PLEASE, DEAR--TAKE JUST ONE SPOONFUL--YOU ALWAYS DID LIKE MAMA'S BEAN SOUP....
NO! NO! I'LL NEVER EAT AGAIN! HE JILTED ME!! I'LL NEVER LOVE ANYONE ELSE BUT LOWHEEL (SOB-SOB)! GO AWAY! LET ME PINE AWAY IN PEACE--SNIF--
JIMMY HATLO

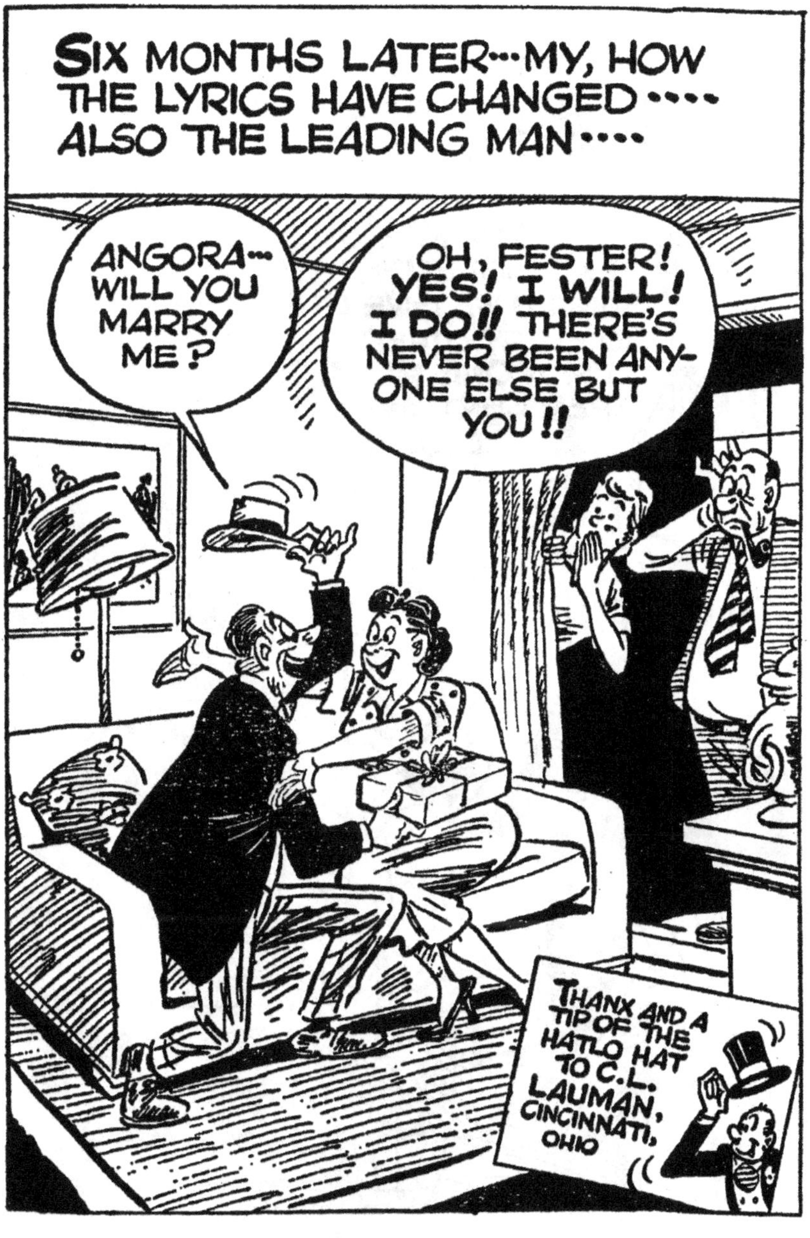
SIX MONTHS LATER--MY, HOW THE LYRICS HAVE CHANGED.... ALSO THE LEADING MAN....
ANGORA-- WILL YOU MARRY ME?
OH, FESTER! YES! I WILL! I DO!! THERE'S NEVER BEEN ANYONE ELSE BUT YOU!!
THANX AND A TIP OF THE HATLO HAT TO C.L. LAUMAN, CINCINNATI, OHIO

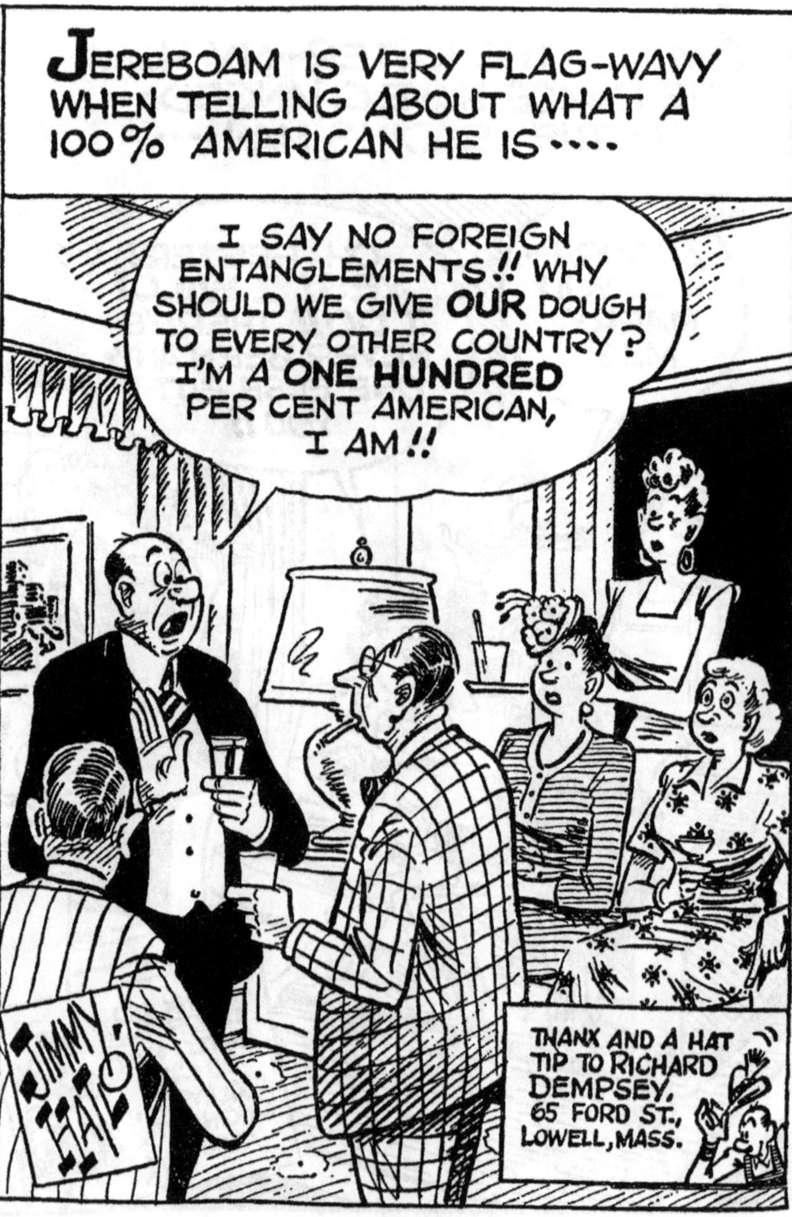
JEREBOAM IS VERY FLAG-WAVY WHEN TELLING ABOUT WHAT A 100% AMERICAN HE IS····
I SAY NO FOREIGN ENTANGLEMENTS!! WHY SHOULD WE GIVE OUR DOUGH TO EVERY OTHER COUNTRY? I'M A ONE HUNDRED PER CENT AMERICAN, I AM!!
JIMMY HATLO
THANX AND A HAT TIP TO RICHARD DEMPSEY, 65 FORD ST., LOWELL, MASS.

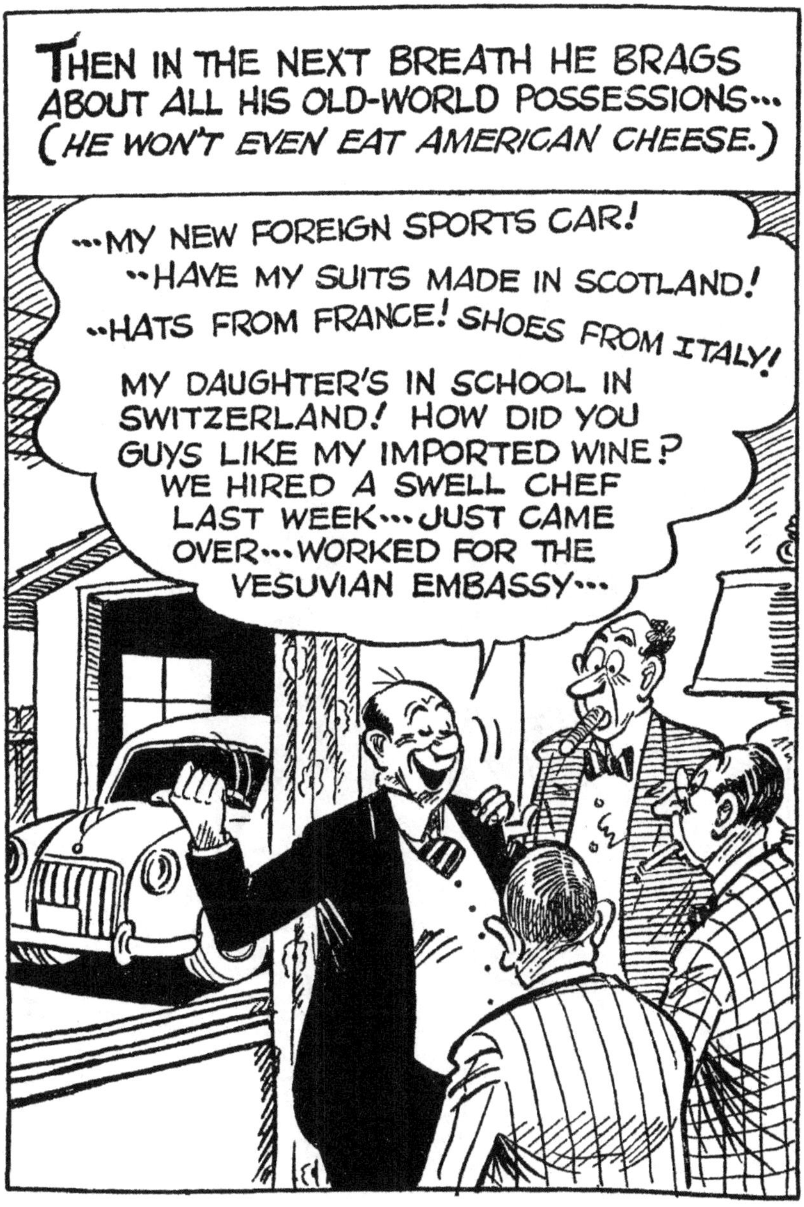
THEN IN THE NEXT BREATH HE BRAGS ABOUT ALL HIS OLD-WORLD POSSESSIONS... (HE WON'T EVEN EAT AMERICAN CHEESE.)
...MY NEW FOREIGN SPORTS CAR! ..HAVE MY SUITS MADE IN SCOTLAND! ..HATS FROM FRANCE! SHOES FROM ITALY! MY DAUGHTER'S IN SCHOOL IN SWITZERLAND! HOW DID YOU GUYS LIKE MY IMPORTED WINE? WE HIRED A SWELL CHEF LAST WEEK... JUST CAME OVER... WORKED FOR THE VESUVIAN EMBASSY...

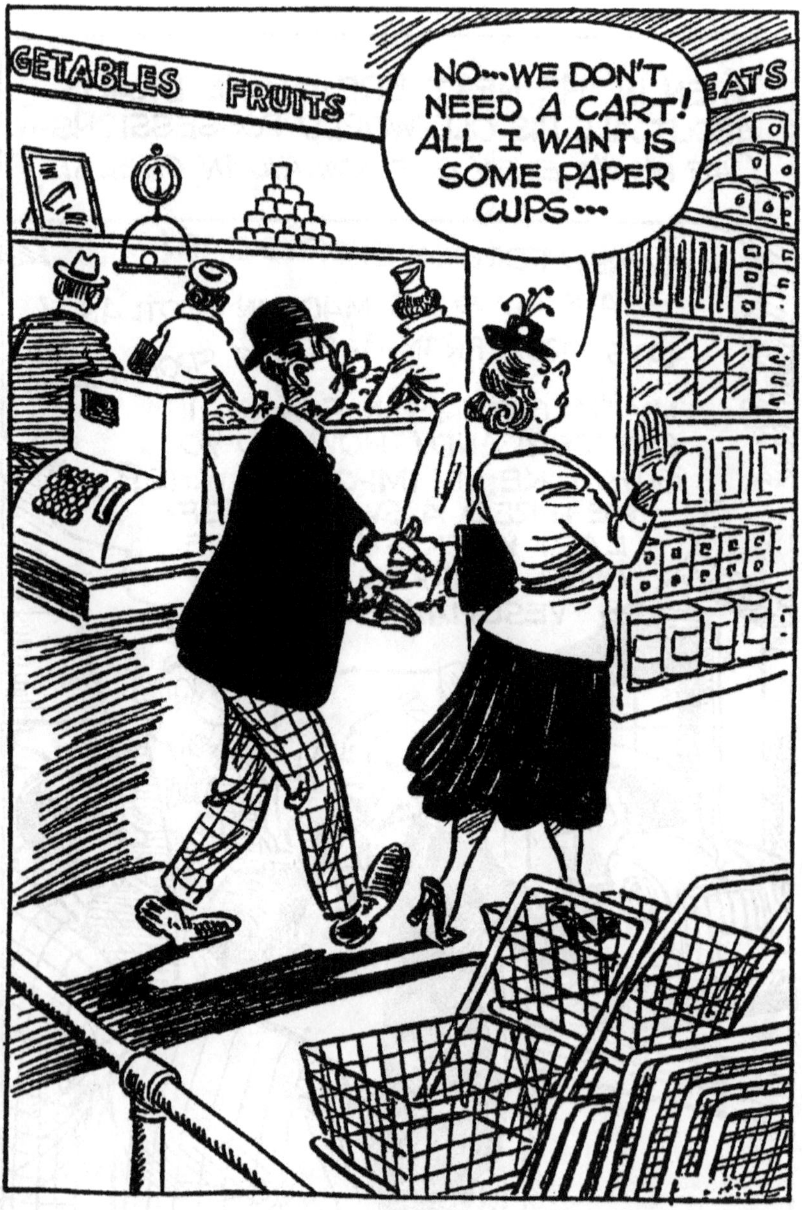
GETABLES
FRUITS
EATS
NO...WE DON'T NEED A CART! ALL I WANT IS SOME PAPER CUPS...

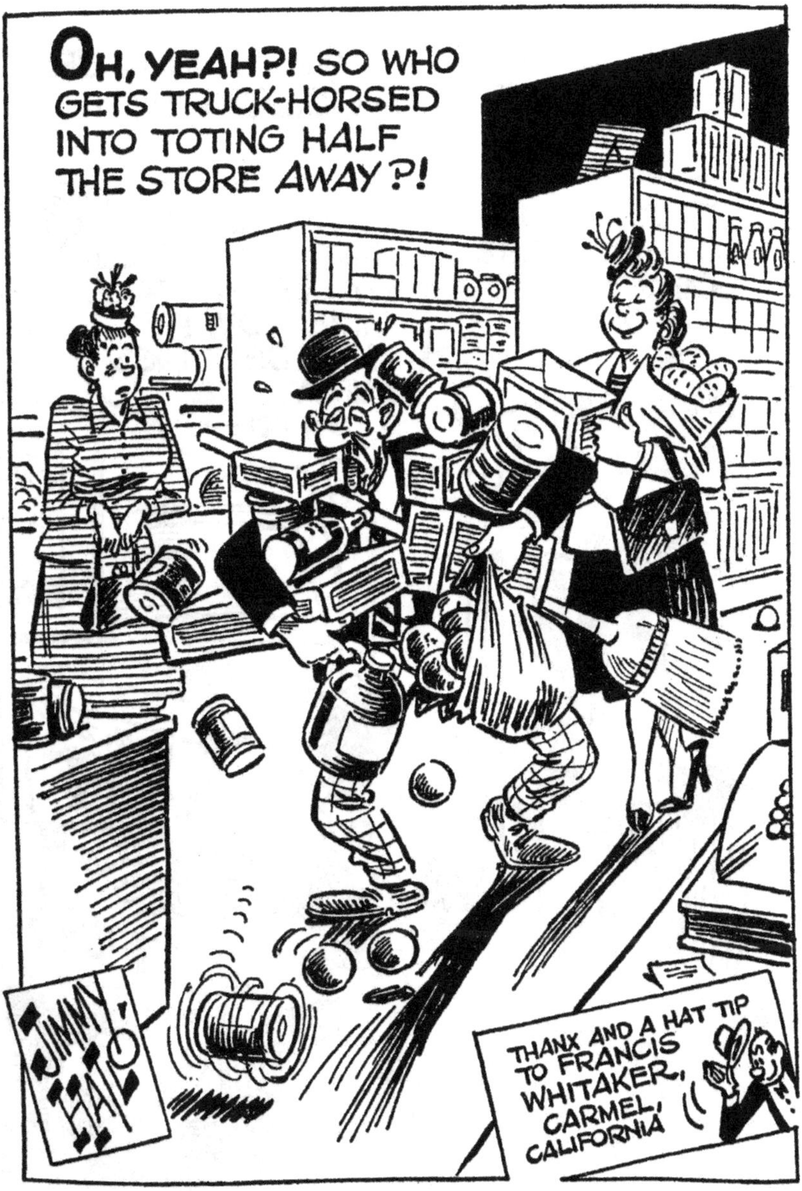
OH, YEAH?! SO WHO GETS TRUCK-HORSED INTO TOTING HALF THE STORE AWAY?!
JIMMY HATLO
THANX AND A HAT TIP TO FRANCIS WHITAKER, CARMEL, CALIFORNIA

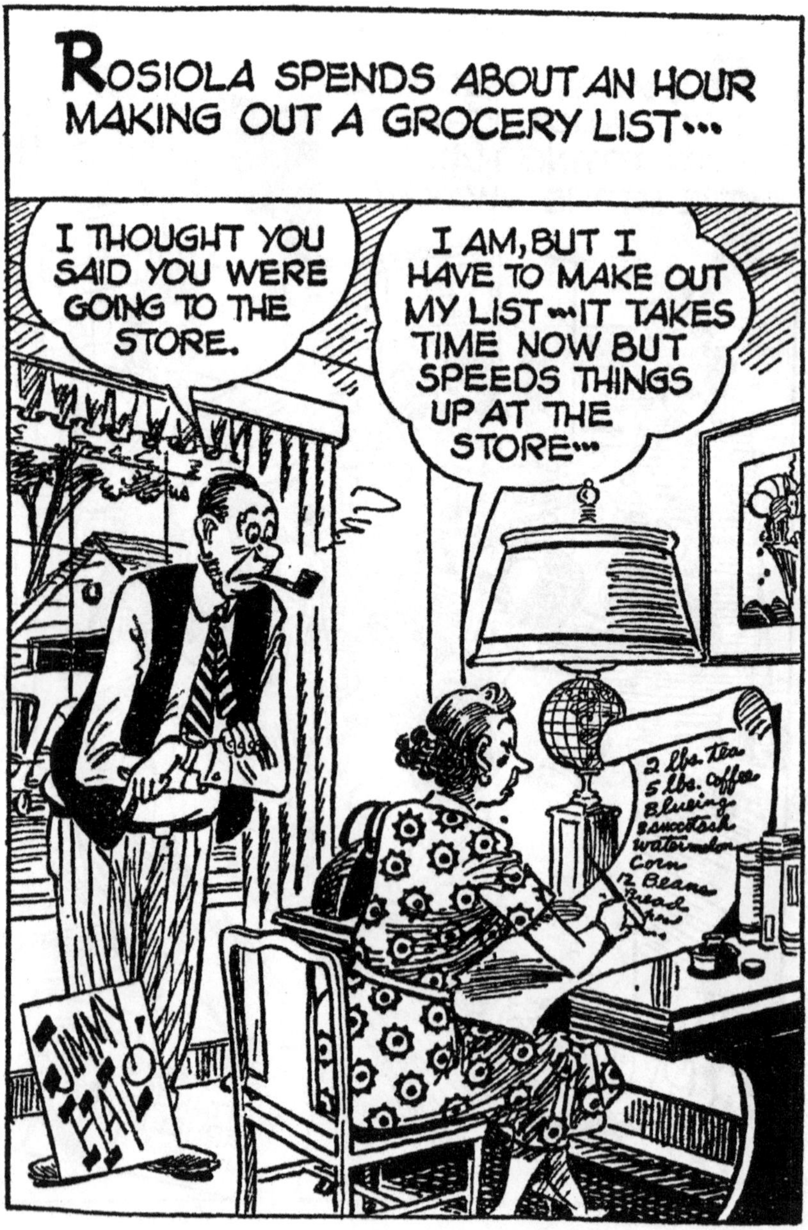
ROSIOLA SPENDS ABOUT AN HOUR MAKING OUT A GROCERY LIST...
I THOUGHT YOU SAID YOU WERE GOING TO THE STORE.
I AM, BUT I HAVE TO MAKE OUT MY LIST...IT TAKES TIME NOW BUT SPEEDS THINGS UP AT THE STORE...
2 lbs. tea
5 lbs. coffee
Bluing
Corn
JIMMY HATLO

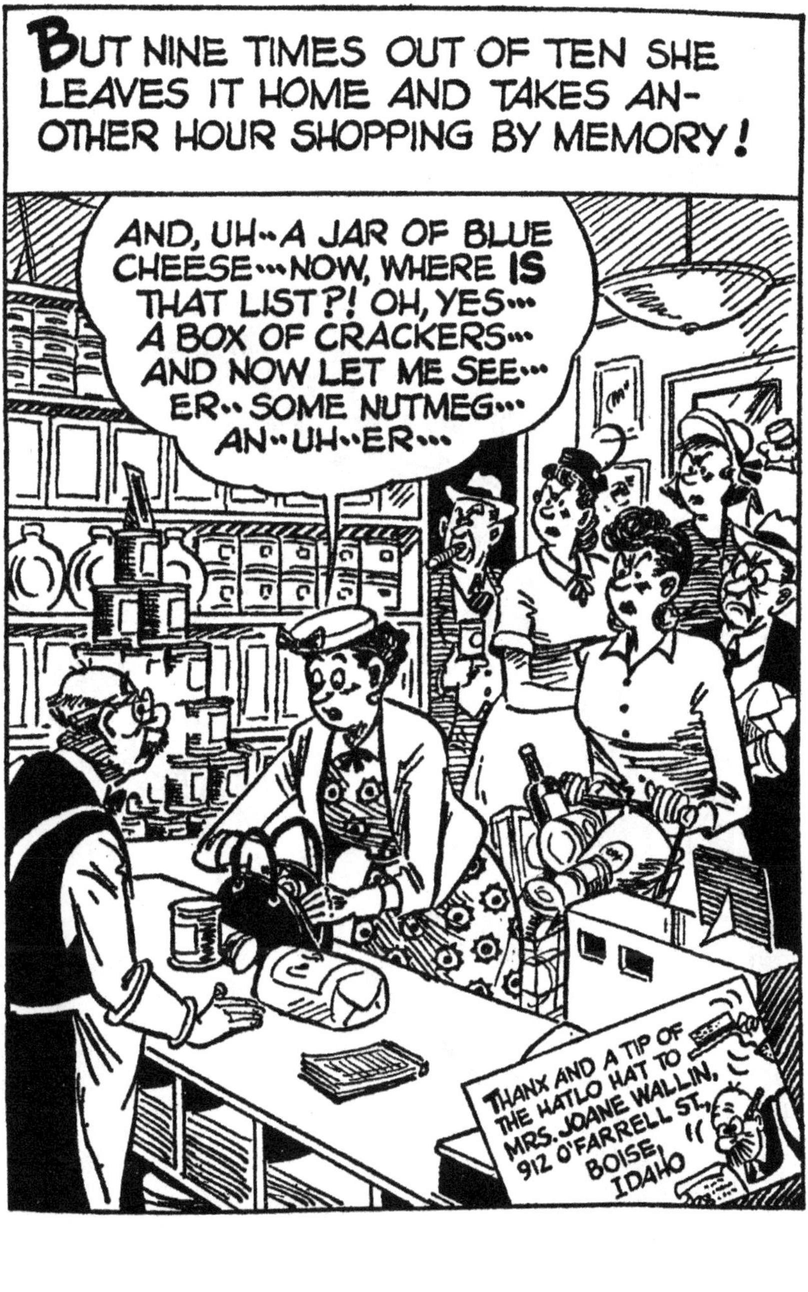
BUT NINE TIMES OUT OF TEN SHE LEAVES IT HOME AND TAKES ANOTHER HOUR SHOPPING BY MEMORY!
AND, UH-- A JAR OF BLUE CHEESE... NOW, WHERE IS THAT LIST?! OH, YES... A BOX OF CRACKERS... AND NOW LET ME SEE... ER.. SOME NUTMEG... AN-- UH-- ER...
THANX AND A TIP OF THE HATLO HAT TO MRS. JOANE WALLIN, 912 O'FARRELL ST., BOISE, IDAHO

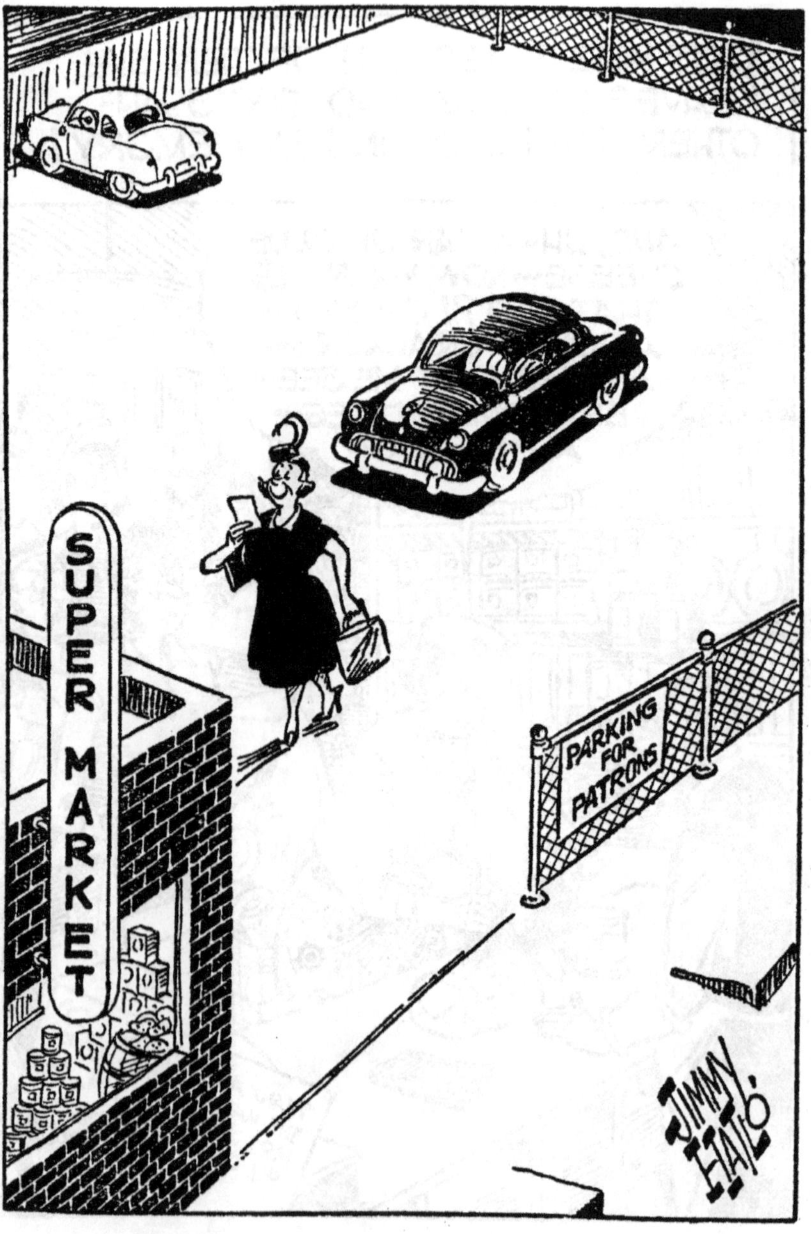
SUPER MARKET
PARKING FOR PATRONS
JIMMY HATLO

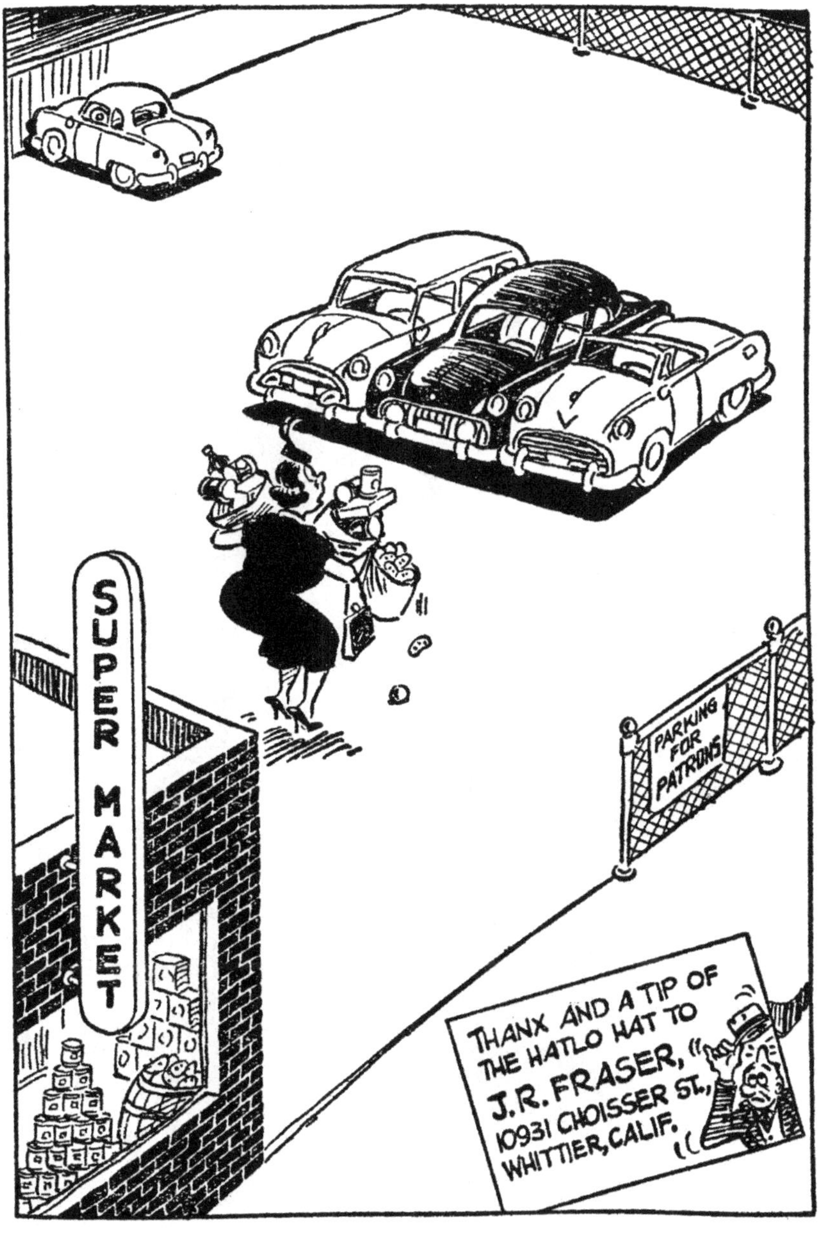
SUPER MARKET
PARKING FOR PATRONS
THANX AND A TIP OF THE HATLO HAT TO J.R. FRASER, 10931 CHOISSER ST., WHITTIER, CALIF.

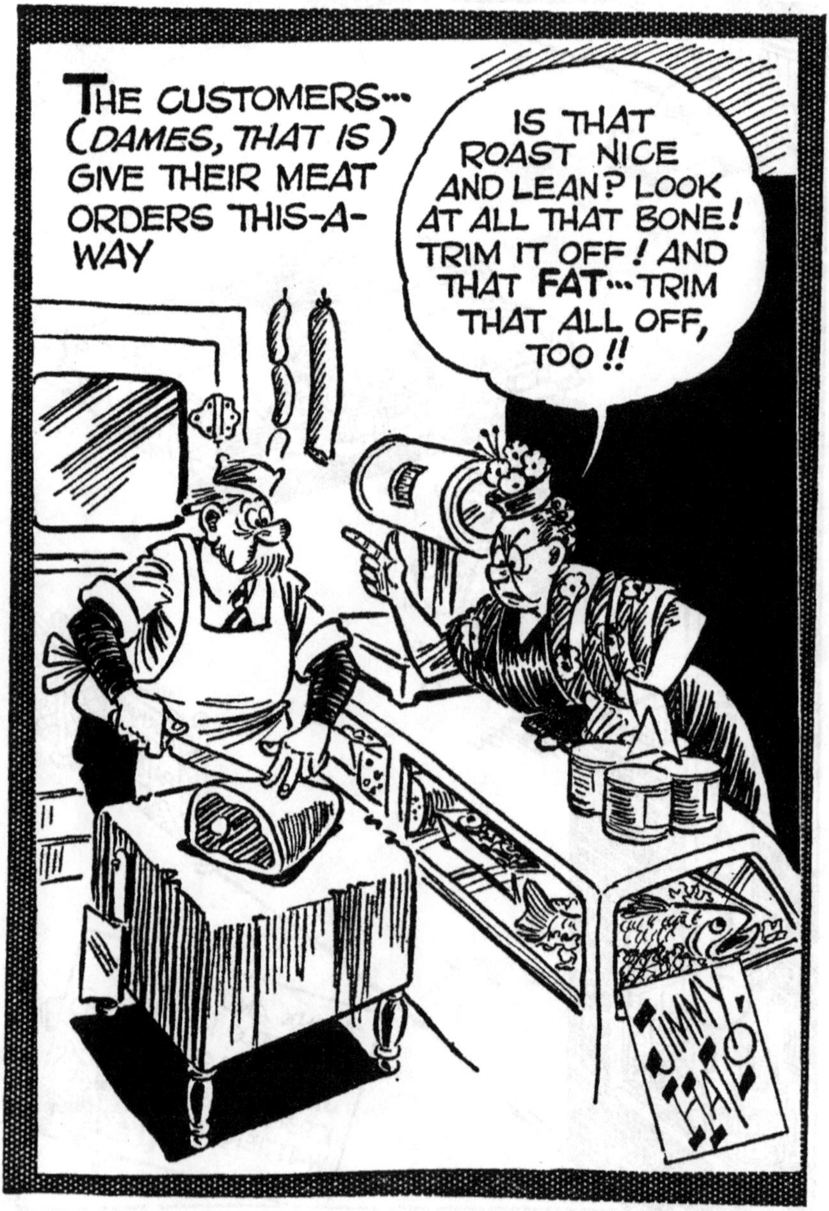
THE CUSTOMERS... (DAMES, THAT IS) GIVE THEIR MEAT ORDERS THIS-A-WAY
IS THAT ROAST NICE AND LEAN? LOOK AT ALL THAT BONE! TRIM IT OFF! AND THAT FAT... TRIM THAT ALL OFF, TOO!!
JIMMY HATLO

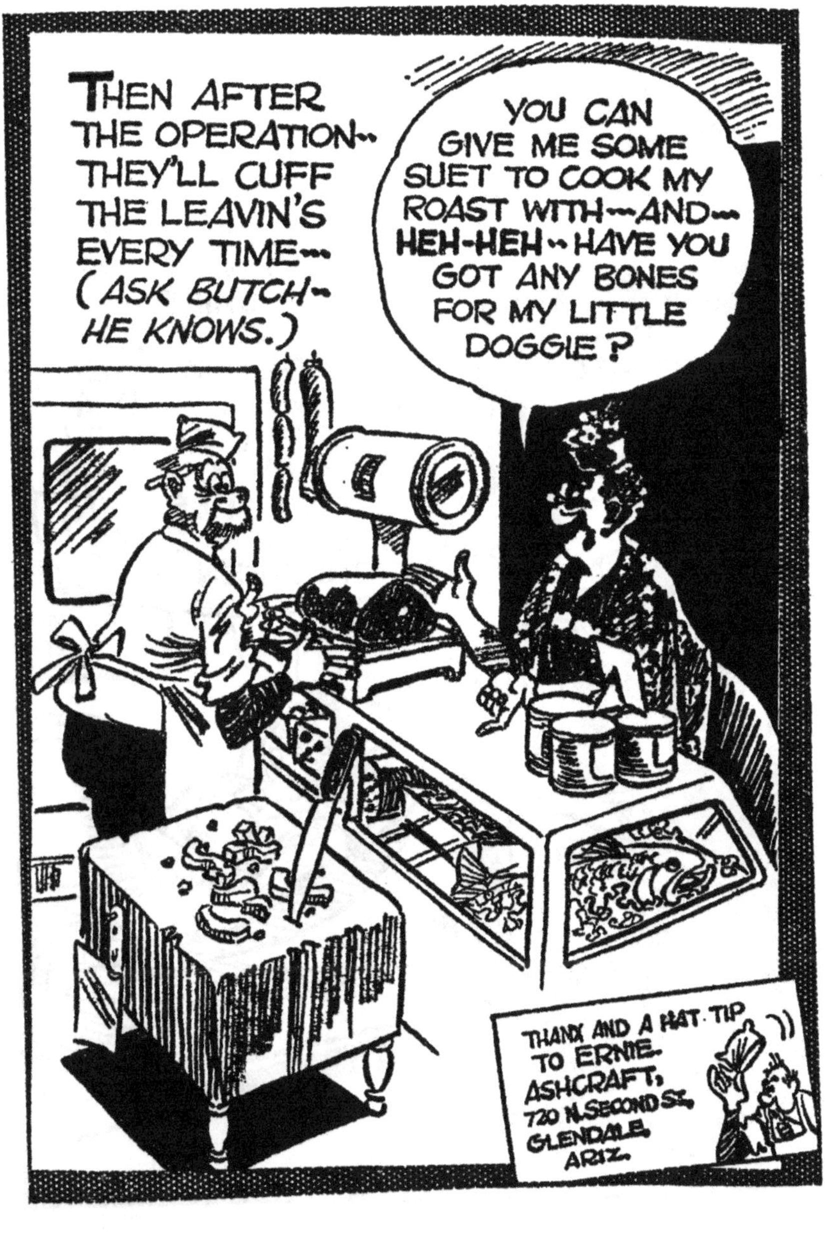
THEN AFTER THE OPERATION.. THEY'LL CUFF THE LEAVIN'S EVERY TIME--- (ASK BUTCH-- HE KNOWS.)
YOU CAN GIVE ME SOME SUET TO COOK MY ROAST WITH---AND--- HEH-HEH -- HAVE YOU GOT ANY BONES FOR MY LITTLE DOGGIE?
THANX AND A HAT-TIP TO ERNIE ASHCRAFT, 720 N. SECOND ST., GLENDALE, ARIZ.

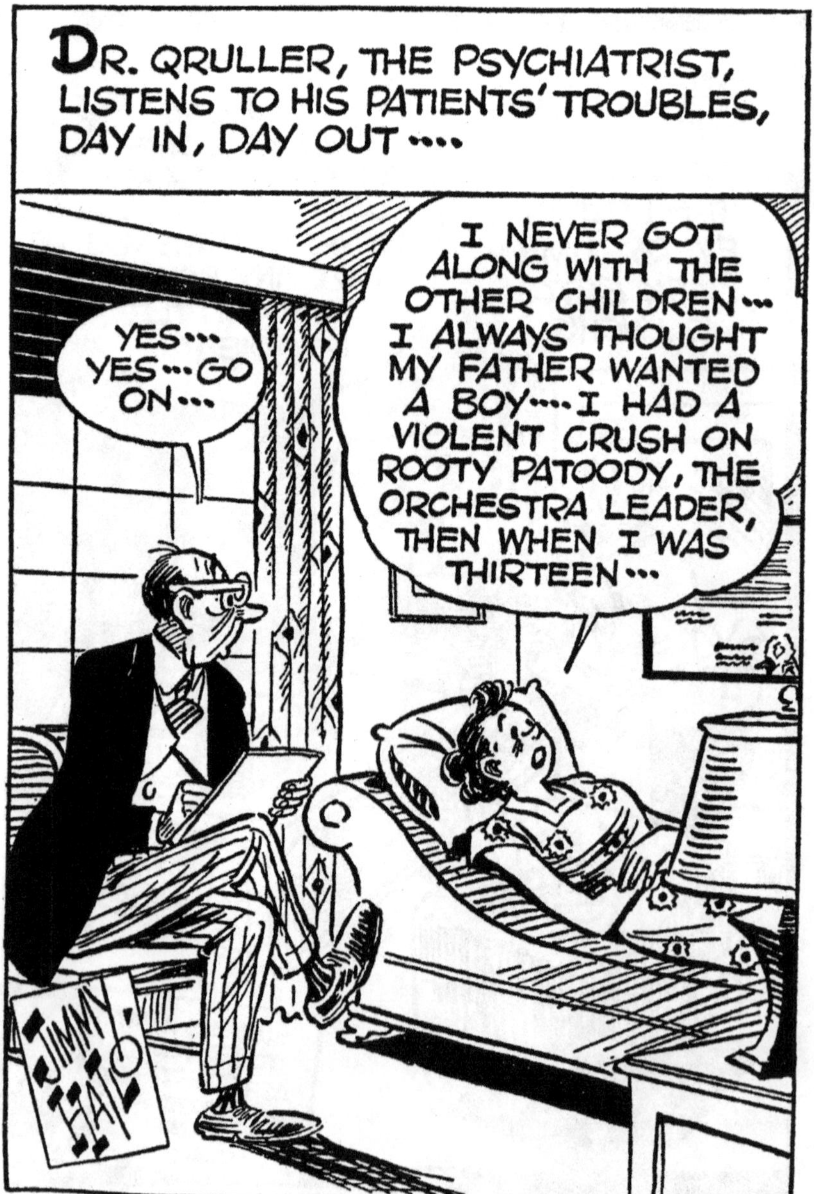
DR. QRULLER, THE PSYCHIATRIST, LISTENS TO HIS PATIENTS' TROUBLES, DAY IN, DAY OUT ....
YES... YES...GO ON...
I NEVER GOT ALONG WITH THE OTHER CHILDREN... I ALWAYS THOUGHT MY FATHER WANTED A BOY.... I HAD A VIOLENT CRUSH ON ROOTY PATOODY, THE ORCHESTRA LEADER, THEN WHEN I WAS THIRTEEN...
JIMMY HATLO

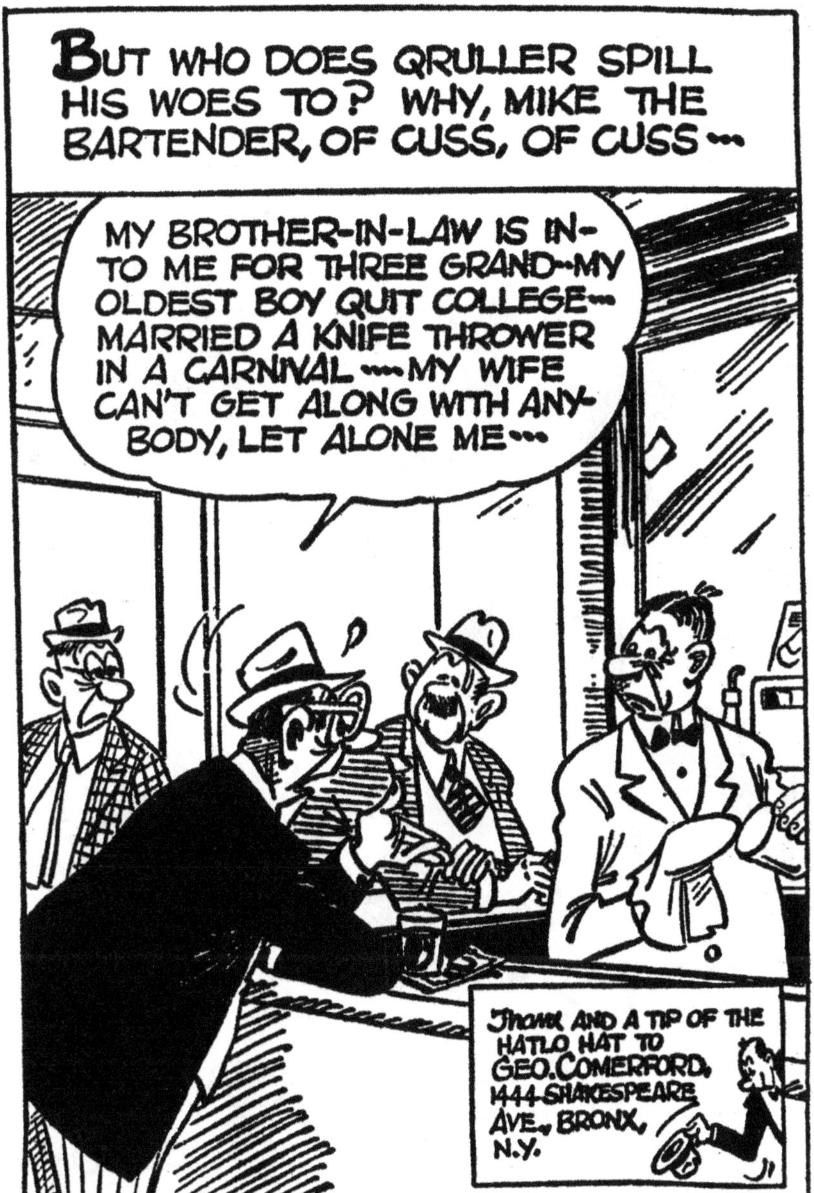
BUT WHO DOES QRULLER SPILL HIS WOES TO? WHY, MIKE THE BARTENDER, OF CUSS, OF CUSS---
MY BROTHER-IN-LAW IS INTO ME FOR THREE GRAND--MY OLDEST BOY QUIT COLLEGE--- MARRIED A KNIFE THROWER IN A CARNIVAL ---MY WIFE CAN'T GET ALONG WITH ANYBODY, LET ALONE ME---
Thanx AND A TIP OF THE HATLO HAT TO GEO. COMERFORD, 1444 SHAKESPEARE AVE., BRONX, N.Y.

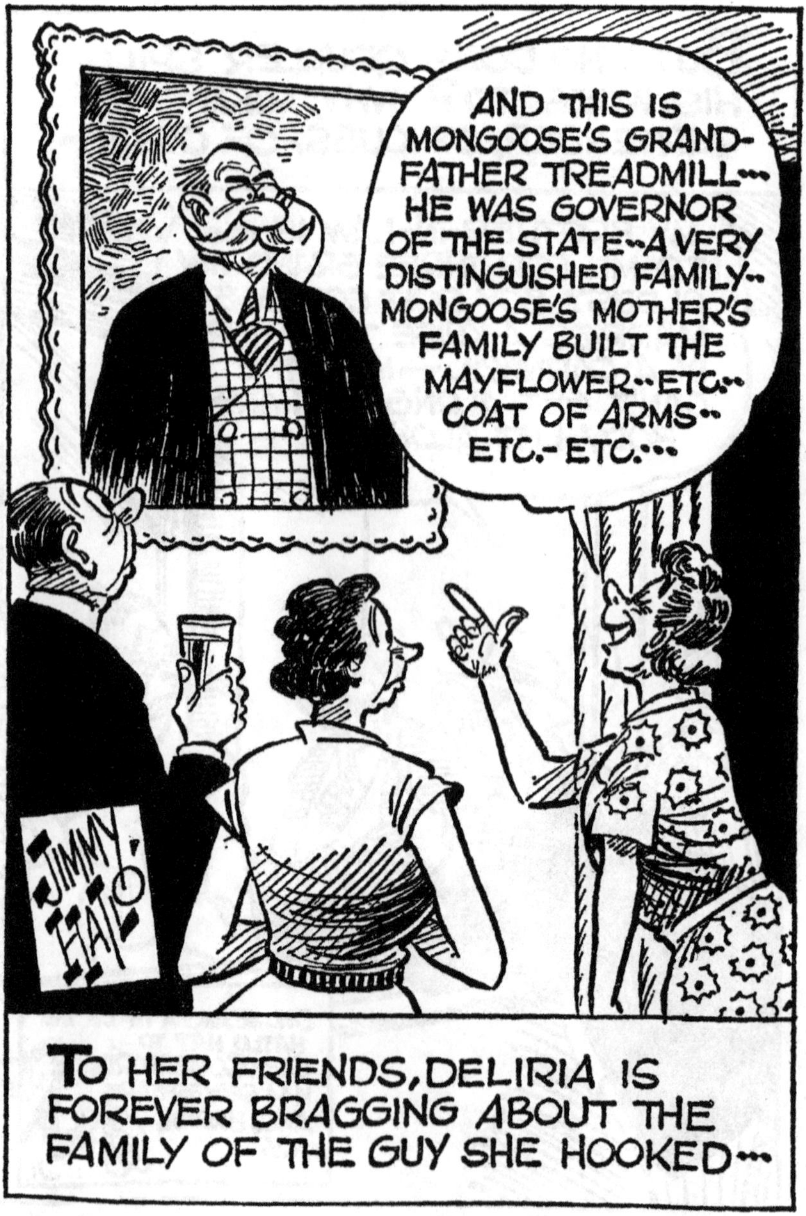
AND THIS IS MONGOOSE'S GRAND-FATHER TREADMILL... HE WAS GOVERNOR OF THE STATE--A VERY DISTINGUISHED FAMILY-- MONGOOSE'S MOTHER'S FAMILY BUILT THE MAYFLOWER--ETC.-- COAT OF ARMS-- ETC.-ETC....
JIMMY HATLO
TO HER FRIENDS, DELIRIA IS FOREVER BRAGGING ABOUT THE FAMILY OF THE GUY SHE HOOKED...

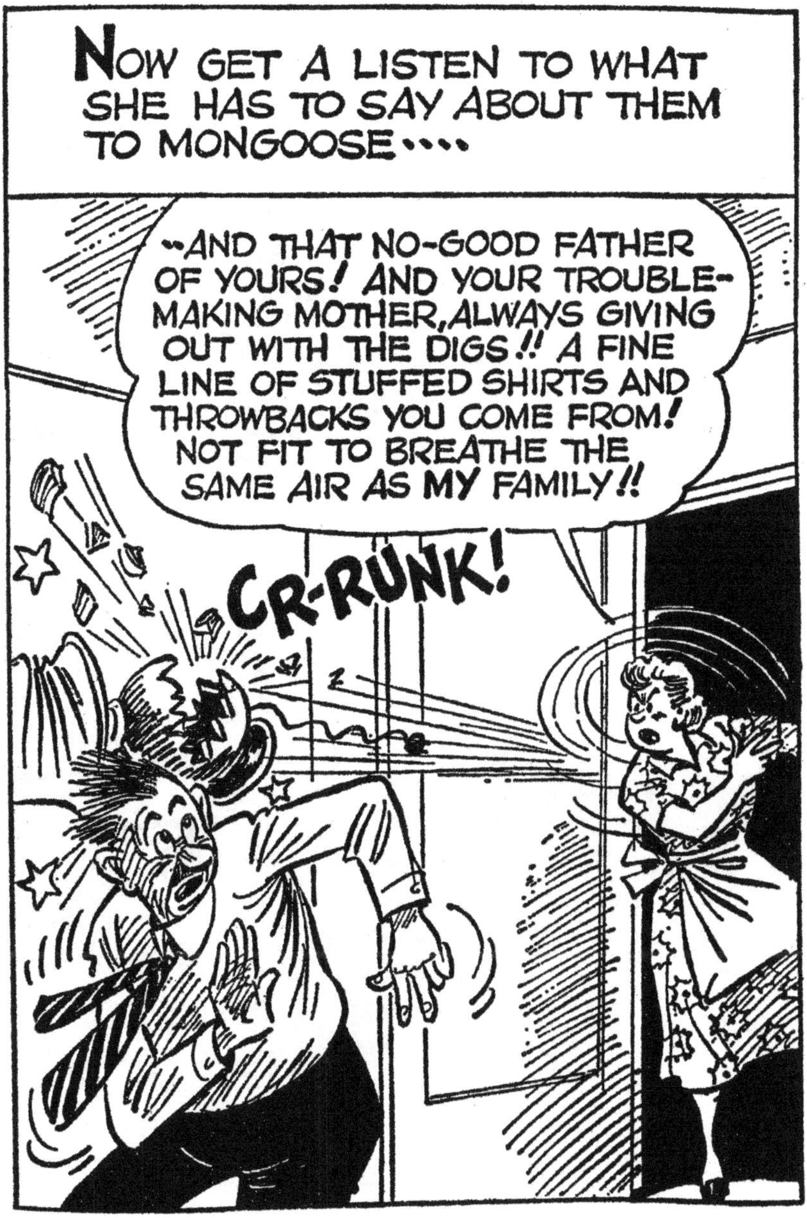
NOW GET A LISTEN TO WHAT SHE HAS TO SAY ABOUT THEM TO MONGOOSE....
--AND THAT NO-GOOD FATHER OF YOURS! AND YOUR TROUBLE-MAKING MOTHER, ALWAYS GIVING OUT WITH THE DIGS!! A FINE LINE OF STUFFED SHIRTS AND THROWBACKS YOU COME FROM! NOT FIT TO BREATHE THE SAME AIR AS MY FAMILY!!
CR-RUNK!

JUNIOR TURNS HIS TOUGH HOMEWORK PROBLEMS OVER TO POP AND KEEPS WATCHING THE BANG-BANG...
POP...WILL YOU HELP ME WITH MY ALGEBRA? WHAT'S THE SQUARE ROOT OF M+7 OVER 67XYB? WILL YOU WORK IT OUT, POP? THANKS...HERE--
JIMMY HATLO
THANX AND A HAT TIP TO E.M. DEIBELE, 905 NE 131 PLACE, PORTLAND 16, ORE.

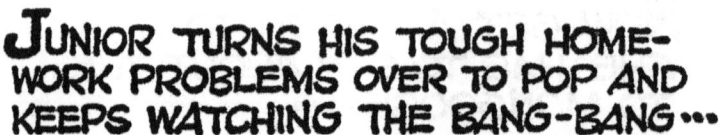

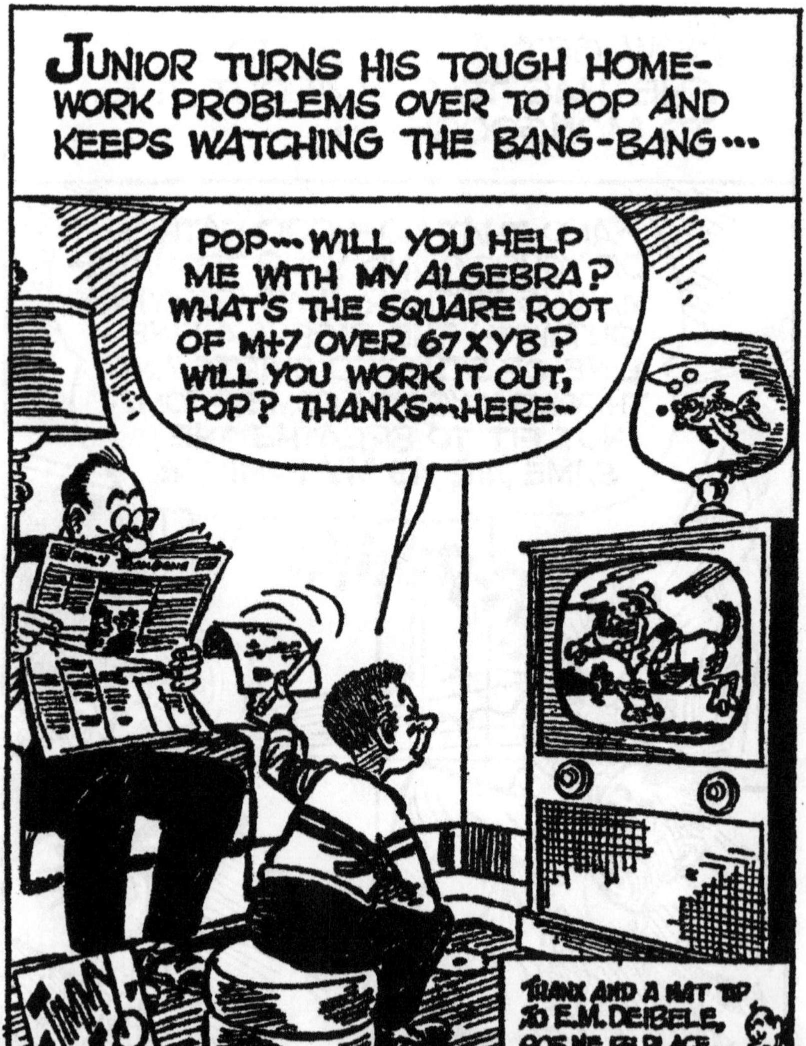

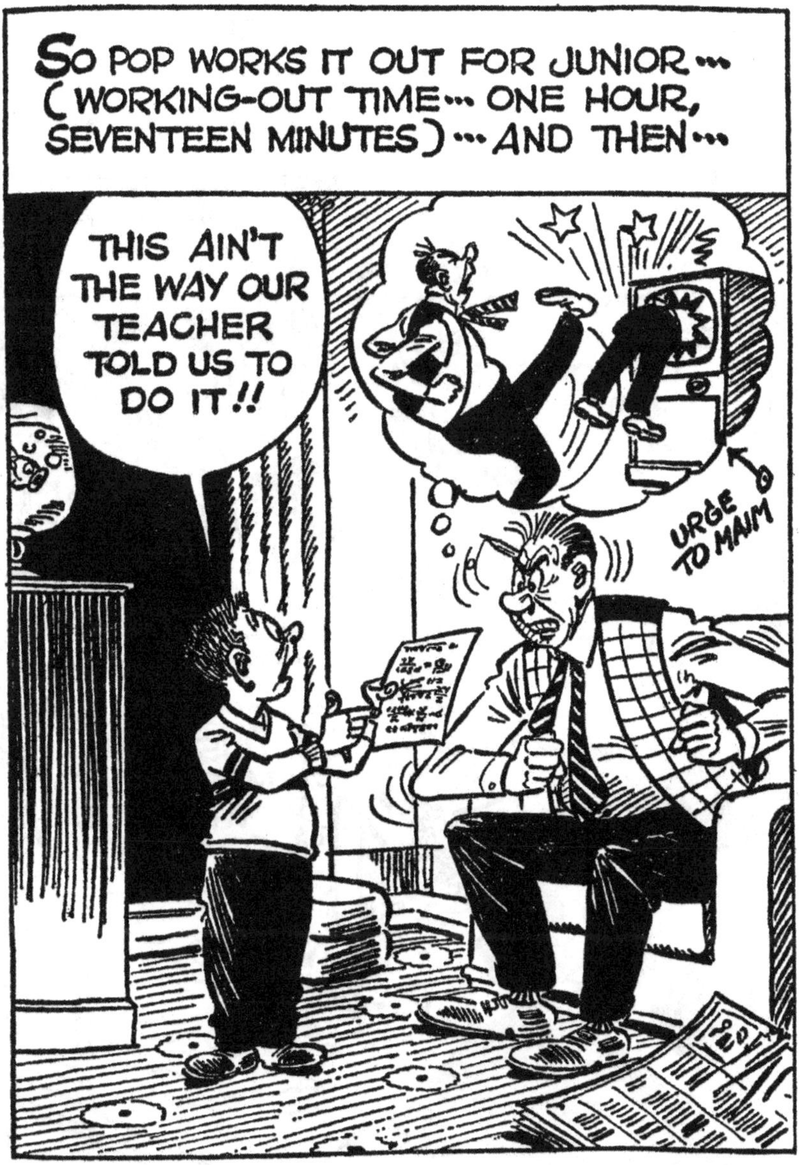
SO POP WORKS IT OUT FOR JUNIOR… (WORKING-OUT TIME… ONE HOUR, SEVENTEEN MINUTES)… AND THEN…
THIS AIN'T THE WAY OUR TEACHER TOLD US TO DO IT!!
URGE TO MAIM

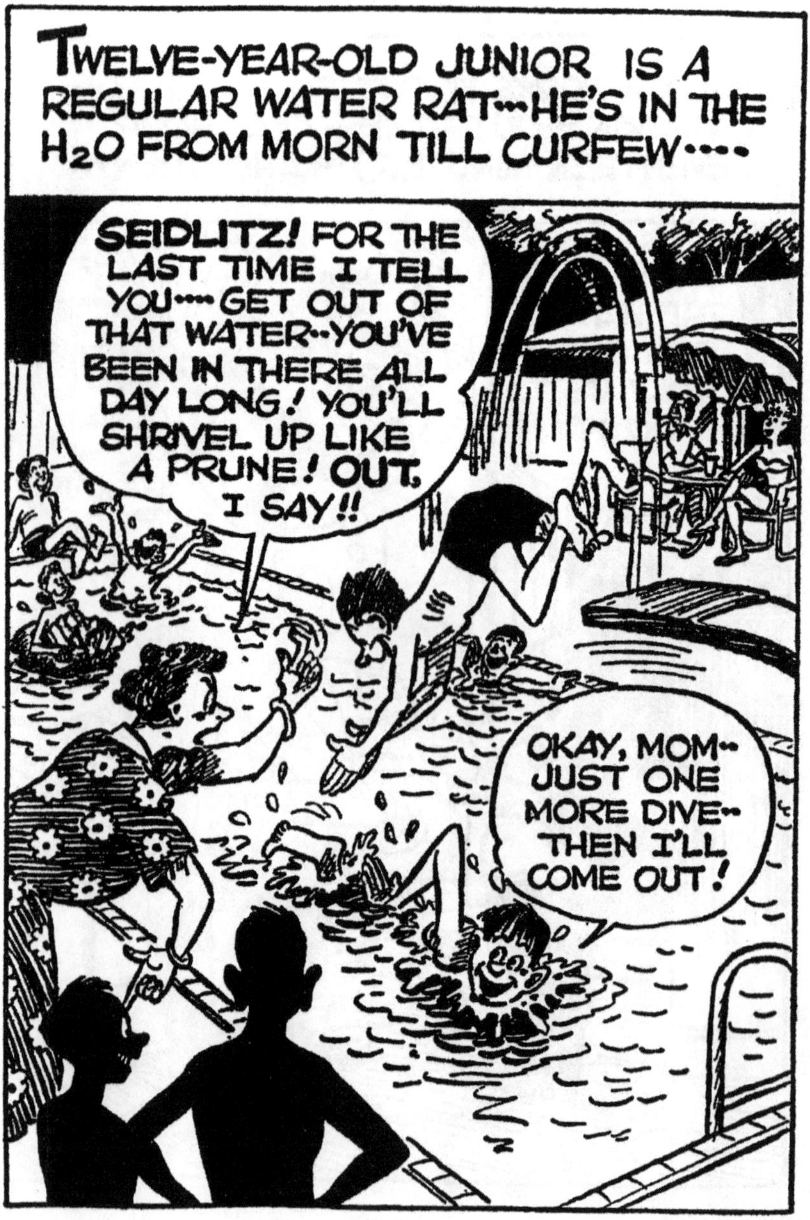

TWELVE-YEAR-OLD JUNIOR IS A REGULAR WATER RAT--HE'S IN THE H_2O FROM MORN TILL CURFEW....
SEIDLITZ! FOR THE LAST TIME I TELL YOU.... GET OUT OF THAT WATER--YOU'VE BEEN IN THERE ALL DAY LONG! YOU'LL SHRIVEL UP LIKE A PRUNE! OUT, I SAY!!
OKAY, MOM-- JUST ONE MORE DIVE-- THEN I'LL COME OUT!

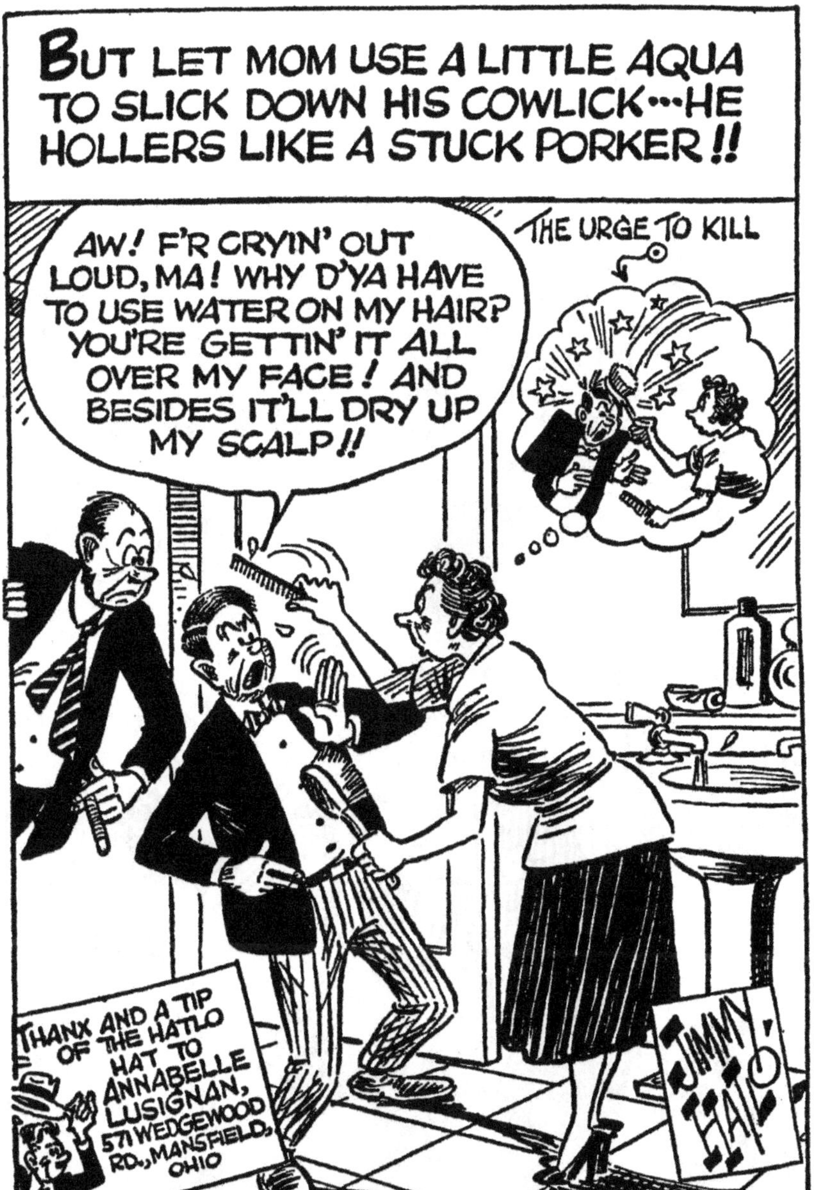
BUT LET MOM USE A LITTLE AQUA TO SLICK DOWN HIS COWLICK···HE HOLLERS LIKE A STUCK PORKER!!
AW! F'R CRYIN' OUT LOUD, MA! WHY D'YA HAVE TO USE WATER ON MY HAIR? YOU'RE GETTIN' IT ALL OVER MY FACE! AND BESIDES IT'LL DRY UP MY SCALP!!
THE URGE TO KILL
THANX AND A TIP OF THE HATLO HAT TO ANNABELLE LUSIGNAN, 571 WEDGEWOOD RD., MANSFIELD, OHIO
JIMMY HATLO

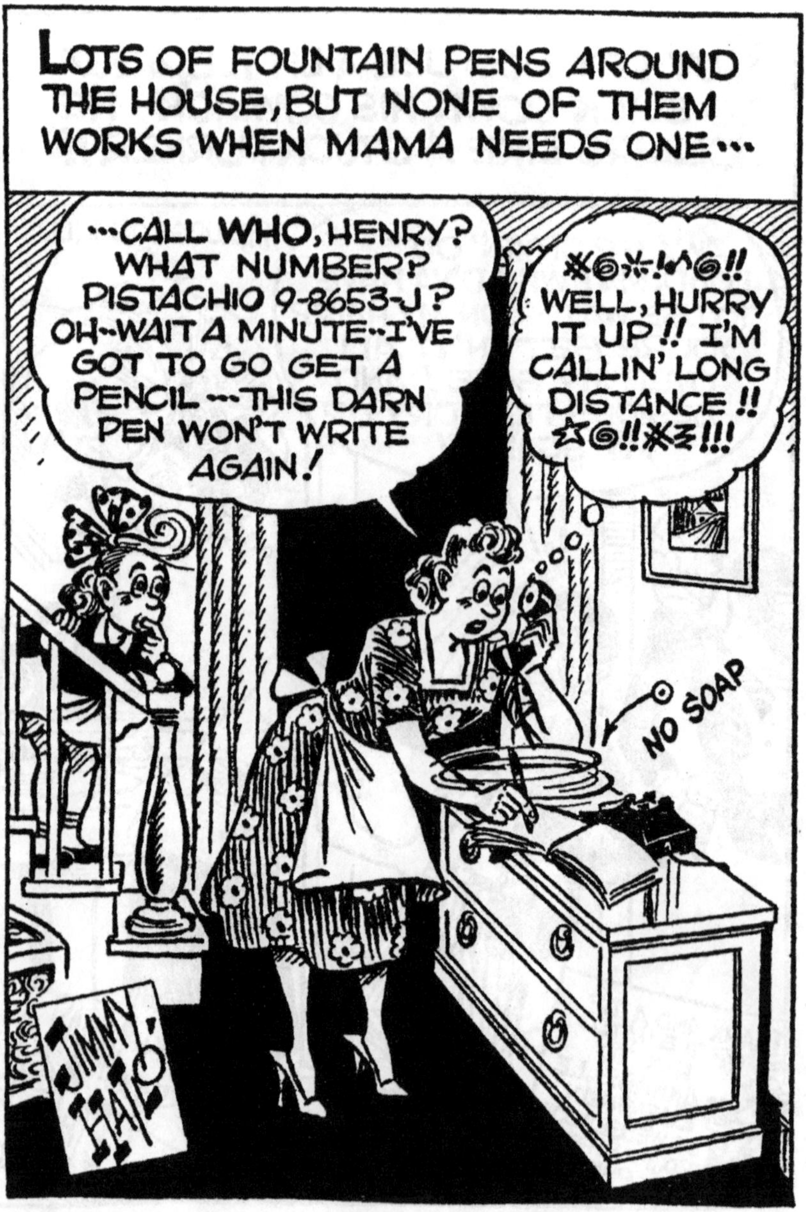
LOTS OF FOUNTAIN PENS AROUND THE HOUSE, BUT NONE OF THEM WORKS WHEN MAMA NEEDS ONE...
...CALL WHO, HENRY? WHAT NUMBER? PISTACHIO 9-8653-J? OH--WAIT A MINUTE--I'VE GOT TO GO GET A PENCIL---THIS DARN PEN WON'T WRITE AGAIN!
WELL, HURRY IT UP!! I'M CALLIN' LONG DISTANCE!!
NO SOAP
JIMMY HATLO

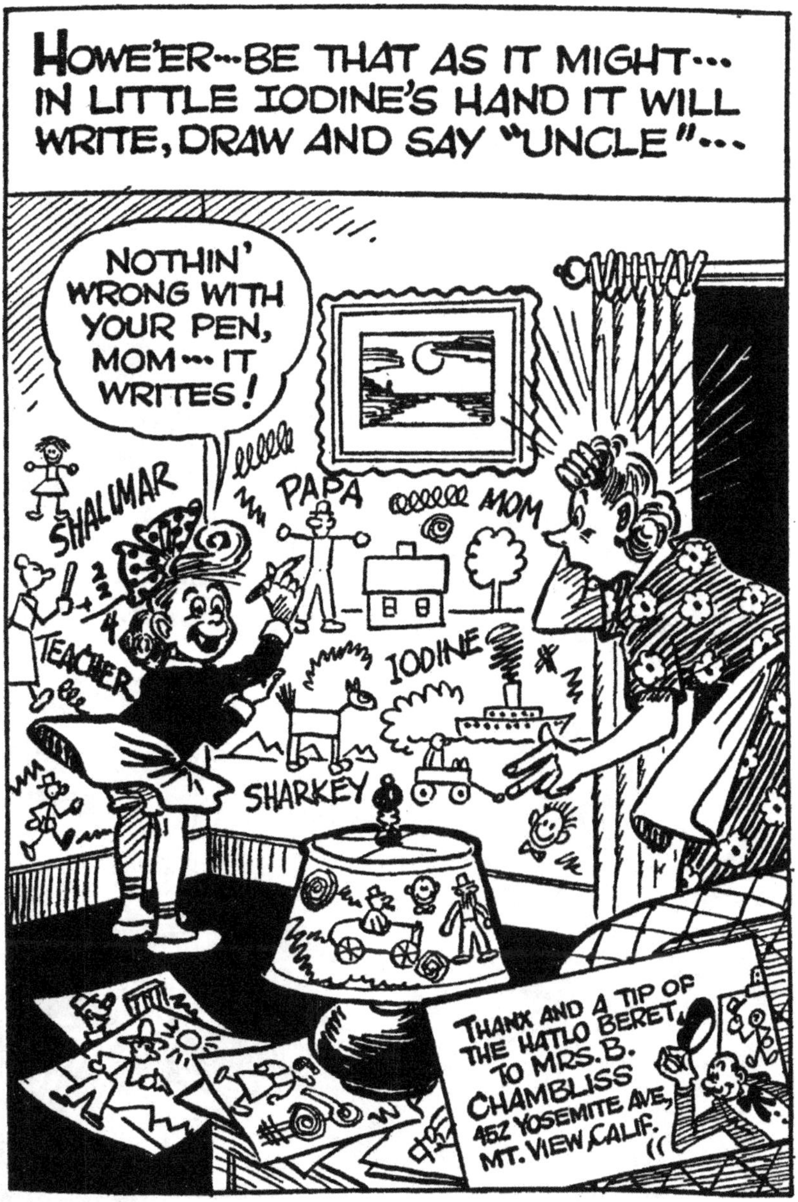
HOWE'ER...BE THAT AS IT MIGHT... IN LITTLE IODINE'S HAND IT WILL WRITE, DRAW AND SAY "UNCLE"...
NOTHIN' WRONG WITH YOUR PEN, MOM... IT WRITES!
SHALIMAR
PAPA
MOM
TEACHER
IODINE
SHARKEY
THANX AND A TIP OF THE HATLO BERET TO MRS. B. CHAMBLISS 452 YOSEMITE AVE, MT. VIEW CALIF.

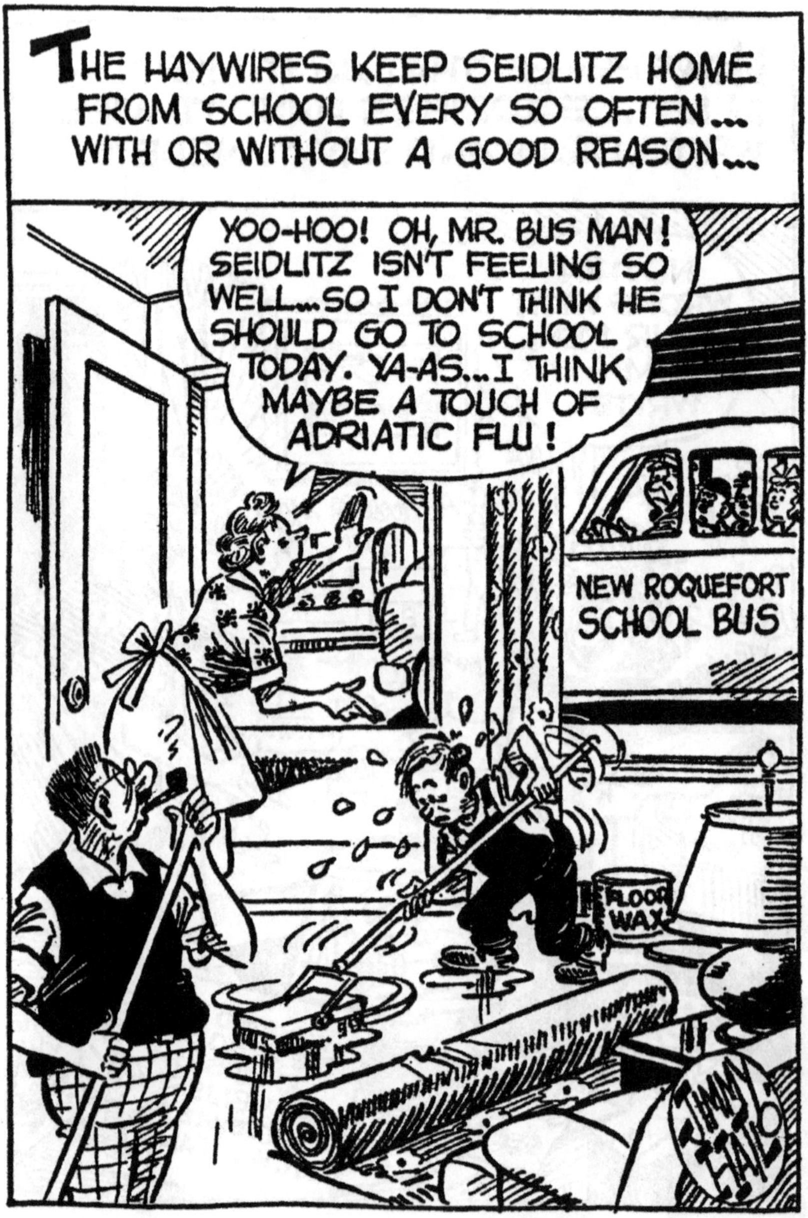
THE HAYWIRES KEEP SEIDLITZ HOME FROM SCHOOL EVERY SO OFTEN... WITH OR WITHOUT A GOOD REASON...
YOO-HOO! OH, MR. BUS MAN! SEIDLITZ ISN'T FEELING SO WELL...SO I DON'T THINK HE SHOULD GO TO SCHOOL TODAY. YA-AS...I THINK MAYBE A TOUCH OF ADRIATIC FLU!
NEW ROQUEFORT SCHOOL BUS
FLOOR WAX
JIMMY HATLO

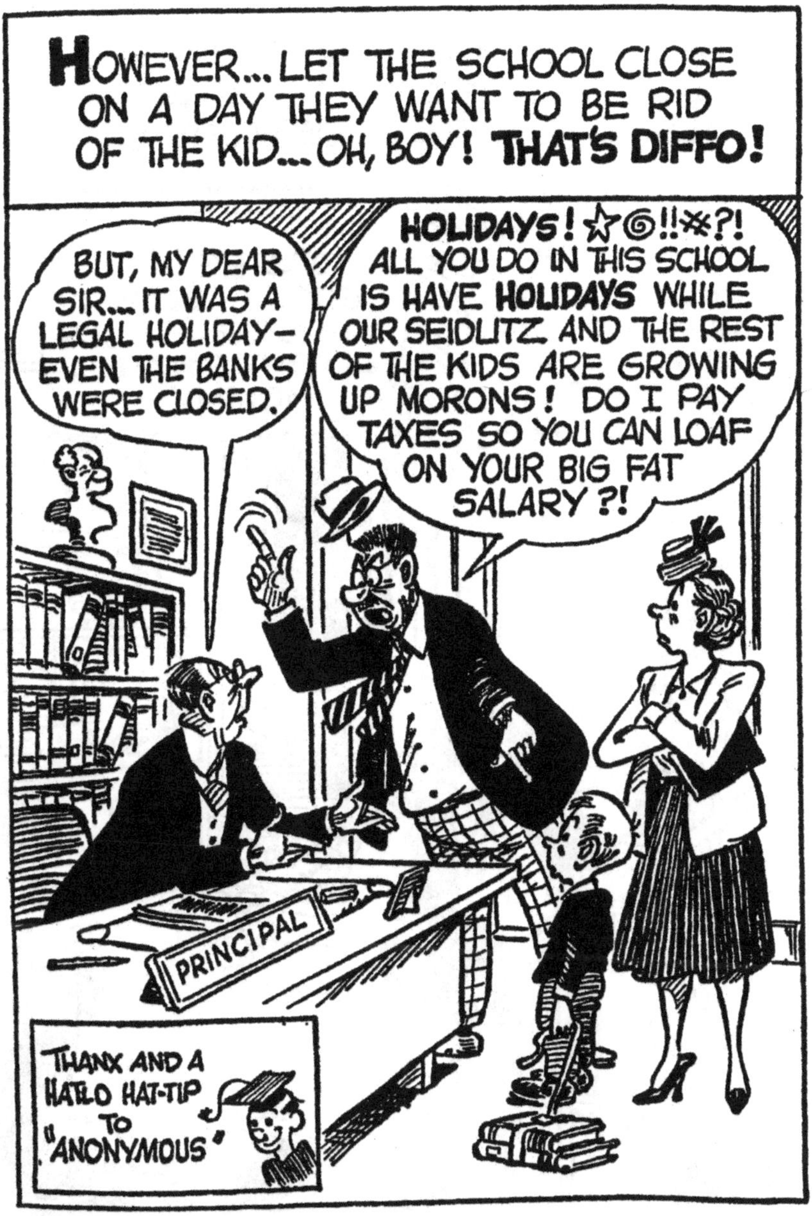
HOWEVER... LET THE SCHOOL CLOSE ON A DAY THEY WANT TO BE RID OF THE KID... OH, BOY! THAT'S DIFFO!
BUT, MY DEAR SIR... IT WAS A LEGAL HOLIDAY— EVEN THE BANKS WERE CLOSED.
HOLIDAYS! ☆@!!✻?! ALL YOU DO IN THIS SCHOOL IS HAVE HOLIDAYS WHILE OUR SEIDLITZ AND THE REST OF THE KIDS ARE GROWING UP MORONS! DO I PAY TAXES SO YOU CAN LOAF ON YOUR BIG FAT SALARY ?!
PRINCIPAL
THANX AND A HATLO HAT-TIP TO "ANONYMOUS"

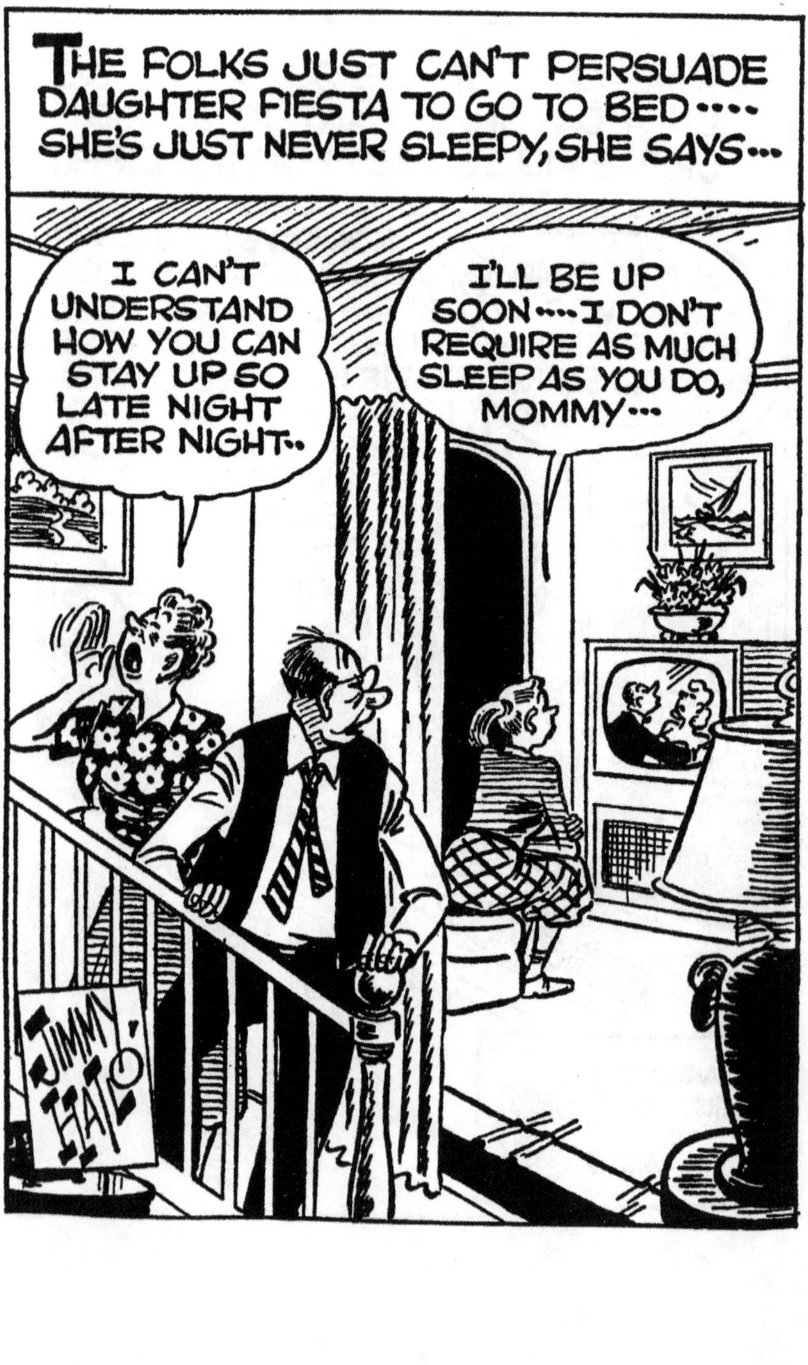
THE FOLKS JUST CAN'T PERSUADE DAUGHTER FIESTA TO GO TO BED···· SHE'S JUST NEVER SLEEPY, SHE SAYS···
I CAN'T UNDERSTAND HOW YOU CAN STAY UP SO LATE NIGHT AFTER NIGHT··
I'LL BE UP SOON····I DON'T REQUIRE AS MUCH SLEEP AS YOU DO, MOMMY···
JIMMY HATLO

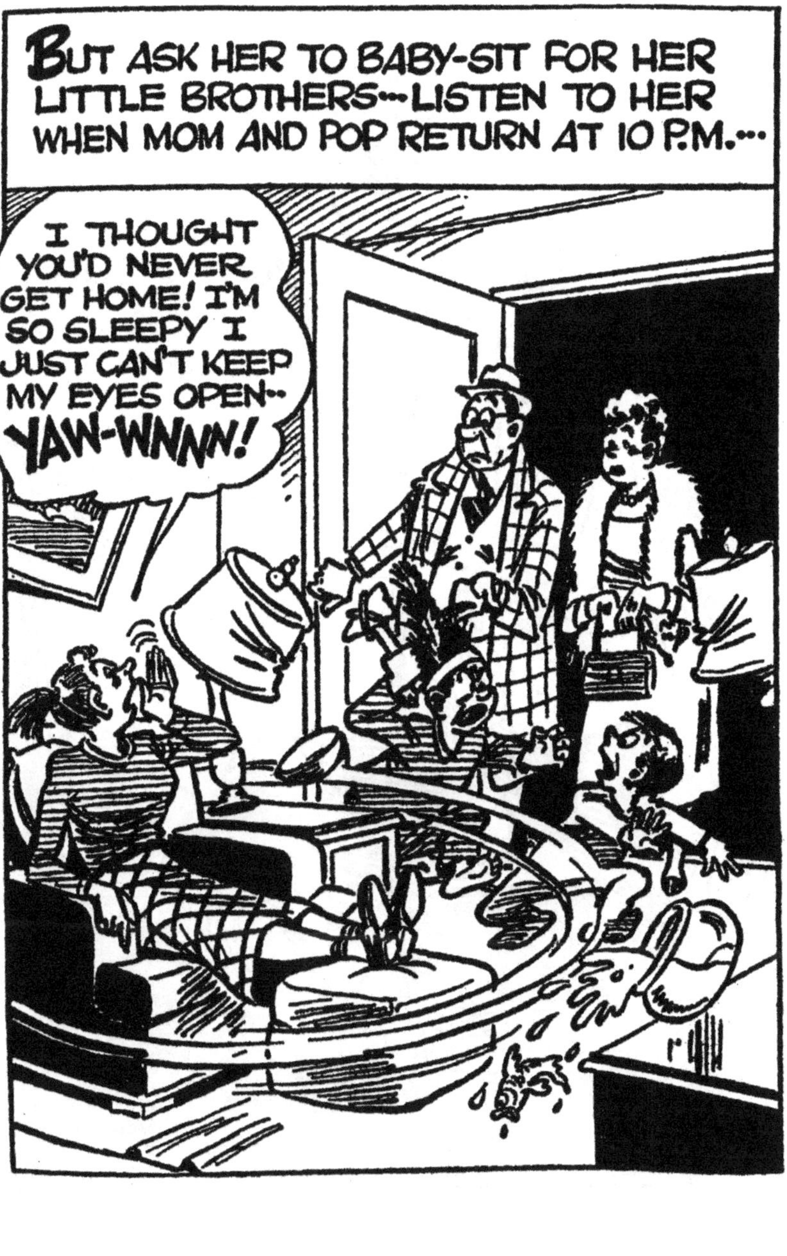
BUT ASK HER TO BABY-SIT FOR HER LITTLE BROTHERS--LISTEN TO HER WHEN MOM AND POP RETURN AT 10 P.M.--
I THOUGHT YOU'D NEVER GET HOME! I'M SO SLEEPY I JUST CAN'T KEEP MY EYES OPEN-- YAW-WNNN!

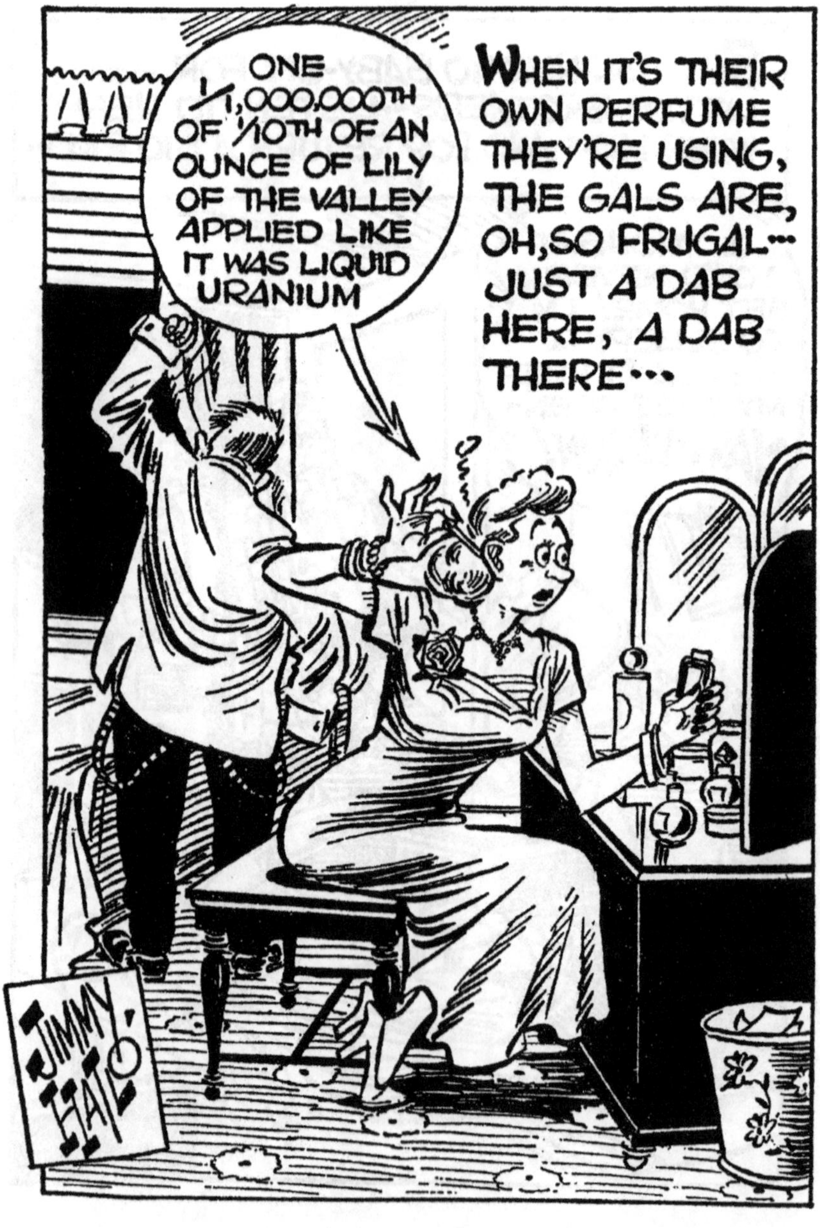

ONE 1/1,000,000TH OF 1/10TH OF AN OUNCE OF LILY OF THE VALLEY APPLIED LIKE IT WAS LIQUID URANIUM
WHEN IT'S THEIR OWN PERFUME THEY'RE USING, THE GALS ARE, OH, SO FRUGAL-- JUST A DAB HERE, A DAB THERE...
JIMMY HATLO

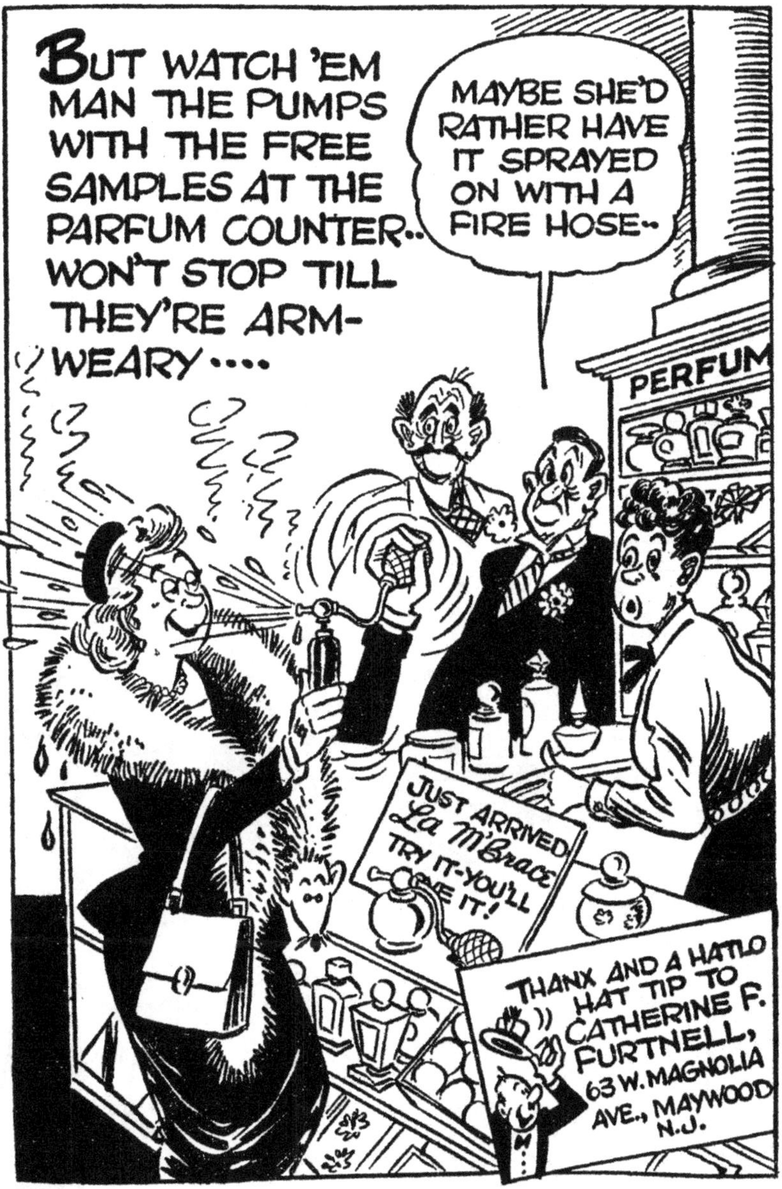
BUT WATCH 'EM MAN THE PUMPS WITH THE FREE SAMPLES AT THE PARFUM COUNTER.. WON'T STOP TILL THEY'RE ARM-WEARY....
MAYBE SHE'D RATHER HAVE IT SPRAYED ON WITH A FIRE HOSE--
PERFUM
JUST ARRIVED La M'Brace TRY IT-YOU'LL LOVE IT!
THANX AND A HATLO HAT TIP TO CATHERINE F. FURTNELL, 63 W. MAGNOLIA AVE., MAYWOOD N.J.

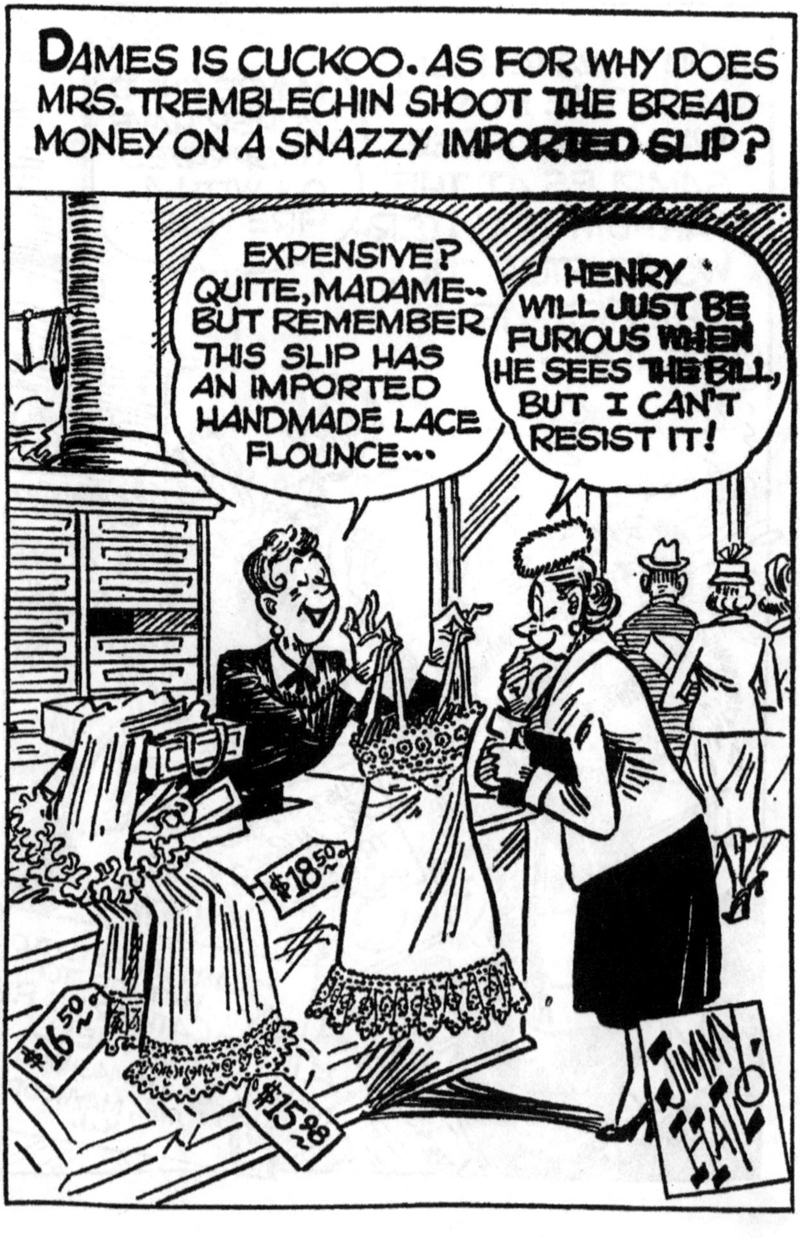
DAMES IS CUCKOO. AS FOR WHY DOES MRS. TREMBLECHIN SHOOT THE BREAD MONEY ON A SNAZZY IMPORTED SLIP?
EXPENSIVE? QUITE, MADAME-- BUT REMEMBER THIS SLIP HAS AN IMPORTED HANDMADE LACE FLOUNCE--
HENRY WILL JUST BE FURIOUS WHEN HE SEES THE BILL, BUT I CAN'T RESIST IT!
$18.50
$16.50
$15.98
JIMMY HATLO

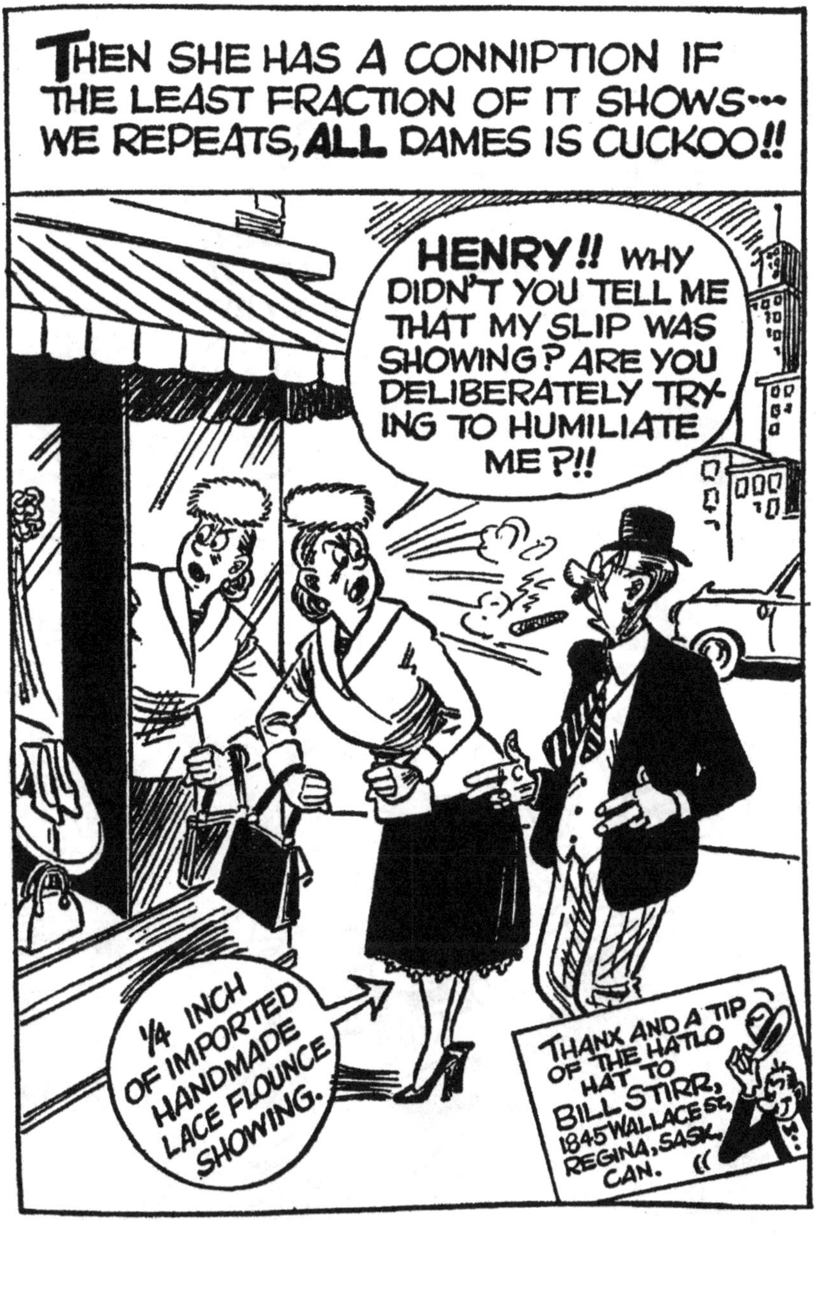
THEN SHE HAS A CONNIPTION IF THE LEAST FRACTION OF IT SHOWS--- WE REPEATS, ALL DAMES IS CUCKOO!!
HENRY!! WHY DIDN'T YOU TELL ME THAT MY SLIP WAS SHOWING? ARE YOU DELIBERATELY TRYING TO HUMILIATE ME?!!
1/4 INCH OF IMPORTED HANDMADE LACE FLOUNCE SHOWING.
THANX AND A TIP OF THE HATLO HAT TO BILL STIRR, 1845 WALLACE St., REGINA, SASK., CAN.

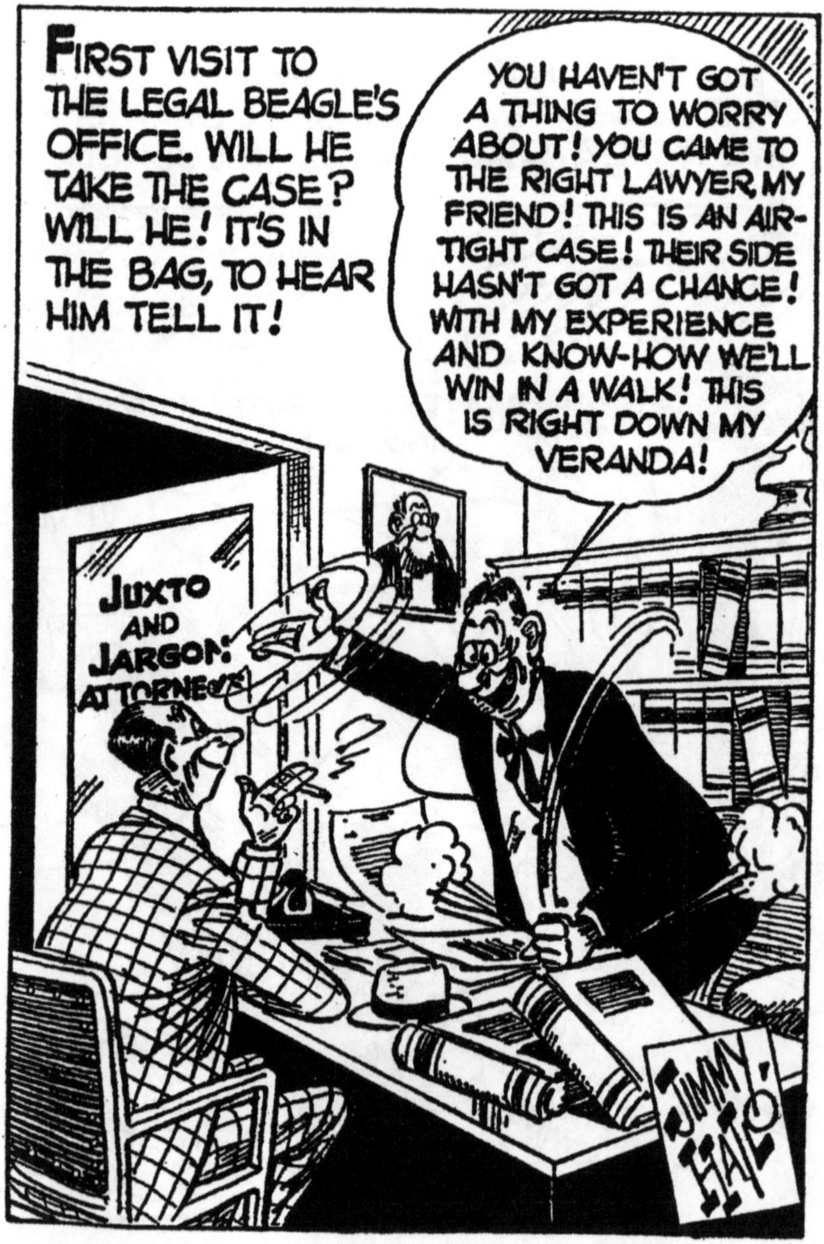
FIRST VISIT TO THE LEGAL BEAGLE'S OFFICE. WILL HE TAKE THE CASE? WILL HE! IT'S IN THE BAG, TO HEAR HIM TELL IT!
YOU HAVEN'T GOT A THING TO WORRY ABOUT! YOU CAME TO THE RIGHT LAWYER, MY FRIEND! THIS IS AN AIR-TIGHT CASE! THEIR SIDE HASN'T GOT A CHANCE! WITH MY EXPERIENCE AND KNOW-HOW WE'LL WIN IN A WALK! THIS IS RIGHT DOWN MY VERANDA!
JUXTO AND JARGON ATTORNEYS
JIMMY HATLO

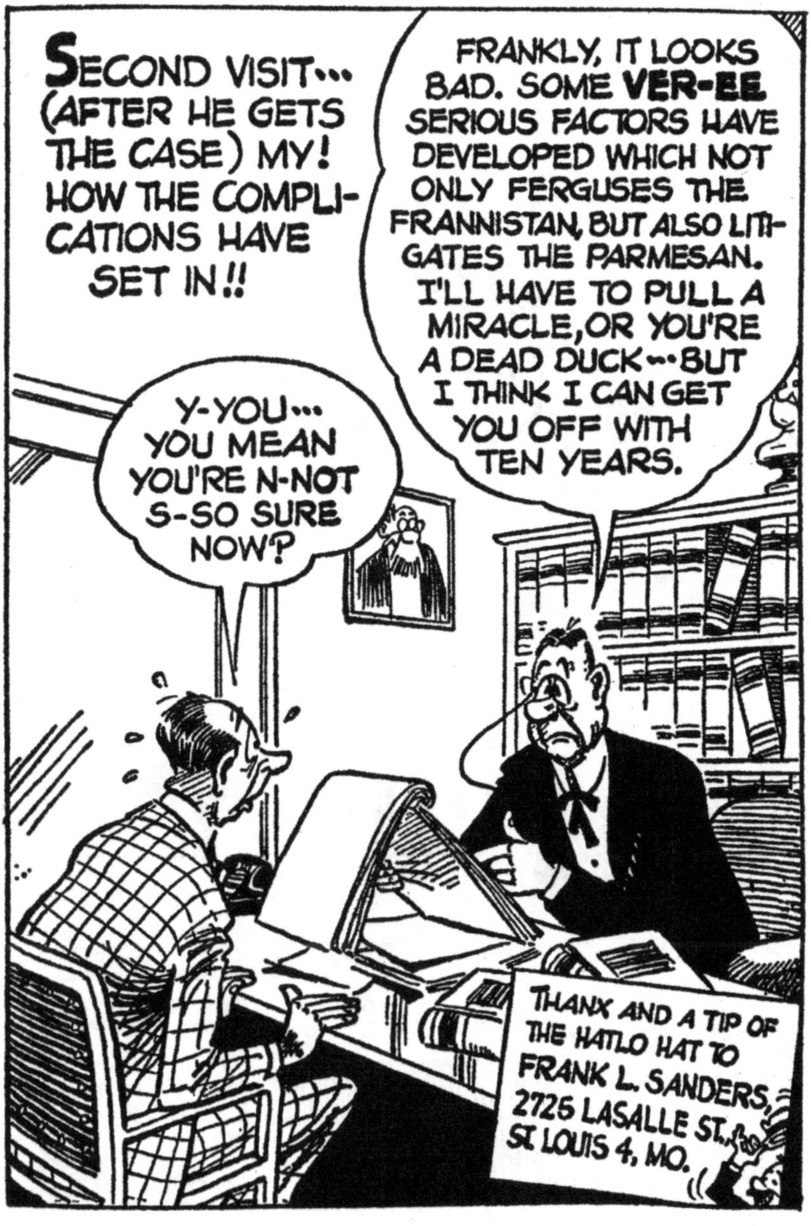
SECOND VISIT... (AFTER HE GETS THE CASE) MY! HOW THE COMPLICATIONS HAVE SET IN!!
FRANKLY, IT LOOKS BAD. SOME VER-EE SERIOUS FACTORS HAVE DEVELOPED WHICH NOT ONLY FERGUSES THE FRANNISTAN, BUT ALSO LITIGATES THE PARMESAN. I'LL HAVE TO PULL A MIRACLE, OR YOU'RE A DEAD DUCK... BUT I THINK I CAN GET YOU OFF WITH TEN YEARS.
Y-YOU... YOU MEAN YOU'RE N-NOT S-SO SURE NOW?
THANX AND A TIP OF THE HATLO HAT TO FRANK L. SANDERS, 2725 LASALLE ST., ST. LOUIS 4, MO.

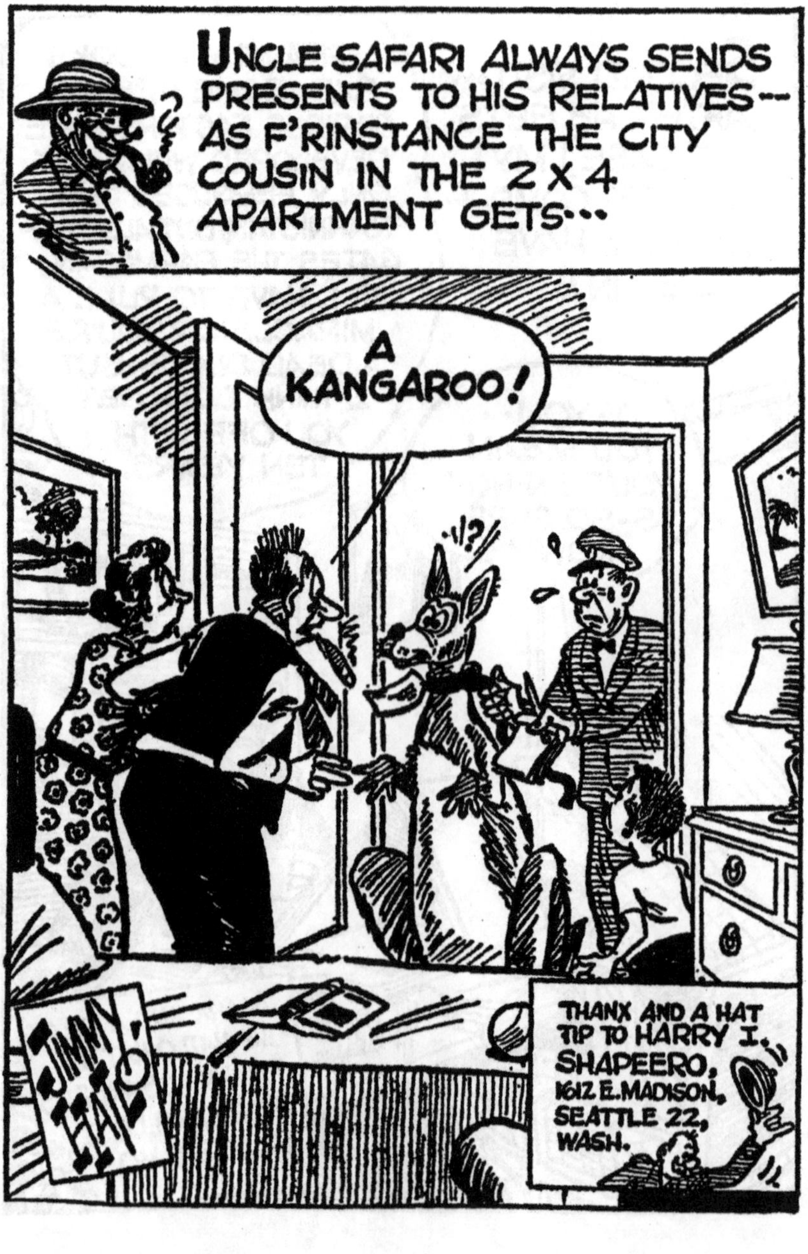
UNCLE SAFARI ALWAYS SENDS PRESENTS TO HIS RELATIVES-- AS F'RINSTANCE THE CITY COUSIN IN THE 2 X 4 APARTMENT GETS...
A KANGAROO!
!?
JIMMY HATLO
THANX AND A HAT TIP TO HARRY I. SHAPEERO, 1612 E. MADISON, SEATTLE 22, WASH.

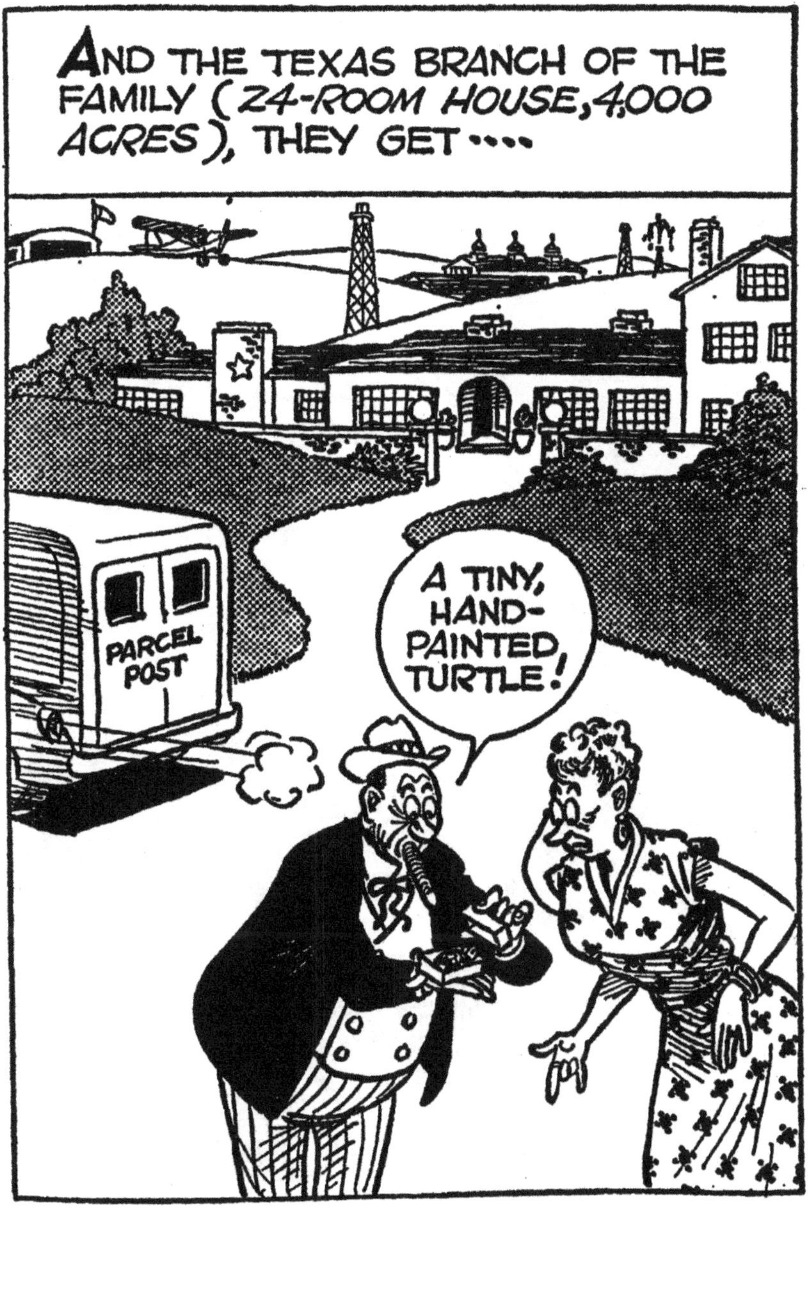
AND THE TEXAS BRANCH OF THE FAMILY (24-ROOM HOUSE, 4,000 ACRES), THEY GET....
PARCEL POST
A TINY, HAND-PAINTED TURTLE!

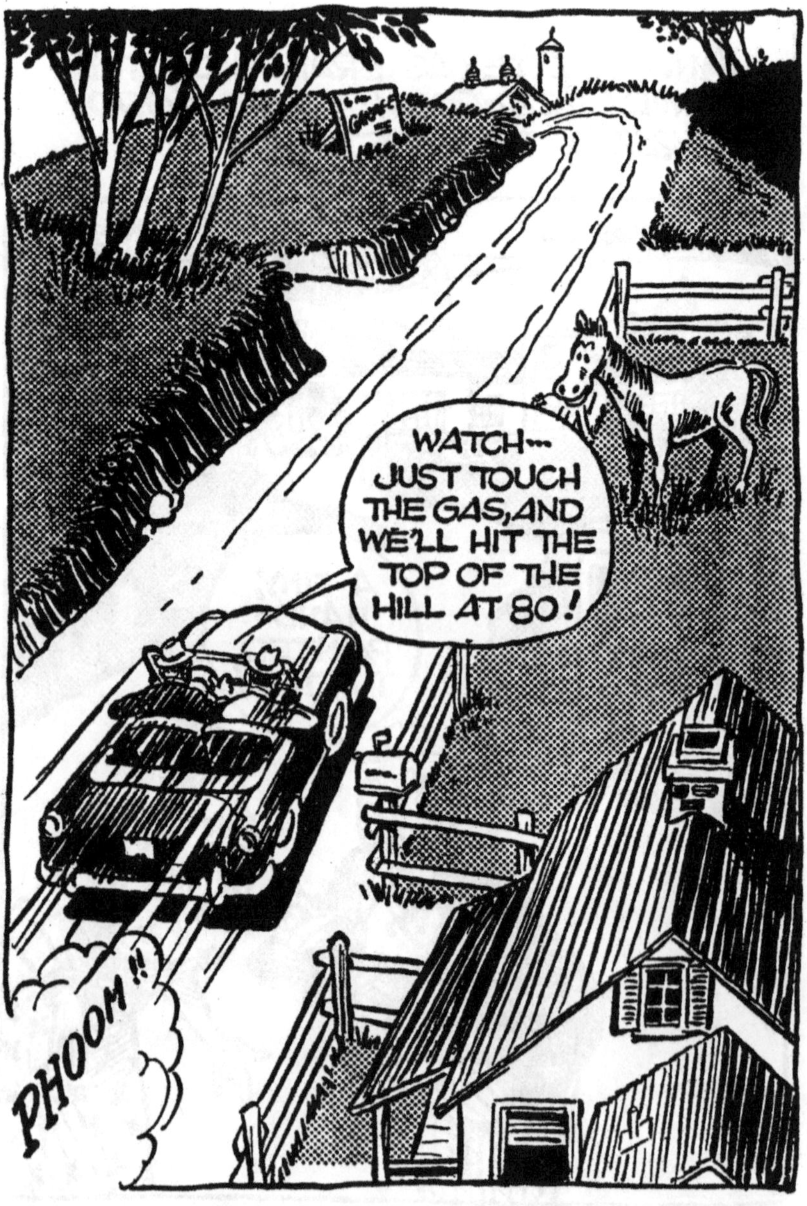
WATCH--
JUST TOUCH
THE GAS, AND
WE'LL HIT THE
TOP OF THE
HILL AT 80!
PHOOM!!

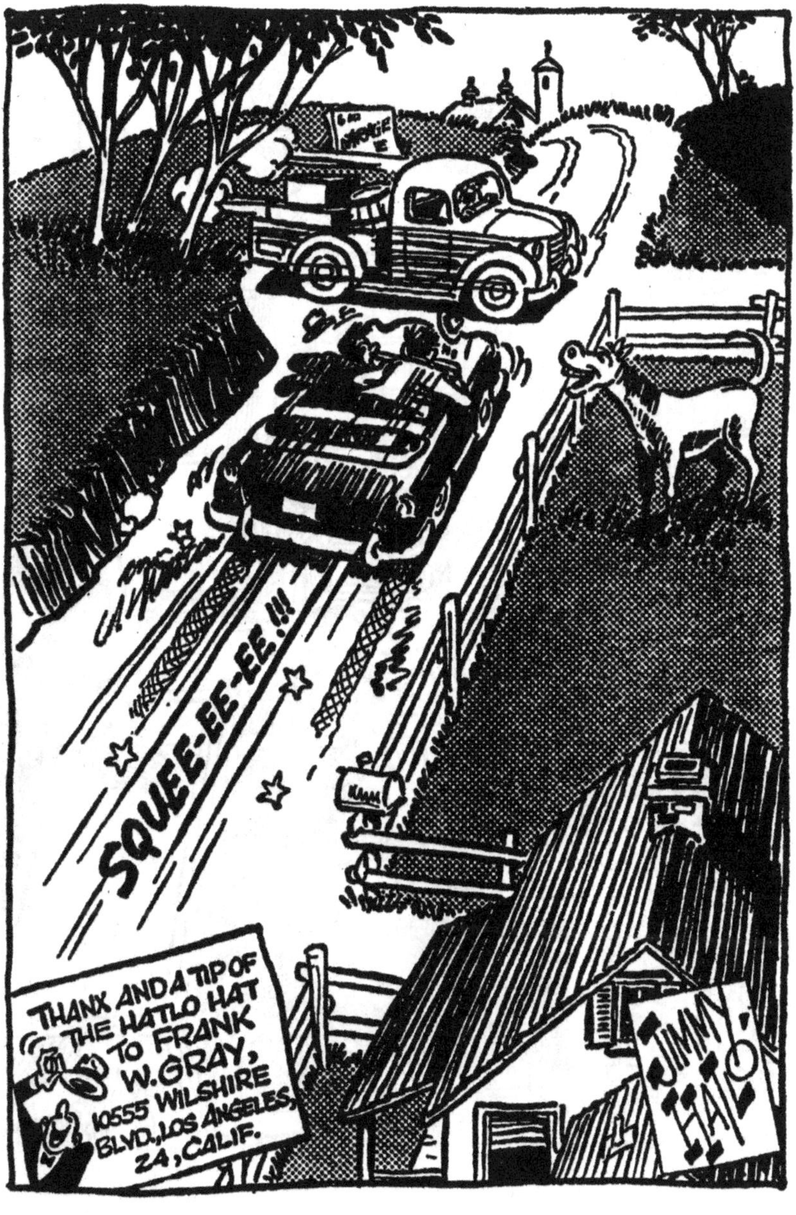
SQUEE-EE-EE!!!
THANX AND A TIP OF THE HATLO HAT TO FRANK W. GRAY, 10555 WILSHIRE BLVD., LOS ANGELES, 24, CALIF.
JIMMY HATLO

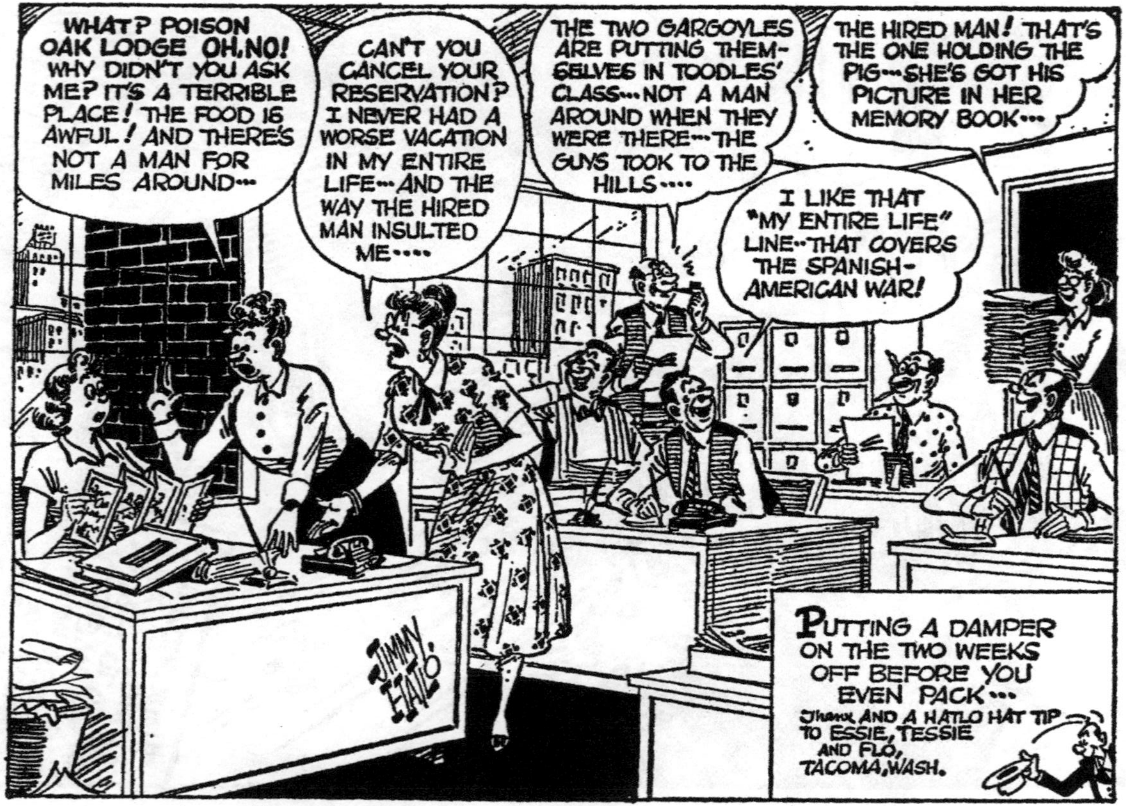
WHAT? POISON OAK LODGE OH, NO! WHY DIDN'T YOU ASK ME? IT'S A TERRIBLE PLACE! THE FOOD IS AWFUL! AND THERE'S NOT A MAN FOR MILES AROUND...
CAN'T YOU CANCEL YOUR RESERVATION? I NEVER HAD A WORSE VACATION IN MY ENTIRE LIFE... AND THE WAY THE HIRED MAN INSULTED ME....
THE TWO GARGOYLES ARE PUTTING THEMSELVES IN TOODLES' CLASS... NOT A MAN AROUND WHEN THEY WERE THERE... THE GUYS TOOK TO THE HILLS....
THE HIRED MAN! THAT'S THE ONE HOLDING THE PIG... SHE'S GOT HIS PICTURE IN HER MEMORY BOOK...
I LIKE THAT "MY ENTIRE LIFE" LINE.. THAT COVERS THE SPANISH-AMERICAN WAR!
JIMMY HATLO
PUTTING A DAMPER ON THE TWO WEEKS OFF BEFORE YOU EVEN PACK...
Thanx AND A HATLO HAT TIP TO ESSIE, TESSIE AND FLO, TACOMA, WASH.

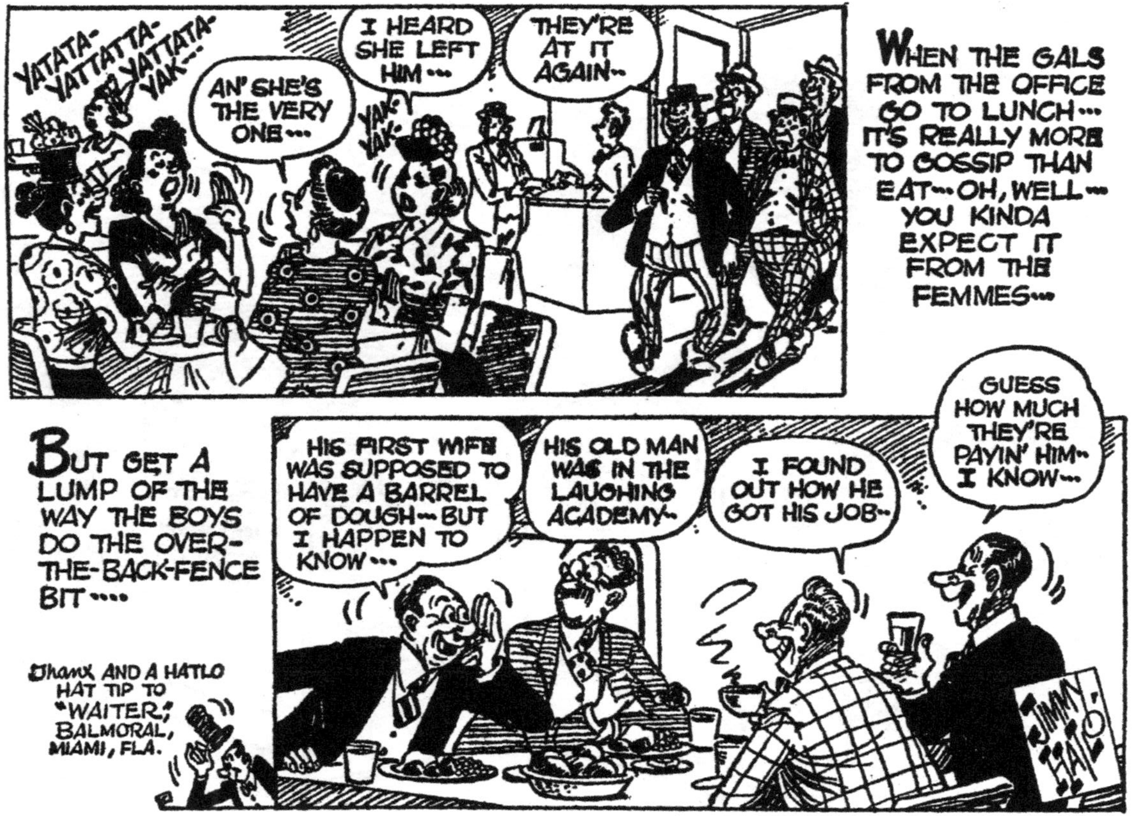
YATATA-YATTATTA-YATTATA-YAK...
AN' SHE'S THE VERY ONE...
I HEARD SHE LEFT HIM...
YAK YAK
THEY'RE AT IT AGAIN..
WHEN THE GALS FROM THE OFFICE GO TO LUNCH... IT'S REALLY MORE TO GOSSIP THAN EAT... OH, WELL... YOU KINDA EXPECT IT FROM THE FEMMES...
BUT GET A LUMP OF THE WAY THE BOYS DO THE OVER-THE-BACK-FENCE BIT....
HIS FIRST WIFE WAS SUPPOSED TO HAVE A BARREL OF DOUGH... BUT I HAPPEN TO KNOW...
HIS OLD MAN WAS IN THE LAUGHING ACADEMY..
I FOUND OUT HOW HE GOT HIS JOB..
GUESS HOW MUCH THEY'RE PAYIN' HIM.. I KNOW...
Thanx AND A HATLO HAT TIP TO "WAITER," BALMORAL, MIAMI, FLA.
JIMMY HATLO

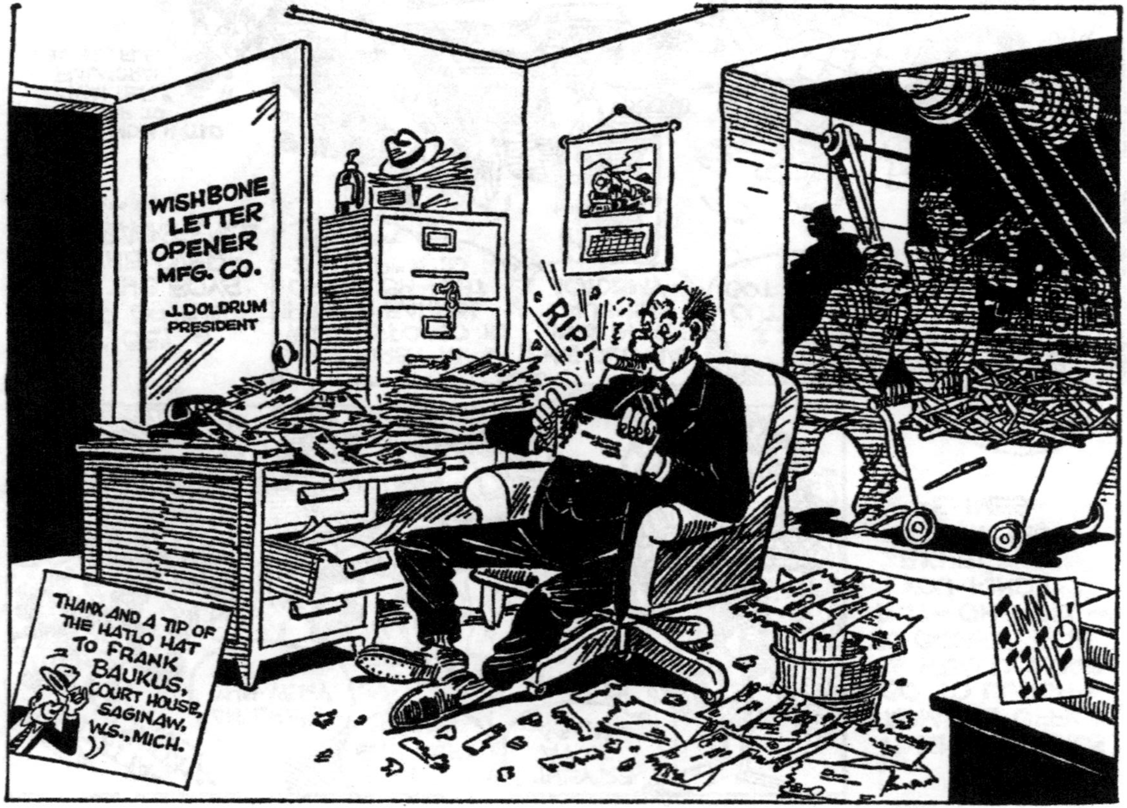
WISHBONE
LETTER
OPENER
MFG. CO.
J. DOLDRUM
PRESIDENT
RIP!
THANX AND A TIP OF THE HATLO HAT TO FRANK BAUKUS, COURT HOUSE, SAGINAW, W.S., MICH.
JIMMY HATLO

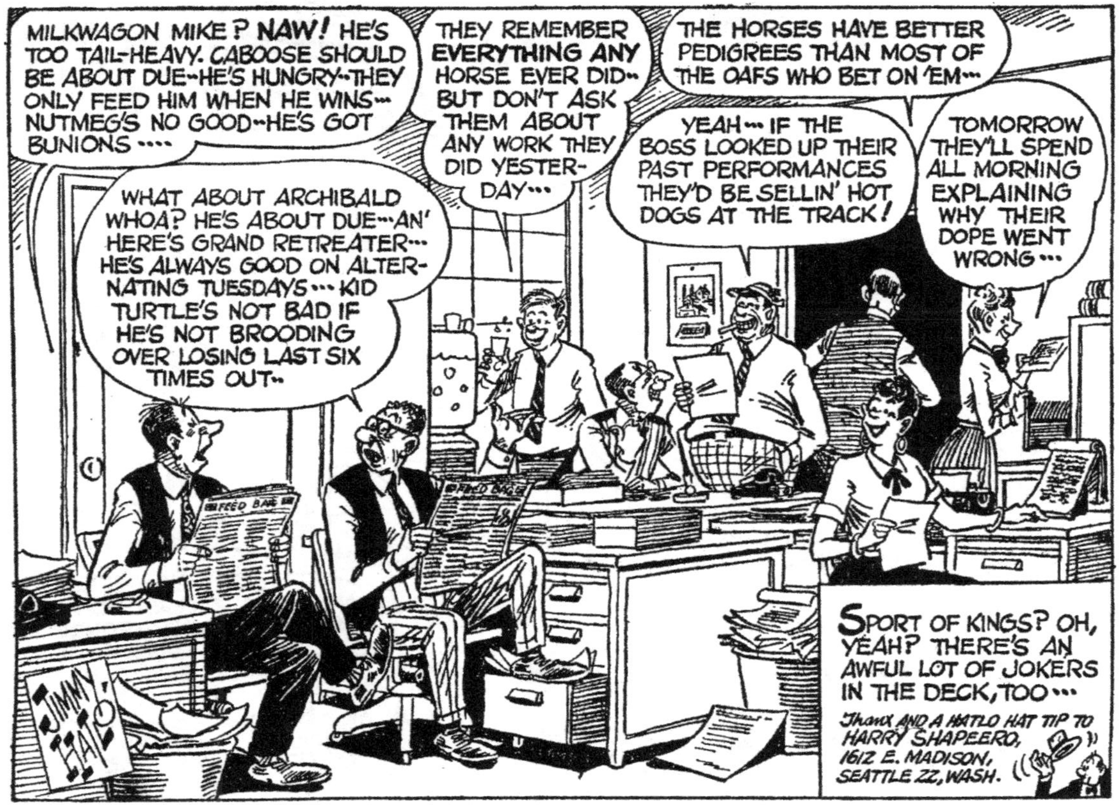
MILKWAGON MIKE? NAW! HE'S TOO TAIL-HEAVY. CABOOSE SHOULD BE ABOUT DUE--HE'S HUNGRY--THEY ONLY FEED HIM WHEN HE WINS... NUTMEG'S NO GOOD--HE'S GOT BUNIONS....
WHAT ABOUT ARCHIBALD WHOA? HE'S ABOUT DUE...AN' HERE'S GRAND RETREATER... HE'S ALWAYS GOOD ON ALTERNATING TUESDAYS... KID TURTLE'S NOT BAD IF HE'S NOT BROODING OVER LOSING LAST SIX TIMES OUT..
THEY REMEMBER EVERYTHING ANY HORSE EVER DID.. BUT DON'T ASK THEM ABOUT ANY WORK THEY DID YESTERDAY...
THE HORSES HAVE BETTER PEDIGREES THAN MOST OF THE OAFS WHO BET ON 'EM...
YEAH... IF THE BOSS LOOKED UP THEIR PAST PERFORMANCES THEY'D BE SELLIN' HOT DOGS AT THE TRACK!
TOMORROW THEY'LL SPEND ALL MORNING EXPLAINING WHY THEIR DOPE WENT WRONG...
FEED BAG
JIMMY HATLO
SPORT OF KINGS? OH, YEAH? THERE'S AN AWFUL LOT OF JOKERS IN THE DECK, TOO...
Thanx AND A HATLO HAT TIP TO HARRY SHAPEERO, 1612 E. MADISON, SEATTLE 22, WASH.

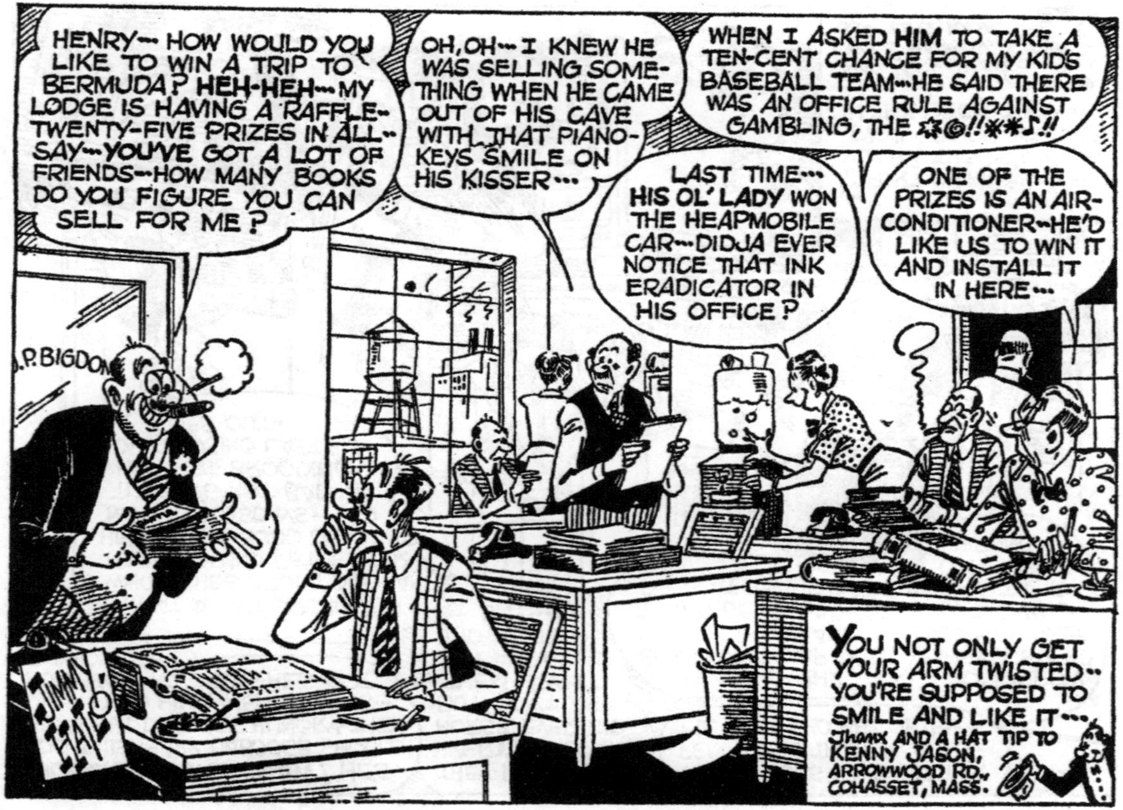
HENRY--- HOW WOULD YOU LIKE TO WIN A TRIP TO BERMUDA? HEH-HEH--- MY LODGE IS HAVING A RAFFLE-- TWENTY-FIVE PRIZES IN ALL-- SAY--- YOU'VE GOT A LOT OF FRIENDS--- HOW MANY BOOKS DO YOU FIGURE YOU CAN SELL FOR ME?
OH, OH--- I KNEW HE WAS SELLING SOMETHING WHEN HE CAME OUT OF HIS CAVE WITH THAT PIANO-KEYS SMILE ON HIS KISSER---
WHEN I ASKED HIM TO TAKE A TEN-CENT CHANCE FOR MY KID'S BASEBALL TEAM--- HE SAID THERE WAS AN OFFICE RULE AGAINST GAMBLING, THE ✿@!!✱✱♪!!
LAST TIME--- HIS OL' LADY WON THE HEAPMOBILE CAR--- DIDJA EVER NOTICE THAT INK ERADICATOR IN HIS OFFICE?
ONE OF THE PRIZES IS AN AIR-CONDITIONER--- HE'D LIKE US TO WIN IT AND INSTALL IT IN HERE---
J.P. BIGDOME
YOU NOT ONLY GET YOUR ARM TWISTED-- YOU'RE SUPPOSED TO SMILE AND LIKE IT---
Thanx AND A HAT TIP TO KENNY JASON, ARROWWOOD RD., COHASSET, MASS.
JIMMY HATLO

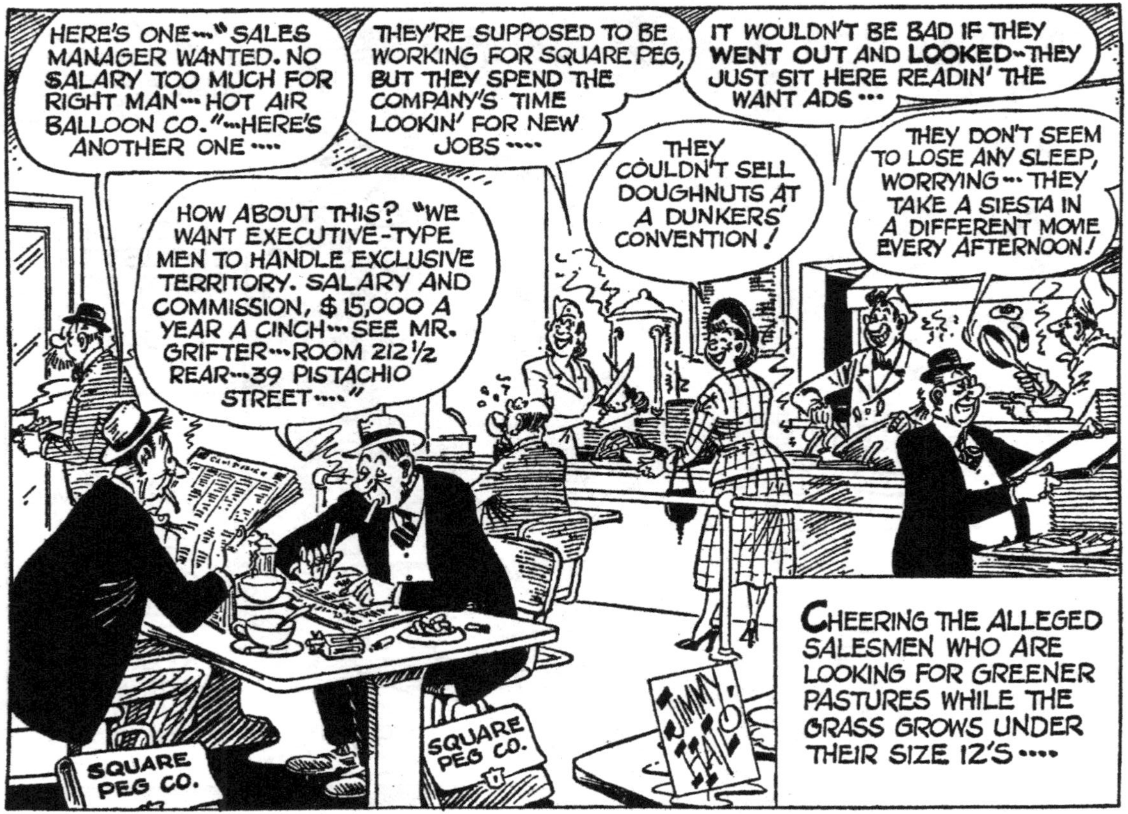
HERE'S ONE... "SALES MANAGER WANTED. NO SALARY TOO MUCH FOR RIGHT MAN... HOT AIR BALLOON CO." ...HERE'S ANOTHER ONE....
HOW ABOUT THIS? "WE WANT EXECUTIVE-TYPE MEN TO HANDLE EXCLUSIVE TERRITORY. SALARY AND COMMISSION, $15,000 A YEAR A CINCH... SEE MR. GRIFTER... ROOM 212 1/2 REAR... 39 PISTACHIO STREET...."
THEY'RE SUPPOSED TO BE WORKING FOR SQUARE PEG, BUT THEY SPEND THE COMPANY'S TIME LOOKIN' FOR NEW JOBS....
THEY COULDN'T SELL DOUGHNUTS AT A DUNKERS' CONVENTION!
IT WOULDN'T BE BAD IF THEY WENT OUT AND LOOKED... THEY JUST SIT HERE READIN' THE WANT ADS...
THEY DON'T SEEM TO LOSE ANY SLEEP, WORRYING... THEY TAKE A SIESTA IN A DIFFERENT MOVIE EVERY AFTERNOON!
SQUARE PEG CO.
SQUARE PEG CO.
JIMMY HATLO
CHEERING THE ALLEGED SALESMEN WHO ARE LOOKING FOR GREENER PASTURES WHILE THE GRASS GROWS UNDER THEIR SIZE 12'S....

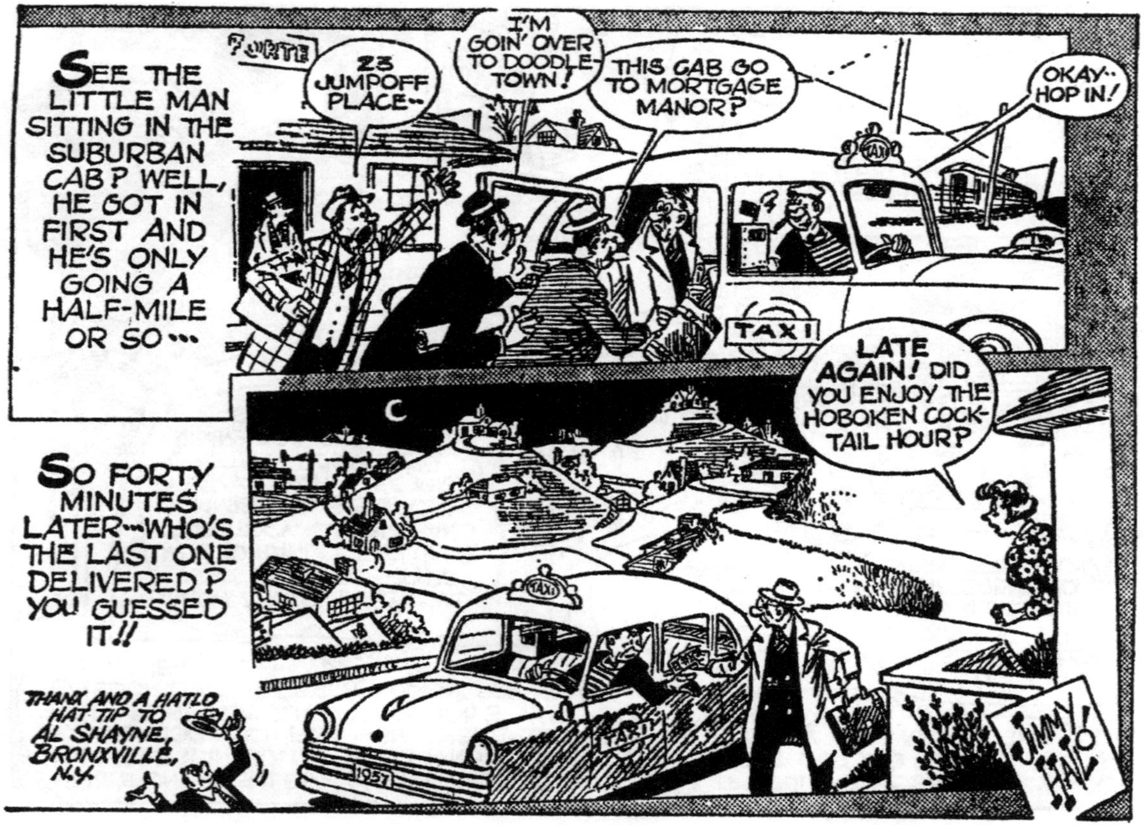
SEE THE LITTLE MAN SITTING IN THE SUBURBAN CAB? WELL, HE GOT IN FIRST AND HE'S ONLY GOING A HALF-MILE OR SO...
23 JUMPOFF PLACE--
I'M GOIN' OVER TO DOODLE-TOWN!
THIS CAB GO TO MORTGAGE MANOR?
OKAY.. HOP IN!
TAXI
SO FORTY MINUTES LATER--WHO'S THE LAST ONE DELIVERED? YOU GUESSED IT!!
LATE AGAIN! DID YOU ENJOY THE HOBOKEN COCK-TAIL HOUR?
TAXI
1957
THANX AND A HATLO HAT TIP TO AL SHAYNE, BRONXVILLE, N.Y.
JIMMY HATLO

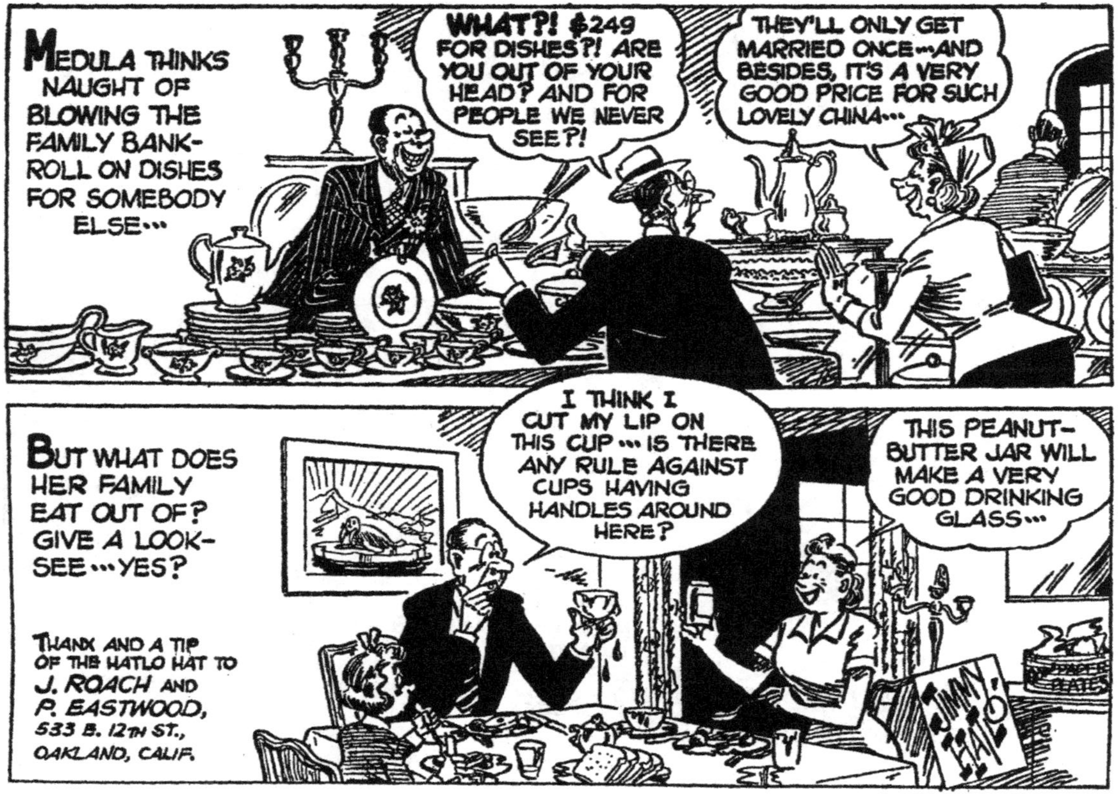
MEDULA THINKS NAUGHT OF BLOWING THE FAMILY BANK-ROLL ON DISHES FOR SOMEBODY ELSE...
WHAT?! $249 FOR DISHES?! ARE YOU OUT OF YOUR HEAD? AND FOR PEOPLE WE NEVER SEE?!
THEY'LL ONLY GET MARRIED ONCE...AND BESIDES, IT'S A VERY GOOD PRICE FOR SUCH LOVELY CHINA...
BUT WHAT DOES HER FAMILY EAT OUT OF? GIVE A LOOK-SEE...YES?
I THINK I CUT MY LIP ON THIS CUP... IS THERE ANY RULE AGAINST CUPS HAVING HANDLES AROUND HERE?
THIS PEANUT-BUTTER JAR WILL MAKE A VERY GOOD DRINKING GLASS...
THANX AND A TIP OF THE HATLO HAT TO J. ROACH AND P. EASTWOOD, 533 B. 12TH ST., OAKLAND, CALIF.
PAPER PLATES

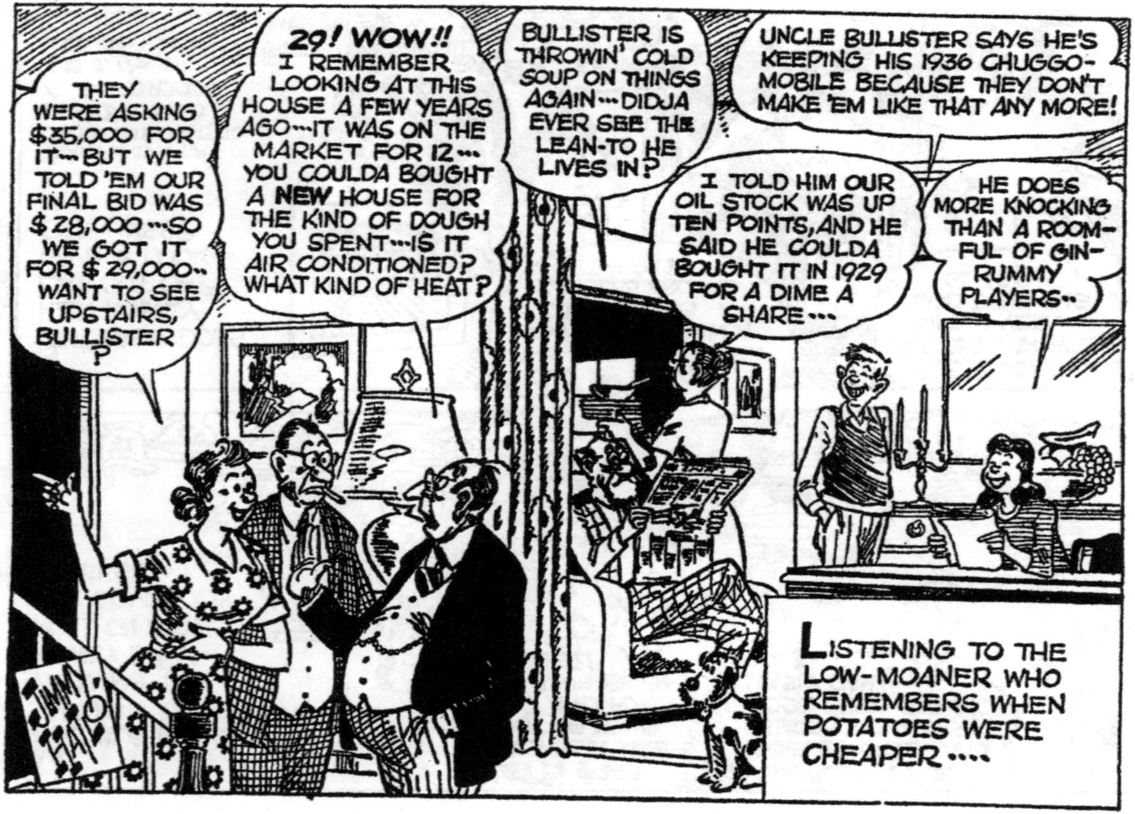

THEY WERE ASKING $35,000 FOR IT... BUT WE TOLD 'EM OUR FINAL BID WAS $28,000... SO WE GOT IT FOR $29,000... WANT TO SEE UPSTAIRS, BULLISTER?
29! WOW!! I REMEMBER LOOKING AT THIS HOUSE A FEW YEARS AGO... IT WAS ON THE MARKET FOR 12... YOU COULDA BOUGHT A NEW HOUSE FOR THE KIND OF DOUGH YOU SPENT... IS IT AIR CONDITIONED? WHAT KIND OF HEAT?
BULLISTER IS THROWIN' COLD SOUP ON THINGS AGAIN... DIDJA EVER SEE THE LEAN-TO HE LIVES IN?
UNCLE BULLISTER SAYS HE'S KEEPING HIS 1936 CHUGGO-MOBILE BECAUSE THEY DON'T MAKE 'EM LIKE THAT ANY MORE!
I TOLD HIM OUR OIL STOCK WAS UP TEN POINTS, AND HE SAID HE COULDA BOUGHT IT IN 1929 FOR A DIME A SHARE...
HE DOES MORE KNOCKING THAN A ROOM-FUL OF GIN-RUMMY PLAYERS..
LISTENING TO THE LOW-MOANER WHO REMEMBERS WHEN POTATOES WERE CHEAPER....
JIMMY HATLO

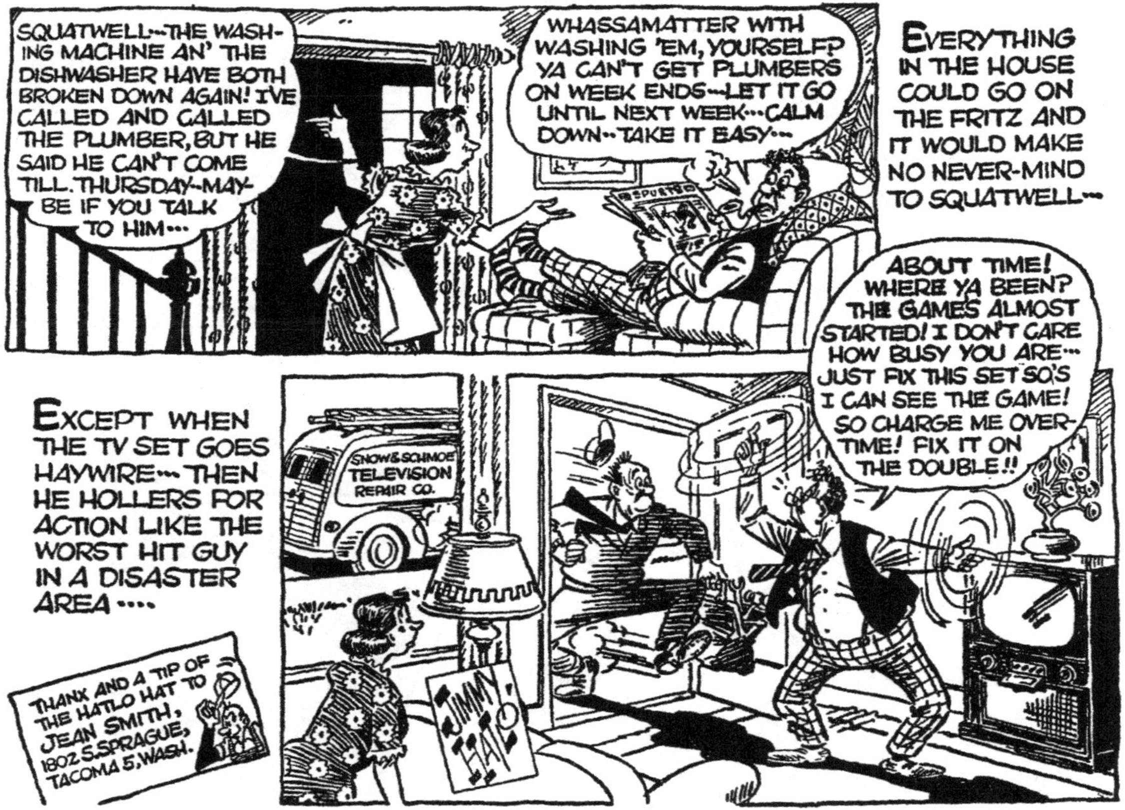
SQUATWELL--THE WASHING MACHINE AN' THE DISHWASHER HAVE BOTH BROKEN DOWN AGAIN! I'VE CALLED AND CALLED THE PLUMBER, BUT HE SAID HE CAN'T COME TILL. THURSDAY--MAYBE IF YOU TALK TO HIM...
WHASSAMATTER WITH WASHING 'EM, YOURSELF? YA CAN'T GET PLUMBERS ON WEEK ENDS--LET IT GO UNTIL NEXT WEEK...CALM DOWN--TAKE IT EASY...
EVERYTHING IN THE HOUSE COULD GO ON THE FRITZ AND IT WOULD MAKE NO NEVER-MIND TO SQUATWELL...
EXCEPT WHEN THE TV SET GOES HAYWIRE...THEN HE HOLLERS FOR ACTION LIKE THE WORST HIT GUY IN A DISASTER AREA....
SNOW & SCHMOE TELEVISION REPAIR CO.
ABOUT TIME! WHERE YA BEEN? THE GAMES ALMOST STARTED! I DON'T CARE HOW BUSY YOU ARE... JUST FIX THIS SET SO'S I CAN SEE THE GAME! SO CHARGE ME OVERTIME! FIX IT ON THE DOUBLE!!
JIMMY HATLO
THANX AND A TIP OF THE HATLO HAT TO JEAN SMITH, 1802 S. SPRAGUE, TACOMA 5, WASH.

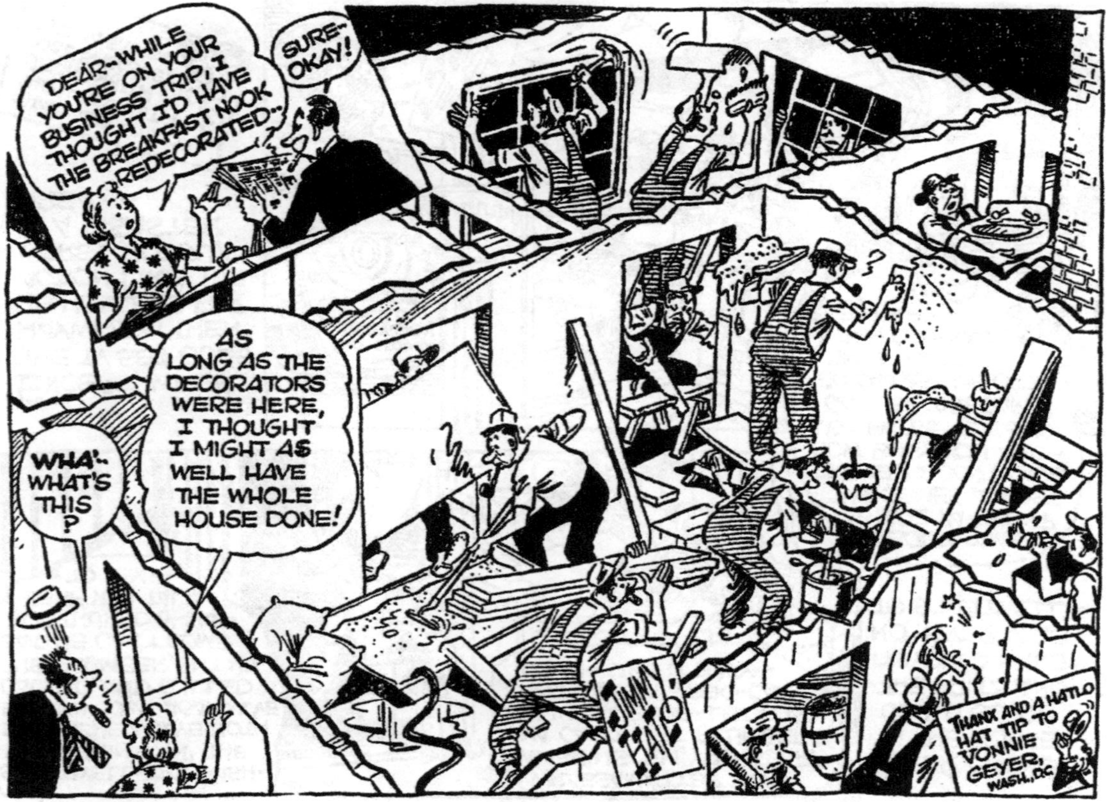
DEAR-WHILE YOU'RE ON YOUR BUSINESS TRIP, I THOUGHT I'D HAVE THE BREAKFAST NOOK REDECORATED-
SURE-OKAY!
AS LONG AS THE DECORATORS WERE HERE, I THOUGHT I MIGHT AS WELL HAVE THE WHOLE HOUSE DONE!
WHA'- WHAT'S THIS ?
JIMMY HATLO
THANX AND A HATLO HAT TIP TO VONNIE GEYER, WASH., D.C.

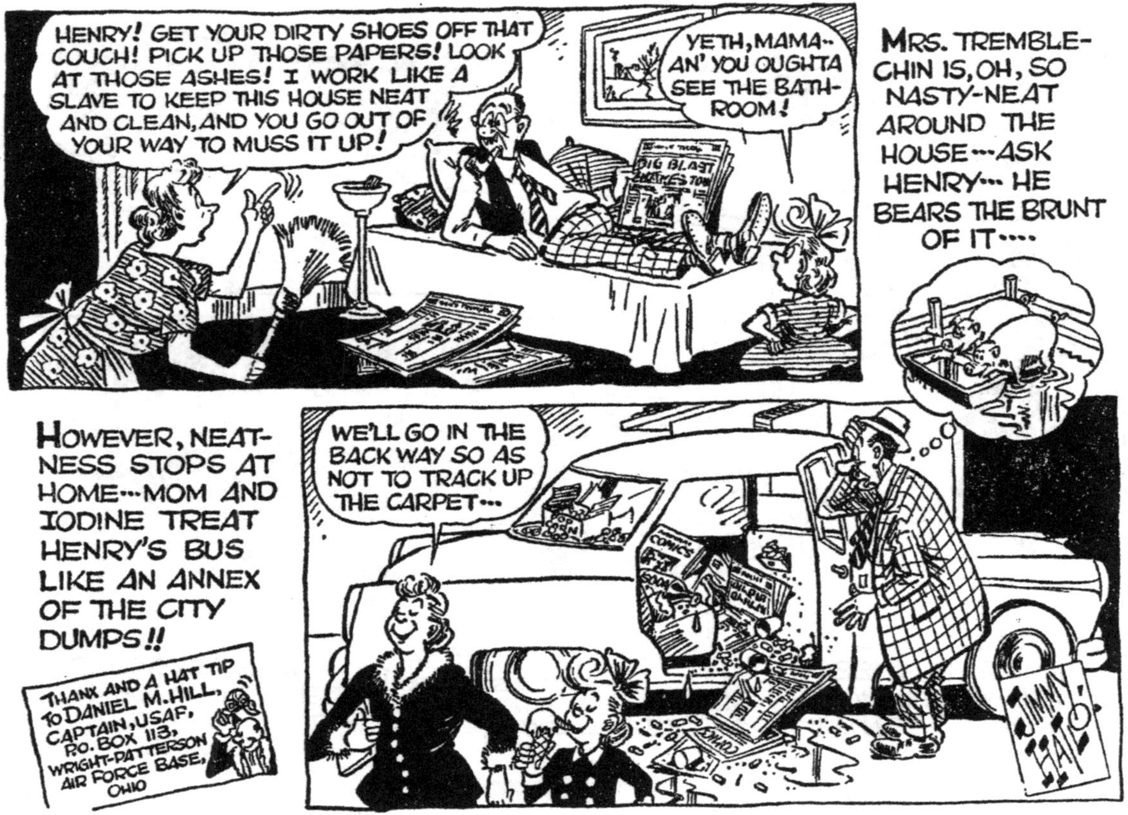
HENRY! GET YOUR DIRTY SHOES OFF THAT COUCH! PICK UP THOSE PAPERS! LOOK AT THOSE ASHES! I WORK LIKE A SLAVE TO KEEP THIS HOUSE NEAT AND CLEAN, AND YOU GO OUT OF YOUR WAY TO MUSS IT UP!
YETH, MAMA-- AN' YOU OUGHTA SEE THE BATH-ROOM!
BIG BLAST
MRS. TREMBLECHIN IS, OH, SO NASTY-NEAT AROUND THE HOUSE---ASK HENRY--- HE BEARS THE BRUNT OF IT....
HOWEVER, NEATNESS STOPS AT HOME---MOM AND IODINE TREAT HENRY'S BUS LIKE AN ANNEX OF THE CITY DUMPS!!
WE'LL GO IN THE BACK WAY SO AS NOT TO TRACK UP THE CARPET---
COMICS
THANX AND A HAT TIP TO DANIEL M. HILL, CAPTAIN, USAF, P.O. BOX 113, WRIGHT-PATTERSON AIR FORCE BASE, OHIO
JIMMY HATLO

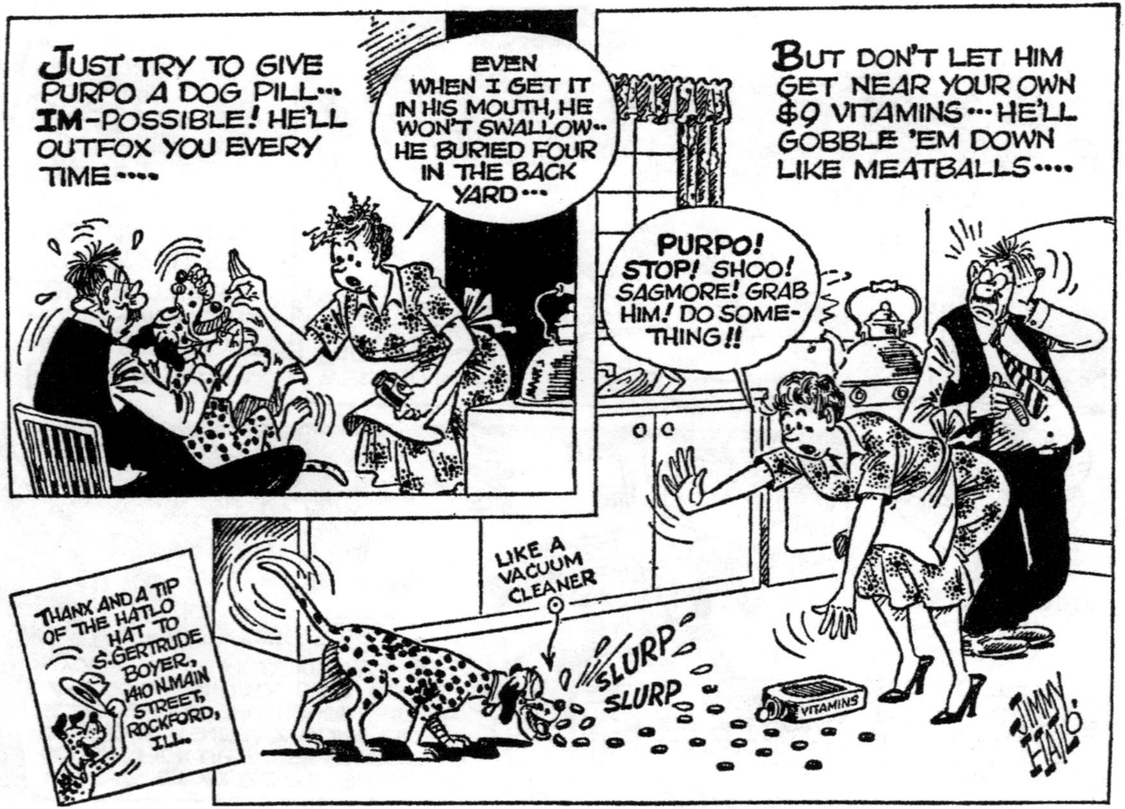
JUST TRY TO GIVE PURPO A DOG PILL... IM-POSSIBLE! HE'LL OUTFOX YOU EVERY TIME....
EVEN WHEN I GET IT IN HIS MOUTH, HE WON'T SWALLOW.. HE BURIED FOUR IN THE BACK YARD...
BUT DON'T LET HIM GET NEAR YOUR OWN $9 VITAMINS... HE'LL GOBBLE 'EM DOWN LIKE MEATBALLS....
PURPO! STOP! SHOO! SAGMORE! GRAB HIM! DO SOME-THING!!
LIKE A VACUUM CLEANER
SLURP
SLURP
VITAMINS
THANX AND A TIP OF THE HATLO HAT TO S.GERTRUDE BOYER, 1410 N.MAIN STREET, ROCKFORD, ILL.
JIMMY HATLO

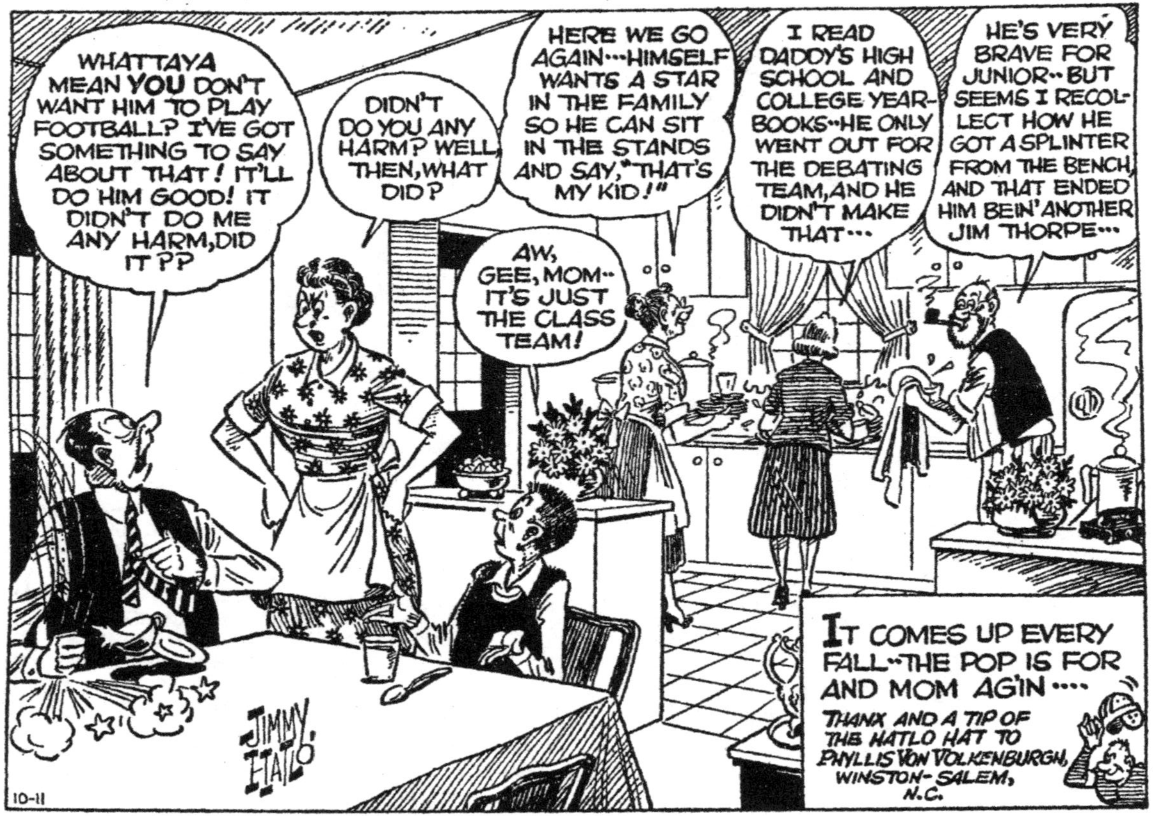
WHATTAYA MEAN YOU DON'T WANT HIM TO PLAY FOOTBALL? I'VE GOT SOMETHING TO SAY ABOUT THAT! IT'LL DO HIM GOOD! IT DIDN'T DO ME ANY HARM, DID IT??
DIDN'T DO YOU ANY HARM? WELL, THEN, WHAT DID?
HERE WE GO AGAIN···HIMSELF WANTS A STAR IN THE FAMILY SO HE CAN SIT IN THE STANDS AND SAY, "THAT'S MY KID!"
AW, GEE, MOM·· IT'S JUST THE CLASS TEAM!
I READ DADDY'S HIGH SCHOOL AND COLLEGE YEAR-BOOKS··HE ONLY WENT OUT FOR THE DEBATING TEAM, AND HE DIDN'T MAKE THAT···
HE'S VERY BRAVE FOR JUNIOR·· BUT SEEMS I RECOL-LECT HOW HE GOT A SPLINTER FROM THE BENCH, AND THAT ENDED HIM BEIN' ANOTHER JIM THORPE···
IT COMES UP EVERY FALL··THE POP IS FOR AND MOM AGIN····
THANX AND A TIP OF THE HATLO HAT TO PHYLLIS VON VOLKENBURGH, WINSTON-SALEM, N.C.
JIMMY HATLO
10-11

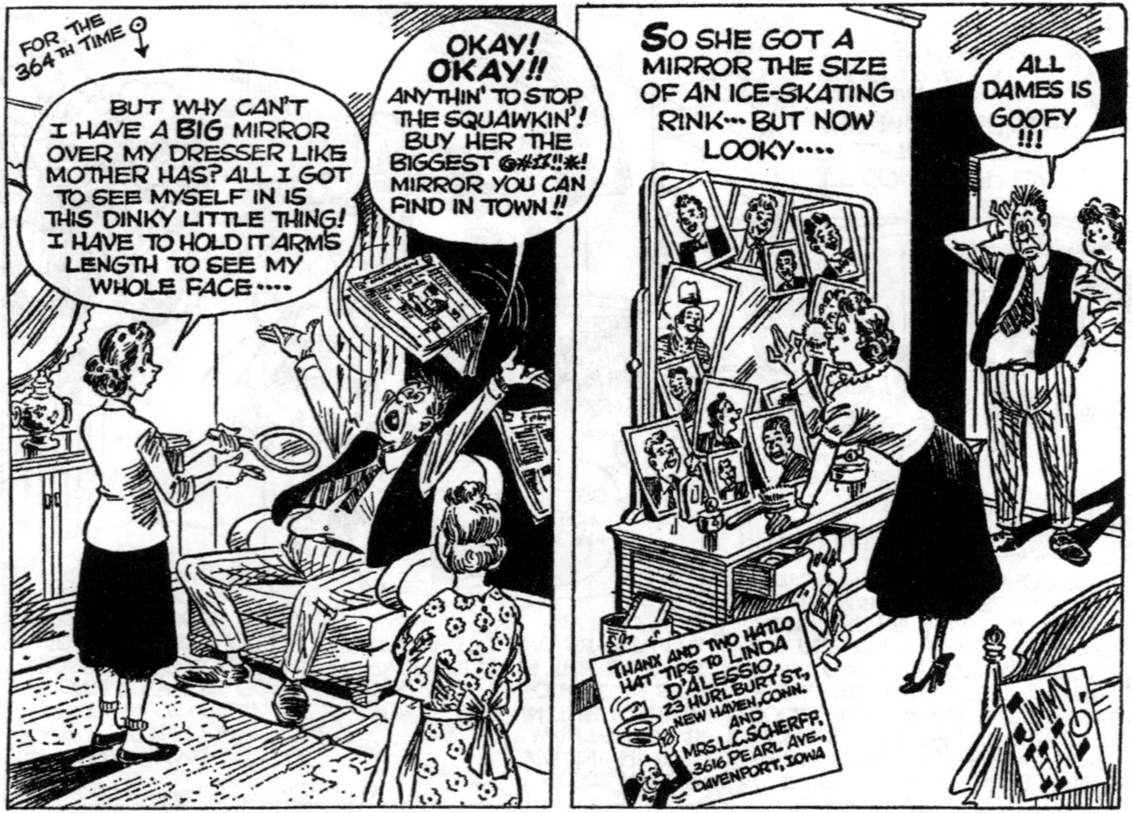
FOR THE 364TH TIME
BUT WHY CAN'T I HAVE A BIG MIRROR OVER MY DRESSER LIKE MOTHER HAS? ALL I GOT TO SEE MYSELF IN IS THIS DINKY LITTLE THING! I HAVE TO HOLD IT ARM'S LENGTH TO SEE MY WHOLE FACE....
OKAY! OKAY!! ANYTHIN' TO STOP THE SQUAWKIN'! BUY HER THE BIGGEST @#‡‡!!✱! MIRROR YOU CAN FIND IN TOWN!!
SO SHE GOT A MIRROR THE SIZE OF AN ICE-SKATING RINK... BUT NOW LOOKY....
ALL DAMES IS GOOFY !!!
THANX AND TWO HATLO HAT TIPS TO LINDA D'ALESSIO, 23 HURLBURT ST., NEW HAVEN, CONN. AND MRS. L.C. SCHERFF, 3616 PEARL AVE., DAVENPORT, IOWA
JIMMY HATLO

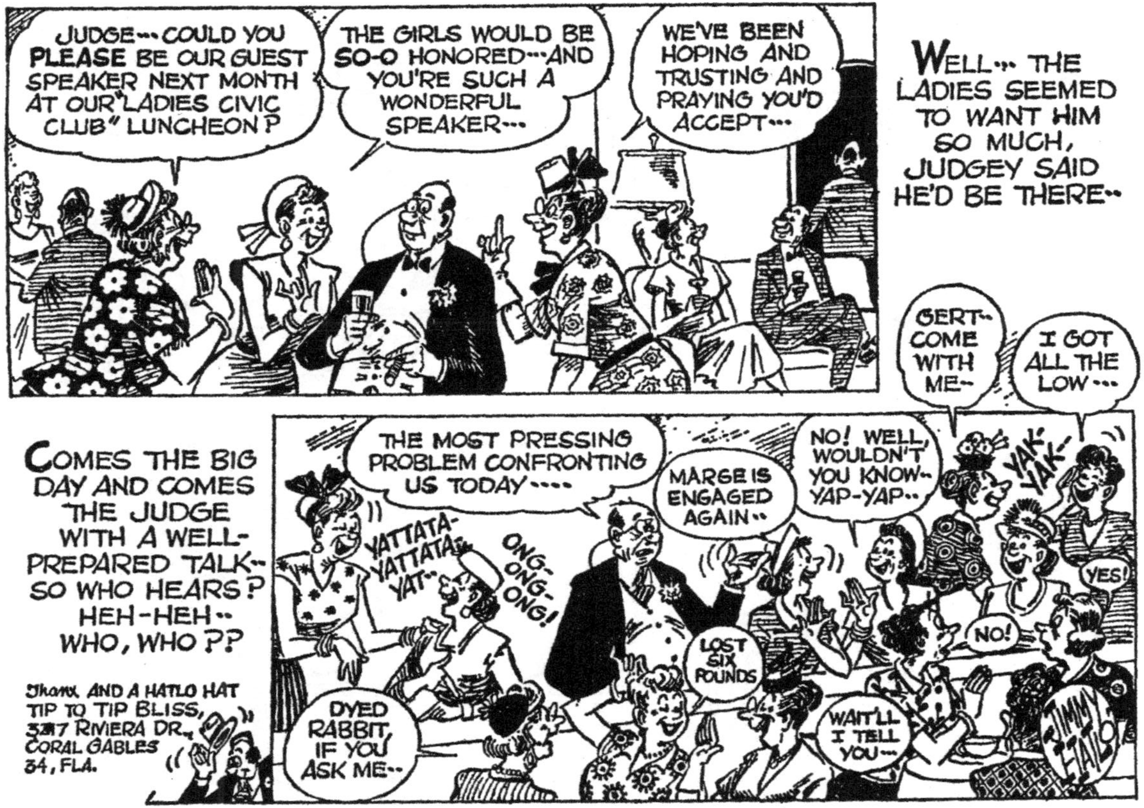
JUDGE--- COULD YOU PLEASE BE OUR GUEST SPEAKER NEXT MONTH AT OUR "LADIES CIVIC CLUB" LUNCHEON?
THE GIRLS WOULD BE SO-O HONORED---AND YOU'RE SUCH A WONDERFUL SPEAKER---
WE'VE BEEN HOPING AND TRUSTING AND PRAYING YOU'D ACCEPT---
WELL-- THE LADIES SEEMED TO WANT HIM SO MUCH, JUDGEY SAID HE'D BE THERE--
COMES THE BIG DAY AND COMES THE JUDGE WITH A WELL-PREPARED TALK-- SO WHO HEARS? HEH-HEH-- WHO, WHO??
THE MOST PRESSING PROBLEM CONFRONTING US TODAY----
YATTATA-YATTATA-YAT--
ONG-ONG-ONG!
DYED RABBIT, IF YOU ASK ME--
MARGE IS ENGAGED AGAIN--
LOST SIX POUNDS
NO! WELL, WOULDN'T YOU KNOW-- YAP-YAP--
WAIT'LL I TELL YOU---
GERT-- COME WITH ME--
I GOT ALL THE LOW---
YAK-YAK!
YES!
NO!
JIMMY HATLO
Thanx AND A HATLO HAT TIP TO TIP BLISS, 3217 RIVIERA DR., CORAL GABLES 34, FLA.

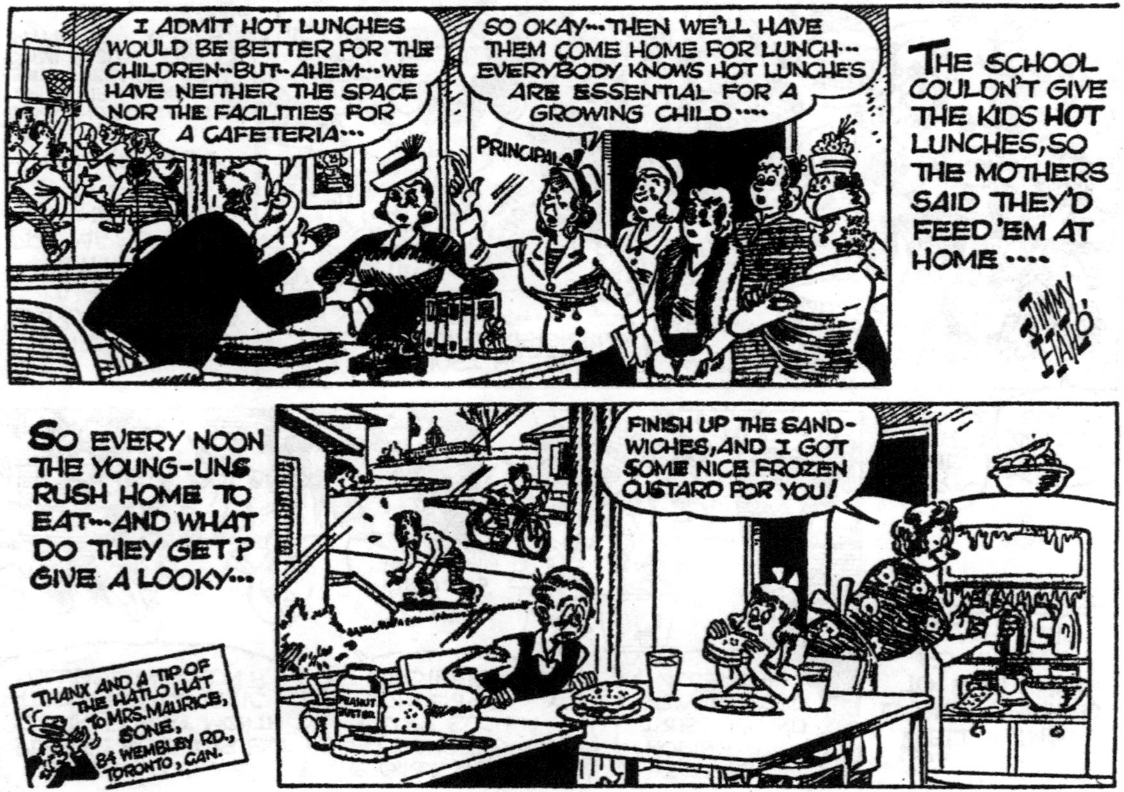

THE SCHOOL COULDN'T GIVE THE KIDS HOT LUNCHES, SO THE MOTHERS SAID THEY'D FEED 'EM AT HOME ....
I ADMIT HOT LUNCHES WOULD BE BETTER FOR THE CHILDREN--BUT--AHEM---WE HAVE NEITHER THE SPACE NOR THE FACILITIES FOR A CAFETERIA---
SO OKAY---THEN WE'LL HAVE THEM COME HOME FOR LUNCH--EVERYBODY KNOWS HOT LUNCHES ARE ESSENTIAL FOR A GROWING CHILD ----
PRINCIPAL
JIMMY HATLO
SO EVERY NOON THE YOUNG-UNS RUSH HOME TO EAT---AND WHAT DO THEY GET? GIVE A LOOKY---
FINISH UP THE SAND-WICHES, AND I GOT SOME NICE FROZEN CUSTARD FOR YOU!
PEANUT BUTTER
THANX AND A TIP OF THE HATLO HAT TO MRS. MAURICE SONE, 84 WEMBLEY RD., TORONTO, CAN.

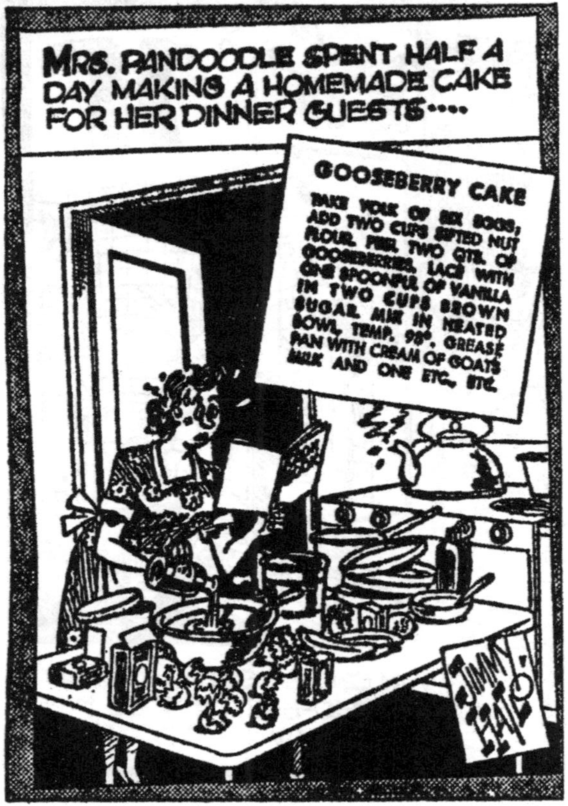
MRS. PANDOODLE SPENT HALF A DAY MAKING A HOMEMADE CAKE FOR HER DINNER GUESTS....
GOOSEBERRY CAKE
TAKE YOLK OF SIX EGGS, ADD TWO CUPS SIFTED NUT FLOUR. PEEL TWO QTS. OF GOOSEBERRIES. LACE WITH ONE SPOONFUL OF VANILLA IN TWO CUPS BROWN SUGAR. MIX IN HEATED BOWL, TEMP. 98°. GREASE PAN WITH CREAM OF GOATS MILK AND ONE ETC., ETC.
JIMMY HATLO

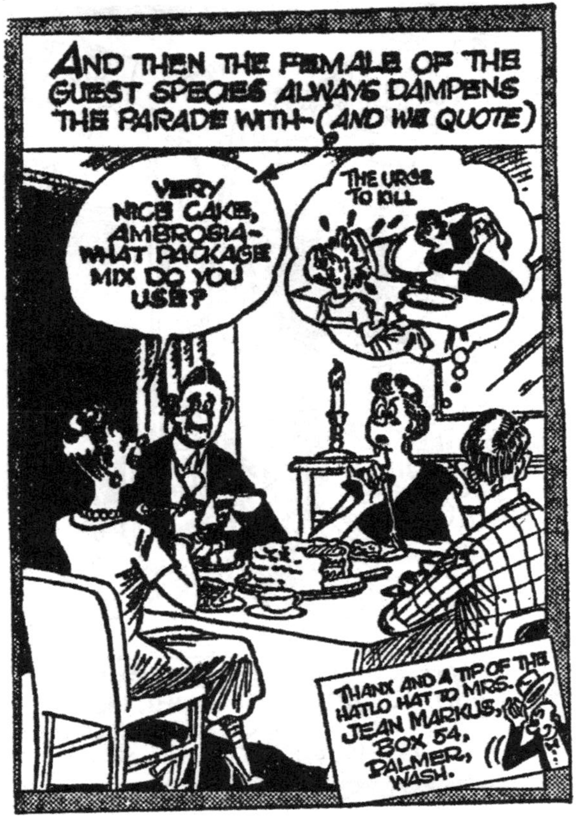
AND THEN THE FEMALE OF THE GUEST SPECIES ALWAYS DAMPENS THE PARADE WITH-(AND WE QUOTE)
VERY NICE CAKE, AMBROSIA-WHAT PACKAGE MIX DO YOU USE?
THE URGE TO KILL
THANX AND A TIP OF THE HATLO HAT TO MRS. JEAN MARKUS, BOX 54, PALMER, WASH.

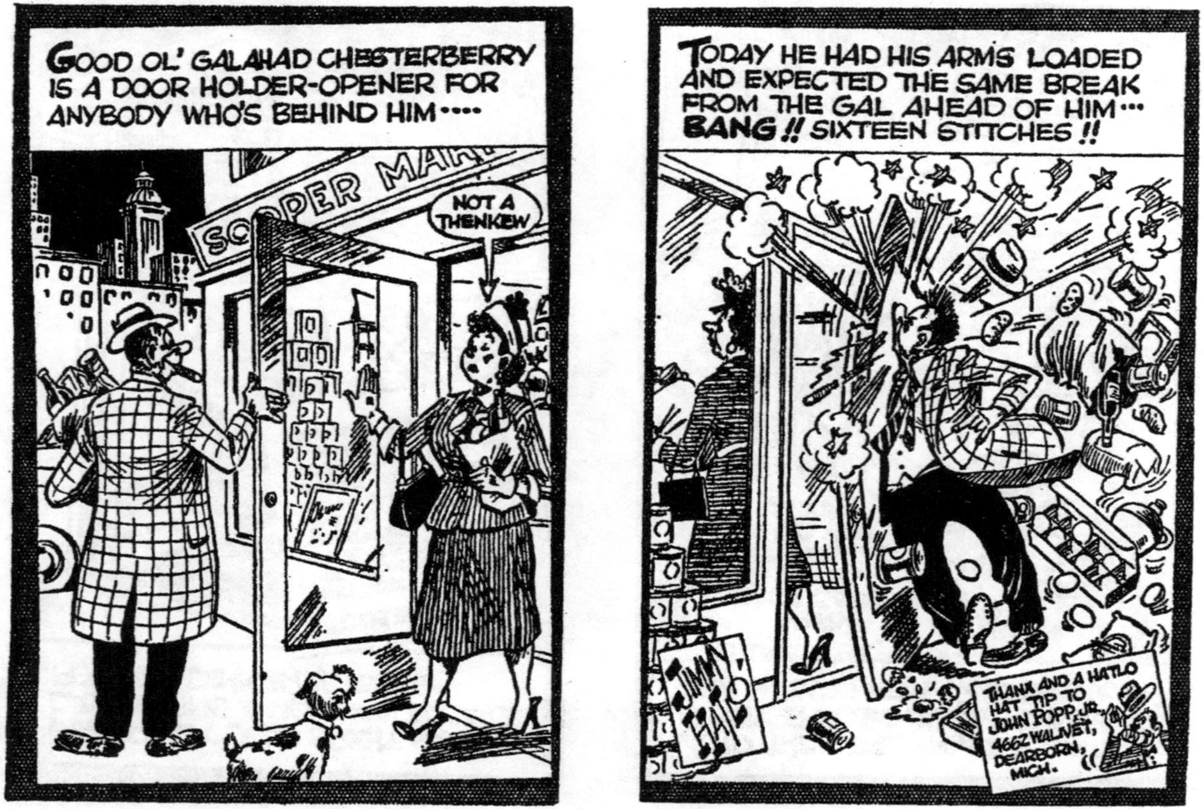
GOOD OL' GALAHAD CHESTERBERRY IS A DOOR HOLDER-OPENER FOR ANYBODY WHO'S BEHIND HIM....
NOT A THENKEW
TODAY HE HAD HIS ARMS LOADED AND EXPECTED THE SAME BREAK FROM THE GAL AHEAD OF HIM... BANG!! SIXTEEN STITCHES!!
THANX AND A HATLO HAT TIP TO JOHN POPP, JR., 4662 WALNUT, DEARBORN, MICH.

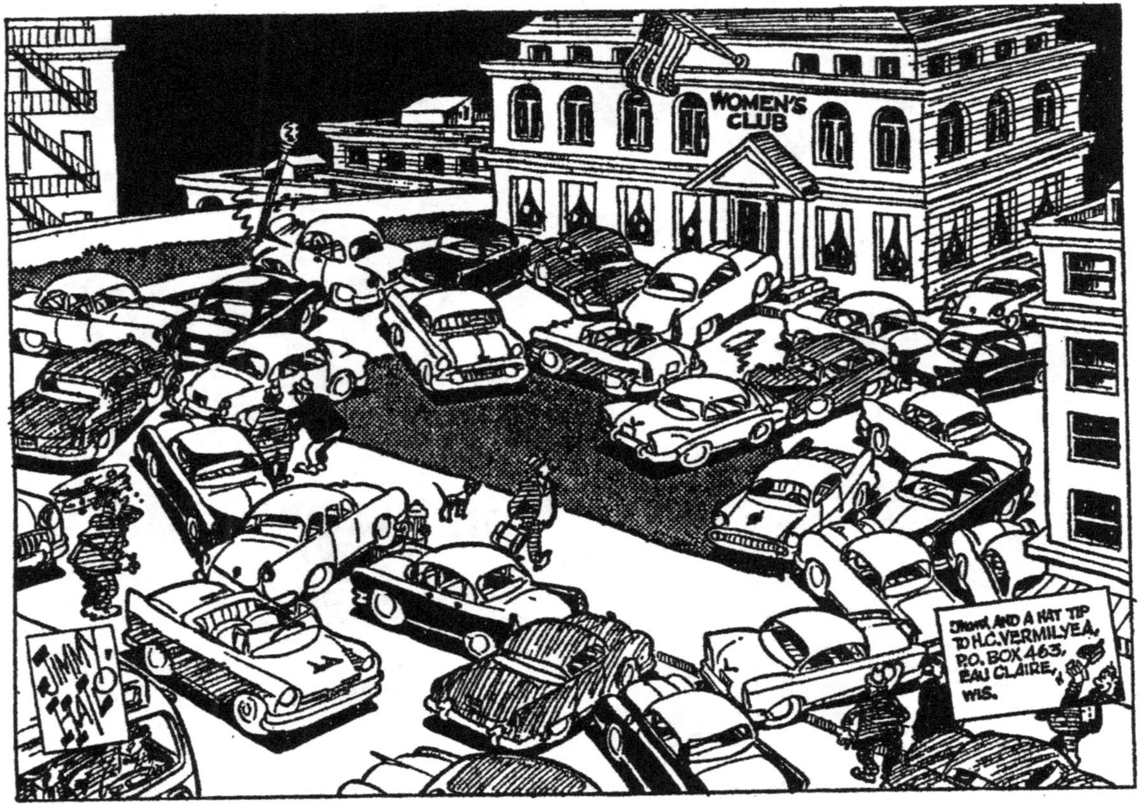
WOMEN'S CLUB
AND A HAT TIP TO H.C. VERMILYEA, P.O. BOX 463, EAU CLAIRE, WIS.
JIMMY

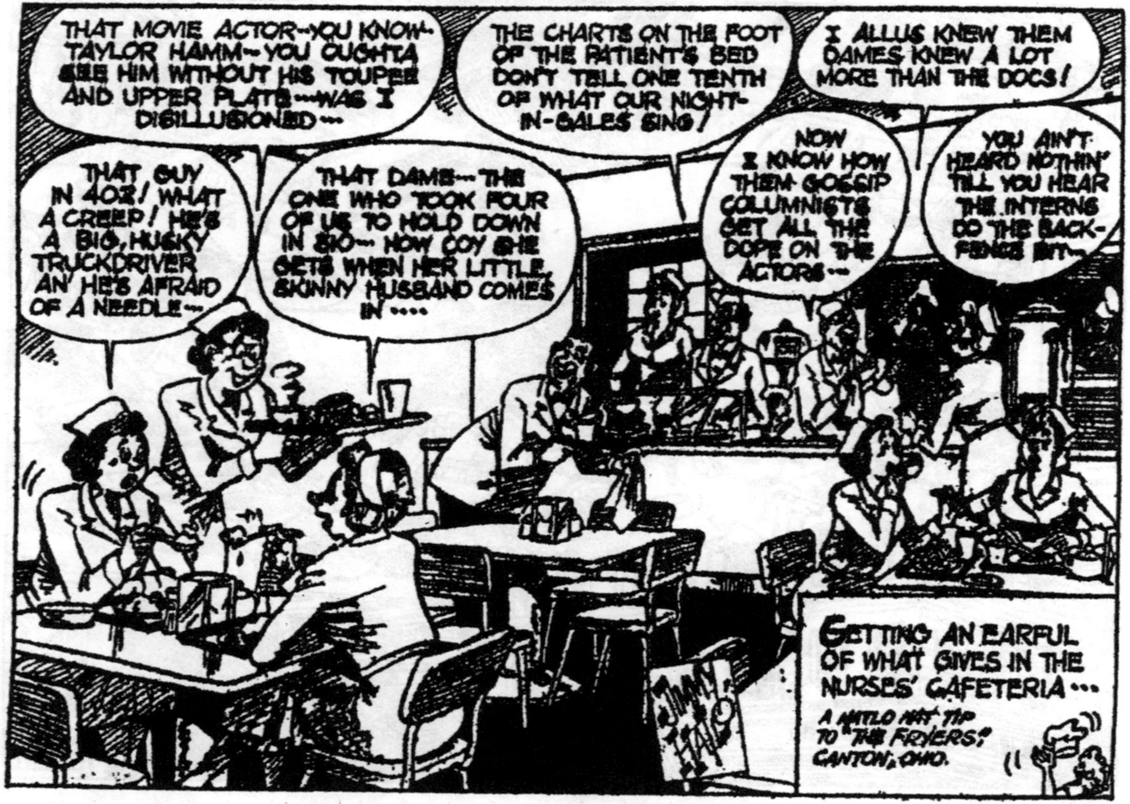
THAT MOVIE ACTOR--YOU KNOW--TAYLOR HAMM--YOU OUGHTA SEE HIM WITHOUT HIS TOUPEE AND UPPER PLATE---WAS I DISILLUSIONED---
THE CHARTS ON THE FOOT OF THE PATIENT'S BED DON'T TELL ONE TENTH OF WHAT OUR NIGHT-IN-GALES SING!
I ALLUS KNEW THEM DAMES KNEW A LOT MORE THAN THE DOCS!
THAT GUY IN 402! WHAT A CREEP! HE'S A BIG, HUSKY TRUCKDRIVER AN' HE'S AFRAID OF A NEEDLE---
THAT DAME--- THE ONE WHO TOOK FOUR OF US TO HOLD DOWN IN 810--- HOW COY SHE GETS WHEN HER LITTLE, SKINNY HUSBAND COMES IN ....
NOW I KNOW HOW THEM GOSSIP COLUMNISTS GET ALL THE DOPE ON THE ACTORS---
YOU AIN'T HEARD NOTHIN' TILL YOU HEAR THE INTERNS DO THE BACK-FENCE BIT---
GETTING AN EARFUL OF WHAT GIVES IN THE NURSES' CAFETERIA ...
A HATLO HAT TIP TO "THE FRYERS," CANTON, OHIO.

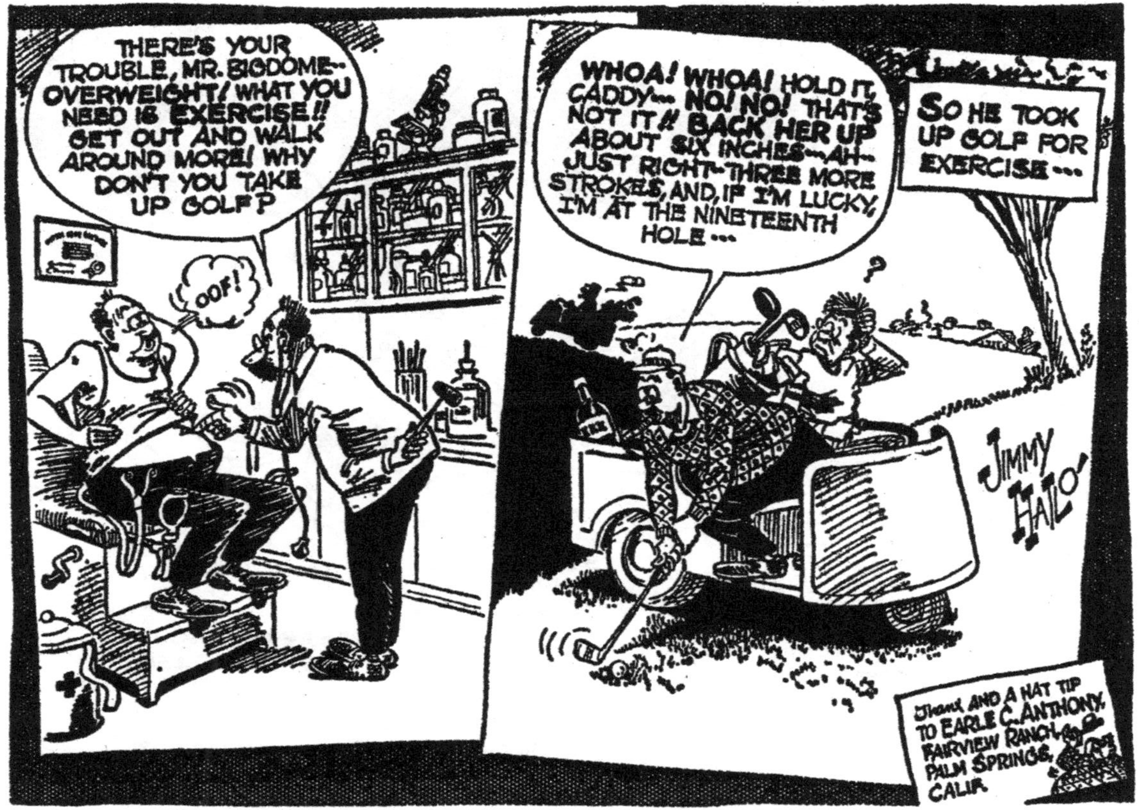
THERE'S YOUR TROUBLE, MR. BIGDOME-- OVERWEIGHT! WHAT YOU NEED IS EXERCISE!! GET OUT AND WALK AROUND MORE! WHY DON'T YOU TAKE UP GOLF?
OOF!
WHOA! WHOA! HOLD IT, CADDY... NO! NO! THAT'S NOT IT!! BACK HER UP ABOUT SIX INCHES--AH-- JUST RIGHT--THREE MORE STROKES, AND, IF I'M LUCKY, I'M AT THE NINETEENTH HOLE...
SO HE TOOK UP GOLF FOR EXERCISE...
JIMMY HATLO
Thanx AND A HAT TIP TO EARLE C. ANTHONY, FAIRVIEW RANCH, PALM SPRINGS, CALIF.

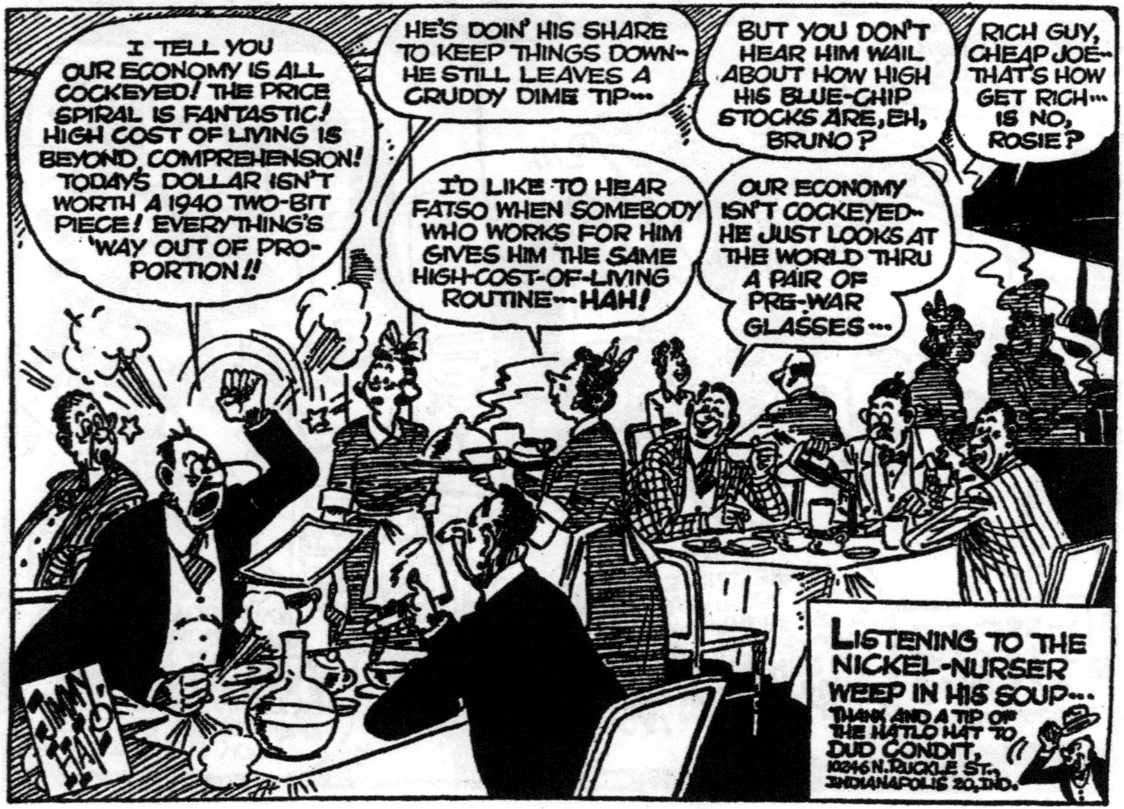
I TELL YOU OUR ECONOMY IS ALL COCKEYED! THE PRICE SPIRAL IS FANTASTIC! HIGH COST OF LIVING IS BEYOND COMPREHENSION! TODAY'S DOLLAR ISN'T WORTH A 1940 TWO-BIT PIECE! EVERYTHING'S 'WAY OUT OF PRO-PORTION!!
HE'S DOIN' HIS SHARE TO KEEP THINGS DOWN-- HE STILL LEAVES A CRUDDY DIME TIP...
I'D LIKE TO HEAR FATSO WHEN SOMEBODY WHO WORKS FOR HIM GIVES HIM THE SAME HIGH-COST-OF-LIVING ROUTINE... HAH!
BUT YOU DON'T HEAR HIM WAIL ABOUT HOW HIGH HIS BLUE-CHIP STOCKS ARE, EH, BRUNO?
OUR ECONOMY ISN'T COCKEYED-- HE JUST LOOKS AT THE WORLD THRU A PAIR OF PRE-WAR GLASSES...
RICH GUY, CHEAP JOE-- THAT'S HOW GET RICH... IS NO, ROSIE?
LISTENING TO THE NICKEL-NURSER WEEP IN HIS SOUP...
THANX AND A TIP OF THE HATLO HAT TO DUD CONDIT, 10246 N. RUCKLE ST., INDIANAPOLIS 20, IND.
JIMMY HATLO

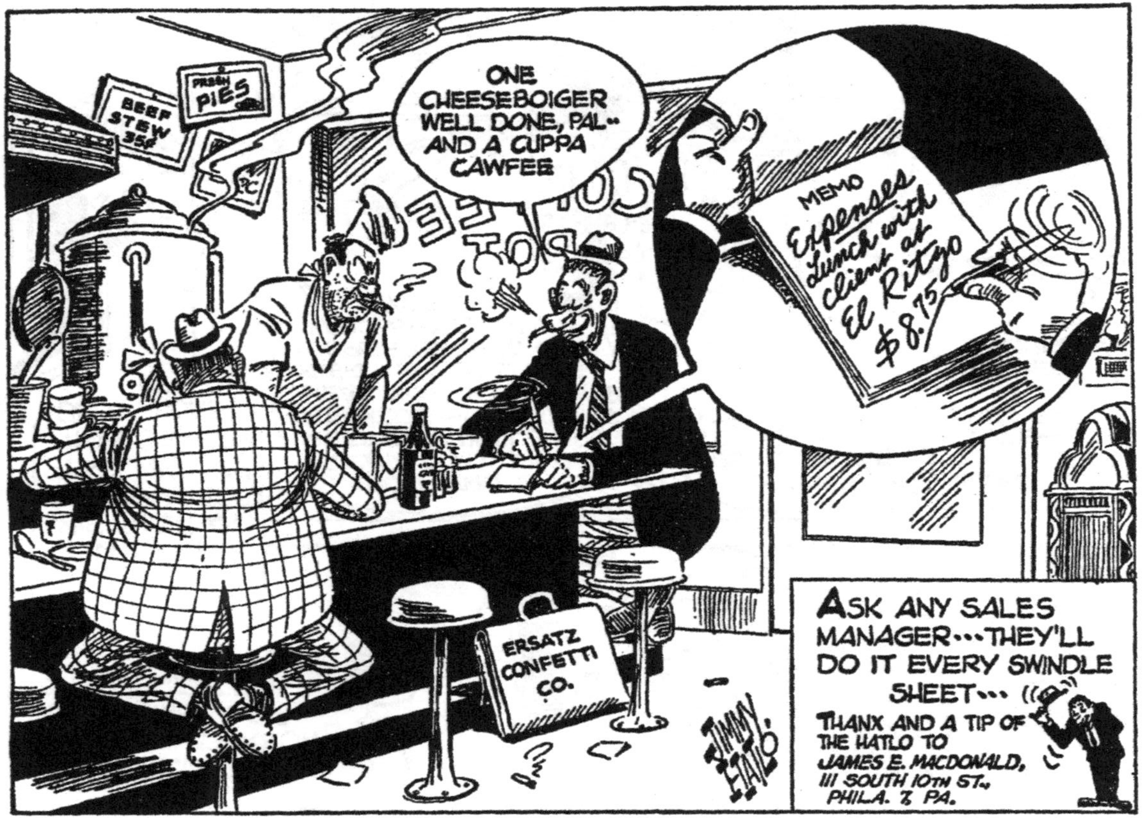
BEEF STEW 35¢
FRESH PIES
ONE CHEESEBOIGER WELL DONE, PAL.. AND A CUPPA CAWFEE
MEMO
Expenses
Lunch with client at El Ritzo
$8.75
ERSATZ CONFETTI CO.
JIMMY HATLO
ASK ANY SALES MANAGER... THEY'LL DO IT EVERY SWINDLE SHEET...
THANX AND A TIP OF THE HATLO TO JAMES E. MACDONALD, 111 SOUTH 10TH ST., PHILA. 7, PA.

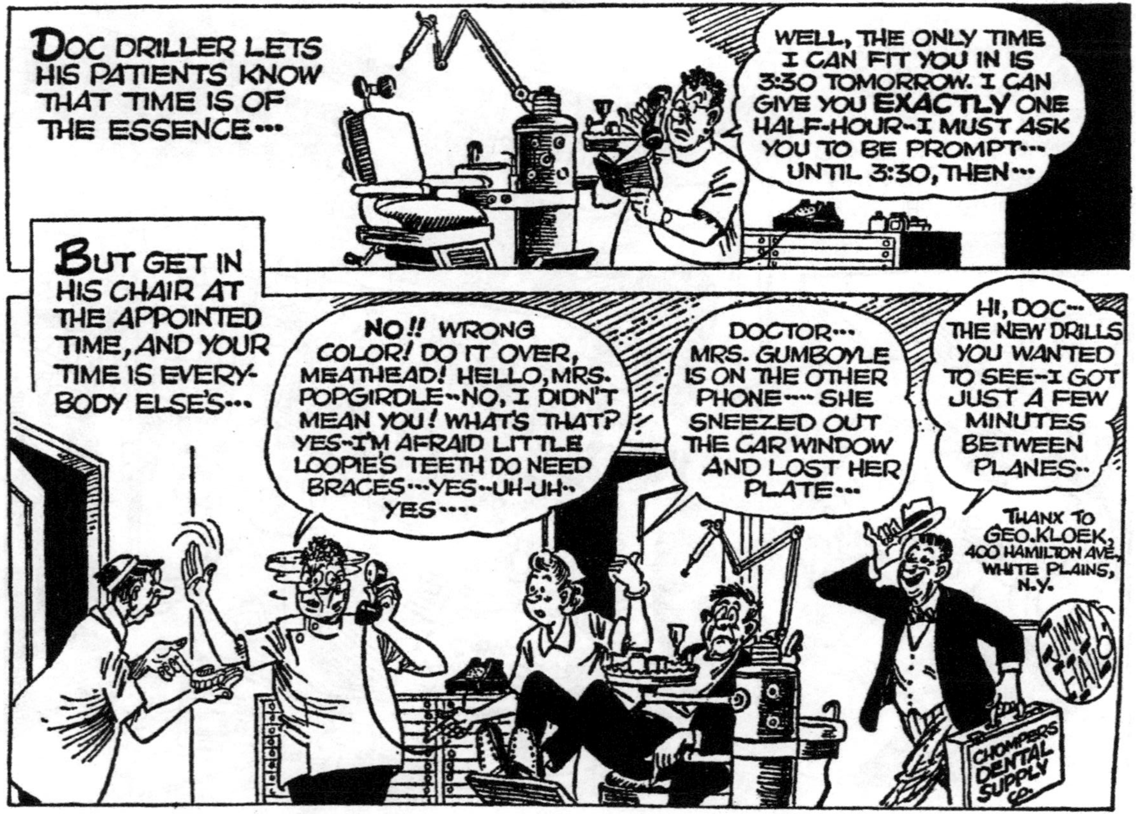
DOC DRILLER LETS HIS PATIENTS KNOW THAT TIME IS OF THE ESSENCE...
WELL, THE ONLY TIME I CAN FIT YOU IN IS 3:30 TOMORROW. I CAN GIVE YOU EXACTLY ONE HALF-HOUR--I MUST ASK YOU TO BE PROMPT... UNTIL 3:30, THEN...
BUT GET IN HIS CHAIR AT THE APPOINTED TIME, AND YOUR TIME IS EVERY-BODY ELSE'S...
NO!! WRONG COLOR! DO IT OVER, MEATHEAD! HELLO, MRS. POPGIRDLE--NO, I DIDN'T MEAN YOU! WHAT'S THAT? YES--I'M AFRAID LITTLE LOOPIE'S TEETH DO NEED BRACES...YES--UH-UH-YES....
DOCTOR... MRS. GUMBOYLE IS ON THE OTHER PHONE.... SHE SNEEZED OUT THE CAR WINDOW AND LOST HER PLATE...
HI, DOC-- THE NEW DRILLS YOU WANTED TO SEE--I GOT JUST A FEW MINUTES BETWEEN PLANES..
THANX TO GEO. KLOEK, 400 HAMILTON AVE., WHITE PLAINS, N.Y.
JIMMY HATLO
CHOMPERS DENTAL SUPPLY CO.

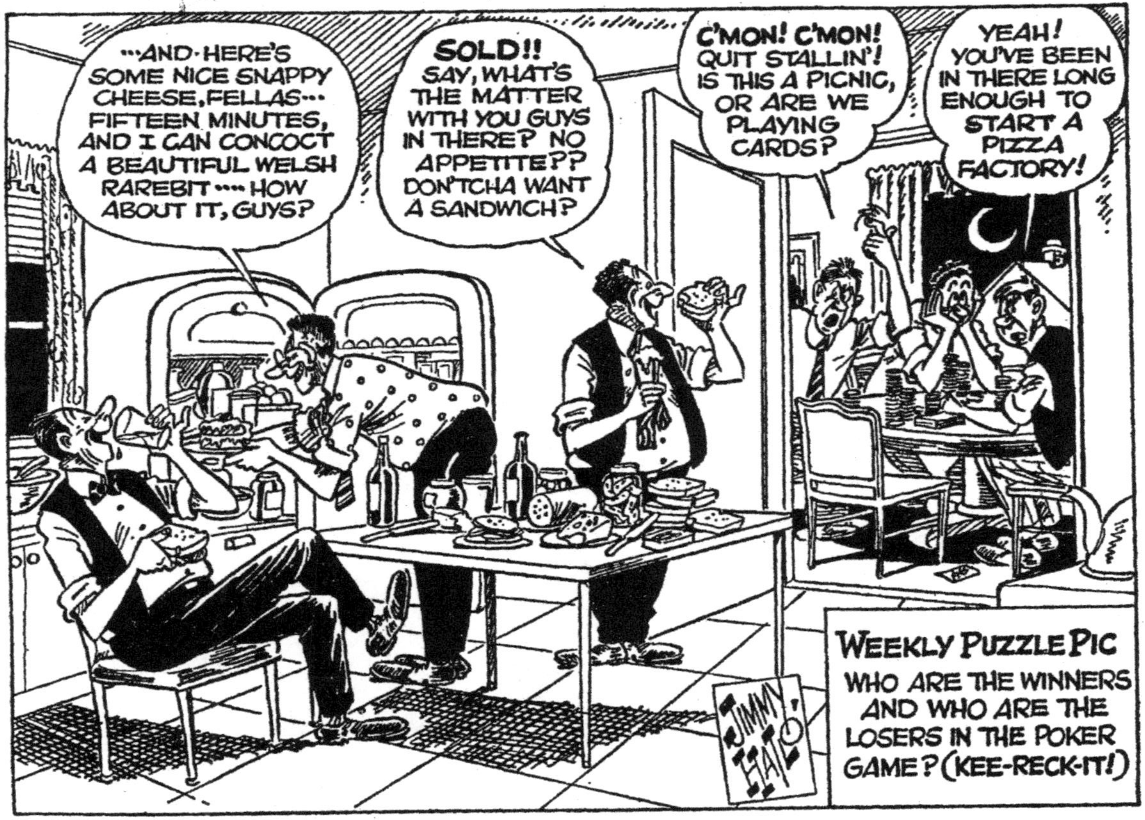

...AND-HERE'S SOME NICE SNAPPY CHEESE, FELLAS... FIFTEEN MINUTES, AND I CAN CONCOCT A BEAUTIFUL WELSH RAREBIT.... HOW ABOUT IT, GUYS?
SOLD!! SAY, WHAT'S THE MATTER WITH YOU GUYS IN THERE? NO APPETITE?? DON'TCHA WANT A SANDWICH?
C'MON! C'MON! QUIT STALLIN'! IS THIS A PICNIC, OR ARE WE PLAYING CARDS?
YEAH! YOU'VE BEEN IN THERE LONG ENOUGH TO START A PIZZA FACTORY!
WEEKLY PUZZLE PIC
WHO ARE THE WINNERS AND WHO ARE THE LOSERS IN THE POKER GAME? (KEE-RECK-IT!)
JIMMY HATLO

A brand new collection of bellylaughs
by America's funniest cartoonist

THE NEWEST
JIMMY HATLO
CARTOON BOOK

NEVER BEFORE IN BOOK FORM

POP BLOWS HIS TOPKNOT IF JUNIOR SO MUCH AS GETS HIS RUBBER HEELS DAMP---
YOU MEAN TO SAY YOU WERE OUT DRESSED LIKE THAT?! DO YOU WANT TO CATCH PNEUMONIA? TAKE OFF THOSE WET SHOES!! TAKE A HOT BATH AND GET INTO BED!!
GEE, POP-- IT'S JUST RAINING A LITTLE BIT---
NOW GET A GANDER AT HIMSELF ENJOYING TWELVE HOURS' MISERY UP TO HIS CLAVICLE IN RAIN AND SLEET---
A-CHOO! THIS IS THE LIFE! A FLOCK IS BOUND TO SHOW UP SOONER OR LATER! A-CHOO!!
JIMMY HATLO
THANX AND A TIP OF THE HATLO HAT TO JIM TOLLEY, 1045 S. WATER, WICHITA 11, KANSAS

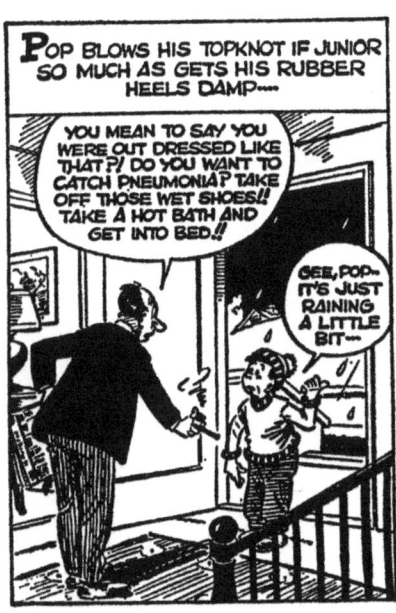

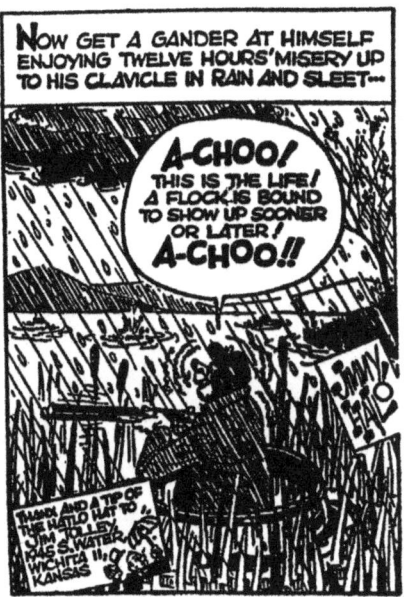

BRING 'EM BACK ALIVE HATLO

When it comes to capturing Whacky Whims, Foolish Foibles, Zanies and Yuks, no one can beat hunter Hatlo!

Armed with nothing except his bare psyche, dogged seeing-eye, and pen-pointed humor, he bags the most riotous specimens of Human Failing ever taken alive!

"You have that touch of high humor which characterizes such American immortals as Mark Twain and Will Rogers."

—*J. Edgar Hoover*

"You make us laugh at ourselves, and you do it every time. I hold my hat high to Hatlo!"

—*Walt Disney*

THE NEWEST JIMMY HATLO CARTOON BOOK

They'll Do It Every Time ®

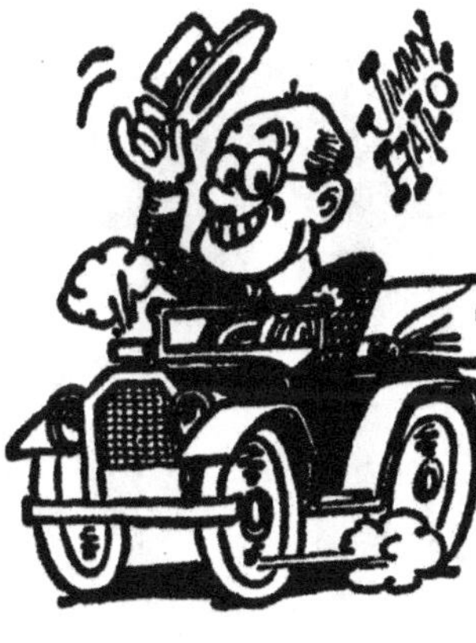
JIMMY HATLO

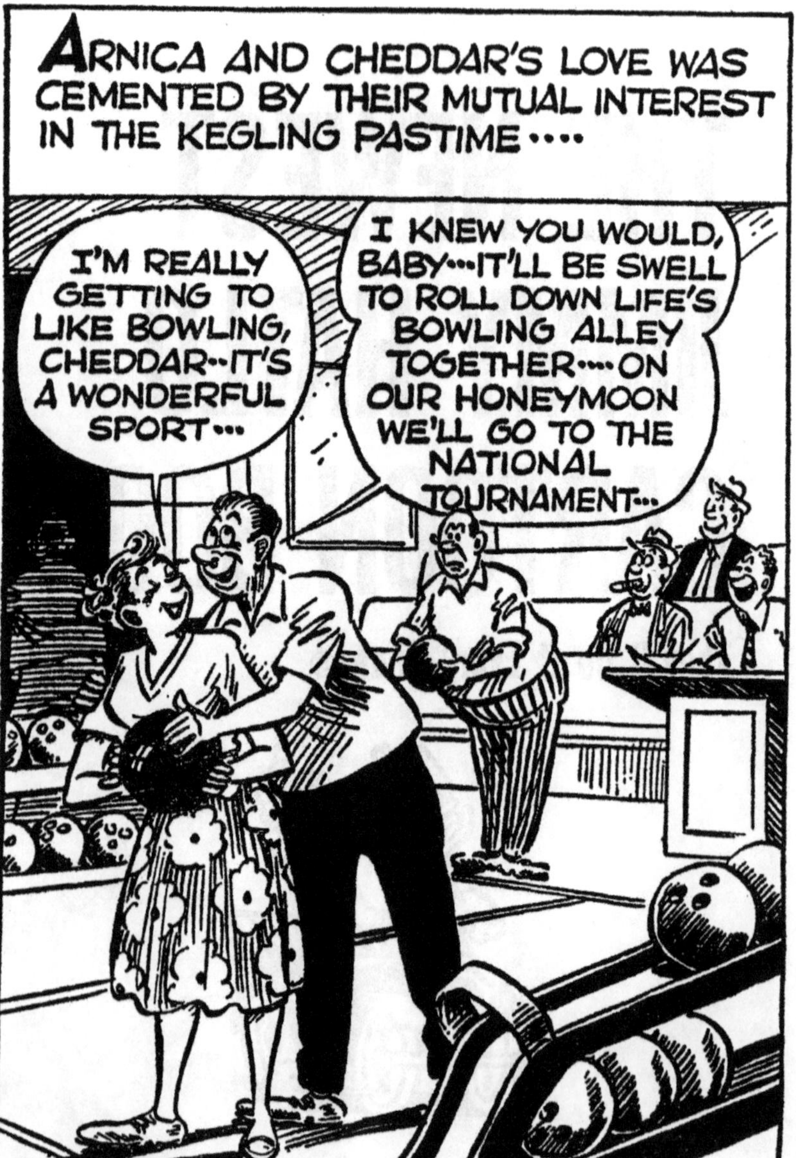
ARNICA AND CHEDDAR'S LOVE WAS CEMENTED BY THEIR MUTUAL INTEREST IN THE KEGLING PASTIME....
I'M REALLY GETTING TO LIKE BOWLING, CHEDDAR--IT'S A WONDERFUL SPORT...
I KNEW YOU WOULD, BABY...IT'LL BE SWELL TO ROLL DOWN LIFE'S BOWLING ALLEY TOGETHER....ON OUR HONEYMOON WE'LL GO TO THE NATIONAL TOURNAMENT...

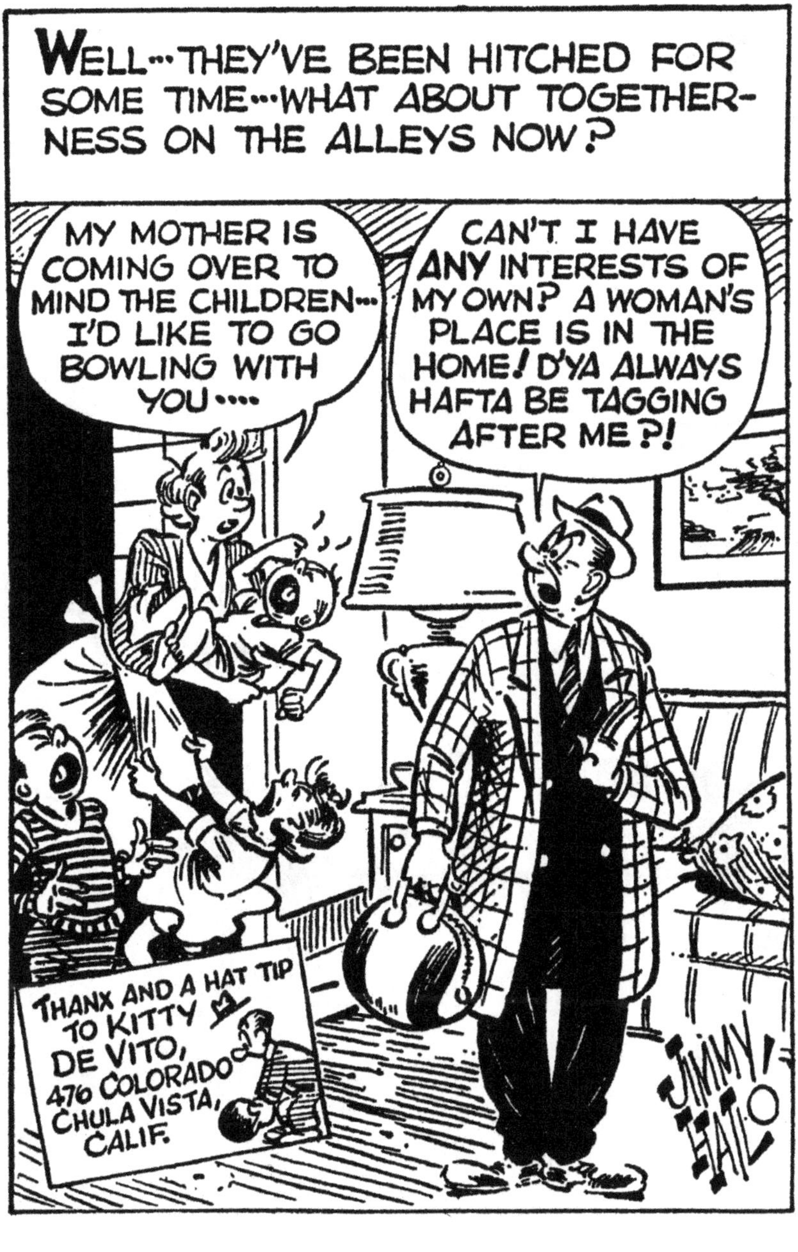
WELL--THEY'VE BEEN HITCHED FOR SOME TIME--WHAT ABOUT TOGETHERNESS ON THE ALLEYS NOW?
MY MOTHER IS COMING OVER TO MIND THE CHILDREN--I'D LIKE TO GO BOWLING WITH YOU....
CAN'T I HAVE ANY INTERESTS OF MY OWN? A WOMAN'S PLACE IS IN THE HOME! D'YA ALWAYS HAFTA BE TAGGING AFTER ME?!
THANX AND A HAT TIP TO KITTY DE VITO, 476 COLORADO CHULA VISTA, CALIF.
JIMMY HATLO

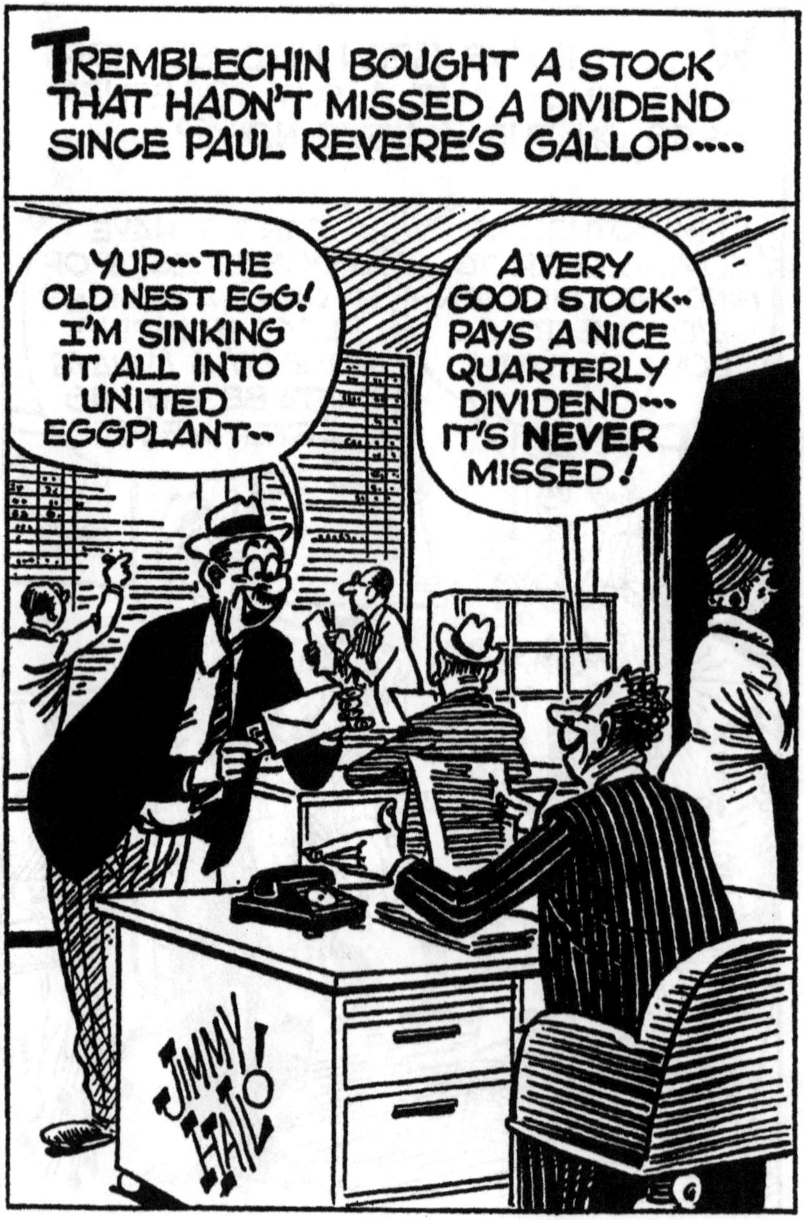
TREMBLECHIN BOUGHT A STOCK THAT HADN'T MISSED A DIVIDEND SINCE PAUL REVERE'S GALLOP....
YUP...THE OLD NEST EGG! I'M SINKING IT ALL INTO UNITED EGGPLANT--
A VERY GOOD STOCK.. PAYS A NICE QUARTERLY DIVIDEND... IT'S NEVER MISSED!
JIMMY HATLO

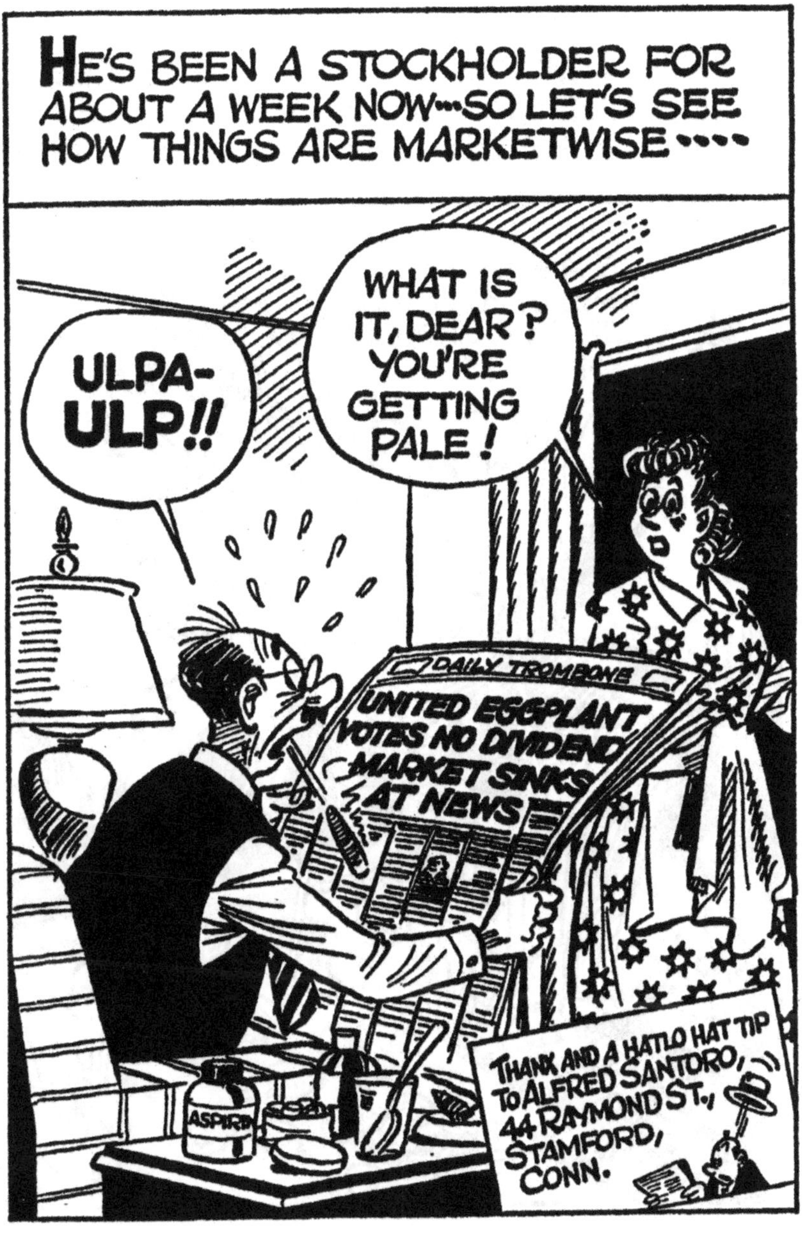
HE'S BEEN A STOCKHOLDER FOR ABOUT A WEEK NOW...SO LET'S SEE HOW THINGS ARE MARKETWISE....
ULPA-ULP!!
WHAT IS IT, DEAR? YOU'RE GETTING PALE!
DAILY TROMBONE
UNITED EGGPLANT VOTES NO DIVIDEND MARKET SINKS AT NEWS
ASPIRIN
THANX AND A HATLO HAT TIP TO ALFRED SANTORO, 44 RAYMOND ST., STAMFORD, CONN.

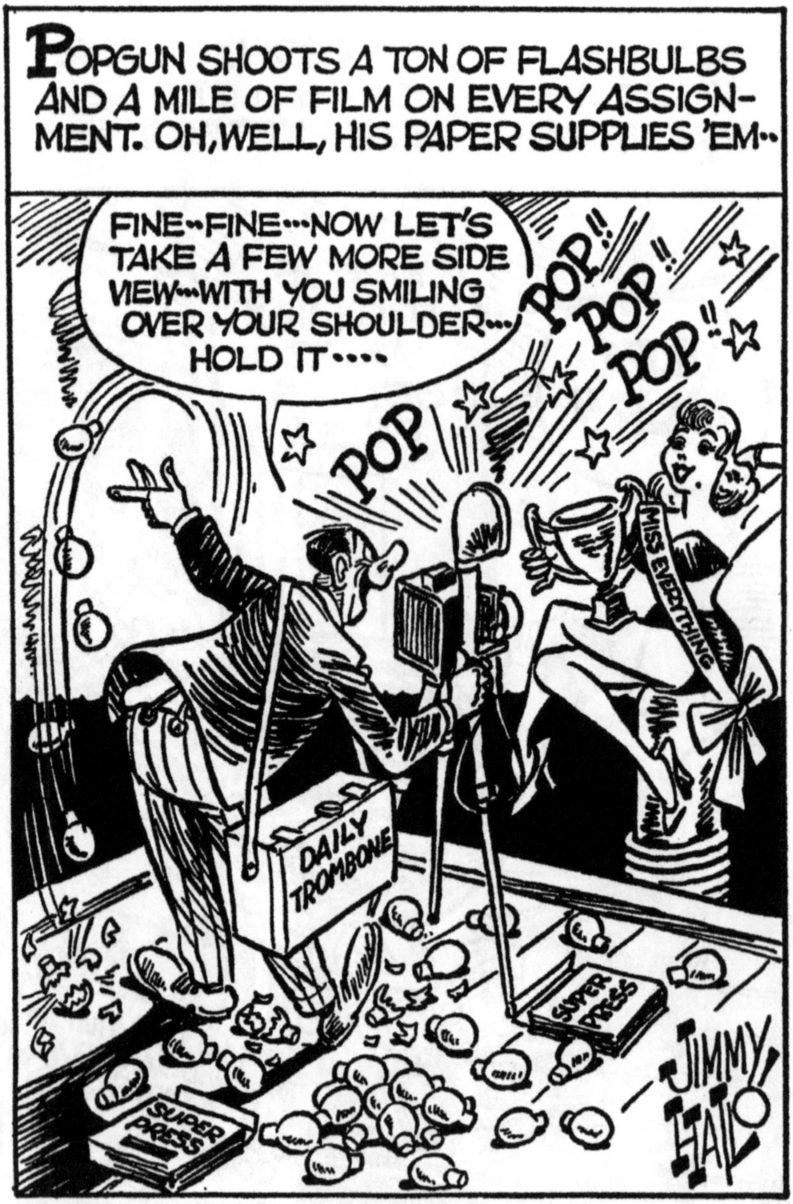
POPGUN SHOOTS A TON OF FLASHBULBS AND A MILE OF FILM ON EVERY ASSIGNMENT. OH, WELL, HIS PAPER SUPPLIES 'EM..
FINE..FINE...NOW LET'S TAKE A FEW MORE SIDE VIEW...WITH YOU SMILING OVER YOUR SHOULDER... HOLD IT....
POP!!
POP!!
POP!!
POP
MISS EVERYTHING
DAILY TROMBONE
SUPER PRESS
SUPER PRESS
JIMMY HATLO

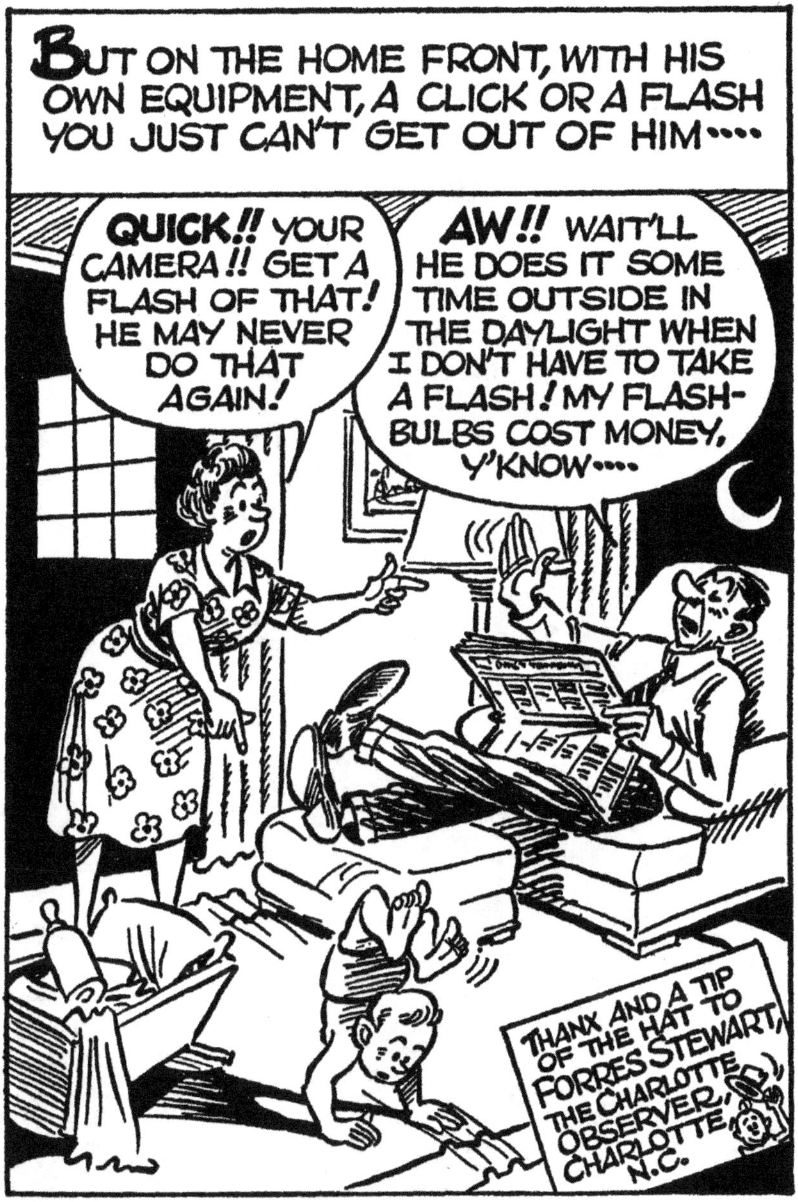
BUT ON THE HOME FRONT, WITH HIS OWN EQUIPMENT, A CLICK OR A FLASH YOU JUST CAN'T GET OUT OF HIM....
QUICK!! YOUR CAMERA!! GET A FLASH OF THAT! HE MAY NEVER DO THAT AGAIN!
AW!! WAIT'LL HE DOES IT SOME TIME OUTSIDE IN THE DAYLIGHT WHEN I DON'T HAVE TO TAKE A FLASH! MY FLASH-BULBS COST MONEY, Y'KNOW....
THANX AND A TIP OF THE HAT TO FORRES STEWART, THE CHARLOTTE OBSERVER, CHARLOTTE, N.C.

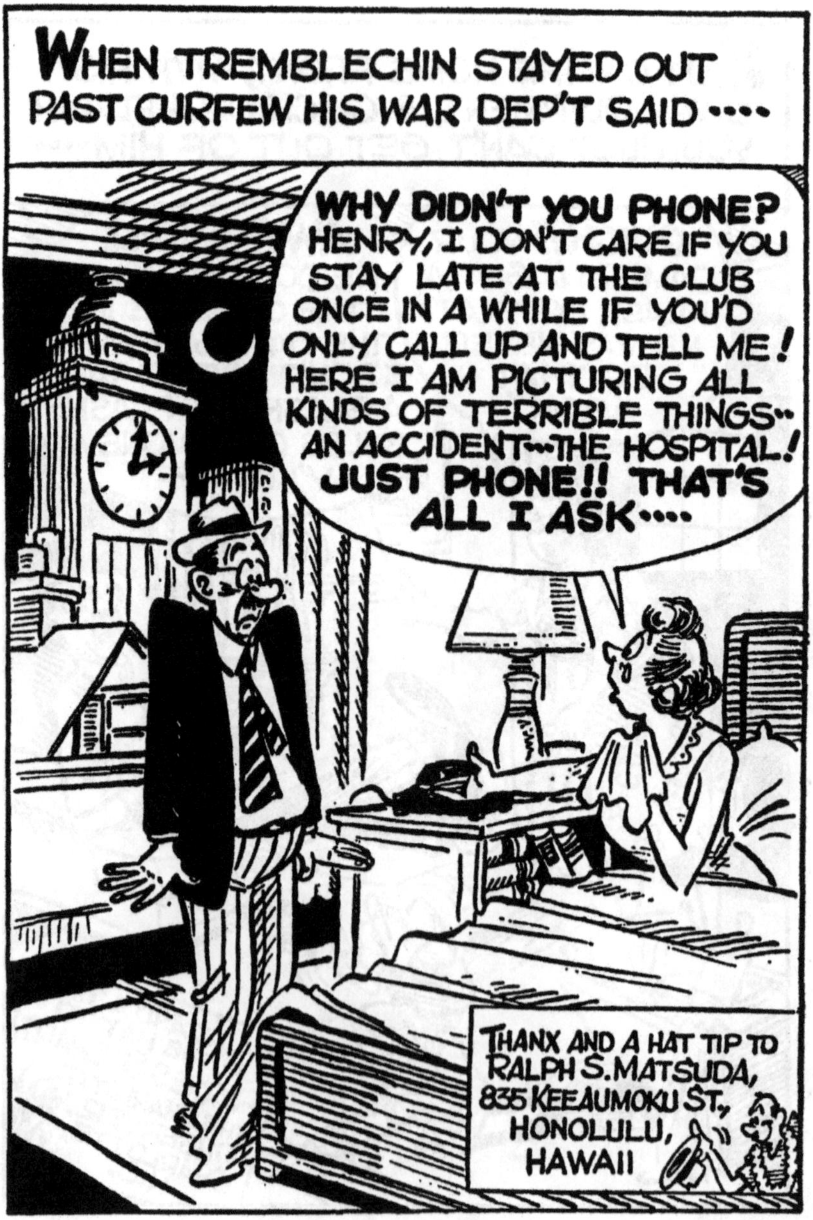
WHEN TREMBLECHIN STAYED OUT PAST CURFEW HIS WAR DEP'T SAID ····
WHY DIDN'T YOU PHONE? HENRY, I DON'T CARE IF YOU STAY LATE AT THE CLUB ONCE IN A WHILE IF YOU'D ONLY CALL UP AND TELL ME! HERE I AM PICTURING ALL KINDS OF TERRIBLE THINGS·· AN ACCIDENT··THE HOSPITAL! JUST PHONE!! THAT'S ALL I ASK····
THANX AND A HAT TIP TO RALPH S. MATSUDA, 835 KEEAUMOKU ST., HONOLULU, HAWAII

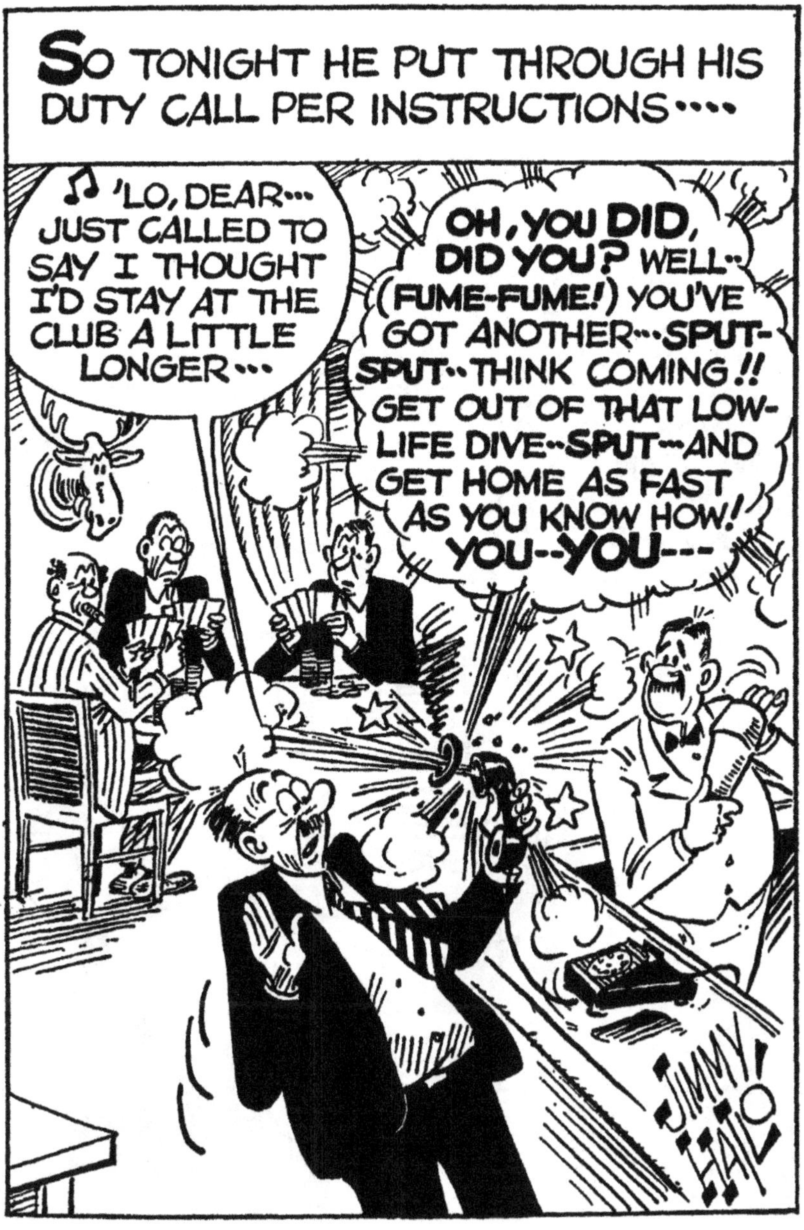
SO TONIGHT HE PUT THROUGH HIS DUTY CALL PER INSTRUCTIONS....
'LO, DEAR... JUST CALLED TO SAY I THOUGHT I'D STAY AT THE CLUB A LITTLE LONGER...
OH, YOU DID, DID YOU? WELL-- (FUME-FUME!) YOU'VE GOT ANOTHER...SPUT-SPUT..THINK COMING!! GET OUT OF THAT LOW-LIFE DIVE--SPUT--AND GET HOME AS FAST AS YOU KNOW HOW! YOU--YOU---
JIMMY HATLO

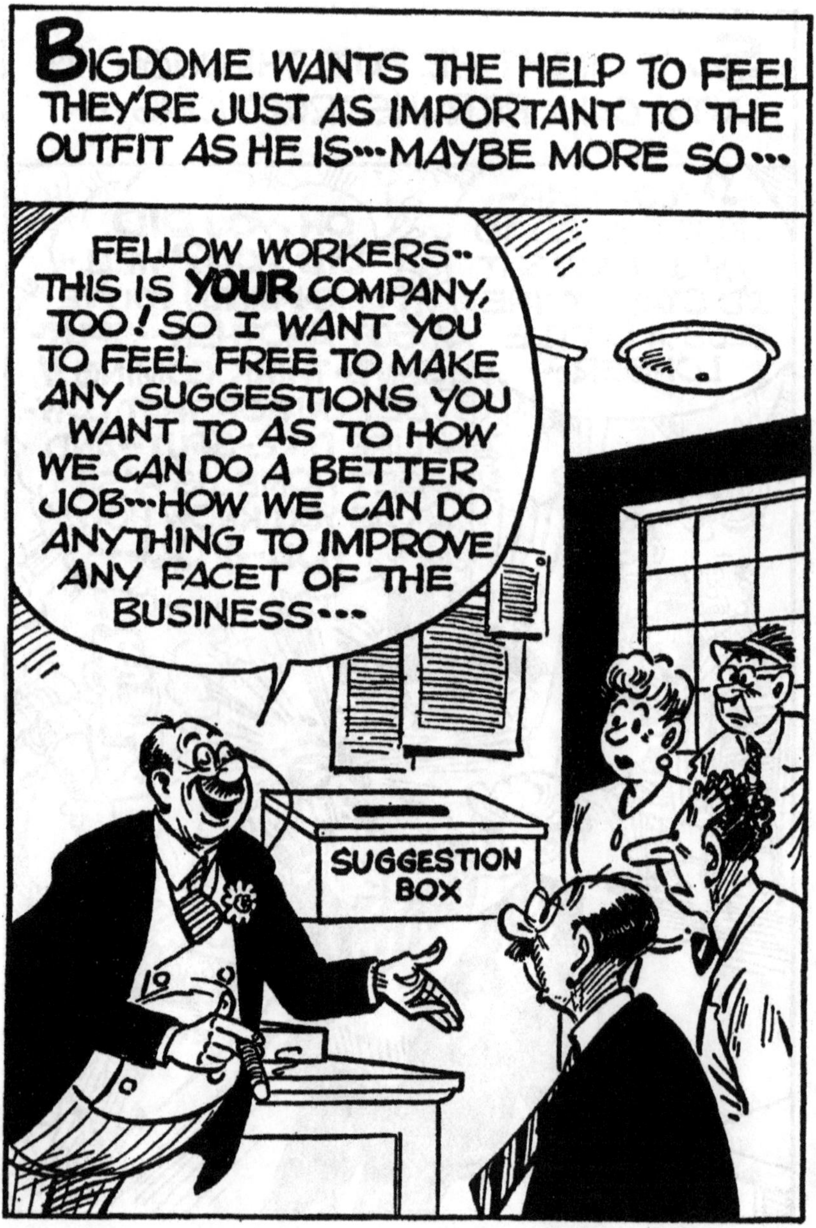
BIGDOME WANTS THE HELP TO FEEL THEY'RE JUST AS IMPORTANT TO THE OUTFIT AS HE IS···MAYBE MORE SO···
FELLOW WORKERS·· THIS IS **YOUR** COMPANY, TOO! SO I WANT YOU TO FEEL FREE TO MAKE ANY SUGGESTIONS YOU WANT TO AS TO HOW WE CAN DO A BETTER JOB···HOW WE CAN DO ANYTHING TO IMPROVE ANY FACET OF THE BUSINESS···
SUGGESTION BOX

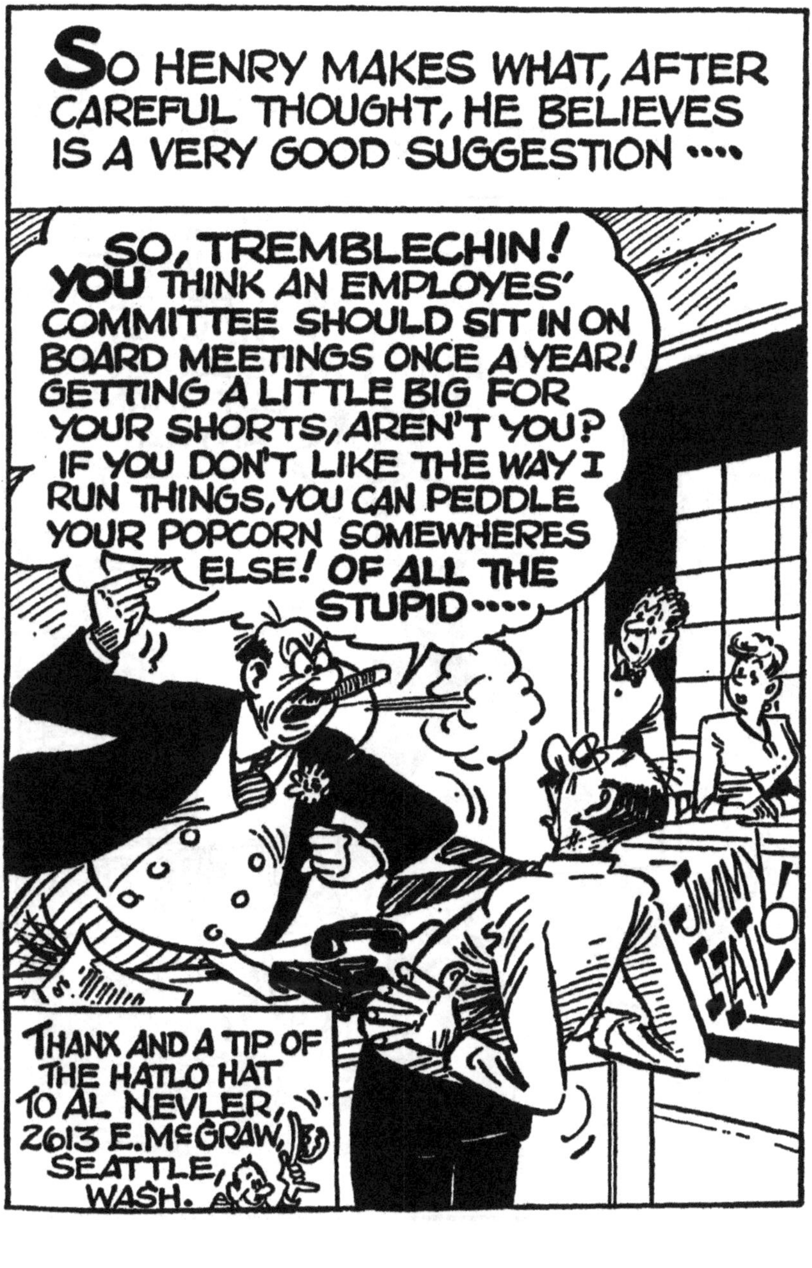
SO HENRY MAKES WHAT, AFTER CAREFUL THOUGHT, HE BELIEVES IS A VERY GOOD SUGGESTION ....
SO, TREMBLECHIN! YOU THINK AN EMPLOYES' COMMITTEE SHOULD SIT IN ON BOARD MEETINGS ONCE A YEAR! GETTING A LITTLE BIG FOR YOUR SHORTS, AREN'T YOU? IF YOU DON'T LIKE THE WAY I RUN THINGS, YOU CAN PEDDLE YOUR POPCORN SOMEWHERES ELSE! OF ALL THE STUPID ....
JIMMY HATLO
THANX AND A TIP OF THE HATLO HAT TO AL NEVLER, 2613 E. McGRAW, SEATTLE, WASH.

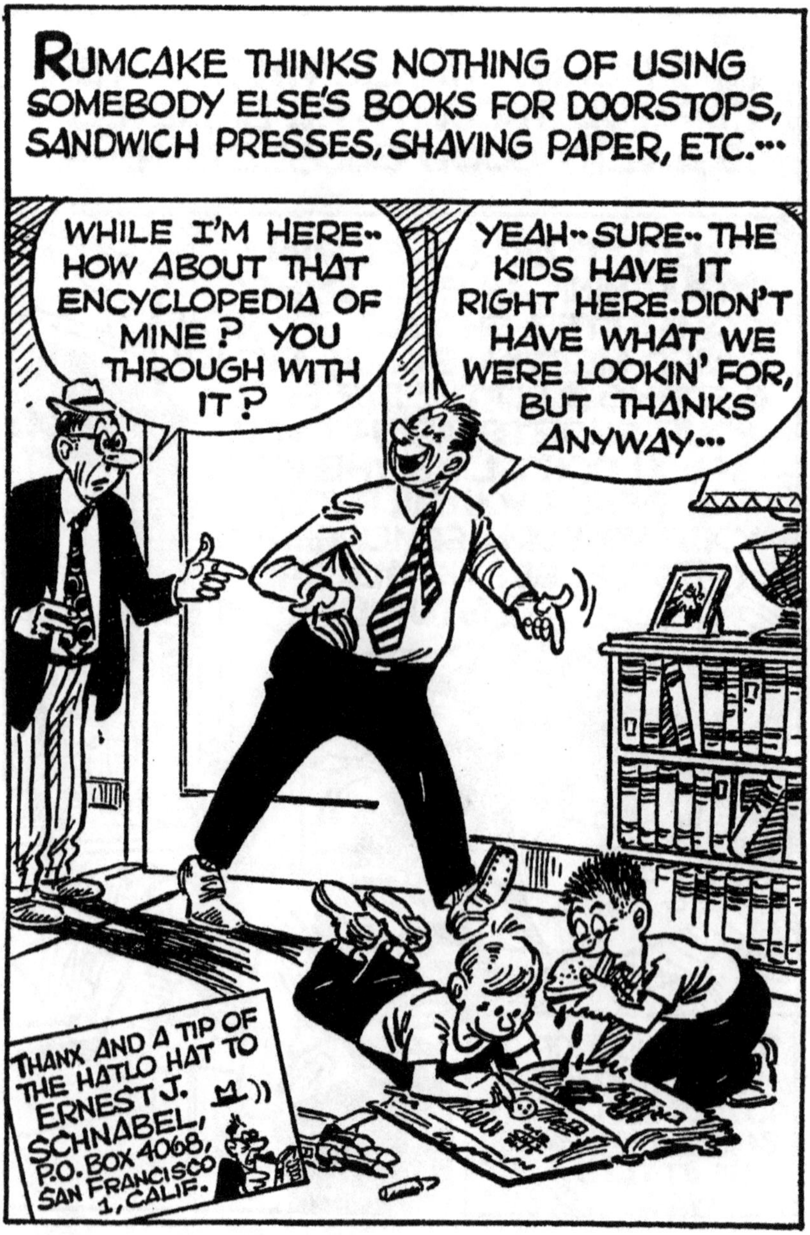
RUMCAKE THINKS NOTHING OF USING SOMEBODY ELSE'S BOOKS FOR DOORSTOPS, SANDWICH PRESSES, SHAVING PAPER, ETC.…
WHILE I'M HERE-- HOW ABOUT THAT ENCYCLOPEDIA OF MINE? YOU THROUGH WITH IT?
YEAH-- SURE-- THE KIDS HAVE IT RIGHT HERE. DIDN'T HAVE WHAT WE WERE LOOKIN' FOR, BUT THANKS ANYWAY…
THANX AND A TIP OF THE HATLO HAT TO ERNEST J. SCHNABEL, P.O. BOX 4068, SAN FRANCISCO 1, CALIF.

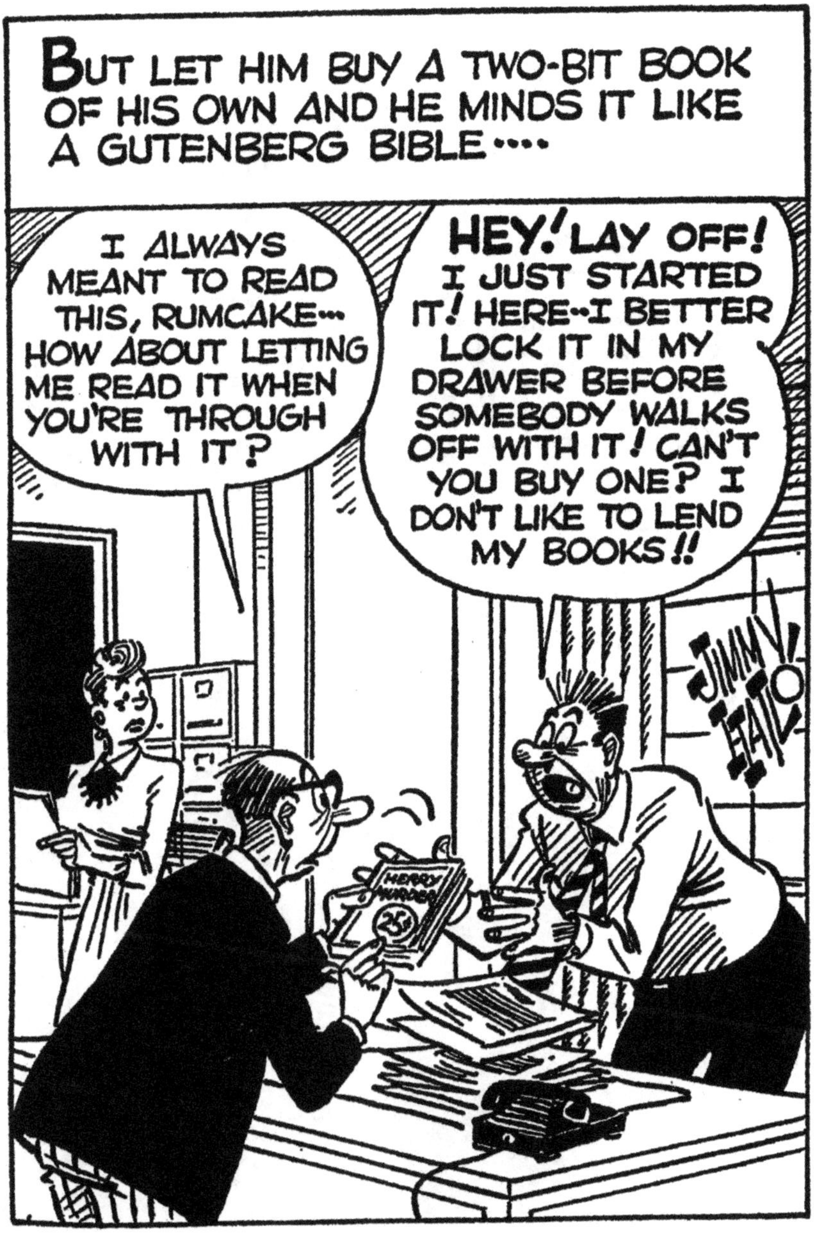

BUT LET HIM BUY A TWO-BIT BOOK OF HIS OWN AND HE MINDS IT LIKE A GUTENBERG BIBLE....
I ALWAYS MEANT TO READ THIS, RUMCAKE--- HOW ABOUT LETTING ME READ IT WHEN YOU'RE THROUGH WITH IT?
HEY! LAY OFF! I JUST STARTED IT! HERE--I BETTER LOCK IT IN MY DRAWER BEFORE SOMEBODY WALKS OFF WITH IT! CAN'T YOU BUY ONE? I DON'T LIKE TO LEND MY BOOKS!!
JIMMY HATLO

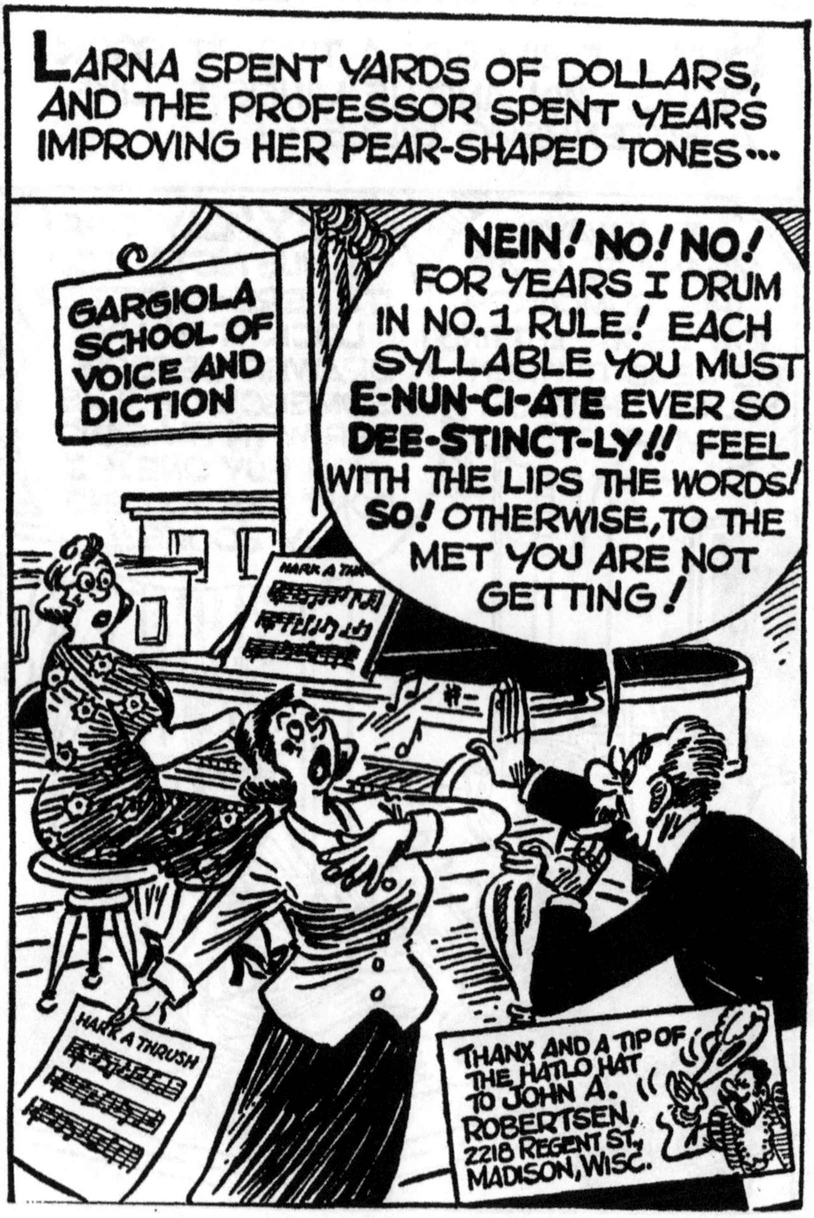
LARNA SPENT YARDS OF DOLLARS, AND THE PROFESSOR SPENT YEARS IMPROVING HER PEAR-SHAPED TONES...
GARGIOLA SCHOOL OF VOICE AND DICTION
NEIN! NO! NO! FOR YEARS I DRUM IN NO.1 RULE! EACH SYLLABLE YOU MUST E-NUN-CI-ATE EVER SO DEE-STINCT-LY!! FEEL WITH THE LIPS THE WORDS! SO! OTHERWISE, TO THE MET YOU ARE NOT GETTING!
HARK A THRUSH
THANX AND A TIP OF THE HATLO HAT TO JOHN A. ROBERTSEN, 2218 REGENT ST., MADISON, WISC.

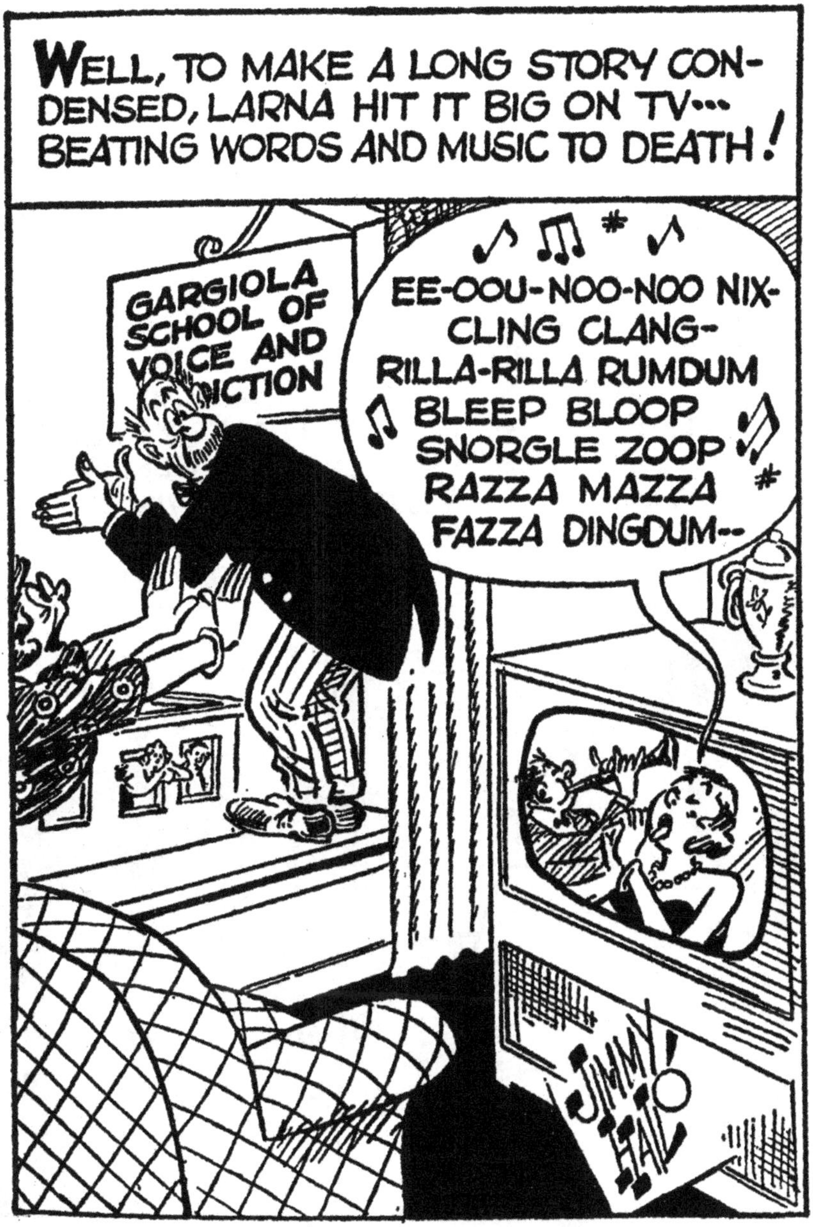
WELL, TO MAKE A LONG STORY CONDENSED, LARNA HIT IT BIG ON TV... BEATING WORDS AND MUSIC TO DEATH!
GARGIOLA SCHOOL OF VOICE AND DICTION
EE-OOU-NOO-NOO NIX-CLING CLANG-RILLA-RILLA RUMDUM BLEEP BLOOP SNORGLE ZOOP RAZZA MAZZA FAZZA DINGDUM--
JIMMY! HAL!

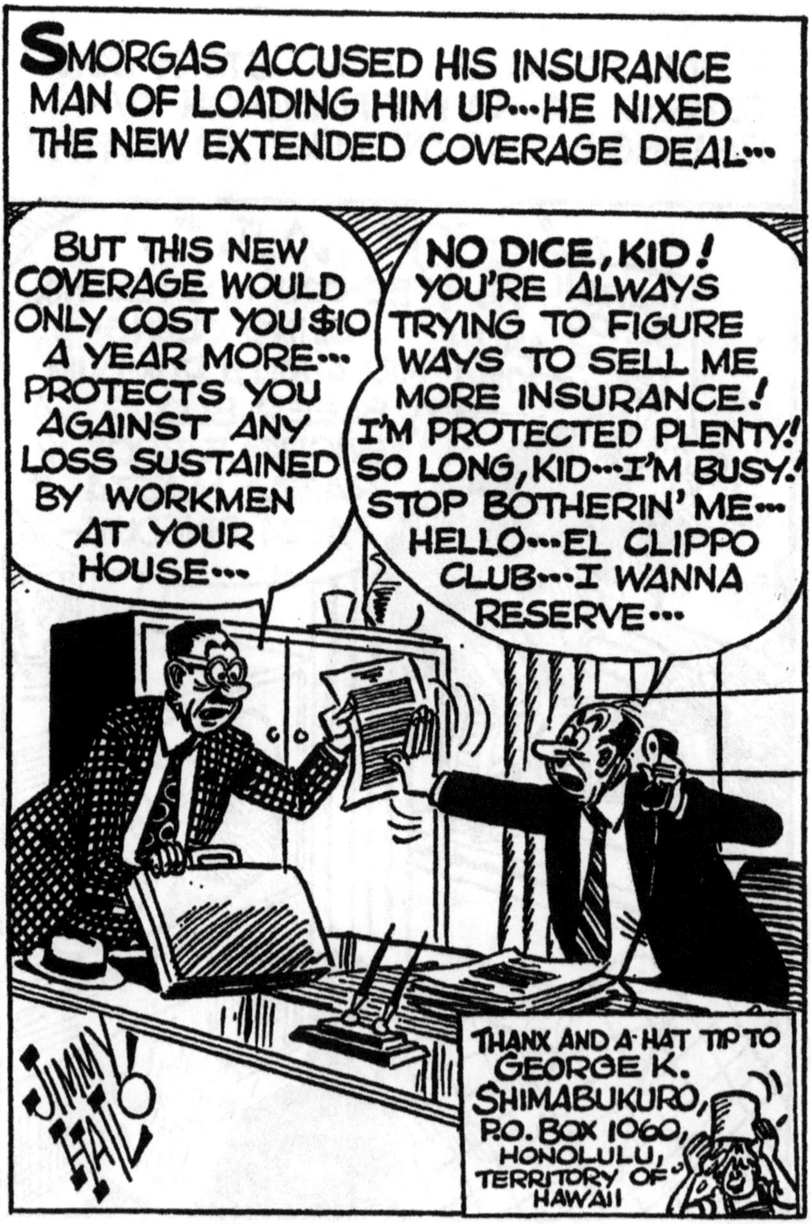
SMORGAS ACCUSED HIS INSURANCE MAN OF LOADING HIM UP···HE NIXED THE NEW EXTENDED COVERAGE DEAL···
BUT THIS NEW COVERAGE WOULD ONLY COST YOU $10 A YEAR MORE··· PROTECTS YOU AGAINST ANY LOSS SUSTAINED BY WORKMEN AT YOUR HOUSE···
NO DICE, KID! YOU'RE ALWAYS TRYING TO FIGURE WAYS TO SELL ME MORE INSURANCE! I'M PROTECTED PLENTY! SO LONG, KID···I'M BUSY! STOP BOTHERIN' ME··· HELLO···EL CLIPPO CLUB···I WANNA RESERVE···
JIMMY HATLO
THANX AND A·HAT TIP TO GEORGE K. SHIMABUKURO, P.O. BOX 1060, HONOLULU, TERRITORY OF HAWAII

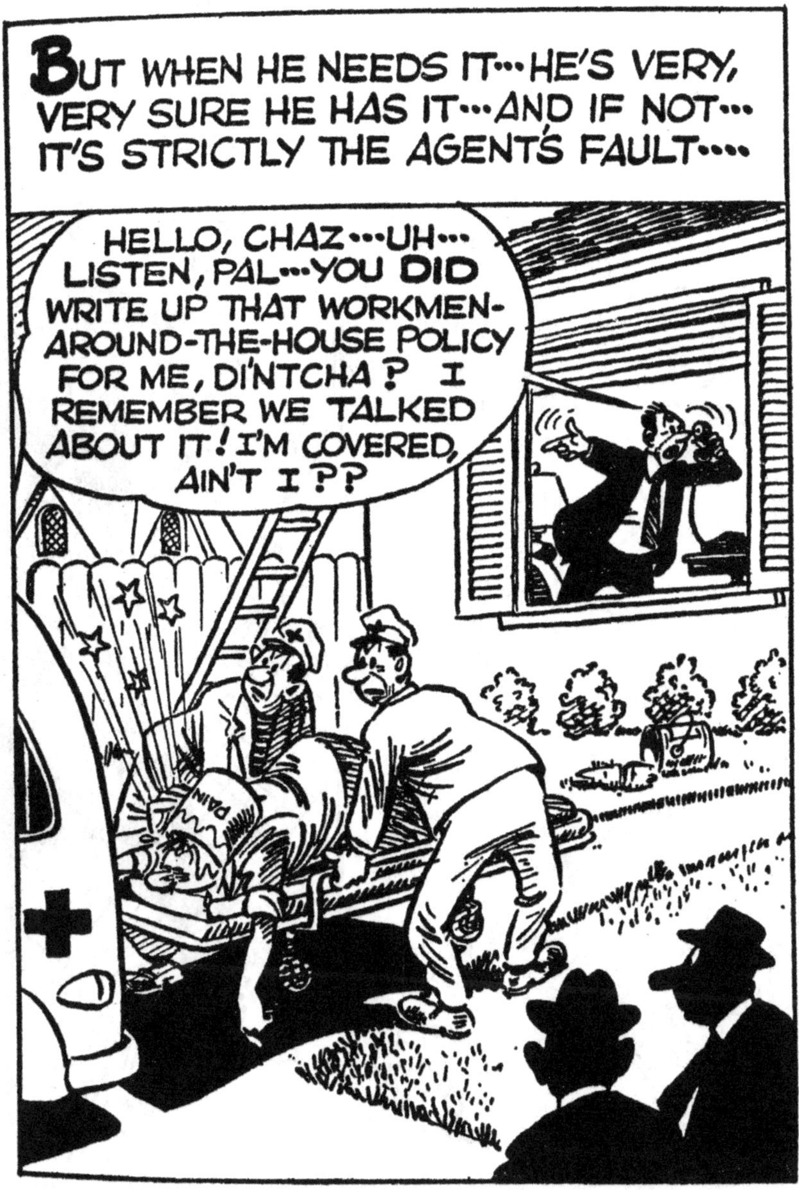
BUT WHEN HE NEEDS IT··· HE'S VERY, VERY SURE HE HAS IT··· AND IF NOT··· IT'S STRICTLY THE AGENT'S FAULT····
HELLO, CHAZ···UH··· LISTEN, PAL···YOU **DID** WRITE UP THAT WORKMEN-AROUND-THE-HOUSE POLICY FOR ME, DI'NTCHA? I REMEMBER WE TALKED ABOUT IT! I'M COVERED, AIN'T I??

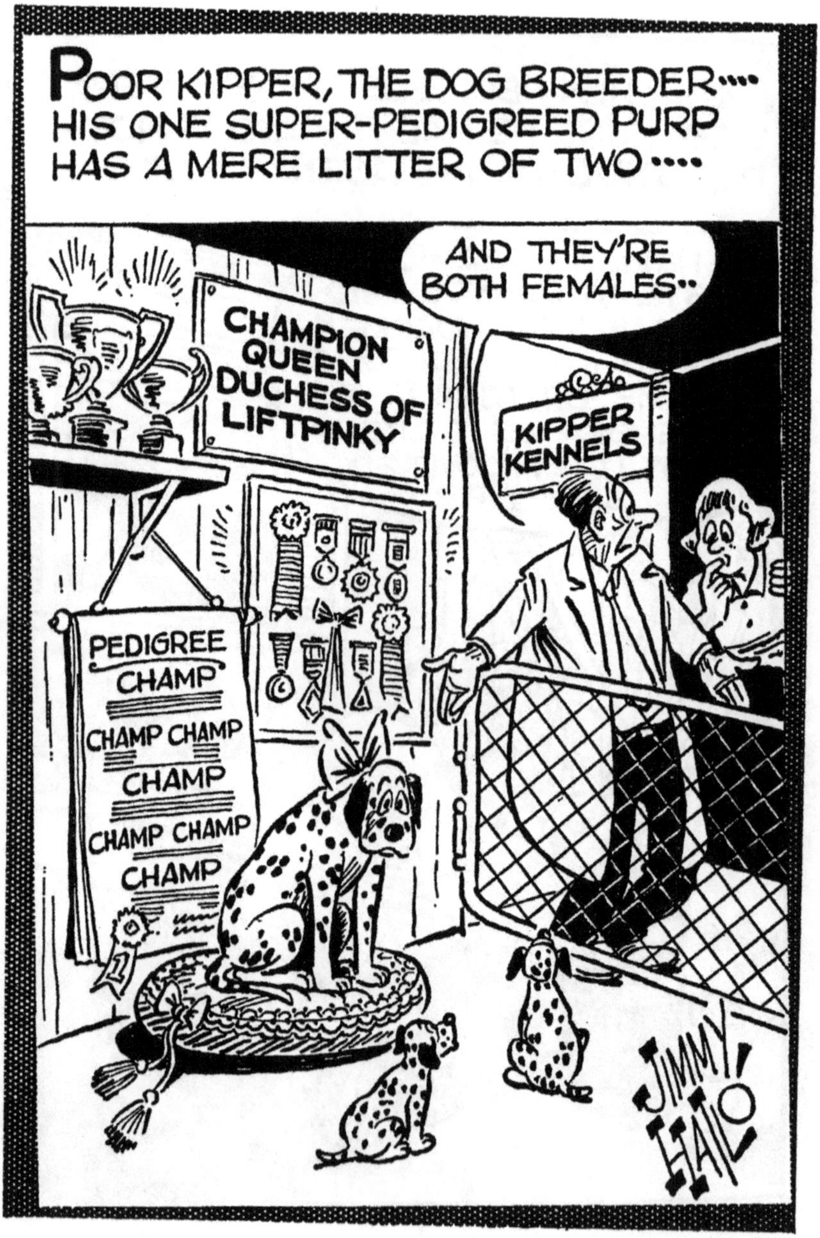
POOR KIPPER, THE DOG BREEDER....
HIS ONE SUPER-PEDIGREED PURP
HAS A MERE LITTER OF TWO....
AND THEY'RE BOTH FEMALES..
CHAMPION QUEEN DUCHESS OF LIFTPINKY
KIPPER KENNELS
PEDIGREE CHAMP
CHAMP CHAMP
CHAMP
CHAMP CHAMP
CHAMP
JIMMY HATLO

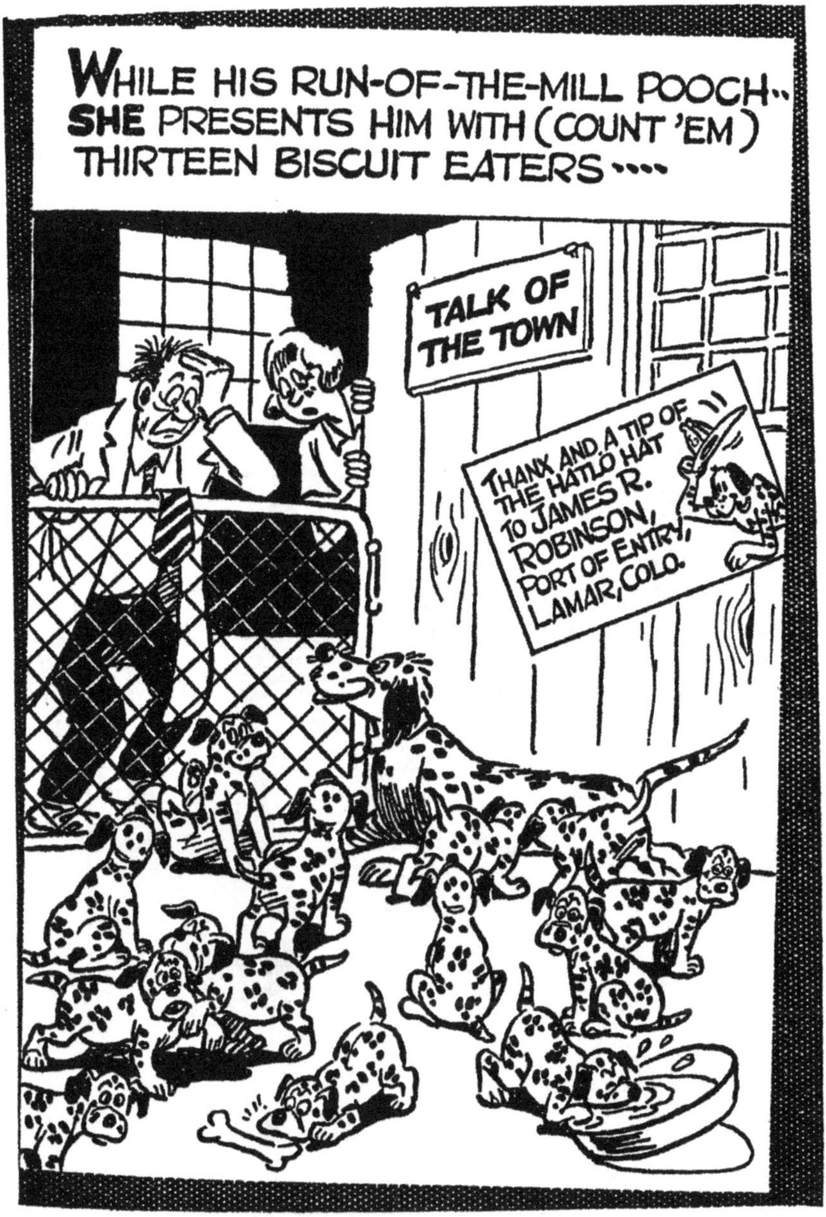
WHILE HIS RUN-OF-THE-MILL POOCH..
SHE PRESENTS HIM WITH (COUNT 'EM)
THIRTEEN BISCUIT EATERS....
TALK OF THE TOWN
THANX AND A TIP OF THE HATLO HAT TO JAMES R. ROBINSON, PORT OF ENTRY, LAMAR, COLO.

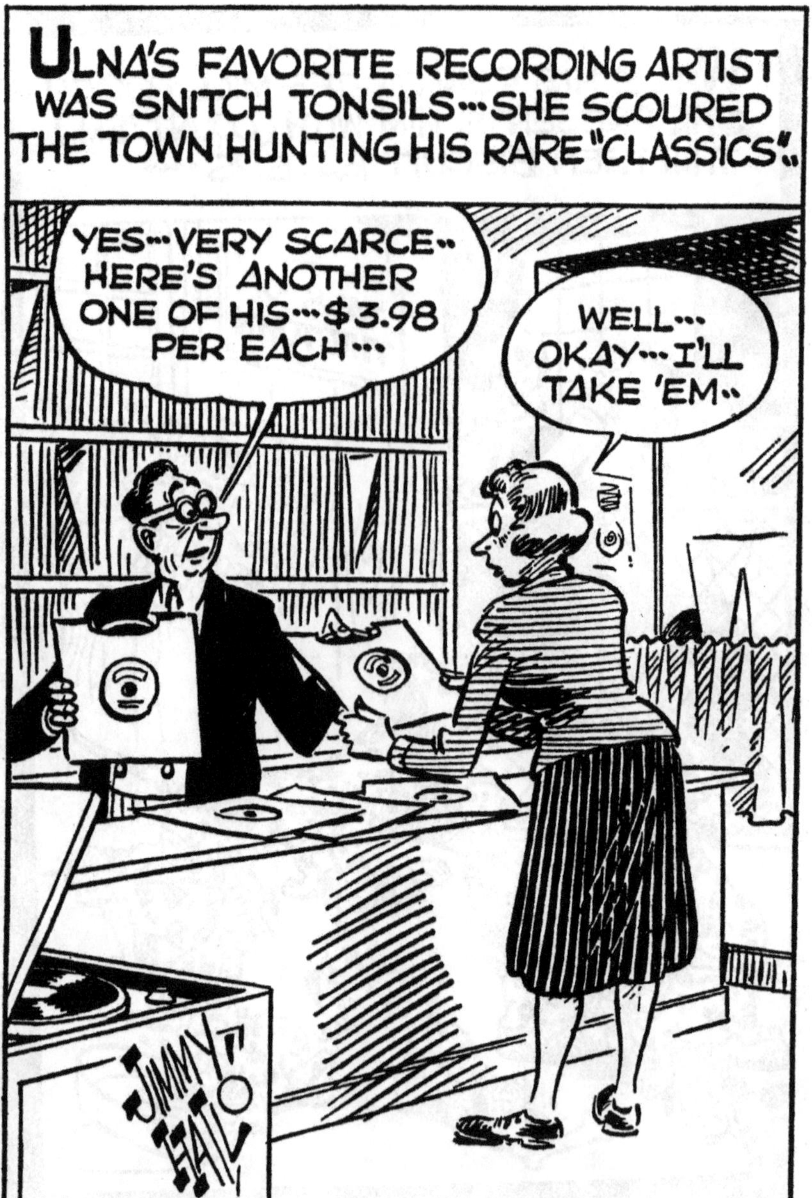
ULNA'S FAVORITE RECORDING ARTIST WAS SNITCH TONSILS--- SHE SCOURED THE TOWN HUNTING HIS RARE "CLASSICS"..
YES--VERY SCARCE.. HERE'S ANOTHER ONE OF HIS--- $3.98 PER EACH---
WELL--- OKAY--- I'LL TAKE 'EM..
JIMMY HATLO

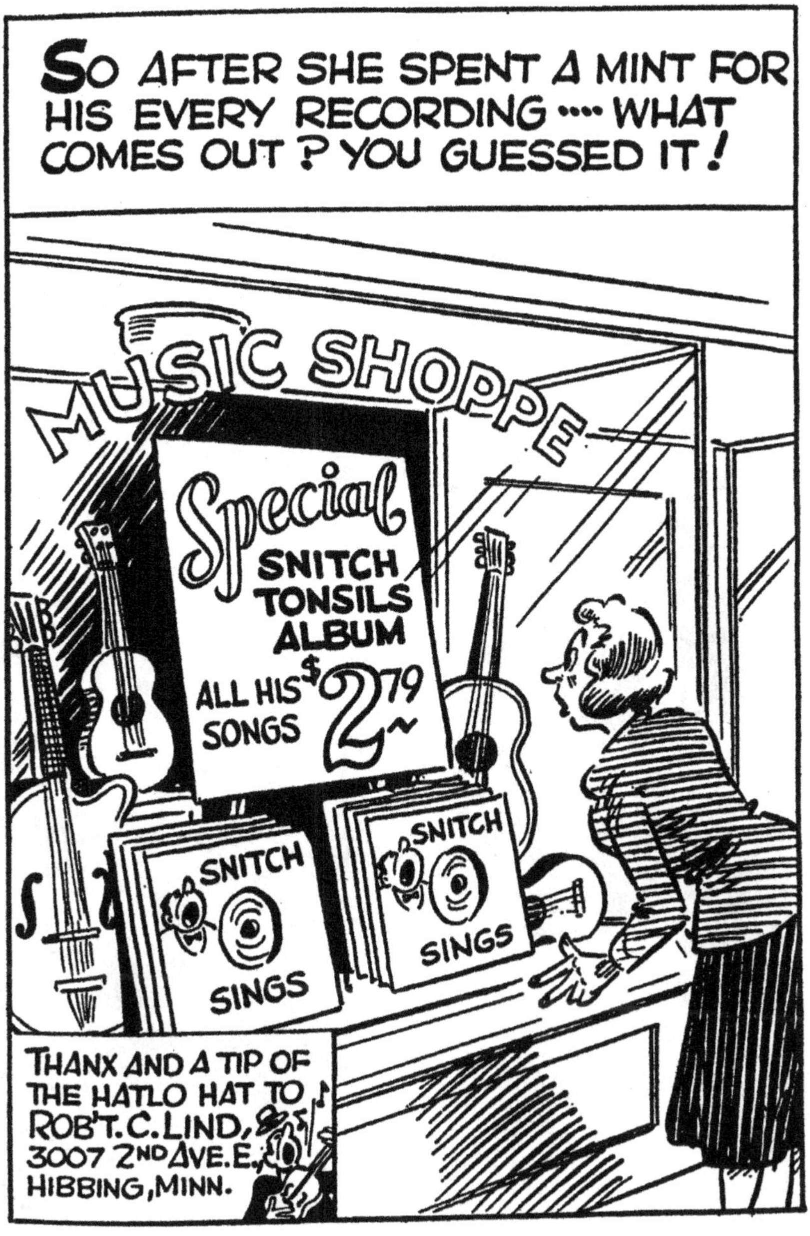
SO AFTER SHE SPENT A MINT FOR HIS EVERY RECORDING .... WHAT COMES OUT ? YOU GUESSED IT !
MUSIC SHOPPE
Special SNITCH TONSILS ALBUM ALL HIS SONGS $2.79
SNITCH SINGS
SNITCH SINGS
THANX AND A TIP OF THE HATLO HAT TO ROB'T. C. LIND, 3007 2ND AVE. E., HIBBING, MINN.

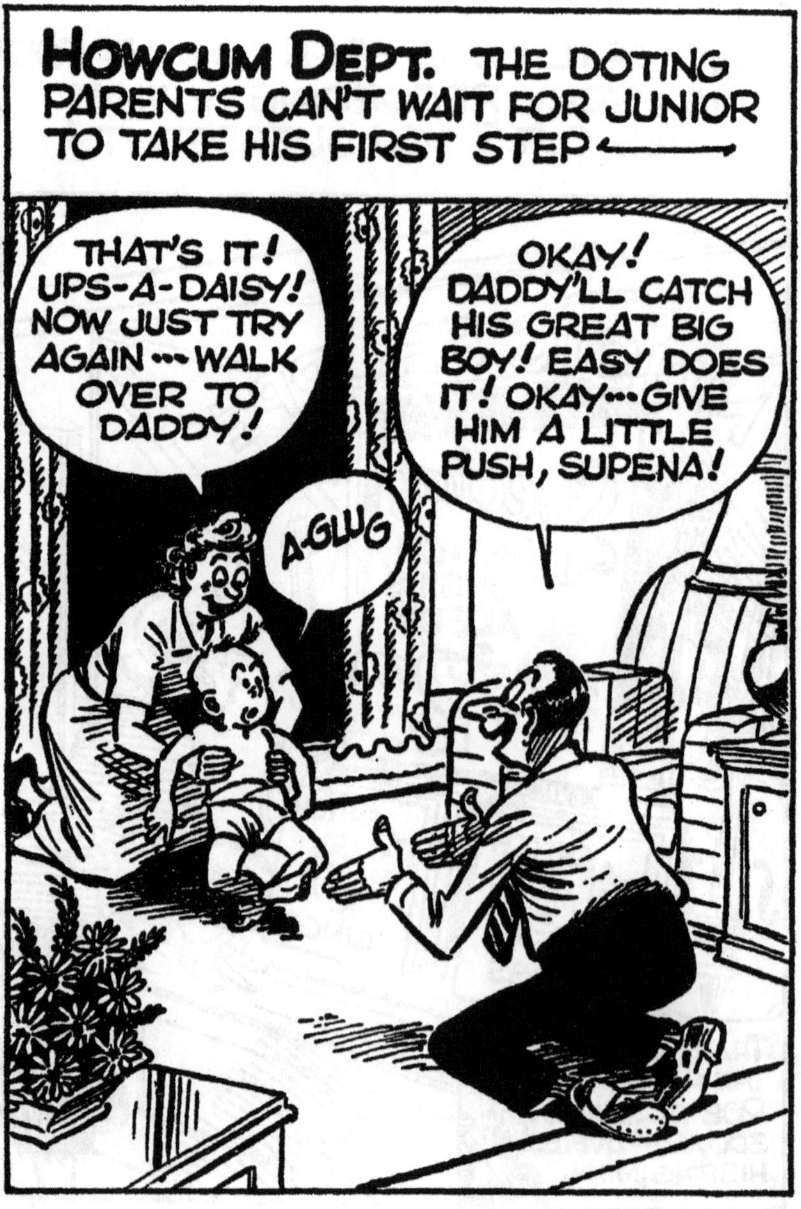
HOWCUM DEPT. THE DOTING PARENTS CAN'T WAIT FOR JUNIOR TO TAKE HIS FIRST STEP
THAT'S IT! UPS-A-DAISY! NOW JUST TRY AGAIN --- WALK OVER TO DADDY!
A-GLUG
OKAY! DADDY'LL CATCH HIS GREAT BIG BOY! EASY DOES IT! OKAY--- GIVE HIM A LITTLE PUSH, SUPENA!

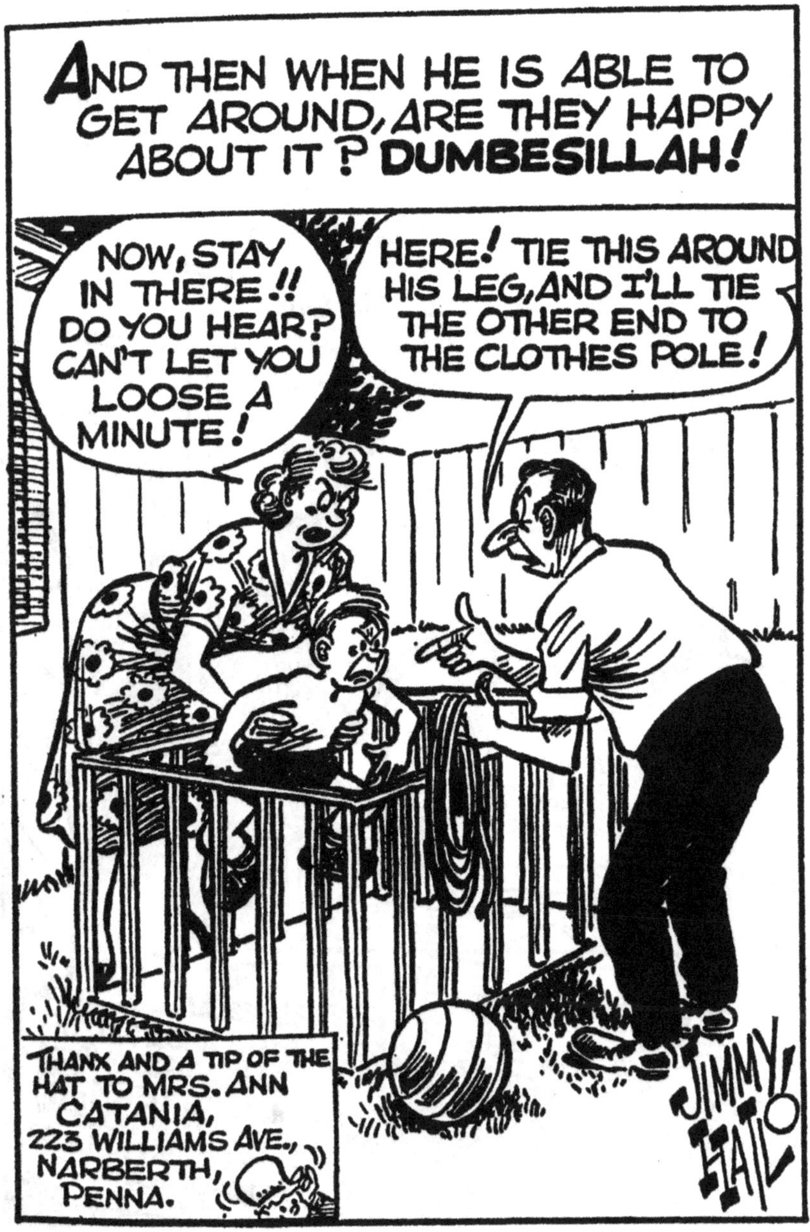
AND THEN WHEN HE IS ABLE TO GET AROUND, ARE THEY HAPPY ABOUT IT? DUMBESILLAH!
NOW, STAY IN THERE!! DO YOU HEAR? CAN'T LET YOU LOOSE A MINUTE!
HERE! TIE THIS AROUND HIS LEG, AND I'LL TIE THE OTHER END TO THE CLOTHES POLE!
THANX AND A TIP OF THE HAT TO MRS. ANN CATANIA, 223 WILLIAMS AVE., NARBERTH, PENNA.
JIMMY HATLO

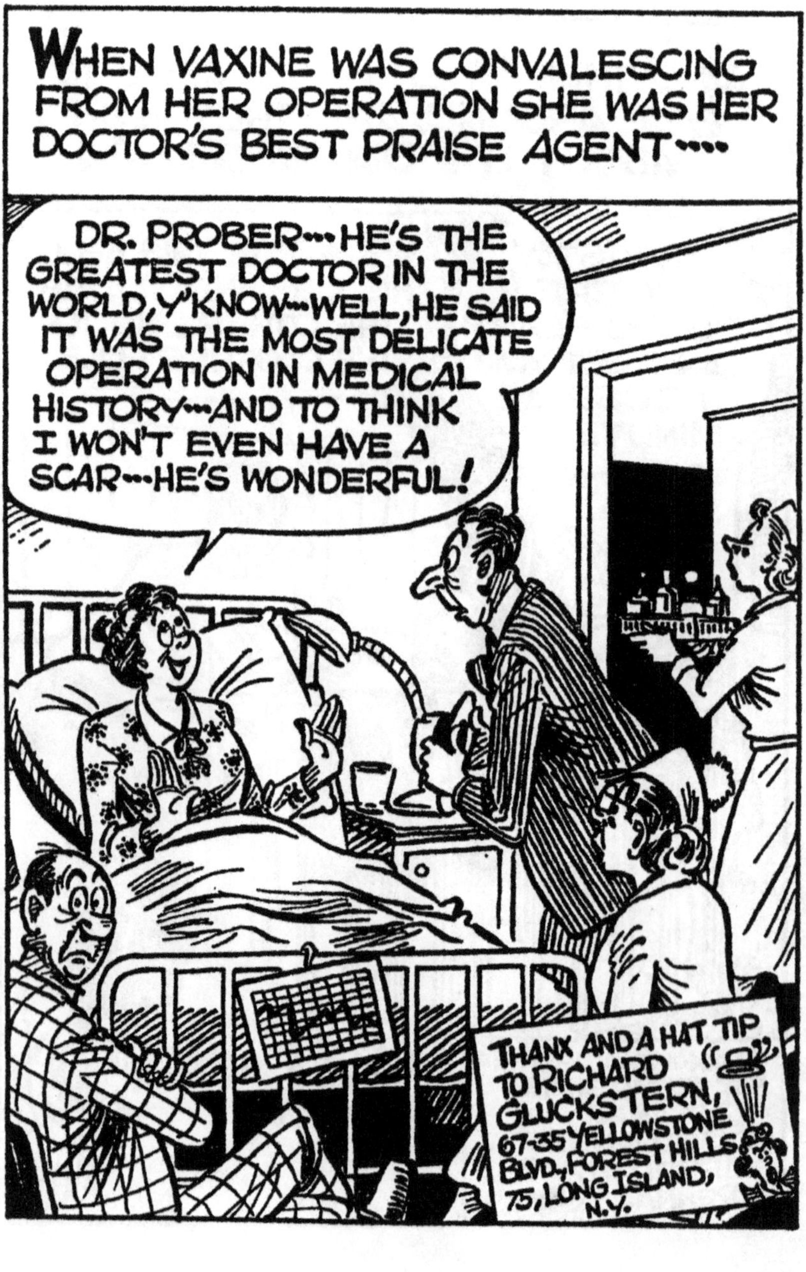
WHEN VAXINE WAS CONVALESCING FROM HER OPERATION SHE WAS HER DOCTOR'S BEST PRAISE AGENT....
DR. PROBER... HE'S THE GREATEST DOCTOR IN THE WORLD, Y'KNOW... WELL, HE SAID IT WAS THE MOST DELICATE OPERATION IN MEDICAL HISTORY... AND TO THINK I WON'T EVEN HAVE A SCAR... HE'S WONDERFUL!
THANX AND A HAT TIP TO RICHARD GLUCKSTERN, 67-35 YELLOWSTONE BLVD., FOREST HILLS 75, LONG ISLAND, N.Y.

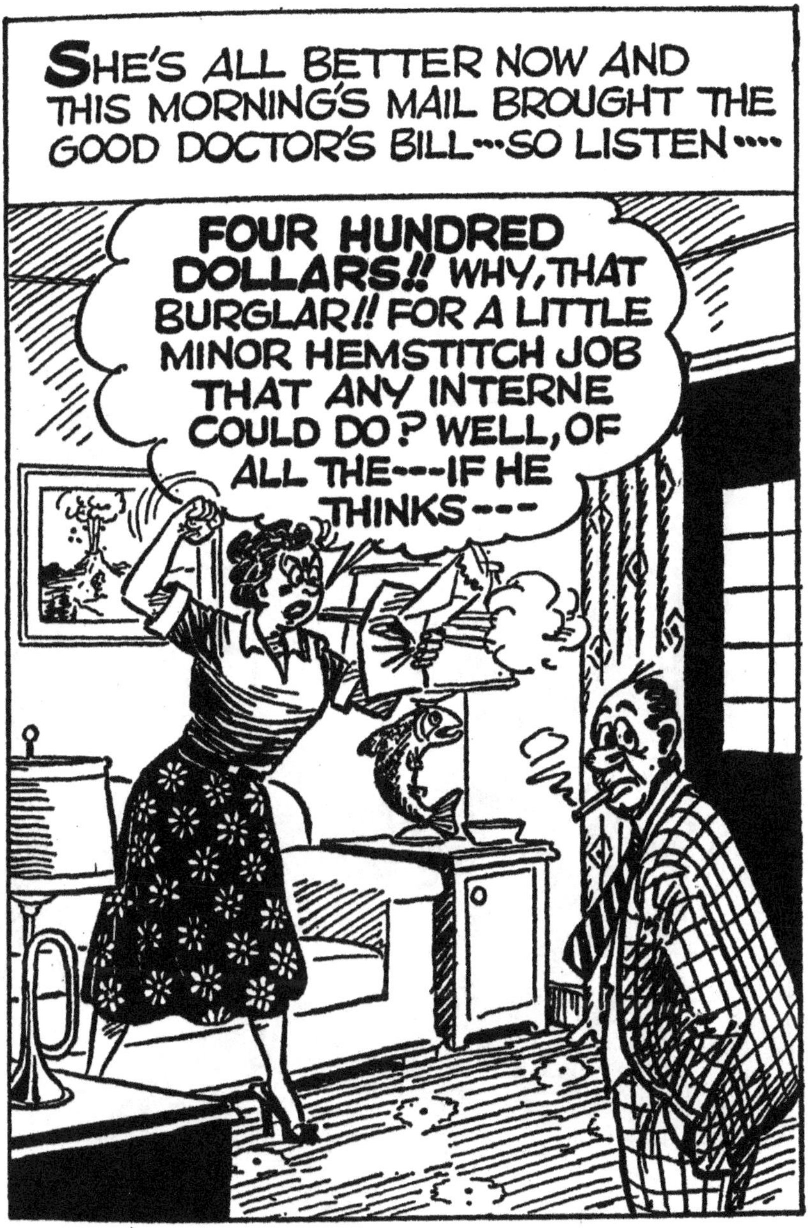
SHE'S ALL BETTER NOW AND THIS MORNING'S MAIL BROUGHT THE GOOD DOCTOR'S BILL--SO LISTEN....
FOUR HUNDRED DOLLARS!! WHY, THAT BURGLAR!! FOR A LITTLE MINOR HEMSTITCH JOB THAT ANY INTERNE COULD DO? WELL, OF ALL THE---IF HE THINKS---

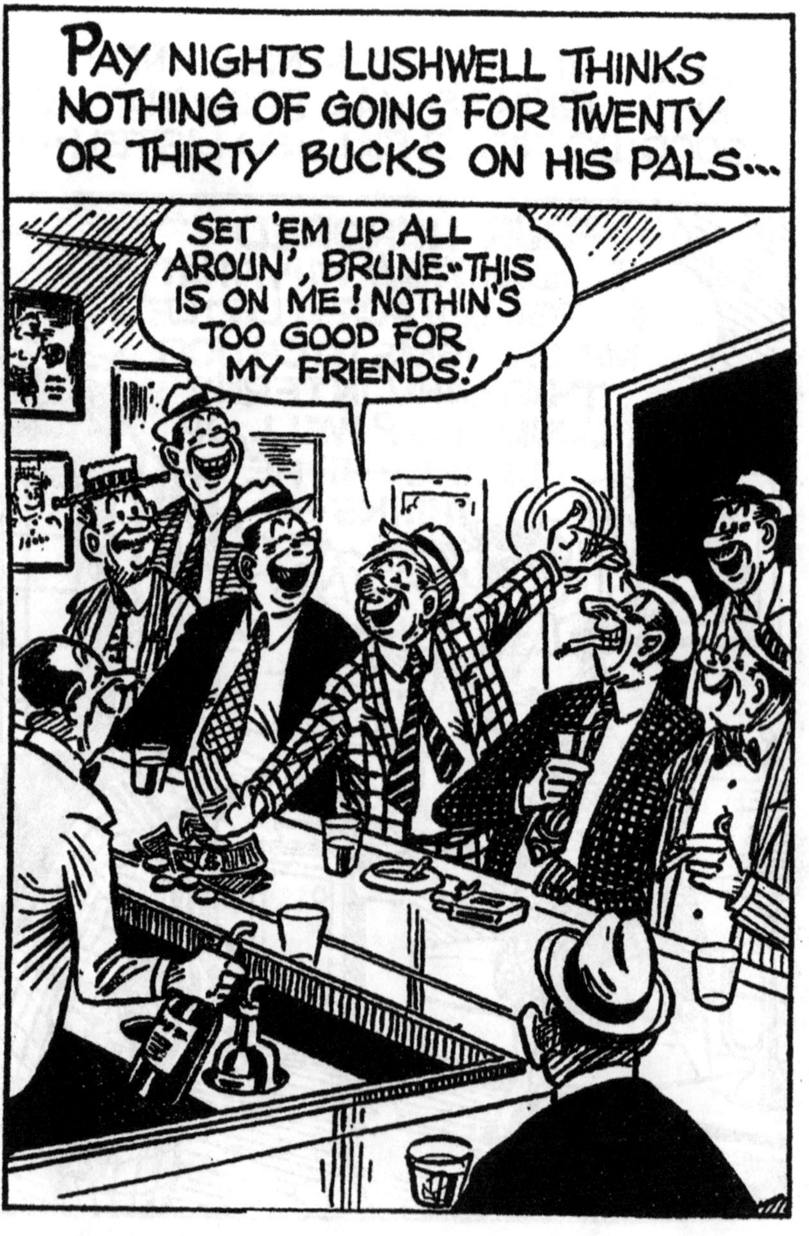
PAY NIGHTS LUSHWELL THINKS NOTHING OF GOING FOR TWENTY OR THIRTY BUCKS ON HIS PALS...
SET 'EM UP ALL AROUN', BRUNE--THIS IS ON ME! NOTHIN'S TOO GOOD FOR MY FRIENDS!

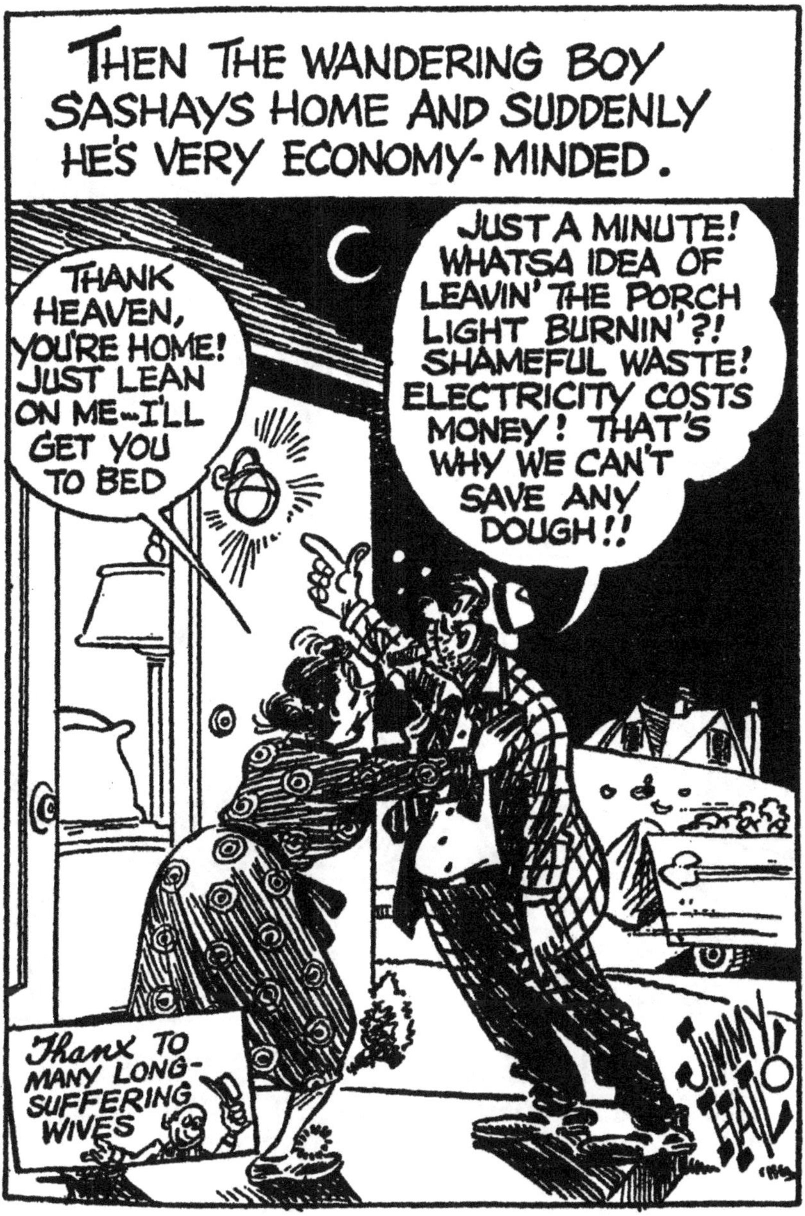
THEN THE WANDERING BOY SASHAYS HOME AND SUDDENLY HE'S VERY ECONOMY-MINDED.
THANK HEAVEN, YOU'RE HOME! JUST LEAN ON ME--I'LL GET YOU TO BED
JUST A MINUTE! WHATSA IDEA OF LEAVIN' THE PORCH LIGHT BURNIN'?! SHAMEFUL WASTE! ELECTRICITY COSTS MONEY! THAT'S WHY WE CAN'T SAVE ANY DOUGH!!
Thanx TO MANY LONG-SUFFERING WIVES
JIMMY HATLO

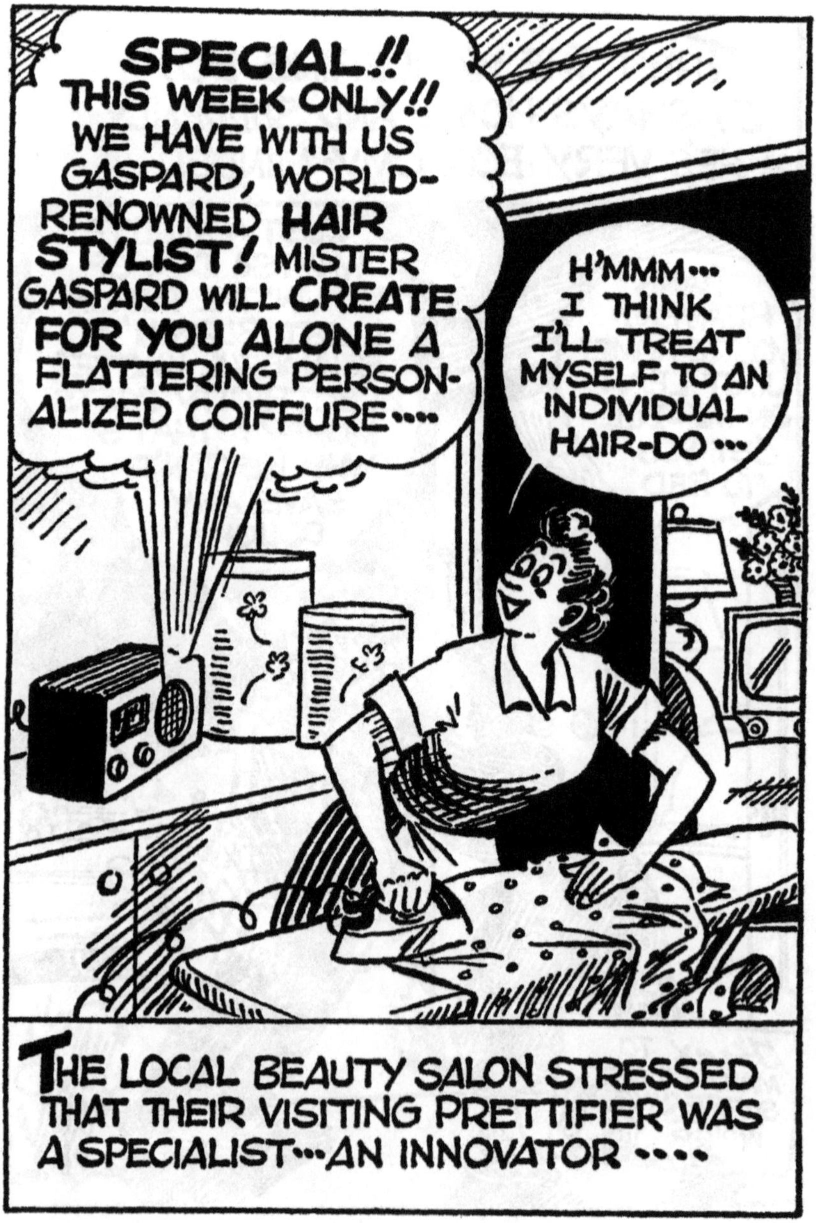
SPECIAL!! THIS WEEK ONLY!! WE HAVE WITH US GASPARD, WORLD-RENOWNED HAIR STYLIST! MISTER GASPARD WILL CREATE FOR YOU ALONE A FLATTERING PERSONALIZED COIFFURE....
H'MMM... I THINK I'LL TREAT MYSELF TO AN INDIVIDUAL HAIR-DO...
THE LOCAL BEAUTY SALON STRESSED THAT THEIR VISITING PRETTIFIER WAS A SPECIALIST...AN INNOVATOR....

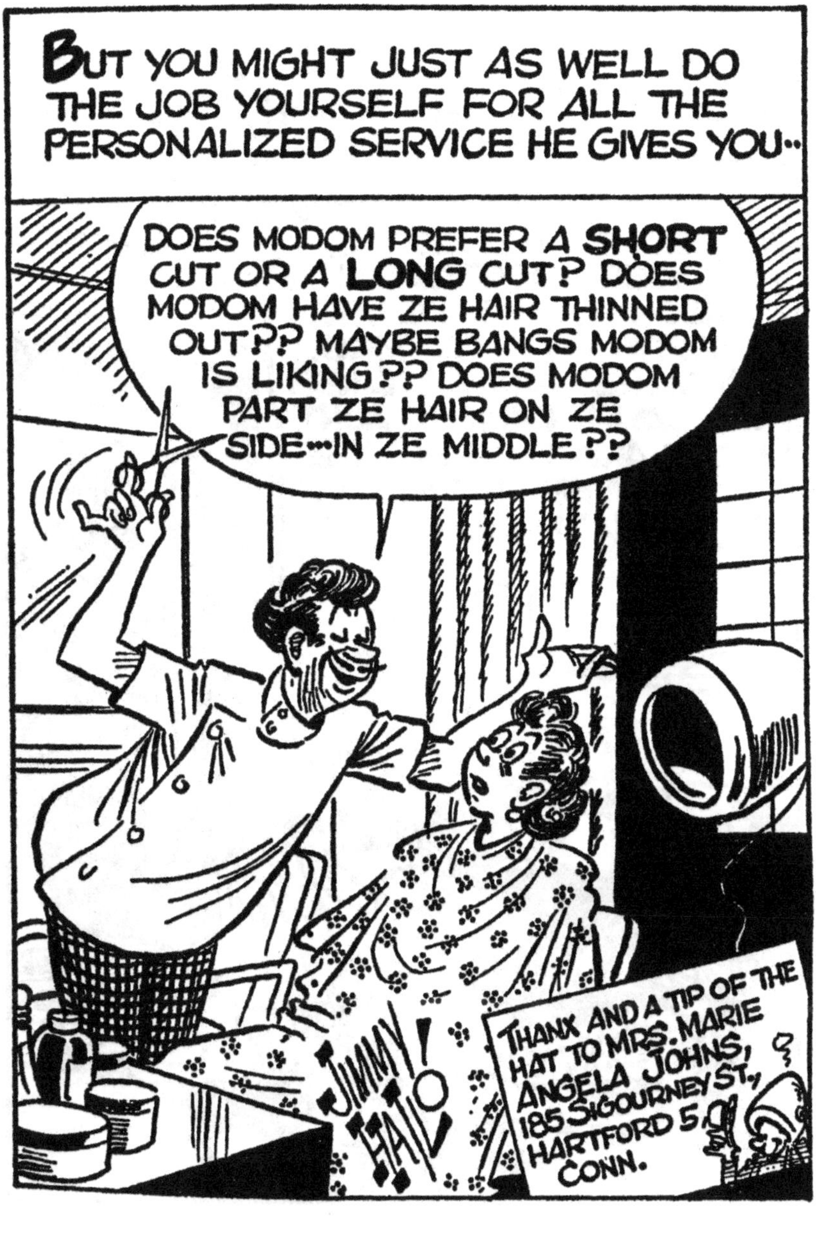
BUT YOU MIGHT JUST AS WELL DO THE JOB YOURSELF FOR ALL THE PERSONALIZED SERVICE HE GIVES YOU..
DOES MODOM PREFER A **SHORT** CUT OR A **LONG** CUT? DOES MODOM HAVE ZE HAIR THINNED OUT?? MAYBE BANGS MODOM IS LIKING?? DOES MODOM PART ZE HAIR ON ZE SIDE---IN ZE MIDDLE??
JIMMY! HALO
THANX AND A TIP OF THE HAT TO MRS. MARIE ANGELA JOHNS, 185 SIGOURNEY ST., HARTFORD 5, CONN.

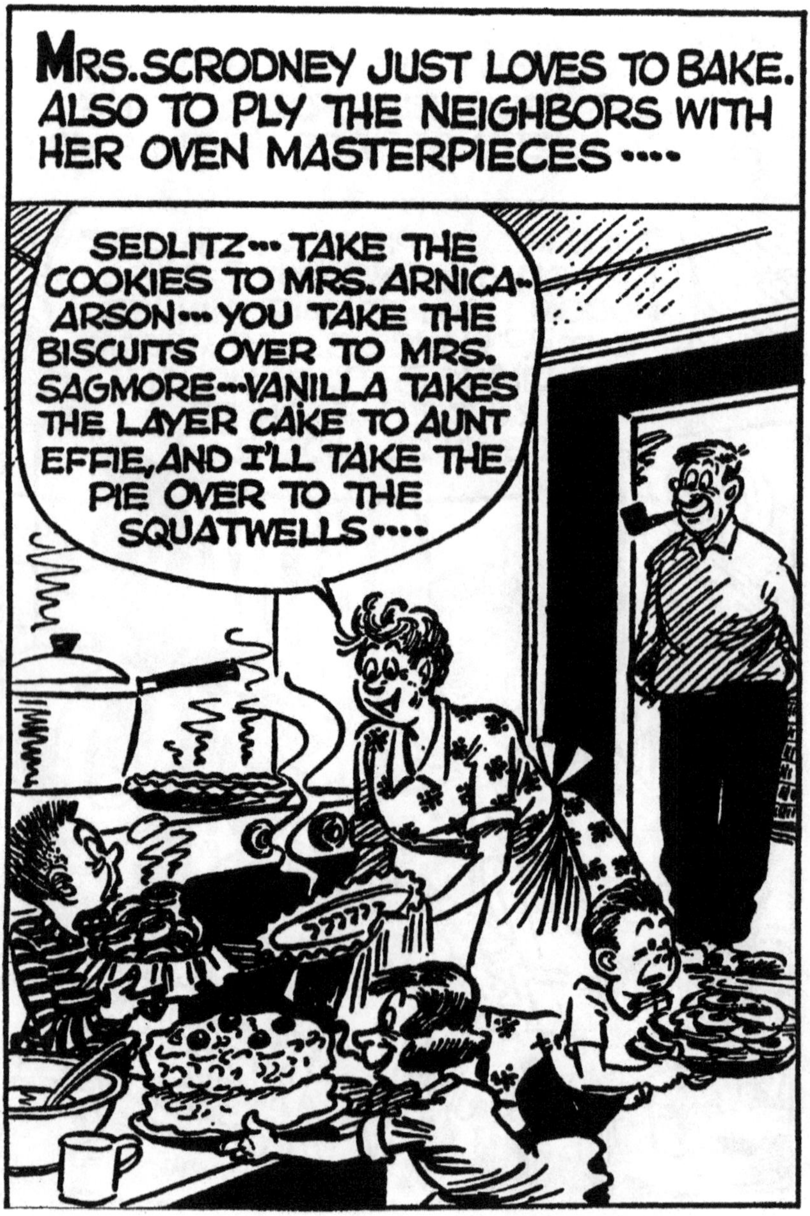
MRS. SCRODNEY JUST LOVES TO BAKE. ALSO TO PLY THE NEIGHBORS WITH HER OVEN MASTERPIECES....
SEDLITZ... TAKE THE COOKIES TO MRS. ARNICA-ARSON... YOU TAKE THE BISCUITS OVER TO MRS. SAGMORE...VANILLA TAKES THE LAYER CAKE TO AUNT EFFIE, AND I'LL TAKE THE PIE OVER TO THE SQUATWELLS....

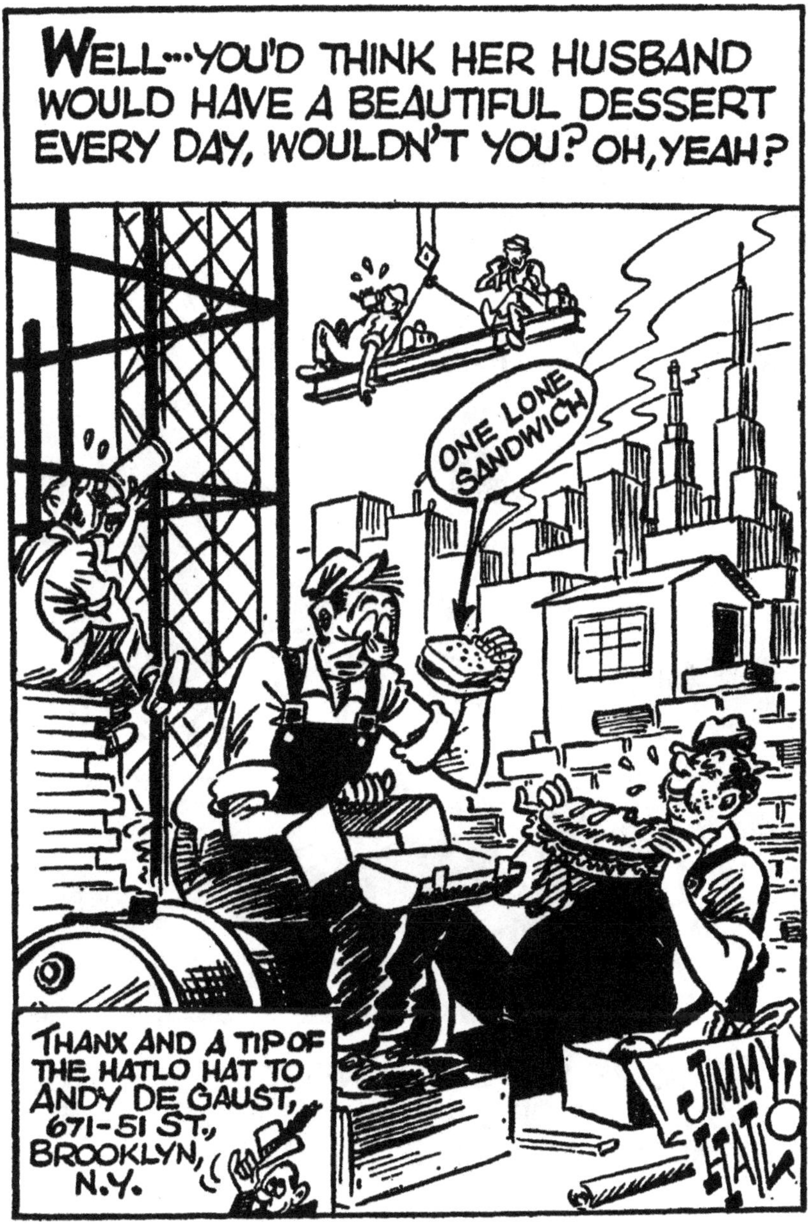
WELL...YOU'D THINK HER HUSBAND WOULD HAVE A BEAUTIFUL DESSERT EVERY DAY, WOULDN'T YOU? OH, YEAH?
ONE LONE SANDWICH
THANX AND A TIP OF THE HATLO HAT TO ANDY DE GAUST, 671-51 ST., BROOKLYN, N.Y.
JIMMY HATLO

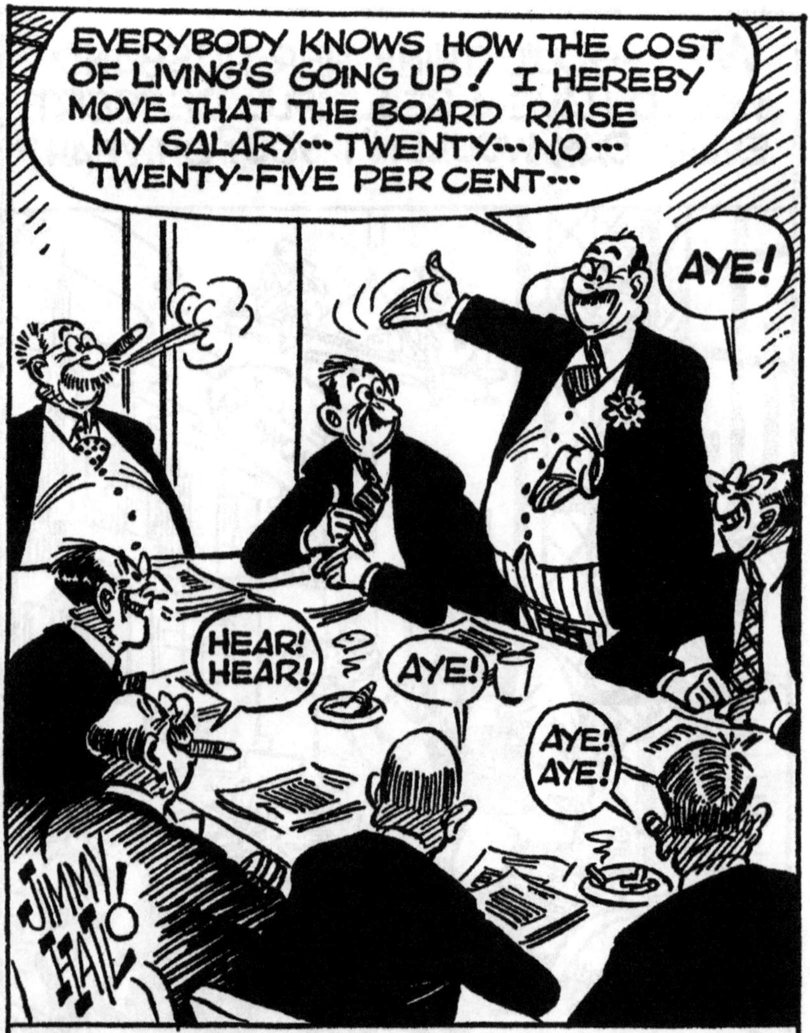
EVERYBODY KNOWS HOW THE COST OF LIVING'S GOING UP! I HEREBY MOVE THAT THE BOARD RAISE MY SALARY··· TWENTY··· NO··· TWENTY-FIVE PER CENT···
AYE!
HEAR! HEAR!
AYE!
AYE! AYE!
JIMMY HATLO

BIGDOME IS VERY CONSCIOUS OF THE HIGH COST OF LIVING, SO HE AND THE BOARD KNOW WHAT TO DO····

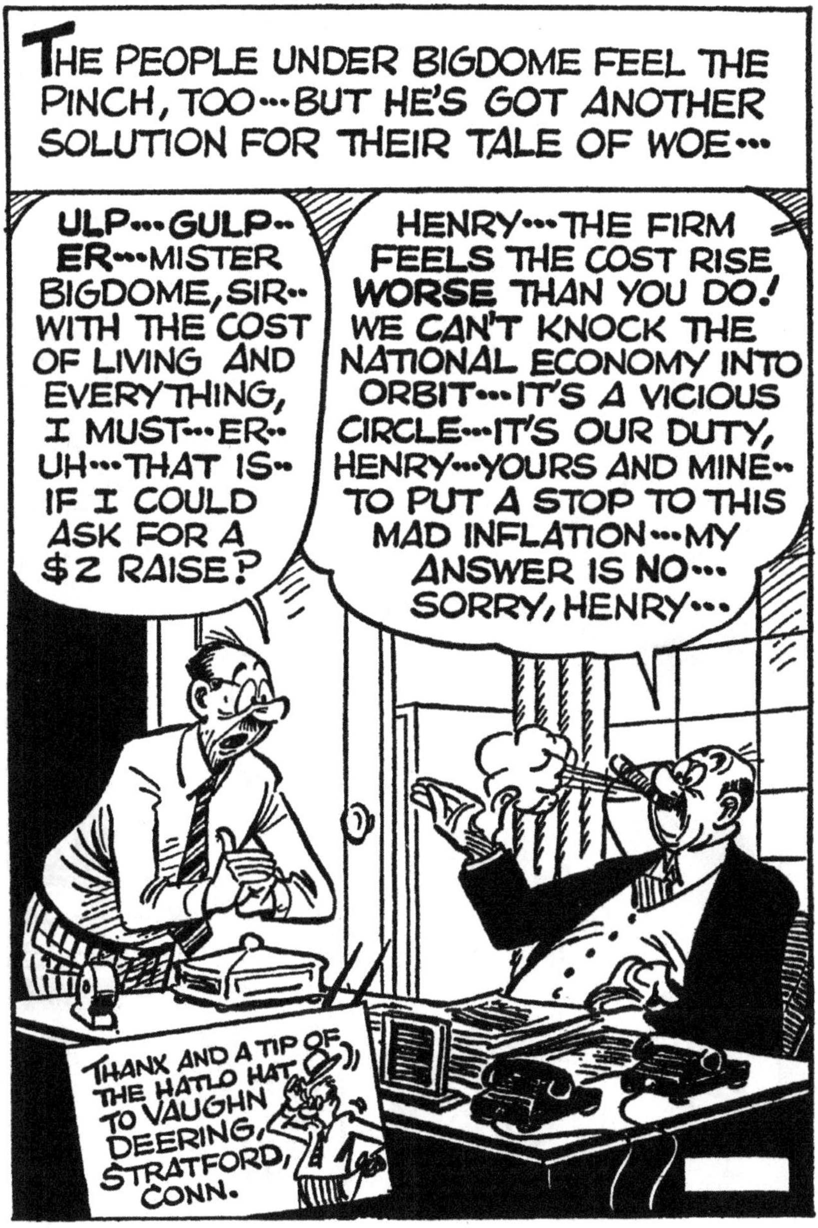
THE PEOPLE UNDER BIGDOME FEEL THE PINCH, TOO...BUT HE'S GOT ANOTHER SOLUTION FOR THEIR TALE OF WOE...
ULP...GULP.. ER...MISTER BIGDOME, SIR.. WITH THE COST OF LIVING AND EVERYTHING, I MUST...ER.. UH...THAT IS.. IF I COULD ASK FOR A $2 RAISE?
HENRY...THE FIRM FEELS THE COST RISE WORSE THAN YOU DO! WE CAN'T KNOCK THE NATIONAL ECONOMY INTO ORBIT...IT'S A VICIOUS CIRCLE...IT'S OUR DUTY, HENRY...YOURS AND MINE.. TO PUT A STOP TO THIS MAD INFLATION...MY ANSWER IS NO... SORRY, HENRY...
THANX AND A TIP OF THE HATLO HAT TO VAUGHN DEERING, STRATFORD, CONN.

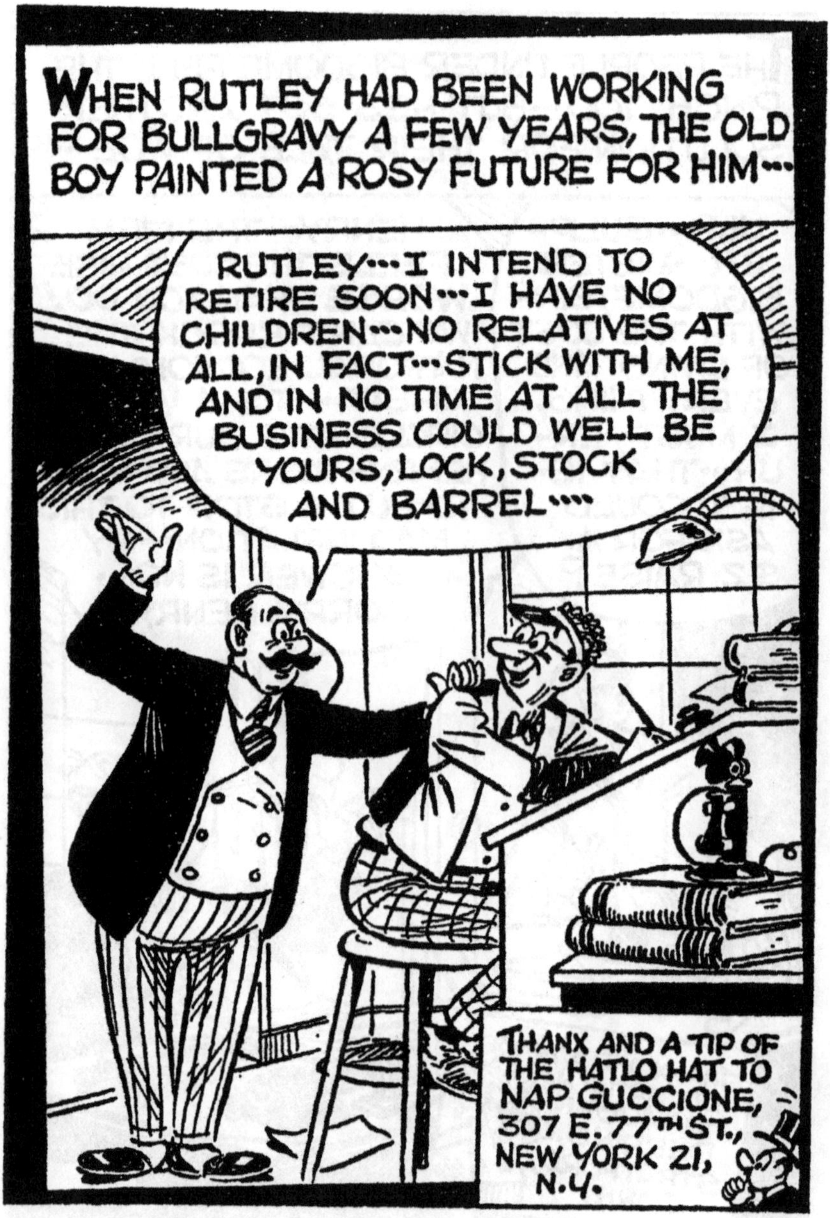
WHEN RUTLEY HAD BEEN WORKING FOR BULLGRAVY A FEW YEARS, THE OLD BOY PAINTED A ROSY FUTURE FOR HIM···
RUTLEY···I INTEND TO RETIRE SOON···I HAVE NO CHILDREN···NO RELATIVES AT ALL, IN FACT···STICK WITH ME, AND IN NO TIME AT ALL THE BUSINESS COULD WELL BE YOURS, LOCK, STOCK AND BARREL····
THANX AND A TIP OF THE HATLO HAT TO NAP GUCCIONE, 307 E. 77TH ST., NEW YORK 21, N.Y.

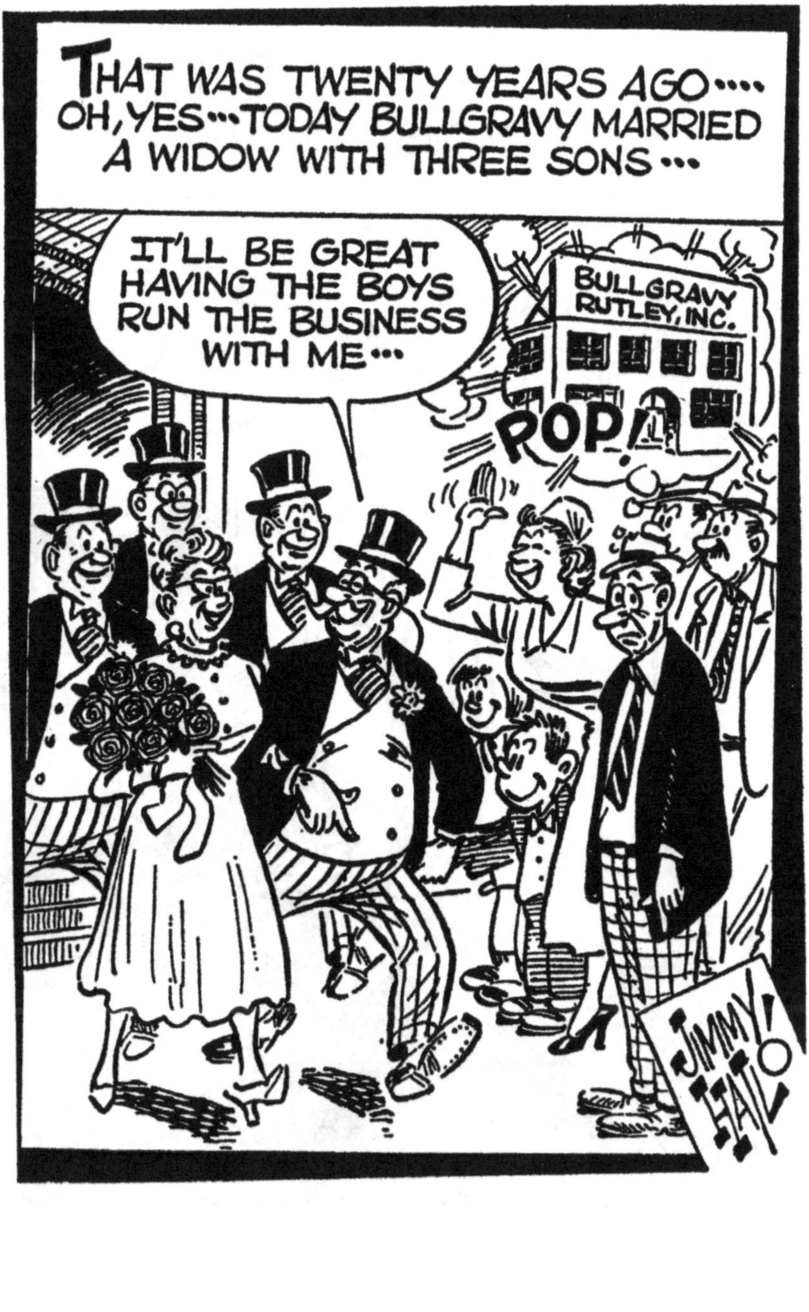
THAT WAS TWENTY YEARS AGO.... OH, YES...TODAY BULLGRAVY MARRIED A WIDOW WITH THREE SONS...
IT'LL BE GREAT HAVING THE BOYS RUN THE BUSINESS WITH ME...
BULLGRAVY RUTLEY, INC.
POP!
JIMMY! HAL!

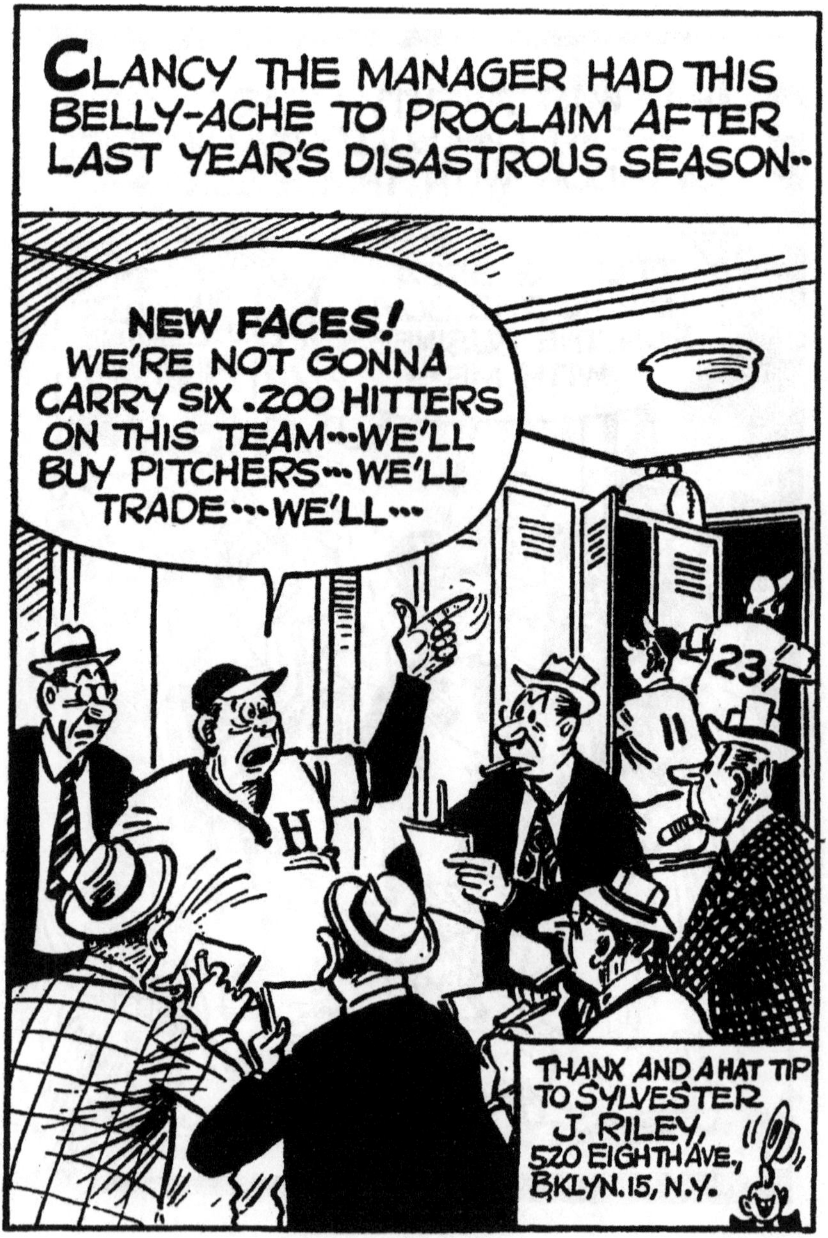

CLANCY THE MANAGER HAD THIS BELLY-ACHE TO PROCLAIM AFTER LAST YEAR'S DISASTROUS SEASON..
NEW FACES! WE'RE NOT GONNA CARRY SIX .200 HITTERS ON THIS TEAM...WE'LL BUY PITCHERS...WE'LL TRADE...WE'LL...
H
23
THANX AND A HAT TIP TO SYLVESTER J. RILEY, 520 EIGHTH AVE., B'KLYN. 15, N.Y.

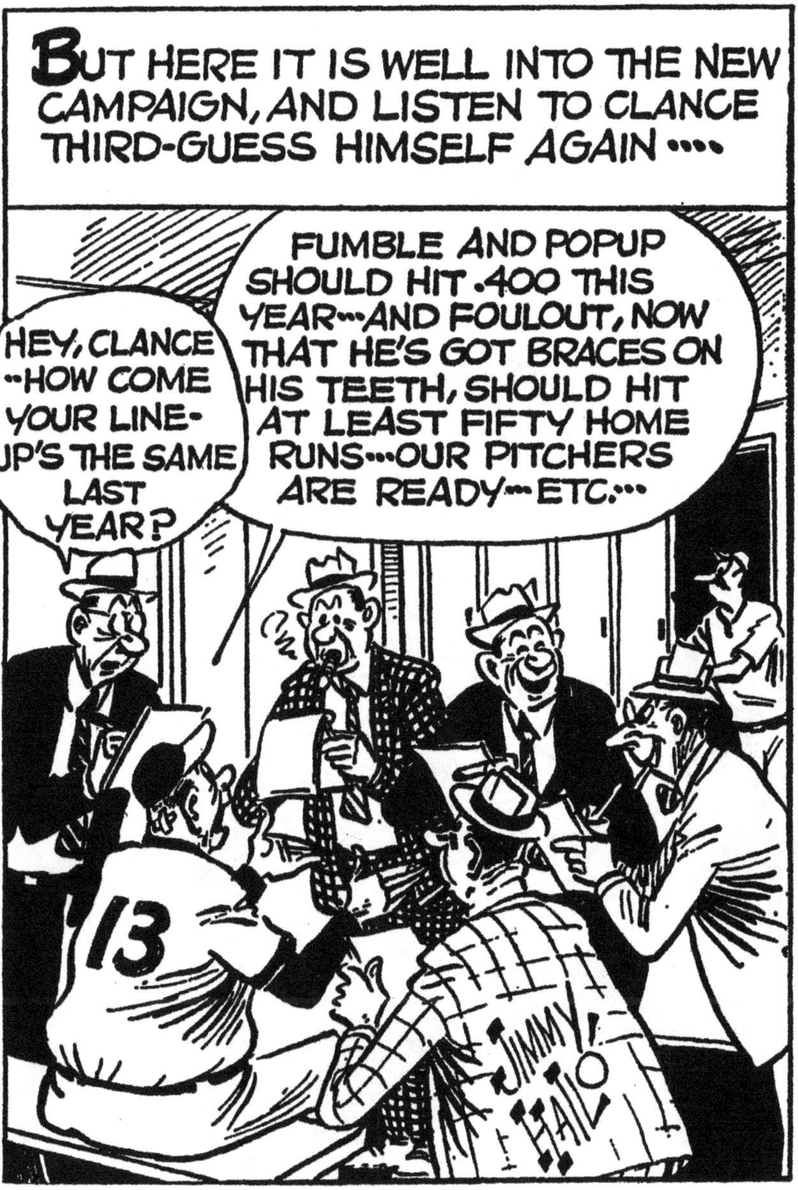
BUT HERE IT IS WELL INTO THE NEW CAMPAIGN, AND LISTEN TO CLANCE THIRD-GUESS HIMSELF AGAIN....
HEY, CLANCE --HOW COME YOUR LINE-UP'S THE SAME LAST YEAR?
FUMBLE AND POPUP SHOULD HIT .400 THIS YEAR...AND FOULOUT, NOW THAT HE'S GOT BRACES ON HIS TEETH, SHOULD HIT AT LEAST FIFTY HOME RUNS...OUR PITCHERS ARE READY...ETC....
13
JIMMY! HALO

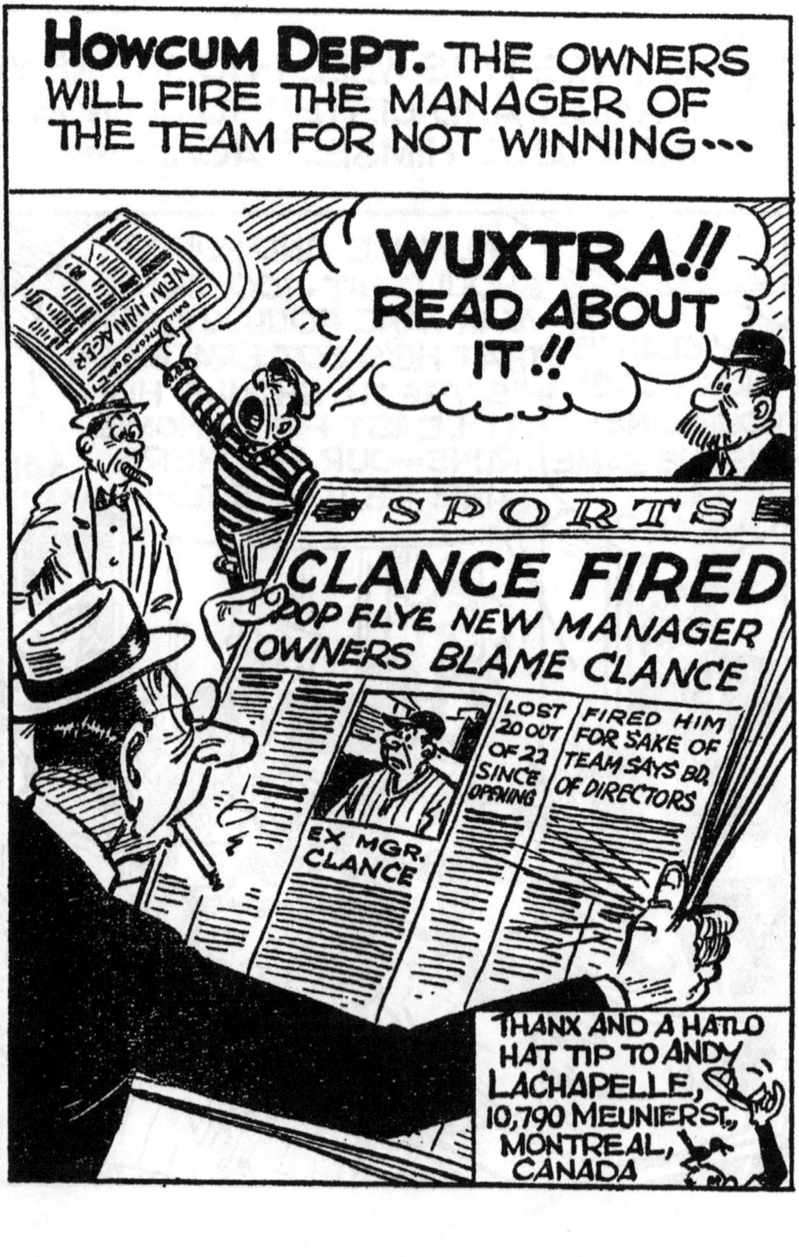
HOWCUM DEPT. THE OWNERS WILL FIRE THE MANAGER OF THE TEAM FOR NOT WINNING---
NEW MANAGER
WUXTRA!! READ ABOUT IT!!
SPORTS
CLANCE FIRED
POP FLYE NEW MANAGER
OWNERS BLAME CLANCE
LOST 20 OUT OF 22 SINCE OPENING
FIRED HIM FOR SAKE OF TEAM SAYS BD. OF DIRECTORS
EX MGR. CLANCE
THANX AND A HATLO HAT TIP TO ANDY LACHAPELLE, 10,790 MEUNIER ST., MONTREAL, CANADA

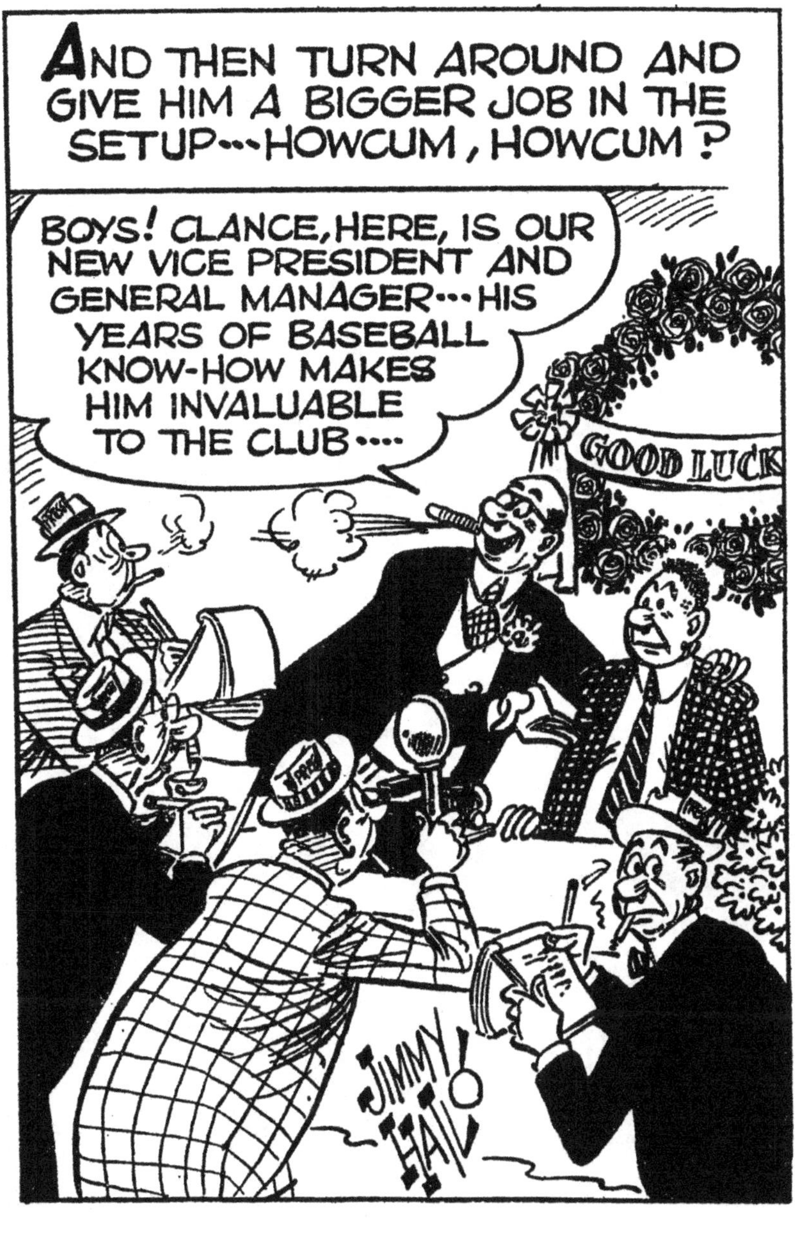
AND THEN TURN AROUND AND GIVE HIM A BIGGER JOB IN THE SETUP---HOWCUM, HOWCUM?
BOYS! CLANCE, HERE, IS OUR NEW VICE PRESIDENT AND GENERAL MANAGER--- HIS YEARS OF BASEBALL KNOW-HOW MAKES HIM INVALUABLE TO THE CLUB----
GOOD LUCK
JIMMY HATLO

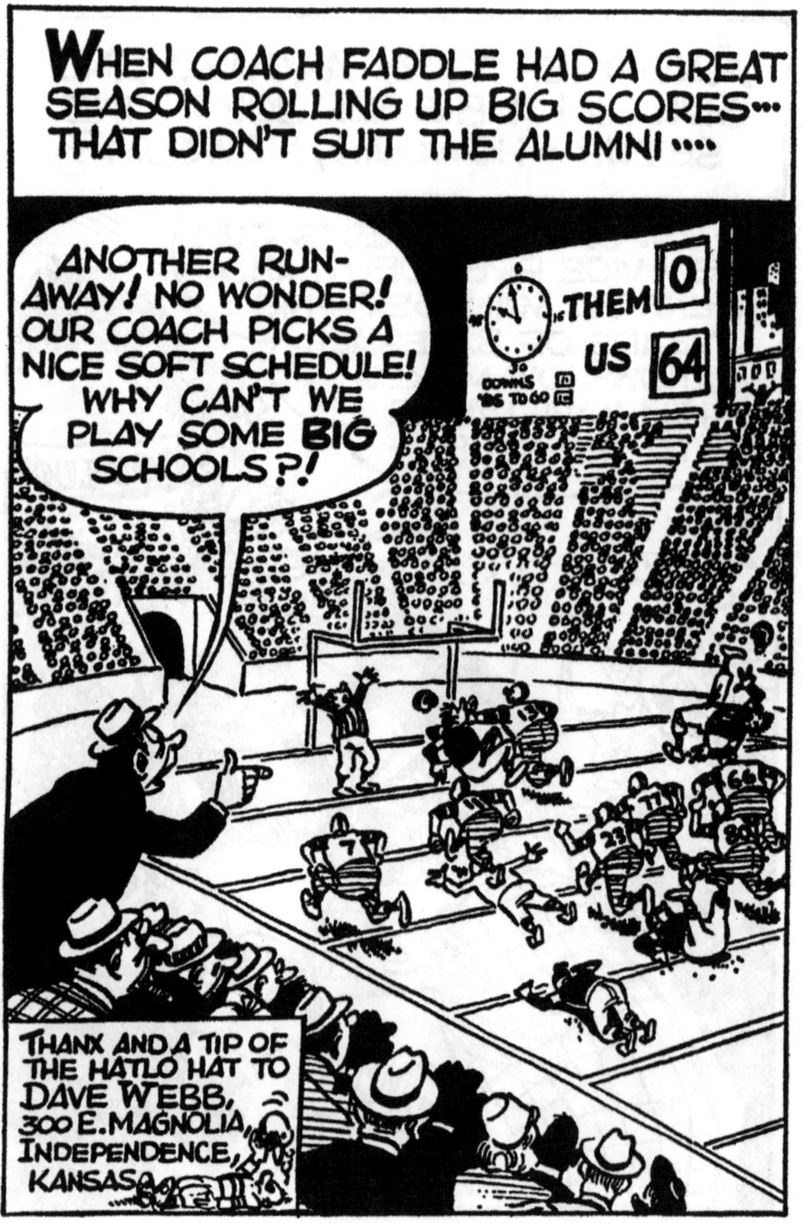
WHEN COACH FADDLE HAD A GREAT SEASON ROLLING UP BIG SCORES... THAT DIDN'T SUIT THE ALUMNI....
ANOTHER RUN-AWAY! NO WONDER! OUR COACH PICKS A NICE SOFT SCHEDULE! WHY CAN'T WE PLAY SOME BIG SCHOOLS?!
THEM 0
US 64
THANX AND A TIP OF THE HATLO HAT TO DAVE WEBB, 300 E. MAGNOLIA, INDEPENDENCE, KANSAS

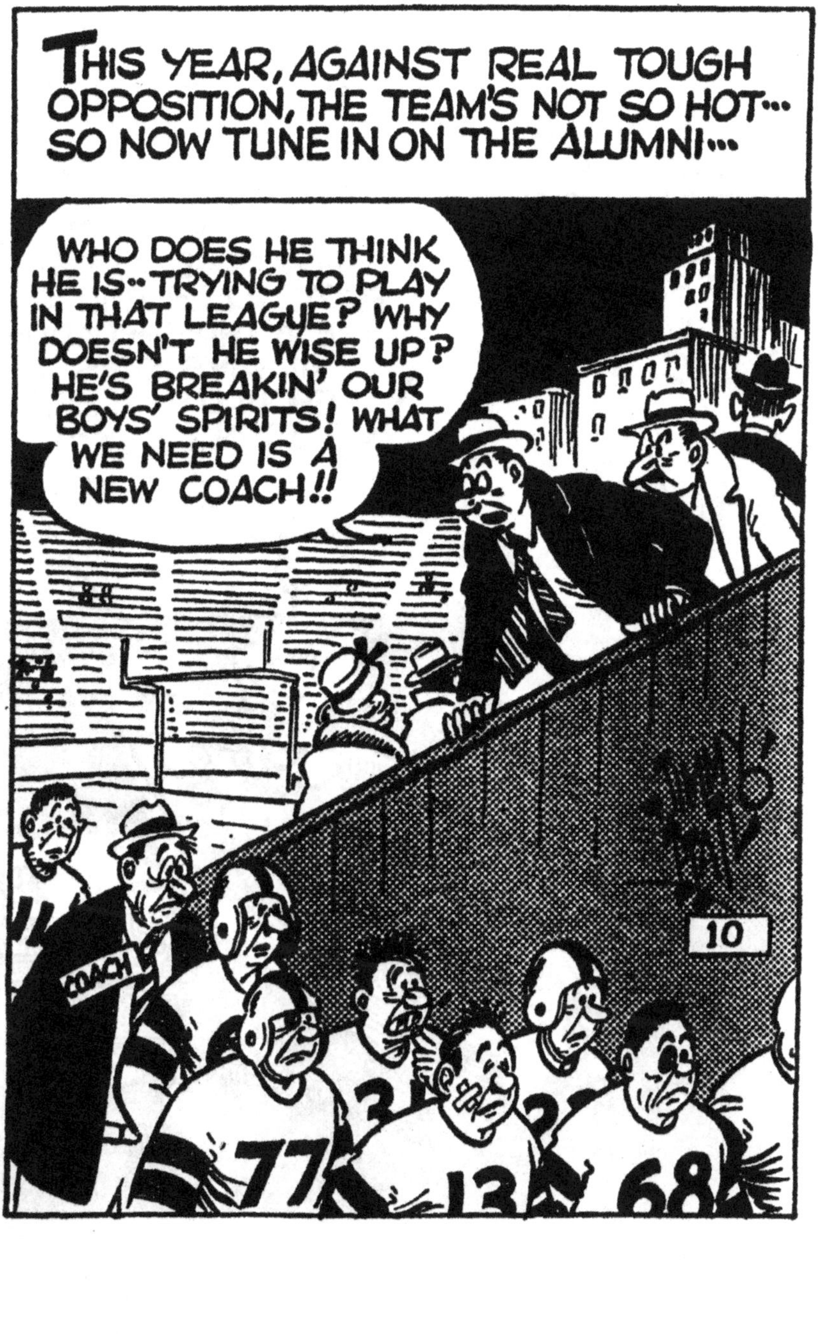
THIS YEAR, AGAINST REAL TOUGH OPPOSITION, THE TEAM'S NOT SO HOT... SO NOW TUNE IN ON THE ALUMNI...
WHO DOES HE THINK HE IS--TRYING TO PLAY IN THAT LEAGUE? WHY DOESN'T HE WISE UP? HE'S BREAKIN' OUR BOYS' SPIRITS! WHAT WE NEED IS A NEW COACH!!
10
COACH
77
13
68

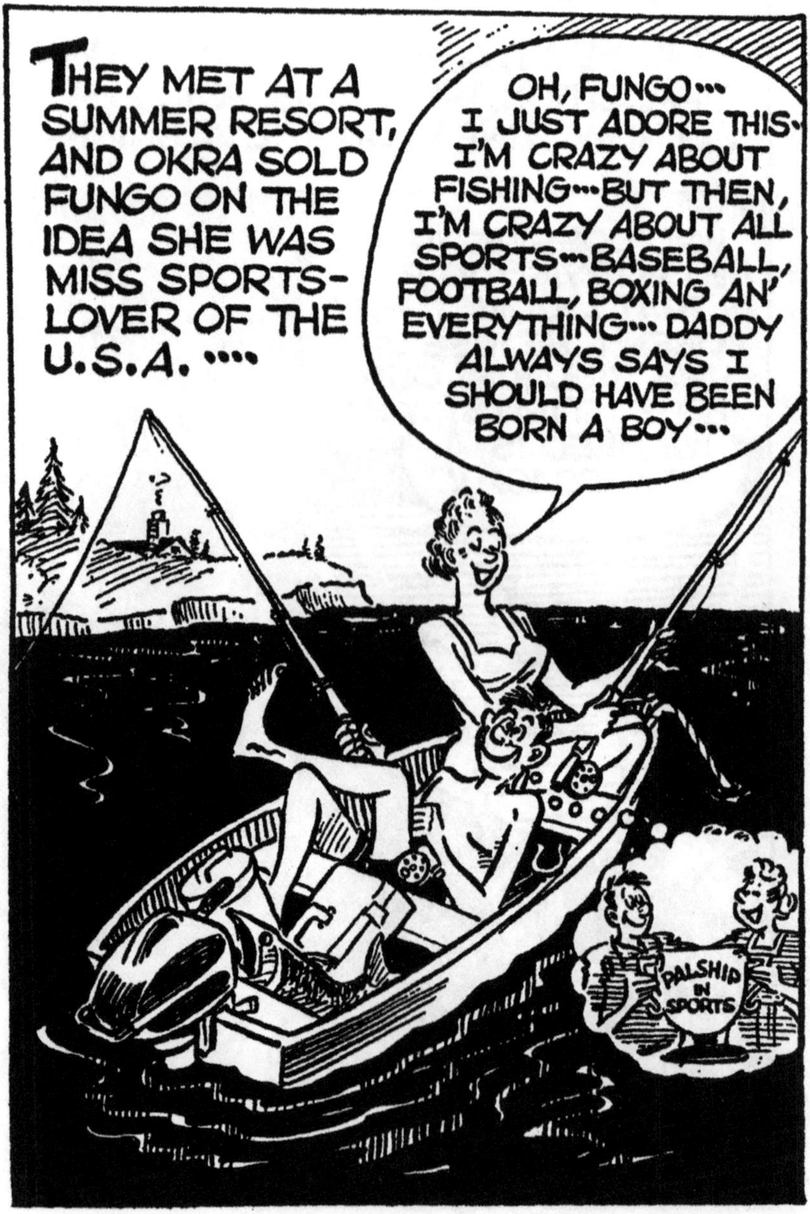
THEY MET AT A SUMMER RESORT, AND OKRA SOLD FUNGO ON THE IDEA SHE WAS MISS SPORTS-LOVER OF THE U.S.A. ....
OH, FUNGO... I JUST ADORE THIS- I'M CRAZY ABOUT FISHING...BUT THEN, I'M CRAZY ABOUT ALL SPORTS...BASEBALL, FOOTBALL, BOXING AN' EVERYTHING... DADDY ALWAYS SAYS I SHOULD HAVE BEEN BORN A BOY...
PALSHIP IN SPORTS

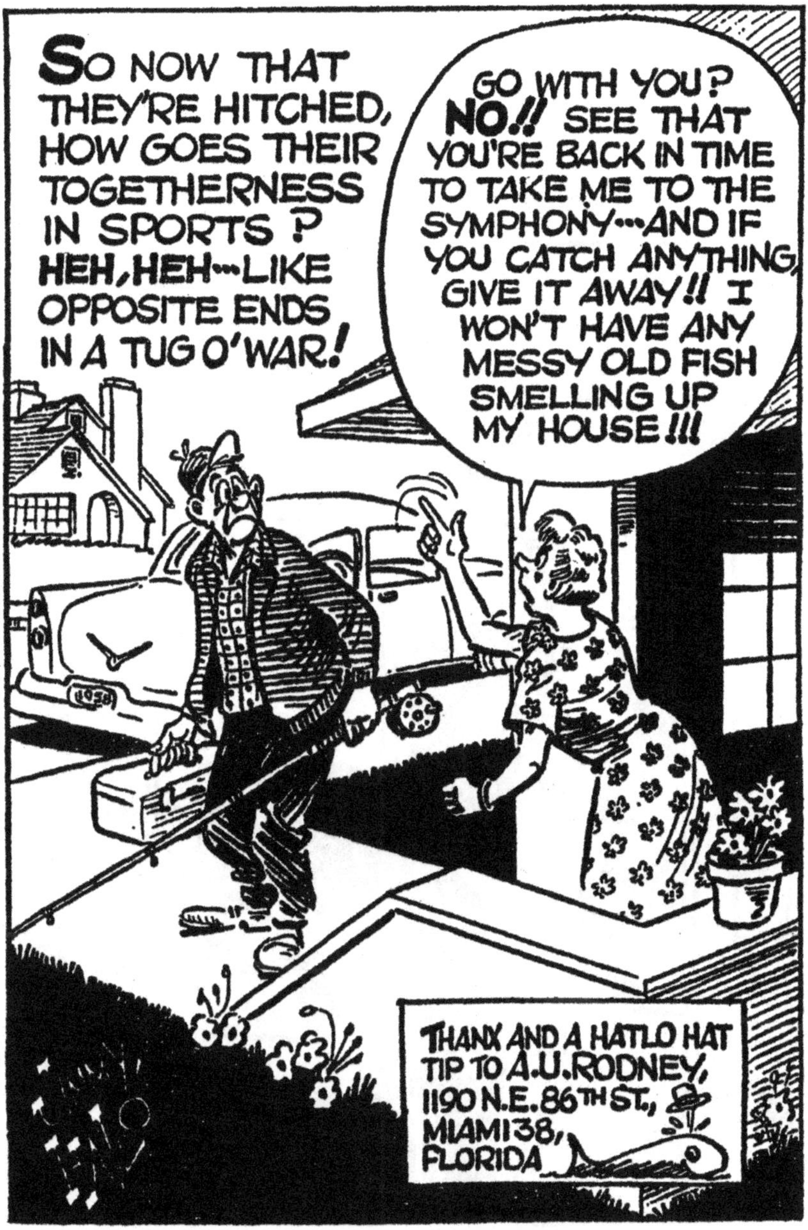
SO NOW THAT THEY'RE HITCHED, HOW GOES THEIR TOGETHERNESS IN SPORTS ? HEH, HEH--LIKE OPPOSITE ENDS IN A TUG O' WAR!
GO WITH YOU? NO!! SEE THAT YOU'RE BACK IN TIME TO TAKE ME TO THE SYMPHONY--AND IF YOU CATCH ANYTHING, GIVE IT AWAY!! I WON'T HAVE ANY MESSY OLD FISH SMELLING UP MY HOUSE!!!
1958
THANX AND A HATLO HAT TIP TO A.U. RODNEY, 1190 N.E. 86TH ST., MIAMI 38, FLORIDA

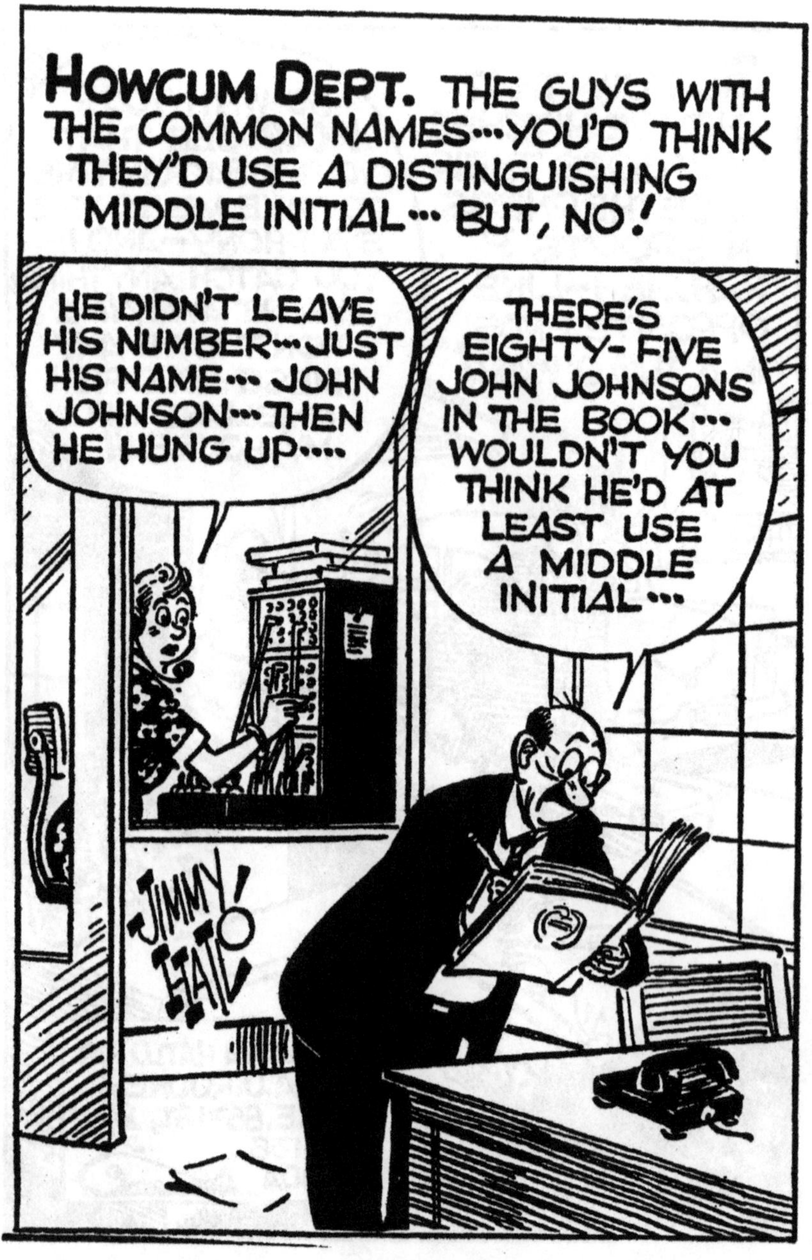
HOWCUM DEPT. THE GUYS WITH THE COMMON NAMES··· YOU'D THINK THEY'D USE A DISTINGUISHING MIDDLE INITIAL··· BUT, NO!
HE DIDN'T LEAVE HIS NUMBER··· JUST HIS NAME··· JOHN JOHNSON··· THEN HE HUNG UP····
THERE'S EIGHTY-FIVE JOHN JOHNSONS IN THE BOOK··· WOULDN'T YOU THINK HE'D AT LEAST USE A MIDDLE INITIAL···
JIMMY! HATLO

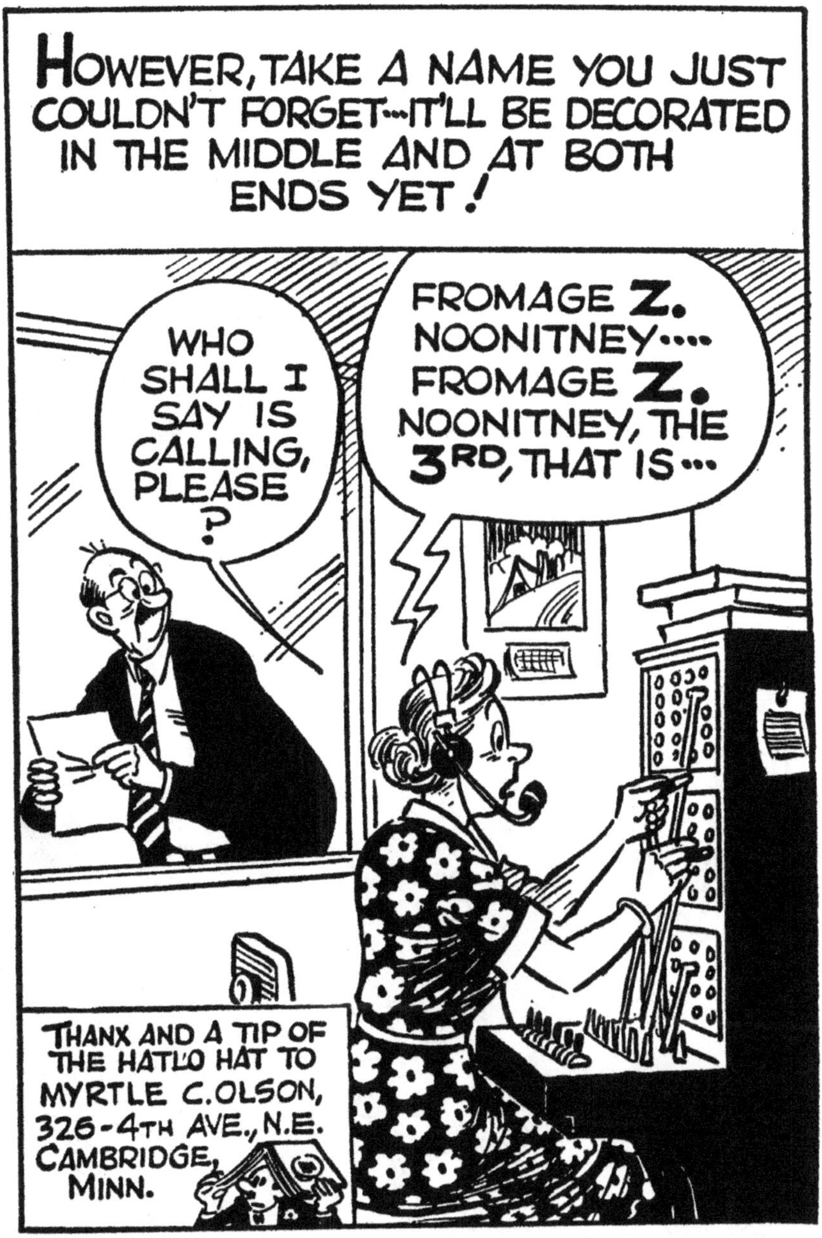
HOWEVER, TAKE A NAME YOU JUST COULDN'T FORGET---IT'LL BE DECORATED IN THE MIDDLE AND AT BOTH ENDS YET!
WHO SHALL I SAY IS CALLING, PLEASE?
FROMAGE Z. NOONITNEY.... FROMAGE Z. NOONITNEY, THE 3RD, THAT IS...
THANX AND A TIP OF THE HATL'O HAT TO MYRTLE C. OLSON, 326-4TH AVE., N.E. CAMBRIDGE, MINN.

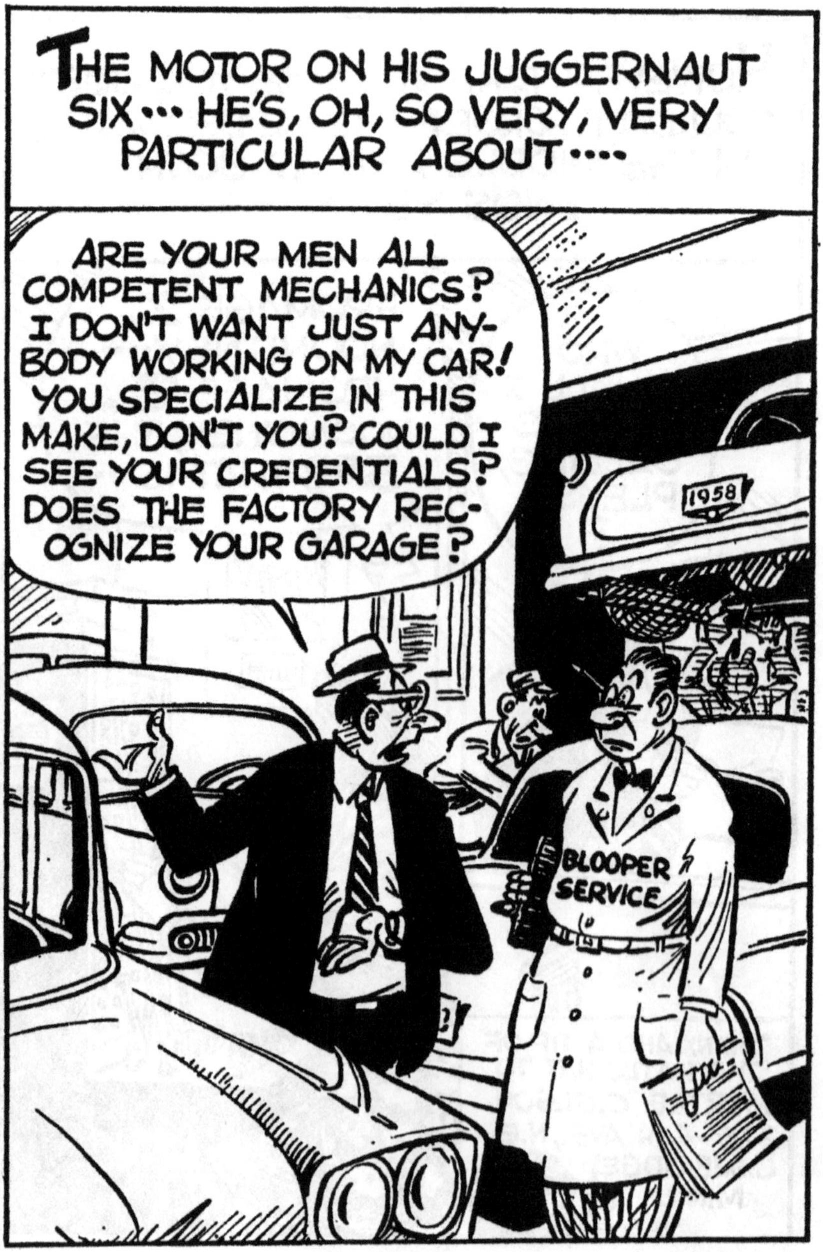
THE MOTOR ON HIS JUGGERNAUT SIX··· HE'S, OH, SO VERY, VERY PARTICULAR ABOUT····
ARE YOUR MEN ALL COMPETENT MECHANICS? I DON'T WANT JUST ANYBODY WORKING ON MY CAR! YOU SPECIALIZE IN THIS MAKE, DON'T YOU? COULD I SEE YOUR CREDENTIALS? DOES THE FACTORY RECOGNIZE YOUR GARAGE?
1958
BLOOPER SERVICE

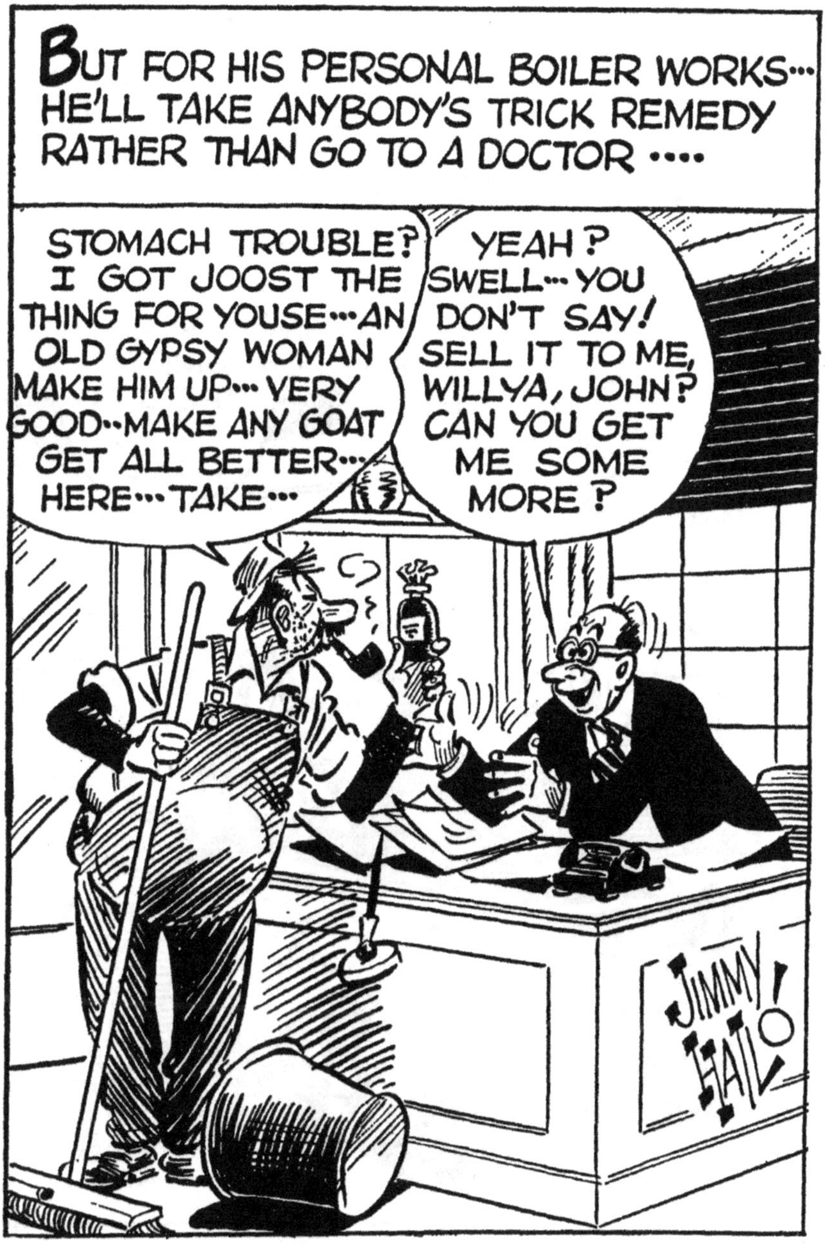
BUT FOR HIS PERSONAL BOILER WORKS... HE'LL TAKE ANYBODY'S TRICK REMEDY RATHER THAN GO TO A DOCTOR ....
STOMACH TROUBLE? I GOT JOOST THE THING FOR YOUSE...AN OLD GYPSY WOMAN MAKE HIM UP... VERY GOOD..MAKE ANY GOAT GET ALL BETTER... HERE... TAKE...
YEAH? SWELL... YOU DON'T SAY! SELL IT TO ME, WILLYA, JOHN? CAN YOU GET ME SOME MORE?
JIMMY HATLO

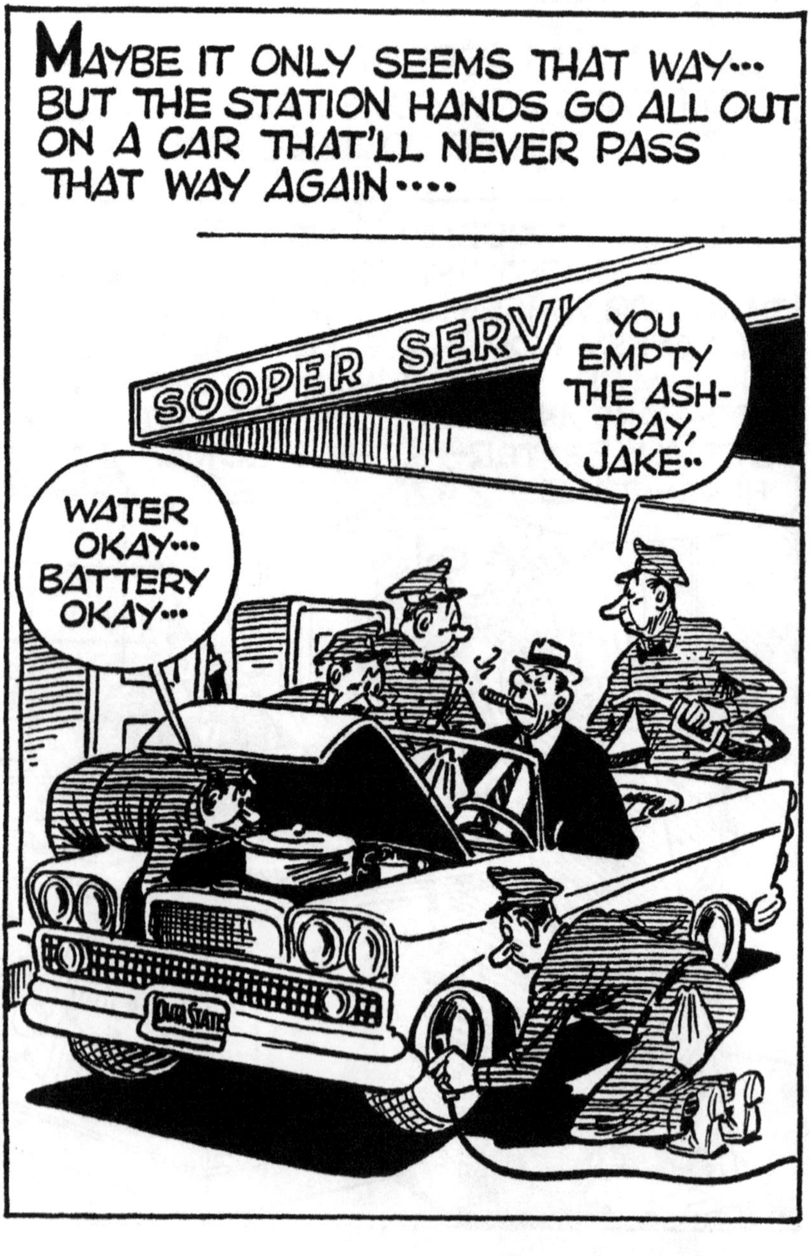
MAYBE IT ONLY SEEMS THAT WAY... BUT THE STATION HANDS GO ALL OUT ON A CAR THAT'LL NEVER PASS THAT WAY AGAIN....
SOOPER SERV
WATER OKAY... BATTERY OKAY...
YOU EMPTY THE ASH-TRAY, JAKE..

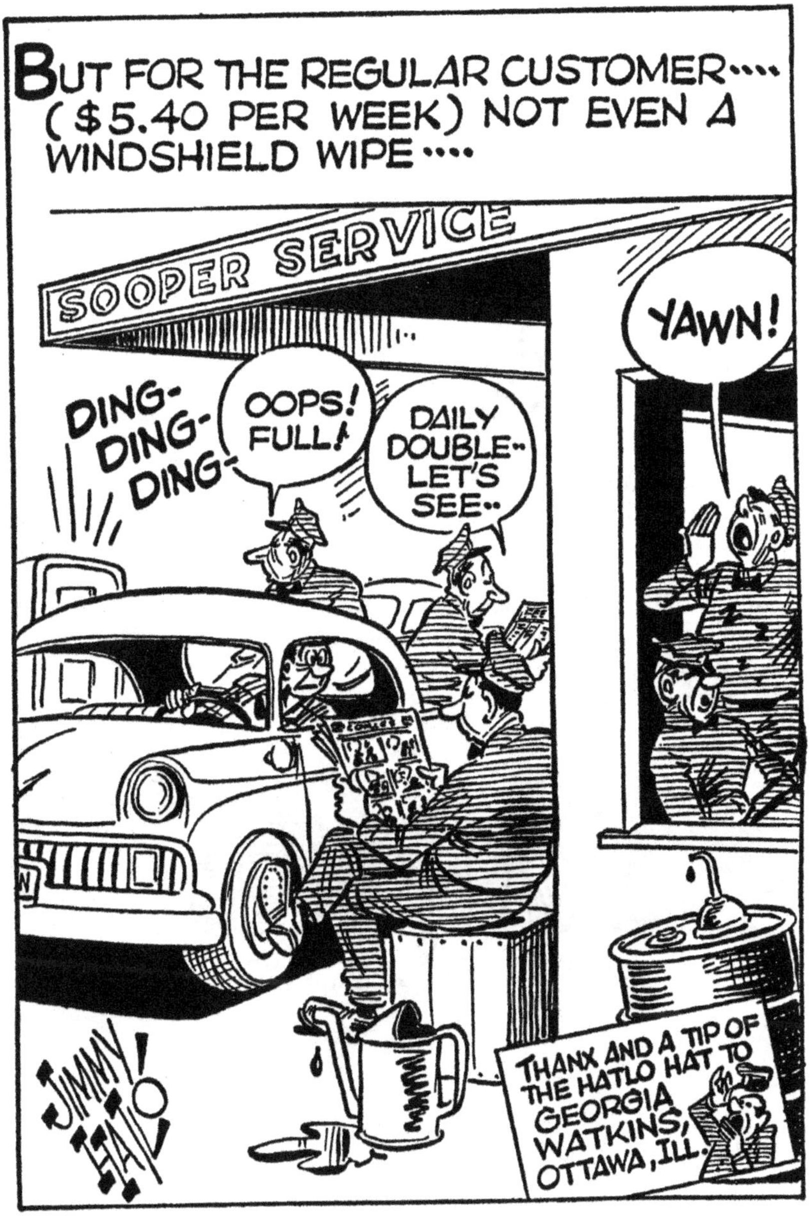
BUT FOR THE REGULAR CUSTOMER....
($5.40 PER WEEK) NOT EVEN A
WINDSHIELD WIPE....
SOOPER SERVICE
DING-
DING-
DING-
OOPS!
FULL!
DAILY
DOUBLE--
LET'S
SEE--
YAWN!
THANX AND A TIP OF
THE HATLO HAT TO
GEORGIA
WATKINS,
OTTAWA, ILL.
JIMMY HATLO

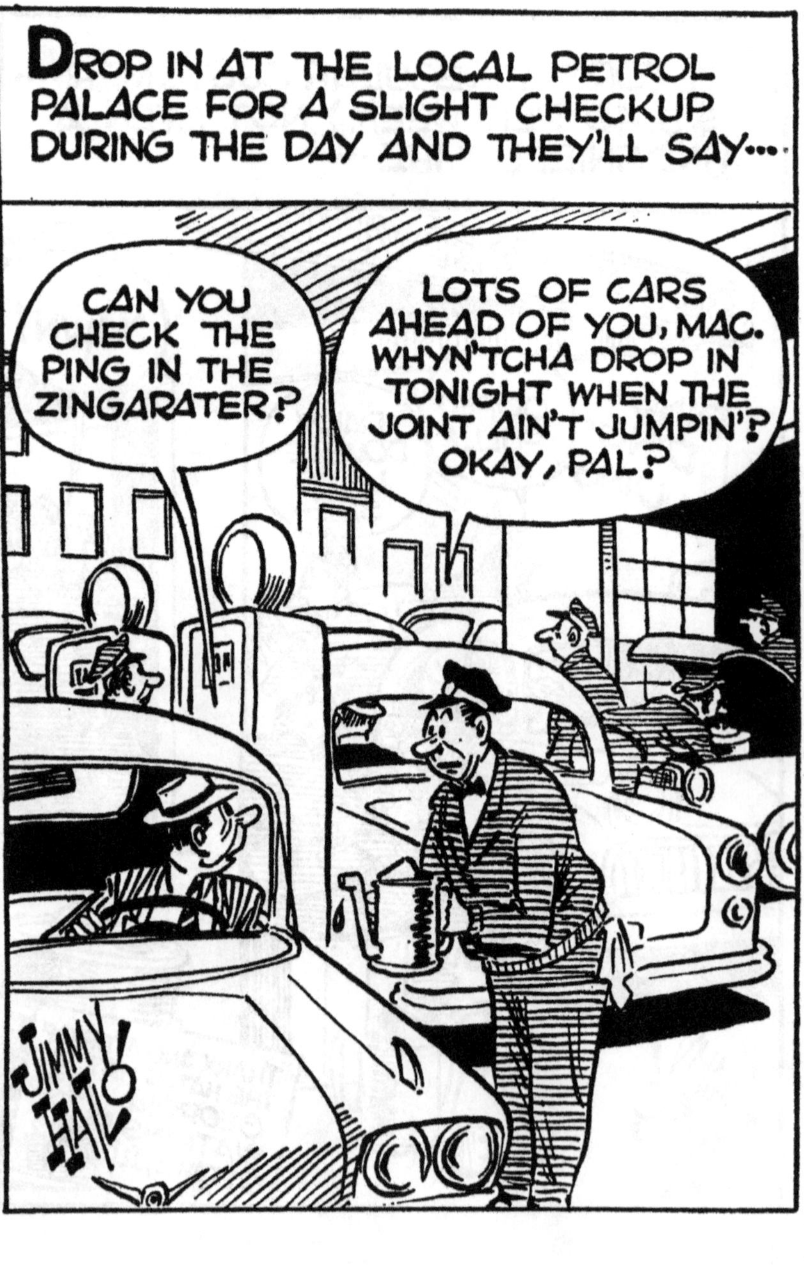
DROP IN AT THE LOCAL PETROL PALACE FOR A SLIGHT CHECKUP DURING THE DAY AND THEY'LL SAY...
CAN YOU CHECK THE PING IN THE ZINGARATER?
LOTS OF CARS AHEAD OF YOU, MAC. WHYN'TCHA DROP IN TONIGHT WHEN THE JOINT AIN'T JUMPIN'? OKAY, PAL?
JIMMY HATLO

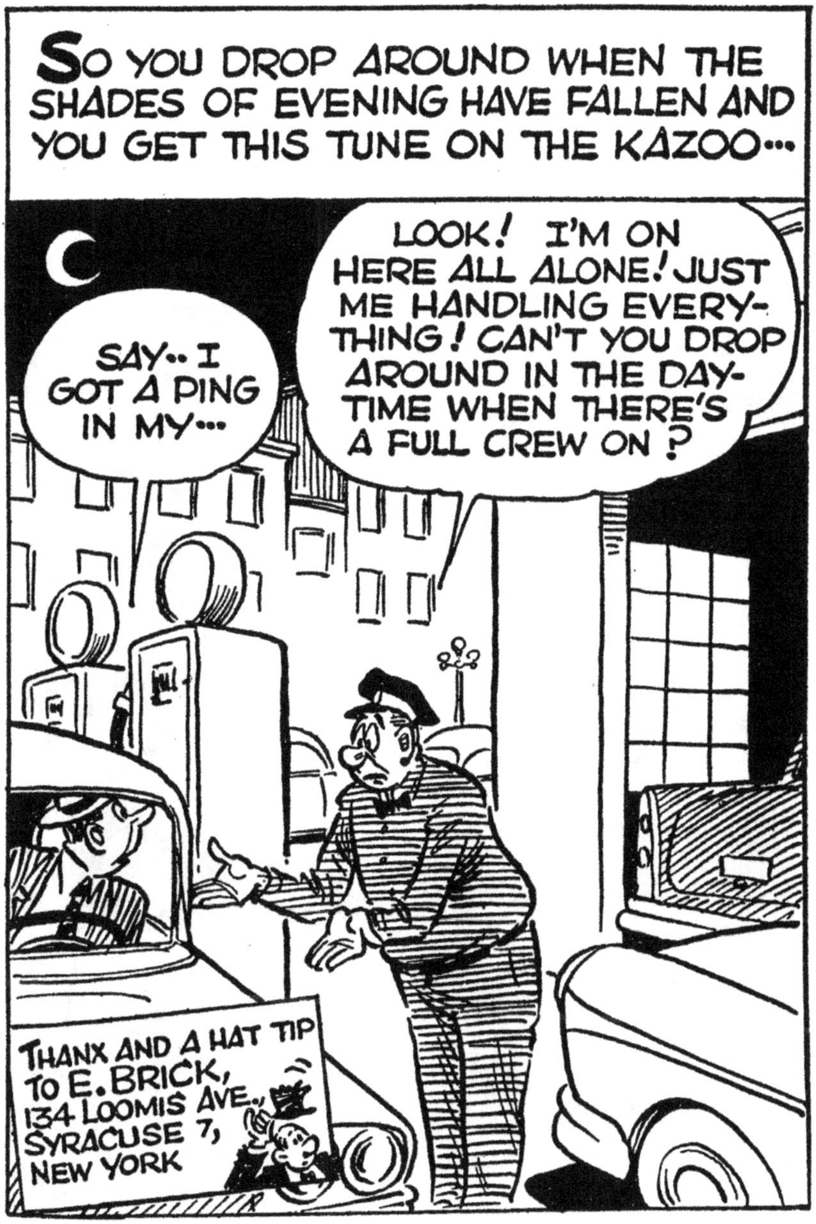
SO YOU DROP AROUND WHEN THE SHADES OF EVENING HAVE FALLEN AND YOU GET THIS TUNE ON THE KAZOO...
SAY.. I GOT A PING IN MY...
LOOK! I'M ON HERE ALL ALONE! JUST ME HANDLING EVERY-THING! CAN'T YOU DROP AROUND IN THE DAY-TIME WHEN THERE'S A FULL CREW ON?
THANX AND A HAT TIP TO E. BRICK, 134 LOOMIS AVE., SYRACUSE 7, NEW YORK

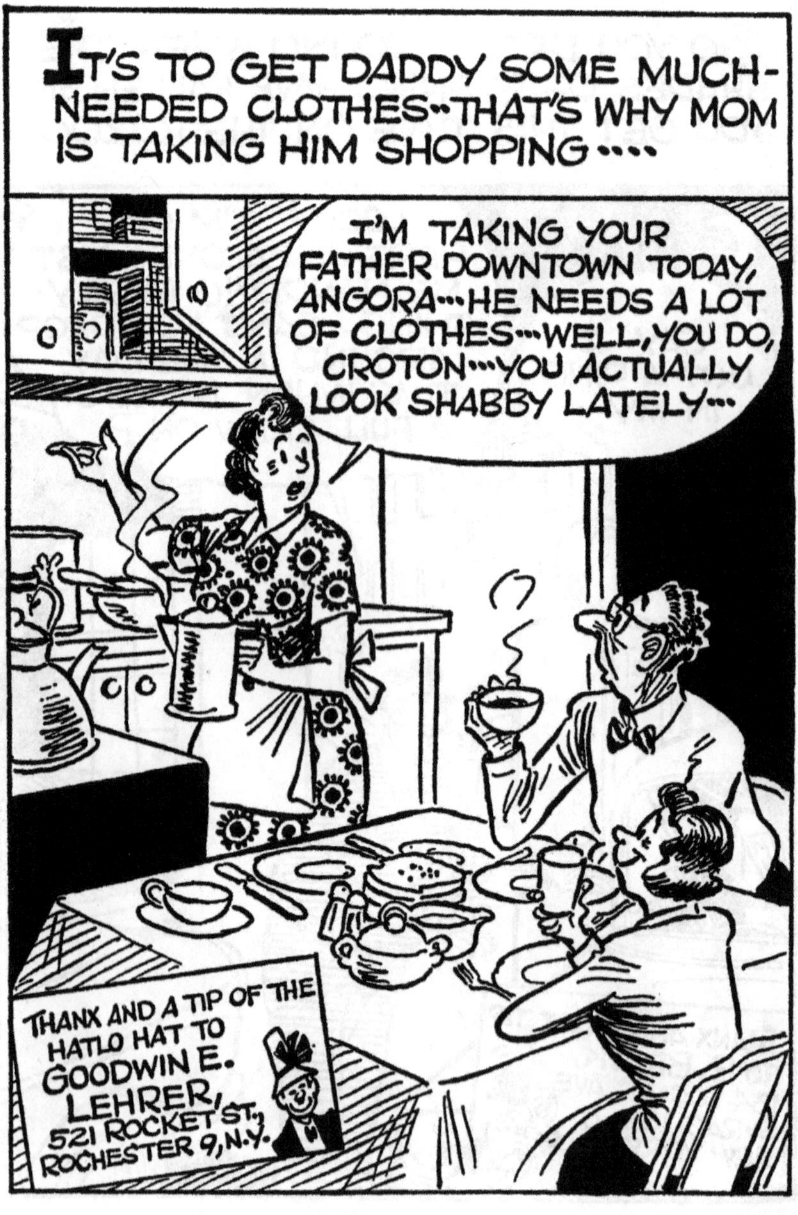
IT'S TO GET DADDY SOME MUCH-NEEDED CLOTHES--THAT'S WHY MOM IS TAKING HIM SHOPPING....
I'M TAKING YOUR FATHER DOWNTOWN TODAY, ANGORA...HE NEEDS A LOT OF CLOTHES...WELL, YOU DO, CROTON...YOU ACTUALLY LOOK SHABBY LATELY...
THANX AND A TIP OF THE HATLO HAT TO GOODWIN E. LEHRER, 521 ROCKET ST., ROCHESTER 9, N.Y.

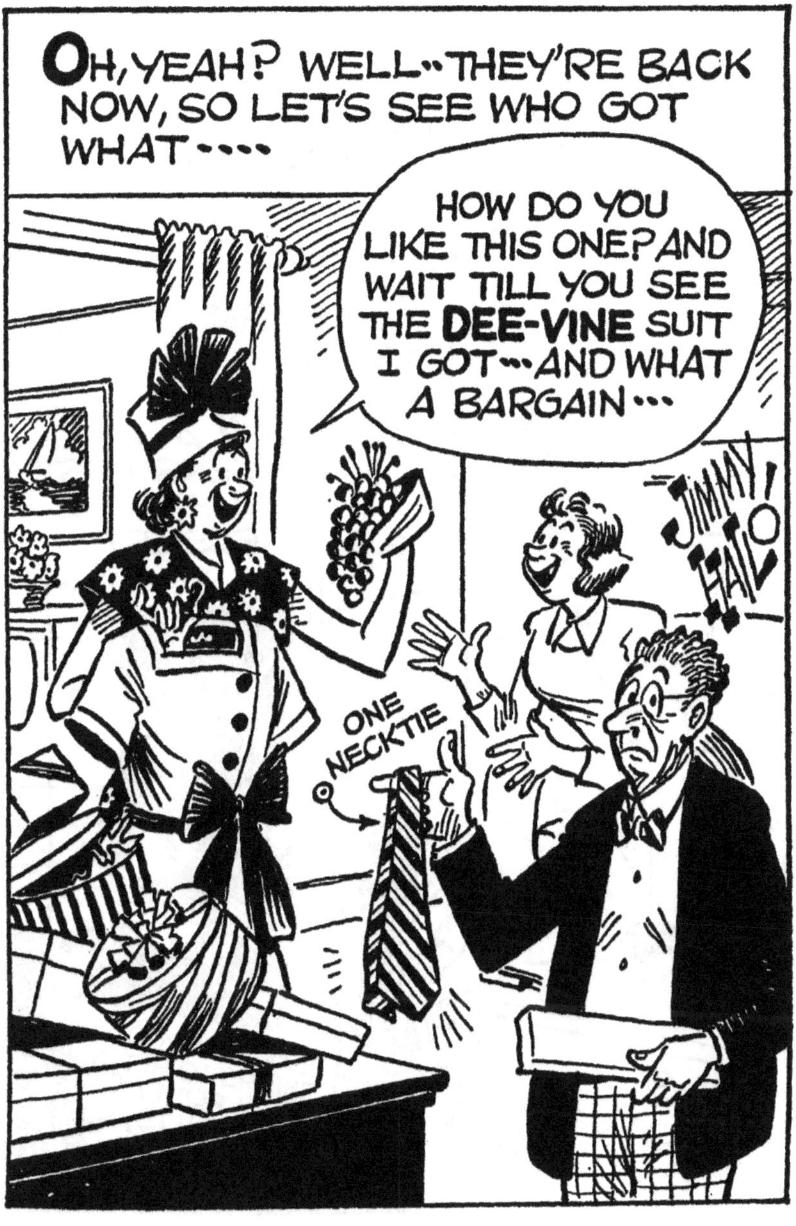

OH, YEAH? WELL.. THEY'RE BACK NOW, SO LET'S SEE WHO GOT WHAT....
HOW DO YOU LIKE THIS ONE? AND WAIT TILL YOU SEE THE DEE-VINE SUIT I GOT...AND WHAT A BARGAIN...
JIMMY HATLO
ONE NECKTIE

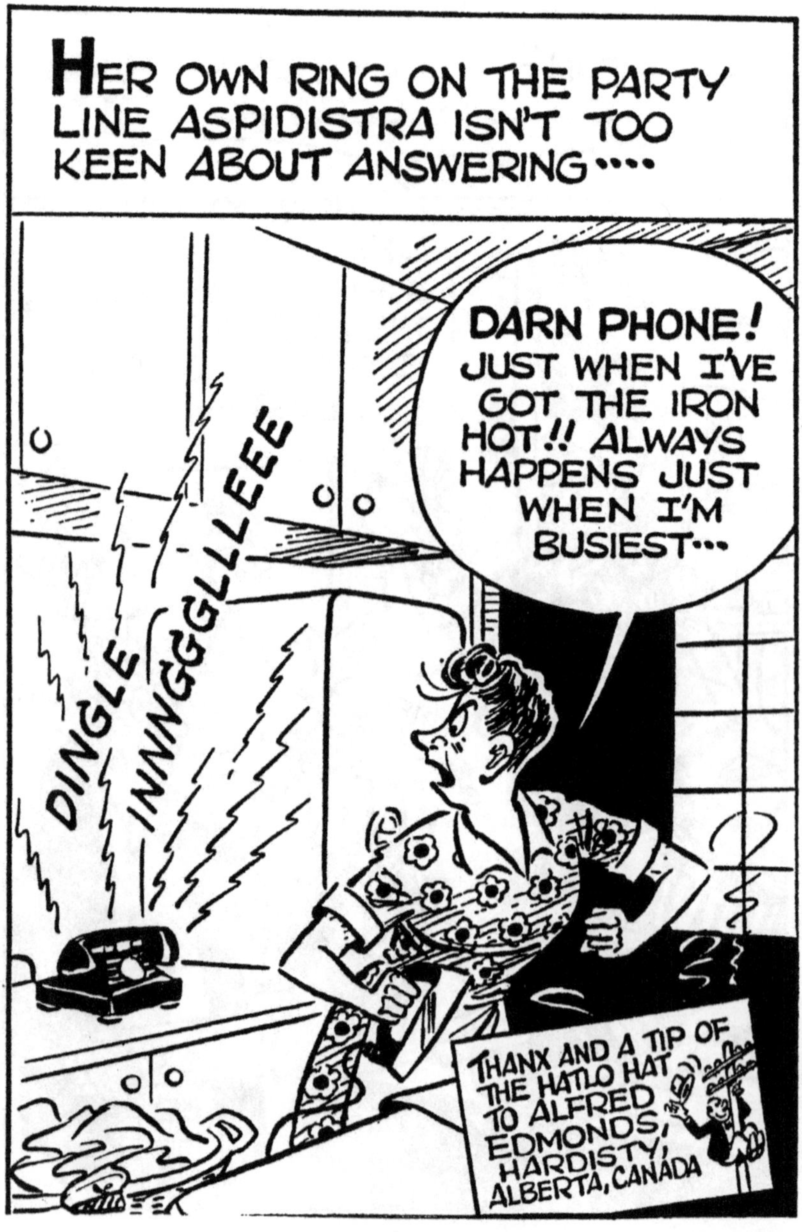
HER OWN RING ON THE PARTY LINE ASPIDISTRA ISN'T TOO KEEN ABOUT ANSWERING....
DARN PHONE! JUST WHEN I'VE GOT THE IRON HOT!! ALWAYS HAPPENS JUST WHEN I'M BUSIEST...
DINGLE
INNNGGGLLLEEE
THANX AND A TIP OF THE HATLO HAT TO ALFRED EDMONDS, HARDISTY, ALBERTA, CANADA

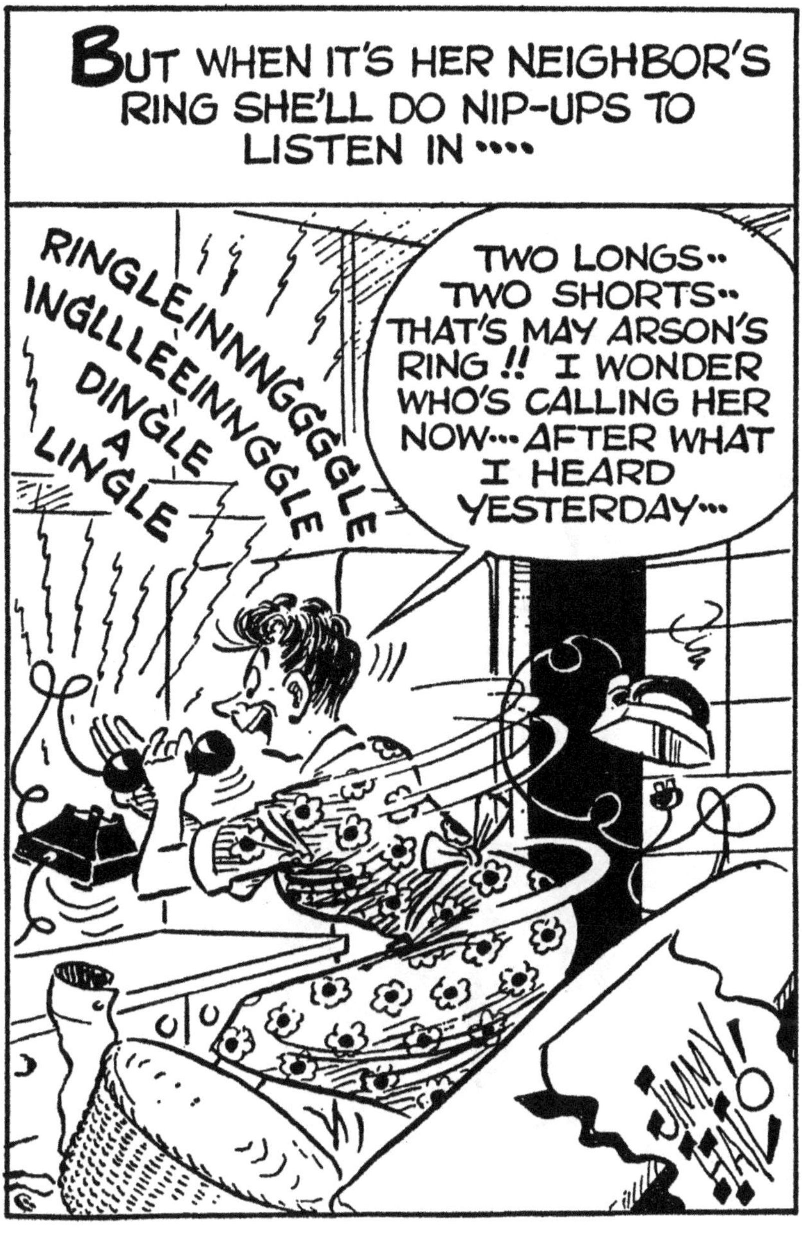
BUT WHEN IT'S HER NEIGHBOR'S RING SHE'LL DO NIP-UPS TO LISTEN IN....
RINGLEINNNGGGGLE
INGLLLEEINNGGLE
DINGLE A LINGLE
TWO LONGS.. TWO SHORTS.. THAT'S MAY ARSON'S RING !! I WONDER WHO'S CALLING HER NOW... AFTER WHAT I HEARD YESTERDAY...
JIMMY HATLO

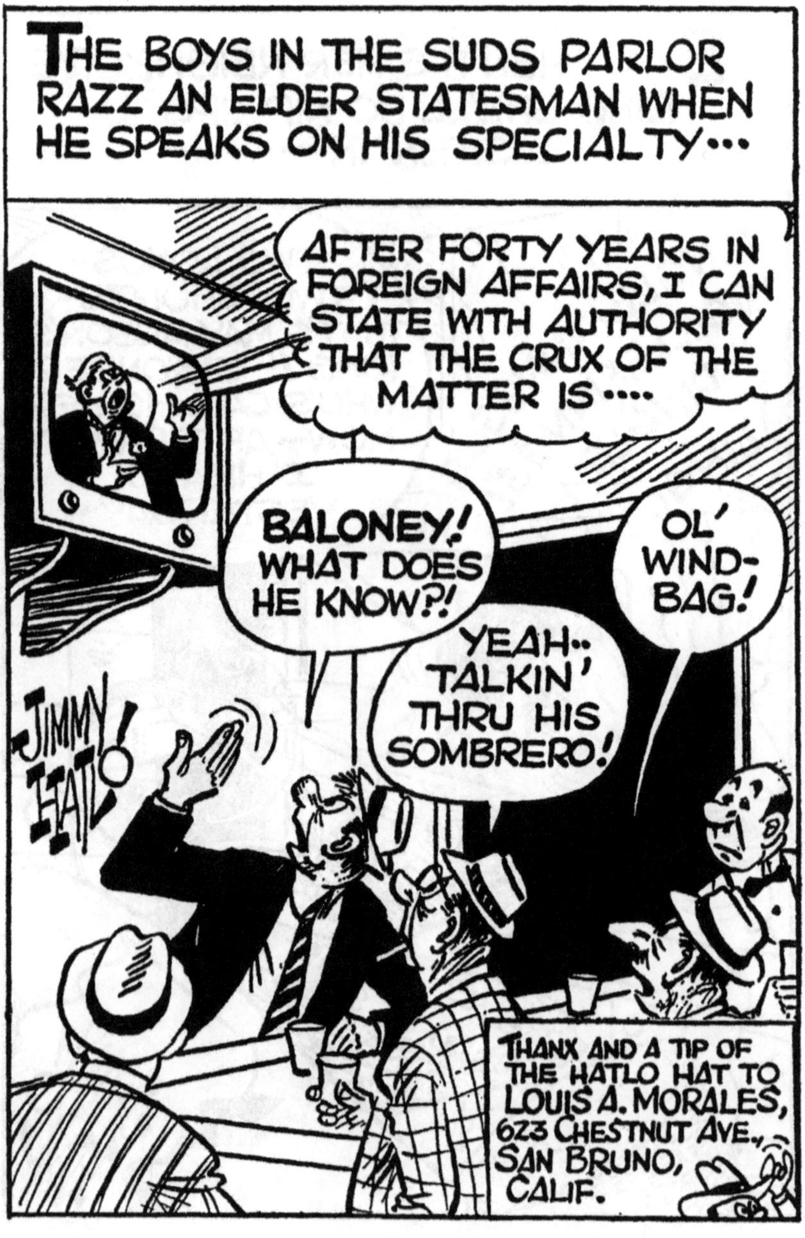
THE BOYS IN THE SUDS PARLOR RAZZ AN ELDER STATESMAN WHEN HE SPEAKS ON HIS SPECIALTY...
AFTER FORTY YEARS IN FOREIGN AFFAIRS, I CAN STATE WITH AUTHORITY THAT THE CRUX OF THE MATTER IS....
BALONEY! WHAT DOES HE KNOW?!
YEAH.. TALKIN' THRU HIS SOMBRERO!
OL' WIND-BAG!
JIMMY HATLO
THANX AND A TIP OF THE HATLO HAT TO LOUIS A. MORALES, 623 CHESTNUT AVE., SAN BRUNO, CALIF.

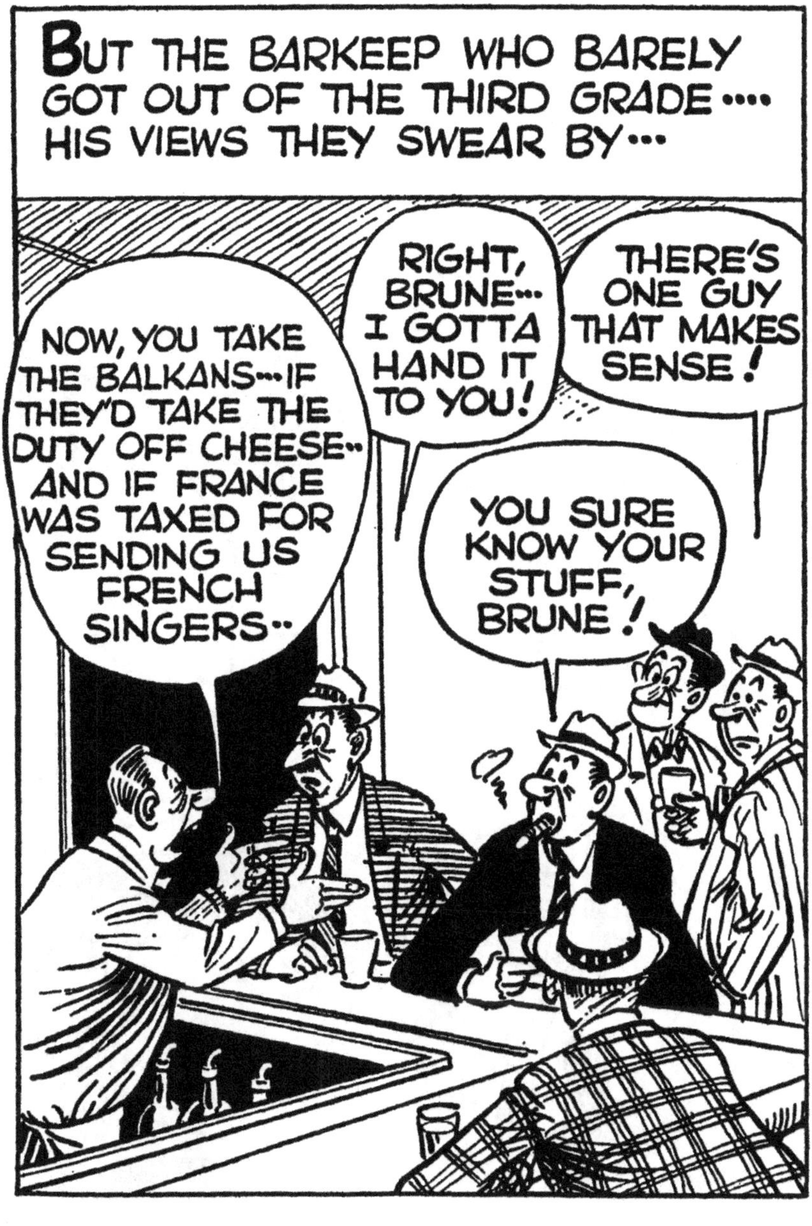

BUT THE BARKEEP WHO BARELY GOT OUT OF THE THIRD GRADE.... HIS VIEWS THEY SWEAR BY...
NOW, YOU TAKE THE BALKANS...IF THEY'D TAKE THE DUTY OFF CHEESE.. AND IF FRANCE WAS TAXED FOR SENDING US FRENCH SINGERS..
RIGHT, BRUNE... I GOTTA HAND IT TO YOU!
THERE'S ONE GUY THAT MAKES SENSE!
YOU SURE KNOW YOUR STUFF, BRUNE!

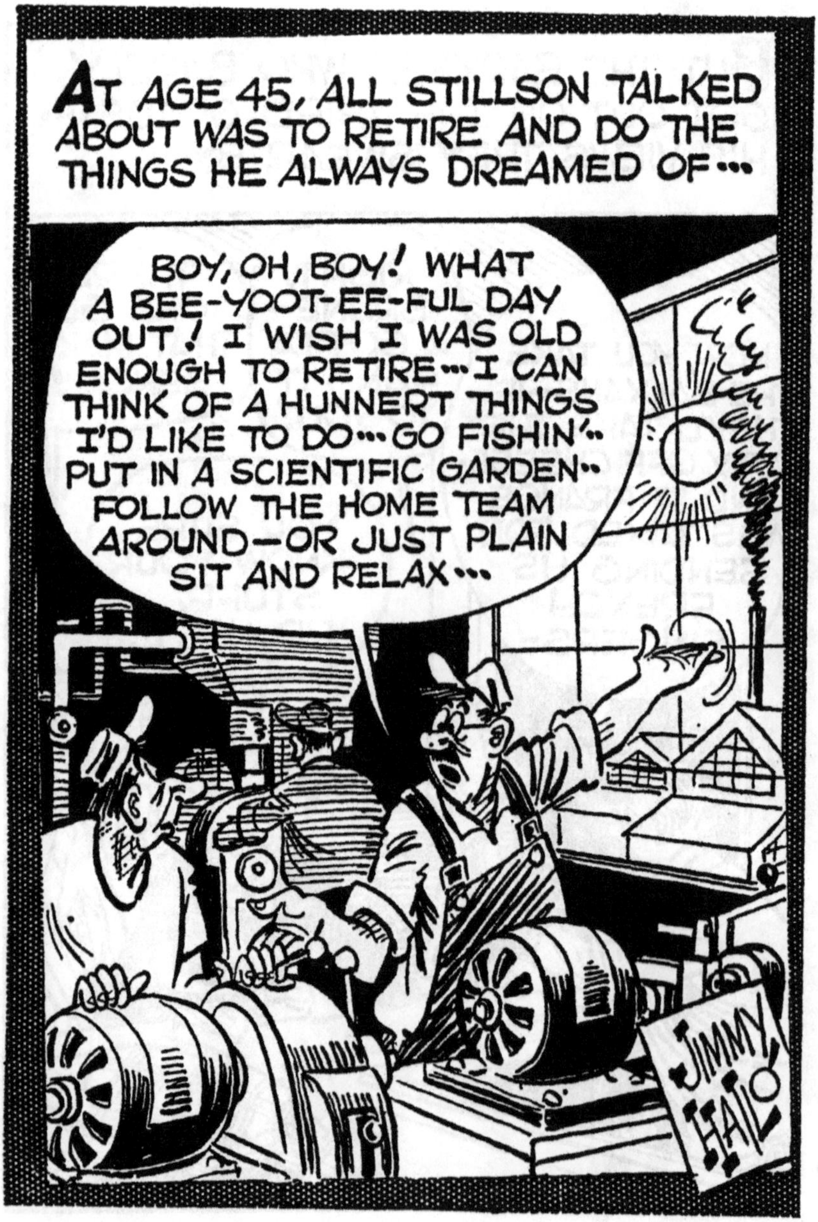
AT AGE 45, ALL STILLSON TALKED ABOUT WAS TO RETIRE AND DO THE THINGS HE ALWAYS DREAMED OF...
BOY, OH, BOY! WHAT A BEE-YOOT-EE-FUL DAY OUT! I WISH I WAS OLD ENOUGH TO RETIRE... I CAN THINK OF A HUNNERT THINGS I'D LIKE TO DO... GO FISHIN'.. PUT IN A SCIENTIFIC GARDEN.. FOLLOW THE HOME TEAM AROUND—OR JUST PLAIN SIT AND RELAX...
JIMMY HATLO

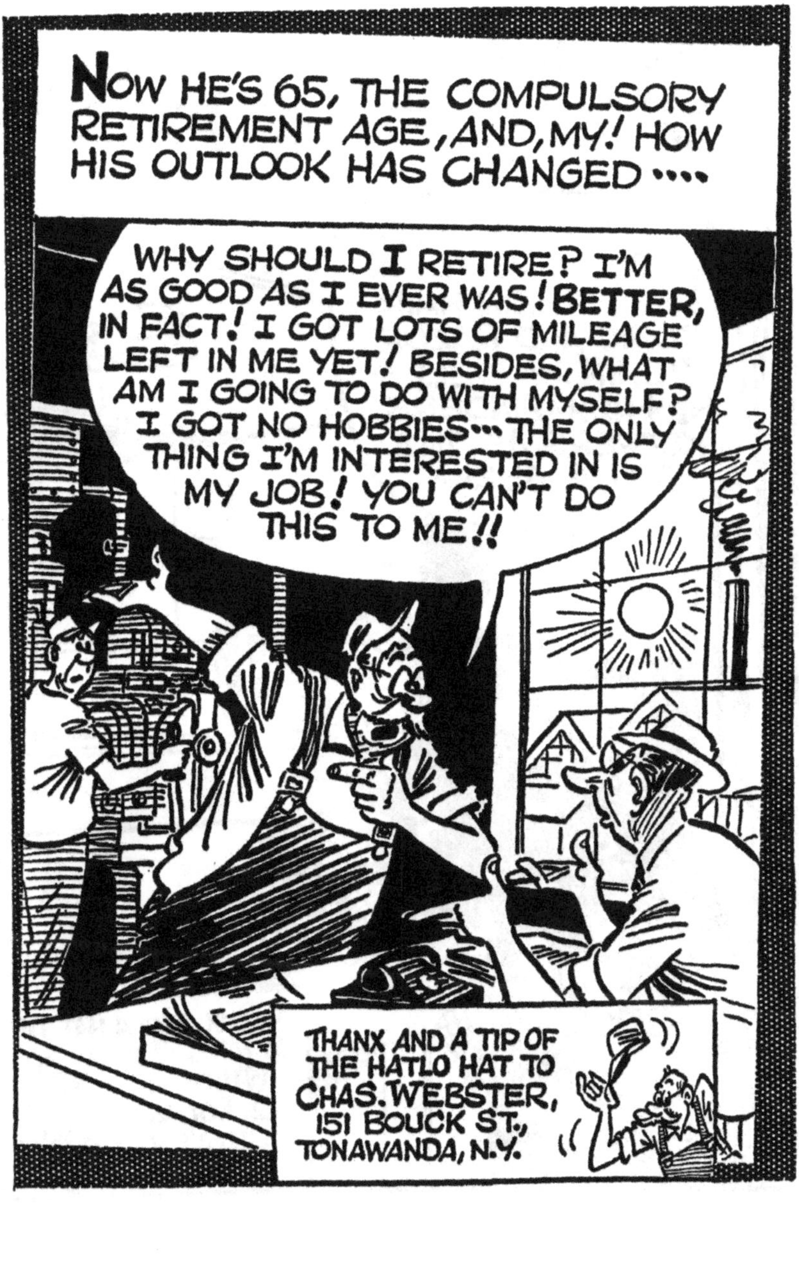
NOW HE'S 65, THE COMPULSORY RETIREMENT AGE, AND, MY! HOW HIS OUTLOOK HAS CHANGED....
WHY SHOULD I RETIRE? I'M AS GOOD AS I EVER WAS! BETTER, IN FACT! I GOT LOTS OF MILEAGE LEFT IN ME YET! BESIDES, WHAT AM I GOING TO DO WITH MYSELF? I GOT NO HOBBIES... THE ONLY THING I'M INTERESTED IN IS MY JOB! YOU CAN'T DO THIS TO ME!!
THANX AND A TIP OF THE HATLO HAT TO CHAS. WEBSTER, 151 BOUCK ST., TONAWANDA, N.Y.

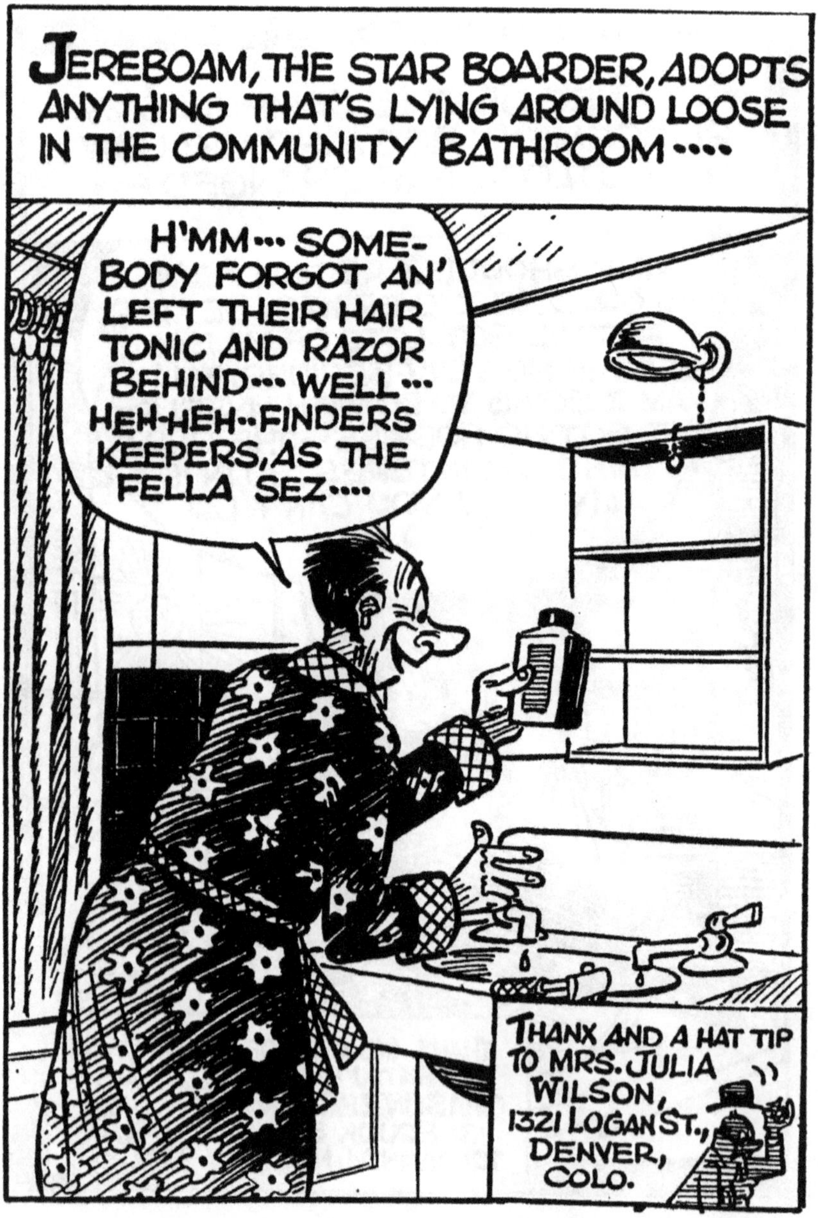
JEREBOAM, THE STAR BOARDER, ADOPTS ANYTHING THAT'S LYING AROUND LOOSE IN THE COMMUNITY BATHROOM....
H'MM... SOMEBODY FORGOT AN' LEFT THEIR HAIR TONIC AND RAZOR BEHIND... WELL... HEH-HEH..FINDERS KEEPERS, AS THE FELLA SEZ....
THANX AND A HAT TIP TO MRS. JULIA WILSON, 1321 LOGAN ST., DENVER, COLO.

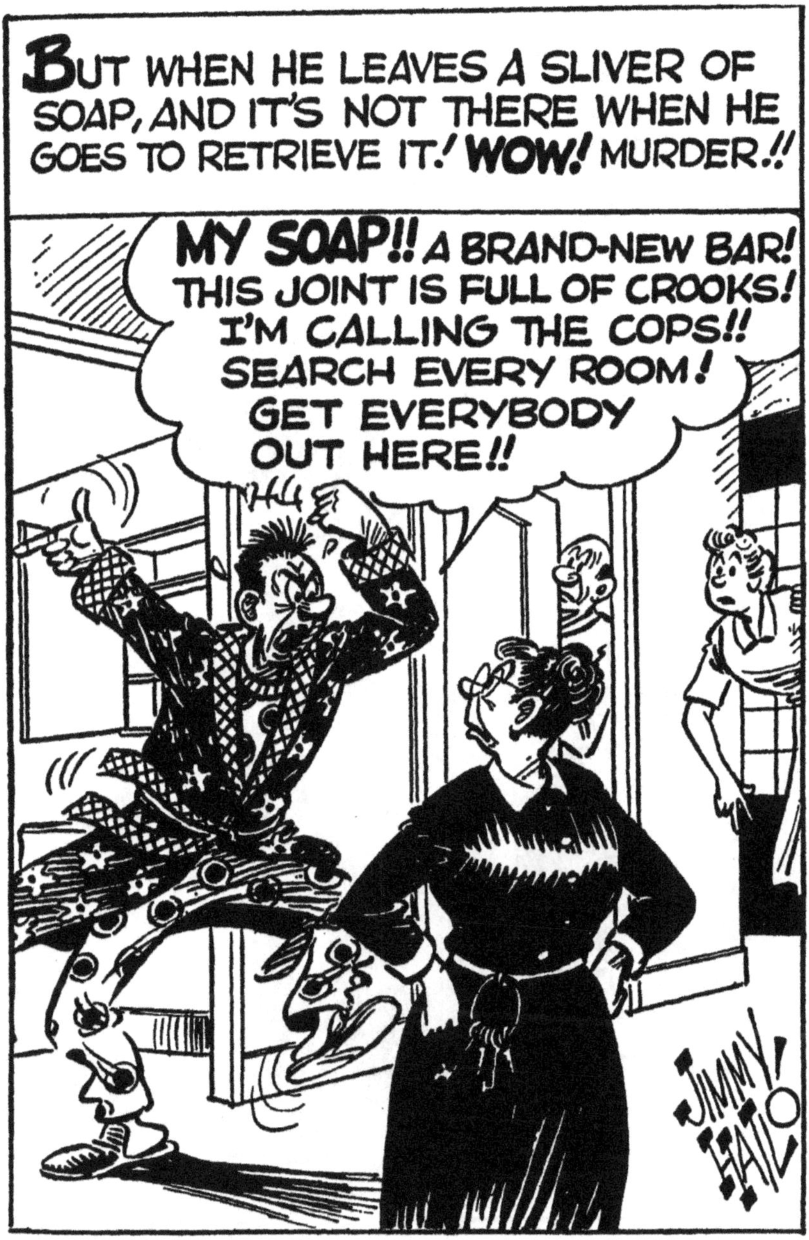
BUT WHEN HE LEAVES A SLIVER OF SOAP, AND IT'S NOT THERE WHEN HE GOES TO RETRIEVE IT! WOW! MURDER.!!
MY SOAP!! A BRAND-NEW BAR! THIS JOINT IS FULL OF CROOKS! I'M CALLING THE COPS!! SEARCH EVERY ROOM! GET EVERYBODY OUT HERE!!
JIMMY HATLO

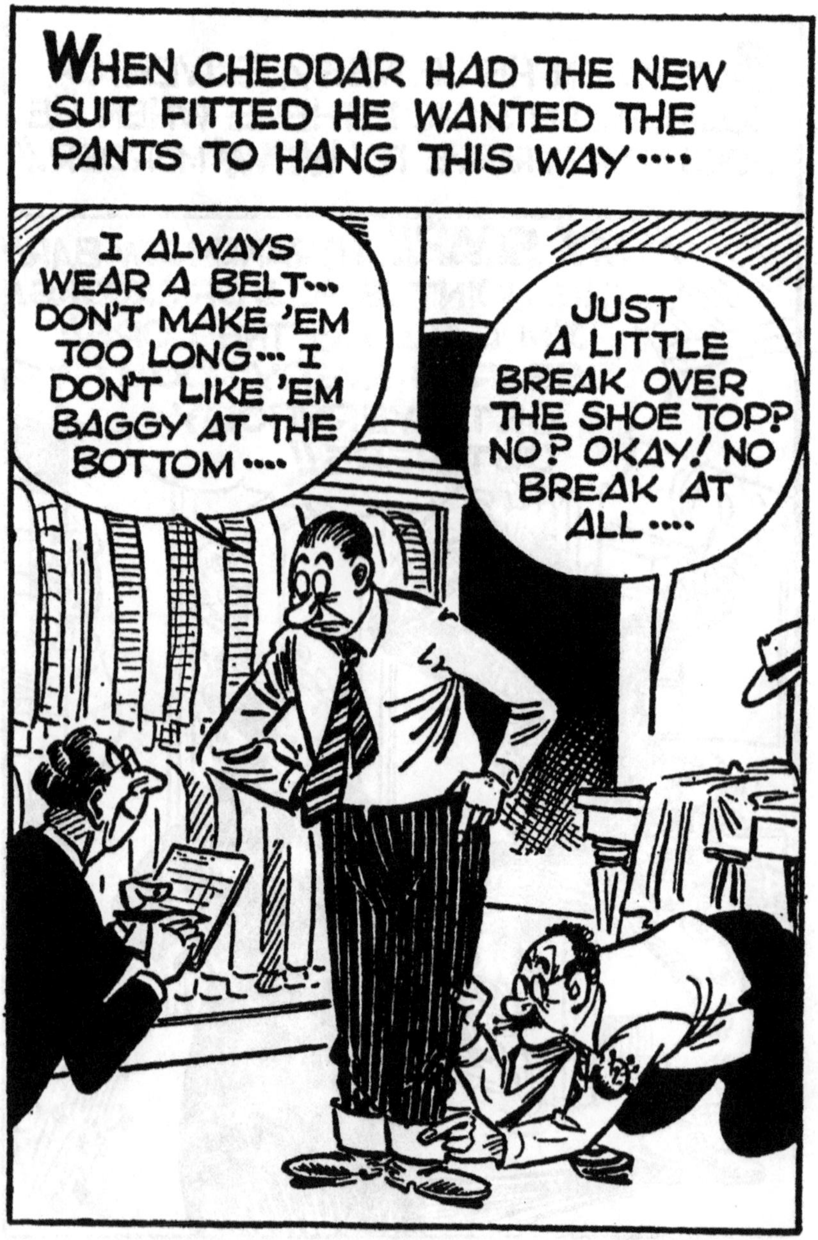
WHEN CHEDDAR HAD THE NEW SUIT FITTED HE WANTED THE PANTS TO HANG THIS WAY....
I ALWAYS WEAR A BELT... DON'T MAKE 'EM TOO LONG... I DON'T LIKE 'EM BAGGY AT THE BOTTOM....
JUST A LITTLE BREAK OVER THE SHOE TOP? NO? OKAY! NO BREAK AT ALL....

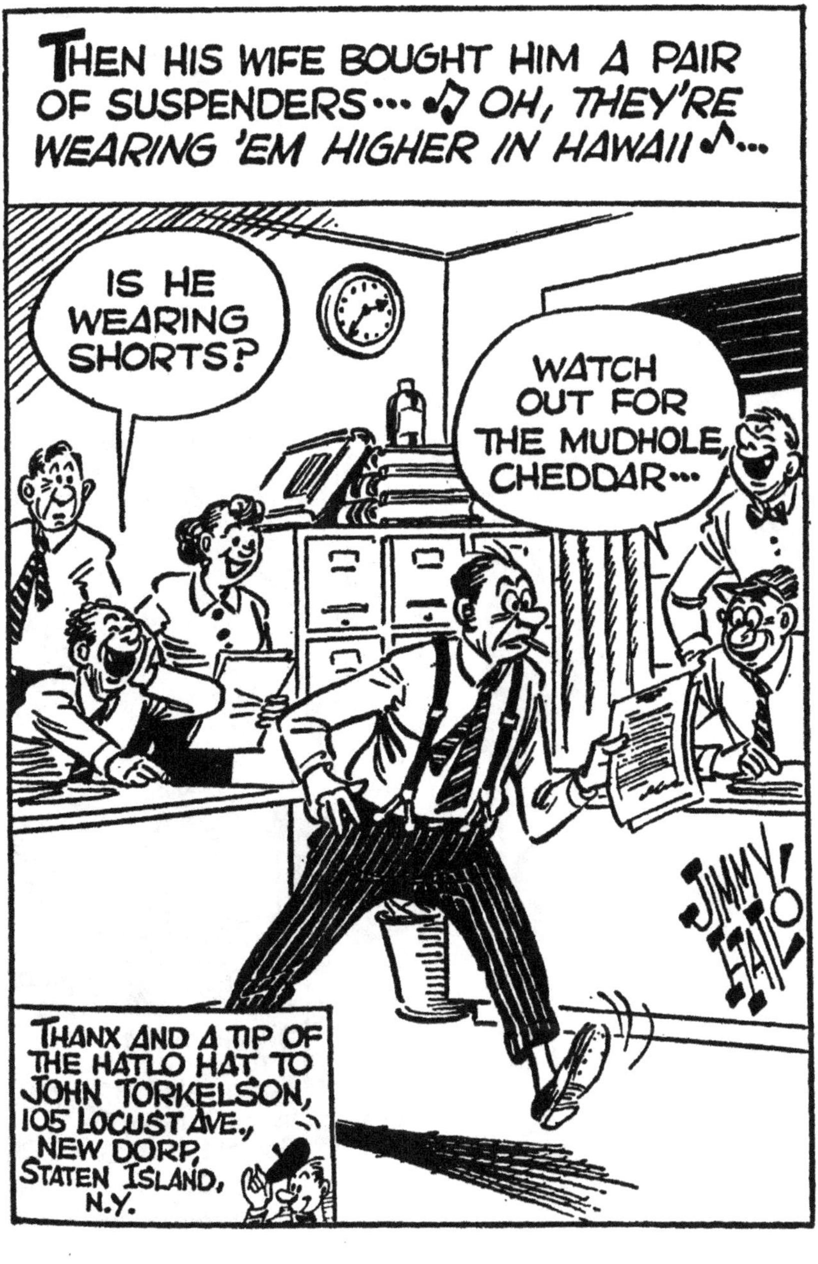
THEN HIS WIFE BOUGHT HIM A PAIR OF SUSPENDERS... ♫ OH, THEY'RE WEARING 'EM HIGHER IN HAWAII ♪...
IS HE WEARING SHORTS?
WATCH OUT FOR THE MUDHOLE, CHEDDAR...
JIMMY HATLO
THANX AND A TIP OF THE HATLO HAT TO JOHN TORKELSON, 105 LOCUST AVE., NEW DORP, STATEN ISLAND, N.Y.

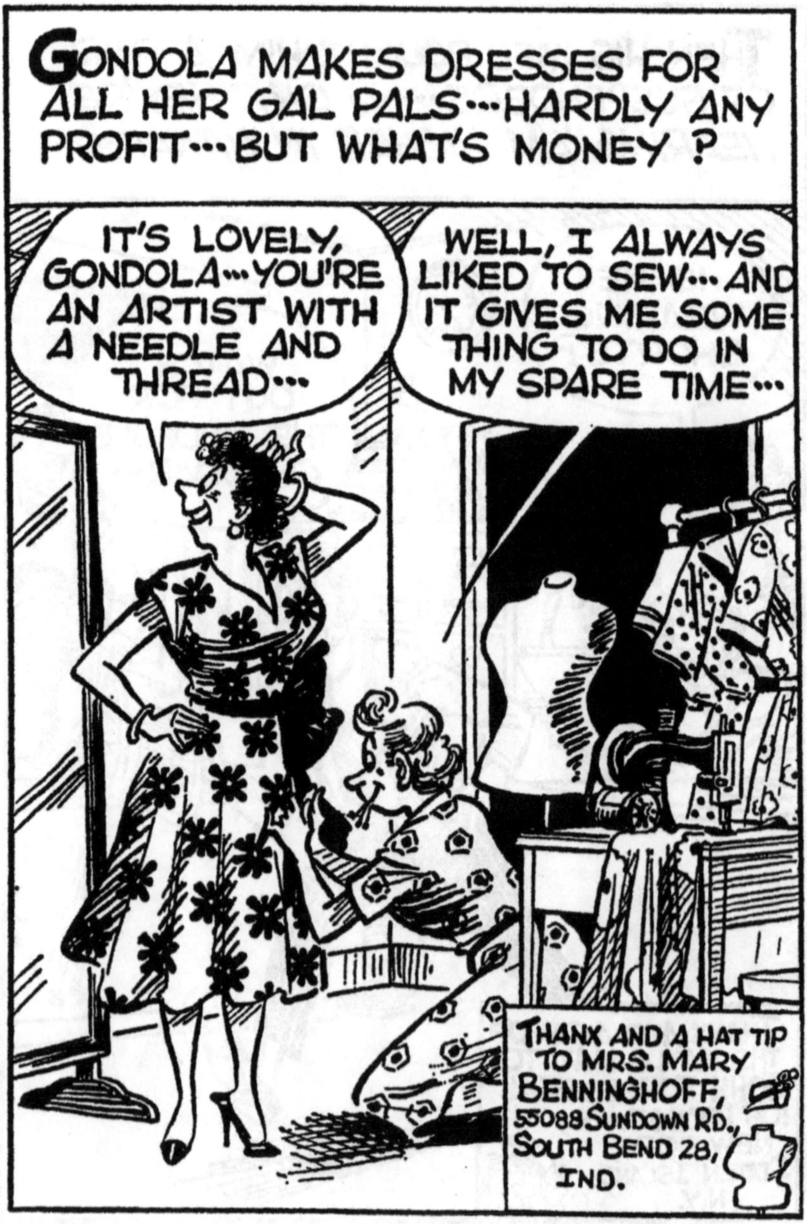
GONDOLA MAKES DRESSES FOR ALL HER GAL PALS···HARDLY ANY PROFIT···BUT WHAT'S MONEY ?
IT'S LOVELY, GONDOLA···YOU'RE AN ARTIST WITH A NEEDLE AND THREAD···
WELL, I ALWAYS LIKED TO SEW···AND IT GIVES ME SOME-THING TO DO IN MY SPARE TIME···
THANX AND A HAT TIP TO MRS. MARY BENNINGHOFF, 55088 SUNDOWN RD., SOUTH BEND 28, IND.

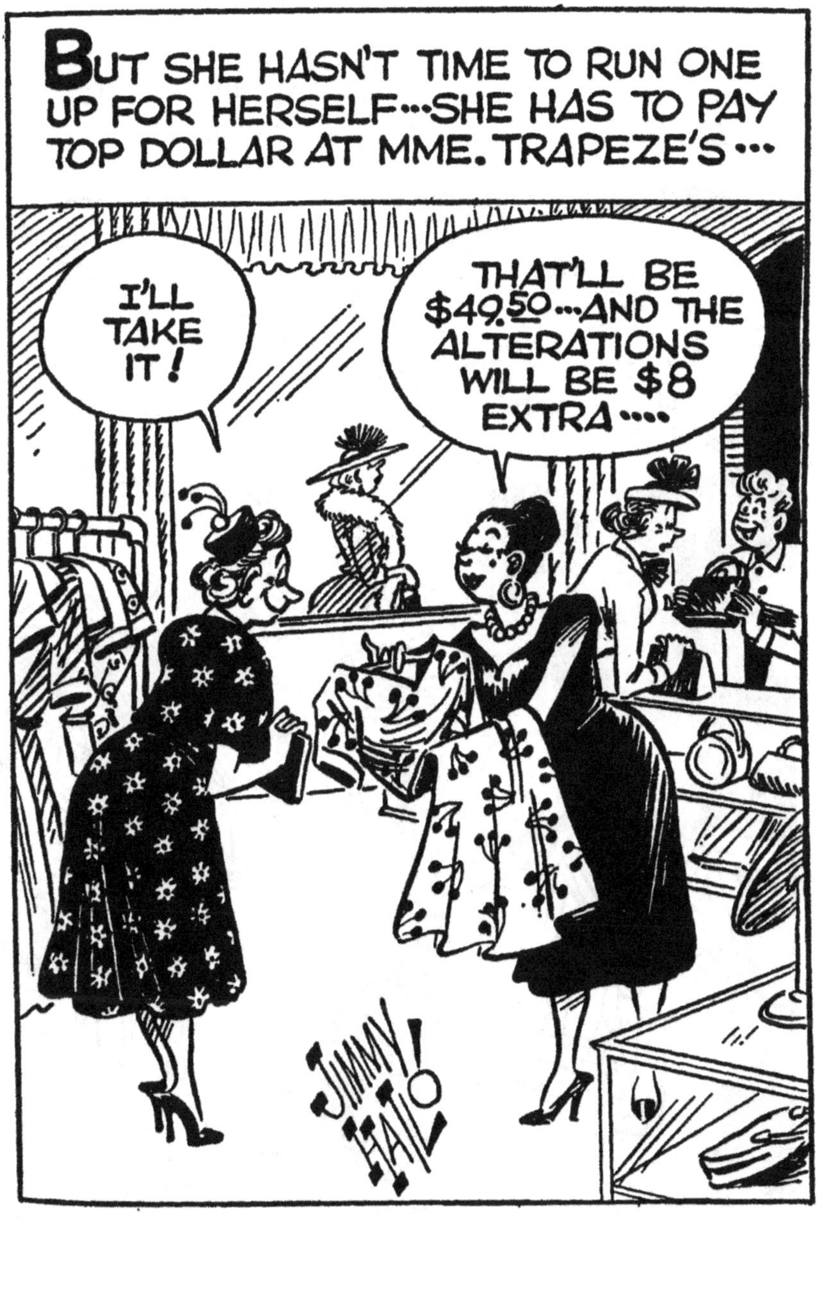
BUT SHE HASN'T TIME TO RUN ONE UP FOR HERSELF---SHE HAS TO PAY TOP DOLLAR AT MME. TRAPEZE'S---
I'LL TAKE IT!
THAT'LL BE $49.50---AND THE ALTERATIONS WILL BE $8 EXTRA----
JIMMY HATLO

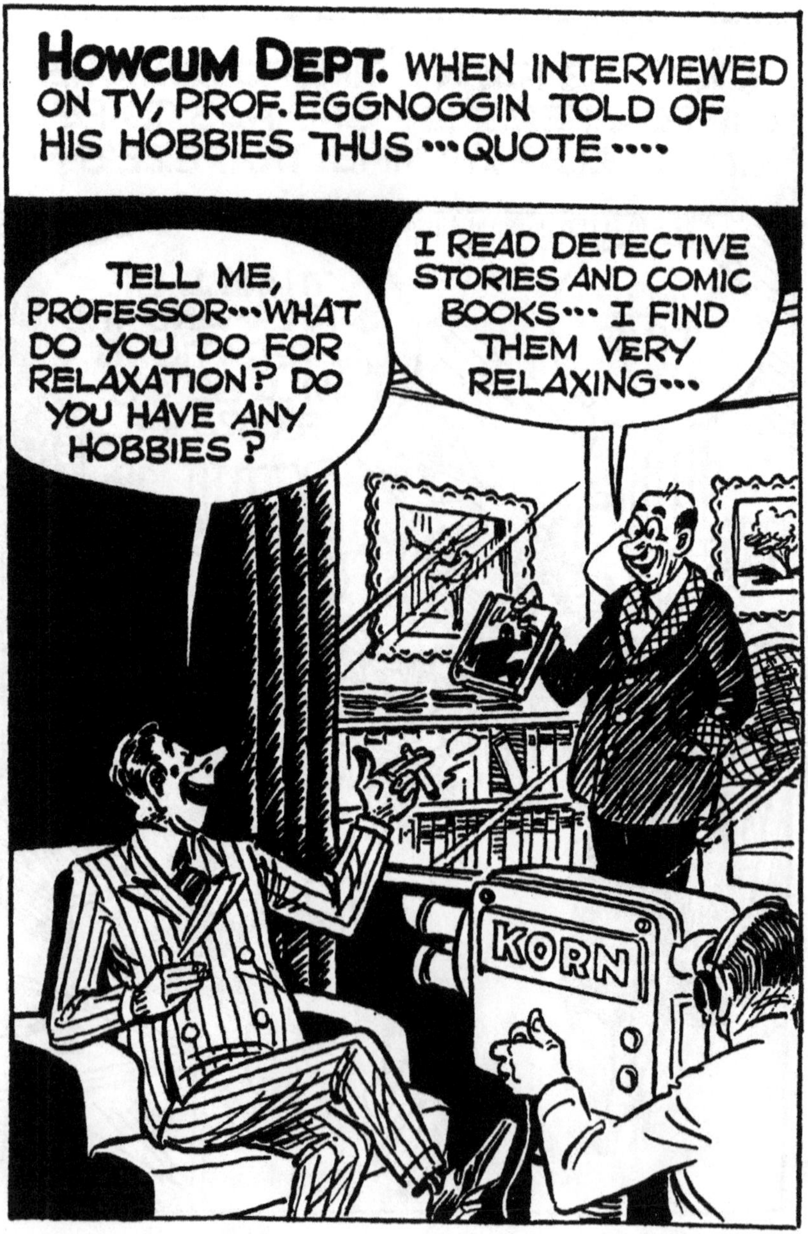
HOWCUM DEPT. WHEN INTERVIEWED ON TV, PROF. EGGNOGGIN TOLD OF HIS HOBBIES THUS ••• QUOTE ••••
TELL ME, PROFESSOR••• WHAT DO YOU DO FOR RELAXATION? DO YOU HAVE ANY HOBBIES?
I READ DETECTIVE STORIES AND COMIC BOOKS••• I FIND THEM VERY RELAXING•••
KORN

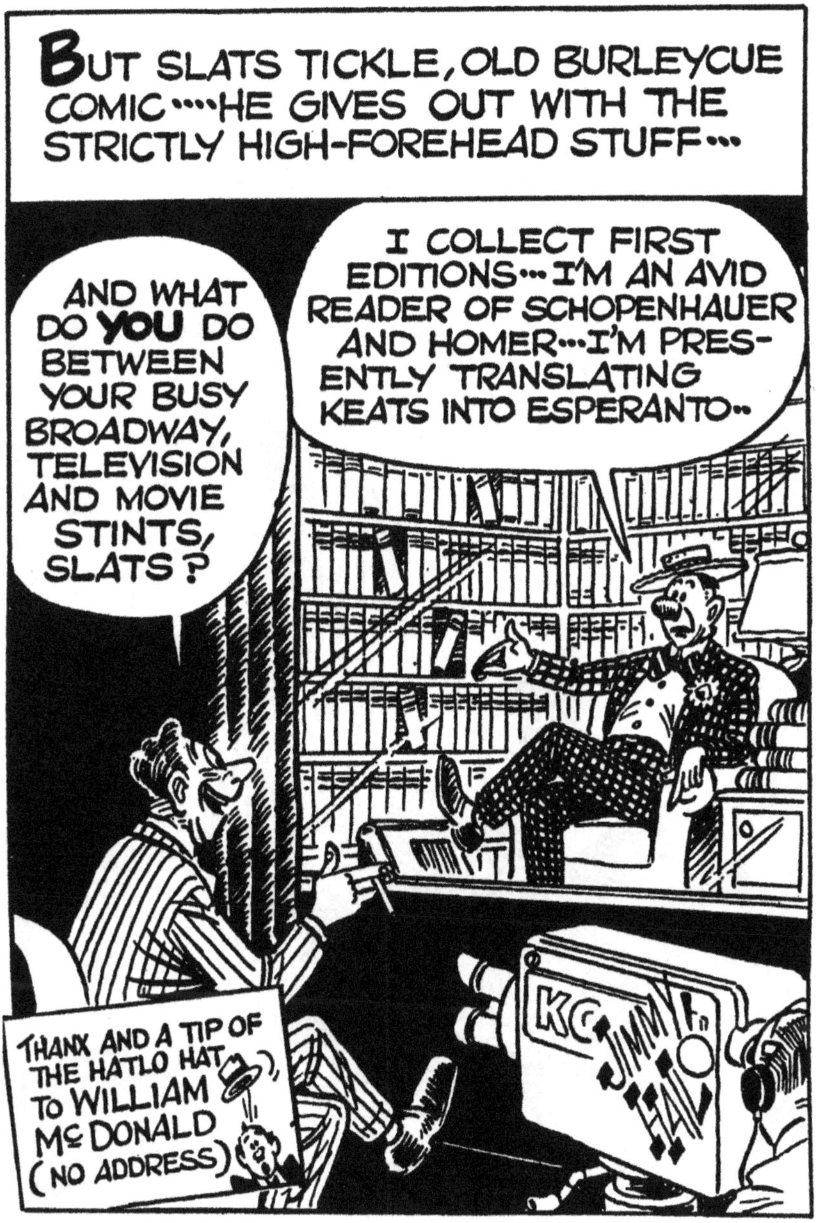
BUT SLATS TICKLE, OLD BURLEYCUE COMIC····HE GIVES OUT WITH THE STRICTLY HIGH-FOREHEAD STUFF···
AND WHAT DO **YOU** DO BETWEEN YOUR BUSY BROADWAY, TELEVISION AND MOVIE STINTS, SLATS?
I COLLECT FIRST EDITIONS···I'M AN AVID READER OF SCHOPENHAUER AND HOMER···I'M PRESENTLY TRANSLATING KEATS INTO ESPERANTO··
THANX AND A TIP OF THE HATLO HAT TO WILLIAM McDONALD (NO ADDRESS)

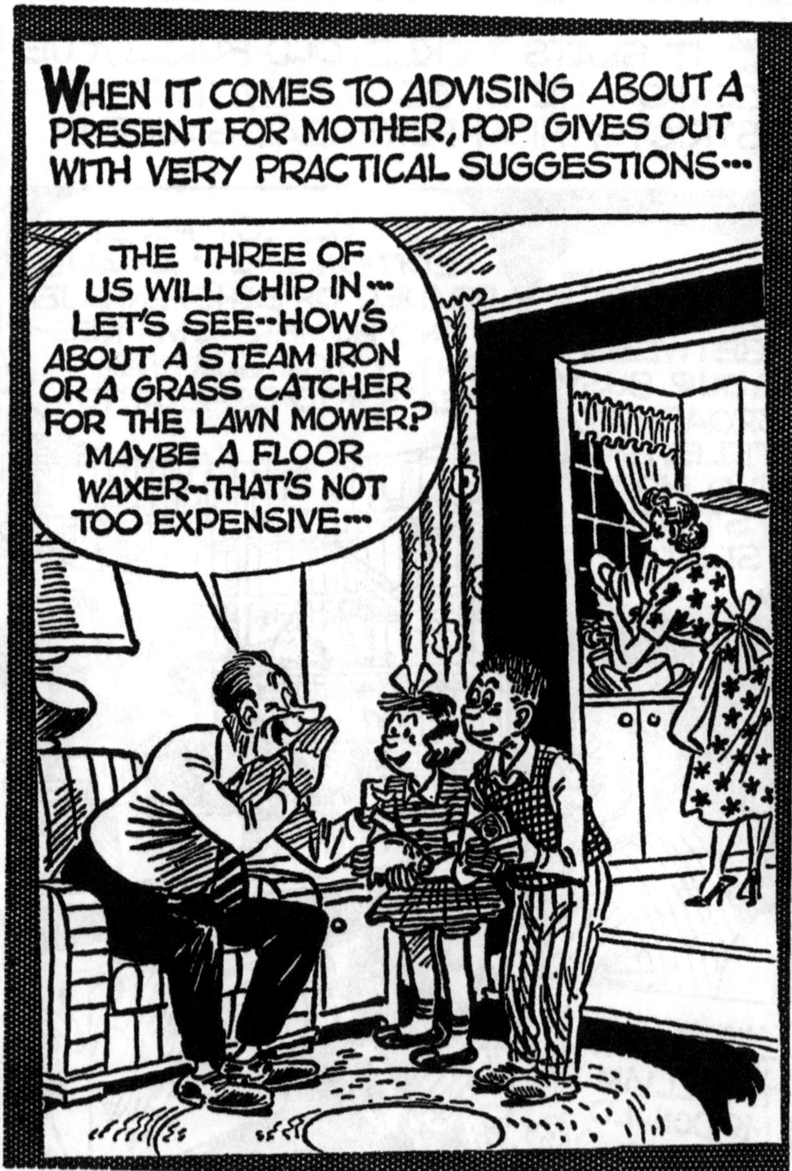
WHEN IT COMES TO ADVISING ABOUT A PRESENT FOR MOTHER, POP GIVES OUT WITH VERY PRACTICAL SUGGESTIONS---
THE THREE OF US WILL CHIP IN--- LET'S SEE--HOW'S ABOUT A STEAM IRON OR A GRASS CATCHER FOR THE LAWN MOWER? MAYBE A FLOOR WAXER--THAT'S NOT TOO EXPENSIVE---

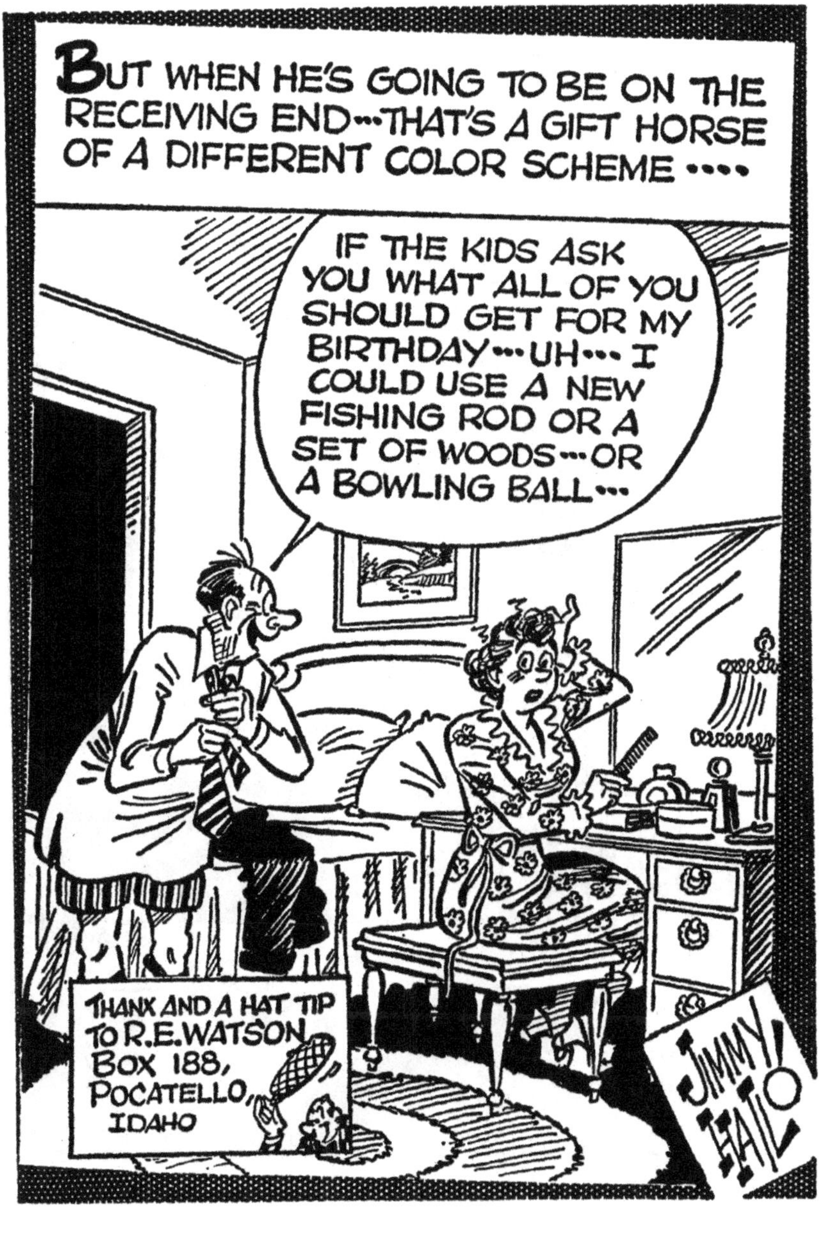
BUT WHEN HE'S GOING TO BE ON THE RECEIVING END···THAT'S A GIFT HORSE OF A DIFFERENT COLOR SCHEME····
IF THE KIDS ASK YOU WHAT ALL OF YOU SHOULD GET FOR MY BIRTHDAY···UH··· I COULD USE A NEW FISHING ROD OR A SET OF WOODS···OR A BOWLING BALL···
THANX AND A HAT TIP TO R.E.WATSON BOX 188, POCATELLO, IDAHO
JIMMY HATLO

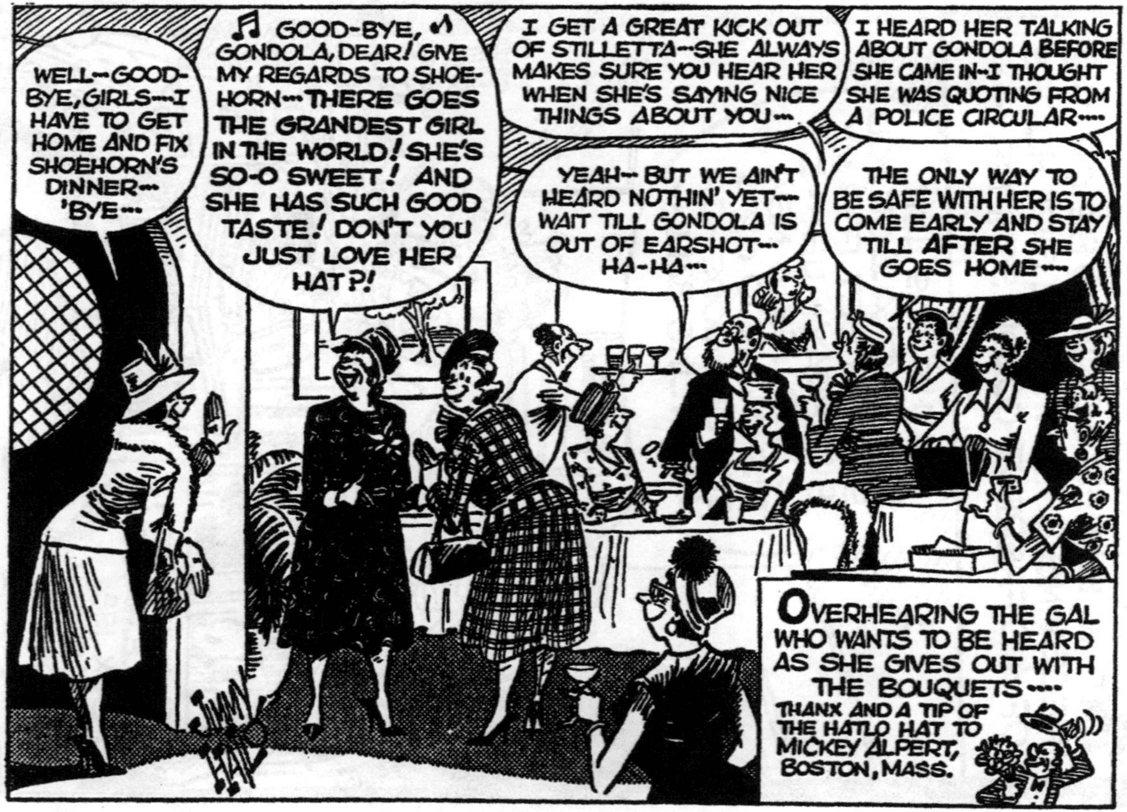
WELL--GOOD-BYE, GIRLS---I HAVE TO GET HOME AND FIX SHOEHORN'S DINNER--- 'BYE---
GOOD-BYE, GONDOLA, DEAR! GIVE MY REGARDS TO SHOE-HORN---THERE GOES THE GRANDEST GIRL IN THE WORLD! SHE'S SO-O SWEET! AND SHE HAS SUCH GOOD TASTE! DON'T YOU JUST LOVE HER HAT?!
I GET A GREAT KICK OUT OF STILLETTA--SHE ALWAYS MAKES SURE YOU HEAR HER WHEN SHE'S SAYING NICE THINGS ABOUT YOU---
I HEARD HER TALKING ABOUT GONDOLA BEFORE SHE CAME IN--I THOUGHT SHE WAS QUOTING FROM A POLICE CIRCULAR----
YEAH-- BUT WE AIN'T HEARD NOTHIN' YET--- WAIT TILL GONDOLA IS OUT OF EARSHOT--- HA-HA---
THE ONLY WAY TO BE SAFE WITH HER IS TO COME EARLY AND STAY TILL AFTER SHE GOES HOME----
OVERHEARING THE GAL WHO WANTS TO BE HEARD AS SHE GIVES OUT WITH THE BOUQUETS----
THANX AND A TIP OF THE HATLO HAT TO MICKEY ALPERT, BOSTON, MASS.
JIMMY HATLO

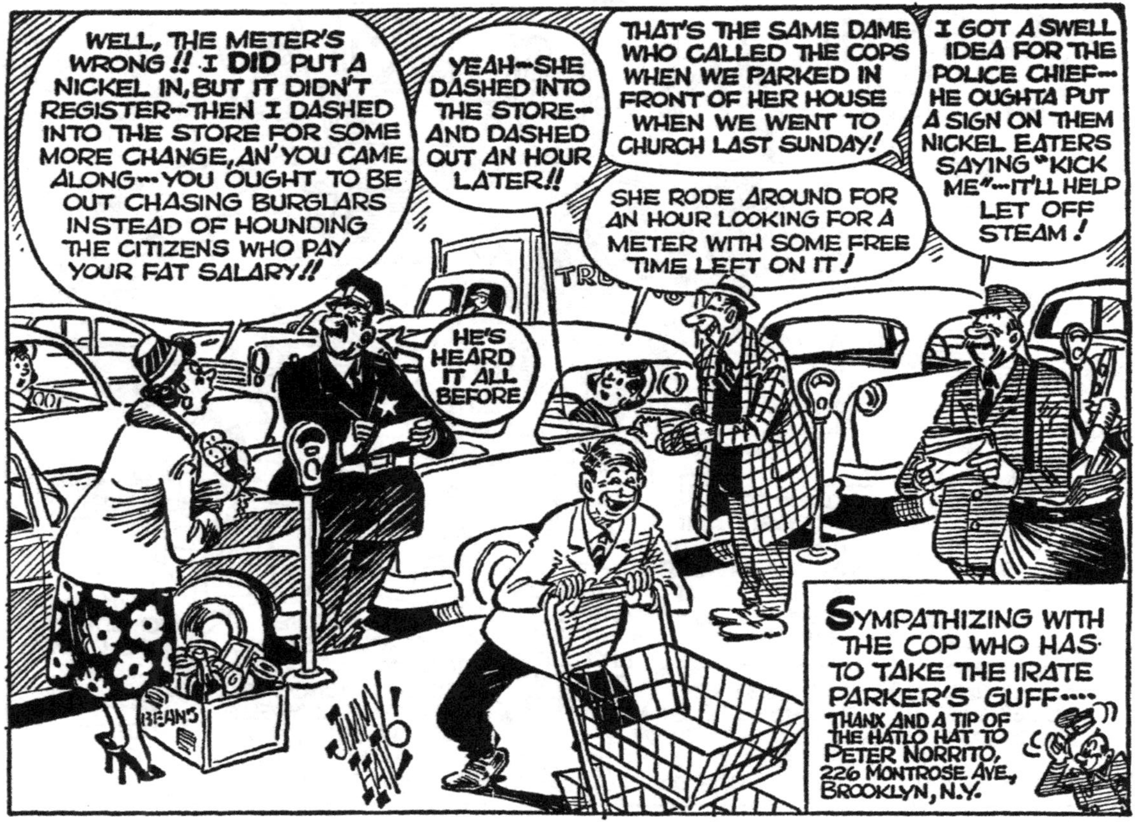
WELL, THE METER'S WRONG!! I DID PUT A NICKEL IN, BUT IT DIDN'T REGISTER--THEN I DASHED INTO THE STORE FOR SOME MORE CHANGE, AN' YOU CAME ALONG--YOU OUGHT TO BE OUT CHASING BURGLARS INSTEAD OF HOUNDING THE CITIZENS WHO PAY YOUR FAT SALARY!!
YEAH--SHE DASHED INTO THE STORE--AND DASHED OUT AN HOUR LATER!!
HE'S HEARD IT ALL BEFORE
THAT'S THE SAME DAME WHO CALLED THE COPS WHEN WE PARKED IN FRONT OF HER HOUSE WHEN WE WENT TO CHURCH LAST SUNDAY!
SHE RODE AROUND FOR AN HOUR LOOKING FOR A METER WITH SOME FREE TIME LEFT ON IT!
I GOT A SWELL IDEA FOR THE POLICE CHIEF--HE OUGHTA PUT A SIGN ON THEM NICKEL EATERS SAYING "KICK ME"--IT'LL HELP LET OFF STEAM!
BEANS
JIMMY HATLO
SYMPATHIZING WITH THE COP WHO HAS TO TAKE THE IRATE PARKER'S GUFF....
THANX AND A TIP OF THE HATLO HAT TO PETER NORRITO, 226 MONTROSE AVE, BROOKLYN, N.Y.

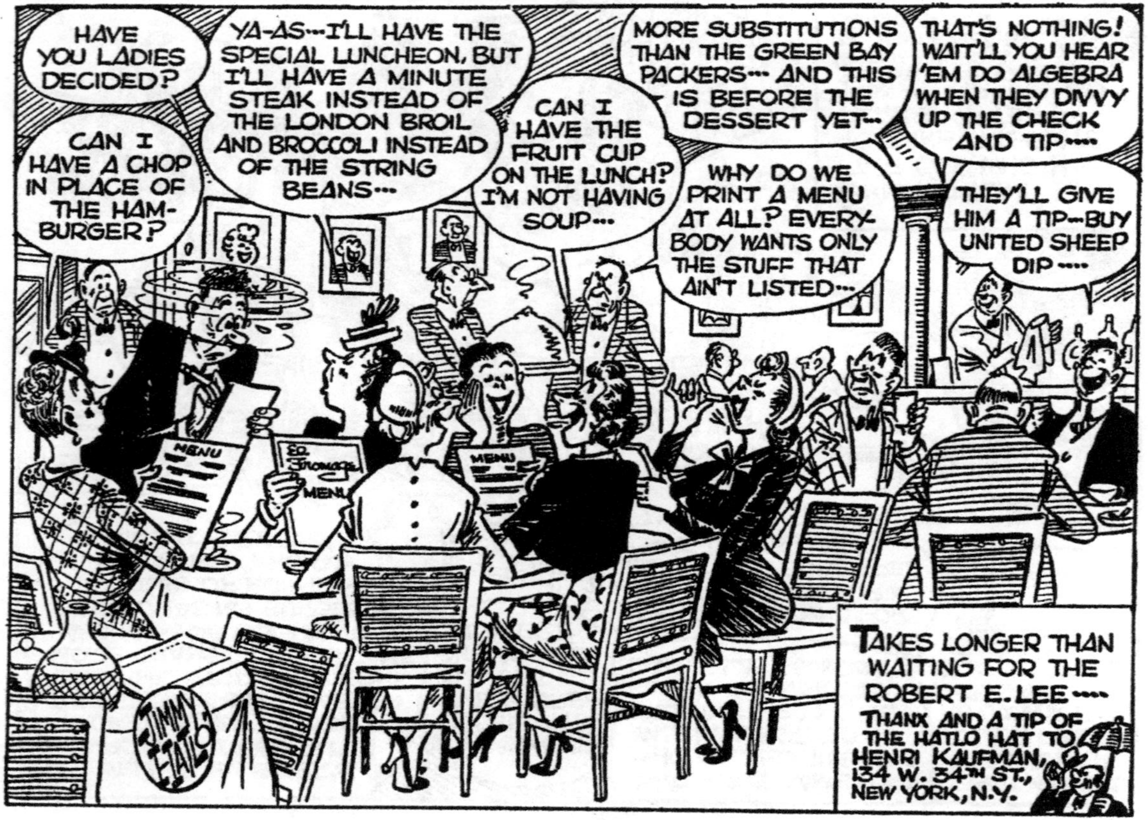
HAVE YOU LADIES DECIDED?
CAN I HAVE A CHOP IN PLACE OF THE HAM-BURGER?
YA-AS---I'LL HAVE THE SPECIAL LUNCHEON, BUT I'LL HAVE A MINUTE STEAK INSTEAD OF THE LONDON BROIL AND BROCCOLI INSTEAD OF THE STRING BEANS---
CAN I HAVE THE FRUIT CUP ON THE LUNCH? I'M NOT HAVING SOUP---
MORE SUBSTITUTIONS THAN THE GREEN BAY PACKERS--- AND THIS IS BEFORE THE DESSERT YET---
WHY DO WE PRINT A MENU AT ALL? EVERY-BODY WANTS ONLY THE STUFF THAT AIN'T LISTED---
THAT'S NOTHING! WAIT'LL YOU HEAR 'EM DO ALGEBRA WHEN THEY DIVVY UP THE CHECK AND TIP----
THEY'LL GIVE HIM A TIP--BUY UNITED SHEEP DIP----
MENU
MENU
MENU
TAKES LONGER THAN WAITING FOR THE ROBERT E. LEE----
THANX AND A TIP OF THE HATLO HAT TO HENRI KAUFMAN, 134 W. 34TH ST., NEW YORK, N.Y.
JIMMY HATLO

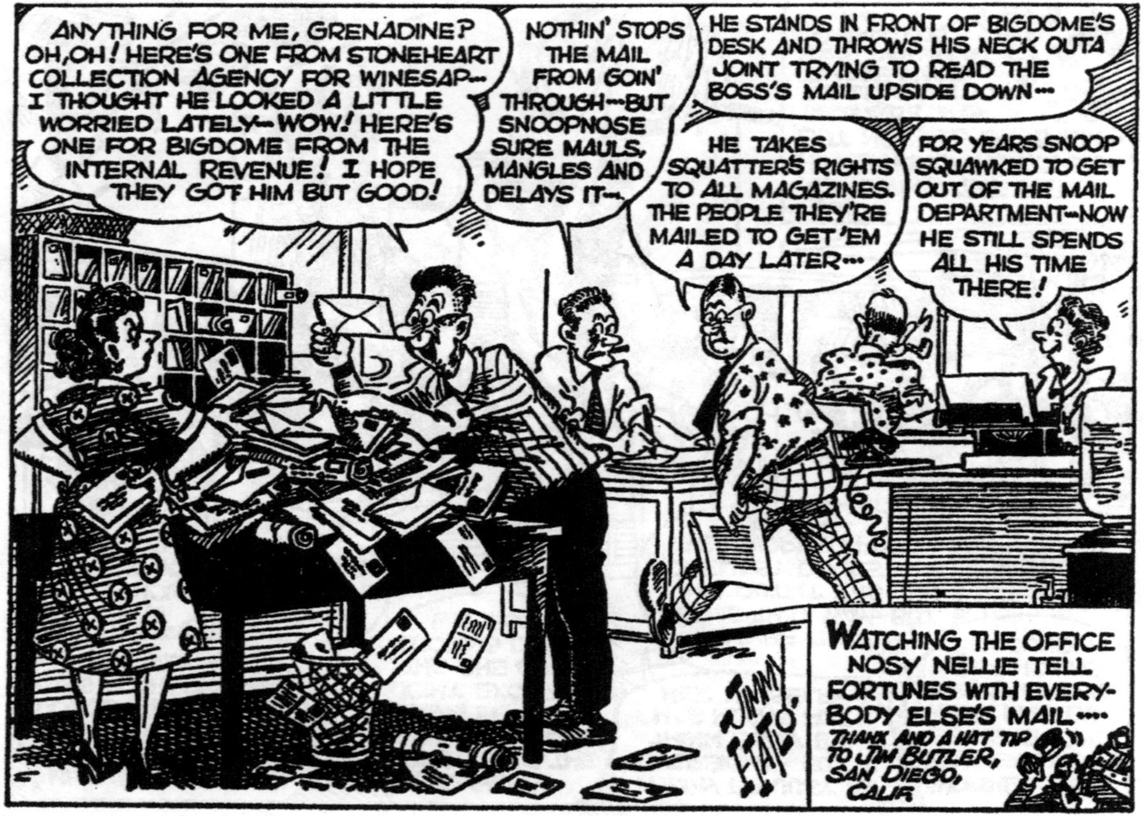
ANYTHING FOR ME, GRENADINE? OH,OH! HERE'S ONE FROM STONEHEART COLLECTION AGENCY FOR WINESAP--- I THOUGHT HE LOOKED A LITTLE WORRIED LATELY--WOW! HERE'S ONE FOR BIGDOME FROM THE INTERNAL REVENUE! I HOPE THEY GOT HIM BUT GOOD!
NOTHIN' STOPS THE MAIL FROM GOIN' THROUGH---BUT SNOOPNOSE SURE MAULS, MANGLES AND DELAYS IT--.
HE STANDS IN FRONT OF BIGDOME'S DESK AND THROWS HIS NECK OUTA JOINT TRYING TO READ THE BOSS'S MAIL UPSIDE DOWN---
HE TAKES SQUATTER'S RIGHTS TO ALL MAGAZINES. THE PEOPLE THEY'RE MAILED TO GET 'EM A DAY LATER---
FOR YEARS SNOOP SQUAWKED TO GET OUT OF THE MAIL DEPARTMENT--NOW HE STILL SPENDS ALL HIS TIME THERE!
JIMMY HATLO
WATCHING THE OFFICE NOSY NELLIE TELL FORTUNES WITH EVERYBODY ELSE'S MAIL....
THANK AND A HAT TIP TO JIM BUTLER, SAN DIEGO, CALIF.

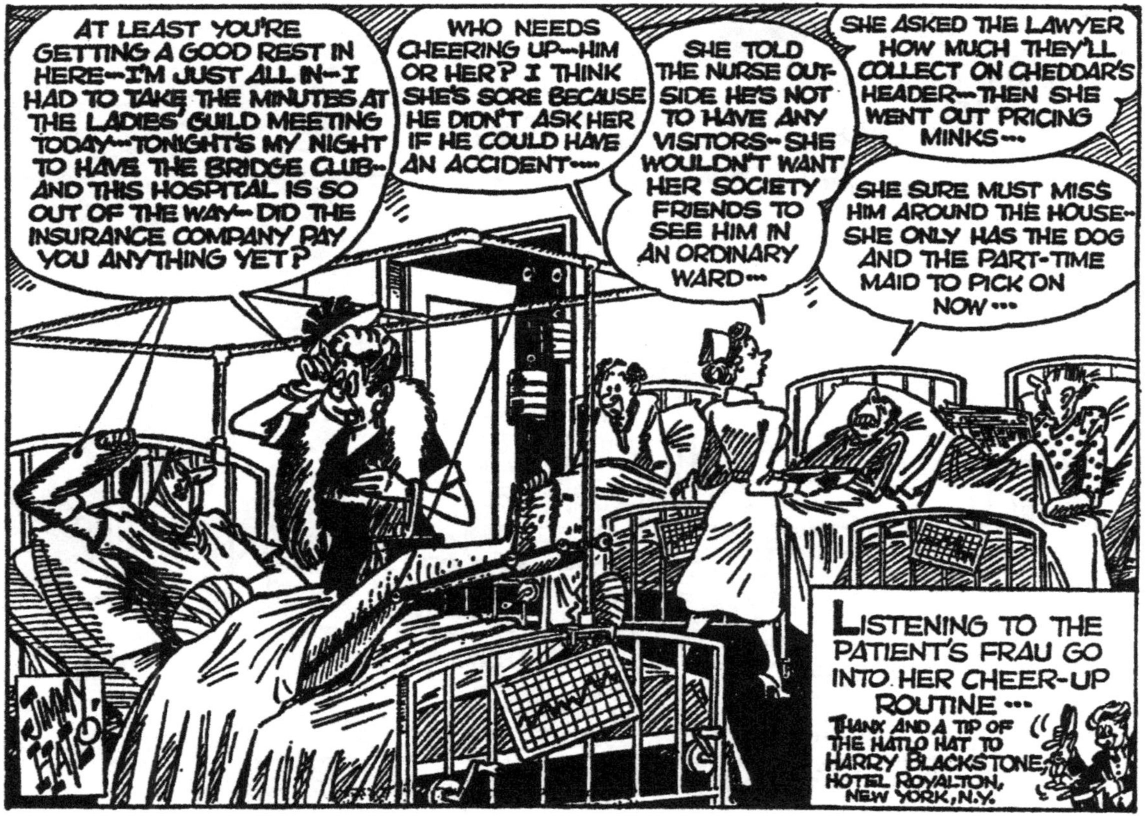
AT LEAST YOU'RE GETTING A GOOD REST IN HERE--I'M JUST ALL IN--I HAD TO TAKE THE MINUTES AT THE LADIES' GUILD MEETING TODAY--TONIGHT'S MY NIGHT TO HAVE THE BRIDGE CLUB--AND THIS HOSPITAL IS SO OUT OF THE WAY--DID THE INSURANCE COMPANY PAY YOU ANYTHING YET?
WHO NEEDS CHEERING UP--HIM OR HER? I THINK SHE'S SORE BECAUSE HE DIDN'T ASK HER IF HE COULD HAVE AN ACCIDENT...
SHE TOLD THE NURSE OUTSIDE HE'S NOT TO HAVE ANY VISITORS--SHE WOULDN'T WANT HER SOCIETY FRIENDS TO SEE HIM IN AN ORDINARY WARD...
SHE ASKED THE LAWYER HOW MUCH THEY'LL COLLECT ON CHEDDAR'S HEADER--THEN SHE WENT OUT PRICING MINKS...
SHE SURE MUST MISS HIM AROUND THE HOUSE--SHE ONLY HAS THE DOG AND THE PART-TIME MAID TO PICK ON NOW...
LISTENING TO THE PATIENT'S FRAU GO INTO HER CHEER-UP ROUTINE...
THANX AND A TIP OF THE HATLO HAT TO HARRY BLACKSTONE, HOTEL ROYALTON, NEW YORK, N.Y.
JIMMY HATLO

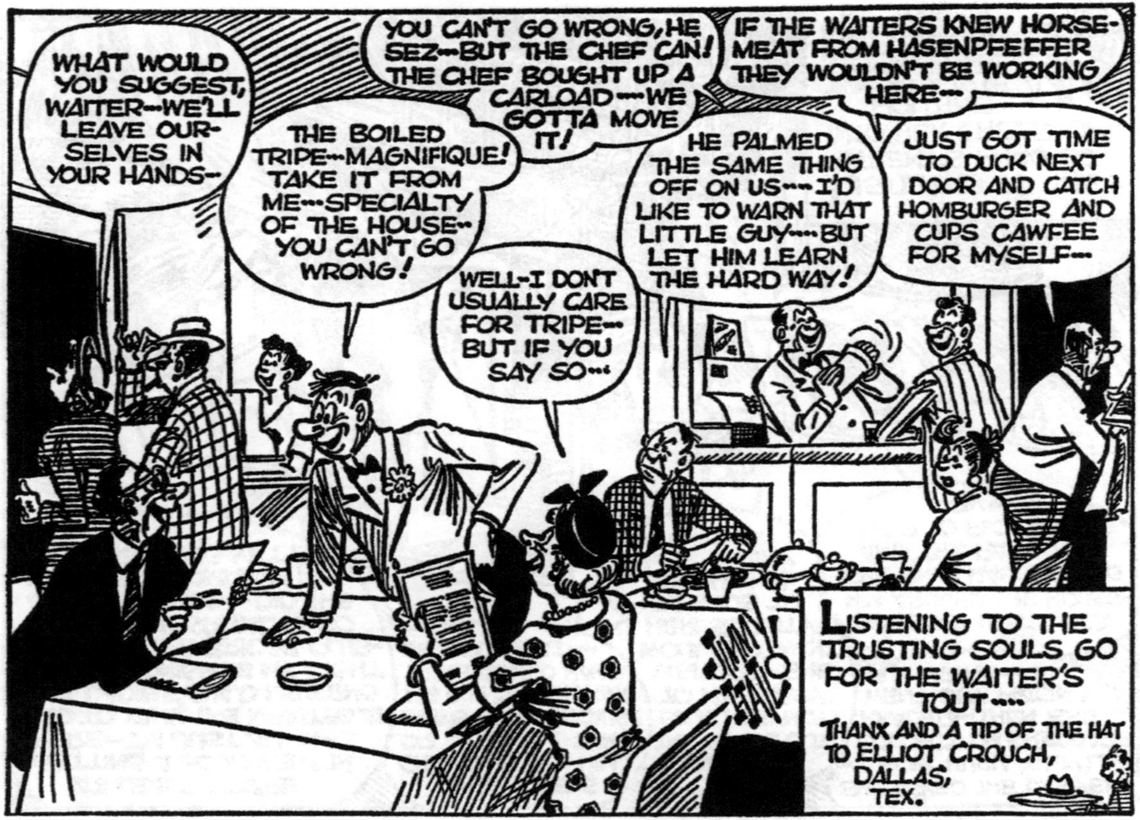
WHAT WOULD YOU SUGGEST, WAITER---WE'LL LEAVE OURSELVES IN YOUR HANDS--
THE BOILED TRIPE--MAGNIFIQUE! TAKE IT FROM ME---SPECIALTY OF THE HOUSE-- YOU CAN'T GO WRONG!
YOU CAN'T GO WRONG, HE SEZ---BUT THE CHEF CAN! THE CHEF BOUGHT UP A CARLOAD---WE GOTTA MOVE IT!
WELL-I DON'T USUALLY CARE FOR TRIPE--- BUT IF YOU SAY SO---
HE PALMED THE SAME THING OFF ON US---I'D LIKE TO WARN THAT LITTLE GUY---BUT LET HIM LEARN THE HARD WAY!
IF THE WAITERS KNEW HORSE-MEAT FROM HASENPFEFFER THEY WOULDN'T BE WORKING HERE---
JUST GOT TIME TO DUCK NEXT DOOR AND CATCH HOMBURGER AND CUPS CAWFEE FOR MYSELF---
LISTENING TO THE TRUSTING SOULS GO FOR THE WAITER'S TOUT---
THANX AND A TIP OF THE HAT TO ELLIOT CROUCH, DALLAS, TEX.

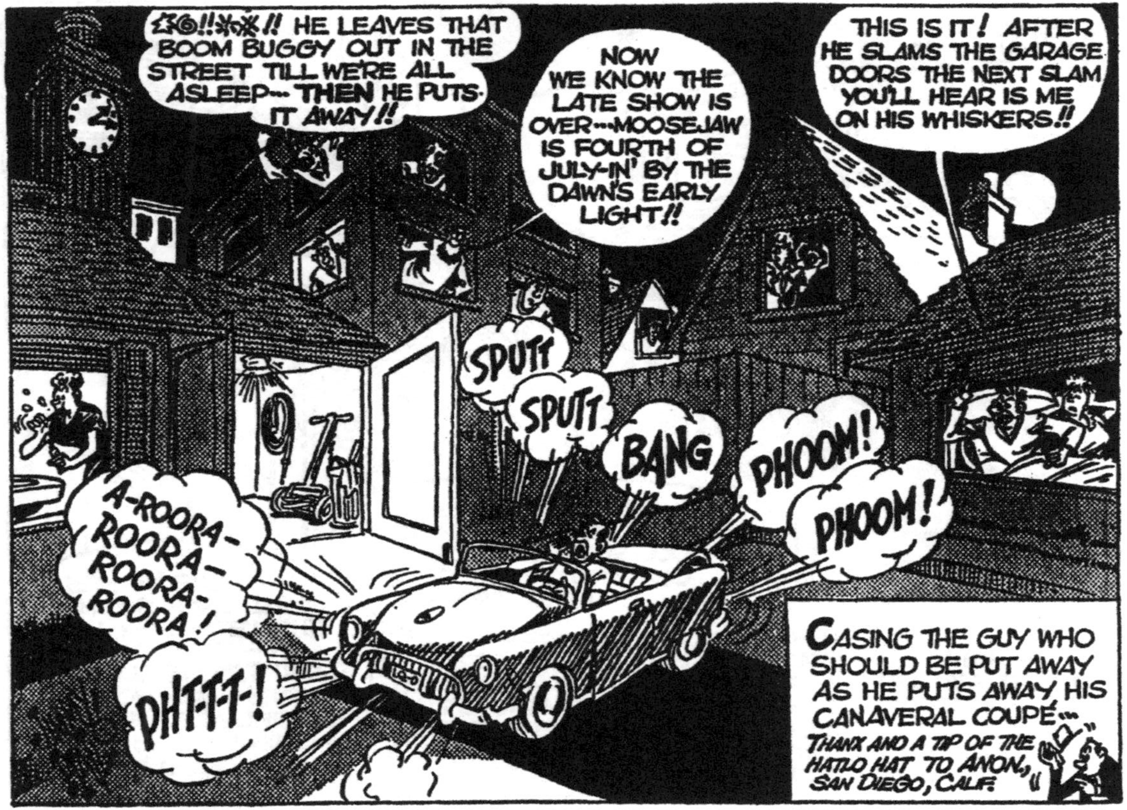

!!!!! HE LEAVES THAT BOOM BUGGY OUT IN THE STREET TILL WE'RE ALL ASLEEP... THEN HE PUTS IT AWAY!!
NOW WE KNOW THE LATE SHOW IS OVER...MOOSEJAW IS FOURTH OF JULY-IN' BY THE DAWN'S EARLY LIGHT!!
THIS IS IT! AFTER HE SLAMS THE GARAGE DOORS THE NEXT SLAM YOU'LL HEAR IS ME ON HIS WHISKERS!!
SPUTT
SPUTT
BANG
PHOOM!
PHOOM!
A-ROORA-ROORA-ROORA-ROORA!
PHT-T-T-!
CASING THE GUY WHO SHOULD BE PUT AWAY AS HE PUTS AWAY HIS CANAVERAL COUPÉ...
THANX AND A TIP OF THE HATLO HAT TO ANON, SAN DIEGO, CALIF.

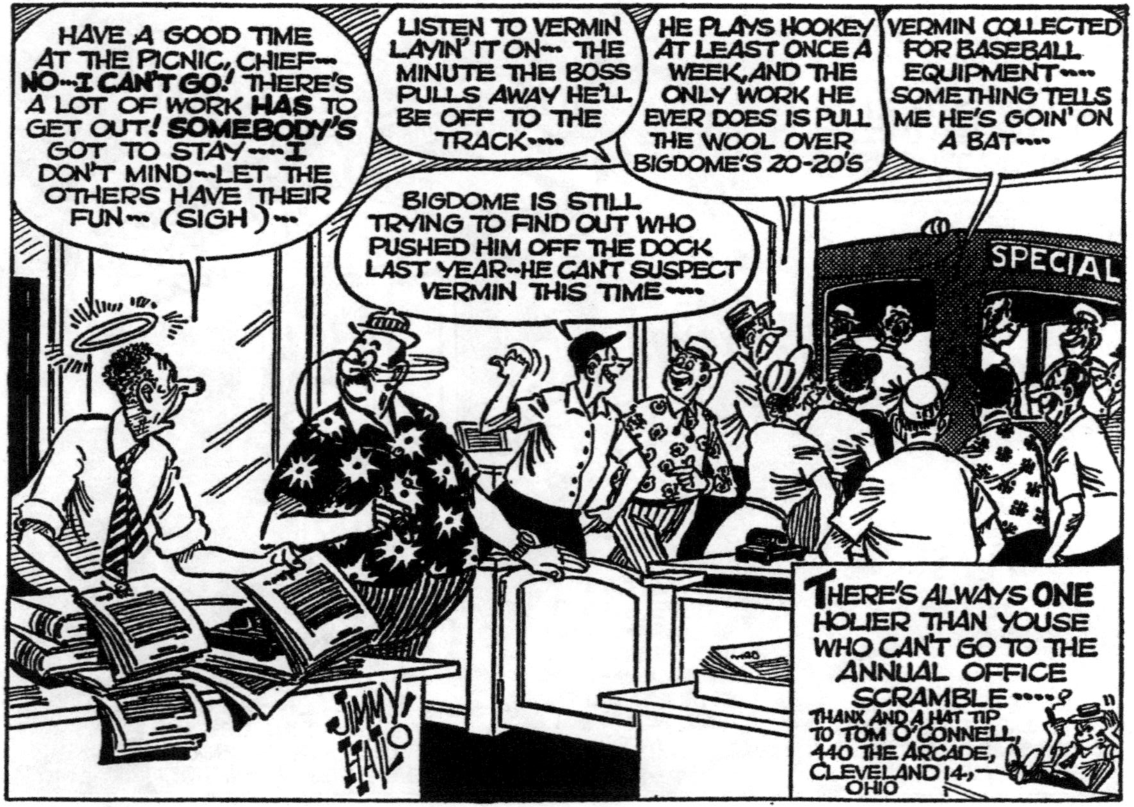

HAVE A GOOD TIME AT THE PICNIC, CHIEF--- NO--I CAN'T GO! THERE'S A LOT OF WORK HAS TO GET OUT! SOMEBODY'S GOT TO STAY----I DON'T MIND--LET THE OTHERS HAVE THEIR FUN--- (SIGH)---
LISTEN TO VERMIN LAYIN' IT ON--- THE MINUTE THE BOSS PULLS AWAY HE'LL BE OFF TO THE TRACK----
BIGDOME IS STILL TRYING TO FIND OUT WHO PUSHED HIM OFF THE DOCK LAST YEAR--HE CAN'T SUSPECT VERMIN THIS TIME----
HE PLAYS HOOKEY AT LEAST ONCE A WEEK, AND THE ONLY WORK HE EVER DOES IS PULL THE WOOL OVER BIGDOME'S 20-20'S
VERMIN COLLECTED FOR BASEBALL EQUIPMENT---- SOMETHING TELLS ME HE'S GOIN' ON A BAT----
SPECIAL
THERE'S ALWAYS ONE HOLIER THAN YOUSE WHO CAN'T GO TO THE ANNUAL OFFICE SCRAMBLE----?
THANX AND A HAT TIP TO TOM O'CONNELL, 440 THE ARCADE, CLEVELAND 14, OHIO
JIMMY HATLO

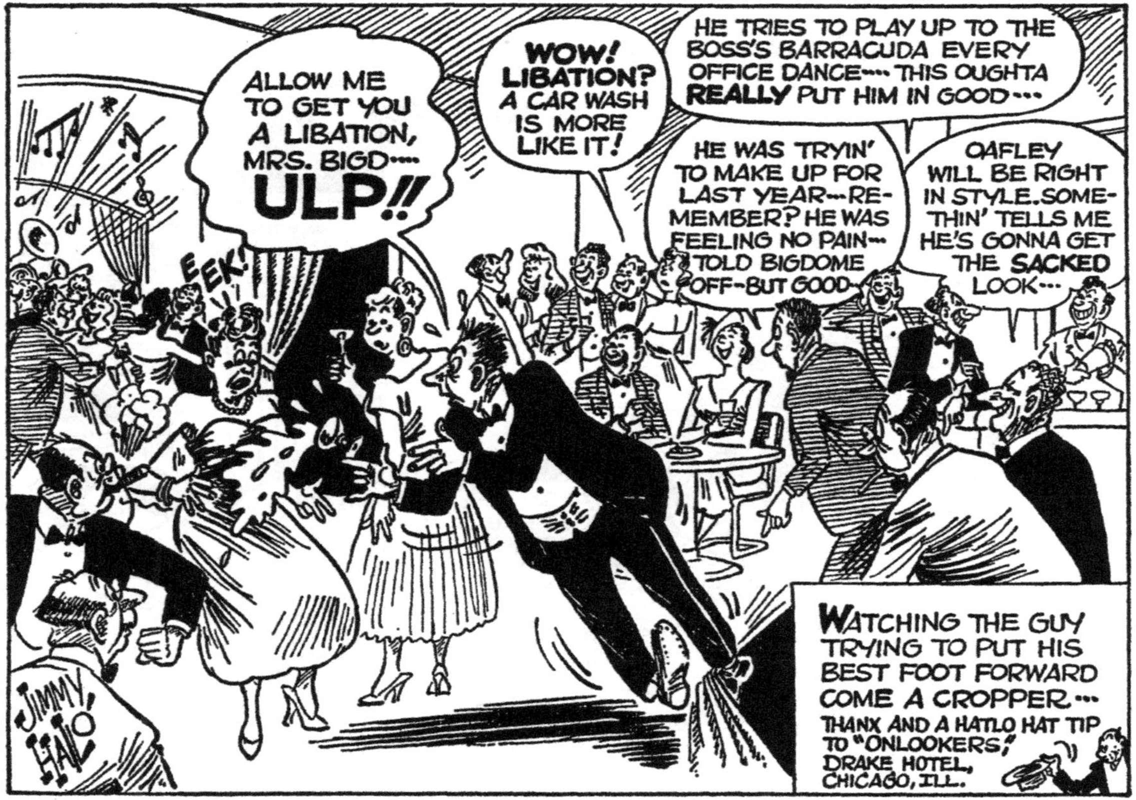
ALLOW ME TO GET YOU A LIBATION, MRS. BIGD---- ULP!!
EEK!
WOW! LIBATION? A CAR WASH IS MORE LIKE IT!
HE TRIES TO PLAY UP TO THE BOSS'S BARRACUDA EVERY OFFICE DANCE---- THIS OUGHTA REALLY PUT HIM IN GOOD---
HE WAS TRYIN' TO MAKE UP FOR LAST YEAR---RE-MEMBER? HE WAS FEELING NO PAIN--- TOLD BIGDOME OFF--BUT GOOD--
OAFLEY WILL BE RIGHT IN STYLE. SOME-THIN' TELLS ME HE'S GONNA GET THE SACKED LOOK---
WATCHING THE GUY TRYING TO PUT HIS BEST FOOT FORWARD COME A CROPPER---
THANX AND A HATLO HAT TIP TO "ONLOOKERS," DRAKE HOTEL, CHICAGO, ILL.
JIMMY HATLO

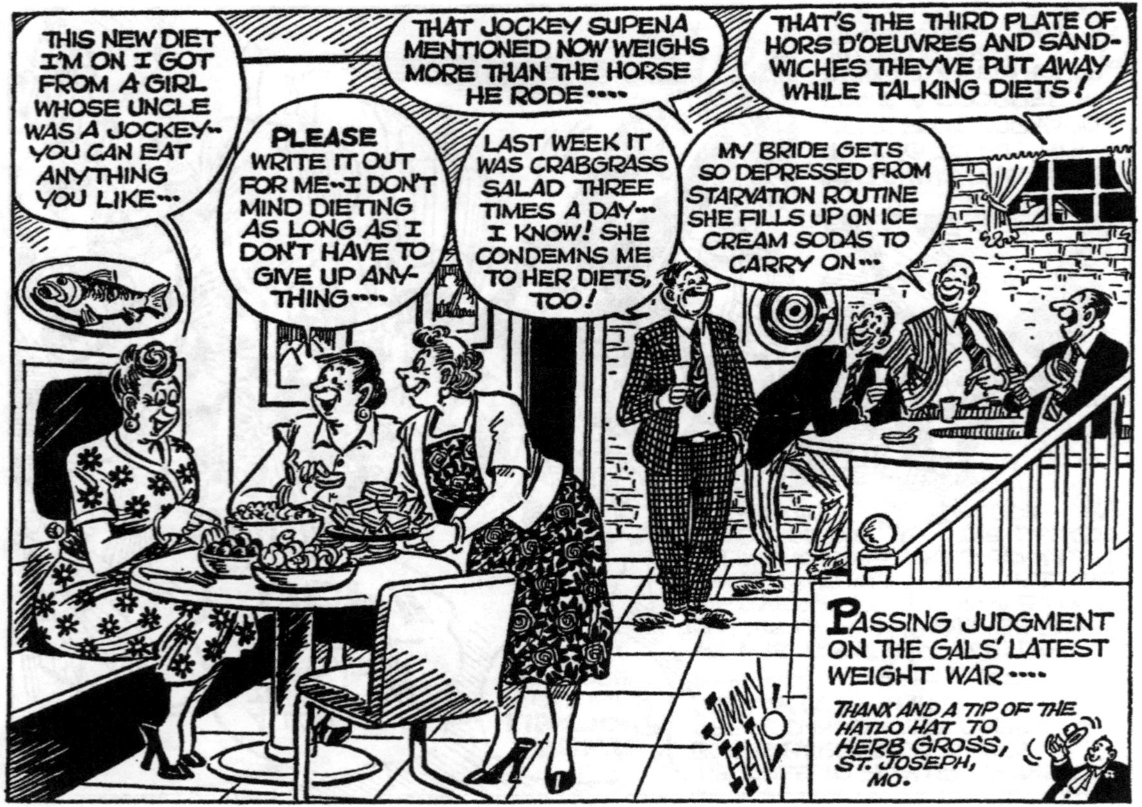
THIS NEW DIET I'M ON I GOT FROM A GIRL WHOSE UNCLE WAS A JOCKEY-- YOU CAN EAT ANYTHING YOU LIKE...
PLEASE WRITE IT OUT FOR ME--I DON'T MIND DIETING AS LONG AS I DON'T HAVE TO GIVE UP ANY-THING....
THAT JOCKEY SUPENA MENTIONED NOW WEIGHS MORE THAN THE HORSE HE RODE....
LAST WEEK IT WAS CRABGRASS SALAD THREE TIMES A DAY... I KNOW! SHE CONDEMNS ME TO HER DIETS, TOO!
THAT'S THE THIRD PLATE OF HORS D'OEUVRES AND SAND-WICHES THEY'VE PUT AWAY WHILE TALKING DIETS!
MY BRIDE GETS SO DEPRESSED FROM STARVATION ROUTINE SHE FILLS UP ON ICE CREAM SODAS TO CARRY ON...
PASSING JUDGMENT ON THE GALS' LATEST WEIGHT WAR....
THANX AND A TIP OF THE HATLO HAT TO HERB GROSS, ST. JOSEPH, MO.
JIMMY HATLO

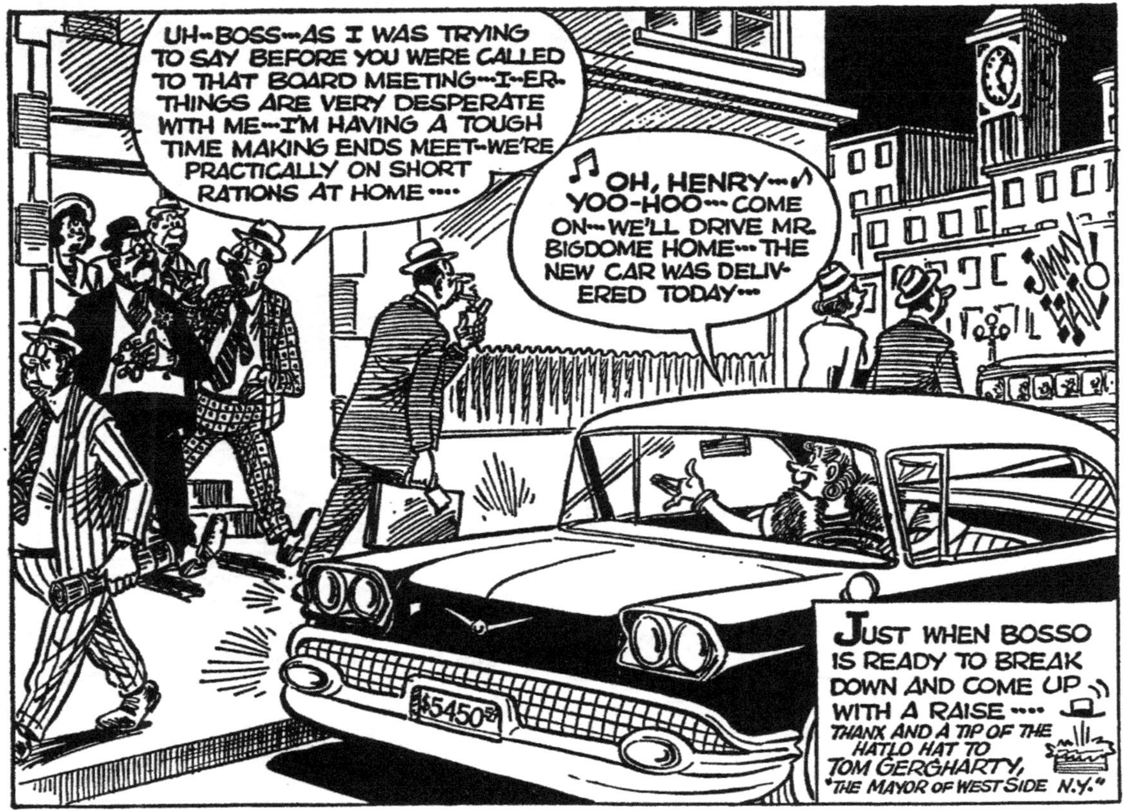
UH--BOSS--AS I WAS TRYING TO SAY BEFORE YOU WERE CALLED TO THAT BOARD MEETING--I--ER-- THINGS ARE VERY DESPERATE WITH ME--I'M HAVING A TOUGH TIME MAKING ENDS MEET--WE'RE PRACTICALLY ON SHORT RATIONS AT HOME....
♫ OH, HENRY--♪ YOO-HOO--COME ON--WE'LL DRIVE MR. BIGDOME HOME--THE NEW CAR WAS DELIVERED TODAY--
JIMMY HATLO
$5450 58
JUST WHEN BOSSO IS READY TO BREAK DOWN AND COME UP WITH A RAISE....
THANX AND A TIP OF THE HATLO HAT TO TOM GERGHARTY, "THE MAYOR OF WEST SIDE N.Y."

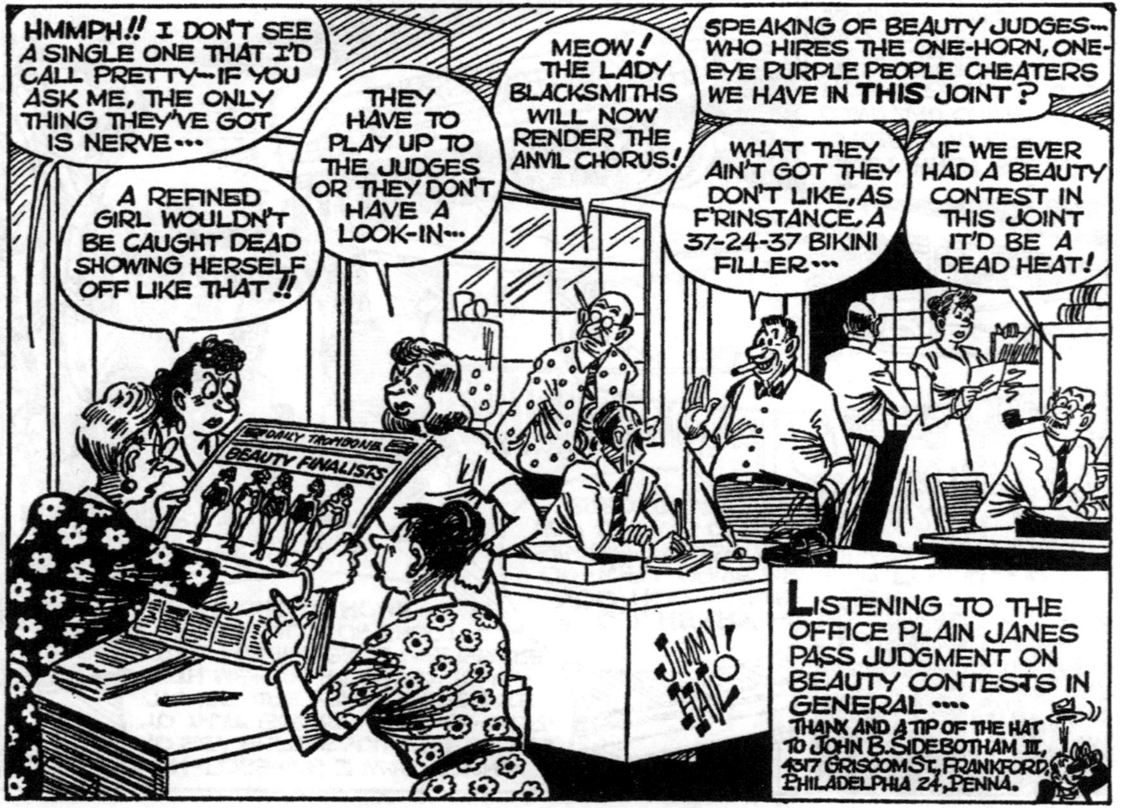
HMMPH!! I DON'T SEE A SINGLE ONE THAT I'D CALL PRETTY--IF YOU ASK ME, THE ONLY THING THEY'VE GOT IS NERVE...
A REFINED GIRL WOULDN'T BE CAUGHT DEAD SHOWING HERSELF OFF LIKE THAT!!
THEY HAVE TO PLAY UP TO THE JUDGES OR THEY DON'T HAVE A LOOK-IN...
MEOW! THE LADY BLACKSMITHS WILL NOW RENDER THE ANVIL CHORUS!
SPEAKING OF BEAUTY JUDGES--WHO HIRES THE ONE-HORN, ONE-EYE PURPLE PEOPLE CHEATERS WE HAVE IN THIS JOINT?
WHAT THEY AIN'T GOT THEY DON'T LIKE, AS F'RINSTANCE, A 37-24-37 BIKINI FILLER...
IF WE EVER HAD A BEAUTY CONTEST IN THIS JOINT IT'D BE A DEAD HEAT!
DAILY TROMBONE
BEAUTY FINALISTS
JIMMY HATLO
LISTENING TO THE OFFICE PLAIN JANES PASS JUDGMENT ON BEAUTY CONTESTS IN GENERAL....
THANX AND A TIP OF THE HAT TO JOHN B. SIDEBOTHAM III, 4317 GRISCOM ST, FRANKFORD, PHILADELPHIA 24, PENNA.

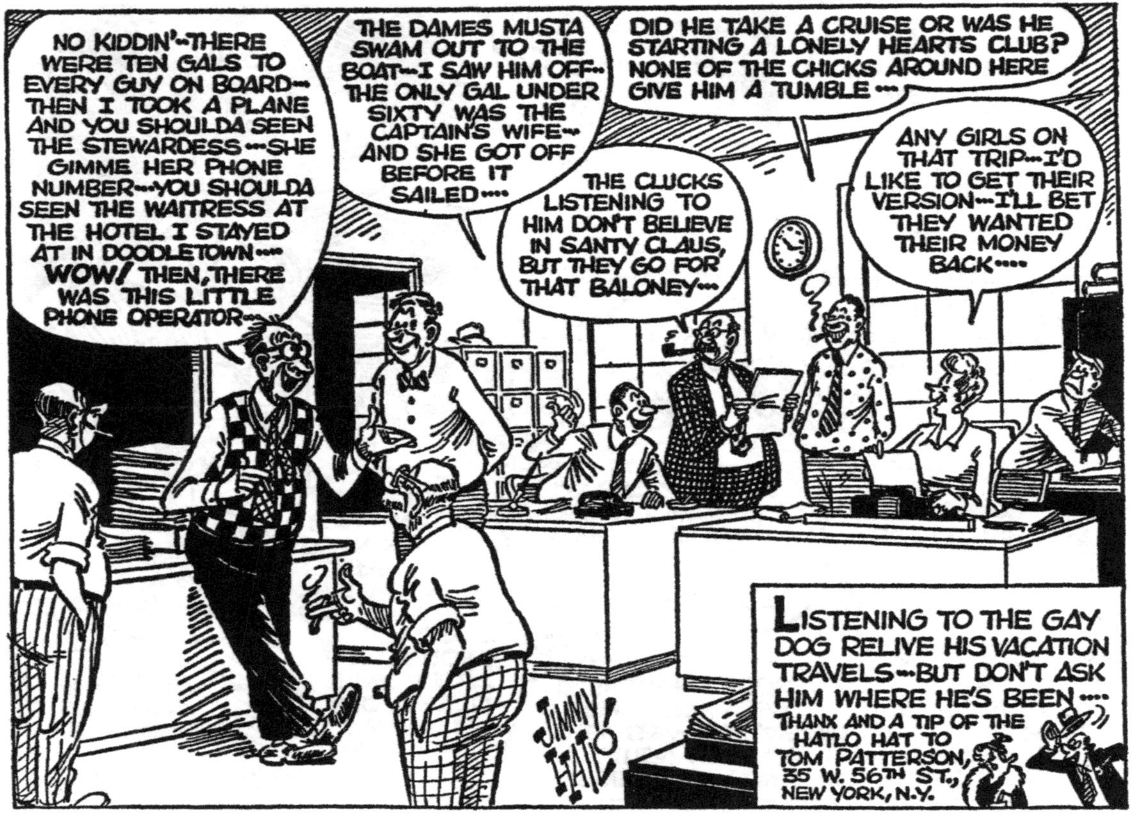
NO KIDDIN'--THERE WERE TEN GALS TO EVERY GUY ON BOARD--THEN I TOOK A PLANE AND YOU SHOULDA SEEN THE STEWARDESS---SHE GIMME HER PHONE NUMBER---YOU SHOULDA SEEN THE WAITRESS AT THE HOTEL I STAYED AT IN DOODLETOWN---- WOW! THEN, THERE WAS THIS LITTLE PHONE OPERATOR--
THE DAMES MUSTA SWAM OUT TO THE BOAT--I SAW HIM OFF--THE ONLY GAL UNDER SIXTY WAS THE CAPTAIN'S WIFE--AND SHE GOT OFF BEFORE IT SAILED----
DID HE TAKE A CRUISE OR WAS HE STARTING A LONELY HEARTS CLUB? NONE OF THE CHICKS AROUND HERE GIVE HIM A TUMBLE---
THE CLUCKS LISTENING TO HIM DON'T BELIEVE IN SANTY CLAUS, BUT THEY GO FOR THAT BALONEY---
ANY GIRLS ON THAT TRIP---I'D LIKE TO GET THEIR VERSION---I'LL BET THEY WANTED THEIR MONEY BACK----
JIMMY HATLO!
LISTENING TO THE GAY DOG RELIVE HIS VACATION TRAVELS--BUT DON'T ASK HIM WHERE HE'S BEEN----
THANX AND A TIP OF THE HATLO HAT TO TOM PATTERSON, 35 W. 56TH ST., NEW YORK, N.Y.

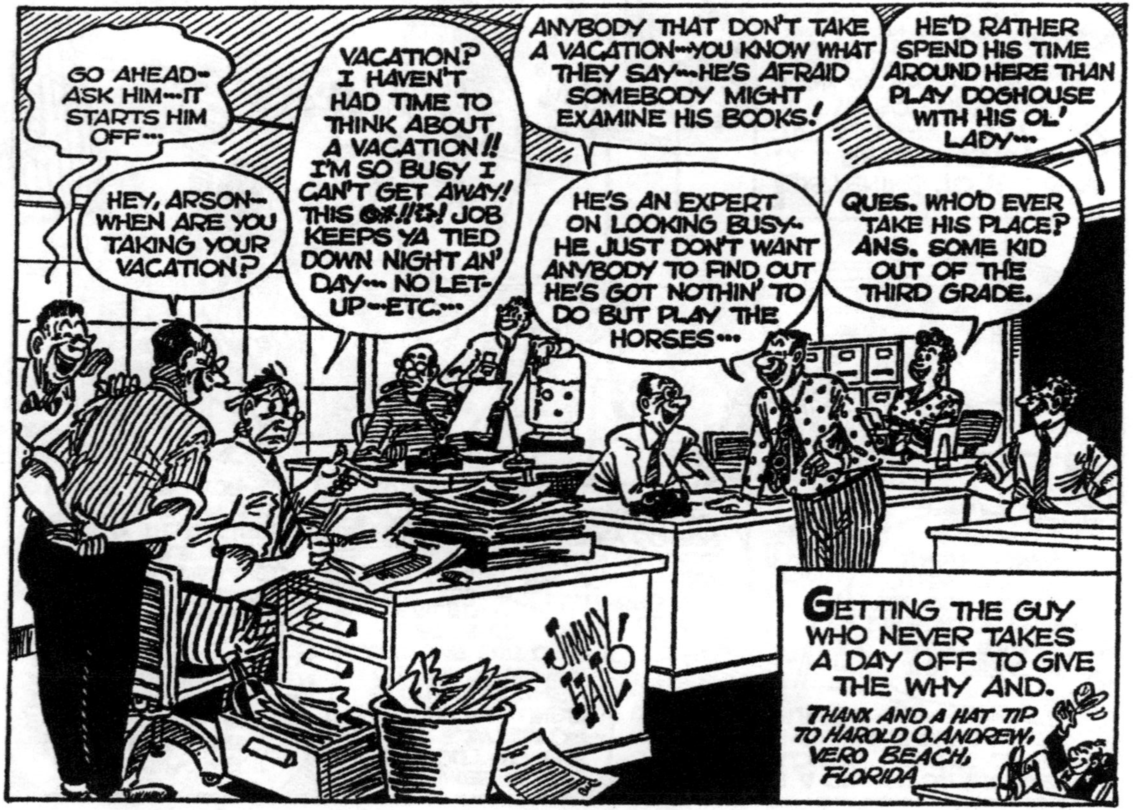

GO AHEAD--ASK HIM---IT STARTS HIM OFF---
HEY, ARSON--WHEN ARE YOU TAKING YOUR VACATION?
VACATION? I HAVEN'T HAD TIME TO THINK ABOUT A VACATION!! I'M SO BUSY I CAN'T GET AWAY! THIS @#!!$! JOB KEEPS YA TIED DOWN NIGHT AN' DAY--- NO LET-UP---ETC.---
ANYBODY THAT DON'T TAKE A VACATION---YOU KNOW WHAT THEY SAY---HE'S AFRAID SOMEBODY MIGHT EXAMINE HIS BOOKS!
HE'S AN EXPERT ON LOOKING BUSY- HE JUST DON'T WANT ANYBODY TO FIND OUT HE'S GOT NOTHIN' TO DO BUT PLAY THE HORSES---
HE'D RATHER SPEND HIS TIME AROUND HERE THAN PLAY DOGHOUSE WITH HIS OL' LADY---
QUES. WHO'D EVER TAKE HIS PLACE? ANS. SOME KID OUT OF THE THIRD GRADE.
JIMMY HATLO!
GETTING THE GUY WHO NEVER TAKES A DAY OFF TO GIVE THE WHY AND.
THANX AND A HAT TIP TO HAROLD O. ANDREW, VERO BEACH, FLORIDA

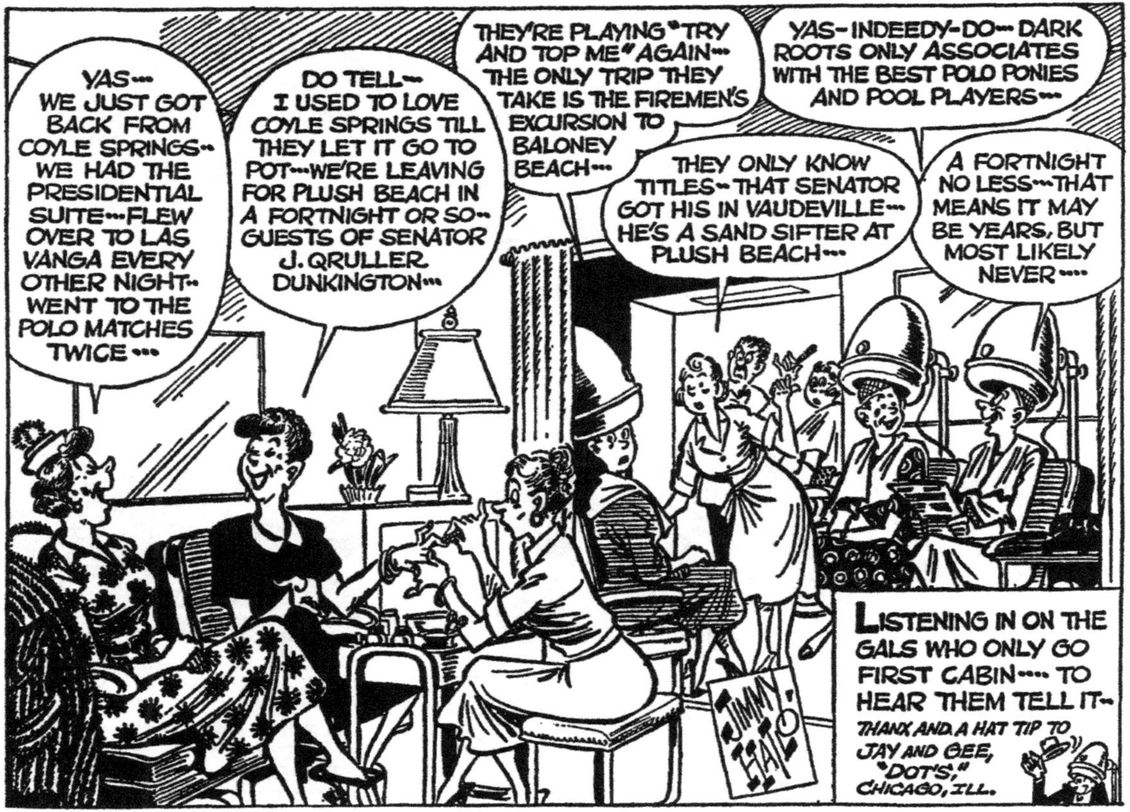
YAS... WE JUST GOT BACK FROM COYLE SPRINGS.. WE HAD THE PRESIDENTIAL SUITE...FLEW OVER TO LAS VANGA EVERY OTHER NIGHT.. WENT TO THE POLO MATCHES TWICE...
DO TELL... I USED TO LOVE COYLE SPRINGS TILL THEY LET IT GO TO POT...WE'RE LEAVING FOR PLUSH BEACH IN A FORTNIGHT OR SO.. GUESTS OF SENATOR J. QRULLER DUNKINGTON...
THEY'RE PLAYING "TRY AND TOP ME" AGAIN... THE ONLY TRIP THEY TAKE IS THE FIREMEN'S EXCURSION TO BALONEY BEACH...
YAS-INDEEDY-DO... DARK ROOTS ONLY ASSOCIATES WITH THE BEST POLO PONIES AND POOL PLAYERS...
THEY ONLY KNOW TITLES.. THAT SENATOR GOT HIS IN VAUDEVILLE... HE'S A SAND SIFTER AT PLUSH BEACH...
A FORTNIGHT NO LESS...THAT MEANS IT MAY BE YEARS, BUT MOST LIKELY NEVER....
JIMMY HAT
LISTENING IN ON THE GALS WHO ONLY GO FIRST CABIN.... TO HEAR THEM TELL IT..
THANX AND A HAT TIP TO JAY AND GEE, "DOT'S," CHICAGO, ILL.

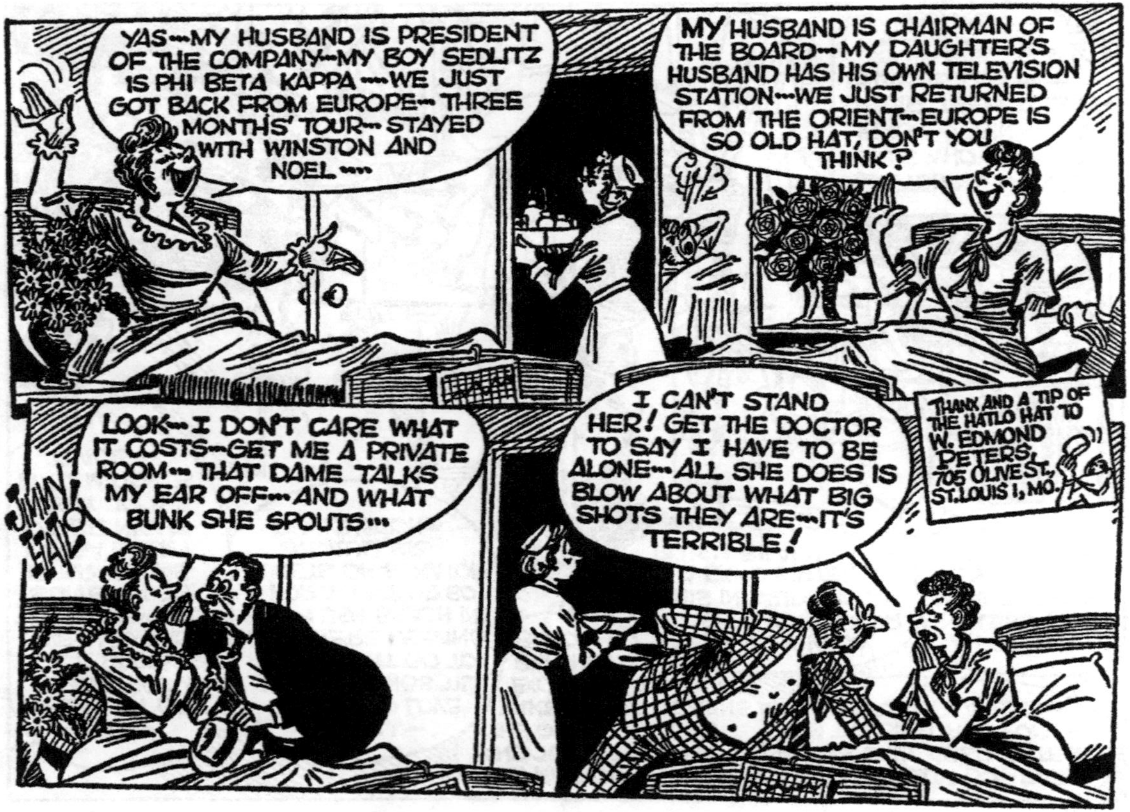
YAS---MY HUSBAND IS PRESIDENT OF THE COMPANY---MY BOY SEDLITZ IS PHI BETA KAPPA ---WE JUST GOT BACK FROM EUROPE--- THREE MONTHS' TOUR--- STAYED WITH WINSTON AND NOEL ---
MY HUSBAND IS CHAIRMAN OF THE BOARD---MY DAUGHTER'S HUSBAND HAS HIS OWN TELEVISION STATION---WE JUST RETURNED FROM THE ORIENT---EUROPE IS SO OLD HAT, DON'T YOU THINK?
LOOK--- I DON'T CARE WHAT IT COSTS---GET ME A PRIVATE ROOM--- THAT DAME TALKS MY EAR OFF--- AND WHAT BUNK SHE SPOUTS---
JIMMY HATLO
I CAN'T STAND HER! GET THE DOCTOR TO SAY I HAVE TO BE ALONE--- ALL SHE DOES IS BLOW ABOUT WHAT BIG SHOTS THEY ARE---IT'S TERRIBLE!
THANX AND A TIP OF THE HATLO HAT TO W. EDMOND PETERS, 705 OLIVE ST, ST. LOUIS 1, MO.

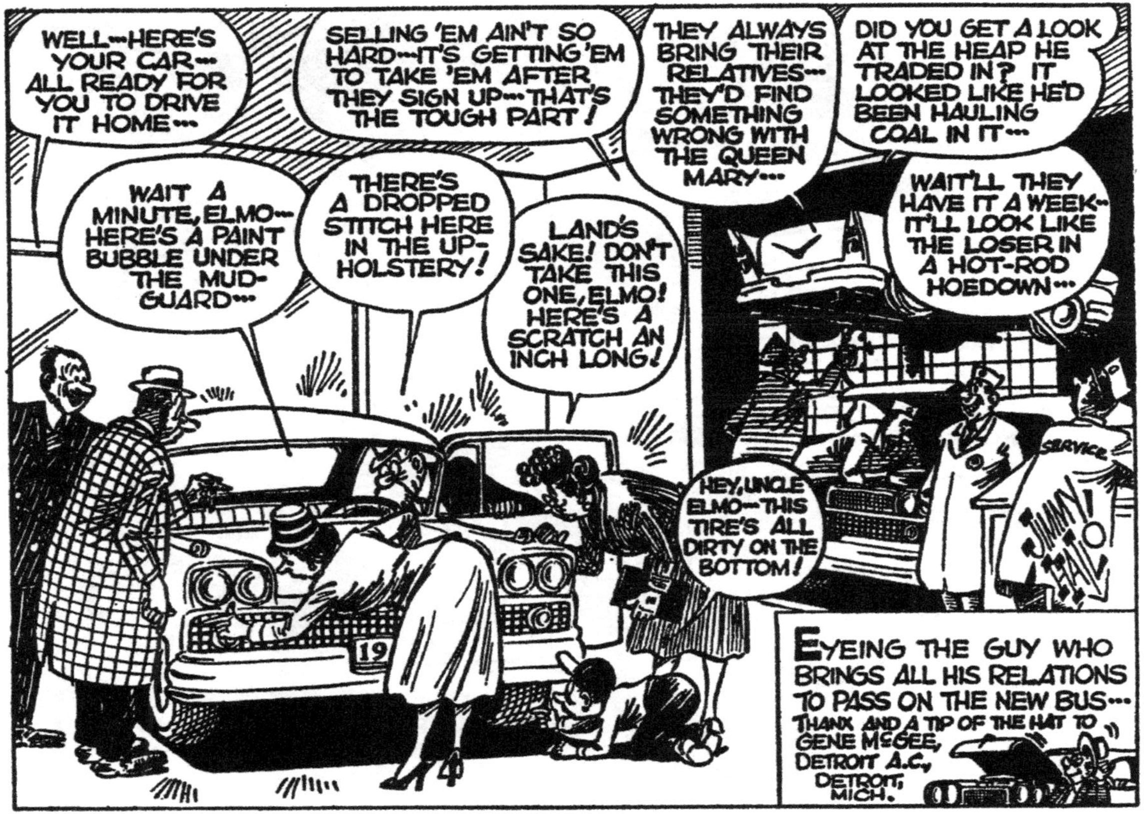
WELL—HERE'S YOUR CAR— ALL READY FOR YOU TO DRIVE IT HOME—
WAIT A MINUTE, ELMO— HERE'S A PAINT BUBBLE UNDER THE MUD-GUARD—
SELLING 'EM AIN'T SO HARD—IT'S GETTING 'EM TO TAKE 'EM AFTER THEY SIGN UP—THAT'S THE TOUGH PART!
THERE'S A DROPPED STITCH HERE IN THE UP-HOLSTERY!
LAND'S SAKE! DON'T TAKE THIS ONE, ELMO! HERE'S A SCRATCH AN INCH LONG!
THEY ALWAYS BRING THEIR RELATIVES— THEY'D FIND SOMETHING WRONG WITH THE QUEEN MARY—
HEY, UNCLE ELMO—THIS TIRE'S ALL DIRTY ON THE BOTTOM!
DID YOU GET A LOOK AT THE HEAP HE TRADED IN? IT LOOKED LIKE HE'D BEEN HAULING COAL IN IT—
WAIT'LL THEY HAVE IT A WEEK— IT'LL LOOK LIKE THE LOSER IN A HOT-ROD HOEDOWN—
SERVICE
JIMMY! HATLO
EYEING THE GUY WHO BRINGS ALL HIS RELATIONS TO PASS ON THE NEW BUS—
THANX AND A TIP OF THE HAT TO GENE McGEE, DETROIT A.C., DETROIT, MICH.

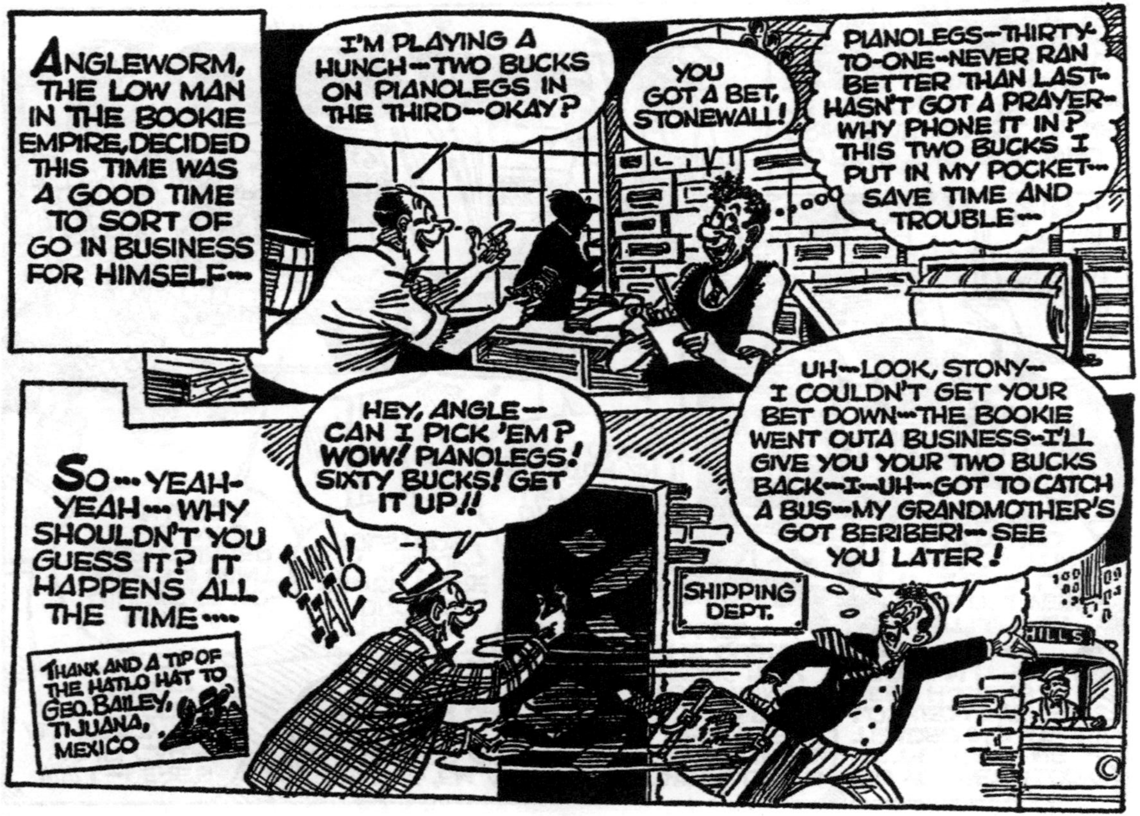
ANGLEWORM, THE LOW MAN IN THE BOOKIE EMPIRE, DECIDED THIS TIME WAS A GOOD TIME TO SORT OF GO IN BUSINESS FOR HIMSELF--
I'M PLAYING A HUNCH--TWO BUCKS ON PIANOLEGS IN THE THIRD--OKAY?
YOU GOT A BET, STONEWALL!
PIANOLEGS--THIRTY-TO-ONE--NEVER RAN BETTER THAN LAST--HASN'T GOT A PRAYER--WHY PHONE IT IN? THIS TWO BUCKS I PUT IN MY POCKET--SAVE TIME AND TROUBLE--
SO--YEAH-YEAH--WHY SHOULDN'T YOU GUESS IT? IT HAPPENS ALL THE TIME----
HEY, ANGLE--CAN I PICK 'EM? WOW! PIANOLEGS! SIXTY BUCKS! GET IT UP!!
UH--LOOK, STONY--I COULDN'T GET YOUR BET DOWN--THE BOOKIE WENT OUTA BUSINESS--I'LL GIVE YOU YOUR TWO BUCKS BACK--I--UH--GOT TO CATCH A BUS--MY GRANDMOTHER'S GOT BERIBERI--SEE YOU LATER!
SHIPPING DEPT.
JIMMY HATLO
THANX AND A TIP OF THE HATLO HAT TO GEO. BAILEY, TIJUANA, MEXICO

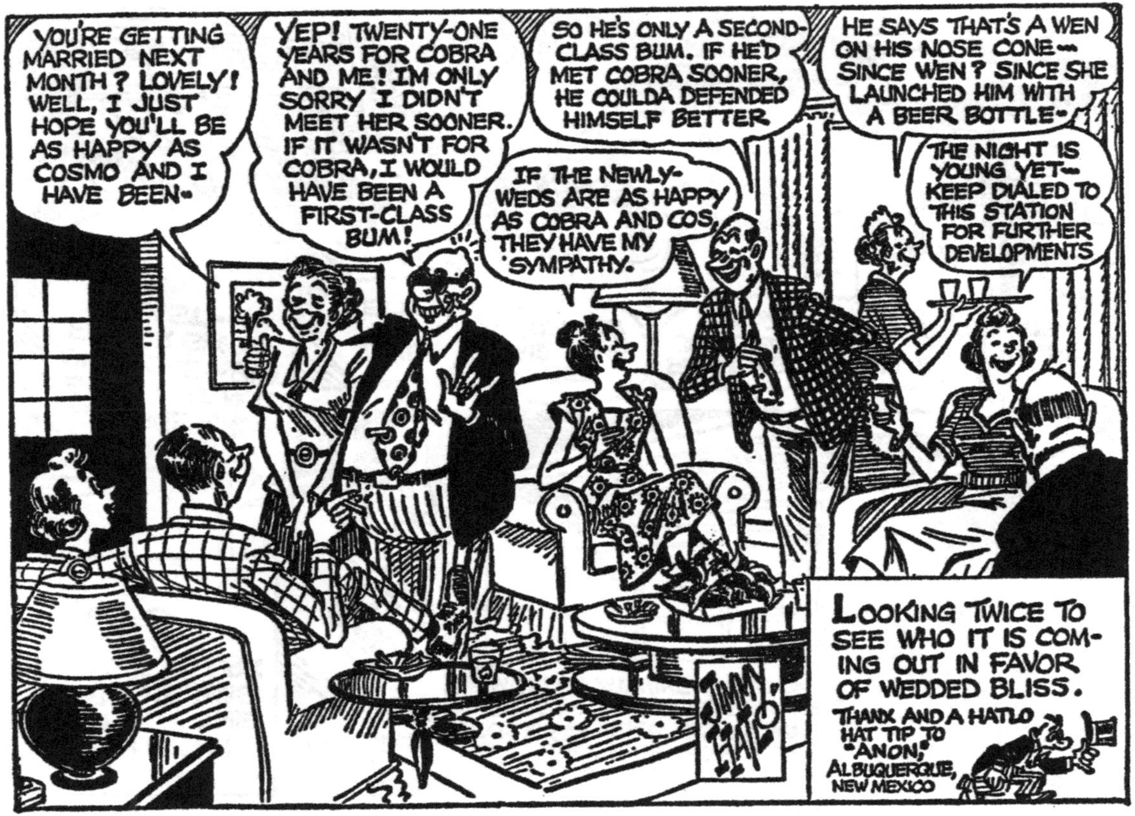
YOU'RE GETTING MARRIED NEXT MONTH? LOVELY! WELL, I JUST HOPE YOU'LL BE AS HAPPY AS COSMO AND I HAVE BEEN.
YEP! TWENTY-ONE YEARS FOR COBRA AND ME! I'M ONLY SORRY I DIDN'T MEET HER SOONER. IF IT WASN'T FOR COBRA, I WOULD HAVE BEEN A FIRST-CLASS BUM!
SO HE'S ONLY A SECOND-CLASS BUM. IF HE'D MET COBRA SOONER, HE COULDA DEFENDED HIMSELF BETTER
IF THE NEWLY-WEDS ARE AS HAPPY AS COBRA AND COS, THEY HAVE MY SYMPATHY.
HE SAYS THAT'S A WEN ON HIS NOSE CONE-- SINCE WEN? SINCE SHE LAUNCHED HIM WITH A BEER BOTTLE.
THE NIGHT IS YOUNG YET-- KEEP DIALED TO THIS STATION FOR FURTHER DEVELOPMENTS
JIMMY HATLO
LOOKING TWICE TO SEE WHO IT IS COMING OUT IN FAVOR OF WEDDED BLISS.
THANX AND A HATLO HAT TIP TO "ANON," ALBUQUERQUE, NEW MEXICO

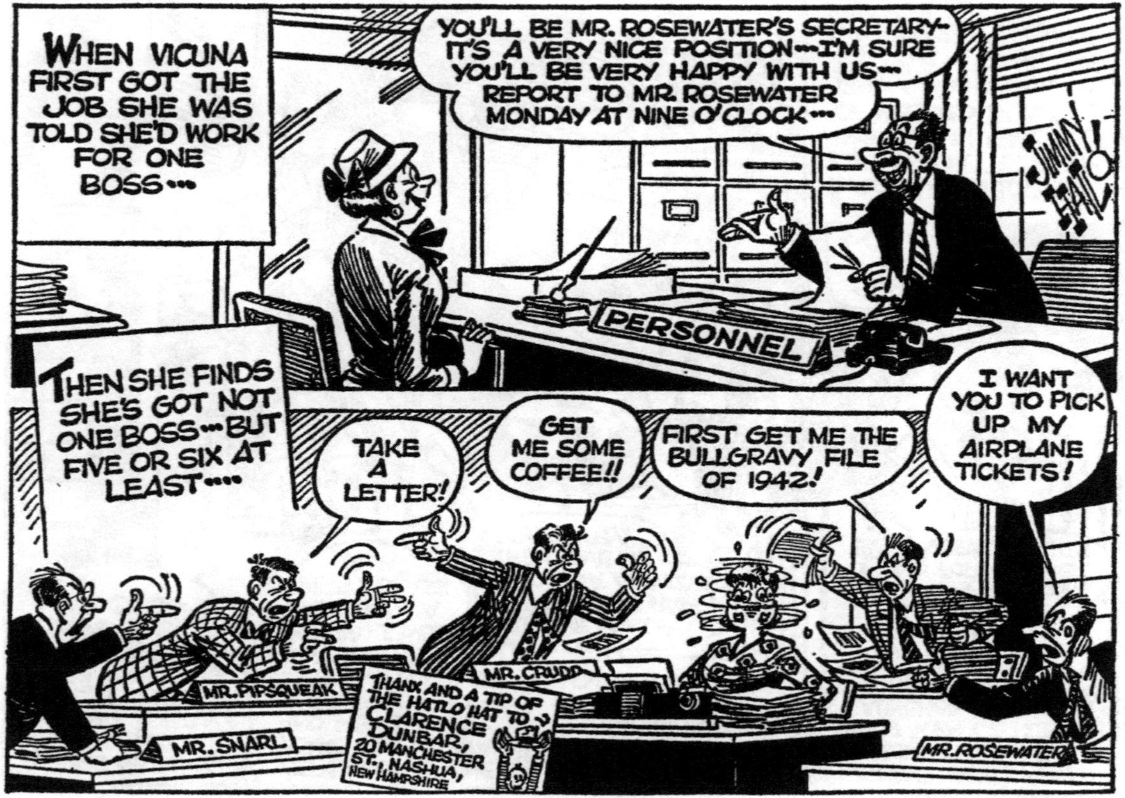
WHEN VICUNA FIRST GOT THE JOB SHE WAS TOLD SHE'D WORK FOR ONE BOSS...
YOU'LL BE MR. ROSEWATER'S SECRETARY-- IT'S A VERY NICE POSITION--I'M SURE YOU'LL BE VERY HAPPY WITH US--- REPORT TO MR. ROSEWATER MONDAY AT NINE O'CLOCK---
PERSONNEL
JIMMY HATLO
THEN SHE FINDS SHE'S GOT NOT ONE BOSS--BUT FIVE OR SIX AT LEAST....
TAKE A LETTER!
GET ME SOME COFFEE!!
FIRST GET ME THE BULLGRAVY FILE OF 1942!
I WANT YOU TO PICK UP MY AIRPLANE TICKETS!
MR. PIPSQUEAK
MR. SNARL
MR. CRUDD
MR. ROSEWATER
THANX AND A TIP OF THE HATLO HAT TO CLARENCE DUNBAR, 20 MANCHESTER ST., NASHUA, NEW HAMPSHIRE

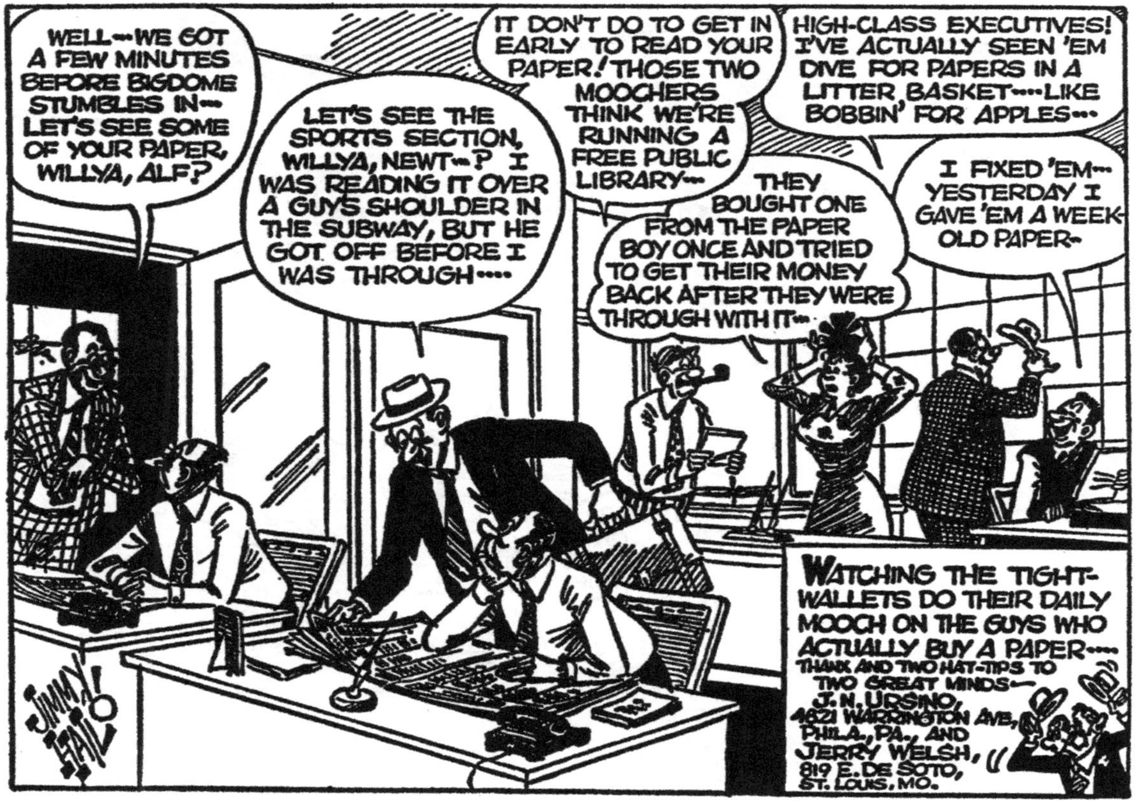
WELL--WE GOT A FEW MINUTES BEFORE BIGDOME STUMBLES IN--LET'S SEE SOME OF YOUR PAPER, WILLYA, ALF?
LET'S SEE THE SPORTS SECTION, WILLYA, NEWT--? I WAS READING IT OVER A GUY'S SHOULDER IN THE SUBWAY, BUT HE GOT OFF BEFORE I WAS THROUGH....
IT DON'T DO TO GET IN EARLY TO READ YOUR PAPER! THOSE TWO MOOCHERS THINK WE'RE RUNNING A FREE PUBLIC LIBRARY--
THEY BOUGHT ONE FROM THE PAPER BOY ONCE AND TRIED TO GET THEIR MONEY BACK AFTER THEY WERE THROUGH WITH IT--
HIGH-CLASS EXECUTIVES! I'VE ACTUALLY SEEN 'EM DIVE FOR PAPERS IN A LITTER BASKET....LIKE BOBBIN' FOR APPLES...
I FIXED 'EM--YESTERDAY I GAVE 'EM A WEEK-OLD PAPER--
WATCHING THE TIGHT-WALLETS DO THEIR DAILY MOOCH ON THE GUYS WHO ACTUALLY BUY A PAPER....
THANX AND TWO HAT-TIPS TO TWO GREAT MINDS--
J. N. URSINO, 4821 WARRINGTON AVE, PHILA., PA., AND JERRY WELSH, 819 E. DE SOTO, ST. LOUIS, MO.
JIMMY HATLO

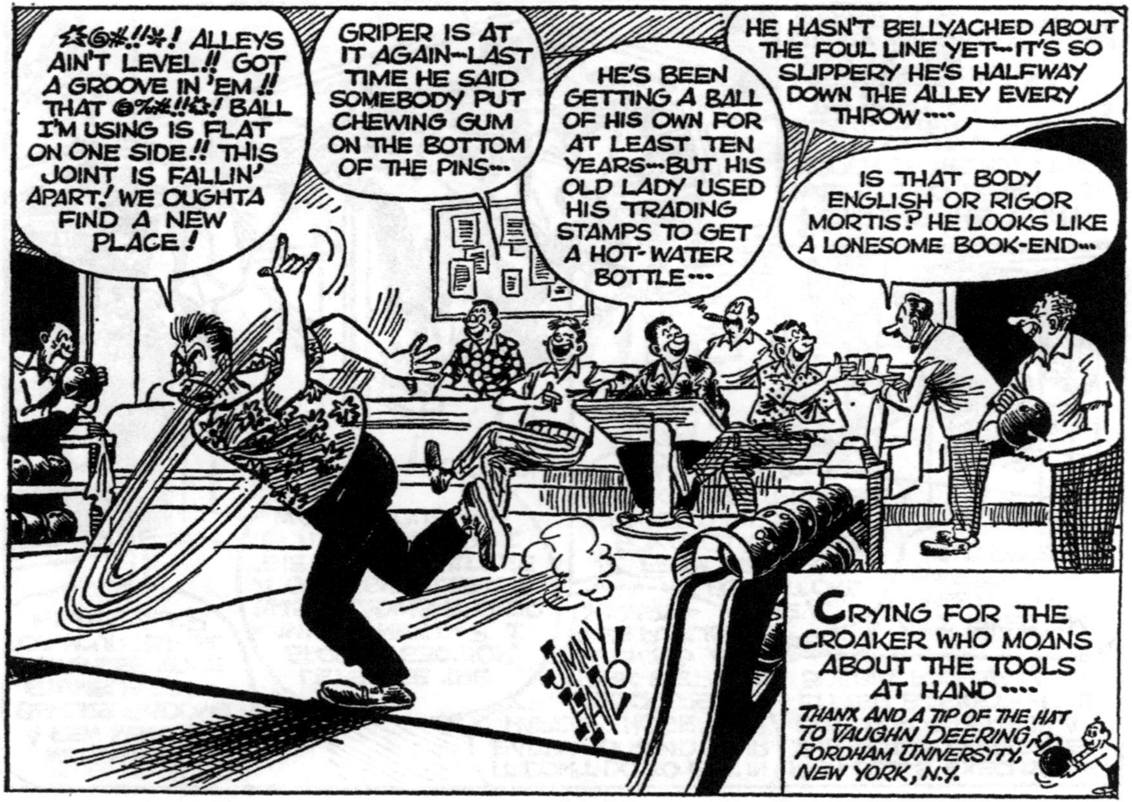
☆@#!!*! ALLEYS AIN'T LEVEL!! GOT A GROOVE IN 'EM!! THAT @%#!!☆! BALL I'M USING IS FLAT ON ONE SIDE!! THIS JOINT IS FALLIN' APART! WE OUGHTA FIND A NEW PLACE!
GRIPER IS AT IT AGAIN--LAST TIME HE SAID SOMEBODY PUT CHEWING GUM ON THE BOTTOM OF THE PINS...
HE'S BEEN GETTING A BALL OF HIS OWN FOR AT LEAST TEN YEARS--BUT HIS OLD LADY USED HIS TRADING STAMPS TO GET A HOT-WATER BOTTLE...
HE HASN'T BELLYACHED ABOUT THE FOUL LINE YET--IT'S SO SLIPPERY HE'S HALFWAY DOWN THE ALLEY EVERY THROW....
IS THAT BODY ENGLISH OR RIGOR MORTIS? HE LOOKS LIKE A LONESOME BOOK-END...
JIMMY HATLO!
CRYING FOR THE CROAKER WHO MOANS ABOUT THE TOOLS AT HAND....
THANX AND A TIP OF THE HAT TO VAUGHN DEERING, FORDHAM UNIVERSITY, NEW YORK, N.Y.

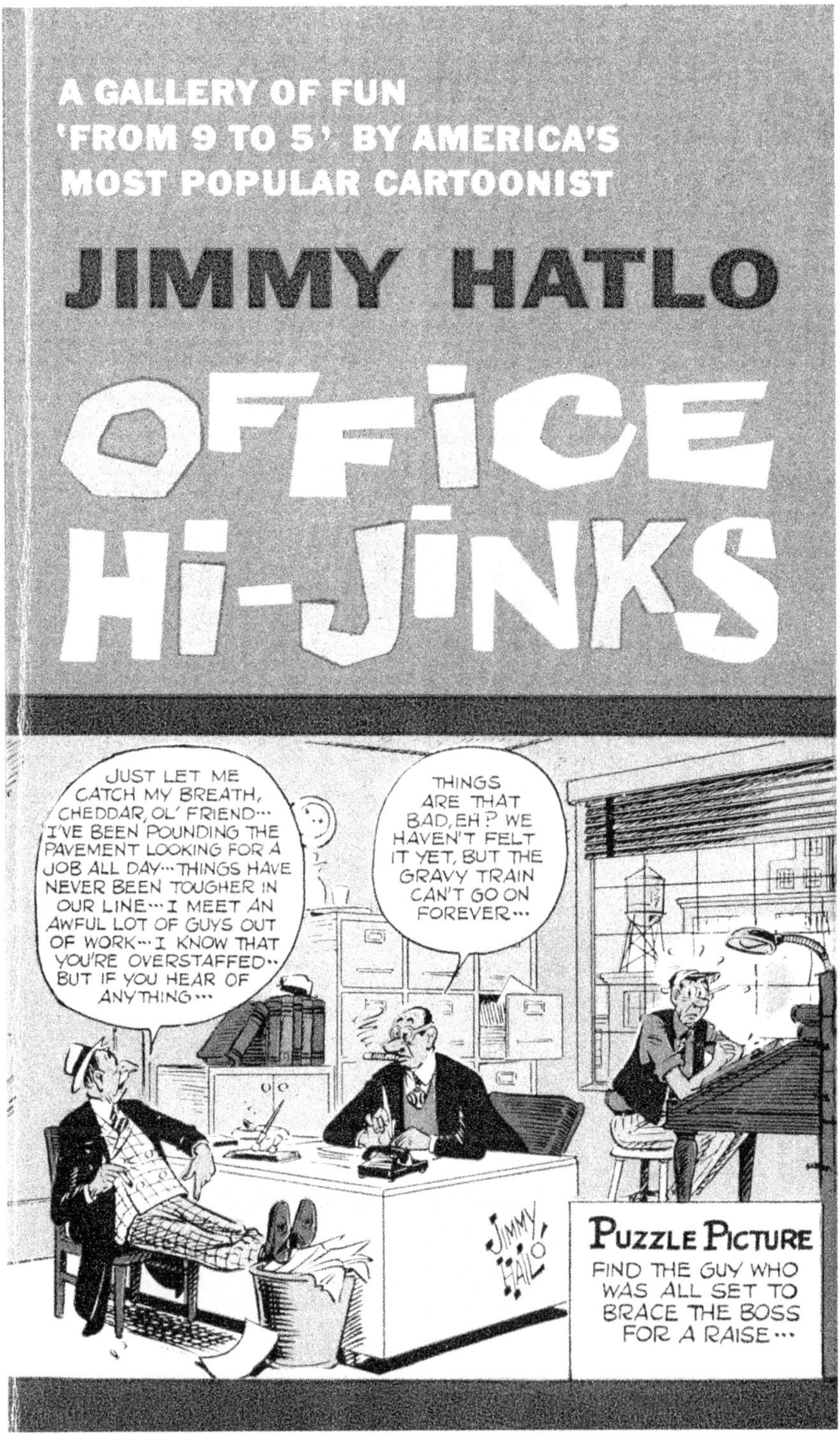
A GALLERY OF FUN
'FROM 9 TO 5' BY AMERICA'S
MOST POPULAR CARTOONIST
JIMMY HATLO
OFFICE HI-JINKS
JUST LET ME CATCH MY BREATH, CHEDDAR, OL' FRIEND... I'VE BEEN POUNDING THE PAVEMENT LOOKING FOR A JOB ALL DAY... THINGS HAVE NEVER BEEN TOUGHER IN OUR LINE... I MEET AN AWFUL LOT OF GUYS OUT OF WORK... I KNOW THAT YOU'RE OVERSTAFFED.. BUT IF YOU HEAR OF ANYTHING...
THINGS ARE THAT BAD, EH? WE HAVEN'T FELT IT YET, BUT THE GRAVY TRAIN CAN'T GO ON FOREVER...
JIMMY HATLO
PUZZLE PICTURE
FIND THE GUY WHO WAS ALL SET TO BRACE THE BOSS FOR A RAISE...

JIMMY HATLO
••••••••••••••••••••••••

OFFICE HI-JINKS

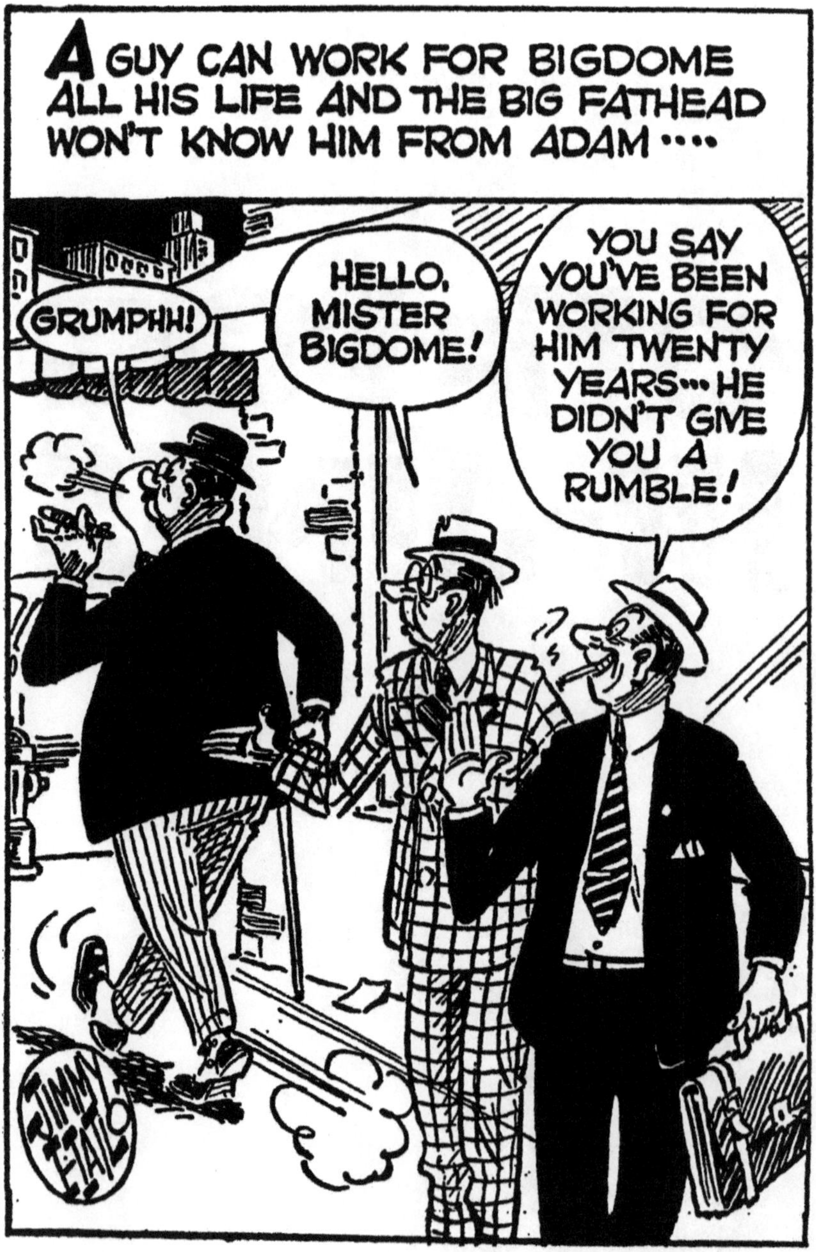
A GUY CAN WORK FOR BIGDOME ALL HIS LIFE AND THE BIG FATHEAD WON'T KNOW HIM FROM ADAM....
GRUMPHH!
HELLO, MISTER BIGDOME!
YOU SAY YOU'VE BEEN WORKING FOR HIM TWENTY YEARS... HE DIDN'T GIVE YOU A RUMBLE!
JIMMY HATLO

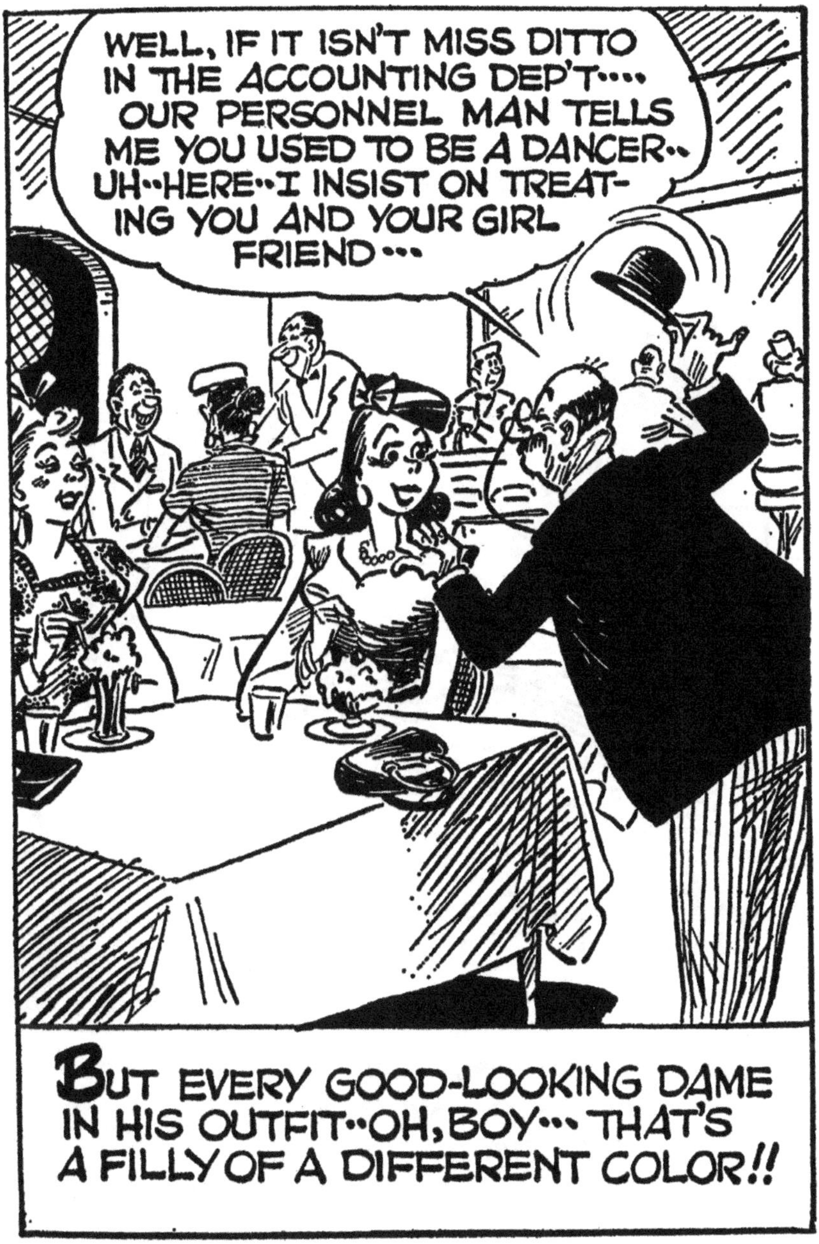
WELL, IF IT ISN'T MISS DITTO IN THE ACCOUNTING DEP'T.... OUR PERSONNEL MAN TELLS ME YOU USED TO BE A DANCER.. UH..HERE..I INSIST ON TREATING YOU AND YOUR GIRL FRIEND...
BUT EVERY GOOD-LOOKING DAME IN HIS OUTFIT..OH, BOY... THAT'S A FILLY OF A DIFFERENT COLOR!!

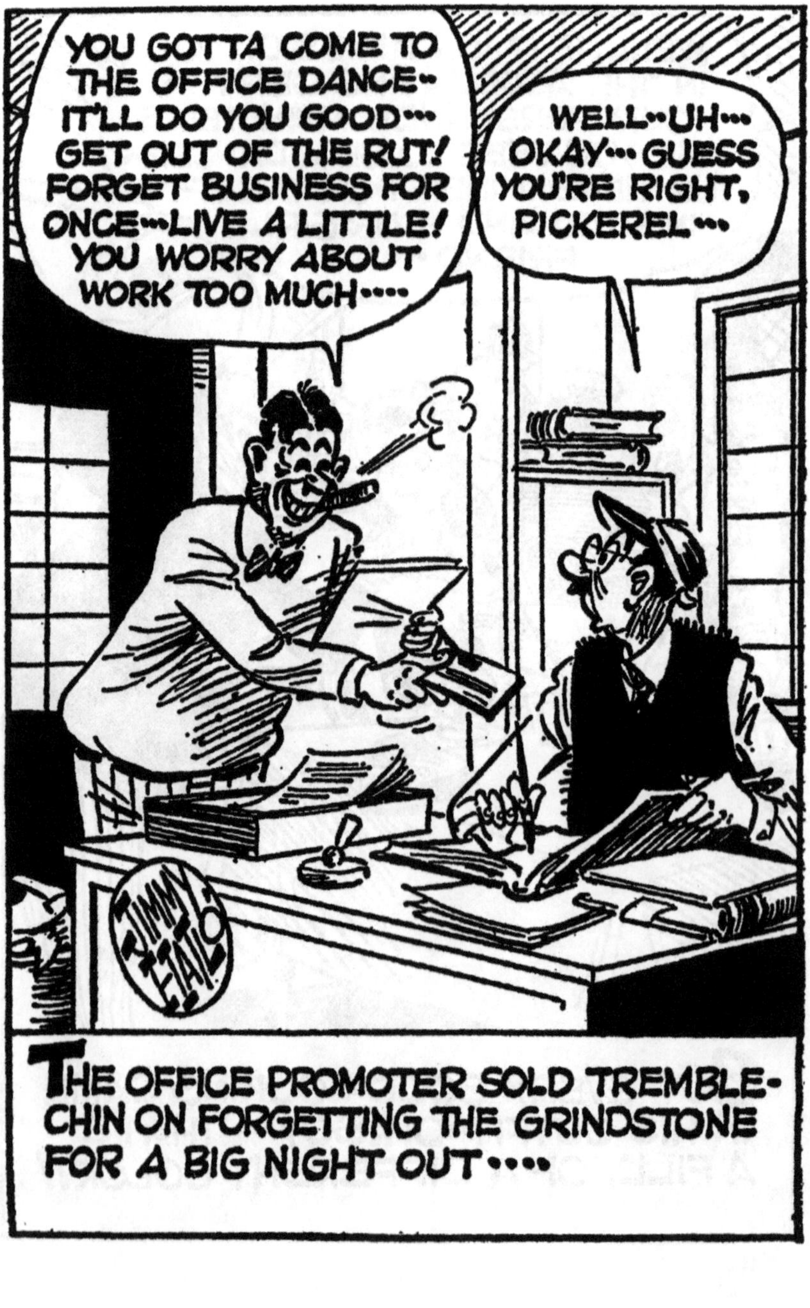
YOU GOTTA COME TO THE OFFICE DANCE-- IT'LL DO YOU GOOD... GET OUT OF THE RUT! FORGET BUSINESS FOR ONCE...LIVE A LITTLE! YOU WORRY ABOUT WORK TOO MUCH....
WELL--UH... OKAY... GUESS YOU'RE RIGHT, PICKEREL...
JIMMY HATLO
THE OFFICE PROMOTER SOLD TREMBLE-CHIN ON FORGETTING THE GRINDSTONE FOR A BIG NIGHT OUT....

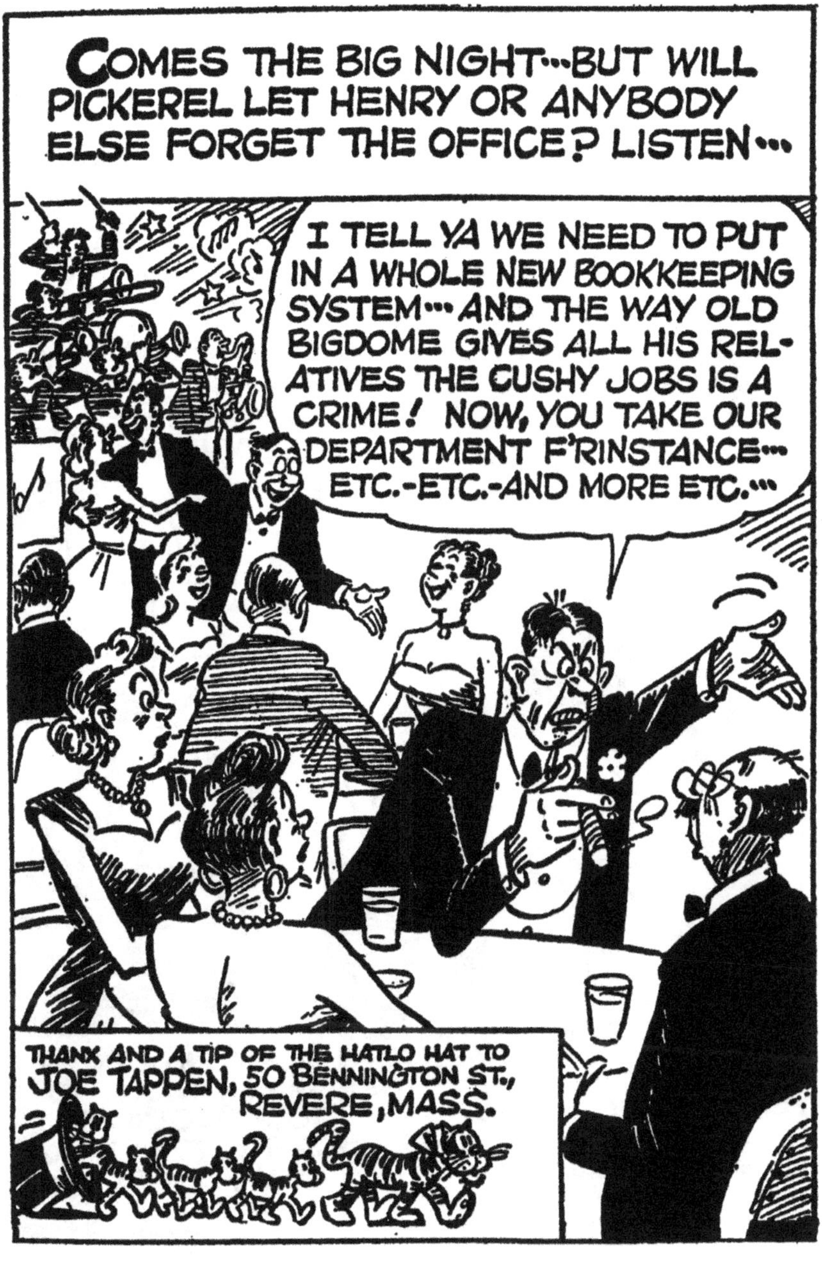
COMES THE BIG NIGHT...BUT WILL PICKEREL LET HENRY OR ANYBODY ELSE FORGET THE OFFICE? LISTEN...
I TELL YA WE NEED TO PUT IN A WHOLE NEW BOOKKEEPING SYSTEM... AND THE WAY OLD BIGDOME GIVES ALL HIS RELATIVES THE CUSHY JOBS IS A CRIME! NOW, YOU TAKE OUR DEPARTMENT F'RINSTANCE... ETC.-ETC.-AND MORE ETC....
THANX AND A TIP OF THE HATLO HAT TO JOE TAPPEN, 50 BENNINGTON ST., REVERE, MASS.

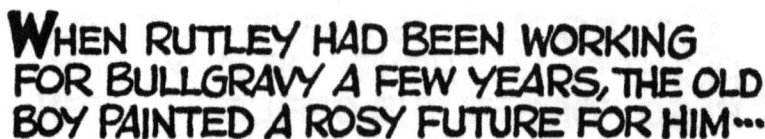

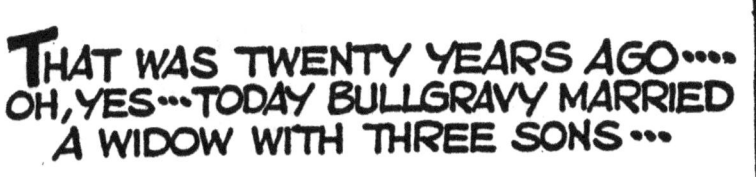

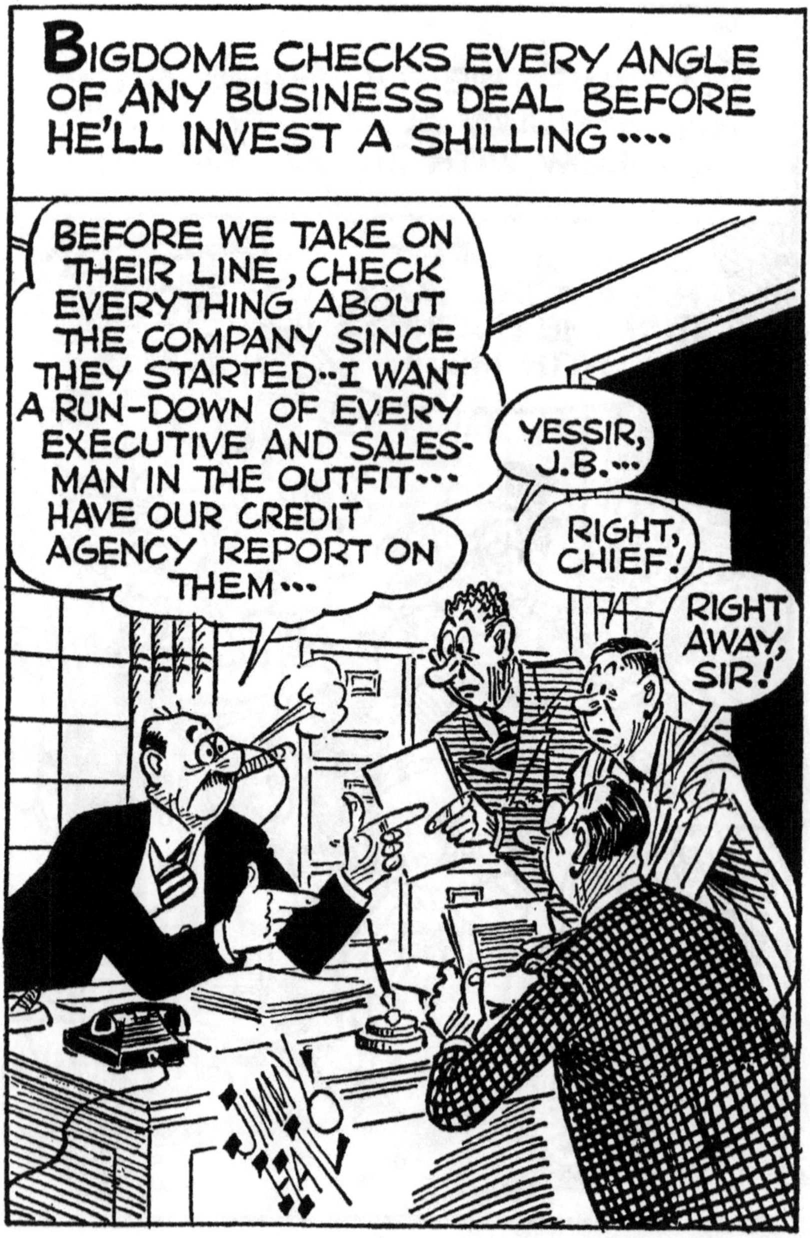
BIGDOME CHECKS EVERY ANGLE OF ANY BUSINESS DEAL BEFORE HE'LL INVEST A SHILLING....
BEFORE WE TAKE ON THEIR LINE, CHECK EVERYTHING ABOUT THE COMPANY SINCE THEY STARTED--I WANT A RUN-DOWN OF EVERY EXECUTIVE AND SALES-MAN IN THE OUTFIT... HAVE OUR CREDIT AGENCY REPORT ON THEM...
YESSIR, J.B....
RIGHT, CHIEF!
RIGHT AWAY, SIR!
JIMMY HATLO

BUT ASK HIM TO BACK A SHOW THAT HASN'T GOT A CHANCE AND HE'LL GO HOOK, LINE AND SAILBOAT...
THIS IS THE AUTHOR... SHE'LL ALSO PLAY THE LEAD... WE CAN GO INTO REHEARSAL IF WE RAISE A HUNNERT GRAND...
A HUNDRED THOUSAND? CAN I GO TO THE REHEARSAL? I ALWAYS DID HAVE A FLAIR FOR THE THEATRE.. GOT A PEN?
THANX AND A TIP OF THE HATLO HAT TO PAUL DEFUR, NORWALK, CONN.

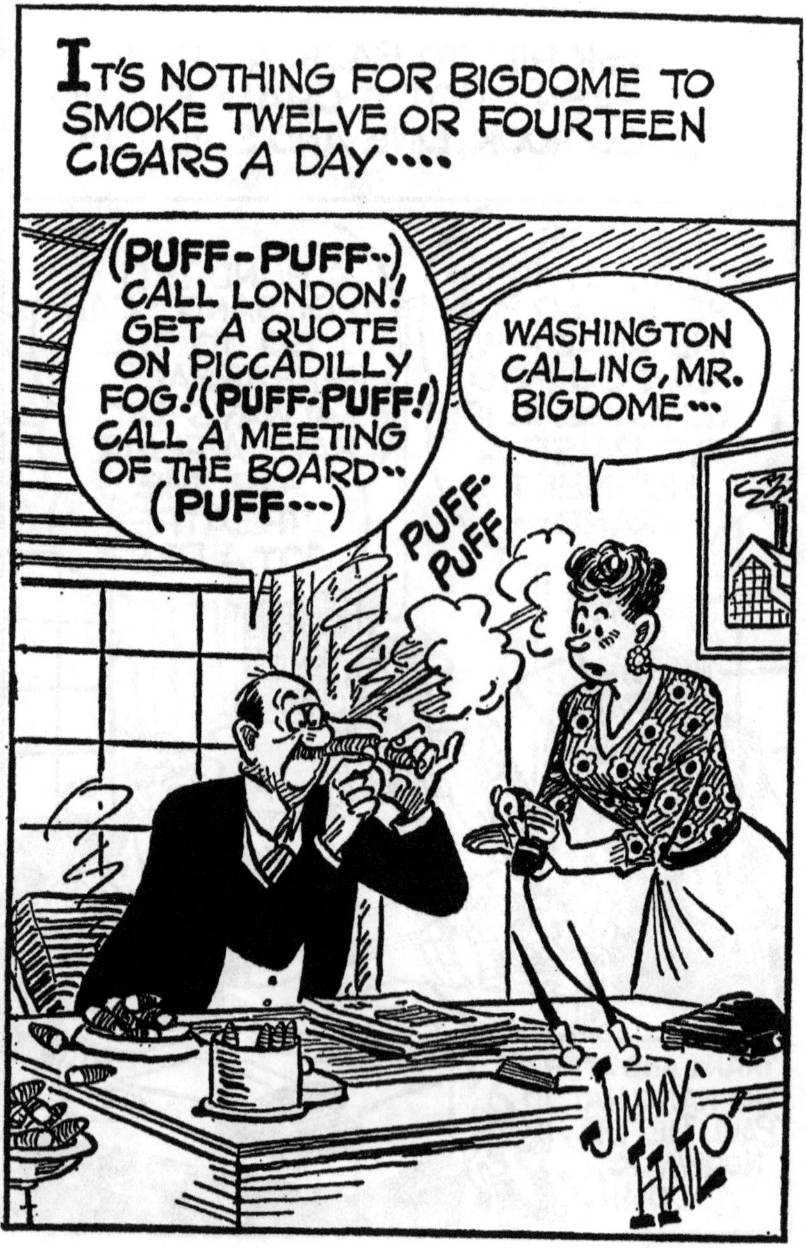
IT'S NOTHING FOR BIGDOME TO SMOKE TWELVE OR FOURTEEN CIGARS A DAY....
(PUFF-PUFF..) CALL LONDON! GET A QUOTE ON PICCADILLY FOG! (PUFF-PUFF!) CALL A MEETING OF THE BOARD.. (PUFF...)
WASHINGTON CALLING, MR. BIGDOME...
PUFF-PUFF
JIMMY HATLO

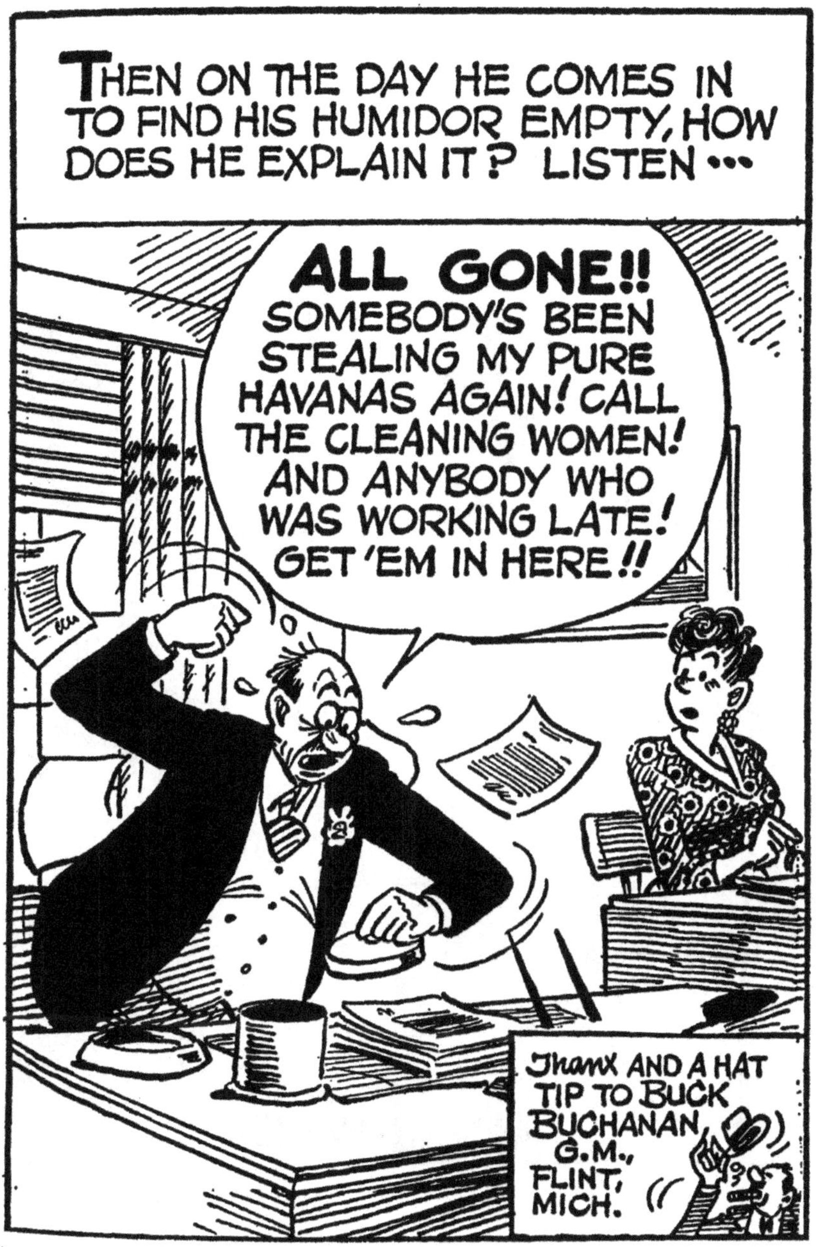
THEN ON THE DAY HE COMES IN TO FIND HIS HUMIDOR EMPTY, HOW DOES HE EXPLAIN IT? LISTEN...
ALL GONE!! SOMEBODY'S BEEN STEALING MY PURE HAVANAS AGAIN! CALL THE CLEANING WOMEN! AND ANYBODY WHO WAS WORKING LATE! GET 'EM IN HERE!!
Thanx AND A HAT TIP TO BUCK BUCHANAN, G.M., FLINT, MICH.

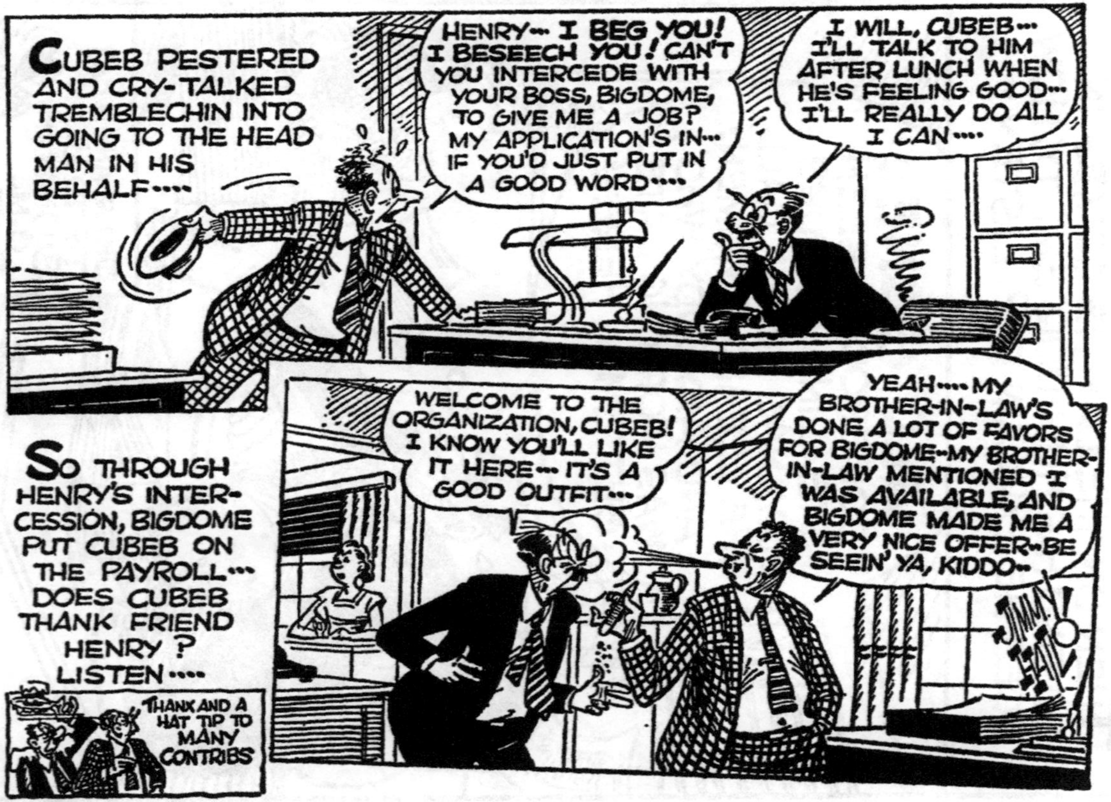
CUBEB PESTERED AND CRY-TALKED TREMBLECHIN INTO GOING TO THE HEAD MAN IN HIS BEHALF....
HENRY... I BEG YOU! I BESEECH YOU! CAN'T YOU INTERCEDE WITH YOUR BOSS, BIGDOME, TO GIVE ME A JOB? MY APPLICATION'S IN... IF YOU'D JUST PUT IN A GOOD WORD....
I WILL, CUBEB... I'LL TALK TO HIM AFTER LUNCH WHEN HE'S FEELING GOOD... I'LL REALLY DO ALL I CAN....
SO THROUGH HENRY'S INTER-CESSION, BIGDOME PUT CUBEB ON THE PAYROLL... DOES CUBEB THANK FRIEND HENRY? LISTEN....
THANX AND A HAT TIP TO MANY CONTRIBS
WELCOME TO THE ORGANIZATION, CUBEB! I KNOW YOU'LL LIKE IT HERE... IT'S A GOOD OUTFIT...
YEAH.... MY BROTHER-IN-LAW'S DONE A LOT OF FAVORS FOR BIGDOME--MY BROTHER-IN-LAW MENTIONED I WAS AVAILABLE, AND BIGDOME MADE ME A VERY NICE OFFER--BE SEEIN' YA, KIDDO--

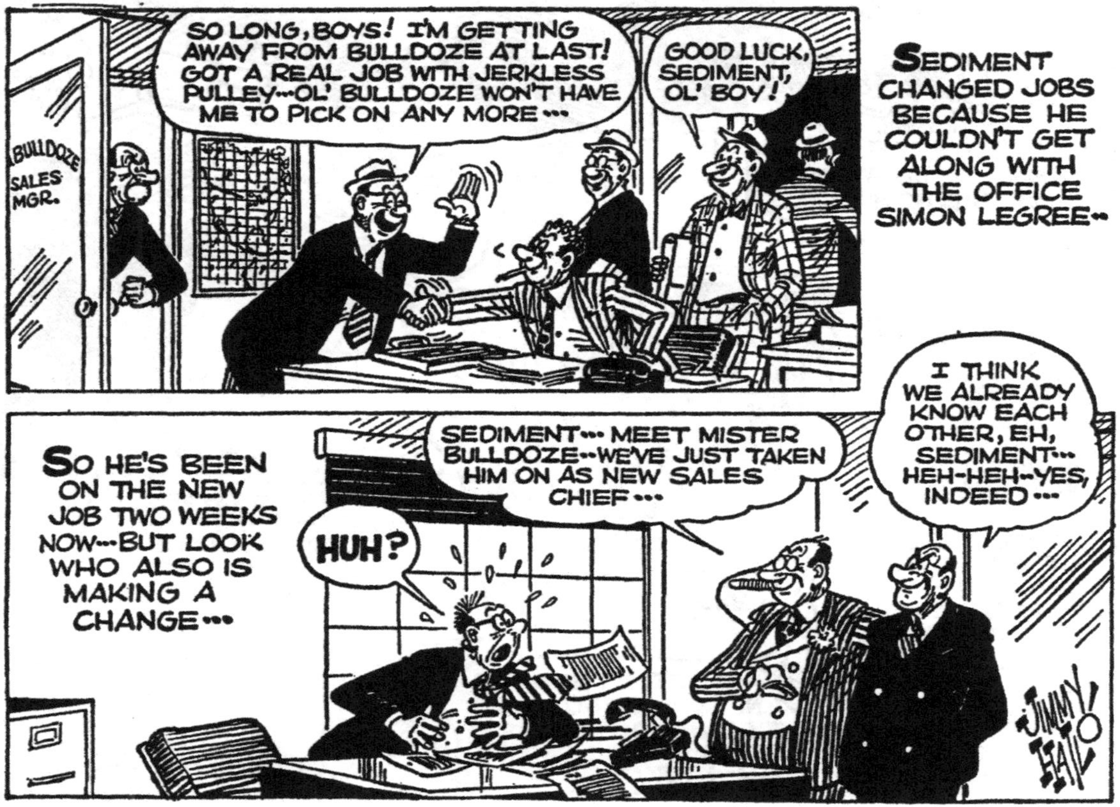

BULLDOZE SALES MGR.
SO LONG, BOYS! I'M GETTING AWAY FROM BULLDOZE AT LAST! GOT A REAL JOB WITH JERKLESS PULLEY--OL' BULLDOZE WON'T HAVE ME TO PICK ON ANY MORE...
GOOD LUCK, SEDIMENT, OL' BOY!
SEDIMENT CHANGED JOBS BECAUSE HE COULDN'T GET ALONG WITH THE OFFICE SIMON LEGREE--
SO HE'S BEEN ON THE NEW JOB TWO WEEKS NOW---BUT LOOK WHO ALSO IS MAKING A CHANGE...
HUH?
SEDIMENT--- MEET MISTER BULLDOZE--WE'VE JUST TAKEN HIM ON AS NEW SALES CHIEF...
I THINK WE ALREADY KNOW EACH OTHER, EH, SEDIMENT-- HEH-HEH--YES, INDEED...
JIMMY HATLO

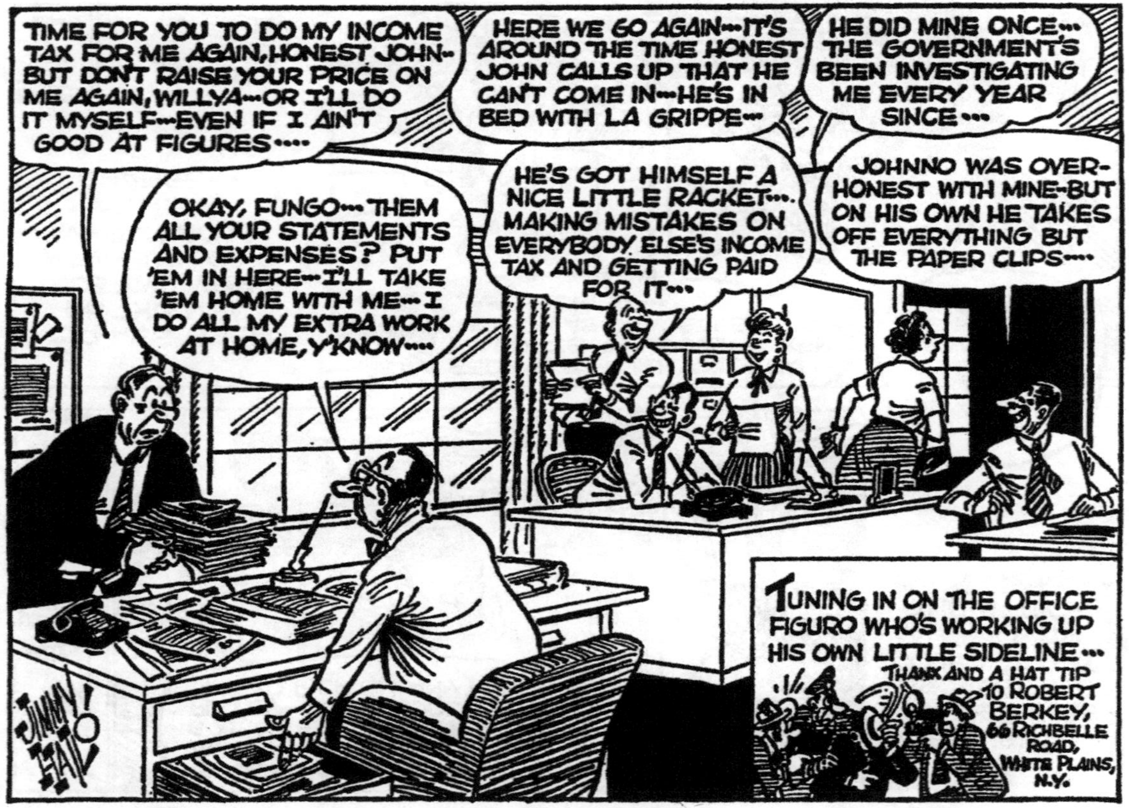
TIME FOR YOU TO DO MY INCOME TAX FOR ME AGAIN, HONEST JOHN-- BUT DON'T RAISE YOUR PRICE ON ME AGAIN, WILLYA--- OR I'LL DO IT MYSELF--- EVEN IF I AIN'T GOOD AT FIGURES....
OKAY, FUNGO--- THEM ALL YOUR STATEMENTS AND EXPENSES? PUT 'EM IN HERE--- I'LL TAKE 'EM HOME WITH ME--- I DO ALL MY EXTRA WORK AT HOME, Y'KNOW....
HERE WE GO AGAIN--- IT'S AROUND THE TIME HONEST JOHN CALLS UP THAT HE CAN'T COME IN--- HE'S IN BED WITH LA GRIPPE---
HE'S GOT HIMSELF A NICE LITTLE RACKET.... MAKING MISTAKES ON EVERYBODY ELSE'S INCOME TAX AND GETTING PAID FOR IT---
HE DID MINE ONCE--- THE GOVERNMENT'S BEEN INVESTIGATING ME EVERY YEAR SINCE---
JOHNNO WAS OVER-HONEST WITH MINE--BUT ON HIS OWN HE TAKES OFF EVERYTHING BUT THE PAPER CLIPS....
TUNING IN ON THE OFFICE FIGURO WHO'S WORKING UP HIS OWN LITTLE SIDELINE---
THANX AND A HAT TIP TO ROBERT BERKEY, 66 RICHBELLE ROAD, WHITE PLAINS, N.Y.
JIMMY HATLO

I WAS ON THE LACROSSE TEAM··· SIXTEEN STITCHES··· GOT MY NOSE BUSTED TWICE ON THE BOXING TEAM··· COULDN'T PLAY FOOTBALL··· HAD A TRICK KNEE FROM POLE VAULTING···
I HAD TO WEAR A BRACE ON MY NECK THREE YEARS·· RAN INTO THE GOAL POSTS THE FIRST DAY OF PRACTICE IN MY SOPHOMORE YEAR···
ARE THEY TALKING ABOUT THEIR ATHLETIC CAREERS OR THEIR HAPPY DAYS IN THE HOSPITAL?
THEY NEVER EVEN WERE ON A TEAM·· THEY WERE ALL-AMERICAN HOT-HOUSE PLANTS IN THE IVY LEAGUE!
THE WORST THING THEM TWO EVER SUFFERED FROM WAS SPLIT INFINITIVES ON THE DEBATING TEAM···
TUNING IN AS THE TWO FISH-STORY BOYS DWELL ON THEIR ATHLETIC DUELING SCARS····
JIMMY HATLO

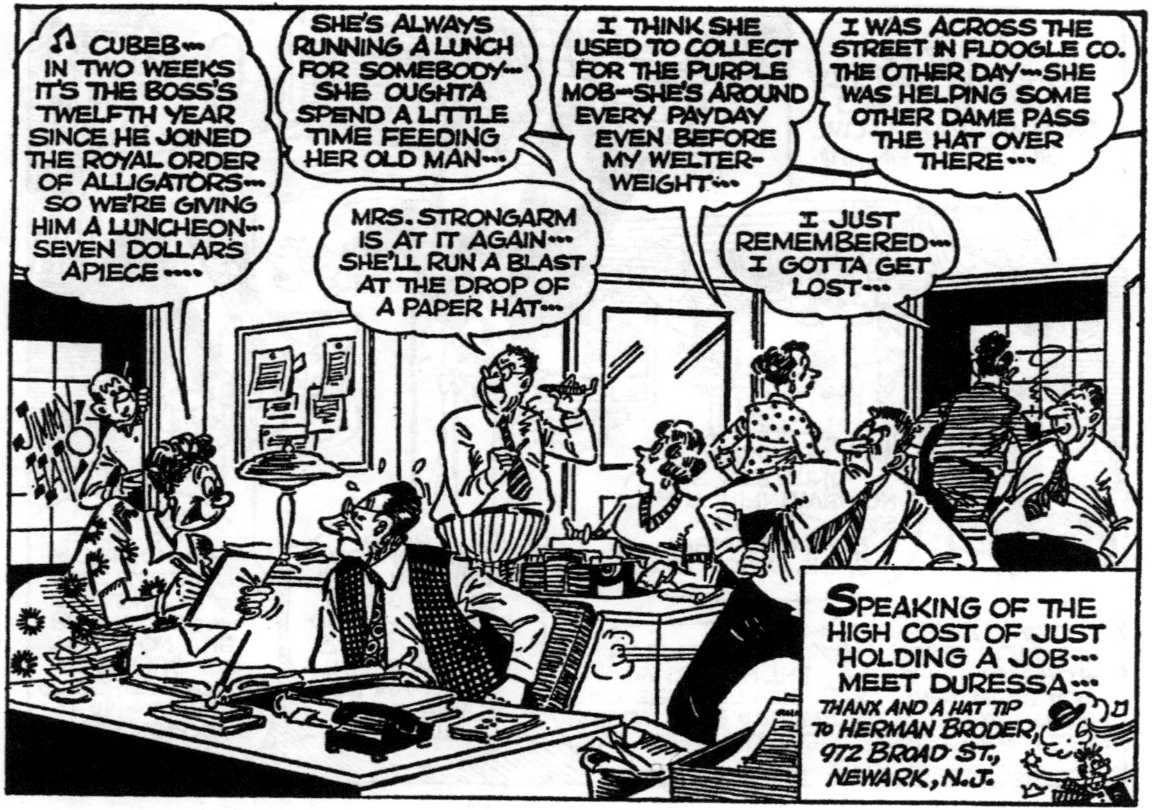
♫ CUBEB... IN TWO WEEKS IT'S THE BOSS'S TWELFTH YEAR SINCE HE JOINED THE ROYAL ORDER OF ALLIGATORS... SO WE'RE GIVING HIM A LUNCHEON... SEVEN DOLLARS APIECE....
SHE'S ALWAYS RUNNING A LUNCH FOR SOMEBODY... SHE OUGHTA SPEND A LITTLE TIME FEEDING HER OLD MAN...
MRS. STRONGARM IS AT IT AGAIN... SHE'LL RUN A BLAST AT THE DROP OF A PAPER HAT...
I THINK SHE USED TO COLLECT FOR THE PURPLE MOB--SHE'S AROUND EVERY PAYDAY EVEN BEFORE MY WELTER-WEIGHT...
I WAS ACROSS THE STREET IN FLOOGLE CO. THE OTHER DAY...SHE WAS HELPING SOME OTHER DAME PASS THE HAT OVER THERE...
I JUST REMEMBERED... I GOTTA GET LOST...
JIMMY HATLO
SPEAKING OF THE HIGH COST OF JUST HOLDING A JOB... MEET DURESSA...
THANX AND A HAT TIP TO HERMAN BRODER, 972 BROAD ST., NEWARK, N.J.

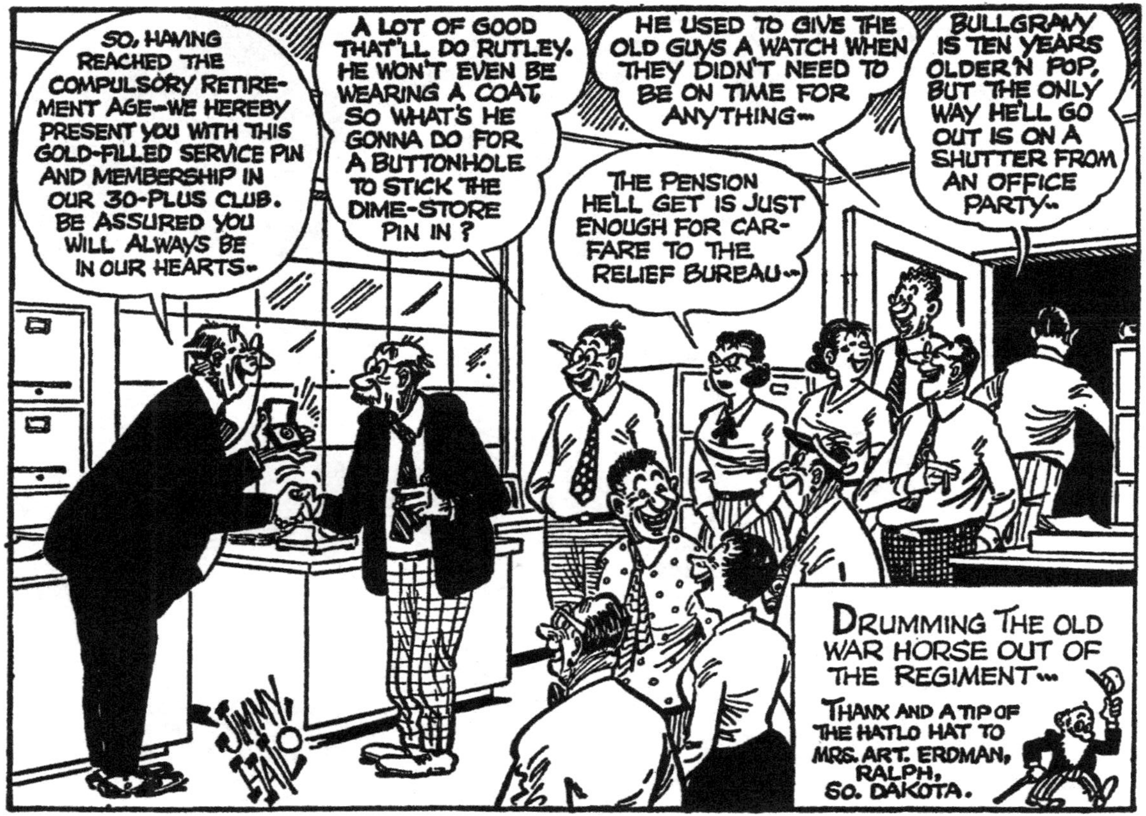
SO, HAVING REACHED THE COMPULSORY RETIREMENT AGE--WE HEREBY PRESENT YOU WITH THIS GOLD-FILLED SERVICE PIN AND MEMBERSHIP IN OUR 30-PLUS CLUB. BE ASSURED YOU WILL ALWAYS BE IN OUR HEARTS..
A LOT OF GOOD THAT'LL DO RUTLEY. HE WON'T EVEN BE WEARING A COAT, SO WHAT'S HE GONNA DO FOR A BUTTONHOLE TO STICK THE DIME-STORE PIN IN?
HE USED TO GIVE THE OLD GUYS A WATCH WHEN THEY DIDN'T NEED TO BE ON TIME FOR ANYTHING...
THE PENSION HE'LL GET IS JUST ENOUGH FOR CARFARE TO THE RELIEF BUREAU...
BULLGRAVY IS TEN YEARS OLDER'N POP, BUT THE ONLY WAY HE'LL GO OUT IS ON A SHUTTER FROM AN OFFICE PARTY..
JIMMY HATLO
DRUMMING THE OLD WAR HORSE OUT OF THE REGIMENT...
THANX AND A TIP OF THE HATLO HAT TO MRS. ART. ERDMAN, RALPH, SO. DAKOTA.

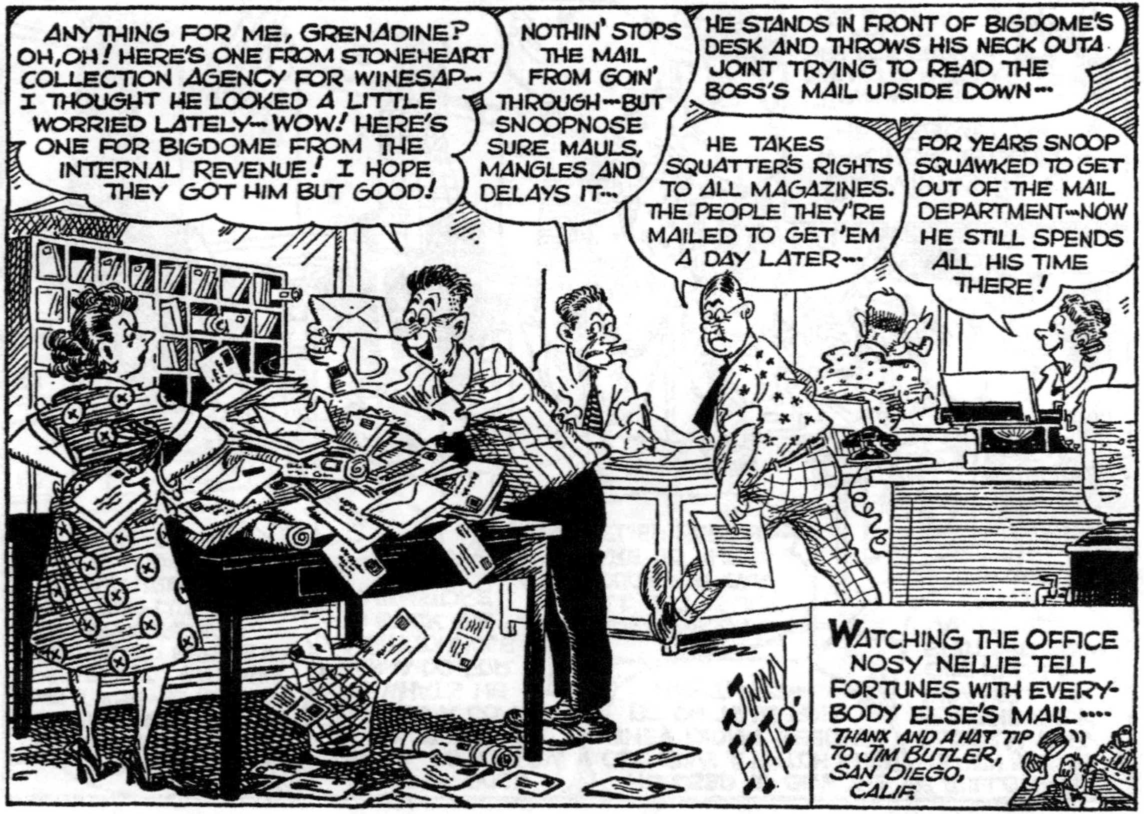
ANYTHING FOR ME, GRENADINE? OH, OH! HERE'S ONE FROM STONEHEART COLLECTION AGENCY FOR WINESAP... I THOUGHT HE LOOKED A LITTLE WORRIED LATELY... WOW! HERE'S ONE FOR BIGDOME FROM THE INTERNAL REVENUE! I HOPE THEY GOT HIM BUT GOOD!
NOTHIN' STOPS THE MAIL FROM GOIN' THROUGH... BUT SNOOPNOSE SURE MAULS, MANGLES AND DELAYS IT...
HE STANDS IN FRONT OF BIGDOME'S DESK AND THROWS HIS NECK OUTA JOINT TRYING TO READ THE BOSS'S MAIL UPSIDE DOWN...
HE TAKES SQUATTER'S RIGHTS TO ALL MAGAZINES. THE PEOPLE THEY'RE MAILED TO GET 'EM A DAY LATER...
FOR YEARS SNOOP SQUAWKED TO GET OUT OF THE MAIL DEPARTMENT... NOW HE STILL SPENDS ALL HIS TIME THERE!
JIMMY HATLO
WATCHING THE OFFICE NOSY NELLIE TELL FORTUNES WITH EVERYBODY ELSE'S MAIL....
THANX AND A HAT TIP TO JIM BUTLER, SAN DIEGO, CALIF.

HEY, CAESAR--HOW MANY APARTMENT HOUSES YOU OWN NOW? DO YOU STILL HAVE YOUR PRIVATE BOX AT THE OPERA?
DON'T BOTHER HIM--HE'S FIGURING OUT HOW MUCH HE'S TAKING IN FROM HIS THREE PARKING LOTS AN' THE STRING OF HASH HOUSES HE BOUGHT LAST YEAR--
LISTEN TO WHO'S KIDDING WHO--CAESAR WOULDN'T OWN HIS SHOE BOX IF HE DEPENDED ON THEM FOR TIPS...
THEY GET ARM SHINES... THEY OWE CEEZE A COUPLE O' BUCKS APIECE... HE'D BETTER COLLECT SOON... I DON'T THINK THEY'RE LONG FOR THIS COMPANY...
THE TWO FLANNEL-MOUTHS SPEND A DIME FOR LUNCH AND THEY GOT HOLES IN THEIR SOLES... BUT THEY GOTTA PUT ON A FRONT WITH A SHINE...
FLIBBERT AND JIBBERT MAY HAVE SOMETHING... I SAW CEEZE DEPOSIT A WHOLE MATTRESSFUL OF DOUGH AT THE BANK YESTERDAY!
SHINE
JIMMY HATLO
KIDDING THE SHOE-SHINE MAN ABOUT FINANCIAL CONDITIONS AND HIDDEN ASSETS...
THANX AND A HATLO HAT TIP TO JOE TUCKER, ST. LOUIS, MO.

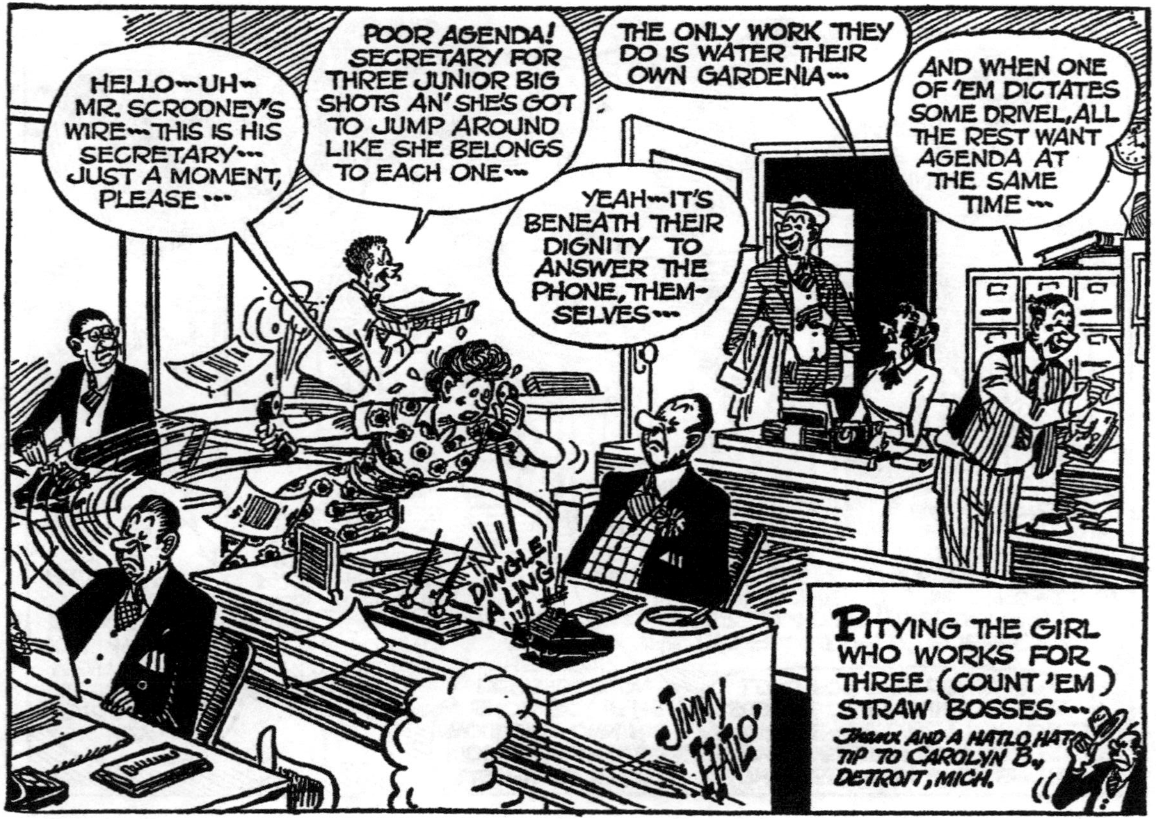
HELLO—UH— MR. SCRODNEY'S WIRE—THIS IS HIS SECRETARY— JUST A MOMENT, PLEASE—
POOR AGENDA! SECRETARY FOR THREE JUNIOR BIG SHOTS AN' SHE'S GOT TO JUMP AROUND LIKE SHE BELONGS TO EACH ONE—
YEAH—IT'S BENEATH THEIR DIGNITY TO ANSWER THE PHONE, THEMSELVES—
THE ONLY WORK THEY DO IS WATER THEIR OWN GARDENIA—
AND WHEN ONE OF 'EM DICTATES SOME DRIVEL, ALL THE REST WANT AGENDA AT THE SAME TIME—
DINGLE A LING
JIMMY HATLO'
PITYING THE GIRL WHO WORKS FOR THREE (COUNT 'EM) STRAW BOSSES—
THANX AND A HATLO HAT TIP TO CAROLYN B., DETROIT, MICH.

BIGDOME DRIVES ME NUTZ WITH THAT NERVOUS COUGH OF HIS··· I ALWAYS FEEL LIKE HITTING HIM ON THE BACK TO RELIEVE HIM····
YEAH···AND THAT NERVOUS WAY HE TWITCHES HIS SHOULDERS··
LISTEN TO WHO'S TALKING! HE SPENDS MORE TIME CRACKIN' HIS KNUCKLES THAN CRACKIN' THE WORK BARRIER···
SST-- SSSST-- SSST--
ZSK- ZSK- ZSK--
AND THAT COIN JINGLER--- HE SOUNDS LIKE THE INSIDE OF A ONE-ARMED BANDIT···
···AND THE TOOTH-ZSKER AND' THE WHISPERING WHISTLER··HOW DID WE ACCUMULATE SUCH FOUL BALLS?
WE OUGHTA PUT THOSE SOUND EFFECTS ON TAPE AND PLAY IT BACK TO THEM···MUSIC TO GO NUTZ BY····
CRACKA
CRACKA
CRACKA
JINGLE
JINGLE
JINGLE
JIMMY HATLO
PUTTING UP WITH THE OFFICE SOUND-EFFECTS BOYS····
THANX AND HATLO'S HAT IS OFF TO JOE TAPPEN, 56 BENNINGTON ST., REVERE, MASS.

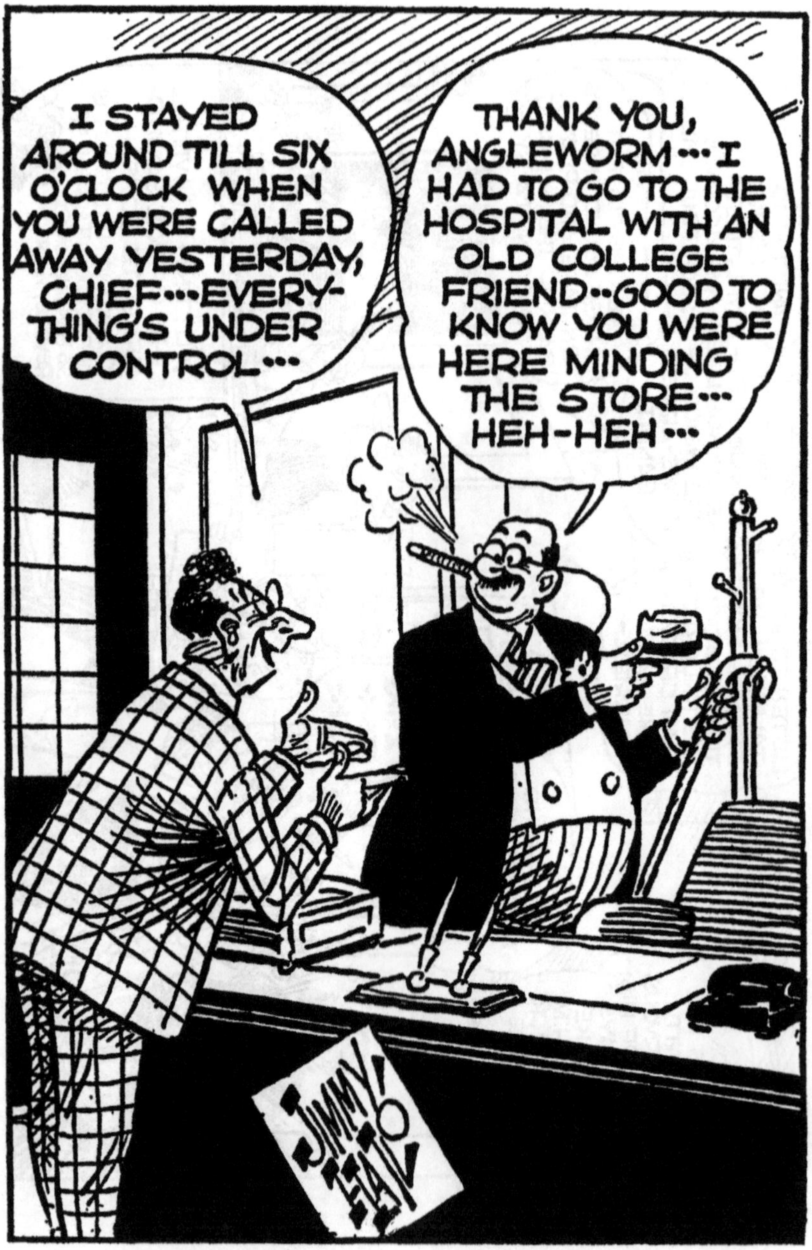
I STAYED AROUND TILL SIX O'CLOCK WHEN YOU WERE CALLED AWAY YESTERDAY, CHIEF··· EVERY-THING'S UNDER CONTROL···
THANK YOU, ANGLEWORM··· I HAD TO GO TO THE HOSPITAL WITH AN OLD COLLEGE FRIEND·· GOOD TO KNOW YOU WERE HERE MINDING THE STORE··· HEH-HEH···

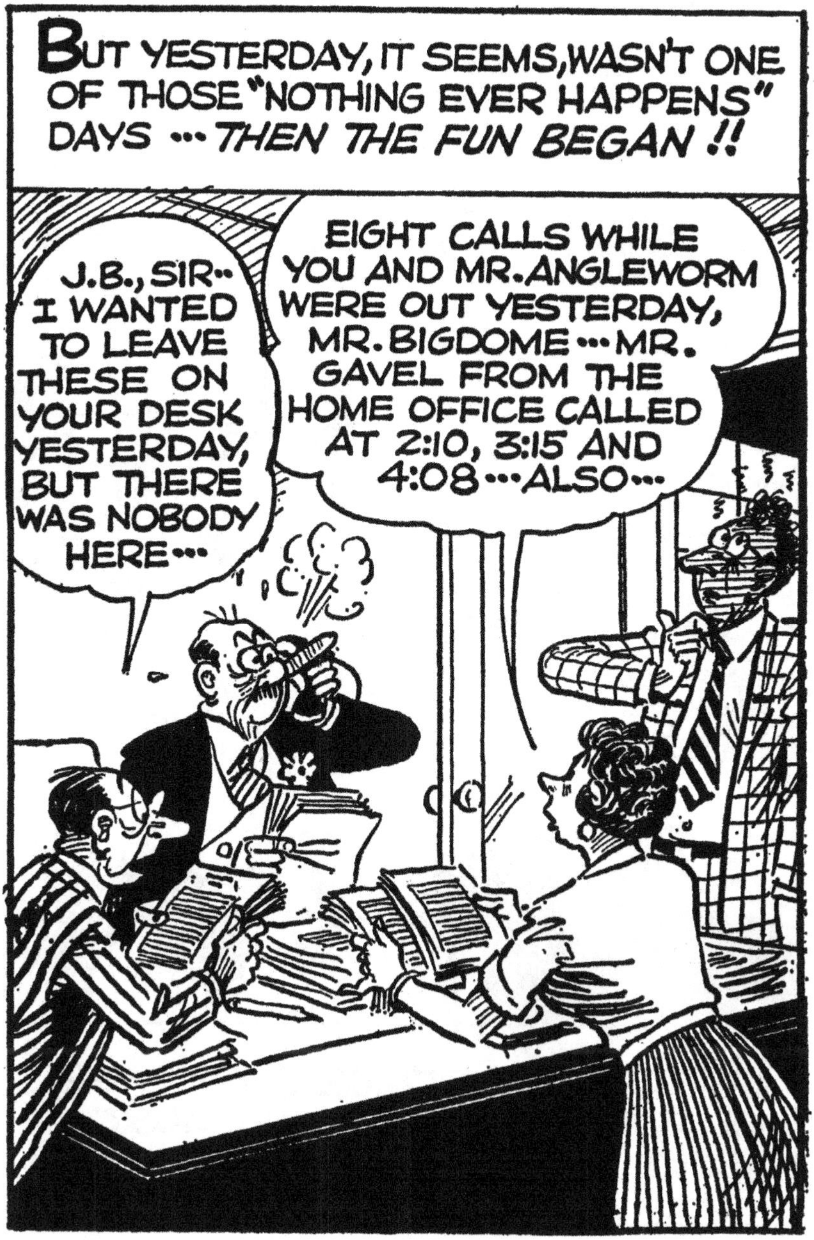
BUT YESTERDAY, IT SEEMS, WASN'T ONE OF THOSE "NOTHING EVER HAPPENS" DAYS ... THEN THE FUN BEGAN !!
J.B., SIR.. I WANTED TO LEAVE THESE ON YOUR DESK YESTERDAY, BUT THERE WAS NOBODY HERE...
EIGHT CALLS WHILE YOU AND MR. ANGLEWORM WERE OUT YESTERDAY, MR. BIGDOME ... MR. GAVEL FROM THE HOME OFFICE CALLED AT 2:10, 3:15 AND 4:08 ... ALSO ...

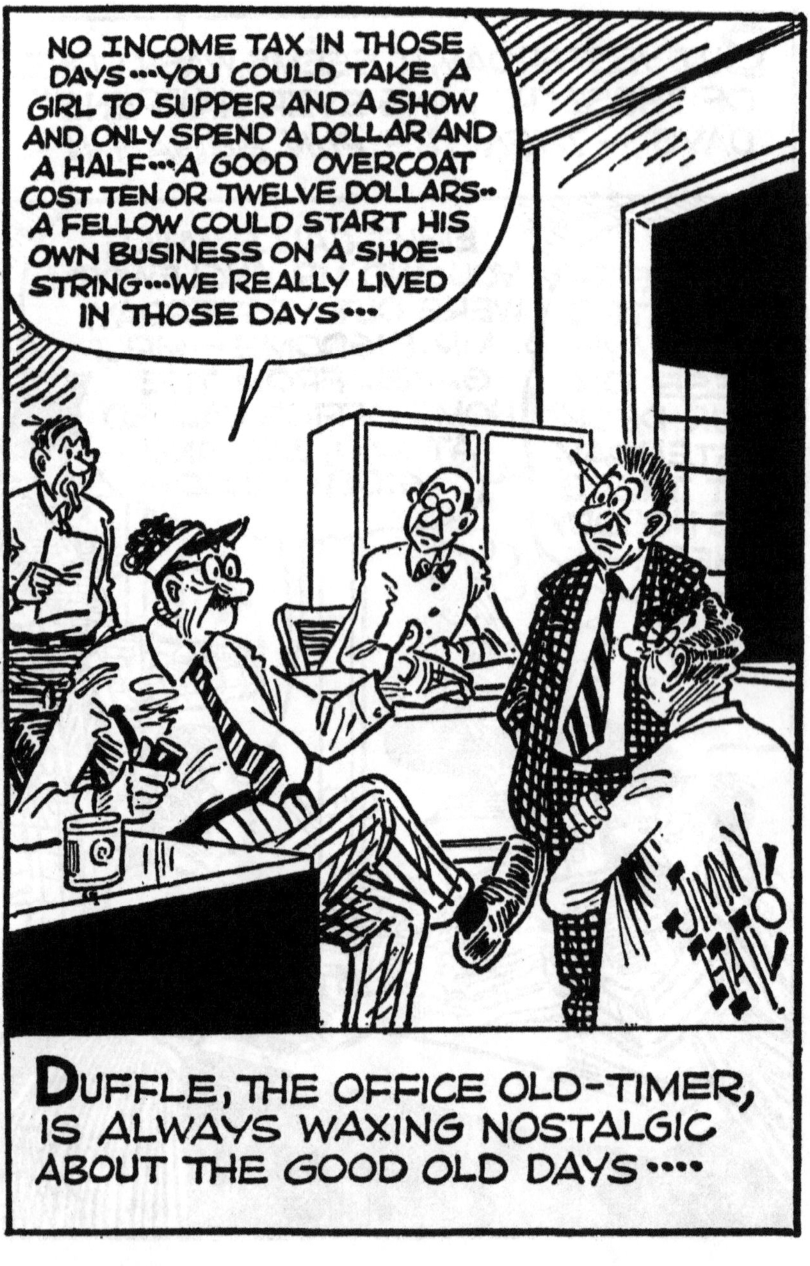
NO INCOME TAX IN THOSE DAYS···YOU COULD TAKE A GIRL TO SUPPER AND A SHOW AND ONLY SPEND A DOLLAR AND A HALF···A GOOD OVERCOAT COST TEN OR TWELVE DOLLARS·· A FELLOW COULD START HIS OWN BUSINESS ON A SHOE-STRING···WE REALLY LIVED IN THOSE DAYS···
JIMMY HATLO
DUFFLE, THE OFFICE OLD-TIMER, IS ALWAYS WAXING NOSTALGIC ABOUT THE GOOD OLD DAYS····

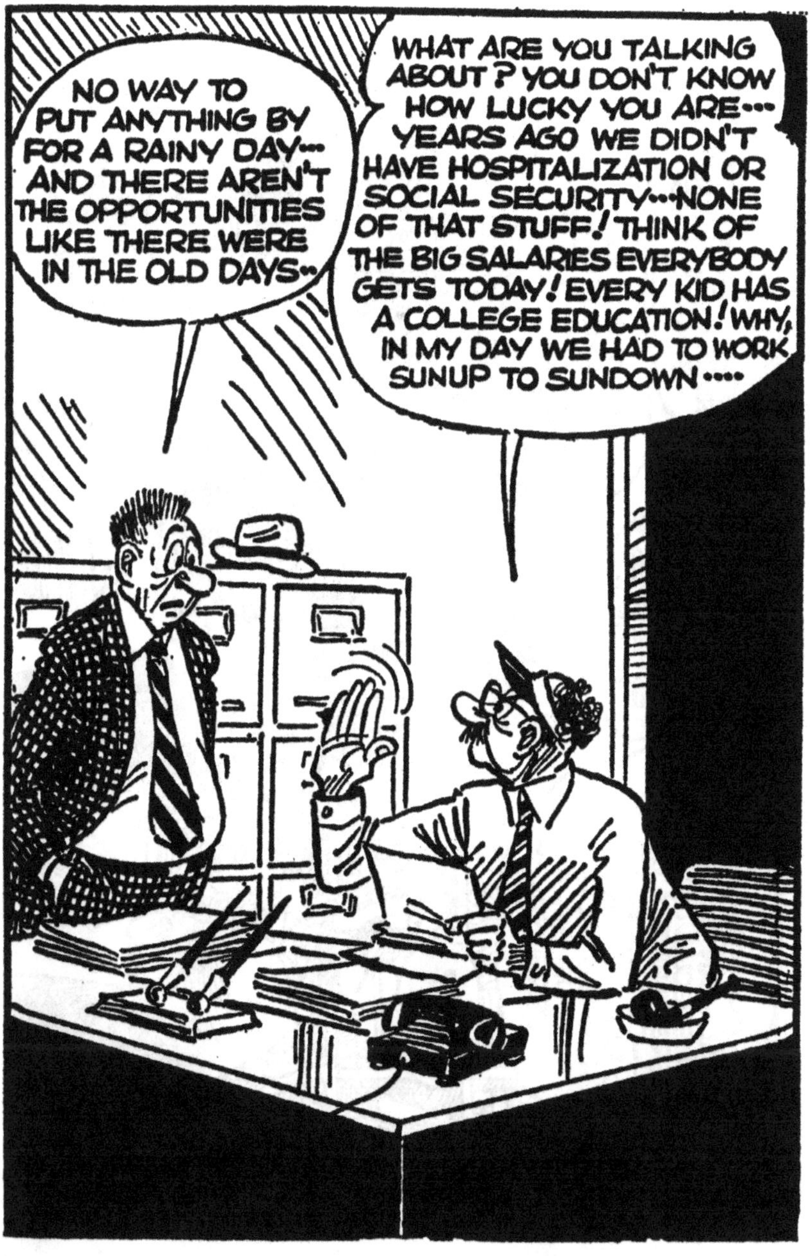
NO WAY TO PUT ANYTHING BY FOR A RAINY DAY... AND THERE AREN'T THE OPPORTUNITIES LIKE THERE WERE IN THE OLD DAYS..
WHAT ARE YOU TALKING ABOUT? YOU DON'T KNOW HOW LUCKY YOU ARE... YEARS AGO WE DIDN'T HAVE HOSPITALIZATION OR SOCIAL SECURITY...NONE OF THAT STUFF! THINK OF THE BIG SALARIES EVERYBODY GETS TODAY! EVERY KID HAS A COLLEGE EDUCATION! WHY, IN MY DAY WE HAD TO WORK SUNUP TO SUNDOWN....

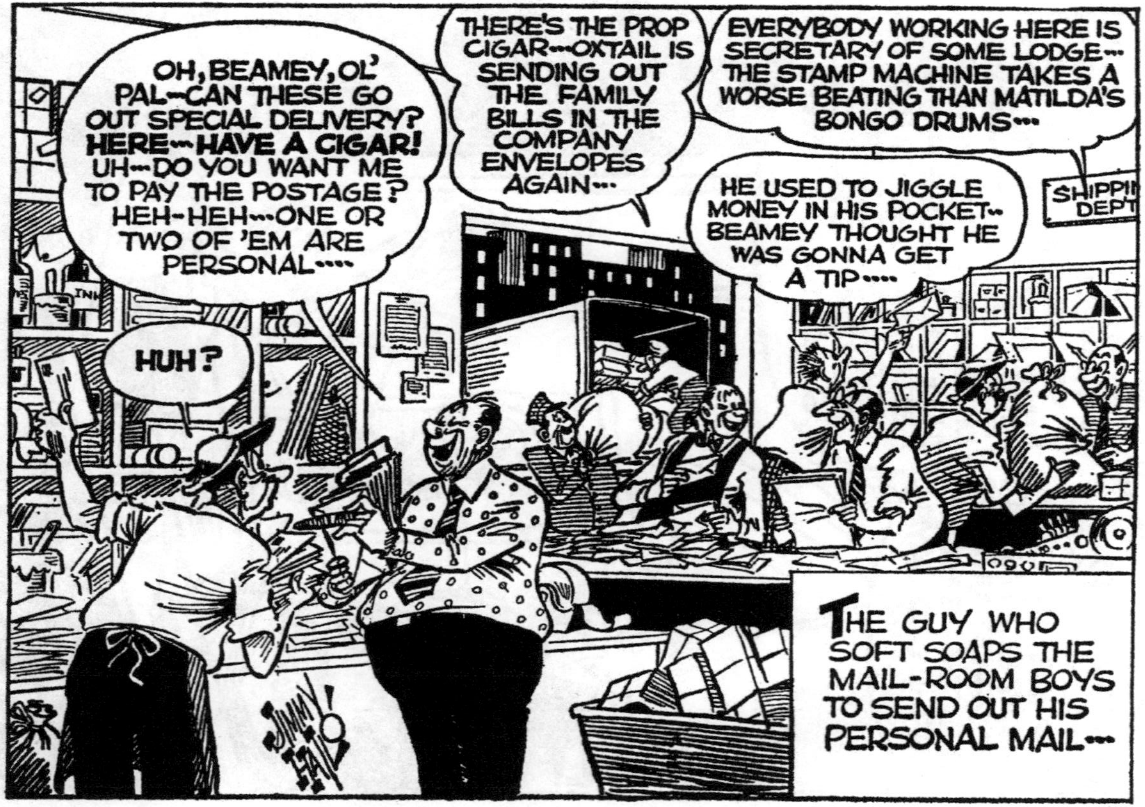
OH, BEAMEY, OL' PAL--CAN THESE GO OUT SPECIAL DELIVERY? HERE--HAVE A CIGAR! UH--DO YOU WANT ME TO PAY THE POSTAGE? HEH-HEH--ONE OR TWO OF 'EM ARE PERSONAL....
HUH?
THERE'S THE PROP CIGAR--OXTAIL IS SENDING OUT THE FAMILY BILLS IN THE COMPANY ENVELOPES AGAIN...
EVERYBODY WORKING HERE IS SECRETARY OF SOME LODGE--THE STAMP MACHINE TAKES A WORSE BEATING THAN MATILDA'S BONGO DRUMS...
HE USED TO JIGGLE MONEY IN HIS POCKET--BEAMEY THOUGHT HE WAS GONNA GET A TIP....
INK
THE GUY WHO SOFT SOAPS THE MAIL-ROOM BOYS TO SEND OUT HIS PERSONAL MAIL...

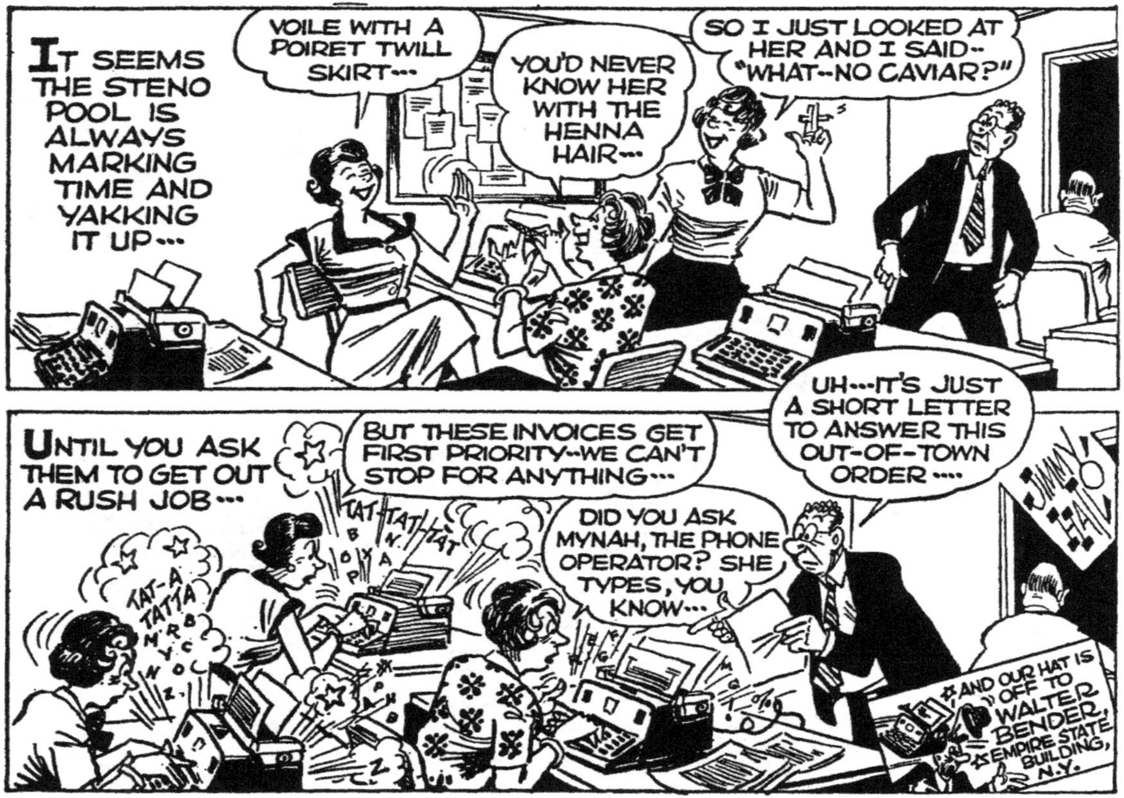

IT SEEMS THE STENO POOL IS ALWAYS MARKING TIME AND YAKKING IT UP...
VOILE WITH A POIRET TWILL SKIRT...
YOU'D NEVER KNOW HER WITH THE HENNA HAIR...
SO I JUST LOOKED AT HER AND I SAID-- "WHAT--NO CAVIAR?"
UNTIL YOU ASK THEM TO GET OUT A RUSH JOB...
BUT THESE INVOICES GET FIRST PRIORITY--WE CAN'T STOP FOR ANYTHING...
UH...IT'S JUST A SHORT LETTER TO ANSWER THIS OUT-OF-TOWN ORDER...
DID YOU ASK MYNAH, THE PHONE OPERATOR? SHE TYPES, YOU KNOW...
TAT-TAT-TAT
TAT-A TAT-A
AND OUR HAT IS OFF TO WALTER BENDER, EMPIRE STATE BUILDING, N.Y.

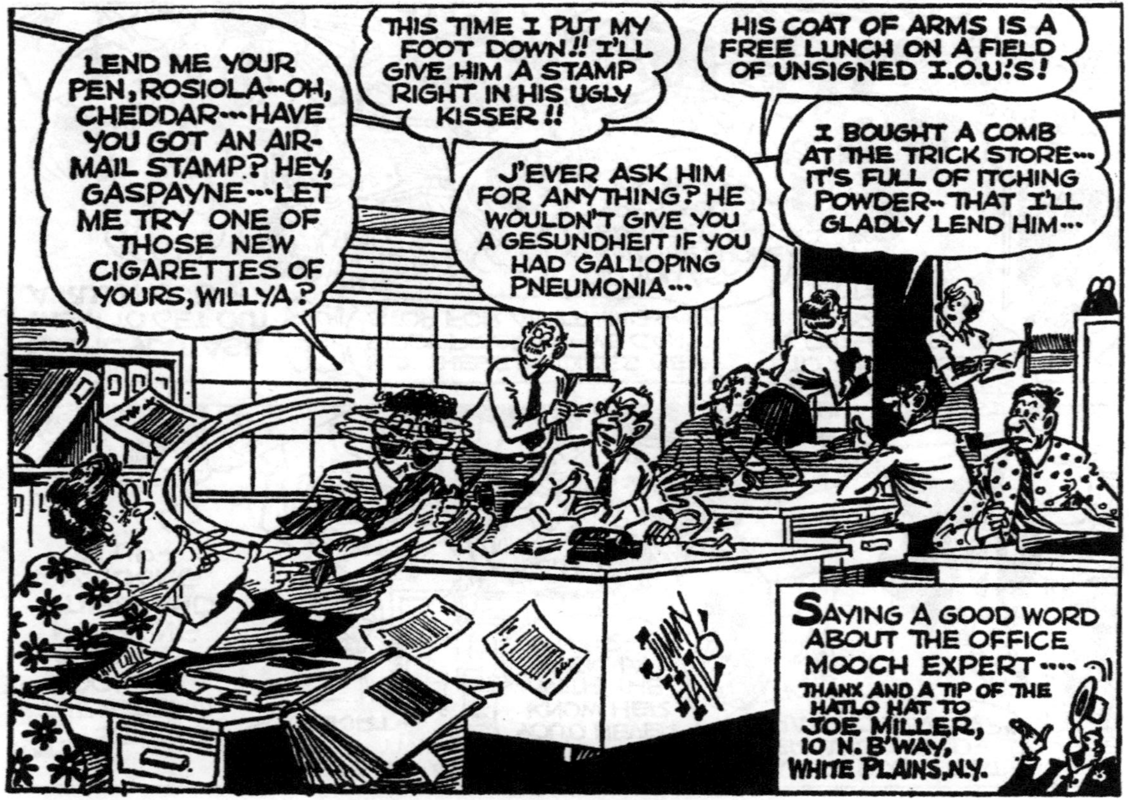
LEND ME YOUR PEN, ROSIOLA---OH, CHEDDAR--- HAVE YOU GOT AN AIR-MAIL STAMP? HEY, GASPAYNE---LET ME TRY ONE OF THOSE NEW CIGARETTES OF YOURS, WILLYA?
THIS TIME I PUT MY FOOT DOWN!! I'LL GIVE HIM A STAMP RIGHT IN HIS UGLY KISSER!!
J'EVER ASK HIM FOR ANYTHING? HE WOULDN'T GIVE YOU A GESUNDHEIT IF YOU HAD GALLOPING PNEUMONIA---
HIS COAT OF ARMS IS A FREE LUNCH ON A FIELD OF UNSIGNED I.O.U.'S!
I BOUGHT A COMB AT THE TRICK STORE--- IT'S FULL OF ITCHING POWDER-- THAT I'LL GLADLY LEND HIM---
SAYING A GOOD WORD ABOUT THE OFFICE MOOCH EXPERT....
THANX AND A TIP OF THE HATLO HAT TO JOE MILLER, 10 N. B'WAY, WHITE PLAINS, N.Y.
JIMMY HATLO

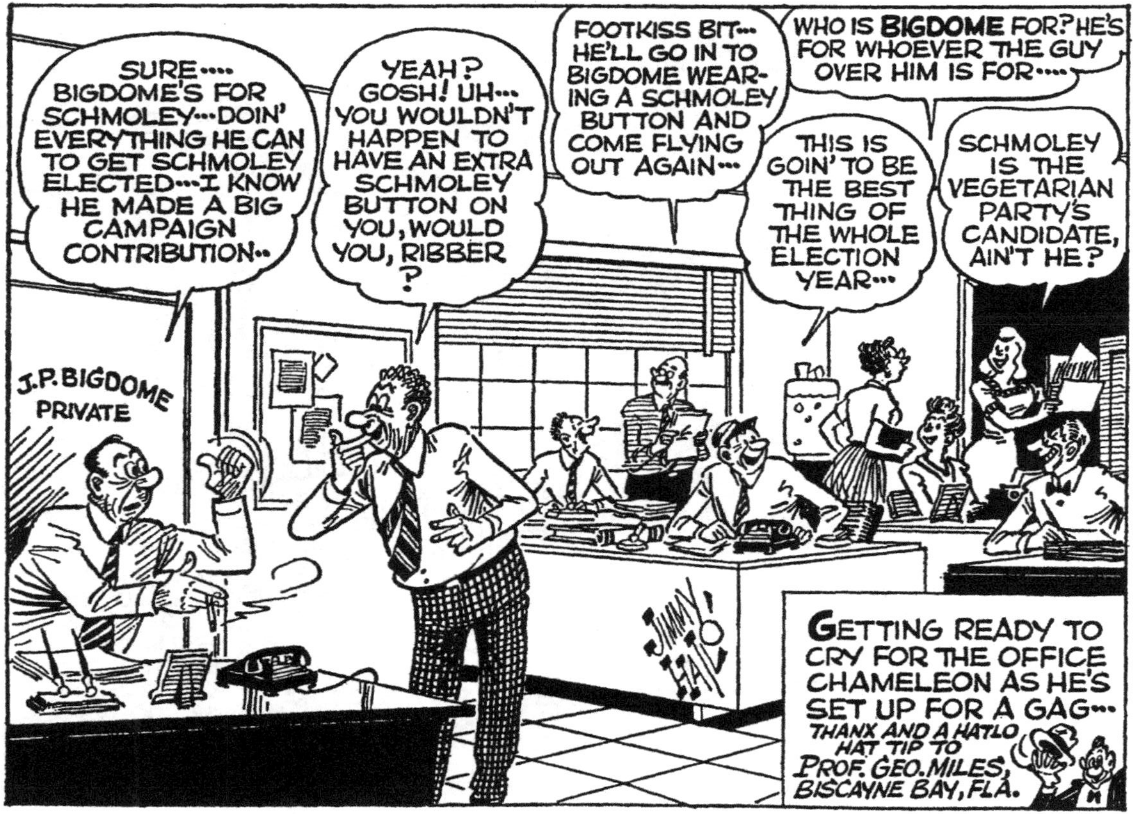
J.P. BIGDOME PRIVATE
SURE.... BIGDOME'S FOR SCHMOLEY...DOIN' EVERYTHING HE CAN TO GET SCHMOLEY ELECTED...I KNOW HE MADE A BIG CAMPAIGN CONTRIBUTION..
YEAH? GOSH! UH... YOU WOULDN'T HAPPEN TO HAVE AN EXTRA SCHMOLEY BUTTON ON YOU, WOULD YOU, RIBBER?
FOOTKISS BIT... HE'LL GO IN TO BIGDOME WEARING A SCHMOLEY BUTTON AND COME FLYING OUT AGAIN...
WHO IS BIGDOME FOR? HE'S FOR WHOEVER THE GUY OVER HIM IS FOR....
THIS IS GOIN' TO BE THE BEST THING OF THE WHOLE ELECTION YEAR...
SCHMOLEY IS THE VEGETARIAN PARTY'S CANDIDATE, AIN'T HE?
JIMMY HATLO
GETTING READY TO CRY FOR THE OFFICE CHAMELEON AS HE'S SET UP FOR A GAG...
THANX AND A HATLO HAT TIP TO PROF. GEO. MILES, BISCAYNE BAY, FLA.

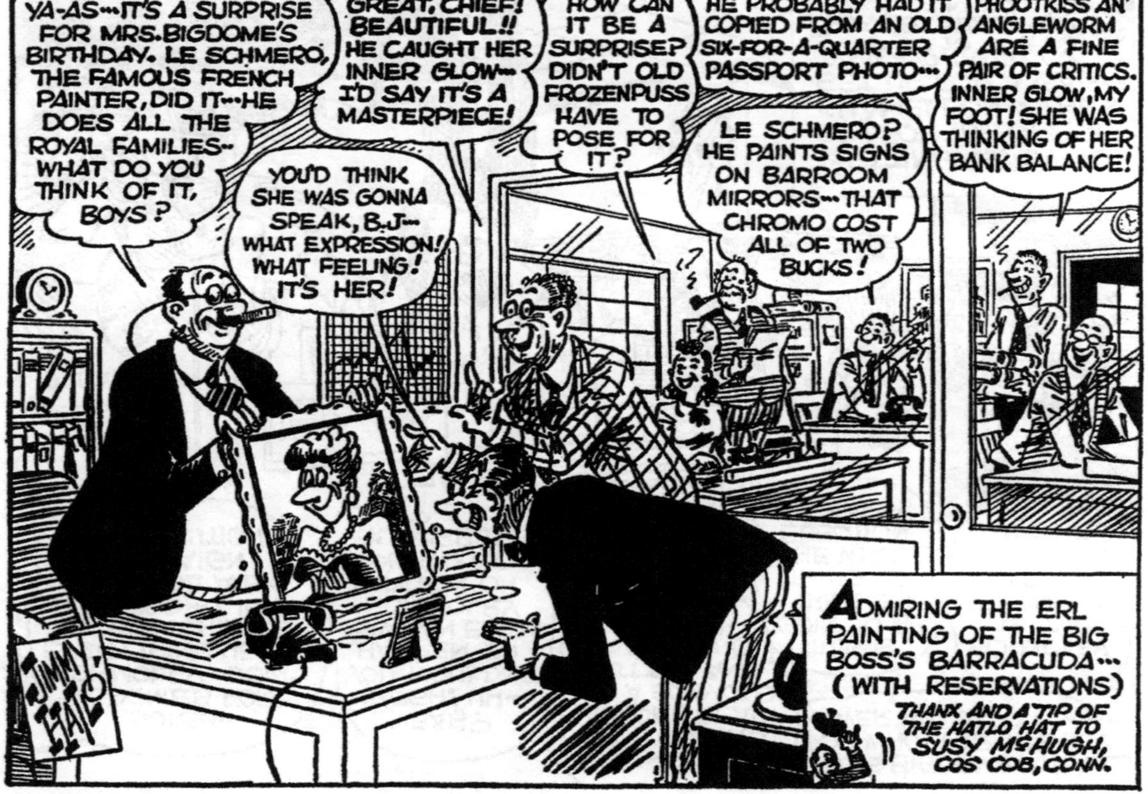
YA-AS··· IT'S A SURPRISE FOR MRS. BIGDOME'S BIRTHDAY. LE SCHMERO, THE FAMOUS FRENCH PAINTER, DID IT···HE DOES ALL THE ROYAL FAMILIES-- WHAT DO YOU THINK OF IT, BOYS?
YOU'D THINK SHE WAS GONNA SPEAK, B.J.··· WHAT EXPRESSION! WHAT FEELING! IT'S HER!
GREAT, CHIEF! BEAUTIFUL!! HE CAUGHT HER INNER GLOW··· I'D SAY IT'S A MASTERPIECE!
HOW CAN IT BE A SURPRISE? DIDN'T OLD FROZENPUSS HAVE TO POSE FOR IT?
HE PROBABLY HAD IT COPIED FROM AN OLD SIX-FOR-A-QUARTER PASSPORT PHOTO···
LE SCHMERO? HE PAINTS SIGNS ON BARROOM MIRRORS··· THAT CHROMO COST ALL OF TWO BUCKS!
PHOOTKISS AN' ANGLEWORM ARE A FINE PAIR OF CRITICS. INNER GLOW, MY FOOT! SHE WAS THINKING OF HER BANK BALANCE!
ADMIRING THE ERL PAINTING OF THE BIG BOSS'S BARRACUDA··· (WITH RESERVATIONS)
THANX AND A TIP OF THE HATLO HAT TO SUSY McHUGH, COS COB, CONN.
JIMMY HATLO

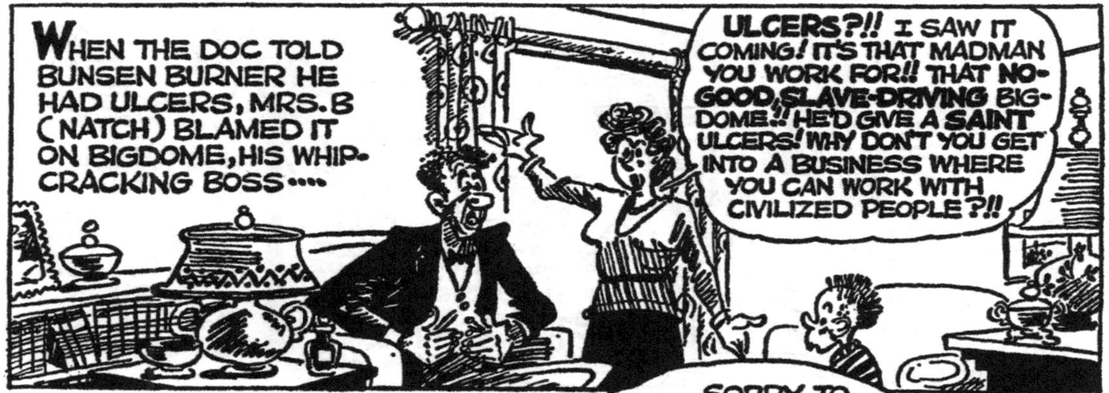
WHEN THE DOC TOLD BUNSEN BURNER HE HAD ULCERS, MRS. B (NATCH) BLAMED IT ON BIGDOME, HIS WHIP-CRACKING BOSS....
ULCERS?!! I SAW IT COMING! IT'S THAT MADMAN YOU WORK FOR!! THAT NO-GOOD, SLAVE-DRIVING BIGDOME!! HE'D GIVE A SAINT ULCERS! WHY DON'T YOU GET INTO A BUSINESS WHERE YOU CAN WORK WITH CIVILIZED PEOPLE?!!

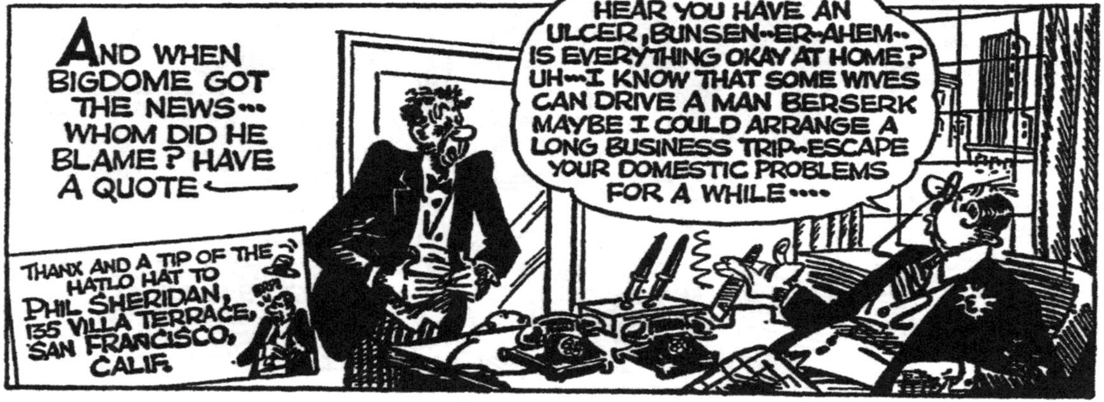
AND WHEN BIGDOME GOT THE NEWS... WHOM DID HE BLAME? HAVE A QUOTE
SORRY TO HEAR YOU HAVE AN ULCER, BUNSEN--ER-AHEM-- IS EVERYTHING OKAY AT HOME? UH--I KNOW THAT SOME WIVES CAN DRIVE A MAN BERSERK MAYBE I COULD ARRANGE A LONG BUSINESS TRIP--ESCAPE YOUR DOMESTIC PROBLEMS FOR A WHILE....
THANX AND A TIP OF THE HATLO HAT TO PHIL SHERIDAN, 135 VILLA TERRACE, SAN FRANCISCO, CALIF.

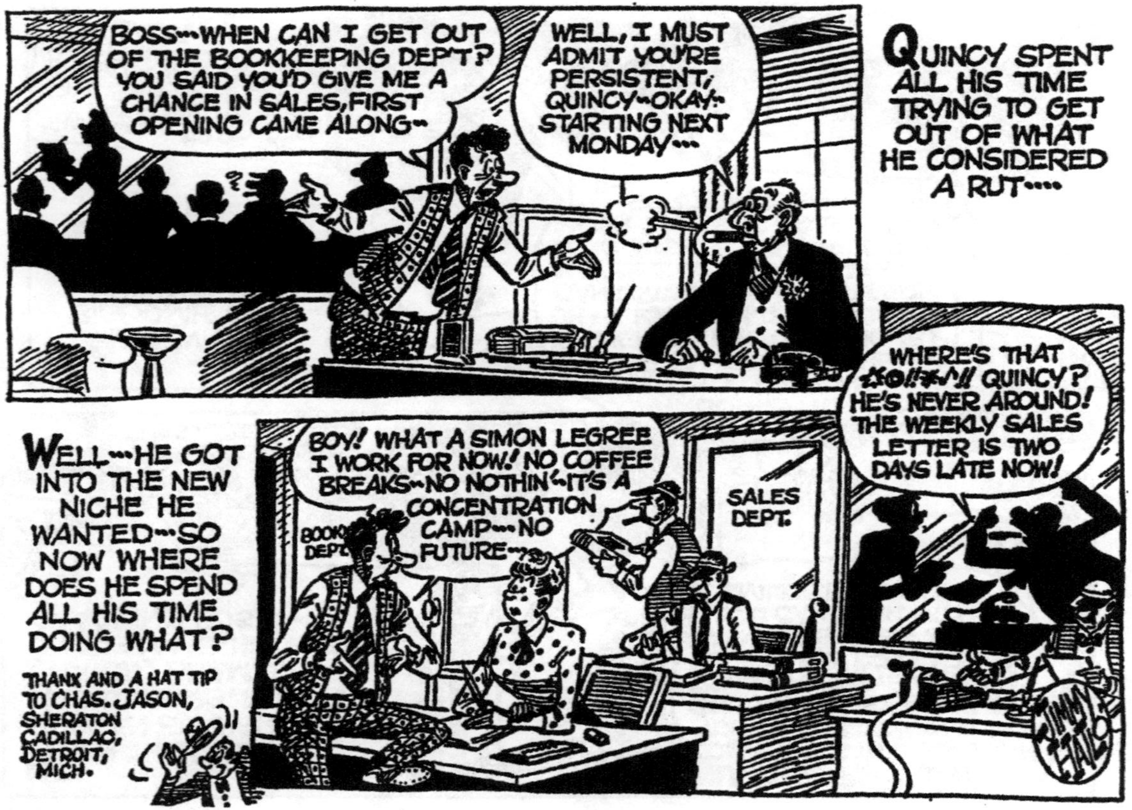
QUINCY SPENT ALL HIS TIME TRYING TO GET OUT OF WHAT HE CONSIDERED A RUT....
BOSS...WHEN CAN I GET OUT OF THE BOOKKEEPING DEP'T? YOU SAID YOU'D GIVE ME A CHANCE IN SALES, FIRST OPENING CAME ALONG..
WELL, I MUST ADMIT YOU'RE PERSISTENT, QUINCY..OKAY.. STARTING NEXT MONDAY...
WELL...HE GOT INTO THE NEW NICHE HE WANTED...SO NOW WHERE DOES HE SPEND ALL HIS TIME DOING WHAT?
BOY! WHAT A SIMON LEGREE I WORK FOR NOW! NO COFFEE BREAKS..NO NOTHIN'..IT'S A CONCENTRATION CAMP...NO FUTURE...
SALES DEPT.
WHERE'S THAT ☆@!!*^!! QUINCY? HE'S NEVER AROUND! THE WEEKLY SALES LETTER IS TWO DAYS LATE NOW!
THANX AND A HAT TIP TO CHAS. JASON, SHERATON CADILLAC, DETROIT, MICH.
JIMMY HATLO

BOYS---I JUST CALLED THIS MEETING TO TELL YOU WHAT A GREAT JOB YOU'RE DOING--YOU'RE THE BEST SALES FORCE IN THE BUSINESS--HOWEVER, YOU SEEM CONTENT TO SIT ON YOUR LAURELS! YOU GUYS OUGHT TO KNOW THAT ORDERS DON'T FLY IN OVER THE TRANSOM!! ANOTHER THING--THERE'S TOO MUCH HORSEPLAY AND GOLD-BRICKING---NOT ONLY THAT, BUT----
HE ALWAYS STARTS WITH TEN SECONDS OF PRAISE, THEN COMES THE HOUR OF SQUAWKS AND ASSORTED COMPLAINTS!
YOU HAVEN'T HEARD ANYTHING YET--WAIT'LL YOU SEE HOW HE ENDS IT--RED NECK--WHITE GILLS AND BLUE IN THE FACE--
WHEN HE GETS THROUGH I DON'T FEEL LIKE SELLING ANYTHING---I JUST WANT TO BUY A GUN----
FIRST HE GIVES YOU A BOUQUET, THEN HE HITS YOU IN THE NOSE SO YOU CAN'T SMELL IT---
JIMMY HATLO
LISTENING TO BIGDOME GIVING OUT THE CANDY BEFORE HE GIVES THE CASTOR OIL ----
THANX AND A HAT TIP TO ORINSKY DE GAUST, 671-51 STREET, BROOKLYN 20, N.Y.

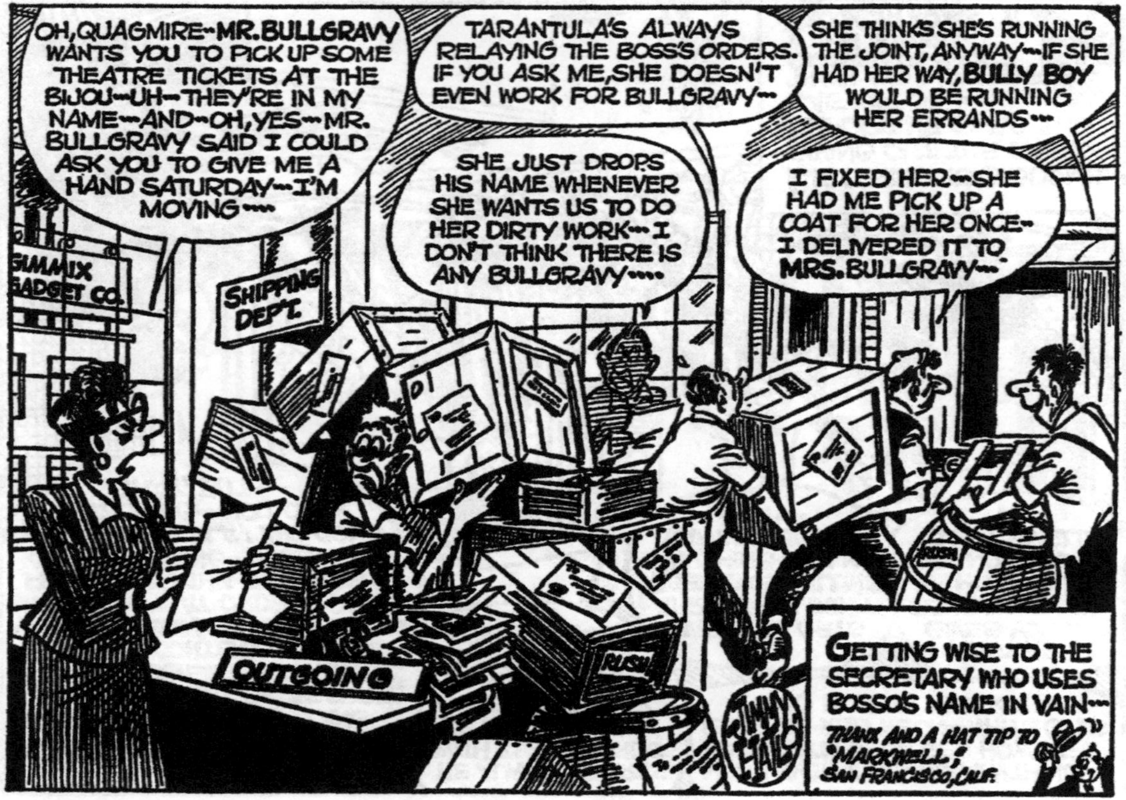
OH, QUAGMIRE--MR. BULLGRAVY WANTS YOU TO PICK UP SOME THEATRE TICKETS AT THE BIJOU--UH--THEY'RE IN MY NAME--AND--OH, YES--MR. BULLGRAVY SAID I COULD ASK YOU TO GIVE ME A HAND SATURDAY--I'M MOVING....
TARANTULA'S ALWAYS RELAYING THE BOSS'S ORDERS. IF YOU ASK ME, SHE DOESN'T EVEN WORK FOR BULLGRAVY--
SHE JUST DROPS HIS NAME WHENEVER SHE WANTS US TO DO HER DIRTY WORK--I DON'T THINK THERE IS ANY BULLGRAVY....
SHE THINKS SHE'S RUNNING THE JOINT, ANYWAY--IF SHE HAD HER WAY, BULLY BOY WOULD BE RUNNING HER ERRANDS--
I FIXED HER--SHE HAD ME PICK UP A COAT FOR HER ONCE--I DELIVERED IT TO MRS. BULLGRAVY--
GIMMIX GADGET CO.
SHIPPING DEPT.
OUTGOING
RUSH
GETTING WISE TO THE SECRETARY WHO USES BOSSO'S NAME IN VAIN--
THANK AND A HAT TIP TO "MARKWELL," SAN FRANCISCO, CALIF.
JIMMY HATLO

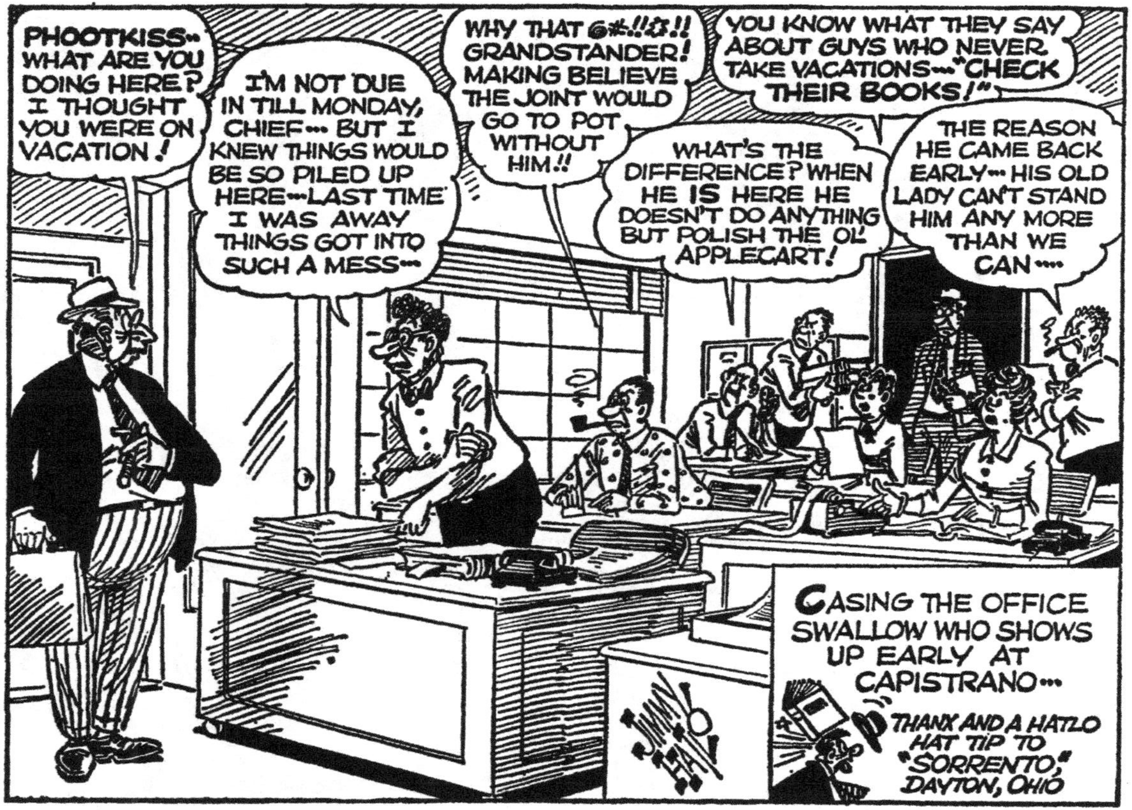
PHOOTKISS.. WHAT ARE YOU DOING HERE? I THOUGHT YOU WERE ON VACATION!
I'M NOT DUE IN TILL MONDAY, CHIEF... BUT I KNEW THINGS WOULD BE SO PILED UP HERE...LAST TIME I WAS AWAY THINGS GOT INTO SUCH A MESS...
WHY THAT 6#!!☆!! GRANDSTANDER! MAKING BELIEVE THE JOINT WOULD GO TO POT WITHOUT HIM!!
WHAT'S THE DIFFERENCE? WHEN HE IS HERE HE DOESN'T DO ANYTHING BUT POLISH THE OL' APPLECART!
YOU KNOW WHAT THEY SAY ABOUT GUYS WHO NEVER TAKE VACATIONS..."CHECK THEIR BOOKS!"
THE REASON HE CAME BACK EARLY... HIS OLD LADY CAN'T STAND HIM ANY MORE THAN WE CAN....
CASING THE OFFICE SWALLOW WHO SHOWS UP EARLY AT CAPISTRANO...
THANX AND A HATLO HAT TIP TO "SORRENTO," DAYTON, OHIO
JIMMY HATLO

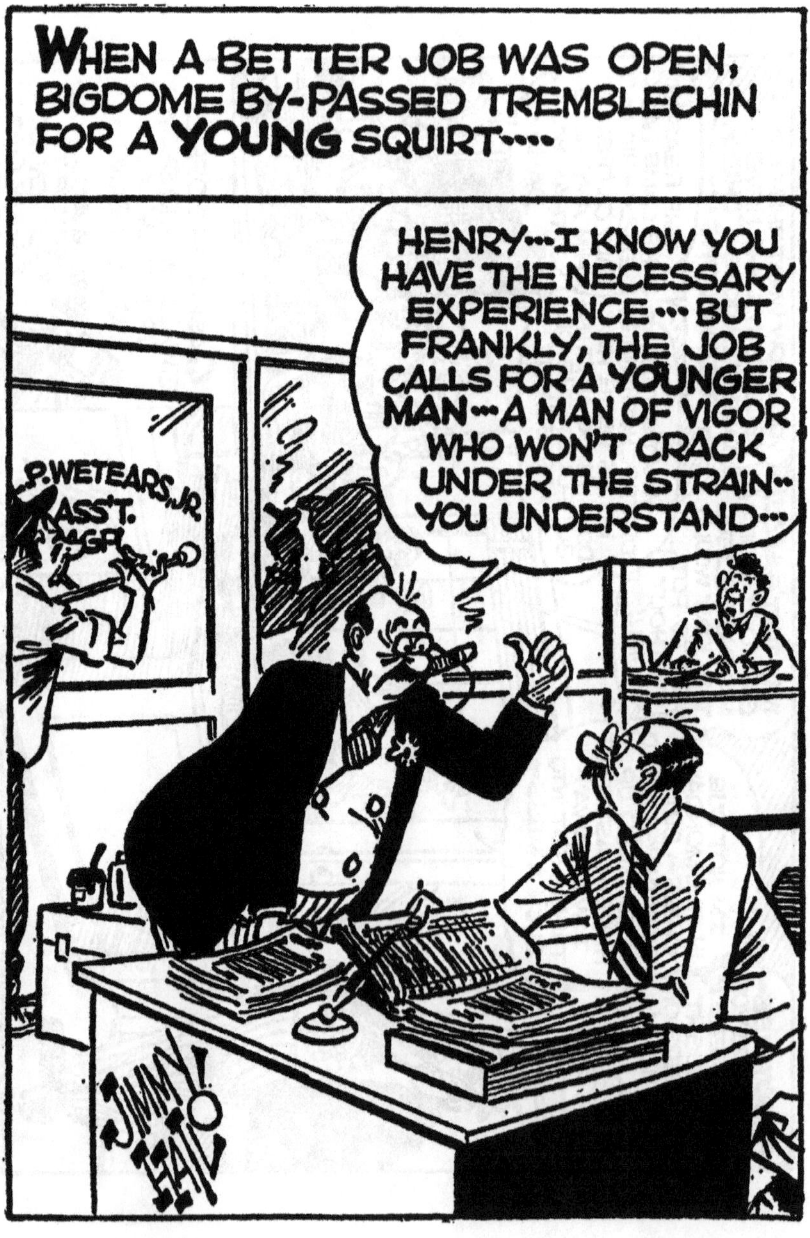
WHEN A BETTER JOB WAS OPEN, BIGDOME BY-PASSED TREMBLECHIN FOR A YOUNG SQUIRT....
HENRY...I KNOW YOU HAVE THE NECESSARY EXPERIENCE ... BUT FRANKLY, THE JOB CALLS FOR A YOUNGER MAN...A MAN OF VIGOR WHO WON'T CRACK UNDER THE STRAIN.. YOU UNDERSTAND...
P. WETEARS, JR. ASS'T. MGR.
JIMMY HATLO

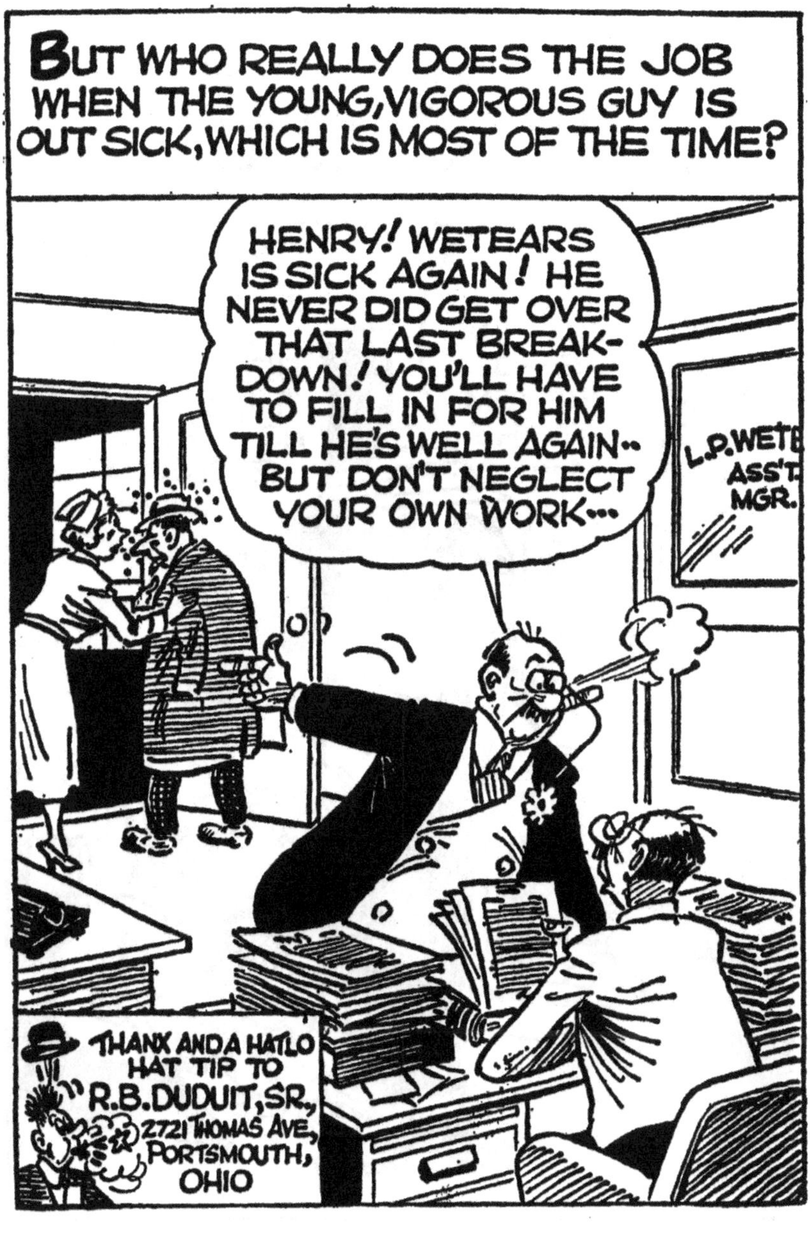
BUT WHO REALLY DOES THE JOB WHEN THE YOUNG, VIGOROUS GUY IS OUT SICK, WHICH IS MOST OF THE TIME?
HENRY! WETEARS IS SICK AGAIN! HE NEVER DID GET OVER THAT LAST BREAK-DOWN! YOU'LL HAVE TO FILL IN FOR HIM TILL HE'S WELL AGAIN-- BUT DON'T NEGLECT YOUR OWN WORK...
L.P.WETE
ASS'T. MGR.
THANX AND A HATLO HAT TIP TO R.B.DUDUIT, SR., 2721 THOMAS AVE, PORTSMOUTH, OHIO

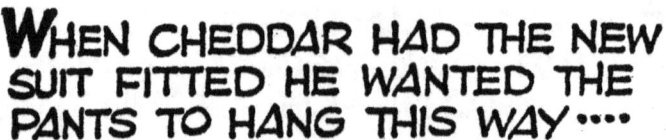

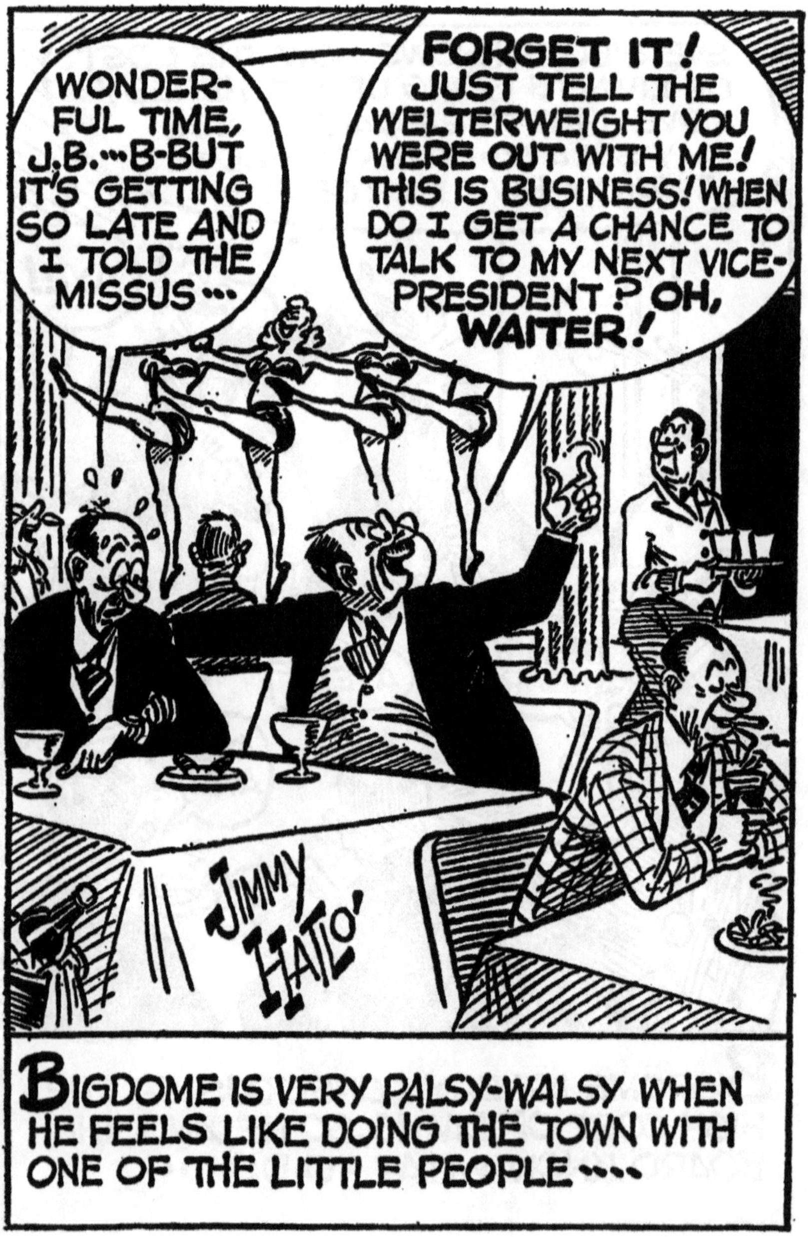
WONDER-FUL TIME, J.B.···B-BUT IT'S GETTING SO LATE AND I TOLD THE MISSUS···
FORGET IT! JUST TELL THE WELTERWEIGHT YOU WERE OUT WITH ME! THIS IS BUSINESS! WHEN DO I GET A CHANCE TO TALK TO MY NEXT VICE-PRESIDENT? OH, WAITER!
JIMMY HATLO'

BIGDOME IS VERY PALSY-WALSY WHEN HE FEELS LIKE DOING THE TOWN WITH ONE OF THE LITTLE PEOPLE····

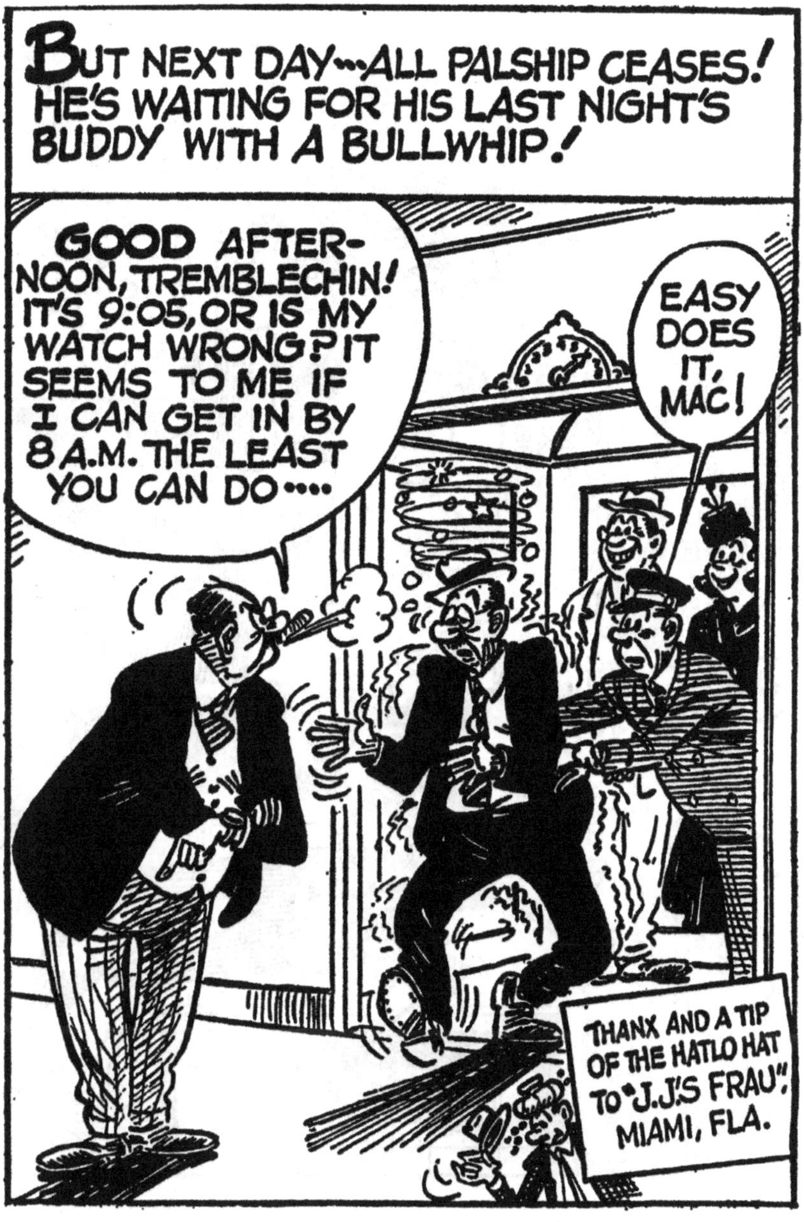
BUT NEXT DAY--ALL PALSHIP CEASES! HE'S WAITING FOR HIS LAST NIGHT'S BUDDY WITH A BULLWHIP!
GOOD AFTERNOON, TREMBLECHIN! IT'S 9:05, OR IS MY WATCH WRONG? IT SEEMS TO ME IF I CAN GET IN BY 8 A.M. THE LEAST YOU CAN DO....
EASY DOES IT, MAC!
THANX AND A TIP OF THE HATLO HAT TO "J.J.'S FRAU", MIAMI, FLA.

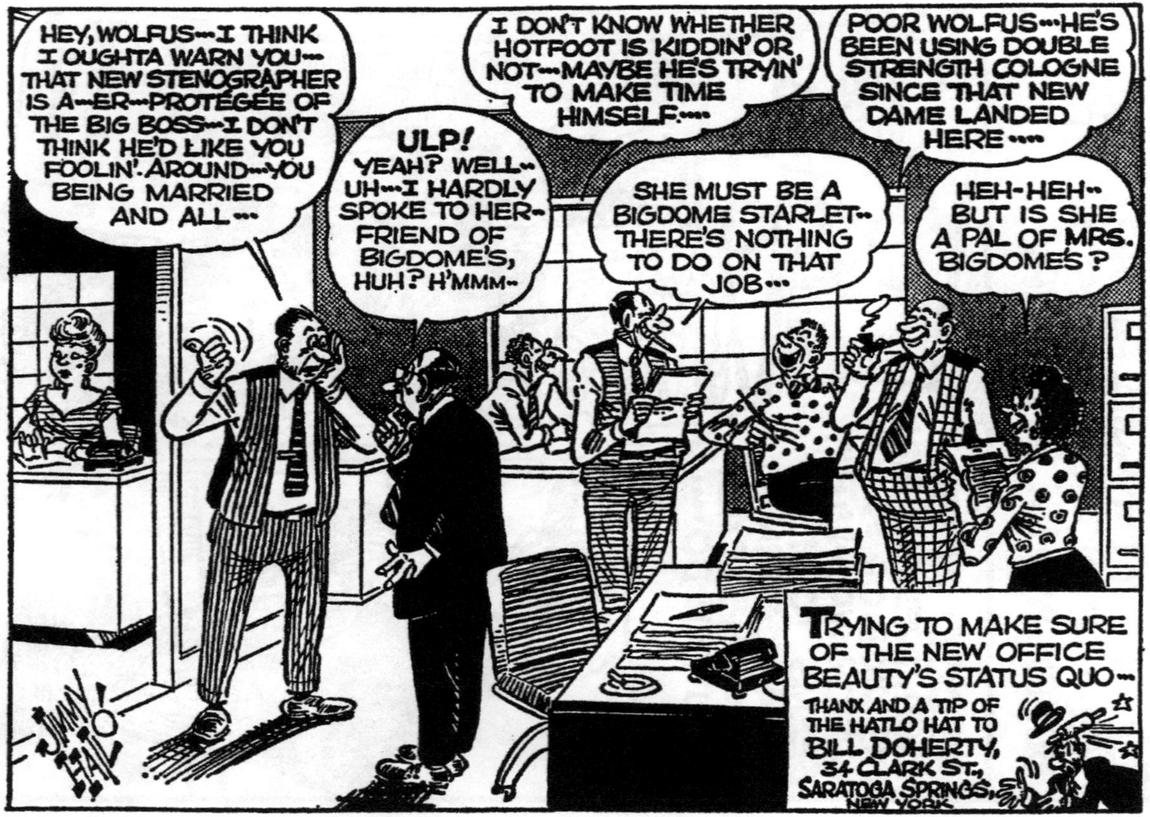
HEY, WOLFUS… I THINK I OUGHTA WARN YOU… THAT NEW STENOGRAPHER IS A…ER…PROTÉGÉE OF THE BIG BOSS…I DON'T THINK HE'D LIKE YOU FOOLIN'. AROUND…YOU BEING MARRIED AND ALL…
ULP! YEAH? WELL.. UH…I HARDLY SPOKE TO HER.. FRIEND OF BIGDOME'S, HUH? H'MMM..
I DON'T KNOW WHETHER HOTFOOT IS KIDDIN' OR NOT…MAYBE HE'S TRYIN' TO MAKE TIME HIMSELF….
SHE MUST BE A BIGDOME STARLET.. THERE'S NOTHING TO DO ON THAT JOB…
POOR WOLFUS…HE'S BEEN USING DOUBLE STRENGTH COLOGNE SINCE THAT NEW DAME LANDED HERE….
HEH-HEH.. BUT IS SHE A PAL OF MRS. BIGDOME'S?
TRYING TO MAKE SURE OF THE NEW OFFICE BEAUTY'S STATUS QUO..
THANX AND A TIP OF THE HATLO HAT TO BILL DOHERTY, 34 CLARK ST., SARATOGA SPRINGS, NEW YORK
JIMMY HATLO

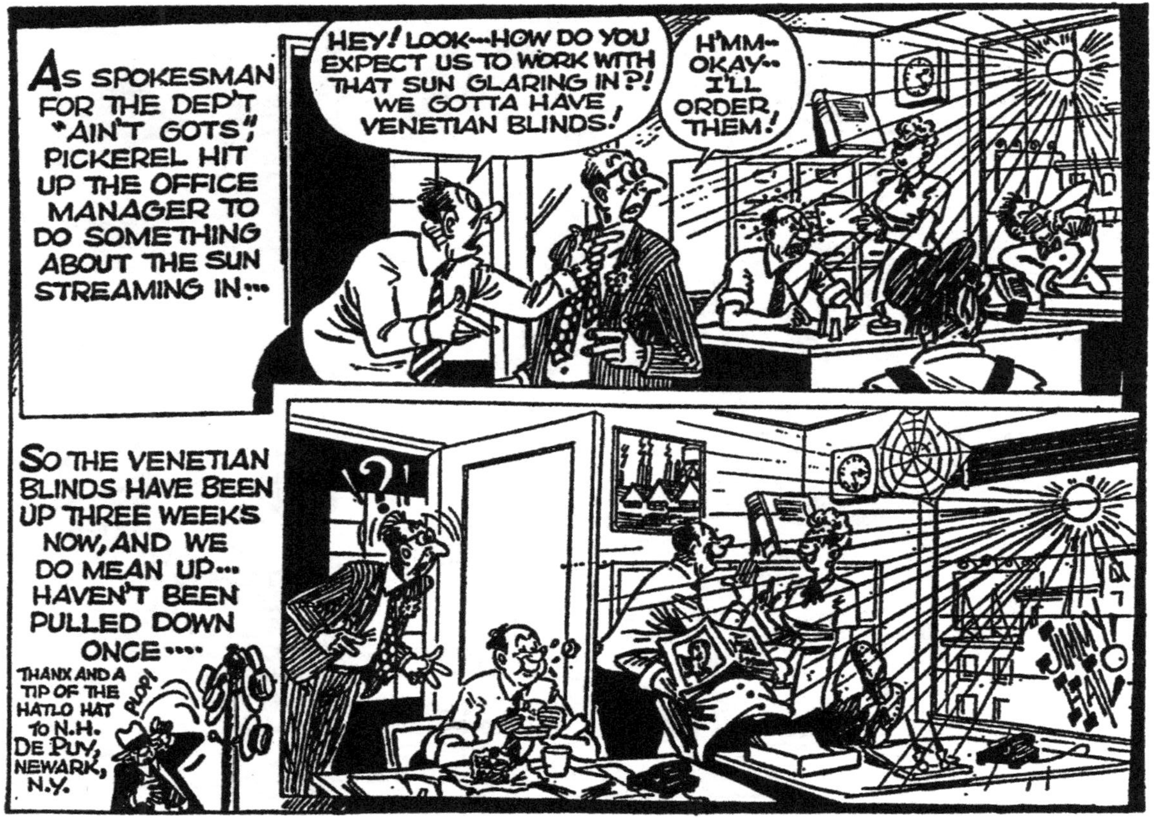
AS SPOKESMAN FOR THE DEP'T "AIN'T GOTS", PICKEREL HIT UP THE OFFICE MANAGER TO DO SOMETHING ABOUT THE SUN STREAMING IN...
HEY! LOOK--HOW DO YOU EXPECT US TO WORK WITH THAT SUN GLARING IN?! WE GOTTA HAVE VENETIAN BLINDS!
H'MM-- OKAY-- I'LL ORDER THEM!
SO THE VENETIAN BLINDS HAVE BEEN UP THREE WEEKS NOW, AND WE DO MEAN UP... HAVEN'T BEEN PULLED DOWN ONCE....
THANX AND A TIP OF THE HATLO HAT TO N.H. DE PUY, NEWARK, N.Y.
PLOP!
JIMMY HATLO

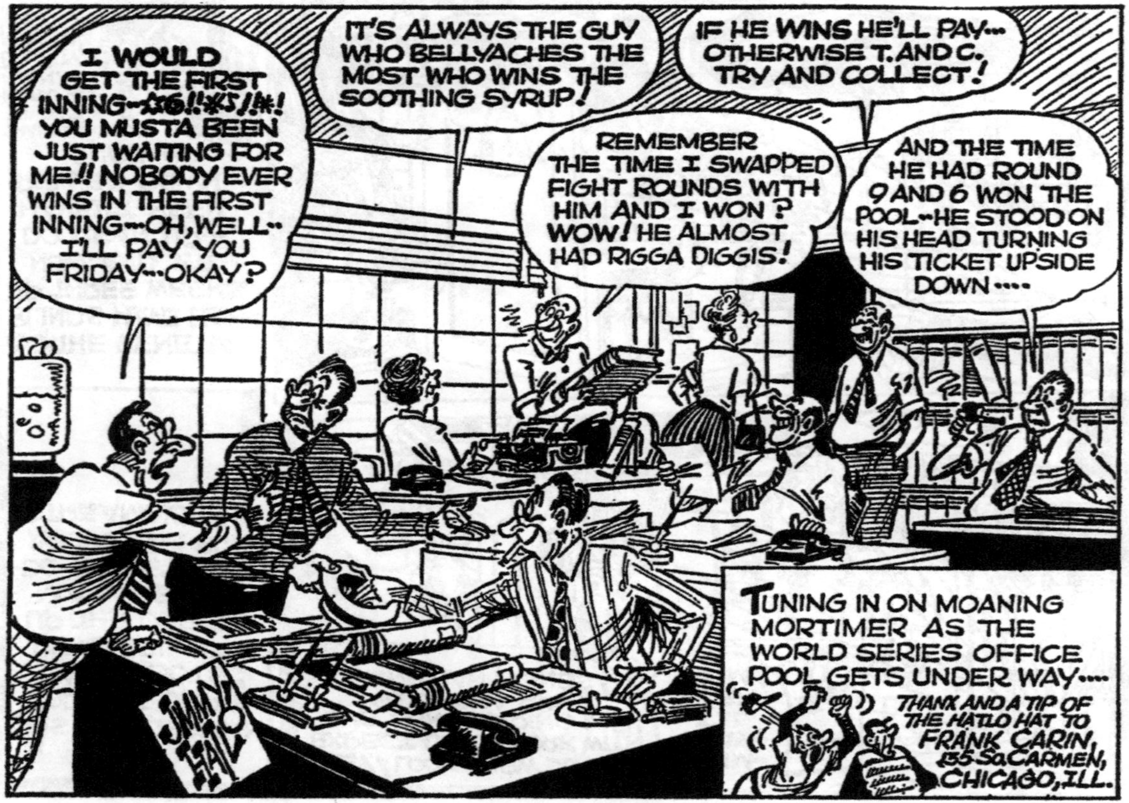
I WOULD GET THE FIRST INNING--☆$!!*$!*! YOU MUSTA BEEN JUST WAITING FOR ME!! NOBODY EVER WINS IN THE FIRST INNING--OH, WELL-- I'LL PAY YOU FRIDAY--OKAY?
IT'S ALWAYS THE GUY WHO BELLYACHES THE MOST WHO WINS THE SOOTHING SYRUP!
IF HE WINS HE'LL PAY-- OTHERWISE T. AND C. TRY AND COLLECT!
REMEMBER THE TIME I SWAPPED FIGHT ROUNDS WITH HIM AND I WON? WOW! HE ALMOST HAD RIGGA DIGGIS!
AND THE TIME HE HAD ROUND 9 AND 6 WON THE POOL--HE STOOD ON HIS HEAD TURNING HIS TICKET UPSIDE DOWN....
TUNING IN ON MOANING MORTIMER AS THE WORLD SERIES OFFICE POOL GETS UNDER WAY....
THANX AND A TIP OF THE HATLO HAT TO FRANK CARIN, 135 So. CARMEN, CHICAGO, ILL.

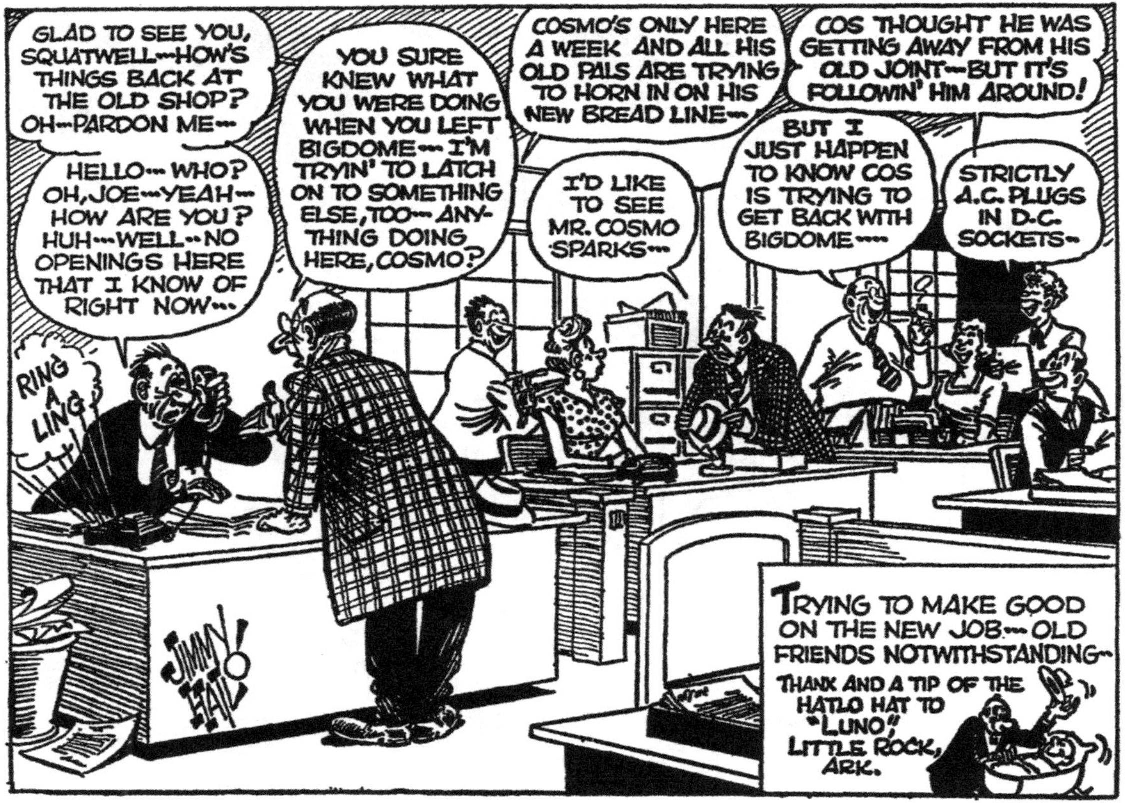
GLAD TO SEE YOU, SQUATWELL—HOW'S THINGS BACK AT THE OLD SHOP? OH—PARDON ME—
HELLO— WHO? OH, JOE—YEAH— HOW ARE YOU? HUH—WELL—NO OPENINGS HERE THAT I KNOW OF RIGHT NOW—
RING A LING
YOU SURE KNEW WHAT YOU WERE DOING WHEN YOU LEFT BIGDOME— I'M TRYIN' TO LATCH ON TO SOMETHING ELSE, TOO— ANYTHING DOING HERE, COSMO?
COSMO'S ONLY HERE A WEEK AND ALL HIS OLD PALS ARE TRYING TO HORN IN ON HIS NEW BREAD LINE—
I'D LIKE TO SEE MR. COSMO SPARKS—
COS THOUGHT HE WAS GETTING AWAY FROM HIS OLD JOINT—BUT IT'S FOLLOWIN' HIM AROUND!
BUT I JUST HAPPEN TO KNOW COS IS TRYING TO GET BACK WITH BIGDOME—
STRICTLY A.C. PLUGS IN D.C. SOCKETS—
JIMMY HATLO
TRYING TO MAKE GOOD ON THE NEW JOB— OLD FRIENDS NOTWITHSTANDING—
THANX AND A TIP OF THE HATLO HAT TO "LUNO," LITTLE ROCK, ARK.

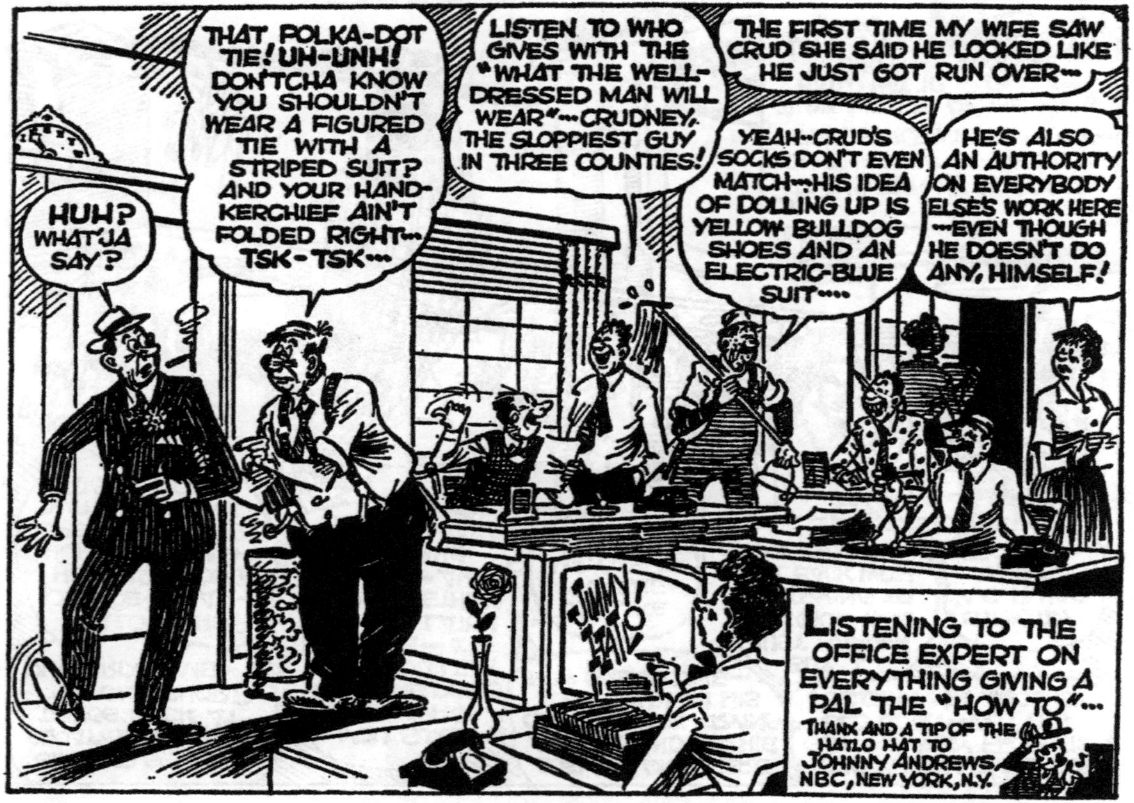
HUH? WHAT'JA SAY?
THAT POLKA-DOT TIE! UH-UNH! DON'TCHA KNOW YOU SHOULDN'T WEAR A FIGURED TIE WITH A STRIPED SUIT? AND YOUR HANDKERCHIEF AIN'T FOLDED RIGHT... TSK-TSK...
LISTEN TO WHO GIVES WITH THE "WHAT THE WELL-DRESSED MAN WILL WEAR"... CRUDNEY, THE SLOPPIEST GUY IN THREE COUNTIES!
THE FIRST TIME MY WIFE SAW CRUD SHE SAID HE LOOKED LIKE HE JUST GOT RUN OVER...
YEAH--CRUD'S SOCKS DON'T EVEN MATCH...HIS IDEA OF DOLLING UP IS YELLOW BULLDOG SHOES AND AN ELECTRIC-BLUE SUIT....
HE'S ALSO AN AUTHORITY ON EVERYBODY ELSE'S WORK HERE ...EVEN THOUGH HE DOESN'T DO ANY, HIMSELF!
JIMMY HATLO!
LISTENING TO THE OFFICE EXPERT ON EVERYTHING GIVING A PAL THE "HOW TO"...
THANX AND A TIP OF THE HATLO HAT TO JOHNNY ANDREWS, NBC, NEW YORK, N.Y.

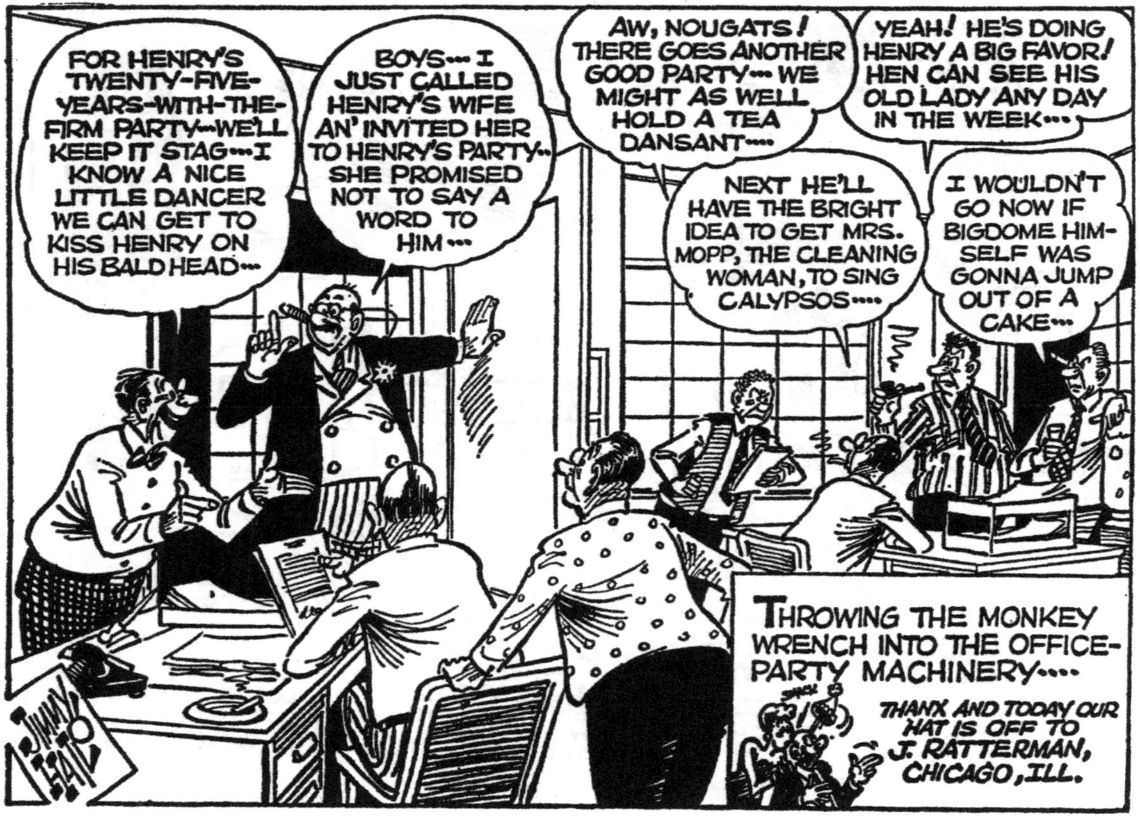
FOR HENRY'S TWENTY-FIVE-YEARS-WITH-THE-FIRM PARTY... WE'LL KEEP IT STAG... I KNOW A NICE LITTLE DANCER WE CAN GET TO KISS HENRY ON HIS BALD HEAD...
BOYS... I JUST CALLED HENRY'S WIFE AN' INVITED HER TO HENRY'S PARTY.. SHE PROMISED NOT TO SAY A WORD TO HIM...
AW, NOUGATS! THERE GOES ANOTHER GOOD PARTY... WE MIGHT AS WELL HOLD A TEA DANSANT....
YEAH! HE'S DOING HENRY A BIG FAVOR! HEN CAN SEE HIS OLD LADY ANY DAY IN THE WEEK...
NEXT HE'LL HAVE THE BRIGHT IDEA TO GET MRS. MOPP, THE CLEANING WOMAN, TO SING CALYPSOS....
I WOULDN'T GO NOW IF BIGDOME HIMSELF WAS GONNA JUMP OUT OF A CAKE...
THROWING THE MONKEY WRENCH INTO THE OFFICE-PARTY MACHINERY....
THANX AND TODAY OUR HAT IS OFF TO J. RATTERMAN, CHICAGO, ILL.
JIMMY HATLO

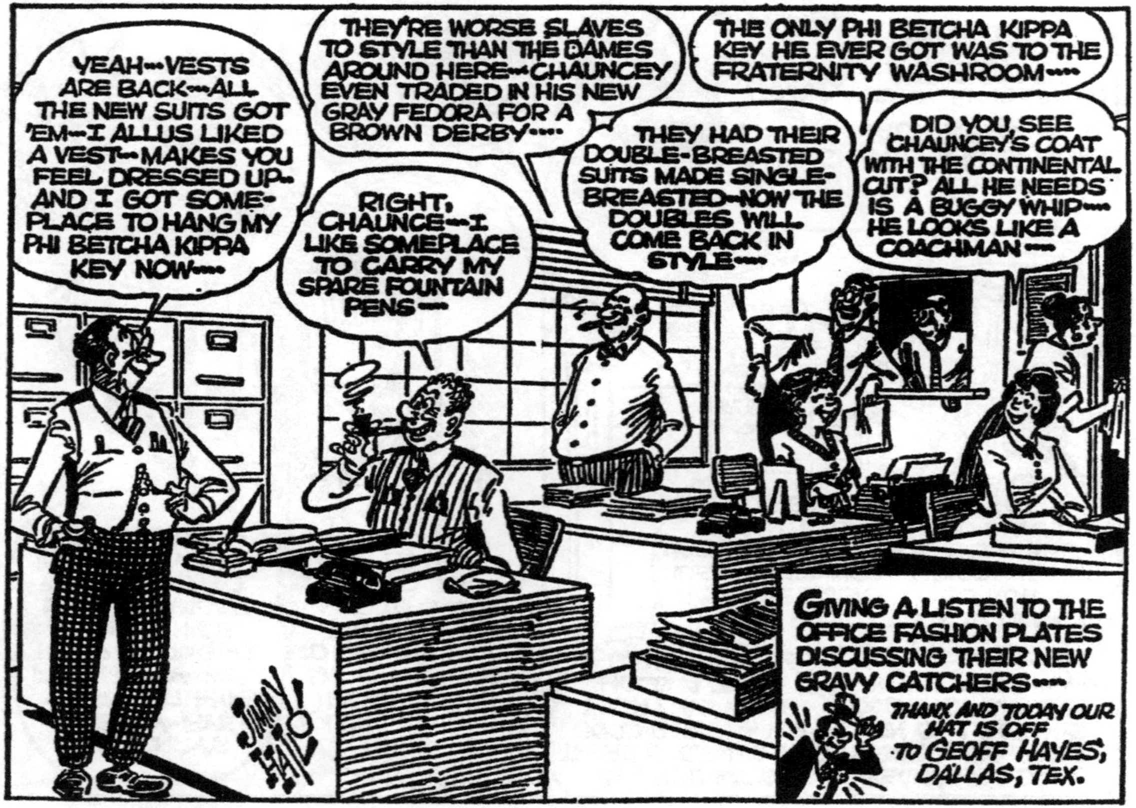
YEAH---VESTS ARE BACK---ALL THE NEW SUITS GOT 'EM---I ALLUS LIKED A VEST--MAKES YOU FEEL DRESSED UP--AND I GOT SOME-PLACE TO HANG MY PHI BETCHA KIPPA KEY NOW----
THEY'RE WORSE SLAVES TO STYLE THAN THE DAMES AROUND HERE--CHAUNCEY EVEN TRADED IN HIS NEW GRAY FEDORA FOR A BROWN DERBY----
RIGHT, CHAUNCE---I LIKE SOMEPLACE TO CARRY MY SPARE FOUNTAIN PENS---
THE ONLY PHI BETCHA KIPPA KEY HE EVER GOT WAS TO THE FRATERNITY WASHROOM----
THEY HAD THEIR DOUBLE-BREASTED SUITS MADE SINGLE-BREASTED--NOW THE DOUBLES WILL COME BACK IN STYLE----
DID YOU SEE CHAUNCEY'S COAT WITH THE CONTINENTAL CUT? ALL HE NEEDS IS A BUGGY WHIP---- HE LOOKS LIKE A COACHMAN---
GIVING A LISTEN TO THE OFFICE FASHION PLATES DISCUSSING THEIR NEW GRAVY CATCHERS----
THANX AND TODAY OUR HAT IS OFF TO GEOFF HAYES, DALLAS, TEX.
JIMMY HATLO

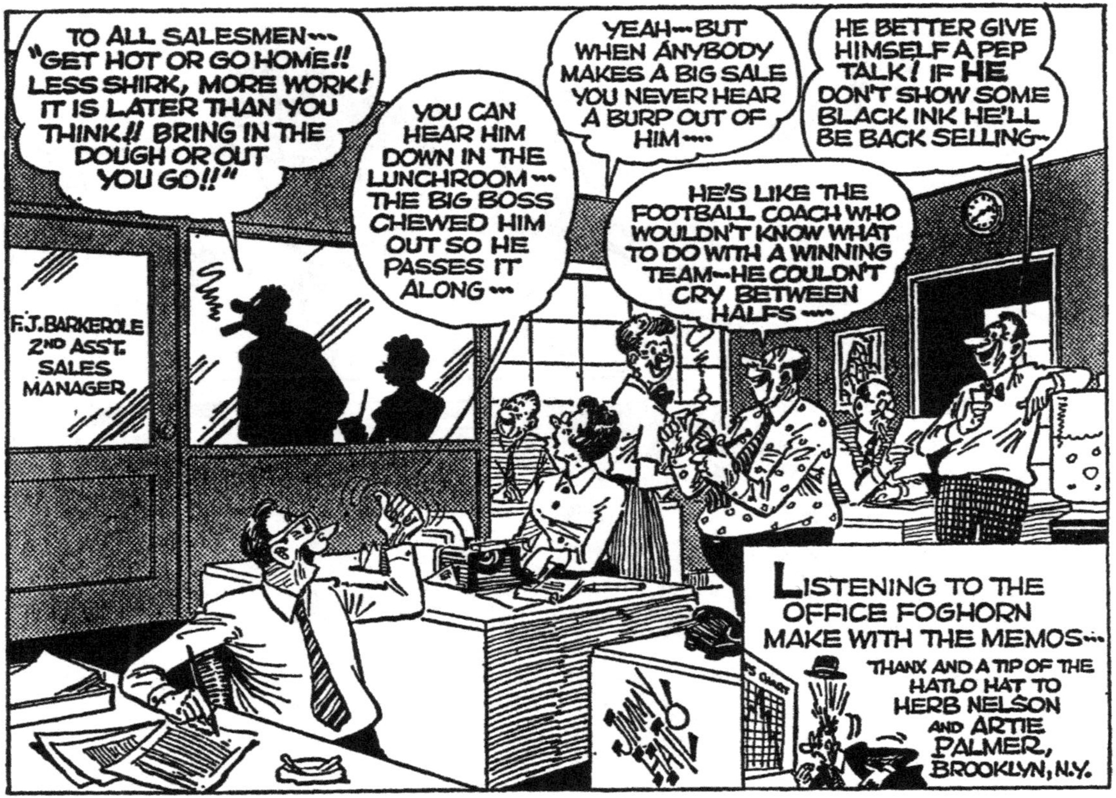
TO ALL SALESMEN... "GET HOT OR GO HOME!! LESS SHIRK, MORE WORK! IT IS LATER THAN YOU THINK!! BRING IN THE DOUGH OR OUT YOU GO!!"
F.J. BARKEROLE 2ND ASS'T. SALES MANAGER
YOU CAN HEAR HIM DOWN IN THE LUNCHROOM... THE BIG BOSS CHEWED HIM OUT SO HE PASSES IT ALONG...
YEAH... BUT WHEN ANYBODY MAKES A BIG SALE YOU NEVER HEAR A BURP OUT OF HIM....
HE BETTER GIVE HIMSELF A PEP TALK! IF HE DON'T SHOW SOME BLACK INK HE'LL BE BACK SELLING...
HE'S LIKE THE FOOTBALL COACH WHO WOULDN'T KNOW WHAT TO DO WITH A WINNING TEAM... HE COULDN'T CRY BETWEEN HALFS....
LISTENING TO THE OFFICE FOGHORN MAKE WITH THE MEMOS...
THANX AND A TIP OF THE HATLO HAT TO HERB NELSON AND ARTIE PALMER, BROOKLYN, N.Y.
JIMMY HATLO

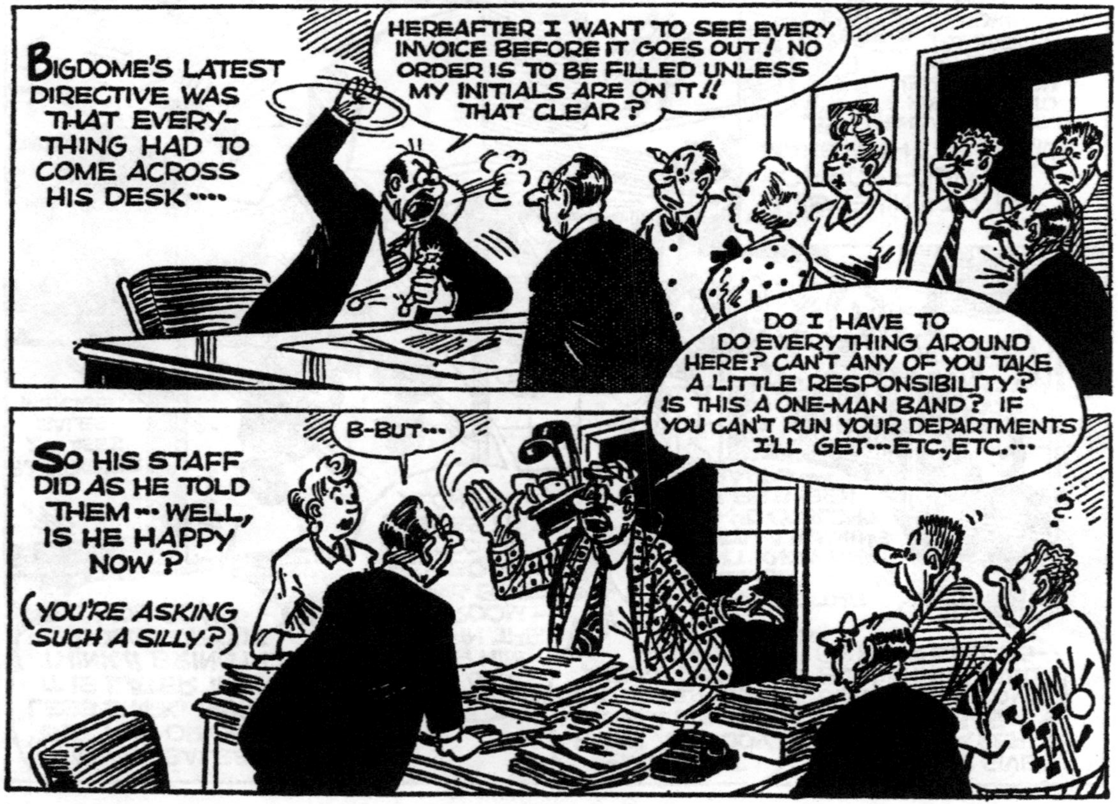
BIGDOME'S LATEST DIRECTIVE WAS THAT EVERYTHING HAD TO COME ACROSS HIS DESK....
HEREAFTER I WANT TO SEE EVERY INVOICE BEFORE IT GOES OUT! NO ORDER IS TO BE FILLED UNLESS MY INITIALS ARE ON IT!! THAT CLEAR?
SO HIS STAFF DID AS HE TOLD THEM... WELL, IS HE HAPPY NOW?
(YOU'RE ASKING SUCH A SILLY?)
B-BUT...
DO I HAVE TO DO EVERYTHING AROUND HERE? CAN'T ANY OF YOU TAKE A LITTLE RESPONSIBILITY? IS THIS A ONE-MAN BAND? IF YOU CAN'T RUN YOUR DEPARTMENTS I'LL GET... ETC., ETC....
JIMMY HATLO

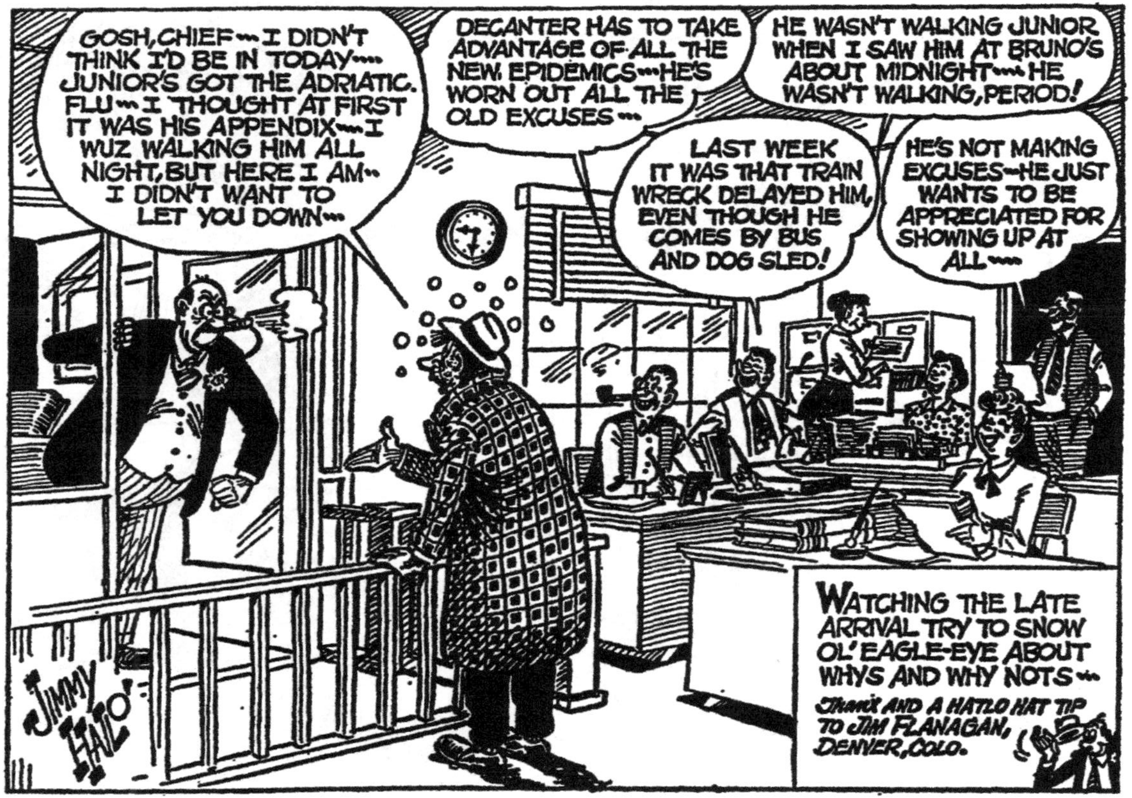
GOSH, CHIEF... I DIDN'T THINK I'D BE IN TODAY.... JUNIOR'S GOT THE ADRIATIC FLU... I THOUGHT AT FIRST IT WAS HIS APPENDIX... I WUZ WALKING HIM ALL NIGHT, BUT HERE I AM.. I DIDN'T WANT TO LET YOU DOWN...
DECANTER HAS TO TAKE ADVANTAGE OF ALL THE NEW EPIDEMICS... HE'S WORN OUT ALL THE OLD EXCUSES...
HE WASN'T WALKING JUNIOR WHEN I SAW HIM AT BRUNO'S ABOUT MIDNIGHT... HE WASN'T WALKING, PERIOD!
LAST WEEK IT WAS THAT TRAIN WRECK DELAYED HIM, EVEN THOUGH HE COMES BY BUS AND DOG SLED!
HE'S NOT MAKING EXCUSES... HE JUST WANTS TO BE APPRECIATED FOR SHOWING UP AT ALL...
WATCHING THE LATE ARRIVAL TRY TO SNOW OL' EAGLE-EYE ABOUT WHYS AND WHY NOTS...
THANX AND A HATLO HAT TIP TO JIM FLANAGAN, DENVER, COLO.
JIMMY HATLO

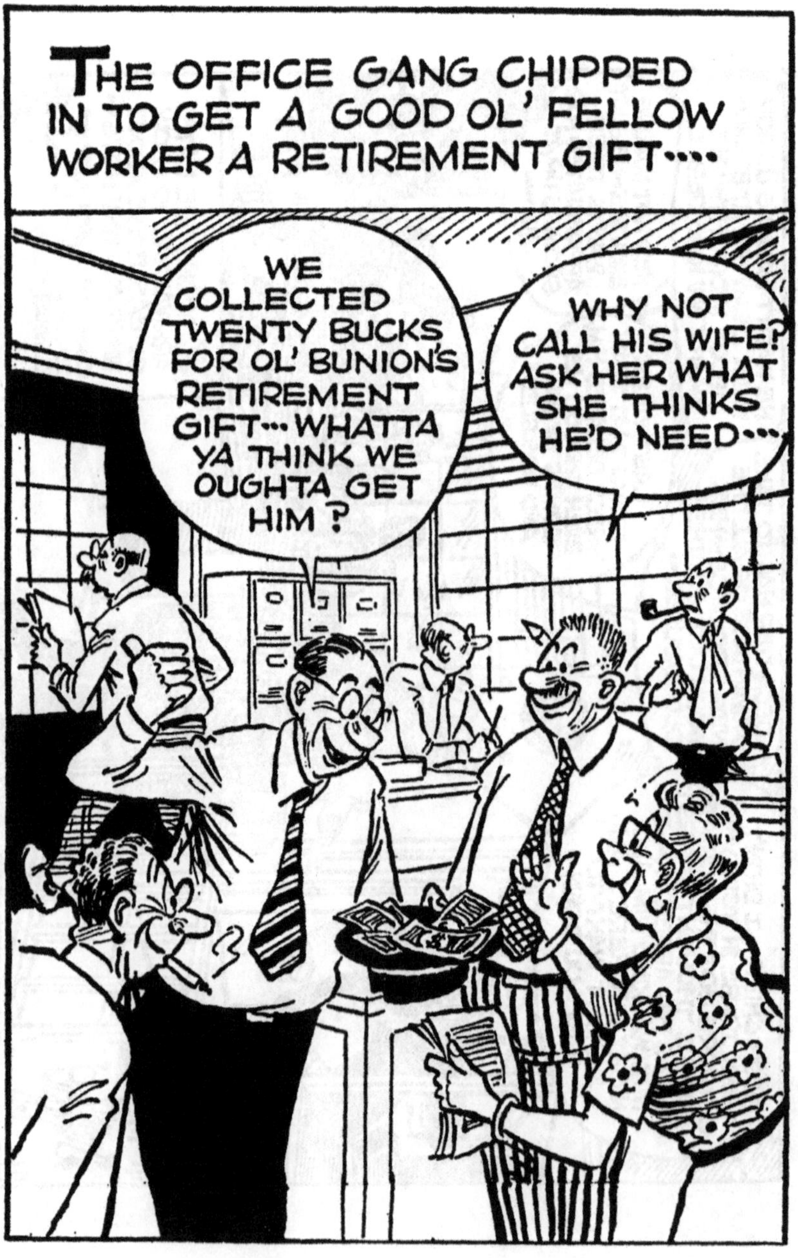
THE OFFICE GANG CHIPPED IN TO GET A GOOD OL' FELLOW WORKER A RETIREMENT GIFT....
WE COLLECTED TWENTY BUCKS FOR OL' BUNION'S RETIREMENT GIFT... WHATTA YA THINK WE OUGHTA GET HIM ?
WHY NOT CALL HIS WIFE? ASK HER WHAT SHE THINKS HE'D NEED...

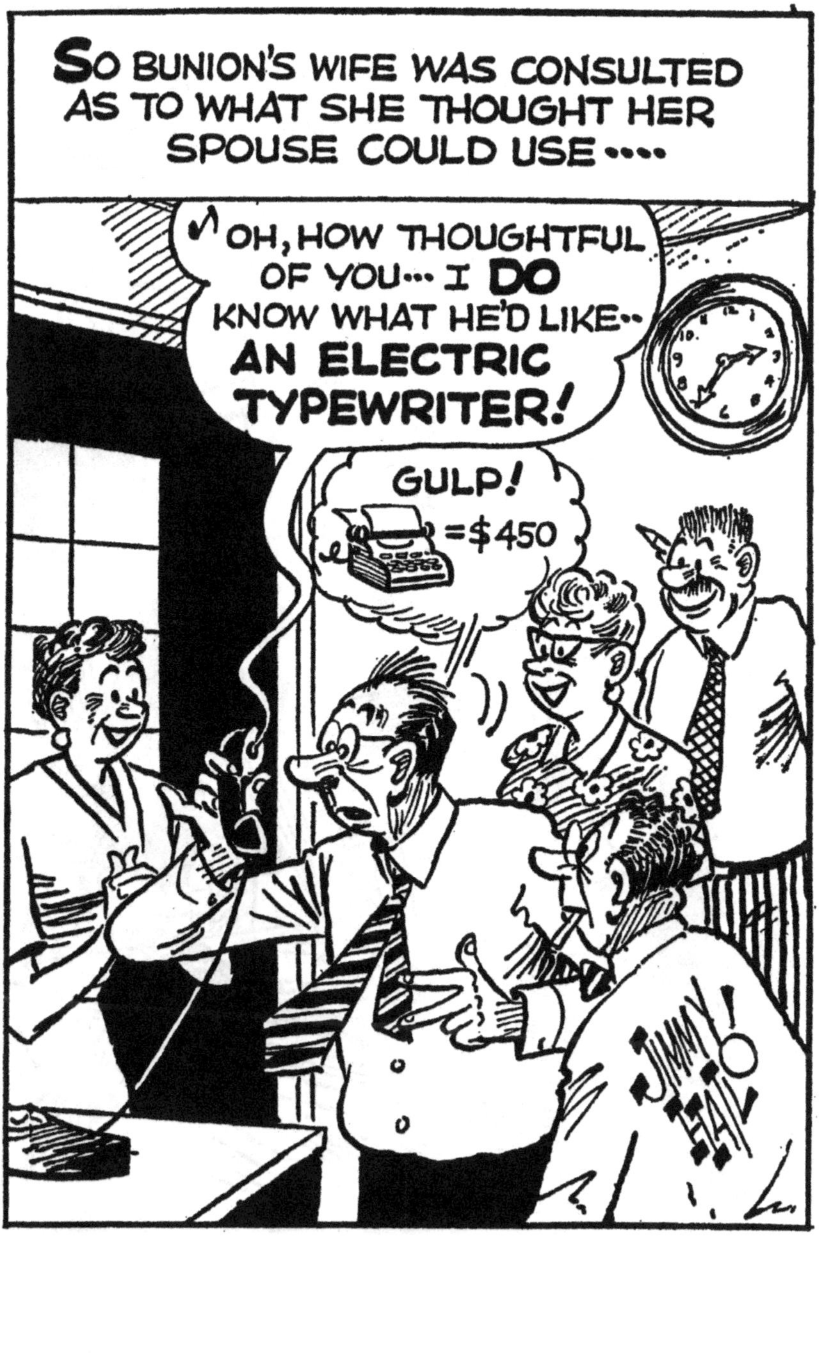
SO BUNION'S WIFE WAS CONSULTED AS TO WHAT SHE THOUGHT HER SPOUSE COULD USE....
OH, HOW THOUGHTFUL OF YOU... I DO KNOW WHAT HE'D LIKE.. AN ELECTRIC TYPEWRITER!
GULP!
=$450

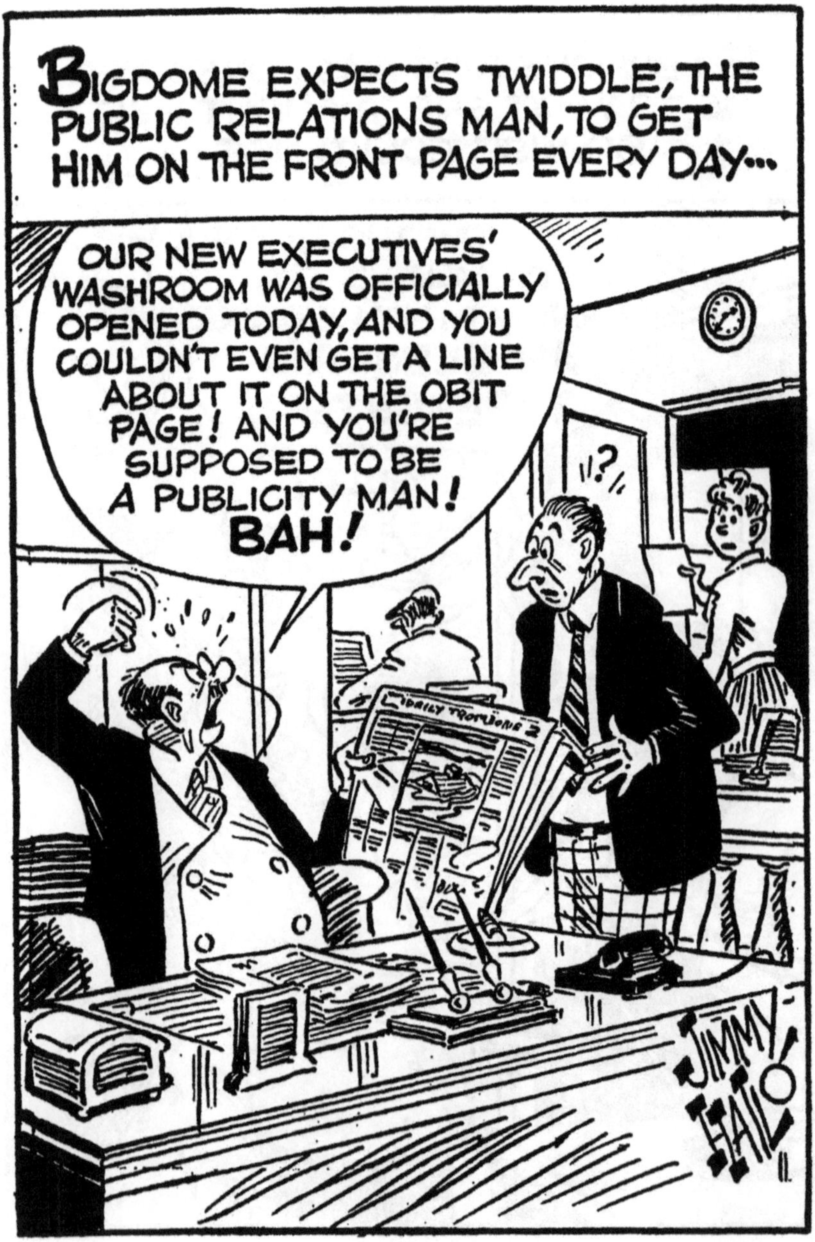
BIGDOME EXPECTS TWIDDLE, THE PUBLIC RELATIONS MAN, TO GET HIM ON THE FRONT PAGE EVERY DAY...
OUR NEW EXECUTIVES' WASHROOM WAS OFFICIALLY OPENED TODAY, AND YOU COULDN'T EVEN GET A LINE ABOUT IT ON THE OBIT PAGE! AND YOU'RE SUPPOSED TO BE A PUBLICITY MAN! BAH!
?
DAILY TROMBONE
JIMMY HATLO

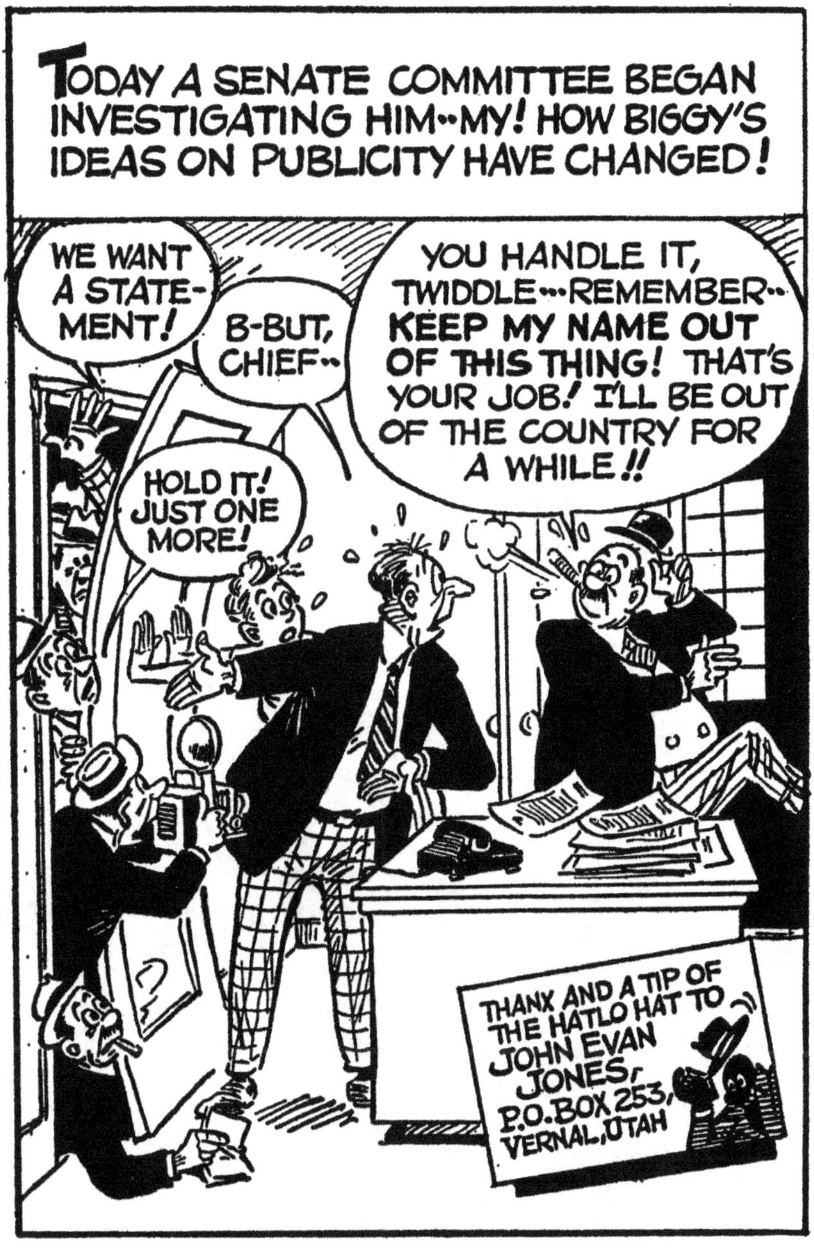
TODAY A SENATE COMMITTEE BEGAN INVESTIGATING HIM--MY! HOW BIGGY'S IDEAS ON PUBLICITY HAVE CHANGED!
WE WANT A STATEMENT!
B-BUT, CHIEF--
YOU HANDLE IT, TWIDDLE---REMEMBER-- KEEP MY NAME OUT OF THIS THING! THAT'S YOUR JOB! I'LL BE OUT OF THE COUNTRY FOR A WHILE!!
HOLD IT! JUST ONE MORE!
THANX AND A TIP OF THE HATLO HAT TO JOHN EVAN JONES, P.O. BOX 253, VERNAL, UTAH

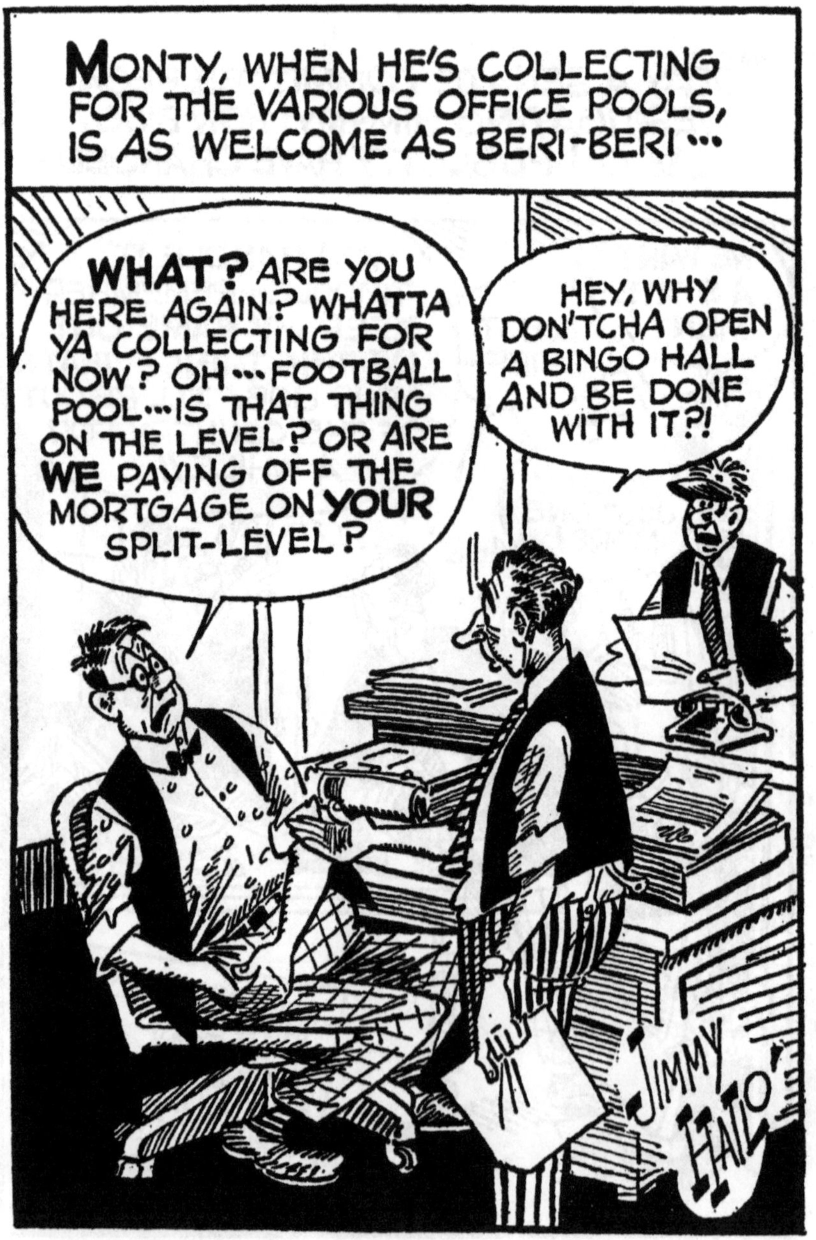
MONTY, WHEN HE'S COLLECTING FOR THE VARIOUS OFFICE POOLS, IS AS WELCOME AS BERI-BERI ...
WHAT? ARE YOU HERE AGAIN? WHATTA YA COLLECTING FOR NOW? OH ... FOOTBALL POOL ... IS THAT THING ON THE LEVEL? OR ARE WE PAYING OFF THE MORTGAGE ON YOUR SPLIT-LEVEL?
HEY, WHY DON'TCHA OPEN A BINGO HALL AND BE DONE WITH IT?!
JIMMY HATLO

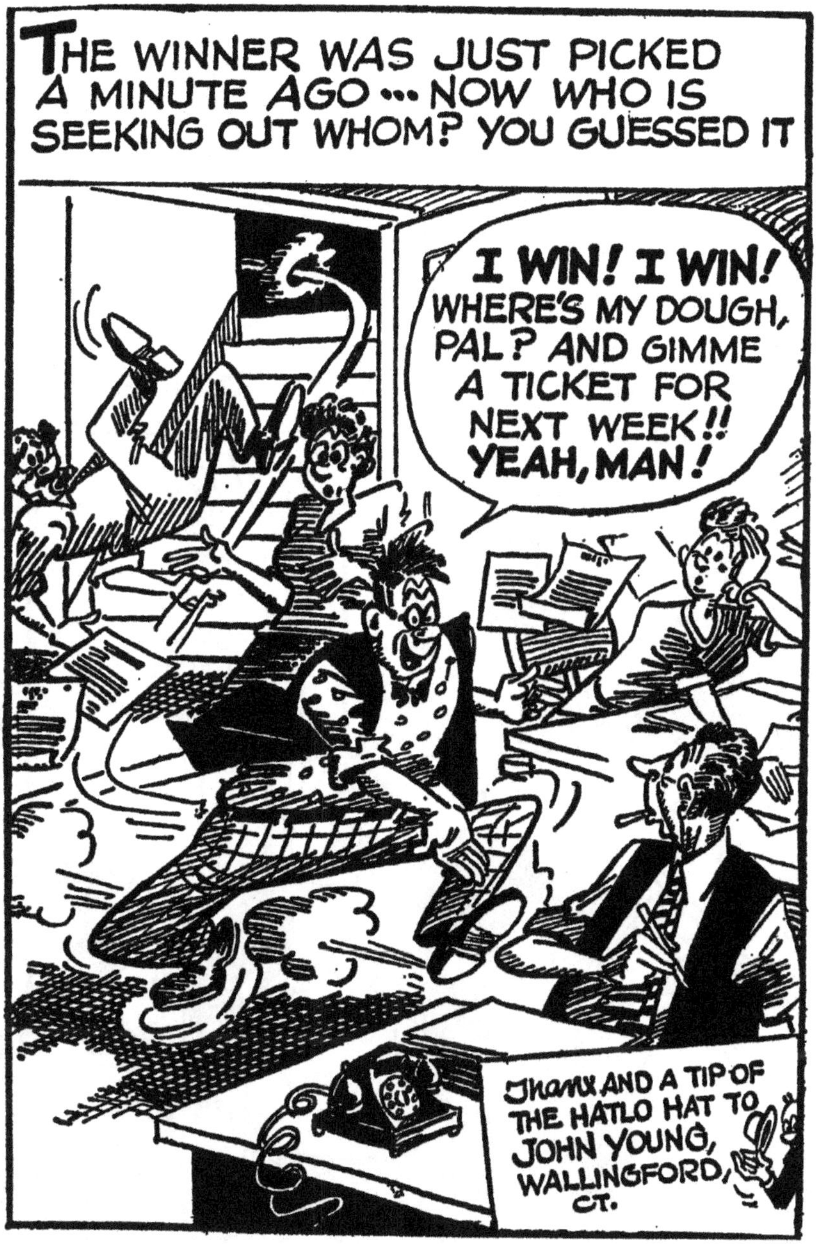
THE WINNER WAS JUST PICKED A MINUTE AGO ... NOW WHO IS SEEKING OUT WHOM? YOU GUESSED IT
I WIN! I WIN! WHERE'S MY DOUGH, PAL? AND GIMME A TICKET FOR NEXT WEEK!! YEAH, MAN!
Thanx AND A TIP OF THE HATLO HAT TO JOHN YOUNG, WALLINGFORD, CT.

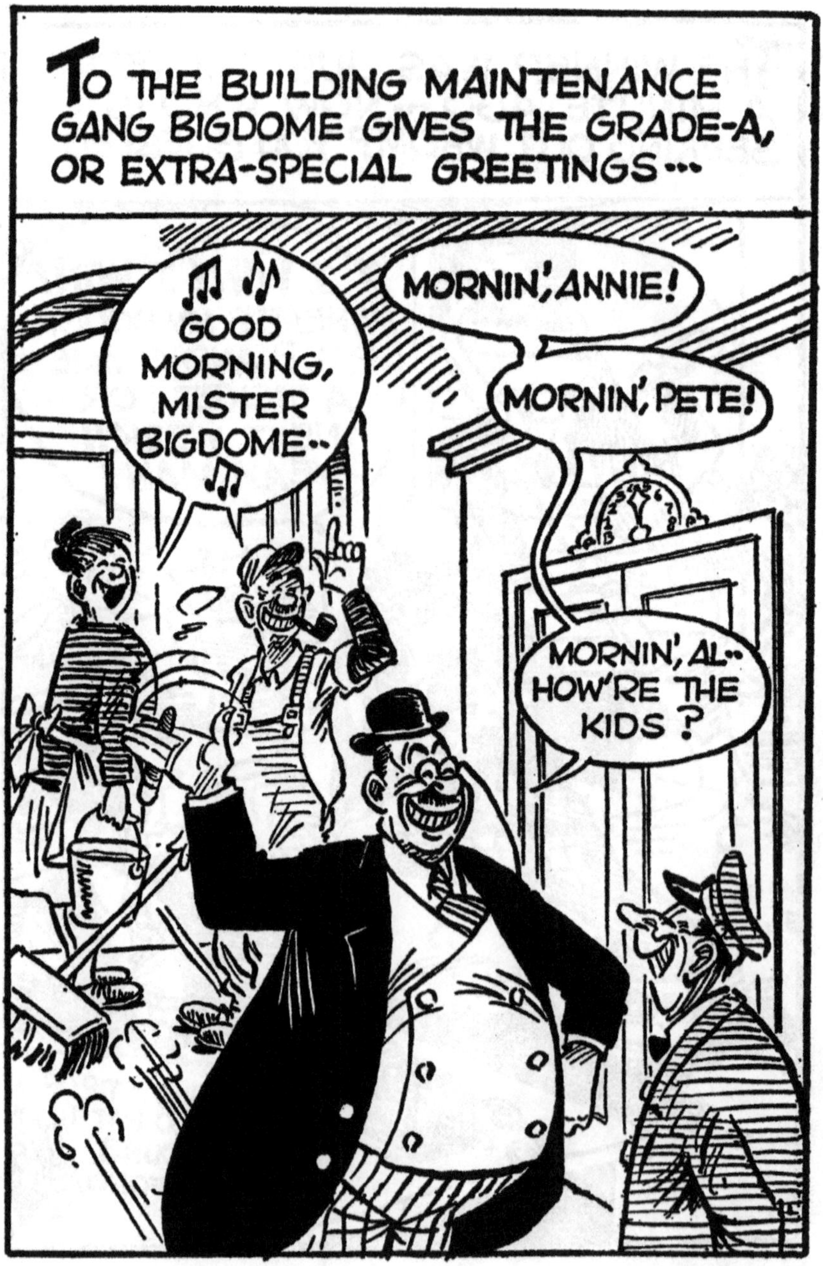
TO THE BUILDING MAINTENANCE GANG BIGDOME GIVES THE GRADE-A, OR EXTRA-SPECIAL GREETINGS...
GOOD MORNING, MISTER BIGDOME..
MORNIN', ANNIE!
MORNIN', PETE!
MORNIN', AL.. HOW'RE THE KIDS?

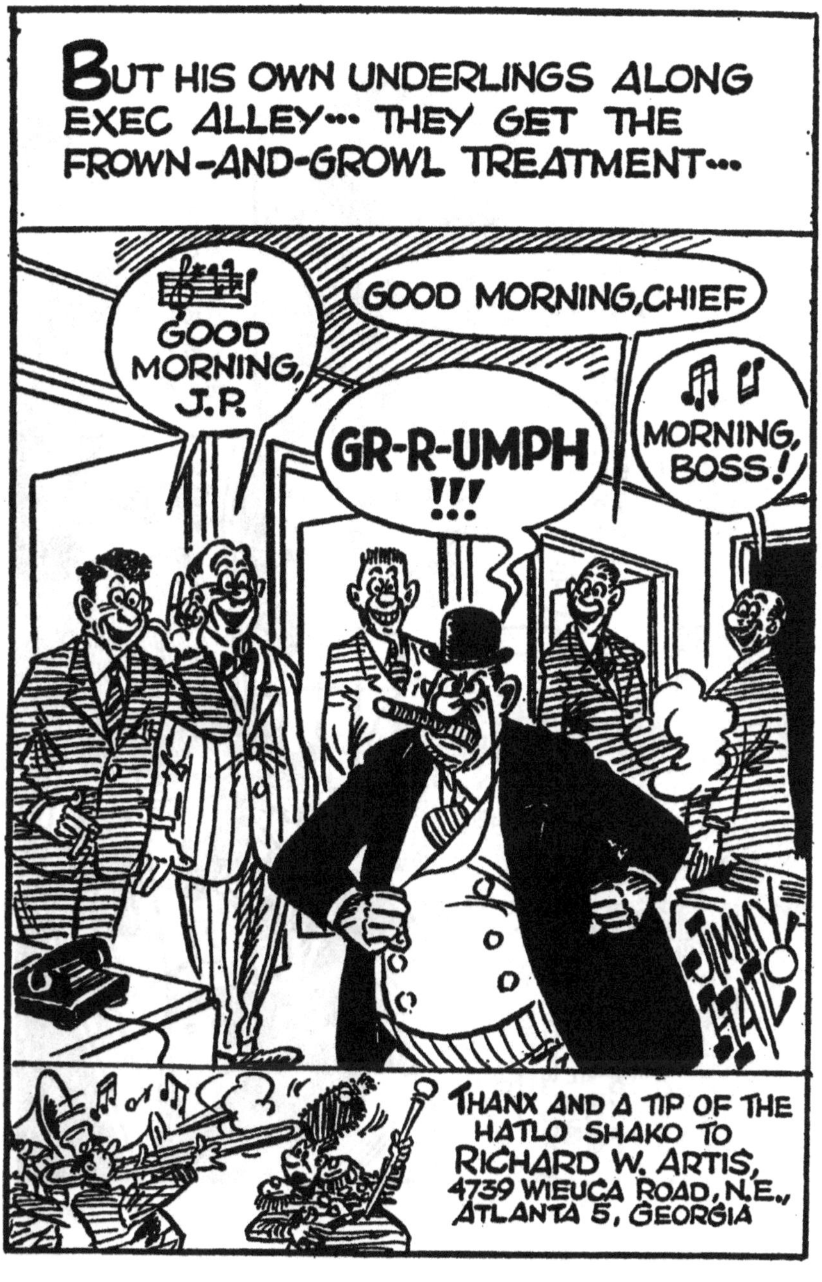

BUT HIS OWN UNDERLINGS ALONG EXEC ALLEY... THEY GET THE FROWN-AND-GROWL TREATMENT...
GOOD MORNING, J.P.
GOOD MORNING, CHIEF
GR-R-UMPH !!!
MORNING, BOSS!
JIMMY HATLO
THANX AND A TIP OF THE HATLO SHAKO TO RICHARD W. ARTIS, 4739 WIEUCA ROAD, N.E., ATLANTA 5, GEORGIA

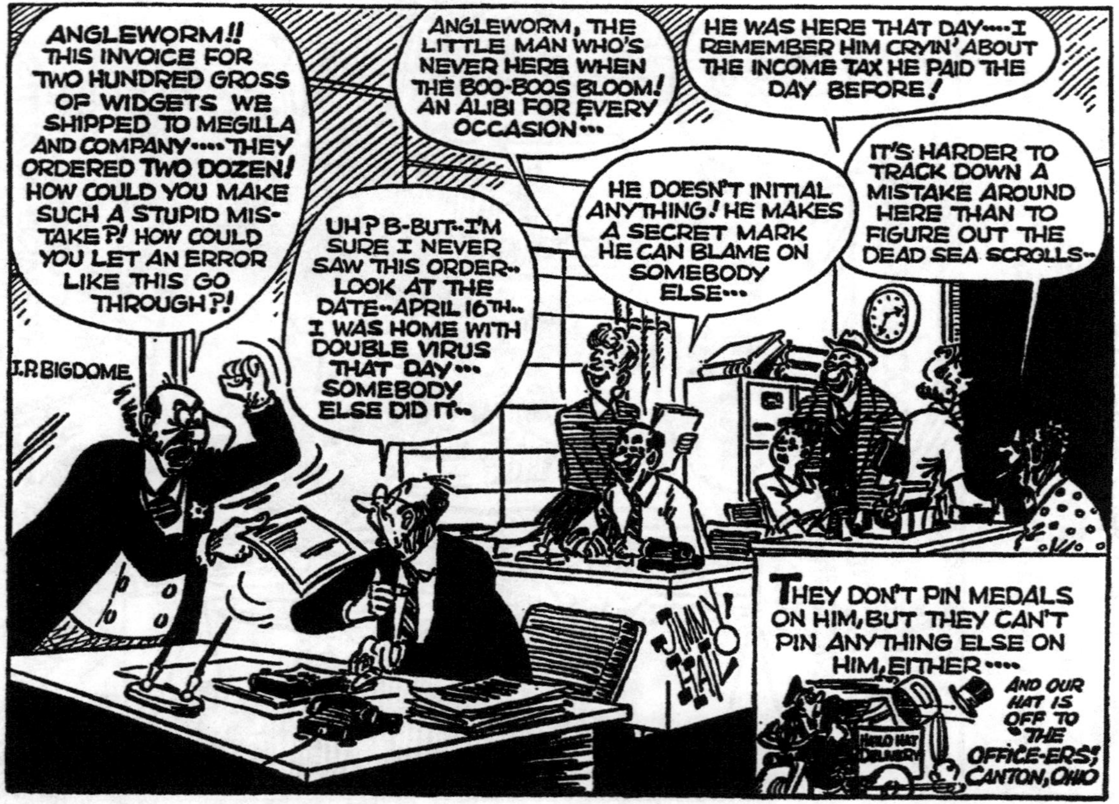
ANGLEWORM!! THIS INVOICE FOR TWO HUNDRED GROSS OF WIDGETS WE SHIPPED TO MEGILLA AND COMPANY.... THEY ORDERED TWO DOZEN! HOW COULD YOU MAKE SUCH A STUPID MISTAKE?! HOW COULD YOU LET AN ERROR LIKE THIS GO THROUGH?!
J.P. BIGDOME
UH? B-BUT--I'M SURE I NEVER SAW THIS ORDER-- LOOK AT THE DATE--APRIL 16TH-- I WAS HOME WITH DOUBLE VIRUS THAT DAY... SOMEBODY ELSE DID IT--
ANGLEWORM, THE LITTLE MAN WHO'S NEVER HERE WHEN THE BOO-BOOS BLOOM! AN ALIBI FOR EVERY OCCASION...
HE DOESN'T INITIAL ANYTHING! HE MAKES A SECRET MARK HE CAN BLAME ON SOMEBODY ELSE...
HE WAS HERE THAT DAY....I REMEMBER HIM CRYIN' ABOUT THE INCOME TAX HE PAID THE DAY BEFORE!
IT'S HARDER TO TRACK DOWN A MISTAKE AROUND HERE THAN TO FIGURE OUT THE DEAD SEA SCROLLS--
JIMMY HATLO!
THEY DON'T PIN MEDALS ON HIM, BUT THEY CAN'T PIN ANYTHING ELSE ON HIM, EITHER....
HATLO HAT DELIVERY
AND OUR HAT IS OFF TO "THE OFFICE-ERS," CANTON, OHIO

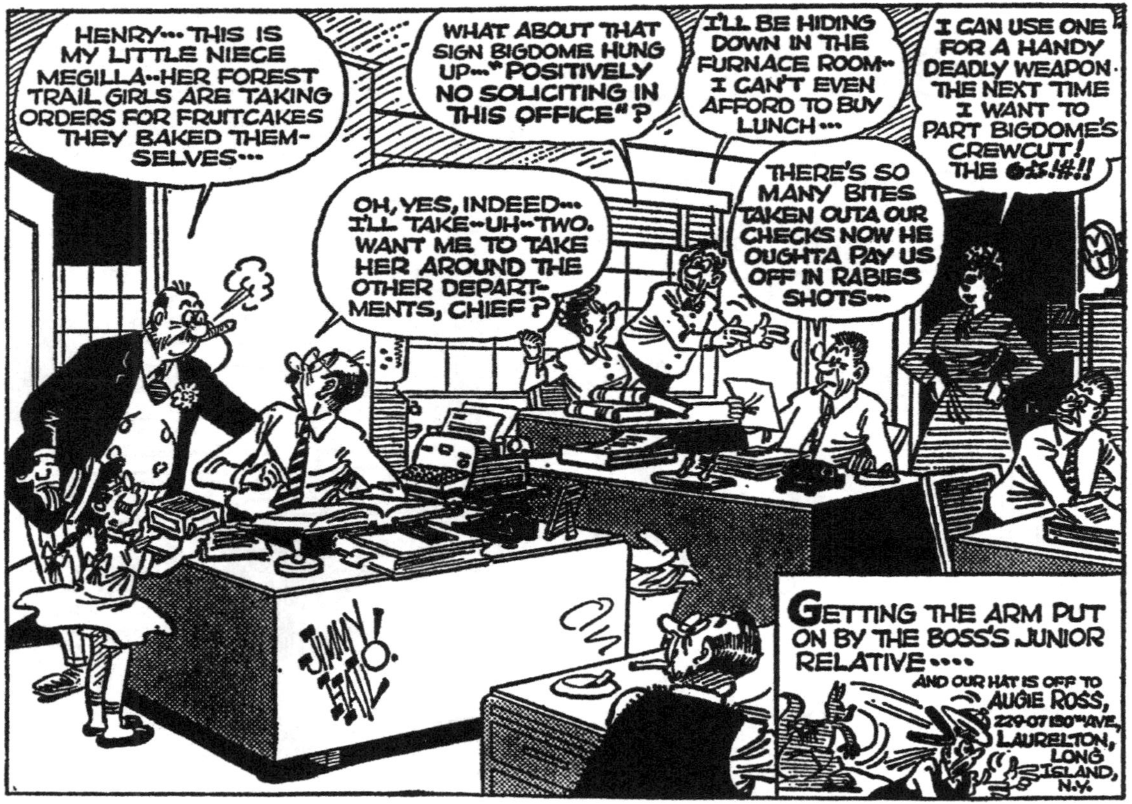
HENRY... THIS IS MY LITTLE NIECE MEGILLA--HER FOREST TRAIL GIRLS ARE TAKING ORDERS FOR FRUITCAKES THEY BAKED THEMSELVES...
OH, YES, INDEED... I'LL TAKE--UH--TWO. WANT ME TO TAKE HER AROUND THE OTHER DEPARTMENTS, CHIEF?
WHAT ABOUT THAT SIGN BIGDOME HUNG UP..."POSITIVELY NO SOLICITING IN THIS OFFICE"?
I'LL BE HIDING DOWN IN THE FURNACE ROOM-- I CAN'T EVEN AFFORD TO BUY LUNCH...
THERE'S SO MANY BITES TAKEN OUTA OUR CHECKS NOW HE OUGHTA PAY US OFF IN RABIES SHOTS...
I CAN USE ONE FOR A HANDY DEADLY WEAPON. THE NEXT TIME I WANT TO PART BIGDOME'S CREWCUT! THE @$!#!!
GETTING THE ARM PUT ON BY THE BOSS'S JUNIOR RELATIVE....
AND OUR HAT IS OFF TO AUGIE ROSS, 229-07 130TH AVE, LAURELTON, LONG ISLAND, N.Y.
JIMMY HATLO

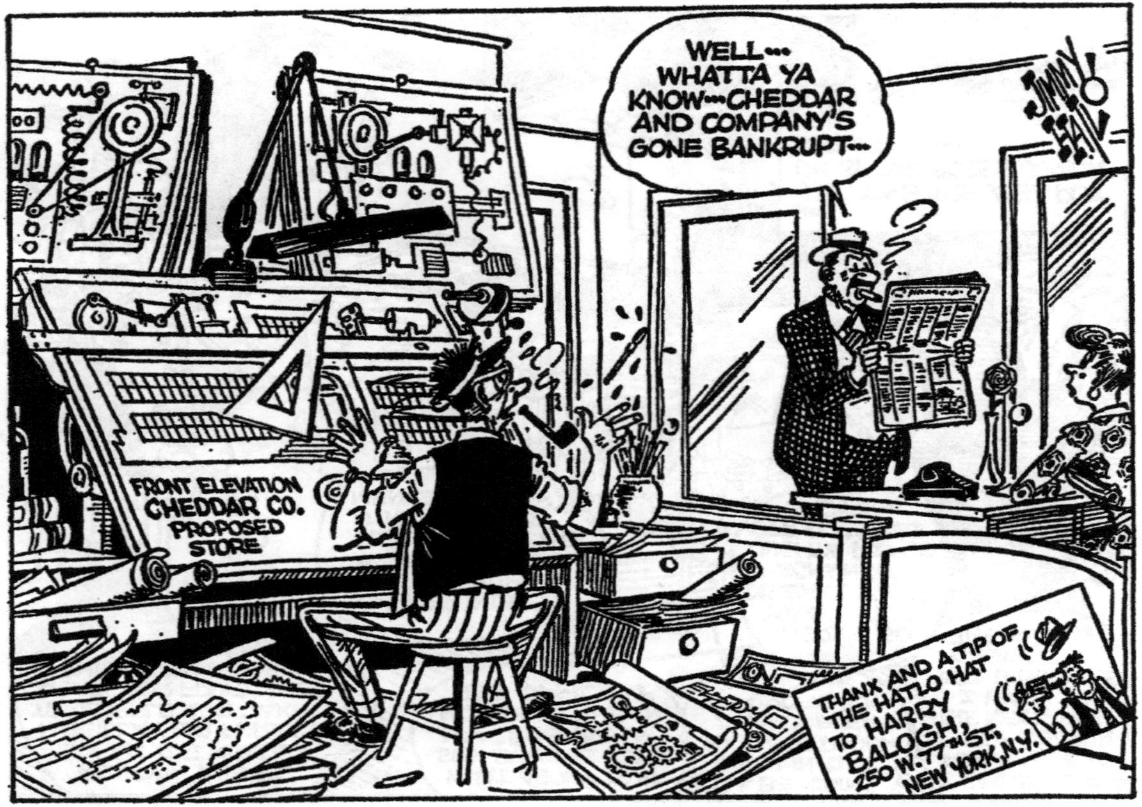
WELL... WHATTA YA KNOW...CHEDDAR AND COMPANY'S GONE BANKRUPT...
FRONT ELEVATION CHEDDAR CO. PROPOSED STORE
THANX AND A TIP OF THE HATLO HAT TO HARRY BALOGH, 250 W. 77TH ST. NEW YORK, N.Y.
JIMMY HATLO

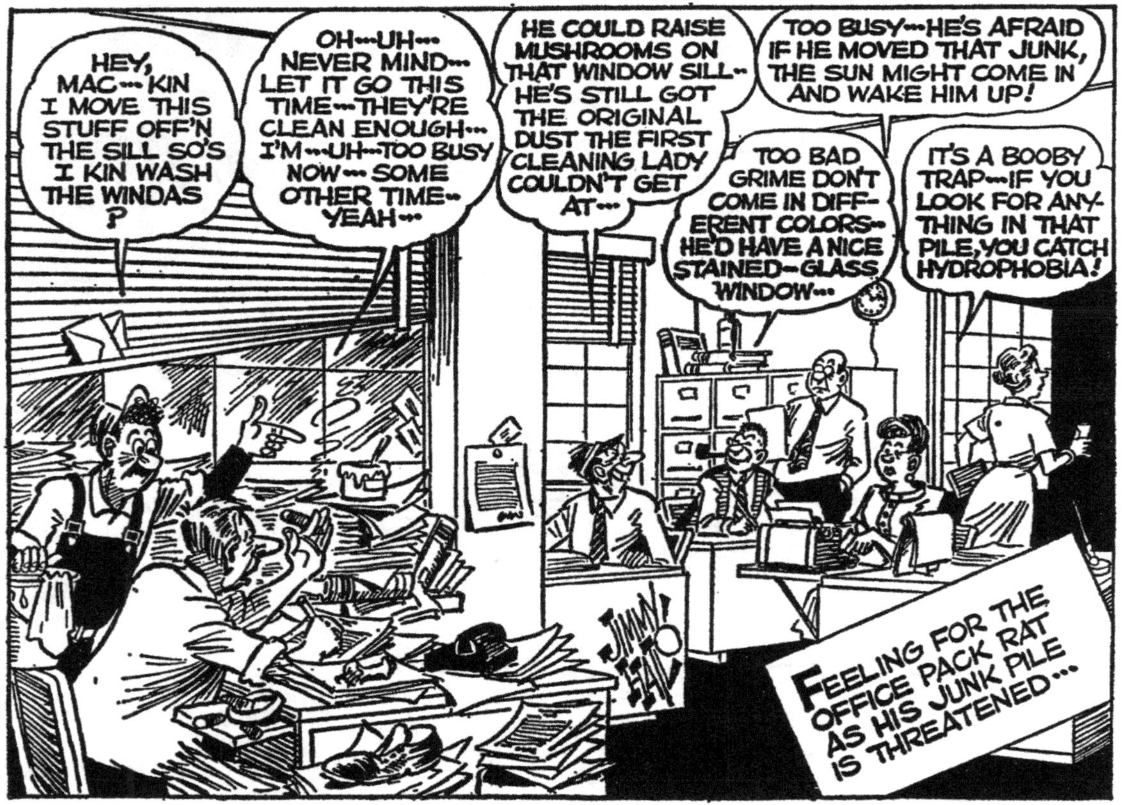
HEY, MAC... KIN I MOVE THIS STUFF OFF'N THE SILL SO'S I KIN WASH THE WINDAS ?
OH...UH... NEVER MIND... LET IT GO THIS TIME...THEY'RE CLEAN ENOUGH... I'M...UH...TOO BUSY NOW... SOME OTHER TIME.. YEAH...
HE COULD RAISE MUSHROOMS ON THAT WINDOW SILL.. HE'S STILL GOT THE ORIGINAL DUST THE FIRST CLEANING LADY COULDN'T GET AT...
TOO BUSY...HE'S AFRAID IF HE MOVED THAT JUNK, THE SUN MIGHT COME IN AND WAKE HIM UP!
TOO BAD GRIME DON'T COME IN DIFF-ERENT COLORS.. HE'D HAVE A NICE STAINED-GLASS WINDOW...
IT'S A BOOBY TRAP...IF YOU LOOK FOR ANY-THING IN THAT PILE, YOU CATCH HYDROPHOBIA!
FEELING FOR THE OFFICE PACK RAT AS HIS JUNK PILE IS THREATENED...

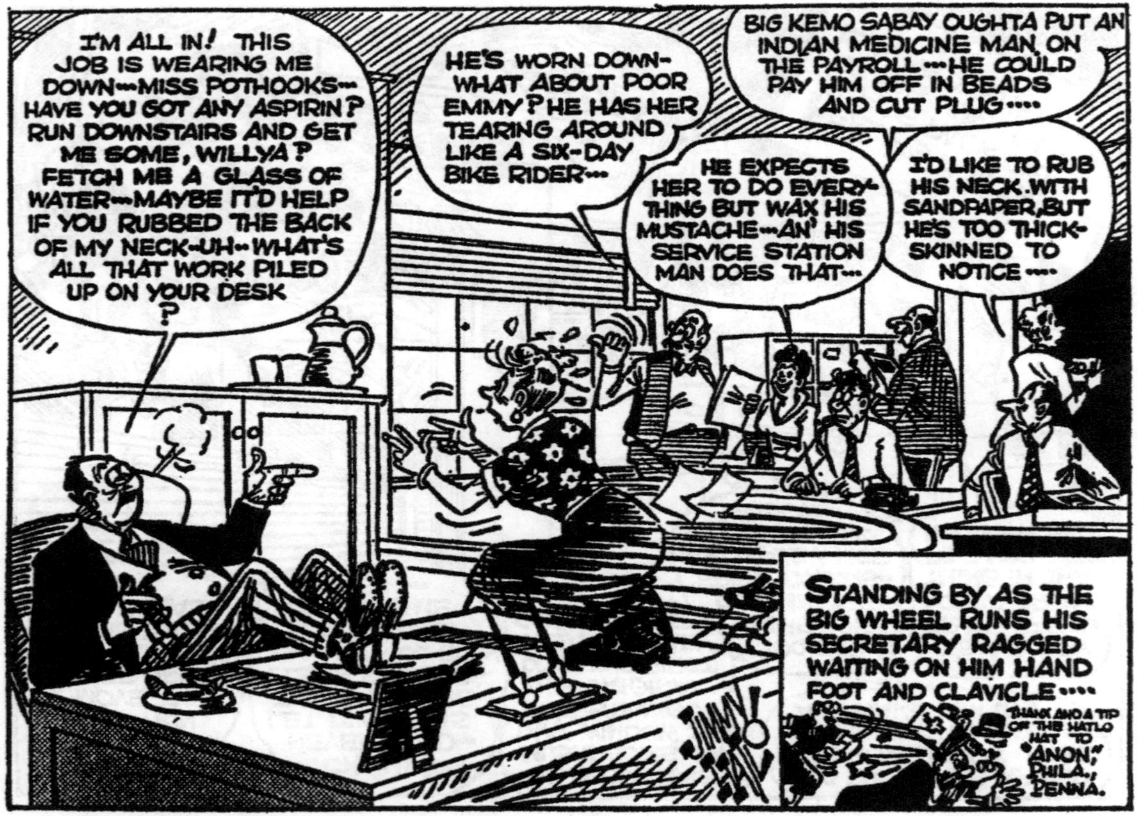
I'M ALL IN! THIS JOB IS WEARING ME DOWN--- MISS POTHOOKS--- HAVE YOU GOT ANY ASPIRIN? RUN DOWNSTAIRS AND GET ME SOME, WILLYA? FETCH ME A GLASS OF WATER--- MAYBE IT'D HELP IF YOU RUBBED THE BACK OF MY NECK--UH-- WHAT'S ALL THAT WORK PILED UP ON YOUR DESK?
HE'S WORN DOWN- WHAT ABOUT POOR EMMY? HE HAS HER TEARING AROUND LIKE A SIX-DAY BIKE RIDER---
HE EXPECTS HER TO DO EVERY-THING BUT WAX HIS MUSTACHE---AN' HIS SERVICE STATION MAN DOES THAT---
BIG KEMO SABAY OUGHTA PUT AN INDIAN MEDICINE MAN ON THE PAYROLL--- HE COULD PAY HIM OFF IN BEADS AND CUT PLUG----
I'D LIKE TO RUB HIS NECK WITH SANDPAPER, BUT HE'S TOO THICK-SKINNED TO NOTICE----
STANDING BY AS THE BIG WHEEL RUNS HIS SECRETARY RAGGED WAITING ON HIM HAND FOOT AND CLAVICLE----
THANX AND A TIP OF THE HATLO HAT TO "ANON," PHILA., PENNA.
JIMMY HATLO

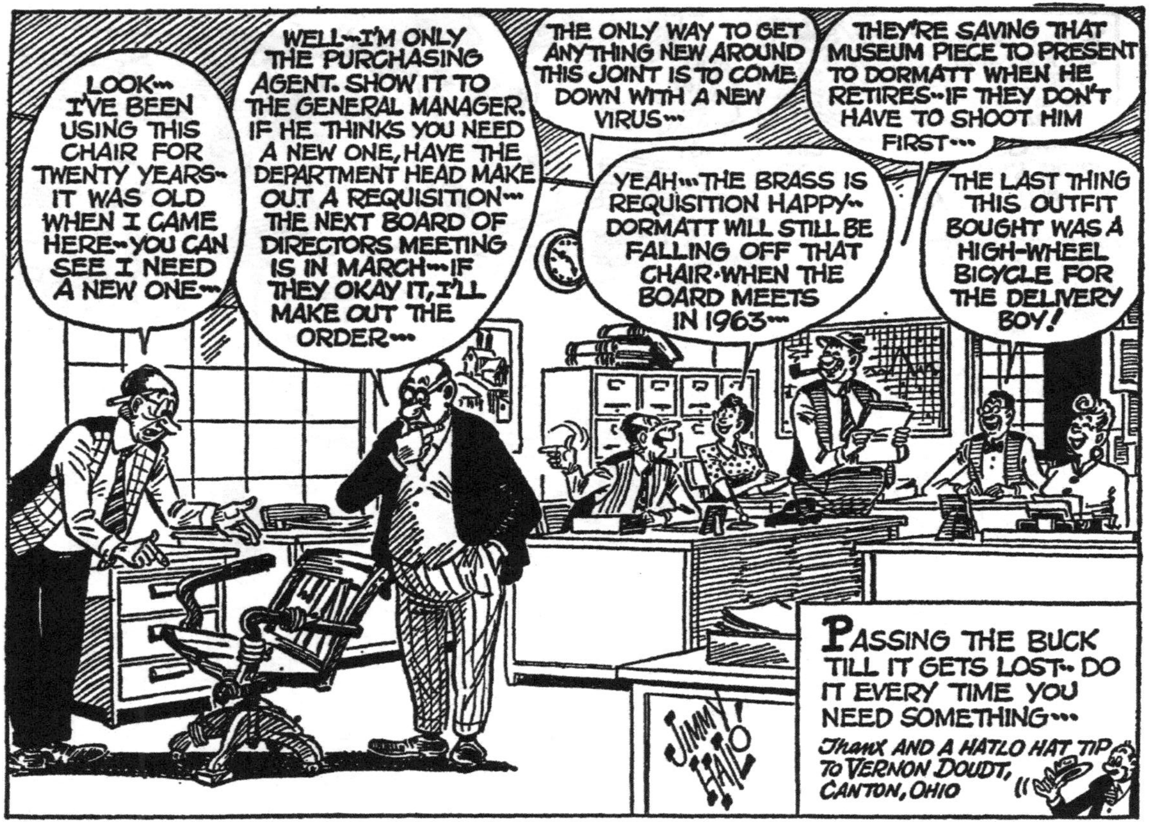
LOOK... I'VE BEEN USING THIS CHAIR FOR TWENTY YEARS.. IT WAS OLD WHEN I CAME HERE.. YOU CAN SEE I NEED A NEW ONE...
WELL...I'M ONLY THE PURCHASING AGENT. SHOW IT TO THE GENERAL MANAGER. IF HE THINKS YOU NEED A NEW ONE, HAVE THE DEPARTMENT HEAD MAKE OUT A REQUISITION... THE NEXT BOARD OF DIRECTORS MEETING IS IN MARCH...IF THEY OKAY IT, I'LL MAKE OUT THE ORDER...
THE ONLY WAY TO GET ANYTHING NEW AROUND THIS JOINT IS TO COME DOWN WITH A NEW VIRUS...
YEAH...THE BRASS IS REQUISITION HAPPY.. DORMATT WILL STILL BE FALLING OFF THAT CHAIR. WHEN THE BOARD MEETS IN 1963...
THEY'RE SAVING THAT MUSEUM PIECE TO PRESENT TO DORMATT WHEN HE RETIRES..IF THEY DON'T HAVE TO SHOOT HIM FIRST...
THE LAST THING THIS OUTFIT BOUGHT WAS A HIGH-WHEEL BICYCLE FOR THE DELIVERY BOY!
PASSING THE BUCK TILL IT GETS LOST.. DO IT EVERY TIME YOU NEED SOMETHING...
THANX AND A HATLO HAT TIP TO VERNON DOUDT, CANTON, OHIO
JIMMY HATLO

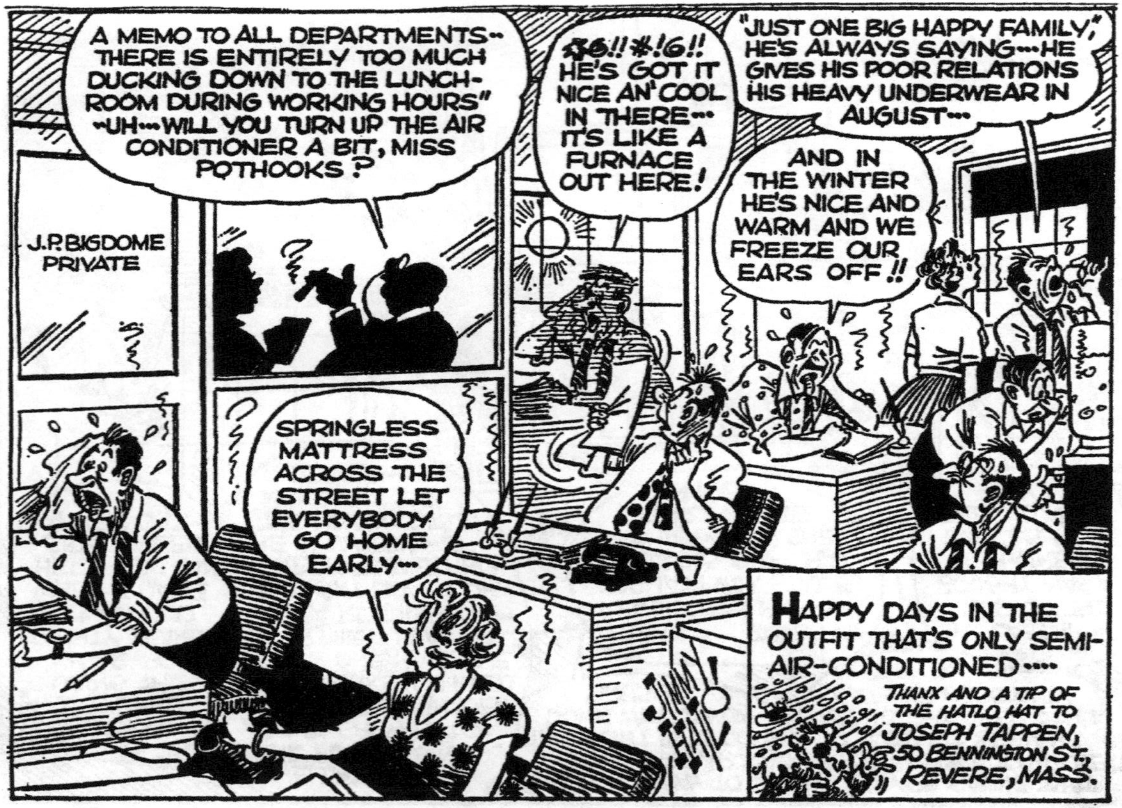
A MEMO TO ALL DEPARTMENTS-- THERE IS ENTIRELY TOO MUCH DUCKING DOWN TO THE LUNCH-ROOM DURING WORKING HOURS" --UH--- WILL YOU TURN UP THE AIR CONDITIONER A BIT, MISS POTHOOKS?
J.P. BIGDOME PRIVATE
HE'S GOT IT NICE AN' COOL IN THERE--- IT'S LIKE A FURNACE OUT HERE!
"JUST ONE BIG HAPPY FAMILY," HE'S ALWAYS SAYING---HE GIVES HIS POOR RELATIONS HIS HEAVY UNDERWEAR IN AUGUST---
AND IN THE WINTER HE'S NICE AND WARM AND WE FREEZE OUR EARS OFF!!
SPRINGLESS MATTRESS ACROSS THE STREET LET EVERYBODY GO HOME EARLY---
HAPPY DAYS IN THE OUTFIT THAT'S ONLY SEMI-AIR-CONDITIONED----
THANX AND A TIP OF THE HATLO HAT TO JOSEPH TAPPEN, 50 BENNINGTON ST., REVERE, MASS.

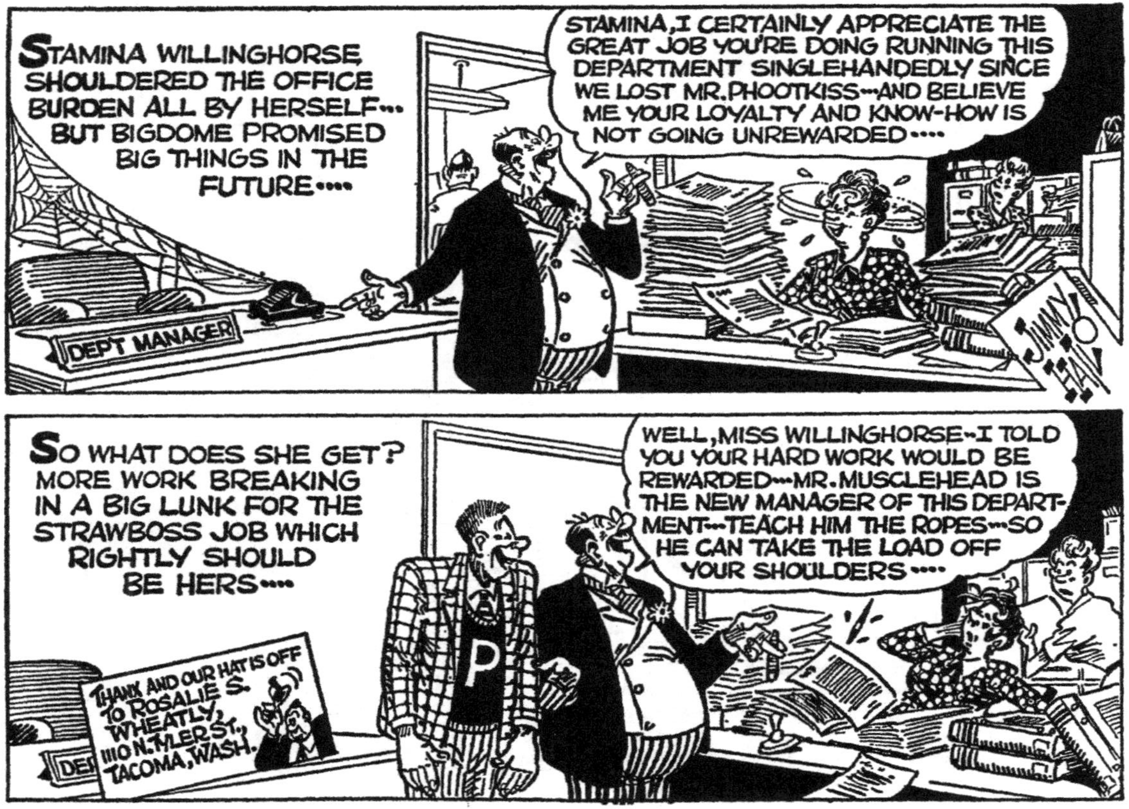

STAMINA WILLINGHORSE, SHOULDERED THE OFFICE BURDEN ALL BY HERSELF... BUT BIGDOME PROMISED BIG THINGS IN THE FUTURE....
STAMINA, I CERTAINLY APPRECIATE THE GREAT JOB YOU'RE DOING RUNNING THIS DEPARTMENT SINGLEHANDEDLY SINCE WE LOST MR. PHOOTKISS---AND BELIEVE ME YOUR LOYALTY AND KNOW-HOW IS NOT GOING UNREWARDED....
DEPT MANAGER
JIMMY HATLO
SO WHAT DOES SHE GET? MORE WORK BREAKING IN A BIG LUNK FOR THE STRAWBOSS JOB WHICH RIGHTLY SHOULD BE HERS....
WELL, MISS WILLINGHORSE--I TOLD YOU YOUR HARD WORK WOULD BE REWARDED---MR. MUSCLEHEAD IS THE NEW MANAGER OF THIS DEPARTMENT---TEACH HIM THE ROPES---SO HE CAN TAKE THE LOAD OFF YOUR SHOULDERS....
THANX AND OUR HAT IS OFF TO ROSALIE S. WHEATLY, 1110 N. TYLER ST., TACOMA, WASH.

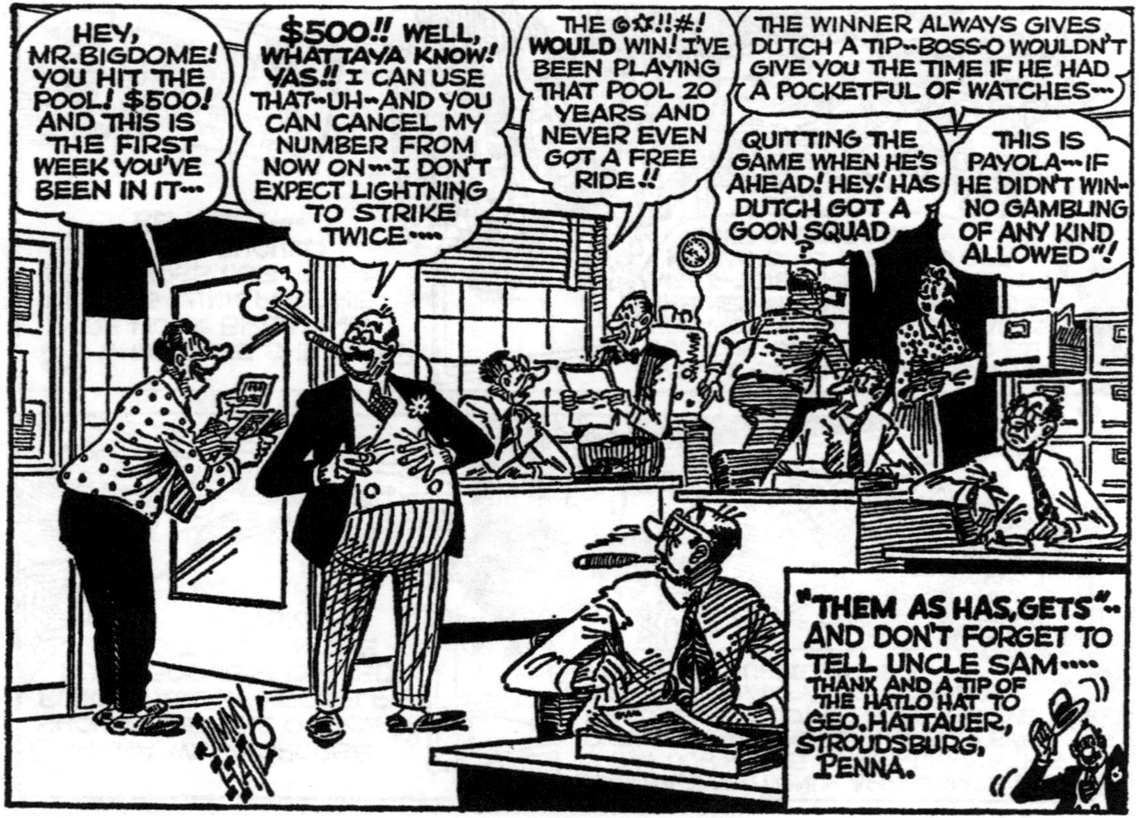
HEY, MR.BIGDOME! YOU HIT THE POOL! $500! AND THIS IS THE FIRST WEEK YOU'VE BEEN IN IT...
$500!! WELL, WHATTAYA KNOW! YAS!! I CAN USE THAT--UH--AND YOU CAN CANCEL MY NUMBER FROM NOW ON...I DON'T EXPECT LIGHTNING TO STRIKE TWICE....
THE @✡!!#! WOULD WIN! I'VE BEEN PLAYING THAT POOL 20 YEARS AND NEVER EVEN GOT A FREE RIDE!!
THE WINNER ALWAYS GIVES DUTCH A TIP--BOSS-O WOULDN'T GIVE YOU THE TIME IF HE HAD A POCKETFUL OF WATCHES...
QUITTING THE GAME WHEN HE'S AHEAD! HEY! HAS DUTCH GOT A GOON SQUAD?
THIS IS PAYOLA...IF HE DIDN'T WIN--NO GAMBLING OF ANY KIND ALLOWED"!
"THEM AS HAS, GETS"-- AND DON'T FORGET TO TELL UNCLE SAM....
THANX AND A TIP OF THE HATLO HAT TO GEO. HATTAUER, STROUDSBURG, PENNA.
JIMMY HATLO

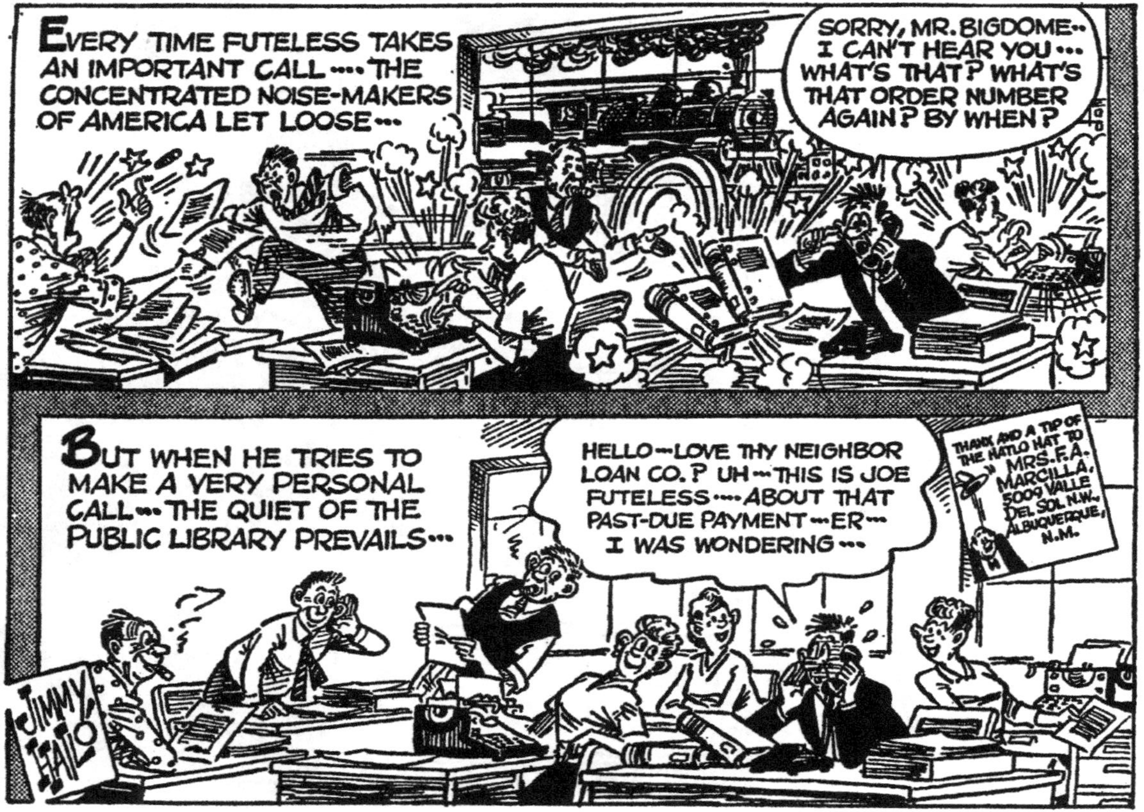
EVERY TIME FUTELESS TAKES AN IMPORTANT CALL .... THE CONCENTRATED NOISE-MAKERS OF AMERICA LET LOOSE ...
SORRY, MR. BIGDOME .. I CAN'T HEAR YOU ... WHAT'S THAT? WHAT'S THAT ORDER NUMBER AGAIN? BY WHEN?
BUT WHEN HE TRIES TO MAKE A VERY PERSONAL CALL ... THE QUIET OF THE PUBLIC LIBRARY PREVAILS ...
HELLO -- LOVE THY NEIGHBOR LOAN CO.? UH -- THIS IS JOE FUTELESS .... ABOUT THAT PAST-DUE PAYMENT -- ER -- I WAS WONDERING ...
THANX AND A TIP OF THE HATLO HAT TO MRS. F.A. MARCILLA, 5009 VALLE DEL SOL N.W., ALBUQUERQUE, N.M.
JIMMY HATLO

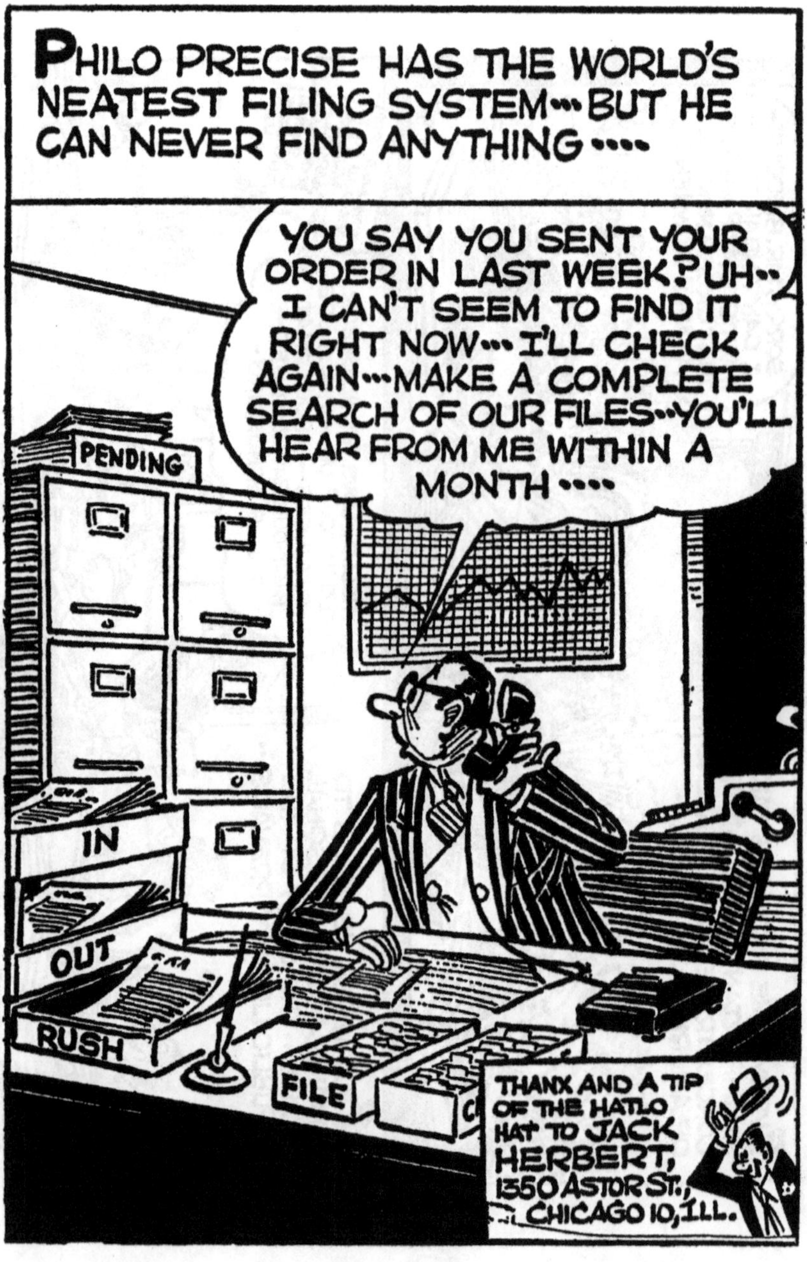
PHILO PRECISE HAS THE WORLD'S NEATEST FILING SYSTEM... BUT HE CAN NEVER FIND ANYTHING....
YOU SAY YOU SENT YOUR ORDER IN LAST WEEK? UH.. I CAN'T SEEM TO FIND IT RIGHT NOW... I'LL CHECK AGAIN...MAKE A COMPLETE SEARCH OF OUR FILES..YOU'LL HEAR FROM ME WITHIN A MONTH....
PENDING
IN
OUT
RUSH
FILE
THANX AND A TIP OF THE HATLO HAT TO JACK HERBERT, 1350 ASTOR ST., CHICAGO 10, ILL.

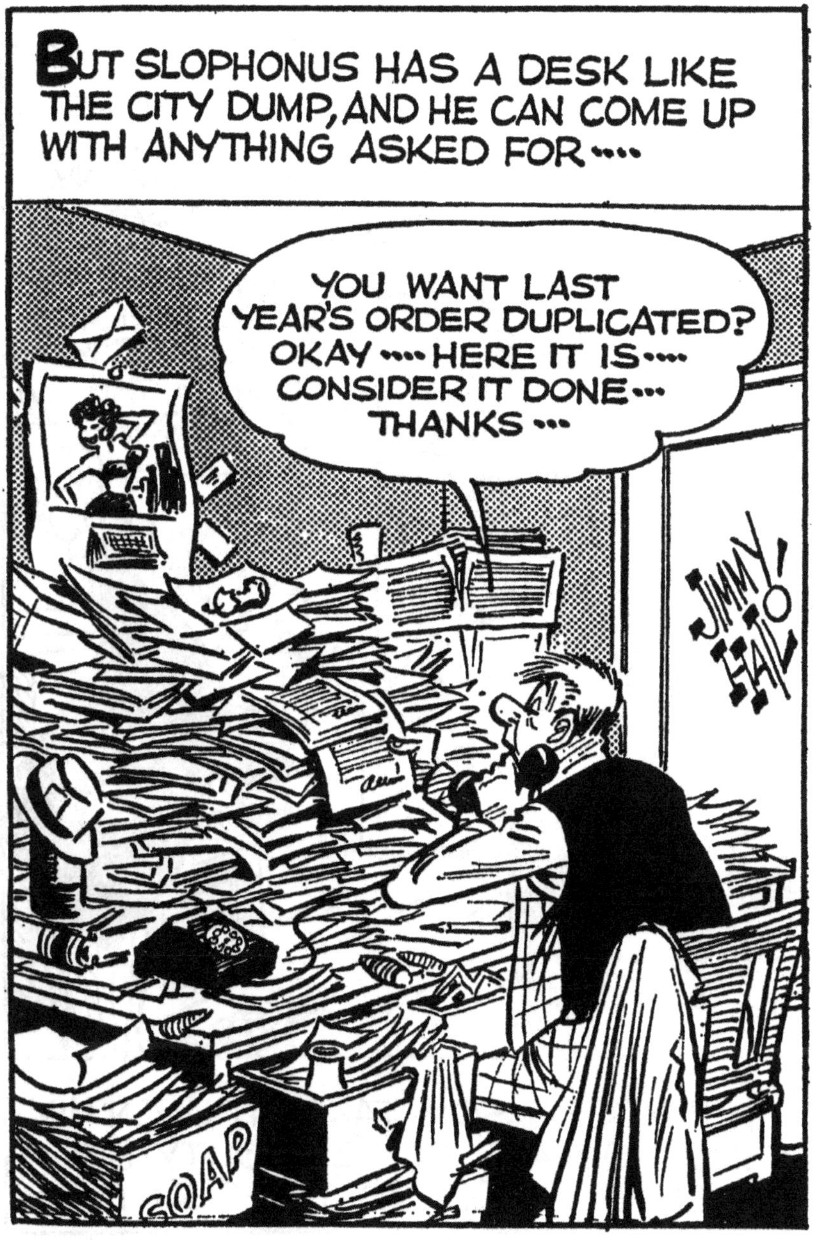
BUT SLOPHONUS HAS A DESK LIKE THE CITY DUMP, AND HE CAN COME UP WITH ANYTHING ASKED FOR....
YOU WANT LAST YEAR'S ORDER DUPLICATED? OKAY .... HERE IT IS.... CONSIDER IT DONE... THANKS ...
JIMMY HATLO!
SOAP

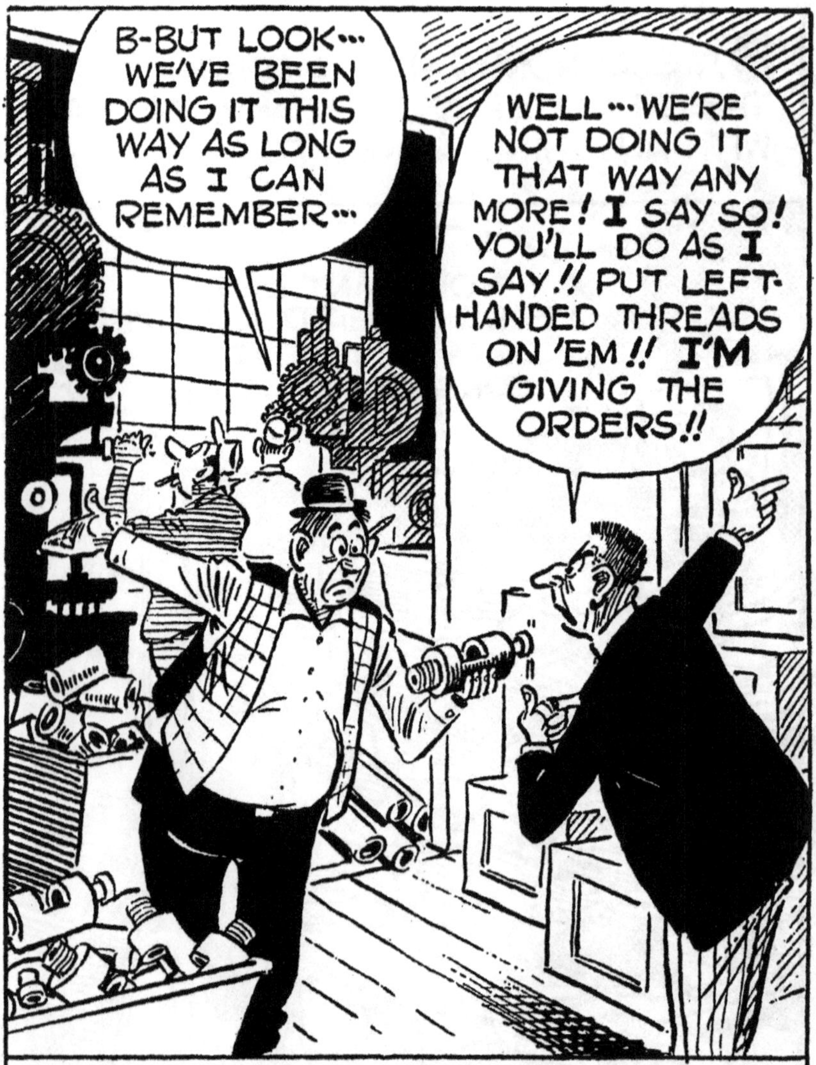
B-BUT LOOK... WE'VE BEEN DOING IT THIS WAY AS LONG AS I CAN REMEMBER...
WELL... WE'RE NOT DOING IT THAT WAY ANY MORE! I SAY SO! YOU'LL DO AS I SAY!! PUT LEFT-HANDED THREADS ON 'EM!! I'M GIVING THE ORDERS!!

THE BOSS'S SON TAKES IT UPON HIMSELF TO MAKE SOME MIGHTY BIG DECISIONS AROUND THE PLANT....

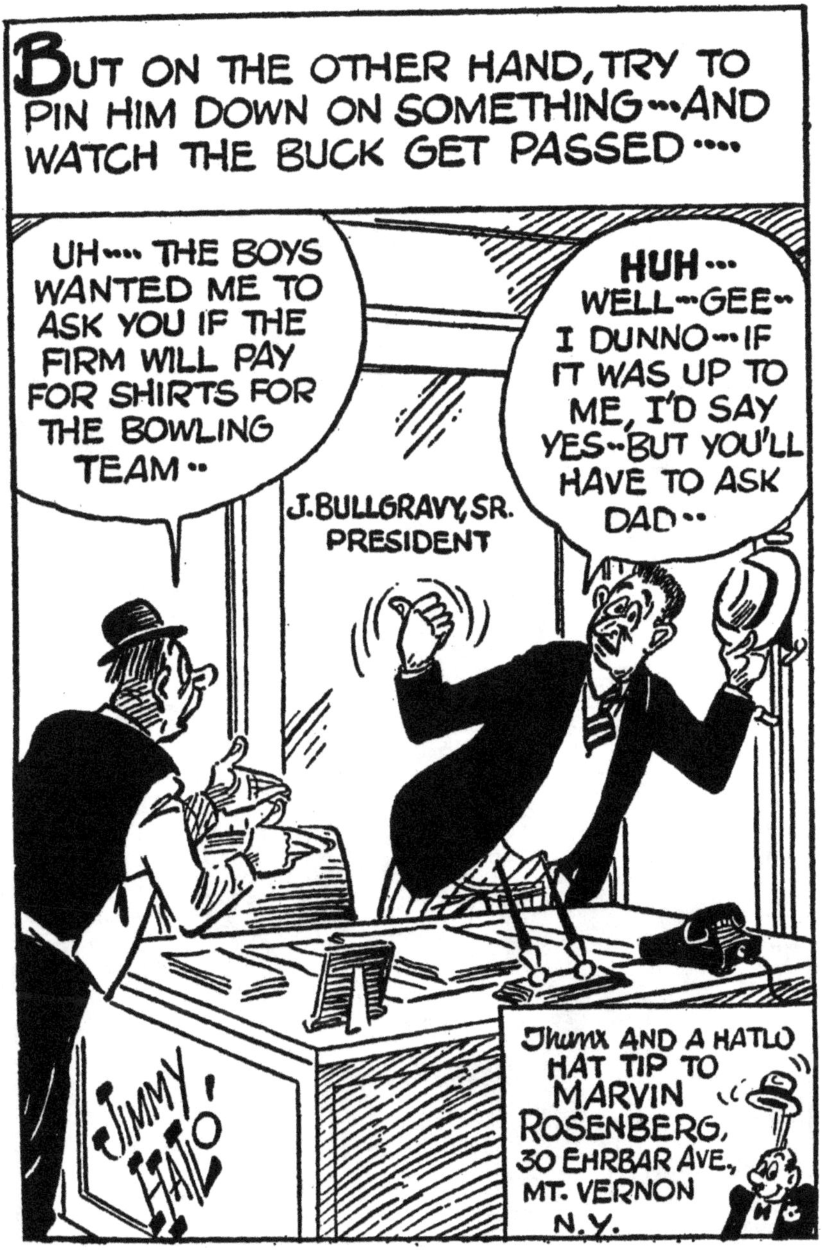
BUT ON THE OTHER HAND, TRY TO PIN HIM DOWN ON SOMETHING...AND WATCH THE BUCK GET PASSED....
UH.... THE BOYS WANTED ME TO ASK YOU IF THE FIRM WILL PAY FOR SHIRTS FOR THE BOWLING TEAM..
J. BULLGRAVY, SR. PRESIDENT
HUH... WELL--GEE-- I DUNNO--IF IT WAS UP TO ME, I'D SAY YES--BUT YOU'LL HAVE TO ASK DAD..
Thanx AND A HATLO HAT TIP TO MARVIN ROSENBERG, 30 EHRBAR AVE., MT. VERNON N.Y.
JIMMY HATLO

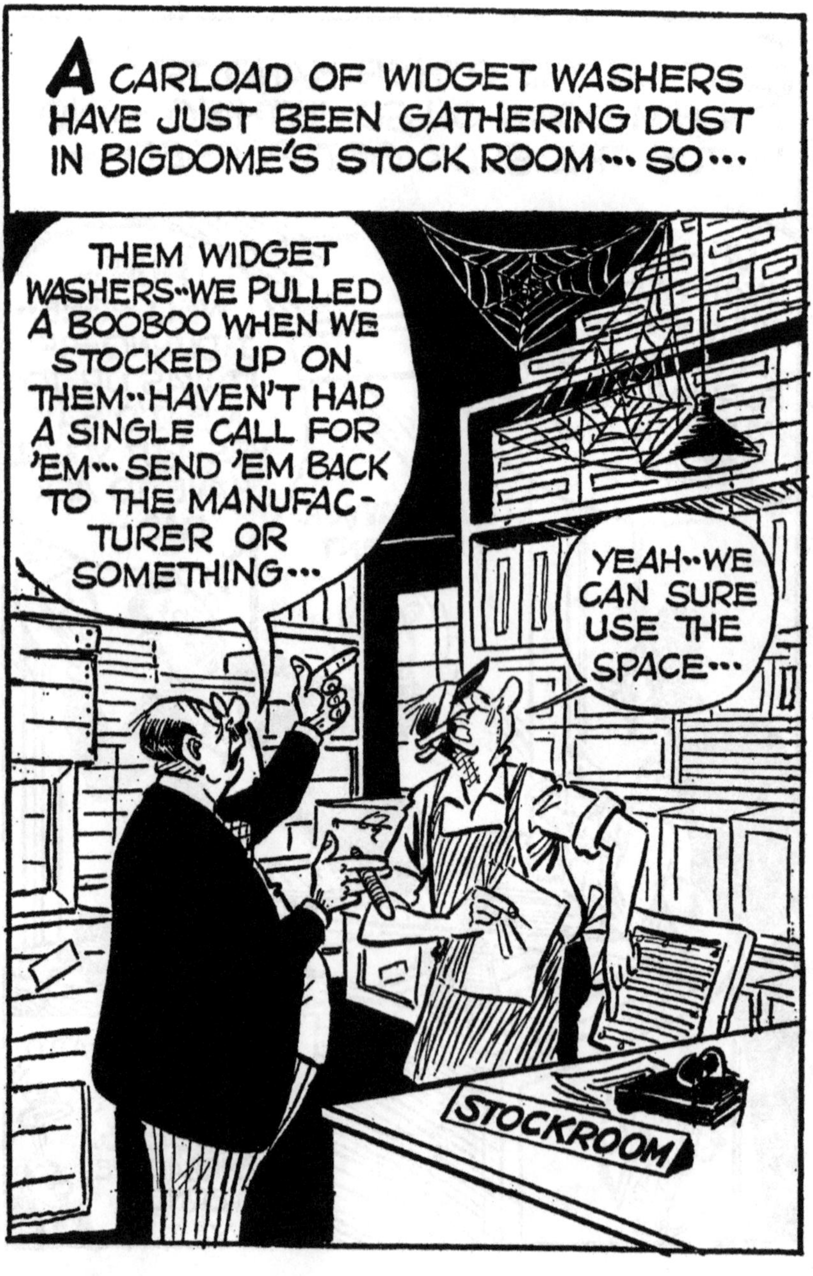
A CARLOAD OF WIDGET WASHERS HAVE JUST BEEN GATHERING DUST IN BIGDOME'S STOCK ROOM ··· SO ···
THEM WIDGET WASHERS··WE PULLED A BOOBOO WHEN WE STOCKED UP ON THEM··HAVEN'T HAD A SINGLE CALL FOR 'EM··· SEND 'EM BACK TO THE MANUFAC-TURER OR SOMETHING···
YEAH··WE CAN SURE USE THE SPACE···
STOCKROOM

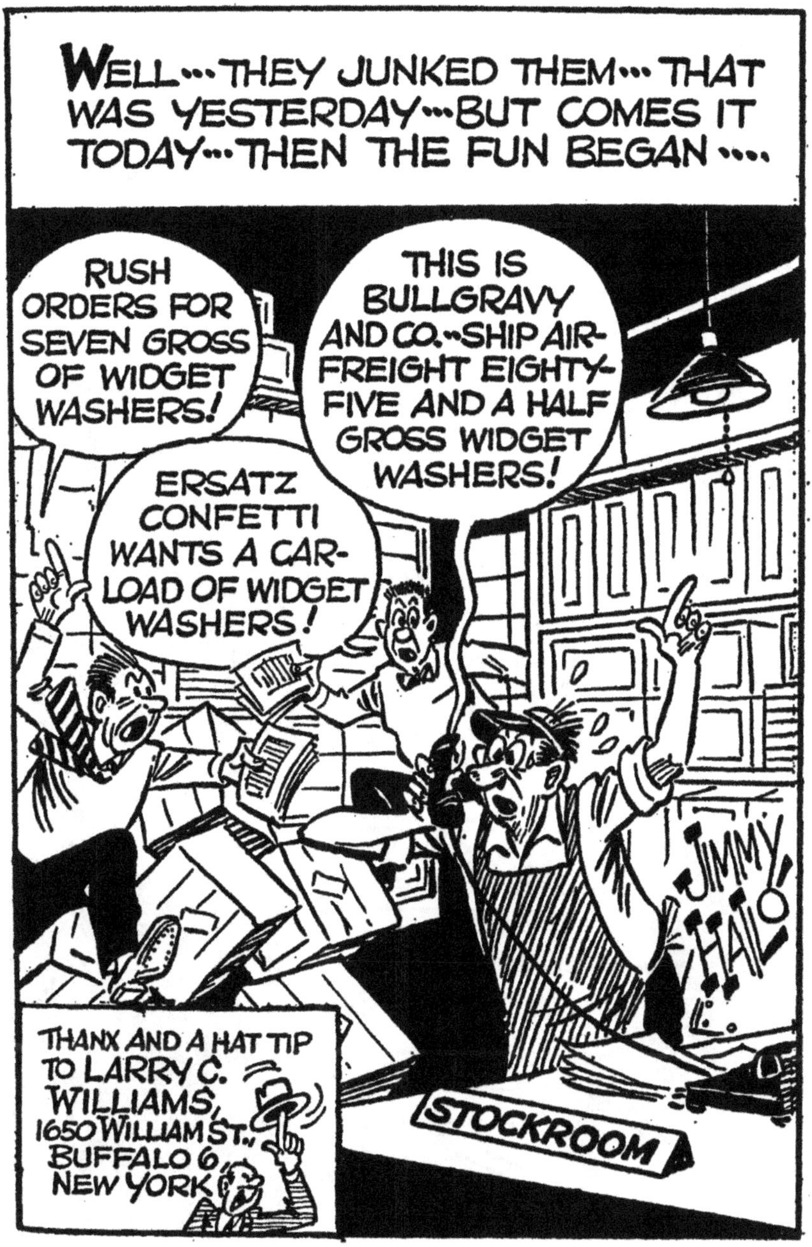
WELL... THEY JUNKED THEM... THAT WAS YESTERDAY...BUT COMES IT TODAY... THEN THE FUN BEGAN....
RUSH ORDERS FOR SEVEN GROSS OF WIDGET WASHERS!
THIS IS BULLGRAVY AND CO.--SHIP AIR-FREIGHT EIGHTY-FIVE AND A HALF GROSS WIDGET WASHERS!
ERSATZ CONFETTI WANTS A CAR-LOAD OF WIDGET WASHERS!
JIMMY HALO
STOCKROOM
THANX AND A HAT TIP TO LARRY C. WILLIAMS, 1650 WILLIAM ST., BUFFALO 6, NEW YORK

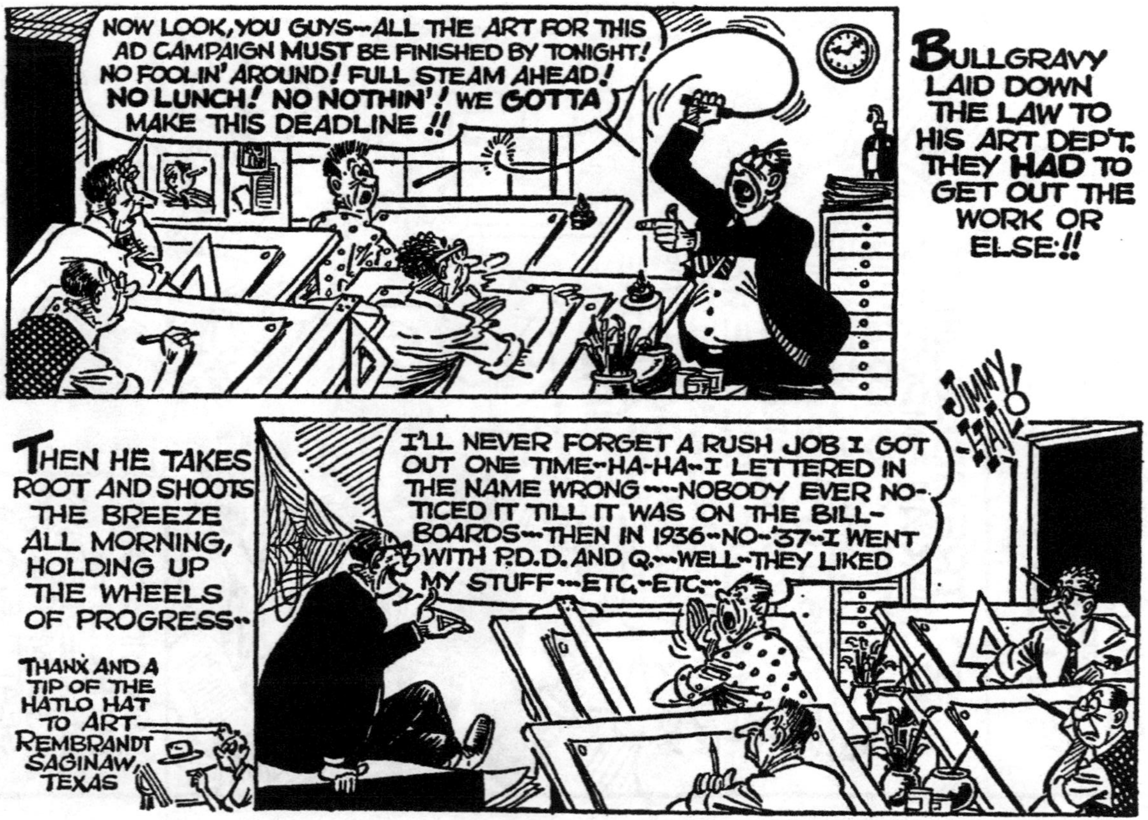
NOW LOOK, YOU GUYS--ALL THE ART FOR THIS AD CAMPAIGN MUST BE FINISHED BY TONIGHT! NO FOOLIN' AROUND! FULL STEAM AHEAD! NO LUNCH! NO NOTHIN'! WE GOTTA MAKE THIS DEADLINE!!
BULLGRAVY LAID DOWN THE LAW TO HIS ART DEP'T. THEY HAD TO GET OUT THE WORK OR ELSE!!
THEN HE TAKES ROOT AND SHOOTS THE BREEZE ALL MORNING, HOLDING UP THE WHEELS OF PROGRESS--
I'LL NEVER FORGET A RUSH JOB I GOT OUT ONE TIME--HA-HA--I LETTERED IN THE NAME WRONG----NOBODY EVER NOTICED IT TILL IT WAS ON THE BILLBOARDS---THEN IN 1936--NO--'37--I WENT WITH P.D.D. AND Q.---WELL--THEY LIKED MY STUFF---ETC.--ETC.--
JIMMY HATLO
THANX AND A TIP OF THE HATLO HAT TO ART REMBRANDT SAGINAW, TEXAS

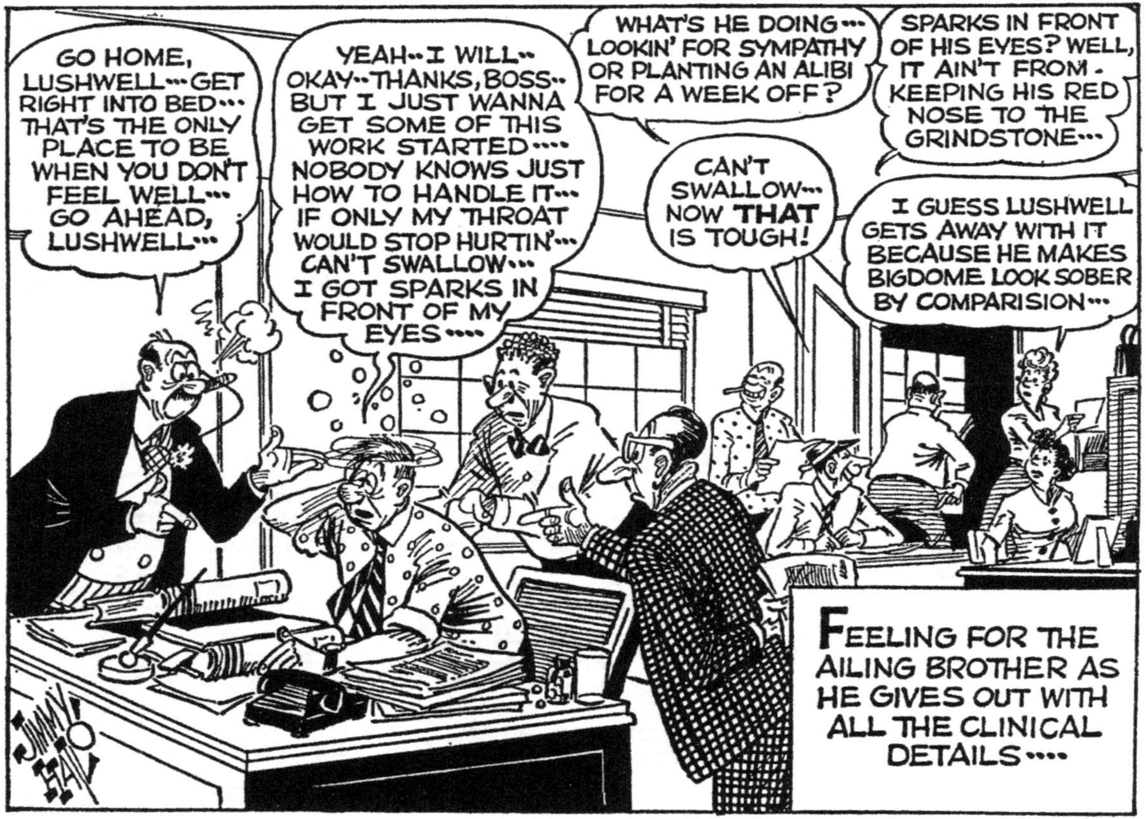
GO HOME, LUSHWELL··· GET RIGHT INTO BED··· THAT'S THE ONLY PLACE TO BE WHEN YOU DON'T FEEL WELL··· GO AHEAD, LUSHWELL···
YEAH·· I WILL·· OKAY·· THANKS, BOSS·· BUT I JUST WANNA GET SOME OF THIS WORK STARTED···· NOBODY KNOWS JUST HOW TO HANDLE IT··· IF ONLY MY THROAT WOULD STOP HURTIN'··· CAN'T SWALLOW··· I GOT SPARKS IN FRONT OF MY EYES····
WHAT'S HE DOING··· LOOKIN' FOR SYMPATHY OR PLANTING AN ALIBI FOR A WEEK OFF?
CAN'T SWALLOW··· NOW **THAT** IS TOUGH!
SPARKS IN FRONT OF HIS EYES? WELL, IT AIN'T FROM - KEEPING HIS RED NOSE TO THE GRINDSTONE···
I GUESS LUSHWELL GETS AWAY WITH IT BECAUSE HE MAKES BIGDOME LOOK SOBER BY COMPARISION···
FEELING FOR THE AILING BROTHER AS HE GIVES OUT WITH ALL THE CLINICAL DETAILS····
JIMMY HATLO

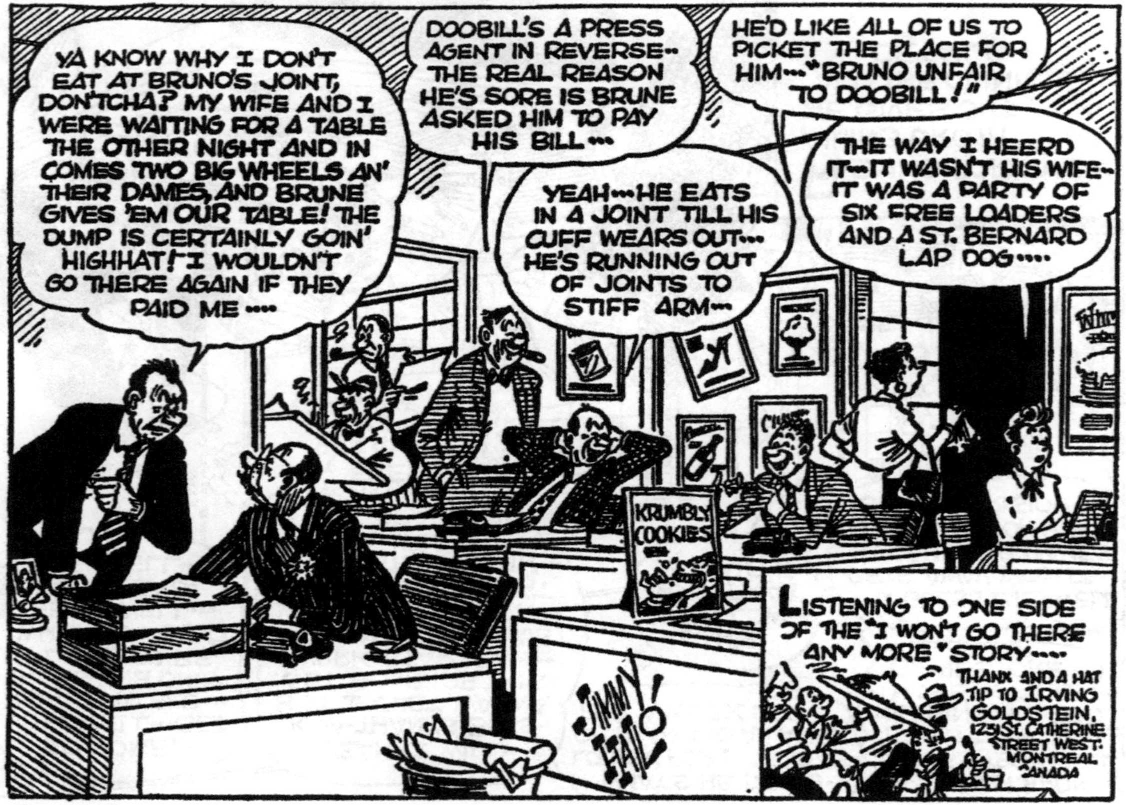
YA KNOW WHY I DON'T EAT AT BRUNO'S JOINT, DON'TCHA? MY WIFE AND I WERE WAITING FOR A TABLE THE OTHER NIGHT AND IN COMES TWO BIG WHEELS AN' THEIR DAMES, AND BRUNE GIVES 'EM OUR TABLE! THE DUMP IS CERTAINLY GOIN' HIGHHAT! I WOULDN'T GO THERE AGAIN IF THEY PAID ME ....
DOOBILL'S A PRESS AGENT IN REVERSE.. THE REAL REASON HE'S SORE IS BRUNE ASKED HIM TO PAY HIS BILL...
YEAH... HE EATS IN A JOINT TILL HIS CUFF WEARS OUT... HE'S RUNNING OUT OF JOINTS TO STIFF ARM...
HE'D LIKE ALL OF US TO PICKET THE PLACE FOR HIM... "BRUNO UNFAIR TO DOOBILL!"
THE WAY I HEERD IT... IT WASN'T HIS WIFE.. IT WAS A PARTY OF SIX FREE LOADERS AND A ST. BERNARD LAP DOG....
KRUMBLY COOKIES
LISTENING TO ONE SIDE OF THE "I WON'T GO THERE ANY MORE" STORY....
THANX AND A HAT TIP TO IRVING GOLDSTEIN, 1231 ST. CATHERINE STREET WEST. MONTREAL CANADA
JIMMY HATLO

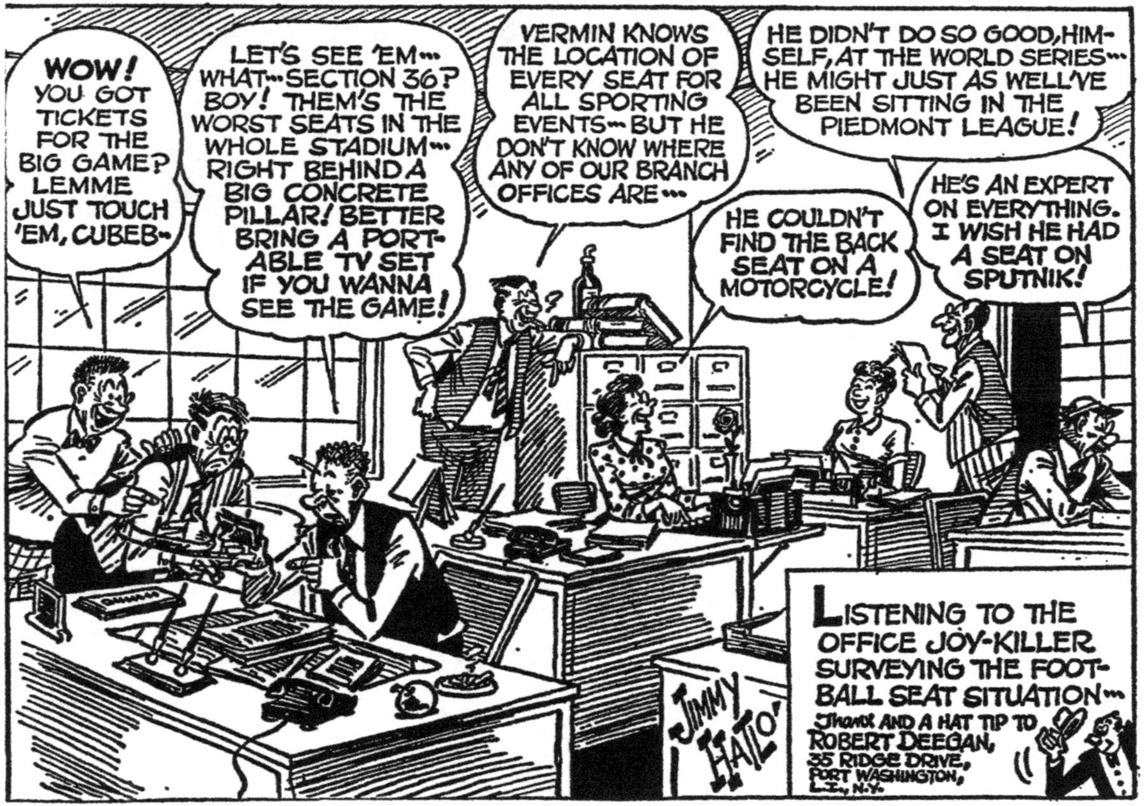
WOW! YOU GOT TICKETS FOR THE BIG GAME? LEMME JUST TOUCH 'EM, CUBEB--
LET'S SEE 'EM--- WHAT---SECTION 36? BOY! THEM'S THE WORST SEATS IN THE WHOLE STADIUM--- RIGHT BEHIND A BIG CONCRETE PILLAR! BETTER BRING A PORTABLE TV SET IF YOU WANNA SEE THE GAME!
VERMIN KNOWS THE LOCATION OF EVERY SEAT FOR ALL SPORTING EVENTS--- BUT HE DON'T KNOW WHERE ANY OF OUR BRANCH OFFICES ARE---
HE DIDN'T DO SO GOOD, HIMSELF, AT THE WORLD SERIES--- HE MIGHT JUST AS WELL'VE BEEN SITTING IN THE PIEDMONT LEAGUE!
HE COULDN'T FIND THE BACK SEAT ON A MOTORCYCLE!
HE'S AN EXPERT ON EVERYTHING. I WISH HE HAD A SEAT ON SPUTNIK!
JIMMY HATLO
LISTENING TO THE OFFICE JOY-KILLER SURVEYING THE FOOTBALL SEAT SITUATION---
Thanx AND A HAT TIP TO ROBERT DEEGAN, 35 RIDGE DRIVE, PORT WASHINGTON, L.I., N.Y.

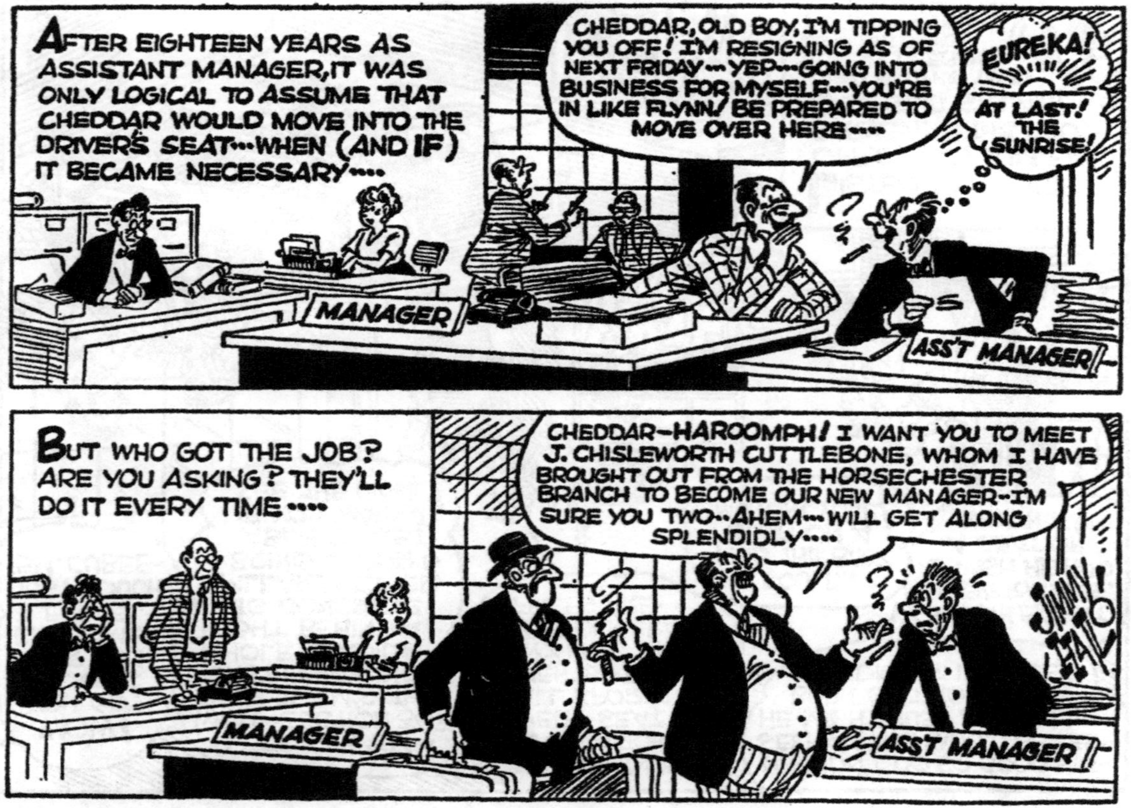
AFTER EIGHTEEN YEARS AS ASSISTANT MANAGER, IT WAS ONLY LOGICAL TO ASSUME THAT CHEDDAR WOULD MOVE INTO THE DRIVER'S SEAT... WHEN (AND IF) IT BECAME NECESSARY....
CHEDDAR, OLD BOY, I'M TIPPING YOU OFF! I'M RESIGNING AS OF NEXT FRIDAY... YEP... GOING INTO BUSINESS FOR MYSELF... YOU'RE IN LIKE FLYNN! BE PREPARED TO MOVE OVER HERE....
EUREKA!
AT LAST! THE SUNRISE!
MANAGER
ASS'T MANAGER
BUT WHO GOT THE JOB? ARE YOU ASKING? THEY'LL DO IT EVERY TIME....
CHEDDAR–HAROOMPH! I WANT YOU TO MEET J. CHISLEWORTH CUTTLEBONE, WHOM I HAVE BROUGHT OUT FROM THE HORSECHESTER BRANCH TO BECOME OUR NEW MANAGER–I'M SURE YOU TWO.. AHEM... WILL GET ALONG SPLENDIDLY....
MANAGER
ASS'T MANAGER
JIMMY HATLO!

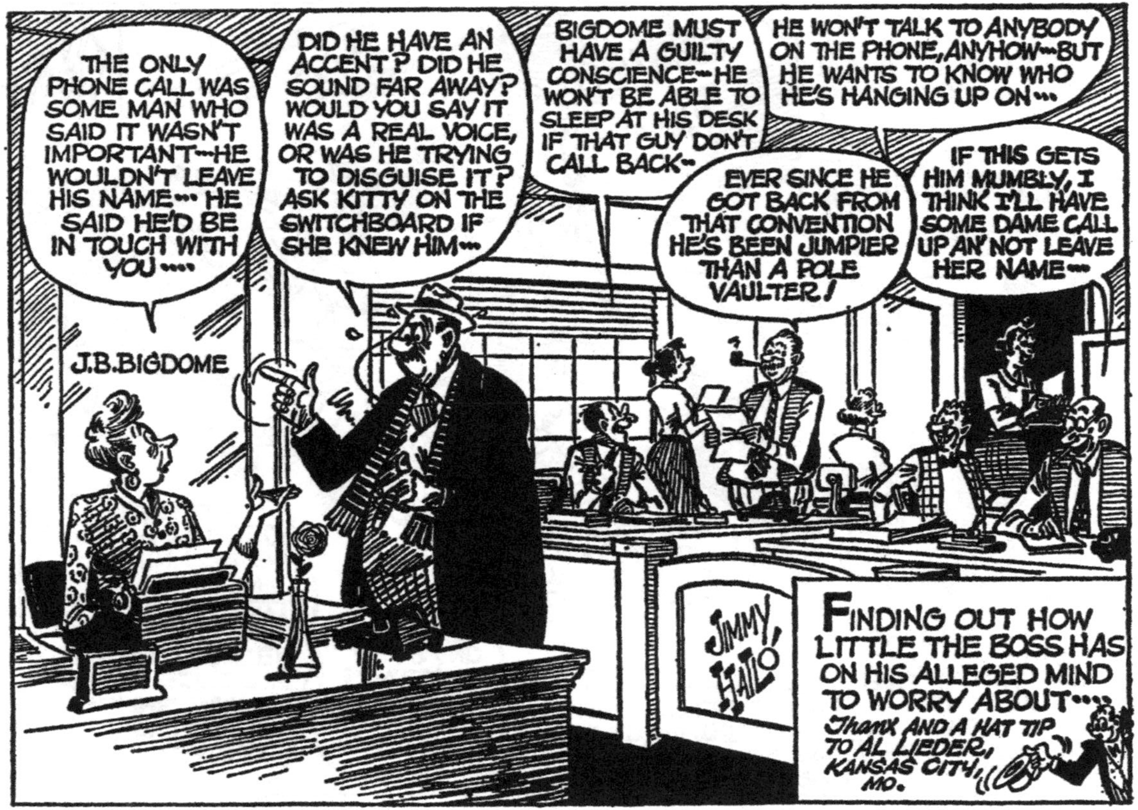
THE ONLY PHONE CALL WAS SOME MAN WHO SAID IT WASN'T IMPORTANT---HE WOULDN'T LEAVE HIS NAME--- HE SAID HE'D BE IN TOUCH WITH YOU....
DID HE HAVE AN ACCENT? DID HE SOUND FAR AWAY? WOULD YOU SAY IT WAS A REAL VOICE, OR WAS HE TRYING TO DISGUISE IT? ASK KITTY ON THE SWITCHBOARD IF SHE KNEW HIM---
BIGDOME MUST HAVE A GUILTY CONSCIENCE--- HE WON'T BE ABLE TO SLEEP AT HIS DESK IF THAT GUY DON'T CALL BACK--
HE WON'T TALK TO ANYBODY ON THE PHONE, ANYHOW---BUT HE WANTS TO KNOW WHO HE'S HANGING UP ON---
EVER SINCE HE GOT BACK FROM THAT CONVENTION HE'S BEEN JUMPIER THAN A POLE VAULTER!
IF THIS GETS HIM MUMBLY, I THINK I'LL HAVE SOME DAME CALL UP AN' NOT LEAVE HER NAME---
J.B.BIGDOME
JIMMY HATLO
FINDING OUT HOW LITTLE THE BOSS HAS ON HIS ALLEGED MIND TO WORRY ABOUT....
THANX AND A HAT TIP TO AL LIEDER, KANSAS CITY, MO.

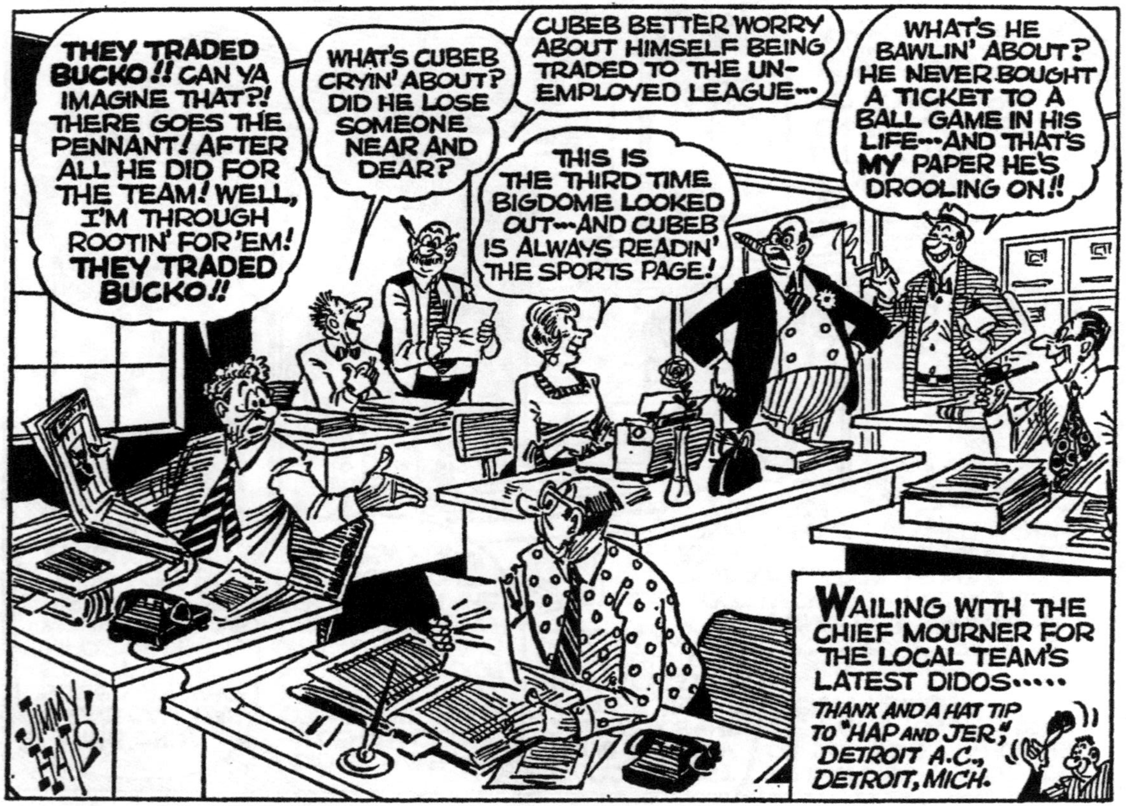
THEY TRADED BUCKO!! CAN YA IMAGINE THAT?! THERE GOES THE PENNANT! AFTER ALL HE DID FOR THE TEAM! WELL, I'M THROUGH ROOTIN' FOR 'EM! THEY TRADED BUCKO!!
WHAT'S CUBEB CRYIN' ABOUT? DID HE LOSE SOMEONE NEAR AND DEAR?
CUBEB BETTER WORRY ABOUT HIMSELF BEING TRADED TO THE UN-EMPLOYED LEAGUE...
THIS IS THE THIRD TIME BIGDOME LOOKED OUT...AND CUBEB IS ALWAYS READIN' THE SPORTS PAGE!
WHAT'S HE BAWLIN' ABOUT? HE NEVER BOUGHT A TICKET TO A BALL GAME IN HIS LIFE...AND THAT'S MY PAPER HE'S DROOLING ON!!
WAILING WITH THE CHIEF MOURNER FOR THE LOCAL TEAM'S LATEST DIDOS.....
THANX AND A HAT TIP TO "HAP AND JER," DETROIT A.C., DETROIT, MICH.
JIMMY HATLO

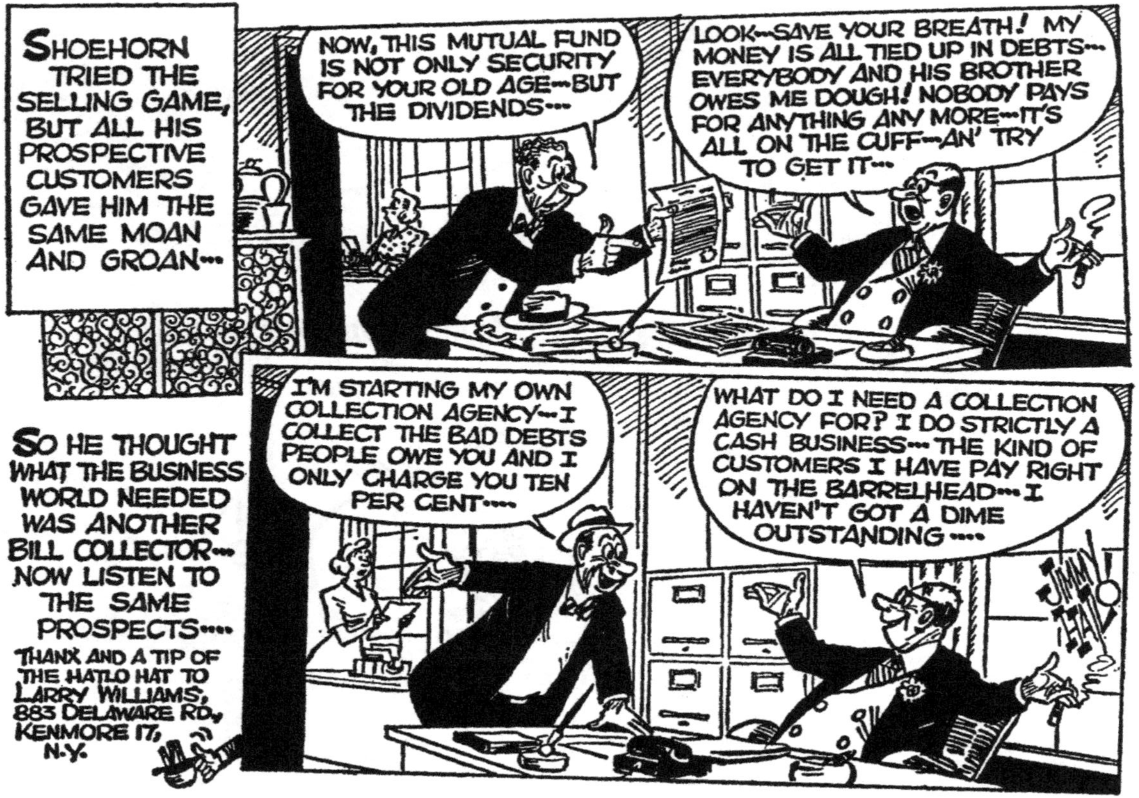
SHOEHORN TRIED THE SELLING GAME, BUT ALL HIS PROSPECTIVE CUSTOMERS GAVE HIM THE SAME MOAN AND GROAN...
NOW, THIS MUTUAL FUND IS NOT ONLY SECURITY FOR YOUR OLD AGE--BUT THE DIVIDENDS...
LOOK--SAVE YOUR BREATH! MY MONEY IS ALL TIED UP IN DEBTS... EVERYBODY AND HIS BROTHER OWES ME DOUGH! NOBODY PAYS FOR ANYTHING ANY MORE--IT'S ALL ON THE CUFF--AN' TRY TO GET IT...
SO HE THOUGHT WHAT THE BUSINESS WORLD NEEDED WAS ANOTHER BILL COLLECTOR... NOW LISTEN TO THE SAME PROSPECTS....
THANX AND A TIP OF THE HATLO HAT TO LARRY WILLIAMS, 883 DELAWARE RD., KENMORE 17, N.Y.
I'M STARTING MY OWN COLLECTION AGENCY--I COLLECT THE BAD DEBTS PEOPLE OWE YOU AND I ONLY CHARGE YOU TEN PER CENT....
WHAT DO I NEED A COLLECTION AGENCY FOR? I DO STRICTLY A CASH BUSINESS--THE KIND OF CUSTOMERS I HAVE PAY RIGHT ON THE BARRELHEAD--I HAVEN'T GOT A DIME OUTSTANDING....
JIMMY HATLO

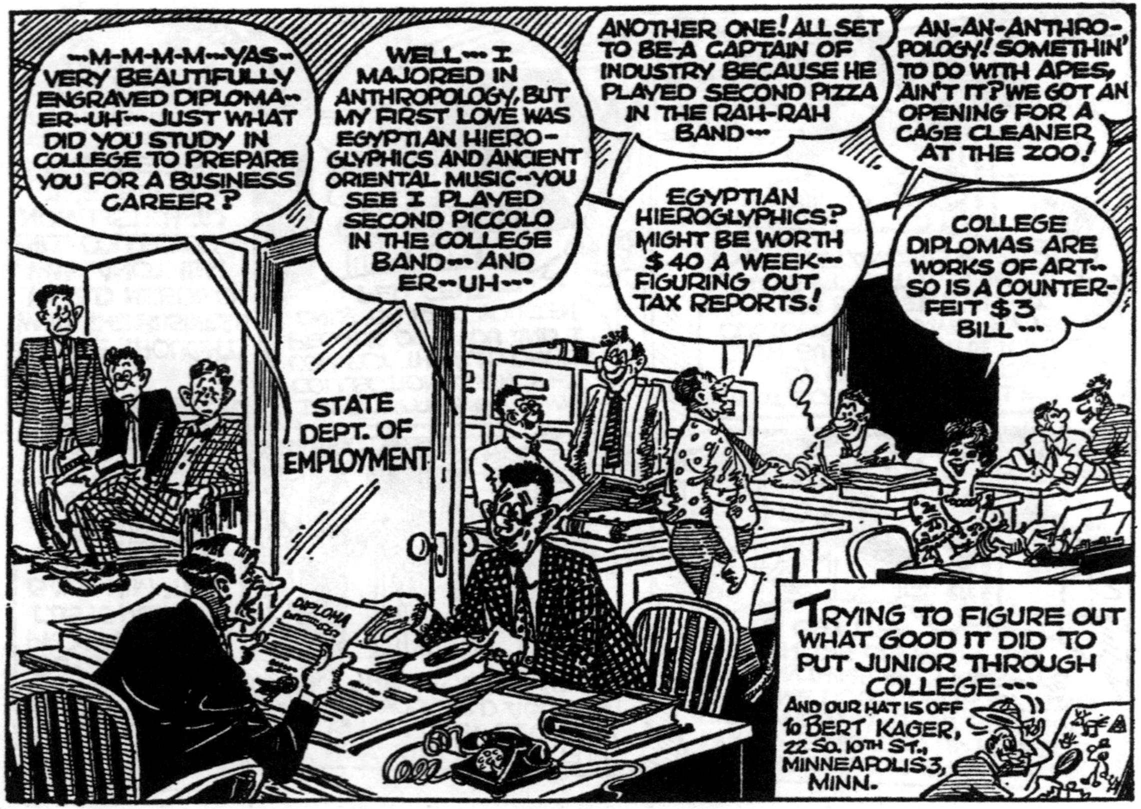
--M-M-M-M--YAS-- VERY BEAUTIFULLY ENGRAVED DIPLOMA-- ER--UH--- JUST WHAT DID YOU STUDY IN COLLEGE TO PREPARE YOU FOR A BUSINESS CAREER?
WELL--- I MAJORED IN ANTHROPOLOGY, BUT MY FIRST LOVE WAS EGYPTIAN HIERO-GLYPHICS AND ANCIENT ORIENTAL MUSIC--YOU SEE I PLAYED SECOND PICCOLO IN THE COLLEGE BAND--- AND ER--UH---
ANOTHER ONE! ALL SET TO BE A CAPTAIN OF INDUSTRY BECAUSE HE PLAYED SECOND PIZZA IN THE RAH-RAH BAND---
EGYPTIAN HIEROGLYPHICS? MIGHT BE WORTH $40 A WEEK--- FIGURING OUT TAX REPORTS!
AN-AN-ANTHRO-POLOGY! SOMETHIN' TO DO WITH APES, AIN'T IT? WE GOT AN OPENING FOR A CAGE CLEANER AT THE ZOO!
COLLEGE DIPLOMAS ARE WORKS OF ART-- SO IS A COUNTER-FEIT $3 BILL---
STATE DEPT. OF EMPLOYMENT
DIPLOMA
TRYING TO FIGURE OUT WHAT GOOD IT DID TO PUT JUNIOR THROUGH COLLEGE---
AND OUR HAT IS OFF TO BERT KAGER, 22 SO. 10TH ST., MINNEAPOLIS 3, MINN.

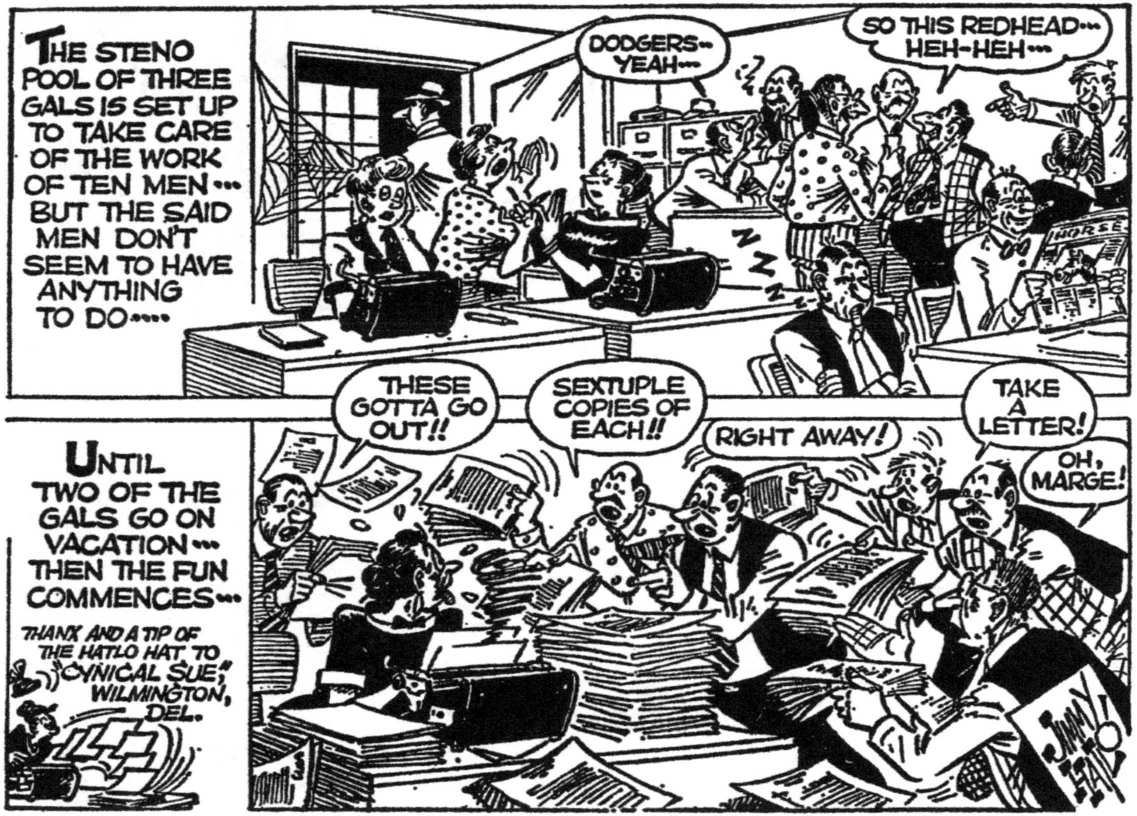
THE STENO POOL OF THREE GALS IS SET UP TO TAKE CARE OF THE WORK OF TEN MEN... BUT THE SAID MEN DON'T SEEM TO HAVE ANYTHING TO DO....
DODGERS-- YEAH...
SO THIS REDHEAD... HEH-HEH...
HORSE
UNTIL TWO OF THE GALS GO ON VACATION... THEN THE FUN COMMENCES...
THANX AND A TIP OF THE HATLO HAT TO "CYNICAL SUE," WILMINGTON, DEL.
THESE GOTTA GO OUT!!
SEXTUPLE COPIES OF EACH!!
RIGHT AWAY!
TAKE A LETTER!
OH, MARGE!
JIMMY HATLO

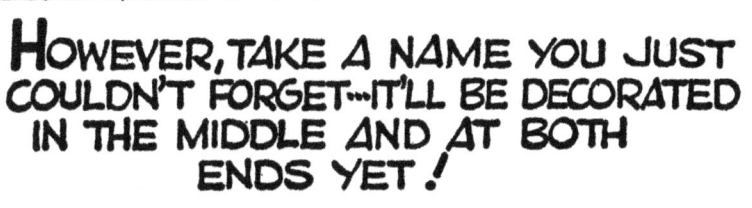

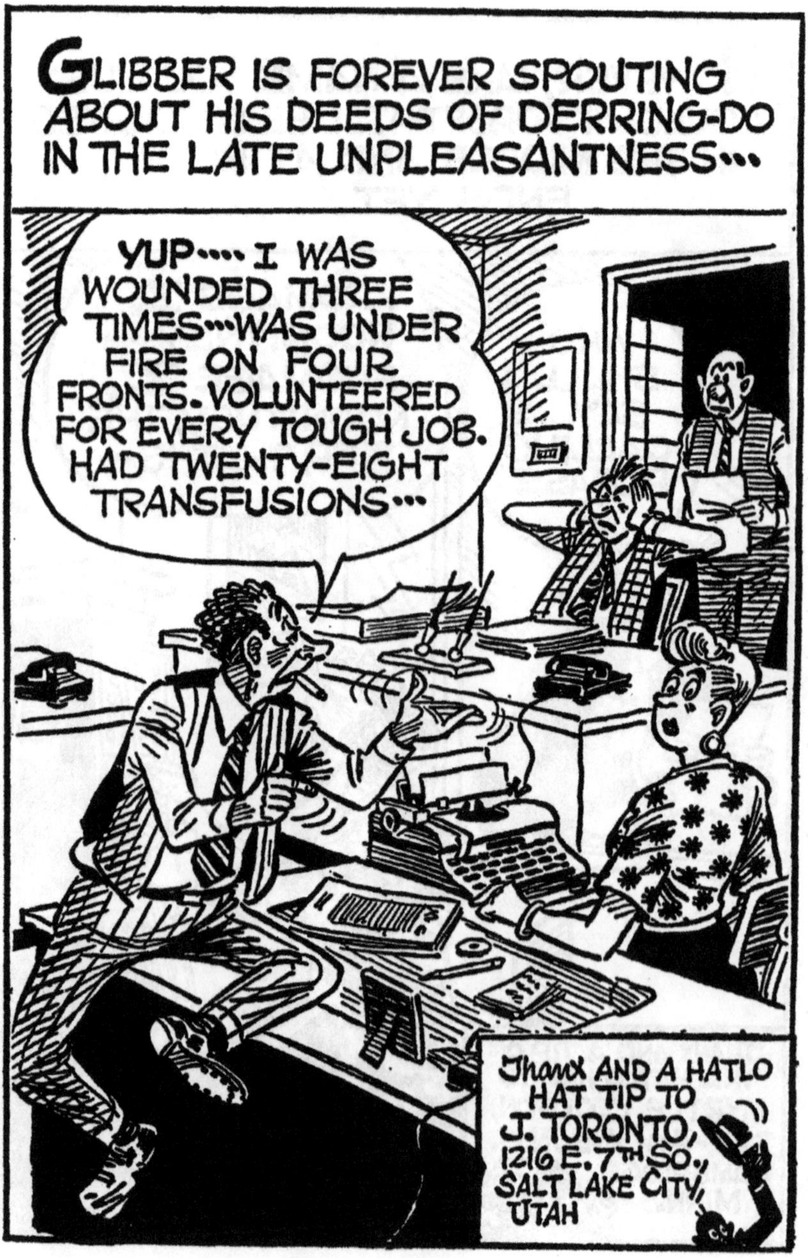
GLIBBER IS FOREVER SPOUTING ABOUT HIS DEEDS OF DERRING-DO IN THE LATE UNPLEASANTNESS...
YUP.... I WAS WOUNDED THREE TIMES...WAS UNDER FIRE ON FOUR FRONTS. VOLUNTEERED FOR EVERY TOUGH JOB. HAD TWENTY-EIGHT TRANSFUSIONS...
Thanx AND A HATLO HAT TIP TO J. TORONTO, 1216 E. 7TH SO., SALT LAKE CITY, UTAH

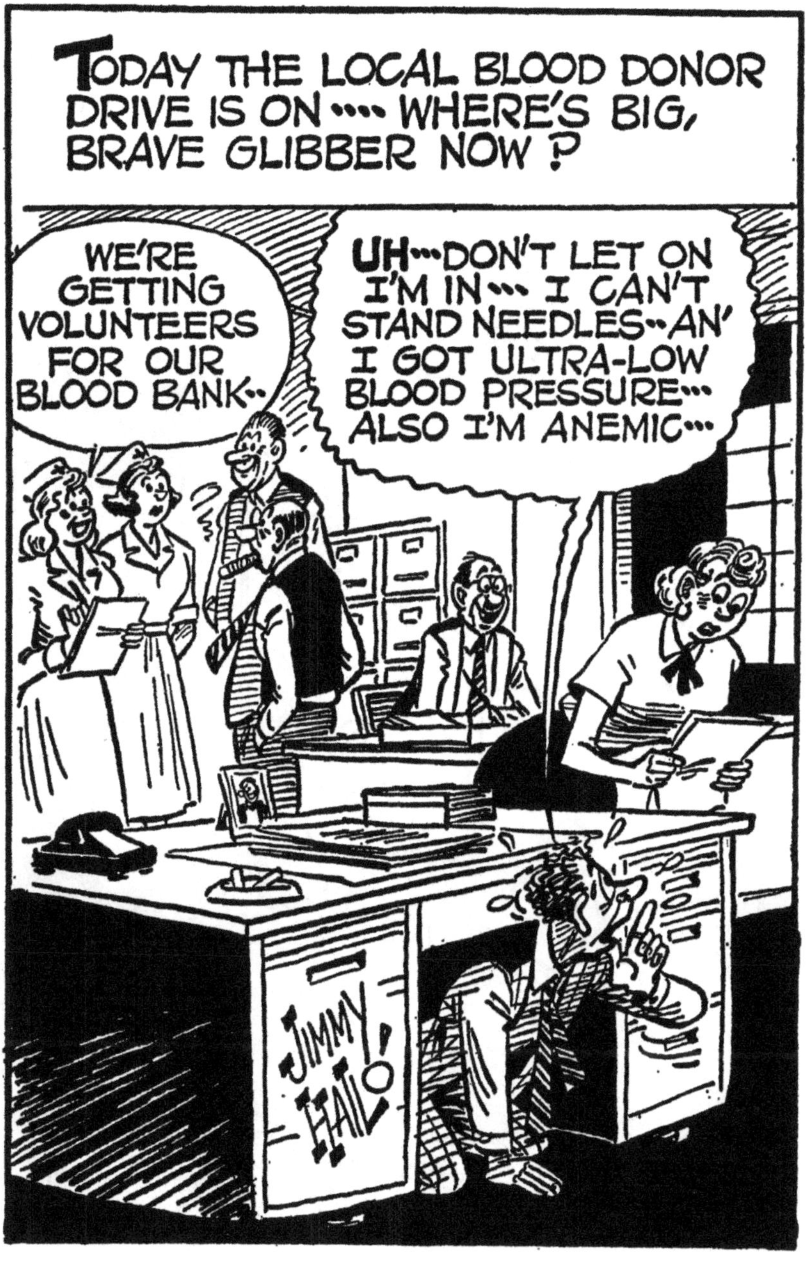
TODAY THE LOCAL BLOOD DONOR DRIVE IS ON.... WHERE'S BIG, BRAVE GLIBBER NOW?
WE'RE GETTING VOLUNTEERS FOR OUR BLOOD BANK..
UH...DON'T LET ON I'M IN... I CAN'T STAND NEEDLES..AN' I GOT ULTRA-LOW BLOOD PRESSURE... ALSO I'M ANEMIC...
JIMMY HATLO!

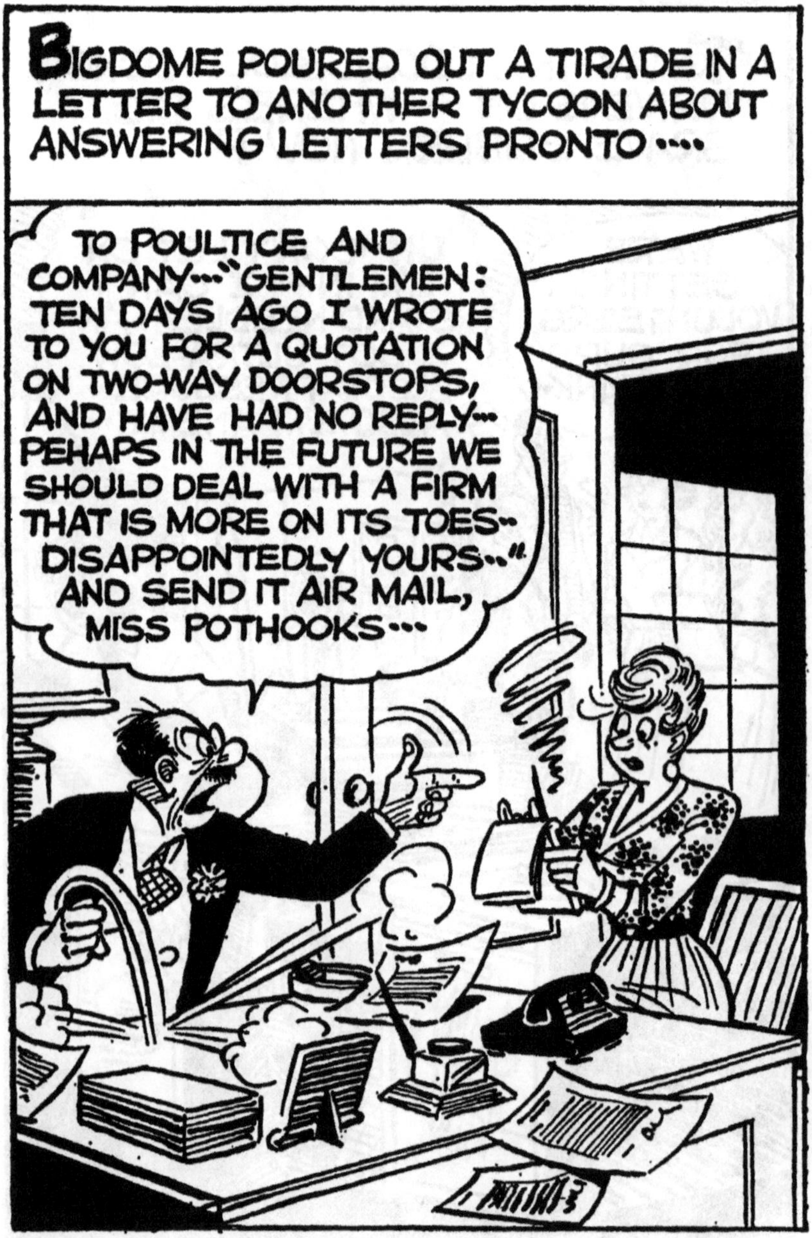
BIGDOME POURED OUT A TIRADE IN A LETTER TO ANOTHER TYCOON ABOUT ANSWERING LETTERS PRONTO ....
TO POULTICE AND COMPANY--- "GENTLEMEN: TEN DAYS AGO I WROTE TO YOU FOR A QUOTATION ON TWO-WAY DOORSTOPS, AND HAVE HAD NO REPLY-- PEHAPS IN THE FUTURE WE SHOULD DEAL WITH A FIRM THAT IS MORE ON ITS TOES-- DISAPPOINTEDLY YOURS--" AND SEND IT AIR MAIL, MISS POTHOOKS---

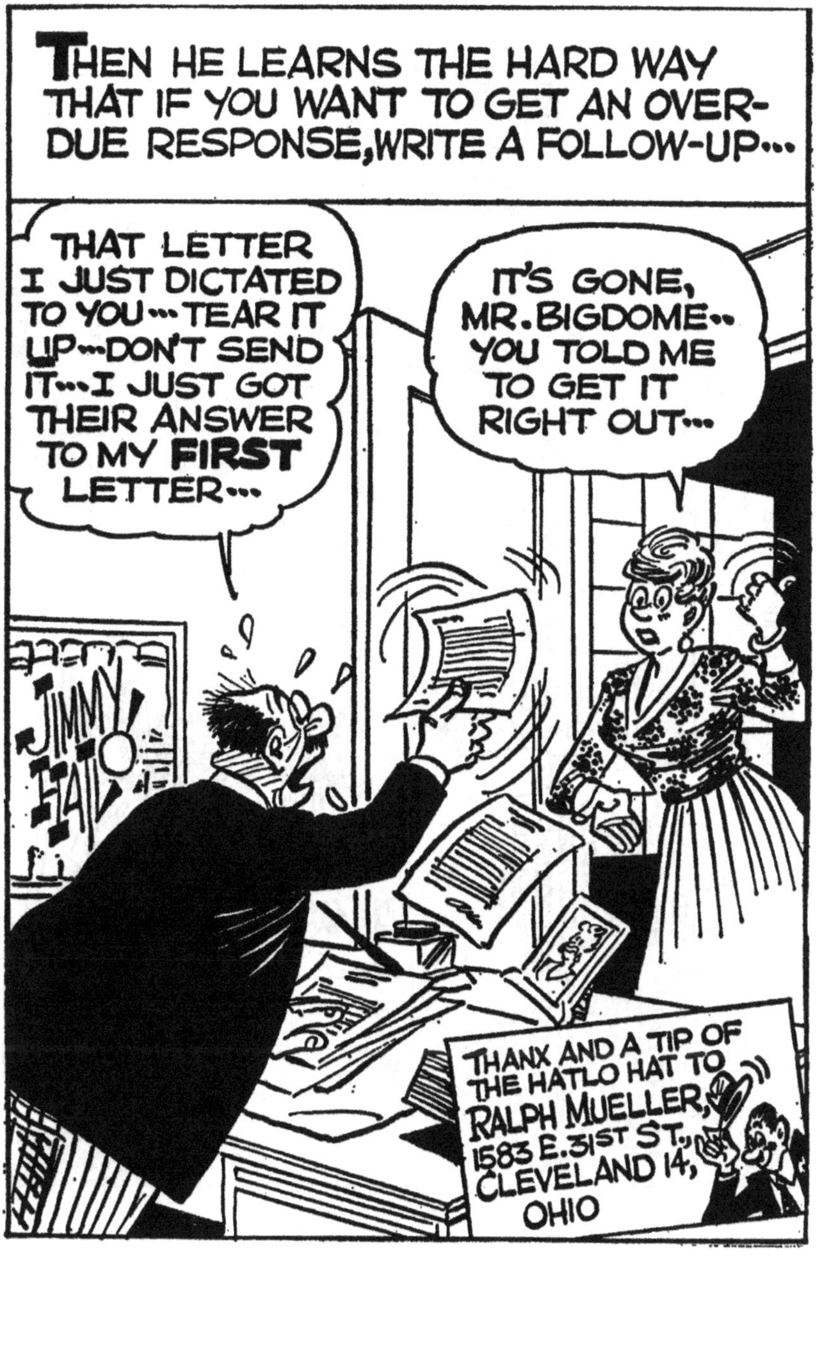
THEN HE LEARNS THE HARD WAY THAT IF YOU WANT TO GET AN OVER-DUE RESPONSE, WRITE A FOLLOW-UP...
THAT LETTER I JUST DICTATED TO YOU... TEAR IT UP... DON'T SEND IT... I JUST GOT THEIR ANSWER TO MY FIRST LETTER...
IT'S GONE, MR. BIGDOME... YOU TOLD ME TO GET IT RIGHT OUT...
THANX AND A TIP OF THE HATLO HAT TO RALPH MUELLER, 1583 E. 31ST ST., CLEVELAND 14, OHIO

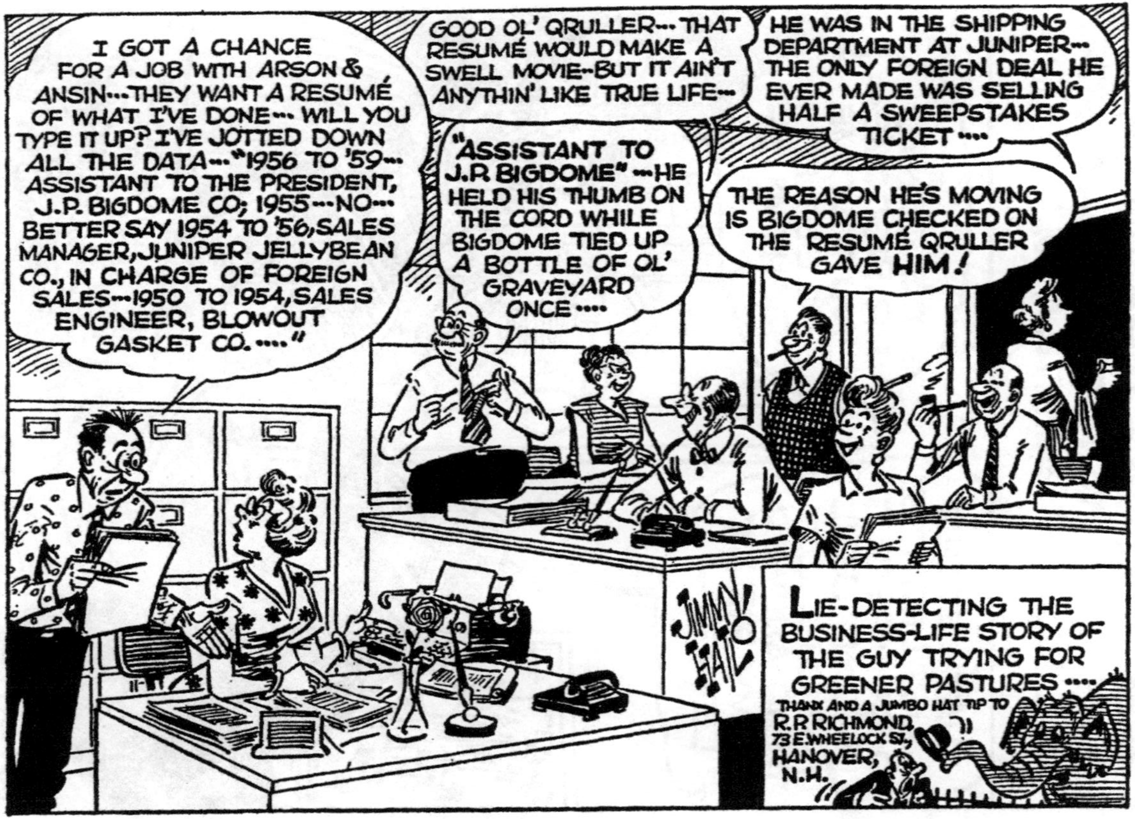
I GOT A CHANCE FOR A JOB WITH ARSON & ANSIN--THEY WANT A RESUMÉ OF WHAT I'VE DONE--- WILL YOU TYPE IT UP? I'VE JOTTED DOWN ALL THE DATA--- "1956 TO '59--- ASSISTANT TO THE PRESIDENT, J.P. BIGDOME CO; 1955---NO--- BETTER SAY 1954 TO '56, SALES MANAGER, JUNIPER JELLYBEAN CO., IN CHARGE OF FOREIGN SALES---1950 TO 1954, SALES ENGINEER, BLOWOUT GASKET CO. ...."
GOOD OL' QRULLER--- THAT RESUMÉ WOULD MAKE A SWELL MOVIE--BUT IT AIN'T ANYTHIN' LIKE TRUE LIFE---
"ASSISTANT TO J.P. BIGDOME"---HE HELD HIS THUMB ON THE CORD WHILE BIGDOME TIED UP A BOTTLE OF OL' GRAVEYARD ONCE ....
HE WAS IN THE SHIPPING DEPARTMENT AT JUNIPER--- THE ONLY FOREIGN DEAL HE EVER MADE WAS SELLING HALF A SWEEPSTAKES TICKET ....
THE REASON HE'S MOVING IS BIGDOME CHECKED ON THE RESUMÉ QRULLER GAVE HIM!
JIMMY HATLO
LIE-DETECTING THE BUSINESS-LIFE STORY OF THE GUY TRYING FOR GREENER PASTURES ....
THANX AND A JUMBO HAT TIP TO R.P. RICHMOND, 73 E. WHEELOCK ST., HANOVER, N.H.

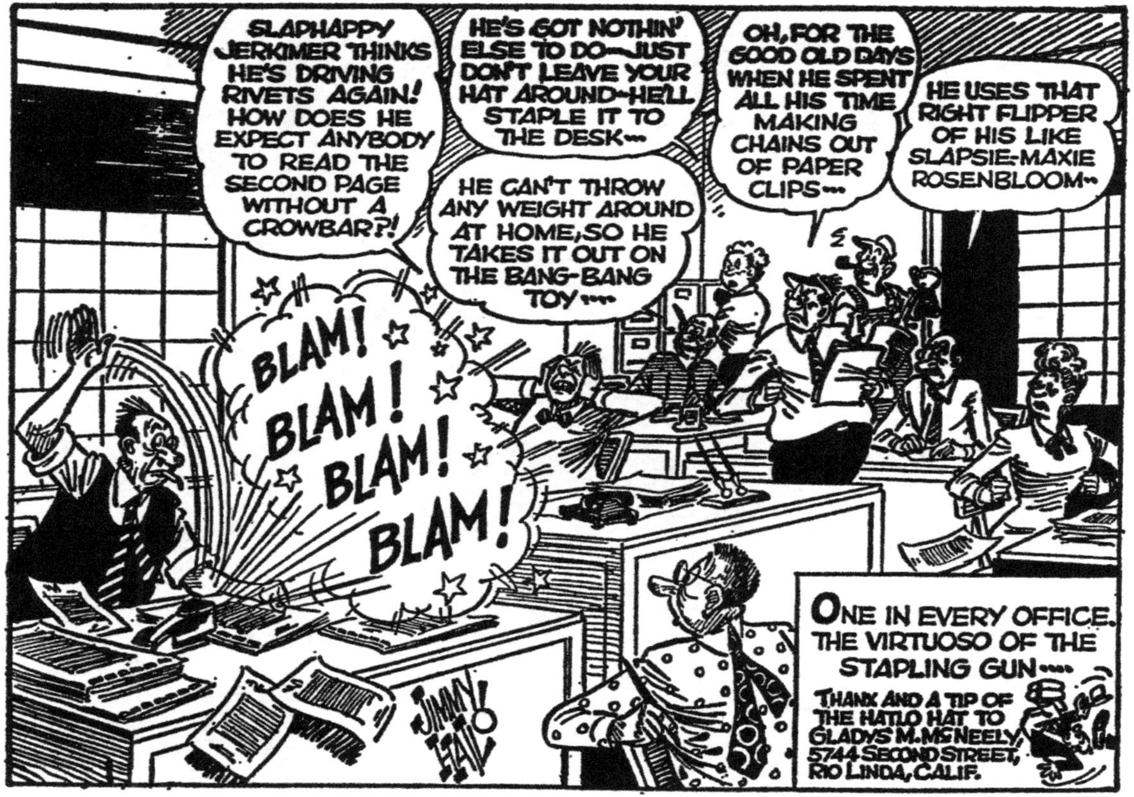
SLAPHAPPY JERKIMER THINKS HE'S DRIVING RIVETS AGAIN! HOW DOES HE EXPECT ANYBODY TO READ THE SECOND PAGE WITHOUT A CROWBAR?!
HE'S GOT NOTHIN' ELSE TO DO—JUST DON'T LEAVE YOUR HAT AROUND—HE'LL STAPLE IT TO THE DESK...
HE CAN'T THROW ANY WEIGHT AROUND AT HOME, SO HE TAKES IT OUT ON THE BANG-BANG TOY....
OH, FOR THE GOOD OLD DAYS WHEN HE SPENT ALL HIS TIME MAKING CHAINS OUT OF PAPER CLIPS...
HE USES THAT RIGHT FLIPPER OF HIS LIKE SLAPSIE-MAXIE ROSENBLOOM..
BLAM! BLAM! BLAM! BLAM!
ONE IN EVERY OFFICE. THE VIRTUOSO OF THE STAPLING GUN....
THANX AND A TIP OF THE HATLO HAT TO GLADYS M. McNEELY, 5744 SECOND STREET, RIO LINDA, CALIF.
JIMMY HATLO

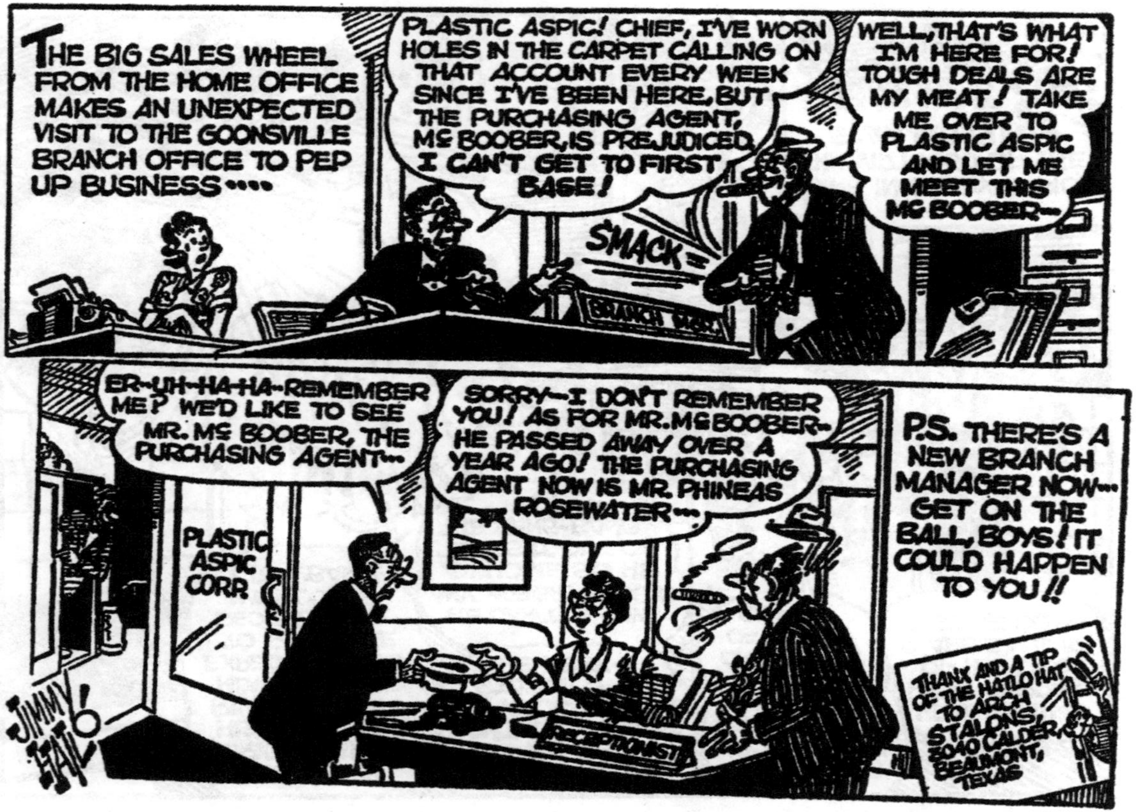
THE BIG SALES WHEEL FROM THE HOME OFFICE MAKES AN UNEXPECTED VISIT TO THE GOONSVILLE BRANCH OFFICE TO PEP UP BUSINESS....
PLASTIC ASPIC! CHIEF, I'VE WORN HOLES IN THE CARPET CALLING ON THAT ACCOUNT EVERY WEEK SINCE I'VE BEEN HERE, BUT THE PURCHASING AGENT, MC BOOBER, IS PREJUDICED. I CAN'T GET TO FIRST BASE!
WELL, THAT'S WHAT I'M HERE FOR! TOUGH DEALS ARE MY MEAT! TAKE ME OVER TO PLASTIC ASPIC AND LET ME MEET THIS MC BOOBER--
SMACK
BRANCH MGR.
ER--UH--HA-HA--REMEMBER ME? WE'D LIKE TO SEE MR. MC BOOBER, THE PURCHASING AGENT...
SORRY--I DON'T REMEMBER YOU! AS FOR MR. MC BOOBER-- HE PASSED AWAY OVER A YEAR AGO! THE PURCHASING AGENT NOW IS MR. PHINEAS ROSEWATER...
PLASTIC ASPIC CORP.
RECEPTIONIST
P.S. THERE'S A NEW BRANCH MANAGER NOW... GET ON THE BALL, BOYS! IT COULD HAPPEN TO YOU!!
THANX AND A TIP OF THE HATLO HAT TO ARCH STALONS, 3040 CALDER, BEAUMONT, TEXAS
JIMMY HATLO

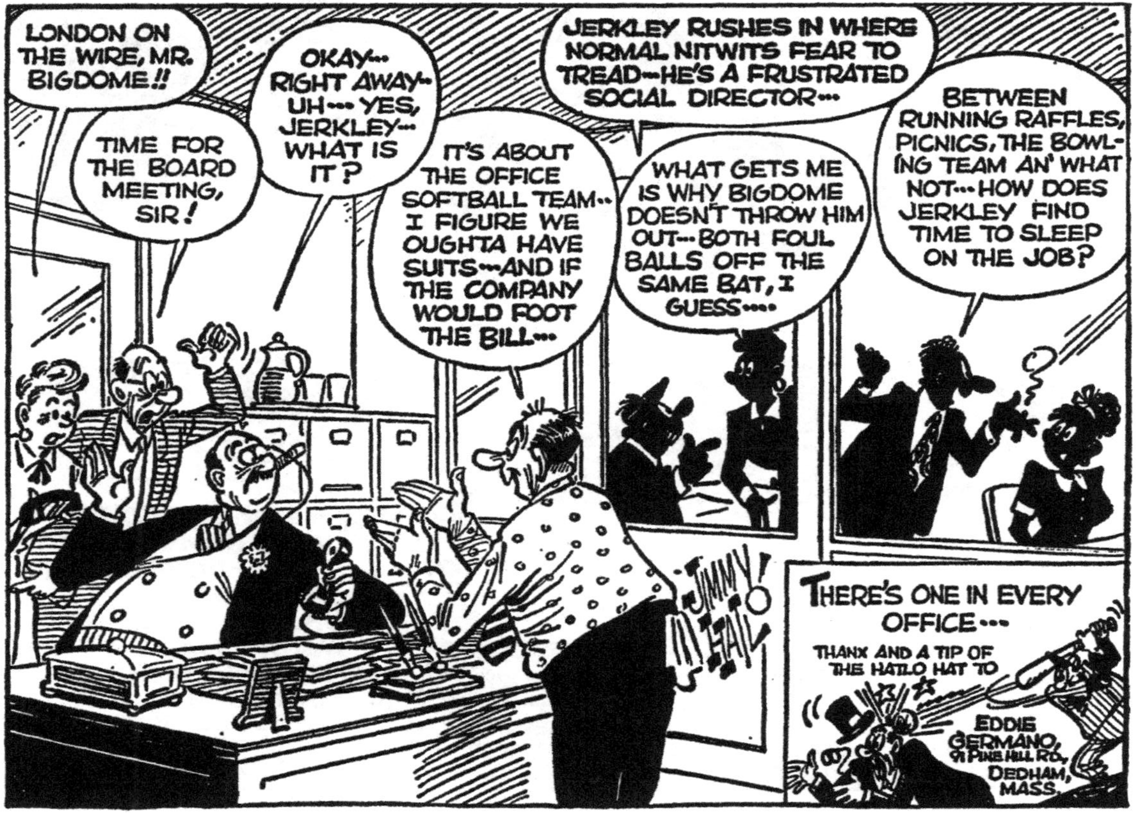
LONDON ON THE WIRE, MR. BIGDOME!!
TIME FOR THE BOARD MEETING, SIR!
OKAY... RIGHT AWAY.. UH... YES, JERKLEY... WHAT IS IT?
IT'S ABOUT THE OFFICE SOFTBALL TEAM.. I FIGURE WE OUGHTA HAVE SUITS...AND IF THE COMPANY WOULD FOOT THE BILL...
JERKLEY RUSHES IN WHERE NORMAL NITWITS FEAR TO TREAD...HE'S A FRUSTRATED SOCIAL DIRECTOR...
WHAT GETS ME IS WHY BIGDOME DOESN'T THROW HIM OUT...BOTH FOUL BALLS OFF THE SAME BAT, I GUESS....
BETWEEN RUNNING RAFFLES, PICNICS, THE BOWLING TEAM AN' WHAT NOT...HOW DOES JERKLEY FIND TIME TO SLEEP ON THE JOB?
JIMMY HATLO
THERE'S ONE IN EVERY OFFICE...
THANX AND A TIP OF THE HATLO HAT TO
EDDIE GERMANO, 91 PINE HILL RD., DEDHAM, MASS.

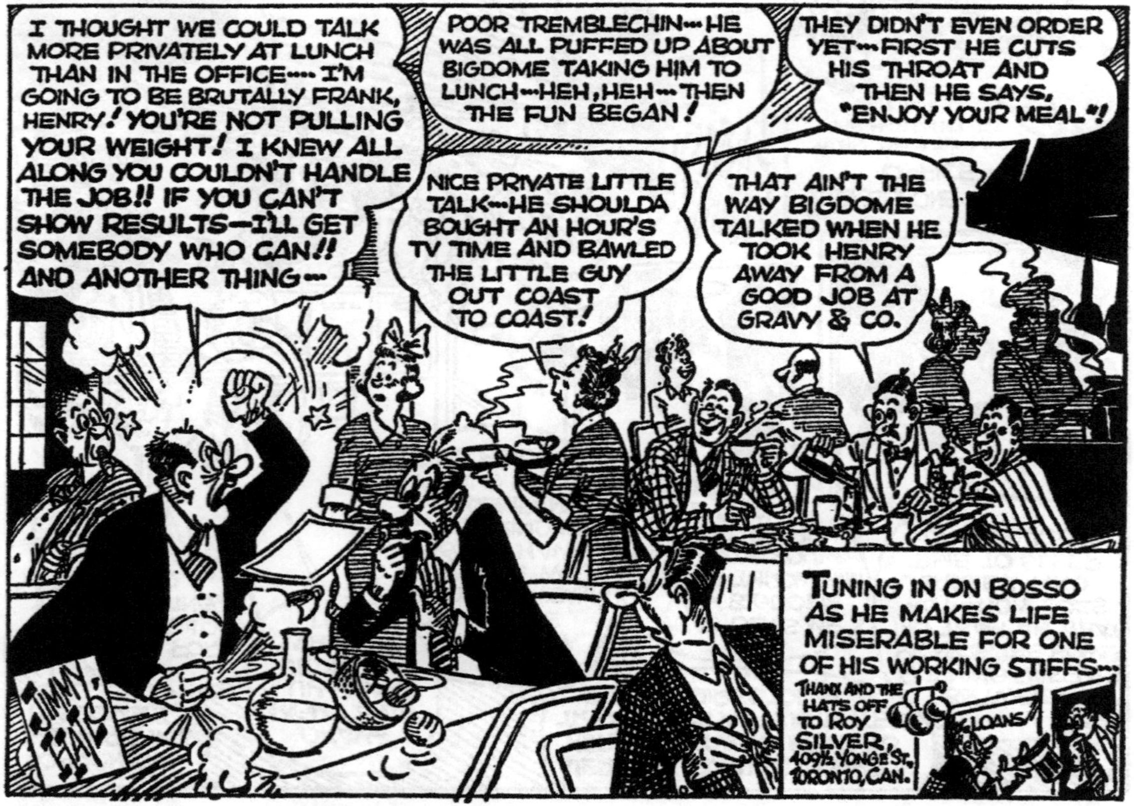
I THOUGHT WE COULD TALK MORE PRIVATELY AT LUNCH THAN IN THE OFFICE.... I'M GOING TO BE BRUTALLY FRANK, HENRY! YOU'RE NOT PULLING YOUR WEIGHT! I KNEW ALL ALONG YOU COULDN'T HANDLE THE JOB!! IF YOU CAN'T SHOW RESULTS—I'LL GET SOMEBODY WHO CAN!! AND ANOTHER THING...
POOR TREMBLECHIN... HE WAS ALL PUFFED UP ABOUT BIGDOME TAKING HIM TO LUNCH... HEH, HEH... THEN THE FUN BEGAN!
THEY DIDN'T EVEN ORDER YET... FIRST HE CUTS HIS THROAT AND THEN HE SAYS, "ENJOY YOUR MEAL"!
NICE PRIVATE LITTLE TALK... HE SHOULDA BOUGHT AN HOUR'S TV TIME AND BAWLED THE LITTLE GUY OUT COAST TO COAST!
THAT AIN'T THE WAY BIGDOME TALKED WHEN HE TOOK HENRY AWAY FROM A GOOD JOB AT GRAVY & CO.
TUNING IN ON BOSSO AS HE MAKES LIFE MISERABLE FOR ONE OF HIS WORKING STIFFS...
THANX AND THE HATS OFF TO ROY SILVER, 409½ YONGE ST., TORONTO, CAN.
LOANS
JIMMY HATLO

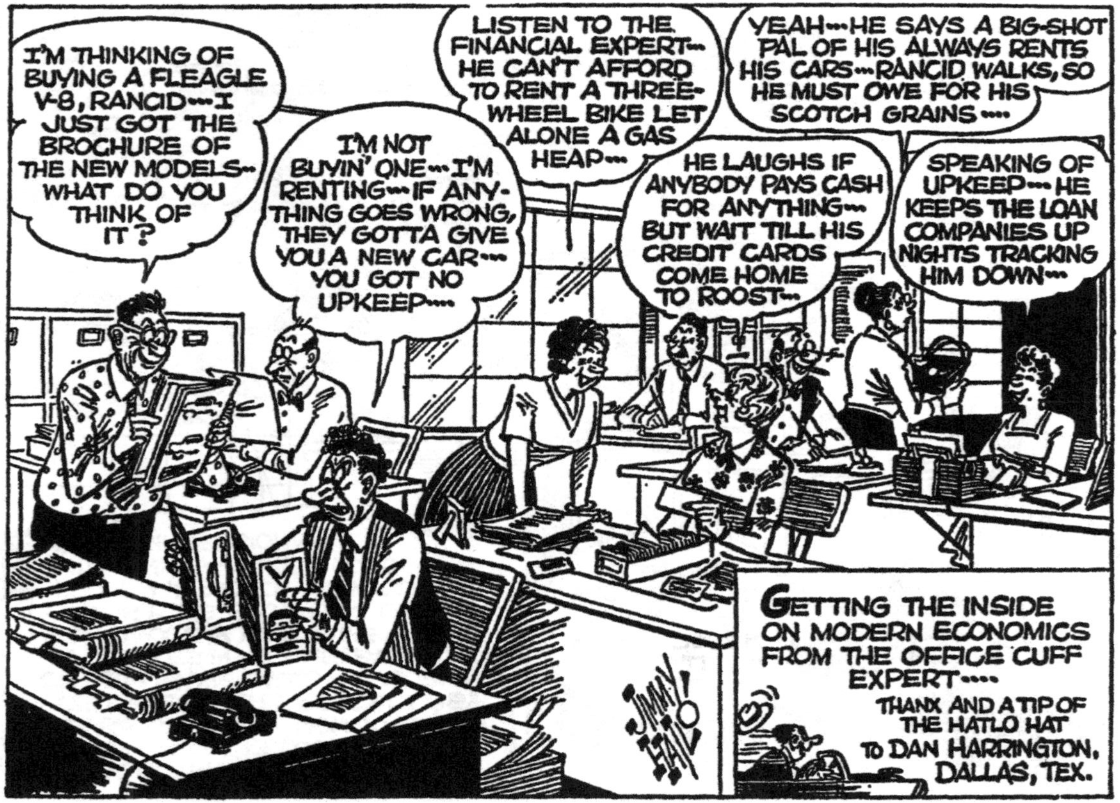
I'M THINKING OF BUYING A FLEAGLE V-8, RANCID---I JUST GOT THE BROCHURE OF THE NEW MODELS-- WHAT DO YOU THINK OF IT?
I'M NOT BUYIN' ONE---I'M RENTING---IF ANY-THING GOES WRONG, THEY GOTTA GIVE YOU A NEW CAR--- YOU GOT NO UPKEEP....
LISTEN TO THE FINANCIAL EXPERT-- HE CAN'T AFFORD TO RENT A THREE-WHEEL BIKE LET ALONE A GAS HEAP---
HE LAUGHS IF ANYBODY PAYS CASH FOR ANYTHING--- BUT WAIT TILL HIS CREDIT CARDS COME HOME TO ROOST---
YEAH---HE SAYS A BIG-SHOT PAL OF HIS ALWAYS RENTS HIS CARS---RANCID WALKS, SO HE MUST OWE FOR HIS SCOTCH GRAINS....
SPEAKING OF UPKEEP---HE KEEPS THE LOAN COMPANIES UP NIGHTS TRACKING HIM DOWN---
JIMMY HATLO
GETTING THE INSIDE ON MODERN ECONOMICS FROM THE OFFICE CUFF EXPERT....
THANX AND A TIP OF THE HATLO HAT TO DAN HARRINGTON, DALLAS, TEX.

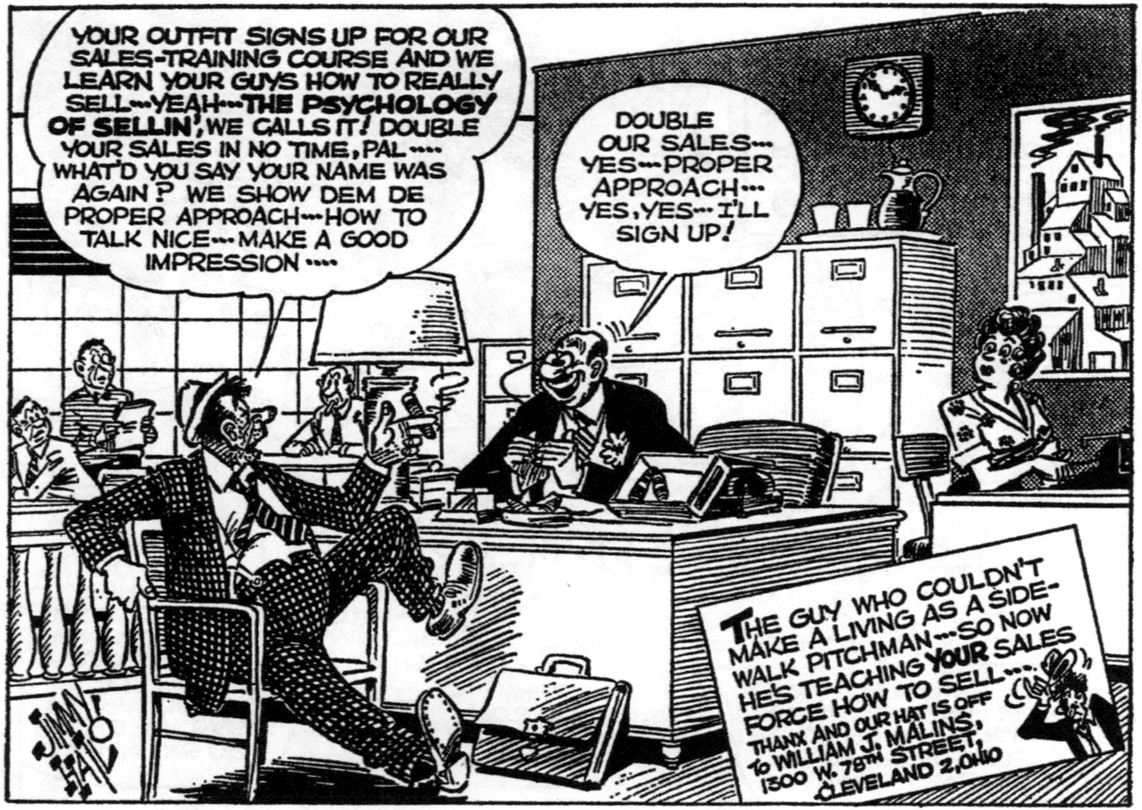
YOUR OUTFIT SIGNS UP FOR OUR SALES-TRAINING COURSE AND WE LEARN YOUR GUYS HOW TO REALLY SELL---YEAH---**THE PSYCHOLOGY OF SELLIN'**, WE CALLS IT! DOUBLE YOUR SALES IN NO TIME, PAL.... WHAT'D YOU SAY YOUR NAME WAS AGAIN? WE SHOW DEM DE PROPER APPROACH---HOW TO TALK NICE---MAKE A GOOD IMPRESSION....
DOUBLE OUR SALES--- YES---PROPER APPROACH--- YES, YES--- I'LL SIGN UP!
THE GUY WHO COULDN'T MAKE A LIVING AS A SIDE-WALK PITCHMAN---SO NOW HE'S TEACHING **YOUR** SALES FORCE HOW TO SELL....
THANX AND OUR HAT IS OFF TO WILLIAM J. MALINS, 1300 W. 78TH STREET, CLEVELAND 2, OHIO
JIMMY HATLO

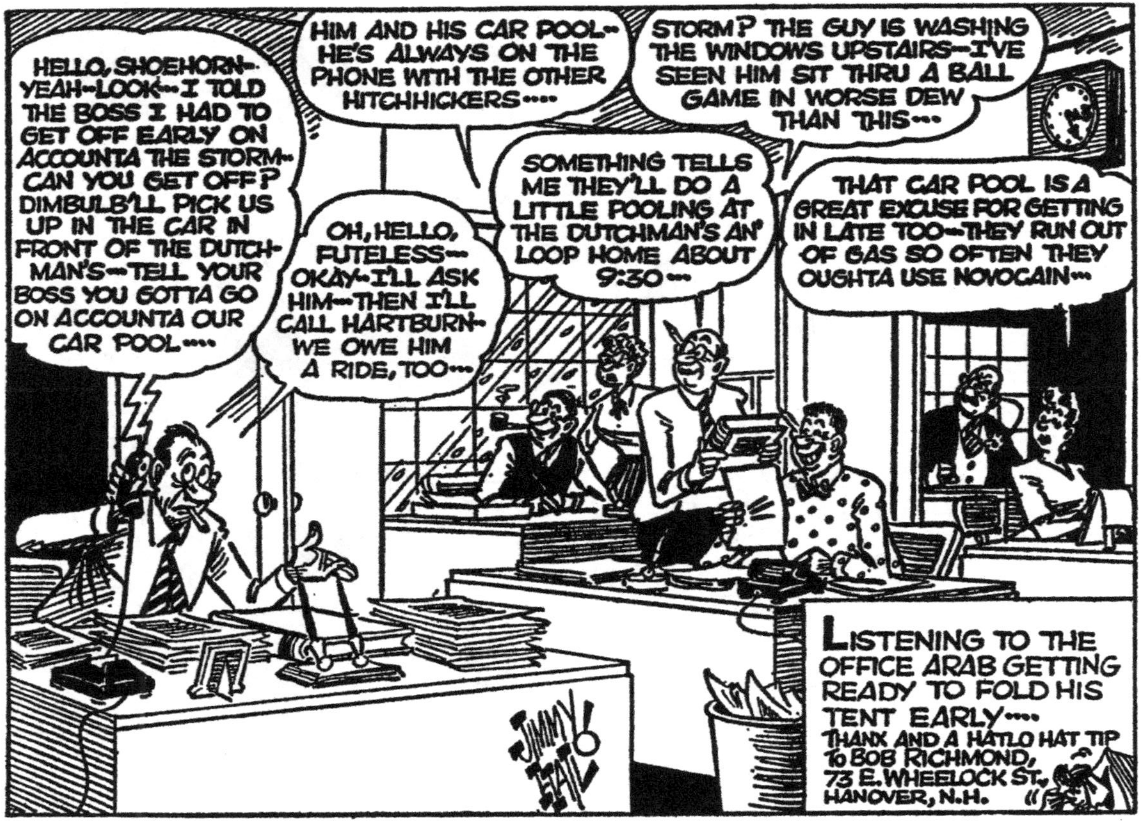
HELLO, SHOEHORN-- YEAH--LOOK--I TOLD THE BOSS I HAD TO GET OFF EARLY ON ACCOUNTA THE STORM-- CAN YOU GET OFF? DIMBULB'LL PICK US UP IN THE CAR IN FRONT OF THE DUTCHMAN'S--TELL YOUR BOSS YOU GOTTA GO ON ACCOUNTA OUR CAR POOL....
HIM AND HIS CAR POOL-- HE'S ALWAYS ON THE PHONE WITH THE OTHER HITCHHICKERS....
OH, HELLO, FUTELESS-- OKAY--I'LL ASK HIM--THEN I'LL CALL HARTBURN-- WE OWE HIM A RIDE, TOO...
SOMETHING TELLS ME THEY'LL DO A LITTLE POOLING AT THE DUTCHMAN'S AN' LOOP HOME ABOUT 9:30...
STORM? THE GUY IS WASHING THE WINDOWS UPSTAIRS--I'VE SEEN HIM SIT THRU A BALL GAME IN WORSE DEW THAN THIS...
THAT CAR POOL IS A GREAT EXCUSE FOR GETTING IN LATE TOO--THEY RUN OUT OF GAS SO OFTEN THEY OUGHTA USE NOVOCAIN...
LISTENING TO THE OFFICE ARAB GETTING READY TO FOLD HIS TENT EARLY....
THANX AND A HATLO HAT TIP TO BOB RICHMOND, 73 E. WHEELOCK ST., HANOVER, N.H.
JIMMY HATLO

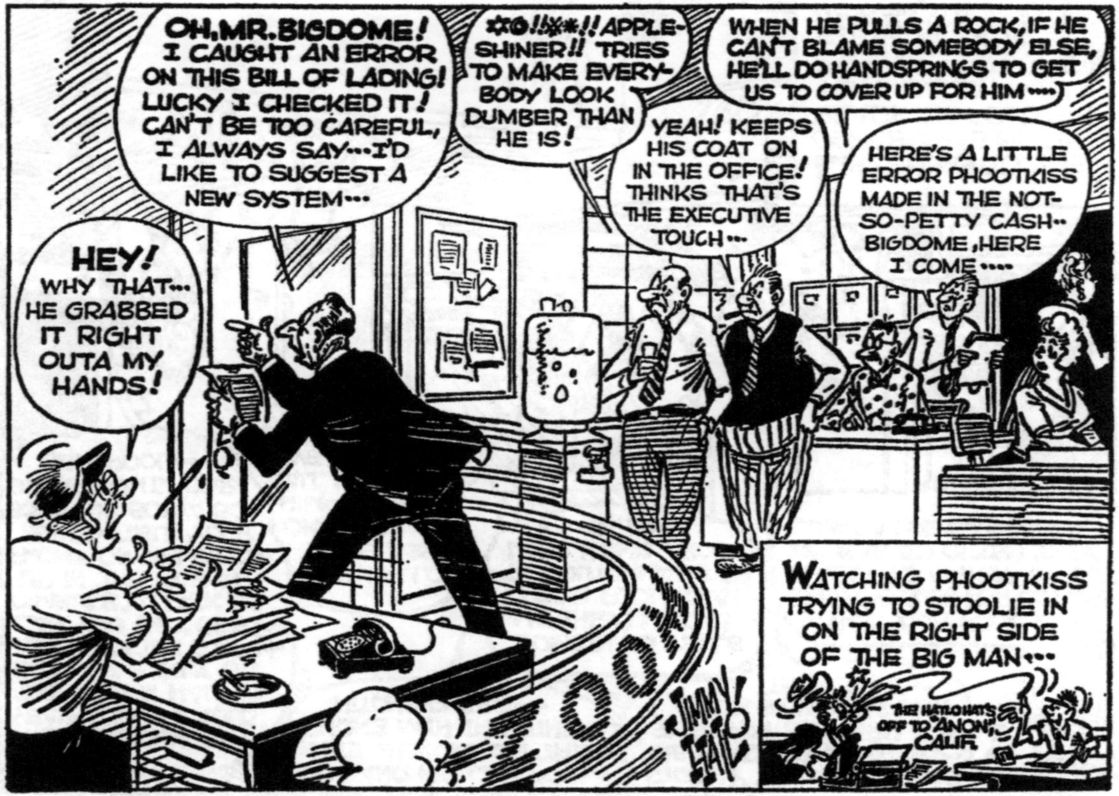
OH, MR. BIGDOME! I CAUGHT AN ERROR ON THIS BILL OF LADING! LUCKY I CHECKED IT! CAN'T BE TOO CAREFUL, I ALWAYS SAY... I'D LIKE TO SUGGEST A NEW SYSTEM...
HEY! WHY THAT... HE GRABBED IT RIGHT OUTA MY HANDS!
☆@!!※*!! APPLE-SHINER!! TRIES TO MAKE EVERYBODY LOOK DUMBER THAN HE IS!
WHEN HE PULLS A ROCK, IF HE CAN'T BLAME SOMEBODY ELSE, HE'LL DO HANDSPRINGS TO GET US TO COVER UP FOR HIM....
YEAH! KEEPS HIS COAT ON IN THE OFFICE! THINKS THAT'S THE EXECUTIVE TOUCH...
HERE'S A LITTLE ERROR PHOOTKISS MADE IN THE NOT-SO-PETTY CASH.. BIGDOME, HERE I COME....
ZOOOM
JIMMY HATLO
WATCHING PHOOTKISS TRYING TO STOOLIE IN ON THE RIGHT SIDE OF THE BIG MAN...
THE HATLO HAT'S OFF TO "ANON," CALIF.

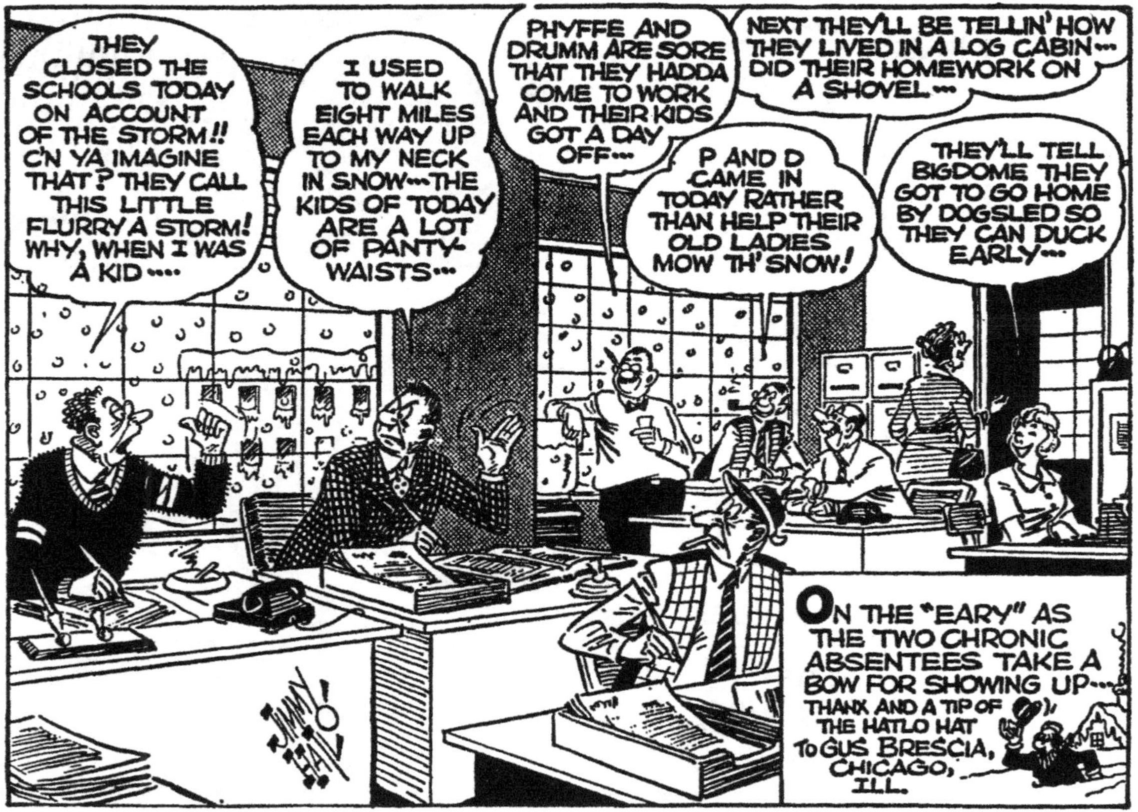
THEY CLOSED THE SCHOOLS TODAY ON ACCOUNT OF THE STORM!! C'N YA IMAGINE THAT? THEY CALL THIS LITTLE FLURRY A STORM! WHY, WHEN I WAS A KID....
I USED TO WALK EIGHT MILES EACH WAY UP TO MY NECK IN SNOW...THE KIDS OF TODAY ARE A LOT OF PANTY-WAISTS...
PHYFFE AND DRUMM ARE SORE THAT THEY HADDA COME TO WORK AND THEIR KIDS GOT A DAY OFF...
NEXT THEY'LL BE TELLIN' HOW THEY LIVED IN A LOG CABIN... DID THEIR HOMEWORK ON A SHOVEL...
P AND D CAME IN TODAY RATHER THAN HELP THEIR OLD LADIES MOW TH' SNOW!
THEY'LL TELL BIGDOME THEY GOT TO GO HOME BY DOGSLED SO THEY CAN DUCK EARLY...
ON THE "EARY" AS THE TWO CHRONIC ABSENTEES TAKE A BOW FOR SHOWING UP...
THANX AND A TIP OF THE HATLO HAT TO GUS BRESCIA, CHICAGO, ILL.
JIMMY HATLO

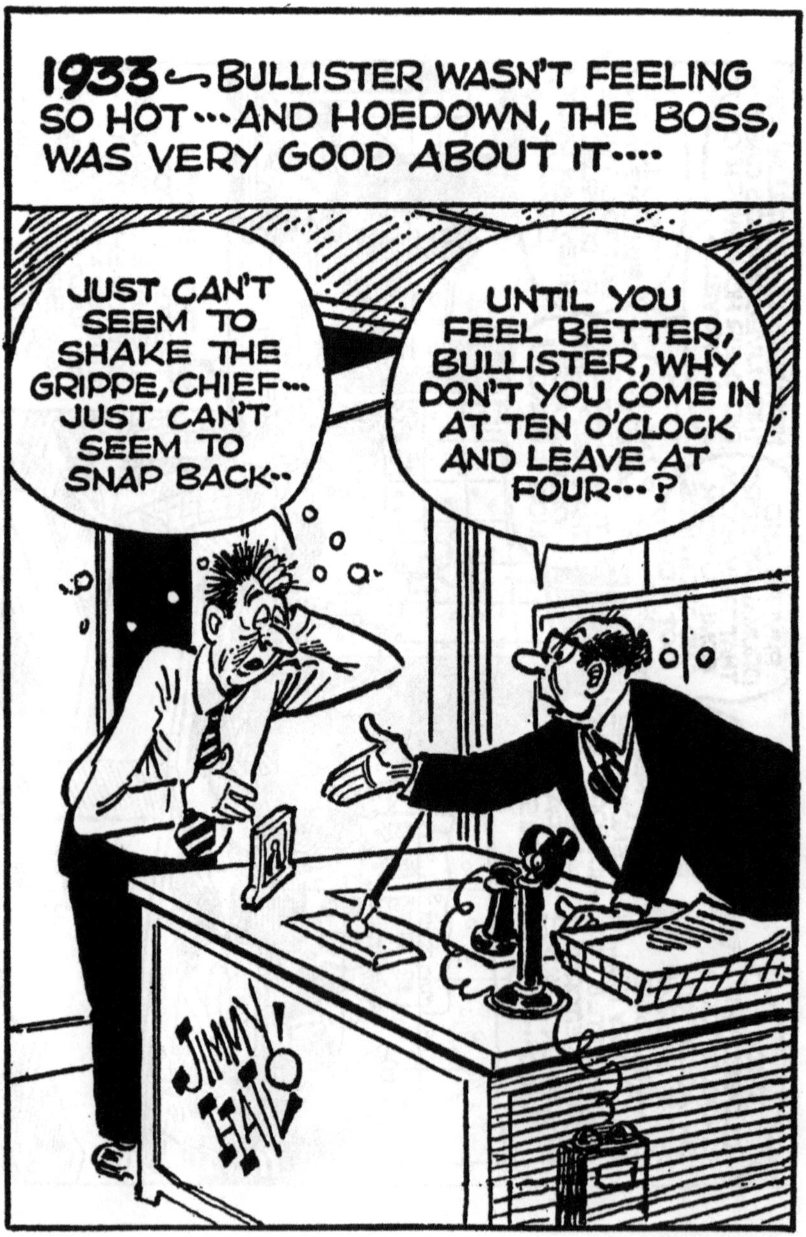
1933 — BULLISTER WASN'T FEELING SO HOT···AND HOEDOWN, THE BOSS, WAS VERY GOOD ABOUT IT····
JUST CAN'T SEEM TO SHAKE THE GRIPPE, CHIEF··· JUST CAN'T SEEM TO SNAP BACK··
UNTIL YOU FEEL BETTER, BULLISTER, WHY DON'T YOU COME IN AT TEN O'CLOCK AND LEAVE AT FOUR···?
JIMMY HATLO

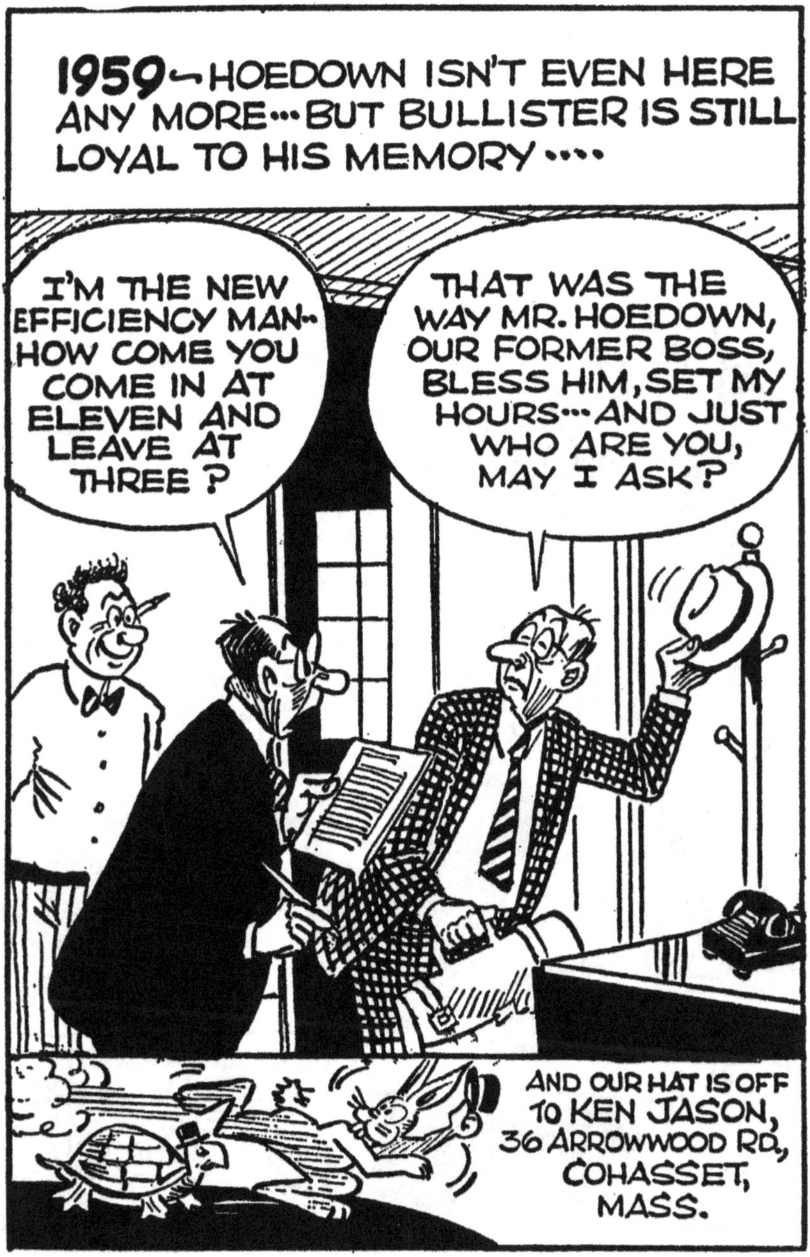
1959—HOEDOWN ISN'T EVEN HERE ANY MORE···BUT BULLISTER IS STILL LOYAL TO HIS MEMORY····
I'M THE NEW EFFICIENCY MAN·· HOW COME YOU COME IN AT ELEVEN AND LEAVE AT THREE?
THAT WAS THE WAY MR. HOEDOWN, OUR FORMER BOSS, BLESS HIM, SET MY HOURS···AND JUST WHO ARE YOU, MAY I ASK?
AND OUR HAT IS OFF TO KEN JASON, 36 ARROWWOOD RD., COHASSET, MASS.

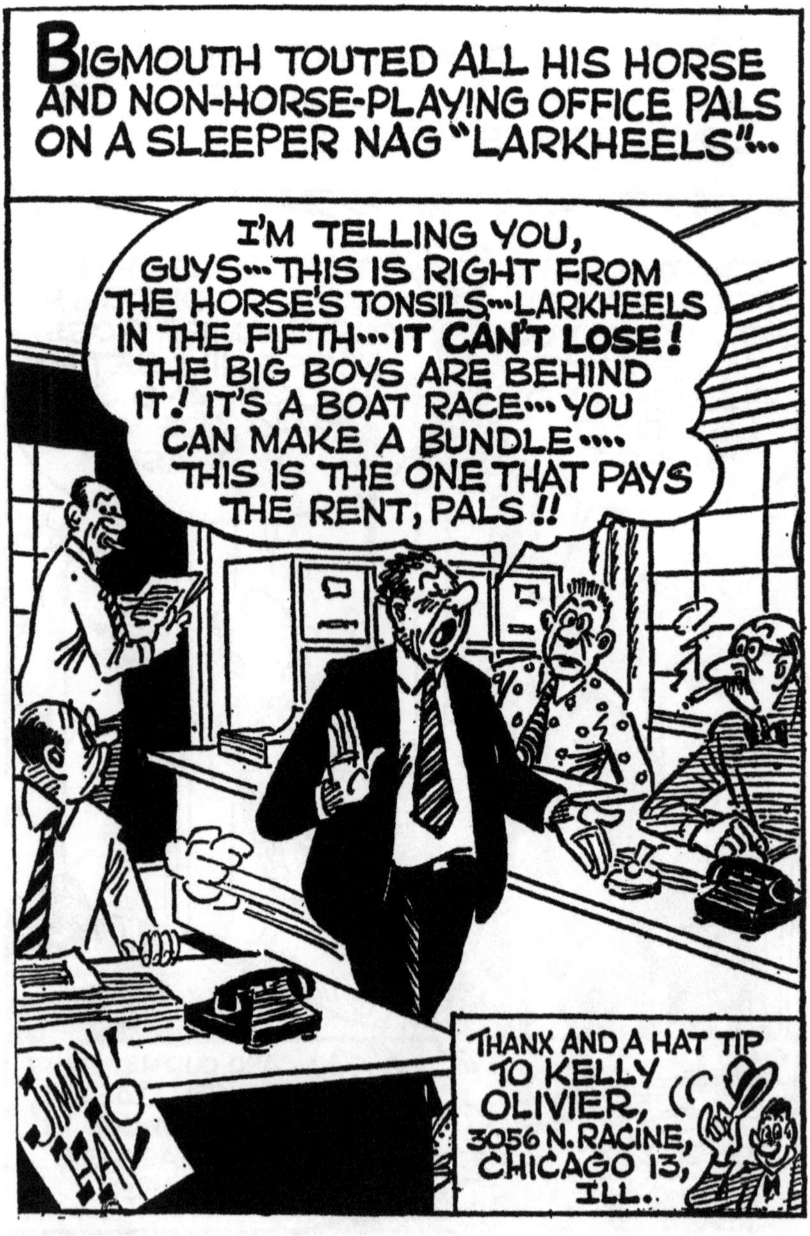
BIGMOUTH TOUTED ALL HIS HORSE AND NON-HORSE-PLAYING OFFICE PALS ON A SLEEPER NAG "LARKHEELS"...
I'M TELLING YOU, GUYS... THIS IS RIGHT FROM THE HORSE'S TONSILS... LARKHEELS IN THE FIFTH... IT CAN'T LOSE! THE BIG BOYS ARE BEHIND IT! IT'S A BOAT RACE... YOU CAN MAKE A BUNDLE.... THIS IS THE ONE THAT PAYS THE RENT, PALS!!
THANX AND A HAT TIP TO KELLY OLIVIER, 3056 N. RACINE, CHICAGO 13, ILL..
JIMMY HATLO

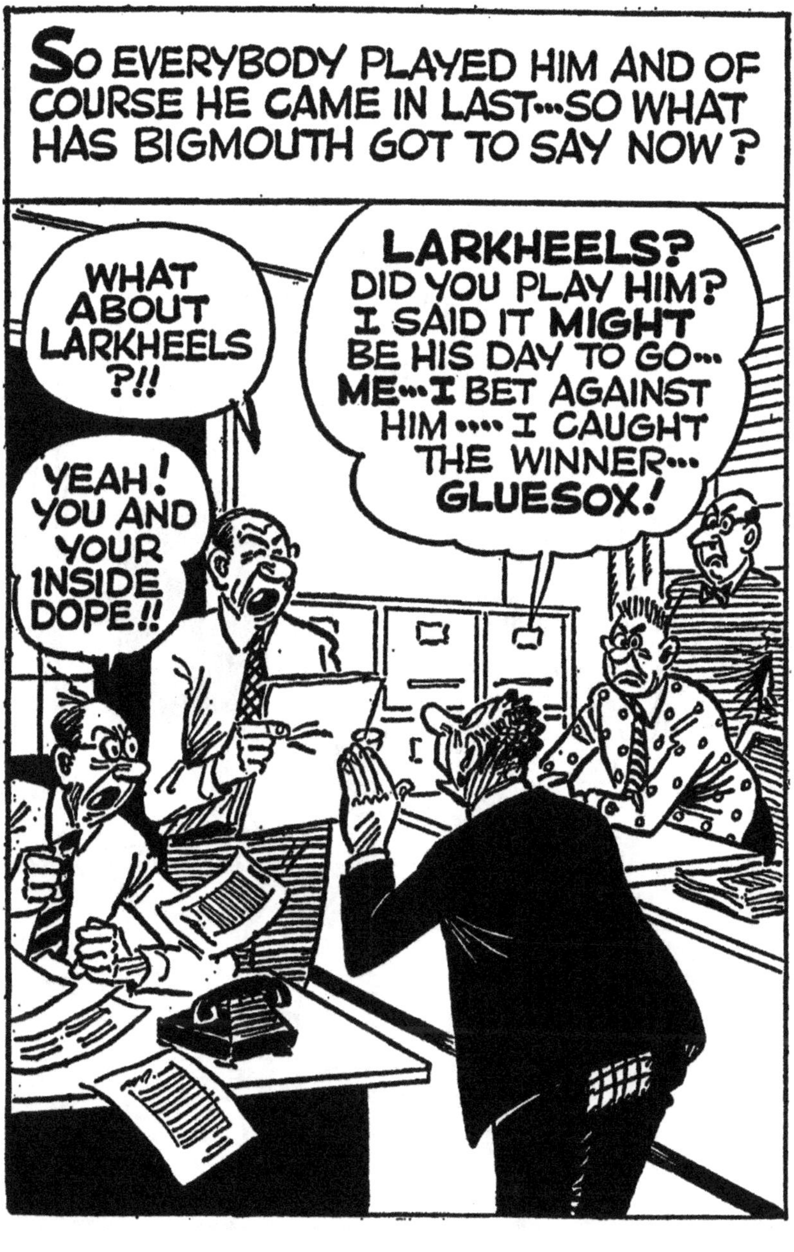

SO EVERYBODY PLAYED HIM AND OF COURSE HE CAME IN LAST...SO WHAT HAS BIGMOUTH GOT TO SAY NOW?
WHAT ABOUT LARKHEELS ?!!
YEAH! YOU AND YOUR INSIDE DOPE!!
LARKHEELS? DID YOU PLAY HIM? I SAID IT MIGHT BE HIS DAY TO GO... ME...I BET AGAINST HIM .... I CAUGHT THE WINNER... GLUESOX!

DOOBILL MOANED AND GROANED TO ONE AND ALL ABOUT THE FIVE DOLLARS HE LENT TO LASAGNA....
LOOK AT THAT FOUR-FLUSHING @☆!?! OWES ME FIVE BUCKS SINCE LAST TUESDAY! I'LL GIVE HIM ONE MORE DAY, THEN I'LL TAKE IT OUTA HIS HIDE!!
THANX AND A TIP OF THE HATLO HAT TO AL TORKELSON, 15 LAYTON AVE., STATEN ISLAND, NEW YORK

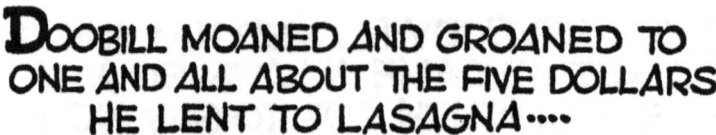

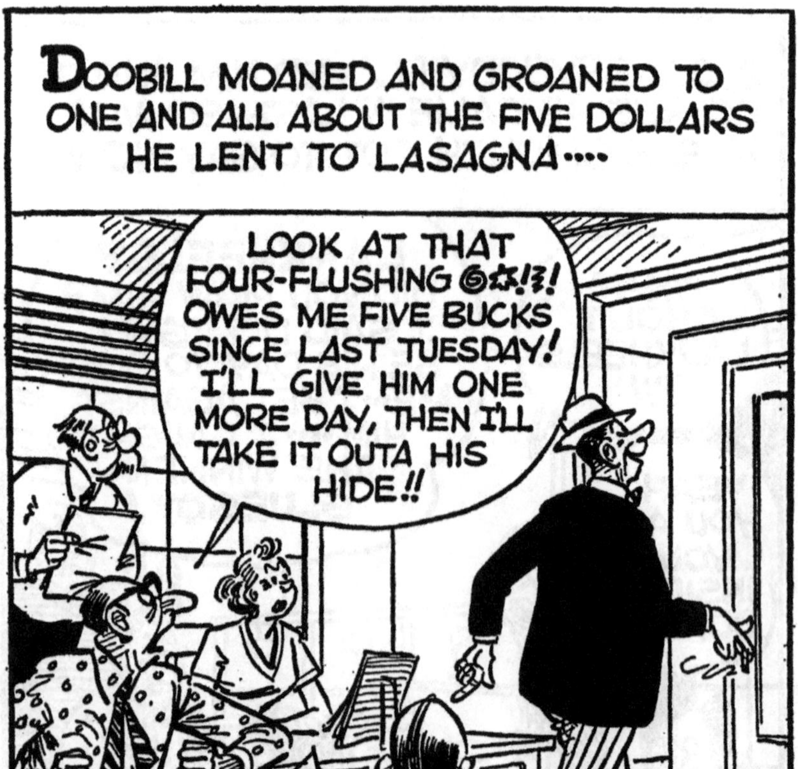

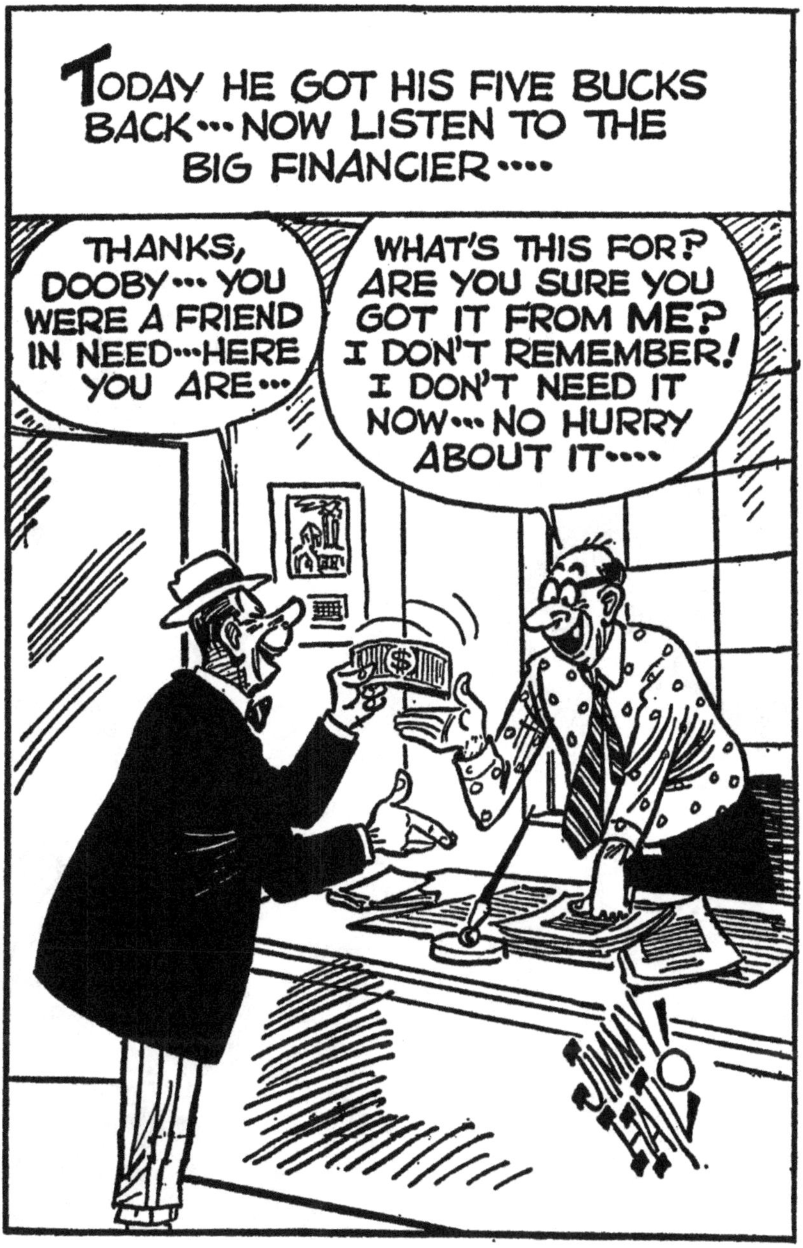
TODAY HE GOT HIS FIVE BUCKS BACK··· NOW LISTEN TO THE BIG FINANCIER····
THANKS, DOOBY··· YOU WERE A FRIEND IN NEED···HERE YOU ARE···
WHAT'S THIS FOR? ARE YOU SURE YOU GOT IT FROM ME? I DON'T REMEMBER! I DON'T NEED IT NOW··· NO HURRY ABOUT IT····
JIMMY HATLO

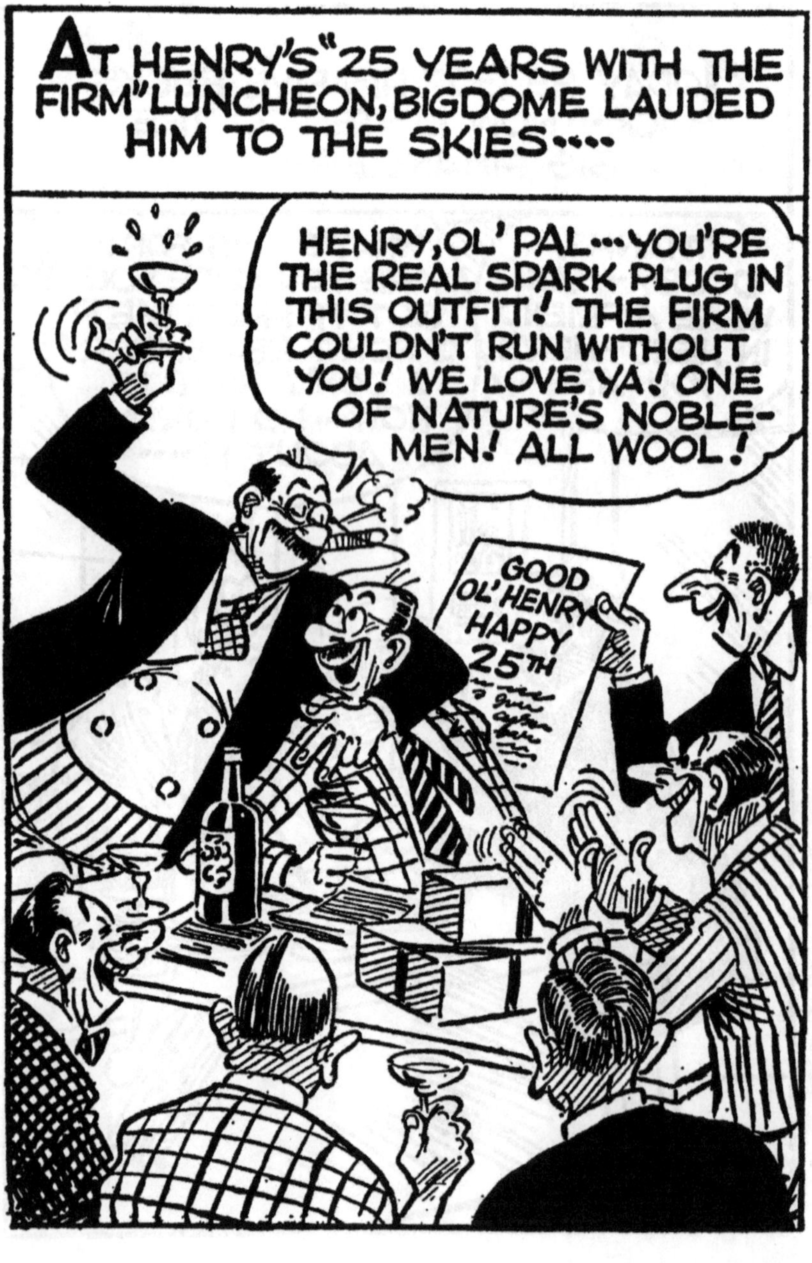
AT HENRY'S "25 YEARS WITH THE FIRM" LUNCHEON, BIGDOME LAUDED HIM TO THE SKIES....
HENRY, OL' PAL...YOU'RE THE REAL SPARK PLUG IN THIS OUTFIT! THE FIRM COULDN'T RUN WITHOUT YOU! WE LOVE YA! ONE OF NATURE'S NOBLEMEN! ALL WOOL!
GOOD OL' HENRY HAPPY 25TH

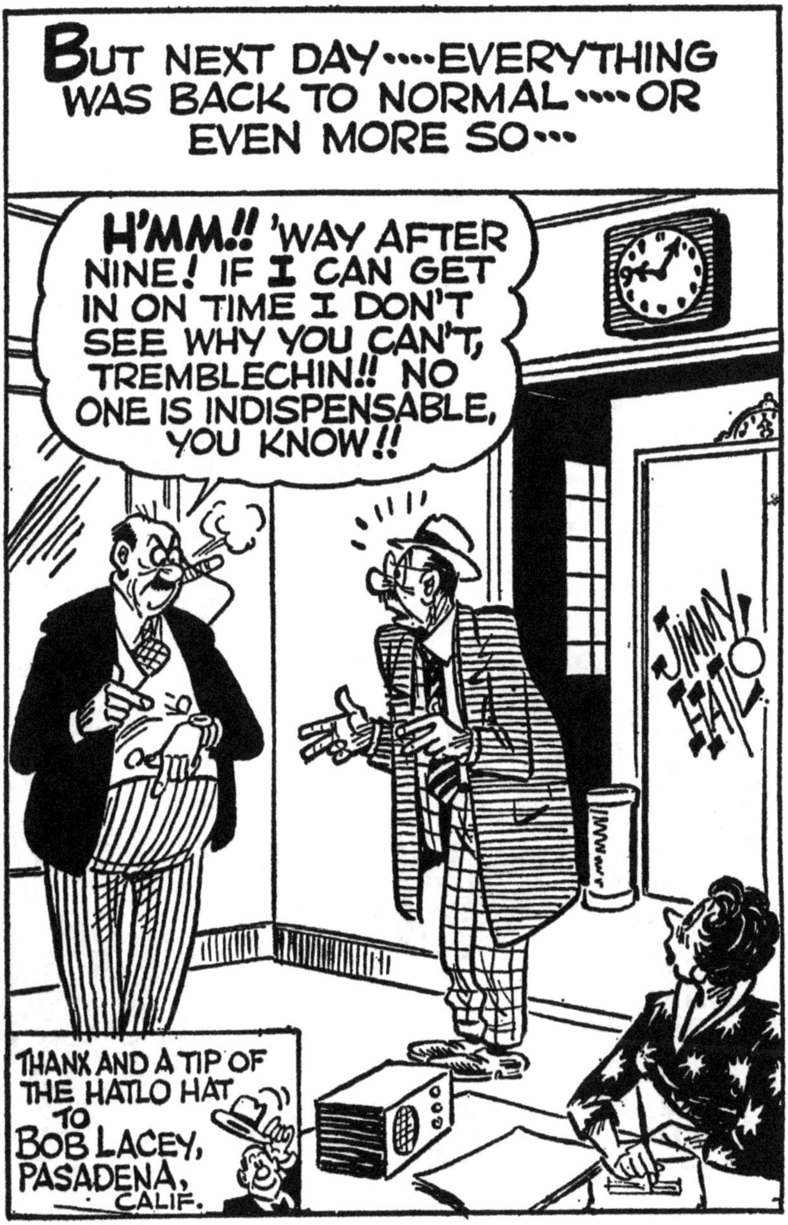

BUT NEXT DAY....EVERYTHING WAS BACK TO NORMAL....OR EVEN MORE SO...
H'MM!! 'WAY AFTER NINE! IF I CAN GET IN ON TIME I DON'T SEE WHY YOU CAN'T, TREMBLECHIN!! NO ONE IS INDISPENSABLE, YOU KNOW!!
JIMMY HATLO
THANX AND A TIP OF THE HATLO HAT TO BOB LACEY, PASADENA, CALIF.

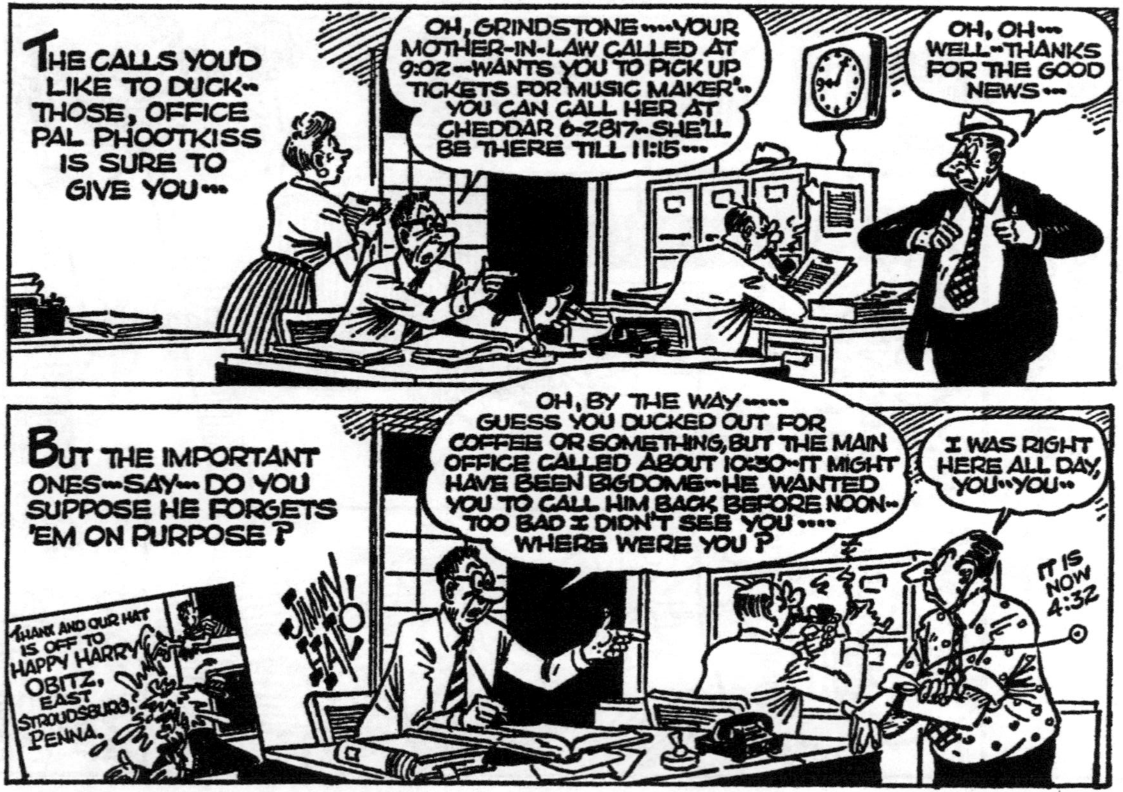
THE CALLS YOU'D LIKE TO DUCK.. THOSE, OFFICE PAL PHOOTKISS IS SURE TO GIVE YOU...
OH, GRINDSTONE....YOUR MOTHER-IN-LAW CALLED AT 9:02 ...WANTS YOU TO PICK UP TICKETS FOR 'MUSIC MAKER'.. YOU CAN CALL HER AT CHEDDAR 6-2817..SHE'LL BE THERE TILL 11:15...
OH, OH... WELL..THANKS FOR THE GOOD NEWS...
BUT THE IMPORTANT ONES...SAY... DO YOU SUPPOSE HE FORGETS 'EM ON PURPOSE?
OH, BY THE WAY..... GUESS YOU DUCKED OUT FOR COFFEE OR SOMETHING, BUT THE MAIN OFFICE CALLED ABOUT 10:30..IT MIGHT HAVE BEEN BIGDOME..HE WANTED YOU TO CALL HIM BACK BEFORE NOON.. TOO BAD I DIDN'T SEE YOU.... WHERE WERE YOU?
I WAS RIGHT HERE ALL DAY, YOU..YOU..
IT IS NOW 4:32
JIMINY! HAL!
THANX AND OUR HAT IS OFF TO HAPPY HARRY OBITZ, EAST STROUDSBURG, PENNA.

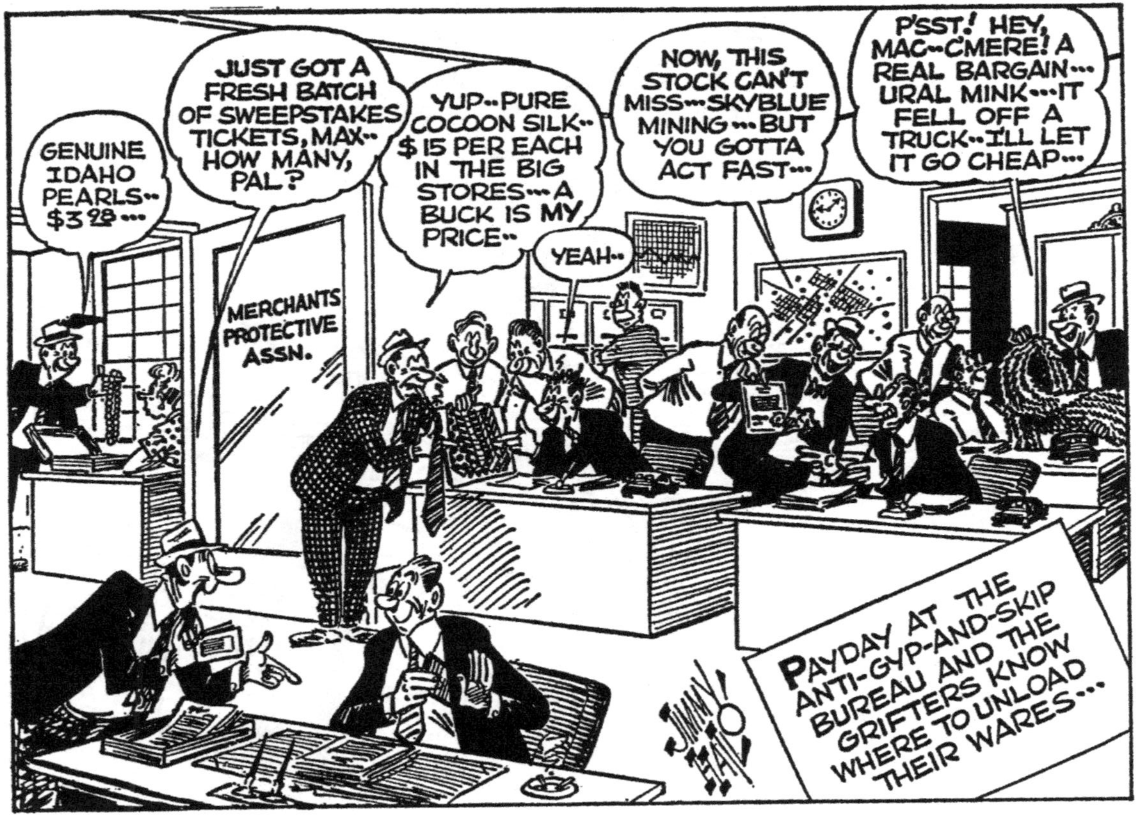
GENUINE IDAHO PEARLS-- $3.98---
JUST GOT A FRESH BATCH OF SWEEPSTAKES TICKETS, MAX-- HOW MANY, PAL?
MERCHANTS PROTECTIVE ASSN.
YUP--PURE COCOON SILK-- $15 PER EACH IN THE BIG STORES---A BUCK IS MY PRICE--
YEAH--
NOW, THIS STOCK CAN'T MISS---SKYBLUE MINING---BUT YOU GOTTA ACT FAST---
P'SST! HEY, MAC--C'MERE! A REAL BARGAIN--- URAL MINK---IT FELL OFF A TRUCK--I'LL LET IT GO CHEAP---
PAYDAY AT THE ANTI-GYP-AND-SKIP BUREAU AND THE GRIFTERS KNOW WHERE TO UNLOAD THEIR WARES---
JIMMY HATLO

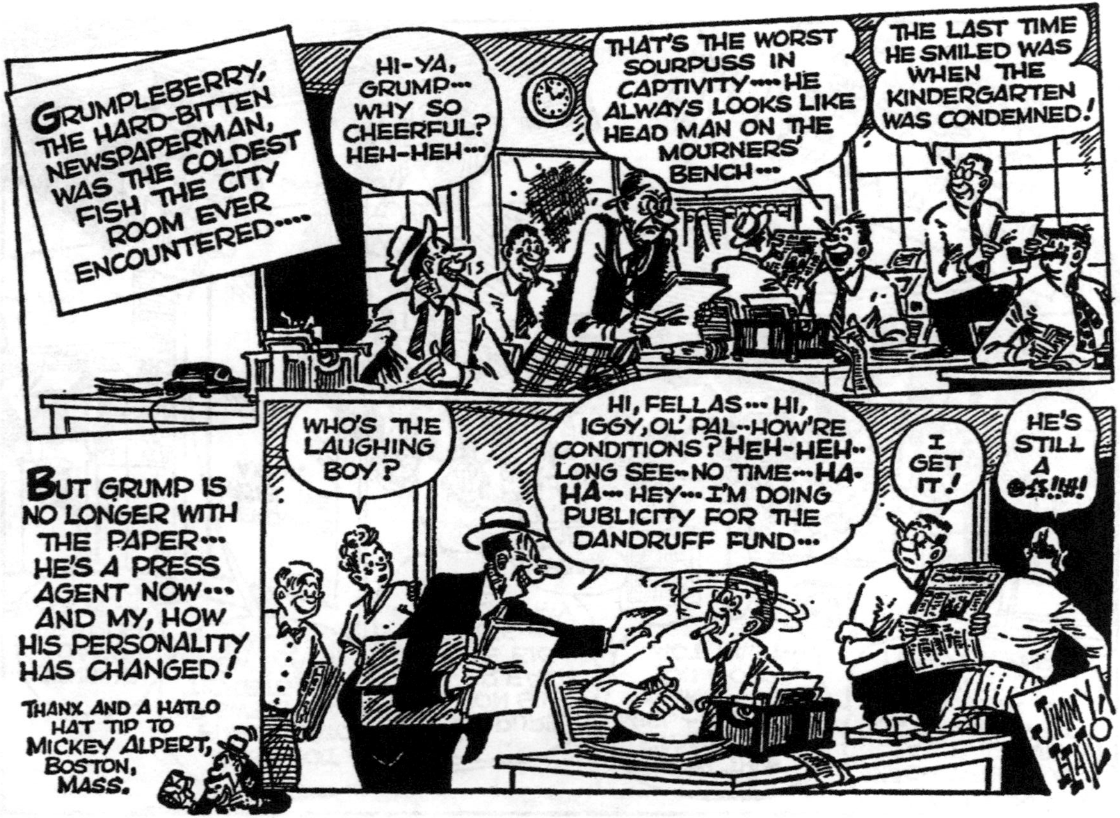
GRUMPLEBERRY, THE HARD-BITTEN NEWSPAPERMAN, WAS THE COLDEST FISH THE CITY ROOM EVER ENCOUNTERED....
HI-YA, GRUMP... WHY SO CHEERFUL? HEH-HEH...
THAT'S THE WORST SOURPUSS IN CAPTIVITY... HE ALWAYS LOOKS LIKE HEAD MAN ON THE MOURNERS' BENCH...
THE LAST TIME HE SMILED WAS WHEN THE KINDERGARTEN WAS CONDEMNED!
BUT GRUMP IS NO LONGER WITH THE PAPER... HE'S A PRESS AGENT NOW... AND MY, HOW HIS PERSONALITY HAS CHANGED!
WHO'S THE LAUGHING BOY?
HI, FELLAS... HI, IGGY, OL' PAL--HOW'RE CONDITIONS? HEH-HEH.. LONG SEE--NO TIME... HA-HA... HEY... I'M DOING PUBLICITY FOR THE DANDRUFF FUND...
I GET IT!
HE'S STILL A @#$!!#!
THANX AND A HATLO HAT TIP TO MICKEY ALPERT, BOSTON, MASS.
JIMMY HATLO

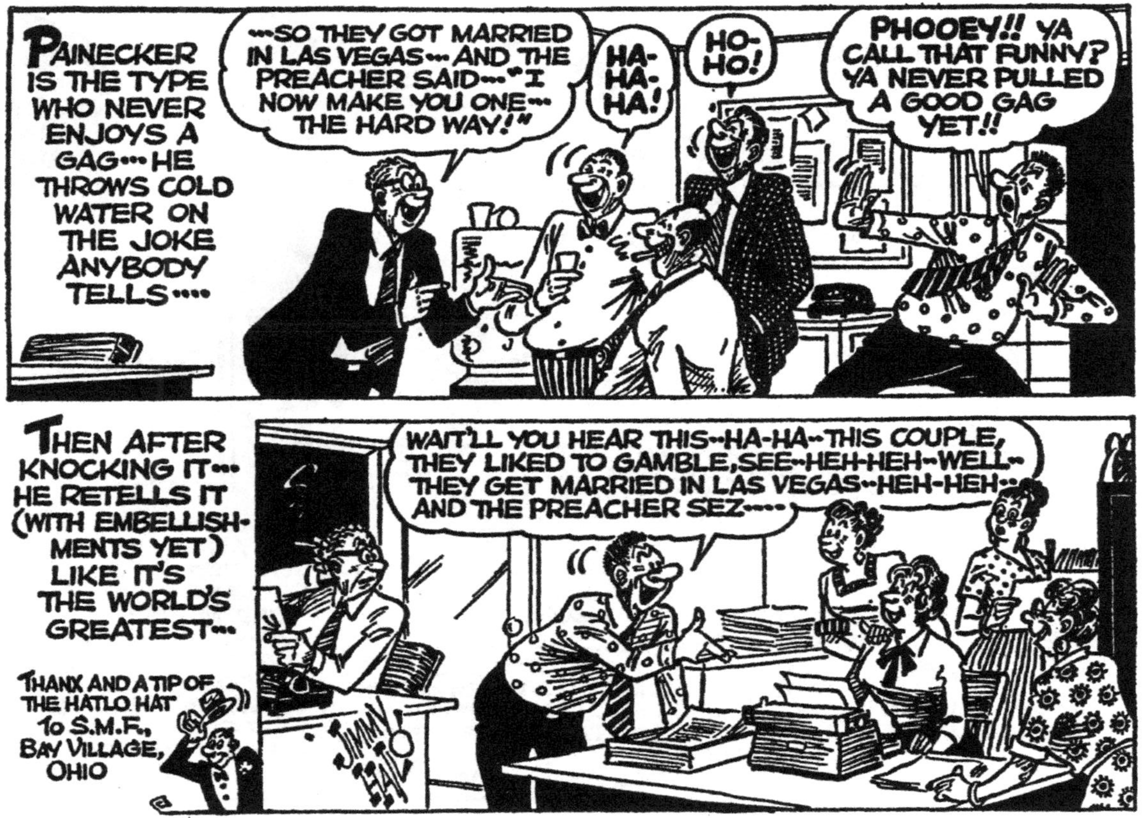
PAINECKER IS THE TYPE WHO NEVER ENJOYS A GAG... HE THROWS COLD WATER ON THE JOKE ANYBODY TELLS....
...SO THEY GOT MARRIED IN LAS VEGAS... AND THE PREACHER SAID... "I NOW MAKE YOU ONE... THE HARD WAY!"
HA-HA-HA!
HO-HO!
PHOOEY!! YA CALL THAT FUNNY? YA NEVER PULLED A GOOD GAG YET!!
THEN AFTER KNOCKING IT... HE RETELLS IT (WITH EMBELLISHMENTS YET) LIKE IT'S THE WORLD'S GREATEST...
WAIT'LL YOU HEAR THIS--HA-HA--THIS COUPLE, THEY LIKED TO GAMBLE, SEE--HEH-HEH--WELL-- THEY GET MARRIED IN LAS VEGAS--HEH-HEH-- AND THE PREACHER SEZ.....
THANX AND A TIP OF THE HATLO HAT TO S.M.F., BAY VILLAGE, OHIO
JIMMY HATLO

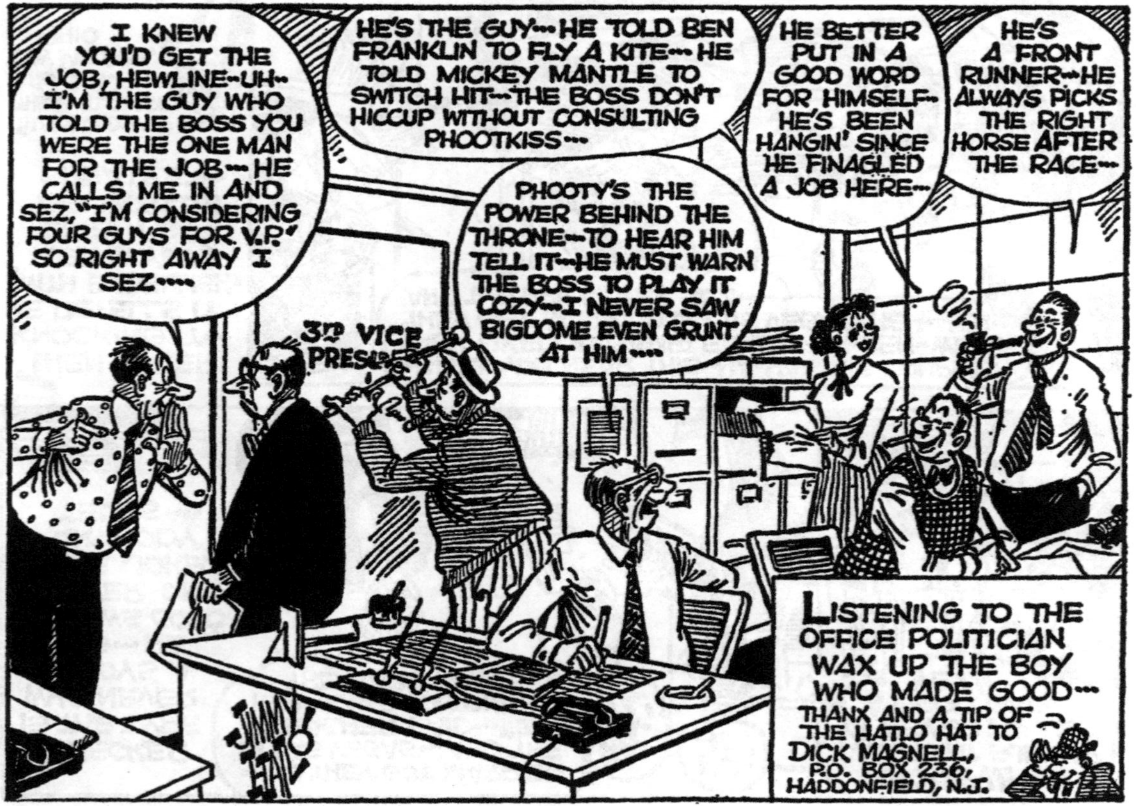
I KNEW YOU'D GET THE JOB, HEWLINE--UH-- I'M THE GUY WHO TOLD THE BOSS YOU WERE THE ONE MAN FOR THE JOB--- HE CALLS ME IN AND SEZ, "I'M CONSIDERING FOUR GUYS FOR V.P." SO RIGHT AWAY I SEZ----
3RD VICE PRES
HE'S THE GUY--- HE TOLD BEN FRANKLIN TO FLY A KITE--- HE TOLD MICKEY MANTLE TO SWITCH HIT--- THE BOSS DON'T HICCUP WITHOUT CONSULTING PHOOTKISS---
PHOOTY'S THE POWER BEHIND THE THRONE--- TO HEAR HIM TELL IT--- HE MUST WARN THE BOSS TO PLAY IT COZY--- I NEVER SAW BIGDOME EVEN GRUNT AT HIM----
HE BETTER PUT IN A GOOD WORD FOR HIMSELF-- HE'S BEEN HANGIN' SINCE HE FINAGLED A JOB HERE---
HE'S A FRONT RUNNER--- HE ALWAYS PICKS THE RIGHT HORSE AFTER THE RACE---
LISTENING TO THE OFFICE POLITICIAN WAX UP THE BOY WHO MADE GOOD---
THANX AND A TIP OF THE HATLO HAT TO DICK MAGNELL, P.O. BOX 236, HADDONFIELD, N.J.
JIMMY HATLO

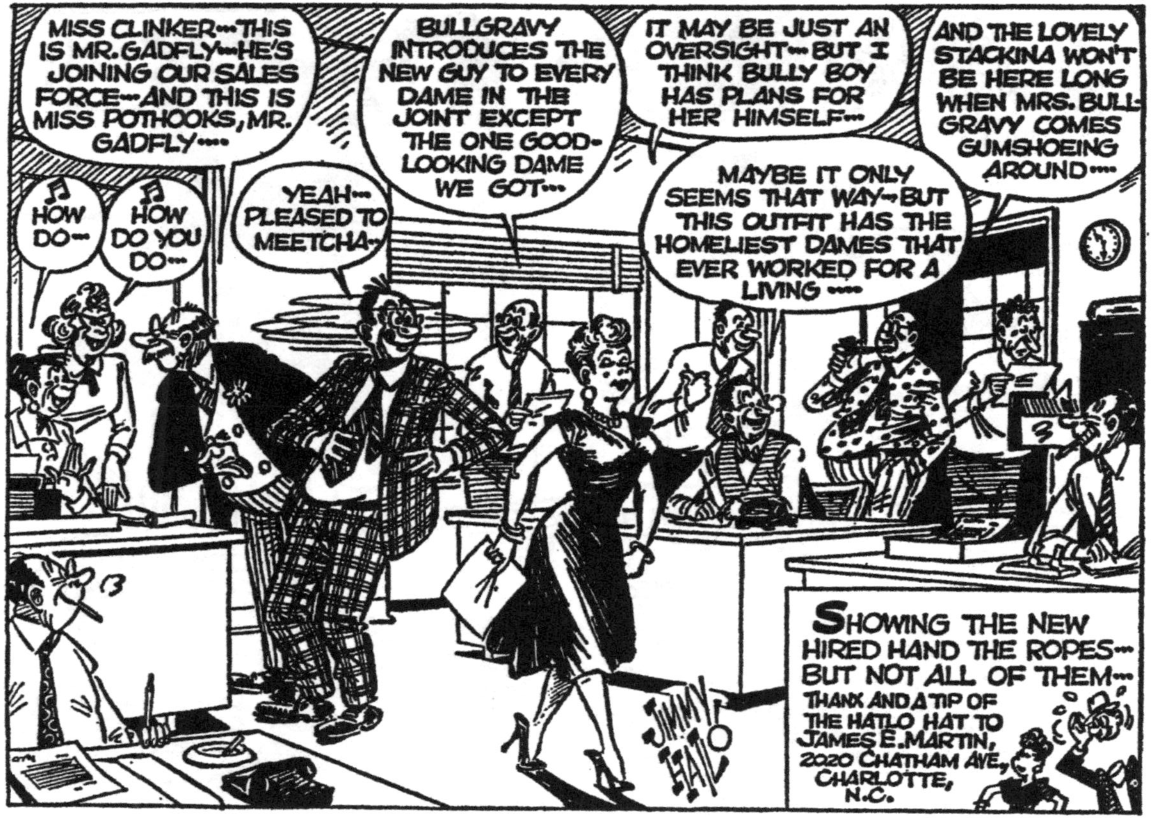
MISS CLINKER••• THIS IS MR. GADFLY••• HE'S JOINING OUR SALES FORCE••• AND THIS IS MISS POTHOOKS, MR. GADFLY••••
♫ HOW DO•••
♫ HOW DO YOU DO•••
YEAH••• PLEASED TO MEETCHA•••
BULLGRAVY INTRODUCES THE NEW GUY TO EVERY DAME IN THE JOINT EXCEPT THE ONE GOOD-LOOKING DAME WE GOT•••
IT MAY BE JUST AN OVERSIGHT••• BUT I THINK BULLY BOY HAS PLANS FOR HER HIMSELF•••
MAYBE IT ONLY SEEMS THAT WAY••• BUT THIS OUTFIT HAS THE HOMELIEST DAMES THAT EVER WORKED FOR A LIVING••••
AND THE LOVELY STACKINA WON'T BE HERE LONG WHEN MRS. BULLGRAVY COMES GUMSHOEING AROUND••••
SHOWING THE NEW HIRED HAND THE ROPES••• BUT NOT ALL OF THEM•••
THANX AND A TIP OF THE HATLO HAT TO JAMES E. MARTIN, 2020 CHATHAM AVE., CHARLOTTE, N.C.
JIMMY HATLO

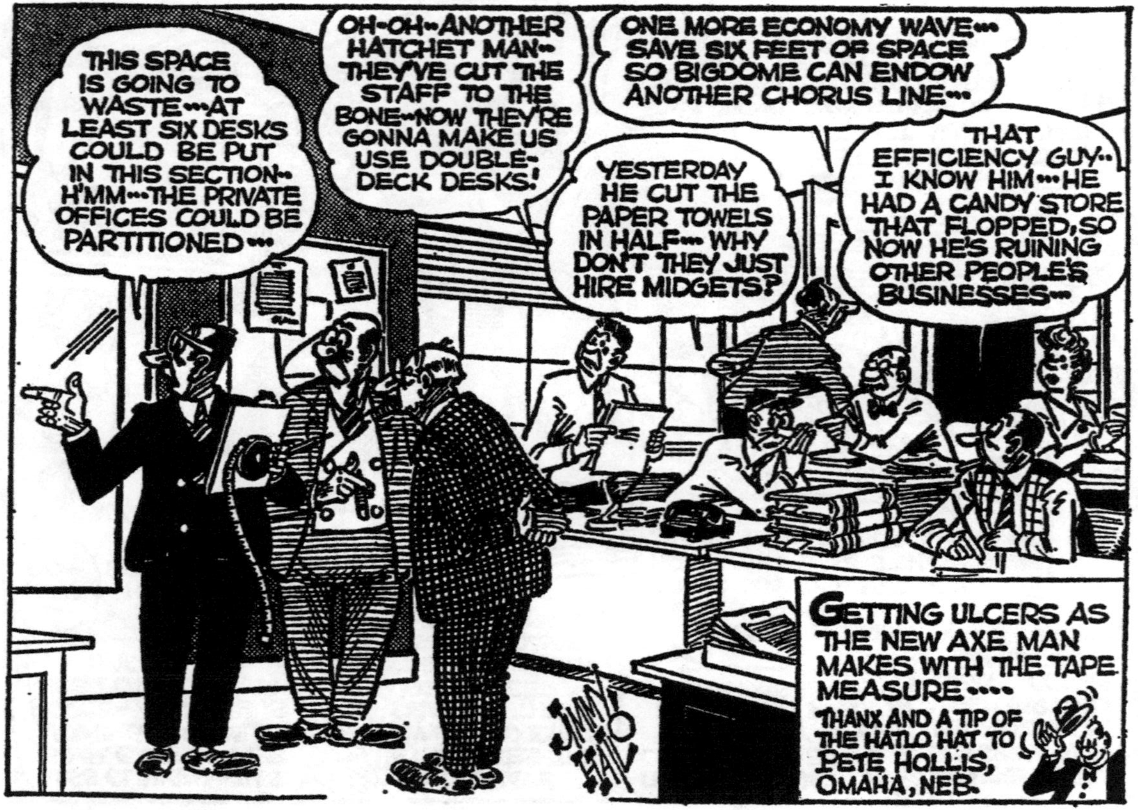
THIS SPACE IS GOING TO WASTE…AT LEAST SIX DESKS COULD BE PUT IN THIS SECTION.. H'MM…THE PRIVATE OFFICES COULD BE PARTITIONED…
OH-OH--ANOTHER HATCHET MAN-- THEY'VE CUT THE STAFF TO THE BONE--NOW THEY'RE GONNA MAKE US USE DOUBLE-DECK DESKS!
ONE MORE ECONOMY WAVE… SAVE SIX FEET OF SPACE SO BIGDOME CAN ENDOW ANOTHER CHORUS LINE…
YESTERDAY HE CUT THE PAPER TOWELS IN HALF… WHY DON'T THEY JUST HIRE MIDGETS?
THAT EFFICIENCY GUY.. I KNOW HIM…HE HAD A CANDY STORE THAT FLOPPED, SO NOW HE'S RUINING OTHER PEOPLE'S BUSINESSES…
GETTING ULCERS AS THE NEW AXE MAN MAKES WITH THE TAPE MEASURE….
THANX AND A TIP OF THE HATLO HAT TO PETE HOLLIS, OMAHA, NEB.
JIMMY HATLO

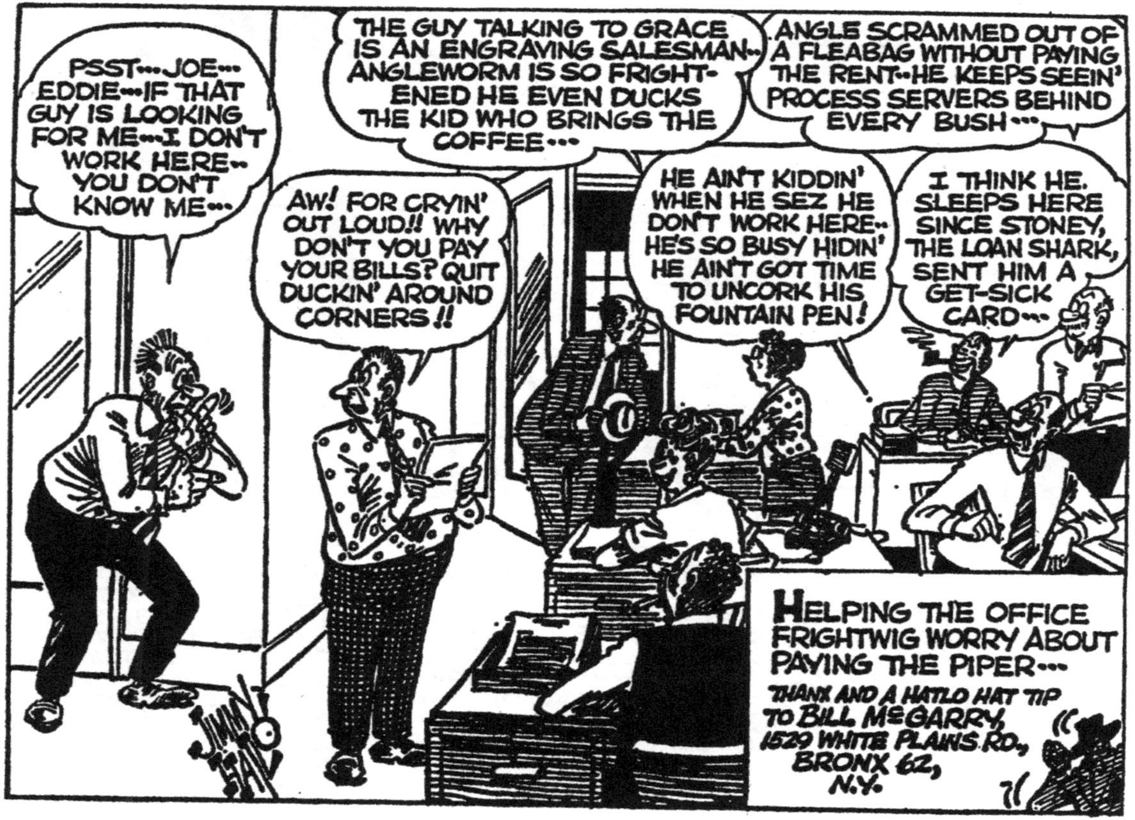
PSST...JOE... EDDIE...IF THAT GUY IS LOOKING FOR ME...I DON'T WORK HERE.. YOU DON'T KNOW ME...
AW! FOR CRYIN' OUT LOUD!! WHY DON'T YOU PAY YOUR BILLS? QUIT DUCKIN' AROUND CORNERS!!
THE GUY TALKING TO GRACE IS AN ENGRAVING SALESMAN.. ANGLEWORM IS SO FRIGHT-ENED HE EVEN DUCKS THE KID WHO BRINGS THE COFFEE...
HE AIN'T KIDDIN' WHEN HE SEZ HE DON'T WORK HERE.. HE'S SO BUSY HIDIN' HE AIN'T GOT TIME TO UNCORK HIS FOUNTAIN PEN!
ANGLE SCRAMMED OUT OF A FLEABAG WITHOUT PAYING THE RENT..HE KEEPS SEEIN' PROCESS SERVERS BEHIND EVERY BUSH...
I THINK HE SLEEPS HERE SINCE STONEY, THE LOAN SHARK, SENT HIM A GET-SICK CARD...
HELPING THE OFFICE FRIGHTWIG WORRY ABOUT PAYING THE PIPER...
THANX AND A HATLO HAT TIP TO BILL McGARRY, 1529 WHITE PLAINS RD., BRONX 62, N.Y.

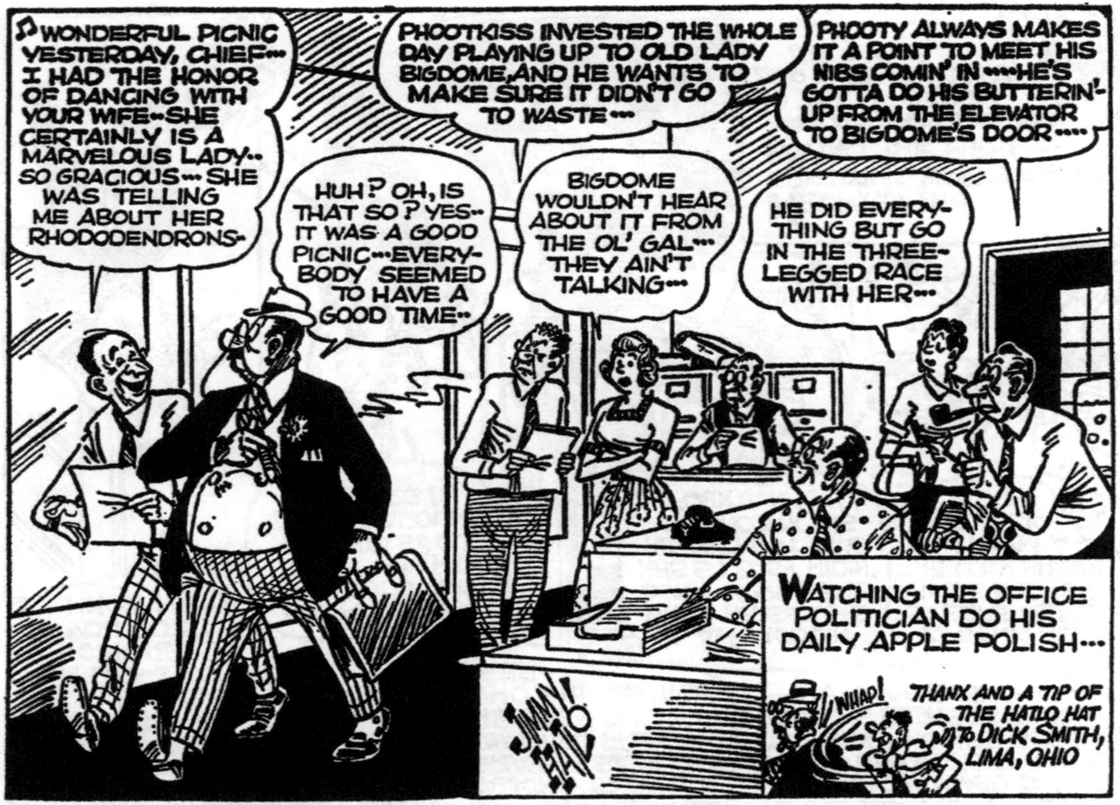
♫ WONDERFUL PICNIC YESTERDAY, CHIEF··· I HAD THE HONOR OF DANCING WITH YOUR WIFE··SHE CERTAINLY IS A MARVELOUS LADY·· SO GRACIOUS··· SHE WAS TELLING ME ABOUT HER RHODODENDRONS·
HUH? OH, IS THAT SO? YES·· IT WAS A GOOD PICNIC···EVERYBODY SEEMED TO HAVE A GOOD TIME··
PHOOTKISS INVESTED THE WHOLE DAY PLAYING UP TO OLD LADY BIGDOME, AND HE WANTS TO MAKE SURE IT DIDN'T GO TO WASTE···
BIGDOME WOULDN'T HEAR ABOUT IT FROM THE OL' GAL··· THEY AIN'T TALKING···
PHOOTY ALWAYS MAKES IT A POINT TO MEET HIS NIBS COMIN' IN ····HE'S GOTTA DO HIS BUTTERIN'-UP FROM THE ELEVATOR TO BIGDOME'S DOOR····
HE DID EVERYTHING BUT GO IN THE THREE-LEGGED RACE WITH HER···
JIMMY! HAL!
WATCHING THE OFFICE POLITICIAN DO HIS DAILY APPLE POLISH···
WHAP!
THANX AND A TIP OF THE HATLO HAT TO DICK SMITH, LIMA, OHIO

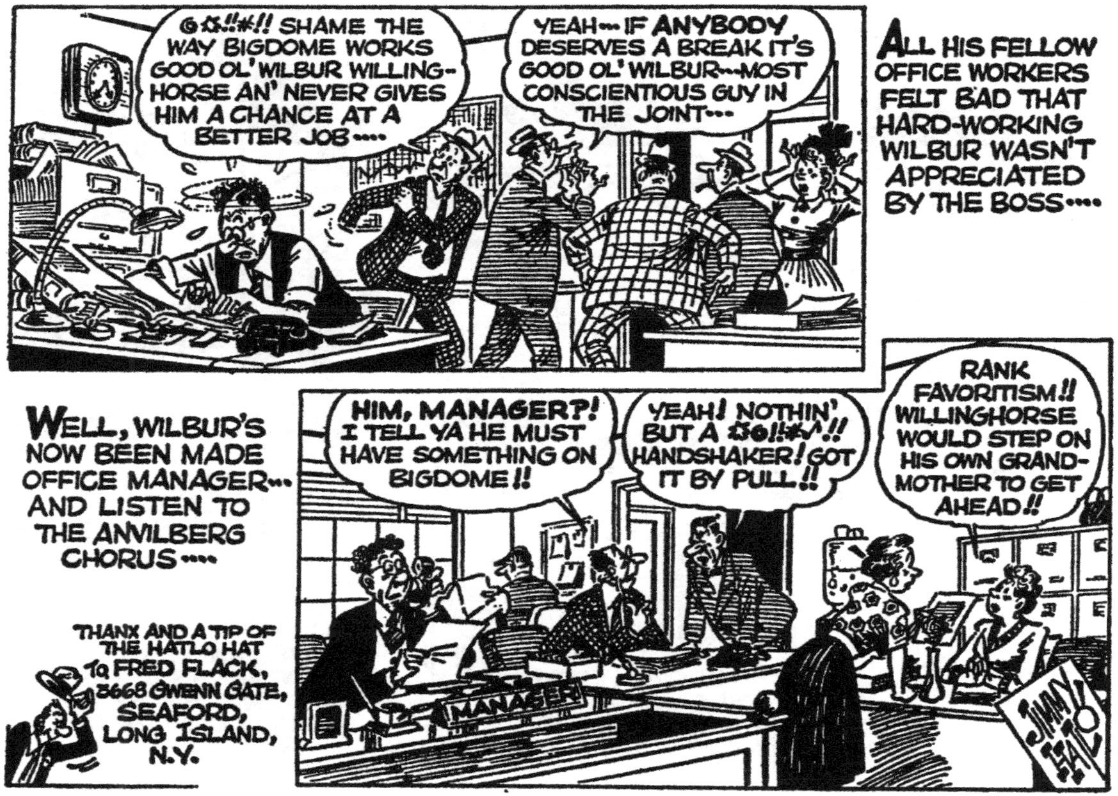
ALL HIS FELLOW OFFICE WORKERS FELT BAD THAT HARD-WORKING WILBUR WASN'T APPRECIATED BY THE BOSS....
@☆!!#!! SHAME THE WAY BIGDOME WORKS GOOD OL' WILBUR WILLINGHORSE AN' NEVER GIVES HIM A CHANCE AT A BETTER JOB....
YEAH... IF ANYBODY DESERVES A BREAK IT'S GOOD OL' WILBUR...MOST CONSCIENTIOUS GUY IN THE JOINT...
WELL, WILBUR'S NOW BEEN MADE OFFICE MANAGER... AND LISTEN TO THE ANVILBERG CHORUS....
HIM, MANAGER?! I TELL YA HE MUST HAVE SOMETHING ON BIGDOME!!
YEAH! NOTHIN' BUT A ☆@!!#^!! HANDSHAKER! GOT IT BY PULL!!
RANK FAVORITISM!! WILLINGHORSE WOULD STEP ON HIS OWN GRANDMOTHER TO GET AHEAD!!
MANAGER
JIMMY HATLO
THANX AND A TIP OF THE HATLO HAT TO FRED FLACK, 3668 GWENN GATE, SEAFORD, LONG ISLAND, N.Y.

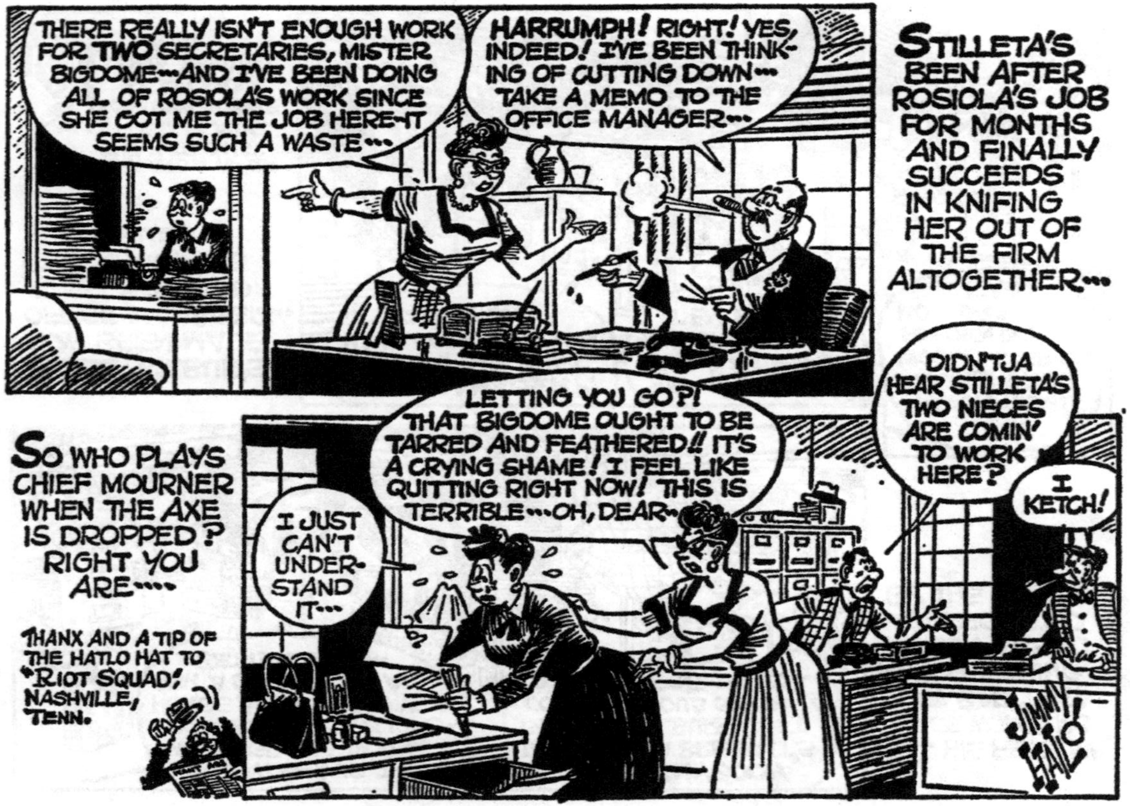
STILLETA'S BEEN AFTER ROSIOLA'S JOB FOR MONTHS AND FINALLY SUCCEEDS IN KNIFING HER OUT OF THE FIRM ALTOGETHER...
THERE REALLY ISN'T ENOUGH WORK FOR TWO SECRETARIES, MISTER BIGDOME...AND I'VE BEEN DOING ALL OF ROSIOLA'S WORK SINCE SHE GOT ME THE JOB HERE--IT SEEMS SUCH A WASTE...
HARRUMPH! RIGHT! YES, INDEED! I'VE BEEN THINKING OF CUTTING DOWN... TAKE A MEMO TO THE OFFICE MANAGER...
SO WHO PLAYS CHIEF MOURNER WHEN THE AXE IS DROPPED? RIGHT YOU ARE....
I JUST CAN'T UNDERSTAND IT...
LETTING YOU GO?! THAT BIGDOME OUGHT TO BE TARRED AND FEATHERED!! IT'S A CRYING SHAME! I FEEL LIKE QUITTING RIGHT NOW! THIS IS TERRIBLE...OH, DEAR--
DIDN'TJA HEAR STILLETA'S TWO NIECES ARE COMIN' TO WORK HERE?
I KETCH!
THANX AND A TIP OF THE HATLO HAT TO "RIOT SQUAD," NASHVILLE, TENN.
JIMMY HATLO

Damon Runyon said: "It is my opinion that Hatlo is one of the greatest cartoonists the newspaper business has ever produced . . ." Every day millions of Americans open their papers to the Hatlo cartoon. Now, Jimmy brings you a book full of jokes, gags, quips, digs and sly gurgles, as he opens the doors of the office—for a million laughs.

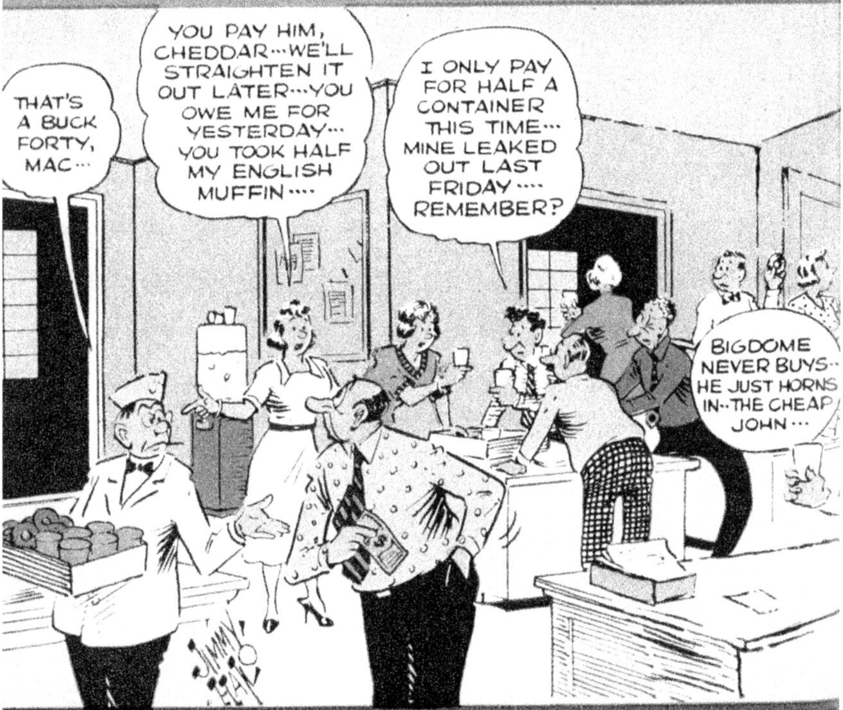
THAT'S A BUCK FORTY, MAC···
YOU PAY HIM, CHEDDAR···WE'LL STRAIGHTEN IT OUT LATER···YOU OWE ME FOR YESTERDAY··· YOU TOOK HALF MY ENGLISH MUFFIN····
I ONLY PAY FOR HALF A CONTAINER THIS TIME··· MINE LEAKED OUT LAST FRIDAY···· REMEMBER?
BIGDOME NEVER BUYS·· HE JUST HORNS IN··THE CHEAP JOHN···
JIMMY HATLO

Printed in the U.S.A.

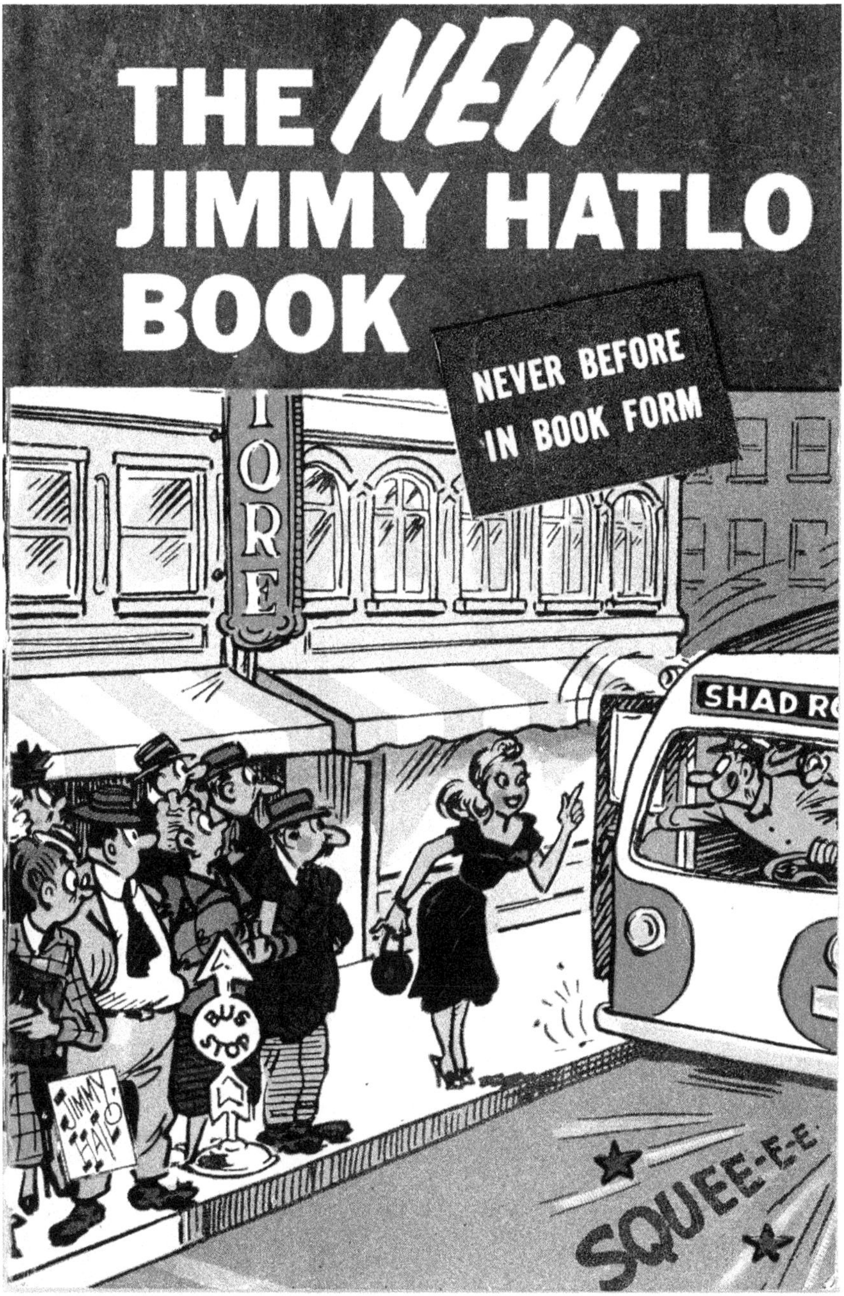
THE NEW JIMMY HATLO BOOK
NEVER BEFORE IN BOOK FORM
ORE
SHAD RO
BUS STOP
JIMMY HATLO
SQUEE-E-E

THE NEW

JIMMY HATLO BOOK

They'll Do It Every Time ®

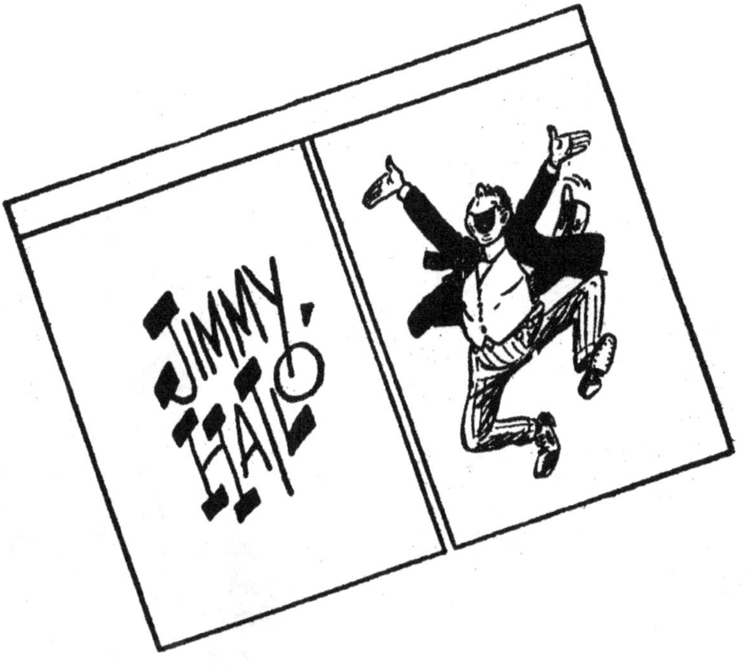

JIMMY HATLO

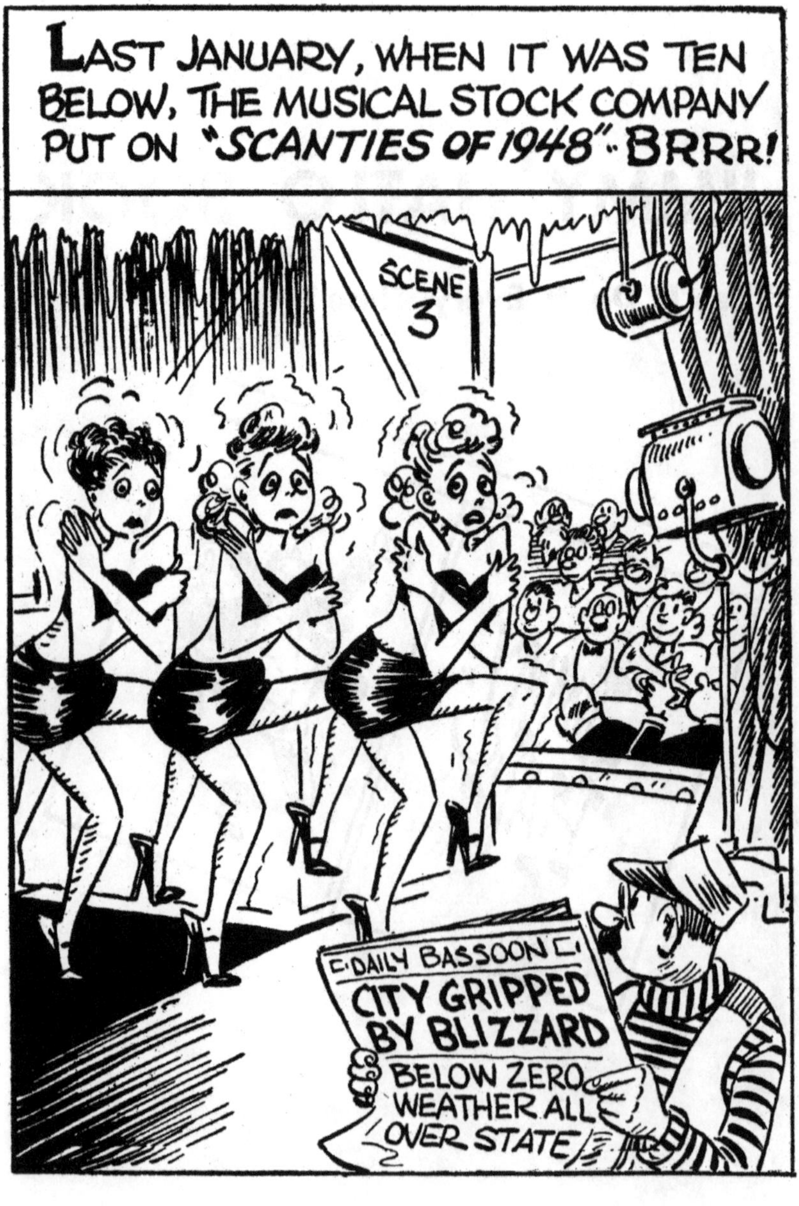
LAST JANUARY, WHEN IT WAS TEN BELOW, THE MUSICAL STOCK COMPANY PUT ON "SCANTIES OF 1948"- BRRRR!
SCENE 3
DAILY BASSOON
CITY GRIPPED BY BLIZZARD
BELOW ZERO WEATHER ALL OVER STATE

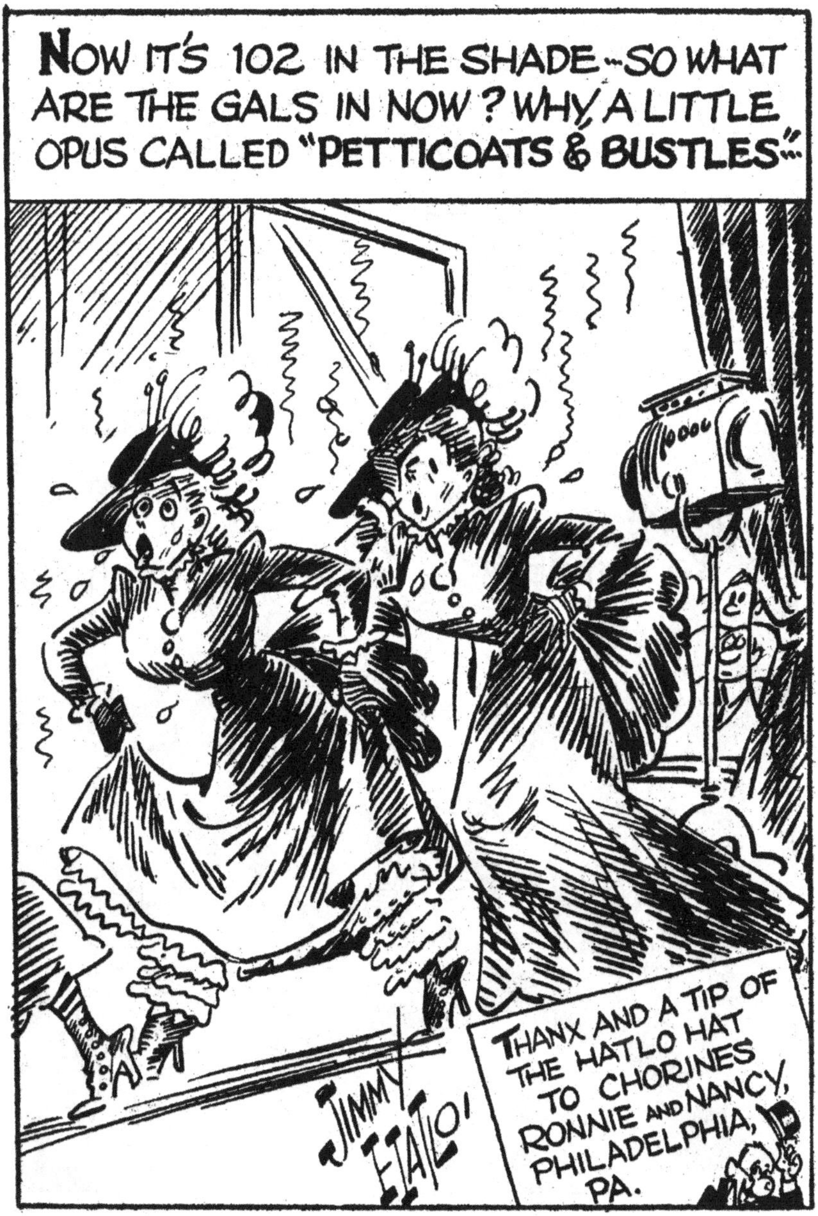
NOW IT'S 102 IN THE SHADE--SO WHAT ARE THE GALS IN NOW? WHY, A LITTLE OPUS CALLED "PETTICOATS & BUSTLES"...
JIMMY HATLO
THANX AND A TIP OF THE HATLO HAT TO CHORINES RONNIE AND NANCY, PHILADELPHIA, PA.

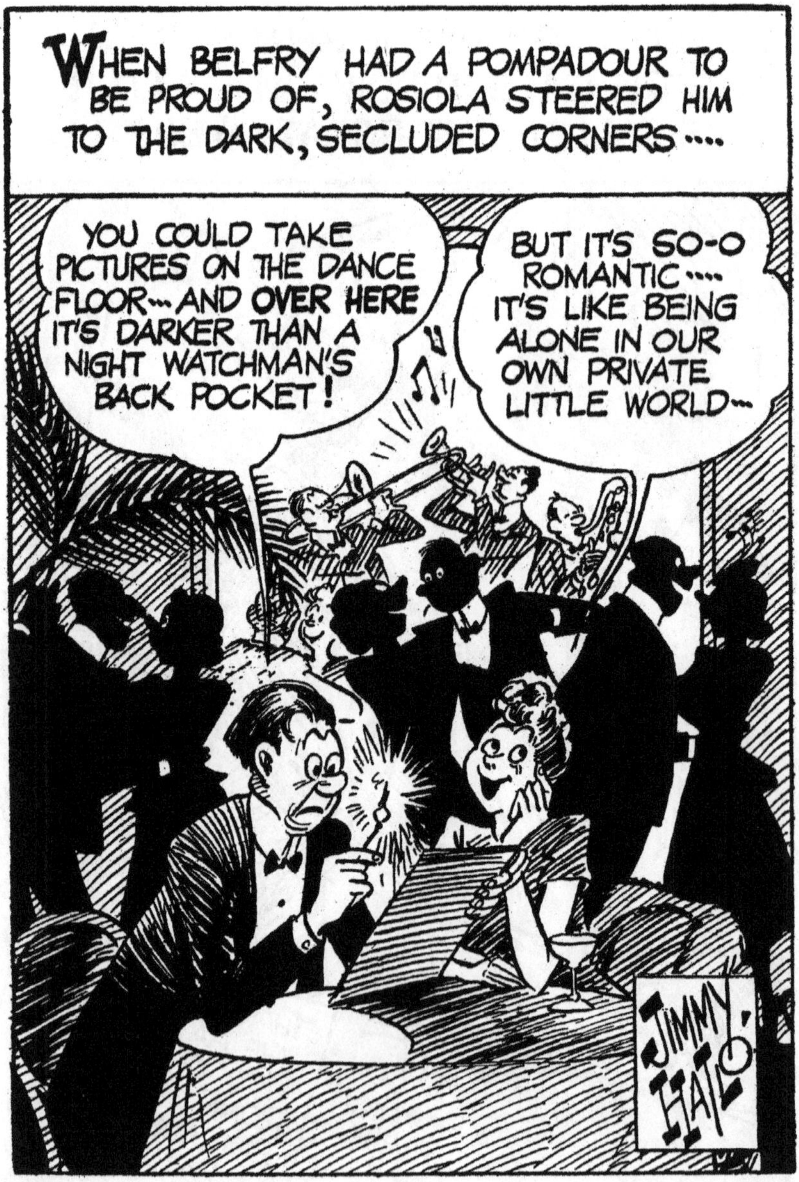
WHEN BELFRY HAD A POMPADOUR TO BE PROUD OF, ROSIOLA STEERED HIM TO THE DARK, SECLUDED CORNERS....
YOU COULD TAKE PICTURES ON THE DANCE FLOOR... AND OVER HERE IT'S DARKER THAN A NIGHT WATCHMAN'S BACK POCKET!
BUT IT'S SO-O ROMANTIC.... IT'S LIKE BEING ALONE IN OUR OWN PRIVATE LITTLE WORLD...
JIMMY HATLO

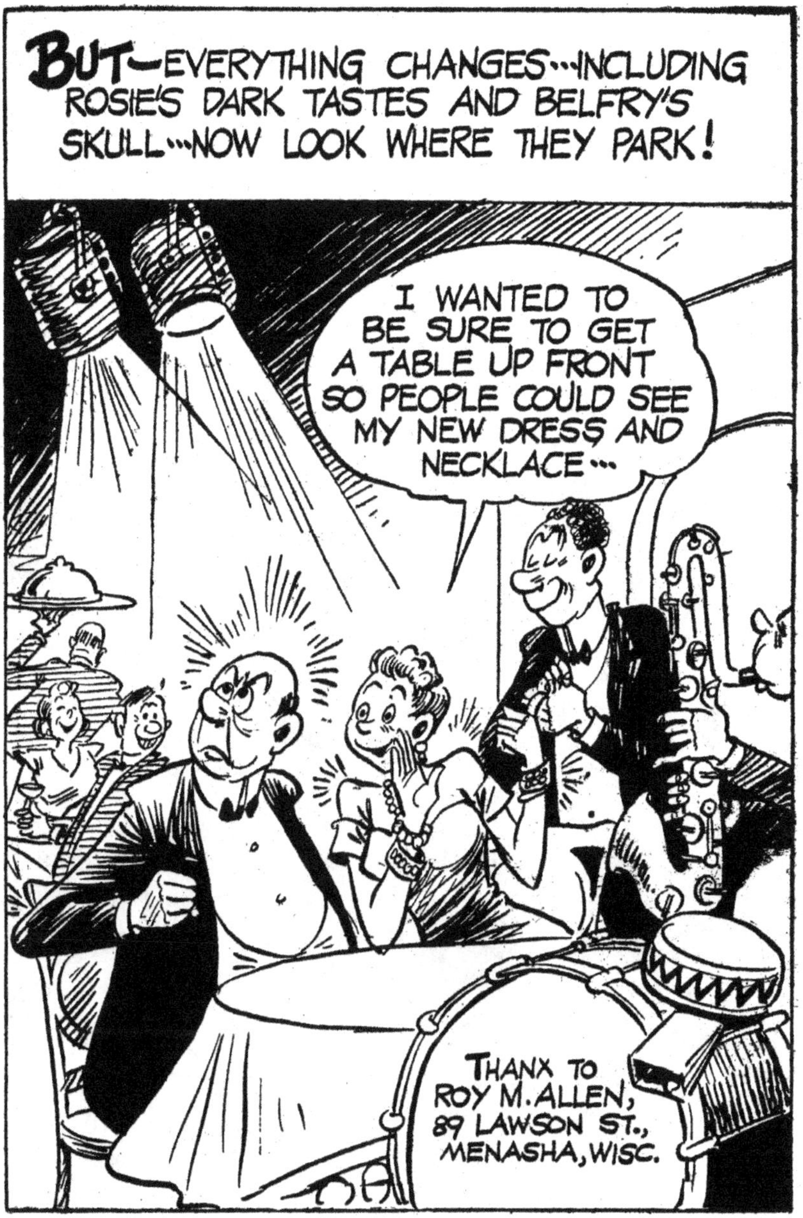
BUT—EVERYTHING CHANGES...INCLUDING ROSIE'S DARK TASTES AND BELFRY'S SKULL...NOW LOOK WHERE THEY PARK!
I WANTED TO BE SURE TO GET A TABLE UP FRONT SO PEOPLE COULD SEE MY NEW DRESS AND NECKLACE...
THANX TO ROY M. ALLEN, 89 LAWSON ST., MENASHA, WISC.

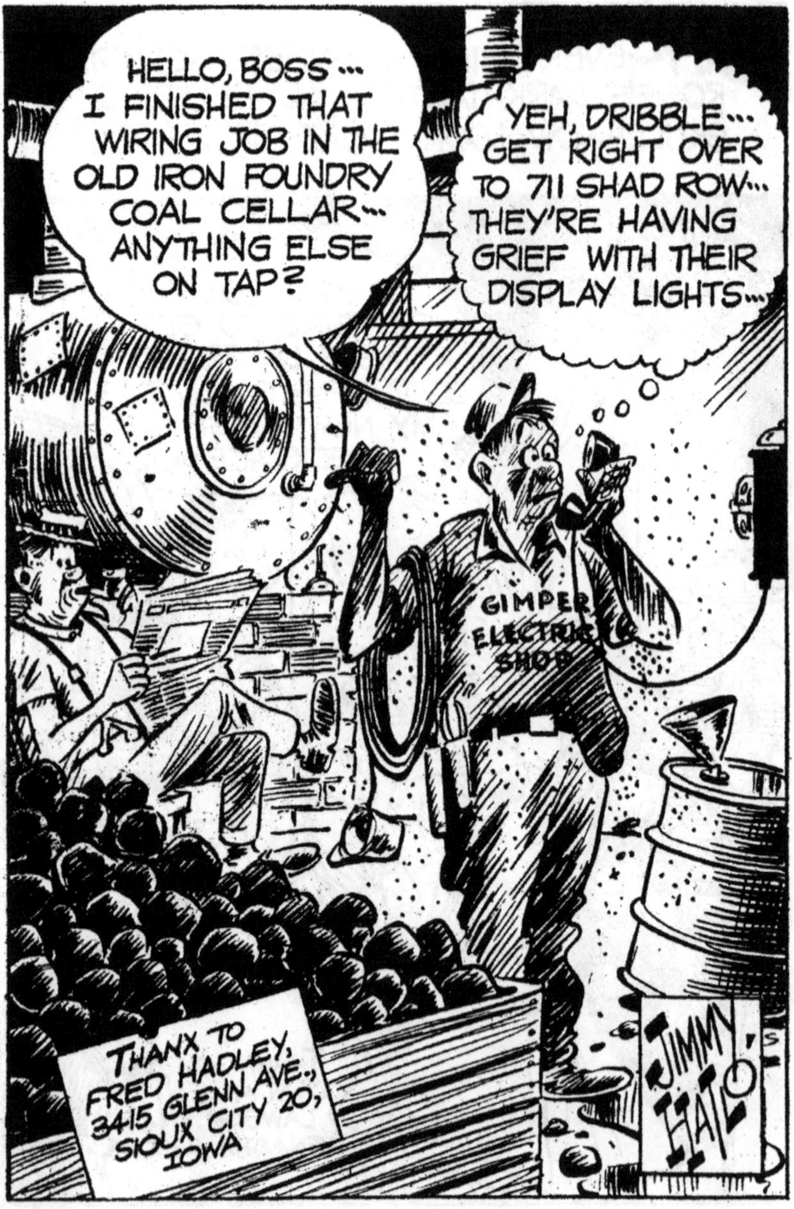
HELLO, BOSS... I FINISHED THAT WIRING JOB IN THE OLD IRON FOUNDRY COAL CELLAR... ANYTHING ELSE ON TAP?
YEH, DRIBBLE... GET RIGHT OVER TO 711 SHAD ROW... THEY'RE HAVING GRIEF WITH THEIR DISPLAY LIGHTS...
GIMPER ELECTRIC SHOP
THANX TO FRED HADLEY, 3415 GLENN AVE., SIOUX CITY 20, IOWA
JIMMY HATLO

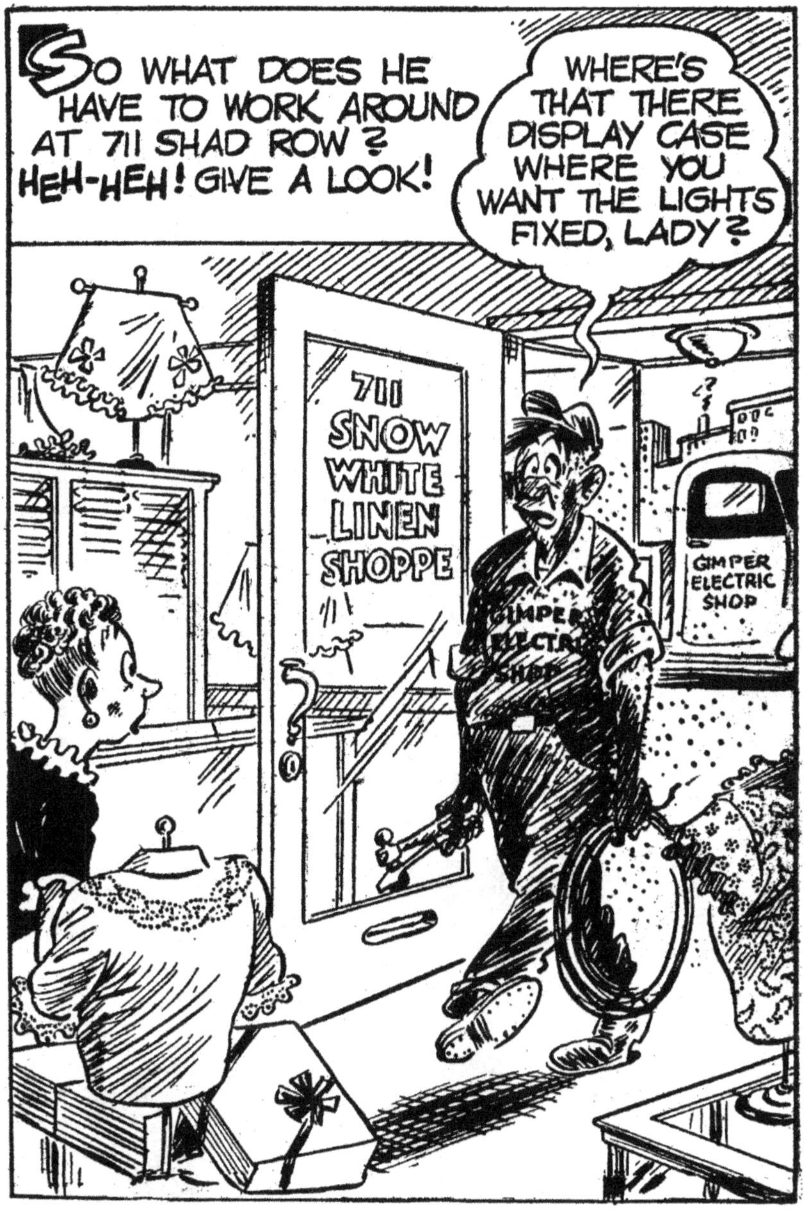
SO WHAT DOES HE HAVE TO WORK AROUND AT 711 SHAD ROW? HEH-HEH! GIVE A LOOK!
WHERE'S THAT THERE DISPLAY CASE WHERE YOU WANT THE LIGHTS FIXED, LADY?
711 SNOW WHITE LINEN SHOPPE
GIMPER ELECTRIC SHOP

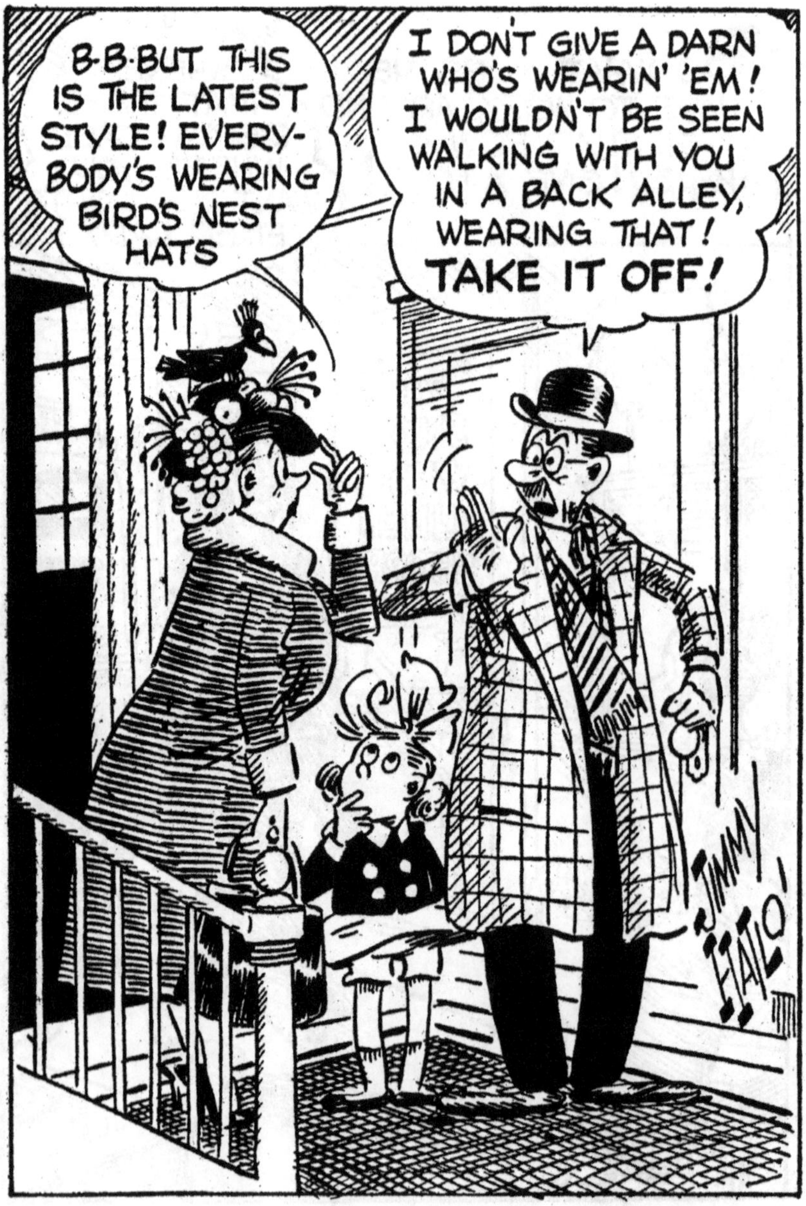
B-B-BUT THIS IS THE LATEST STYLE! EVERY-BODY'S WEARING BIRD'S NEST HATS
I DON'T GIVE A DARN WHO'S WEARIN' 'EM! I WOULDN'T BE SEEN WALKING WITH YOU IN A BACK ALLEY, WEARING THAT! TAKE IT OFF!
JIMMY HATLO

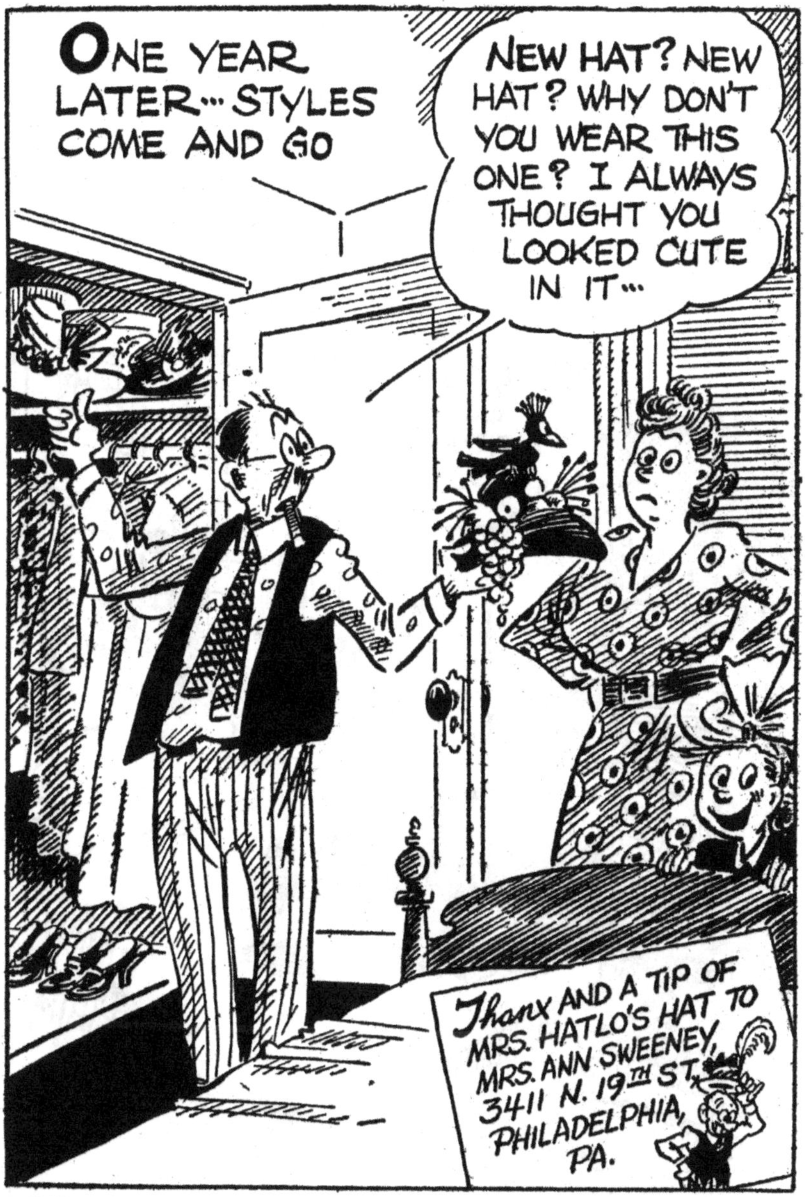
ONE YEAR LATER... STYLES COME AND GO
NEW HAT? NEW HAT? WHY DON'T YOU WEAR THIS ONE? I ALWAYS THOUGHT YOU LOOKED CUTE IN IT...
Thanx AND A TIP OF MRS. HATLO'S HAT TO MRS. ANN SWEENEY, 3411 N. 19TH ST., PHILADELPHIA, PA.

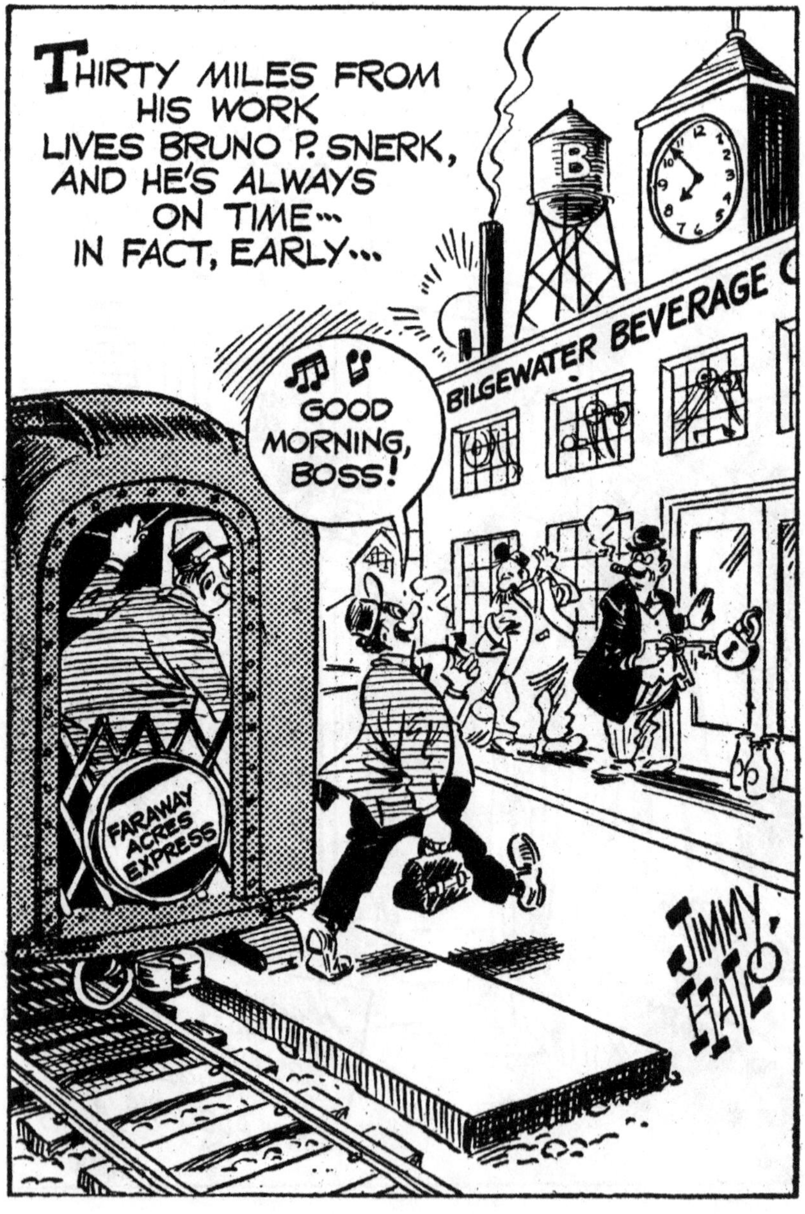
THIRTY MILES FROM HIS WORK LIVES BRUNO P. SNERK, AND HE'S ALWAYS ON TIME... IN FACT, EARLY...
GOOD MORNING, BOSS!
BILGEWATER BEVERAGE C
FARAWAY ACRES EXPRESS
JIMMY HATLO

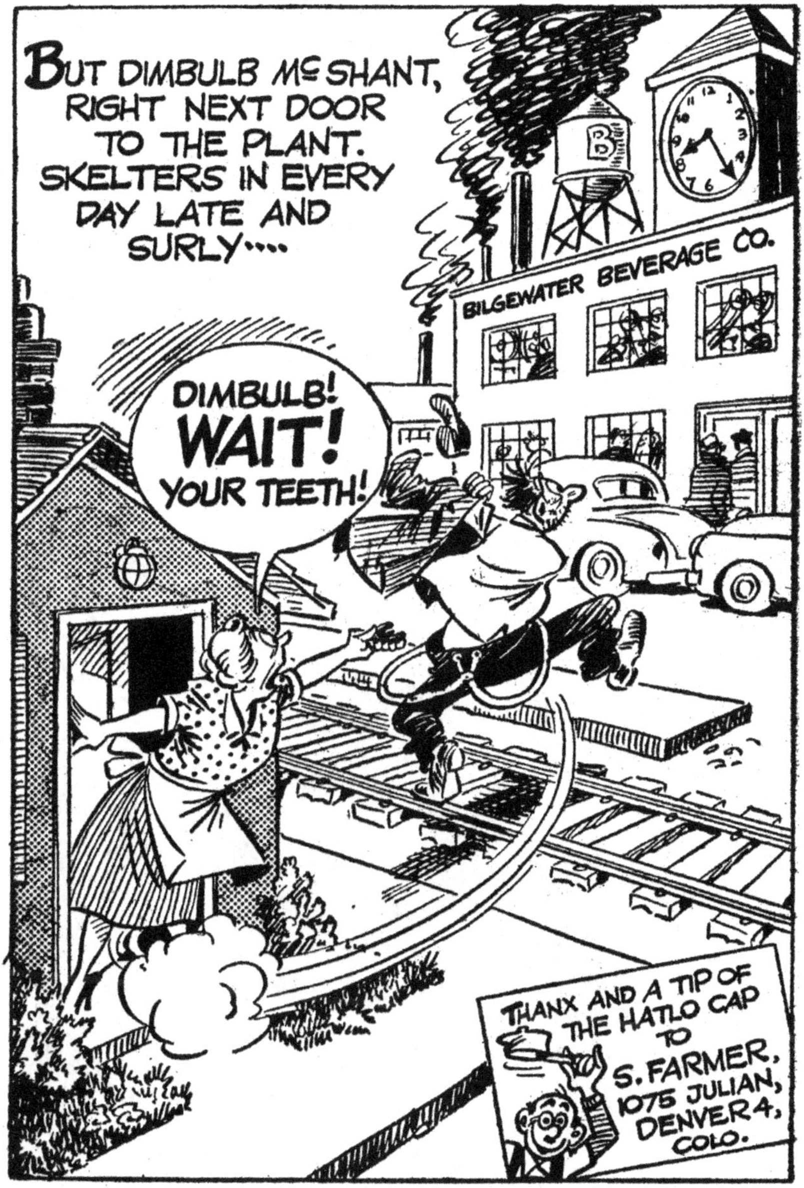

BUT DIMBULB MᶜSHANT, RIGHT NEXT DOOR TO THE PLANT. SKELTERS IN EVERY DAY LATE AND SURLY....
BILGEWATER BEVERAGE CO.
DIMBULB! WAIT! YOUR TEETH!
THANX AND A TIP OF THE HATLO CAP TO S. FARMER, 1075 JULIAN, DENVER 4, COLO.

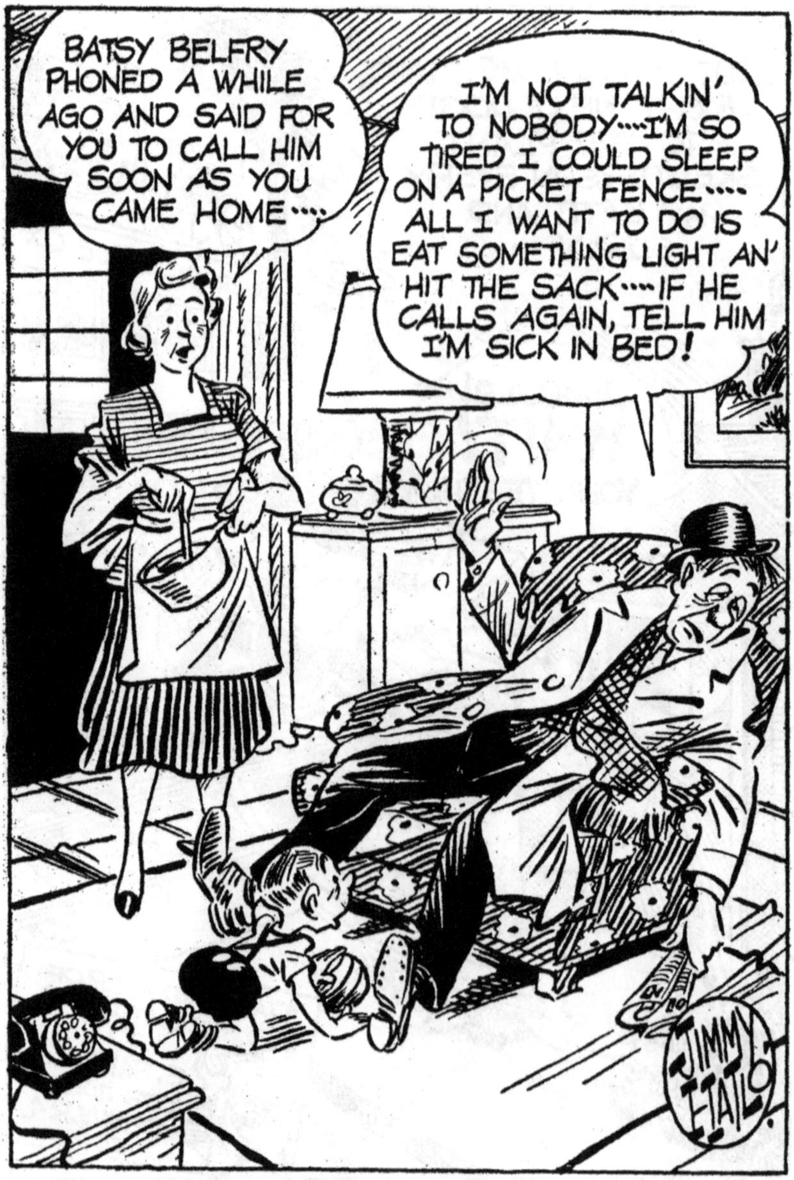
BATSY BELFRY PHONED A WHILE AGO AND SAID FOR YOU TO CALL HIM SOON AS YOU CAME HOME....
I'M NOT TALKIN' TO NOBODY....I'M SO TIRED I COULD SLEEP ON A PICKET FENCE.... ALL I WANT TO DO IS EAT SOMETHING LIGHT AN' HIT THE SACK....IF HE CALLS AGAIN, TELL HIM I'M SICK IN BED!
JIMMY HATLO

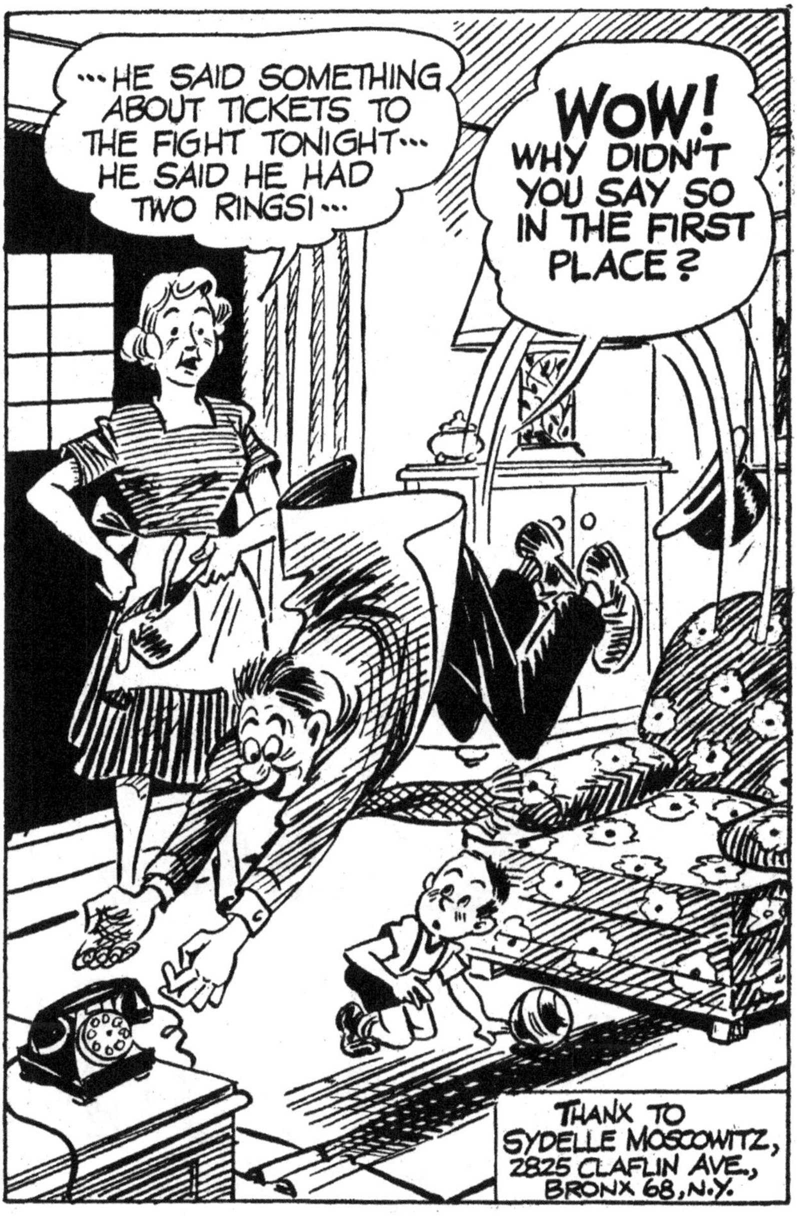
...HE SAID SOMETHING ABOUT TICKETS TO THE FIGHT TONIGHT... HE SAID HE HAD TWO RINGSI...
WOW! WHY DIDN'T YOU SAY SO IN THE FIRST PLACE?
THANX TO SYDELLE MOSCOWITZ, 2825 CLAFLIN AVE., BRONX 68, N.Y.

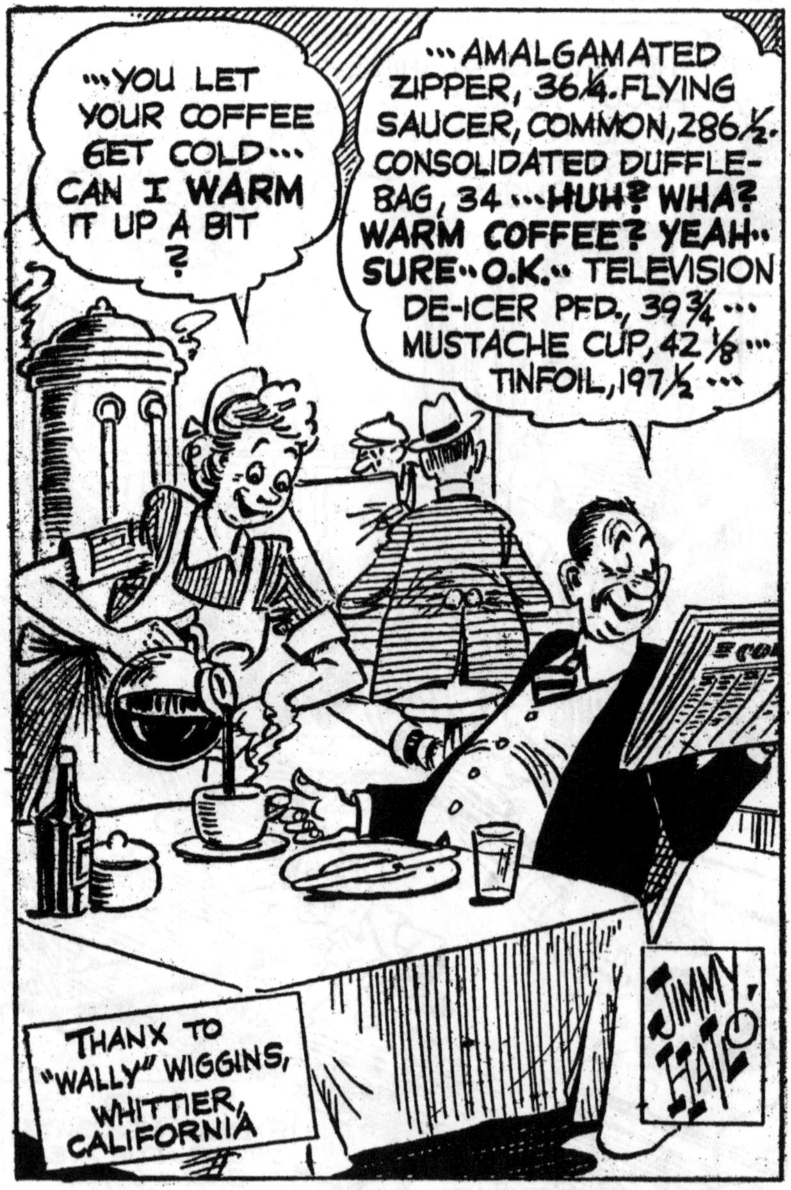
...YOU LET YOUR COFFEE GET COLD... CAN I WARM IT UP A BIT ?
...AMALGAMATED ZIPPER, 36¼. FLYING SAUCER, COMMON, 286½. CONSOLIDATED DUFFLE-BAG, 34 ...HUH? WHA? WARM COFFEE? YEAH.. SURE.. O.K... TELEVISION DE-ICER PFD., 39¾ ... MUSTACHE CUP, 42⅛ ... TINFOIL, 197½ ...
THANX TO "WALLY" WIGGINS, WHITTIER, CALIFORNIA
JIMMY HATLO

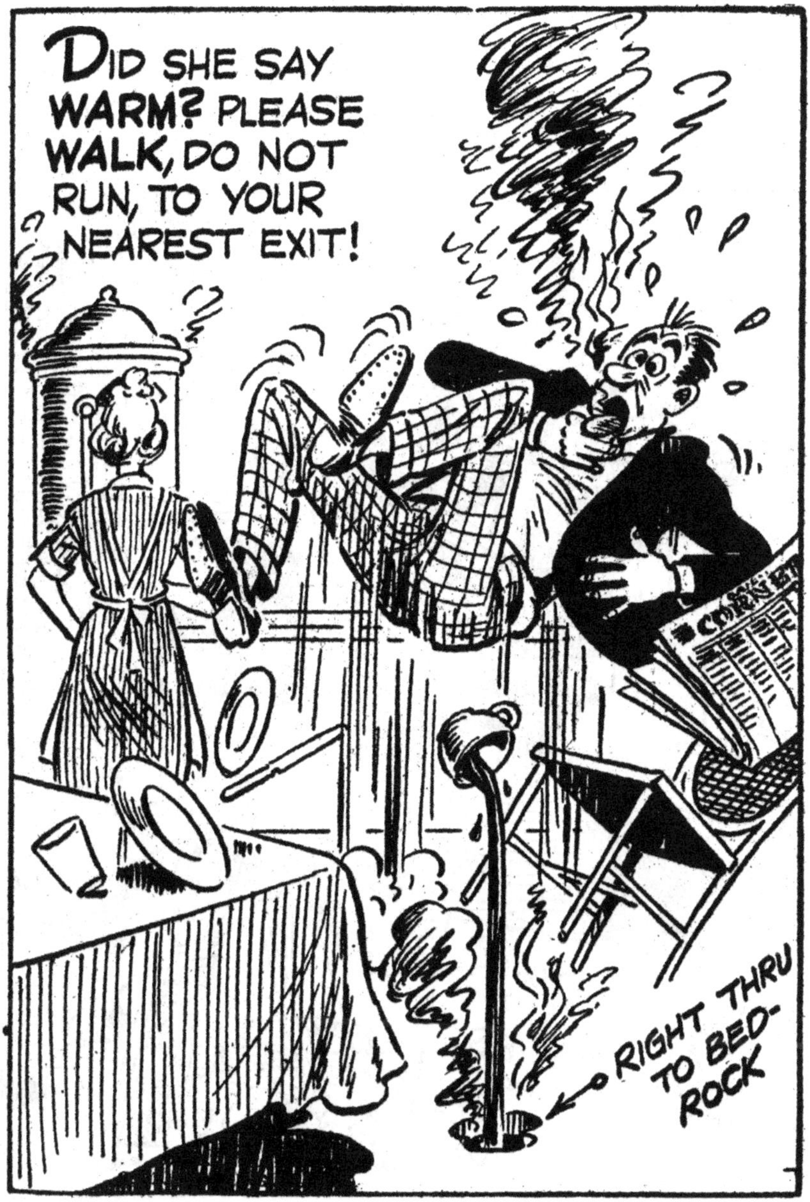
DID SHE SAY WARM? PLEASE WALK, DO NOT RUN, TO YOUR NEAREST EXIT!
RIGHT THRU TO BED-ROCK

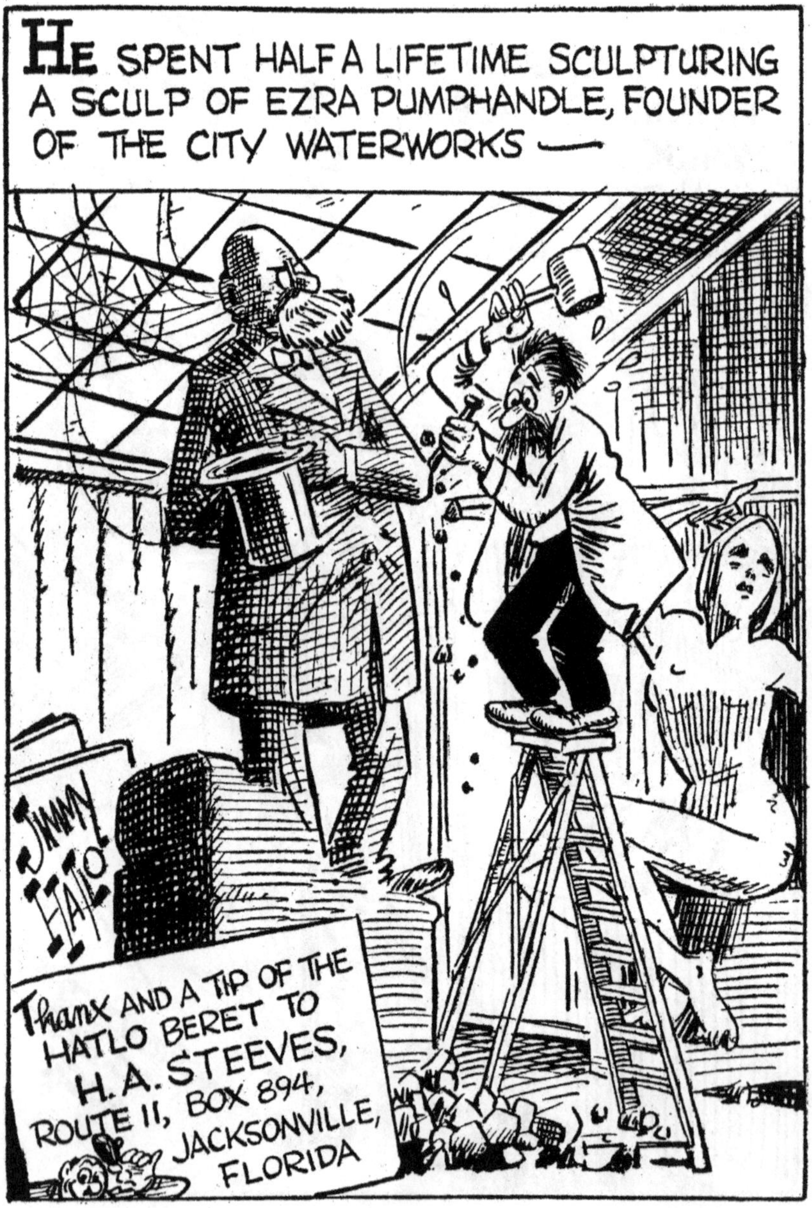
HE SPENT HALF A LIFETIME SCULPTURING A SCULP OF EZRA PUMPHANDLE, FOUNDER OF THE CITY WATERWORKS —
JIMMY HATLO
Thanx AND A TIP OF THE HATLO BERET TO H. A. STEEVES, ROUTE 11, BOX 894, JACKSONVILLE, FLORIDA

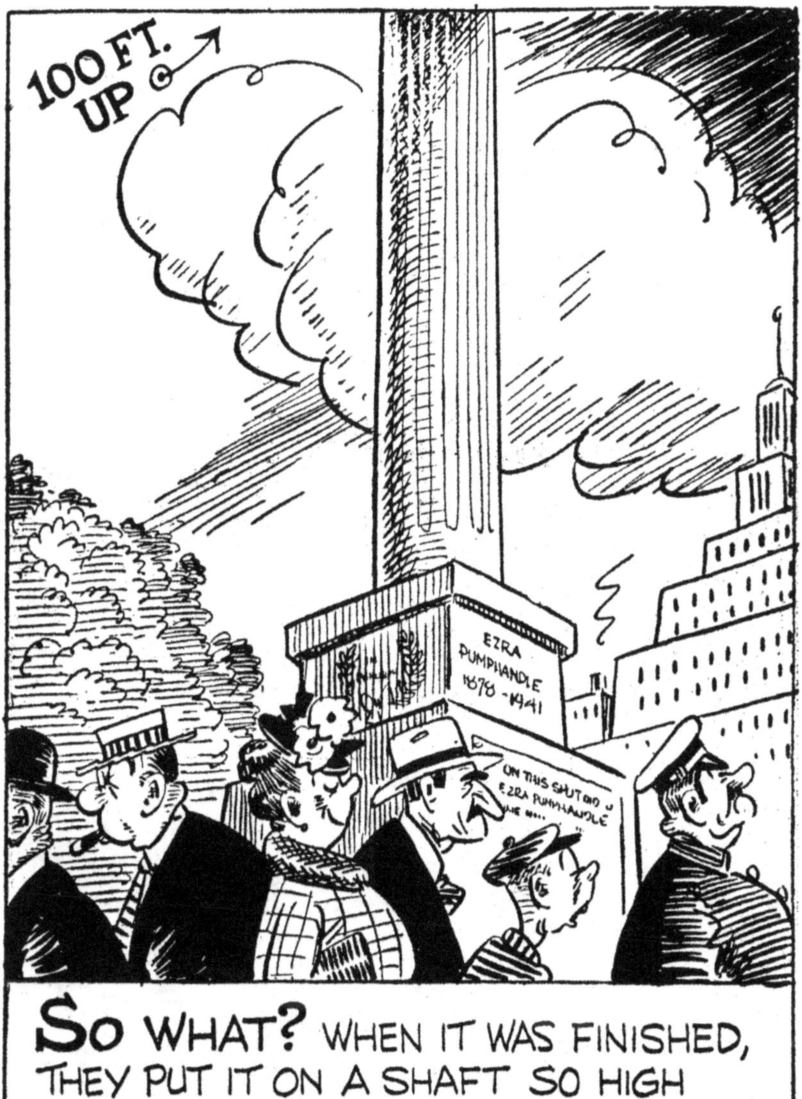
100 FT. UP
EZRA PUMPHANDLE 1878-1941

SO WHAT? WHEN IT WAS FINISHED, THEY PUT IT ON A SHAFT SO HIGH NOBODY EVER TOOK A GANDER AT IT.. BUT THE PIGEONS ...

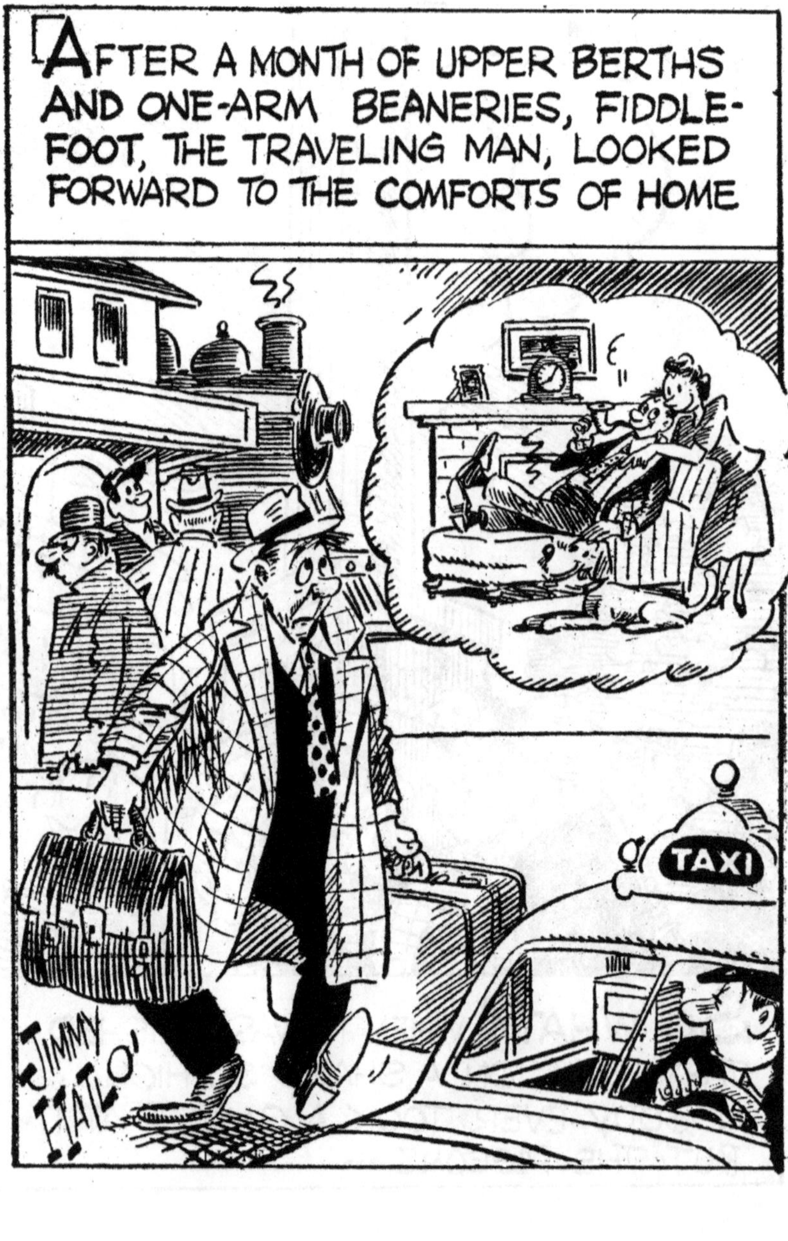
AFTER A MONTH OF UPPER BERTHS AND ONE-ARM BEANERIES, FIDDLE-FOOT, THE TRAVELING MAN, LOOKED FORWARD TO THE COMFORTS OF HOME
TAXI
JIMMY HATLO

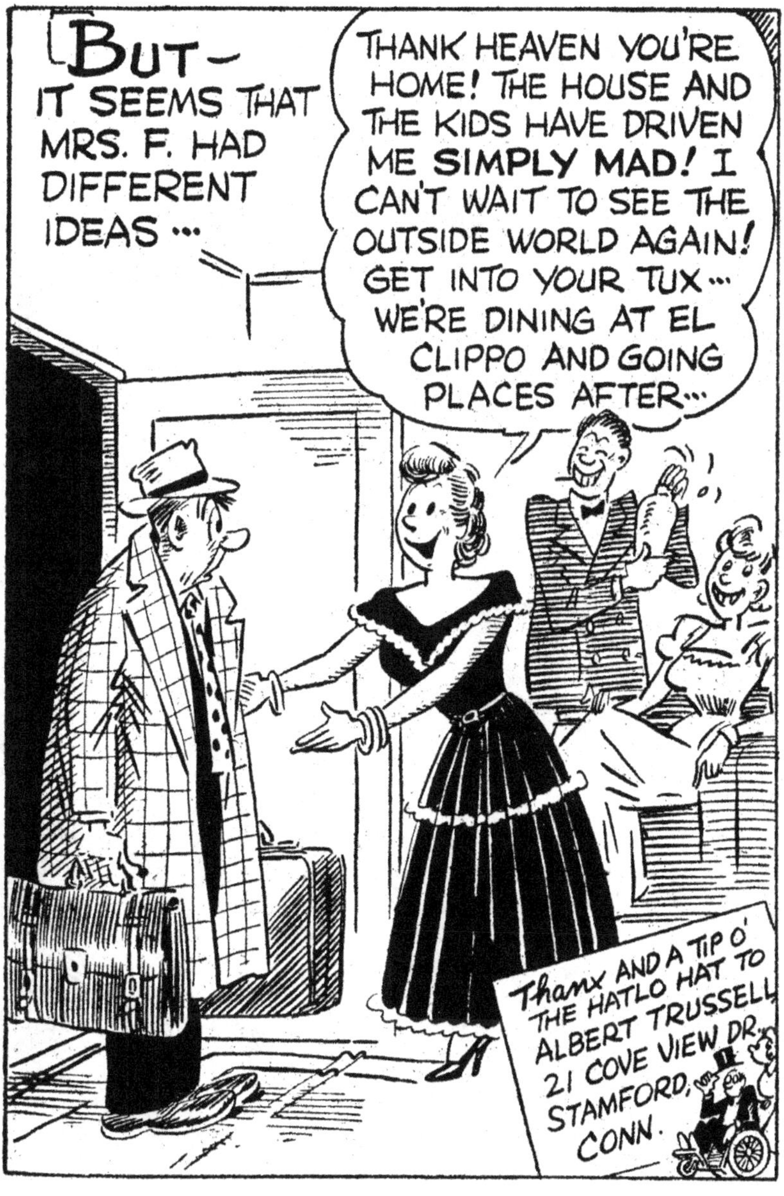
BUT-
IT SEEMS THAT MRS. F. HAD DIFFERENT IDEAS ...
THANK HEAVEN YOU'RE HOME! THE HOUSE AND THE KIDS HAVE DRIVEN ME SIMPLY MAD! I CAN'T WAIT TO SEE THE OUTSIDE WORLD AGAIN! GET INTO YOUR TUX... WE'RE DINING AT EL CLIPPO AND GOING PLACES AFTER...
Thanx AND A TIP O' THE HATLO HAT TO ALBERT TRUSSELL, 21 COVE VIEW DR., STAMFORD, CONN.

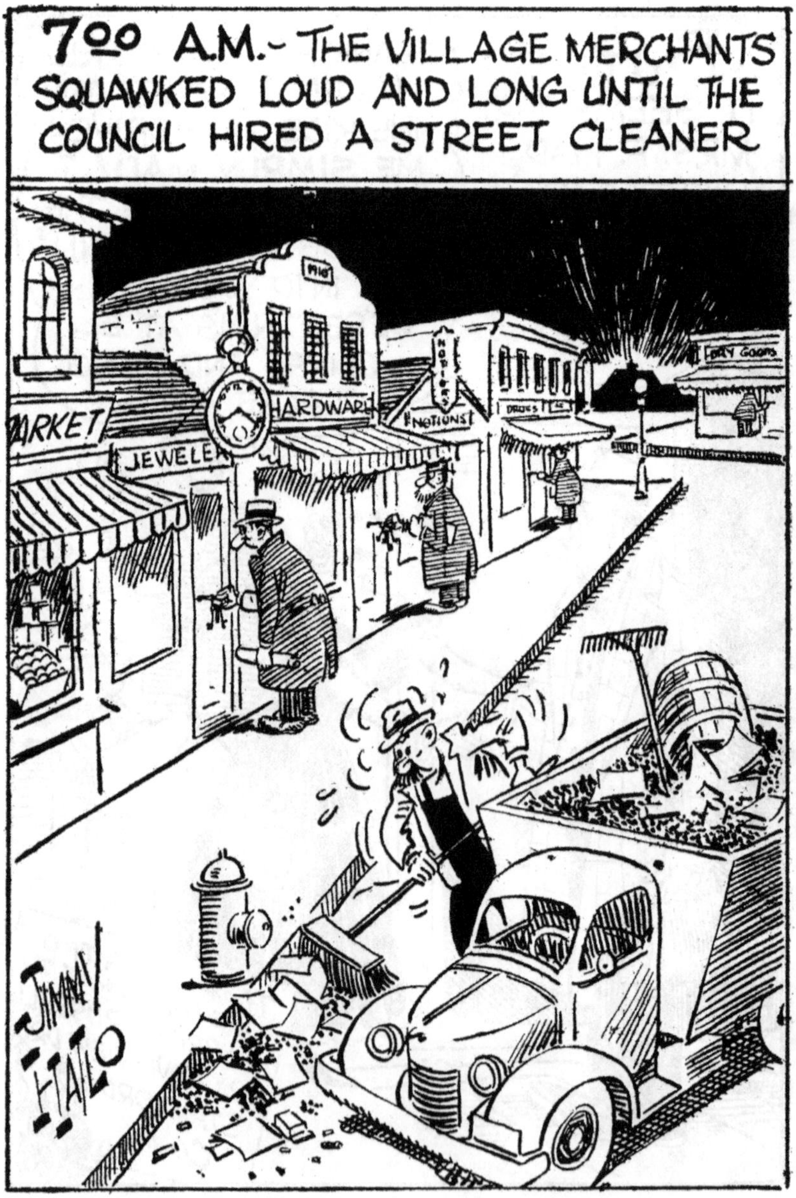

7^00 A.M.- THE VILLAGE MERCHANTS SQUAWKED LOUD AND LONG UNTIL THE COUNCIL HIRED A STREET CLEANER
ARKET
JEWELE
HARDWAR
NOTIONS
DRUGS
DRY GOODS
JIMMY HATLO

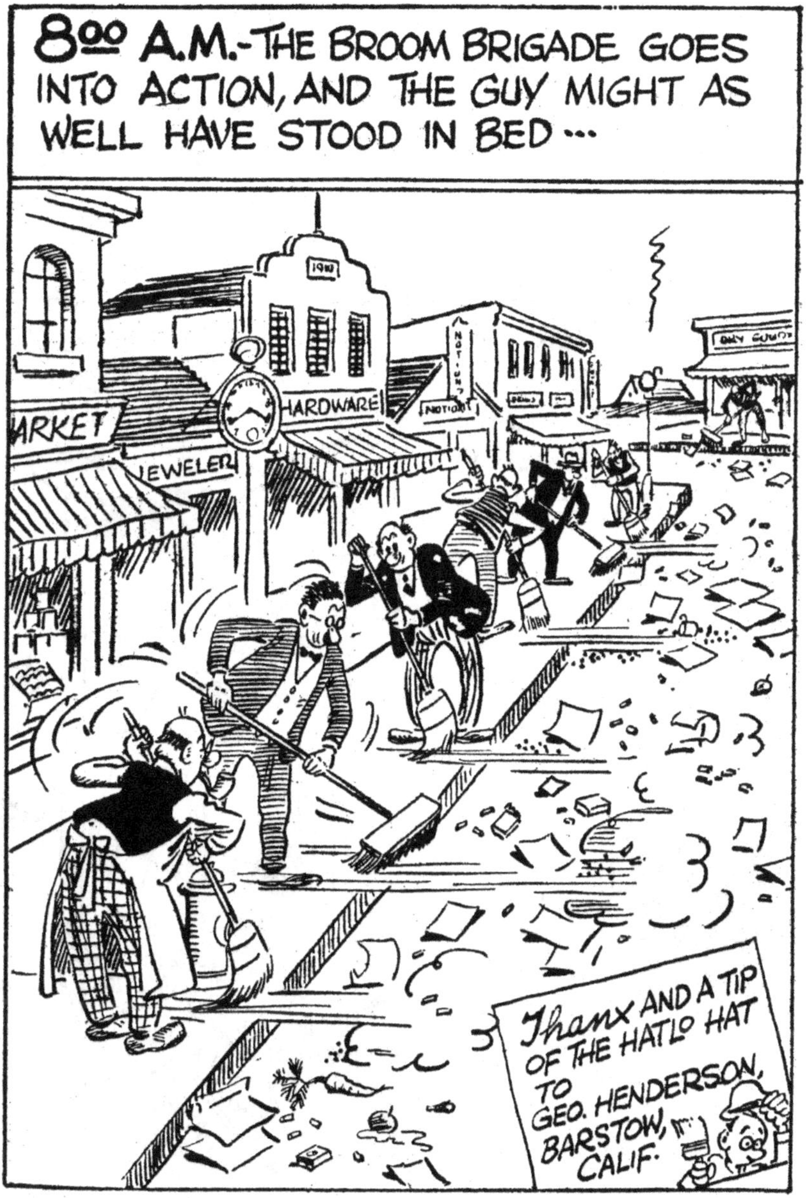
8⁰⁰ A.M.-THE BROOM BRIGADE GOES INTO ACTION, AND THE GUY MIGHT AS WELL HAVE STOOD IN BED...
ARKET
EWELER
HARDWARE
Thanx AND A TIP OF THE HATLO HAT TO GEO. HENDERSON, BARSTOW, CALIF.

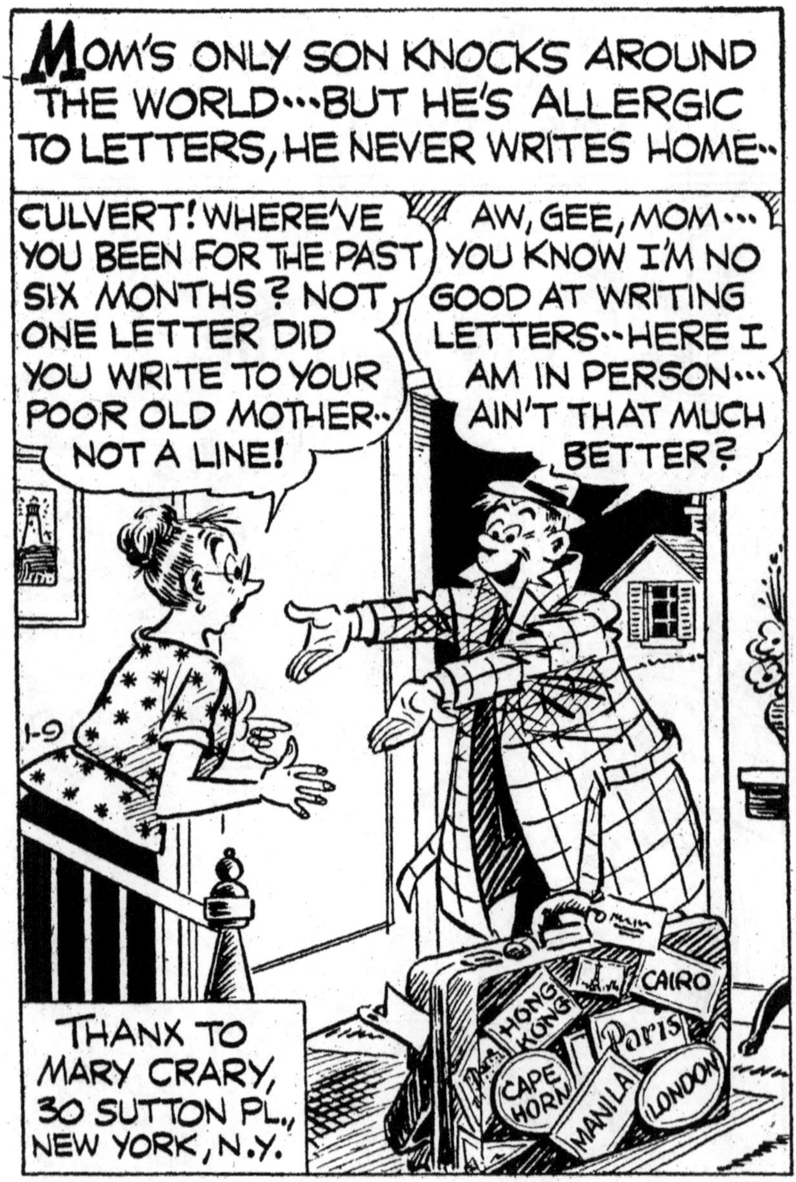
MOM'S ONLY SON KNOCKS AROUND THE WORLD···BUT HE'S ALLERGIC TO LETTERS, HE NEVER WRITES HOME··
CULVERT! WHERE'VE YOU BEEN FOR THE PAST SIX MONTHS? NOT ONE LETTER DID YOU WRITE TO YOUR POOR OLD MOTHER·· NOT A LINE!
AW, GEE, MOM··· YOU KNOW I'M NO GOOD AT WRITING LETTERS··HERE I AM IN PERSON··· AIN'T THAT MUCH BETTER?
1-9
CAIRO
HONG KONG
Paris
CAPE HORN
MANILA
LONDON
THANX TO MARY CRARY, 30 SUTTON PL., NEW YORK, N.Y.

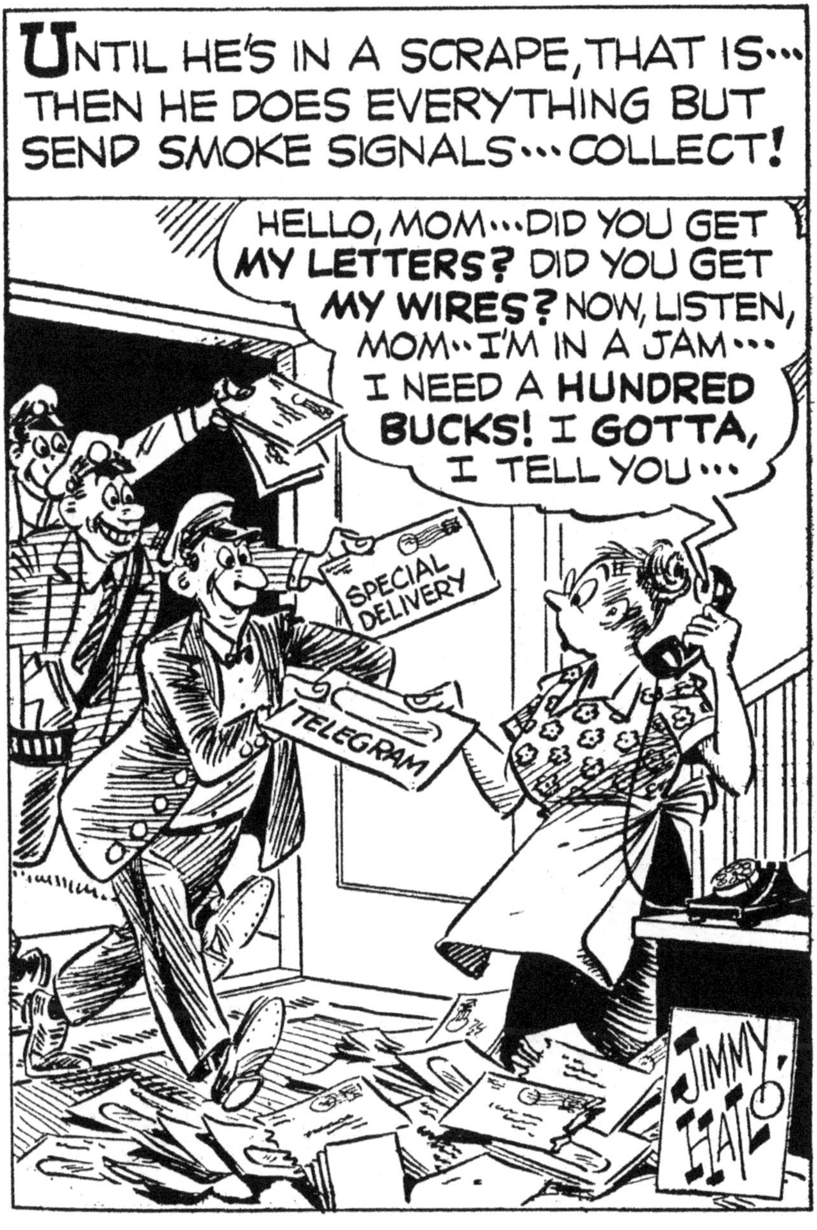
UNTIL HE'S IN A SCRAPE, THAT IS... THEN HE DOES EVERYTHING BUT SEND SMOKE SIGNALS... COLLECT!
HELLO, MOM...DID YOU GET MY LETTERS? DID YOU GET MY WIRES? NOW, LISTEN, MOM.. I'M IN A JAM... I NEED A HUNDRED BUCKS! I GOTTA, I TELL YOU...
SPECIAL DELIVERY
TELEGRAM
JIMMY HATLO

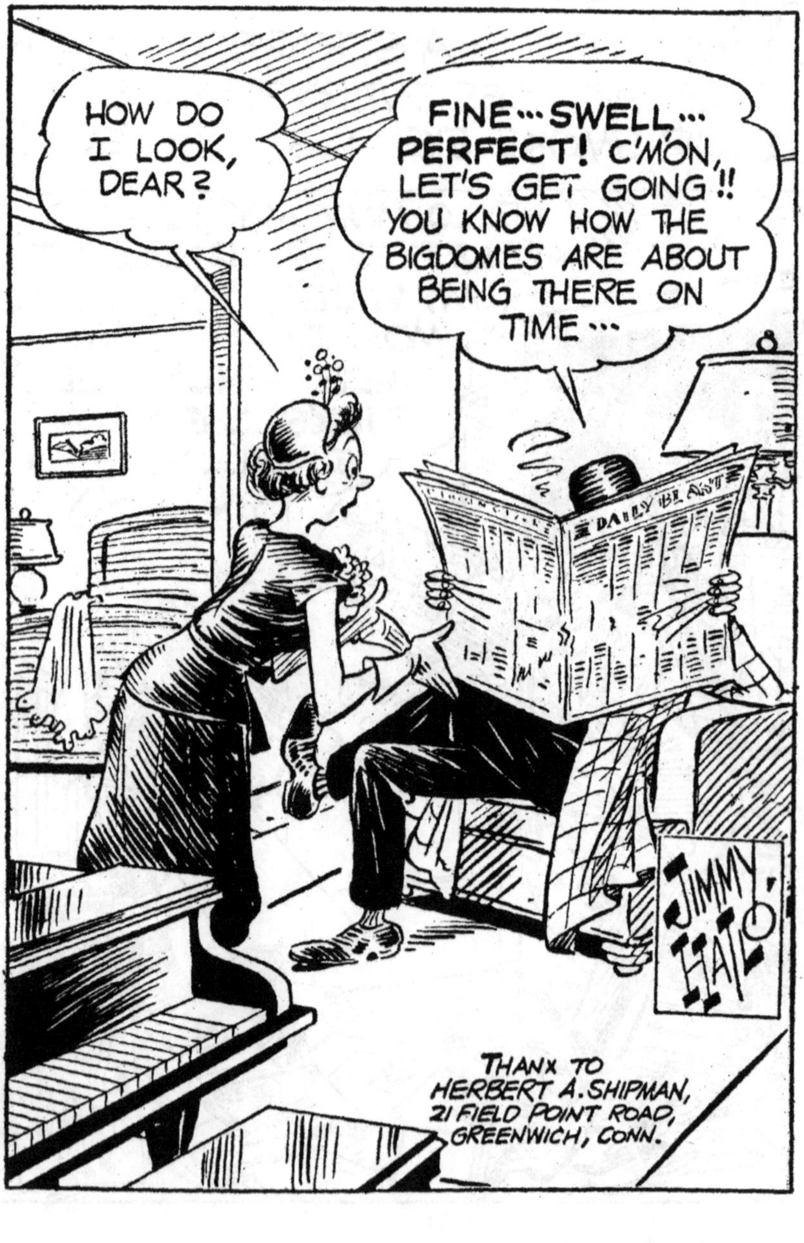
HOW DO I LOOK, DEAR?
FINE... SWELL... PERFECT! C'MON, LET'S GET GOING!! YOU KNOW HOW THE BIGDOMES ARE ABOUT BEING THERE ON TIME...
DAILY BLAST
JIMMY HATLO
THANX TO HERBERT A. SHIPMAN, 21 FIELD POINT ROAD, GREENWICH, CONN.

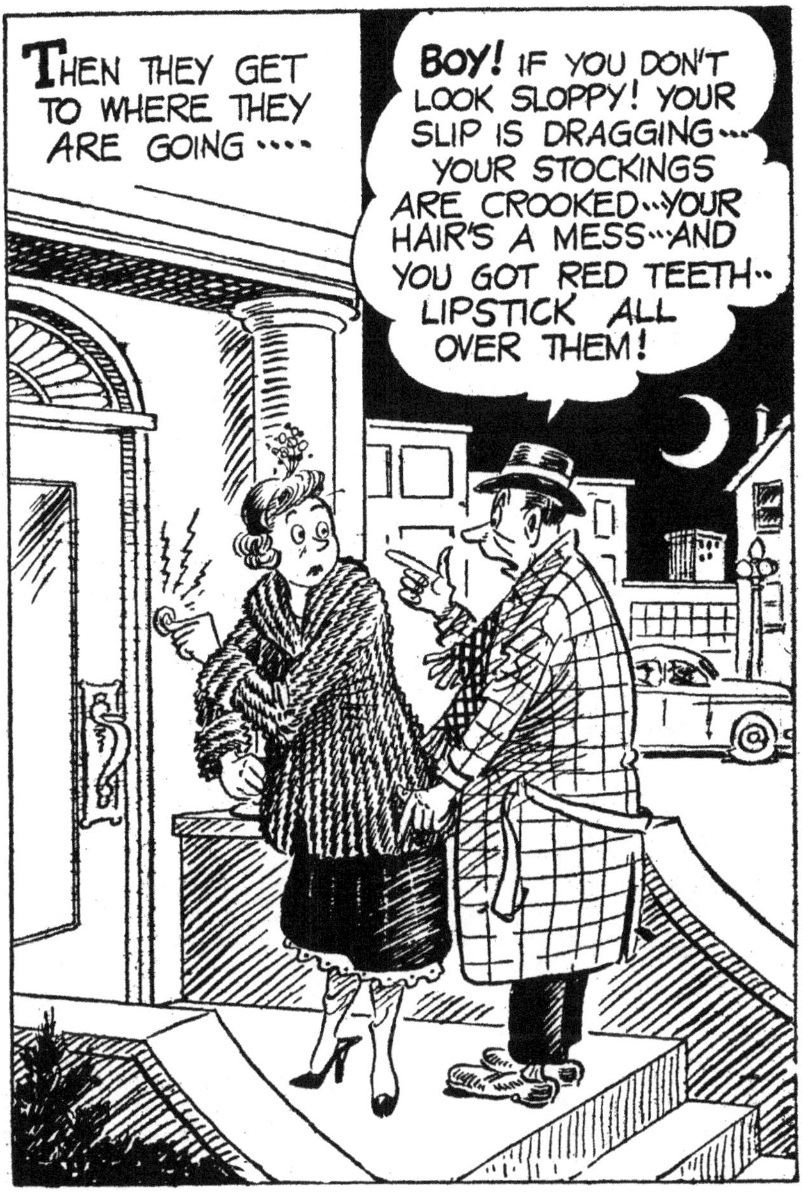
THEN THEY GET TO WHERE THEY ARE GOING....
BOY! IF YOU DON'T LOOK SLOPPY! YOUR SLIP IS DRAGGING... YOUR STOCKINGS ARE CROOKED...YOUR HAIR'S A MESS...AND YOU GOT RED TEETH.. LIPSTICK ALL OVER THEM!

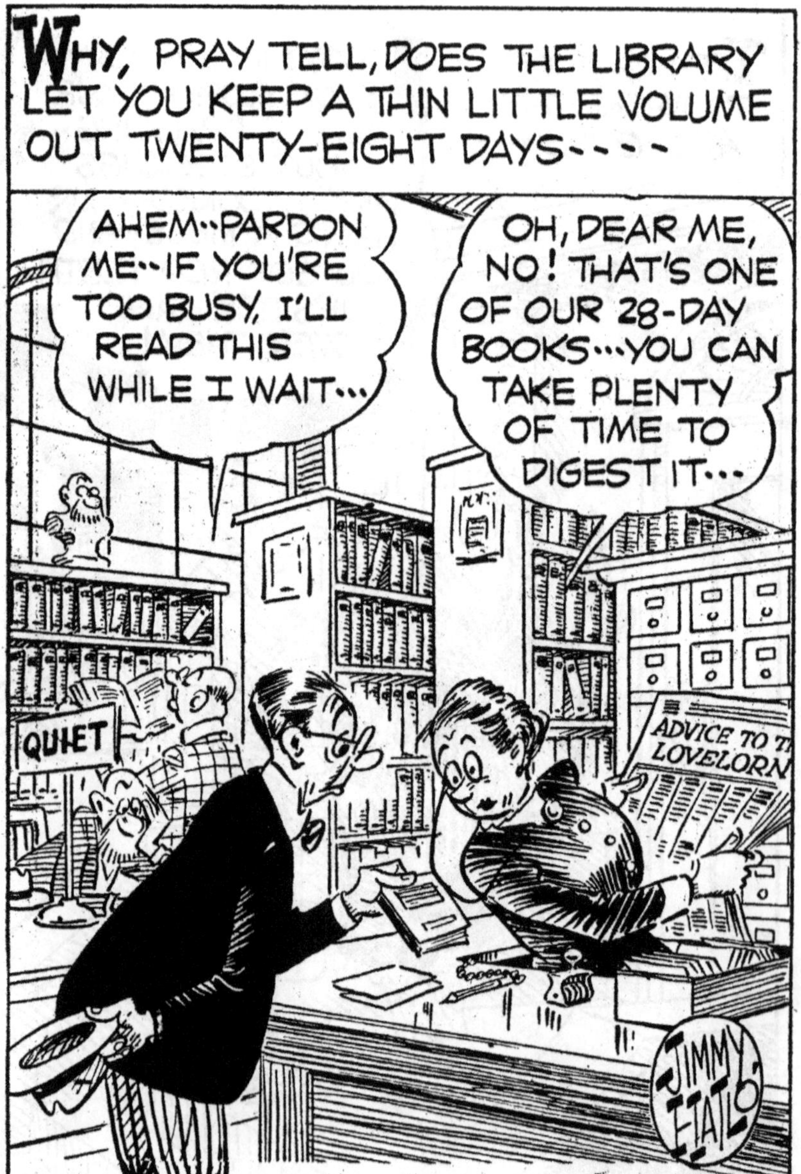
WHY, PRAY TELL, DOES THE LIBRARY LET YOU KEEP A THIN LITTLE VOLUME OUT TWENTY-EIGHT DAYS----
AHEM--PARDON ME--IF YOU'RE TOO BUSY, I'LL READ THIS WHILE I WAIT...
OH, DEAR ME, NO! THAT'S ONE OF OUR 28-DAY BOOKS...YOU CAN TAKE PLENTY OF TIME TO DIGEST IT...
QUIET
ADVICE TO T
LOVELORN
JIMMY HATLO

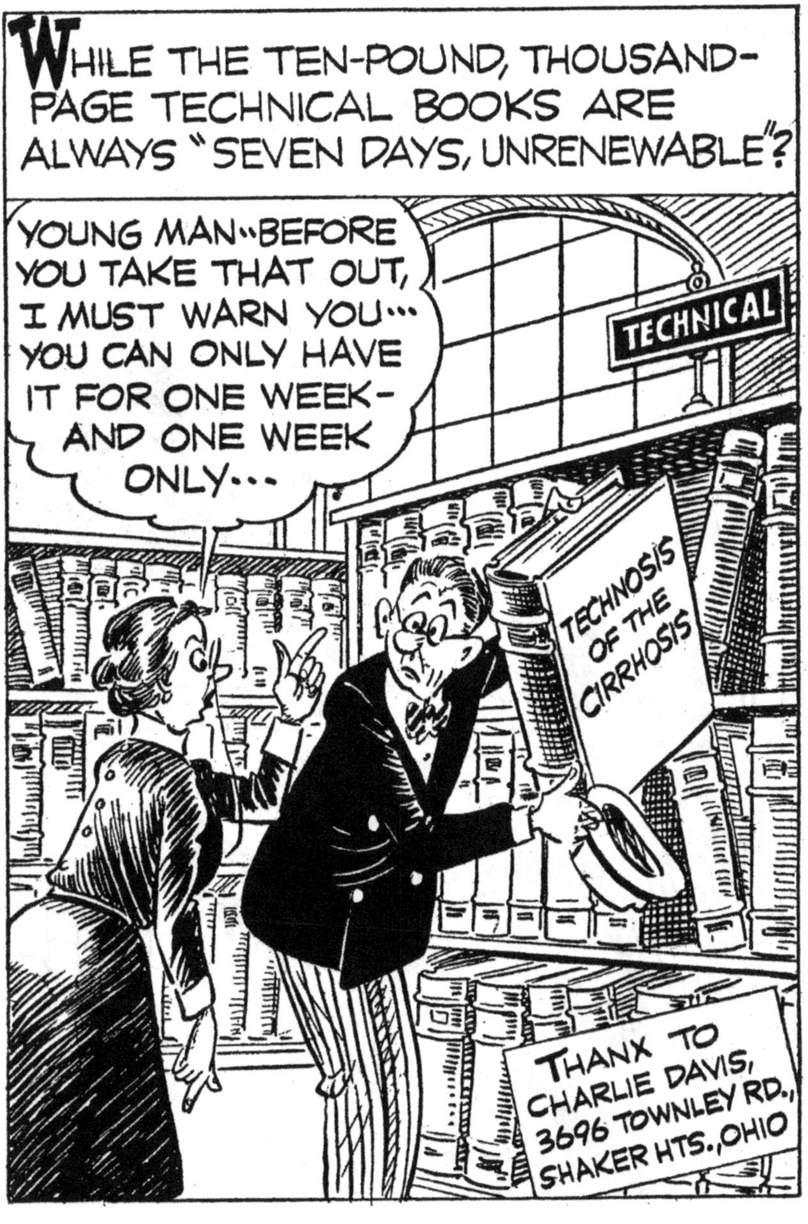
WHILE THE TEN-POUND, THOUSAND-PAGE TECHNICAL BOOKS ARE ALWAYS "SEVEN DAYS, UNRENEWABLE"?
YOUNG MAN.. BEFORE YOU TAKE THAT OUT, I MUST WARN YOU... YOU CAN ONLY HAVE IT FOR ONE WEEK- AND ONE WEEK ONLY...
TECHNICAL
TECHNOSIS OF THE CIRRHOSIS
THANX TO CHARLIE DAVIS, 3696 TOWNLEY RD., SHAKER HTS., OHIO

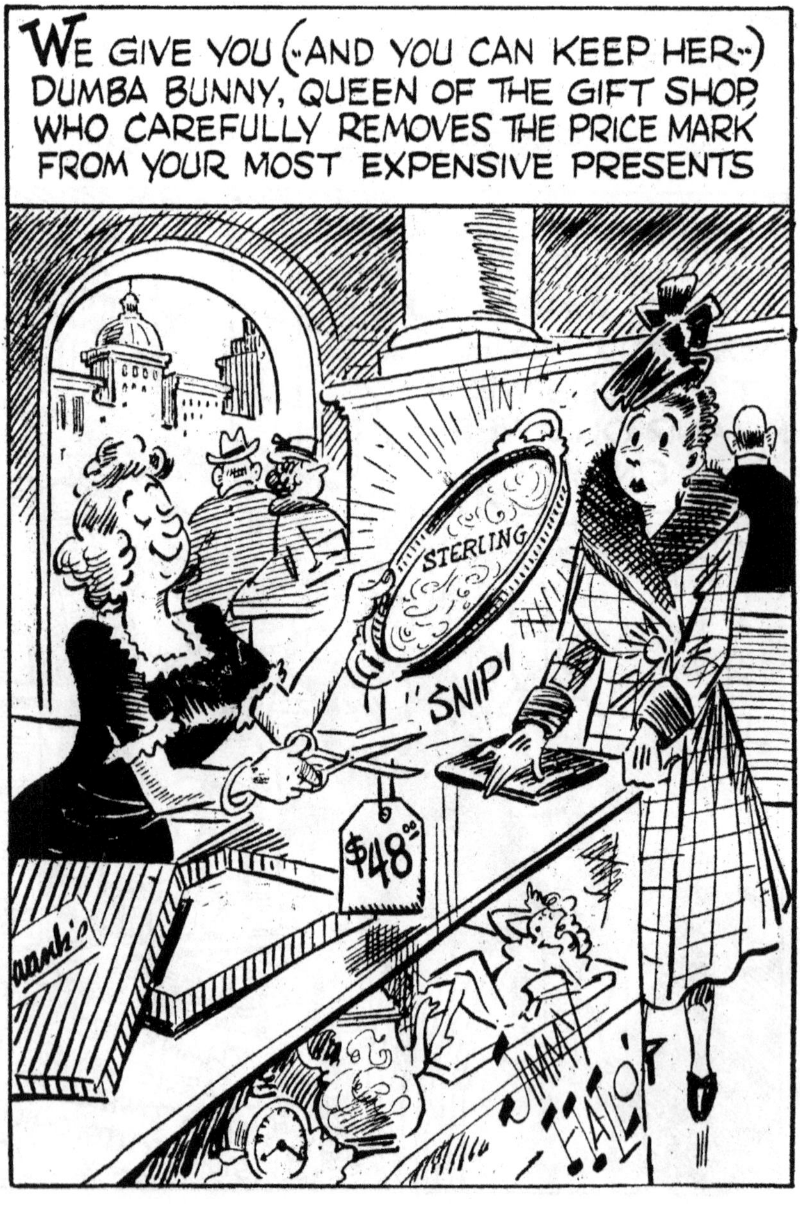
WE GIVE YOU (..AND YOU CAN KEEP HER..) DUMBA BUNNY, QUEEN OF THE GIFT SHOP, WHO CAREFULLY REMOVES THE PRICE MARK FROM YOUR MOST EXPENSIVE PRESENTS
STERLING
SNIP!
$48.00
JIMMY HATLO

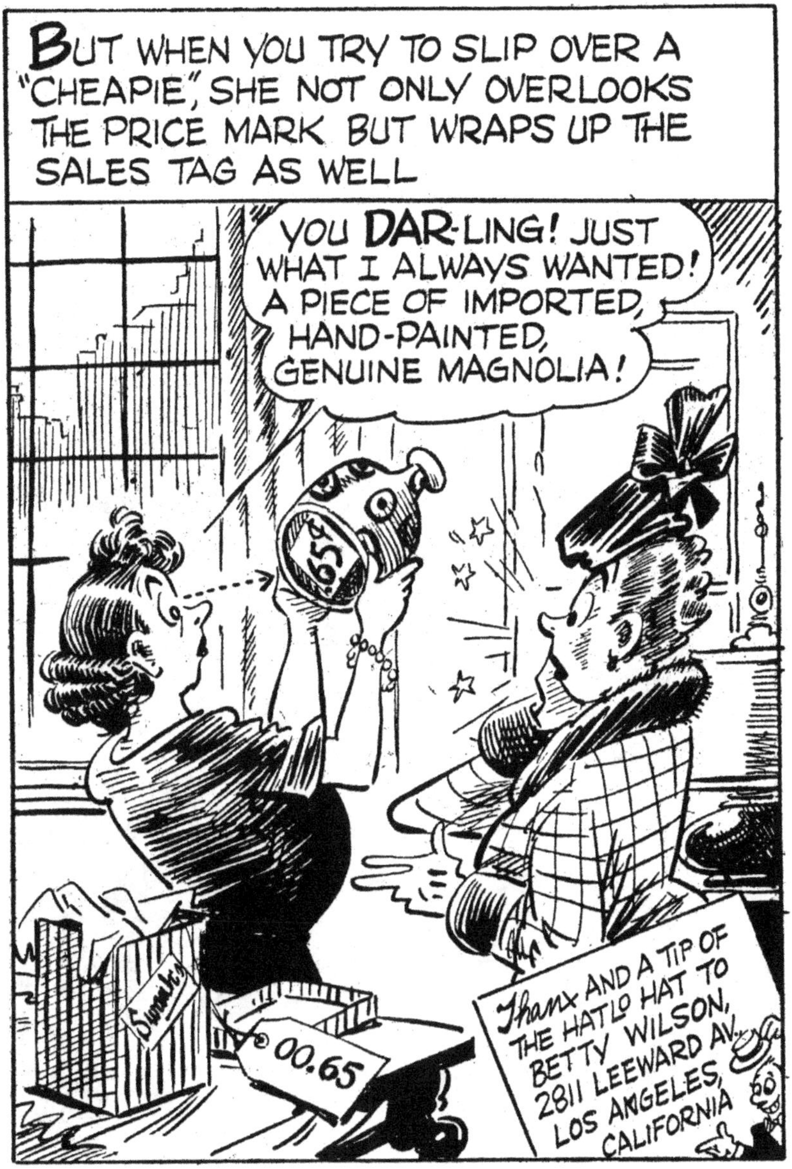
BUT WHEN YOU TRY TO SLIP OVER A "CHEAPIE", SHE NOT ONLY OVERLOOKS THE PRICE MARK BUT WRAPS UP THE SALES TAG AS WELL
YOU DAR-LING! JUST WHAT I ALWAYS WANTED! A PIECE OF IMPORTED, HAND-PAINTED, GENUINE MAGNOLIA!
65¢
00.65
Thanx AND A TIP OF THE HATLO HAT TO BETTY WILSON, 2811 LEEWARD AV., LOS ANGELES, CALIFORNIA

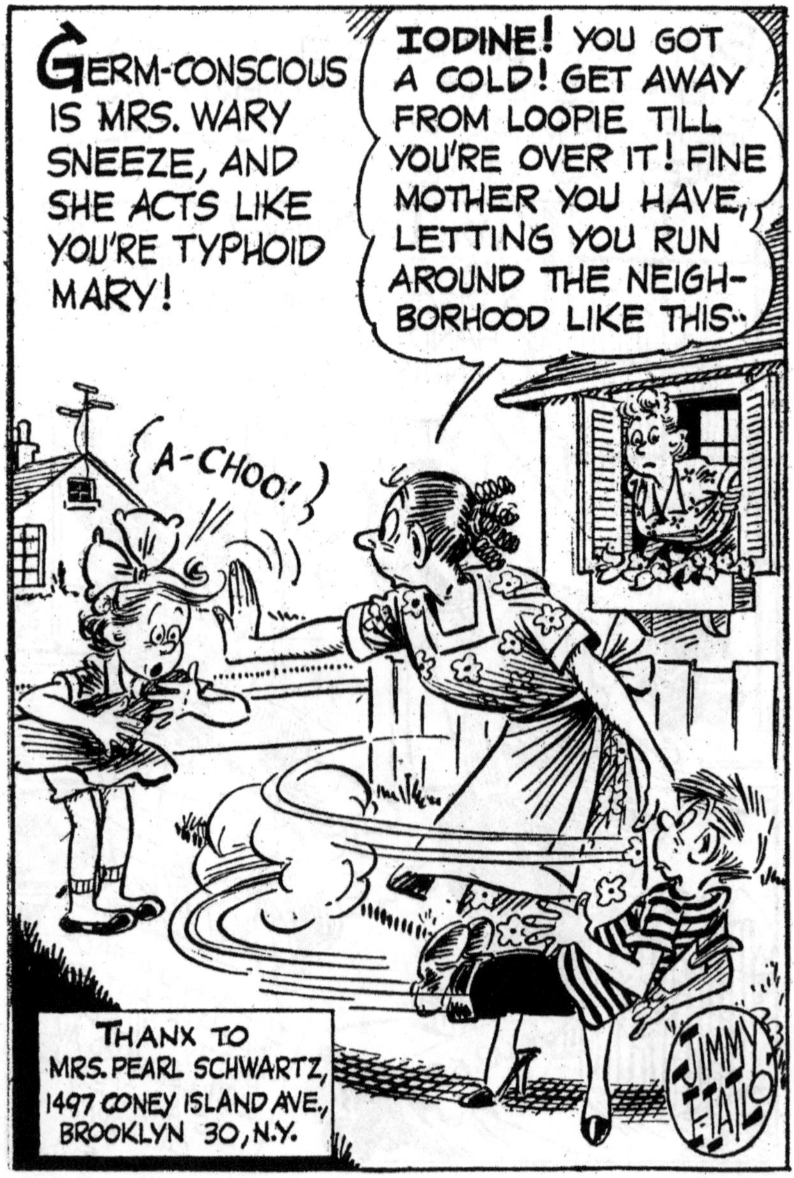
GERM-CONSCIOUS IS MRS. WARY SNEEZE, AND SHE ACTS LIKE YOU'RE TYPHOID MARY!
IODINE! YOU GOT A COLD! GET AWAY FROM LOOPIE TILL YOU'RE OVER IT! FINE MOTHER YOU HAVE, LETTING YOU RUN AROUND THE NEIGH-BORHOOD LIKE THIS..
A-CHOO!
THANX TO MRS. PEARL SCHWARTZ, 1497 CONEY ISLAND AVE., BROOKLYN 30, N.Y.
JIMMY HATLO

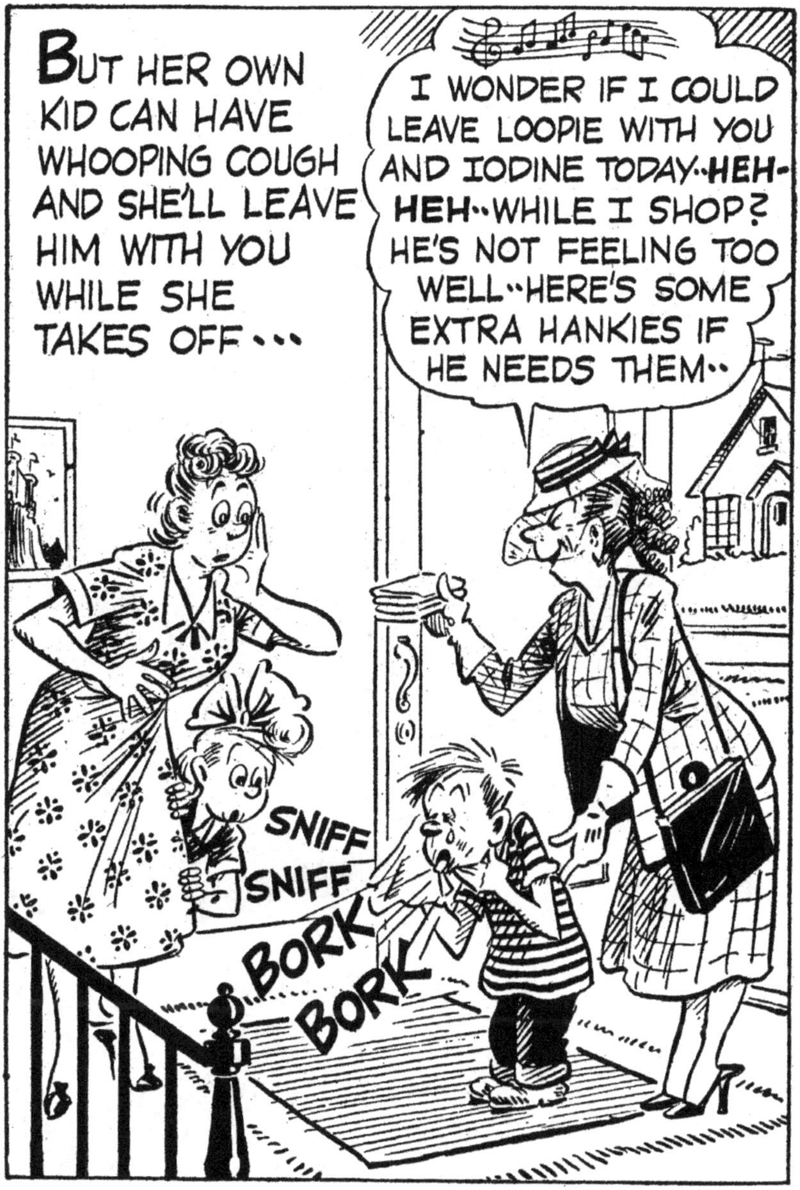
BUT HER OWN KID CAN HAVE WHOOPING COUGH AND SHE'LL LEAVE HIM WITH YOU WHILE SHE TAKES OFF...
I WONDER IF I COULD LEAVE LOOPIE WITH YOU AND IODINE TODAY..HEH-HEH..WHILE I SHOP? HE'S NOT FEELING TOO WELL..HERE'S SOME EXTRA HANKIES IF HE NEEDS THEM..
SNIFF
SNIFF
BORK
BORK

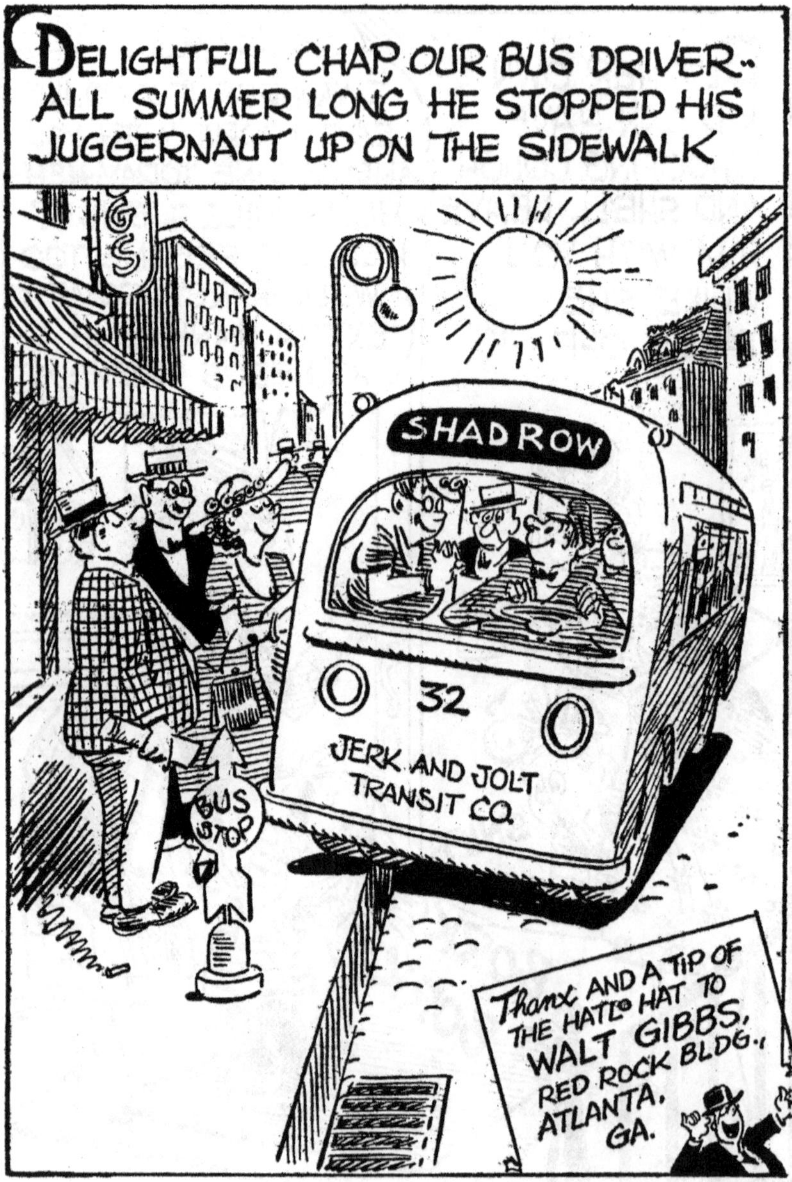
DELIGHTFUL CHAP, OUR BUS DRIVER.. ALL SUMMER LONG HE STOPPED HIS JUGGERNAUT UP ON THE SIDEWALK
SHADROW
32
JERK AND JOLT TRANSIT CO.
BUS STOP
Thanx AND A TIP OF THE HATLO HAT TO WALT GIBBS, RED ROCK BLDG., ATLANTA, GA.

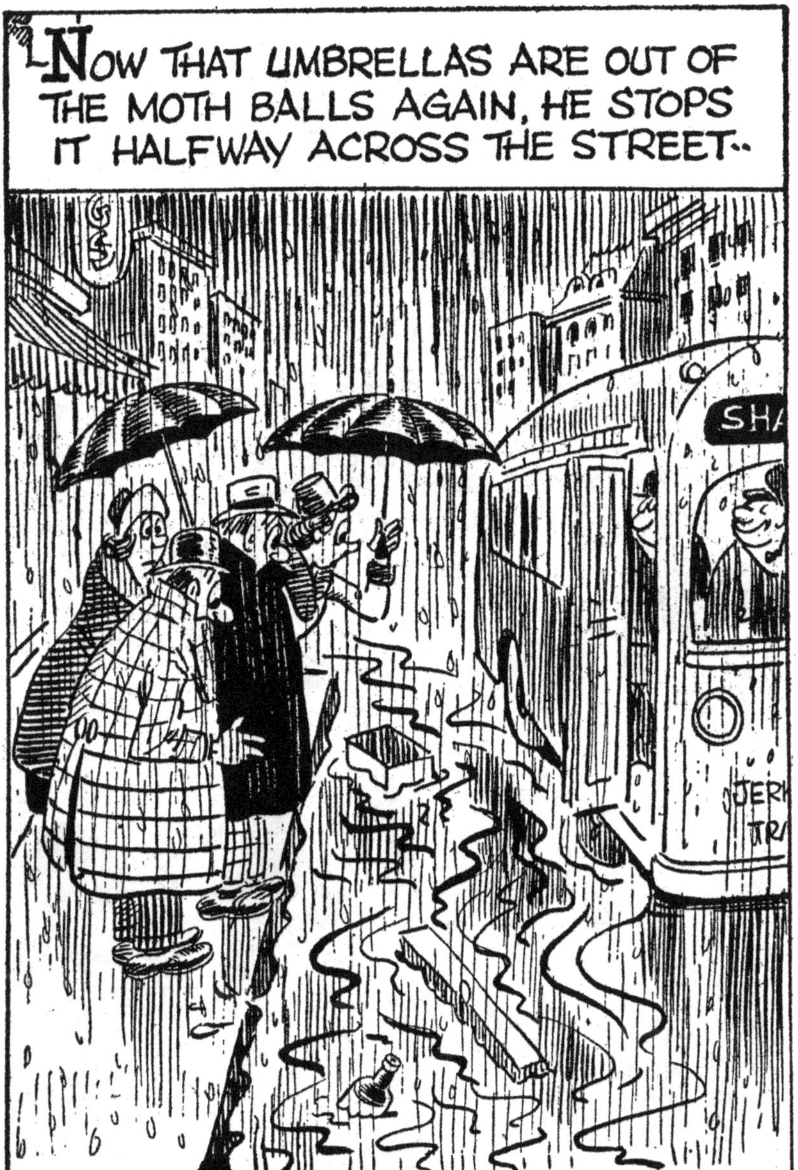
NOW THAT UMBRELLAS ARE OUT OF THE MOTH BALLS AGAIN, HE STOPS IT HALFWAY ACROSS THE STREET--

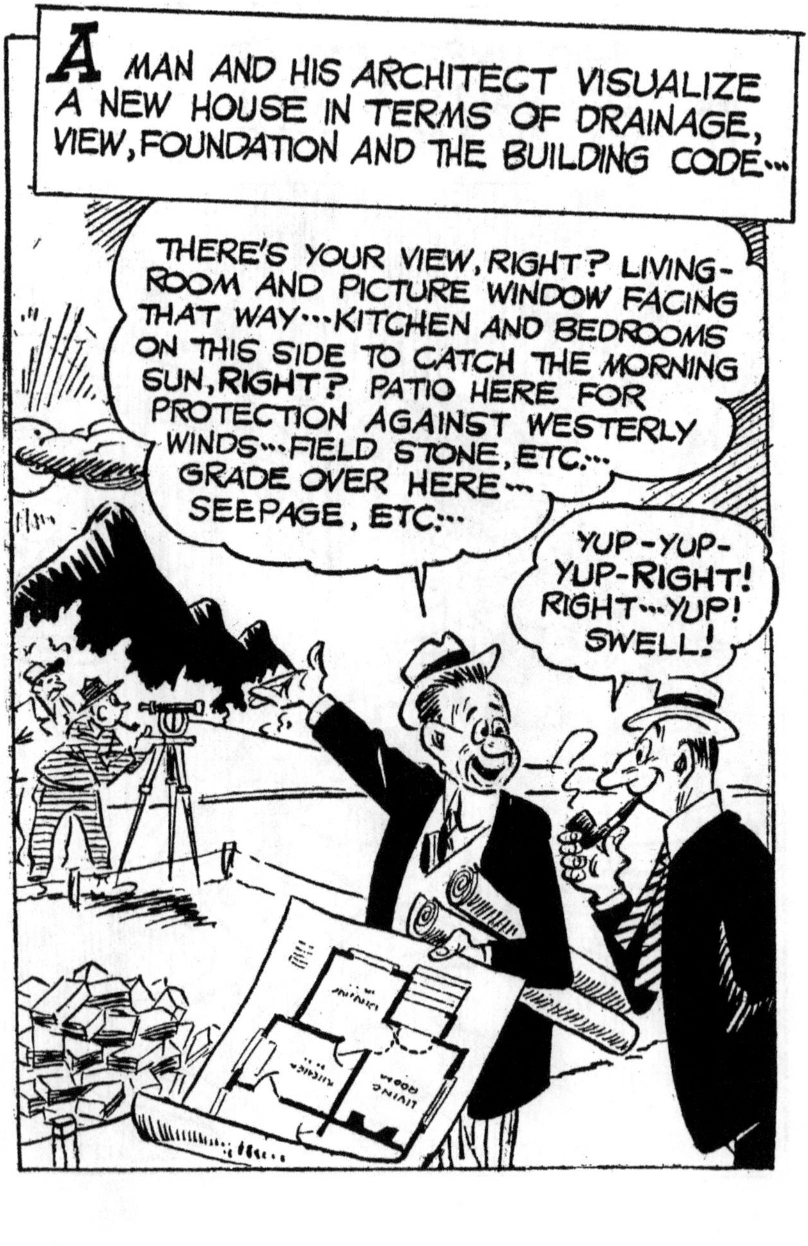
A MAN AND HIS ARCHITECT VISUALIZE A NEW HOUSE IN TERMS OF DRAINAGE, VIEW, FOUNDATION AND THE BUILDING CODE...
THERE'S YOUR VIEW, RIGHT? LIVING-ROOM AND PICTURE WINDOW FACING THAT WAY...KITCHEN AND BEDROOMS ON THIS SIDE TO CATCH THE MORNING SUN, RIGHT? PATIO HERE FOR PROTECTION AGAINST WESTERLY WINDS...FIELD STONE, ETC... GRADE OVER HERE... SEEPAGE, ETC...
YUP-YUP-YUP-RIGHT! RIGHT...YUP! SWELL!

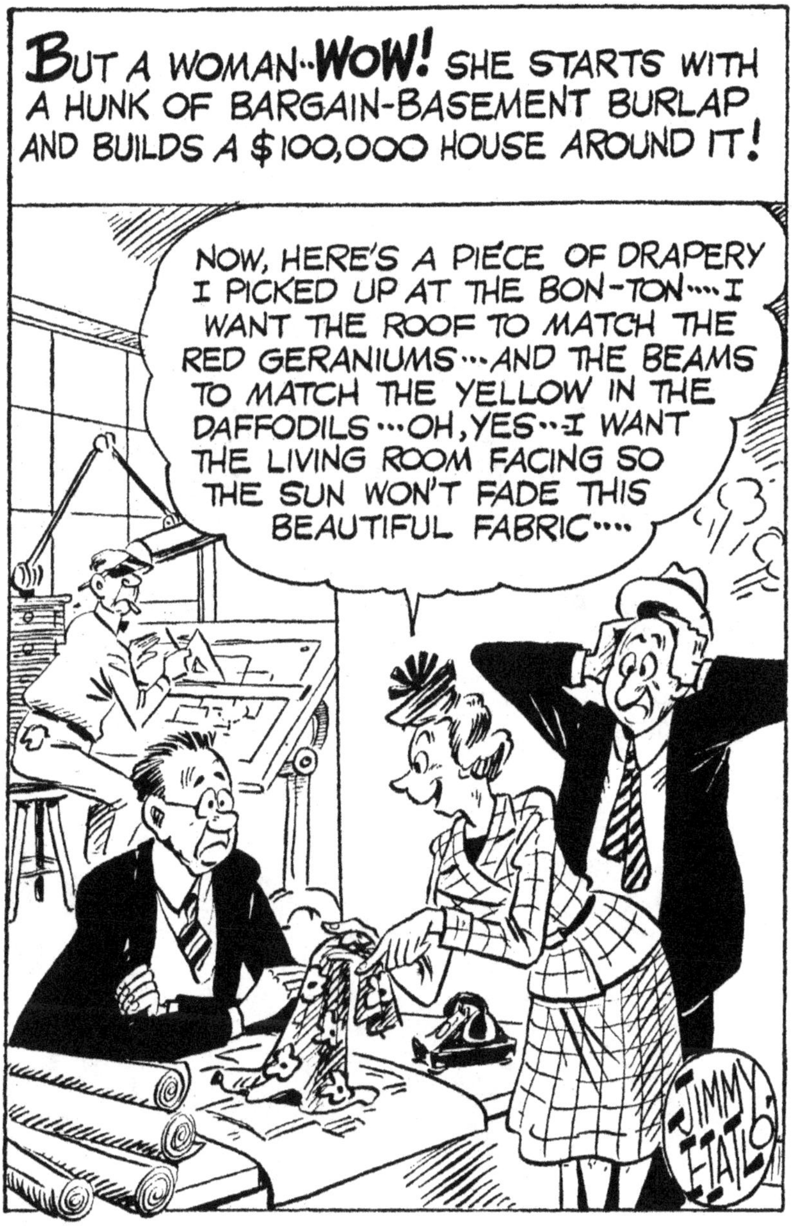
BUT A WOMAN..WOW! SHE STARTS WITH A HUNK OF BARGAIN-BASEMENT BURLAP AND BUILDS A $100,000 HOUSE AROUND IT!
NOW, HERE'S A PIECE OF DRAPERY I PICKED UP AT THE BON-TON....I WANT THE ROOF TO MATCH THE RED GERANIUMS...AND THE BEAMS TO MATCH THE YELLOW IN THE DAFFODILS...OH, YES..I WANT THE LIVING ROOM FACING SO THE SUN WON'T FADE THIS BEAUTIFUL FABRIC....
JIMMY HATLO

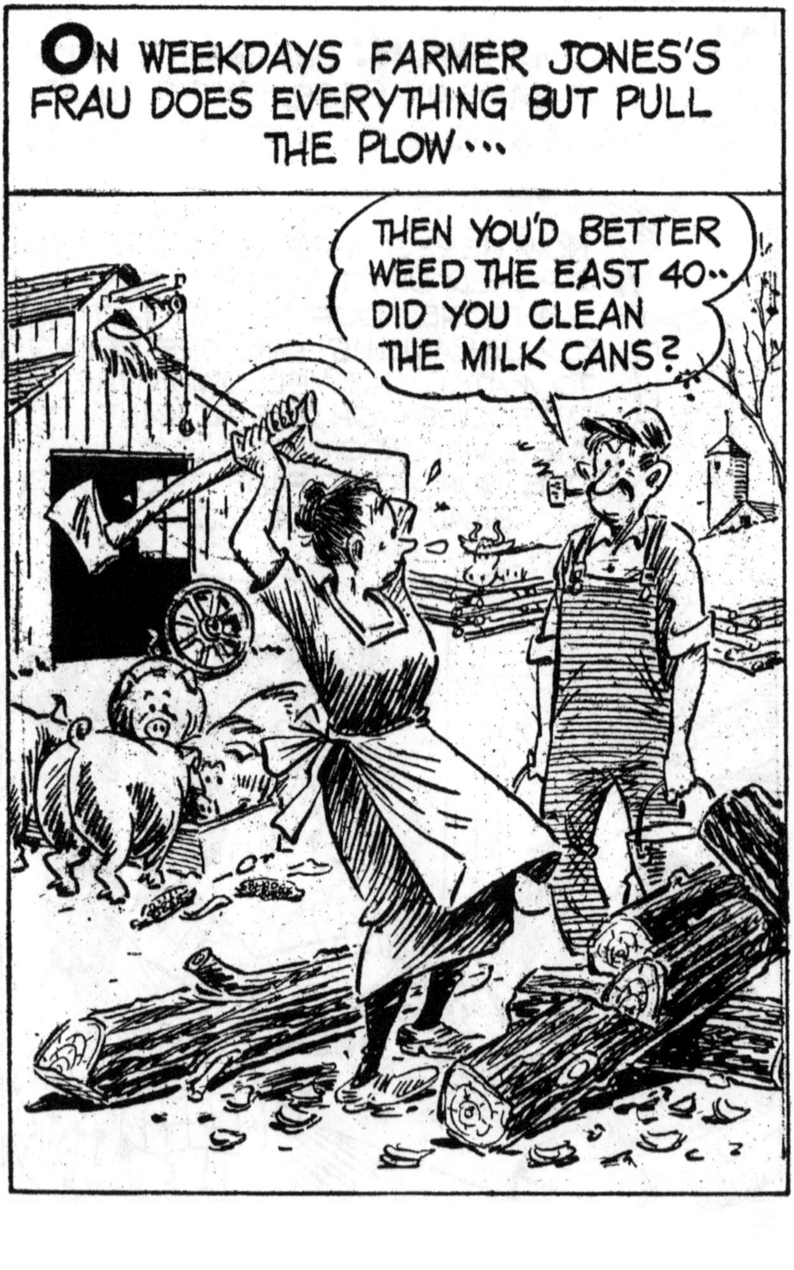
ON WEEKDAYS FARMER JONES'S FRAU DOES EVERYTHING BUT PULL THE PLOW...
THEN YOU'D BETTER WEED THE EAST 40.. DID YOU CLEAN THE MILK CANS?

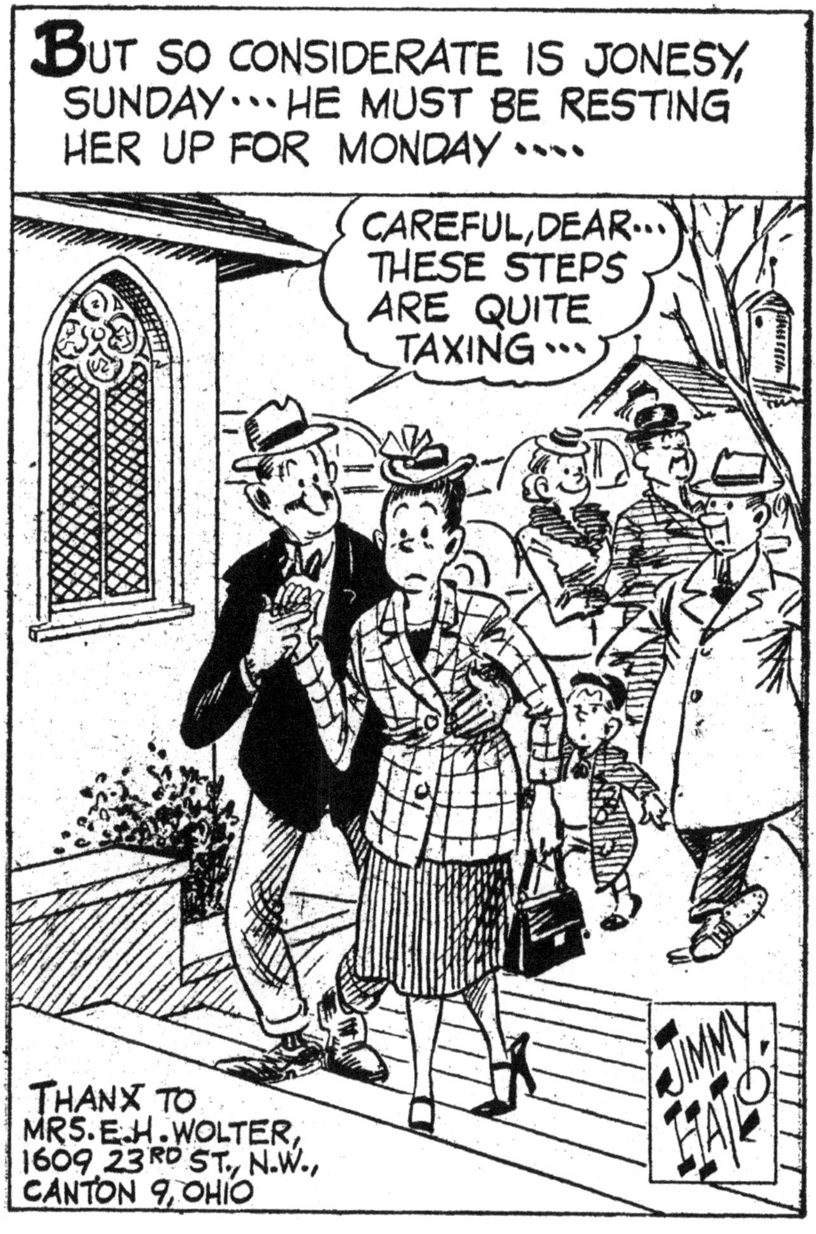
BUT SO CONSIDERATE IS JONESY, SUNDAY··· HE MUST BE RESTING HER UP FOR MONDAY····
CAREFUL, DEAR··· THESE STEPS ARE QUITE TAXING···
THANX TO MRS. E.H. WOLTER, 1609 23RD ST., N.W., CANTON 9, OHIO
JIMMY HATLO

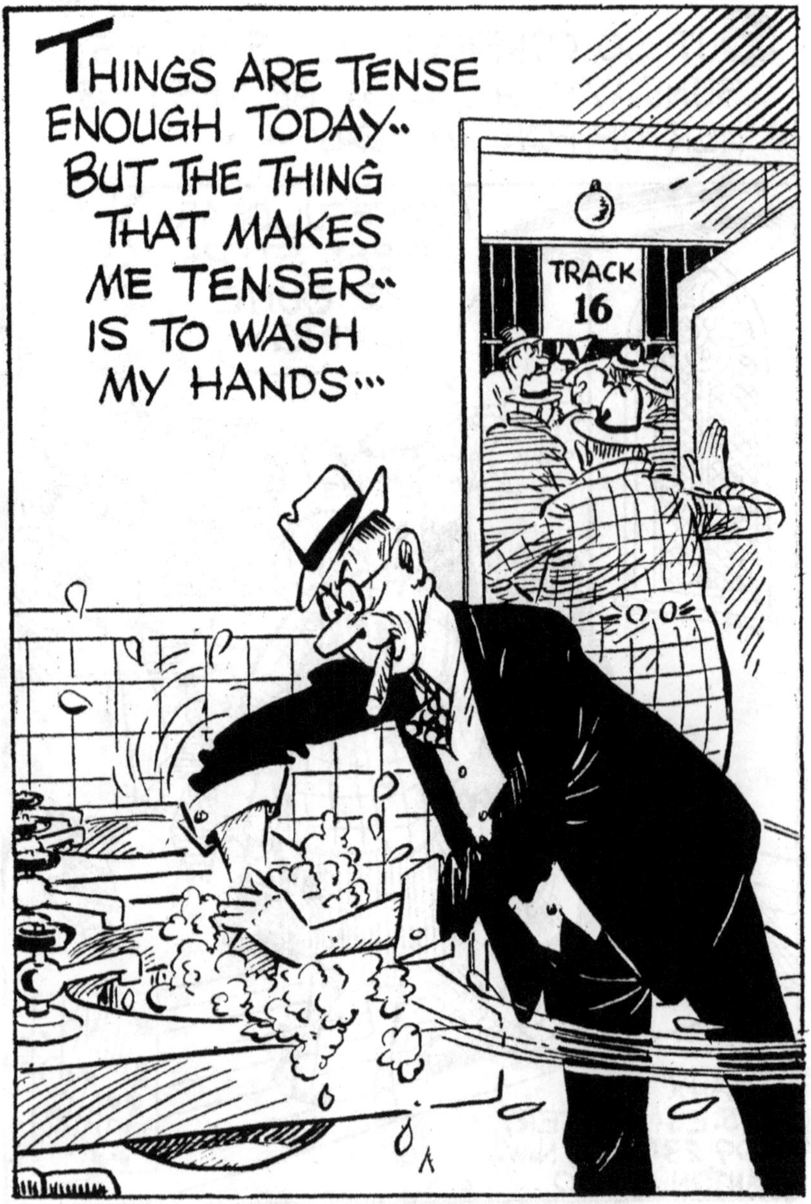

THINGS ARE TENSE ENOUGH TODAY.. BUT THE THING THAT MAKES ME TENSER.. IS TO WASH MY HANDS...
TRACK 16

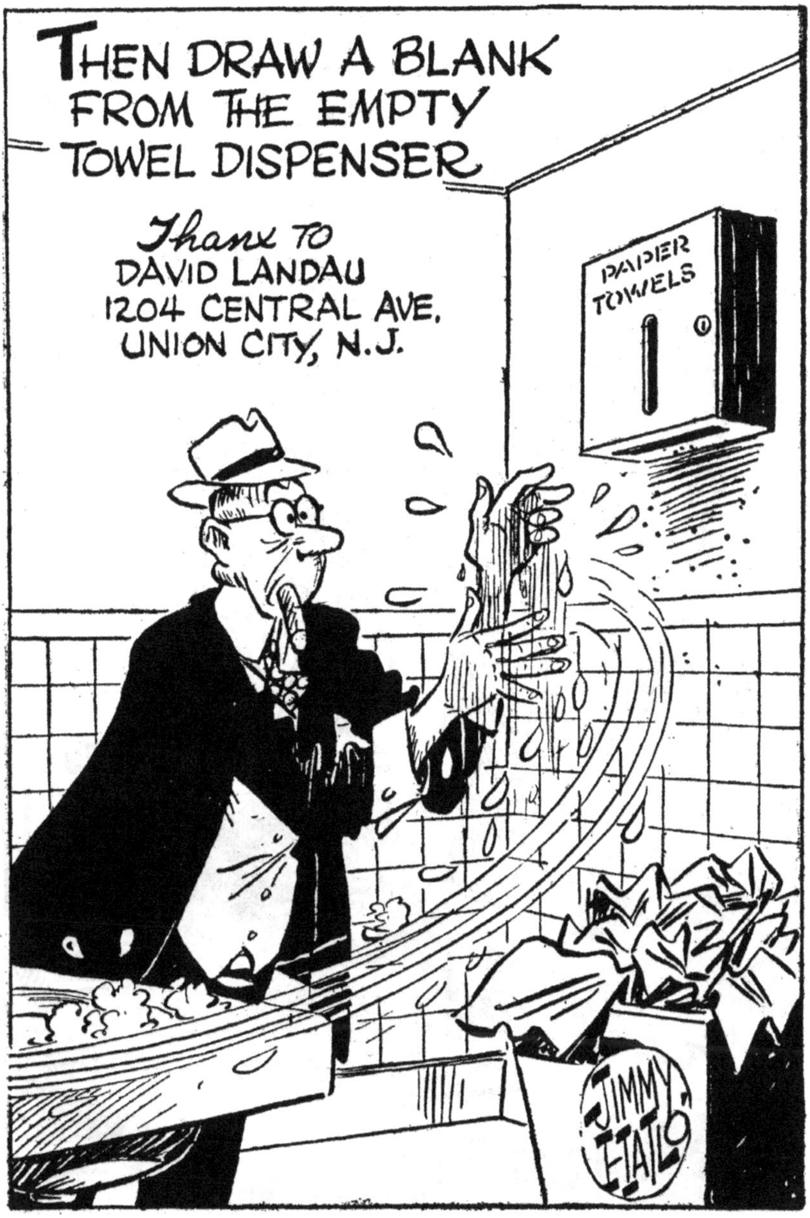
THEN DRAW A BLANK FROM THE EMPTY TOWEL DISPENSER
Thanx TO DAVID LANDAU 1204 CENTRAL AVE. UNION CITY, N.J.
PAPER TOWELS
JIMMY HATLO

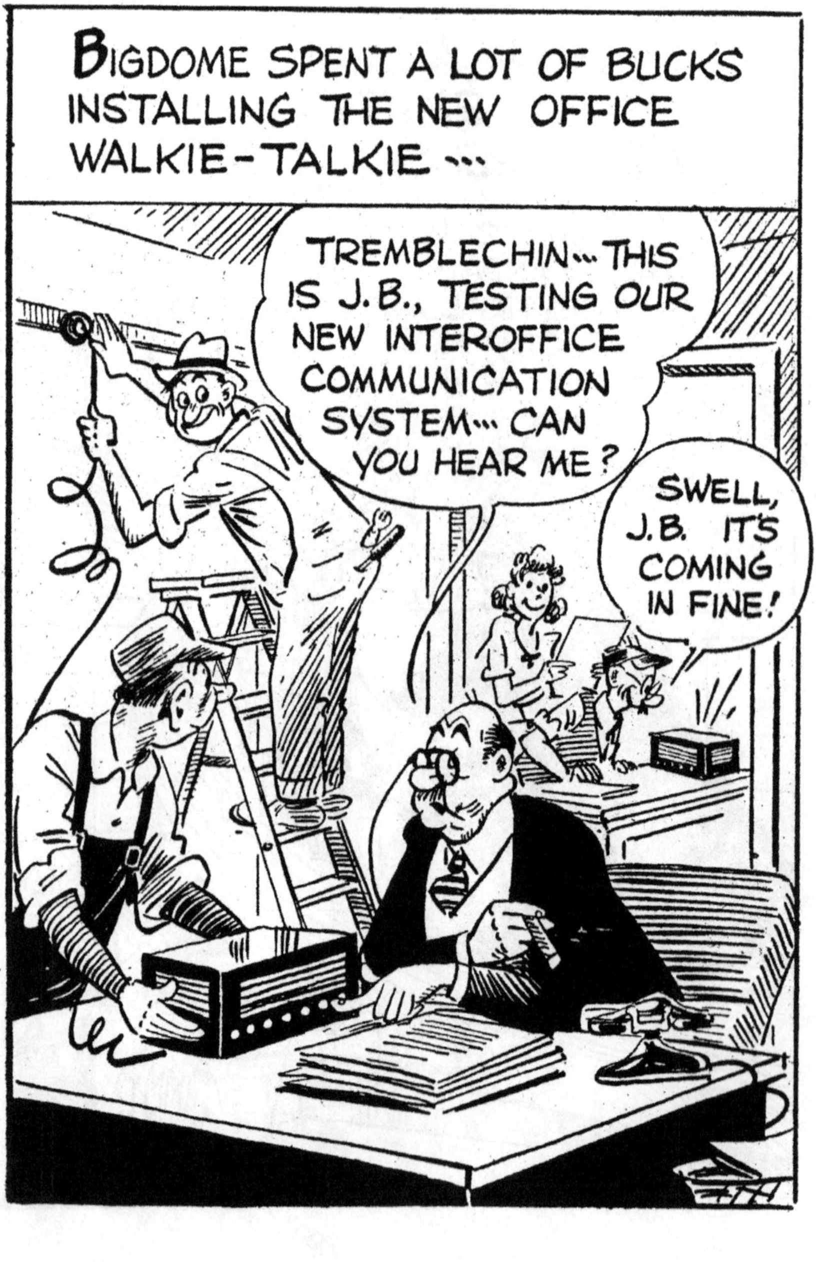
BIGDOME SPENT A LOT OF BUCKS INSTALLING THE NEW OFFICE WALKIE-TALKIE ...
TREMBLECHIN ... THIS IS J.B., TESTING OUR NEW INTEROFFICE COMMUNICATION SYSTEM ... CAN YOU HEAR ME?
SWELL, J.B. IT'S COMING IN FINE!

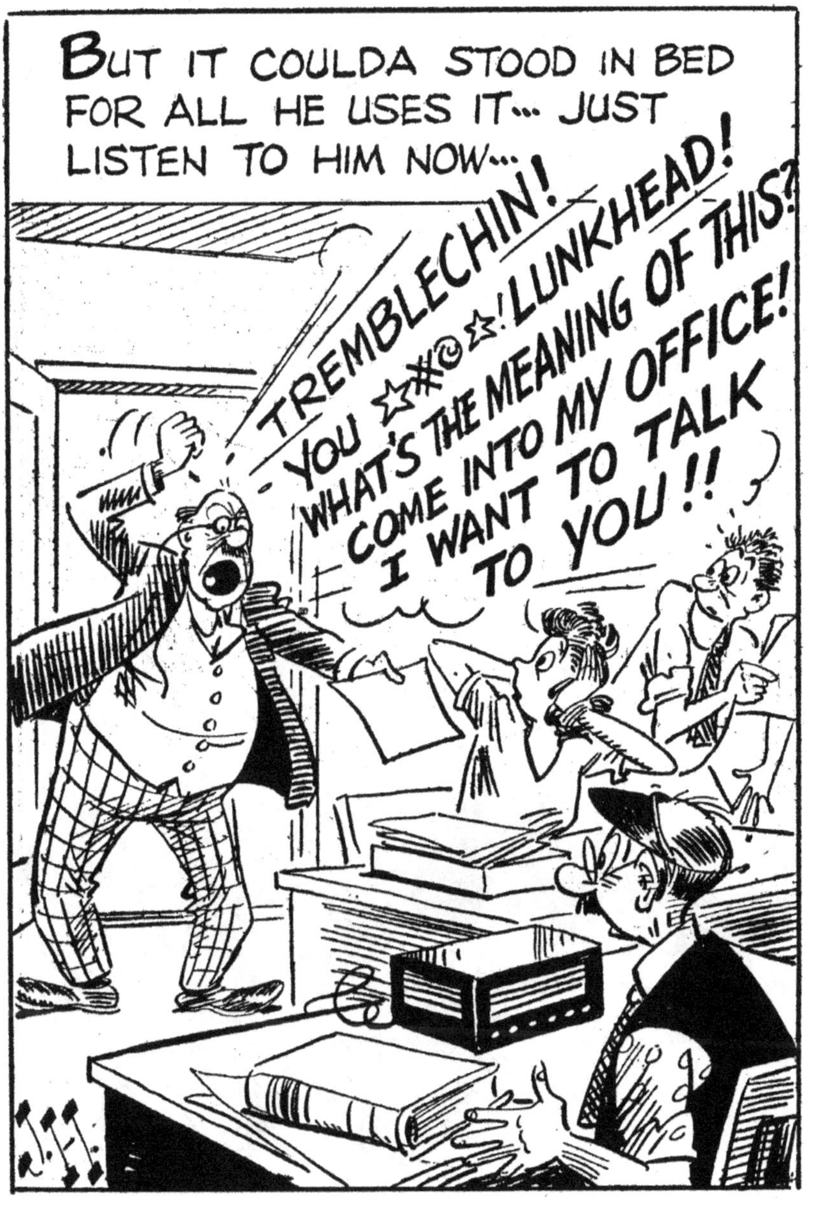
BUT IT COULDA STOOD IN BED FOR ALL HE USES IT... JUST LISTEN TO HIM NOW...
TREMBLECHIN! YOU ☆#@☆! LUNKHEAD! WHAT'S THE MEANING OF THIS? COME INTO MY OFFICE! I WANT TO TALK TO YOU!!

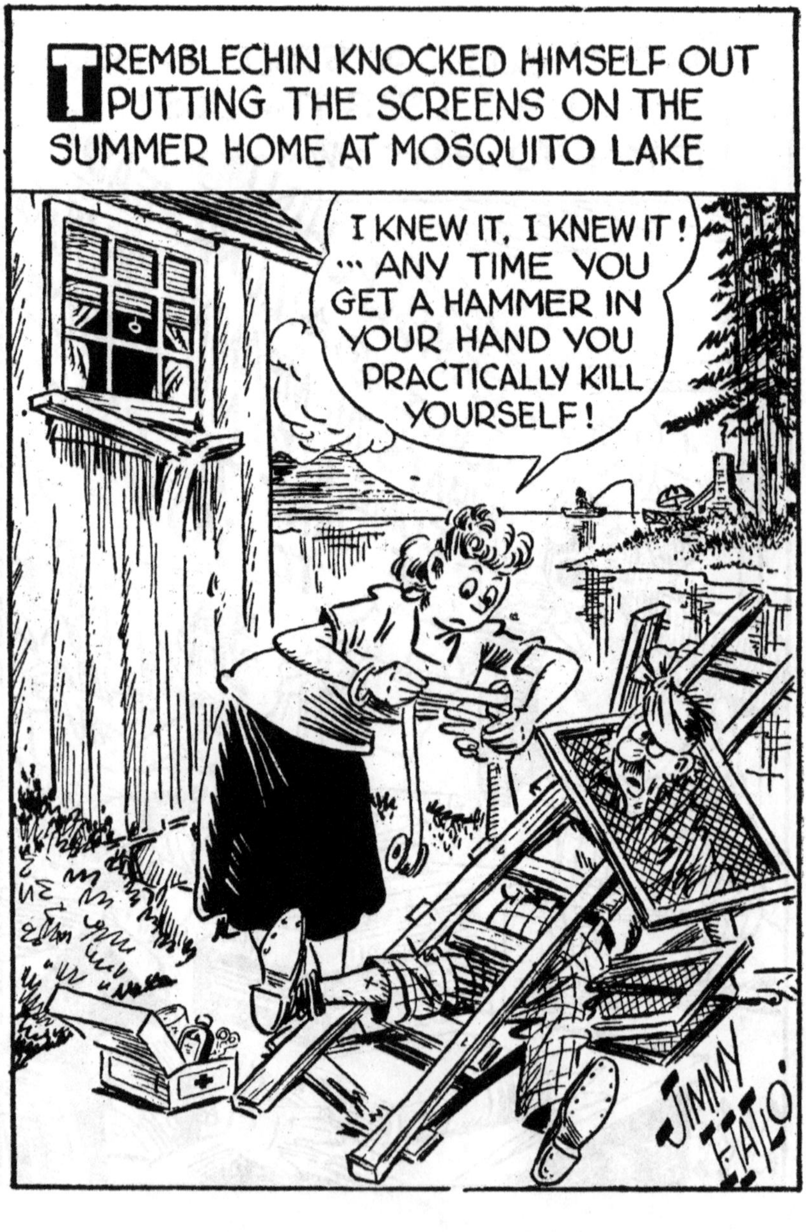
TREMBLECHIN KNOCKED HIMSELF OUT PUTTING THE SCREENS ON THE SUMMER HOME AT MOSQUITO LAKE
I KNEW IT, I KNEW IT! ... ANY TIME YOU GET A HAMMER IN YOUR HAND YOU PRACTICALLY KILL YOURSELF!
JIMMY HATLO

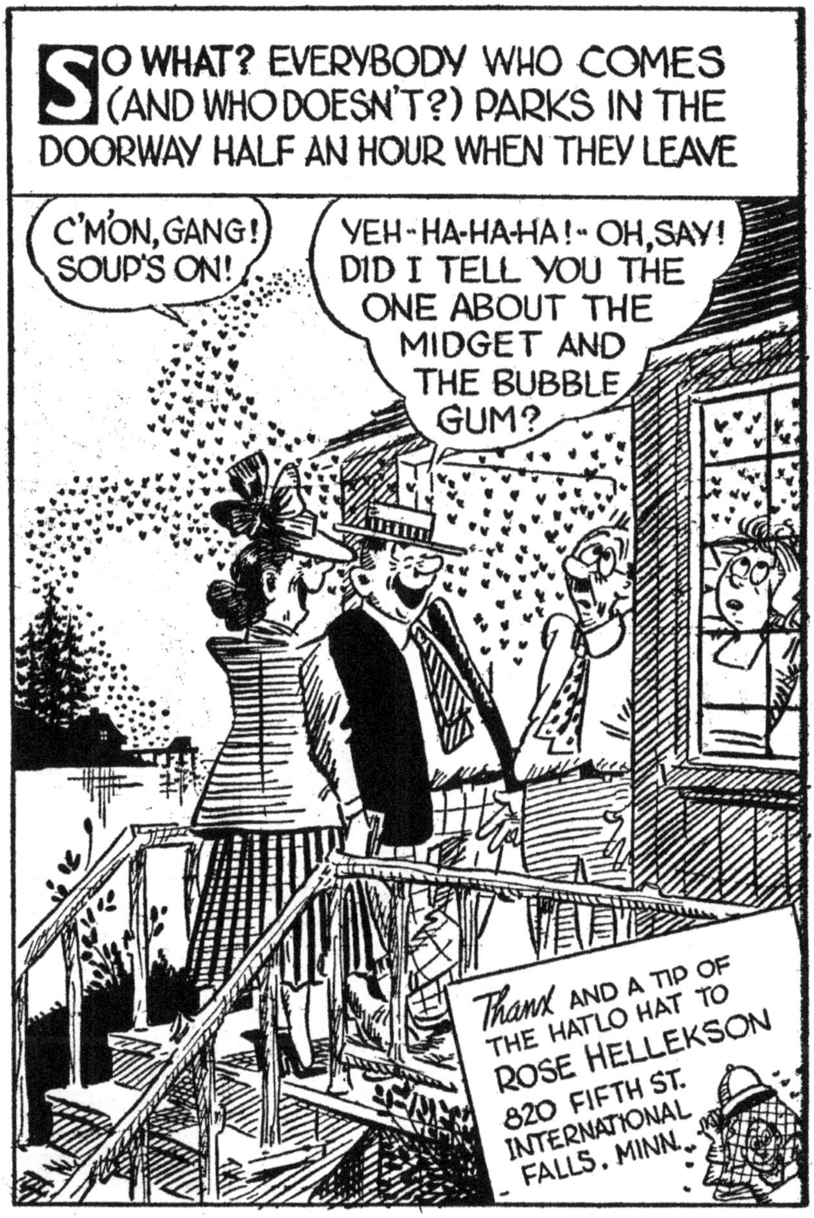
SO WHAT? EVERYBODY WHO COMES (AND WHO DOESN'T?) PARKS IN THE DOORWAY HALF AN HOUR WHEN THEY LEAVE
C'M'ON, GANG! SOUP'S ON!
YEH-HA-HA-HA!- OH, SAY! DID I TELL YOU THE ONE ABOUT THE MIDGET AND THE BUBBLE GUM?
Thanx AND A TIP OF THE HATLO HAT TO ROSE HELLEKSON 820 FIFTH ST. INTERNATIONAL FALLS. MINN.

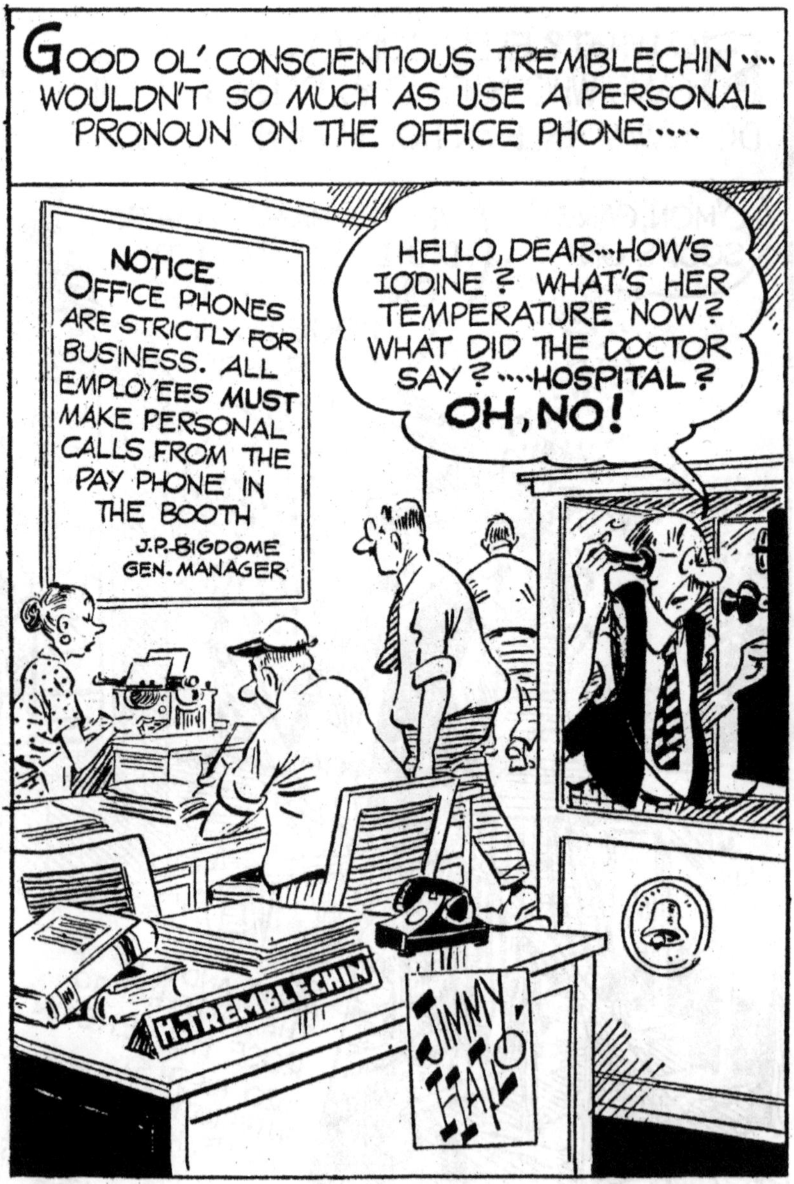
GOOD OL' CONSCIENTIOUS TREMBLECHIN.... WOULDN'T SO MUCH AS USE A PERSONAL PRONOUN ON THE OFFICE PHONE....
NOTICE
OFFICE PHONES ARE STRICTLY FOR BUSINESS. ALL EMPLOYEES MUST MAKE PERSONAL CALLS FROM THE PAY PHONE IN THE BOOTH
J.P. BIGDOME
GEN. MANAGER
HELLO, DEAR...HOW'S IODINE? WHAT'S HER TEMPERATURE NOW? WHAT DID THE DOCTOR SAY?....HOSPITAL? OH, NO!
H.TREMBLECHIN
JIMMY HATLO

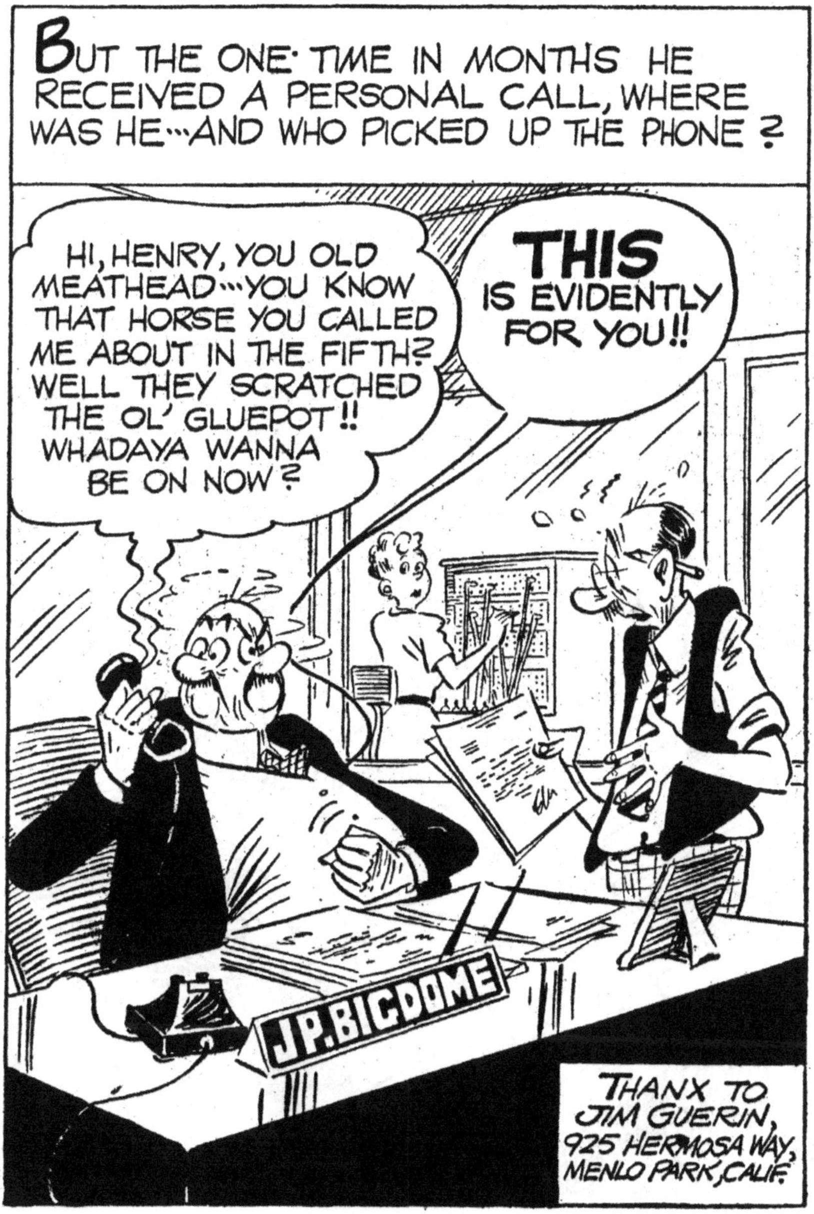
BUT THE ONE TIME IN MONTHS HE RECEIVED A PERSONAL CALL, WHERE WAS HE···AND WHO PICKED UP THE PHONE?
HI, HENRY, YOU OLD MEATHEAD···YOU KNOW THAT HORSE YOU CALLED ME ABOUT IN THE FIFTH? WELL THEY SCRATCHED THE OL' GLUEPOT!! WHADAYA WANNA BE ON NOW?
THIS IS EVIDENTLY FOR YOU!!
J.P. BIGDOME
THANX TO JIM GUERIN, 925 HERMOSA WAY, MENLO PARK, CALIF.

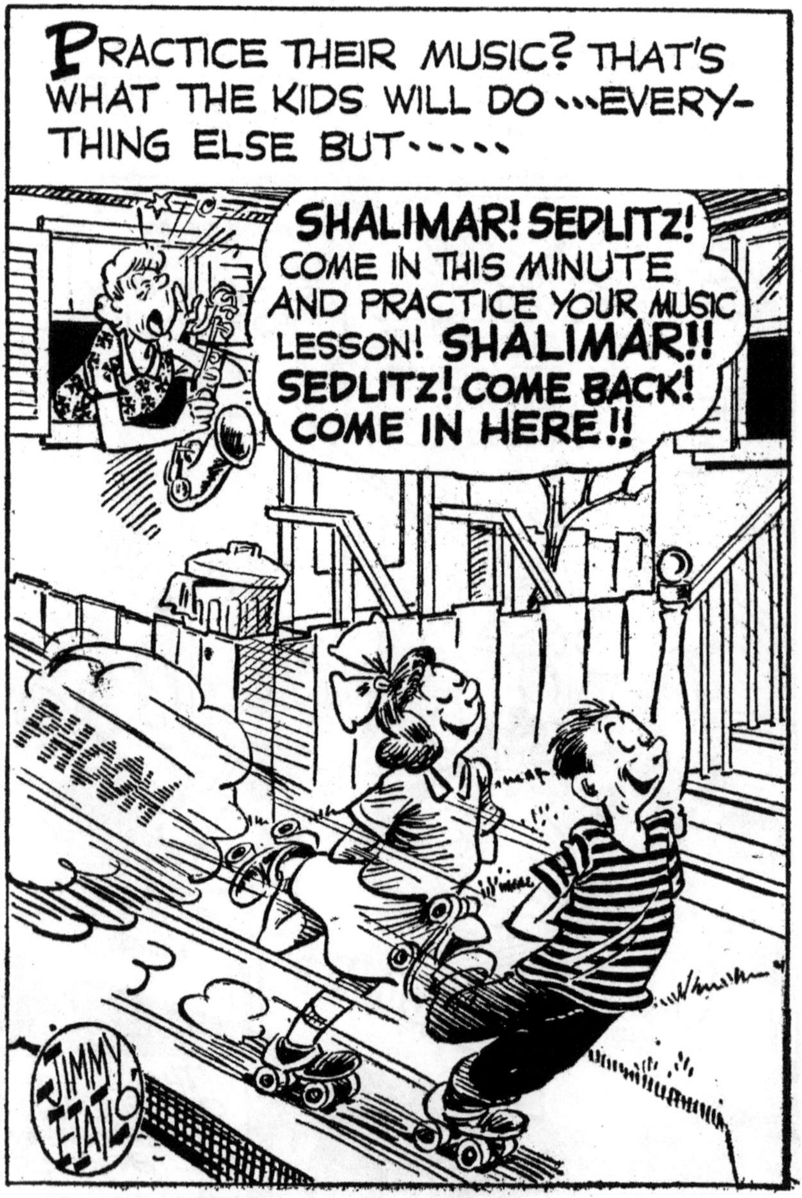
PRACTICE THEIR MUSIC? THAT'S WHAT THE KIDS WILL DO ... EVERYTHING ELSE BUT .....
SHALIMAR! SEDLITZ! COME IN THIS MINUTE AND PRACTICE YOUR MUSIC LESSON! SHALIMAR!! SEDLITZ! COME BACK! COME IN HERE!!

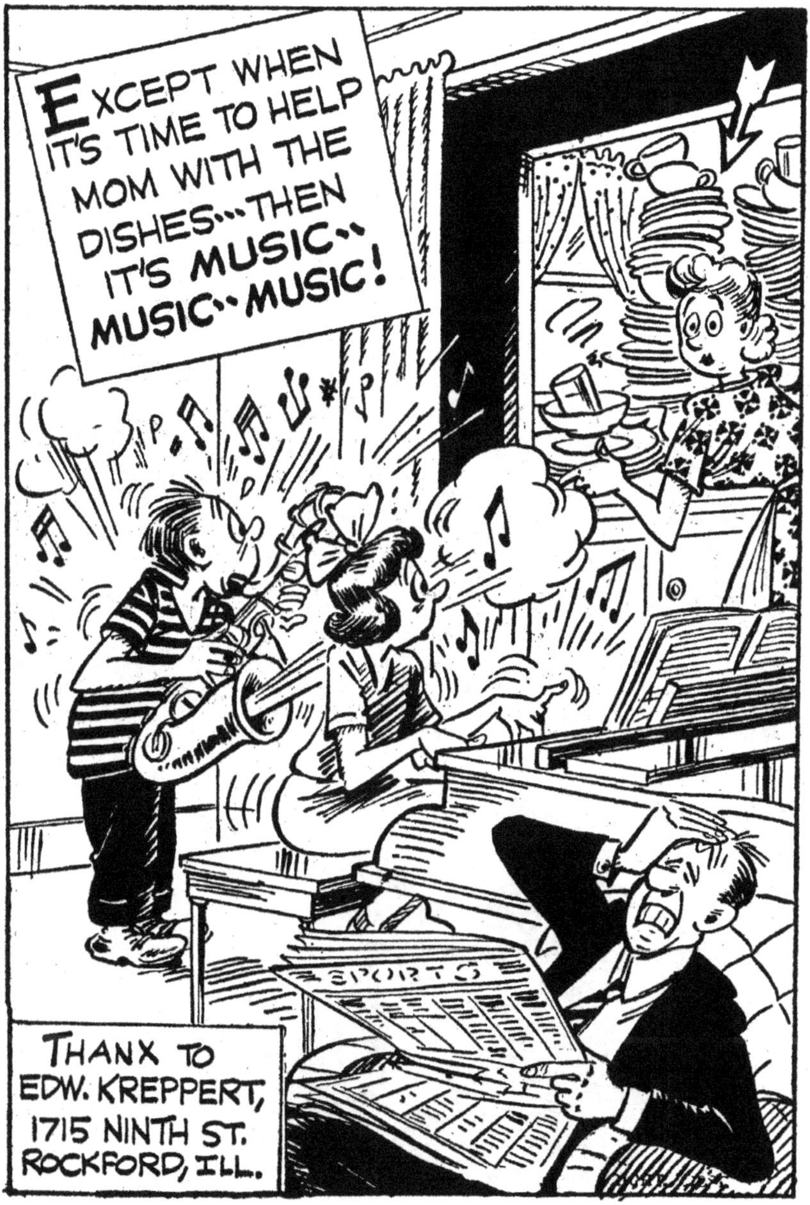
EXCEPT WHEN IT'S TIME TO HELP MOM WITH THE DISHES...THEN IT'S MUSIC.. MUSIC.. MUSIC!
SPORTS
THANX TO EDW. KREPPERT, 1715 NINTH ST. ROCKFORD, ILL.

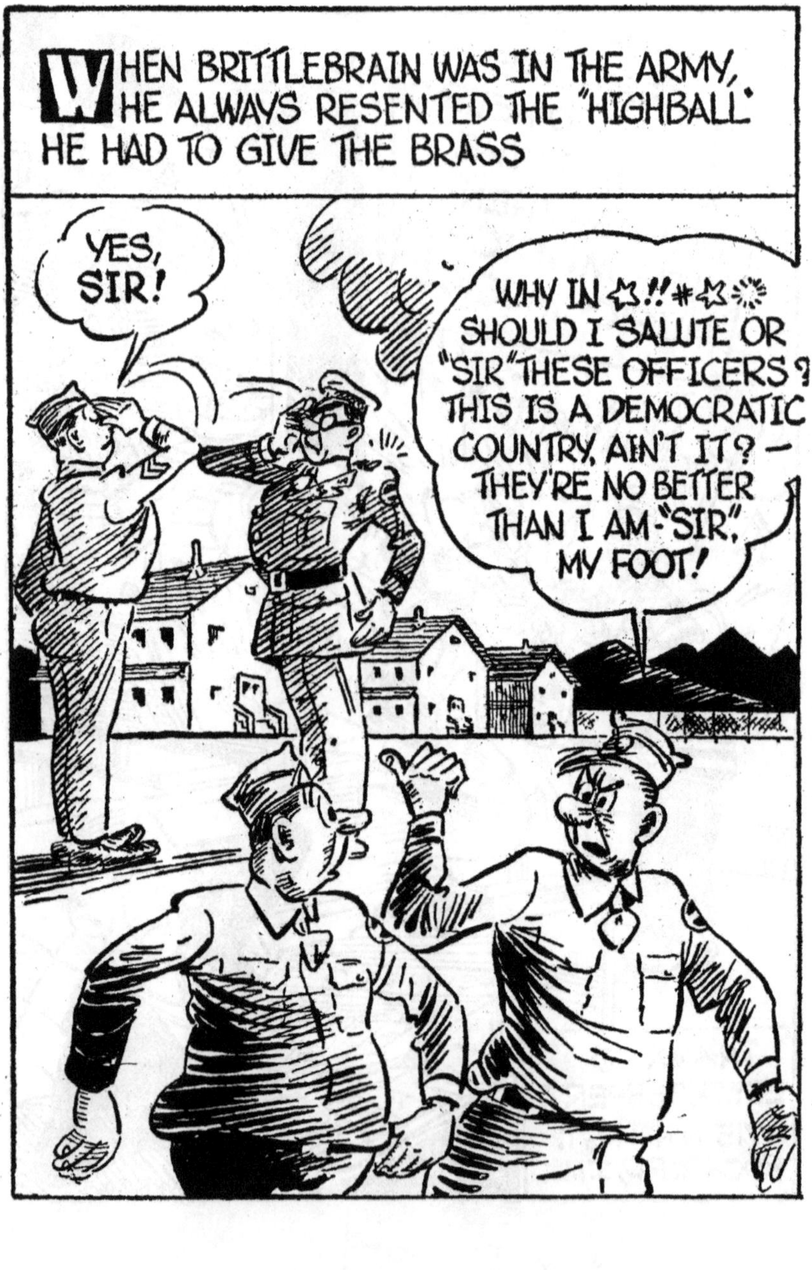
WHEN BRITTLEBRAIN WAS IN THE ARMY, HE ALWAYS RESENTED THE "HIGHBALL" HE HAD TO GIVE THE BRASS
YES, SIR!
WHY IN ☆!!#☆☼ SHOULD I SALUTE OR "SIR" THESE OFFICERS? THIS IS A DEMOCRATIC COUNTRY, AIN'T IT? — THEY'RE NO BETTER THAN I AM - "SIR", MY FOOT!

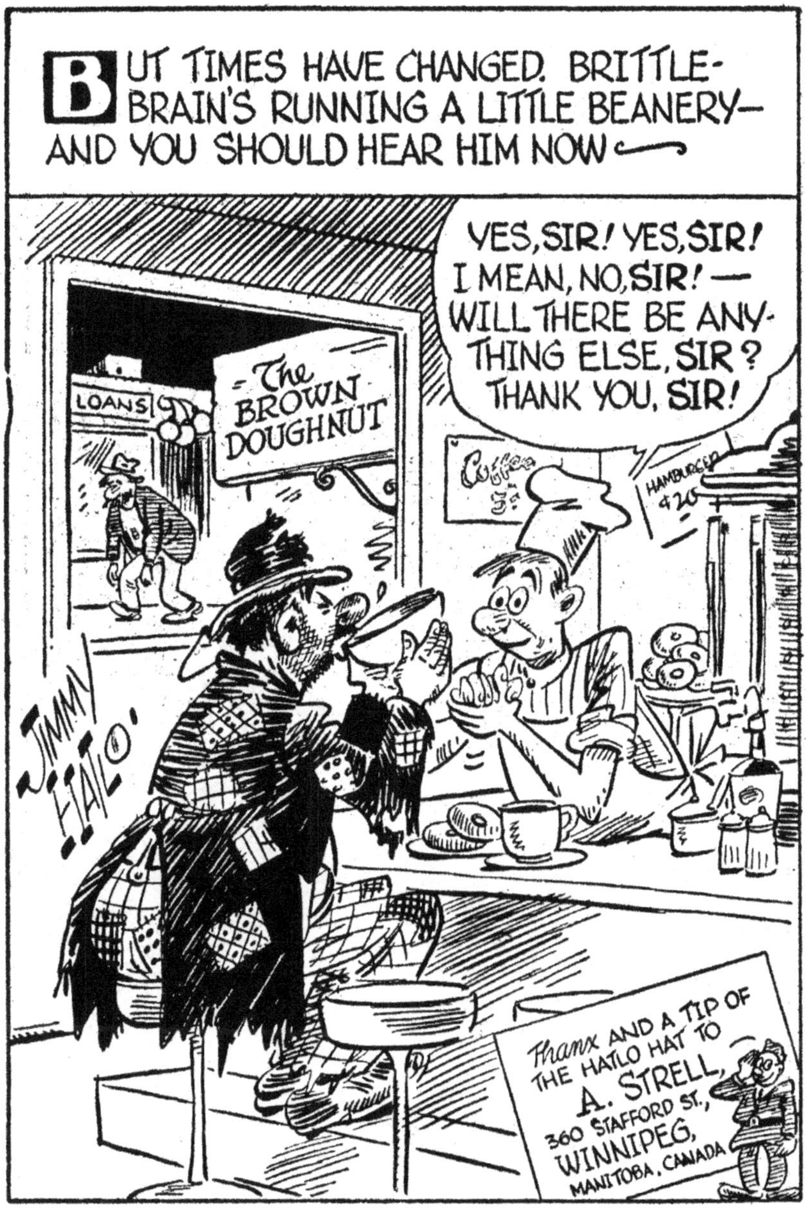
BUT TIMES HAVE CHANGED. BRITTLE-BRAIN'S RUNNING A LITTLE BEANERY—AND YOU SHOULD HEAR HIM NOW—
YES, SIR! YES, SIR! I MEAN, NO, SIR!— WILL THERE BE ANY-THING ELSE, SIR? THANK YOU, SIR!
LOANS
The BROWN DOUGHNUT
HAMBURGER 42¢
JIMMY HATLO
Thanx AND A TIP OF THE HATLO HAT TO A. STRELL, 360 STAFFORD ST., WINNIPEG, MANITOBA, CANADA

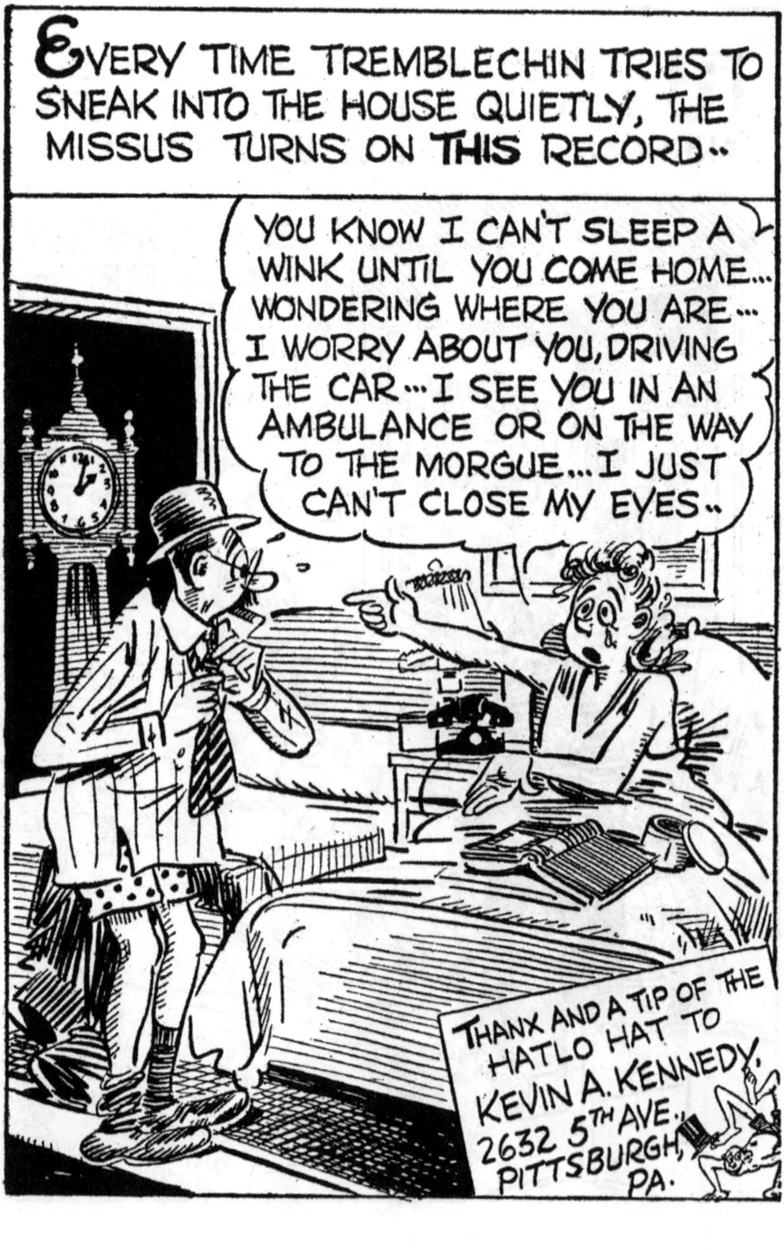
EVERY TIME TREMBLECHIN TRIES TO SNEAK INTO THE HOUSE QUIETLY, THE MISSUS TURNS ON THIS RECORD..
YOU KNOW I CAN'T SLEEP A WINK UNTIL YOU COME HOME... WONDERING WHERE YOU ARE... I WORRY ABOUT YOU, DRIVING THE CAR... I SEE YOU IN AN AMBULANCE OR ON THE WAY TO THE MORGUE... I JUST CAN'T CLOSE MY EYES..
THANX AND A TIP OF THE HATLO HAT TO KEVIN A. KENNEDY, 2632 5TH AVE., PITTSBURGH, PA.

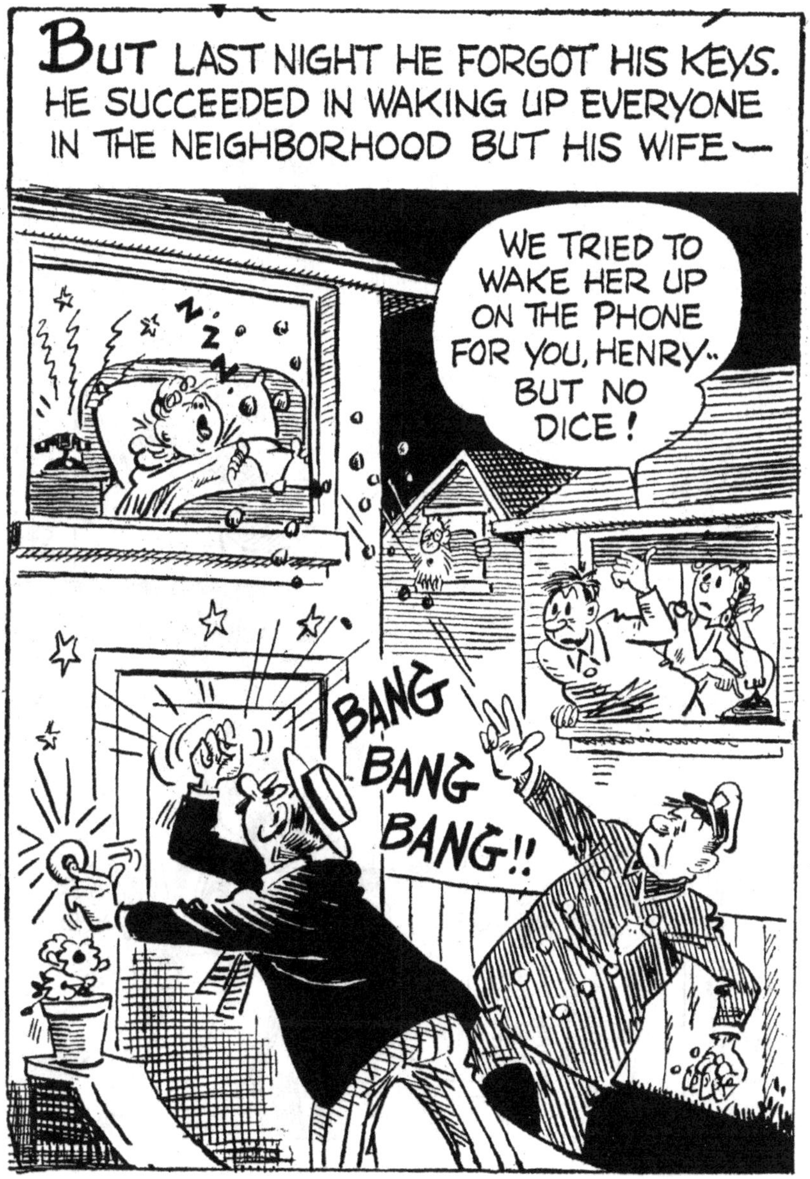
BUT LAST NIGHT HE FORGOT HIS KEYS. HE SUCCEEDED IN WAKING UP EVERYONE IN THE NEIGHBORHOOD BUT HIS WIFE—
WE TRIED TO WAKE HER UP ON THE PHONE FOR YOU, HENRY.. BUT NO DICE!
BANG
BANG
BANG!!

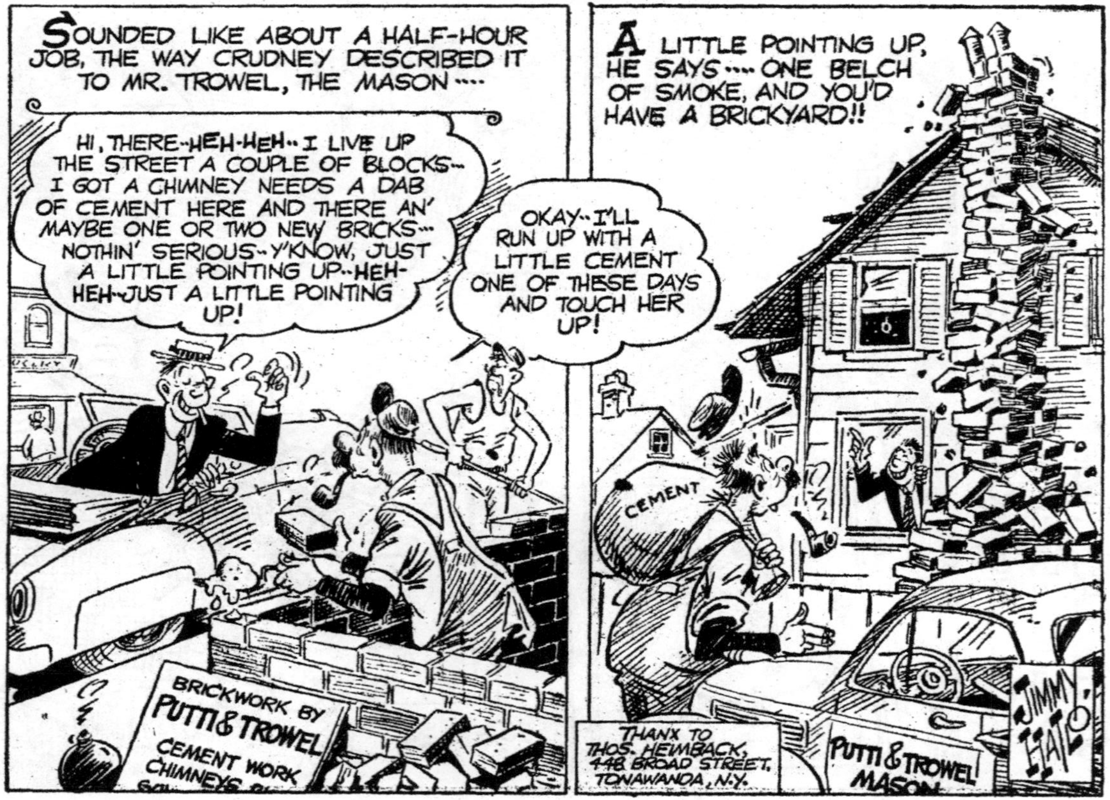
SOUNDED LIKE ABOUT A HALF-HOUR JOB, THE WAY CRUDNEY DESCRIBED IT TO MR. TROWEL, THE MASON....
HI, THERE--HEH-HEH-- I LIVE UP THE STREET A COUPLE OF BLOCKS-- I GOT A CHIMNEY NEEDS A DAB OF CEMENT HERE AND THERE AN' MAYBE ONE OR TWO NEW BRICKS--- NOTHIN' SERIOUS--Y'KNOW, JUST A LITTLE POINTING UP--HEH-HEH--JUST A LITTLE POINTING UP!
OKAY-- I'LL RUN UP WITH A LITTLE CEMENT ONE OF THESE DAYS AND TOUCH HER UP!
BRICKWORK BY PUTTI & TROWEL
CEMENT WORK
A LITTLE POINTING UP, HE SAYS.... ONE BELCH OF SMOKE, AND YOU'D HAVE A BRICKYARD!!
CEMENT
PUTTI & TROWEL MASON
THANX TO THOS. HEIMBACK, 448 BROAD STREET, TONAWANDA, N.Y.
JIMMY HATLO

THOSE RESORT-COUNTRY MAPS MAKE THE LAKES LOOK SO CLOSE TOGETHER YOU COULD BROAD-JUMP FROM ONE TO ANOTHER...
WE START AT TOP LAKE AND FISH AND FLOAT THROUGH SIX LAKES FOR 100 MILES! WHADDYAMEAN, CARRY THE CANOE? THE ONLY PORTAGE IS NO MORE'N TEN MINUTES! LOOK! ALL YOU HAVE TO DO IS STEP FROM DEERFLY LAKE INTO LAKE GABOON....
CHAIN LAKE DISTRICT
TOP LAKE
DEERFLY LAKE
LAKE GABOON
SOUPY LAKE
LAKE ECZEMA
JIMMY HATLO
HOWEVER....
WHAT FUN
DEERFLY LAKE 22 MILES
LAKE GABOON 45 MILES
WELL, HOW FAR DOES IT SAY NOW, NATURE BOY?
THANX TO WILLIAM HIESTAND, 711 HILLCREST ROAD, WEST LAFAYETTE, IND.

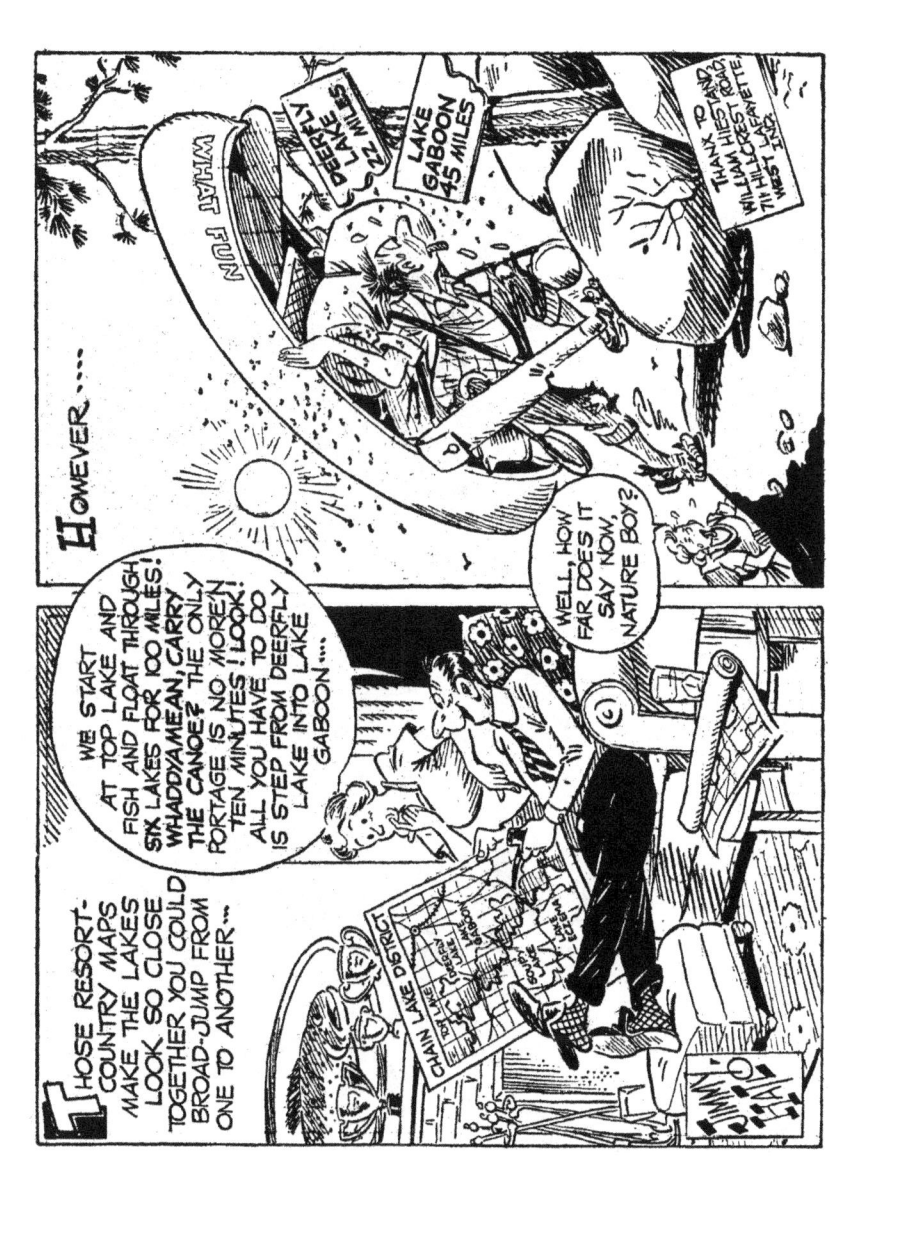

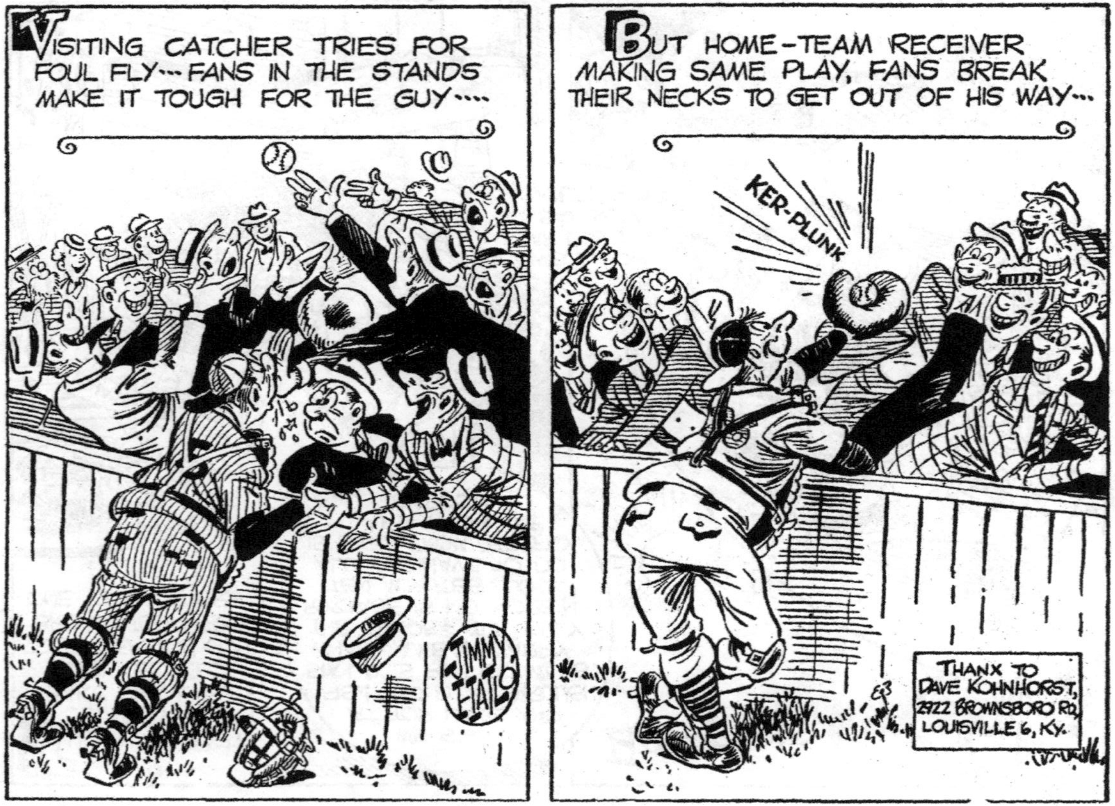
VISITING CATCHER TRIES FOR FOUL FLY--- FANS IN THE STANDS MAKE IT TOUGH FOR THE GUY....
JIMMY HATLO
BUT HOME-TEAM RECEIVER MAKING SAME PLAY, FANS BREAK THEIR NECKS TO GET OUT OF HIS WAY...
KER-PLUNK
THANX TO DAVE KOHNHORST, 2922 BROWNSBORO RD, LOUISVILLE 6, KY.

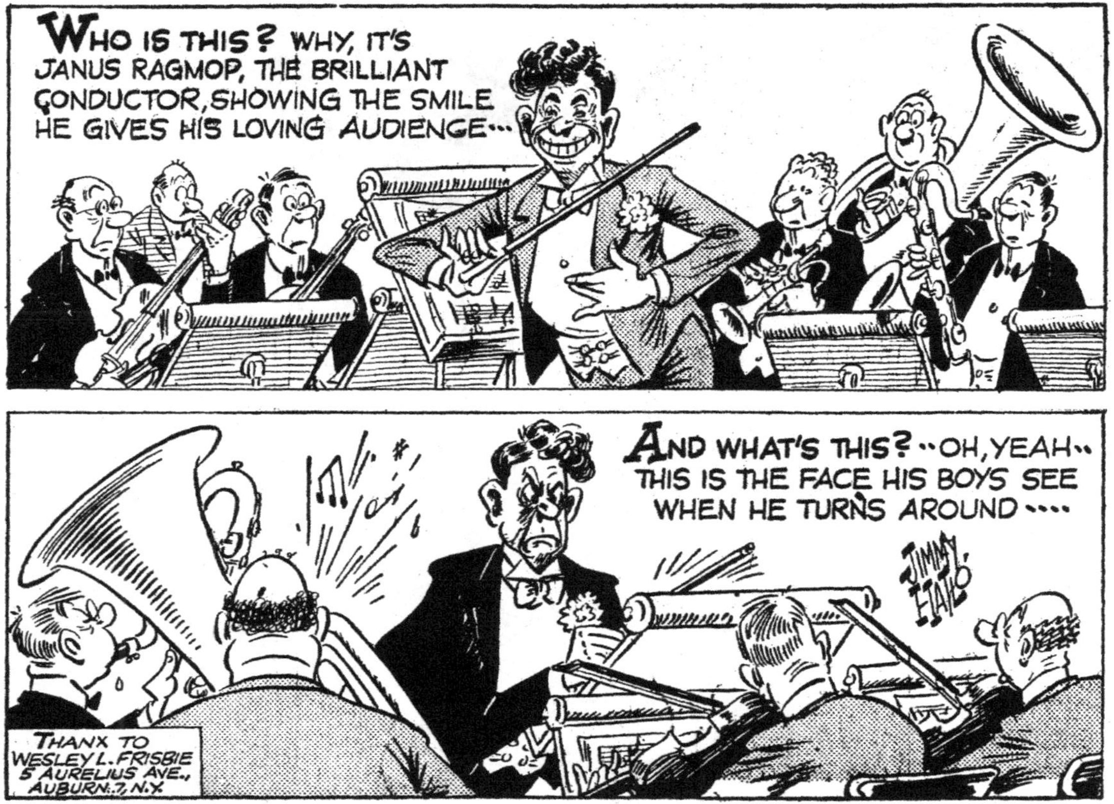
WHO IS THIS? WHY, IT'S JANUS RAGMOP, THE BRILLIANT CONDUCTOR, SHOWING THE SMILE HE GIVES HIS LOVING AUDIENCE...
AND WHAT'S THIS? ..OH, YEAH.. THIS IS THE FACE HIS BOYS SEE WHEN HE TURNS AROUND....
JIMMY HATLO
THANX TO WESLEY L. FRISBIE 5 AURELIUS AVE., AUBURN, 7, N.Y.

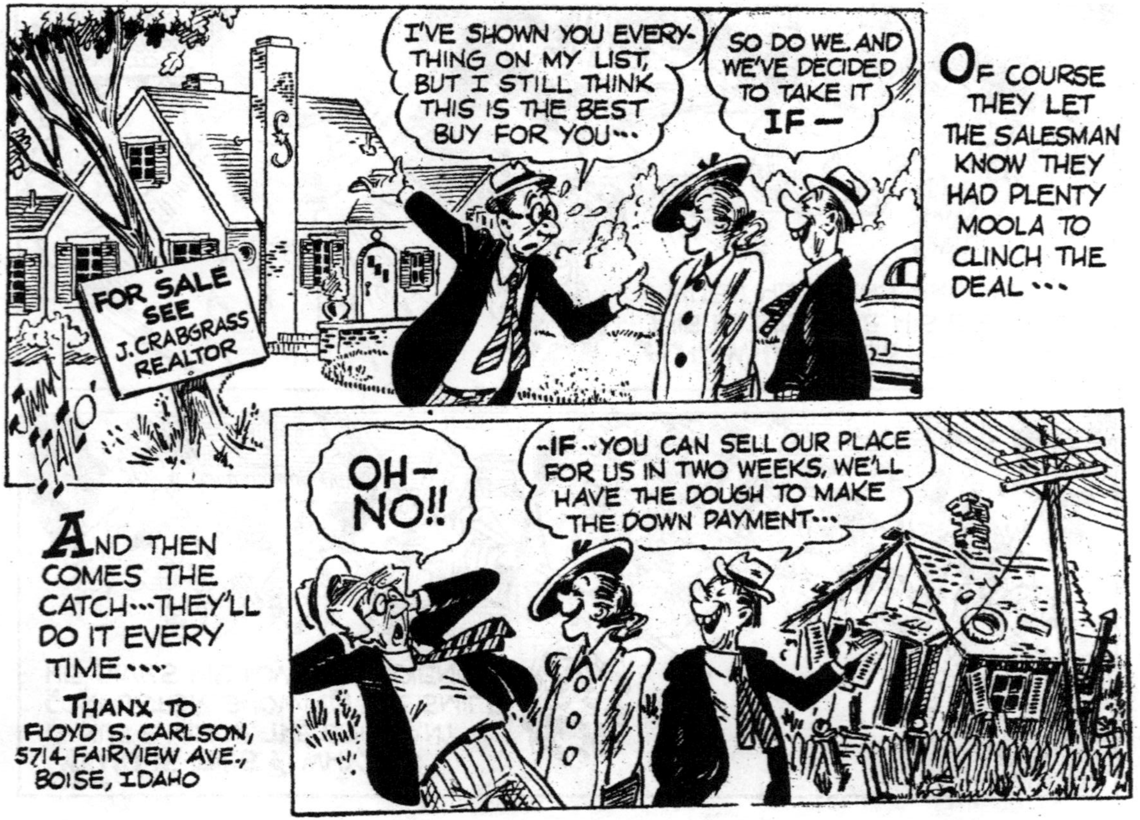
OF COURSE THEY LET THE SALESMAN KNOW THEY HAD PLENTY MOOLA TO CLINCH THE DEAL...
FOR SALE SEE J. CRABGRASS REALTOR
I'VE SHOWN YOU EVERYTHING ON MY LIST, BUT I STILL THINK THIS IS THE BEST BUY FOR YOU...
SO DO WE. AND WE'VE DECIDED TO TAKE IT IF—
JIMMY HATLO
AND THEN COMES THE CATCH...THEY'LL DO IT EVERY TIME...
THANX TO FLOYD S. CARLSON, 5714 FAIRVIEW AVE., BOISE, IDAHO
-IF..YOU CAN SELL OUR PLACE FOR US IN TWO WEEKS, WE'LL HAVE THE DOUGH TO MAKE THE DOWN PAYMENT...
OH—NO!!

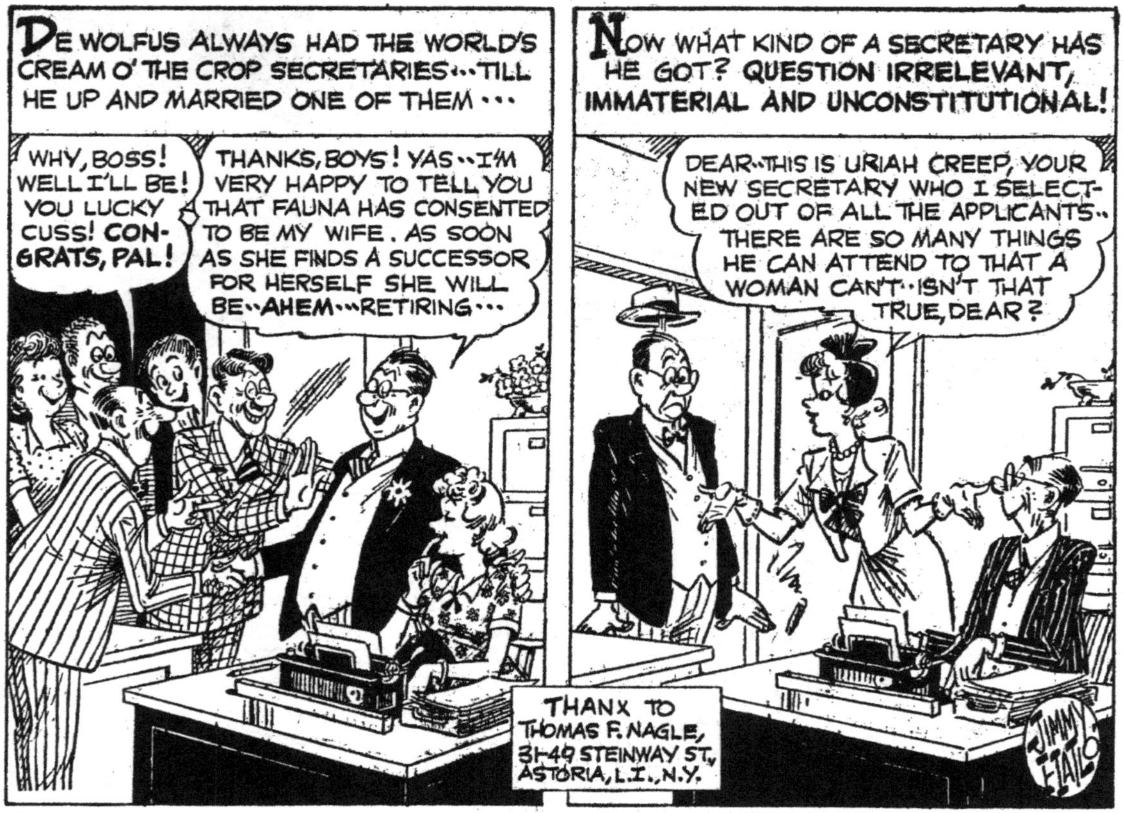
DE WOLFUS ALWAYS HAD THE WORLD'S CREAM O' THE CROP SECRETARIES... TILL HE UP AND MARRIED ONE OF THEM...
WHY, BOSS! WELL I'LL BE! YOU LUCKY CUSS! CONGRATS, PAL!
THANKS, BOYS! YAS.. I'M VERY HAPPY TO TELL YOU THAT FAUNA HAS CONSENTED TO BE MY WIFE. AS SOON AS SHE FINDS A SUCCESSOR FOR HERSELF SHE WILL BE.. AHEM... RETIRING...
NOW WHAT KIND OF A SECRETARY HAS HE GOT? QUESTION IRRELEVANT, IMMATERIAL AND UNCONSTITUTIONAL!
DEAR.. THIS IS URIAH CREEP, YOUR NEW SECRETARY WHO I SELECTED OUT OF ALL THE APPLICANTS.. THERE ARE SO MANY THINGS HE CAN ATTEND TO THAT A WOMAN CAN'T.. ISN'T THAT TRUE, DEAR?
THANX TO THOMAS F. NAGLE, 31-49 STEINWAY ST., ASTORIA, L.I., N.Y.
JIMMY HATLO

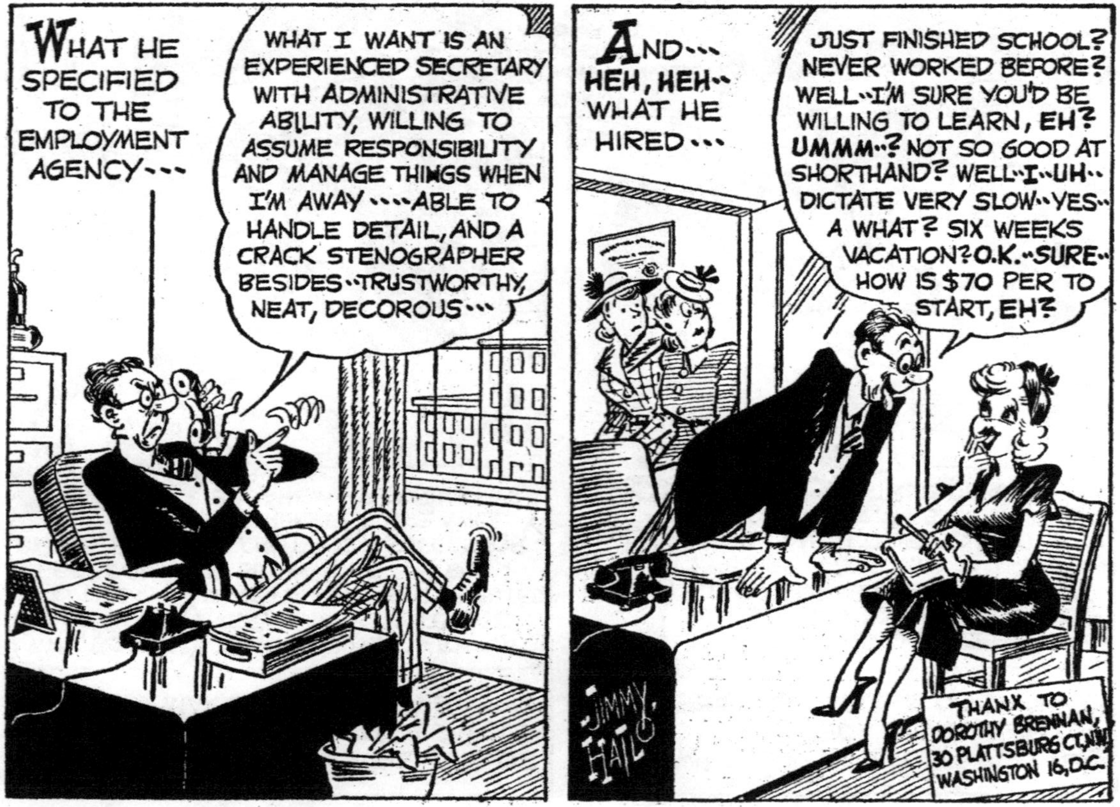
WHAT HE SPECIFIED TO THE EMPLOYMENT AGENCY...
WHAT I WANT IS AN EXPERIENCED SECRETARY WITH ADMINISTRATIVE ABILITY, WILLING TO ASSUME RESPONSIBILITY AND MANAGE THINGS WHEN I'M AWAY....ABLE TO HANDLE DETAIL, AND A CRACK STENOGRAPHER BESIDES..TRUSTWORTHY, NEAT, DECOROUS...
AND... HEH, HEH.. WHAT HE HIRED...
JUST FINISHED SCHOOL? NEVER WORKED BEFORE? WELL..I'M SURE YOU'D BE WILLING TO LEARN, EH? UMMM..? NOT SO GOOD AT SHORTHAND? WELL..I..UH.. DICTATE VERY SLOW..YES.. A WHAT? SIX WEEKS VACATION? O.K..SURE.. HOW IS $70 PER TO START, EH?
JIMMY HATLO
THANX TO DOROTHY BRENNAN, 30 PLATTSBURG CT.,N.W. WASHINGTON 16, D.C.

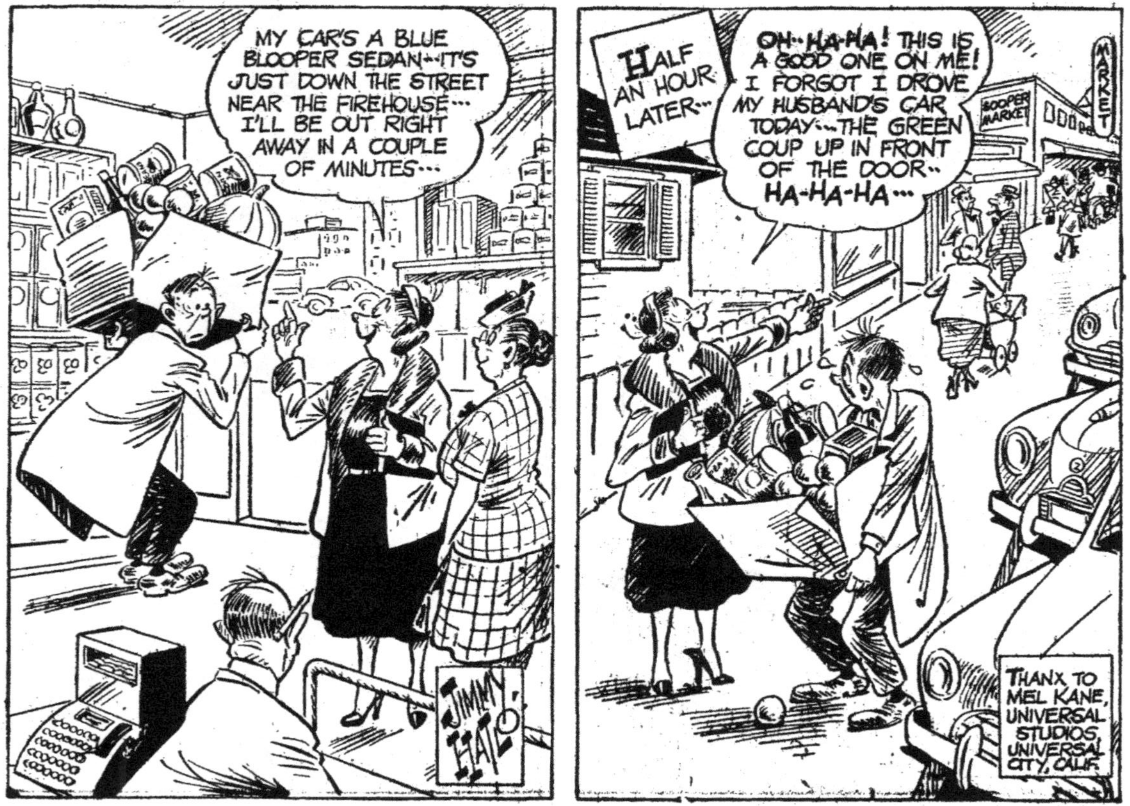
MY CAR'S A BLUE BLOOPER SEDAN--IT'S JUST DOWN THE STREET NEAR THE FIREHOUSE... I'LL BE OUT RIGHT AWAY IN A COUPLE OF MINUTES...
JIMMY HATLO
HALF AN HOUR LATER...
OH--HA-HA! THIS IS A GOOD ONE ON ME! I FORGOT I DROVE MY HUSBAND'S CAR TODAY...THE GREEN COUP UP IN FRONT OF THE DOOR-- HA-HA-HA...
BOOPER MARKET
MARKET
THANX TO MEL KANE, UNIVERSAL STUDIOS, UNIVERSAL CITY, CALIF.

BURPERTON FELL HOOK-LINE-AND-DOUGHNUT FOR HEPPY'S CULINARY SKILL.
YOU DO THINGS TO ME, BABY... YOU COOK JUST LIKE MY MOTHER USED TO. WHAT DO YOU SAY? LET'S GET HITCHED!
JIMMY HATLO
THANX AND A TIP OF THE HATLO HAT TO LANK McCALL, EAST 86TH ST, NEW YORK, N.Y.
SO THEY TIED THE KNOT... AND POOR OLD BURPY HASN'T HAD A SQUARE MEAL SINCE
IF I NEVER SEE A KITCHEN AGAIN, IT'LL BE TOO SOON! WHEN ARE YOU GONNA MAKE ENOUGH DOUGH SO WE CAN HIRE A COOK?

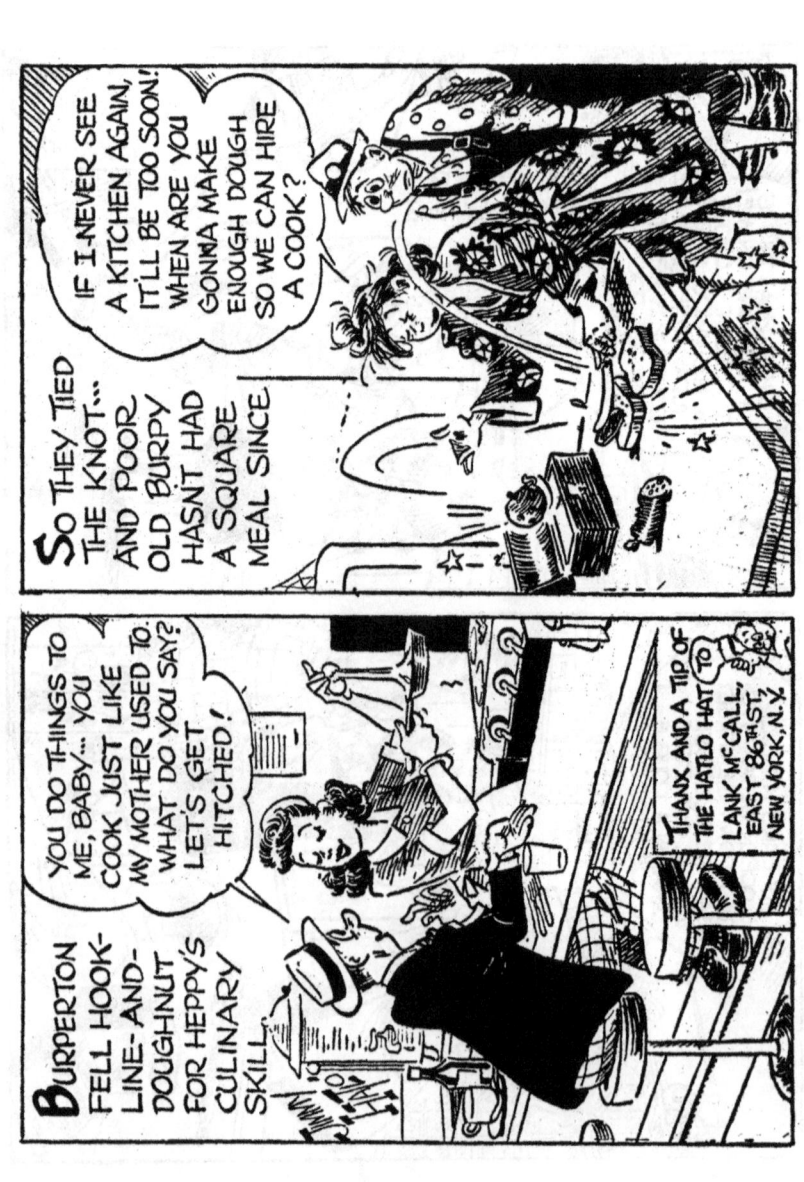

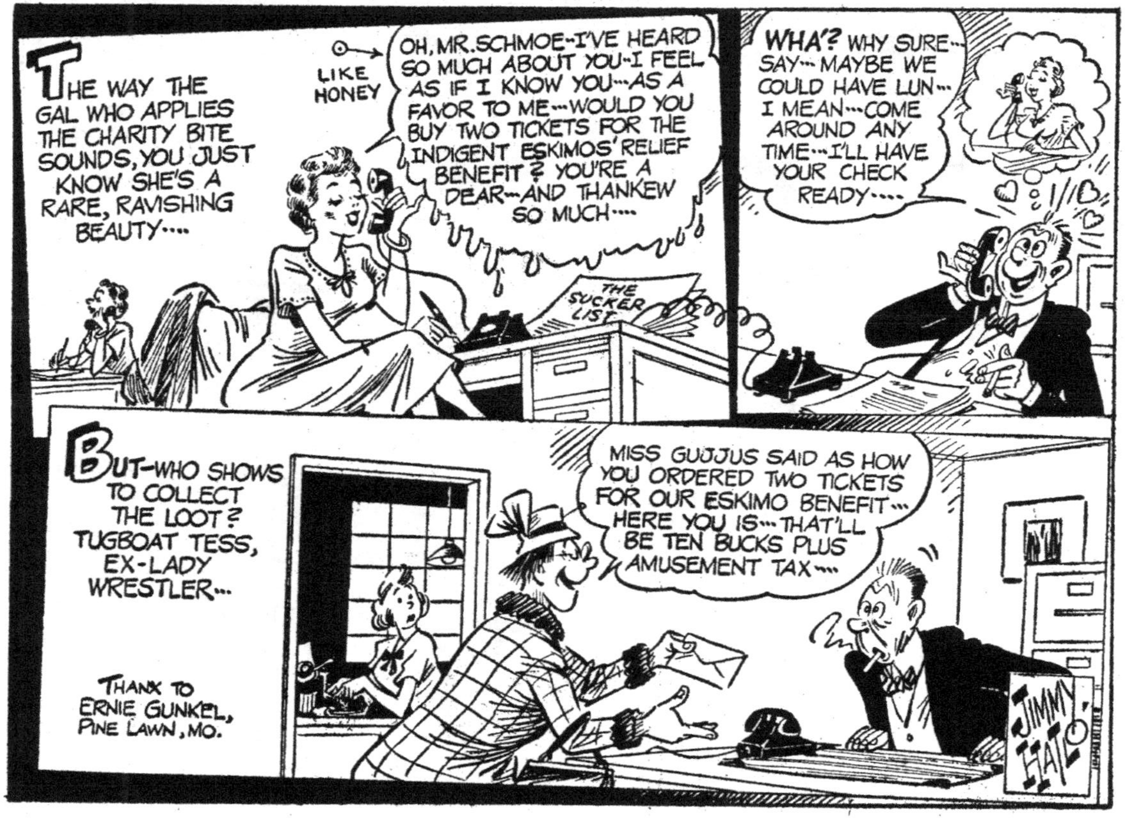
THE WAY THE GAL WHO APPLIES THE CHARITY BITE SOUNDS, YOU JUST KNOW SHE'S A RARE, RAVISHING BEAUTY....
LIKE HONEY
OH, MR. SCHMOE--I'VE HEARD SO MUCH ABOUT YOU--I FEEL AS IF I KNOW YOU---AS A FAVOR TO ME---WOULD YOU BUY TWO TICKETS FOR THE INDIGENT ESKIMOS' RELIEF BENEFIT? YOU'RE A DEAR---AND THANKEW SO MUCH....
THE SUCKER LIST
WHA'? WHY SURE... SAY--- MAYBE WE COULD HAVE LUN--- I MEAN---COME AROUND ANY TIME---I'LL HAVE YOUR CHECK READY....
BUT-WHO SHOWS TO COLLECT THE LOOT? TUGBOAT TESS, EX-LADY WRESTLER...
MISS GUJJUS SAID AS HOW YOU ORDERED TWO TICKETS FOR OUR ESKIMO BENEFIT--- HERE YOU IS--- THAT'LL BE TEN BUCKS PLUS AMUSEMENT TAX....
THANX TO ERNIE GUNKEL, PINE LAWN, MO.
JIMMY HATLO

HOW COME? THE TRUCK JOCKEY NEEDS ONLY 1/16 OF AN INCH CLEARANCE TO BACK INTO AN ALLEY IN THE CITY..
WOW! TALK ABOUT DELICATE OPERATIONS !!
BUT IN THE SUBURBS WITH PLENTY ROOM TO SPARE --- BYE-BYE, TWO NICE HEDGES ---
LOOK OUT! PULL YOUR HEAD IN!
THANX TO MARGARET AND BEV POST, MT. VIEW RD., FRANKLIN, N.J.
JIMMY HATLO

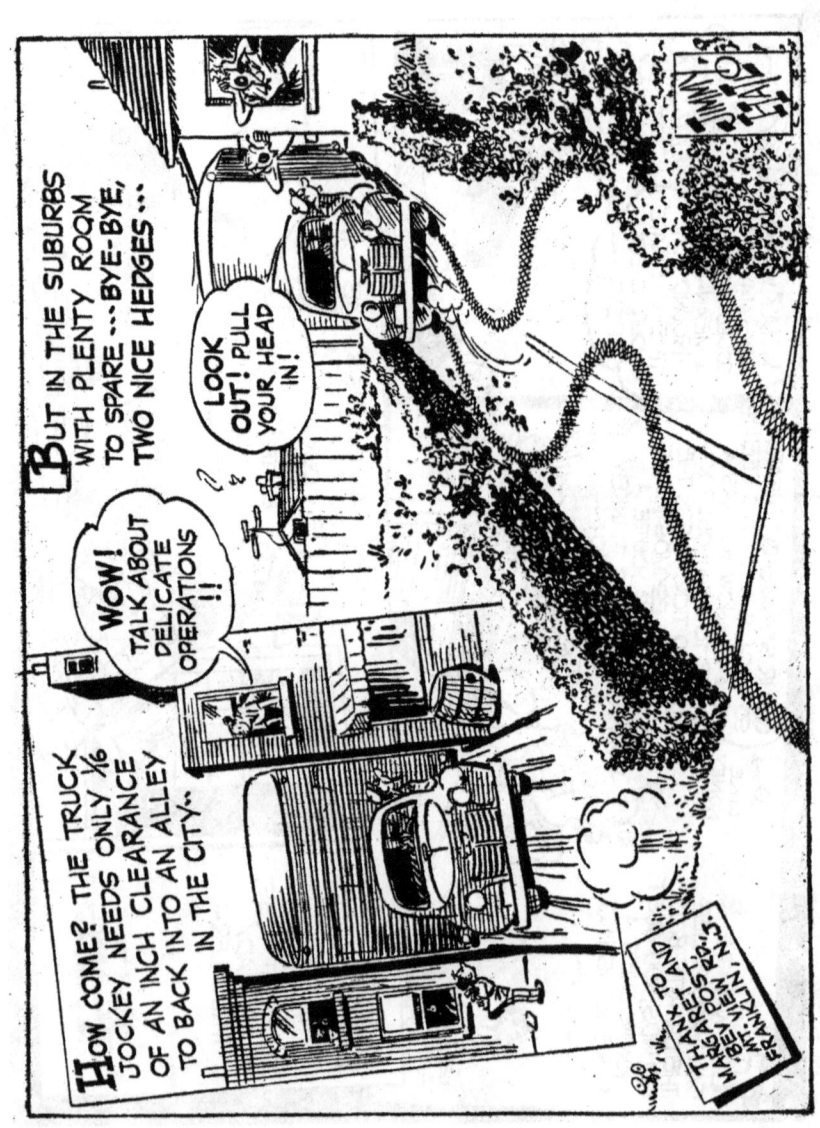

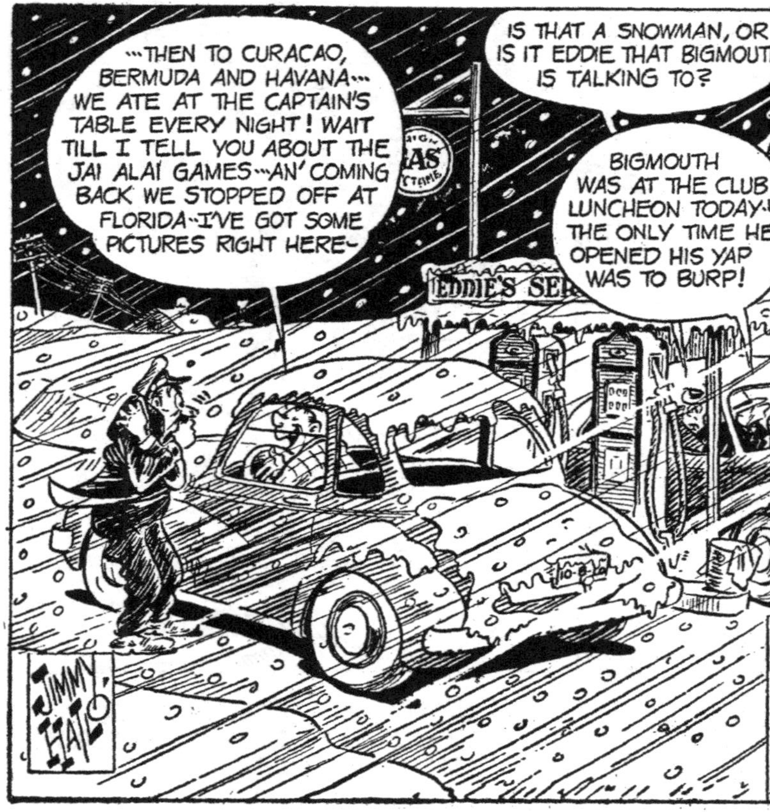

ANOTHER HEADACHE IN THE GAS BUSINESS, WITH CHILBLAINS THROWN IN…

THANX TO CARL M. BAEHR, HARDING WAY, W. AND STATE RD, GALION, OHIO

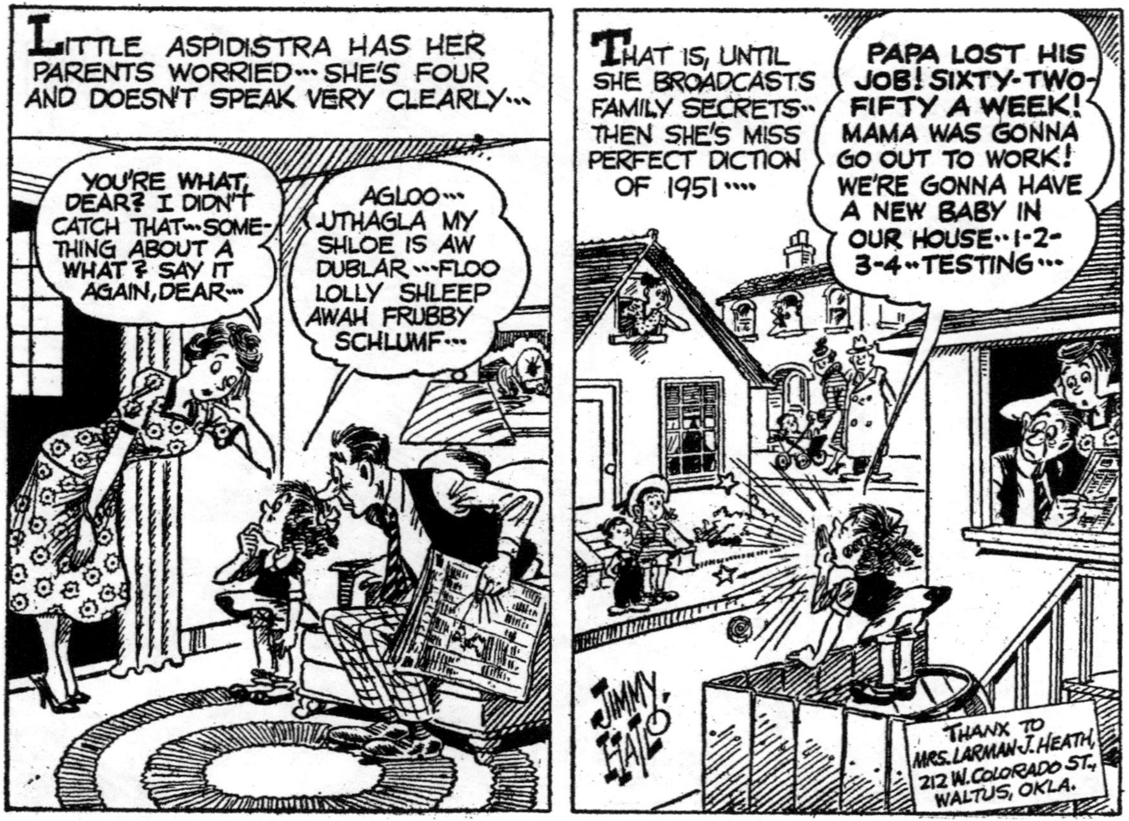
LITTLE ASPIDISTRA HAS HER PARENTS WORRIED... SHE'S FOUR AND DOESN'T SPEAK VERY CLEARLY...
YOU'RE WHAT, DEAR? I DIDN'T CATCH THAT...SOMETHING ABOUT A WHAT? SAY IT AGAIN, DEAR...
AGLOO... UTHAGLA MY SHLOE IS AW DUBLAR...FLOO LOLLY SHLEEP AWAH FRUBBY SCHLUMF...
THAT IS, UNTIL SHE BROADCASTS FAMILY SECRETS.. THEN SHE'S MISS PERFECT DICTION OF 1951....
PAPA LOST HIS JOB! SIXTY-TWO-FIFTY A WEEK! MAMA WAS GONNA GO OUT TO WORK! WE'RE GONNA HAVE A NEW BABY IN OUR HOUSE..1-2-3-4..TESTING...
JIMMY HATLO
THANX TO MRS. LARMAN J. HEATH, 212 W. COLORADO ST., WALTUS, OKLA.

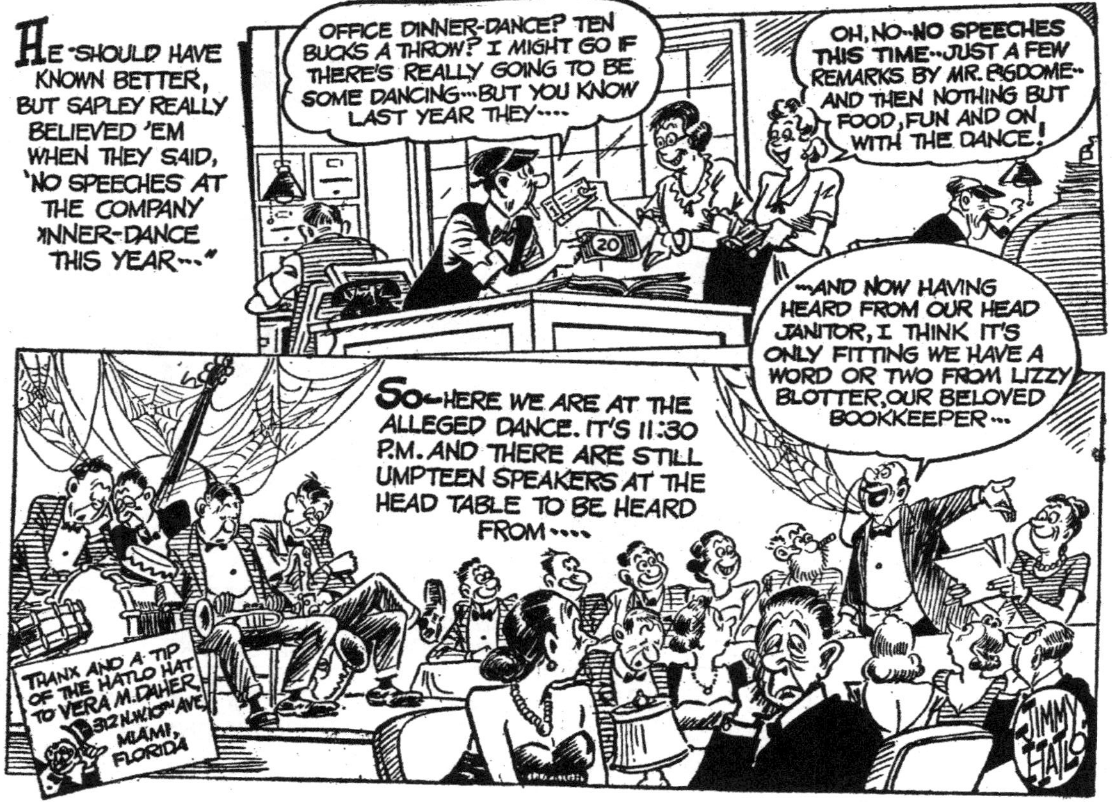

HE SHOULD HAVE KNOWN BETTER, BUT SAPLEY REALLY BELIEVED 'EM WHEN THEY SAID, 'NO SPEECHES AT THE COMPANY DINNER-DANCE THIS YEAR...'
OFFICE DINNER-DANCE? TEN BUCKS A THROW? I MIGHT GO IF THERE'S REALLY GOING TO BE SOME DANCING...BUT YOU KNOW LAST YEAR THEY....
OH, NO--NO SPEECHES THIS TIME--JUST A FEW REMARKS BY MR. BIGDOME-- AND THEN NOTHING BUT FOOD, FUN AND ON WITH THE DANCE!
20
SO-- HERE WE ARE AT THE ALLEGED DANCE. IT'S 11:30 P.M. AND THERE ARE STILL UMPTEEN SPEAKERS AT THE HEAD TABLE TO BE HEARD FROM....
...AND NOW HAVING HEARD FROM OUR HEAD JANITOR, I THINK IT'S ONLY FITTING WE HAVE A WORD OR TWO FROM LIZZY BLOTTER, OUR BELOVED BOOKKEEPER...
THANX AND A TIP OF THE HATLO HAT TO VERA M. DAHER, 312 N.W. 10TH AVE, MIAMI, FLORIDA
JIMMY HATLO

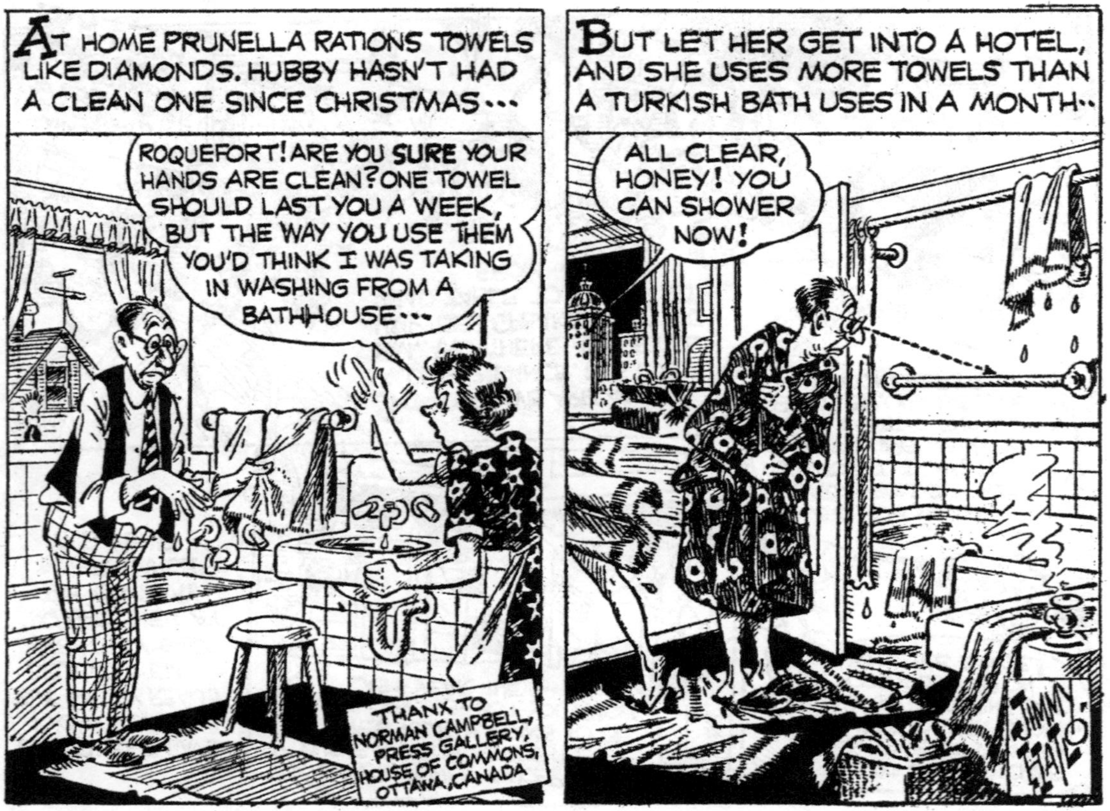
AT HOME PRUNELLA RATIONS TOWELS LIKE DIAMONDS. HUBBY HASN'T HAD A CLEAN ONE SINCE CHRISTMAS...
ROQUEFORT! ARE YOU SURE YOUR HANDS ARE CLEAN? ONE TOWEL SHOULD LAST YOU A WEEK, BUT THE WAY YOU USE THEM YOU'D THINK I WAS TAKING IN WASHING FROM A BATHHOUSE...
THANX TO NORMAN CAMPBELL, PRESS GALLERY, HOUSE OF COMMONS, OTTAWA, CANADA
BUT LET HER GET INTO A HOTEL, AND SHE USES MORE TOWELS THAN A TURKISH BATH USES IN A MONTH..
ALL CLEAR, HONEY! YOU CAN SHOWER NOW!
JIMMY HATLO

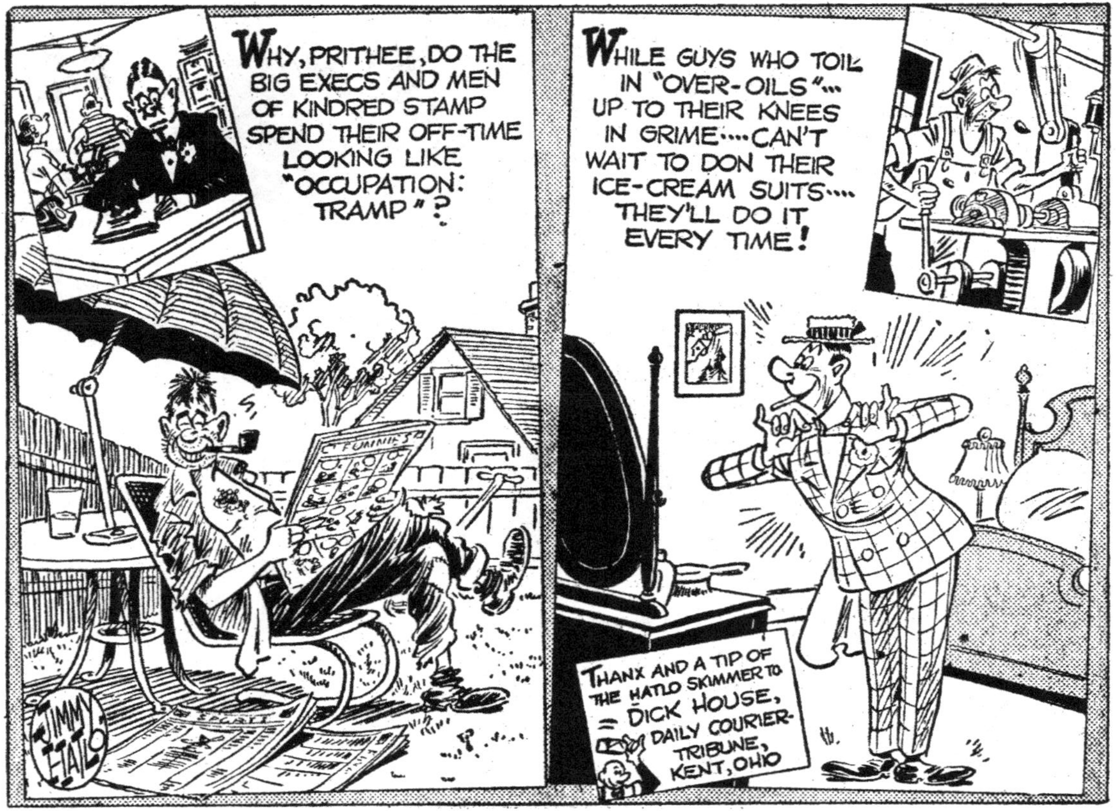
WHY, PRITHEE, DO THE BIG EXECS AND MEN OF KINDRED STAMP SPEND THEIR OFF-TIME LOOKING LIKE "OCCUPATION: TRAMP"?
FUNNIES
SPORTS
JIMMY HATLO
WHILE GUYS WHO TOIL IN "OVER-OILS"... UP TO THEIR KNEES IN GRIME.... CAN'T WAIT TO DON THEIR ICE-CREAM SUITS.... THEY'LL DO IT EVERY TIME!
THANX AND A TIP OF THE HATLO SKIMMER TO = DICK HOUSE, DAILY COURIER-TRIBUNE, KENT, OHIO

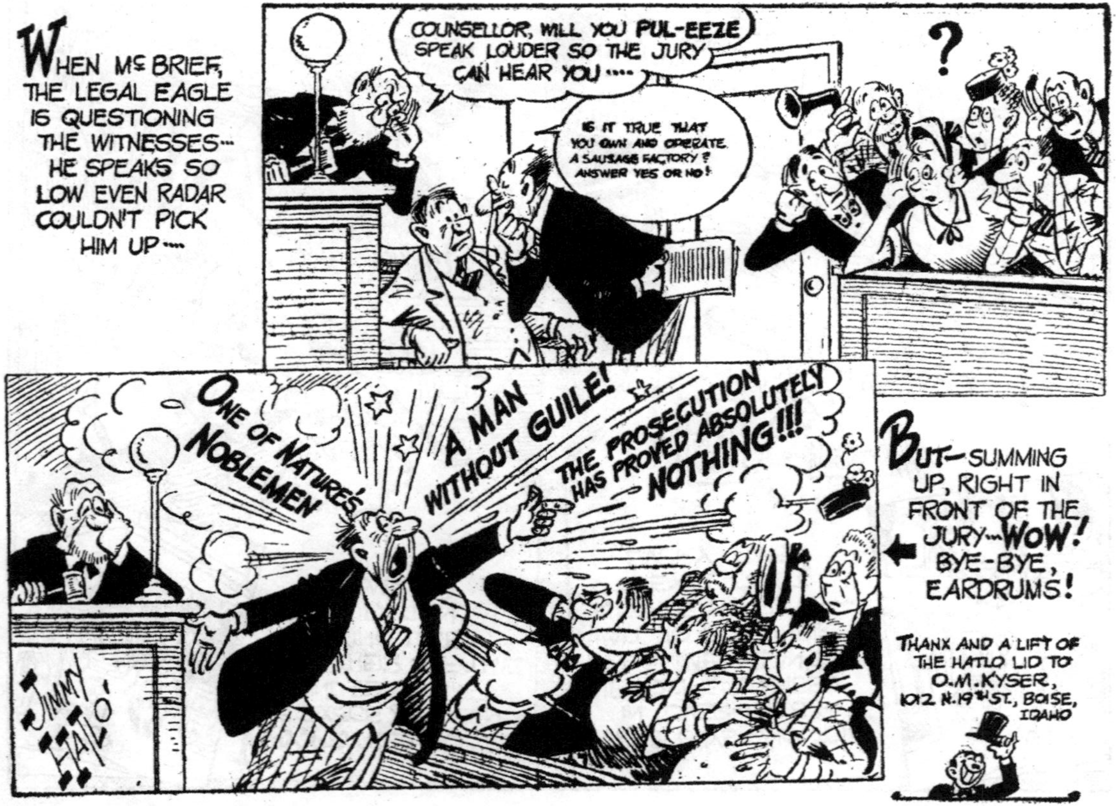
WHEN MC BRIEF, THE LEGAL EAGLE IS QUESTIONING THE WITNESSES... HE SPEAKS SO LOW EVEN RADAR COULDN'T PICK HIM UP....
COUNSELLOR, WILL YOU PUL-EEZE SPEAK LOUDER SO THE JURY CAN HEAR YOU....
IS IT TRUE THAT YOU OWN AND OPERATE A SAUSAGE FACTORY? ANSWER YES OR NO!
?
ONE OF NATURE'S NOBLEMEN
A MAN WITHOUT GUILE!
THE PROSECUTION HAS PROVED ABSOLUTELY NOTHING!!!
JIMMY HATLO
BUT—SUMMING UP, RIGHT IN FRONT OF THE JURY... WOW! BYE-BYE, EARDRUMS!
THANX AND A LIFT OF THE HATLO LID TO O.M. KYSER, 1012 N. 19TH ST., BOISE, IDAHO

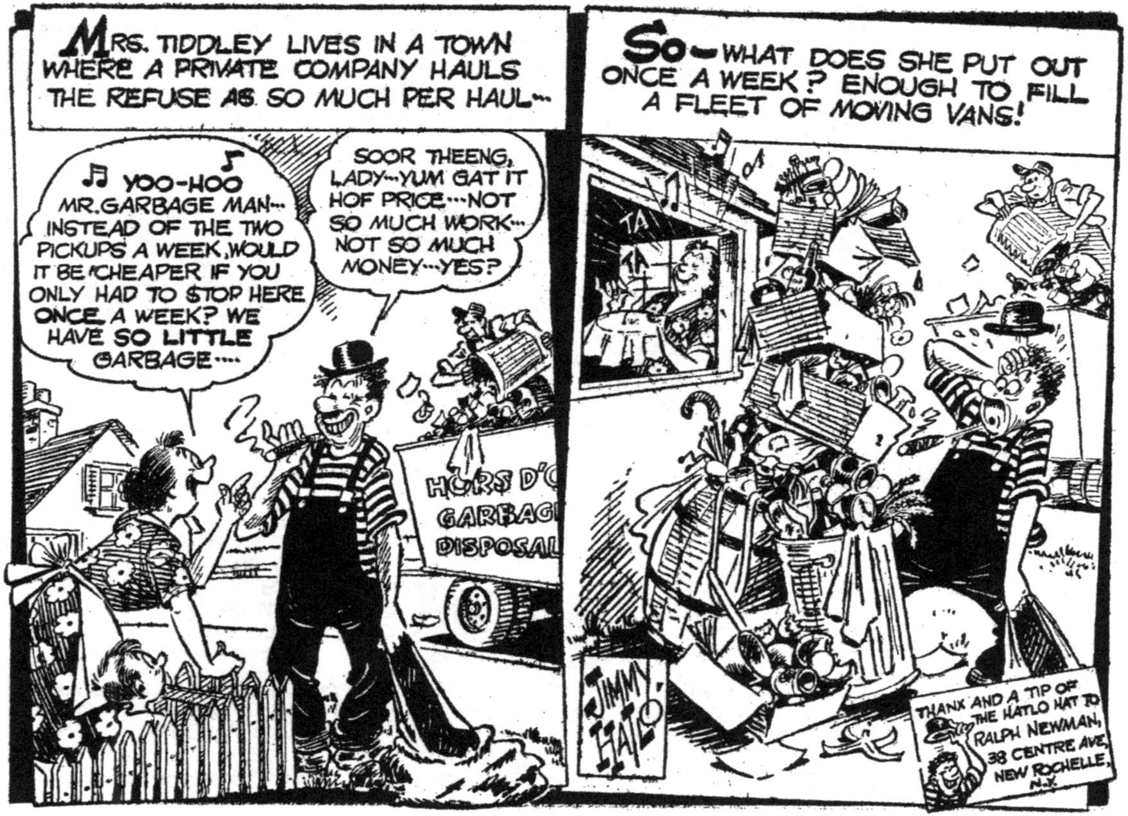
MRS. TIDDLEY LIVES IN A TOWN WHERE A PRIVATE COMPANY HAULS THE REFUSE AS SO MUCH PER HAUL...
YOO-HOO MR. GARBAGE MAN... INSTEAD OF THE TWO PICKUPS A WEEK, WOULD IT BE CHEAPER IF YOU ONLY HAD TO STOP HERE ONCE A WEEK? WE HAVE SO LITTLE GARBAGE....
SOOR THEENG, LADY... YUM GAT IT HOF PRICE... NOT SO MUCH WORK... NOT SO MUCH MONEY... YES?
HORS D'O GARBAG DISPOSAL
SO— WHAT DOES SHE PUT OUT ONCE A WEEK? ENOUGH TO FILL A FLEET OF MOVING VANS!
TA TA
JIMMY HATLO
THANX AND A TIP OF THE HATLO HAT TO RALPH NEWMAN, 38 CENTRE AVE, NEW ROCHELLE, N.Y.

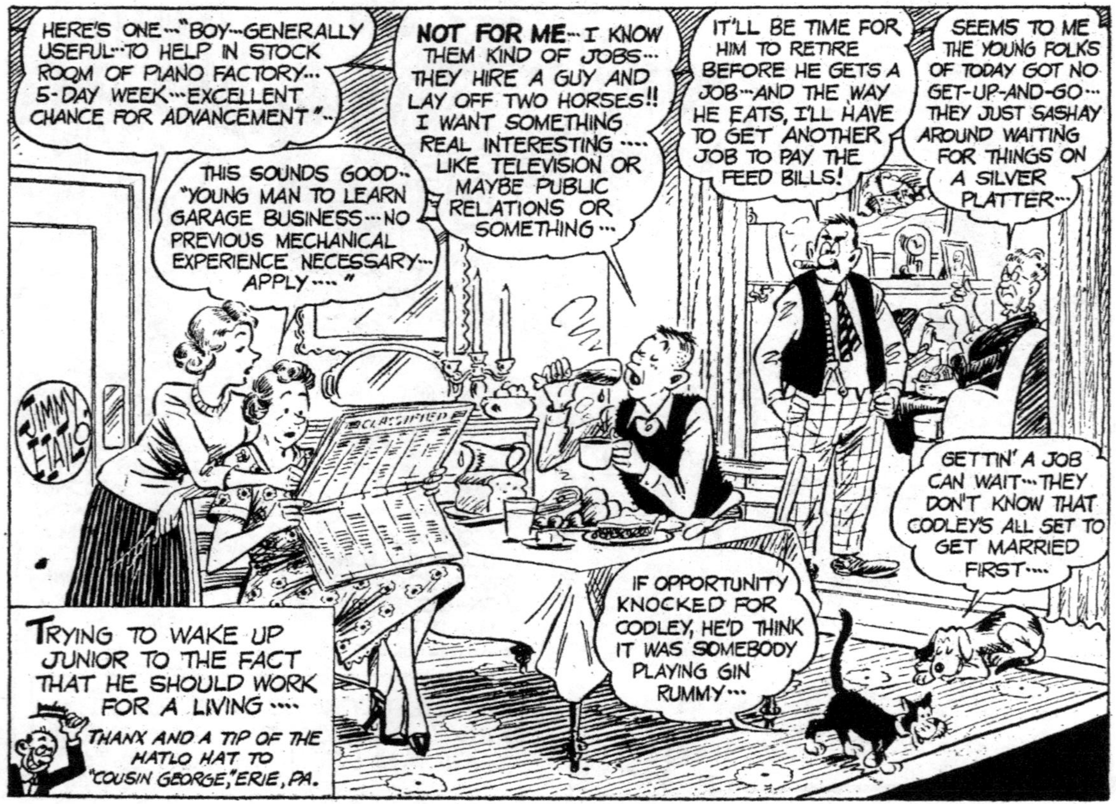
HERE'S ONE... "BOY...GENERALLY USEFUL...TO HELP IN STOCK ROOM OF PIANO FACTORY... 5-DAY WEEK...EXCELLENT CHANCE FOR ADVANCEMENT"...
THIS SOUNDS GOOD... "YOUNG MAN TO LEARN GARAGE BUSINESS...NO PREVIOUS MECHANICAL EXPERIENCE NECESSARY... APPLY...."
NOT FOR ME... I KNOW THEM KIND OF JOBS... THEY HIRE A GUY AND LAY OFF TWO HORSES!! I WANT SOMETHING REAL INTERESTING.... LIKE TELEVISION OR MAYBE PUBLIC RELATIONS OR SOMETHING...
IT'LL BE TIME FOR HIM TO RETIRE BEFORE HE GETS A JOB...AND THE WAY HE EATS, I'LL HAVE TO GET ANOTHER JOB TO PAY THE FEED BILLS!
SEEMS TO ME THE YOUNG FOLKS OF TODAY GOT NO GET-UP-AND-GO... THEY JUST SASHAY AROUND WAITING FOR THINGS ON A SILVER PLATTER...
GETTIN' A JOB CAN WAIT...THEY DON'T KNOW THAT CODLEY'S ALL SET TO GET MARRIED FIRST....
IF OPPORTUNITY KNOCKED FOR CODLEY, HE'D THINK IT WAS SOMEBODY PLAYING GIN RUMMY...
JIMMY HATLO
CLASSIFIED
TRYING TO WAKE UP JUNIOR TO THE FACT THAT HE SHOULD WORK FOR A LIVING....
THANX AND A TIP OF THE HATLO HAT TO "COUSIN GEORGE," ERIE, PA.

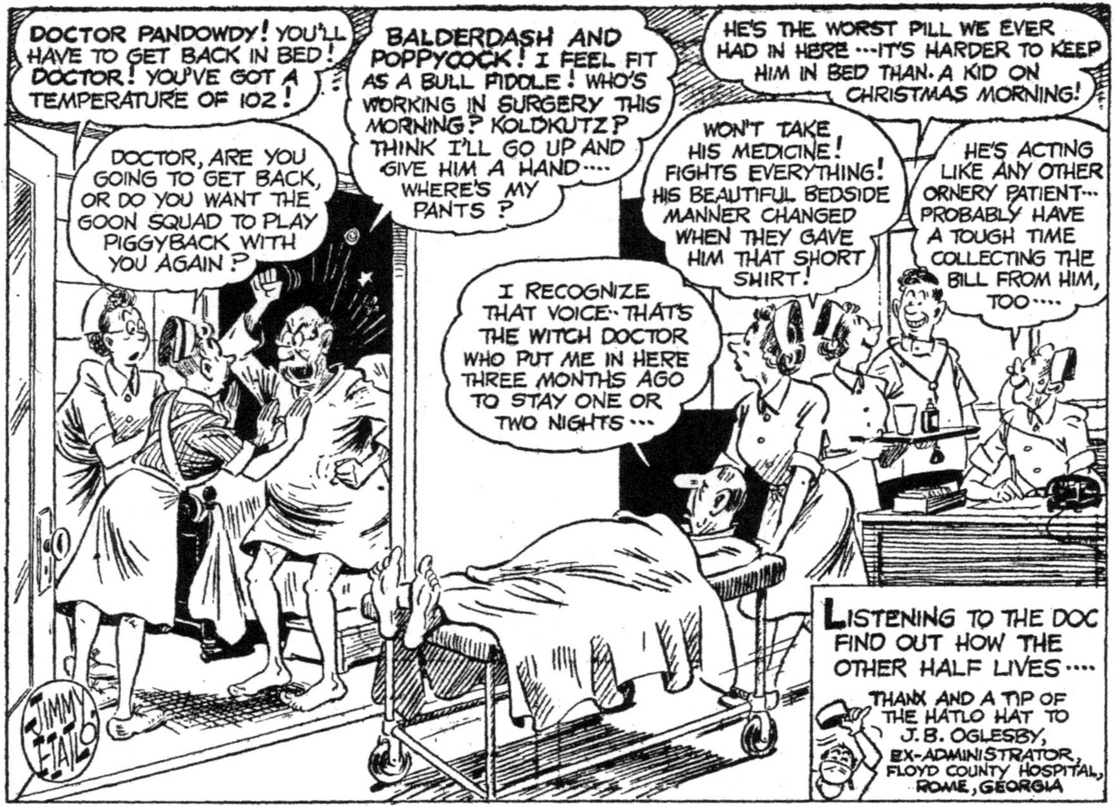
DOCTOR PANDOWDY! YOU'LL HAVE TO GET BACK IN BED! DOCTOR! YOU'VE GOT A TEMPERATURE OF 102!
DOCTOR, ARE YOU GOING TO GET BACK, OR DO YOU WANT THE GOON SQUAD TO PLAY PIGGYBACK WITH YOU AGAIN?
BALDERDASH AND POPPYCOCK! I FEEL FIT AS A BULL FIDDLE! WHO'S WORKING IN SURGERY THIS MORNING? KOLDKUTZ? THINK I'LL GO UP AND GIVE HIM A HAND.... WHERE'S MY PANTS?
I RECOGNIZE THAT VOICE-THAT'S THE WITCH DOCTOR WHO PUT ME IN HERE THREE MONTHS AGO TO STAY ONE OR TWO NIGHTS...
WON'T TAKE HIS MEDICINE! FIGHTS EVERYTHING! HIS BEAUTIFUL BEDSIDE MANNER CHANGED WHEN THEY GAVE HIM THAT SHORT SHIRT!
HE'S THE WORST PILL WE EVER HAD IN HERE ...IT'S HARDER TO KEEP HIM IN BED THAN A KID ON CHRISTMAS MORNING!
HE'S ACTING LIKE ANY OTHER ORNERY PATIENT... PROBABLY HAVE A TOUGH TIME COLLECTING THE BILL FROM HIM, TOO....
LISTENING TO THE DOC FIND OUT HOW THE OTHER HALF LIVES....
THANX AND A TIP OF THE HATLO HAT TO J. B. OGLESBY, EX-ADMINISTRATOR, FLOYD COUNTY HOSPITAL, ROME, GEORGIA
JIMMY HATLO

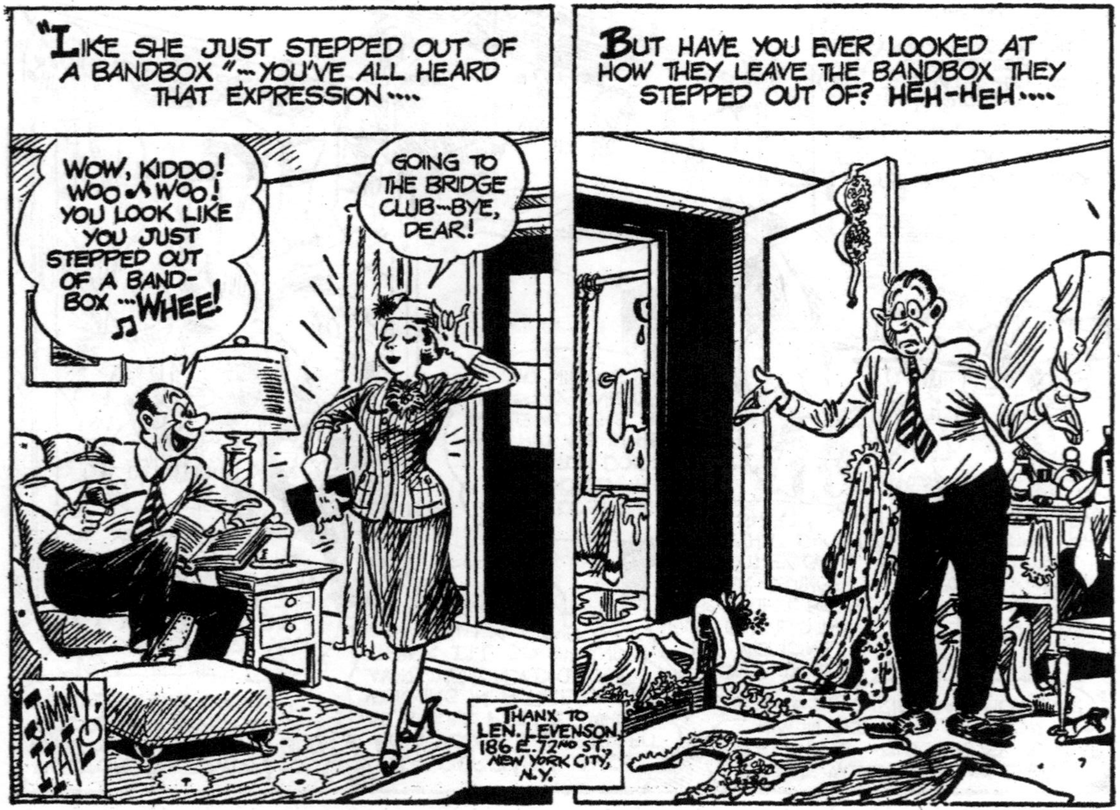
"LIKE SHE JUST STEPPED OUT OF A BANDBOX"...YOU'VE ALL HEARD THAT EXPRESSION....
WOW, KIDDO! WOO WOO! YOU LOOK LIKE YOU JUST STEPPED OUT OF A BAND-BOX ...WHEE!
GOING TO THE BRIDGE CLUB...BYE, DEAR!
JIMMY HATLO
THANX TO LEN. LEVENSON 186 E. 72ND ST., NEW YORK CITY, N.Y.
BUT HAVE YOU EVER LOOKED AT HOW THEY LEAVE THE BANDBOX THEY STEPPED OUT OF? HEH-HEH....

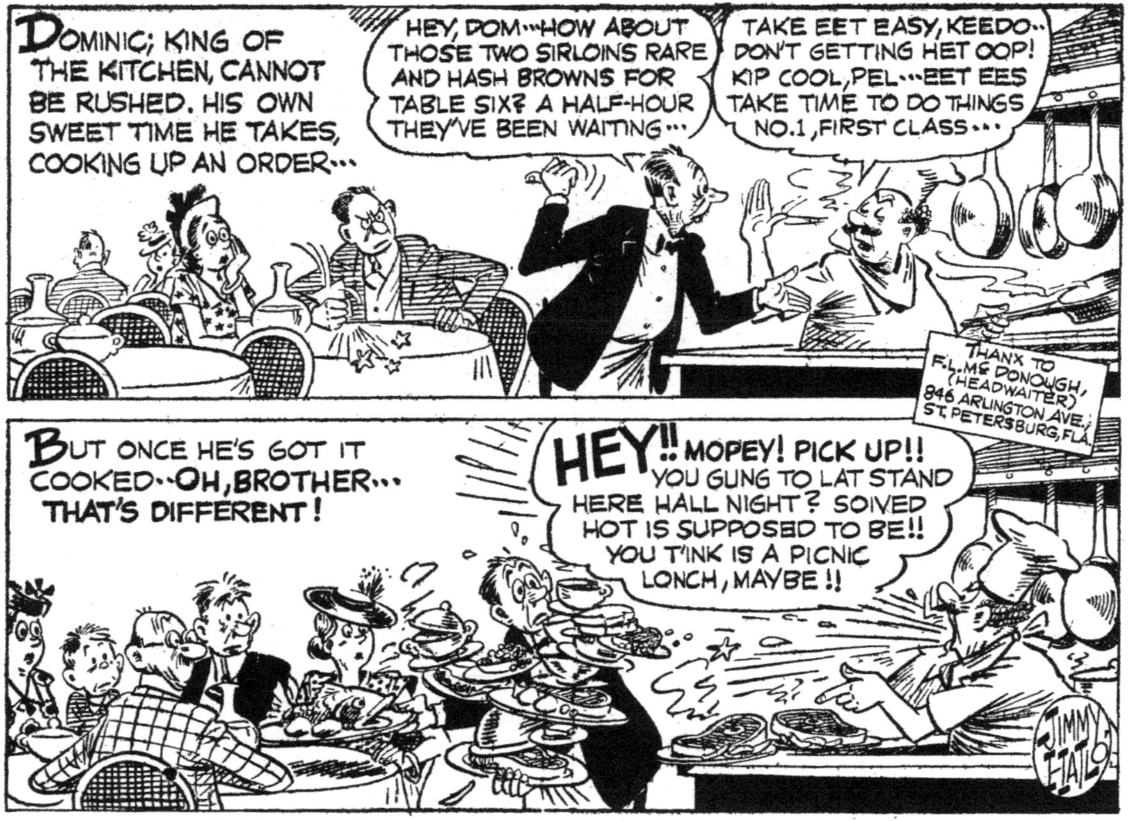
DOMINIC; KING OF THE KITCHEN, CANNOT BE RUSHED. HIS OWN SWEET TIME HE TAKES, COOKING UP AN ORDER...
HEY, DOM...HOW ABOUT THOSE TWO SIRLOINS RARE AND HASH BROWNS FOR TABLE SIX? A HALF-HOUR THEY'VE BEEN WAITING...
TAKE EET EASY, KEEDO.. DON'T GETTING HET OOP! KIP COOL, PEL...EET EES TAKE TIME TO DO THINGS NO.1, FIRST CLASS...
THANX TO F.L. MC DONOUGH, (HEADWAITER) 846 ARLINGTON AVE., ST. PETERSBURG, FLA.
BUT ONCE HE'S GOT IT COOKED..OH, BROTHER... THAT'S DIFFERENT!
HEY!! MOPEY! PICK UP!! YOU GUNG TO LAT STAND HERE HALL NIGHT? SOIVED HOT IS SUPPOSED TO BE!! YOU T'INK IS A PICNIC LONCH, MAYBE!!
JIMMY HATLO

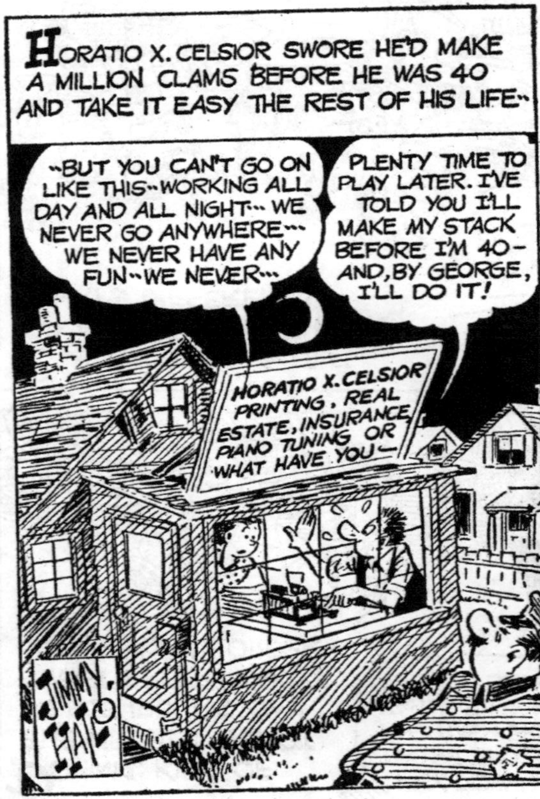
HORATIO X. CELSIOR SWORE HE'D MAKE A MILLION CLAMS BEFORE HE WAS 40 AND TAKE IT EASY THE REST OF HIS LIFE--
--BUT YOU CAN'T GO ON LIKE THIS--WORKING ALL DAY AND ALL NIGHT--- WE NEVER GO ANYWHERE--- WE NEVER HAVE ANY FUN--WE NEVER---
PLENTY TIME TO PLAY LATER. I'VE TOLD YOU I'LL MAKE MY STACK BEFORE I'M 40- AND, BY GEORGE, I'LL DO IT!
HORATIO X. CELSIOR PRINTING, REAL ESTATE, INSURANCE, PIANO TUNING OR WHAT HAVE YOU-
JIMMY HATLO
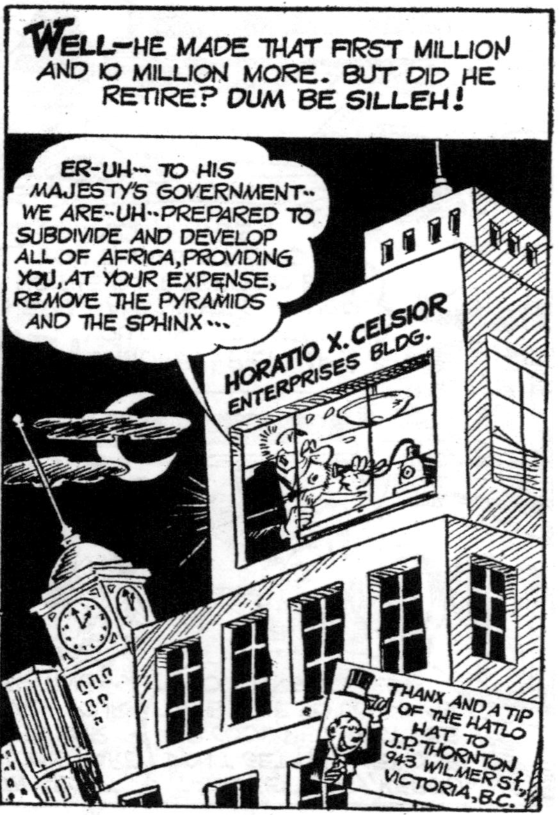
WELL-HE MADE THAT FIRST MILLION AND 10 MILLION MORE.. BUT DID HE RETIRE? DUM BE SILLEH!
ER-UH--- TO HIS MAJESTY'S GOVERNMENT-- WE ARE--UH--PREPARED TO SUBDIVIDE AND DEVELOP ALL OF AFRICA, PROVIDING YOU, AT YOUR EXPENSE, REMOVE THE PYRAMIDS AND THE SPHINX---
HORATIO X. CELSIOR ENTERPRISES BLDG.
THANX AND A TIP OF THE HATLO HAT TO J.P. THORNTON, 943 WILMER ST., VICTORIA, B.C.

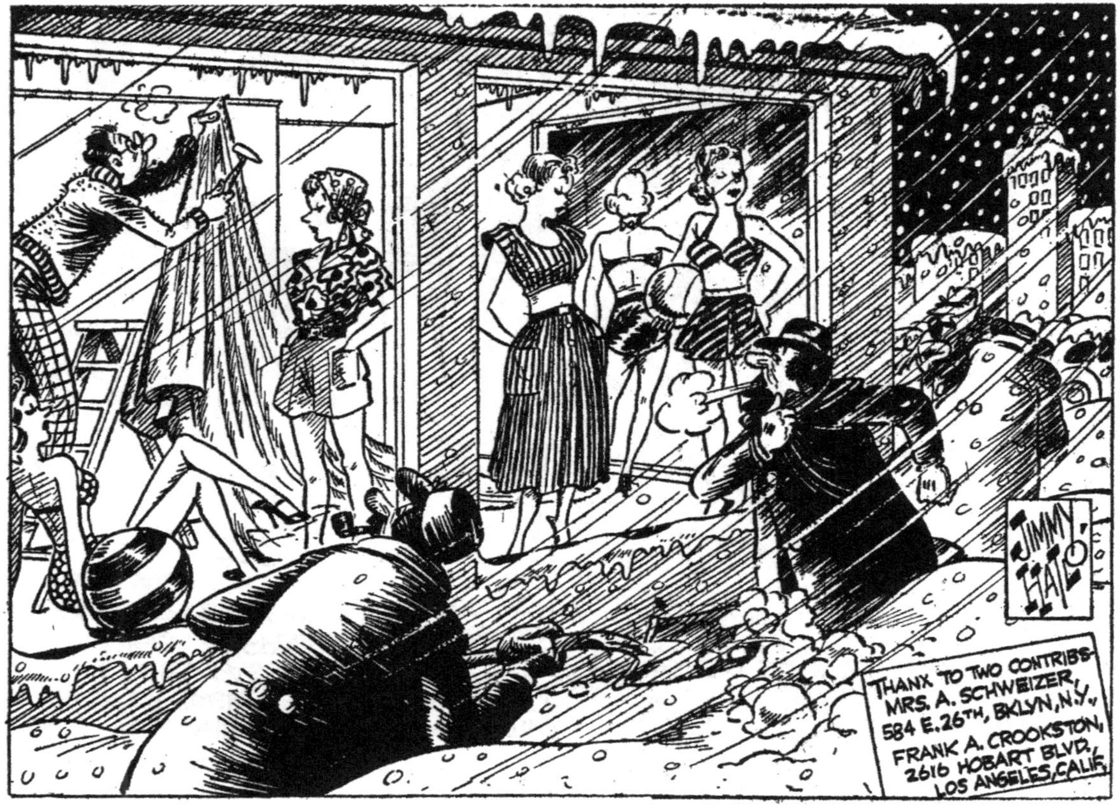
JIMMY HATLO
THANX TO TWO CONTRIBS- MRS. A. SCHWEIZER, 584 E. 26TH, BKLYN, N.Y., FRANK A. CROOKSTON, 2616 HOBART BLVD, LOS ANGELES, CALIF.

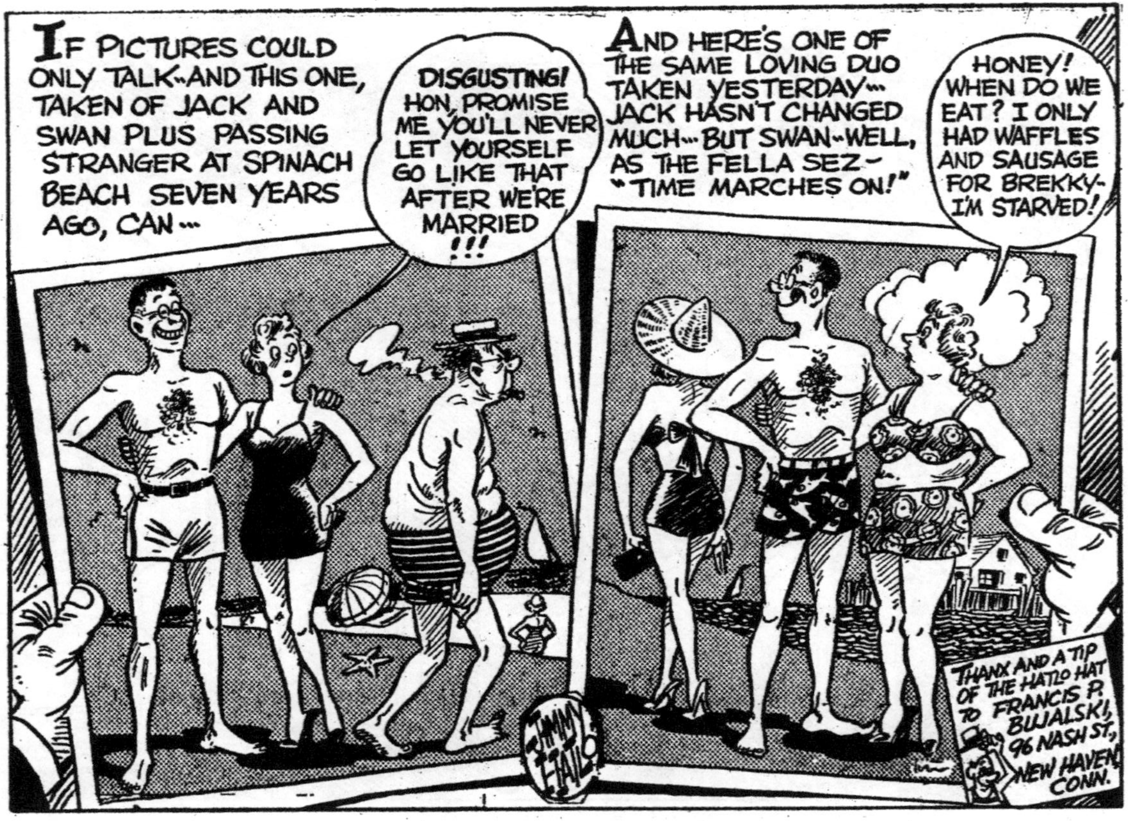
IF PICTURES COULD ONLY TALK--AND THIS ONE, TAKEN OF JACK AND SWAN PLUS PASSING STRANGER AT SPINACH BEACH SEVEN YEARS AGO, CAN...
DISGUSTING! HON, PROMISE ME YOU'LL NEVER LET YOURSELF GO LIKE THAT AFTER WE'RE MARRIED !!!
AND HERE'S ONE OF THE SAME LOVING DUO TAKEN YESTERDAY... JACK HASN'T CHANGED MUCH... BUT SWAN--WELL, AS THE FELLA SEZ-- "TIME MARCHES ON!"
HONEY! WHEN DO WE EAT? I ONLY HAD WAFFLES AND SAUSAGE FOR BREKKY-- I'M STARVED!
JIMMY HATLO
THANX AND A TIP OF THE HATLO HAT TO FRANCIS P. BUJALSKI, 96 NASH ST, NEW HAVEN, CONN.

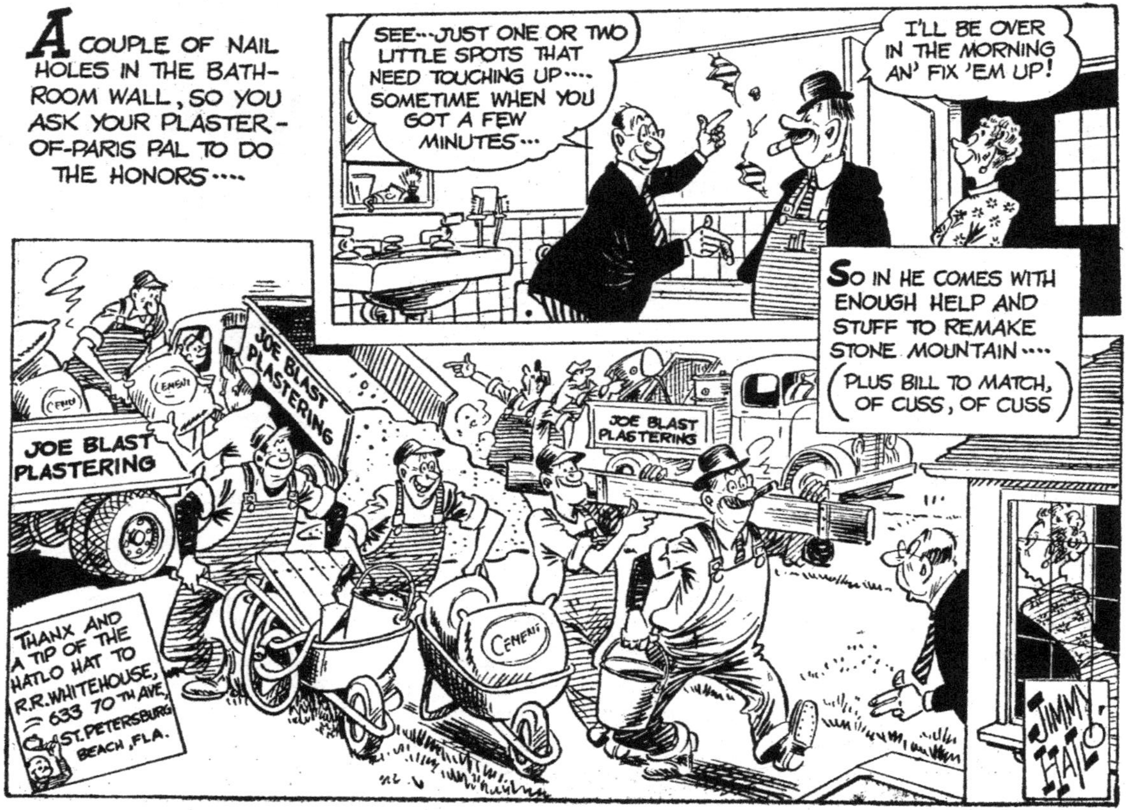
A COUPLE OF NAIL HOLES IN THE BATH-ROOM WALL, SO YOU ASK YOUR PLASTER-OF-PARIS PAL TO DO THE HONORS....
SEE...JUST ONE OR TWO LITTLE SPOTS THAT NEED TOUCHING UP.... SOMETIME WHEN YOU GOT A FEW MINUTES...
I'LL BE OVER IN THE MORNING AN' FIX 'EM UP!
SO IN HE COMES WITH ENOUGH HELP AND STUFF TO REMAKE STONE MOUNTAIN....
(PLUS BILL TO MATCH, OF CUSS, OF CUSS)
JOE BLAST PLASTERING
JOE BLAST PLASTERING
JOE BLAST PLASTERING
THANX AND A TIP OF THE HATLO HAT TO R.R.WHITEHOUSE, 633 70TH AVE, ST. PETERSBURG BEACH, FLA.
JIMMY HATLO

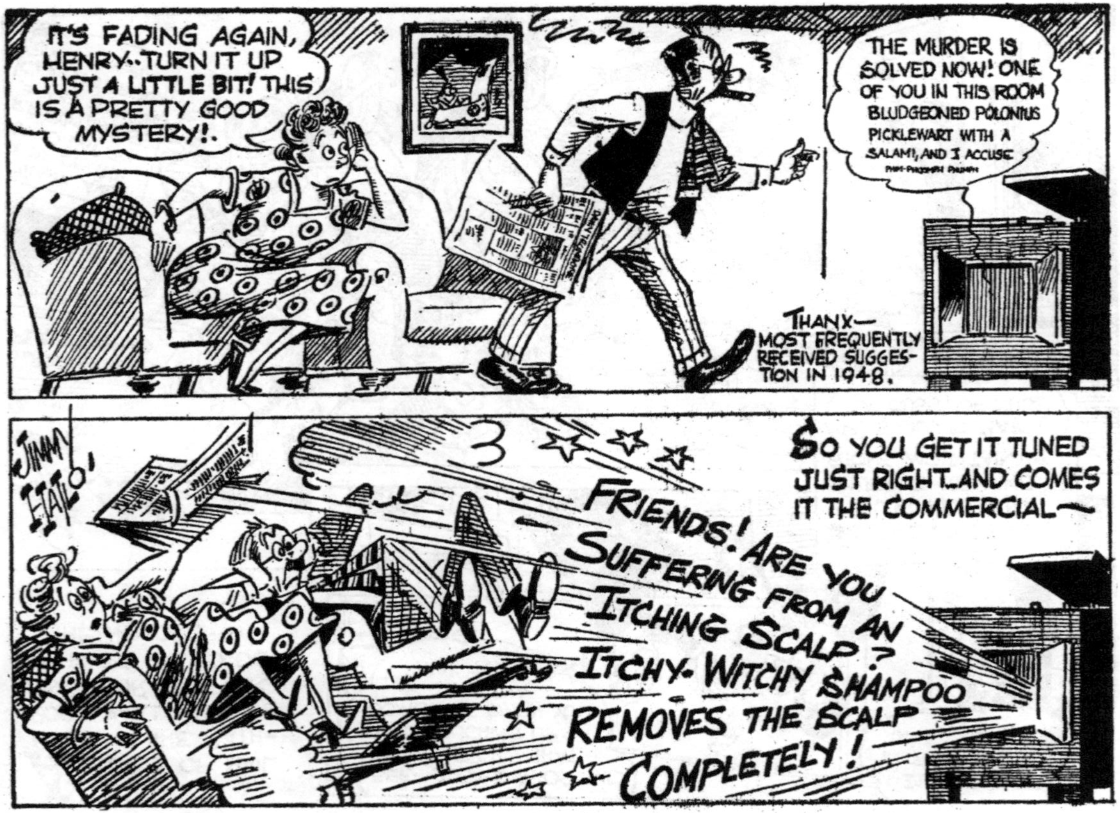
IT'S FADING AGAIN, HENRY.. TURN IT UP JUST A LITTLE BIT! THIS IS A PRETTY GOOD MYSTERY!.
THE MURDER IS SOLVED NOW! ONE OF YOU IN THIS ROOM BLUDGEONED POLONIUS PICKLEWART WITH A SALAMI, AND I ACCUSE
THANX— MOST FREQUENTLY RECEIVED SUGGESTION IN 1948.
SO YOU GET IT TUNED JUST RIGHT.. AND COMES IT THE COMMERCIAL—
FRIENDS! ARE YOU SUFFERING FROM AN ITCHING SCALP? ITCHY-WITCHY SHAMPOO REMOVES THE SCALP COMPLETELY!
JIMMY HATLO

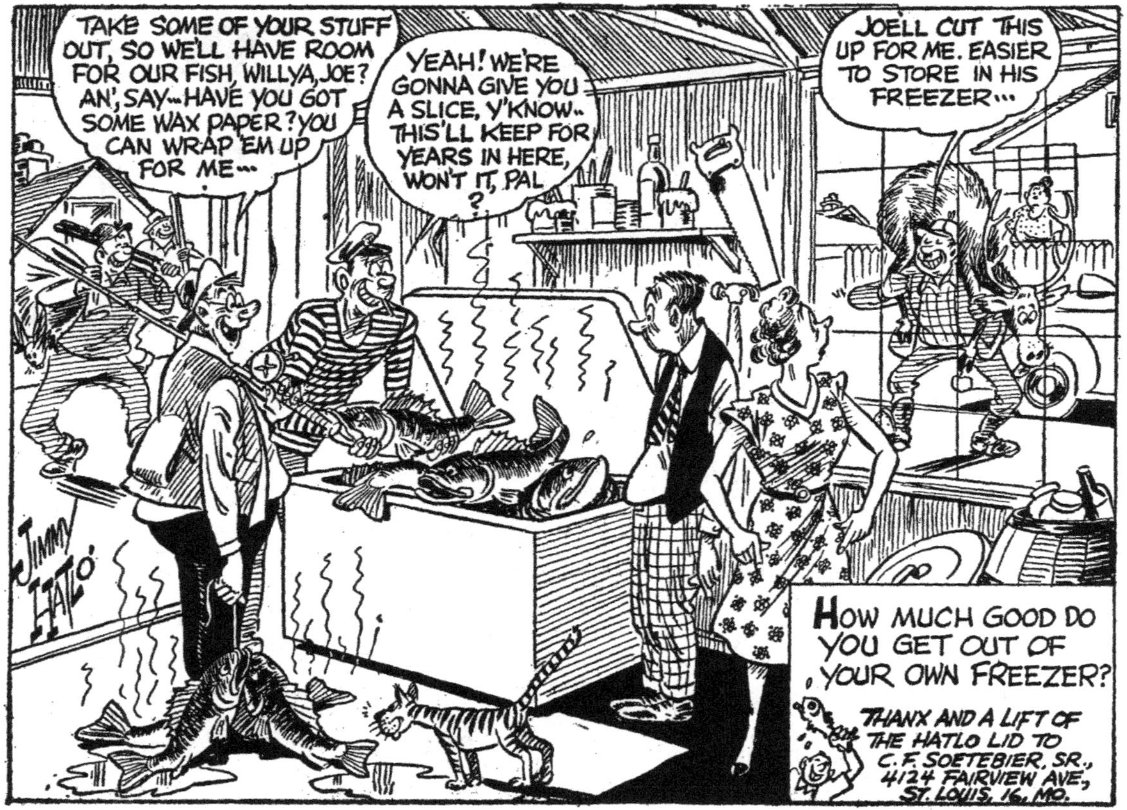
TAKE SOME OF YOUR STUFF OUT, SO WE'LL HAVE ROOM FOR OUR FISH, WILLYA, JOE? AN', SAY... HAVE YOU GOT SOME WAX PAPER? YOU CAN WRAP 'EM UP FOR ME...
YEAH! WE'RE GONNA GIVE YOU A SLICE, Y'KNOW.. THIS'LL KEEP FOR YEARS IN HERE, WON'T IT, PAL?
JOE'LL CUT THIS UP FOR ME. EASIER TO STORE IN HIS FREEZER...
JIMMY HATLO
HOW MUCH GOOD DO YOU GET OUT OF YOUR OWN FREEZER?
THANX AND A LIFT OF THE HATLO LID TO C. F. SOETEBIER, SR., 4124 FAIRVIEW AVE, ST. LOUIS, 16, MO.

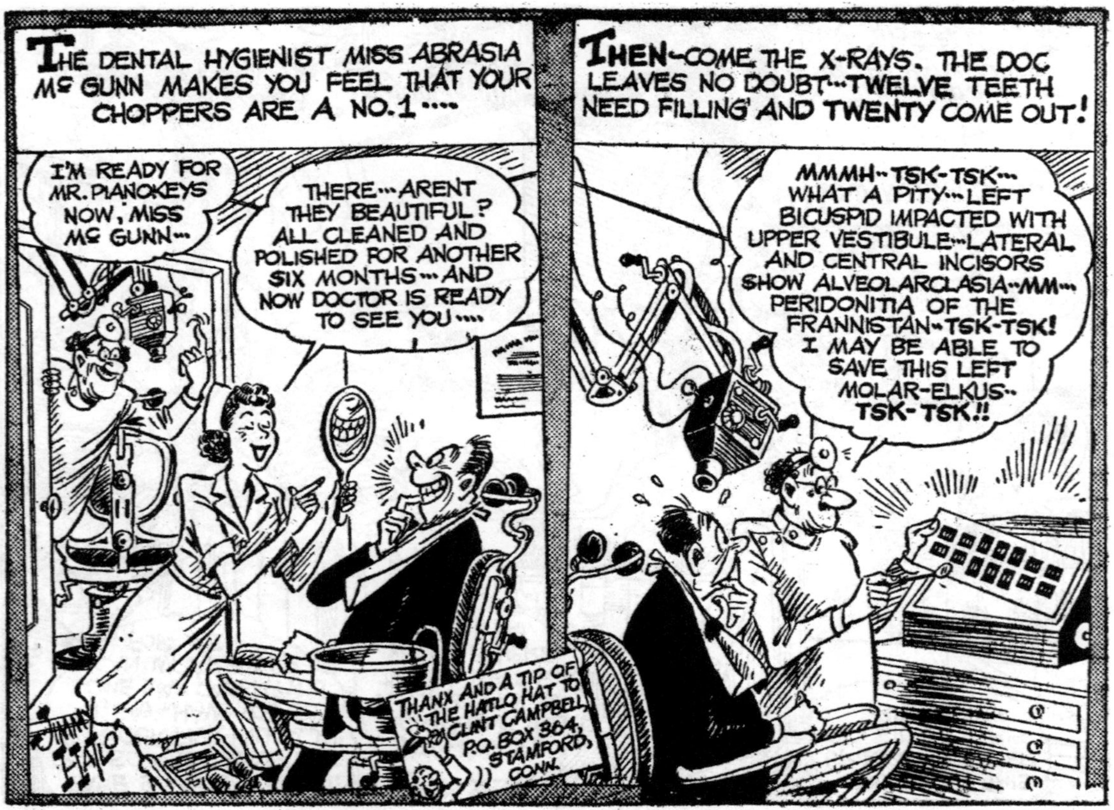
THE DENTAL HYGIENIST MISS ABRASIA McGUNN MAKES YOU FEEL THAT YOUR CHOPPERS ARE A NO.1....
I'M READY FOR MR. PIANOKEYS NOW, MISS McGUNN...
THERE...ARENT THEY BEAUTIFUL? ALL CLEANED AND POLISHED FOR ANOTHER SIX MONTHS...AND NOW DOCTOR IS READY TO SEE YOU....
THANX AND A TIP OF THE HATLO HAT TO CLINT CAMPBELL, P.O. BOX 364, STAMFORD, CONN.
JIMMY HATLO
THEN-COME THE X-RAYS. THE DOC LEAVES NO DOUBT--TWELVE TEETH NEED FILLING AND TWENTY COME OUT!
MMMH--TSK-TSK... WHAT A PITY...LEFT BICUSPID IMPACTED WITH UPPER VESTIBULE...LATERAL AND CENTRAL INCISORS SHOW ALVEOLARCLASIA--MM... PERIDONITIA OF THE FRANNISTAN--TSK-TSK! I MAY BE ABLE TO SAVE THIS LEFT MOLAR-ELKUS-- TSK-TSK!!

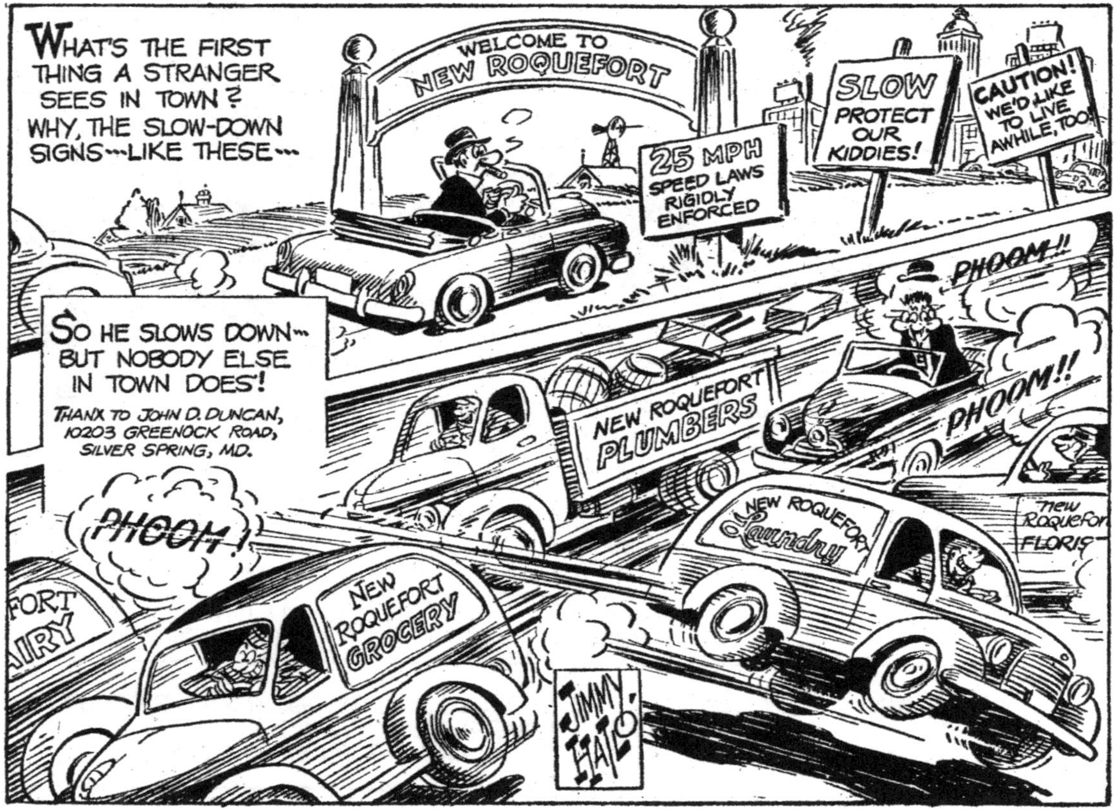
WHAT'S THE FIRST THING A STRANGER SEES IN TOWN? WHY, THE SLOW-DOWN SIGNS---LIKE THESE---
WELCOME TO NEW ROQUEFORT
25 MPH SPEED LAWS RIGIDLY ENFORCED
SLOW PROTECT OUR KIDDIES!
CAUTION! WE'D LIKE TO LIVE AWHILE, TOO!
SO HE SLOWS DOWN--- BUT NOBODY ELSE IN TOWN DOES!
THANX TO JOHN D. DUNCAN, 10203 GREENOCK ROAD, SILVER SPRING, MD.
PHOOM!!
PHOOM!!
NEW ROQUEFORT PLUMBERS
PHOOM!
NEW ROQUEFORT Laundry
New Roquefor FLORIS
New Roquefort GROCERY
FORT AIRY
JIMMY HATLO

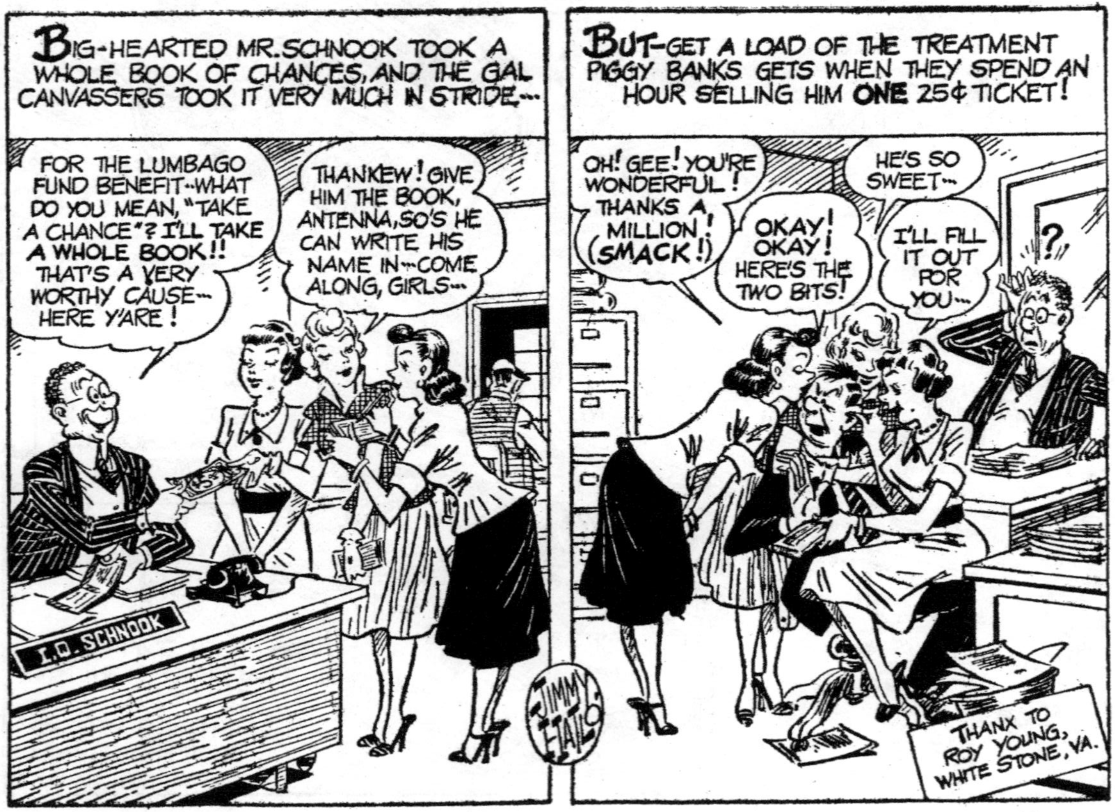
BIG-HEARTED MR. SCHNOOK TOOK A WHOLE BOOK OF CHANCES, AND THE GAL CANVASSERS TOOK IT VERY MUCH IN STRIDE...
FOR THE LUMBAGO FUND BENEFIT--WHAT DO YOU MEAN, "TAKE A CHANCE"? I'LL TAKE A WHOLE BOOK!! THAT'S A VERY WORTHY CAUSE--HERE Y'ARE!
THANKEW! GIVE HIM THE BOOK, ANTENNA, SO'S HE CAN WRITE HIS NAME IN--COME ALONG, GIRLS--
I.Q. SCHNOOK
JIMMY HATLO
BUT-GET A LOAD OF THE TREATMENT PIGGY BANKS GETS WHEN THEY SPEND AN HOUR SELLING HIM ONE 25¢ TICKET!
OH! GEE! YOU'RE WONDERFUL! THANKS A MILLION! (SMACK!)
OKAY! OKAY! HERE'S THE TWO BITS!
HE'S SO SWEET--
I'LL FILL IT OUT FOR YOU--
?
THANX TO ROY YOUNG, WHITE STONE, VA.

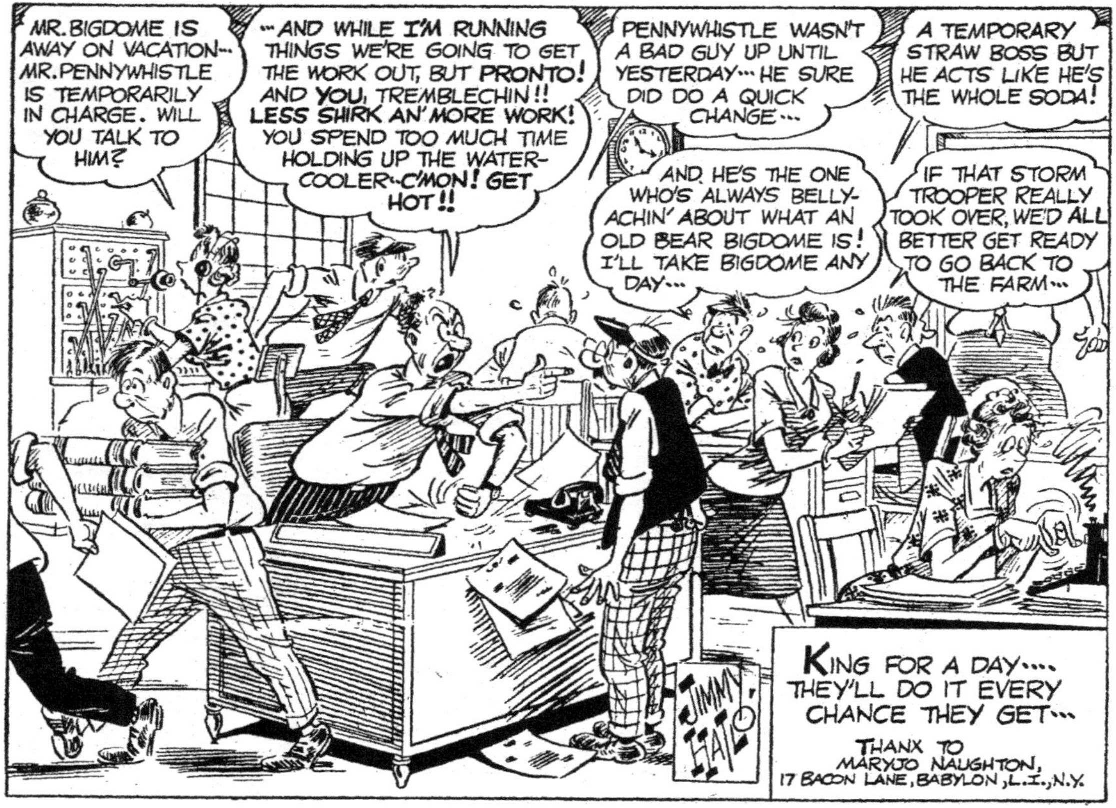
MR. BIGDOME IS AWAY ON VACATION... MR. PENNYWHISTLE IS TEMPORARILY IN CHARGE. WILL YOU TALK TO HIM?
...AND WHILE I'M RUNNING THINGS WE'RE GOING TO GET THE WORK OUT, BUT PRONTO! AND YOU, TREMBLECHIN!! LESS SHIRK AN' MORE WORK! YOU SPEND TOO MUCH TIME HOLDING UP THE WATER-COOLER--C'MON! GET HOT!!
PENNYWHISTLE WASN'T A BAD GUY UP UNTIL YESTERDAY... HE SURE DID DO A QUICK CHANGE...
AND HE'S THE ONE WHO'S ALWAYS BELLY-ACHIN' ABOUT WHAT AN OLD BEAR BIGDOME IS! I'LL TAKE BIGDOME ANY DAY...
A TEMPORARY STRAW BOSS BUT HE ACTS LIKE HE'S THE WHOLE SODA!
IF THAT STORM TROOPER REALLY TOOK OVER, WE'D ALL BETTER GET READY TO GO BACK TO THE FARM...
KING FOR A DAY.... THEY'LL DO IT EVERY CHANCE THEY GET...
THANX TO MARYJO NAUGHTON, 17 BACON LANE, BABYLON, L.I., N.Y.
JIMMY HATLO

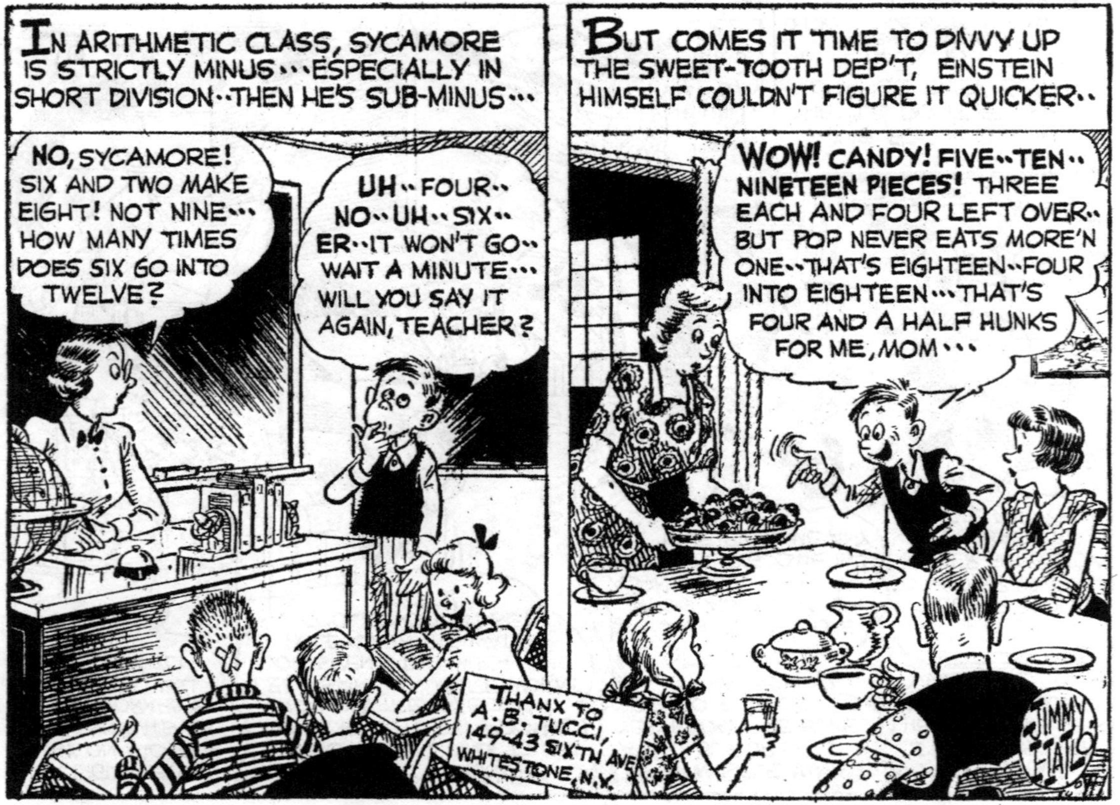
IN ARITHMETIC CLASS, SYCAMORE IS STRICTLY MINUS···ESPECIALLY IN SHORT DIVISION··THEN HE'S SUB-MINUS···
NO, SYCAMORE! SIX AND TWO MAKE EIGHT! NOT NINE··· HOW MANY TIMES DOES SIX GO INTO TWELVE?
UH··FOUR·· NO··UH··SIX·· ER··IT WON'T GO·· WAIT A MINUTE··· WILL YOU SAY IT AGAIN, TEACHER?
THANX TO A.B. TUCCI, 149-43 SIXTH AVE WHITESTONE, N.Y.
BUT COMES IT TIME TO DIVVY UP THE SWEET-TOOTH DEP'T, EINSTEIN HIMSELF COULDN'T FIGURE IT QUICKER··
WOW! CANDY! FIVE··TEN·· NINETEEN PIECES! THREE EACH AND FOUR LEFT OVER·· BUT POP NEVER EATS MORE'N ONE··THAT'S EIGHTEEN··FOUR INTO EIGHTEEN···THAT'S FOUR AND A HALF HUNKS FOR ME, MOM···
JIMMY HATLO

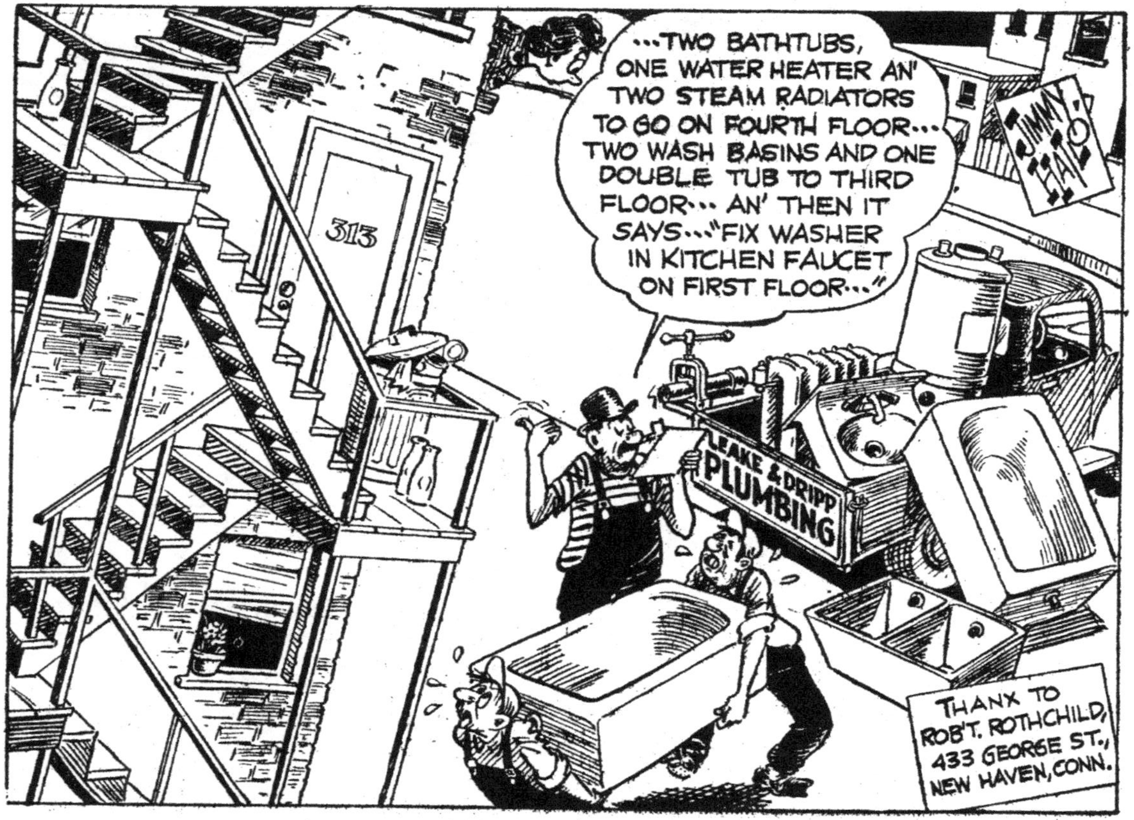
...TWO BATHTUBS, ONE WATER HEATER AN' TWO STEAM RADIATORS TO GO ON FOURTH FLOOR... TWO WASH BASINS AND ONE DOUBLE TUB TO THIRD FLOOR... AN' THEN IT SAYS..."FIX WASHER IN KITCHEN FAUCET ON FIRST FLOOR..."
313
LEAKE & DRIPP PLUMBING
THANX TO ROB'T. ROTHCHILD, 433 GEORGE ST., NEW HAVEN, CONN.

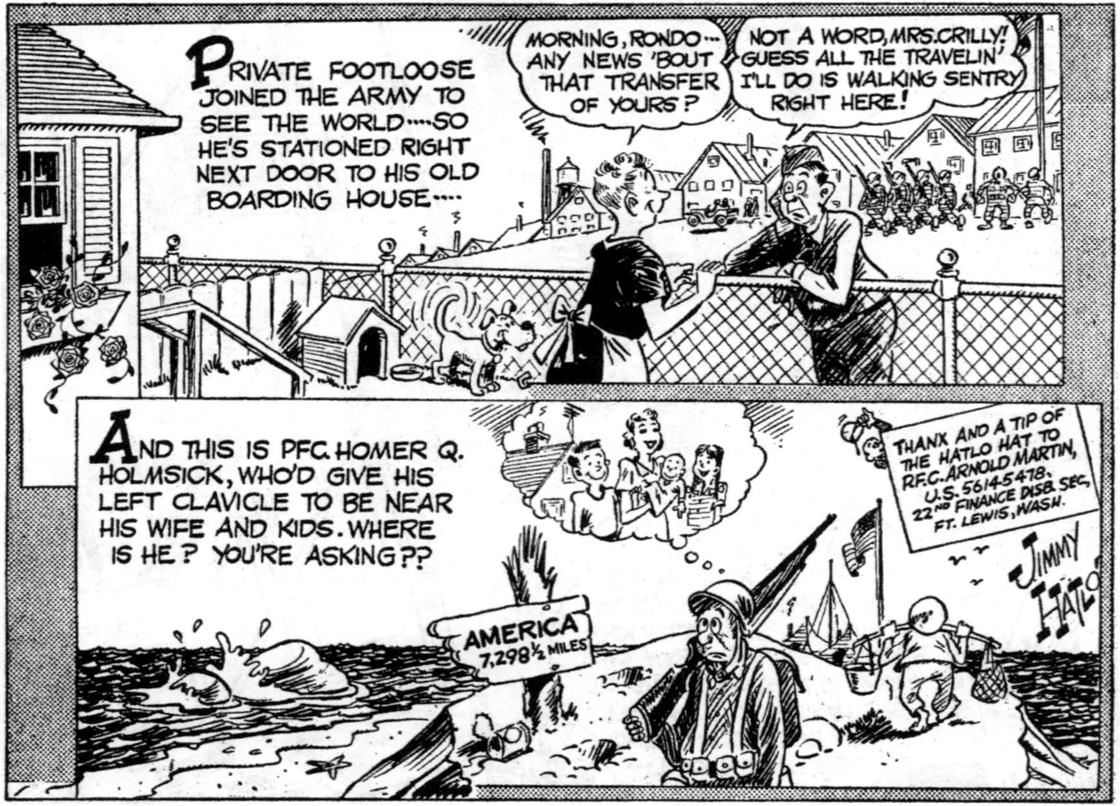
PRIVATE FOOTLOOSE JOINED THE ARMY TO SEE THE WORLD....SO HE'S STATIONED RIGHT NEXT DOOR TO HIS OLD BOARDING HOUSE....
MORNING, RONDO... ANY NEWS 'BOUT THAT TRANSFER OF YOURS?
NOT A WORD, MRS. CRILLY! GUESS ALL THE TRAVELIN' I'LL DO IS WALKING SENTRY RIGHT HERE!
AND THIS IS PFC. HOMER Q. HOLMSICK, WHO'D GIVE HIS LEFT CLAVICLE TO BE NEAR HIS WIFE AND KIDS. WHERE IS HE? YOU'RE ASKING??
AMERICA 7,298½ MILES
THANX AND A TIP OF THE HATLO HAT TO P.F.C. ARNOLD MARTIN, U.S. 56145478, 22ND FINANCE DISB. SEC, FT. LEWIS, WASH.
JIMMY HATLO

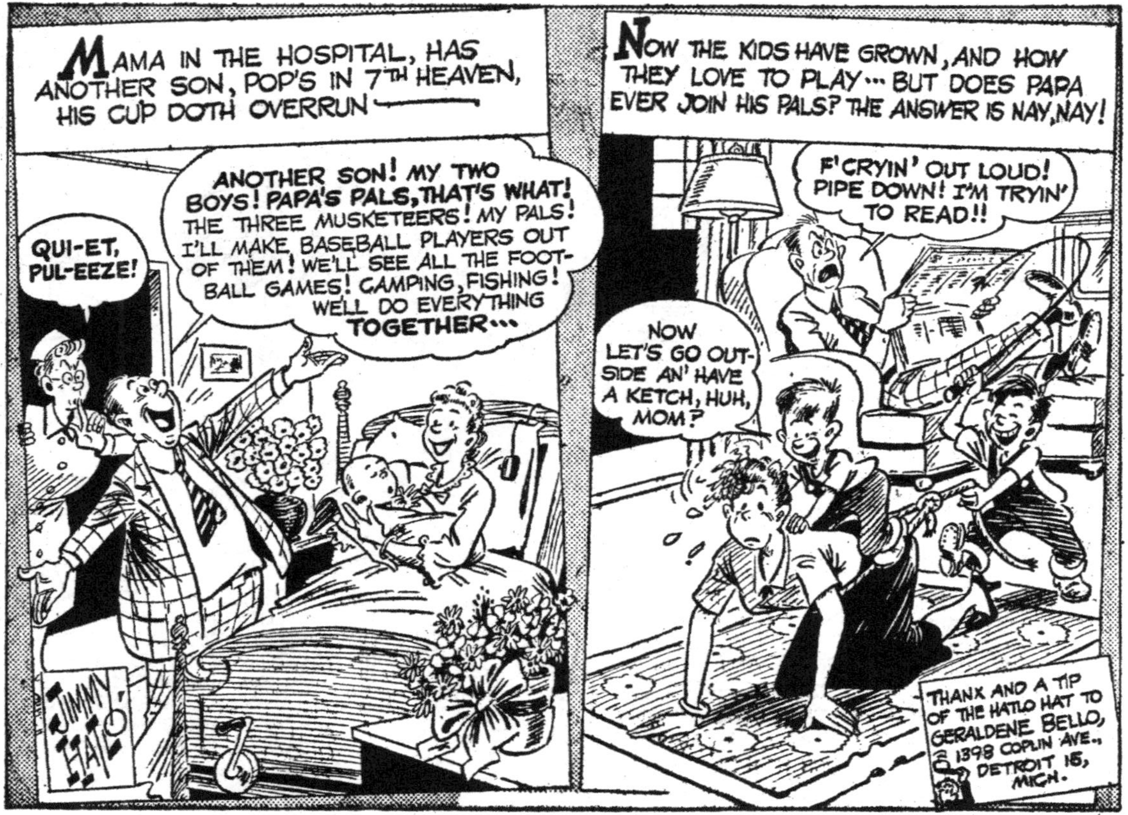
MAMA IN THE HOSPITAL, HAS ANOTHER SON, POP'S IN 7TH HEAVEN, HIS CUP DOTH OVERRUN
QUI-ET, PUL-EEZE!
ANOTHER SON! MY TWO BOYS! PAPA'S PALS, THAT'S WHAT! THE THREE MUSKETEERS! MY PALS! I'LL MAKE BASEBALL PLAYERS OUT OF THEM! WE'LL SEE ALL THE FOOT-BALL GAMES! CAMPING, FISHING! WE'LL DO EVERYTHING TOGETHER...
JIMMY HATLO
NOW THE KIDS HAVE GROWN, AND HOW THEY LOVE TO PLAY... BUT DOES PAPA EVER JOIN HIS PALS? THE ANSWER IS NAY, NAY!
F'CRYIN' OUT LOUD! PIPE DOWN! I'M TRYIN' TO READ!!
NOW LET'S GO OUT-SIDE AN' HAVE A KETCH, HUH, MOM?
THANX AND A TIP OF THE HATLO HAT TO GERALDENE BELLO, 1398 COPLIN AVE., DETROIT 15, MICH.

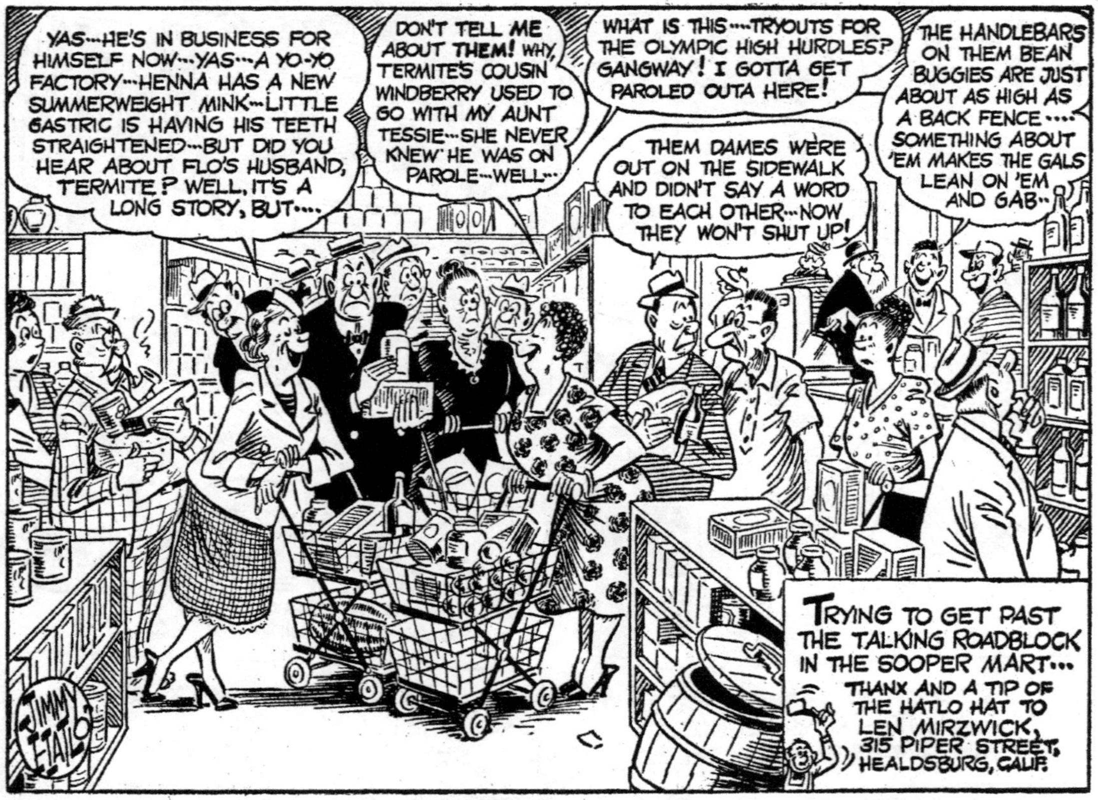
YAS…HE'S IN BUSINESS FOR HIMSELF NOW…YAS…A YO-YO FACTORY…HENNA HAS A NEW SUMMERWEIGHT MINK…LITTLE GASTRIC IS HAVING HIS TEETH STRAIGHTENED…BUT DID YOU HEAR ABOUT FLO'S HUSBAND, TERMITE? WELL, IT'S A LONG STORY, BUT….
DON'T TELL ME ABOUT THEM! WHY, TERMITE'S COUSIN WINDBERRY USED TO GO WITH MY AUNT TESSIE…SHE NEVER KNEW HE WAS ON PAROLE…WELL…
WHAT IS THIS….TRYOUTS FOR THE OLYMPIC HIGH HURDLES? GANGWAY! I GOTTA GET PAROLED OUTA HERE!
THEM DAMES WERE OUT ON THE SIDEWALK AND DIDN'T SAY A WORD TO EACH OTHER…NOW THEY WON'T SHUT UP!
THE HANDLEBARS ON THEM BEAN BUGGIES ARE JUST ABOUT AS HIGH AS A BACK FENCE…. SOMETHING ABOUT 'EM MAKES THE GALS LEAN ON 'EM AND GAB…
TRYING TO GET PAST THE TALKING ROADBLOCK IN THE SOOPER MART…
THANX AND A TIP OF THE HATLO HAT TO LEN MIRZWICK, 315 PIPER STREET, HEALDSBURG, CALIF.
JIMMY HATLO

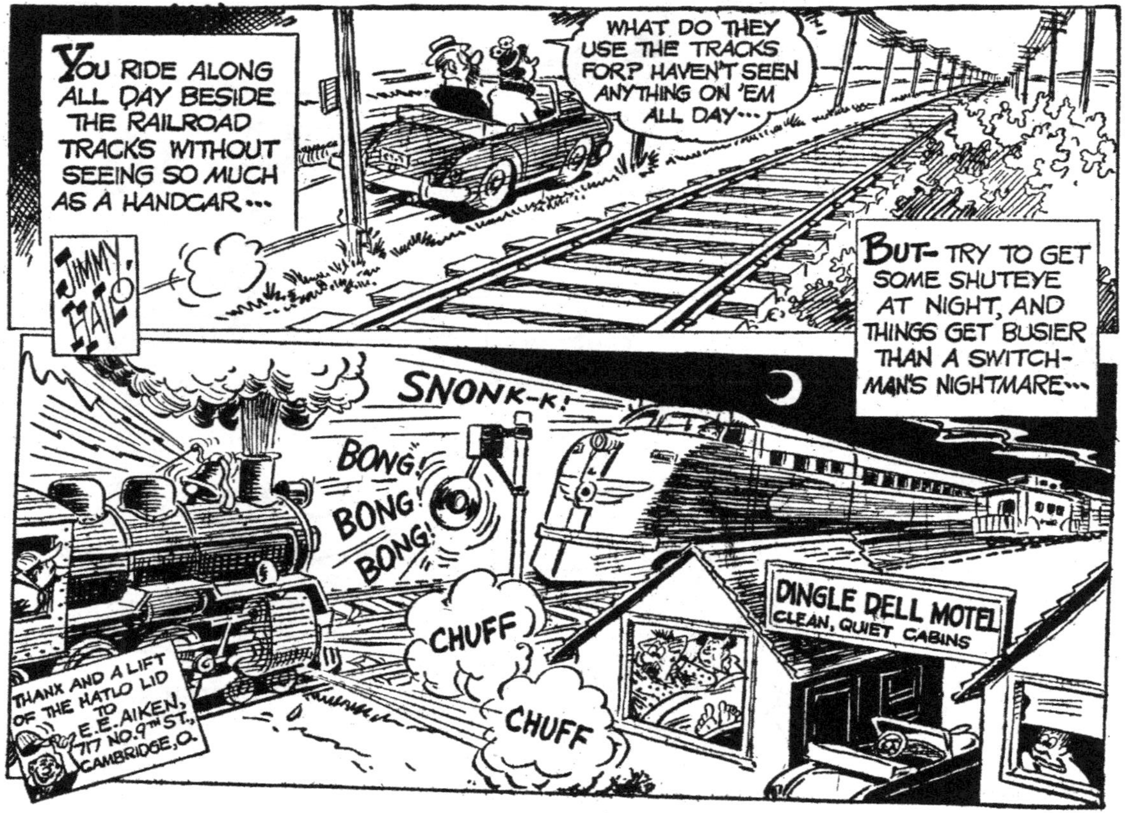
YOU RIDE ALONG ALL DAY BESIDE THE RAILROAD TRACKS WITHOUT SEEING SO MUCH AS A HANDCAR...
WHAT DO THEY USE THE TRACKS FOR? HAVEN'T SEEN ANYTHING ON 'EM ALL DAY...
JIMMY HATLO
BUT- TRY TO GET SOME SHUTEYE AT NIGHT, AND THINGS GET BUSIER THAN A SWITCHMAN'S NIGHTMARE...
SNONK-K!
BONG! BONG! BONG!
CHUFF
CHUFF
DINGLE DELL MOTEL
CLEAN, QUIET CABINS
THANX AND A LIFT OF THE HATLO LID TO E.E. AIKEN, 717 NO. 9TH ST., CAMBRIDGE, O.

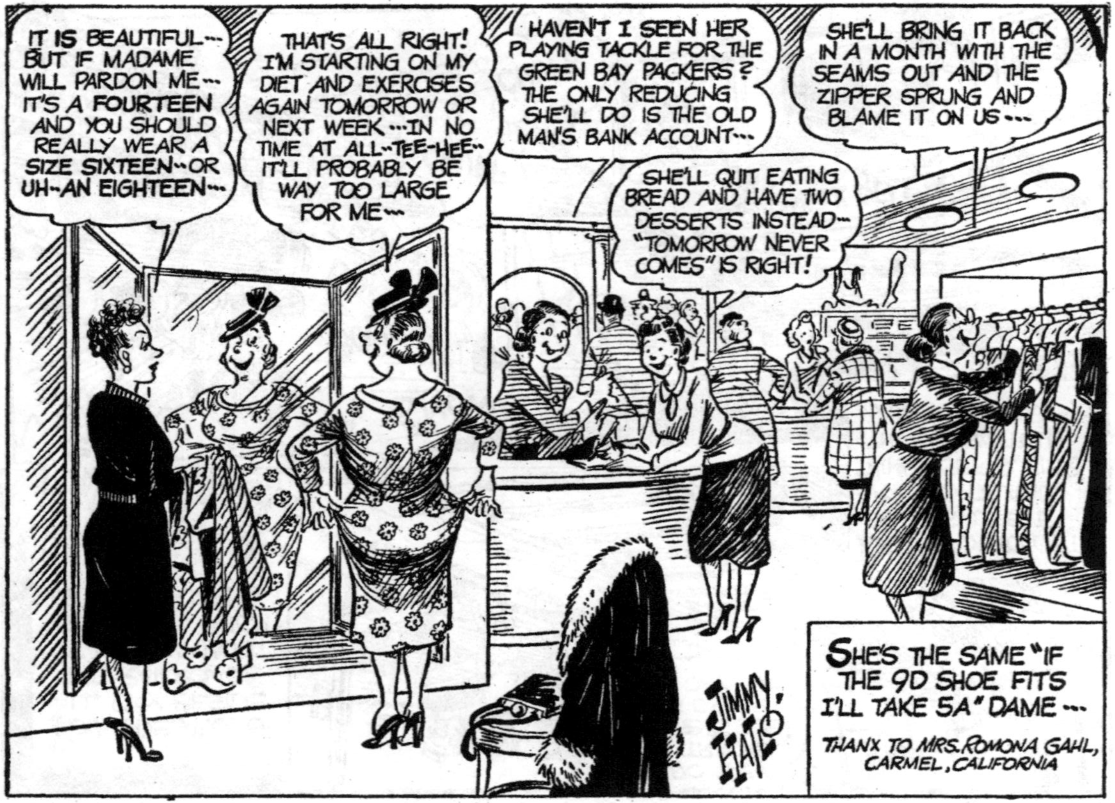
IT IS BEAUTIFUL--- BUT IF MADAME WILL PARDON ME--- IT'S A FOURTEEN AND YOU SHOULD REALLY WEAR A SIZE SIXTEEN--OR UH--AN EIGHTEEN---
THAT'S ALL RIGHT! I'M STARTING ON MY DIET AND EXERCISES AGAIN TOMORROW OR NEXT WEEK---IN NO TIME AT ALL--TEE-HEE-- IT'LL PROBABLY BE WAY TOO LARGE FOR ME---
HAVEN'T I SEEN HER PLAYING TACKLE FOR THE GREEN BAY PACKERS? THE ONLY REDUCING SHE'LL DO IS THE OLD MAN'S BANK ACCOUNT---
SHE'LL QUIT EATING BREAD AND HAVE TWO DESSERTS INSTEAD--- "TOMORROW NEVER COMES" IS RIGHT!
SHE'LL BRING IT BACK IN A MONTH WITH THE SEAMS OUT AND THE ZIPPER SPRUNG AND BLAME IT ON US---
JIMMY HATLO
SHE'S THE SAME "IF THE 9D SHOE FITS I'LL TAKE 5A" DAME---
THANX TO MRS. ROMONA GAHL, CARMEL, CALIFORNIA

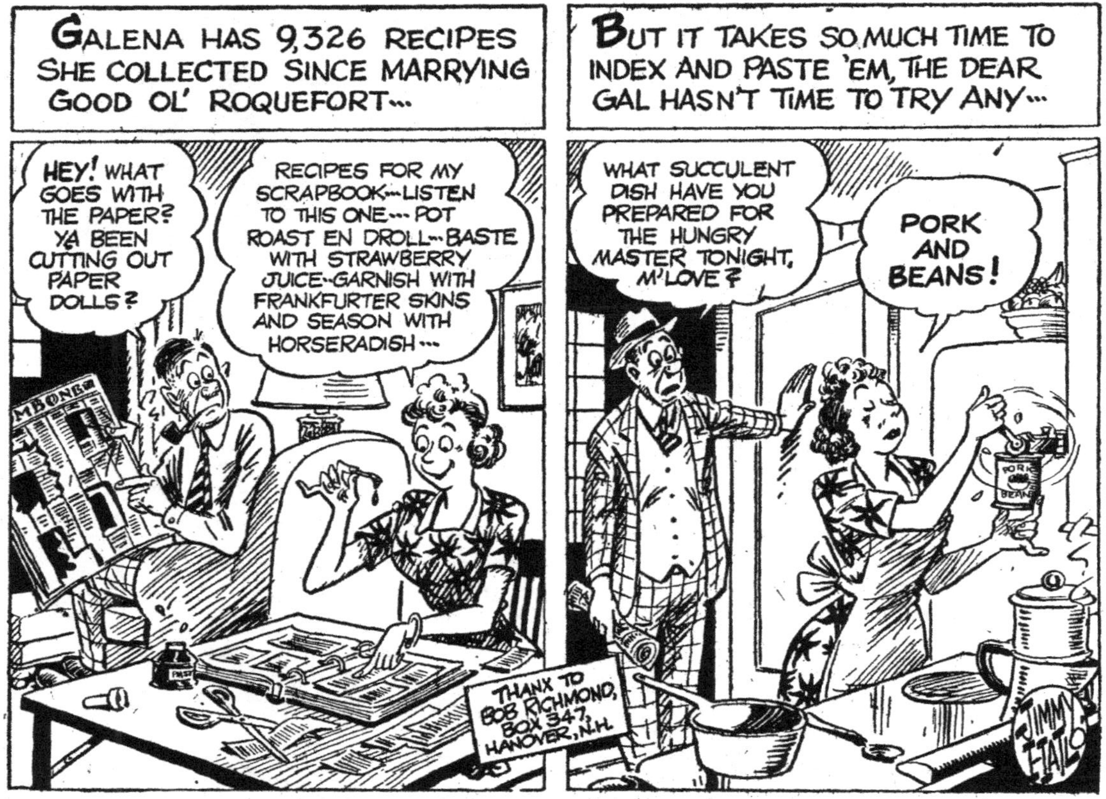
GALENA HAS 9,326 RECIPES SHE COLLECTED SINCE MARRYING GOOD OL' ROQUEFORT...
HEY! WHAT GOES WITH THE PAPER? YA BEEN CUTTING OUT PAPER DOLLS?
RECIPES FOR MY SCRAPBOOK...LISTEN TO THIS ONE...POT ROAST EN DROLL...BASTE WITH STRAWBERRY JUICE...GARNISH WITH FRANKFURTER SKINS AND SEASON WITH HORSERADISH...
THANX TO BOB RICHMOND, BOX 347, HANOVER, N.H.
BUT IT TAKES SO MUCH TIME TO INDEX AND PASTE 'EM, THE DEAR GAL HASN'T TIME TO TRY ANY...
WHAT SUCCULENT DISH HAVE YOU PREPARED FOR THE HUNGRY MASTER TONIGHT, M'LOVE?
PORK AND BEANS!
JIMMY HATLO

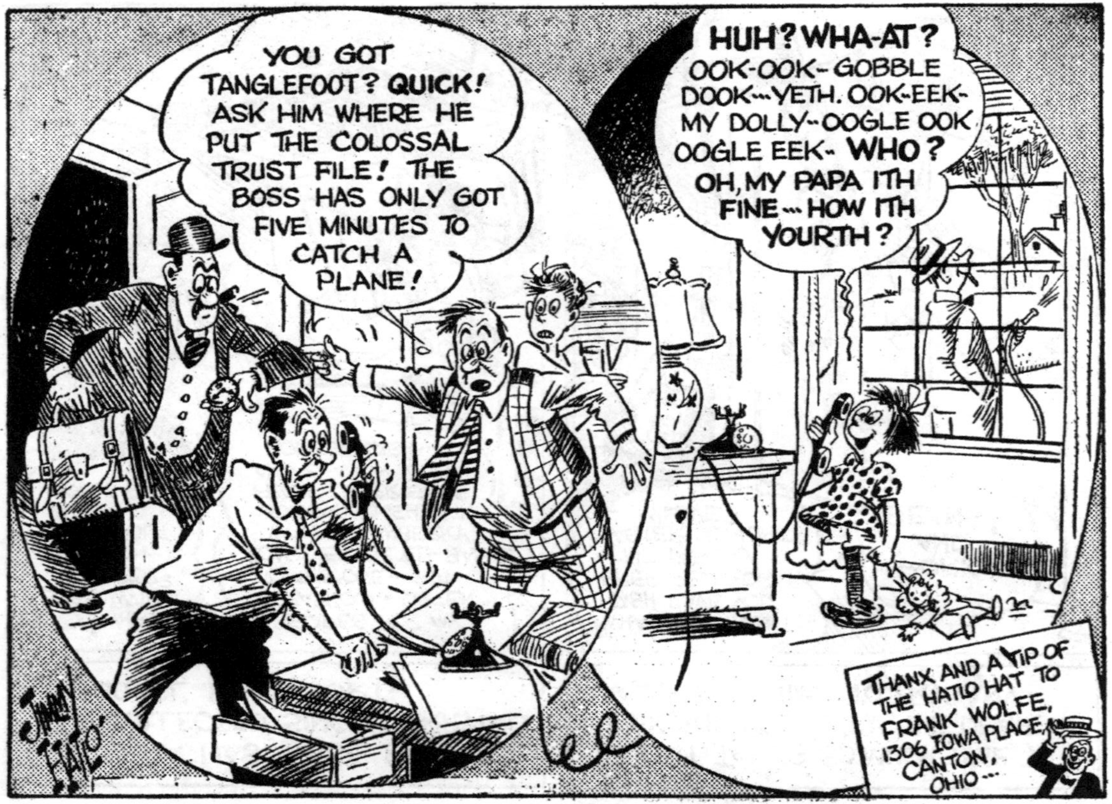
YOU GOT TANGLEFOOT? QUICK! ASK HIM WHERE HE PUT THE COLOSSAL TRUST FILE! THE BOSS HAS ONLY GOT FIVE MINUTES TO CATCH A PLANE!
HUH? WHA-AT? OOK-OOK-GOBBLE DOOK--- YETH. OOK-EEK- MY DOLLY-OOGLE OOK OOGLE EEK- WHO? OH, MY PAPA ITH FINE--- HOW ITH YOURTH?
THANX AND A TIP OF THE HATLO HAT TO FRANK WOLFE, 1306 IOWA PLACE, CANTON, OHIO---
JIMMY HATLO

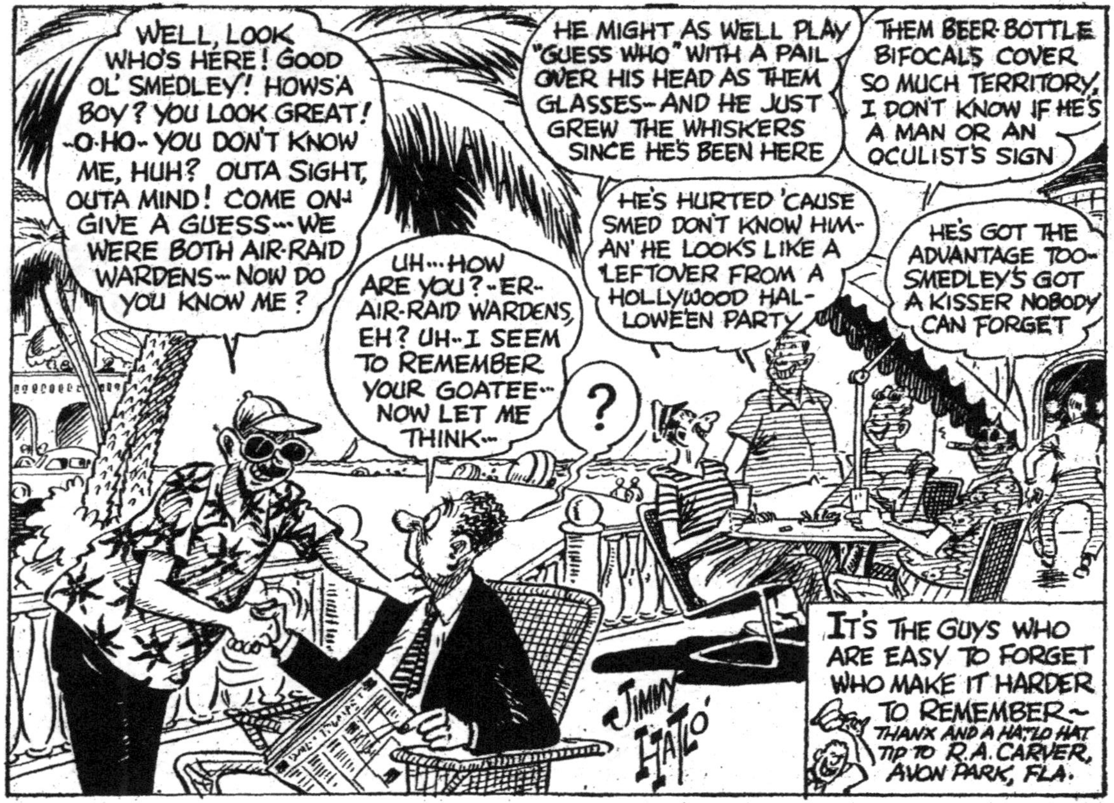

WELL, LOOK WHO'S HERE! GOOD OL' SMEDLEY! HOWS'A BOY? YOU LOOK GREAT! -O-HO- YOU DON'T KNOW ME, HUH? OUTA SIGHT, OUTA MIND! COME ON- GIVE A GUESS--- WE WERE BOTH AIR-RAID WARDENS--- NOW DO YOU KNOW ME?
UH---HOW ARE YOU?--ER- AIR-RAID WARDENS, EH? UH--I SEEM TO REMEMBER YOUR GOATEE-- NOW LET ME THINK--
?
HE MIGHT AS WELL PLAY "GUESS WHO" WITH A PAIL OVER HIS HEAD AS THEM GLASSES-- AND HE JUST GREW THE WHISKERS SINCE HE'S BEEN HERE
HE'S HURTED 'CAUSE SMED DON'T KNOW HIM-- AN' HE LOOKS LIKE A 'LEFTOVER FROM A HOLLYWOOD HAL-LOWE'EN PARTY
THEM BEER-BOTTLE BIFOCALS COVER SO MUCH TERRITORY, I DON'T KNOW IF HE'S A MAN OR AN OCULIST'S SIGN
HE'S GOT THE ADVANTAGE TOO- SMEDLEY'S GOT A KISSER NOBODY CAN FORGET
JIMMY HATLO
IT'S THE GUYS WHO ARE EASY TO FORGET WHO MAKE IT HARDER TO REMEMBER~
THANX AND A HATLO HAT TIP TO R.A. CARVER, AVON PARK, FLA.

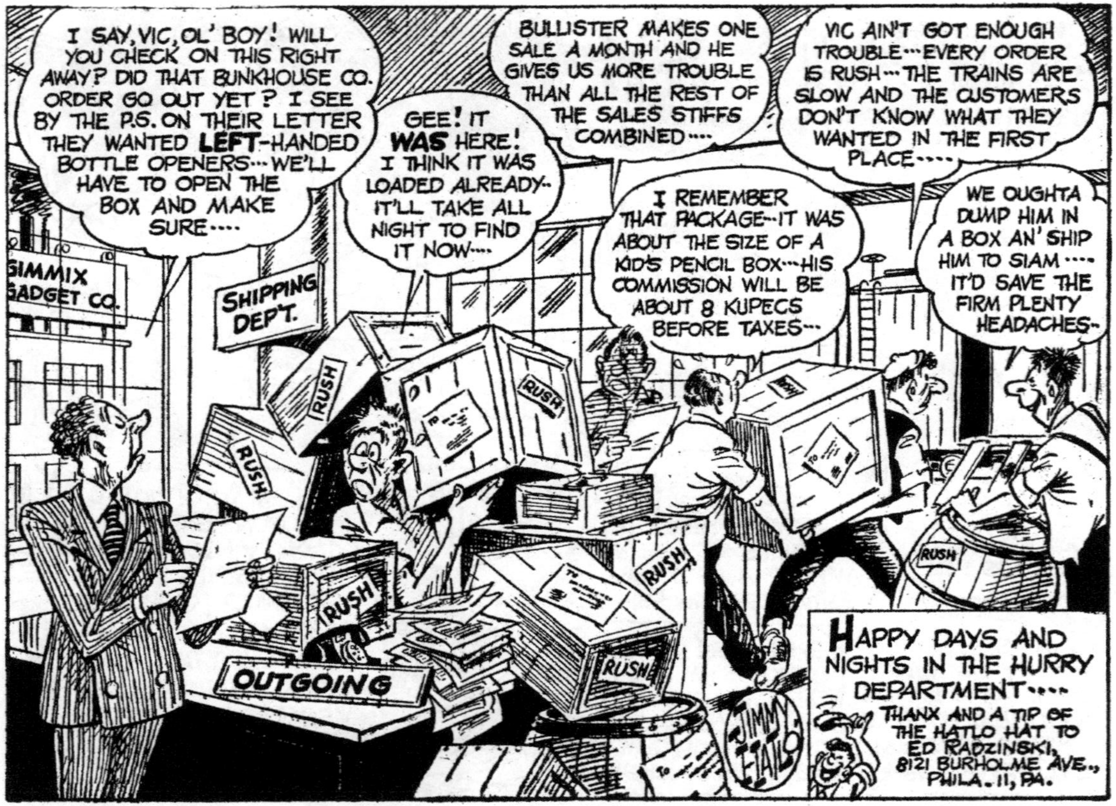
I SAY, VIC, OL' BOY! WILL YOU CHECK ON THIS RIGHT AWAY? DID THAT BUNKHOUSE CO. ORDER GO OUT YET? I SEE BY THE P.S. ON THEIR LETTER THEY WANTED **LEFT**-HANDED BOTTLE OPENERS··· WE'LL HAVE TO OPEN THE BOX AND MAKE SURE····
GEE! IT **WAS** HERE! I THINK IT WAS LOADED ALREADY·· IT'LL TAKE ALL NIGHT TO FIND IT NOW····
BULLISTER MAKES ONE SALE A MONTH AND HE GIVES US MORE TROUBLE THAN ALL THE REST OF THE SALES STIFFS COMBINED····
VIC AIN'T GOT ENOUGH TROUBLE··· EVERY ORDER IS RUSH··· THE TRAINS ARE SLOW AND THE CUSTOMERS DON'T KNOW WHAT THEY WANTED IN THE FIRST PLACE····
I REMEMBER THAT PACKAGE··· IT WAS ABOUT THE SIZE OF A KID'S PENCIL BOX··· HIS COMMISSION WILL BE ABOUT 8 KUPECS BEFORE TAXES···
WE OUGHTA DUMP HIM IN A BOX AN' SHIP HIM TO SIAM···· IT'D SAVE THE FIRM PLENTY HEADACHES··
SIMMIX GADGET CO.
SHIPPING DEP'T.
RUSH
OUTGOING
HAPPY DAYS AND NIGHTS IN THE HURRY DEPARTMENT····
THANX AND A TIP OF THE HATLO HAT TO ED RADZINSKI, 8121 BURHOLME AVE., PHILA. 11, PA.
JIMMY HATLO

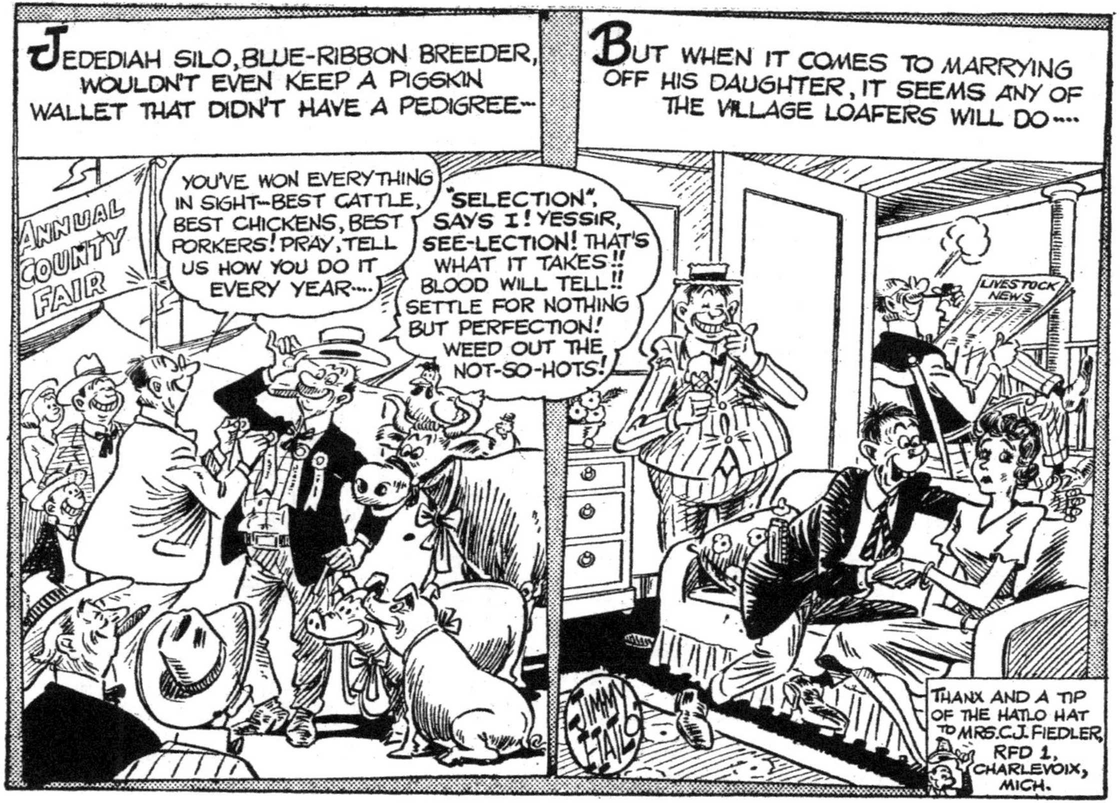
JEDEDIAH SILO, BLUE-RIBBON BREEDER, WOULDN'T EVEN KEEP A PIGSKIN WALLET THAT DIDN'T HAVE A PEDIGREE--
ANNUAL COUNTY FAIR
YOU'VE WON EVERYTHING IN SIGHT--BEST CATTLE, BEST CHICKENS, BEST PORKERS! PRAY, TELL US HOW YOU DO IT EVERY YEAR....
"SELECTION", SAYS I! YESSIR, SEE-LECTION! THAT'S WHAT IT TAKES!! BLOOD WILL TELL!! SETTLE FOR NOTHING BUT PERFECTION! WEED OUT THE NOT-SO-HOTS!
BUT WHEN IT COMES TO MARRYING OFF HIS DAUGHTER, IT SEEMS ANY OF THE VILLAGE LOAFERS WILL DO....
LIVESTOCK NEWS
JIMMY HATLO
THANX AND A TIP OF THE HATLO HAT TO MRS. C.J. FIEDLER, RFD 1, CHARLEVOIX, MICH.

ER-UH-CHIEF...I...UH... HEAR YOU NEED A NEW MANAGER IN THE TIN-FOIL DEP'T....AND...UH... ON ACCOUNT OF MY EXPERIENCE...I...UH... THOUGHT THAT-WELL... THAT...I...UH... WOULD....
YOU'VE GOT LOTS OF TIME, GRINDSTONE. WE'RE KEEPING AN EYE ON YOU....BUT YOU'RE TOO YOUNG FOR THIS JOB. WE'RE GIVING IT TO GOOBER.. HE'S BEEN HERE A LITTLE LONGER THAN YOU...AGE, SENIORITY... IT ALL COUNTS, M'BOY....
NON-RISE YEAST CO.
THANX AND A TIP OF THE HATLO HAT TO GERALD PRICE, 37-25 81ST ST., JACKSON HTS., N.Y.
AND 25 YEARS LATER—YOU GUESSED IT!
CHIEF...I HEAR OLD GOOBER HAS REACHED THE RETIREMENT AGE AND IS BEING PUT OUT TO PASTURE... I THOUGHT THAT MAYBE I...UH...
SORRY, GRINDSTONE... JOB CALLS FOR YOUTH! WHILE YOU'RE NOT EXACTLY AN OLD WARHORSE....ON THE OTHER HAND GOOBER'S SON HAS A LOT OF VINEGAR....THE BOY DESERVES HIS CHANCE. YOUTH WILL BE SERVED, Y'KNOW....
NON-RISE YEAST CO.
JIMMY HATLO

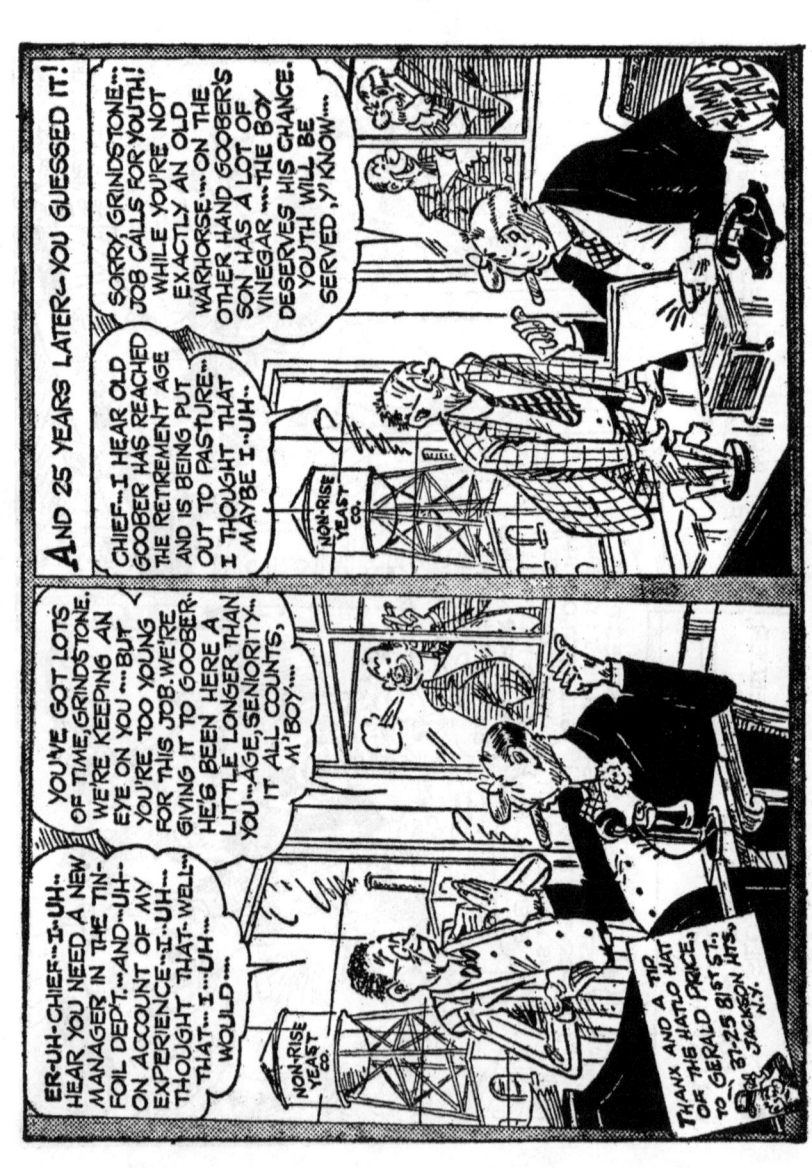

...FIFTY YEARS OF LOYAL SERVICE AND DEVOTION TO THIS CLUB IN WHICH HE NEVER SHIRKED A SINGLE ASSIGNMENT! I'M SURE YOU WILL BE GLAD TO KNOW YOUR BOARD OF DIRECTORS HAS MADE GOOD OLD JOE WILLINGHORSE A LIFE MEMBER!
WHAT A BREAK FOR GOOD OLD JOE. HE WON'T HAVE TO PAY ANY DUES NEXT MONTH..THAT IS...IF HE HOLDS OUT TILL NEXT MONTH!
SIX TERMS AS SECRETARY.. THREE TIMES PRESIDENT... AND THEY WAIT UNTIL GABRIEL IS TUNING UP THE TRUMPET BEFORE THEY FINALLY PAY OFF!
WE REALLY GOT SOME BIGHEARTED GUYS ON THE BOARD...LOOKS TO ME LIKE THEY'D HAVE DONE BETTER TO BUY JOE A HARP AND A PAIR OF WINGS....
IT'S WHAT I ALWAYS SAY ABOUT THIS CLUB...IT GETS AROUND TO DOING EVERYTHING FIFTY YEARS TOO LATE...
ALSO...THEY ONLY GIVE DINNERS TO GUYS WHO DON'T NEED A FREE MEAL..
THANX AND A TIP OF THE HATLO HAT TO LUCY P. MASON, 3108 DEVONSHIRE RD, CLEVELAND, 9 OHIO
JIMMY HATLO

DOES SILO, THE CONSIDERATE GROCER, LET A LADY TOTE THAT BIG BOX ? NO, SIR!
ER... THAT'S SO MUCH IN ONE LOAD... WOULDN'T IT BE BETTER TO PUT IT INTO TWO OR MAYBE THREE SMALLER CARTONS ?
YOU DON'T THINK WED LET YOU TRY TO LIFT THIS!? PERISH, FORBID!! HO-HO! WE'RE GONNA CARRY IT OUT TO YOUR CAR, AREN'T WE, WILBUR?
SURE THING-- WHERE ARE YOU PARKED, LADY?
JIMMY HATLO
SO-- TWO GUYS LUG IT TO HER CHARIOT.... THEN SHE ALONE HAS GOT TO CARRY IT!
THANX AND A TIP OF THE HATLO HAT TO VIRGINIA MERRITT, 250 GRANT ST., GENEVA, OHIO

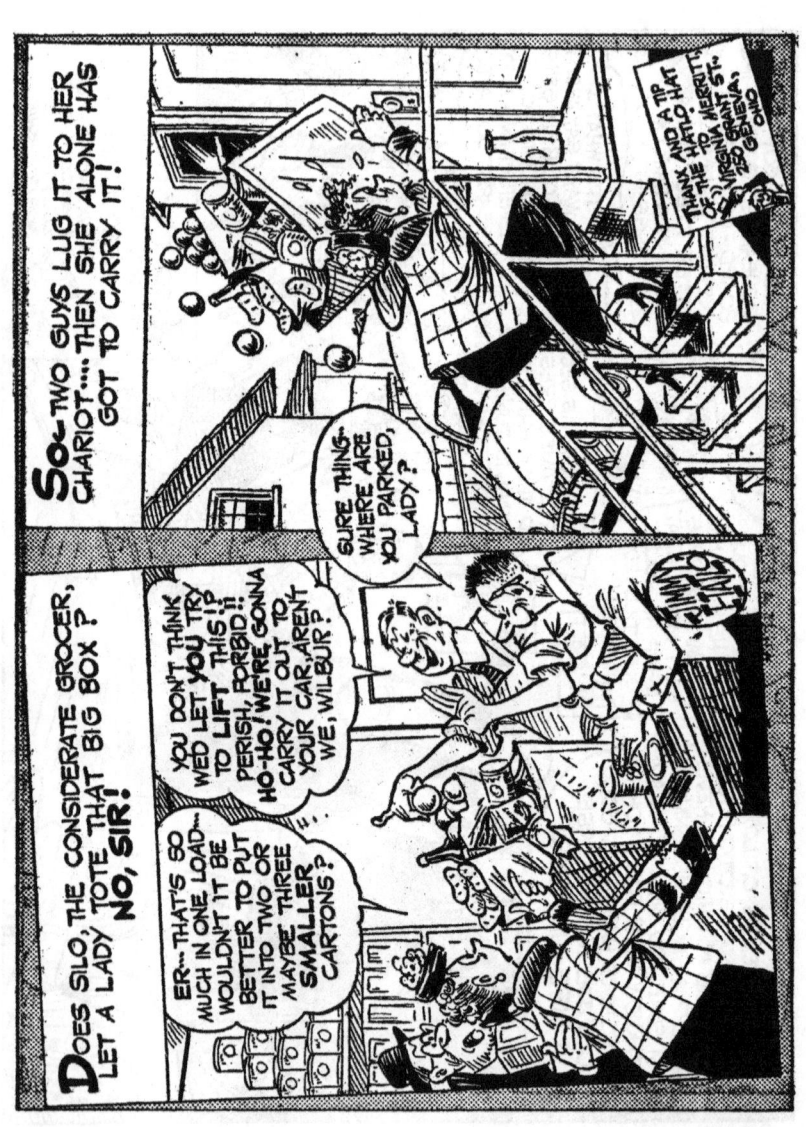

NOW, DON'T FORGET.... I GOT YOU THOSE COWBOY OUTFITS BECAUSE YOU PROMISED YOU'D PRACTICE PIANO EVERY DAY....
YIPPEE-HI-HO! RUSTLER RED IS HOLED UP HERE IN DRY GULCH CANYON... COME OUT, VARMINT, OR WE COME IN SHOOTIN'!
CLUMP
CLUMP!
CLUMP!
CLUMP!
CLUMP!
1A
THOSE HEELS! IT'S LIKE LIVING UNDER THE ARMORY WHERE A GERMAN REGIMENT IS LEARNING TO GOOSESTEP....
WHAT ARE THEY DOING...RIDING A COUPLE OF BREWERY HORSES UP THOSE STAIRS?
SHE CAN'T AFFORD TO BUY RUGS, BUT SHE'LL PROBABLY INSTALL A BOWLING ALLEY FOR THOSE BRATS NEXT...
AND SHE'S THE ONE WHO KNOCKS ON THE FLOOR IF OUR CAT MEOWS....
JIMMY HATLO
IT'S BEEN BAD ENOUGH... THIS IS THE END ....
THANX AND A TIP OF THE HATLO HAT TO SHIRLEY MARKERT, WARNERS, N.Y.

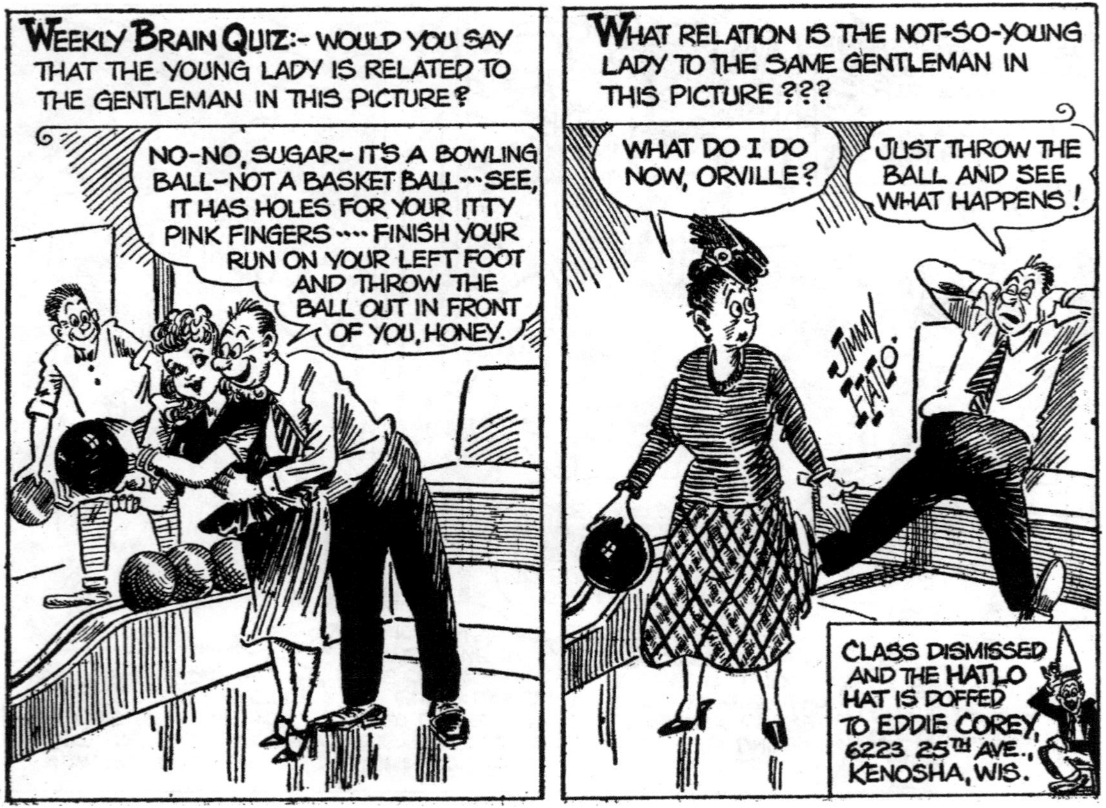
WEEKLY BRAIN QUIZ:- WOULD YOU SAY THAT THE YOUNG LADY IS RELATED TO THE GENTLEMAN IN THIS PICTURE?
NO-NO, SUGAR- IT'S A BOWLING BALL-NOT A BASKET BALL ··· SEE, IT HAS HOLES FOR YOUR ITTY PINK FINGERS ···· FINISH YOUR RUN ON YOUR LEFT FOOT AND THROW THE BALL OUT IN FRONT OF YOU, HONEY.
WHAT RELATION IS THE NOT-SO-YOUNG LADY TO THE SAME GENTLEMAN IN THIS PICTURE???
WHAT DO I DO NOW, ORVILLE?
JUST THROW THE BALL AND SEE WHAT HAPPENS!
JIMMY HATLO
CLASS DISMISSED AND THE HATLO HAT IS DOFFED TO EDDIE COREY, 6223 25TH AVE., KENOSHA, WIS.

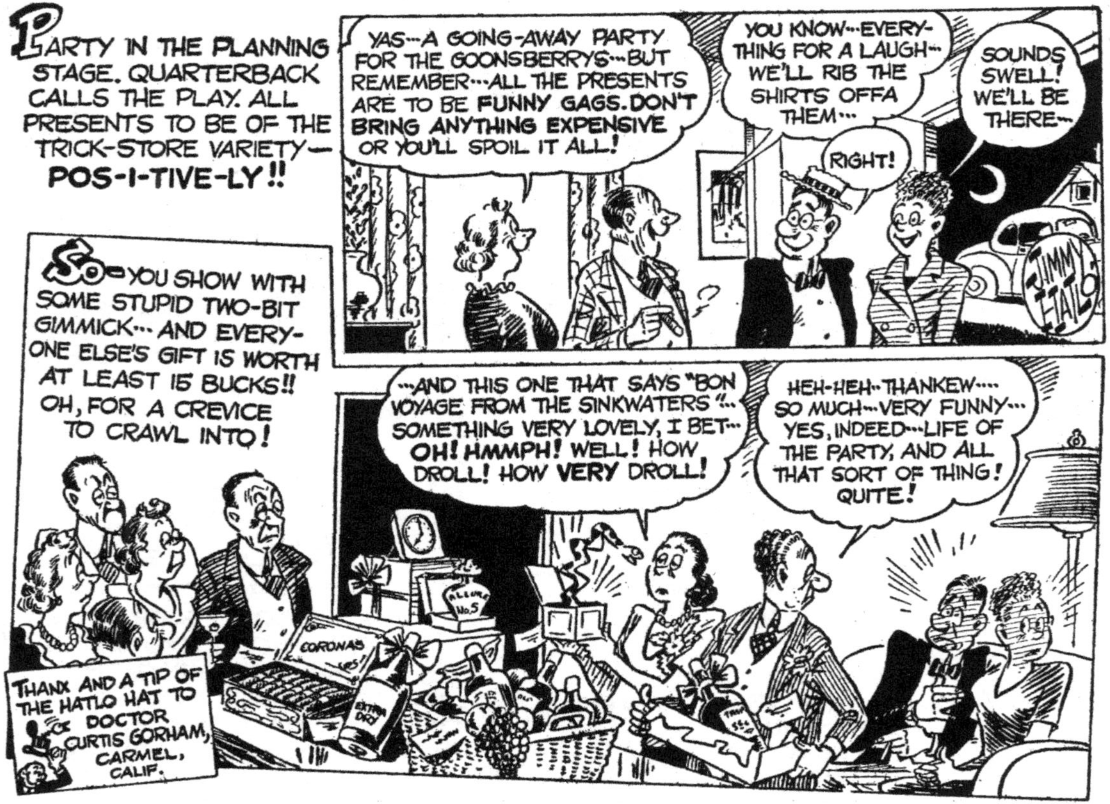
PARTY IN THE PLANNING STAGE. QUARTERBACK CALLS THE PLAY. ALL PRESENTS TO BE OF THE TRICK-STORE VARIETY—POS-I-TIVE-LY!!
YAS···A GOING-AWAY PARTY FOR THE GOONSBERRYS···BUT REMEMBER···ALL THE PRESENTS ARE TO BE FUNNY GAGS. DON'T BRING ANYTHING EXPENSIVE OR YOU'LL SPOIL IT ALL!
YOU KNOW···EVERYTHING FOR A LAUGH··· WE'LL RIB THE SHIRTS OFFA THEM···
RIGHT!
SOUNDS SWELL! WE'LL BE THERE···
JIMMY HATLO
SO-YOU SHOW WITH SOME STUPID TWO-BIT GIMMICK··· AND EVERYONE ELSE'S GIFT IS WORTH AT LEAST 15 BUCKS!! OH, FOR A CREVICE TO CRAWL INTO!
···AND THIS ONE THAT SAYS "BON VOYAGE FROM THE SINKWATERS"··· SOMETHING VERY LOVELY, I BET··· OH! HMMPH! WELL! HOW DROLL! HOW VERY DROLL!
HEH-HEH-THANKEW···· SO MUCH···VERY FUNNY··· YES, INDEED···LIFE OF THE PARTY, AND ALL THAT SORT OF THING! QUITE!
CORONAS
EXTRA DRY
ALLURE No.5
THANX AND A TIP OF THE HATLO HAT TO DOCTOR CURTIS GORHAM, CARMEL, CALIF.

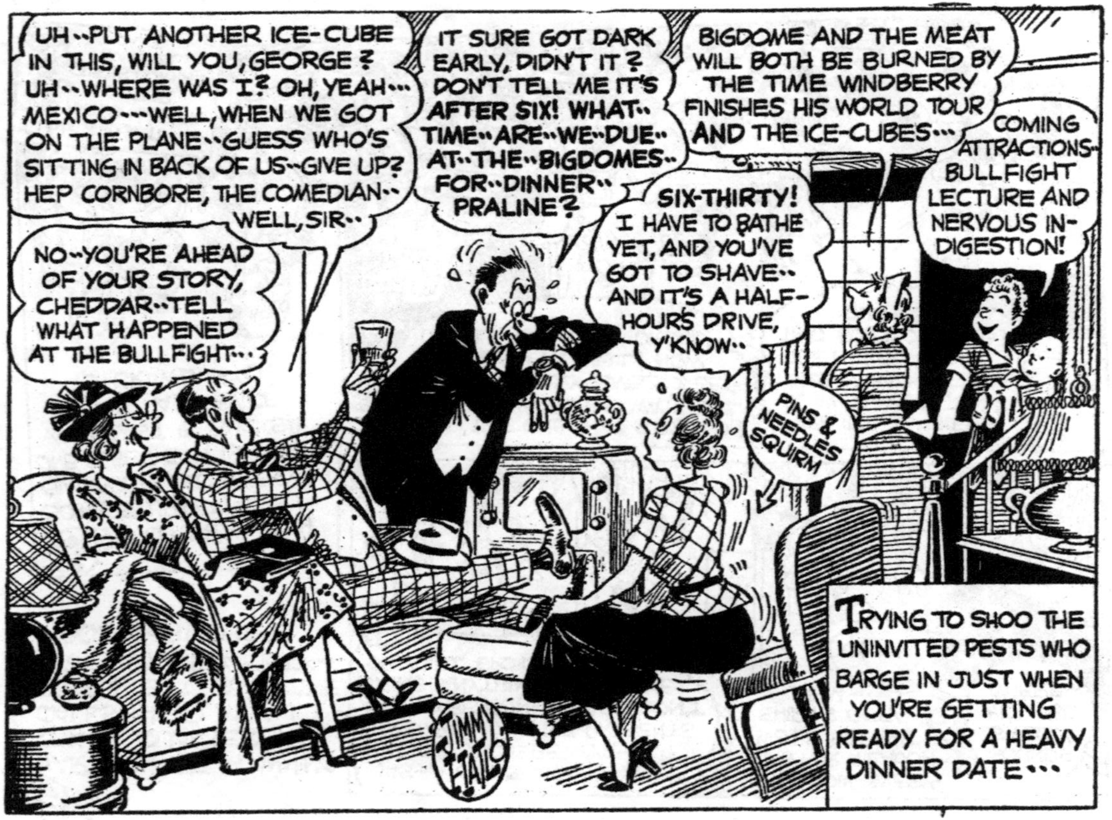
UH··PUT ANOTHER ICE-CUBE IN THIS, WILL YOU, GEORGE? UH··WHERE WAS I? OH, YEAH··· MEXICO···WELL, WHEN WE GOT ON THE PLANE··GUESS WHO'S SITTING IN BACK OF US··GIVE UP? HEP CORNBORE, THE COMEDIAN·· WELL, SIR··
NO··YOU'RE AHEAD OF YOUR STORY, CHEDDAR··TELL WHAT HAPPENED AT THE BULLFIGHT···
IT SURE GOT DARK EARLY, DIDN'T IT? DON'T TELL ME IT'S AFTER SIX! WHAT·· TIME··ARE··WE··DUE·· AT··THE··BIGDOMES·· FOR··DINNER·· PRALINE?
SIX-THIRTY! I HAVE TO BATHE YET, AND YOU'VE GOT TO SHAVE·· AND IT'S A HALF-HOUR'S DRIVE, Y'KNOW··
BIGDOME AND THE MEAT WILL BOTH BE BURNED BY THE TIME WINDBERRY FINISHES HIS WORLD TOUR AND THE ICE-CUBES···
COMING ATTRACTIONS·· BULLFIGHT LECTURE AND NERVOUS INDIGESTION!
PINS & NEEDLES SQUIRM
JIMMY HATLO
TRYING TO SHOO THE UNINVITED PESTS WHO BARGE IN JUST WHEN YOU'RE GETTING READY FOR A HEAVY DINNER DATE···

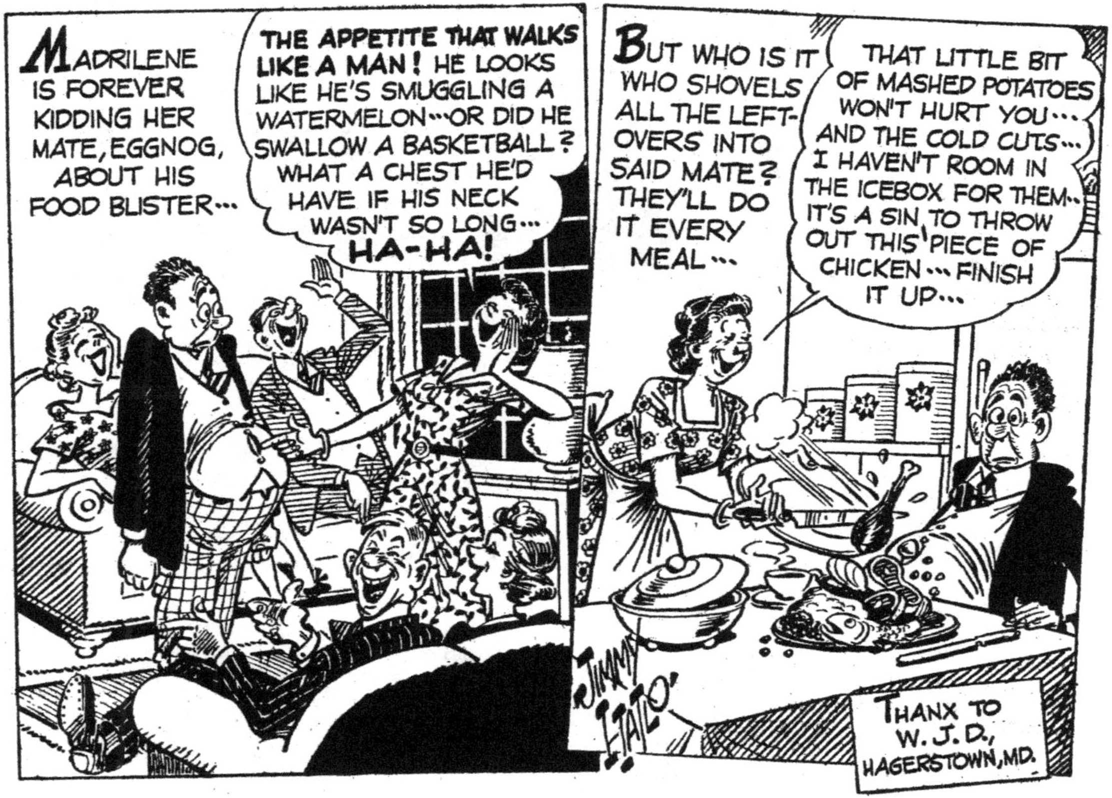
MADRILENE IS FOREVER KIDDING HER MATE, EGGNOG, ABOUT HIS FOOD BLISTER...
THE APPETITE THAT WALKS LIKE A MAN! HE LOOKS LIKE HE'S SMUGGLING A WATERMELON...OR DID HE SWALLOW A BASKETBALL? WHAT A CHEST HE'D HAVE IF HIS NECK WASN'T SO LONG... HA-HA!
BUT WHO IS IT WHO SHOVELS ALL THE LEFT-OVERS INTO SAID MATE? THEY'LL DO IT EVERY MEAL...
THAT LITTLE BIT OF MASHED POTATOES WON'T HURT YOU... AND THE COLD CUTS... I HAVEN'T ROOM IN THE ICEBOX FOR THEM... IT'S A SIN TO THROW OUT THIS PIECE OF CHICKEN... FINISH IT UP...
JIMMY HATLO
THANX TO W. J. D., HAGERSTOWN, MD.

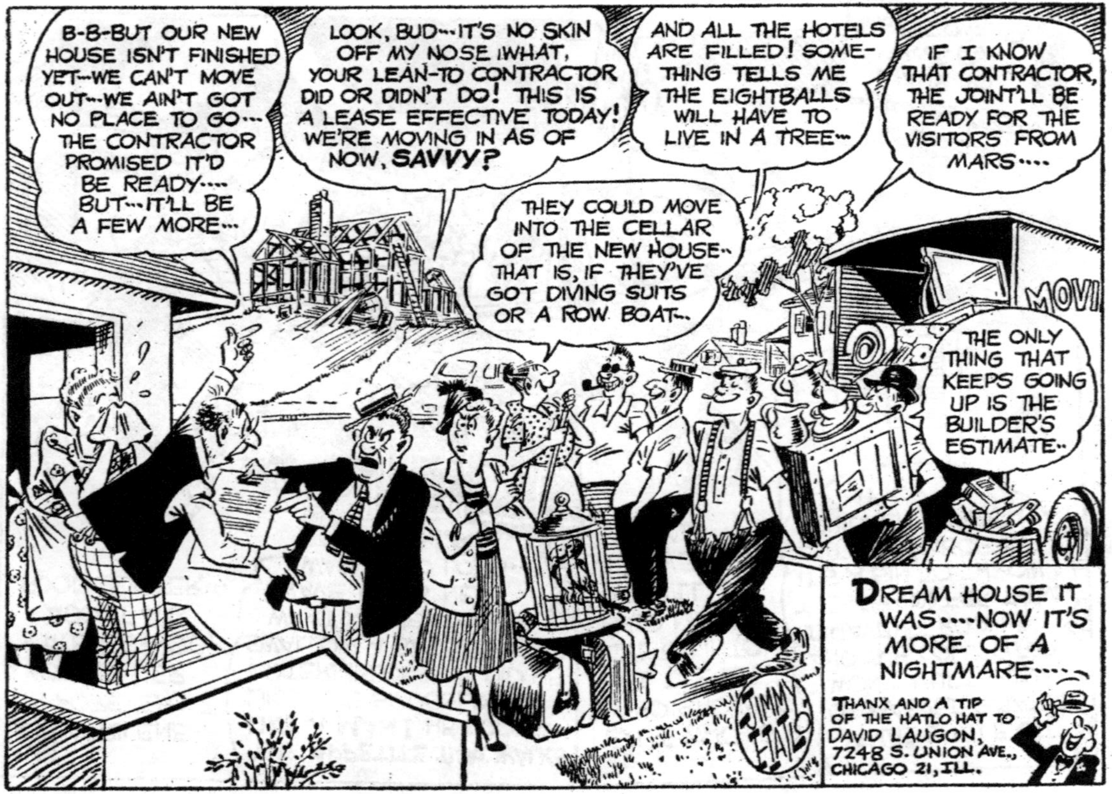
B-B-BUT OUR NEW HOUSE ISN'T FINISHED YET--WE CAN'T MOVE OUT--WE AIN'T GOT NO PLACE TO GO--- THE CONTRACTOR PROMISED IT'D BE READY---- BUT--IT'LL BE A FEW MORE---
LOOK, BUD--IT'S NO SKIN OFF MY NOSE WHAT, YOUR LEAN-TO CONTRACTOR DID OR DIDN'T DO! THIS IS A LEASE EFFECTIVE TODAY! WE'RE MOVING IN AS OF NOW, SAVVY?
AND ALL THE HOTELS ARE FILLED! SOMETHING TELLS ME THE EIGHTBALLS WILL HAVE TO LIVE IN A TREE--
IF I KNOW THAT CONTRACTOR, THE JOINT'LL BE READY FOR THE VISITORS FROM MARS....
THEY COULD MOVE INTO THE CELLAR OF THE NEW HOUSE-- THAT IS, IF THEY'VE GOT DIVING SUITS OR A ROW BOAT--
MOVI
THE ONLY THING THAT KEEPS GOING UP IS THE BUILDER'S ESTIMATE--
DREAM HOUSE IT WAS....NOW IT'S MORE OF A NIGHTMARE....
THANX AND A TIP OF THE HATLO HAT TO DAVID LAUGON, 7248 S. UNION AVE., CHICAGO 21, ILL.
JIMMY HATLO

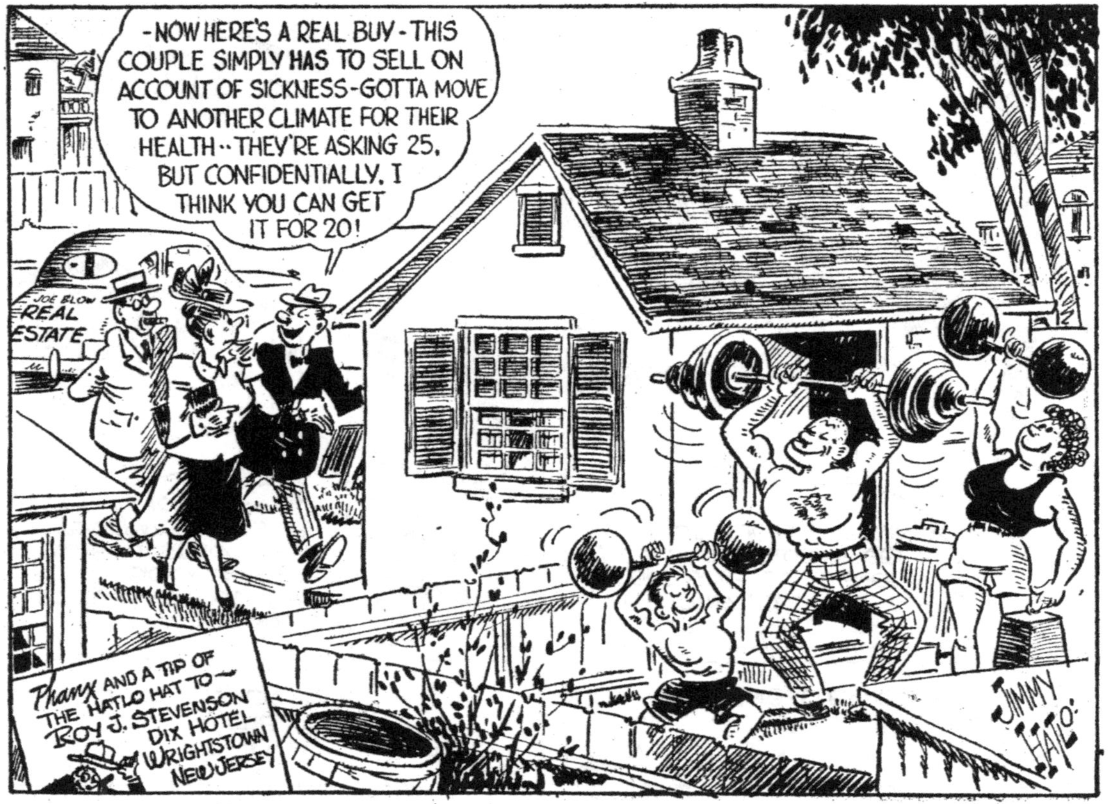
-NOW HERE'S A REAL BUY - THIS COUPLE SIMPLY HAS TO SELL ON ACCOUNT OF SICKNESS-GOTTA MOVE TO ANOTHER CLIMATE FOR THEIR HEALTH -- THEY'RE ASKING 25, BUT CONFIDENTIALLY, I THINK YOU CAN GET IT FOR 20!
JOE BLOW REAL ESTATE
Thanx AND A TIP OF THE HATLO HAT TO— ROY J. STEVENSON DIX HOTEL WRIGHTSTOWN NEW JERSEY
JIMMY HATLO

WURRA, WURRA! WIFEY'S SICK....
SEND FOR THE DOCTOR,
QUICK, QUICK, QUICK....
COME AS FAST AS YOU CAN, DOCTOR! NO FOOLIN', SHE'S REALLY SICK...CAN'T HARDLY MOVE...JUST TOOK HER TEMPERATURE...IT'S UP TO 104 3/10....
THANX TO ELIZABETH STURNS, 4569 ZENOBIA ST., DENVER 12, COLO.
JIMMY HATLO
DOWN THE ROAD COMES DOC, CAREENING,
WHILE WIFEY DOES HER WHOLE
SPRING-CLEANING....
I CAN'T LET THE DOCTOR SEE ME AND MY HOUSE LIKE THIS...GET SOME CLEAN SHEETS OUT OF THE CLOSET...GET MY BEST SILK NIGHTGOWN...GET....
WHAT THE-?

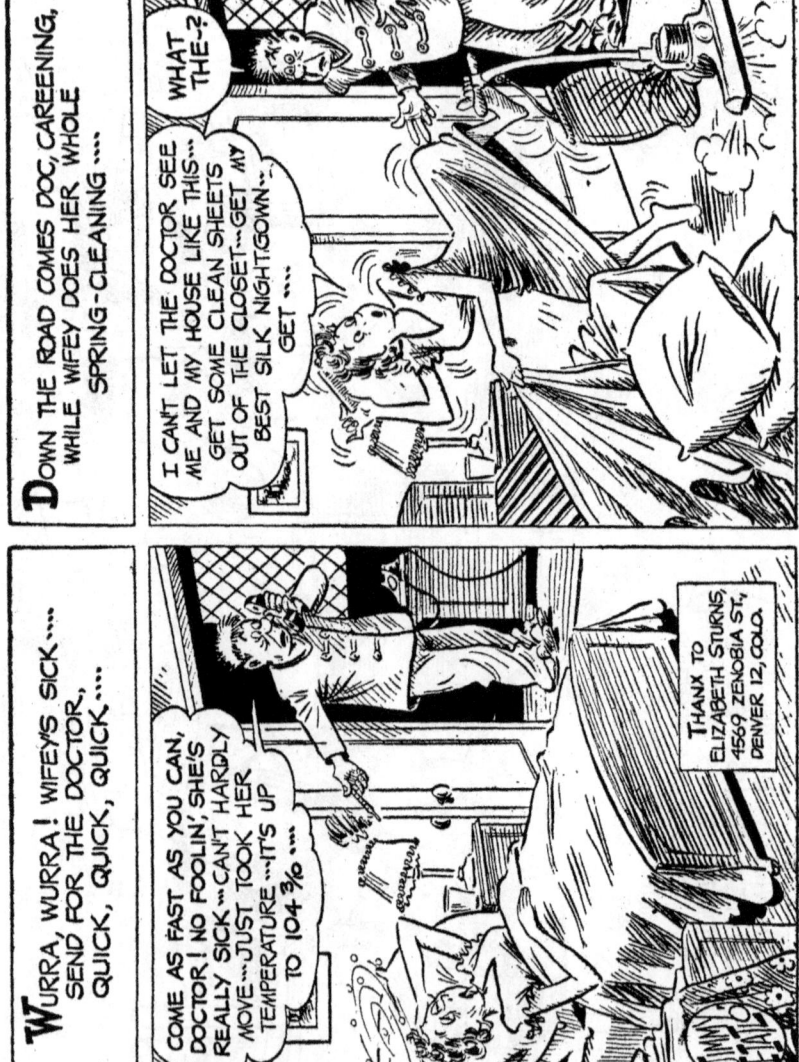

NAH- I STILL SAY I DON'T NEED A FENCE... TOO EXPENSIVE. YOU GUYS GO AHEAD... BUT NOT ME!!
HEY- HAVE ONE OF YOU GUYS GOT A COUPLA MORE SCRAPS ABOUT 3 FEET LONG ?
JIMMY HATLO
THANX TO M/SGT. ROB'T E. ROBINSON, 14810 IRVING AVE, DOLTON, ILL.

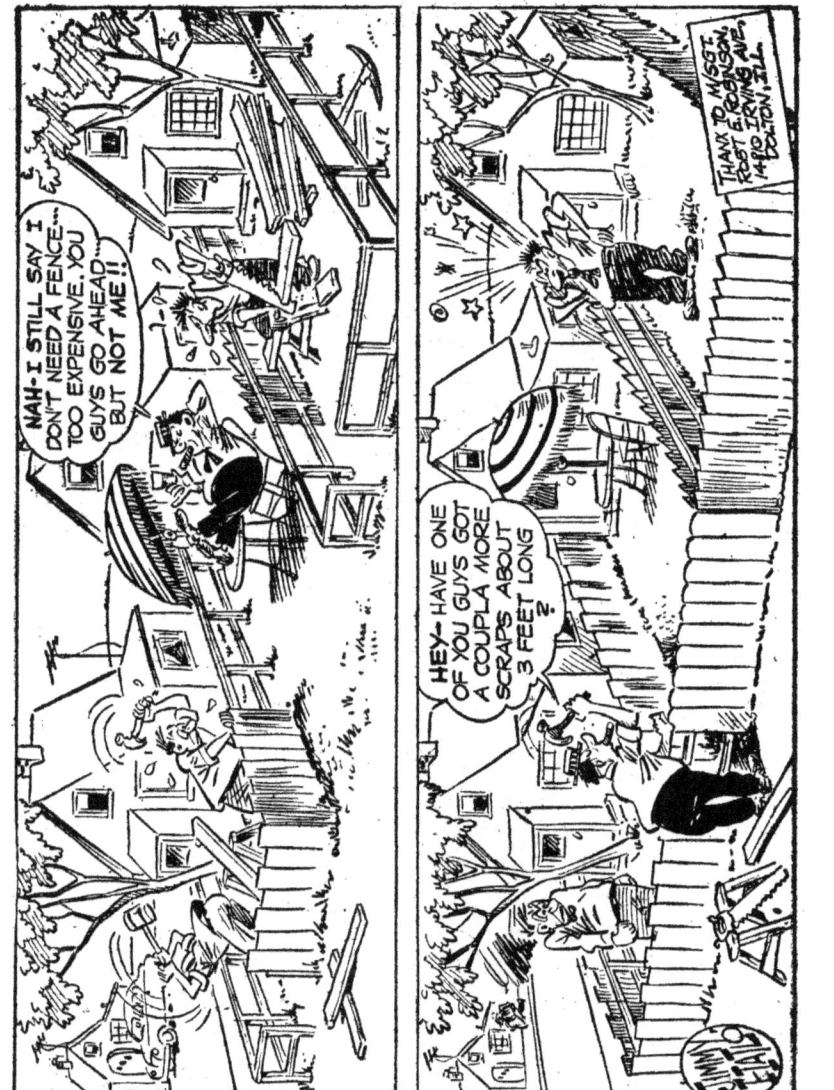

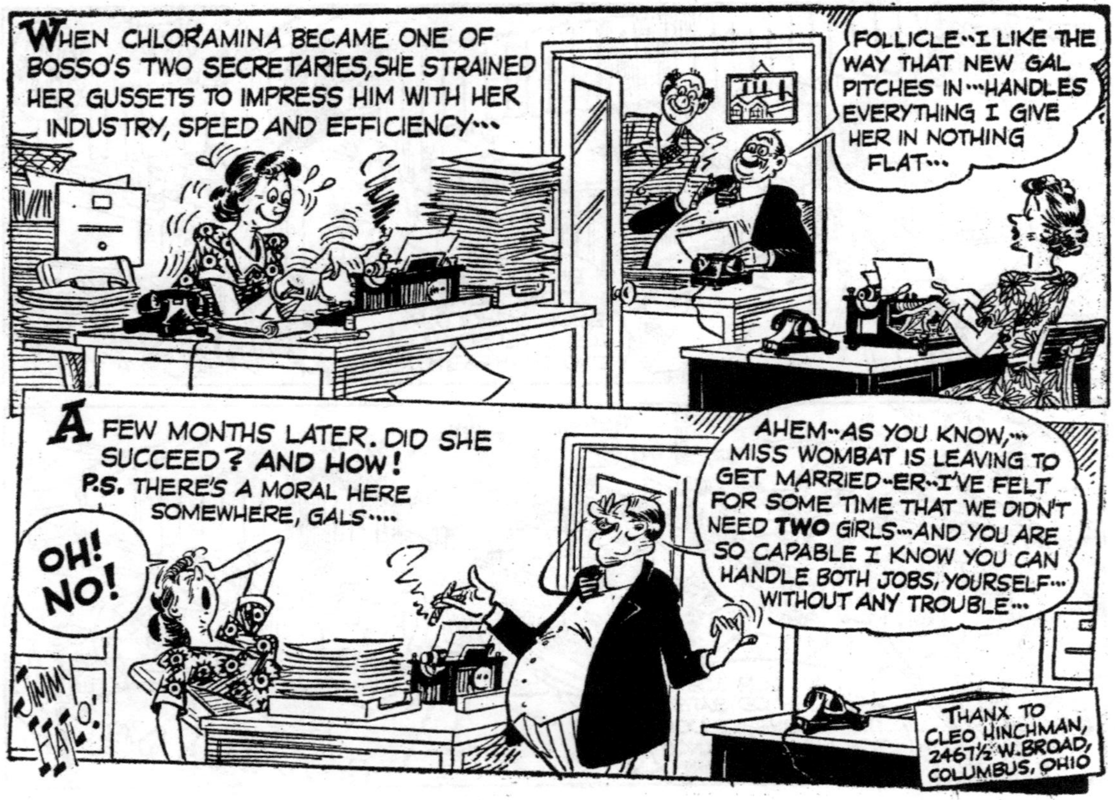
WHEN CHLORAMINA BECAME ONE OF BOSSO'S TWO SECRETARIES, SHE STRAINED HER GUSSETS TO IMPRESS HIM WITH HER INDUSTRY, SPEED AND EFFICIENCY...
FOLLICLE--I LIKE THE WAY THAT NEW GAL PITCHES IN---HANDLES EVERYTHING I GIVE HER IN NOTHING FLAT...
A FEW MONTHS LATER. DID SHE SUCCEED? AND HOW! P.S. THERE'S A MORAL HERE SOMEWHERE, GALS....
AHEM--AS YOU KNOW,... MISS WOMBAT IS LEAVING TO GET MARRIED--ER--I'VE FELT FOR SOME TIME THAT WE DIDN'T NEED TWO GIRLS---AND YOU ARE SO CAPABLE I KNOW YOU CAN HANDLE BOTH JOBS, YOURSELF... WITHOUT ANY TROUBLE...
OH! NO!
JIMMY HATLO!
THANX TO CLEO HINCHMAN, 2467½ W. BROAD, COLUMBUS, OHIO

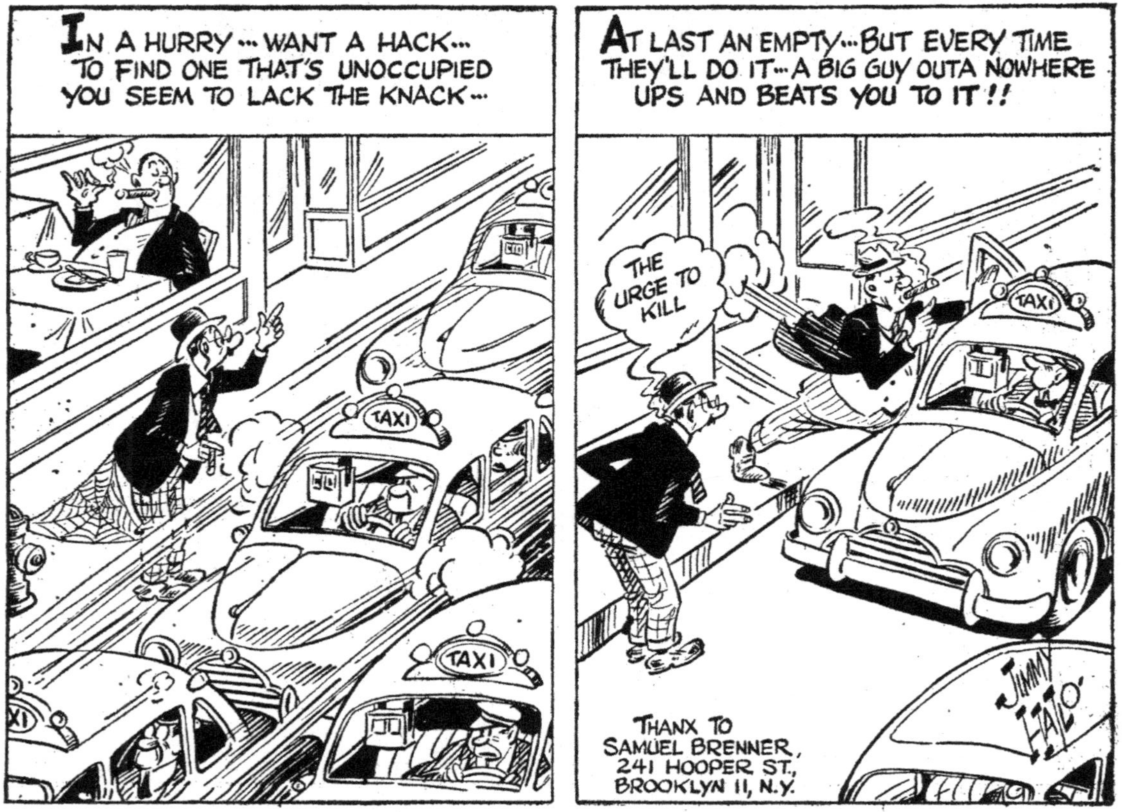
IN A HURRY ··· WANT A HACK···
TO FIND ONE THAT'S UNOCCUPIED
YOU SEEM TO LACK THE KNACK···
TAXI
TAXI
AT LAST AN EMPTY···BUT EVERY TIME
THEY'LL DO IT···A BIG GUY OUTA NOWHERE
UPS AND BEATS YOU TO IT!!
THE URGE TO KILL
TAXI
THANX TO
SAMUEL BRENNER,
241 HOOPER ST.,
BROOKLYN 11, N.Y.
JIMMY HATLO

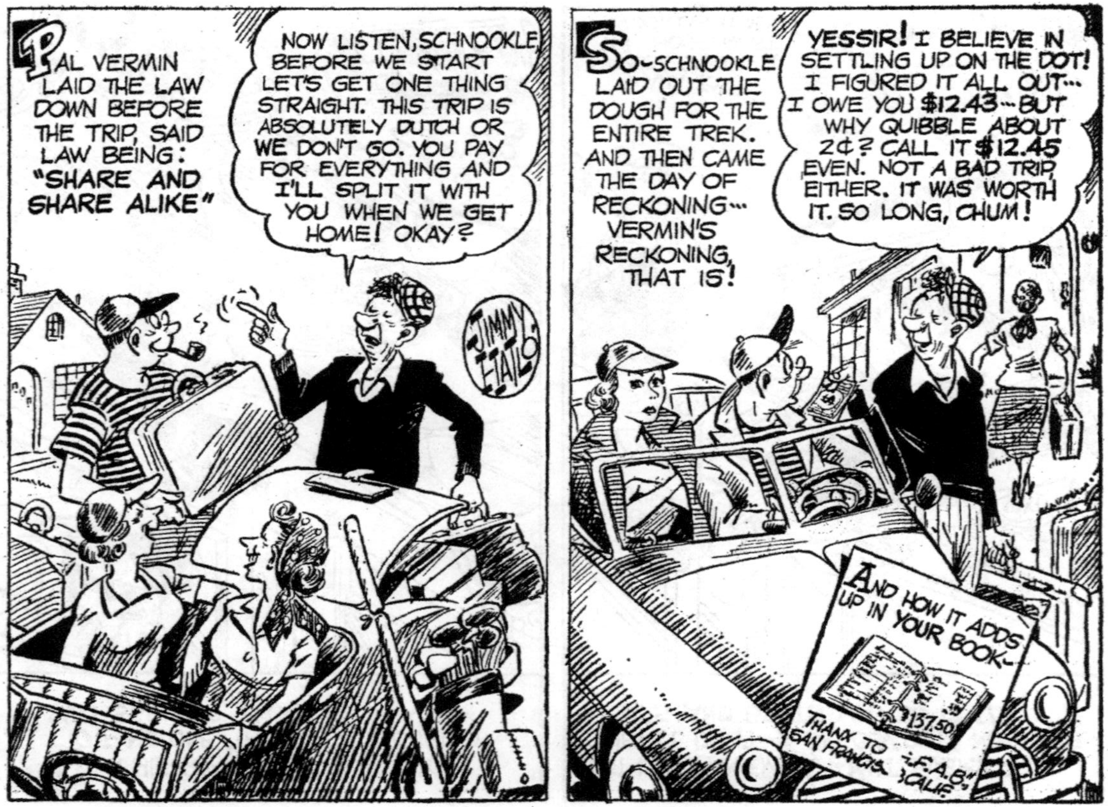
PAL VERMIN LAID THE LAW DOWN BEFORE THE TRIP, SAID LAW BEING: "SHARE AND SHARE ALIKE"
NOW LISTEN, SCHNOOKLE, BEFORE WE START LET'S GET ONE THING STRAIGHT. THIS TRIP IS ABSOLUTELY DUTCH OR WE DON'T GO. YOU PAY FOR EVERYTHING AND I'LL SPLIT IT WITH YOU WHEN WE GET HOME! OKAY?
JIMMY HATLO
SO-SCHNOOKLE LAID OUT THE DOUGH FOR THE ENTIRE TREK. AND THEN CAME THE DAY OF RECKONING... VERMIN'S RECKONING, THAT IS!
YESSIR! I BELIEVE IN SETTLING UP ON THE DOT! I FIGURED IT ALL OUT... I OWE YOU $12.43... BUT WHY QUIBBLE ABOUT 2¢? CALL IT $12.45 EVEN. NOT A BAD TRIP, EITHER. IT WAS WORTH IT. SO LONG, CHUM!
AND HOW IT ADDS UP IN YOUR BOOK-
137.50
THANX TO "F.A.B." SAN FRANCISCO, CALIF.

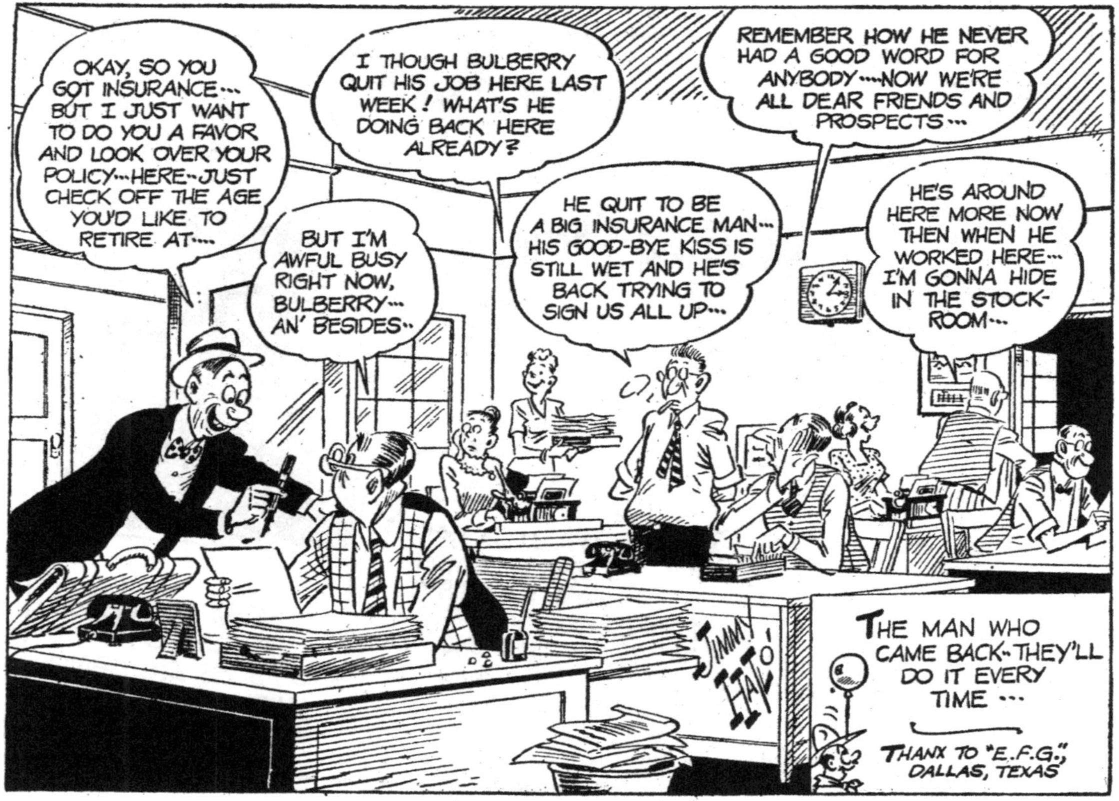
OKAY, SO YOU GOT INSURANCE... BUT I JUST WANT TO DO YOU A FAVOR AND LOOK OVER YOUR POLICY...HERE..JUST CHECK OFF THE AGE YOU'D LIKE TO RETIRE AT...
BUT I'M AWFUL BUSY RIGHT NOW, BULBERRY... AN' BESIDES..
I THOUGH BULBERRY QUIT HIS JOB HERE LAST WEEK! WHAT'S HE DOING BACK HERE ALREADY?
HE QUIT TO BE A BIG INSURANCE MAN... HIS GOOD-BYE KISS IS STILL WET AND HE'S BACK TRYING TO SIGN US ALL UP...
REMEMBER HOW HE NEVER HAD A GOOD WORD FOR ANYBODY...NOW WE'RE ALL DEAR FRIENDS AND PROSPECTS...
HE'S AROUND HERE MORE NOW THEN WHEN HE WORKED HERE... I'M GONNA HIDE IN THE STOCK-ROOM...
JIMMY HATLO
THE MAN WHO CAME BACK..THEY'LL DO IT EVERY TIME...
THANX TO "E.F.G.," DALLAS, TEXAS

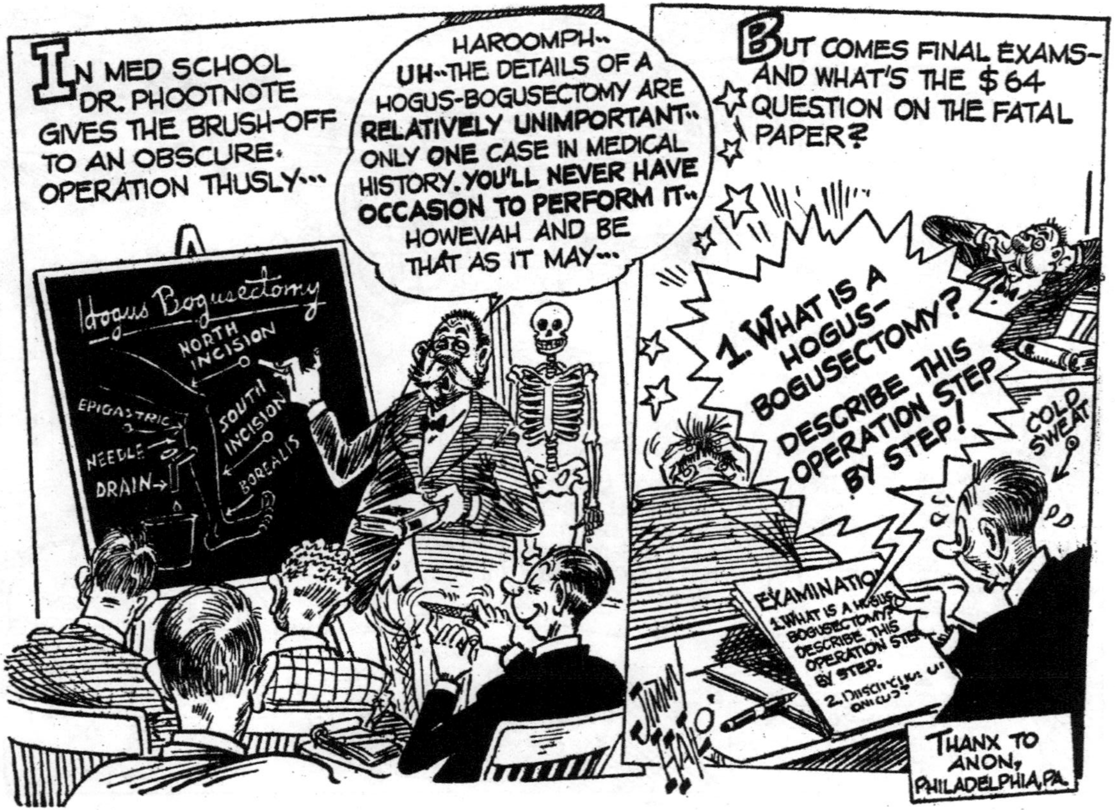
IN MED SCHOOL DR. PHOOTNOTE GIVES THE BRUSH-OFF TO AN OBSCURE OPERATION THUSLY...
HAROOMPH.. UH..THE DETAILS OF A HOGUS-BOGUSECTOMY ARE RELATIVELY UNIMPORTANT.. ONLY ONE CASE IN MEDICAL HISTORY. YOU'LL NEVER HAVE OCCASION TO PERFORM IT.. HOWEVAH AND BE THAT AS IT MAY...
Hogus Bogusectomy
NORTH INCISION
EPIGASTRIC
NEEDLE
DRAIN
SOUTH INCISION
BOREALIS
BUT COMES FINAL EXAMS- AND WHAT'S THE $64 QUESTION ON THE FATAL PAPER?
1. WHAT IS A HOGUS-BOGUSECTOMY? DESCRIBE THIS OPERATION STEP BY STEP!
COLD SWEAT
EXAMINATION
1. WHAT IS A HOGUS-BOGUSECTOMY? DESCRIBE THIS OPERATION STEP BY STEP.
JIMINY
HALO!
THANX TO ANON, PHILADELPHIA, PA.

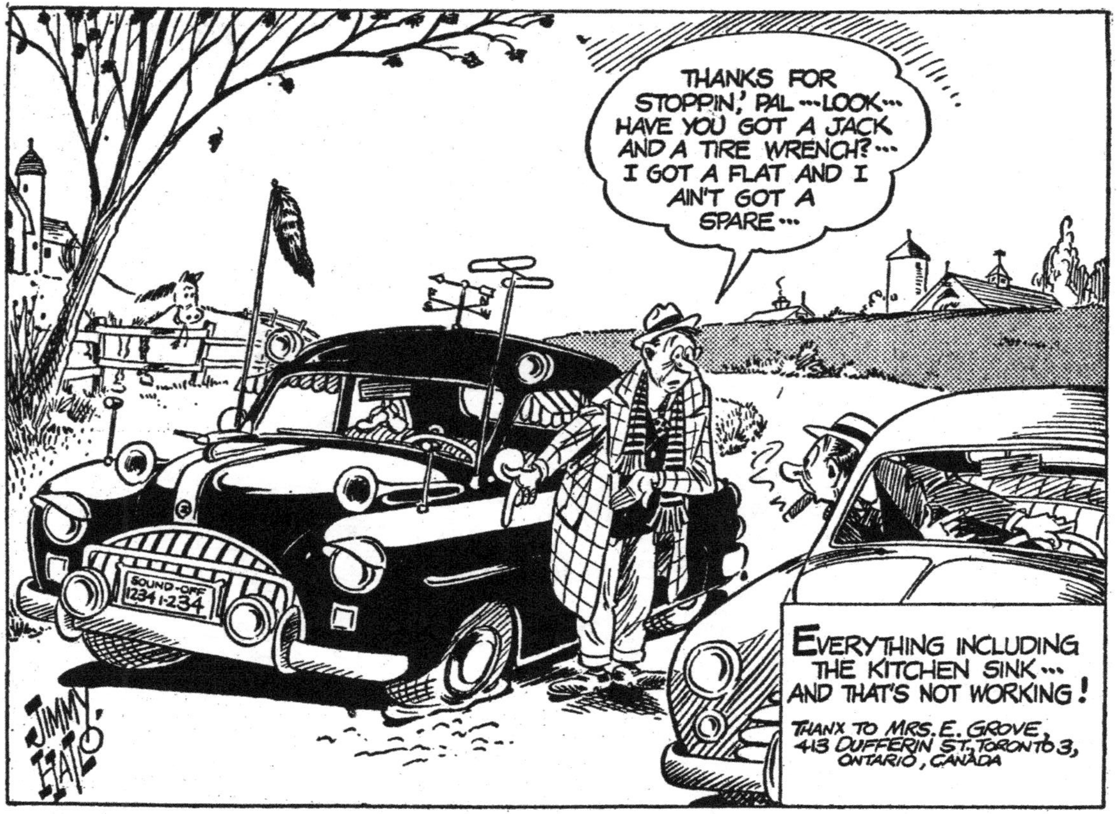
THANKS FOR STOPPIN,' PAL --- LOOK--- HAVE YOU GOT A JACK AND A TIRE WRENCH?--- I GOT A FLAT AND I AIN'T GOT A SPARE---
SOUND-OFF 12341-234
EVERYTHING INCLUDING THE KITCHEN SINK--- AND THAT'S NOT WORKING!
THANX TO MRS. E. GROVE, 413 DUFFERIN ST., TORONTO 3, ONTARIO, CANADA
JIMMY HATLO

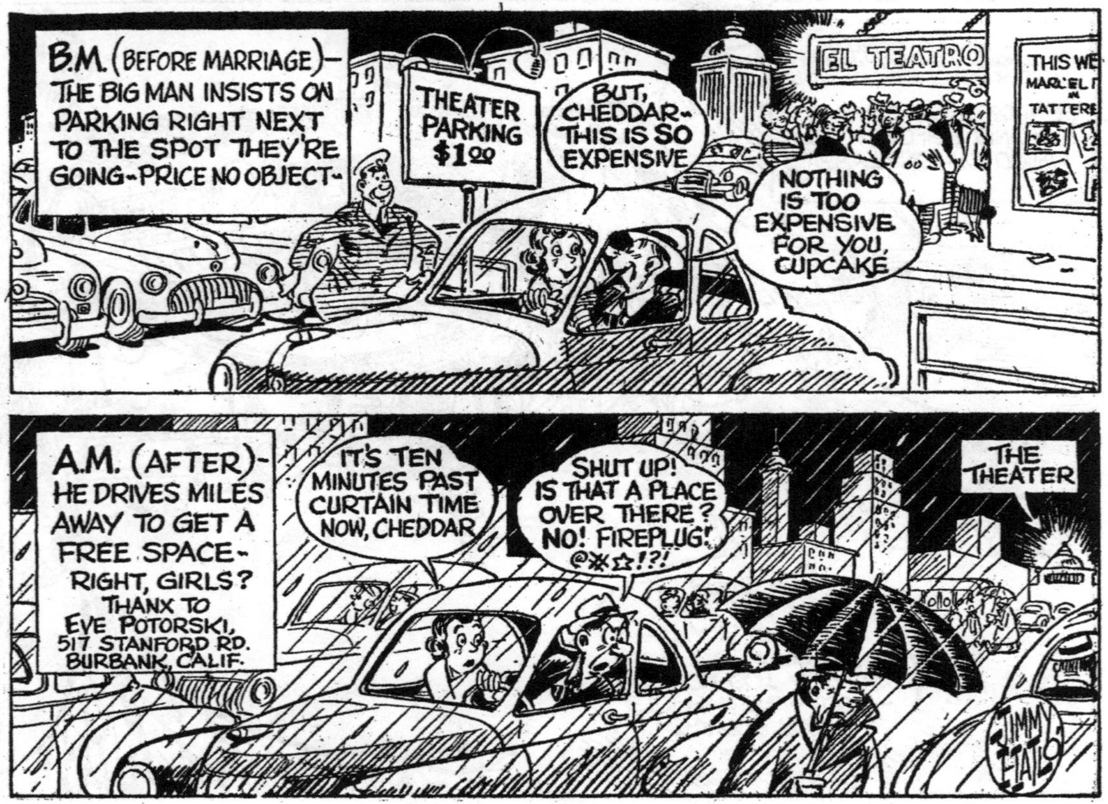
B.M. (BEFORE MARRIAGE)– THE BIG MAN INSISTS ON PARKING RIGHT NEXT TO THE SPOT THEY'RE GOING–PRICE NO OBJECT–
THEATER PARKING $1.00
BUT, CHEDDAR– THIS IS SO EXPENSIVE
EL TEATRO
NOTHING IS TOO EXPENSIVE FOR YOU, CUPCAKE
A.M. (AFTER)– HE DRIVES MILES AWAY TO GET A FREE SPACE– RIGHT, GIRLS?
THANX TO EVE POTORSKI, 517 STANFORD RD. BURBANK, CALIF.
IT'S TEN MINUTES PAST CURTAIN TIME NOW, CHEDDAR
SHUT UP! IS THAT A PLACE OVER THERE? NO! FIREPLUG! @✻☆!?!
THE THEATER
JIMMY HATLO

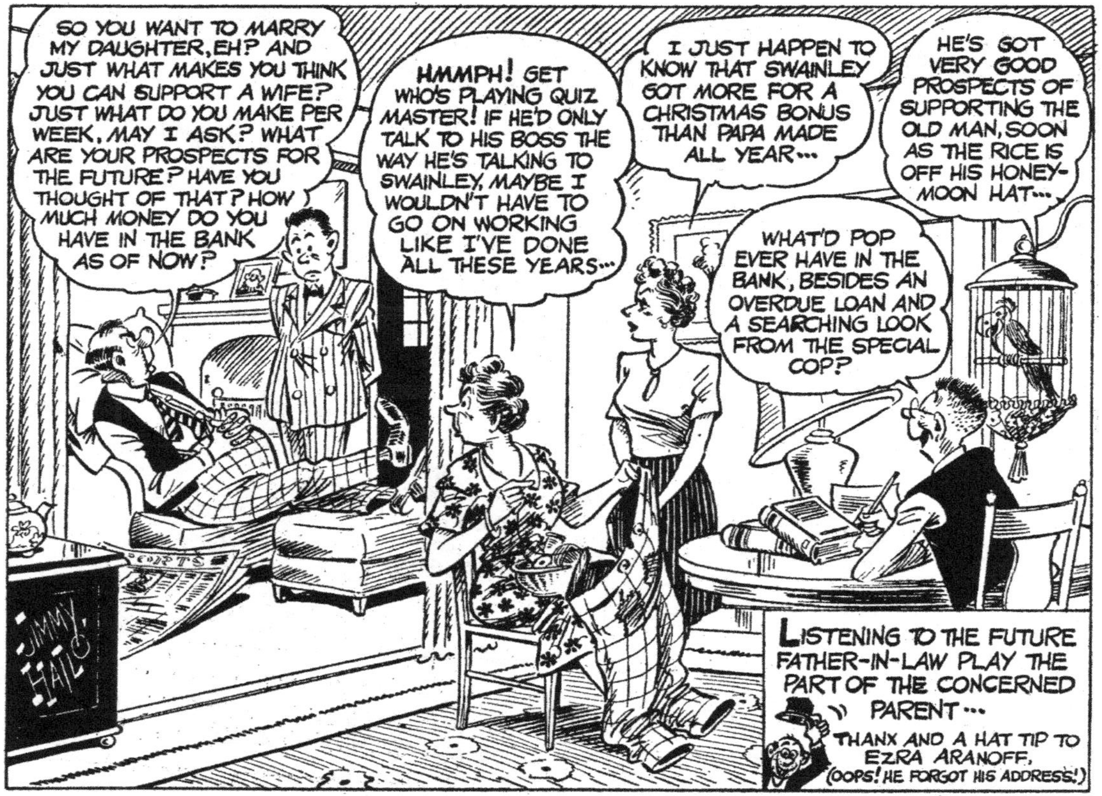
SO YOU WANT TO MARRY MY DAUGHTER, EH? AND JUST WHAT MAKES YOU THINK YOU CAN SUPPORT A WIFE? JUST WHAT DO YOU MAKE PER WEEK, MAY I ASK? WHAT ARE YOUR PROSPECTS FOR THE FUTURE? HAVE YOU THOUGHT OF THAT? HOW MUCH MONEY DO YOU HAVE IN THE BANK AS OF NOW?
HMMPH! GET WHO'S PLAYING QUIZ MASTER! IF HE'D ONLY TALK TO HIS BOSS THE WAY HE'S TALKING TO SWAINLEY, MAYBE I WOULDN'T HAVE TO GO ON WORKING LIKE I'VE DONE ALL THESE YEARS...
I JUST HAPPEN TO KNOW THAT SWAINLEY GOT MORE FOR A CHRISTMAS BONUS THAN PAPA MADE ALL YEAR...
HE'S GOT VERY GOOD PROSPECTS OF SUPPORTING THE OLD MAN, SOON AS THE RICE IS OFF HIS HONEY-MOON HAT...
WHAT'D POP EVER HAVE IN THE BANK, BESIDES AN OVERDUE LOAN AND A SEARCHING LOOK FROM THE SPECIAL COP?
LISTENING TO THE FUTURE FATHER-IN-LAW PLAY THE PART OF THE CONCERNED PARENT...
THANX AND A HAT TIP TO EZRA ARANOFF.
(OOPS! HE FORGOT HIS ADDRESS!)
JIMMY HATLO

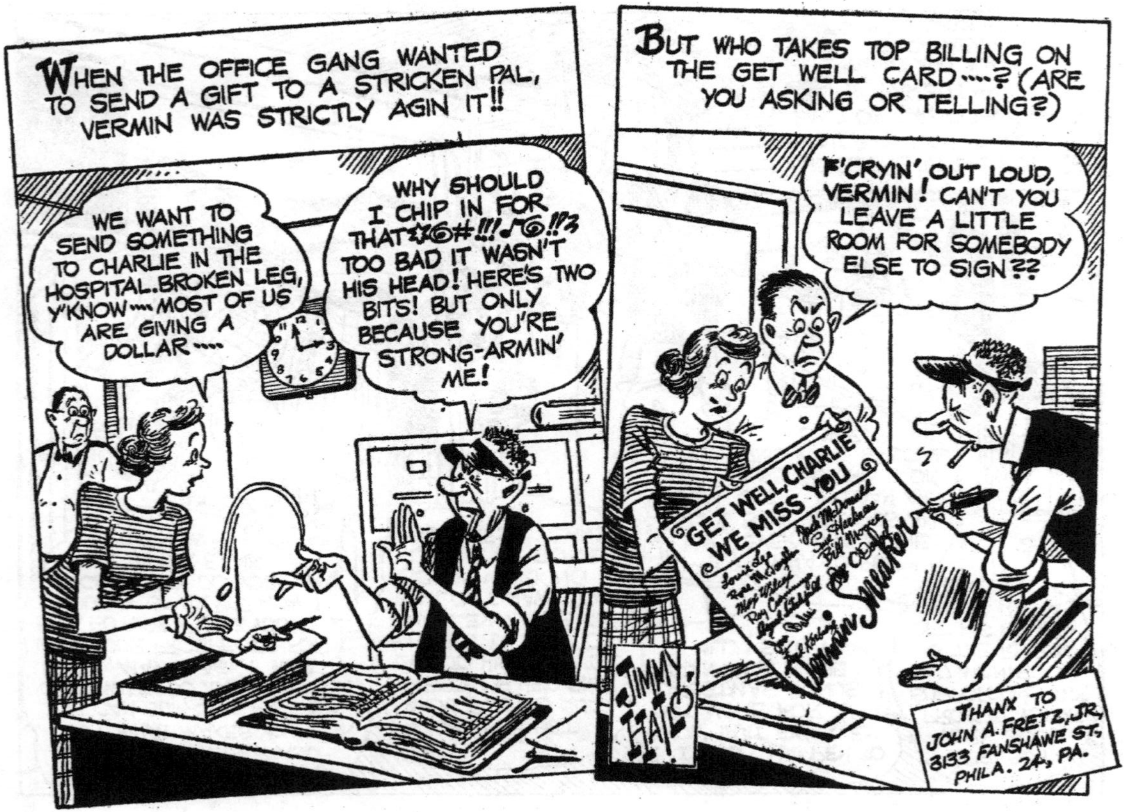
WHEN THE OFFICE GANG WANTED TO SEND A GIFT TO A STRICKEN PAL, VERMIN WAS STRICTLY AGIN IT!!
WE WANT TO SEND SOMETHING TO CHARLIE IN THE HOSPITAL. BROKEN LEG, Y'KNOW.... MOST OF US ARE GIVING A DOLLAR....
WHY SHOULD I CHIP IN FOR THAT☆⊚#!!!♪⊚!!? TOO BAD IT WASN'T HIS HEAD! HERE'S TWO BITS! BUT ONLY BECAUSE YOU'RE STRONG-ARMIN' ME!
BUT WHO TAKES TOP BILLING ON THE GET WELL CARD....? (ARE YOU ASKING OR TELLING?)
F'CRYIN' OUT LOUD, VERMIN! CAN'T YOU LEAVE A LITTLE ROOM FOR SOMEBODY ELSE TO SIGN??
GET WELL, CHARLIE
WE MISS YOU
JIMMY HATLO
THANX TO JOHN A. FRETZ, JR, 3133 FANSHAWE ST, PHILA. 24, PA.

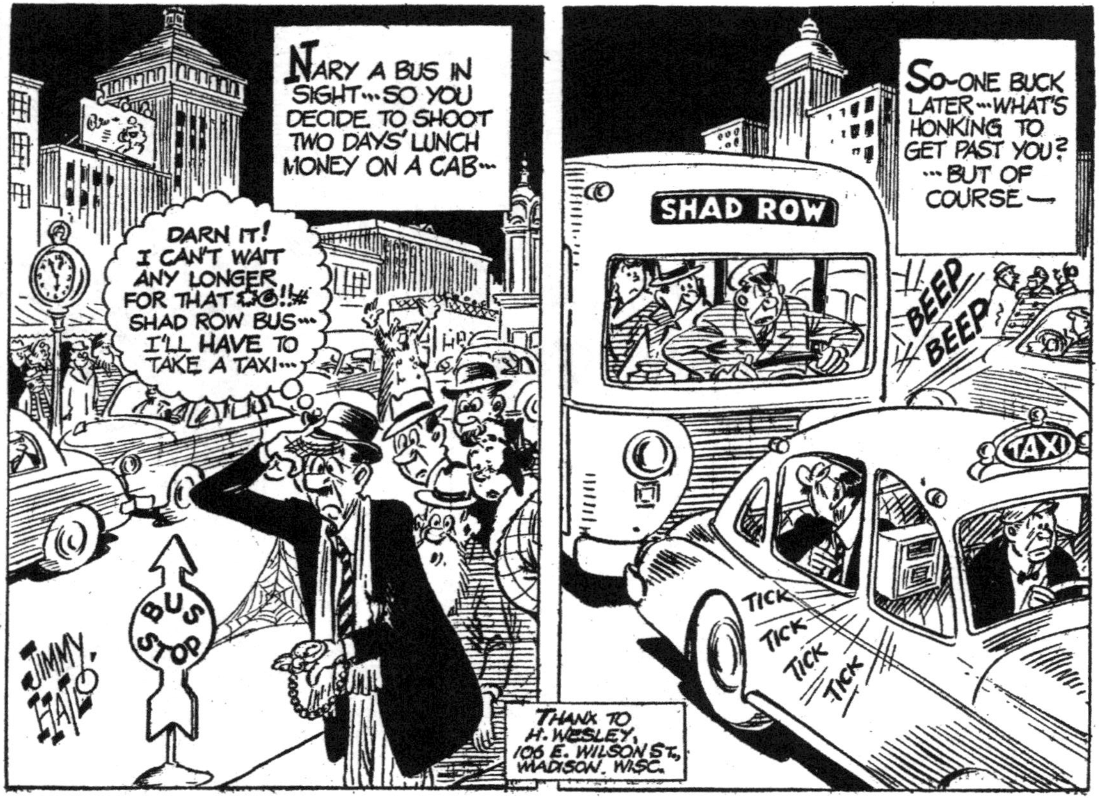
NARY A BUS IN SIGHT ... SO YOU DECIDE TO SHOOT TWO DAYS' LUNCH MONEY ON A CAB ...
DARN IT! I CAN'T WAIT ANY LONGER FOR THAT ☼@!!# SHAD ROW BUS ... I'LL HAVE TO TAKE A TAXI ...
BUS STOP
JIMMY HATLO
THANX TO H. WESLEY, 106 E. WILSON ST., MADISON, WISC.
SO-ONE BUCK LATER ... WHAT'S HONKING TO GET PAST YOU? ... BUT OF COURSE —
SHAD ROW
BEEP
BEEP
TAXI
TICK
TICK
TICK
TICK

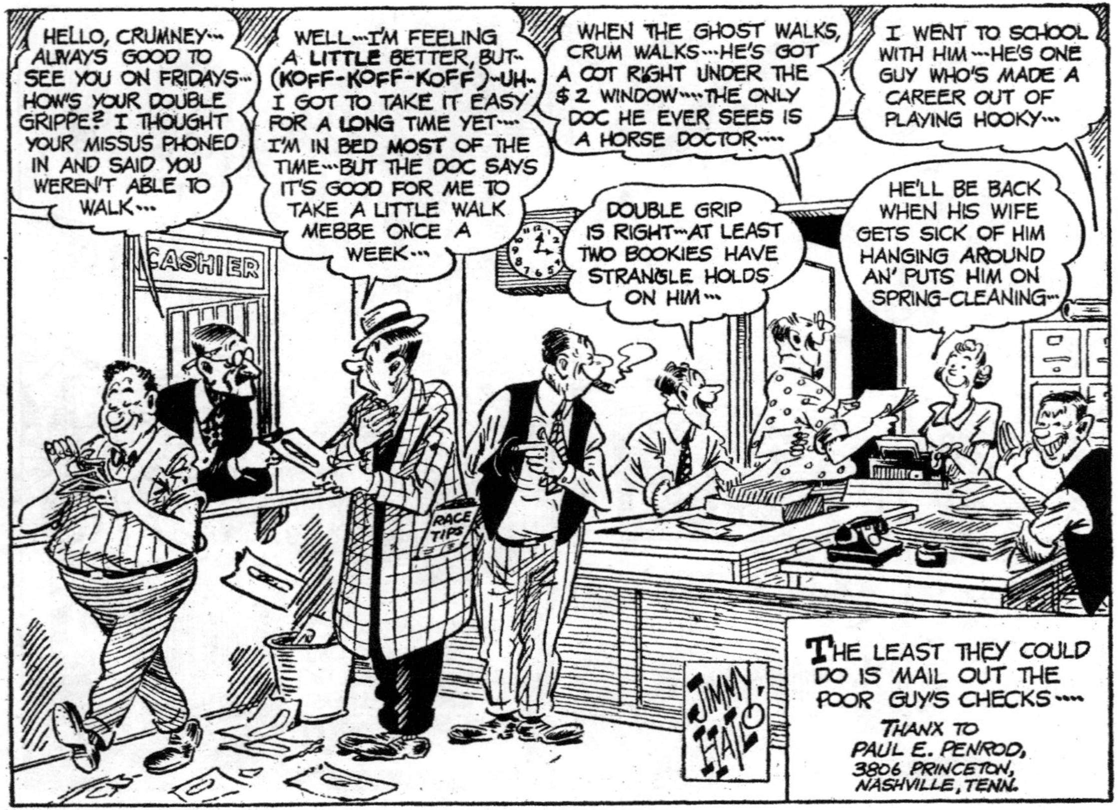
HELLO, CRUMNEY... ALWAYS GOOD TO SEE YOU ON FRIDAYS... HOW'S YOUR DOUBLE GRIPPE? I THOUGHT YOUR MISSUS PHONED IN AND SAID YOU WEREN'T ABLE TO WALK...
CASHIER
WELL...I'M FEELING A LITTLE BETTER, BUT-- (KOFF-KOFF-KOFF)--UH-- I GOT TO TAKE IT EASY FOR A LONG TIME YET.... I'M IN BED MOST OF THE TIME...BUT THE DOC SAYS IT'S GOOD FOR ME TO TAKE A LITTLE WALK MEBBE ONCE A WEEK...
RACE TIPS
WHEN THE GHOST WALKS, CRUM WALKS...HE'S GOT A COT RIGHT UNDER THE $2 WINDOW....THE ONLY DOC HE EVER SEES IS A HORSE DOCTOR....
DOUBLE GRIP IS RIGHT...AT LEAST TWO BOOKIES HAVE STRANGLE HOLDS ON HIM...
I WENT TO SCHOOL WITH HIM ...HE'S ONE GUY WHO'S MADE A CAREER OUT OF PLAYING HOOKY...
HE'LL BE BACK WHEN HIS WIFE GETS SICK OF HIM HANGING AROUND AN' PUTS HIM ON SPRING-CLEANING...
JIMMY HATLO
THE LEAST THEY COULD DO IS MAIL OUT THE POOR GUY'S CHECKS....
THANX TO PAUL E. PENROD, 3806 PRINCETON, NASHVILLE, TENN.

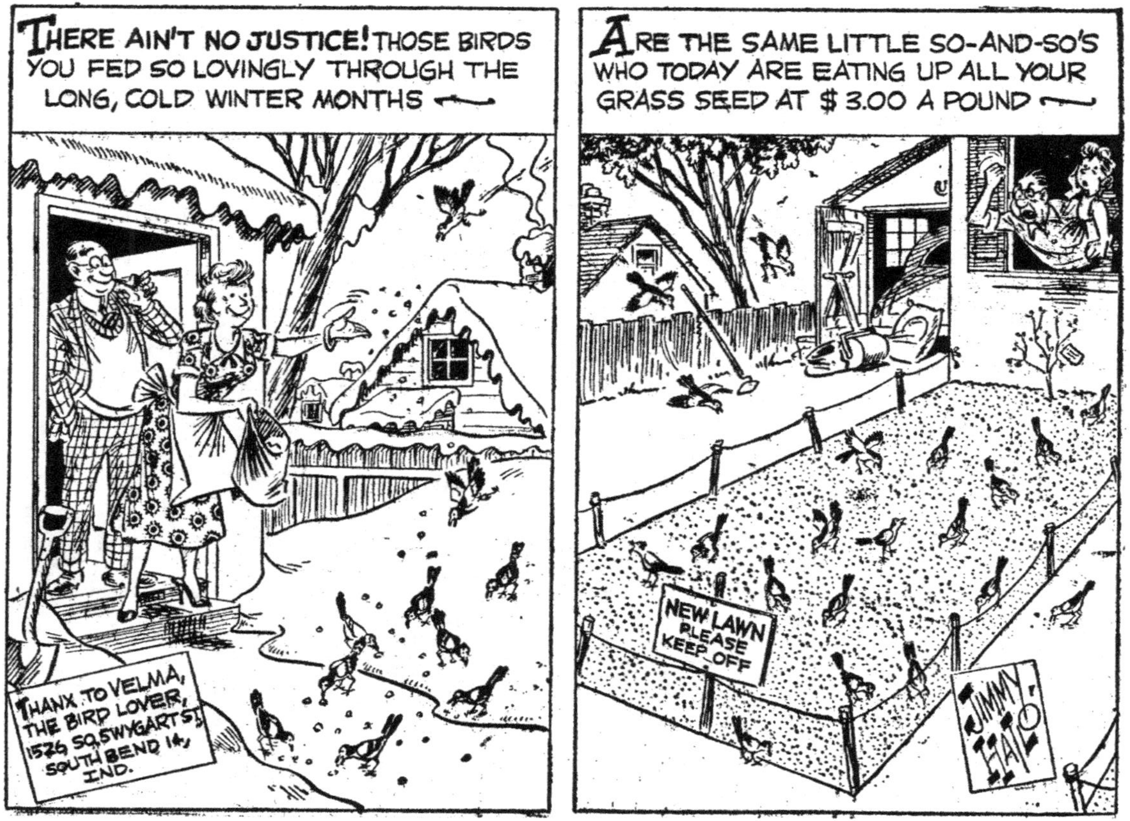
THERE AIN'T NO JUSTICE! THOSE BIRDS YOU FED SO LOVINGLY THROUGH THE LONG, COLD WINTER MONTHS
THANX TO VELMA, THE BIRD LOVER, 1526 SO. SWYGART ST. SOUTH BEND 14, IND.
ARE THE SAME LITTLE SO-AND-SO'S WHO TODAY ARE EATING UP ALL YOUR GRASS SEED AT $ 3.00 A POUND
NEW LAWN PLEASE KEEP OFF
JIMMY HATLO

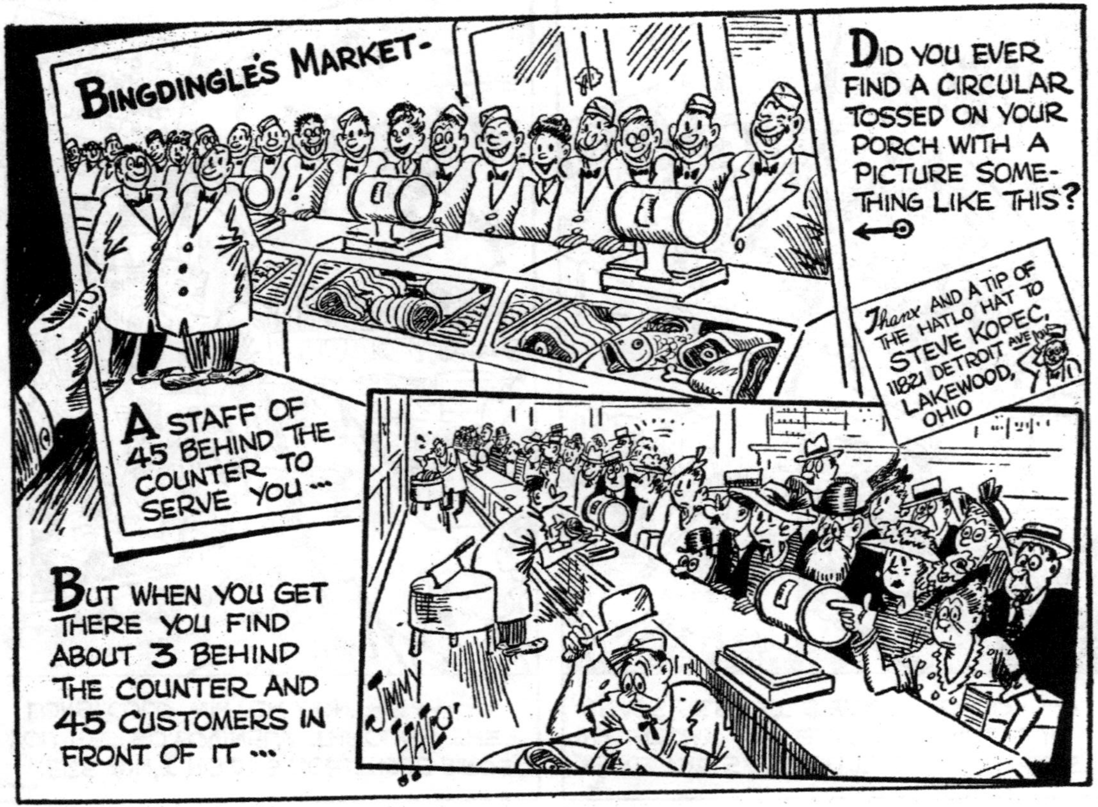
DID YOU EVER FIND A CIRCULAR TOSSED ON YOUR PORCH WITH A PICTURE SOMETHING LIKE THIS?
BINGDINGLE'S MARKET-
A STAFF OF 45 BEHIND THE COUNTER TO SERVE YOU...
Thanx AND A TIP OF THE HATLO HAT TO STEVE KOPEC, 11821 DETROIT AVE LAKEWOOD, OHIO
BUT WHEN YOU GET THERE YOU FIND ABOUT 3 BEHIND THE COUNTER AND 45 CUSTOMERS IN FRONT OF IT...
JIMMY HATLO

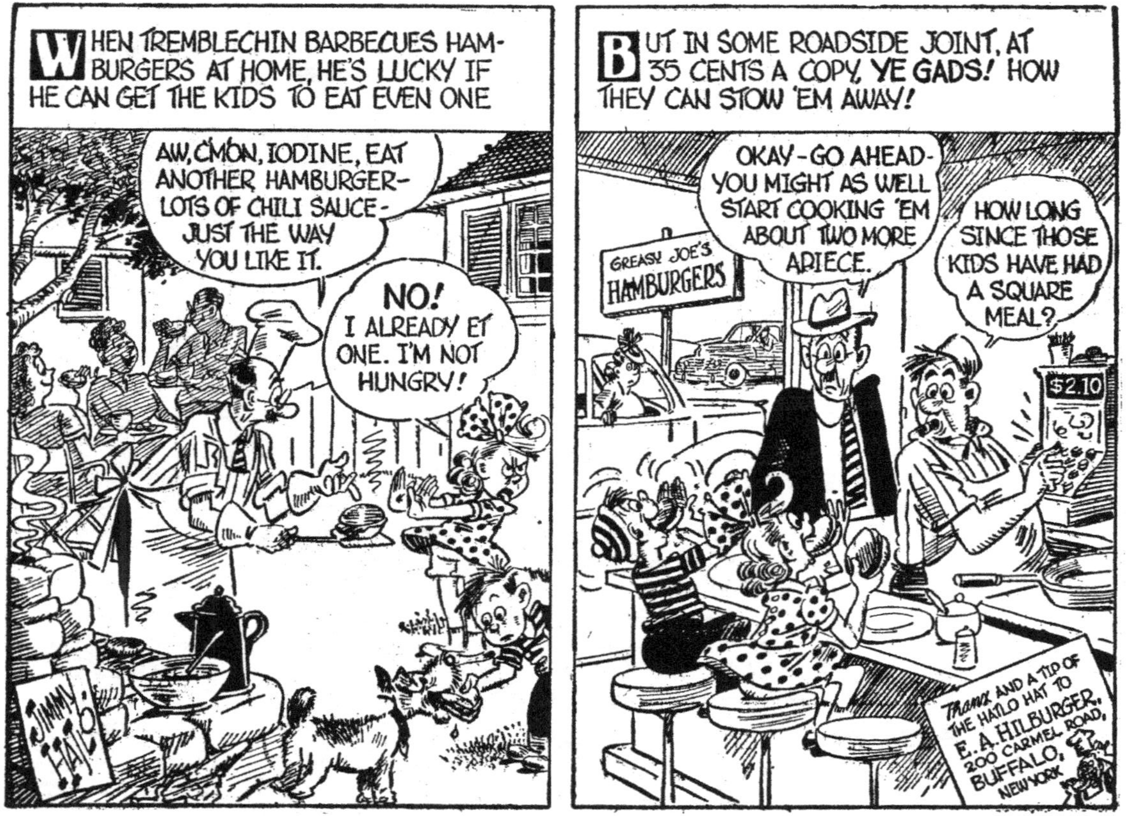
WHEN TREMBLECHIN BARBECUES HAMBURGERS AT HOME, HE'S LUCKY IF HE CAN GET THE KIDS TO EAT EVEN ONE
AW, C'MON, IODINE, EAT ANOTHER HAMBURGER- LOTS OF CHILI SAUCE- JUST THE WAY YOU LIKE IT.
NO! I ALREADY ET ONE. I'M NOT HUNGRY!
JIMMY HATLO
BUT IN SOME ROADSIDE JOINT, AT 35 CENTS A COPY, YE GADS! HOW THEY CAN STOW 'EM AWAY!
GREASY JOE'S HAMBURGERS
OKAY-GO AHEAD- YOU MIGHT AS WELL START COOKING 'EM ABOUT TWO MORE APIECE.
HOW LONG SINCE THOSE KIDS HAVE HAD A SQUARE MEAL?
$2.10
Thanx AND A TIP OF THE HATLO HAT TO E. A. HILBURGER, 200 CARMEL ROAD, BUFFALO, NEW YORK

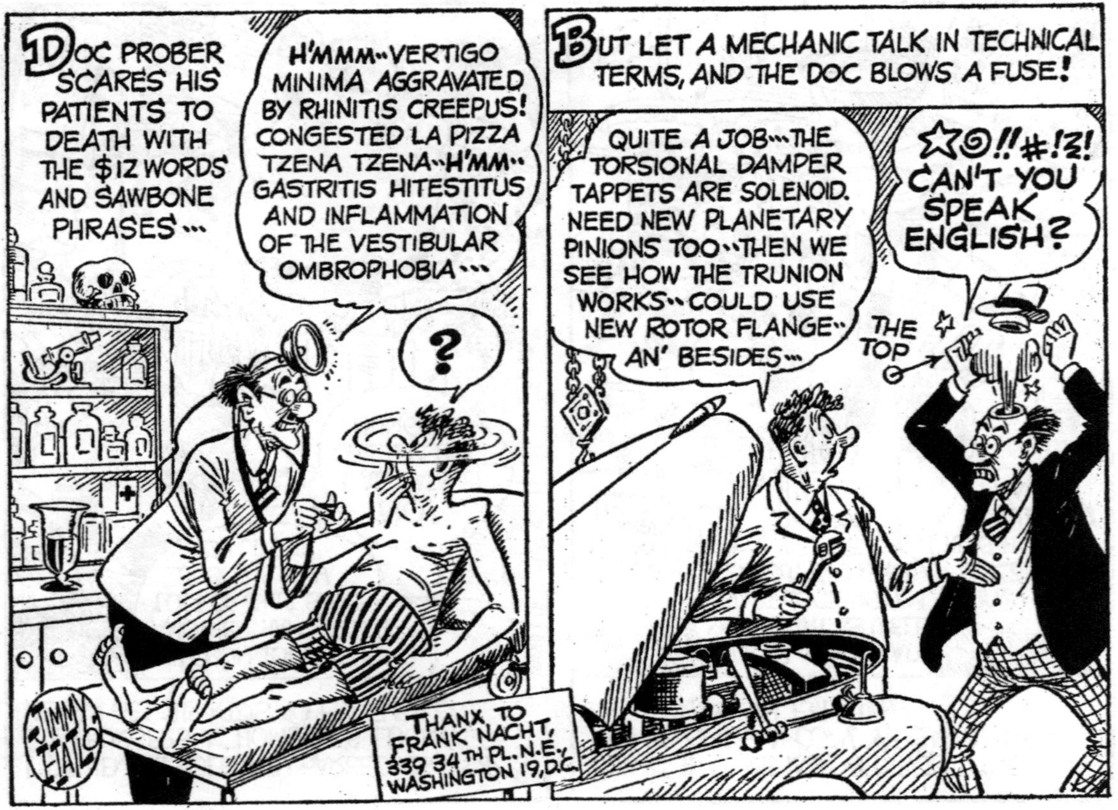
DOC PROBER SCARES HIS PATIENTS TO DEATH WITH THE $IZ WORDS AND SAWBONE PHRASES...
H'MMM..VERTIGO MINIMA AGGRAVATED BY RHINITIS CREEPUS! CONGESTED LA PIZZA TZENA TZENA..H'MM.. GASTRITIS HITESTITUS AND INFLAMMATION OF THE VESTIBULAR OMBROPHOBIA...
?
JIMMY HATLO
THANX TO FRANK NACHT, 339 34TH PL. N.E., WASHINGTON 19, D.C.
BUT LET A MECHANIC TALK IN TECHNICAL TERMS, AND THE DOC BLOWS A FUSE!
QUITE A JOB...THE TORSIONAL DAMPER TAPPETS ARE SOLENOID. NEED NEW PLANETARY PINIONS TOO..THEN WE SEE HOW THE TRUNION WORKS..COULD USE NEW ROTOR FLANGE.. AN' BESIDES...
!!#!?! CAN'T YOU SPEAK ENGLISH?
THE TOP

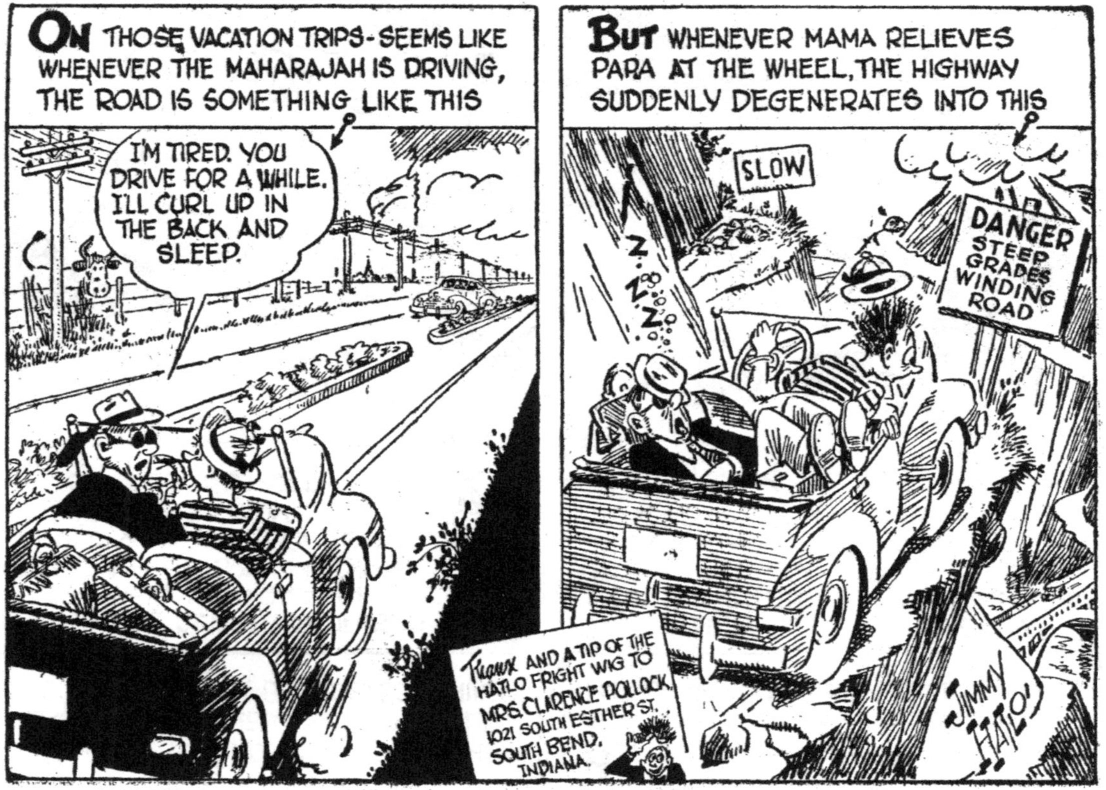
ON THOSE VACATION TRIPS - SEEMS LIKE WHENEVER THE MAHARAJAH IS DRIVING, THE ROAD IS SOMETHING LIKE THIS
I'M TIRED. YOU DRIVE FOR A WHILE. I'LL CURL UP IN THE BACK AND SLEEP.
BUT WHENEVER MAMA RELIEVES PAPA AT THE WHEEL, THE HIGHWAY SUDDENLY DEGENERATES INTO THIS
SLOW
DANGER STEEP GRADES WINDING ROAD
Z Z Z
THANX AND A TIP OF THE HATLO FRIGHT WIG TO MRS. CLARENCE POLLOCK, 1021 SOUTH ESTHER ST. SOUTH BEND, INDIANA.
JIMMY HATLO

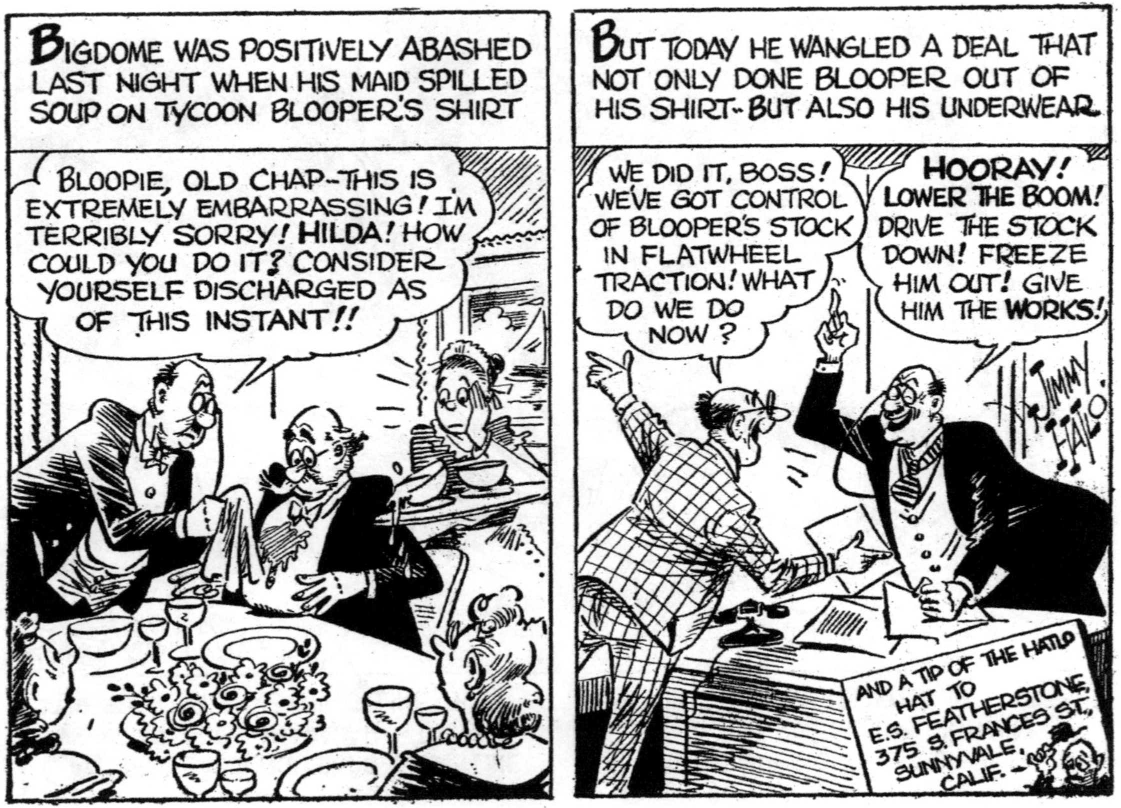
BIGDOME WAS POSITIVELY ABASHED LAST NIGHT WHEN HIS MAID SPILLED SOUP ON TYCOON BLOOPER'S SHIRT
BLOOPIE, OLD CHAP-THIS IS EXTREMELY EMBARRASSING! I'M TERRIBLY SORRY! HILDA! HOW COULD YOU DO IT? CONSIDER YOURSELF DISCHARGED AS OF THIS INSTANT!!
BUT TODAY HE WANGLED A DEAL THAT NOT ONLY DONE BLOOPER OUT OF HIS SHIRT-BUT ALSO HIS UNDERWEAR
WE DID IT, BOSS! WE'VE GOT CONTROL OF BLOOPER'S STOCK IN FLATWHEEL TRACTION! WHAT DO WE DO NOW?
HOORAY! LOWER THE BOOM! DRIVE THE STOCK DOWN! FREEZE HIM OUT! GIVE HIM THE WORKS!
JIMMY HATLO
AND A TIP OF THE HATLO HAT TO E.S. FEATHERSTONE, 375 S. FRANCES ST., SUNNYVALE, CALIF.

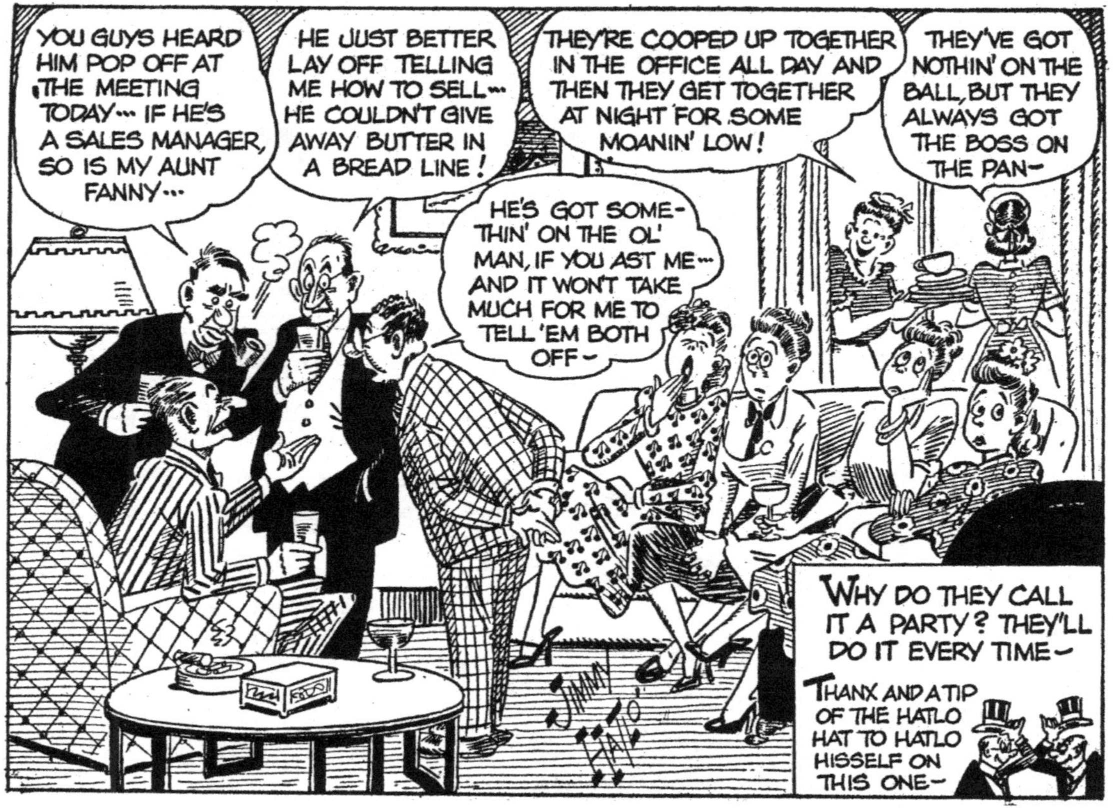
YOU GUYS HEARD HIM POP OFF AT THE MEETING TODAY··· IF HE'S A SALES MANAGER, SO IS MY AUNT FANNY···
HE JUST BETTER LAY OFF TELLING ME HOW TO SELL··· HE COULDN'T GIVE AWAY BUTTER IN A BREAD LINE!
THEY'RE COOPED UP TOGETHER IN THE OFFICE ALL DAY AND THEN THEY GET TOGETHER AT NIGHT FOR SOME MOANIN' LOW!
THEY'VE GOT NOTHIN' ON THE BALL, BUT THEY ALWAYS GOT THE BOSS ON THE PAN–
HE'S GOT SOME-THIN' ON THE OL' MAN, IF YOU AST ME··· AND IT WON'T TAKE MUCH FOR ME TO TELL 'EM BOTH OFF–
JIMMY HATLO
WHY DO THEY CALL IT A PARTY? THEY'LL DO IT EVERY TIME–
THANX AND A TIP OF THE HATLO HAT TO HATLO HISSELF ON THIS ONE–

IT SEEMS TREMBLECHIN IS ALWAYS READING ABOUT THOSE CON MEN WHO ARE ABLE TO CASH GREAT BIG POGO CHECKS FROM COAST TO COAST....
DAILY BAZOOKA
RUBBER CHECK CHARLIE FLEECES MERCHANTS! PASSES OVER $5,000 IN WORTHLESS CHECKS TO 15 LEADING STORES!!
IS WANTED FROM COAST TO COAST
BUT-JUST LET HIM TRY TO CASH A PERFECTLY GOOD $5 CHECK IN A STORE HE'S PATRONIZED FOR YEARS--AND--
JIMMY, HATLO
THANX TO VINCENT M. BYRNE, 61-17 WOODSIDE AVE, WOODSIDE, N.Y.

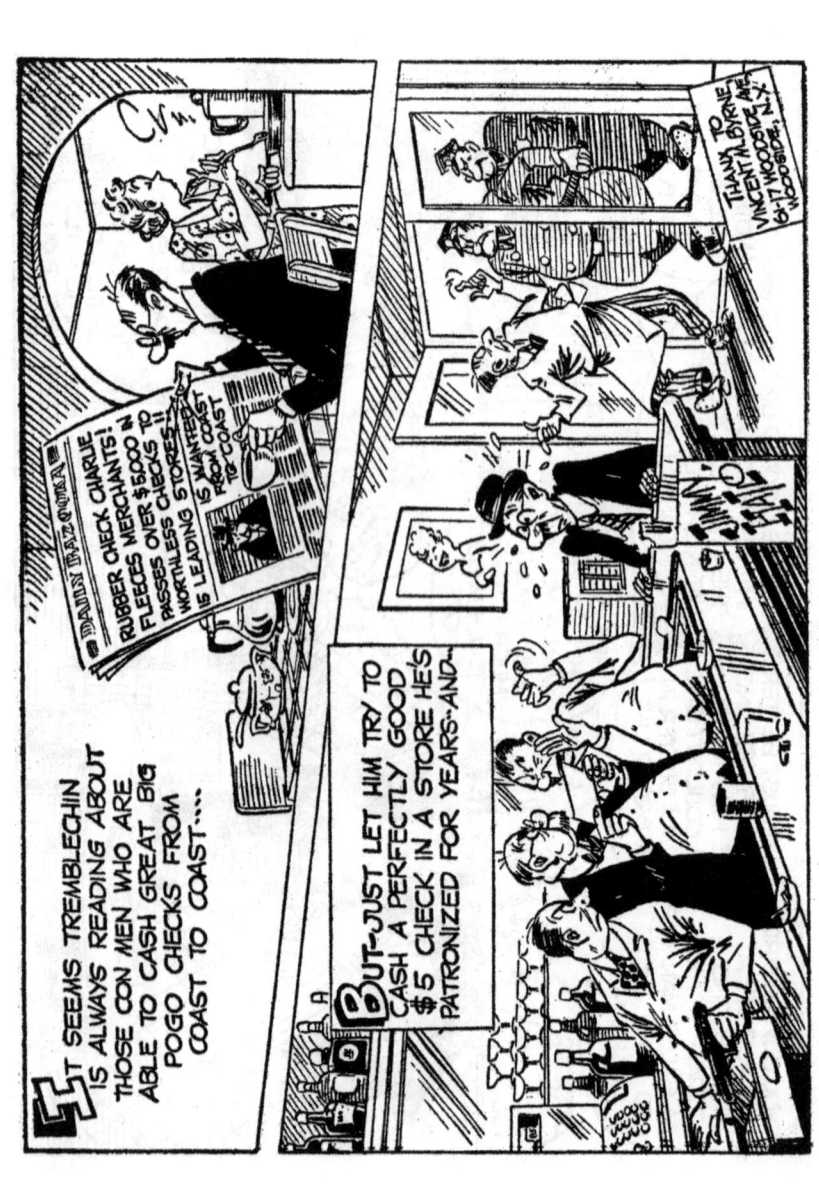

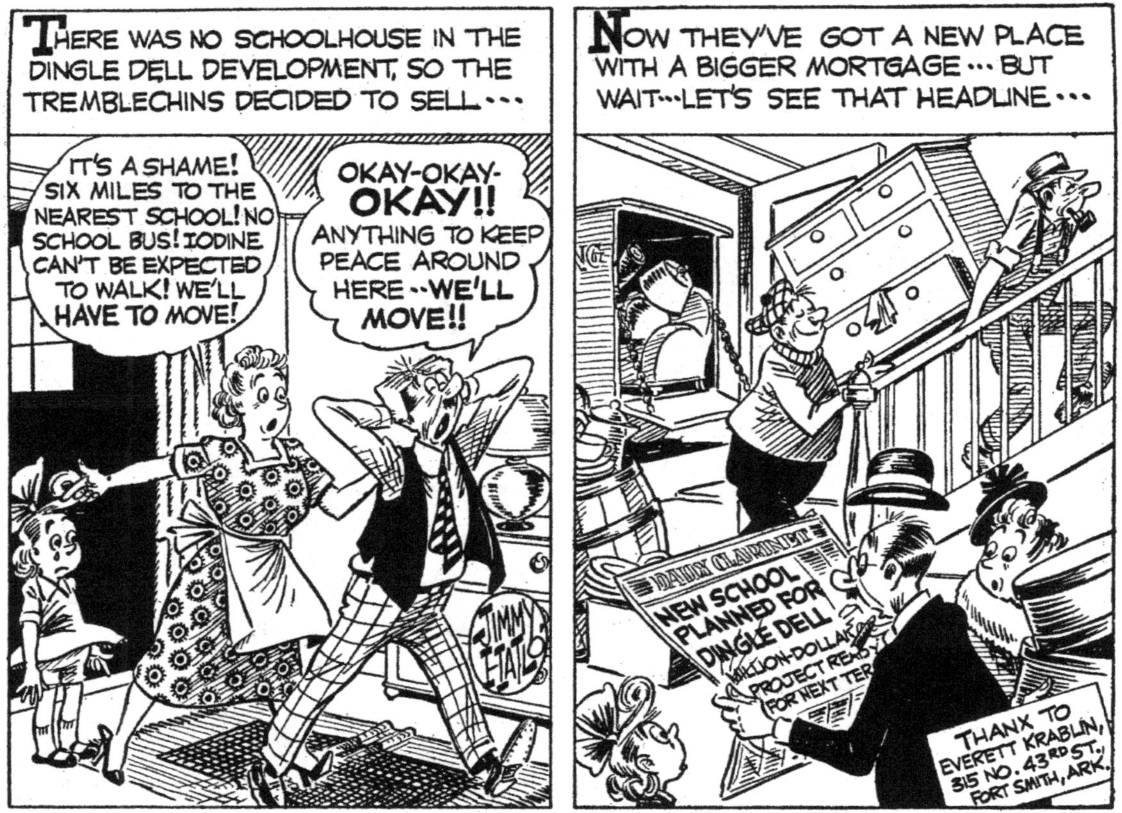
THERE WAS NO SCHOOLHOUSE IN THE DINGLE DELL DEVELOPMENT, SO THE TREMBLECHINS DECIDED TO SELL···
IT'S A SHAME! SIX MILES TO THE NEAREST SCHOOL! NO SCHOOL BUS! IODINE CAN'T BE EXPECTED TO WALK! WE'LL HAVE TO MOVE!
OKAY-OKAY-OKAY!! ANYTHING TO KEEP PEACE AROUND HERE --WE'LL MOVE!!
JIMMY HATLO
NOW THEY'VE GOT A NEW PLACE WITH A BIGGER MORTGAGE ··· BUT WAIT···LET'S SEE THAT HEADLINE ···
DAILY CLARINET
NEW SCHOOL PLANNED FOR DINGLE DELL
MILLION-DOLLAR PROJECT READY FOR NEXT TER
THANX TO EVERETT KRABLIN, 315 NO. 43RD ST., FORT SMITH, ARK.

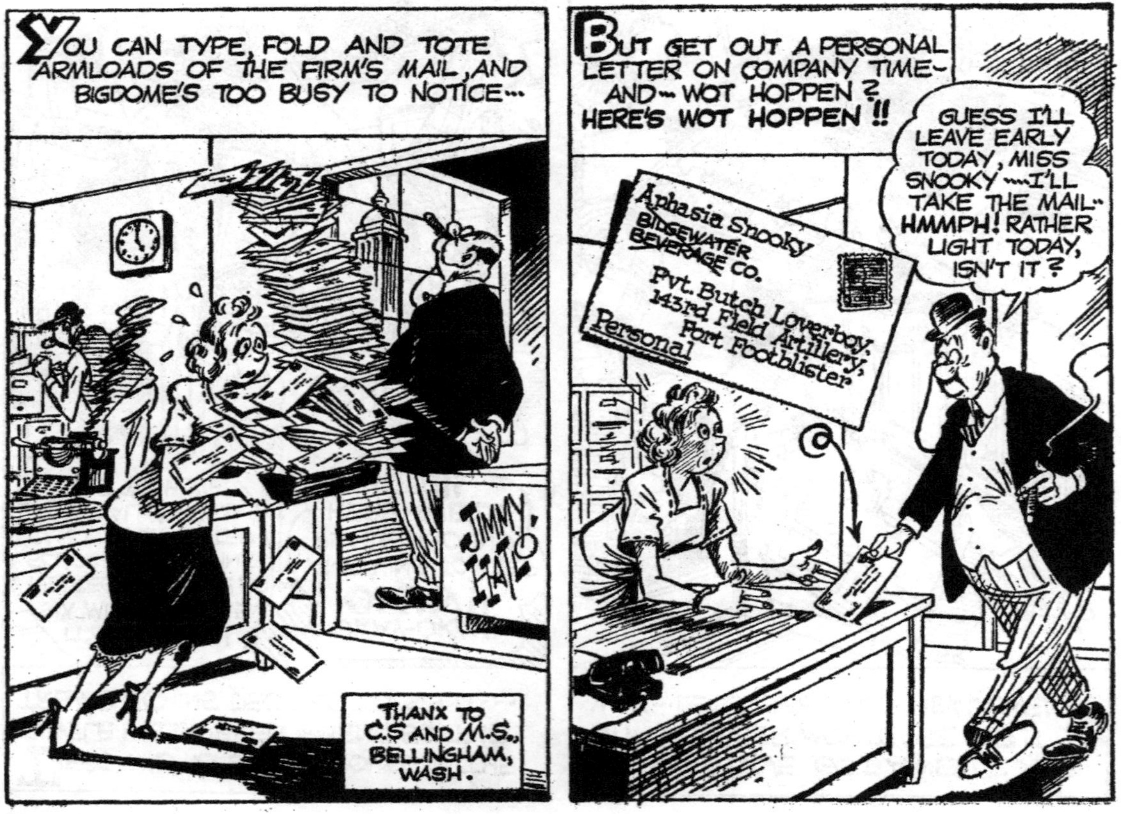
YOU CAN TYPE, FOLD AND TOTE ARMLOADS OF THE FIRM'S MAIL, AND BIGDOME'S TOO BUSY TO NOTICE...
JIMMY HATLO
THANX TO C.S AND M.S., BELLINGHAM, WASH.
BUT GET OUT A PERSONAL LETTER ON COMPANY TIME-- AND-- WOT HOPPEN ? HERE'S WOT HOPPEN !!
Aphasia Snooky
BIDGEWATER BEVERAGE CO.
Pvt. Butch Loverboy,
143rd Field Artillery,
Fort Footblister
Personal
GUESS I'LL LEAVE EARLY TODAY, MISS SNOOKY ....I'LL TAKE THE MAIL-- HMMPH! RATHER LIGHT TODAY, ISN'T IT ?

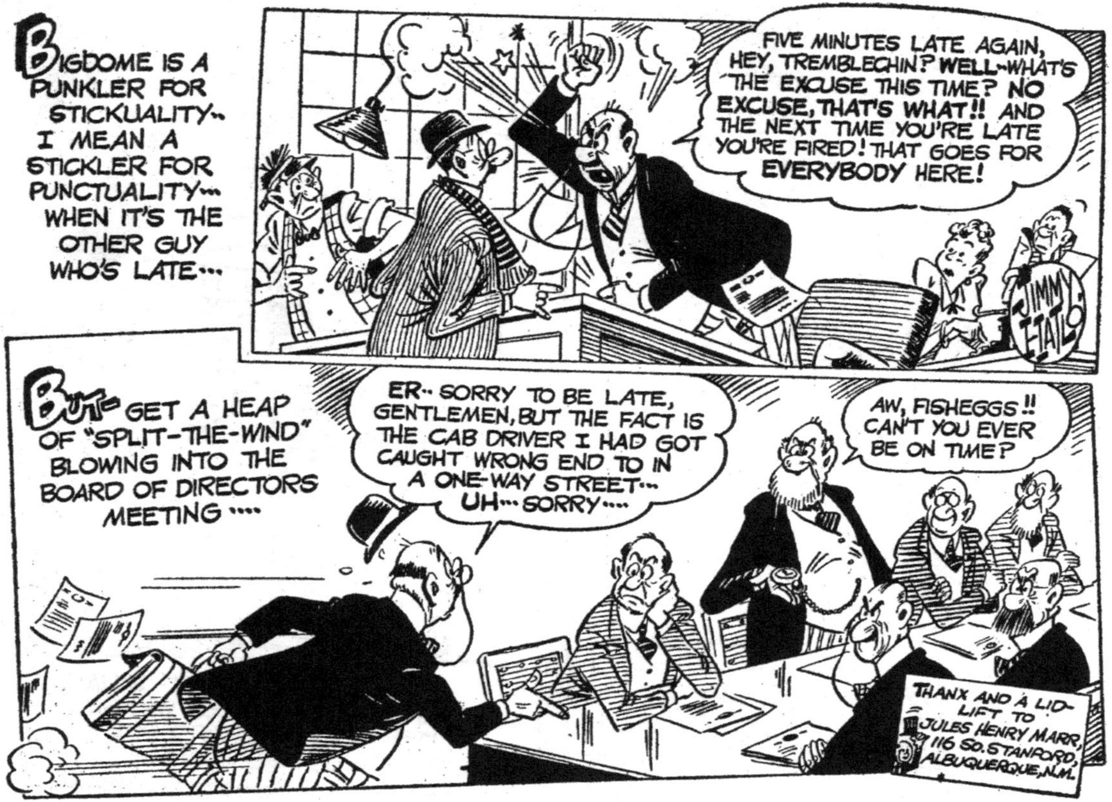
BIGDOME IS A PUNKLER FOR STICKUALITY.. I MEAN A STICKLER FOR PUNCTUALITY... WHEN IT'S THE OTHER GUY WHO'S LATE...
FIVE MINUTES LATE AGAIN, HEY, TREMBLECHIN? WELL-WHAT'S THE EXCUSE THIS TIME? NO EXCUSE, THAT'S WHAT!! AND THE NEXT TIME YOU'RE LATE YOU'RE FIRED! THAT GOES FOR EVERYBODY HERE!
JIMMY HATLO
BUT- GET A HEAP OF "SPLIT-THE-WIND" BLOWING INTO THE BOARD OF DIRECTORS MEETING....
ER.. SORRY TO BE LATE, GENTLEMEN, BUT THE FACT IS THE CAB DRIVER I HAD GOT CAUGHT WRONG END TO IN A ONE-WAY STREET... UH... SORRY....
AW, FISHEGGS!! CAN'T YOU EVER BE ON TIME?
THANX AND A LID-LIFT TO JULES HENRY MARR, 116 SO. STANFORD, ALBUQUERQUE, N.M.

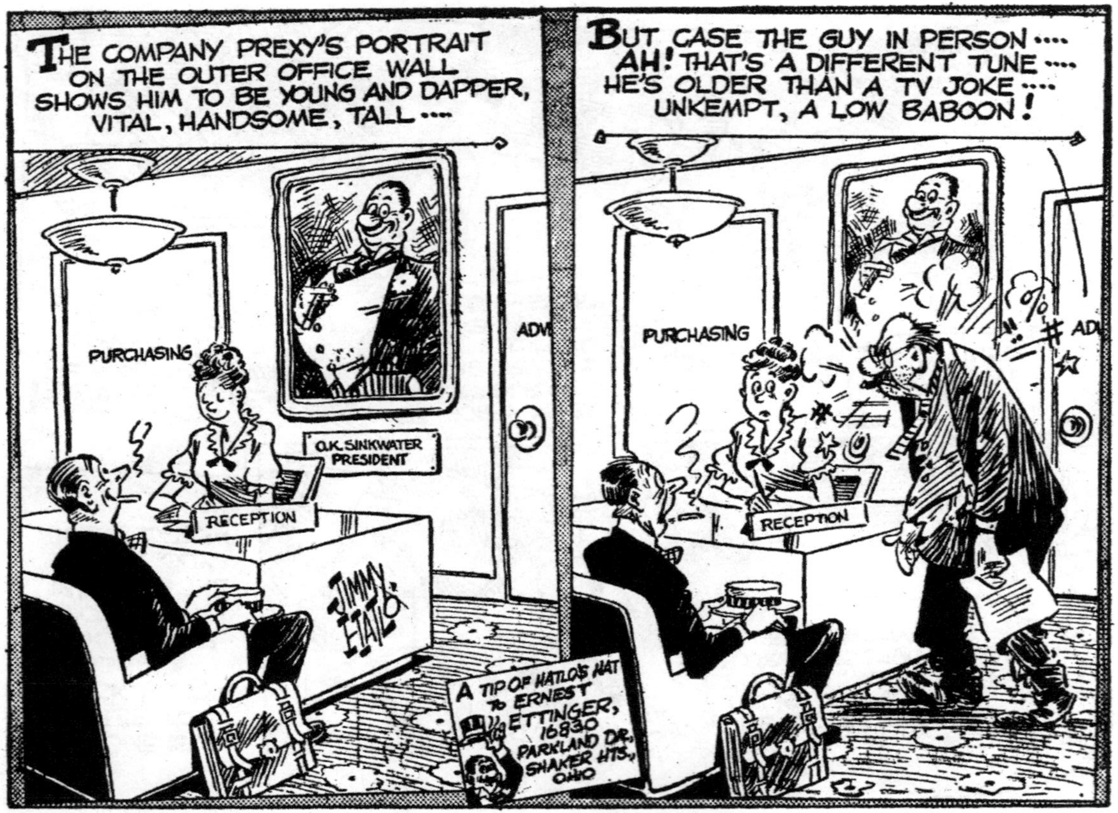
THE COMPANY PREXY'S PORTRAIT ON THE OUTER OFFICE WALL SHOWS HIM TO BE YOUNG AND DAPPER, VITAL, HANDSOME, TALL ....
PURCHASING
O.K. SINKWATER PRESIDENT
RECEPTION
ADV
JIMMY HATLO
BUT CASE THE GUY IN PERSON .... AH! THAT'S A DIFFERENT TUNE .... HE'S OLDER THAN A TV JOKE .... UNKEMPT, A LOW BABOON!
PURCHASING
RECEPTION
AD
A TIP OF HATLO'S HAT TO ERNEST ETTINGER, 16830 PARKLAND DR. SHAKER HTS., OHIO

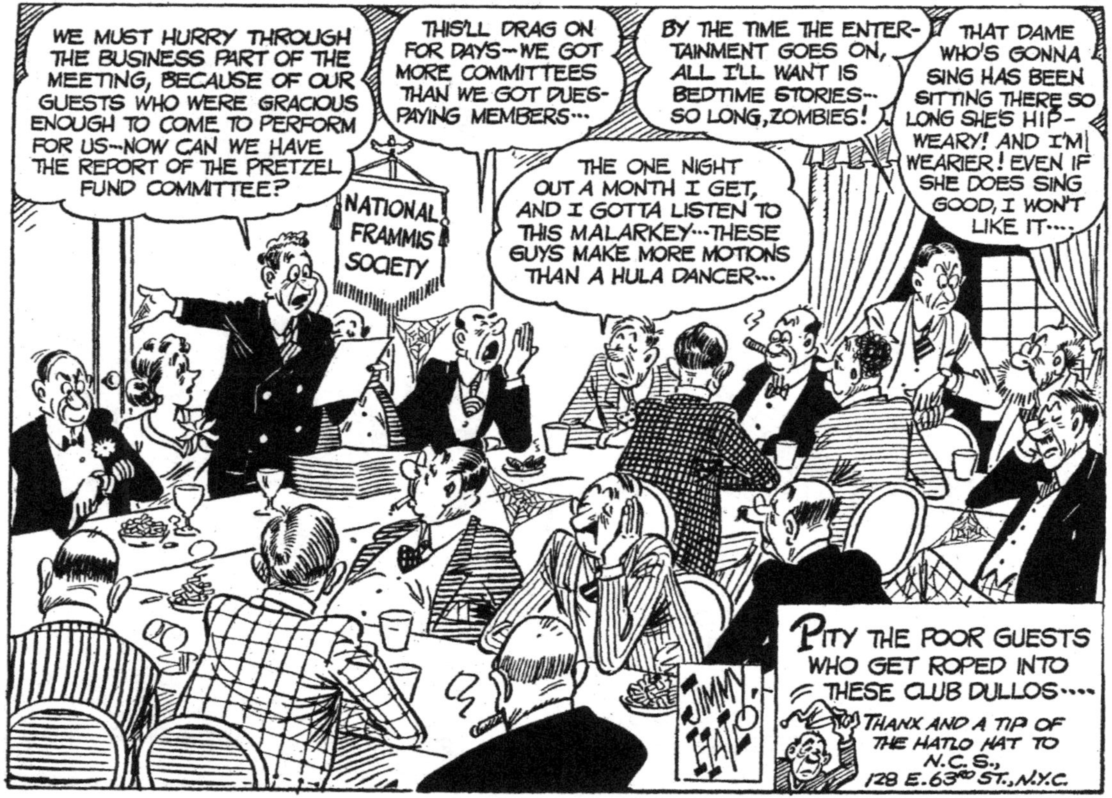
WE MUST HURRY THROUGH THE BUSINESS PART OF THE MEETING, BECAUSE OF OUR GUESTS WHO WERE GRACIOUS ENOUGH TO COME TO PERFORM FOR US--NOW CAN WE HAVE THE REPORT OF THE PRETZEL FUND COMMITTEE?
NATIONAL FRAMMIS SOCIETY
THIS'LL DRAG ON FOR DAYS--WE GOT MORE COMMITTEES THAN WE GOT DUES-PAYING MEMBERS...
BY THE TIME THE ENTERTAINMENT GOES ON, ALL I'LL WANT IS BEDTIME STORIES-- SO LONG, ZOMBIES!
THE ONE NIGHT OUT A MONTH I GET, AND I GOTTA LISTEN TO THIS MALARKEY...THESE GUYS MAKE MORE MOTIONS THAN A HULA DANCER...
THAT DAME WHO'S GONNA SING HAS BEEN SITTING THERE SO LONG SHE'S HIP-WEARY! AND I'M WEARIER! EVEN IF SHE DOES SING GOOD, I WON'T LIKE IT....
JIMMY HATLO
PITY THE POOR GUESTS WHO GET ROPED INTO THESE CLUB DULLOS....
THANX AND A TIP OF THE HATLO HAT TO N.C.S., 128 E. 63RD ST., N.Y.C.

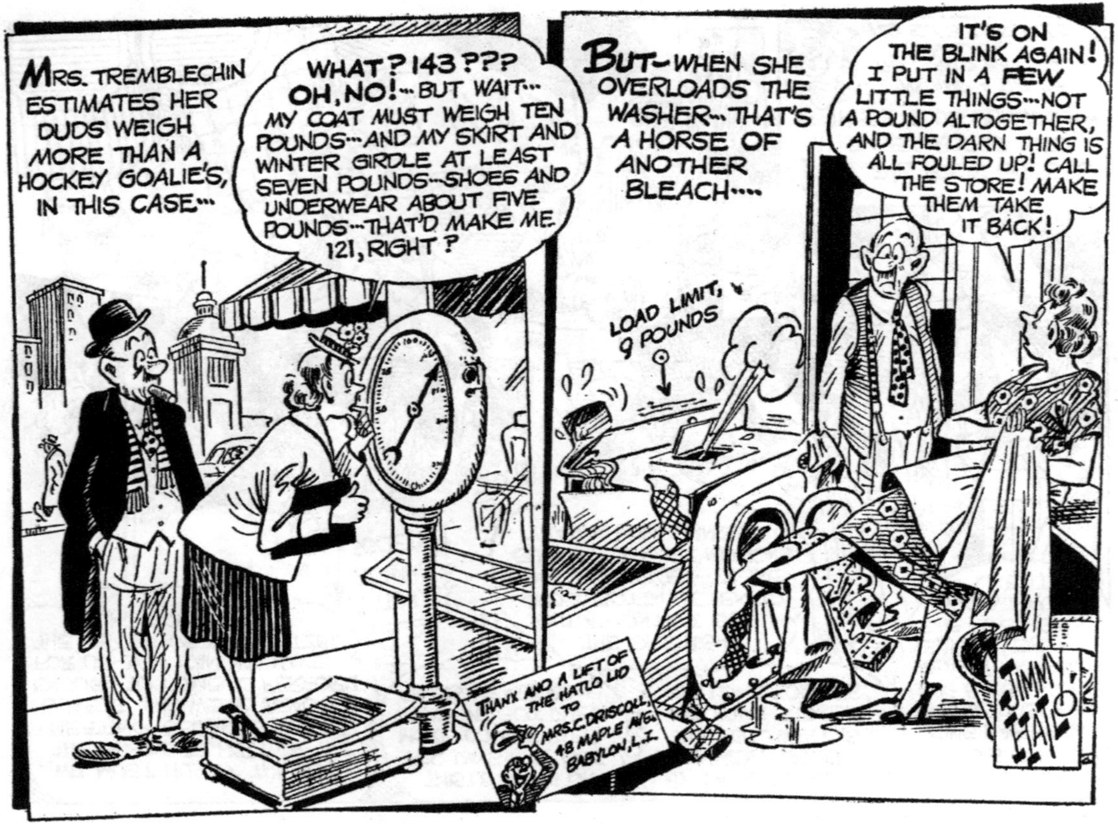
MRS. TREMBLECHIN ESTIMATES HER DUDS WEIGH MORE THAN A HOCKEY GOALIE'S, IN THIS CASE...
WHAT? 143??? OH, NO!... BUT WAIT... MY COAT MUST WEIGH TEN POUNDS... AND MY SKIRT AND WINTER GIRDLE AT LEAST SEVEN POUNDS... SHOES AND UNDERWEAR ABOUT FIVE POUNDS... THAT'D MAKE ME 121, RIGHT?
BUT—WHEN SHE OVERLOADS THE WASHER... THAT'S A HORSE OF ANOTHER BLEACH....
LOAD LIMIT, 9 POUNDS
IT'S ON THE BLINK AGAIN! I PUT IN A FEW LITTLE THINGS... NOT A POUND ALTOGETHER, AND THE DARN THING IS ALL FOULED UP! CALL THE STORE! MAKE THEM TAKE IT BACK!
THANX AND A LIFT OF THE HATLO LID TO MRS. C. DRISCOLL, 48 MAPLE AVE. BABYLON, L.I.
JIMMY HATLO

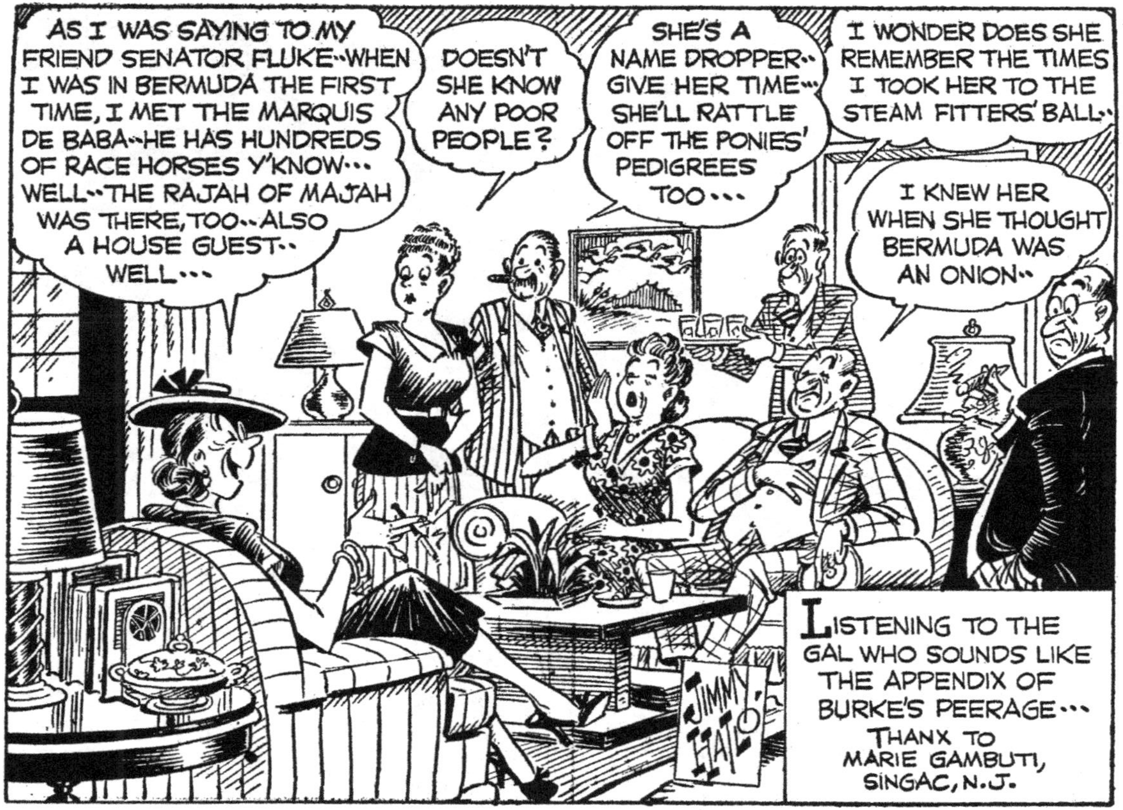
AS I WAS SAYING TO MY FRIEND SENATOR FLUKE--WHEN I WAS IN BERMUDA THE FIRST TIME, I MET THE MARQUIS DE BABA--HE HAS HUNDREDS OF RACE HORSES Y'KNOW... WELL--THE RAJAH OF MAJAH WAS THERE, TOO--ALSO A HOUSE GUEST-- WELL...
DOESN'T SHE KNOW ANY POOR PEOPLE?
SHE'S A NAME DROPPER-- GIVE HER TIME--- SHE'LL RATTLE OFF THE PONIES' PEDIGREES TOO...
I WONDER DOES SHE REMEMBER THE TIMES I TOOK HER TO THE STEAM FITTERS' BALL--
I KNEW HER WHEN SHE THOUGHT BERMUDA WAS AN ONION--
JIMMY HATLO
LISTENING TO THE GAL WHO SOUNDS LIKE THE APPENDIX OF BURKE'S PEERAGE...
THANX TO MARIE GAMBUTI, SINGAC, N.J.

DILLDOCK WORKS LIKE A BEAVER, WIRING BIG CONTROL PANELS FOR HECTIC ELECTRIC, BUT NONE OF THE BIG SHOTS EVER COMES AROUND TO WATCH HIM ...
TODAY HE BROUGHT HIS KITCHEN RADIO DOWN TO THE PLANT FOR A MINOR REPAIR— AND... YOU GUESSED IT! THREE (3) OF HIS BOSSES
THANX AND A TIP OF THE HATLO HAT TO ED FARLEY 267 FULTON AV. JERSEY CITY N. J.
JIMMY HATLO

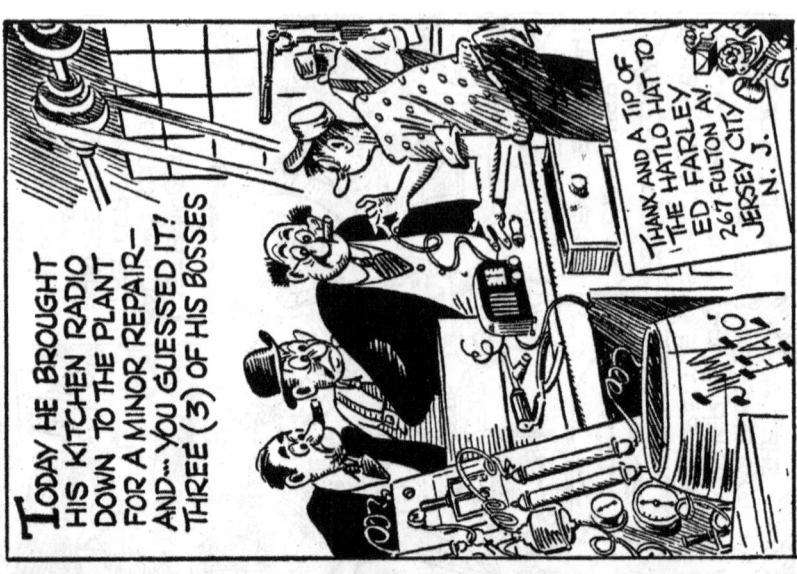

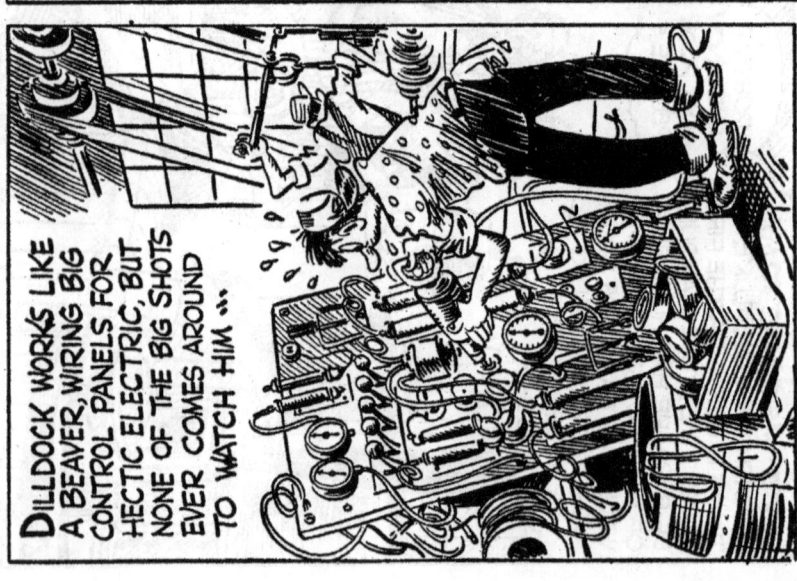

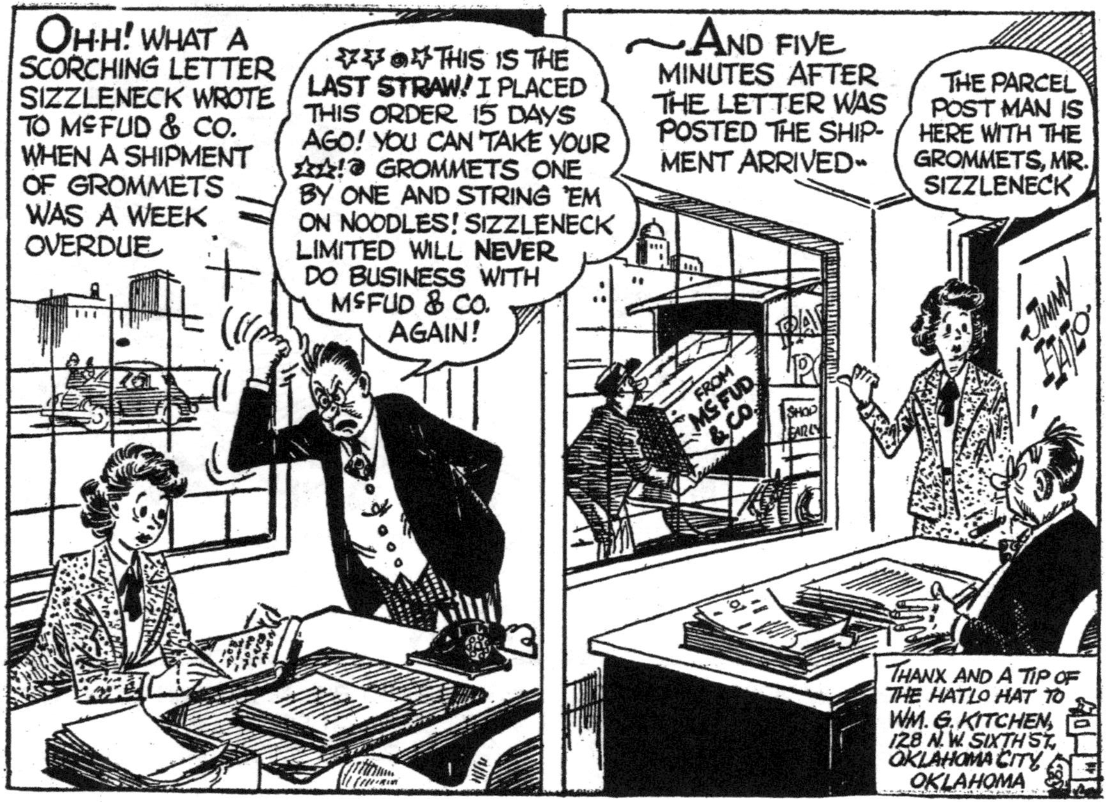
OH-H! WHAT A SCORCHING LETTER SIZZLENECK WROTE TO McFUD & CO. WHEN A SHIPMENT OF GROMMETS WAS A WEEK OVERDUE
THIS IS THE LAST STRAW! I PLACED THIS ORDER 15 DAYS AGO! YOU CAN TAKE YOUR GROMMETS ONE BY ONE AND STRING 'EM ON NOODLES! SIZZLENECK LIMITED WILL NEVER DO BUSINESS WITH McFUD & CO. AGAIN!
~AND FIVE MINUTES AFTER THE LETTER WAS POSTED THE SHIPMENT ARRIVED–
THE PARCEL POST MAN IS HERE WITH THE GROMMETS, MR. SIZZLENECK
FROM McFUD & CO.
SHOP EARLY
JIMMY HATLO
THANX AND A TIP OF THE HATLO HAT TO WM. G. KITCHEN, 128 N.W. SIXTH ST, OKLAHOMA CITY, OKLAHOMA

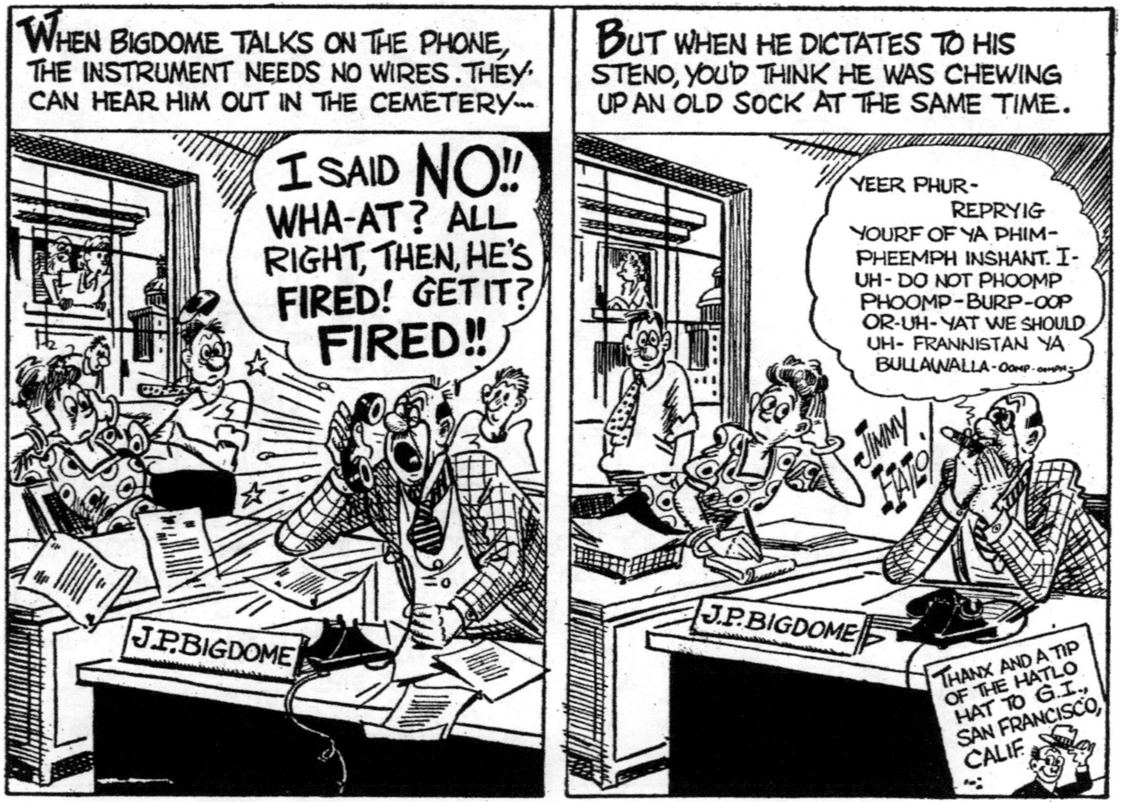
WHEN BIGDOME TALKS ON THE PHONE, THE INSTRUMENT NEEDS NO WIRES. THEY CAN HEAR HIM OUT IN THE CEMETERY---
I SAID NO!! WHA-AT? ALL RIGHT, THEN, HE'S FIRED! GET IT? FIRED!!
J.P. BIGDOME
BUT WHEN HE DICTATES TO HIS STENO, YOU'D THINK HE WAS CHEWING UP AN OLD SOCK AT THE SAME TIME.
YEER PHUR- REPRYIG YOURF OF YA PHIM-PHEEMPH INSHANT. I-UH- DO NOT PHOOMP PHOOMP-BURP-OOP OR-UH-YAT WE SHOULD UH- FRANNISTAN YA BULLAWALLA-OOMP-OOMPH-
JIMMY HATLO
J.P. BIGDOME
THANX AND A TIP OF THE HATLO HAT TO G.I., SAN FRANCISCO, CALIF.

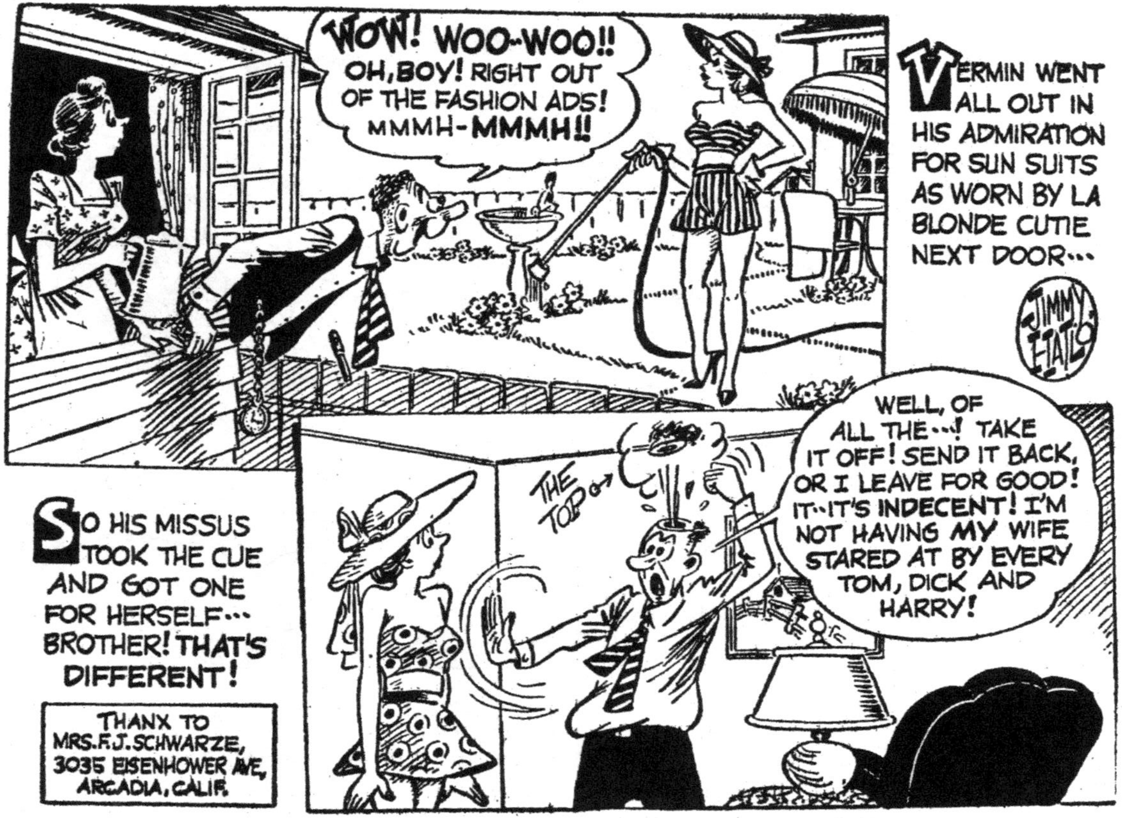
VERMIN WENT ALL OUT IN HIS ADMIRATION FOR SUN SUITS AS WORN BY LA BLONDE CUTIE NEXT DOOR...
WOW! WOO-WOO!! OH, BOY! RIGHT OUT OF THE FASHION ADS! MMMH-MMMH!!
JIMMY HATLO
SO HIS MISSUS TOOK THE CUE AND GOT ONE FOR HERSELF... BROTHER! THAT'S DIFFERENT!
THE TOP
WELL, OF ALL THE...! TAKE IT OFF! SEND IT BACK, OR I LEAVE FOR GOOD! IT--IT'S INDECENT! I'M NOT HAVING MY WIFE STARED AT BY EVERY TOM, DICK AND HARRY!
THANX TO MRS. F. J. SCHWARZE, 3035 EISENHOWER AVE, ARCADIA, CALIF.

OLD SALTY McMUSSEL, THE TECHNICOLOR GOB, HAS BEEN JAMMED WITH TATTOO NEEDLES FROM BROOKLYN TO HONG KONG
PROF. SPUMONI
Artistic TATTOOING
ACE HOTEL
HURT A LITTLE, SAILOR?
NAH-LET 'ER FLICKER-YOU KNOW ME, PROF -TOUGH AS NAILS!
McMUSSEL
DOLLY
BUT HE WENT OUT LIKE AN ASBESTOS MATCH WHEN HE LINED UP FOR A LITTLE TETANUS INJECTION
ONE GANDER AT THAT NEEDLE, SIR, KNOCKED HIM COLDER THAN A MACKEREL
JIMMY HATLO
Thanx AND A TIP OF THE HATLO HAT TO
EUNICE S. SMITH,
1159 CHELSEA AVENUE,
MEMPHIS,
TENNESSEE

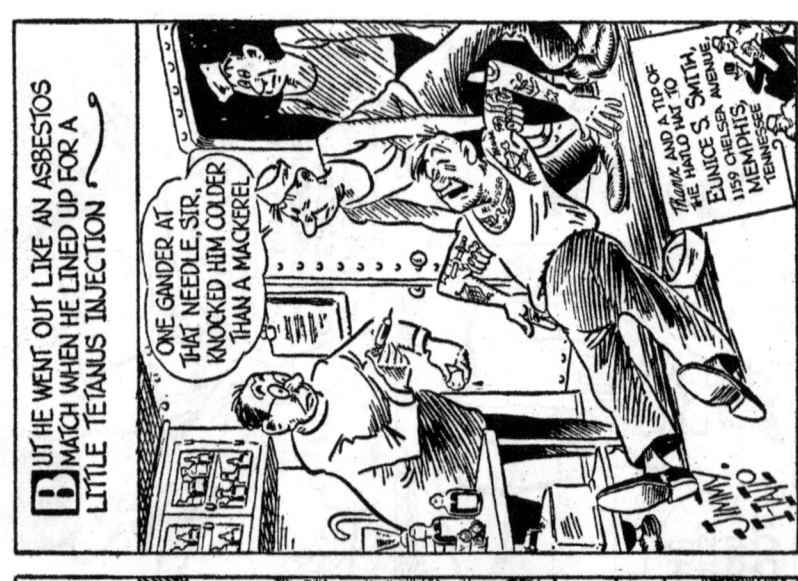

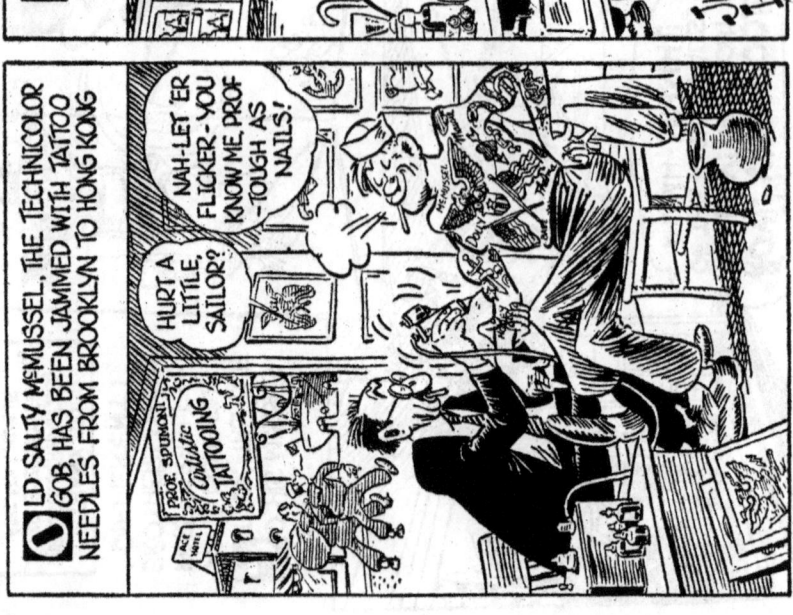

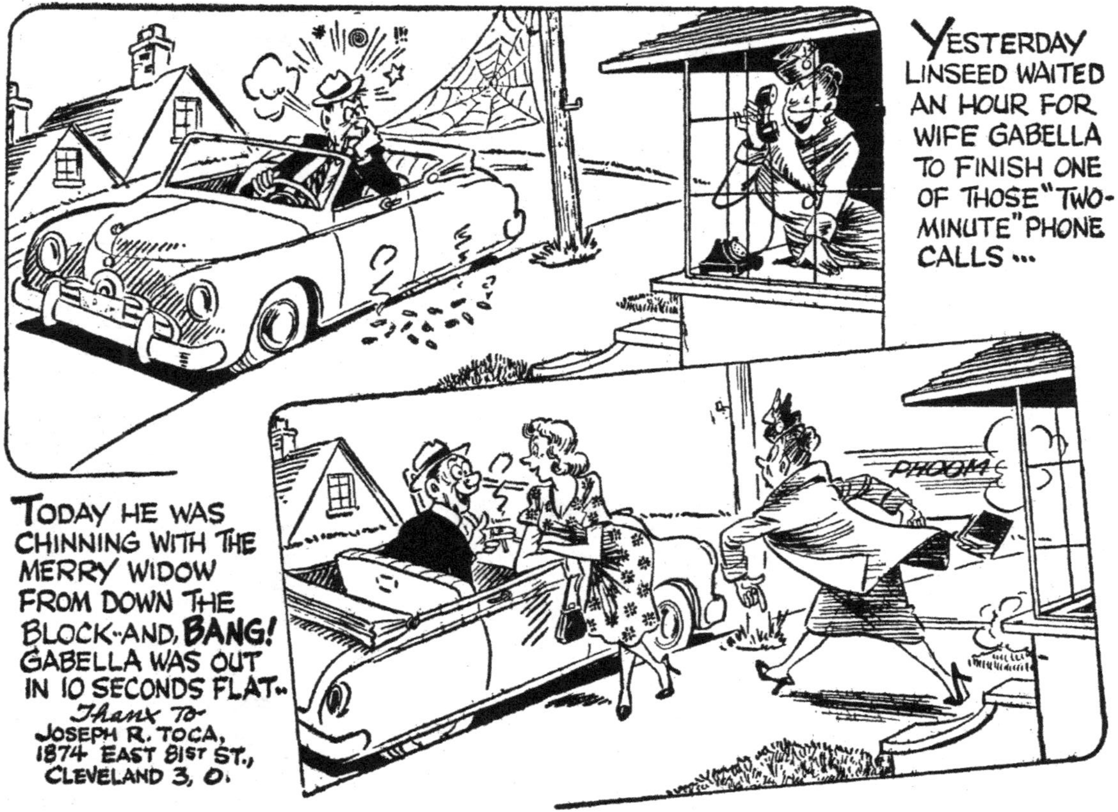
YESTERDAY LINSEED WAITED AN HOUR FOR WIFE GABELLA TO FINISH ONE OF THOSE "TWO-MINUTE" PHONE CALLS...
TODAY HE WAS CHINNING WITH THE MERRY WIDOW FROM DOWN THE BLOCK--AND, BANG! GABELLA WAS OUT IN 10 SECONDS FLAT..
PHOOM
Thanx to-
JOSEPH R. TOCA,
1874 EAST 81ST ST.,
CLEVELAND 3, O.

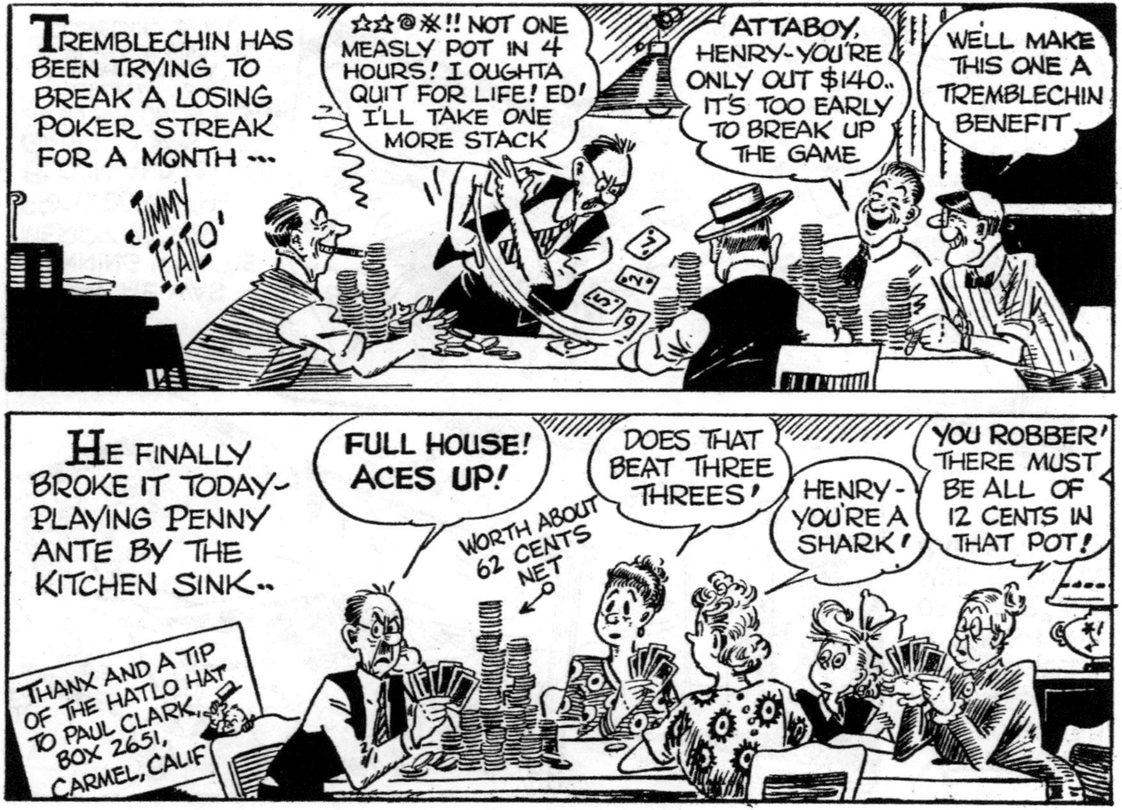
TREMBLECHIN HAS BEEN TRYING TO BREAK A LOSING POKER STREAK FOR A MONTH ...
☆☆@※!! NOT ONE MEASLY POT IN 4 HOURS! I OUGHTA QUIT FOR LIFE! ED! I'LL TAKE ONE MORE STACK
ATTABOY, HENRY- YOU'RE ONLY OUT $140.. IT'S TOO EARLY TO BREAK UP THE GAME
WE'LL MAKE THIS ONE A TREMBLECHIN BENEFIT
JIMMY HATLO'
HE FINALLY BROKE IT TODAY- PLAYING PENNY ANTE BY THE KITCHEN SINK..
FULL HOUSE! ACES UP!
WORTH ABOUT 62 CENTS NET
DOES THAT BEAT THREE THREES!
HENRY- YOU'RE A SHARK!
YOU ROBBER! THERE MUST BE ALL OF 12 CENTS IN THAT POT!
THANX AND A TIP OF THE HATLO HAT TO PAUL CLARK, BOX 2651, CARMEL, CALIF

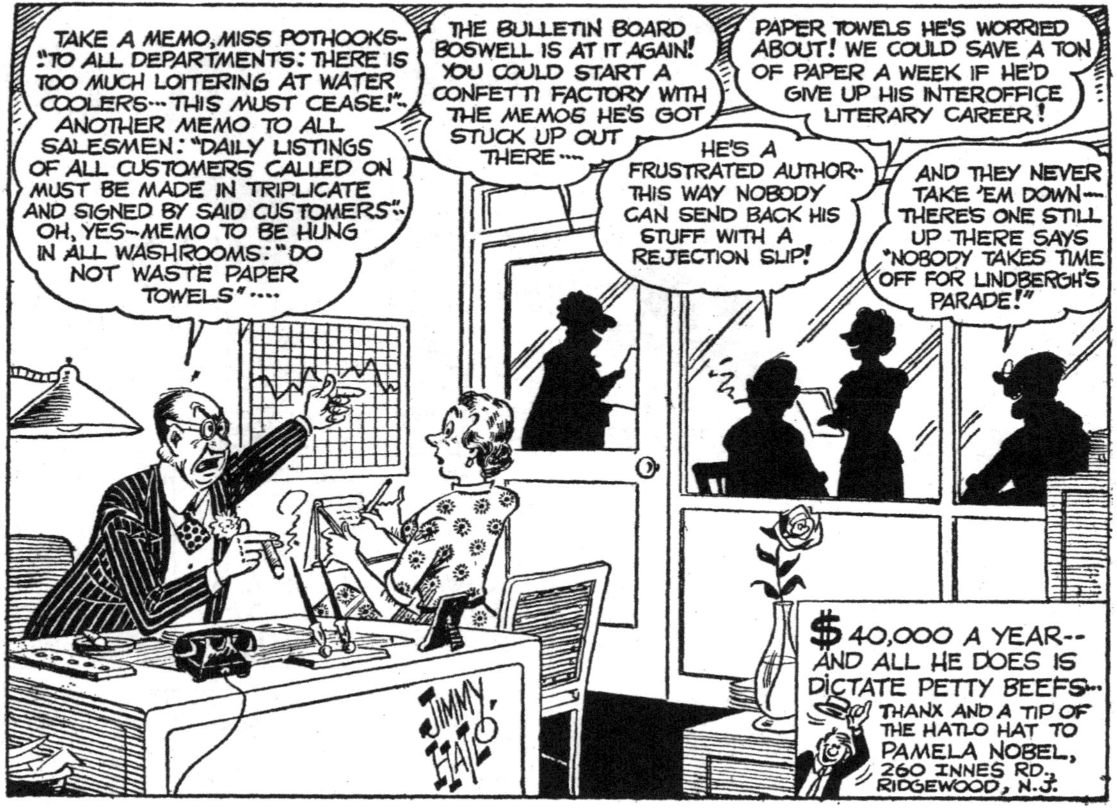
TAKE A MEMO, MISS POTHOOKS--"TO ALL DEPARTMENTS: THERE IS TOO MUCH LOITERING AT WATER COOLERS--- THIS MUST CEASE!"-- ANOTHER MEMO TO ALL SALESMEN: "DAILY LISTINGS OF ALL CUSTOMERS CALLED ON MUST BE MADE IN TRIPLICATE AND SIGNED BY SAID CUSTOMERS"-- OH, YES--MEMO TO BE HUNG IN ALL WASHROOMS: "DO NOT WASTE PAPER TOWELS"....
THE BULLETIN BOARD BOSWELL IS AT IT AGAIN! YOU COULD START A CONFETTI FACTORY WITH THE MEMOS HE'S GOT STUCK UP OUT THERE....
PAPER TOWELS HE'S WORRIED ABOUT! WE COULD SAVE A TON OF PAPER A WEEK IF HE'D GIVE UP HIS INTEROFFICE LITERARY CAREER!
HE'S A FRUSTRATED AUTHOR-- THIS WAY NOBODY CAN SEND BACK HIS STUFF WITH A REJECTION SLIP!
AND THEY NEVER TAKE 'EM DOWN--- THERE'S ONE STILL UP THERE SAYS "NOBODY TAKES TIME OFF FOR LINDBERGH'S PARADE!"
JIMMY HATLO
$40,000 A YEAR-- AND ALL HE DOES IS DICTATE PETTY BEEFS...
THANX AND A TIP OF THE HATLO HAT TO PAMELA NOBEL, 260 INNES RD., RIDGEWOOD, N.J.

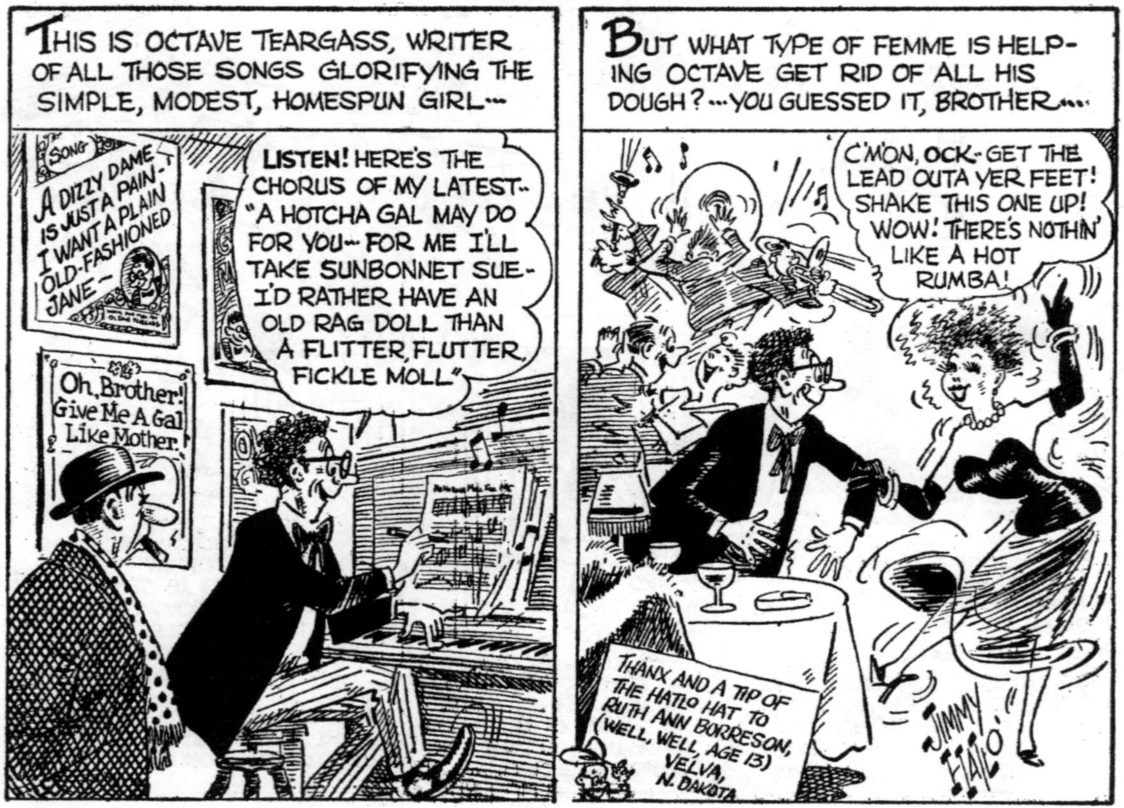
THIS IS OCTAVE TEARGASS, WRITER OF ALL THOSE SONGS GLORIFYING THE SIMPLE, MODEST, HOMESPUN GIRL—
SONG
A DIZZY DAME IS JUST A PAIN- I WANT A PLAIN OLD-FASHIONED JANE—
Oh, Brother! Give Me A Gal Like Mother.
LISTEN! HERE'S THE CHORUS OF MY LATEST— "A HOTCHA GAL MAY DO FOR YOU— FOR ME I'LL TAKE SUNBONNET SUE- I'D RATHER HAVE AN OLD RAG DOLL THAN A FLITTER, FLUTTER, FICKLE MOLL"
BUT WHAT TYPE OF FEMME IS HELPING OCTAVE GET RID OF ALL HIS DOUGH? ... YOU GUESSED IT, BROTHER....
C'MON, OCK- GET THE LEAD OUTA YER FEET! SHAKE THIS ONE UP! WOW! THERE'S NOTHIN' LIKE A HOT RUMBA!
THANX AND A TIP OF THE HATLO HAT TO RUTH ANN BORRESON, (WELL, WELL, AGE 13) VELVA, N. DAKOTA
JIMMY HATLO

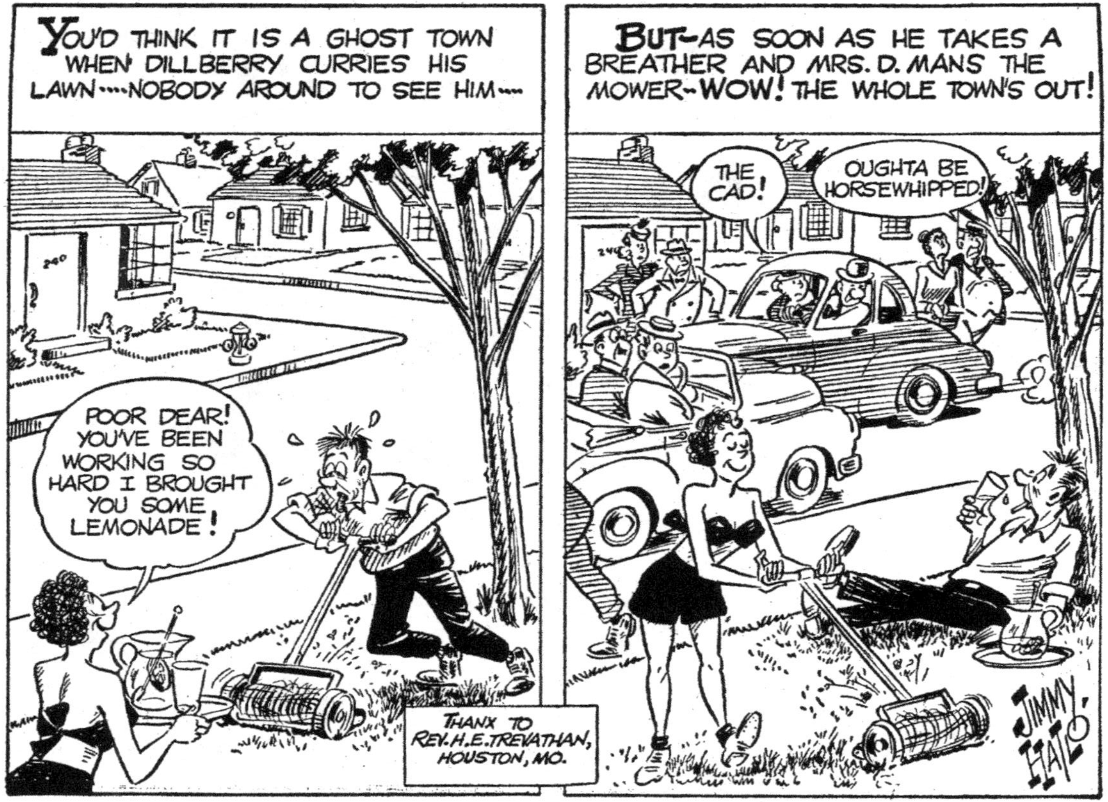
YOU'D THINK IT IS A GHOST TOWN WHEN DILLBERRY CURRIES HIS LAWN....NOBODY AROUND TO SEE HIM....
POOR DEAR! YOU'VE BEEN WORKING SO HARD I BROUGHT YOU SOME LEMONADE!
THANX TO REV. H.E. TREVATHAN, HOUSTON, MO.
BUT-AS SOON AS HE TAKES A BREATHER AND MRS. D. MANS THE MOWER-WOW! THE WHOLE TOWN'S OUT!
THE CAD!
OUGHTA BE HORSEWHIPPED!
JIMMY HATLO

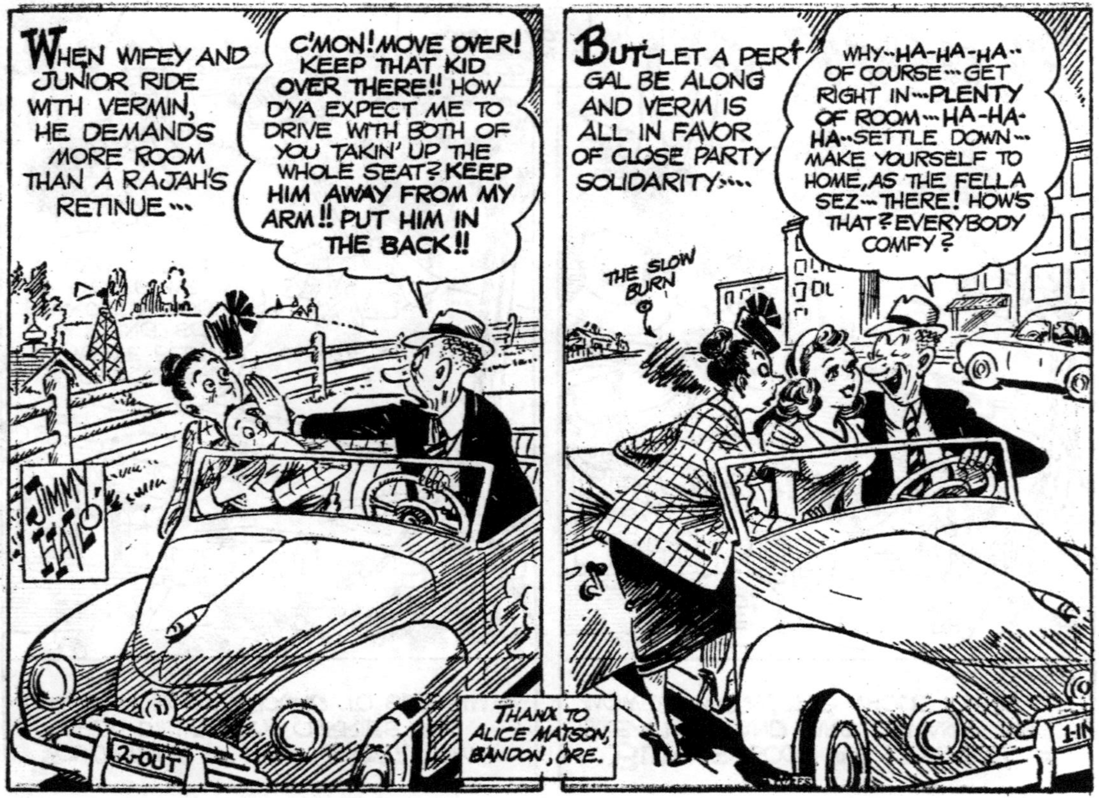
WHEN WIFEY AND JUNIOR RIDE WITH VERMIN, HE DEMANDS MORE ROOM THAN A RAJAH'S RETINUE...
C'MON! MOVE OVER! KEEP THAT KID OVER THERE!! HOW D'YA EXPECT ME TO DRIVE WITH BOTH OF YOU TAKIN' UP THE WHOLE SEAT? KEEP HIM AWAY FROM MY ARM!! PUT HIM IN THE BACK!!
JIMMY HATLO
2-OUT
THANX TO ALICE MATSON, BANDON, ORE.
BUT-LET A PERT GAL BE ALONG AND VERM IS ALL IN FAVOR OF CLOSE PARTY SOLIDARITY...
WHY-HA-HA-HA- OF COURSE... GET RIGHT IN... PLENTY OF ROOM... HA-HA-HA-SETTLE DOWN... MAKE YOURSELF TO HOME, AS THE FELLA SEZ... THERE! HOW'S THAT? EVERYBODY COMFY?
THE SLOW BURN

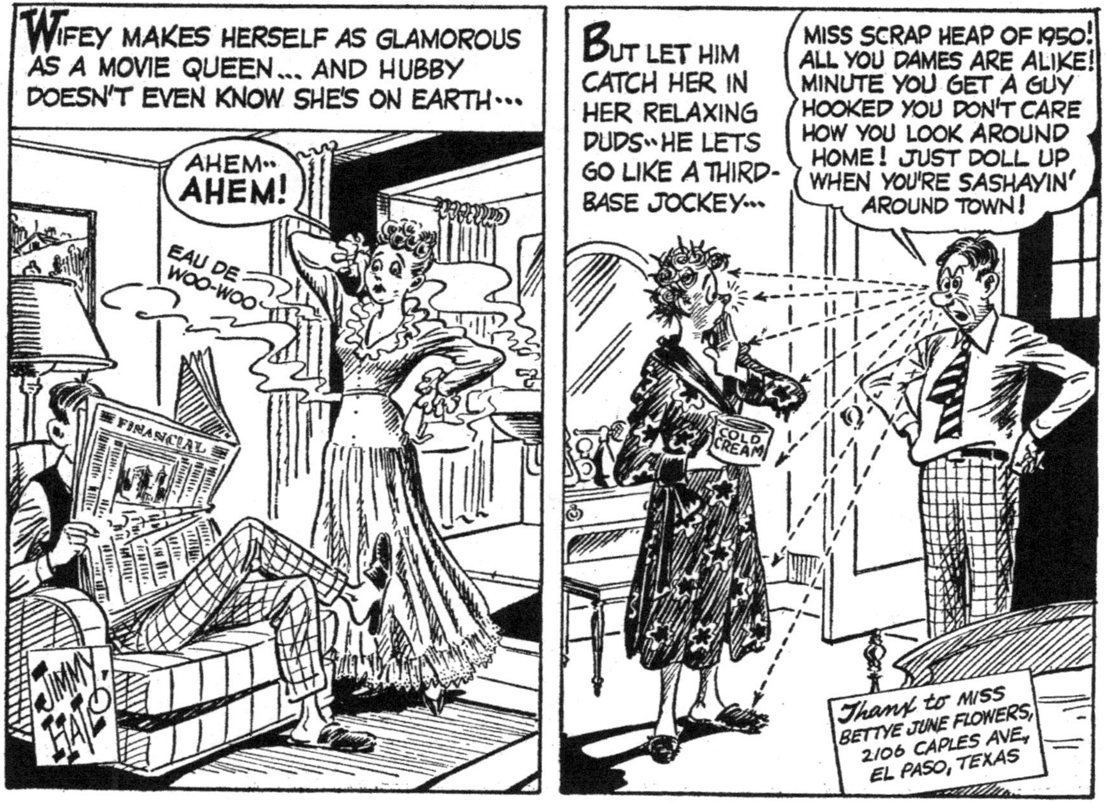
WIFEY MAKES HERSELF AS GLAMOROUS AS A MOVIE QUEEN... AND HUBBY DOESN'T EVEN KNOW SHE'S ON EARTH...
AHEM.. AHEM!
EAU DE WOO-WOO
FINANCIAL
JIMMY HATLO
BUT LET HIM CATCH HER IN HER RELAXING DUDS.. HE LETS GO LIKE A THIRD-BASE JOCKEY...
MISS SCRAP HEAP OF 1950! ALL YOU DAMES ARE ALIKE! MINUTE YOU GET A GUY HOOKED YOU DON'T CARE HOW YOU LOOK AROUND HOME! JUST DOLL UP WHEN YOU'RE SASHAYIN' AROUND TOWN!
COLD CREAM
Thanx to MISS BETTYE JUNE FLOWERS, 2106 CAPLES AVE, EL PASO, TEXAS

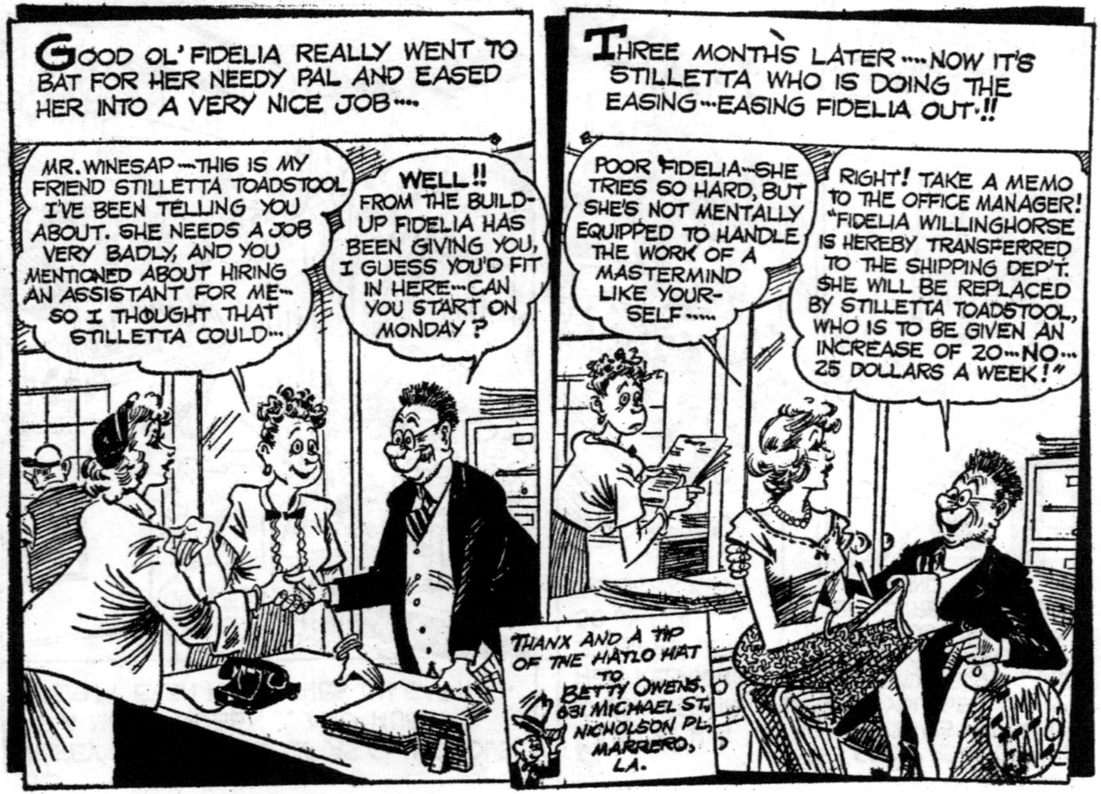
GOOD OL' FIDELIA REALLY WENT TO BAT FOR HER NEEDY PAL AND EASED HER INTO A VERY NICE JOB....
MR. WINESAP---THIS IS MY FRIEND STILLETTA TOADSTOOL I'VE BEEN TELLING YOU ABOUT. SHE NEEDS A JOB VERY BADLY, AND YOU MENTIONED ABOUT HIRING AN ASSISTANT FOR ME--- SO I THOUGHT THAT STILLETTA COULD...
WELL!! FROM THE BUILD-UP FIDELIA HAS BEEN GIVING YOU, I GUESS YOU'D FIT IN HERE---CAN YOU START ON MONDAY?
THREE MONTHS LATER.... NOW IT'S STILLETTA WHO IS DOING THE EASING---EASING FIDELIA OUT.!!
POOR FIDELIA---SHE TRIES SO HARD, BUT SHE'S NOT MENTALLY EQUIPPED TO HANDLE THE WORK OF A MASTERMIND LIKE YOURSELF.....
RIGHT! TAKE A MEMO TO THE OFFICE MANAGER! "FIDELIA WILLINGHORSE IS HEREBY TRANSFERRED TO THE SHIPPING DEP'T. SHE WILL BE REPLACED BY STILLETTA TOADSTOOL, WHO IS TO BE GIVEN AN INCREASE OF 20...NO... 25 DOLLARS A WEEK!"
THANX AND A TIP OF THE HATLO HAT TO BETTY OWENS, 631 MICHAEL ST., NICHOLSON PL., MARRERO, LA.
JIMMY HATLO

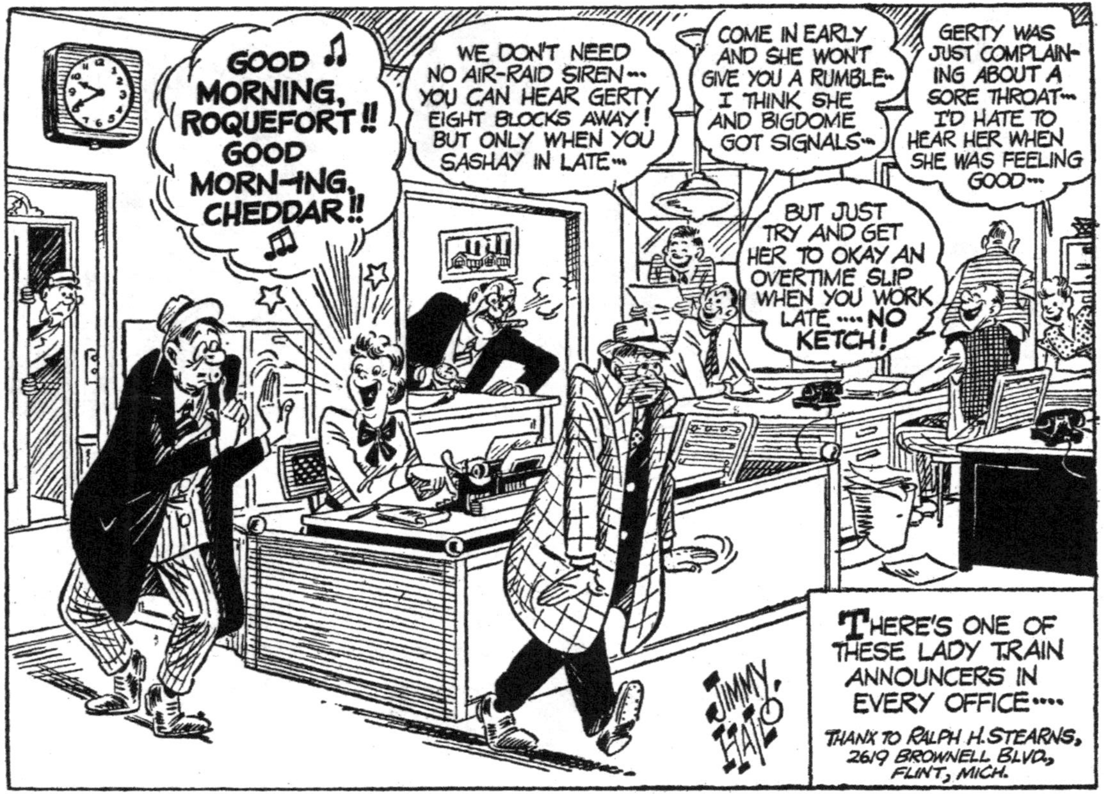
GOOD MORNING, ROQUEFORT!! GOOD MORN-ING, CHEDDAR!!
WE DON'T NEED NO AIR-RAID SIREN... YOU CAN HEAR GERTY EIGHT BLOCKS AWAY! BUT ONLY WHEN YOU SASHAY IN LATE...
COME IN EARLY AND SHE WON'T GIVE YOU A RUMBLE.. I THINK SHE AND BIGDOME GOT SIGNALS...
GERTY WAS JUST COMPLAINING ABOUT A SORE THROAT... I'D HATE TO HEAR HER WHEN SHE WAS FEELING GOOD...
BUT JUST TRY AND GET HER TO OKAY AN OVERTIME SLIP WHEN YOU WORK LATE.... NO KETCH!
JIMMY HATLO
THERE'S ONE OF THESE LADY TRAIN ANNOUNCERS IN EVERY OFFICE....
THANX TO RALPH H. STEARNS, 2619 BROWNELL BLVD., FLINT, MICH.

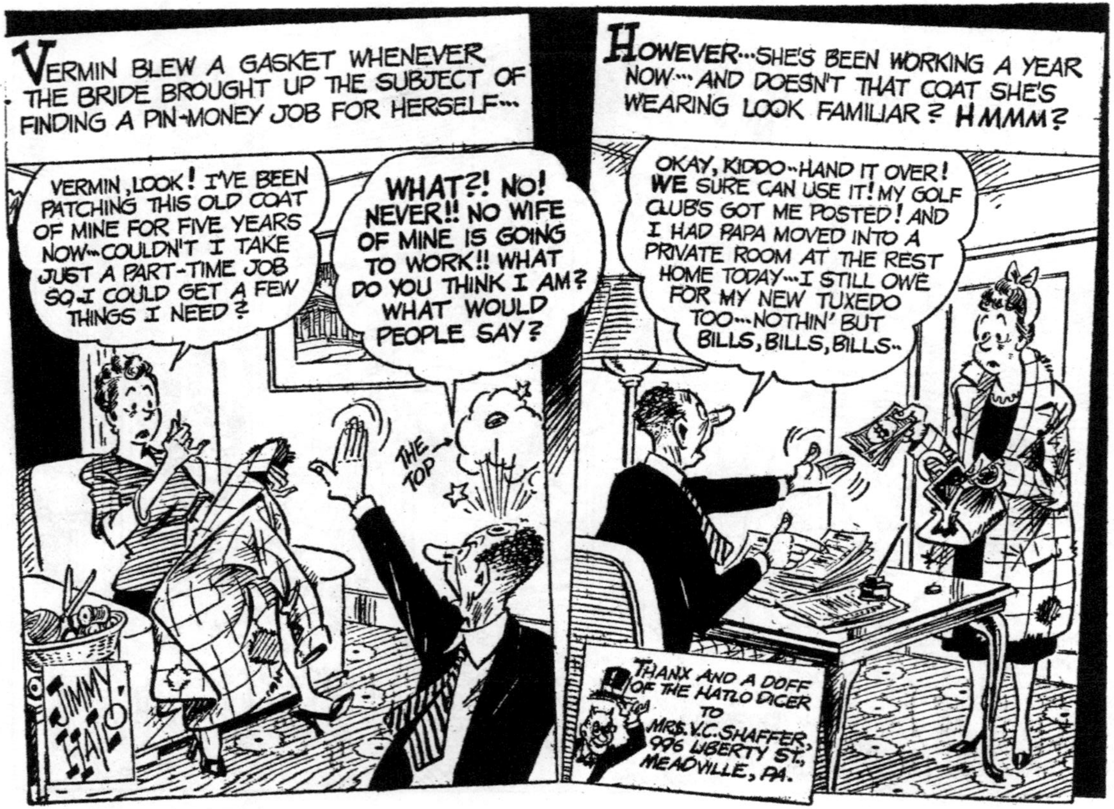
VERMIN BLEW A GASKET WHENEVER THE BRIDE BROUGHT UP THE SUBJECT OF FINDING A PIN-MONEY JOB FOR HERSELF...
VERMIN, LOOK! I'VE BEEN PATCHING THIS OLD COAT OF MINE FOR FIVE YEARS NOW...COULDN'T I TAKE JUST A PART-TIME JOB SO I COULD GET A FEW THINGS I NEED?
WHAT?! NO! NEVER!! NO WIFE OF MINE IS GOING TO WORK!! WHAT DO YOU THINK I AM? WHAT WOULD PEOPLE SAY?
THE TOP
JIMMY HATLO
HOWEVER...SHE'S BEEN WORKING A YEAR NOW...AND DOESN'T THAT COAT SHE'S WEARING LOOK FAMILIAR? HMMM?
OKAY, KIDDO...HAND IT OVER! WE SURE CAN USE IT! MY GOLF CLUB'S GOT ME POSTED! AND I HAD PAPA MOVED INTO A PRIVATE ROOM AT THE REST HOME TODAY...I STILL OWE FOR MY NEW TUXEDO TOO...NOTHIN' BUT BILLS, BILLS, BILLS..
THANX AND A DOFF OF THE HATLO DICER TO MRS. V.C. SHAFFER, 996 LIBERTY ST., MEADVILLE, PA.

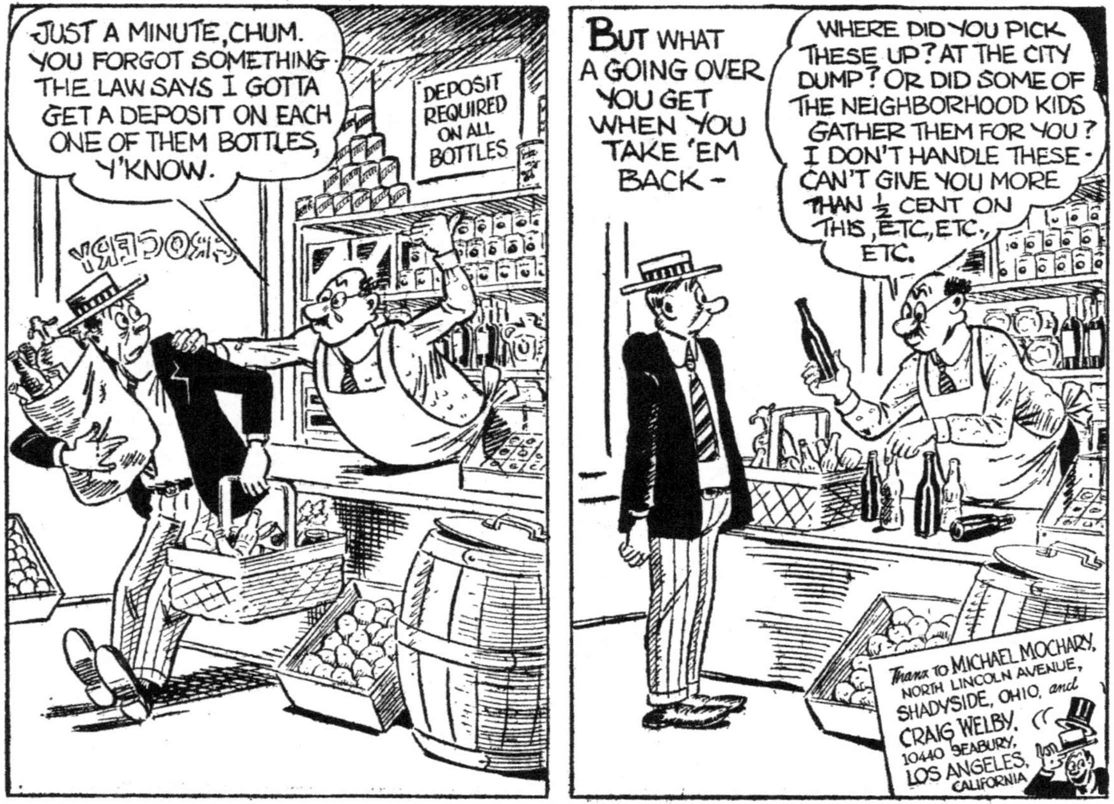
JUST A MINUTE, CHUM. YOU FORGOT SOMETHING. THE LAW SAYS I GOTTA GET A DEPOSIT ON EACH ONE OF THEM BOTTLES, Y'KNOW.
DEPOSIT REQUIRED ON ALL BOTTLES
BUT WHAT A GOING OVER YOU GET WHEN YOU TAKE 'EM BACK -
WHERE DID YOU PICK THESE UP? AT THE CITY DUMP? OR DID SOME OF THE NEIGHBORHOOD KIDS GATHER THEM FOR YOU? I DON'T HANDLE THESE - CAN'T GIVE YOU MORE THAN ½ CENT ON THIS, ETC, ETC., ETC.
Thanx to MICHAEL MOCHARY, NORTH LINCOLN AVENUE, SHADYSIDE, OHIO, and CRAIG WELBY, 10440 SEABURY, LOS ANGELES, CALIFORNIA

FINES ARE FOR SISSIES.... NO SELF-RESPECTING TOUGH GUY WILL PAY...AS PER EXAMPLE, KNUCKLES Mc COOL....
$ 10 FINE OR TEN DAYS IN JAIL!
FINE, MY FOOT! I AIN'T PAYIN' NO TEN BUCKS! MAKE THAT THIRTY DAYS... I'LL DO IT STANDIN' ON MY HEAD! GO AHEAD, CONTEMPT ME!!
JIMMY HATLO
THANX AND A FLIP OF THE FEZ TO SGT. CLEM PATRICK, POLICE DEP'T, MT. CARMEL, PA.
BUT, OH, BROTHER! HOW 24 HOURS IN THE SNEEZER WILL CHANGE HIS TUNE...
LEMME OUTA HERE! GET ME A LAWYER! I'M NOT STAYIN' HERE ANOTHER MINUTE! I KNOW MY RIGHTS!! YOU CAN'T DO THIS TO ME! I WANT TO PAY MY FINE!!
SHADDAP! LEAVE ME GET SOME SLEEP!

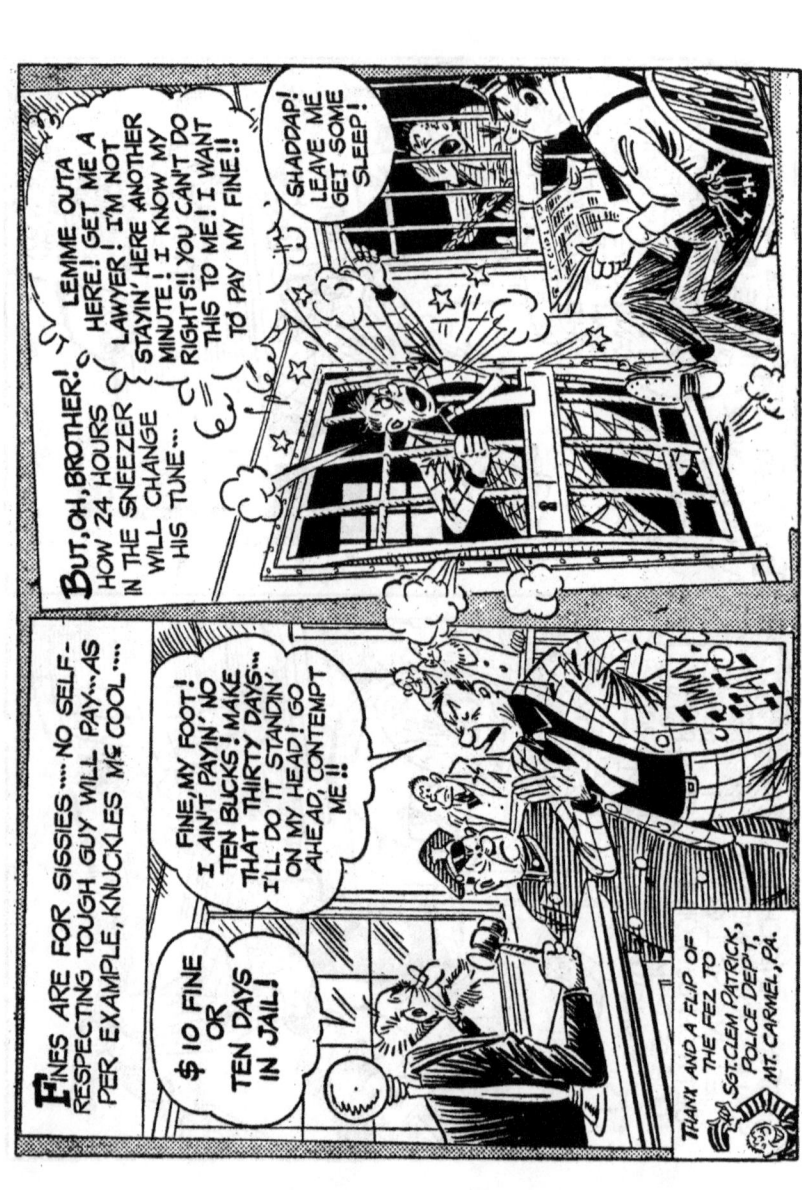

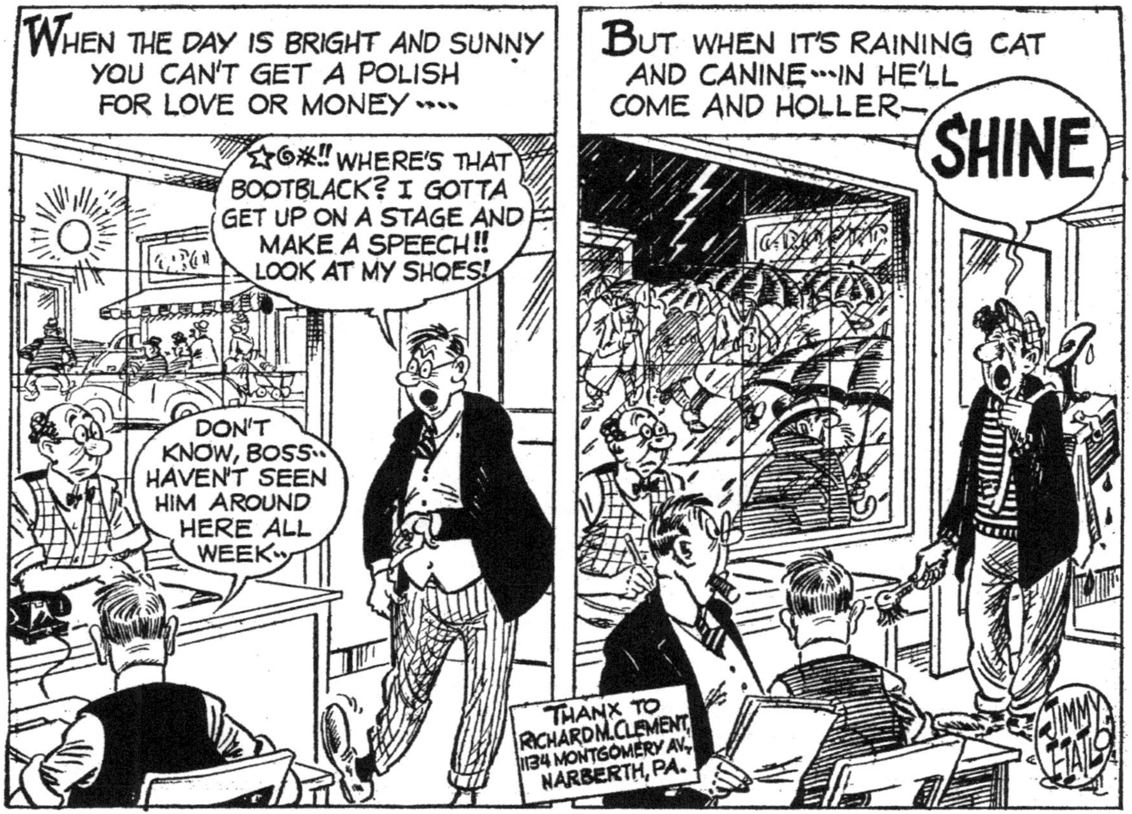
WHEN THE DAY IS BRIGHT AND SUNNY YOU CAN'T GET A POLISH FOR LOVE OR MONEY ....
☆@✱!! WHERE'S THAT BOOTBLACK? I GOTTA GET UP ON A STAGE AND MAKE A SPEECH!! LOOK AT MY SHOES!
DON'T KNOW, BOSS.. HAVEN'T SEEN HIM AROUND HERE ALL WEEK..
BUT WHEN IT'S RAINING CAT AND CANINE...IN HE'LL COME AND HOLLER—
SHINE
THANX TO RICHARD M. CLEMENT, 1134 MONTGOMERY AV., NARBERTH, PA.
JIMMY HATLO

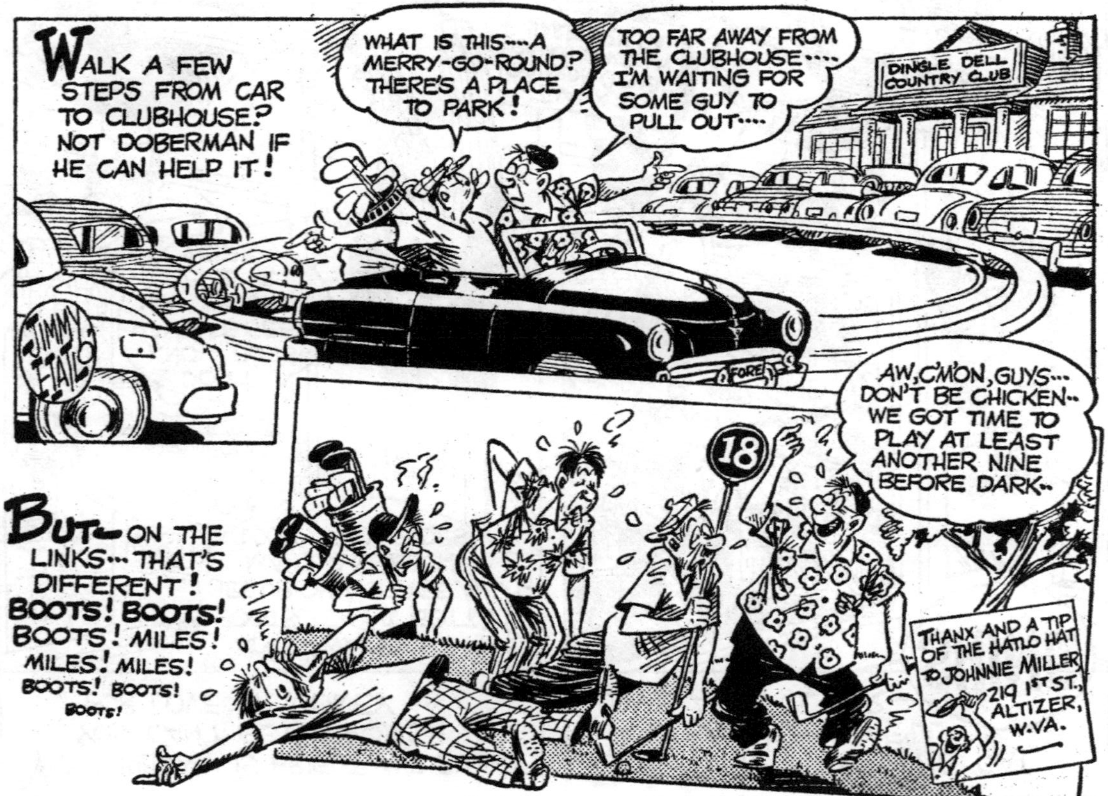
WALK A FEW STEPS FROM CAR TO CLUBHOUSE? NOT DOBERMAN IF HE CAN HELP IT!
WHAT IS THIS---A MERRY-GO-ROUND? THERE'S A PLACE TO PARK!
TOO FAR AWAY FROM THE CLUBHOUSE.... I'M WAITING FOR SOME GUY TO PULL OUT....
DINGLE DELL COUNTRY CLUB
FORE
JIMMY HATLO
BUT— ON THE LINKS... THAT'S DIFFERENT!
BOOTS! BOOTS! BOOTS! MILES! MILES! MILES! BOOTS! BOOTS! BOOTS!
18
AW, C'MON, GUYS... DON'T BE CHICKEN.. WE GOT TIME TO PLAY AT LEAST ANOTHER NINE BEFORE DARK..
THANX AND A TIP OF THE HATLO HAT TO JOHNNIE MILLER, 219 1ST ST., ALTIZER, W.VA.

YA-AS, POOR ROQUEFORT-
SINCE THEY MADE HIM
AN EXECUTIVE AT THE
PLANT, HE BRINGS HOME
A BRIEF CASE FULL OF
WORK EVERY NIGHT..
JIMMY HATLO
Thanx AND A TIP OF
THE HATLO HAT TO
IRWIN BLOCK,
185 WASHINGTON AV.,
KENMORE, 17
NEW YORK

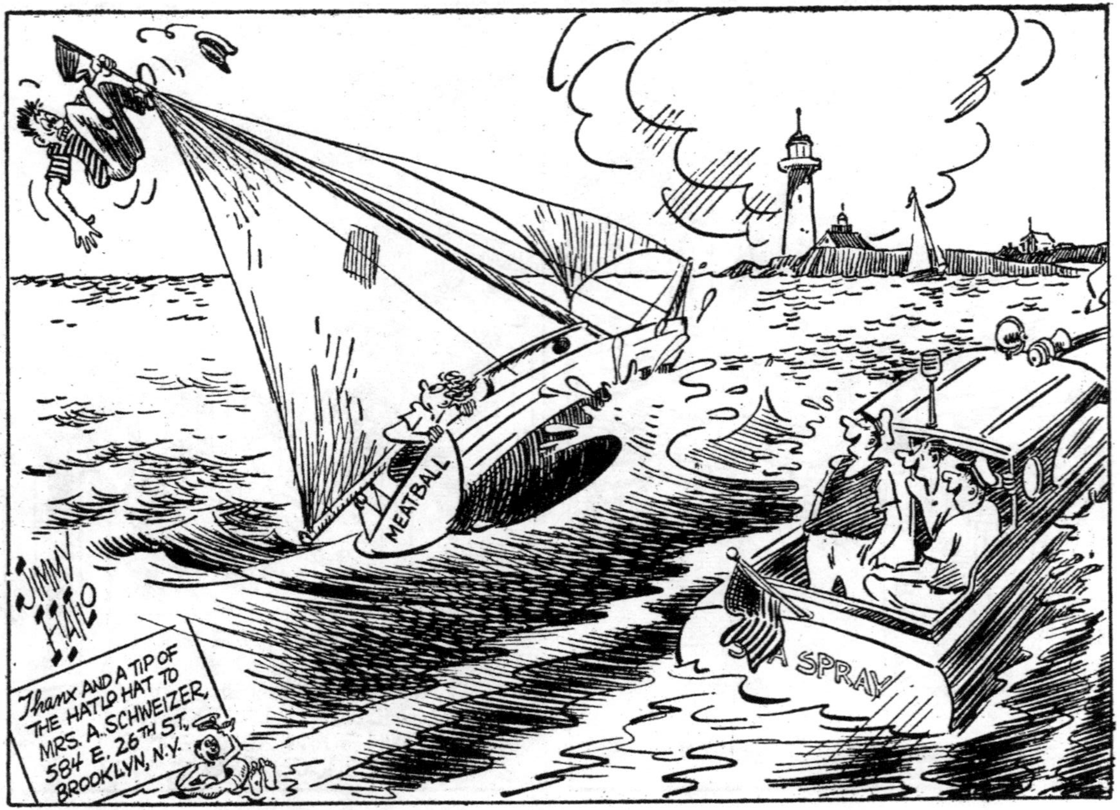
MEATBALL
SEA SPRAY
JIMMY HATLO
Thanx AND A TIP OF THE HATLO HAT TO MRS. A. SCHWEIZER, 584 E. 26TH ST., BROOKLYN, N.Y.

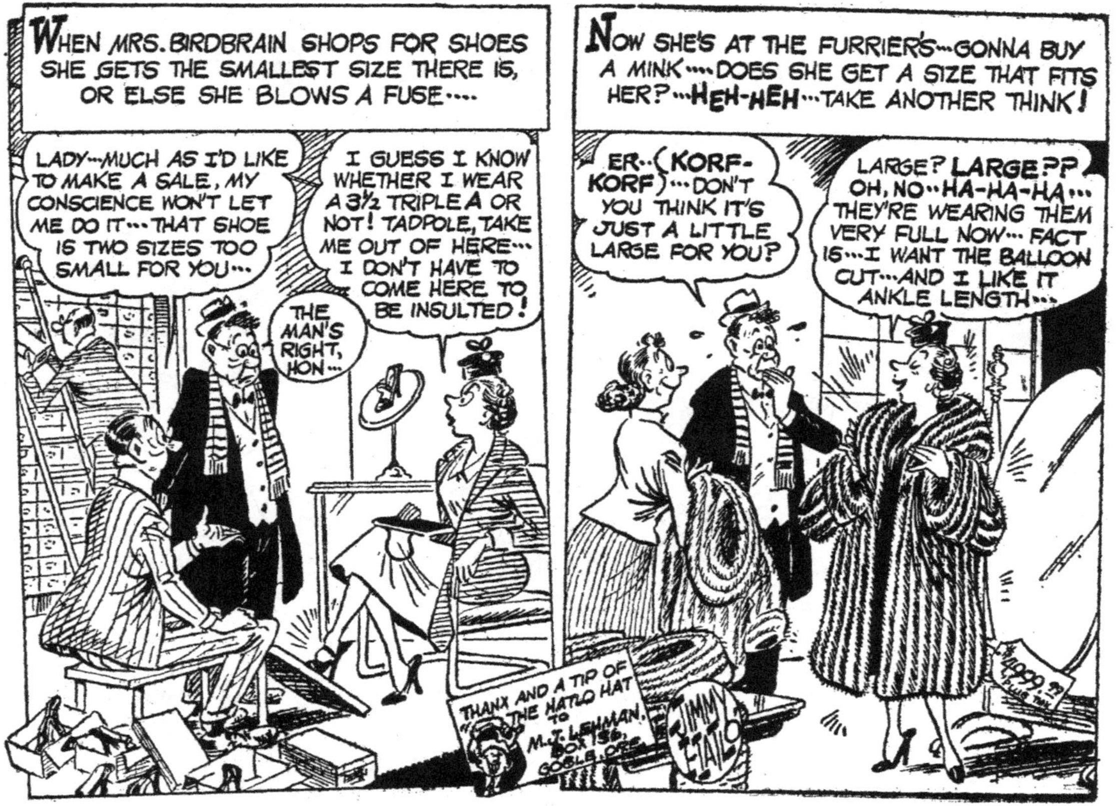
WHEN MRS. BIRDBRAIN SHOPS FOR SHOES SHE GETS THE SMALLEST SIZE THERE IS, OR ELSE SHE BLOWS A FUSE....
LADY...MUCH AS I'D LIKE TO MAKE A SALE, MY CONSCIENCE WON'T LET ME DO IT...THAT SHOE IS TWO SIZES TOO SMALL FOR YOU...
I GUESS I KNOW WHETHER I WEAR A 3½ TRIPLE A OR NOT! TADPOLE, TAKE ME OUT OF HERE... I DON'T HAVE TO COME HERE TO BE INSULTED!
THE MAN'S RIGHT, HON...
NOW SHE'S AT THE FURRIER'S...GONNA BUY A MINK....DOES SHE GET A SIZE THAT FITS HER?...HEH-HEH...TAKE ANOTHER THINK!
ER..(KORF-KORF)...DON'T YOU THINK IT'S JUST A LITTLE LARGE FOR YOU?
LARGE? LARGE?? OH, NO..HA-HA-HA... THEY'RE WEARING THEM VERY FULL NOW... FACT IS...I WANT THE BALLOON CUT...AND I LIKE IT ANKLE LENGTH...
$4999.99 PLUS TAX
THANX AND A TIP OF "THE NATLO HAT" TO M.T. LEHMAN, BOX 136, GOBLE, ORE.
JIMMY HATLO

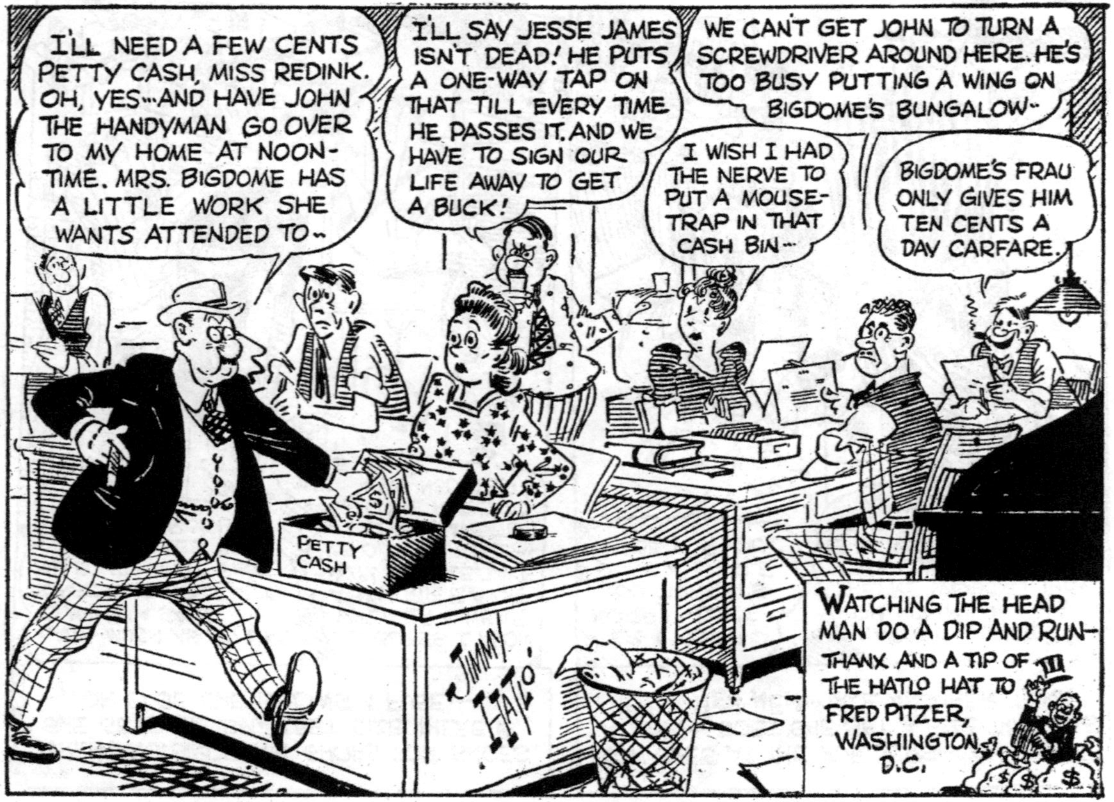
I'LL NEED A FEW CENTS PETTY CASH, MISS REDINK. OH, YES...AND HAVE JOHN THE HANDYMAN GO OVER TO MY HOME AT NOON-TIME. MRS. BIGDOME HAS A LITTLE WORK SHE WANTS ATTENDED TO..
I'LL SAY JESSE JAMES ISN'T DEAD! HE PUTS A ONE-WAY TAP ON THAT TILL EVERY TIME HE PASSES IT. AND WE HAVE TO SIGN OUR LIFE AWAY TO GET A BUCK!
WE CAN'T GET JOHN TO TURN A SCREWDRIVER AROUND HERE. HE'S TOO BUSY PUTTING A WING ON BIGDOME'S BUNGALOW..
I WISH I HAD THE NERVE TO PUT A MOUSE-TRAP IN THAT CASH BIN...
BIGDOME'S FRAU ONLY GIVES HIM TEN CENTS A DAY CARFARE.
PETTY CASH
JIMMY HATLO
WATCHING THE HEAD MAN DO A DIP AND RUN—
THANX AND A TIP OF THE HATLO HAT TO FRED PITZER, WASHINGTON, D.C.

DID I EVER TELL YOU HOW I GOT MY FIRST JOB? WELL···AFTER I'D WORKED MY WAY THRU COLLEGE I WAS ALL SET TO PLAY PRO BALL, WHEN I SAW AN AD··"EXPERIENCED SALESMAN WANTED." I WENT TO THE ADDRESS··SAW A CROWD AND DECIDED TO GO IN THE BACK WAY·· WELL···
THE LAST TIME HE TOLD HIS LIFE STORY··· WE GOT HOME AT EIGHT O'CLOCK··AN' NO OVERTIME···
CHAPTER ONE. MY LIFE AND HARD TIMES···OR THRU LIFE'S TROUBLED WATERS WITH GALL AND SWINDLE SHEET···
THE ONLY BALL HE EVER PLAYED WAS WITH A SHADY POLITICIAN·····
COLLEGE! HAWH! HE GOT TOSSED OUT OF THE BARBERS' INSTITUTE FOR SHARP PRACTICES···
··BUT HE NEVER MENTIONS ABOUT MARRYIN' THE OLD BOSS'S HOMELY DAUGHTER··
BIGDOME ALWAYS PICKS A SWELL TIME TO GET CHUMMY AND GIVE OUT WITH HIS LIFE'S HISTORY···
JIMMY HATLO

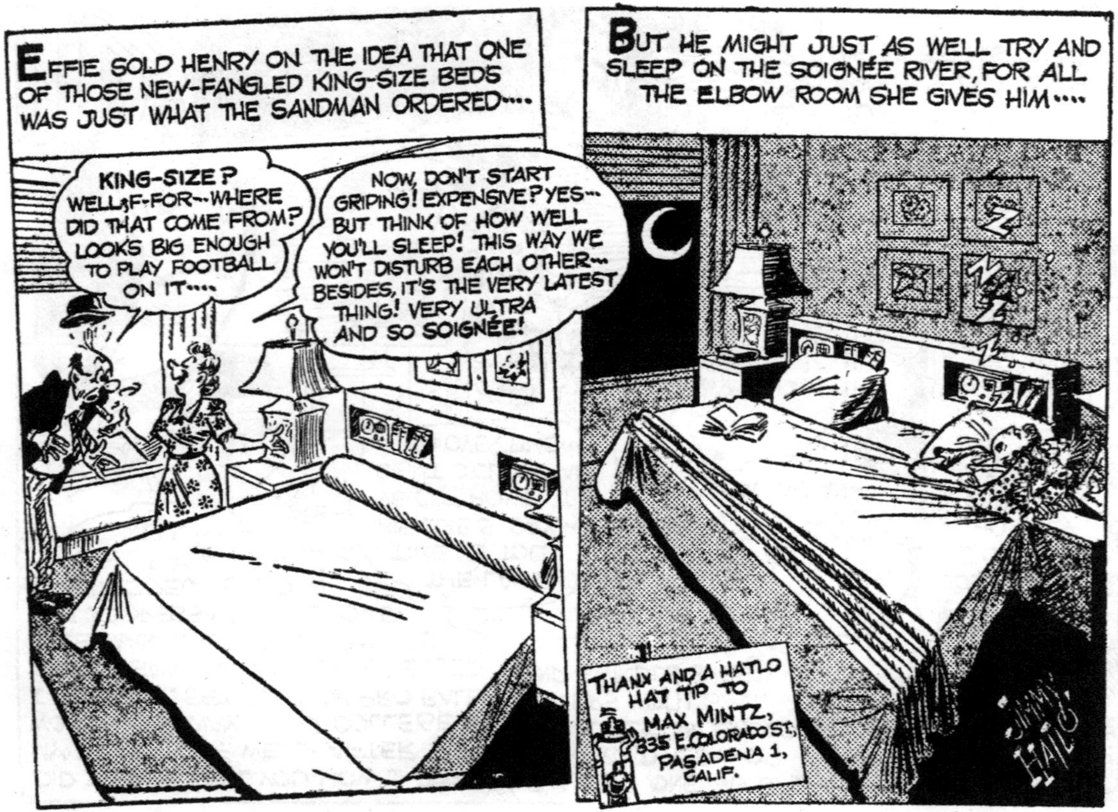
EFFIE SOLD HENRY ON THE IDEA THAT ONE OF THOSE NEW-FANGLED KING-SIZE BEDS WAS JUST WHAT THE SANDMAN ORDERED....
KING-SIZE? WELL,F-FOR--WHERE DID THAT COME FROM? LOOKS BIG ENOUGH TO PLAY FOOTBALL ON IT....
NOW, DON'T START GRIPING! EXPENSIVE? YES--BUT THINK OF HOW WELL YOU'LL SLEEP! THIS WAY WE WON'T DISTURB EACH OTHER--BESIDES, IT'S THE VERY LATEST THING! VERY ULTRA AND SO SOIGNÉE!
BUT HE MIGHT JUST AS WELL TRY AND SLEEP ON THE SOIGNÉE RIVER, FOR ALL THE ELBOW ROOM SHE GIVES HIM....
THANX AND A HATLO HAT TIP TO MAX MINTZ, 335 E. COLORADO ST., PASADENA 1, CALIF.
JIMMY HATLO

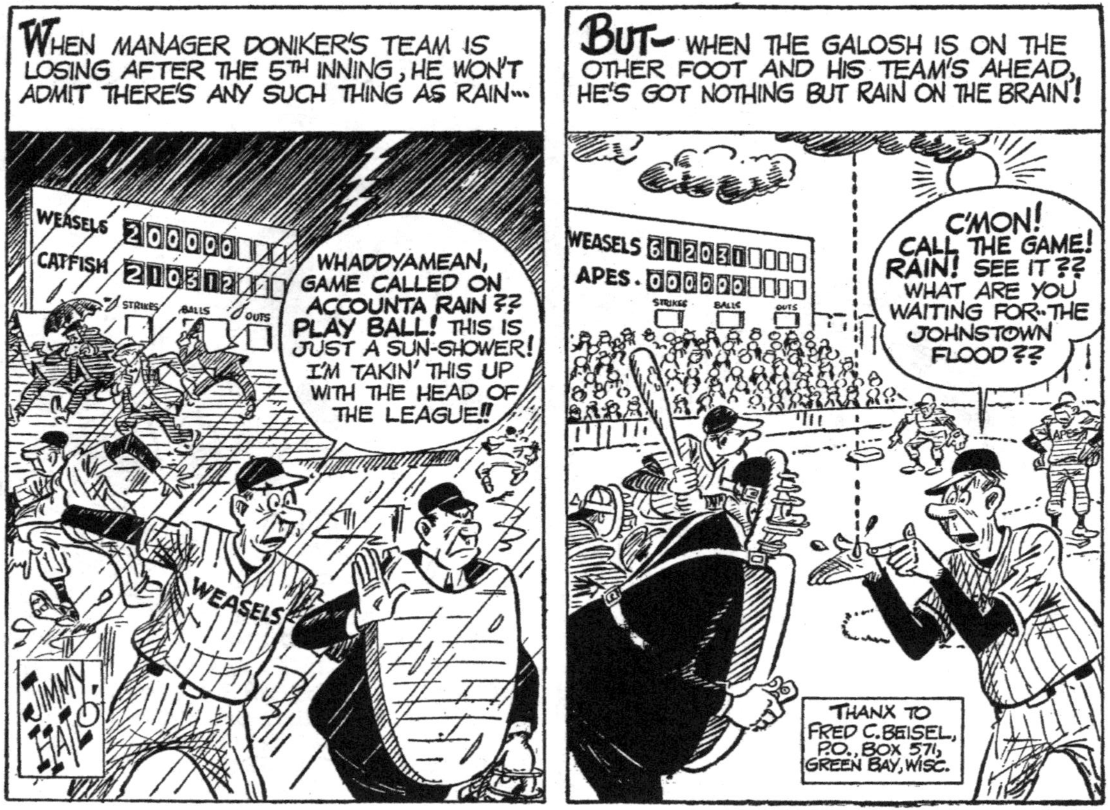
WHEN MANAGER DONIKER'S TEAM IS LOSING AFTER THE 5TH INNING, HE WON'T ADMIT THERE'S ANY SUCH THING AS RAIN...
WEASELS 2 0 0 0 0 0
CATFISH 2 1 0 3 1 2
STRIKES BALLS OUTS
WHADDYAMEAN, GAME CALLED ON ACCOUNTA RAIN ?? PLAY BALL! THIS IS JUST A SUN-SHOWER! I'M TAKIN' THIS UP WITH THE HEAD OF THE LEAGUE!!
WEASELS
JIMMY HATLO
BUT– WHEN THE GALOSH IS ON THE OTHER FOOT AND HIS TEAM'S AHEAD, HE'S GOT NOTHING BUT RAIN ON THE BRAIN!
WEASELS 6 1 2 0 3 1
APES. 0 0 0 0 0 0
STRIKES BALLS OUTS
C'MON! CALL THE GAME! RAIN! SEE IT ?? WHAT ARE YOU WAITING FOR–THE JOHNSTOWN FLOOD ??
APES
THANX TO FRED C. BEISEL, P.O., BOX 571, GREEN BAY, WISC.

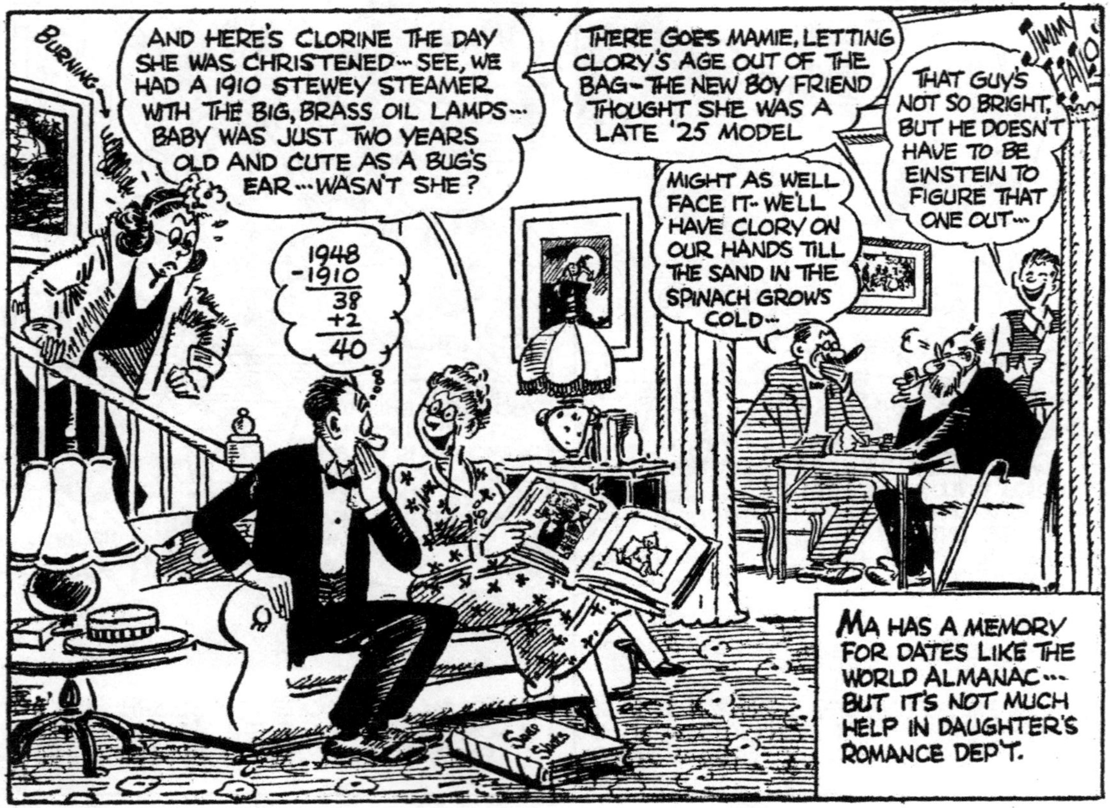
BURNING
AND HERE'S CLORINE THE DAY SHE WAS CHRISTENED... SEE, WE HAD A 1910 STEWEY STEAMER WITH THE BIG, BRASS OIL LAMPS... BABY WAS JUST TWO YEARS OLD AND CUTE AS A BUG'S EAR... WASN'T SHE?
1948 -1910 38 +2 40
THERE GOES MAMIE, LETTING CLORY'S AGE OUT OF THE BAG-- THE NEW BOY FRIEND THOUGHT SHE WAS A LATE '25 MODEL
MIGHT AS WELL FACE IT-- WE'LL HAVE CLORY ON OUR HANDS TILL THE SAND IN THE SPINACH GROWS COLD...
THAT GUY'S NOT SO BRIGHT, BUT HE DOESN'T HAVE TO BE EINSTEIN TO FIGURE THAT ONE OUT...
JIMMY HATLO
MA HAS A MEMORY FOR DATES LIKE THE WORLD ALMANAC... BUT IT'S NOT MUCH HELP IN DAUGHTER'S ROMANCE DEP'T.

TRY TO PUSH A LOAD ON, AND WHERE DOES THE ELEVATOR STOP? ABOUT A FOOT ABOVE FLOOR LEVEL...
JIMMY HATLO
BUT ONCE ABOARD, WHERE DOES THE WALL TROLLEY STOP WHEN YOU WANT OFF? A FOOT BELOW NORMAL, OF COURSE!
THANX TO CLEO HINDMAN, 60 N. OAKLEY, COLUMBUS, OHIO

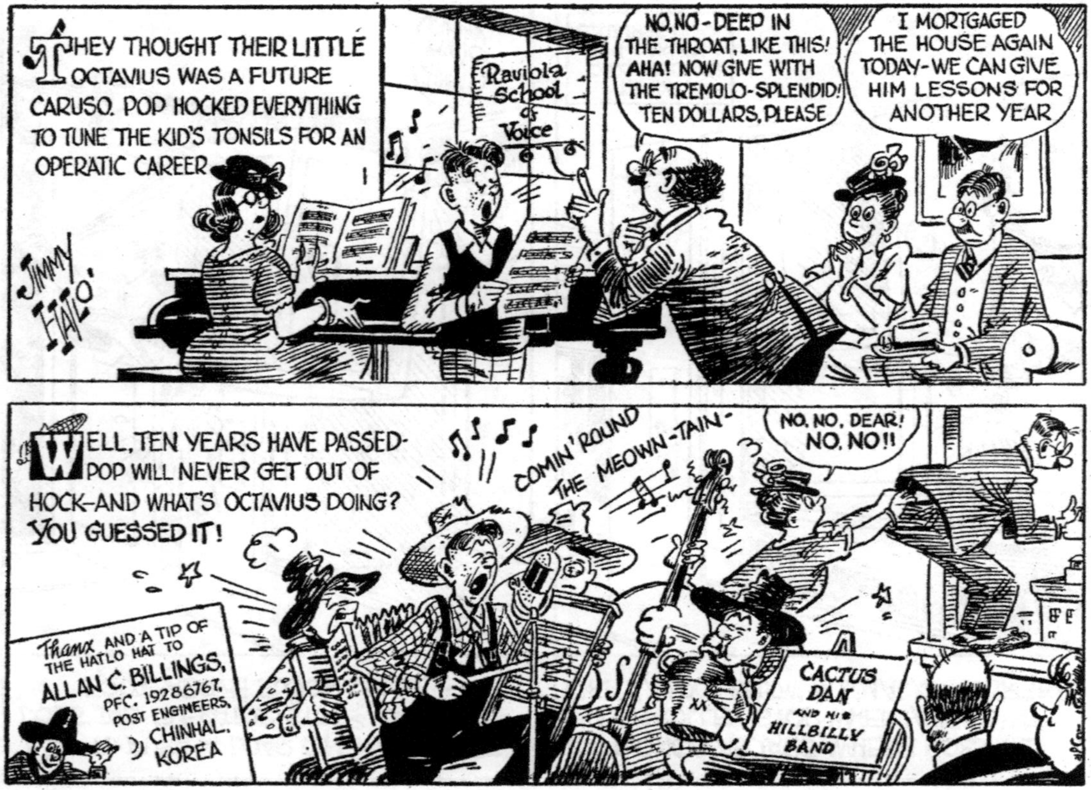
THEY THOUGHT THEIR LITTLE OCTAVIUS WAS A FUTURE CARUSO. POP HOCKED EVERYTHING TO TUNE THE KID'S TONSILS FOR AN OPERATIC CAREER
JIMMY HATLO
Raviola School of Voice
NO, NO - DEEP IN THE THROAT, LIKE THIS! AHA! NOW GIVE WITH THE TREMOLO-SPLENDID! TEN DOLLARS, PLEASE
I MORTGAGED THE HOUSE AGAIN TODAY - WE CAN GIVE HIM LESSONS FOR ANOTHER YEAR
WELL, TEN YEARS HAVE PASSED - POP WILL NEVER GET OUT OF HOCK - AND WHAT'S OCTAVIUS DOING? YOU GUESSED IT!
COMIN' ROUND THE MEOWN-TAIN-
NO, NO, DEAR! NO, NO!!
CACTUS DAN AND HIS HILLBILLY BAND
Thanx AND A TIP OF THE HATLO HAT TO ALLAN C. BILLINGS, PFC. 19286767, POST ENGINEERS, CHINHAL, KOREA

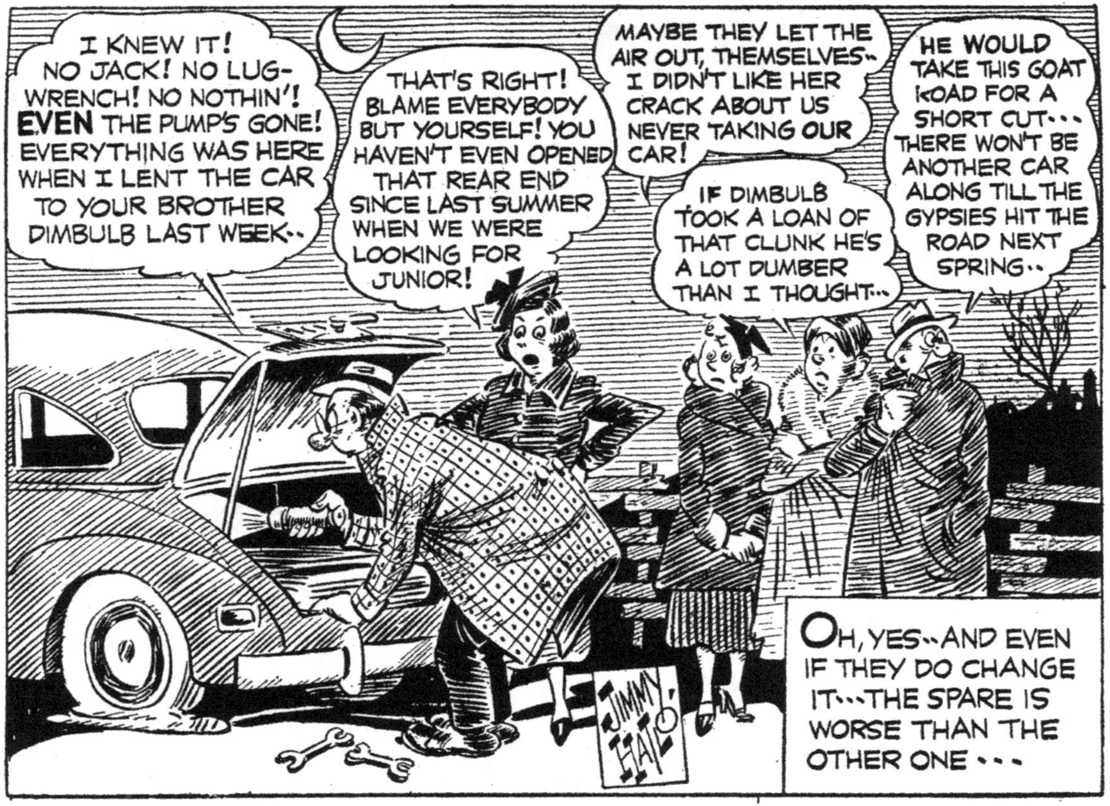
I KNEW IT! NO JACK! NO LUG-WRENCH! NO NOTHIN'! EVEN THE PUMP'S GONE! EVERYTHING WAS HERE WHEN I LENT THE CAR TO YOUR BROTHER DIMBULB LAST WEEK..
THAT'S RIGHT! BLAME EVERYBODY BUT YOURSELF! YOU HAVEN'T EVEN OPENED THAT REAR END SINCE LAST SUMMER WHEN WE WERE LOOKING FOR JUNIOR!
MAYBE THEY LET THE AIR OUT, THEMSELVES.. I DIDN'T LIKE HER CRACK ABOUT US NEVER TAKING OUR CAR!
IF DIMBULB TOOK A LOAN OF THAT CLUNK HE'S A LOT DUMBER THAN I THOUGHT...
HE WOULD TAKE THIS GOAT ROAD FOR A SHORT CUT... THERE WON'T BE ANOTHER CAR ALONG TILL THE GYPSIES HIT THE ROAD NEXT SPRING..
OH, YES..AND EVEN IF THEY DO CHANGE IT...THE SPARE IS WORSE THAN THE OTHER ONE...
JIMMY HATLO

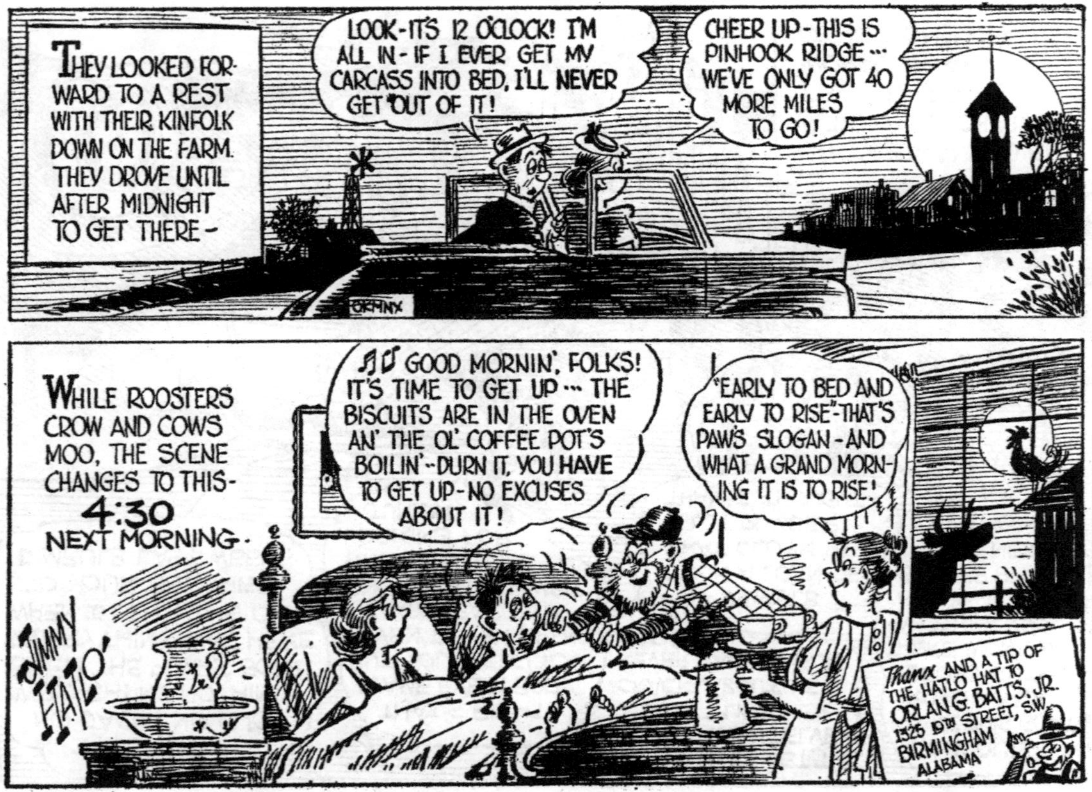
THEY LOOKED FORWARD TO A REST WITH THEIR KINFOLK DOWN ON THE FARM. THEY DROVE UNTIL AFTER MIDNIGHT TO GET THERE -
LOOK - IT'S 12 O'CLOCK! I'M ALL IN - IF I EVER GET MY CARCASS INTO BED, I'LL NEVER GET OUT OF IT!
CHEER UP - THIS IS PINHOOK RIDGE ... WE'VE ONLY GOT 40 MORE MILES TO GO!
WHILE ROOSTERS CROW AND COWS MOO, THE SCENE CHANGES TO THIS - 4:30 NEXT MORNING -
GOOD MORNIN', FOLKS! IT'S TIME TO GET UP ... THE BISCUITS ARE IN THE OVEN AN' THE OL' COFFEE POT'S BOILIN' - DURN IT, YOU HAVE TO GET UP - NO EXCUSES ABOUT IT!
"EARLY TO BED AND EARLY TO RISE" - THAT'S PAW'S SLOGAN - AND WHAT A GRAND MORNING IT IS TO RISE!
THANX AND A TIP OF THE HATLO HAT TO ORLAN G. BATTS, JR. 1325 19TH STREET, S.W. BIRMINGHAM ALABAMA
JIMMY HATLO

HOTTEST DAY IN HISTORY MAKES POOR PAPA DROOP... WHAT'S MOM GOT FOR SUPPER? RED-HOT PEPPER-POT SOUP!
OH, HELLO, HENRY... SIT DOWN... YOU MUST BE TIRED OUT... HOW'S THIS? BRAND-NEW RECIPE....
DAILY DUZZEN
HEAT WAVE SETS ALL-TIME RECORD
FRY EGGS ON SIDEWALK HERE!
JIMMY HATLO
TIME SASHAYS ON... IT'S WINTER... 23 BELOW.... HE GETS COLD CUTS AND FROZEN ASPIC, AS IF YOU DIDN'T KNOW!
A GRATEFUL TIP OF THE HATLO BEANIE TO "N.O.," ST. LOUIS, MISSOURI

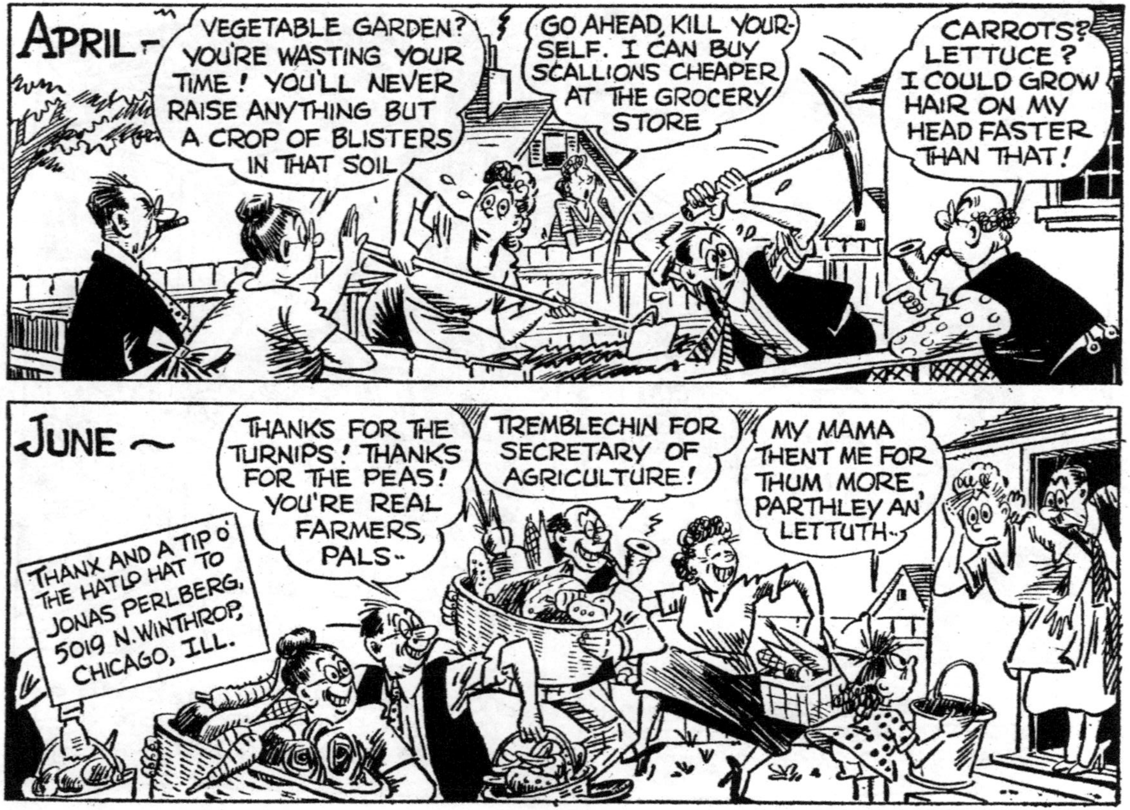
APRIL –
VEGETABLE GARDEN? YOU'RE WASTING YOUR TIME! YOU'LL NEVER RAISE ANYTHING BUT A CROP OF BLISTERS IN THAT SOIL
GO AHEAD, KILL YOURSELF. I CAN BUY SCALLIONS CHEAPER AT THE GROCERY STORE
CARROTS? LETTUCE? I COULD GROW HAIR ON MY HEAD FASTER THAN THAT!
JUNE ~
THANKS FOR THE TURNIPS! THANKS FOR THE PEAS! YOU'RE REAL FARMERS, PALS..
TREMBLECHIN FOR SECRETARY OF AGRICULTURE!
MY MAMA THENT ME FOR THUM MORE PARTHLEY AN' LETTUTH..
THANX AND A TIP O' THE HATLO HAT TO JONAS PERLBERG, 5019 N. WINTHROP, CHICAGO, ILL.

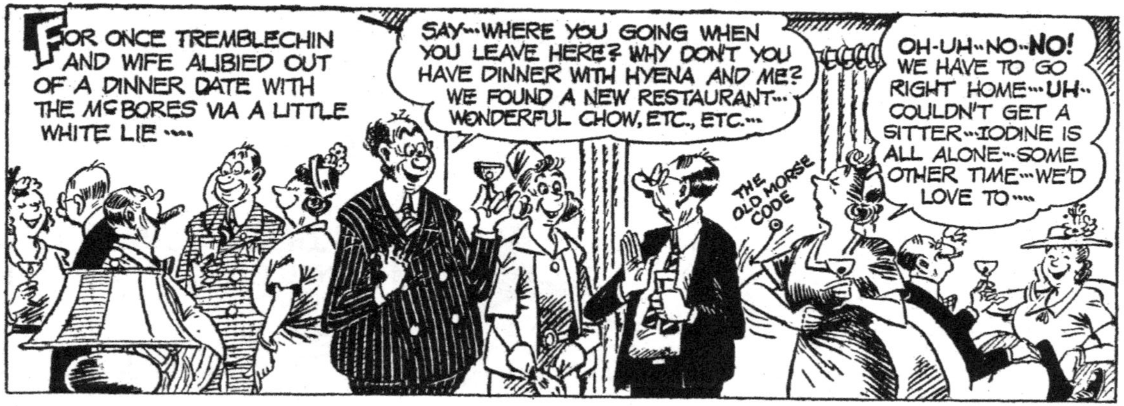
FOR ONCE TREMBLECHIN AND WIFE ALIBIED OUT OF A DINNER DATE WITH THE McBORES VIA A LITTLE WHITE LIE ....
SAY... WHERE YOU GOING WHEN YOU LEAVE HERE? WHY DON'T YOU HAVE DINNER WITH HYENA AND ME? WE FOUND A NEW RESTAURANT... WONDERFUL CHOW, ETC., ETC....
THE OLD MORSE CODE
OH-UH.. NO.. NO! WE HAVE TO GO RIGHT HOME... UH.. COULDN'T GET A SITTER.. IODINE IS ALL ALONE.. SOME OTHER TIME... WE'D LOVE TO....

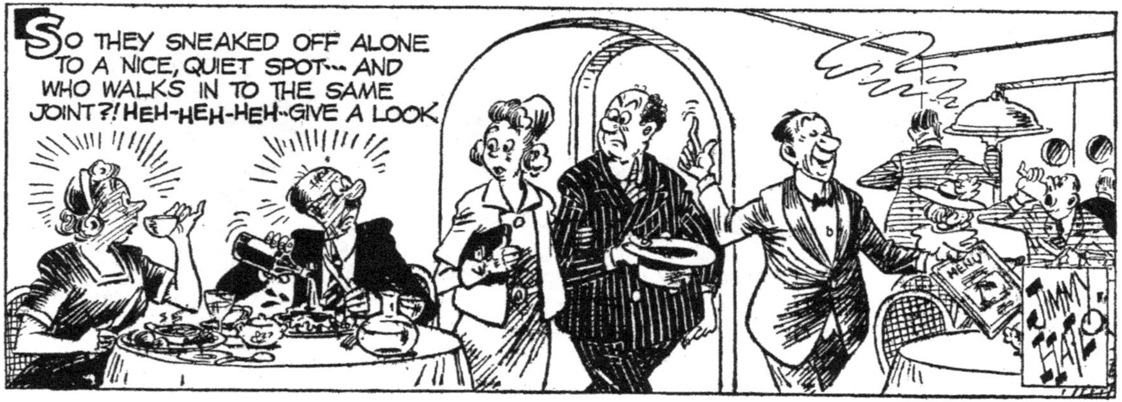
SO THEY SNEAKED OFF ALONE TO A NICE, QUIET SPOT... AND WHO WALKS IN TO THE SAME JOINT?! HEH-HEH-HEH.. GIVE A LOOK
MENU
JIMMY HATLO

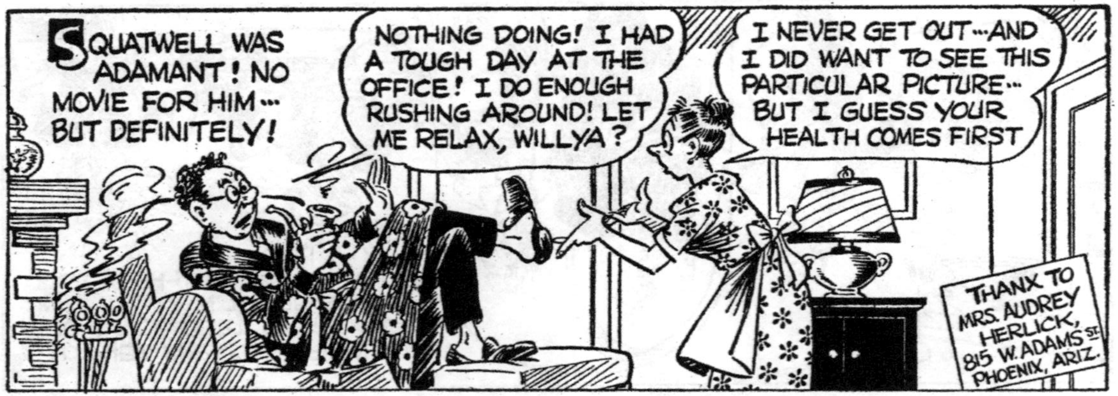
SQUATWELL WAS ADAMANT! NO MOVIE FOR HIM... BUT DEFINITELY!
NOTHING DOING! I HAD A TOUGH DAY AT THE OFFICE! I DO ENOUGH RUSHING AROUND! LET ME RELAX, WILLYA?
I NEVER GET OUT...AND I DID WANT TO SEE THIS PARTICULAR PICTURE... BUT I GUESS YOUR HEALTH COMES FIRST
THANX TO MRS. AUDREY HERLICK, 815 W. ADAMS ST. PHOENIX, ARIZ.

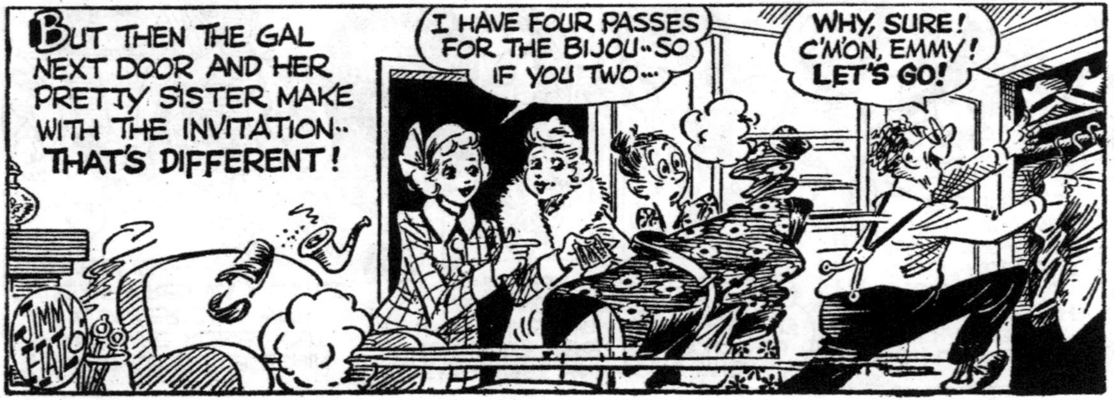
BUT THEN THE GAL NEXT DOOR AND HER PRETTY SISTER MAKE WITH THE INVITATION.. THAT'S DIFFERENT!
I HAVE FOUR PASSES FOR THE BIJOU..SO IF YOU TWO...
WHY, SURE! C'MON, EMMY! LET'S GO!
JIMMY HATLO

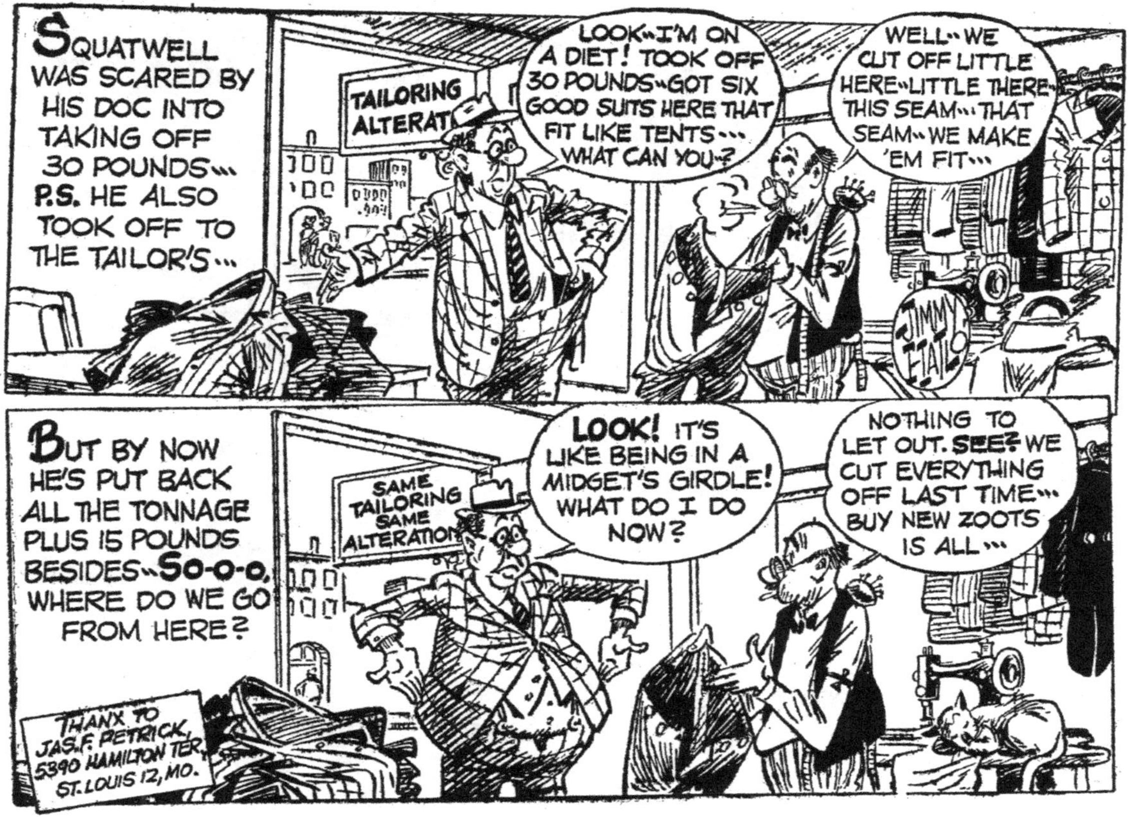
SQUATWELL WAS SCARED BY HIS DOC INTO TAKING OFF 30 POUNDS... P.S. HE ALSO TOOK OFF TO THE TAILOR'S...
TAILORING ALTERAT
LOOK.. I'M ON A DIET! TOOK OFF 30 POUNDS.. GOT SIX GOOD SUITS HERE THAT FIT LIKE TENTS... WHAT CAN YOU..?
WELL.. WE CUT OFF LITTLE HERE.. LITTLE THERE.. THIS SEAM... THAT SEAM.. WE MAKE 'EM FIT...
JIMMY FTALO
BUT BY NOW HE'S PUT BACK ALL THE TONNAGE PLUS 15 POUNDS BESIDES.. SO-O-O, WHERE DO WE GO FROM HERE?
SAME TAILORING SAME ALTERATION
LOOK! IT'S LIKE BEING IN A MIDGET'S GIRDLE! WHAT DO I DO NOW?
NOTHING TO LET OUT. SEE? WE CUT EVERYTHING OFF LAST TIME... BUY NEW ZOOTS IS ALL...
THANX TO JAS.F. PETRICK, 5390 HAMILTON TER., ST. LOUIS 12, MO.

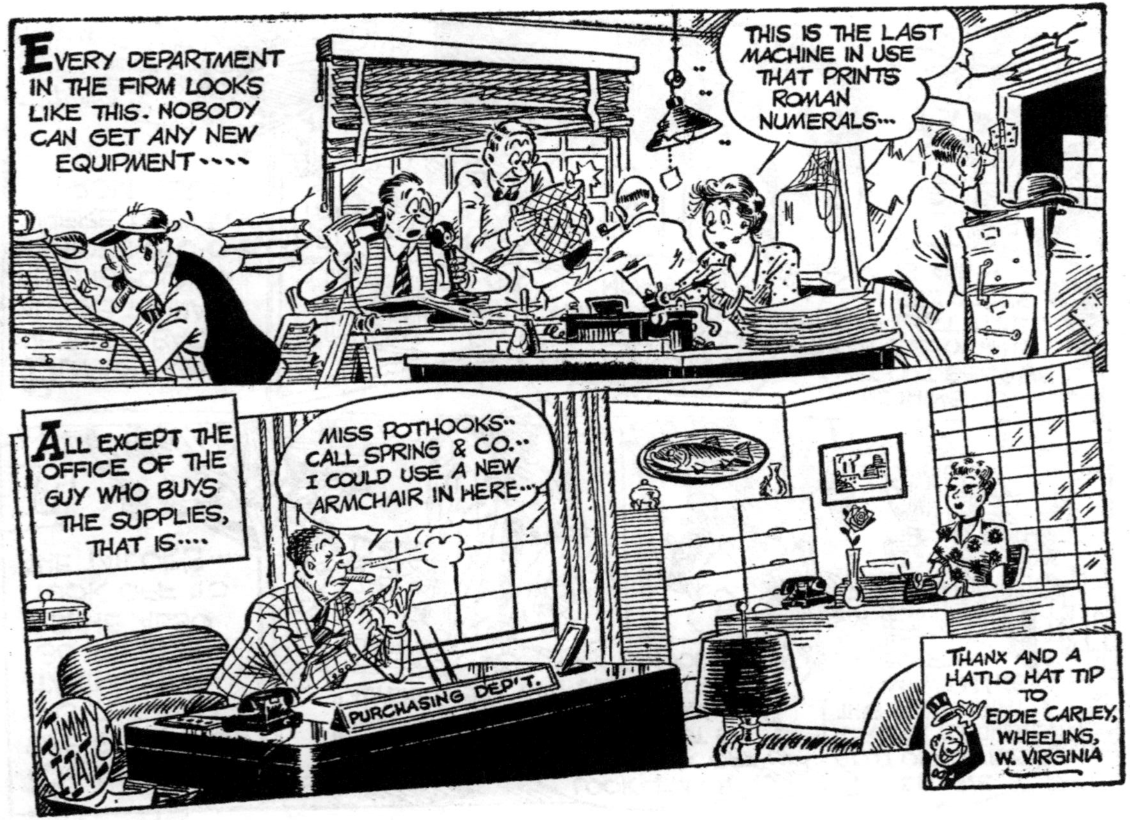
EVERY DEPARTMENT IN THE FIRM LOOKS LIKE THIS. NOBODY CAN GET ANY NEW EQUIPMENT....
THIS IS THE LAST MACHINE IN USE THAT PRINTS ROMAN NUMERALS...
ALL EXCEPT THE OFFICE OF THE GUY WHO BUYS THE SUPPLIES, THAT IS....
MISS POTHOOKS.. CALL SPRING & CO.. I COULD USE A NEW ARMCHAIR IN HERE...
PURCHASING DEP'T.
THANX AND A HATLO HAT TIP TO EDDIE CARLEY, WHEELING, W. VIRGINIA
JIMMY HATLO

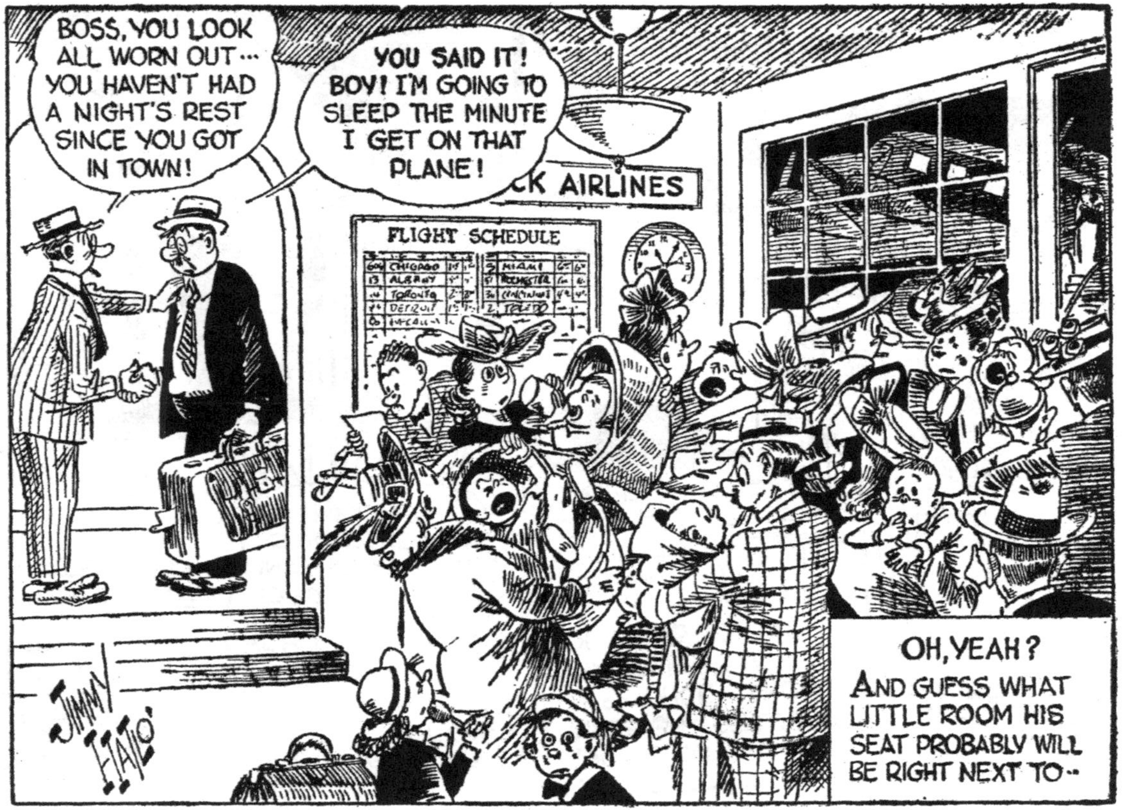
BOSS, YOU LOOK ALL WORN OUT... YOU HAVEN'T HAD A NIGHT'S REST SINCE YOU GOT IN TOWN!
YOU SAID IT! BOY! I'M GOING TO SLEEP THE MINUTE I GET ON THAT PLANE!
CK AIRLINES
FLIGHT SCHEDULE
OH, YEAH?
AND GUESS WHAT LITTLE ROOM HIS SEAT PROBABLY WILL BE RIGHT NEXT TO--
JIMMY HATLO

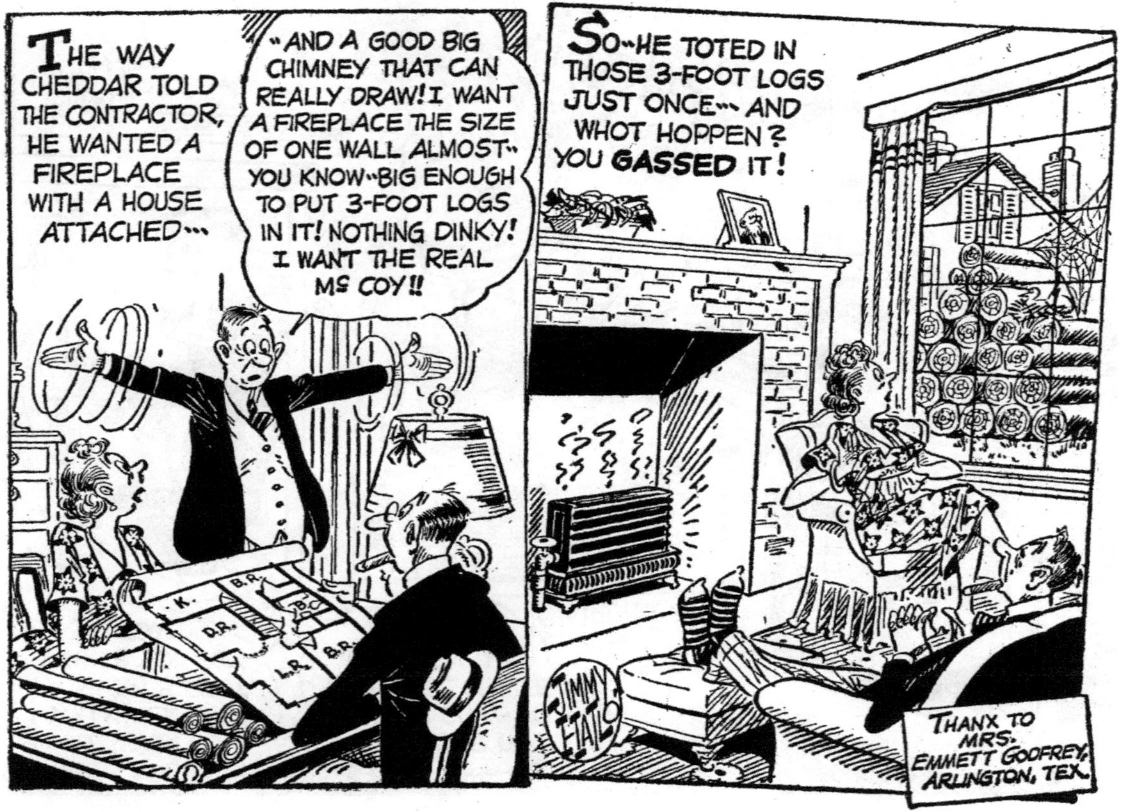
THE WAY CHEDDAR TOLD THE CONTRACTOR, HE WANTED A FIREPLACE WITH A HOUSE ATTACHED…
"AND A GOOD BIG CHIMNEY THAT CAN REALLY DRAW! I WANT A FIREPLACE THE SIZE OF ONE WALL ALMOST" YOU KNOW-BIG ENOUGH TO PUT 3-FOOT LOGS IN IT! NOTHING DINKY! I WANT THE REAL Mc COY!!
K.
B.R.
D.R.
L.R.
B.R.
SO-HE TOTED IN THOSE 3-FOOT LOGS JUST ONCE… AND WHOT HOPPEN? YOU GASSED IT!
JIMMY HATLO
THANX TO MRS. EMMETT GODFREY, ARLINGTON, TEX.

THE RESORT TOWN OF STINGAREE BEACH IS PRACTICALLY DEAD FROM EARLY SEPTEMBER TO ABOUT MAY 29TH...
DRUGS
STARFISH HOTEL
HOTEL
BOWLING
BAIT
POOL
JIMMY HATLO
SO — WHEN DO THE TOWN FATHERS DIG UP THE STREETS? WHY, ALL JULY AND AUGUST, OF COURSE...
THANX TO LEROY C. SHRONK, 3864 INDIAN QUEEN LANE, PHILADELPHIA 29, PA.
STREET CLOSED FOR REPAIRS

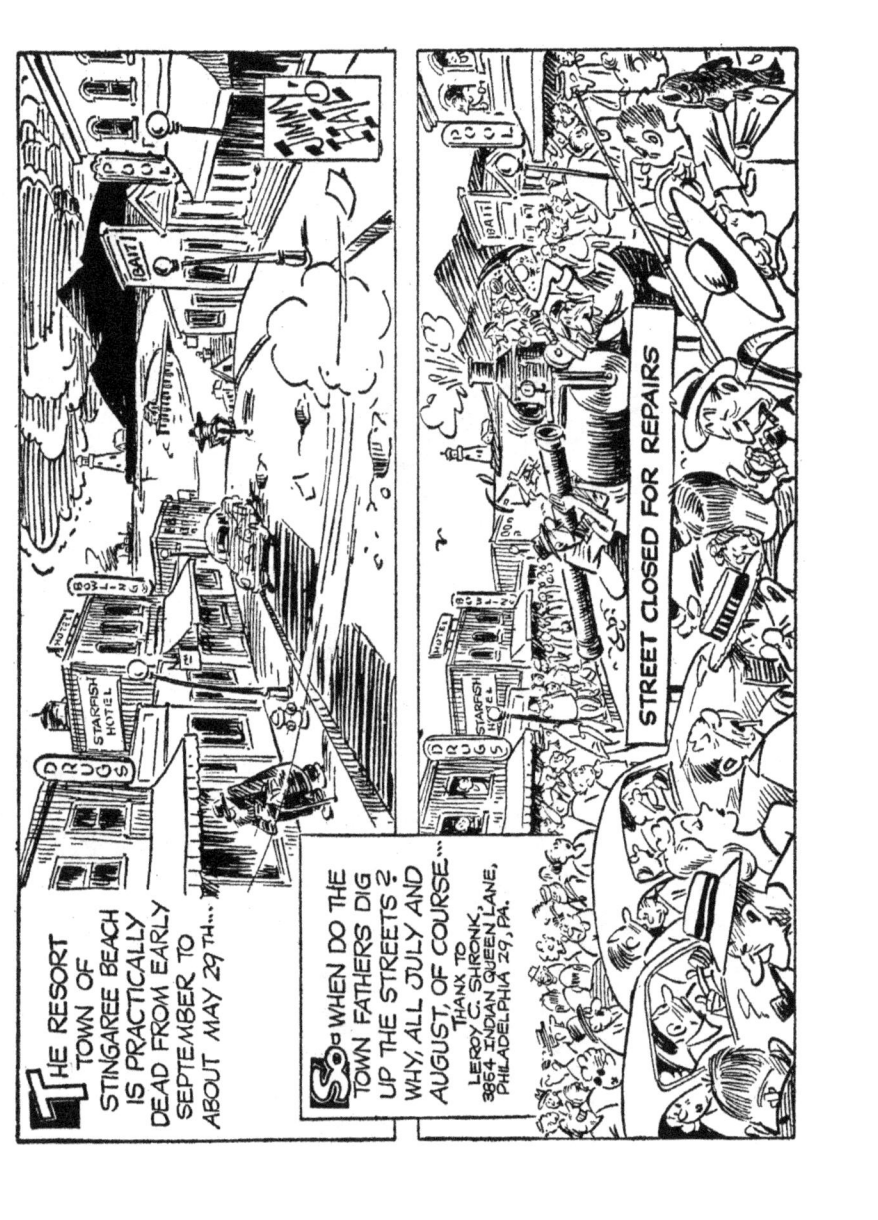

DROOPINA PRESERVES EVERYTHING BUT THE OLD MAN'S EQUILIBRIUM.... AND IT'S SO ECONOMICAL...(SHE SAYS)
GOOD GRIEF! ARE YOU STILL EMBALMING THEM DINGLEBERRIES? WHY DON'T YOU SAVE TIME AND TROUBLE? YOU CAN BUY 'EM CANNED!!
JUST YOU WAIT UNTIL YOU SEE HOW MUCH I SAVE... I'VE FIGURED OUT I'LL SAVE 22¢ A JAR OVER WHAT I'VE BEEN PAYING FOR JAM...
BUT TO THIS DAY HUBBY HASN'T TASTED ONE OF HER PUT-UP JOBS! AND HE'S THE ONLY ONE IN TOWN WHO HASN'T!
I INSIST YOU TAKE A JAR, DERMA... HERE'S ONE FOR YOUR MOTHER TOO.... LET ME KNOW HOW YOU LIKE IT... THERE'S MORE WHERE THIS CAME FROM...
MY MAMMA SENT ME OVER.. SHE WANTS YOU TO TASTE THIS....
THANX AND A TIP OF THE HATLO HAT TO MADELINE SHERIDAN, 135 VILLA TER., SAN FRANCISCO, CALIF.
JIMMY HATLO

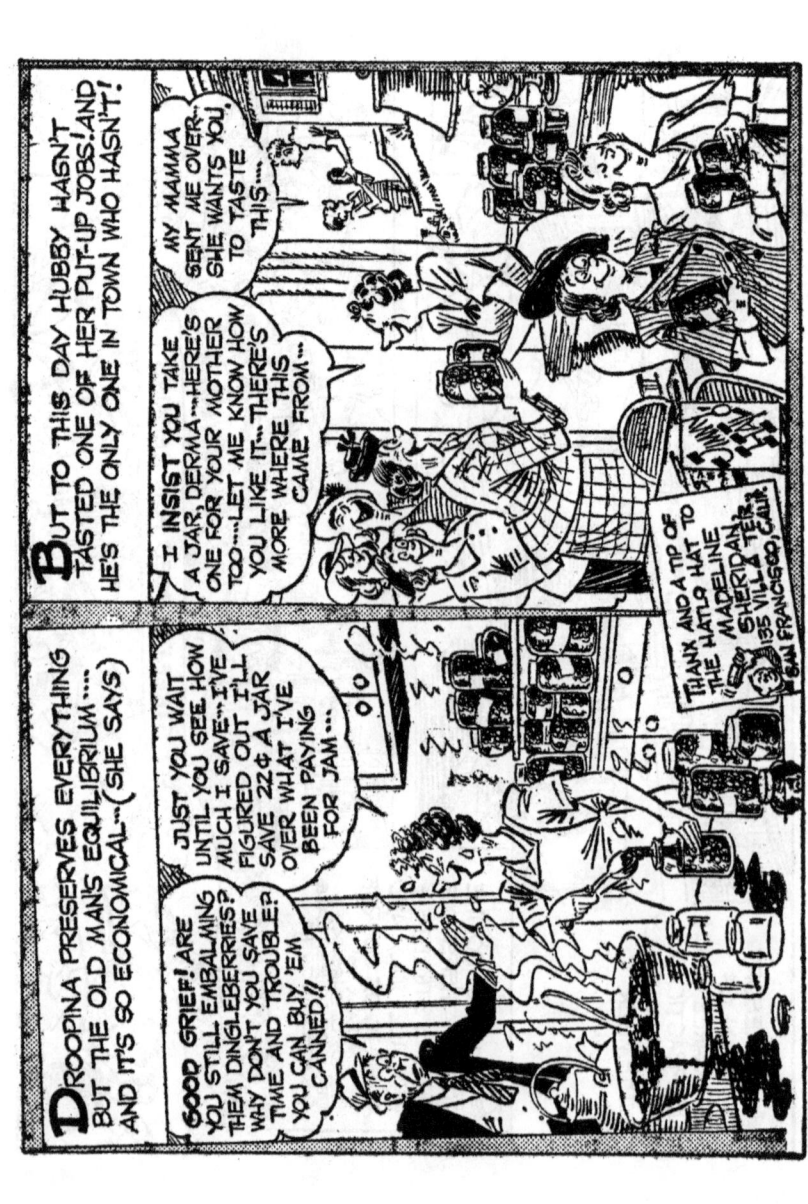

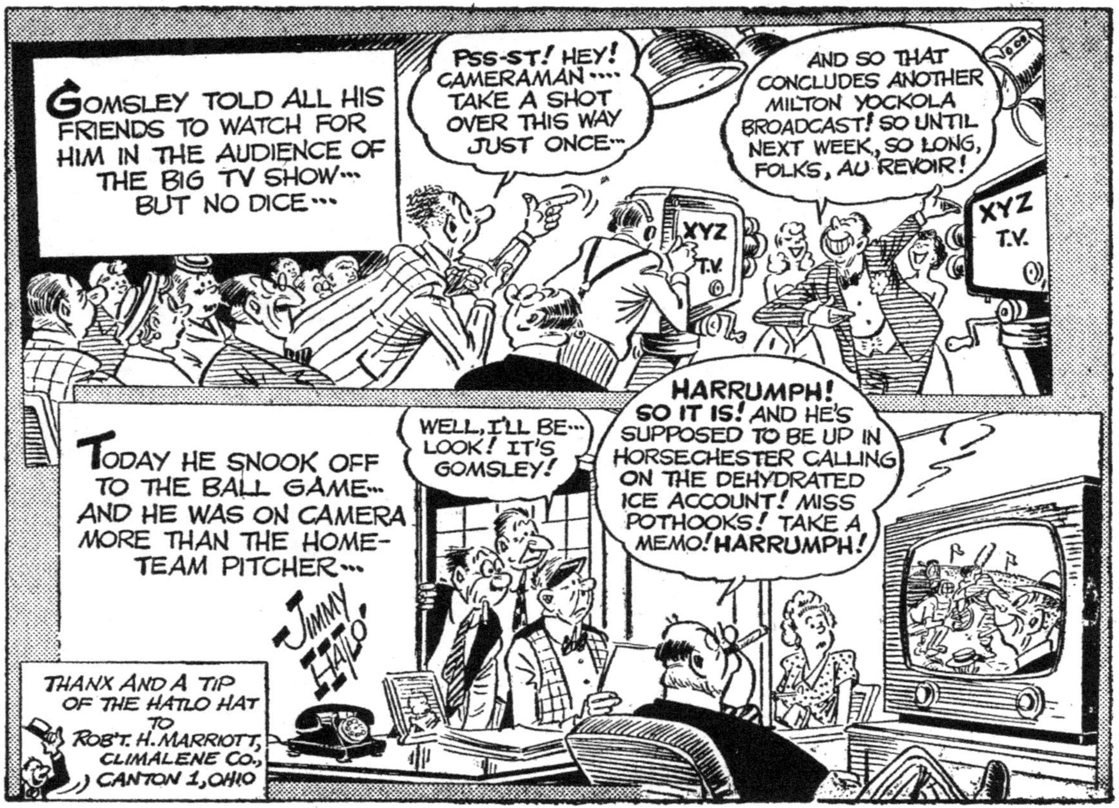
GOMSLEY TOLD ALL HIS FRIENDS TO WATCH FOR HIM IN THE AUDIENCE OF THE BIG TV SHOW... BUT NO DICE...
PSS-ST! HEY! CAMERAMAN.... TAKE A SHOT OVER THIS WAY JUST ONCE...
AND SO THAT CONCLUDES ANOTHER MILTON YOCKOLA BROADCAST! SO UNTIL NEXT WEEK, SO LONG, FOLKS, AU REVOIR!
XYZ T.V.
XYZ T.V.
TODAY HE SNOOK OFF TO THE BALL GAME... AND HE WAS ON CAMERA MORE THAN THE HOME-TEAM PITCHER...
WELL, I'LL BE... LOOK! IT'S GOMSLEY!
HARRUMPH! SO IT IS! AND HE'S SUPPOSED TO BE UP IN HORSECHESTER CALLING ON THE DEHYDRATED ICE ACCOUNT! MISS POTHOOKS! TAKE A MEMO! HARRUMPH!
JIMMY HATLO
THANX AND A TIP OF THE HATLO HAT TO ROB'T. H. MARRIOTT, CLIMALENE CO., CANTON 1, OHIO

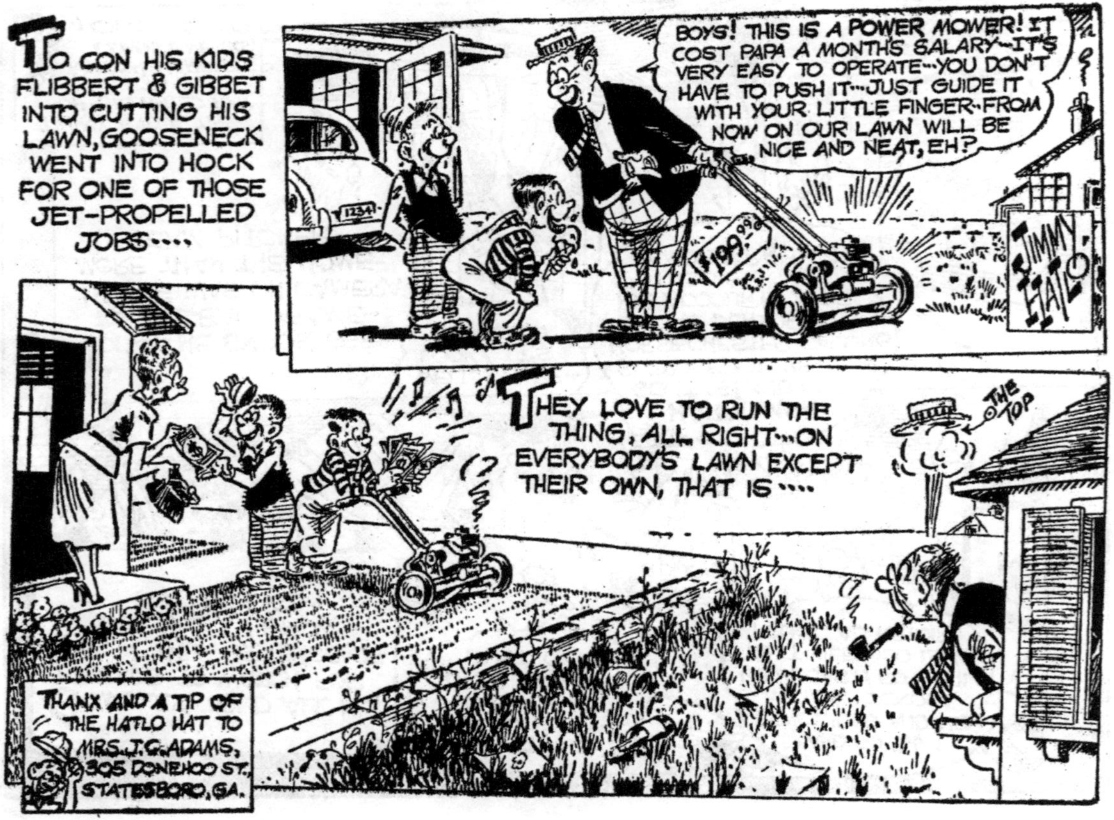
TO CON HIS KIDS FLIBBERT & GIBBET INTO CUTTING HIS LAWN, GOOSENECK WENT INTO HOCK FOR ONE OF THOSE JET-PROPELLED JOBS....
BOYS! THIS IS A POWER MOWER! IT COST PAPA A MONTH'S SALARY--IT'S VERY EASY TO OPERATE--YOU DON'T HAVE TO PUSH IT--JUST GUIDE IT WITH YOUR LITTLE FINGER--FROM NOW ON OUR LAWN WILL BE NICE AND NEAT, EH?
$199.99
JIMMY HATLO
THEY LOVE TO RUN THE THING, ALL RIGHT...ON EVERYBODY'S LAWN EXCEPT THEIR OWN, THAT IS....
THE TOP
THANX AND A TIP OF THE HATLO HAT TO MRS. J.C. ADAMS, 305 DONEHOO ST., STATESBORO, GA.

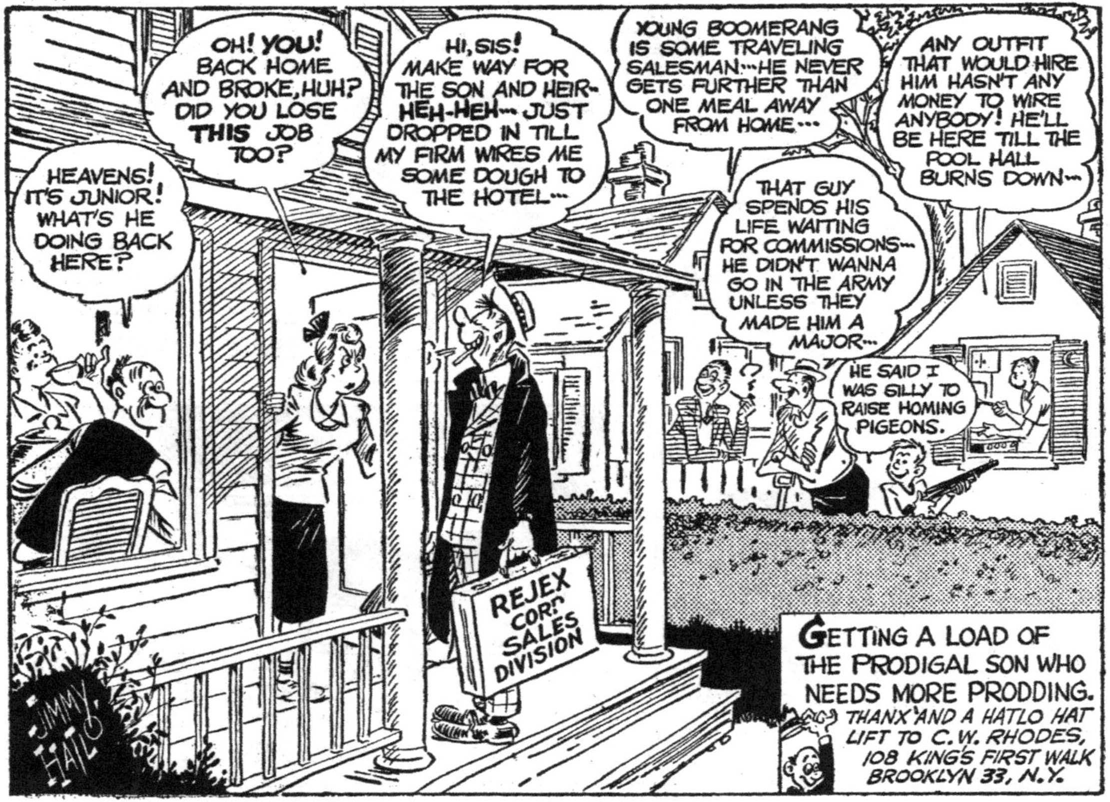
HEAVENS! IT'S JUNIOR! WHAT'S HE DOING BACK HERE?
OH! YOU! BACK HOME AND BROKE, HUH? DID YOU LOSE THIS JOB TOO?
HI, SIS! MAKE WAY FOR THE SON AND HEIR-HEH-HEH... JUST DROPPED IN TILL MY FIRM WIRES ME SOME DOUGH TO THE HOTEL...
REJEX CORP. SALES DIVISION
YOUNG BOOMERANG IS SOME TRAVELING SALESMAN... HE NEVER GETS FURTHER THAN ONE MEAL AWAY FROM HOME...
THAT GUY SPENDS HIS LIFE WAITING FOR COMMISSIONS... HE DIDN'T WANNA GO IN THE ARMY UNLESS THEY MADE HIM A MAJOR...
ANY OUTFIT THAT WOULD HIRE HIM HASN'T ANY MONEY TO WIRE ANYBODY! HE'LL BE HERE TILL THE POOL HALL BURNS DOWN...
HE SAID I WAS SILLY TO RAISE HOMING PIGEONS.
GETTING A LOAD OF THE PRODIGAL SON WHO NEEDS MORE PRODDING.
THANX AND A HATLO HAT LIFT TO C.W. RHODES, 108 KING'S FIRST WALK BROOKLYN 33, N.Y.
JIMMY HATLO

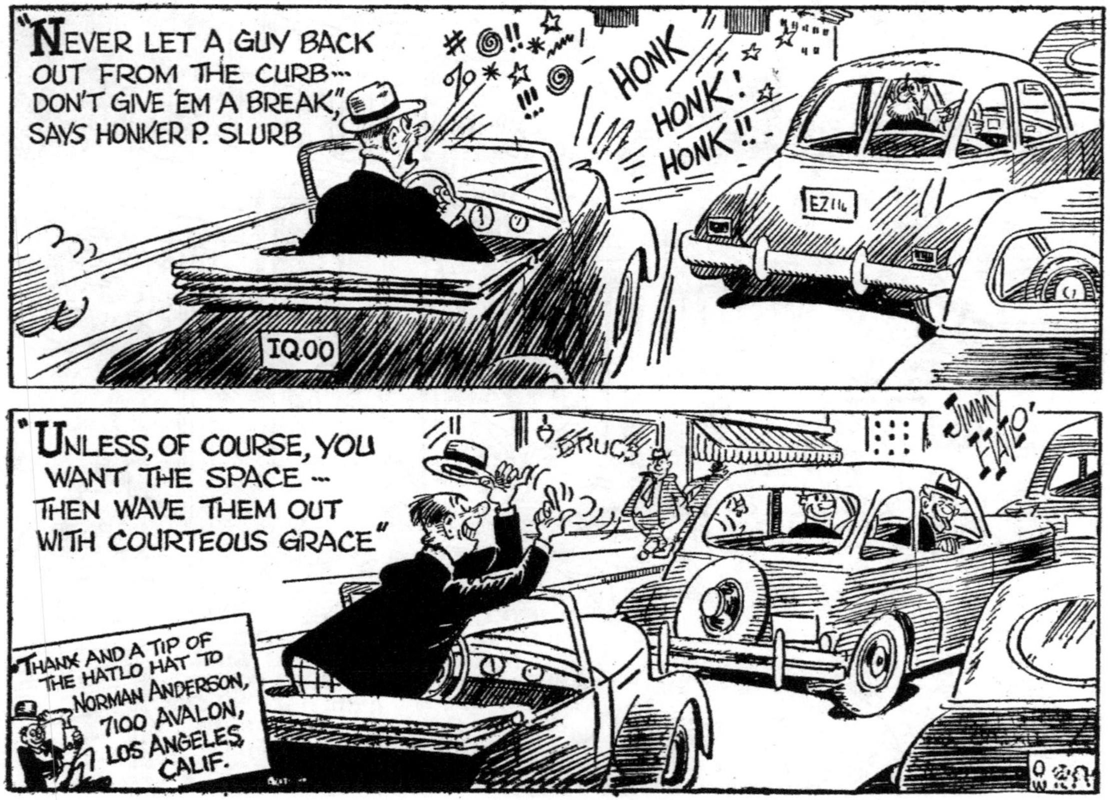
"NEVER LET A GUY BACK OUT FROM THE CURB... DON'T GIVE 'EM A BREAK," SAYS HONKER P. SLURB
HONK
HONK!
HONK!!
EZ116
IQ.00
"UNLESS, OF COURSE, YOU WANT THE SPACE... THEN WAVE THEM OUT WITH COURTEOUS GRACE"
DRUGS
JIMMY HATLO
THANX AND A TIP OF THE HATLO HAT TO NORMAN ANDERSON, 7100 AVALON, LOS ANGELES, CALIF.

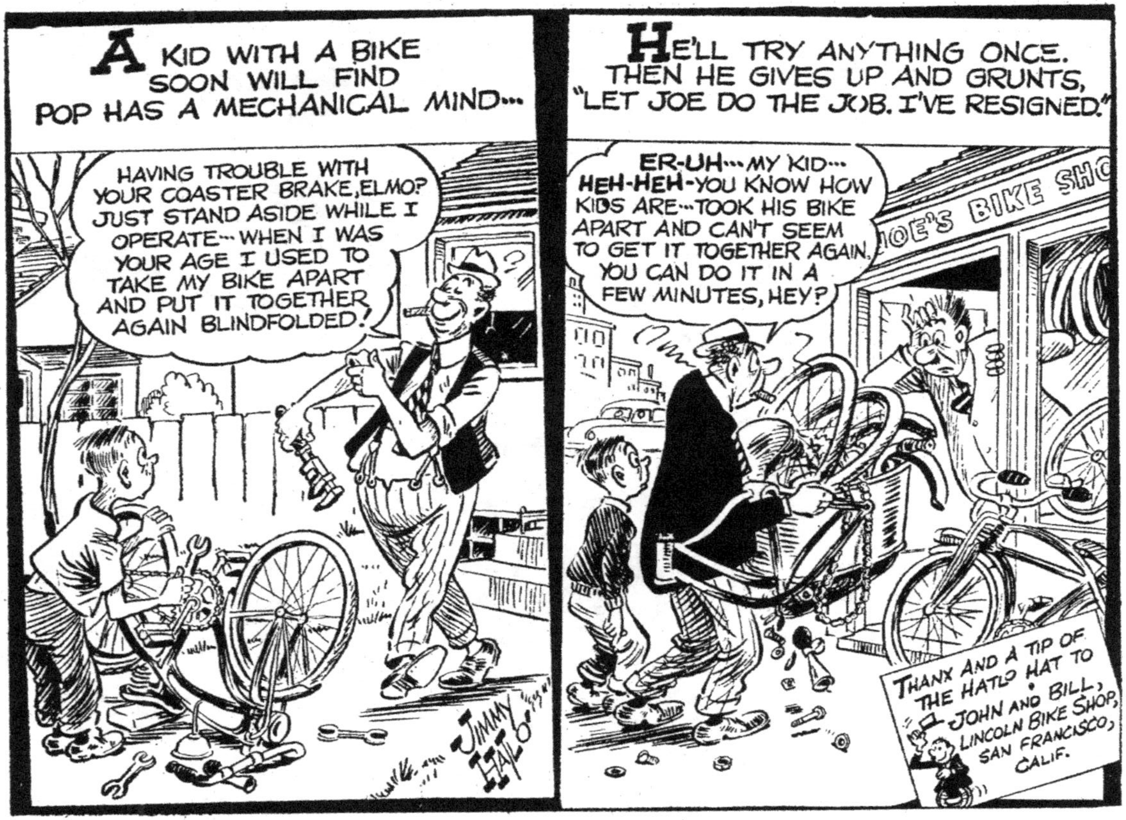
A KID WITH A BIKE SOON WILL FIND POP HAS A MECHANICAL MIND...
HAVING TROUBLE WITH YOUR COASTER BRAKE, ELMO? JUST STAND ASIDE WHILE I OPERATE... WHEN I WAS YOUR AGE I USED TO TAKE MY BIKE APART AND PUT IT TOGETHER AGAIN BLINDFOLDED!
JIMMY HATLO
HE'LL TRY ANYTHING ONCE. THEN HE GIVES UP AND GRUNTS, "LET JOE DO THE JOB. I'VE RESIGNED."
ER-UH... MY KID... HEH-HEH-YOU KNOW HOW KIDS ARE...TOOK HIS BIKE APART AND CAN'T SEEM TO GET IT TOGETHER AGAIN. YOU CAN DO IT IN A FEW MINUTES, HEY?
JOE'S BIKE SHO
THANX AND A TIP OF THE HATLO HAT TO JOHN AND BILL, LINCOLN BIKE SHOP, SAN FRANCISCO, CALIF.

THE FAMILY MEETS THE GOOD DOCTOR AT THE DOOR THUS…AND WE QUOTE…:
OH, DOCTOR…WE'RE SO GLAD YOU'VE COME…LITTLE YORICK IS SO-O-O SICK HE CAN HARDLY HOLD HIS LITTLE HEAD UP!
BUT BE THAT AS IT MAY…IT TAKES FIVE OF THEM TO HOLD LI'L' YORICK DOWN SO'S DOC CAN GET A THERMOMETER IN HIS KISSER
JIMMY HATLO
MD
MD
THANX TO DR. ROB'T A. SCHLESS, MEDICAL ARTS BLDG., PHILADELPHIA, PA.

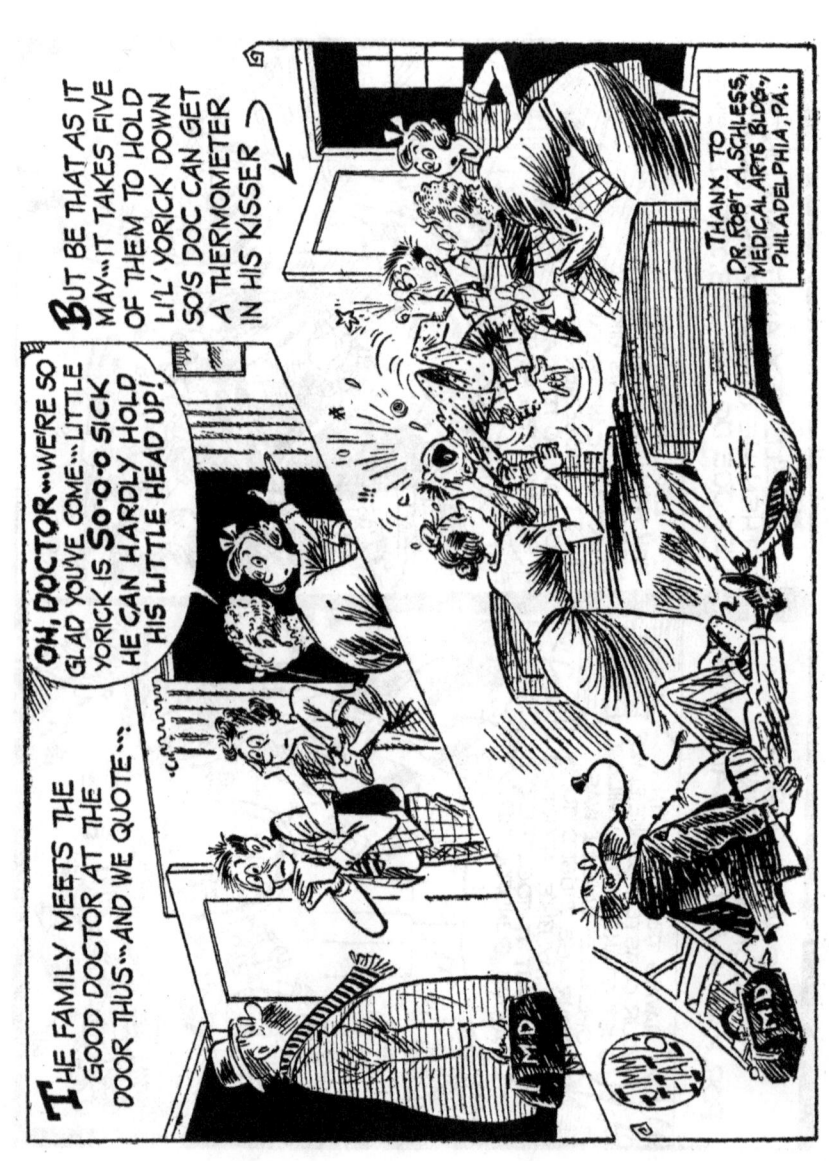

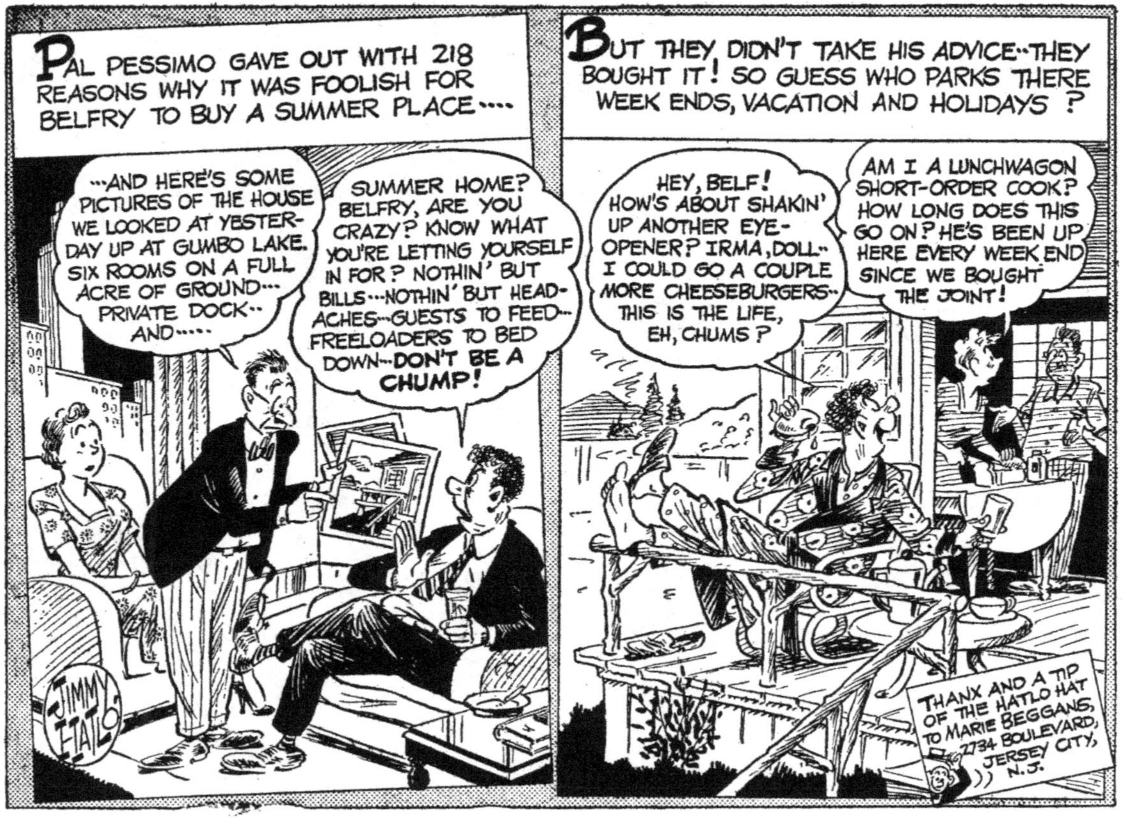
PAL PESSIMO GAVE OUT WITH 218 REASONS WHY IT WAS FOOLISH FOR BELFRY TO BUY A SUMMER PLACE....
...AND HERE'S SOME PICTURES OF THE HOUSE WE LOOKED AT YESTERDAY UP AT GUMBO LAKE. SIX ROOMS ON A FULL ACRE OF GROUND... PRIVATE DOCK.. AND.....
SUMMER HOME? BELFRY, ARE YOU CRAZY? KNOW WHAT YOU'RE LETTING YOURSELF IN FOR? NOTHIN' BUT BILLS...NOTHIN' BUT HEADACHES...GUESTS TO FEED... FREELOADERS TO BED DOWN...DON'T BE A CHUMP!
JIMMY HATLO
BUT THEY DIDN'T TAKE HIS ADVICE..THEY BOUGHT IT! SO GUESS WHO PARKS THERE WEEK ENDS, VACATION AND HOLIDAYS ?
HEY, BELF! HOW'S ABOUT SHAKIN' UP ANOTHER EYE-OPENER? IRMA, DOLL.. I COULD GO A COUPLE MORE CHEESEBURGERS.. THIS IS THE LIFE, EH, CHUMS ?
AM I A LUNCHWAGON SHORT-ORDER COOK? HOW LONG DOES THIS GO ON? HE'S BEEN UP HERE EVERY WEEK END SINCE WE BOUGHT THE JOINT!
THANX AND A TIP OF THE HATLO HAT TO MARIE BEGGANS, 2734 BOULEVARD, JERSEY CITY, N.J.

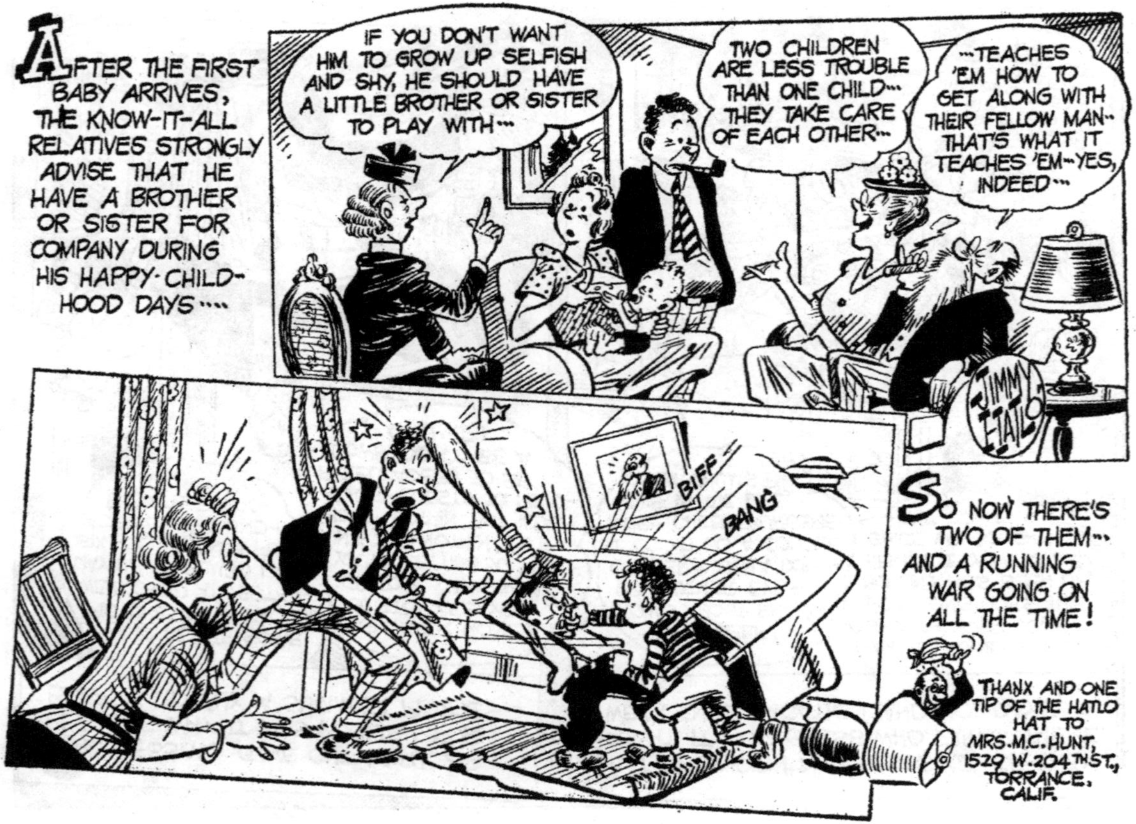
AFTER THE FIRST BABY ARRIVES, THE KNOW-IT-ALL RELATIVES STRONGLY ADVISE THAT HE HAVE A BROTHER OR SISTER FOR COMPANY DURING HIS HAPPY-CHILDHOOD DAYS....
IF YOU DON'T WANT HIM TO GROW UP SELFISH AND SHY, HE SHOULD HAVE A LITTLE BROTHER OR SISTER TO PLAY WITH...
TWO CHILDREN ARE LESS TROUBLE THAN ONE CHILD... THEY TAKE CARE OF EACH OTHER...
...TEACHES 'EM HOW TO GET ALONG WITH THEIR FELLOW MAN.. THAT'S WHAT IT TEACHES 'EM--YES, INDEED...
JIMMY HATLO
BIFF
BANG
SO NOW THERE'S TWO OF THEM... AND A RUNNING WAR GOING ON ALL THE TIME!
THANX AND ONE TIP OF THE HATLO HAT TO MRS. M.C. HUNT, 1529 W. 204TH ST., TORRANCE, CALIF.

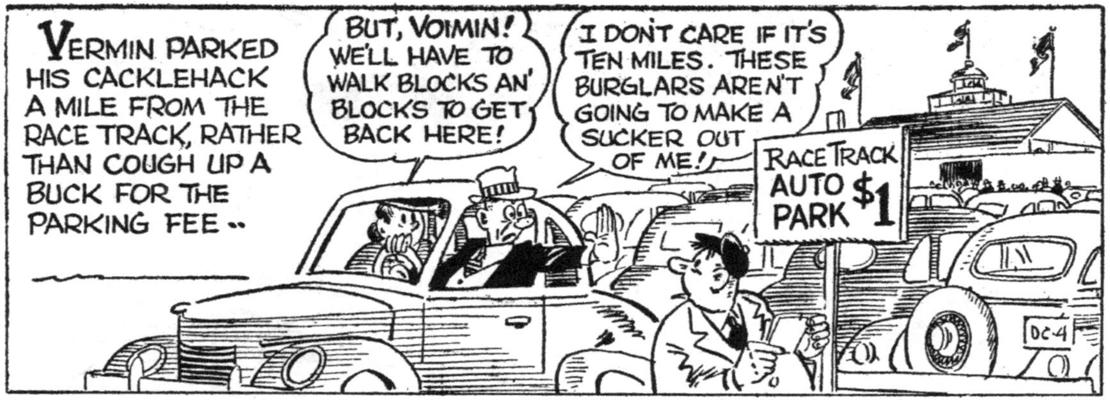
VERMIN PARKED HIS CACKLEHACK A MILE FROM THE RACE TRACK, RATHER THAN COUGH UP A BUCK FOR THE PARKING FEE --
BUT, VOIMIN! WE'LL HAVE TO WALK BLOCKS AN' BLOCKS TO GET BACK HERE!
I DON'T CARE IF IT'S TEN MILES. THESE BURGLARS AREN'T GOING TO MAKE A SUCKER OUT OF ME!
RACE TRACK AUTO PARK $1
DC-4

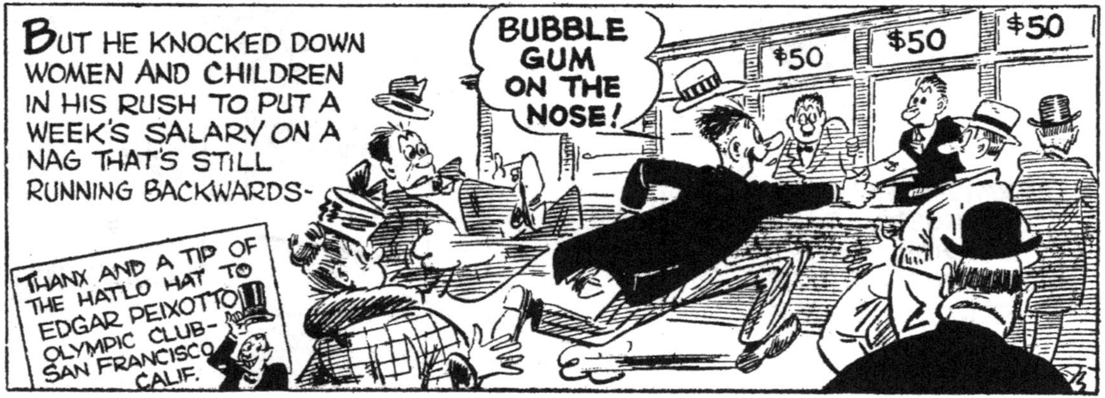
BUT HE KNOCKED DOWN WOMEN AND CHILDREN IN HIS RUSH TO PUT A WEEK'S SALARY ON A NAG THAT'S STILL RUNNING BACKWARDS-
BUBBLE GUM ON THE NOSE!
$50
$50
$50
THANX AND A TIP OF THE HATLO HAT TO EDGAR PEIXOTTO OLYMPIC CLUB- SAN FRANCISCO CALIF.

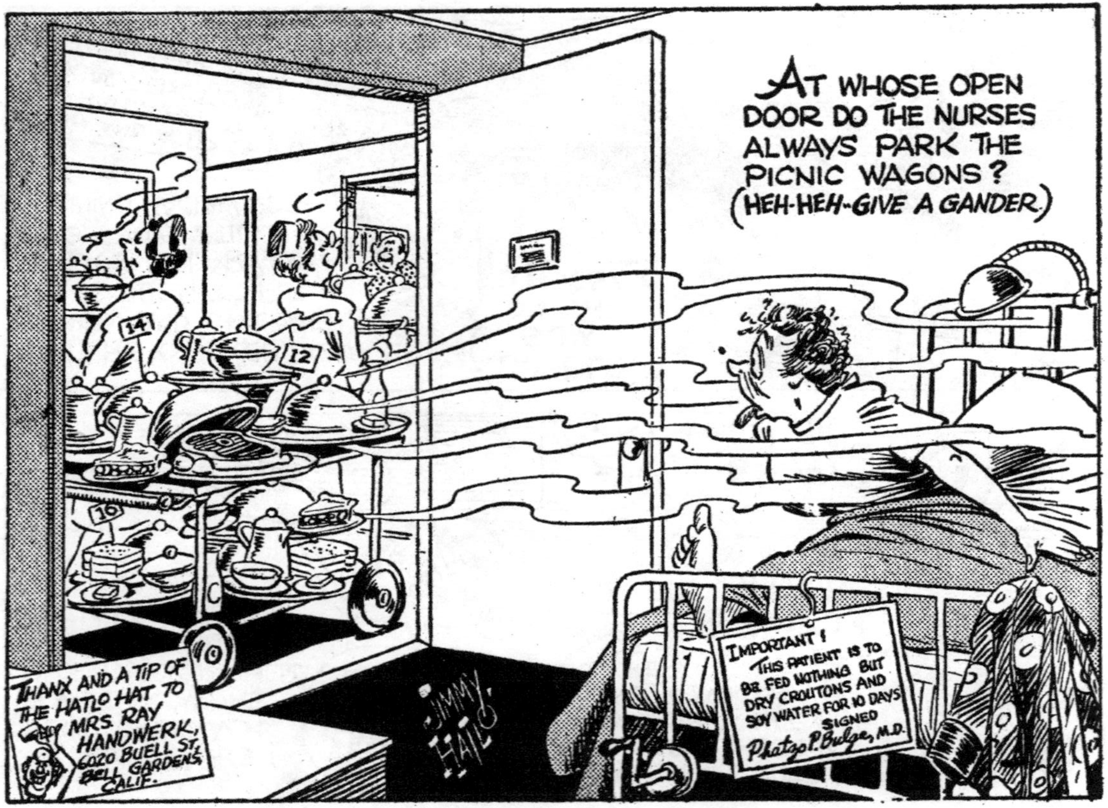
AT WHOSE OPEN DOOR DO THE NURSES ALWAYS PARK THE PICNIC WAGONS? (HEH-HEH-GIVE A GANDER)
14
12
16
IMPORTANT! THIS PATIENT IS TO BE FED NOTHING BUT DRY CROUTONS AND SOY WATER FOR 10 DAYS SIGNED Phatzo P. Bulge, M.D.
THANX AND A TIP OF THE HATLO HAT TO MRS. RAY HANDWERK, 6020 BUELL ST, BELL GARDENS, CALIF.
JIMMY HATLO

HEY, FRANK··YOU CAN' STRAIGHTEN ME OUT ON SOMETHING··· PHOTOGRAPHY IS MY HOBBY···CAN I DEDUCT PART OF THE RENT FROM MY INCOME TAX ON ACCOUNT OF I GOT A DARK-ROOM IN THE CELLAR ?
I'VE BEEN WANTING TO ASK YOU, FRANKIE··· CAN ANYBODY USE THE SHORT FORM? MY SON WORKS FOR THE GOVERNMENT··· IS THAT A CAPITAL GAIN? AND HOW ABOUT····
THAT FELLOW EMPTION SURE IS POPULAR·· HE'S HAD A CROWD AROUND HIM ALL NIGHT···
YEAH, F.X., OL' BOY··HOW'S ABOUT LUNCH NEXT WEEK? I WANT TO GET A LITTLE FRIENDLY ADVICE···
YEAH··THE SAME GUYS WHO WATCH A CORN DOCTOR BUT DON'T BUY ANY SALVE···
AFTER MARCH 15TH HE CAN GO BACK TO SITTING ALL ALONE BY HIS NON-DEDUCTIBLE TELEVISION SET···
JIMMY HATLO
TRYING TO MILK SOME "FOR FREE" INFO FROM FRANCIS X. EMPTION, THE INCOME TAX EXPERT····

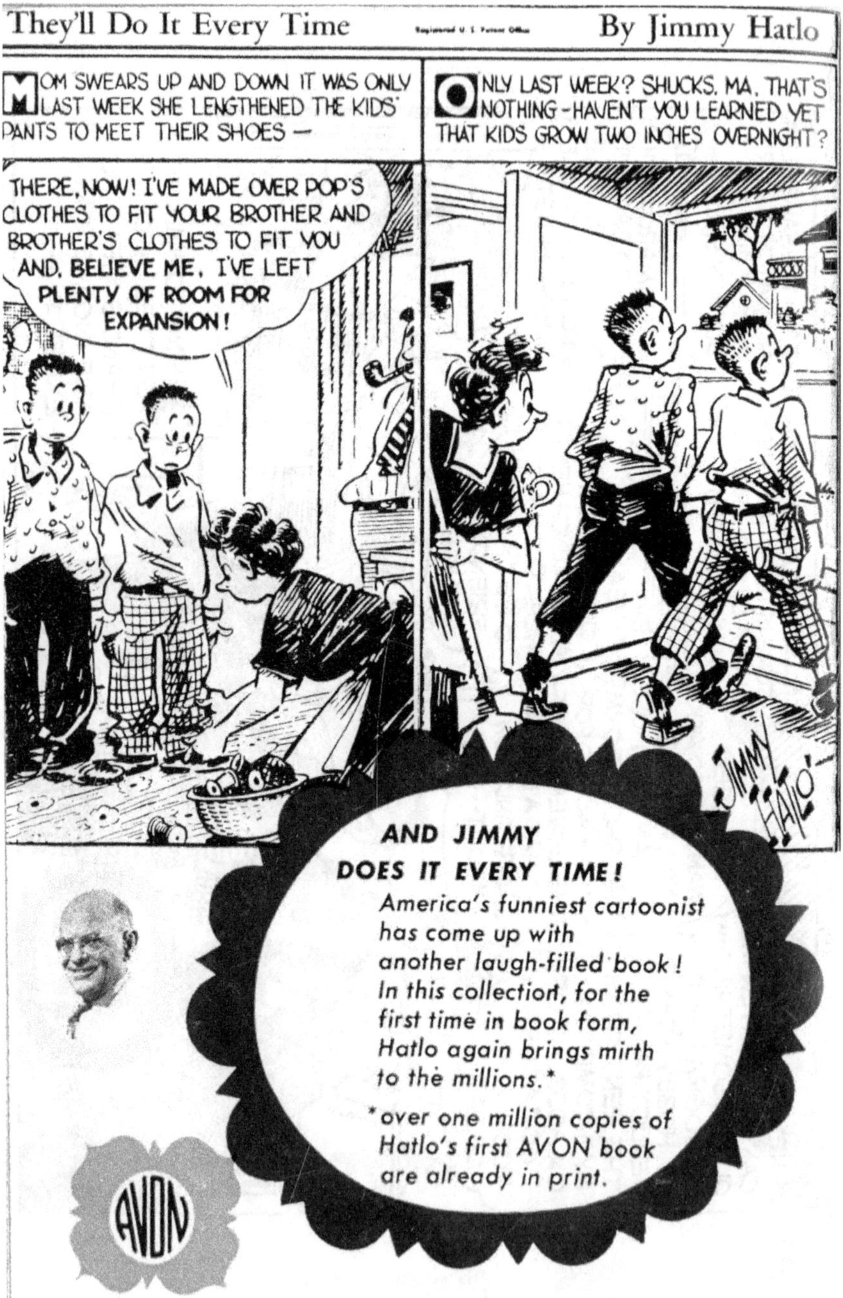
They'll Do It Every Time
By Jimmy Hatlo
MOM SWEARS UP AND DOWN IT WAS ONLY LAST WEEK SHE LENGTHENED THE KIDS' PANTS TO MEET THEIR SHOES —
THERE, NOW! I'VE MADE OVER POP'S CLOTHES TO FIT YOUR BROTHER AND BROTHER'S CLOTHES TO FIT YOU AND, BELIEVE ME, I'VE LEFT PLENTY OF ROOM FOR EXPANSION!
ONLY LAST WEEK? SHUCKS, MA, THAT'S NOTHING - HAVEN'T YOU LEARNED YET THAT KIDS GROW TWO INCHES OVERNIGHT?
JIMMY HATLO
AND JIMMY DOES IT EVERY TIME!
America's funniest cartoonist has come up with another laugh-filled book! In this collection, for the first time in book form, Hatlo again brings mirth to the millions.*
*over one million copies of Hatlo's first AVON book are already in print.
AVON

COACHWHIP PUBLICATIONS
CoachwhipBooks.com

THE GOOD OLD DAYS
ERWIN L. HESS

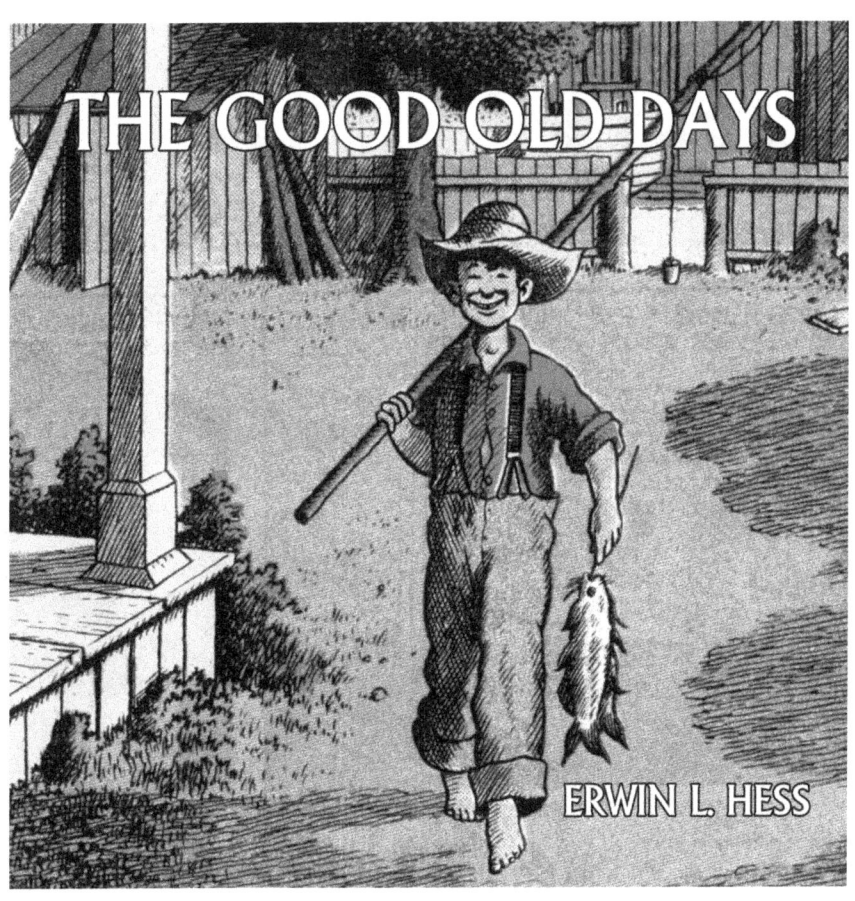

COACHWHIP PUBLICATIONS
CoachwhipBooks.com

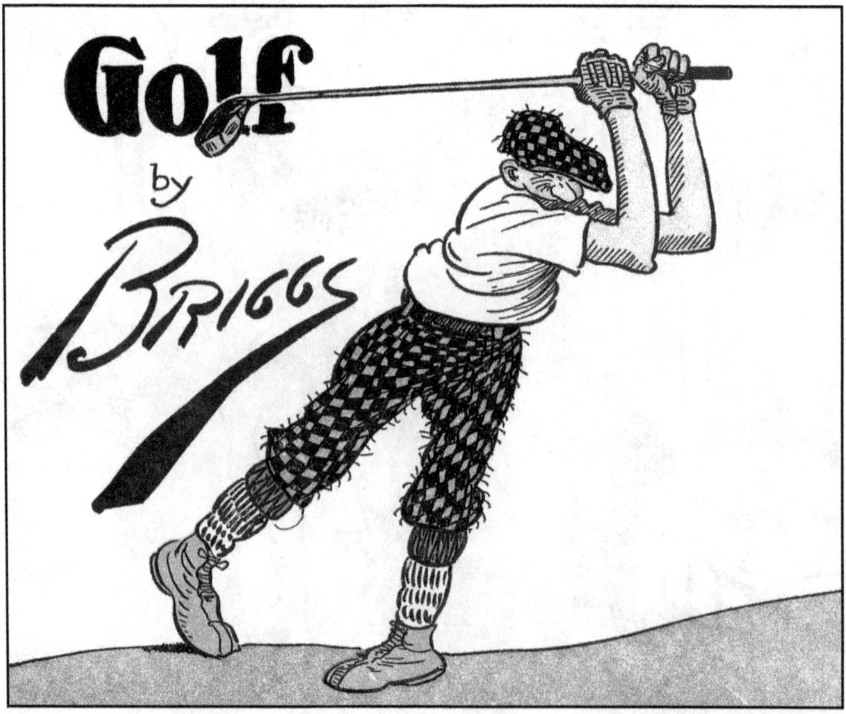
Golf
by
Briggs

COACHWHIP PUBLICATIONS
CoachwhipBooks.com

That Little Game

BERT LINK

COACHWHIP PUBLICATIONS
CoachwhipBooks.com

COACHWHIP PUBLICATIONS

COACHWHIPBOOKS.COM

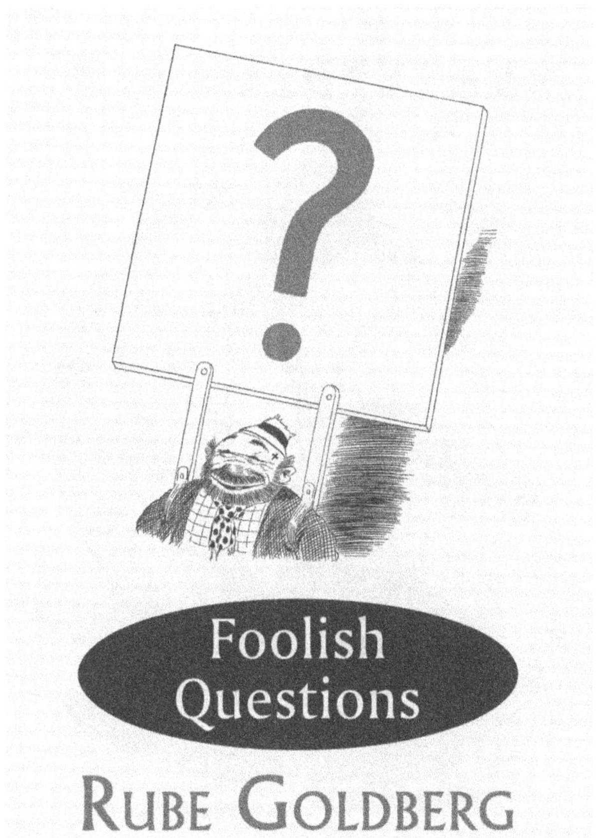
Foolish Questions
RUBE GOLDBERG

COACHWHIP PUBLICATIONS
CoachwhipBooks.com

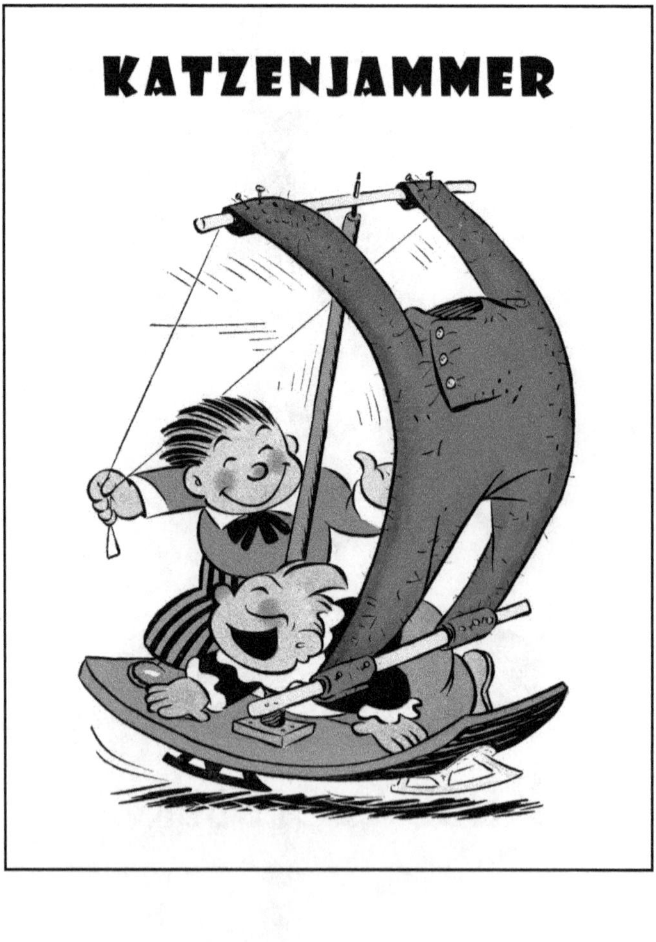
KATZENJAMMER

COACHWHIP PUBLICATIONS
CoachwhipBooks.com

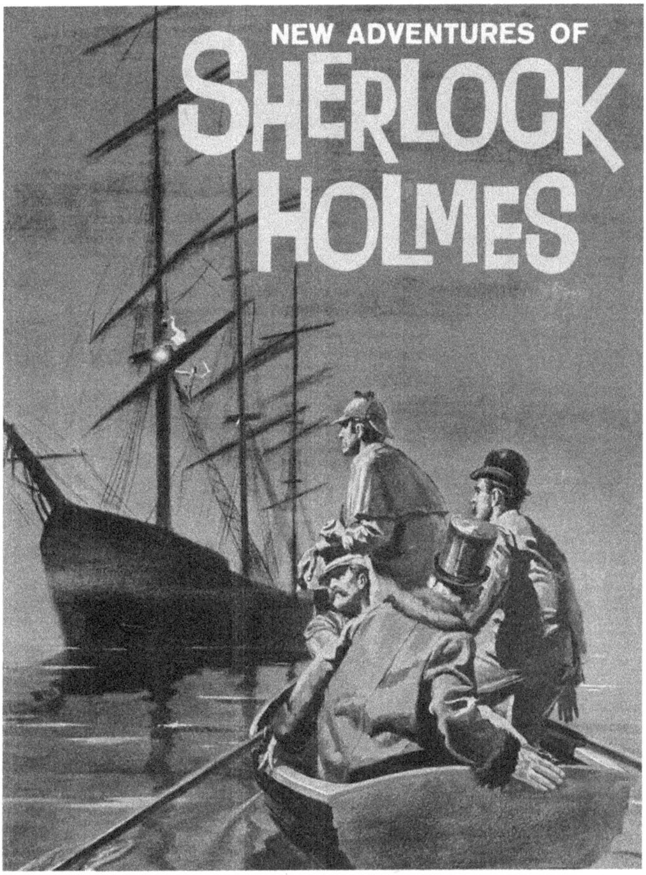
NEW ADVENTURES OF
SHERLOCK
HOLMES

COACHWHIP PUBLICATIONS
CoachwhipBooks.com

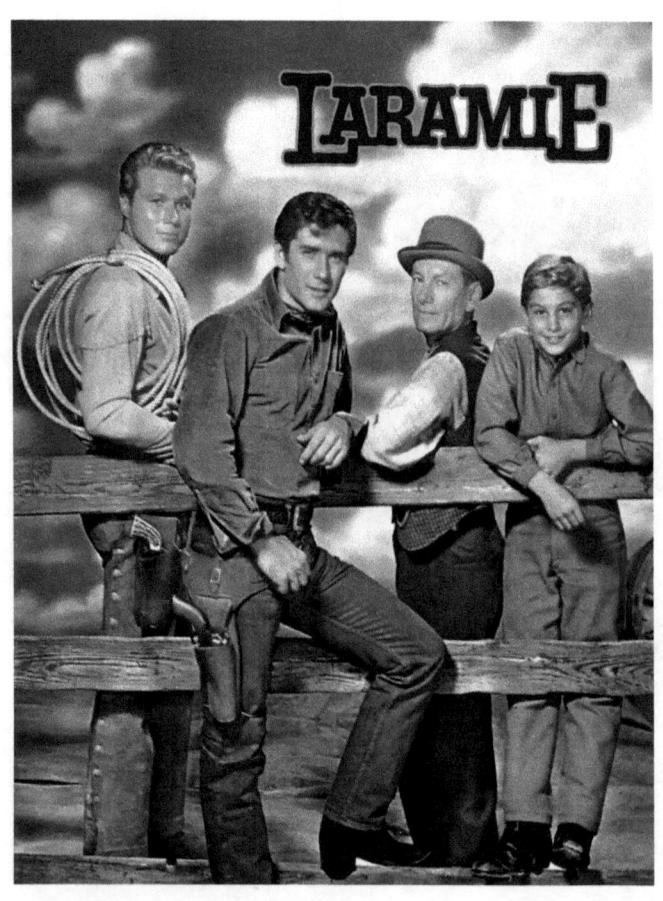

COACHWHIP PUBLICATIONS

COACHWHIPBOOKS.COM

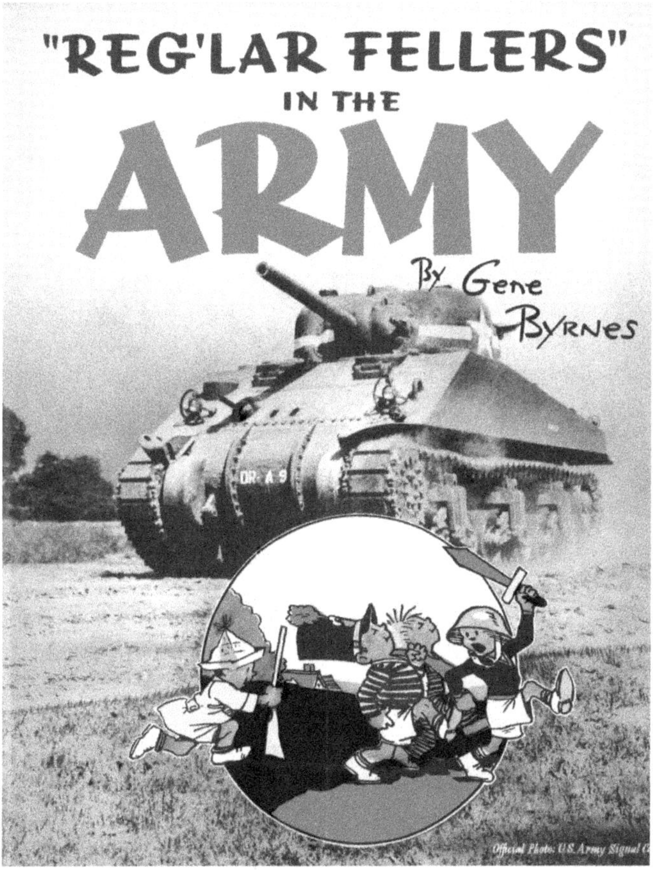
"REG'LAR FELLERS"
IN THE
ARMY
By Gene Byrnes
DR-A-9
Official Photo: U.S. Army Signal C

www.ingramcontent.com/pod-product-compliance
Lightning Source LLC
Chambersburg PA
CBHW071501160426
43195CB00013B/2178